THE BASIC WORKS OF ARISTOTLE

ARISTOTLE

THE BASIC WORKS OF ARISTOTLE

Edited by Richard McKeon

Introduction by C.D.C. Reeve

UNIVERSITY OF NORTH CAROLINA AT
CHAPEL HILL

THE MODERN LIBRARY

NEW YORK

The numbers in the margin of this edition refer to the corresponding lines of the Greek text in the great modern edition of Aristotle's work published between 1831 and 1870 by the Berlin Academy. The pagination of the Berlin edition has become the customary means by which to locate a passage of Aristotle. A reference to, say, *Metaphysics* xii. 10. 1075ª25 would place the passage in question in Chapter 10 of Book 12 of the *Metaphysics,* on line 25 of the first column, i.e., column a, of page 1075 of the Berlin edition.

2001 Modern Library Paperback Edition

LIBRARY OF CONGRESS CATALOGING-IN-PUBLICATION DATA
Aristotle.
[Selections. English. 2001]
The basic works of Aristotle / edited by Richard McKeon; introduction by C.D.C. Reeve
p.   cm.—(Modern Library classics)
Originally published: New York: Random House, © 1941. With new intro.
ISBN 0-375-75799-6 (pbk.)
1. Philosophy.   I. McKeon, Richard Peter, 1900– II. Title. III. Series.
B407 .A2713 2001   185—dc21   2001030607

Modern Library website address: www.modernlibrary.com

Printed in the United States of America

30 29 28 27 26 25 24

ARISTOTLE

Aristotle was born in 384/3 B.C. in the little town of Stagira on the eastern coast of the peninsula of Chalcidice in Thrace. His father, Nicomachus, was court physician and, according to tradition, friend of Amyntas II, king of Macedon and father of Philip the Great. Nicomachus died while Aristotle was still a child, and he was raised by Proxenus of Atarneus, whose son Nicanor was later adopted, in turn, by Aristotle and was married to Aristotle's daughter. In 368/7, at the age of eighteen, Aristotle was sent to Athens, where he remained in close association with the Academy of Plato for twenty years, until the death of Plato in 348/7. After Plato's death he left Athens and, together with Xenocrates, visited the court of Hermias, a former member of the Academy who had become tyrant of Assos and Atarneus in Mysia in Asia Minor. Aristotle married Hermias' niece Pythias, and he probably taught at a kind of Academic center in Assos. Somewhat later he went to Mitylene in Lesbos, where he doubtless engaged in biological research. In 343/2, on the invitation of Philip of Macedon, he became tutor to Alexander. The instruction probably extended only to 340, when Alexander was appointed regent for his father, but his tutor did not return to Athens until 335/4, a year after the death of Philip.

The next twelve years Aristotle devoted with extraordinary industry to the establishment of a school, the Lyceum, to the institution and pursuit of a program of investigation, speculation, and teaching in almost every branch of knowledge, and to the composition of all, or most, or at least the more scientific portions, of those of his writings which are now extant. When Alexander died in 323, Aristotle's Macedonian connections brought him under suspicion and he fled Athens lest, as he is said to have remarked, the Athenians sin twice against philosophy. An accusation of impiety was brought against him, not unlike those which had been brought against Anaxagoras and Protagoras or that on which Socrates had been condemned. The specific charge was that he had instituted a private cult in the memory of his friend Hermias, since he had erected a statue to him at Delphi and had composed a poem, in what was alleged to be the manner of a paean, in his honor. He took refuge under the protection of Antipater, viceroy to Alexander, in Chalcis in Euboea, where he died in 322 a short time before the death of Demosthenes.

Most of the scant information that has come to us concerning the life of Aristotle is suggestive, but there is little positive evidence, in his works or in external sources, to support inferences concerning the formative forces that influenced his work. Since his father was a physician, he was a hereditary member of the guild of Asclepiads, and it is tempting to speculate on the youthful beginnings of his interest in biological investigations and his possible training in dissection, pharmacology, and medicine; but his father died when he was young, and there is no evidence in his works of an early training in medicine. He spent twenty years in the Academy; that period has been used as evidence of a close association with Plato which resulted in a deep impress on his thought, but it has also been argued, by scholars like Burnet and Taylor, that Plato was not in the Academy at the time of Aristotle's arrival, that he was away for repeated and lengthy periods during Aristotle's stay, and that Aristotle's knowledge of Platonism was acquired at second-hand and was never accurate. We do not know how he spent his time at the Academy: there is an ancient tradition that he undertook the teaching of rhetoric in opposition to the flourishing school of Isocrates; it seems probable that he participated in the biological research which was flourishing at the Academy; the fragments of his early dialogues suggest that he wrote works intended to popularize Platonism. His reasons for leaving Athens on the death of Plato can only be conjectured: he may have been dissatisfied with the prospects of the Academy under Plato's nephew and successor Speusippus, who seemed to Aristotle to have reduced metaphysics to mathematics, or Speusippus may have charged Aristotle and Xenocrates to open a branch of the Academy in Asia Minor. He probably taught in Assos; there is evidence in his biological writings that he collected specimens of animals and fish in Lesbos and in the waters adjacent to the island; he doubtless began the composition of some of the works that have survived during his travels.

In spite of the fact that the relation between Aristotle and Alexander has been a tempting subject for speculation since Plutarch and that the ambition to influence kings through philosophy was deeply implanted in the Academy, there is no evidence that Aristotle had any influence on the moral ideals or political ambitions of his royal pupil, and Aristotle in turn seems to have taken no account of the effects of the ideal of world empire on the forms of political association and on the possible survival of the Greek city-state. There is good reason to doubt the accuracy of the legend that Alexander sent records of astronomical observations and biological specimens to his former master from the East. His writings contain interesting sidelights on the methods and adjuncts of teaching in the Lyceum, but the relation of his writings to the work of the Lyceum, and even the order of their composition, are far from clear. Since they are obviously not "published" works, it has been supposed that they are "lecture-notes," notes of students, or records of research and thought, brought periodically up to date, for consultation by advanced students. Since the structure of his doctrines is complex, and since he was long associated with the Academy and later a persistent critic of the doctrines of the Academy, his works have been chopped into pieces by critics seeking an evolution in them from Platonic idealism to scientific empiricism.

The period of Aristotle's manhood coincided with the reduction of the Greek city-states to the hegemony of Macedonia and the twelve or thirteen years of his work in the Lyceum with the campaigns of Alexander the Great. Hermias was doubtless a kind of advance-guard of Philip's projects against the Persians; Philip's choice of Aristotle as tutor to Alexander associated him closely with the political fortunes of Macedonia; and Alexander doubtless suspected him of complicity in the plot against his life for which Aristotle's nephew Callisthenes was executed; it is highly probable that the Lyceum received support and endowments from Callisthenes, Antipater, or even Alexander. In an important sense an epoch of Greek history was brought to a close when Alexander, Aristotle, and Demosthenes all died within somewhat more than a year.

The life of Aristotle was thus spent in a period which has seemed confused and dim to historians who have learned from Demosthenes to see it as the time of the loss of Greek liberties and the decline of Greek ideals; it has seemed a period of stirring action which came close to the fulfillment of an ambitious hope to those who see in the growth of panhellenism preached by Isocrates the beginnings of more stable political organizations and in the exploits of Alexander the spread of Greek ideals. Aristotle spent a large part of his life as an alien in Athens, and he seems to have been unsympathetic with, if not unmindful of, the ambitions of Alexander. Contemporary political events and social changes left few marks on his political and moral philosophy, and the search for effects of social conditions in his metaphysics and in his contributions to science has led only to speculative generalizations concerning the influence of environment on thought: to the conclusion that the existence of classes in society suggested hierarchies in his conception of the universe, that slave labor led him to neglect the mechanical arts and prefer the theoretic to the practical sciences, that his theories were therefore verbal rather than based on the resources of experience, and that his physical principles reflected his conception of political rule. Apart from such speculations, it is clear that the peace which was forced on Athens by Macedonian domination permitted Aristotle to organize a course of studies and to initiate a vast scheme of research into the history of political organizations, of science, and philosophy—the study of constitutions of Greek states, of the history of mathematics and medicine, and of the opinions of philosophers—as well as into the natural history of minerals, plants, and animals, and to lay the foundations thereby for one of the first attempts at an encyclopedic organization of human knowledge.

Richard McKeon

CONTENTS

PREFACE

The study of an ancient writer might appropriately envisage one or more of three objectives: the re-discovery and appreciation of past accomplishments and thoughts, the assemblage for present employment of odd, edifying, or useful items of information or knowledge, or the inquiry into truths whose specifications do not change with time. Although these three ends sometimes coincide in the reading of a philosopher who has been studied for centuries, the usual fate of philosophers, notwithstanding the concern for truth evinced in their writings, is to suffer doctrinal dismemberment by later philosophers and to undergo at the hands of historians and philologists reconstructions in which doctrine is barely discernible. As a result of the possible diversification of these ends, the influences that have been attributed to the thoughts of philosophers are not always easily calculable from examination of their own statements, yet the paradoxes, no less than the cumulative lines of progress, in intellectual history suggest the three ideals relevant to an introduction to the philosophy of Aristotle and selections from his works.

An introduction to the works of a philosopher should, first, since it is intended to supply aids to understanding the man and his thought, be specific and clear in its authentication of the information it conveys. The words of the philosopher himself are the best means by which to achieve such authenticity, and therefore the works of Aristotle have been reproduced intact and unabridged so far as the generous limits of space in this large volume have made such reproduction practicable and, where omissions have been unavoidable, the fact of the omission and the character of the omitted portions have been indicated as explicitly as possible. To select and rearrange small fragments of a philosopher's works is to recompose them and often to alter the doctrines they express. Therefore instead of parcels and snatches selected and pieced together with an eye to what seems more likely to catch the interest of the reader, the entire texts of seven of the most important books are included, and even when omissions have been made from the other seven works of which parts are published in this edition, entire books or entire chapters have been retained.

The vast labors which have been expended on the text of Aristotle during the last century have greatly facilitated the study of his philosophy. The monumental Oxford translation of his works into English, completed in 1931, was made possible by antecedent scholarly efforts, in which philologists have engaged at least since the publication of the great modern edition of Aristotle's works by the Berlin Academy between 1831 and 1870, to determine and to clarify what Aristotle says. That translation is readable and makes Aristotle's philosophy available to readers untrained in Greek as no previous English translation had. The eleven volumes of the Oxford translation can be reduced to a single volume, once the clearly inauthentic works have been excluded from consideration, without too serious loss of portions that bear on problems of general philosophic interest. The texts of seven works are complete: the *Physics, On generation and corruption, On the soul,* the *Metaphysics,* the *Nicomachean ethics,* the *Politics,* and the *Poetics.* For the most part omissions are from the four biological works; several of the *Short natural treatises* are omitted; of the physical works only the *Meteorology* and a portion of one of the four books of *On the heavens* are omitted; similarly three of the six books of the *Organon* and one of the three books of the *Rhetoric* are in part omitted; the *Constitution of Athens* is not included. Of the works which are commonly held to be authentic only three are not reproduced even in partial selection—the *Meteorology, On the progression of animals,* and the *Constitution of Athens;* or, if the tendency to accept *On the motion of animals* and the *Eudemian ethics* as genuine is justified, the number omitted is five, although it might be held, since three books of the *Nicomachean ethics* appear without alteration in the *Eudemian ethics,* that selections from the latter work may be found in the text of the former.

Explanatory notes and cross references by which difficult passages and interrelations have been elucidated by the translators have for the most part been retained. Purely philological notes, on the other hand, have been omitted, although major problems which have led to emendations, interpolations, and transpositions are indicated. The pagination of the Bekker edition of the Greek text of Aristotle, which is published in the first two of the five volumes of the Berlin edition, has become the customary means to locate a passage in Aristotle, and it has therefore been reproduced in the margins of the present edition. Thus, a reference to, say, *Metaphysics* xiii. 4. 1078^{b}27, would place the passage in question in Chapter 4 of Book 13 (or Book M) of the *Metaphysics,* on line 27 of the second column, i.e. column b, of page 1078 of the Berlin edition. Since the two volumes are paged continuously, no special designation of the volumes is needed; since the line references are to lines in the Greek text, they are of course only approximate in the English translation.

To make a difficult writer like Aristotle available in translation without, in the second place, supplying the dubious reader with more specific and urgent motivation for study than the recommendation that Aristotle is of the select group of timelessly great philosophers would scarcely constitute adequate introduction to his philosophy. For good or evil our interests and our erudition are grounded in the age in which we live, and the justice of our view of the past is moderated by the contemporary angle which can never be wholly removed from the perspective in which we see it. The words, the aphorisms, the distinctions, and even the ideas of Aristotle have in many instances become commonplaces in our culture and in other instances have been made the familiar whipping horses by which we castigate old errors and so boast of our own advances. It is wise to profit by our limitations and to make the familiar vestiges of a philosopher's thoughts in present-day inquiries and interests the beginning point of the study of his philosophy. The ordered presentation of Aristotle's doctrines in the *Introduction* finds its emphases precisely in such vestigial remains selected as points of interest for the reader who comes to Aristotle for renewed acquaintance or for the first time.

An introduction to a philosopher which did no more than confirm the student in established opinions, or an edition whose apparatus did no more than supply the reader with instruments by which to find what he had conceived to be useful prior to his reading of the philosopher and prior to philosophic analysis of his standards of utility, would aid the reader to find what he was looking for but at the expense of its subject, for the philosophy would almost certainly not be understood, and misconceived philosophic doctrines, however ingeniously contrived, are of doubtful ultimate utility. The third objective of an introduction to the works of a philosopher, to which the preceding two must be subordinate since there is no adequate reason for reading the works of a philosopher other than the philosophy they express, is more easily obscured than achieved by aids to reading or to philosophy. Some aid is needed, however, and therefore a method of reading Aristotle's works is suggested in the *Introduction* by a brief statement of the interrelations and continuity of his doctrines. The reader is advised to treat this interpretation skeptically until and unless he can find it confirmed in his own reading of the text, for it is useful only as a device by which to permit Aristotle to speak for himself. The achievement of Aristotle can be discovered only by reading and rereading his works, and the appreciation of that achievement depends quite as much on the deepened sense of value and the precision of criteria which he inculcates as on the materials he treats. The Middle Ages may seem to have exaggerated in calling him the Philosopher, but the understanding of what he said is still an unparalleled introduction to philosophy.

It is as difficult to reconstruct some notion of the appearance of Aristotle as to determine the lineaments and characteristics of his thought. The representation of him which was most familiar a generation ago, the statue in the Palazzo Spada in Rome, is almost certainly not a portrait of Aristotle. It was long supposed to be Aristotle because of its fragmentary inscription which should in all probability be restored more correctly as "Aristippos," and in any case the head does not belong to the statue. The portrait reproduced as the frontispiece, a bust in the Kunsthistorisches Museum in Vienna, has rather better claim to rank as a genuine portrait of Aristotle, although the identification rests on a tortuous argument. As proposed by Studniczka (*Das Bildnis des Aristoteles;* Leipzig, 1908), the identification goes back to a bust which was found in Rome about 1590 and which was bought by the learned antiquary Fulvio Orsini. It was identified by an inscription on its base. This bust is lost, but two drawings, one of them by Rubens, have survived. A family of twelve busts, varying in quality, preservation, and probable date, has been assembled, which seem, from their close correspondence, not only to represent one man but to imitate one original portrait, and which further, from their similarity to two drawings of the lost bust, may be portraits of Aristotle. The identification is plausible, though by no means certain. The style places the original portrait approximately in the time of Aristotle, and of the twelve extant busts the Vienna head probably gives the best idea of the original. The nose is almost entirely modern, but there is little other restoration. Several features ascribed to Aristotle by ancient tradition may be seen in these portraits: small eyes, short beard, and thinning hair.

Grateful acknowledgment is hereby extended to the Oxford University Press for permission to reprint the translation of the works of Aristotle prepared under the editorship of W. D. Ross. The arduous task of reading proof, checking quotations, and preparing the enormous materials of this volume for publication was rendered manageable by the assistance of Dr. Herbert Lamm and Dr. Meyer W. Isenberg, while the actual consummation of the task was not only facilitated by the co-operation of the staff of Random House, but is largely due to the jogging encouragement and reproaches of Mr. Bennett A. Cerf and Mr. Saxe Commins.

RICHARD McKEON

INTRODUCTION
C.D.C. Reeve

Aristotle's Writings

A list of Aristotle's papers, probably made in the third century B.C., seems to describe most of his extant writings, as well as a number of works—some in dialogue form—that are now lost. When Sulla captured Athens in 87 B.C., these papers were brought to Rome, where they were edited, organized into different treatises, and arranged in a logical sequence by Andronicus of Rhodes in around 30 B.C. Most of the writings he thought to be genuinely Aristotelian have been transmitted to us via manuscript copies produced between the ninth and the sixteenth centuries.

These writings, of which the present volume include a rich selection, may be classified as follows: logic, dialectic, metaphysics: *Categories, On Interpretation, Prior Analytics, Topics, On Sophistical Refutations, Metaphysics;* science and philosophy of science: *Posterior Analytics, Physics, On the Heavens, On Generation and Corruption, Meteorology, History of Animals, On the Parts of Animals, On the Motion of Animals, On the Progression of Animals, On the Generation of Animals;* psychology and philosophy of mind: *On the Soul, Sense and Sensibilia, On Memory and Reminiscence, On Sleep, On Dreams, On Prophesying by Dreams, On Length and Shortness of Life, On Youth, Old Age, Life and Death, Respiration;* ethics and politics: *Nicomachean Ethics, Magna Moralia, Eudemian Ethics, Politics, Rhetoric, Constitution of Athens;* aesthetics: *Poetics.*

The most credible view of these writings is that they are lecture notes written or dictated by Aristotle himself and not intended for publication. Their organization into treatises and the internal organization of the treatises into books and chapters may, however, not be his. No doubt this accounts for some, though not all, of their legendary and manifest difficulty.

The Aristotelian World

Of the various things that exist in the world described in Aristotle's writings, "some exist by nature, some from other causes" (*Physics* 192^{b}8–9). Those that exist by nature have a nature of their own, an internal source of movement, growth, and alteration (192^{b}13–15). Thus, for example, a feline embryo has within it a source that explains why it grows into a cat, why that cat moves and alters in the ways it does, and why it eventually decays and dies. A house or any other artifact, by contrast, has no such source within it;

instead, the source is "in something else external to the thing," namely, the craftsman who manufactures it (*Physics* 192ᵇ30–31; also *Metaphysics* 1032ᵃ32–ᵇ10).

A thing's nature is the same as its essence or function, which is the same as its end, or that for the sake of which it exists. For its end just is to actualize its nature by performing its function (*Nicomachean Ethics* 1168ᵃ6–9), and something that cannot perform its function ceases to be what it is except in name (*On the Parts of Animals* 640ᵇ33–641ᵃ6, *Politics* 1253ᵃ23–25). Aristotle's view of natural beings is therefore teleological: He sees them as being defined by an end *(telos)* for which they are striving, and as needing to have their behavior explained by reference to it. It is this end, essence, or function that fixes what the good for that being consists in, and what its virtues or excellences are (*Nicomachean Ethics* 1098ᵃ7–20, *Physics* 195ᵃ23–25).

Most natural things, as well as the products of art or craft, are hylomorphic compounds, compounds of matter *(hulê)* and form *(morphê)*. Statues are examples: Their matter is the stone or metal from which they are made; their form is their shape. Human beings are also examples: Their matter is (roughly speaking) their body; their soul is their form. Thus a person's soul is not something separable from his body, but is more like the structural organization responsible for his body's being alive and functioning appropriately.

While the natures of such compounds owe something to their matter and something to their form, what they owe to form is more important (*Metaphysics* 1025ᵇ26–1026ᵃ6, *Physics* 193ᵇ6–7). For example, a human being can survive through change in his matter (we are constantly metabolizing), but if his form is changed, he ceases to exist (*Politics* 1276ᵇ1–13). That is why the sort of investigation into human beings we find in *De Anima* and in ethical and political treatises focuses on souls rather than bodies.

These souls consist of distinct, hierarchically organized constituents (*Nicomachean Ethics,* bk. I, ch. 13). The lowest rung in the hierarchy is the vegetative soul, which is responsible for nutrition and growth, and which is also found in plants and other animals. At the next rung up, we find appetitive soul, which is responsible for perception, imagination, and movement, and so is present in other animals too, but not in plants. This sort of soul lacks reason but, unlike the vegetative, can be influenced by it. The third element in the human soul is reason. It is divided into the scientific element, which enables us to contemplate or engage in theoretical activity, and the calculative or deliberative element, which enables us to engage in practical and political activity (*Nicomachean Ethics* 1097ᵇ33–1098ᵃ8, 1139ᵃ3–ᵇ5).

Because the human soul contains these different elements, the human good might be defined by properties exemplified by all three of them or by properties exemplified by only some of them. In the famous function argument from the *Nicomachean Ethics,* bk. I, ch. 7, Aristotle argues for the latter alternative: The human good is happiness, which is "an active life of the element that has a rational principle" (1098ª3–4). The problem is that the scientific and the deliberative element both fit this description. Human happiness might, therefore, consist in practical political activity, or in contemplative theorizing, or in a mixture of both. Even a brief glance at *Nicomachean Ethics,* bk. X, chs. 6–8 will reveal how hard it is to determine which of these Aristotle has in mind.

Aristotelian Sciences

The Aristotelian sciences provide us with knowledge of the world, how to live successfully in it, and how to produce what we need to do so. Hence they fall into three distinct types:

I.   *Theoretical sciences:* theology, philosophy, mathematics, natural sciences.

II. *Practical sciences:* ethics, household management, statesmanship, which is divided into legislation and politics, with politics being further divided into deliberative science and judicial science (*Nicomachean Ethics* 1141ᵇ29–32).

III. *Productive sciences* (crafts, arts): medicine, building, etc.

Of these, the theoretical ones are the Aristotelian paradigm, since they provide us with knowledge of universal necessary truths. The extent to which ethics or statesmanship fit the paradigm, however, is less clear. One reason for this is that a huge part of these sciences has to do not with universal principles of the sort one finds in physics, but with particular cases, whose near infinite variety cannot easily be summed up in a formula (*Nicomachean Ethics* 1109ᵇ21, *Rhetoric* 1374ª18–ᵇ23). The knowledge of what justice is may well be scientific knowledge, but to know what justice requires in a particular case one also needs equity, which is a combination of virtue and a trained eye (*Nicomachean Ethics,* bk. V, ch. 10). Perhaps, then, we should think of practical sciences as having something like a theoretically scientific core, but as not being reducible to it.

Theoretical Science

Each Aristotelian theoretical science deals with a genus—a natural class of beings that have forms or essences (*Posterior Analytics* 87ª38–39, *Metaphysics* 1003ᵇ19–21). When appropriately regimented, it may be set out as a structure of demonstrations, the indemonstrable first principles of which are definitions of those essences. More precisely, the first principles special to biology, or to some other science that applies to only a part of reality, are like this. Others that are common to all sciences—such as the principle of non-contradiction and other logical principles—have a somewhat different character. Since all these first principles are necessary truths, and demonstration is a type of deductive inference, scientific theorems are also necessary.

Though we cannot grasp a *first* principle by demonstrating it from yet more primitive principles, it must—if we are to have any unqualified scientific knowledge at all—be "better known" to us than any of the science's theorems (*Nicomachean Ethics* 1139^{b}33–34). This better knowledge is provided by intuition *(nous),* and the process by which principles come within intuition's ken is induction (1139^{b}28–29, 1141^{a}7–8).

Induction begins with perception of particulars, which gives rise to retention of perceptual contents, or memories (*Posterior Analytics* 100^{a}1–3). From a unified set of such memories experience arises (100^{a}3–6), "when, from many notions gained by experience, one universal supposition about similar objects is produced" (*Metaphysics* 981^{a}1–7). Getting from particulars to universals, therefore, is a largely noninferential process. If we simply attend to particular cases—perhaps to all, perhaps to just one—and have some acumen, we will get there (*Prior Analytics* 68^{b}15–29, *Posterior Analytics* 88^{a}12–17, 89^{b}10–13). When these universals are appropriately analyzed into their "elements *(stoicheia)* and first principles," they become intrinsically clear and unqualifiedly known (*Physics* 184^{a}16–21).

A universal essence is something out there in the world. Its analogue in a scientific theory, however, is a definition similar in structure to it (*Metaphysics* 1034^{b}20–22). That is why the first principles of the sciences are not essences, but definitions of them.

The inductive path to first principles and scientific knowledge begins with perception of particulars and of perceptually accessible, unanalyzed universals, and leads eventually to analyzed universal essences (first principles) and definitions of them. At this point, induction gives way to deduction, as we descend from these essences to other principles. Perception alone cannot reach the end of this journey, but without perception it cannot so much as begin. Perception, elaborated in theory, is the soul's window on the Aristotelian world (*Prior Analytics* 46^{a}17–18, *On the Soul* 432^{a}7–9).

Dialectic

The first principles proper to a science cannot be demonstrated within that science. If they could, they would not be genuine *first* principles. They can, however, be defended by dialectic. For, since it "examines," and does so by appeal not to scientific principles but to common or generally accepted opinions *(endoxa),* "dialectic is a process of criticism wherein lies the path to the [first] principles of all inquiries" *(Topics* 101ᵃ36–ᵇ4).

Now opinions are endoxa when they are accepted without demurral "by every one or by the majority or by the wise, either by all of them, or by most or by the most notable and illustrious of them" *(Topics* 100ᵇ21–23), so that the majority do not disagree with the wise about them, nor do either group disagree among themselves (104ᵃ8–11). Generally accepted opinions, therefore, are beliefs to which there is simply no worthwhile opposition. Apparent endoxa, by contrast, are beliefs that mistakenly appear to have this uncontested status (100ᵇ23–25, 104ᵃ15–33).

Defending first principles on the basis of endoxa is a matter of going through the difficulties *(aporiai)* "on both sides of a subject" until they are solved *(Topics* 101ᵃ35). Suppose, then, that the topic to be dialectically investigated is this: Is being a single unchanging thing, or not? A competent dialectician will, first, follow out the consequences of each alternative to see what difficulties they face. Second, he will go through the difficulties he has uncovered to determine which can be solved and which cannot. As a result, he will be well placed to attack or defend either alternative in the strongest possible way.

Aporematic, which is the part of philosophy that deals with such difficulties, is like dialectic in its methods, but differs from it in important respects. In a dialectical argument, for example, the opponent may refuse to accept a proposition that a philosopher would accept: "The premises of the philosopher's deductions or those of the one investigating by himself, though true and familiar, may be refused by . . . [an opponent] because they lie too near to the original proposition, and so he sees what will happen if he grants them. But the philosopher is unconcerned about this. Indeed, he will presumably be eager that his axioms should be as familiar and as near to the question at hand as possible, since it is from premises of this sort that scientific deductions proceed" *(Topics* 155ᵇ10–16). Since the truth may well hinge on propositions whose status is just like these premises, there is no guarantee that what a dialectician considers most defensible will be true.

Drawing on this new class of endoxa, then, the philosopher examines both the claim that being is a single unchanging thing, and the claim that it is not, in just the way that the dialectician does. As a result, he determines, let us suppose, that the most defensible, or least problematic, conclusion is that in some senses of the terms, being is one and unchanging, in others, not. To reach this conclusion, however, he will have to disambiguate and reformulate endoxa on both sides, partly accepting and partly rejecting them. Others, he may well have to reject outright, so that beliefs that initially seemed to be endoxa—that seemed to be unproblematic—will have emerged as only apparently such *(Topics* 100ᵇ23–25). These he will have to explain away: "We should state not only the truth, but also the cause of error—for this contributes towards producing conviction, since when a reasonable explanation is given of why the false view appears true, this tends to produce belief in the true view" (*Nicomachean Ethics* 1154ᵃ22–25). If, at the end of this process, the difficulties are solved and most of the most-authoritative endoxa are left, that, Aristotle claims, will be a sufficient proof of the philosopher's conclusion (1145ᵇ6–7).

But in that claim lies a problem. For while dialectic treats things "only with an eye to general opinion," philosophy must treat them "according to their truth" (*Topics* 105ᵇ30–31). Endoxa, however, are just generally accepted and unobjectionable opinions. Since even such unopposed opinions may nevertheless be false, how can an argument that relies on them be guaranteed to reach the truth? The answer lies in aporematic philosophy's dialectical capacity to criticize or examine (101ᵇ3).

Because he is a generally educated person, an aporematic philosopher knows what it takes to be a genuine science of whatever sort (*On the Parts of Animals* 639ᵃ1–8). Hence he will know, for example, what level of exactness a science should have, given its subject matter, and what we should and should not seek to have demonstrated (*Nicomachean Ethics* 1094ᵇ23–27, *Metaphysics* 1006ᵃ5–11). Using his dialectical capacity to examine, therefore, a philosopher can, for example, determine whether a person, A, has any sort of mathematical knowledge, or is simply a charlatan. If A passes the examination, the philosopher can use his own knowledge of what a mathematical science must be like to determine whether A's mathematical knowledge is genuinely scientific. If he finds that it is, he knows that the undemonstrated mathematical first principles A accepts are true. If, in particular, A accepts that magnitudes are divisible without limit, the philosopher knows that this is true.

When he uses his dialectical skill to draw out the consequences of this principle and of its negation, however, he sees difficulties and supporting arguments based on endoxa on both sides. Since he knows the principle is true, however, his goal will be to resolve the difficulties it faces and undo the arguments that seem to support its negation. If he is successful, he will have refuted all the objections to it, and so will have provided a negative demonstration, or demonstration by refutation, of it (*Metaphysics* 1006ᵃ12). Such a demonstration is aporematic philosophy's way to a scientific first principle, and constitutes the sufficient proof of it to which Aristotle refers.

In many texts, Aristotle characterizes problems as knots in our understanding that dialectic enables us to untie, in others, he characterizes dialectic itself as enabling us to make first principles clear. What aporematic philosophy offers us in regard to the first principles of the sciences, then, is no knots—no impediments to clear and exact intuitive grasp. And with such clarity comes scientific knowledge of the most excellent and unqualified sort—knowledge that manifests the virtue of theoretical wisdom (*Nicomachean Ethics* 1141ª16–17).

———

The marginal numbers accompanying the text correspond to the page number, column (represented by the letters a and b), and line of the edition of Aristotle's works published in Berlin by Immanuel Bekker in 1831. Line numbers given in citations are those of the Greek text and correspond only approximately to lines in translations.

Organon

CATEGORIAE

Translated by E. M. Edghill

CONTENTS

CATEGORIAE

(*Categories*)

1   Things are said to be named 'equivocally' when, though they
have a common name, the definition corresponding with the name
differs for each. Thus, a real man and a figure in a picture can both
lay claim to the name 'animal'; yet these are equivocally so named,
for, though they have a common name, the definition corresponding
with the name differs for each. For should any one define in what
sense each is an animal, his definition in the one case will be ap- 5
propriate to that case only.

On the other hand, things are said to be named 'univocally' which
have both the name and the definition answering to the name in
common. A man and an ox are both 'animal', and these are univocally so named, inasmuch as not only the name, but also the
definition, is the same in both cases: for if a man should state in 10
what sense each is an animal, the statement in the one case would be
identical with that in the other.

Things are said to be named 'derivatively', which derive their name
from some other name, but differ from it in termination. Thus the
grammarian derives his name from the word 'grammar', and the 15
courageous man from the word 'courage'.

2   Forms of speech are either simple or composite. Examples of the
latter are such expressions as 'the man runs', 'the man wins'; of the
former 'man', 'ox', 'runs', 'wins'.

Of things themselves some are predicable of a subject, and are 20
never present in a subject. Thus 'man' is predicable of the individual
man, and is never present in a subject.

By being 'present in a subject' I do not mean present as parts are
present in a whole, but being incapable of existence apart from the
said subject.

Some things, again, are present in a subject, but are never predicable of a subject. For instance, a certain point of grammatical 25
knowledge is present in the mind, but is not predicable of any
subject; or again, a certain whiteness may be present in the body
(for colour requires a material basis), yet it is never predicable of
anything.

Other things, again, are both predicable of a subject and present
1ᵇ in a subject. Thus while knowledge is present in the human mind,
it is predicable of grammar.

There is, lastly, a class of things which are neither present in a
subject nor predicable of a subject, such as the individual man or
5 the individual horse. But, to speak more generally, that which is
individual and has the character of a unit is never predicable of a
subject. Yet in some cases there is nothing to prevent such being
present in a subject. Thus a certain point of grammatical knowledge
is present in a subject.

10 **3** When one thing is predicated of another, all that which is predicable of the predicate will be predicable also of the subject. Thus,
'man' is predicated of the individual man; but 'animal' is predicated
of 'man'; it will, therefore, be predicable of the individual man also:
15 for the individual man is both 'man' and 'animal'.

If genera are different and co-ordinate, their differentiae are themselves different in kind. Take as an instance the genus 'animal' and the
genus 'knowledge'. 'With feet', 'two-footed', 'winged', 'aquatic', are
differentiae of 'animal'; the species of knowledge are not distinguished
by the same differentiae. One species of knowledge does not differ from
another in being 'two-footed'.

20 But where one genus is subordinate to another, there is nothing to
prevent their having the same differentiae: for the greater class
is predicated of the lesser, so that all the differentiae of the
predicate will be differentiae also of the subject.

25 **4** Expressions which are in no way composite signify substance,
quantity, quality, relation, place, time, position, state, action, or
affection. To sketch my meaning roughly, examples of substance are
'man' or 'the horse', of quantity, such terms as 'two cubits long' or
'three cubits long', of quality, such attributes as 'white', 'grammatical'. 'Double', 'half', 'greater', fall under the category of relation;
2ᵃ 'in the market place', 'in the Lyceum', under that of place; 'yesterday', 'last year', under that of time. 'Lying', 'sitting', are terms
indicating position; 'shod', 'armed', state; 'to lance', 'to cauterize',
action; 'to be lanced', 'to be cauterized', affection.

No one of these terms, in and by itself, involves an affirmation;
5 it is by the combination of such terms that positive or negative statements arise. For every assertion must, as is admitted, be either true
or false, whereas expressions which are not in any way composite,
10 such as 'man', 'white', 'runs', 'wins', cannot be either true or false.

5 Substance, in the truest and primary and most definite sense of
the word, is that which is neither predicable of a subject nor present
in a subject; for instance, the individual man or horse. But in a
secondary sense those things are called substances within which, as
species, the primary substances are included; also those which, as 15
genera, include the species. For instance, the individual man is
included in the species 'man', and the genus to which the species
belongs is 'animal'; these, therefore—that is to say, the species 'man'
and the genus 'animal'—are termed secondary substances.

It is plain from what has been said that both the name and the
definition of the predicate must be predicable of the subject. For 20
instance, 'man' is predicated of the individual man. Now in this case
the name of the species 'man' is applied to the individual, for we use
the term 'man' in describing the individual; and the definition of
'man' will also be predicated of the individual man, for the individual man is both man and animal. Thus, both the name and the 25
definition of the species are predicable of the individual.

With regard, on the other hand, to those things which are present
in a subject, it is generally the case that neither their name nor their
definition is predicable of that in which they are present. Though,
however, the definition is never predicable, there is nothing in certain 30
cases to prevent the name being used. For instance, 'white' being
present in a body is predicated of that in which it is present, for
a body is called white: the definition, however, of the color 'white'
is never predicable of the body.

Everything except primary substances is either predicable of a
primary substance or present in a primary substance. This becomes
evident by reference to particular instances which occur. 'Animal' 35
is predicated of the species 'man', therefore of the individual man,
for if there were no individual man of whom it could be predicated,
it could not be predicated of the species 'man' at all. Again, colour is 2ᵇ
present in body, therefore in individual bodies, for if there were no
individual body in which it was present, it could not be present in
body at all. Thus everything except primary substances is either
predicated of primary substances, or is present in them, and if these 5
last did not exist, it would be impossible for anything else to exist.

Of secondary substances, the species is more truly substance than
the genus, being more nearly related to primary substance. For if
any one should render an account of what a primary substance is,
he would render a more instructive account, and one more proper to
the subject, by stating the species than by stating the genus. Thus, he 10
would give a more instructive account of an individual man by stating

that he was man than by stating that he was animal, for the former description is peculiar to the individual in a greater degree, while the latter is too general. Again, the man who gives an account of the nature of an individual tree will give a more instructive account by mentioning the species 'tree' than by mentioning the genus 'plant'.

15　　Moreover, primary substances are most properly called substances in virtue of the fact that they are the entities which underlie everything else, and that everything else is either predicated of them or present in them. Now the same relation which subsists between primary substance and everything else subsists also between the species and the genus: for the species is to the genus as subject is to predi-
20　cate, since the genus is predicated of the species, whereas the species cannot be predicated of the genus. Thus we have a second ground for asserting that the species is more truly substance than the genus.

Of species themselves, except in the case of such as are genera, no one is more truly substance than another. We should not give a more appropriate account of the individual man by stating the
25　species to which he belonged, than we should of an individual horse by adopting the same method of definition. In the same way, of primary substances, no one is more truly substance than another; an individual man is not more truly substance than an individual ox.

It is, then, with good reason that of all that remains, when we exclude primary substances, we concede to species and genera alone
30　the name 'secondary substance', for these alone of all the predicates convey a knowledge of primary substance. For it is by stating the species or the genus that we appropriately define any individual man; and we shall make our definition more exact by stating the former than by stating the latter. All other things that we state,
35　such as that he is white, that he runs, and so on, are irrelevant to the definition. Thus it is just that these alone, apart from primary substances, should be called substances.

Further, primary substances are most properly so called because they underlie and are the subjects of everything else. Now the same
3ᵃ　relation that subsists between primary substance and everything else subsists also between the species and the genus to which the primary substance belongs, on the one hand, and every attribute which is not included within these, on the other. For these are the subjects of all such. If we call an individual man 'skilled in grammar', the predicate is applicable also to the species and to the genus to
5　which he belongs. This law holds good in all cases.

It is a common characteristic of all substance that it is never present in a subject. For primary substance is neither present in a subject nor predicated of a subject; while, with regard to secondary substances, it is clear from the following arguments (apart from others) that they are not present in a subject. For 'man' is predicated of the individual man, but is not present in any subject: for manhood is not present in the individual man. In the same way, 'animal' is also predicated of the individual man, but is not present in him. Again, when a thing is present in a subject, though the name may quite well be applied to that in which it is present, the definition cannot be applied. Yet of secondary substances, not only the name, but also the definition, applies to the subject: we should use both the definition of the species and that of the genus with reference to the individual man. Thus substance cannot be present in a subject.

Yet this is not peculiar to substance, for it is also the case that differentiae cannot be present in subjects. The characteristics 'terrestrial' and 'two-footed' are predicated of the species 'man', but not present in it. For they are not *in* man. Moreover, the definition of the differentia may be predicated of that of which the differentia itself is predicated. For instance, if the characteristic 'terrestrial' is predicated of the species 'man', the definition also of that characteristic may be used to form the predicate of the species 'man': for 'man' is terrestrial.

The fact that the parts of substances appear to be present in the whole, as in a subject, should not make us apprehensive lest we should have to admit that such parts are not substances: for in explaining the phrase 'being present in a subject', we stated [1] that we meant 'otherwise than as parts in a whole'.

It is the mark of substances and of differentiae that, in all propositions of which they form the predicate, they are predicated univocally. For all such propositions have for their subject either the individual or the species. It is true that, inasmuch as primary substance is not predicable of anything, it can never form the predicate of any proposition. But of secondary substances, the species is predicated of the individual, the genus both of the species and of the individual. Similarly the differentiae are predicated of the species and of the individuals. Moreover, the definition of the species and that of the genus are applicable to the primary substance, and that of the genus to the species. For all that is predicated of the predicate will be predicated also of the subject. Similarly, the definition of the differentiae will be applicable to the species and to the individuals. But it was stated above [2] that the word 'univocal' was applied to those things which had both name and definition in common. It is,

[1] 1ᵃ 24.　　　　　　　　　　　　　　　　[2] 1ᵃ 6.

therefore, established that in every proposition, of which either substance or a differentia forms the predicate, these are predicated
univocally.

10   All substance appears to signify that which is individual. In the
case of primary substance this is indisputably true, for the thing
is a unit. In the case of secondary substances, when we speak,
for instance, of 'man' or 'animal', our form of speech gives the impression that we are here also indicating that which is individual,
15 but the impression is not strictly true; for a secondary substance
is not an individual, but a class with a certain qualification; for it is
not one and single as a primary substance is; the words 'man',
'animal', are predicable of more than one subject.

Yet species and genus do not merely indicate quality, like the term
'white'; 'white' indicates quality and nothing further, but species
and genus determine the quality with reference to a substance: they
20 signify substance qualitatively differentiated. The determinate qualification covers a larger field in the case of the genus than in that of
the species: he who uses the word 'animal' is herein using a word
of wider extension than he who uses the word 'man'.

Another mark of substance is that it has no contrary. What could
25 be the contrary of any primary substance, such as the individual
man or animal? It has none. Nor can the species or the genus have
a contrary. Yet this characteristic is not peculiar to substance, but is
true of many other things, such as quantity. There is nothing that
forms the contrary of 'two cubits long' or of 'three cubits long', or of
30 'ten', or of any such term. A man may contend that 'much' is the
contrary of 'little', or 'great' of 'small', but of definite quantitative
terms no contrary exists.

Substance, again, does not appear to admit of variation of degree.
I do not mean by this that one substance cannot be more or less truly
substance than another, for it has already been stated [3] that this
35 is the case; but that no single substance admits of varying degrees
within itself. For instance, one particular substance, 'man', cannot be
more or less man either than himself at some other time or than
some other man. One man cannot be more man than another, as that
which is white may be more or less white than some other white
4ᵃ object, or as that which is beautiful may be more or less beautiful
than some other beautiful object. The same quality, moreover, is said
to subsist in a thing in varying degrees at different times. A body,
being white, is said to be whiter at one time than it was before, or,
being warm, is said to be warmer or less warm than at some other

[3] 2ᵃ 11—ᵇ 22.

time. But substance is not said to be more or less that which it is: 5
a man is not more truly a man at one time than he was before, nor is
anything, if it is substance, more or less what it is. Substance, then,
does not admit of variation of degree.

The most distinctive mark of substance appears to be that, while 10
remaining numerically one and the same, it is capable of admitting
contrary qualities. From among things other than substance, we
should find ourselves unable to bring forward any which possessed
this mark. Thus, one and the same colour cannot be white and black. 15
Nor can the same one action be good and bad: this law holds good
with everything that is not substance. But one and the self-same
substance, while retaining its identity, is yet capable of admitting
contrary qualities. The same individual person is at one time white,
at another black, at one time warm, at another cold, at one time good, 20
at another bad. This capacity is found nowhere else, though it might
be maintained that a statement or opinion was an exception to the
rule. The same statement, it is agreed, can be both true and false.
For if the statement 'he is sitting' is true, yet, when the person in 25
question has risen, the same statement will be false. The same applies
to opinions. For if any one thinks truly that a person is sitting, yet,
when that person has risen, this same opinion, if still held, will be
false. Yet although this exception may be allowed, there is, nevertheless, a difference in the manner in which the thing takes place.
It is by themselves changing that substances admit contrary quali- 30
ties. It is thus that that which was hot becomes cold, for it has
entered into a different state. Similarly that which was white becomes black, and that which was bad good, by a process of change;
and in the same way in all other cases it is by changing that substances are capable of admitting contrary qualities. But statements
and opinions themselves remain unaltered in all respects: it is by the 35
alteration in the facts of the case that the contrary quality comes to
be theirs. The statement 'he is sitting' remains unaltered, but it is
at one time true, at another false, according to circumstances. What 4ᵇ
has been said of statements applies also to opinions. Thus, in respect
of the manner in which the thing takes place, it is the peculiar mark
of substance that it should be capable of admitting contrary qualities; for it is by itself changing that it does so.

If, then, a man should make this exception and contend that
statements and opinions are capable of admitting contrary qualities, his contention is unsound. For statements and opinions are said 5
to have this capacity, not because they themselves undergo modifi-

cation, but because this modification occurs in the case of something else. The truth or falsity of a statement depends on facts, and not on any power on the part of the statement itself of admitting
10 contrary qualities. In short, there is nothing which can alter the nature of statements and opinions. As, then, no change takes place in themselves, these cannot be said to be capable of admitting contrary qualities.

But it is by reason of the modification which takes place within the substance itself that a substance is said to be capable of admitting contrary qualities; for a substance admits within itself either
15 disease or health, whiteness or blackness. It is in this sense that it is said to be capable of admitting contrary qualities.

To sum up, it is a distinctive mark of substance, that, while remaining numerically one and the same, it is capable of admitting contrary qualities, the modification taking place through a change in the substance itself.

Let these remarks suffice on the subject of substance.

20 6   Quantity is either discrete or continuous. Moreover, some quantities are such that each part of the whole has a relative position to the other parts: others have within them no such relation of part to part.

Instances of discrete quantities are number and speech; of continuous, lines, surfaces, solids, and, besides these, time and place.
25   In the case of the parts of a number, there is no common boundary at which they join. For example: two fives make ten, but the two fives have no common boundary, but are separate; the parts three and seven also do not join at any boundary. Nor, to generalize, would it ever be possible in the case of number that there should
30 be a common boundary among the parts; they are always separate. Number, therefore, is a discrete quantity.

The same is true of speech. That speech is a quantity is evident: for it is measured in long and short syllables. I mean here that speech which is vocal. Moreover, it is a discrete quantity, for its parts
35 have no common boundary. There is no common boundary at which the syllables join, but each is separate and distinct from the rest.
5ᵃ   A line, on the other hand, is a continuous quantity, for it is possible to find a common boundary at which its parts join. In the case of the line, this common boundary is the point; in the case of the plane, it is the line: for the parts of the plane have also a common boundary. Similarly you can find a common boundary in the case of
5 the parts of a solid, namely either a line or a plane.

Space and time also belong to this class of quantities. Time, past, present, and future, forms a continuous whole. Space, likewise, is a continuous quantity: for the parts of a solid occupy a certain space, and these have a common boundary; it follows that the parts of space also, which are occupied by the parts of the solid, 10 have the same common boundary as the parts of the solid. Thus, not only time, but space also, is a continuous quantity, for its parts have a common boundary.

Quantities consist either of parts which bear a relative position 15 each to each, or of parts which do not. The parts of a line bear a relative position to each other, for each lies somewhere, and it would be possible to distinguish each, and to state the position of each on the plane and to explain to what sort of part among the rest each was contiguous. Similarly the parts of a plane have position, 20 for it could similarly be stated what was the position of each and what sort of parts were contiguous. The same is true with regard to the solid and to space. But it would be impossible to show that the parts of a number had a relative position each to each, or a par- 25 ticular position, or to state what parts were contiguous. Nor could this be done in the case of time, for none of the parts of time has an abiding existence, and that which does not abide can hardly have position. It would be better to say that such parts had a rela- tive order, in virtue of one being prior to another. Similarly with number: in counting, 'one' is prior to 'two', and 'two' to 'three', 30 and thus the parts of number may be said to possess a relative order, though it would be impossible to discover any distinct posi- tion for each. This holds good also in the case of speech. None of its parts has an abiding existence: when once a syllable is pro- nounced, it is not possible to retain it, so that, naturally, as the parts 35 do not abide, they cannot have position. Thus, some quantities con- sist of parts which have position, and some of those which have not.

Strictly speaking, only the things which I have mentioned belong to the category of quantity: everything else that is called quantita- tive is a quantity in a secondary sense. It is because we have in mind some one of these quantities, properly so called, that we apply quantitative terms to other things. We speak of what is white 5ᵇ as large, because the surface over which the white extends is large; we speak of an action or a process as lengthy, because the time covered is long; these things cannot in their own right claim the quantitative epithet. For instance, should any one explain how long an action was, his statement would be made in terms of the 5

time taken, to the effect that it lasted a year, or something of that sort. In the same way, he would explain the size of a white object in terms of surface, for he would state the area which it covered. Thus the things already mentioned, and these alone, are in their intrinsic nature quantities; nothing else can claim the name in its
10 own right, but, if at all, only in a secondary sense.

Quantities have no contraries. In the case of definite quantities this is obvious; thus, there is nothing that is the contrary of 'two cubits long' or of 'three cubits long', or of a surface, or of any such quantities. A man might, indeed, argue that 'much' was the con-
15 trary of 'little', and 'great' of 'small'. But these are not quantitative, but relative; things are not great or small absolutely, they are so called rather as the result of an act of comparison. For instance, a mountain is called small, a grain large, in virtue of the fact that the latter is greater than others of its kind, the former less. Thus
20 there is a reference here to an external standard, for if the terms 'great' and 'small' were used absolutely, a mountain would never be called small or a grain large. Again, we say that there are many people in a village, and few in Athens, although those in the city are many times as numerous as those in the village: or we say
25 that a house has many in it, and a theatre few, though those in the theatre far outnumber those in the house. The terms 'two cubits long', 'three cubits long', and so on indicate quantity, the terms 'great' and 'small' indicate relation, for they have reference to an external standard. It is, therefore, plain that these are to be classed as relative.
30   Again, whether we define them as quantitative or not, they have no contraries: for how can there be a contrary of an attribute which is not to be apprehended in or by itself, but only by reference to something external? Again, if 'great' and 'small' are contraries, it will come about that the same subject can admit contrary qualities at one and the same time, and that things will themselves be
35 contrary to themselves. For it happens at times that the same thing is both small and great. For the same thing may be small in comparison with one thing, and great in comparison with another, so that the same thing comes to be both small and great at one and the same time, and is of such a nature as to admit contrary qualities at one and the same moment. Yet it was agreed, when substance was being discussed, that nothing admits contrary qualities
6ᵃ at one and the same moment. For though substance is capable of admitting contrary qualities, yet no one is at the same time both sick and healthy, nothing is at the same time both white and black.

Nor is there anything which is qualified in contrary ways at one and the same time.

Moreover, if these were contraries, they would themselves be contrary to themselves. For if 'great' is the contrary of 'small', and 5 the same thing is both great and small at the same time, then 'small' or 'great' is the contrary of itself. But this is impossible. The term 'great', therefore, is not the contrary of the term 'small', nor 'much' of 'little'. And even though a man should call these terms not relative, but quantitative, they would not have contraries.   10

It is in the case of space that quantity most plausibly appears to admit of a contrary. For men define the term 'above' as the contrary of 'below', when it is the region at the centre they mean by 'below'; and this is so, because nothing is farther from the extremities of the universe than the region at the centre. Indeed, it seems that 15 in defining contraries of every kind men have recourse to a spatial metaphor, for they say that those things are contraries which, within the same class, are separated *by the greatest possible distance.*

Quantity does not, it appears, admit of variation of degree. One thing cannot be two cubits long in a greater degree than another. 20 Similarly with regard to number: what is 'three' is not more truly three than what is 'five' is five; nor is one set of three more truly three than another set. Again, one period of time is not said to be more truly time than another. Nor is there any other kind of quantity, of all that have been mentioned, with regard to which variation of degree can be predicated. The category of quantity, therefore, 25 does not admit of variation of degree.

The most distinctive mark of quantity is that equality and inequality are predicated of it. Each of the aforesaid quantities is said to be equal or unequal. For instance, one solid is said to be equal or unequal to another; number, too, and time can have these terms applied to them, as indeed can all those kinds of quantity that have 30 been mentioned.

That which is not a quantity can by no means, it would seem, be termed equal or unequal to anything else. One particular disposition or one particular quality, such as whiteness, is by no means compared with another in terms of equality and inequality but rather in terms of similarity. Thus it is the distinctive mark of quantity that it can be called equal and unequal.   35

7   Those things are called relative, which, being either said to be *of* something else or *related to* something else, are explained by reference to that other thing. For instance, the word 'superior' is

explained by reference to something else, for it is superiority *over something else* that is meant. Similarly, the expression 'double' has this external reference, for it is the double *of something else* that is 6^b meant. So it is with everything else of this kind. There are, moreover, other relatives, e. g. habit, disposition, perception, knowledge, and attitude. The significance of all these is explained by a reference to something else and in no other way. Thus, a habit is a habit *of* 5 *something,* knowledge is knowledge *of something,* attitude is the attitude *of something.* So it is with all other relatives that have been mentioned. Those terms, then, are called relative, the nature of which is explained by reference to something else, the preposition 'of' or some other preposition being used to indicate the relation. Thus, one mountain is called great *in comparison with another*; for the mountain claims this attribute *by comparison with* something.
10 Again, that which is called similar must be similar *to something else,* and all other such attributes have this external reference. It is to be noted that lying and standing and sitting are particular attitudes, but attitude is itself a relative term. To lie, to stand, to be seated, are not themselves attitudes, but take their name from the aforesaid attitudes.
15   It is possible for relatives to have contraries. Thus virtue has a contrary, vice, these both being relatives; knowledge, too, has a contrary, ignorance. But this is not the mark of all relatives; 'double' and 'triple' have no contrary, nor indeed has any such term.
20   It also appears that relatives can admit of variation of degree. For 'like' and 'unlike', 'equal' and 'unequal', have the modifications 'more' and 'less' applied to them, and each of these is relative in character: for the terms 'like' and 'unequal' bear a reference to something external. Yet, again, it is not every relative term that 25 admits of variation of degree. No term such as 'double' admits of this modification. All relatives have correlatives: by the term 'slave' we mean the slave *of a master*; by the term 'master', the master *of a* 30 *slave*; by 'double', the double *of its half*; by 'half', the half *of its double*; by 'greater', greater *than that which is less*; by 'less', less *than that which is greater*.
So it is with every other relative term; but the case we use to express the correlation differs in some instances. Thus, by knowledge we mean knowledge *of* the knowable; by the knowable, that which is to be apprehended *by* knowledge; by perception, perception 35 *of* the perceptible; by the perceptible, that which is apprehended *by* perception.

Sometimes, however, reciprocity of correlation does not appear to exist. This comes about when a blunder is made, and that to which the relative is related is not accurately stated. If a man states that a wing is necessarily relative to a bird, the connexion between these two will not be reciprocal, for it will not be possible to say that a bird is a bird by reason of its wings. The reason is that the original statement was inaccurate, for the wing is not said 7ᵃ to be relative to the bird *qua* bird, since many creatures besides birds have wings, but *qua* winged creature. If, then, the statement is made accurate, the connexion will be reciprocal, for we can speak of a wing having reference necessarily to a winged creature, and of a winged creature as being such because of its wings.

Occasionally, perhaps, it is necessary to coin words, if no word 5 exists by which a correlation can adequately be explained. If we define a rudder as necessarily having reference to a boat, our definition will not be appropriate, for the rudder does not have this reference to a boat *qua* boat, as there are boats which have no rudders. 10 Thus we cannot use the terms reciprocally, for the word 'boat' cannot be said to find its explanation in the word 'rudder'. As there is no existing word, our definition would perhaps be more accurate if we coined some word like 'ruddered' as the correlative of 'rudder'. If we express ourselves thus accurately, at any rate the terms are reciprocally connected, for the 'ruddered' thing is 'ruddered' in virtue of its rudder. So it is in all other cases. A head will be more 15 accurately defined as the correlative of that which is 'headed', than as that of an animal, for the animal does not have a head *qua* animal, since many animals have no head.

Thus we may perhaps most easily comprehend that to which a thing is related, when a name does not exist, if, from that which has a name, we derive a new name, and apply it to that with which the first is reciprocally connected, as in the aforesaid instances, 20 when we derived the word 'winged' from 'wing' and 'ruddered' from 'rudder'.

All relatives, then, if properly defined, have a correlative. I add this condition because, if that to which they are related is stated at haphazard and not accurately, the two are not found to be interdependent. Let me state what I mean more clearly. Even in the 25 case of acknowledged correlatives, and where names exist for each, there will be no interdependence if one of the two is denoted, not by that name which expresses the correlative notion, but by one of irrelevant significance. The term 'slave', if defined as related, not to a master, but to a man, or a biped, or anything of that sort, is not

reciprocally connected with that in relation to which it is defined,
30 for the statement is not exact. Further, if one thing is said to be
correlative with another, and the terminology used is correct, then,
though all irrelevant attributes should be removed, and only that
one attribute left in virtue of which it was correctly stated to be
correlative with that other, the stated correlation will still exist.
If the correlative of 'the slave' is said to be 'the master', then, though
35 all irrelevant attributes of the said 'master', such as 'biped', 'receptive of knowledge', 'human', should be removed, and the attribute
'master' alone left, the stated correlation existing between him and
the slave will remain the same, for it is *of a master* that a slave is
7ᵇ said to be the slave. On the other hand, if, of two correlatives,
one is not correctly termed, then, when all other attributes are
removed and that alone is left in virtue of which it was stated to be
correlative, the stated correlation will be found to have disappeared.

For suppose the correlative of 'the slave' should be said to be
'the man', or the correlative of 'the wing' 'the bird'; if the attribute
5 'master' be withdrawn from 'the man', the correlation between
'the man' and 'the slave' will cease to exist, for if the man is not a
master, the slave is not a slave. Similarly, if the attribute 'winged'
be withdrawn from 'the bird', 'the wing' will no longer be relative;
for if the so-called correlative is not winged, it follows that 'the
wing' has no correlative.

10 Thus it is essential that the correlated terms should be exactly designated; if there is a name existing, the statement will be easy; if
not, it is doubtless our duty to construct names. When the terminology is thus correct, it is evident that all correlatives are interdependent.

15 Correlatives are thought to come into existence simultaneously.
This is for the most part true, as in the case of the double and the
half. The existence of the half necessitates the existence of that of
which it is a half. Similarly the existence of a master necessitates
the existence of a slave, and that of a slave implies that of a master;
these are merely instances of a general rule. Moreover, they cancel
20 one another; for if there is no double it follows that there is no
half, and vice versa; this rule also applies to all such correlatives.
Yet it does not appear to be true in all cases that correlatives come
into existence simultaneously. The object of knowledge would appear to exist before knowledge itself, for it is usually the case that
25 we acquire knowledge of objects already existing; it would be difficult, if not impossible, to find a branch of knowledge the beginning
of the existence of which was contemporaneous with that of its object.

Again, while the object of knowledge, if it ceases to exist, cancels at the same time the knowledge which was its correlative, the converse of this is not true. It is true that if the object of knowledge does not exist there can be no knowledge: for there will no longer be anything to know. Yet it is equally true that, if the knowl- 30 edge of a certain object does not exist, the object may nevertheless quite well exist. Thus, in the case of the squaring of the circle, if indeed that process is an object of knowledge, though it itself exists as an object of knowledge, yet the knowledge of it has not yet come into existence. Again, if all animals ceased to exist, there would be no knowledge, but there might yet be many objects of knowledge.

This is likewise the case with regard to perception: for the object 35 of perception is, it appears, prior to the act of perception. If the perceptible is annihilated, perception also will cease to exist; but the annihilation of perception does not cancel the existence of the perceptible. For perception implies a body perceived and a body in which perception takes place. Now if that which is perceptible is annihilated, it follows that the body is annihilated, for the body is a perceptible thing; and if the body does not exist, it follows that 8ᵃ perception also ceases to exist. Thus the annihilation of the perceptible involves that of perception.

But the annihilation of perception does not involve that of the perceptible. For if the animal is annihilated, it follows that perception also is annihilated, but perceptibles such as body, heat, sweet- 5 ness, bitterness, and so on, will remain.

Again, perception is generated at the same time as the perceiving subject, for it comes into existence at the same time as the animal. But the perceptible surely exists before perception; for fire and water and such elements, out of which the animal is itself 10 composed, exist before the animal is an animal at all, and before perception. Thus it would seem that the perceptible exists before perception.

It may be questioned whether it is true that no substance is relative, as seems to be the case, or whether exception is to be made in the case of certain secondary substances. With regard to primary substances, it is quite true that there is no such possibility, for 15 neither wholes nor parts of primary substances are relative. The individual man or ox is not defined with reference to something external. Similarly with the parts: a particular hand or head is not defined as a particular hand or head of a particular person, but as 20 the hand or head of a particular person. It is true also, for the

most part at least, in the case of secondary substances; the species 'man' and the species 'ox' are not defined with reference to anything outside themselves. Wood, again, is only relative in so far as it is some one's property, not in so far as it is wood. It is plain, then,
25 that in the cases mentioned substance is not relative. But with regard to some secondary substances there is a difference of opinion; thus, such terms as 'head' and 'hand' are defined with reference to that of which the things indicated are a part, and so it comes about that these appear to have a relative character. Indeed, if our defini-
30 tion of that which is relative was complete, it is very difficult, if not impossible, to prove that no substance is relative. If, however, our definition was not complete, if those things only are properly called relative in the case of which relation to an external object is a necessary condition of existence, perhaps some explanation of the dilemma may be found.

The former definition does indeed apply to all relatives, but the fact that a thing is explained with reference to something else does not make it essentially relative.
35 From this it is plain that, if a man definitely apprehends a relative thing, he will also definitely apprehend that to which it is relative. Indeed this is self-evident: for if a man knows that some particular thing is relative, assuming that we call that a relative in the case of
8ᵇ which relation to something is a necessary condition of existence, he knows that also to which it is related. For if he does not know at all that to which it is related, he will not know whether or not it is relative. This is clear, moreover, in particular instances. If a man
5 knows definitely that such and such a thing is 'double', he will also forthwith know definitely that of which it is the double. For if there is nothing definite of which he knows it to be the double, he does not know at all that it is double. Again, if he knows that a thing is more beautiful, it follows necessarily that he will forthwith definitely know that also than which it is more beautiful. He will not merely know indefinitely that it is more beautiful than some-
10 thing which is less beautiful, for this would be supposition, not knowledge. For if he does not know definitely that than which it is more beautiful, he can no longer claim to know definitely that it is more beautiful than something else which is less beautiful: for it might be that nothing was less beautiful. It is, therefore, evident that if a man apprehends some relative thing definitely, he necessarily knows that also definitely to which it is related.
15 Now the head, the hand, and such things are substances, and it is possible to know their essential character definitely, but it does

not necessarily follow that we should know that to which they are related. It is not possible to know forthwith whose head or hand is meant. Thus these are not relatives, and, this being the case, it 20 would be true to say that no substance is relative in character. It is perhaps a difficult matter, in such cases, to make a positive statement without more exhaustive examination, but to have raised questions with regard to details is not without advantage.

8 By 'quality' I mean that in virtue of which people are said to be 25 such and such.

Quality is a term that is used in many senses. One sort of quality let us call 'habit' or 'disposition'. Habit differs from disposition in being more lasting and more firmly established. The various kinds of knowledge and of virtue are habits, for knowledge, even when acquired only in a moderate degree, is, it is agreed, abiding in its 30 character and difficult to displace, unless some great mental upheaval takes place, through disease or any such cause. The virtues, also, such as justice, self-restraint, and so on, are not easily dislodged or dismissed, so as to give place to vice.

By a disposition, on the other hand, we mean a condition that is 35 easily changed and quickly gives place to its opposite. Thus, heat, cold, disease, health, and so on are dispositions. For a man is disposed in one way or another with reference to these, but quickly changes, becoming cold instead of warm, ill instead of well. So it is 9ᵃ with all other dispositions also, unless through lapse of time a disposition has itself become inveterate and almost impossible to dislodge: in which case we should perhaps go so far as to call it a habit.

It is evident that men incline to call those conditions habits which are of a more or less permanent type and difficult to displace; for those who are not retentive of knowledge, but volatile, are not 5 said to have such and such a 'habit' as regards knowledge, yet they are *disposed,* we may say, either better or worse, towards knowledge. Thus habit differs from disposition in this, that while the latter is ephemeral, the former is permanent and difficult to alter.

Habits are at the same time dispositions, but dispositions are not 10 necessarily habits. For those who have some specific habit may be said also, in virtue of that habit, to be thus or thus disposed; but those who are disposed in some specific way have not in all cases the corresponding habit.

Another sort of quality is that in virtue of which, for example, we call men good boxers or runners, or healthy or sickly: in fact it

15 includes all those terms which refer to inborn capacity or incapacity. Such things are not predicated of a person in virtue of his disposition, but in virtue of his inborn capacity or incapacity to do something with ease or to avoid defeat of any kind. Persons are called good boxers or good runners, not in virtue of such and such a dis-
20 position, but in virtue of an inborn capacity to accomplish something with ease. Men are called healthy in virtue of the inborn capacity of easy resistance to those unhealthy influences that may ordinarily arise; unhealthy, in virtue of the lack of this capacity.
25 Similarly with regard to softness and hardness. Hardness is predicated of a thing because it has that capacity of resistance which enables it to withstand disintegration; softness, again, is predicated of a thing by reason of the lack of that capacity.

A third class within this category is that of affective qualities and affections. Sweetness, bitterness, sourness, are examples of this sort
30 of quality, together with all that is akin to these; heat, moreover, and cold, whiteness, and blackness are affective qualities. It is evident that these are qualities, for those things that possess them are themselves said to be such and such by reason of their presence. Honey is called sweet because it contains sweetness; the body is called white because it contains whiteness; and so in all other cases.
35 The term 'affective quality' is not used as indicating that those things which admit these qualities are affected in any way. Honey
9ᵇ is not called sweet because it is affected in a specific way, nor is this what is meant in any other instance. Similarly heat and cold are called affective qualities, not because those things which admit them
5 are affected. What is meant is that these said qualities are capable of producing an 'affection' in the way of perception. For sweetness has the power of affecting the sense of taste; heat, that of touch; and so it is with the rest of these qualities.

Whiteness and blackness, however, and the other colours, are not
10 said to be affective qualities in this sense, but because they themselves are the results of an affection. It is plain that many changes of colour take place because of affections. When a man is ashamed, he blushes; when he is afraid, he becomes pale, and so on. So true is
15 this, that when a man is by nature liable to such affections, arising from some concomitance of elements in his constitution, it is a probable inference that he has the corresponding complexion of skin. For the same disposition of bodily elements, which in the former instance was momentarily present in the case of an access of shame, might be a result of a man's natural temperament, so as to produce the corresponding colouring also as a natural characteristic. All con-

ditions, therefore, of this kind, if caused by certain permanent and 20 lasting affections, are called affective qualities. For pallor and duskiness of complexion are called qualities, inasmuch as we are said to be such and such in virtue of them, not only if they originate in natural constitution, but also if they come about through long disease or 25 sunburn, and are difficult to remove, or indeed remain throughout life. For in the same way we are said to be such and such because of these.

Those conditions, however, which arise from causes which may easily be rendered ineffective or speedily removed, are called, not qualities, but affections: for we are not said to be such and such in virtue of them. The man who blushes through shame is not said 30 to be a constitutional blusher, nor is the man who becomes pale through fear said to be constitutionally pale. He is said rather to have been affected. Thus such conditions are called affections, not qualities.

In like manner there are affective qualities and affections of the 35 soul. That temper with which a man is born and which has its origin in certain deep-seated affections is called a quality. I mean such 10ᵃ conditions as insanity, irascibility, and so on: for people are said to be mad or irascible in virtue of these. Similarly those abnormal psychic states which are not inborn, but arise from the concomitance of certain other elements, and are difficult to remove, or altogether permanent, are called qualities, for in virtue of them men are said 5 to be such and such.

Those, however, which arise from causes easily rendered ineffective are called affections, not qualities. Suppose that a man is irritable when vexed: he is not even spoken of as a bad-tempered man, when in such circumstances he loses his temper somewhat, but rather is said to be affected. Such conditions are therefore termed, not qualities, but affections.   10

The fourth sort of quality is figure and the shape that belongs to a thing; and besides this, straightness and curvedness and any other qualities of this type; each of these defines a thing as being such and such. Because it is triangular or quadrangular a thing is said to have a specific character, or again because it is straight or curved; 15 in fact a thing's shape in every case gives rise to a qualification of it.

Rarity and density, roughness and smoothness, seem to be terms indicating quality: yet these, it would appear, really belong to a class different from that of quality. For it is rather a certain relative position of the parts composing the thing thus qualified which, it appears, is indicated by each of these terms. A thing is dense, owing 20 to the fact that its parts are closely combined with one another; rare, because there are interstices between the parts; smooth, because its parts lie, so to speak, evenly; rough, because some parts project beyond others.

25 There may be other sorts of quality, but those that are most properly so called have, we may safely say, been enumerated.

These, then, are qualities, and the things that take their name from them as derivatives, or are in some other way dependent on them, are said to be qualified in some specific way. In most, indeed in almost all cases, the name of that which is qualified is derived 30 from that of the quality. Thus the terms 'whiteness', 'grammar', 'justice', give us the adjectives 'white', 'grammatical', 'just', and so on.

There are some cases, however, in which, as the quality under consideration has no name, it is impossible that those possessed of it should have a name that is derivative. For instance, the name 35 given to the runner or boxer, who is so called in virtue of an inborn 10^b capacity, is not derived from that of any quality; for those capacities have no name assigned to them. In this, the inborn capacity is distinct from the science, with reference to which men are called, e. g., boxers or wrestlers. Such a science is classed as a disposition; it has a name, and is called 'boxing' or 'wrestling' as the case may be, and the name given to those disposed in this way is derived from that of the science.

5 Sometimes, even though a name exists for the quality, that which takes its character from the quality has a name that is not a derivative. For instance, the upright man takes his character from the possession of the quality of integrity, but the name given him is not derived from the word 'integrity'. Yet this does not occur often.

We may therefore state that those things are said to be possessed 10 of some specific quality which have a name derived from that of the aforesaid quality, or which are in some other way dependent on it.

One quality may be the contrary of another; thus justice is the contrary of injustice, whiteness of blackness, and so on. The things, also, which are said to be such and such in virtue of these qualities, may be contrary the one to the other; for that which is unjust is 15 contrary to that which is just, that which is white to that which is black. This, however, is not always the case. Red, yellow, and such colours, though qualities, have no contraries.

If one of two contraries is a quality, the other will also be a quality. This will be evident from particular instances, if we apply the names used to denote the other categories; for instance, granted that 20 justice is the contrary of injustice and justice is a quality, injustice will also be a quality: neither quantity, nor relation, nor place, nor indeed any other category but that of quality, will be applicable properly to injustice. So it is with all other contraries falling under the category of quality.   25

Qualities admit of variation of degree. Whiteness is predicated of one thing in a greater or less degree than of another. This is also the case with reference to justice. Moreover, one and the same thing may exhibit a quality in a greater degree than it did before: if a thing is white, it may become whiter.

Though this is generally the case, there are exceptions. For if we should say that justice admitted of variation of degree, difficulties 30 might ensue, and this is true with regard to all those qualities which are dispositions. There are some, indeed, who dispute the possibility of variation here. They maintain that justice and health cannot very well admit of variation of degree themselves, but that people vary 35 in the degree in which they possess these qualities, and that this is the case with grammatical learning and all those qualities which 11ᵃ are classed as dispositions. However that may be, it is an incontrovertible fact that the things which in virtue of these qualities are said to be what they are vary in the degree in which they possess them; for one man is said to be better versed in grammar, or more healthy or just, than another, and so on.

The qualities expressed by the terms 'triangular' and 'quadrangu- 5 lar' do not appear to admit of variation of degree, nor indeed do any that have to do with figure. For those things to which the definition of the triangle or circle is applicable are all equally triangular or circular. Those, on the other hand, to which the same definition is not applicable, cannot be said to differ from one another in degree; the square is no more a circle than the rectangle, for to neither is 10 the definition of the circle appropriate. In short, if the definition of the term proposed is not applicable to both objects, they cannot be compared. Thus it is not all qualities which admit of variation of degree.

Whereas none of the characteristics I have mentioned are peculiar 15 to quality, the fact that likeness and unlikeness can be predicated with reference to quality only, gives to that category its distinctive feature. One thing is like another only with reference to that in virtue of which it is such and such; thus this forms the peculiar mark of quality.

We must not be disturbed because it may be argued that, though 20 proposing to discuss the category of quality, we have included in it

many relative terms. We did say that habits and dispositions were relative. In practically all such cases the genus is relative, the individual not. Thus knowledge, as a genus, is explained by reference to
25 something else, for we mean a knowledge *of something*. But particular branches of knowledge are not thus explained. The knowledge of grammar is not relative to anything external, nor is the knowledge of music, but these, if relative at all, are relative only in
30 virtue of their genera; thus grammar is said to be the *knowledge* of something, not the grammar of something; similarly music is the *knowledge* of something, not the music of something.

Thus individual branches of knowledge are not relative. And it is because we possess these individual branches of knowledge that we are said to be such and such. It is these that we actually possess: we are called experts because we possess knowledge in some particular
35 branch. Those particular branches, therefore, of knowledge, in virtue of which we are sometimes said to be such and such, are themselves qualities, and are not relative. Further, if anything should happen to fall within both the category of quality and that of relation, there would be nothing extraordinary in classing it under both these heads.

11ᵇ 9   Action and affection both admit of contraries and also of variation of degree. Heating is the contrary of cooling, being heated of being cooled, being glad of being vexed. Thus they admit of con-
5 traries. They also admit of variation of degree: for it is possible to heat in a greater or less degree; also to be heated in a greater or less degree. Thus action and affection also admit of variation of degree. So much, then, is stated with regard to these categories.

We spoke, moreover, of the category of position when we were dealing with that of relation, and stated that such terms derived their names from those of the corresponding attitudes.
10   As for the rest, time, place, state, since they are easily intelligible, I say no more about them than was said at the beginning, that in the category of state are included such states as 'shod', 'armed', in that of place 'in the Lyceum' and so on, as was explained before.

15 10   The proposed categories have, then, been adequately dealt with.

We must next explain the various senses in which the term 'opposite' is used. Things are said to be opposed in four senses: (i) as correlatives to one another, (ii) as contraries to one another, (iii) as privatives to positives, (iv) as affirmatives to negatives.

Let me sketch my meaning in outline. An instance of the use of the word 'opposite' with reference to correlatives is afforded by the expressions 'double' and 'half'; with reference to contraries by 'bad' 20 and 'good'. Opposites in the sense of 'privatives' and 'positives' are 'blindness' and 'sight'; in the sense of affirmatives and negatives, the propositions 'he sits', 'he does not sit'.

(i) Pairs of opposites which fall under the category of relation are explained by a reference of the one to the other, the reference being indicated by the preposition 'of' or by some other preposition. 25 Thus, double is a relative term, for that which is double is explained as the double *of something*. Knowledge, again, is the opposite of the thing known, in the same sense; and the thing known also is explained by its relation to its opposite, knowledge. For the thing 30 known is explained as that which is known *by something;* that is, by knowledge. Such things, then, as are opposite the one to the other in the sense of being correlatives are explained by a reference of the one to the other.

(ii) Pairs of opposites which are contraries are not in any way interdependent, but are contrary the one to the other. The good is not spoken of as the good *of the bad,* but as *the contrary of the bad,* 35 nor is white spoken of as the white *of the black,* but as *the contrary of the black.* These two types of opposition are therefore dis- 12ᵃ tinct. Those contraries which are such that the subjects in which they are naturally present, or of which they are predicated, must necessarily contain either the one or the other of them, have no intermediate, but those in the case of which no such necessity obtains, always have an intermediate. Thus disease and health are naturally present in the body of an animal, and it is necessary that 5 either the one or the other should be present in the body of an animal. Odd and even, again, are predicated of number, and it is necessary that the one or the other should be present in numbers. Now there is no intermediate between the terms of either of these two pairs. On the other hand, in those contraries with regard to which no such necessity obtains, we find an intermediate. Blackness and 10 whiteness are naturally present in the body, but it is not necessary that either the one or the other should be present in the body, inasmuch as it is not true to say that everybody must be white or black. Badness and goodness, again, are predicated of man, and of many 15 other things, but it is not necessary that either the one quality or the other should be present in that of which they are predicated: it is not true to say that everything that may be good or bad must be either good or bad. These pairs of contraries have intermediates: the intermediates between white and black are grey, sallow, and all the other colours that come between; the intermediate between good and bad is that which is neither the one nor the other.

20   Some intermediate qualities have names, such as grey and sallow and all the other colours that come between white and black; in other cases, however, it is not easy to name the intermediate, but we must define it as that which is *not* either extreme, as in the case 25 of that which is neither good nor bad, neither just nor unjust.

(iii) 'Privatives' and 'positives' have reference to the same subject. Thus, sight and blindness have reference to the eye. It is a universal rule that each of a pair of opposites of this type has reference to that to which the particular 'positive' is natural. We say that that which is capable of some particular faculty or possession has 30 suffered privation when the faculty or possession in question is in no way present in that in which, and at the time at which, it should naturally be present. We do not call that toothless which has not teeth, or that blind which has not sight, but rather that which has not teeth or sight at the time when by nature it should. For there are some creatures which from birth are without sight, or without teeth, but these are not called toothless or blind.

35   To be without some faculty or to possess it is not the same as the corresponding 'privative' or 'positive'. 'Sight' is a 'positive', 'blindness' a 'privative', but 'to possess sight' is not equivalent to 'sight', 'to be blind' is not equivalent to 'blindness'. Blindness is a 'privative', to be blind is to be in a state of privation, but is not a 'privative'. Moreover, if 'blindness' were equivalent to 'being blind', 40 both would be predicated of the same subject; but though a man is said to be blind, he is by no means said to be blindness.

12ᵇ   To be in a state of 'possession' is, it appears, the opposite of being in a state of 'privation', just as 'positives' and 'privatives' themselves are opposite. There is the same type of antithesis in both cases; for just as blindness is opposed to sight, so is being blind 5 opposed to having sight.

That which is affirmed or denied is not itself affirmation or denial. By 'affirmation' we mean an affirmative proposition, by 'denial' a negative. Now, those facts which form the matter of the affirmation or denial are not propositions; yet these two are said to be opposed 10 in the same sense as the affirmation and denial, for in this case also the type of antithesis is the same. For as the affirmation is opposed to the denial, as in the two propositions 'he sits', 'he does not sit', so also the fact which constitutes the matter of the proposition in one case is opposed to that in the other, his sitting, that is to say, to his 15 not sitting.

It is evident that 'positives' and 'privatives' are not opposed each to each in the same sense as relatives. The one is not explained by reference to the other; sight is not sight *of blindness,* nor is any other preposition used to indicate the relation. Similarly blindness is not said to be blindness *of sight,* but rather, privation of sight. 20 Relatives, moreover, reciprocate; if blindness, therefore, were a relative, there would be a reciprocity of relation between it and that with which it was correlative. But this is not the case. Sight is not called the sight *of blindness.* 25

That those terms which fall under the heads of 'positives' and 'privatives' are not opposed each to each as contraries, either, is plain from the following facts: Of a pair of contraries such that they have *no* intermediate, one or the other must needs be present in the subject in which they naturally subsist, or of which they are predi- 30 cated; for it is those, as we proved, in the case of which this necessity obtains, that have no intermediate. Moreover, we cited health and disease, odd and even, as instances. But those contraries which *have* an intermediate are not subject to any such necessity. It is not necessary that every substance, receptive of such qualities, should be either black or white, cold or hot, for something intermediate between these contraries may very well be present in the subject. 35 We proved, moreover, that those contraries have an intermediate in the case of which the said necessity does not obtain. Yet when one of the two contraries is a constitutive property of the subject, as it is a constitutive property of fire to be hot, of snow to be white, it is necessary determinately that one of the two contraries, not one *or* the other, should be present in the subject; for fire cannot be cold, 40 or snow black. Thus, it is not the case here that one of the two must needs be present in every subject receptive of these qualities, but only in that subject of which the one forms a constitutive property. 13ª Moreover, in such cases it is one member of the pair determinately, and not either the one or the other, which must be present.

In the case of 'positives' and 'privatives', on the other hand, neither of the aforesaid statements holds good. For it is not necessary that a subject receptive of the qualities should always have either the one or the other; that which has not yet advanced to 5 the state when sight is natural is not said either to be blind or to see. Thus 'positives' and 'privatives' do not belong to that class of contraries which consists of those which have no intermediate. On the other hand, they do not belong either to that class which consists of contraries which have an intermediate. For under certain

conditions it is necessary that either the one or the other should form part of the constitution of every appropriate subject. For when a thing has reached the stage when it is by nature capable of
10 sight, it will be said either to see or to be blind, and that in an indeterminate sense, signifying that the capacity may be either present or absent; for it is not necessary either that it should see or that it should be blind, but that it should be either in the one state or in the other. Yet in the case of those contraries which have an intermediate we found that it was never necessary that either the one or the other should be present in every appropriate subject, but only that in certain subjects one of the pair should be present,
15 and that in a determinate sense. It is, therefore, plain that 'positives' and 'privatives' are not opposed each to each in either of the senses in which contraries are opposed.

Again, in the case of contraries, it is possible that there should be changes from either into the other, while the subject retains its identity, unless indeed one of the contraries is a constitutive prop-
20 erty of that subject, as heat is of fire. For it is possible that that which is healthy should become diseased, that which is white, black, that which is cold, hot, that which is good, bad, that which is bad, good. The bad man, if he is being brought into a better way of life and thought, may make some advance, however slight, and if he
25 should once improve, even ever so little, it is plain that he might change completely, or at any rate make very great progress; for a man becomes more and more easily moved to virtue, however small the improvement was at first. It is, therefore, natural to suppose that he will make yet greater progress than he has made in the past; and as this process goes on, it will change him completely and establish
30 him in the contrary state, provided he is not hindered by lack of time. In the case of 'positives' and 'privatives', however, change in both directions is impossible. There may be a change from possession to privation, but not from privation to possession. The man who
35 has become blind does not regain his sight; the man who has become bald does not regain his hair; the man who has lost his teeth does not grow a new set.

13ᵇ   (iv) Statements opposed as affirmation and negation belong manifestly to a class which is distinct, for in this case, and in this case only, it is necessary for the one opposite to be true and the other false.

Neither in the case of contraries, nor in the case of correlatives, nor in the case of 'positives' and 'privatives', is it necessary for one to be true and the other false. Health and disease are contraries:

neither of them is true or false. 'Double' and 'half' are opposed to each other as correlatives: neither of them is true or false. The case is the same, of course, with regard to 'positives' and 'privatives' such as 'sight' and 'blindness'. In short, where there is no sort of combination of words, truth and falsity have no place, and all the opposites we have mentioned so far consist of simple words.

At the same time, when the words which enter into opposed statements are contraries, these, more than any other set of opposites, would seem to claim this characteristic. 'Socrates is ill' is the contrary of 'Socrates is well', but not even of such composite expressions is it true to say that one of the pair must always be true and the other false. For if Socrates exists, one will be true and the other false, but if he does not exist, both will be false; for neither 'Socrates is ill' nor 'Socrates is well' is true, if Socrates does not exist at all.

In the case of 'positives' and 'privatives', if the subject does not exist at all, neither proposition is true, but even if the subject exists, it is not always the fact that one is true and the other false. For 'Socrates has sight' is the opposite of 'Socrates is blind' in the sense of the word 'opposite' which applies to possession and privation. Now if Socrates exists, it is not necessary that one should be true and the other false, for when he is not yet able to acquire the power of vision, both are false, as also if Socrates is altogether non-existent.

But in the case of affirmation and negation, whether the subject exists or not, one is always false and the other true. For manifestly, if Socrates exists, one of the two propositions 'Socrates is ill', 'Socrates is not ill', is true, and the other false. This is likewise the case if he does not exist; for if he does not exist, to say that he is ill is false, to say that he is not ill is true. Thus it is in the case of those opposites only, which are opposite in the sense in which the term is used with reference to affirmation and negation, that the rule holds good, that one of the pair must be true and the other false.

11   That the contrary of a good is an evil is shown by induction: the contrary of health is disease, of courage, cowardice, and so on. But the contrary of an evil is sometimes a good, sometimes an evil. For defect, which is an evil, has excess for its contrary, this also being an evil, and the mean, which is a good, is equally the contrary of the one and of the other. It is only in a few cases, however, that we see instances of this: in most, the contrary of an evil is a good.

In the case of contraries, it is not always necessary that if one

exists the other should also exist: for if all become healthy there will
be health and no disease, and again, if everything turns white, there
10 will be white, but no black. Again, since the fact that Socrates is
ill is the contrary of the fact that Socrates is well, and two contrary
conditions cannot both obtain in one and the same individual at the
same time, both these contraries could not exist at once: for if that
Socrates was well was a fact, then that Socrates was ill could not
possibly be one.

15   It is plain that contrary attributes must needs be present in subjects which belong to the same species or genus. Disease and health
require as their subject the body of an animal; white and black
require a body, without further qualification; justice and injustice
require as their subject the human soul.

Moreover, it is necessary that pairs of contraries should in all
20 cases either belong to the same genus or belong to contrary genera
or be themselves genera. White and black belong to the same genus,
colour; justice and injustice, to contrary genera, virtue and vice;
while good and evil do not belong to genera, but are themselves
25 actual genera, with terms under them.

12   There are four senses in which one thing can be said to be
'prior' to another. Primarily and most properly the term has reference to time: in this sense the word is used to indicate that one
thing is older or more ancient than another, for the expressions
'older' and 'more ancient' imply greater length of time.

Secondly, one thing is said to be 'prior' to another when the
30 sequence of their being cannot be reversed. In this sense 'one' is
'prior' to 'two'. For if 'two' exists, it follows directly that 'one' must
exist, but if 'one' exists, it does not follow necessarily that 'two'
exists: thus the sequence subsisting cannot be reversed. It is agreed,
then, that when the sequence of two things cannot be reversed, then
35 that one on which the other depends is called 'prior' to that other.

In the third place, the term 'prior' is used with reference to any
order, as in the case of science and of oratory. For in sciences
which use demonstration there is that which is prior and that which
is posterior in order; in geometry, the elements are prior to the
14b propositions; in reading and writing, the letters of the alphabet
are prior to the syllables. Similarly, in the case of speeches, the
exordium is prior in order to the narrative.

Besides these senses of the word, there is a fourth. That which is
better and more honourable is said to have a natural priority. In
5 common parlance men speak of those whom they honour and love

as 'coming first' with them. This sense of the word is perhaps the most far-fetched.

Such, then, are the different senses in which the term 'prior' is used.

Yet it would seem that besides those mentioned there is yet an- 10 other. For in those things, the being of each of which implies that of the other, that which is in any way the cause may reasonably be said to be by nature 'prior' to the effect. It is plain that there are instances of this. The fact of the being of a man carries with it the truth of the proposition that he is, and the implication is recip- 15 rocal: for if a man is, the proposition wherein we allege that he is is true, and conversely, if the proposition wherein we allege that he is is true, then he is. The true proposition, however, is in no way the cause of the being of the man, but the fact of the man's being does seem somehow to be the cause of the truth of the proposition, 20 for the truth or falsity of the proposition depends on the fact of the man's being or not being.

Thus the word 'prior' may be used in five senses.

13 The term 'simultaneous' is primarily and most appropriately applied to those things the genesis of the one of which is simul- taneous with that of the other; for in such cases neither is prior or 25 posterior to the other. Such things are said to be simultaneous in point of time. Those things, again, are 'simultaneous' in point of nature, the being of each of which involves that of the other, while at the same time neither is the cause of the other's being. This is the case with regard to the double and the half, for these are reciprocally dependent, since, if there is a double, there is also a half, and if 30 there is a half, there is also a double, while at the same time neither is the cause of the being of the other.

Again, those species which are distinguished one from another and opposed one to another within the same genus are said to be 'simultaneous' in nature. I mean those species which are dis- tinguished each from each by one and the same method of division. 35 Thus the 'winged' species is simultaneous with the 'terrestrial' and the 'water' species. These are distinguished within the same genus, and are opposed each to each, for the genus 'animal' has the 'winged', the 'terrestrial', and the 'water' species, and no one of these is prior or posterior to another; on the contrary, all such things appear to be 'simultaneous' in nature. Each of these also, the terrestrial, 15ᵃ the winged, and the water species, can be divided again into sub- species. Those species, then, also will be 'simultaneous' in point of nature, which, belonging to the same genus, are distinguished each from each by one and the same method of differentiation.

5   But genera are prior to species, for the sequence of their being cannot be reversed. If there is the species 'water-animal', there will be the genus 'animal', but granted the being of the genus 'animal', it does not follow necessarily that there will be the species 'water-animal'.

Those things, therefore, are said to be 'simultaneous' in nature, the being of each of which involves that of the other, while at the same time neither is in any way the cause of the other's being;

10   those species, also, which are distinguished each from each and opposed within the same genus. Those things, moreover, are 'simultaneous' in the unqualified sense of the word which come into being at the same time.

14   There are six sorts of movement: generation, destruction, increase, diminution, alteration, and change of place.

15   It is evident in all but one case that all these sorts of movement are distinct each from each. Generation is distinct from destruction, increase and change of place from diminution, and so on. But in the case of alteration it may be argued that the process necessarily

20   implies one or other of the other five sorts of motion. This is not true, for we may say that all affections, or nearly all, produce in us an alteration which is distinct from all other sorts of motion, for that which is affected need not suffer either increase or diminution or any of the other sorts of motion. Thus alteration is a distinct

25   sort of motion; for, if it were not, the thing altered would not only be altered, but would forthwith necessarily suffer increase or diminution or some one of the other sorts of motion in addition; which as a matter of fact is not the case. Similarly that which was undergoing the process of increase or was subject to some other sort of motion would, if alteration were not a distinct form of motion, necessarily be subject to alteration also. But there are some things which undergo increase but yet not alteration. The square, for

30   instance, if a gnomon is applied to it, undergoes increase but not alteration, and so it is with all other figures of this sort. Alteration and increase, therefore, are distinct.

15b   Speaking generally, rest is the contrary of motion. But the different forms of motion have their own contraries in other forms; thus destruction is the contrary of generation, diminution of increase, rest in a place, of change of place. As for this last, change in the reverse direction would seem to be most truly its contrary;

thus motion upwards is the contrary of motion downwards and 5 vice versa.

In the case of that sort of motion which yet remains, of those that have been enumerated, it is not easy to state what is its contrary. It appears to have no contrary, unless one should define the contrary here also either as 'rest in its quality' or as 'change in the direction of the contrary quality', just as we defined the con- 10 trary of change of place either as rest in a place or as change in the reverse direction. For a thing is altered when change of quality takes place; therefore either rest in its quality or change in the direction of the contrary quality may be called the contrary of this qualitative form of motion. In this way becoming white is the contrary of becoming black; there is alteration in the contrary direc- 15 tion, since a change of a qualitative nature takes place.

15 The term 'to have' is used in various senses. In the first place it is used with reference to habit or disposition or any other quality, for we are said to 'have' a piece of knowledge or a virtue. Then, again, it has reference to quantity, as, for instance, in the case of 20 a man's height; for he is said to 'have' a height of three cubits or four cubits. It is used, moreover, with regard to apparel, a man being said to 'have' a coat or tunic; or in respect of something which we have on a part of ourselves, as a ring on the hand: or in respect of something which is a part of us, as hand or foot. The term refers also to content, as in the case of a vessel and wheat, or of a jar and wine; a jar is said to 'have' wine, and a corn-measure wheat. The 25 expression in such cases has reference to content. Or it refers to that which has been acquired; we are said to 'have' a house or a field. A man is also said to 'have' a wife, and a wife a husband, and this appears to be the most remote meaning of the term, for by the use of it we mean simply that the husband lives with the wife.   30

Other senses of the word might perhaps be found, but the most ordinary ones have all been enumerated.

DE INTERPRETATIONE

Translated by E. M. Edghill

CONTENTS

DE INTERPRETATIONE

(*On Interpretation*)

16ᵃ 1   First we must define the terms 'noun' and 'verb', then the terms 'denial' and 'affirmation', then 'proposition' and 'sentence'.

Spoken words are the symbols of mental experience and written words are the symbols of spoken words. Just as all men have not 5 the same writing, so all men have not the same speech sounds, but the mental experiences, which these directly symbolize, are the same for all, as also are those things of which our experiences are the images. This matter has, however, been discussed in my treatise about the soul, for it belongs to an investigation distinct from that which lies before us.

As there are in the mind thoughts which do not involve truth or 10 falsity, and also those which must be either true or false, so it is in speech. For truth and falsity imply combination and separation. Nouns and verbs, provided nothing is added, are like thoughts without combination or separation; 'man' and 'white', as isolated 15 terms, are not yet either true or false. In proof of this, consider the word 'goat-stag'. It has significance, but there is no truth or falsity about it, unless 'is' or 'is not' is added, either in the present or in some other tense.

2   By a noun we mean a sound significant by convention, which has 20 no reference to time, and of which no part is significant apart from the rest. In the noun 'Fairsteed', the part 'steed' has no significance in and by itself, as in the phrase 'fair steed'. Yet there is a difference between simple and composite nouns; for in the former the part 25 is in no way significant, in the latter it contributes to the meaning of the whole, although it has not an independent meaning. Thus in the word 'pirate-boat' the word 'boat' has no meaning except as part of the whole word.

The limitation 'by convention' was introduced because nothing is by nature a noun or name—it is only so when it becomes a symbol; inarticulate sounds, such as those which brutes produce, are significant, yet none of these constitutes a noun.

The expression 'not-man' is not a noun. There is indeed no 30
recognized term by which we may denote such an expression, for it is
not a sentence or a denial. Let it then be called an indefinite noun.

The expressions 'of Philo', 'to Philo', and so on, constitute not
nouns, but cases of a noun. The definition of these cases of a noun 16[b]
is in other respects the same as that of the noun proper, but, when
coupléd with 'is', 'was', or 'will be', they do not, as they are, form a
proposition either true or false, and this the noun proper always
does, under these conditions. Take the words 'of Philo is' or 'of
Philo is not'; these words do not, as they stand, form either a true
or a false proposition.   5

3 A verb is that which, in addition to its proper meaning, carries
with it the notion of time. No part of it has any independent meaning, and it is a sign of something said of something else.

I will explain what I mean by saying that it carries with it the
notion of time. 'Health' is a noun, but 'is healthy' is a verb; for
besides its proper meaning it indicates the present existence of the
state in question.

Moreover, a verb is always a sign of something said of something 10
else, i.e. of something either predicable of or present in some other
thing.

Such expressions as 'is not-healthy', 'is not-ill', I do not describe
as verbs; for though they carry the additional note of time, and
always form a predicate, there is no specified name for this variety;
but let them be called indefinite verbs, since they apply equally 15
well to that which exists and to that which does not.

Similarly 'he was healthy', 'he will be healthy', are not verbs,
but tenses of a verb; the difference lies in the fact that the verb
indicates present time, while the tenses of the verb indicate those
times which lie outside the present.

Verbs in and by themselves are substantial and have significance,
for he who uses such expressions arrests the hearer's mind, and fixes 20
his attention; but they do not, as they stand, express any judgement,
either positive or negative. For neither are 'to be' and 'not to be'
and the participle 'being' significant of any fact, unless something
is added; for they do not themselves indicate anything, but imply a
copulation, of which we cannot form a conception apart from the 25
things coupled.

4 A sentence is a significant portion of speech, some parts of
which have an independent meaning, that is to say, as an utterance,

though not as the expression of any positive judgement. Let me explain. The word 'human' has meaning, but does not constitute a proposition, either positive or negative. It is only when other words

30 are added that the whole will form an affirmation or denial. But if we separate one syllable of the word 'human' from the other, it has no meaning; similarly in the word 'mouse', the part '-ouse' has no meaning in itself, but is merely a sound. In composite words, indeed, the parts contribute to the meaning of the whole; yet, as has been pointed out,[1] they have not an independent meaning.

17ª   Every sentence has meaning, not as being the natural means by which a physical faculty is realized, but, as we have said, by convention. Yet every sentence is not a proposition; only such are propositions as have in them either truth or falsity. Thus a prayer is a sentence, but is neither true nor false.

5   Let us therefore dismiss all other types of sentence but the proposition, for this last concerns our present inquiry, whereas the investigation of the others belongs rather to the study of rhetoric or of poetry.[2]

5 The first class of simple propositions is the simple affirmation, the next, the simple denial; all others are only one by conjunction.

10   Every proposition must contain a verb or the tense of a verb. The phrase which defines the species 'man', if no verb in present, past, or future time be added, is not a proposition. It may be asked how the expression 'a footed animal with two feet' can be called single; for it is not the circumstance that the words follow in unbroken succession that effects the unity. This inquiry, however, finds its place in an investigation foreign to that before us.

15   We call those propositions single which indicate a single fact, or the conjunction of the parts of which results in unity: those propositions, on the other hand, are separate and many in number, which indicate many facts, or whose parts have no conjunction.

Let us, moreover, consent to call a noun or a verb an expression only, and not a proposition, since it is not possible for a man to speak in this way when he is expressing something, in such a way as to make a statement, whether his utterance is an answer to a question or an act of his own initiation.

20   To return: of propositions one kind is simple, i.e. that which asserts or denies something of something, the other composite, i.e. that which is compounded of simple propositions. A simple proposition is a statement, with meaning, as to the presence of something

[1] Cf. 16ª 22–26.   [2] Cf. *Poet.* 1456ᵇ 11.

in a subject or its absence, in the present, past, or future, according to the divisions of time.

6　An affirmation is a positive assertion of something about some- 25 thing, a denial a negative assertion.

Now it is possible both to affirm and to deny the presence of something which is present or of something which is not, and since these same affirmations and denials are possible with reference to those times which lie outside the present, it would be possible to contradict 30 any affirmation or denial. Thus it is plain that every affirmation has an opposite denial, and similarly every denial an opposite affirmation.

We will call such a pair of propositions a pair of contradictories. Those positive and negative propositions are said to be contradictory which have the same subject and predicate. The identity of subject 35 and of predicate must not be 'equivocal'. Indeed there are definitive qualifications besides this, which we make to meet the casuistries of sophists.

7　Some things are universal, others individual. By the term 'universal' I mean that which is of such a nature as to be predicated of many subjects, by 'individual' that which is not thus predicated. Thus 'man' is a universal, 'Callias' an individual.　　　　　　　40

Our propositions necessarily sometimes concern a universal sub- 17ᵇ ject, sometimes an individual.

If, then, a man states a positive and a negative proposition of universal character with regard to a universal, these two propositions are 'contrary'. By the expression 'a proposition of universal character 5 with regard to a universal', such propositions as 'every man is white', 'no man is white' are meant. When, on the other hand, the positive and negative propositions, though they have regard to a universal, are yet not of universal character, they will not be contrary, albeit the meaning intended is sometimes contrary. As instances of propositions made with regard to a universal, but not of universal character, we may take the propositions 'man is white', 'man is not white'. 10 'Man' is a universal, but the proposition is not made as of universal character; for the word 'every' does not make the subject a universal, but rather gives the proposition a universal character. If, however, both predicate and subject are distributed, the proposition thus constituted is contrary to truth; no affirmation will, under such circumstances, be true. The proposition 'every man is every 15 animal' is an example of this type.

An affirmation is opposed to a denial in the sense which I denote by the term 'contradictory', when, while the subject remains the same, the affirmation is of universal character and the denial is not. The affirmation 'every man is white' is the *contradictory* of the denial 'not every man is white', or again, the proposition 'no man is white' is the *contradictory* of the proposition 'some men are white'.

20 But propositions are opposed as *contraries* when both the affirmation and the denial are universal, as in the sentences 'every man is white', 'no man is white', 'every man is just', 'no man is just'.

We see that in a pair of this sort both propositions cannot be true, but the contradictories of a pair of contraries can sometimes both be
25 true with reference to the same subject; for instance 'not every man is white' and 'some men are white' are both true. Of such corresponding positive and negative propositions as refer to universals and have a universal character, one must be true and the other false. This is the case also when the reference is to individuals, as in the propositions 'Socrates is white', 'Socrates is not white'.

When, on the other hand, the reference is to universals, but the propositions are not universal, it is not always the case that one is
30 true and the other false, for it is possible to state truly that man is white and that man is not white and that man is beautiful and that man is not beautiful; for if a man is deformed he is the reverse of beautiful, also if he is progressing towards beauty he is not yet beautiful.

This statement might seem at first sight to carry with it a con-
35 tradiction, owing to the fact that the proposition 'man is not white' appears to be equivalent to the proposition 'no man is white'. This, however, is not the case, nor are they necessarily at the same time true or false.

It is evident also that the denial corresponding to a single affirmation is itself single; for the denial must deny just that which the affirmation affirms concerning the same subject, and must correspond with the affirmation both in the universal or particular char-
18ᵃ acter of the subject and in the distributed or undistributed sense in which it is understood.

For instance, the affirmation 'Socrates is white' has its proper denial in the proposition 'Socrates is not white'. If anything else be negatively predicated of the subject or if anything else be the subject though the predicate remain the same, the denial will not be the denial proper to that affirmation, but one that is distinct.

The denial proper to the affirmation 'every man is white' is 'not
5 every man is white'; that proper to the affirmation 'some men are

white' is 'no man is white', while that proper to the affirmation 'man is white' is 'man is not white'.

We have shown further that a single denial is contradictorily opposite to a single affirmation and we have explained which these are; we have also stated that contrary are distinct from contradictory propositions and which the contrary are; also that with re- 10 gard to a pair of opposite propositions it is not always the case that one is true and the other false. We have pointed out, moreover, what the reason of this is and under what circumstances the truth of the one involves the falsity of the other.

8 An affirmation or denial is single, if it indicates some one fact about some one subject; it matters not whether the subject is universal and whether the statement has a universal character, or whether this is not so. Such single propositions are: 'every man is white', 'not every man is white'; 'man is white', 'man is not white'; 15 'no man is white', 'some men are white'; provided the word 'white' has one meaning. If, on the other hand, one word has two meanings which do not combine to form one, the affirmation is not single. For instance, if a man should establish the symbol 'garment' as significant both of a horse and of a man, the proposition 'garment 20 is white' would not be a single affirmation, nor its opposite a single denial. For it is equivalent to the proposition 'horse and man are white', which, again, is equivalent to the two propositions 'horse is white', 'man is white'. If, then, these two propositions have more than a single significance, and do not form a single proposition, it is plain that the first proposition either has more than one significance 25 or else has none; for a particular man is not a horse.

This, then, is another instance of those propositions of which both the positive and the negative forms may be true or false simultaneously.

9 In the case of that which is or which has taken place, propositions, whether positive or negative, must be true or false. Again, in the case of a pair of contradictories, either when the subject is universal and the propositions are of a universal character, or when it 30 is individual, as has been said,[3] one of the two must be true and the other false; whereas when the subject is universal, but the propositions are not of a universal character, there is no such necessity. We have discussed this type also in a previous chapter.[4]

When the subject, however, is individual, and that which is predi-

[3] Cf. 17^b 26–9.   [4] Cf. 17^b 29–37.

cated of it relates to the future, the case is altered. For if all propositions whether positive or negative are either true or false,
35 then any given predicate must either belong to the subject or not, so that if one man affirms that an event of a given character will take place and another denies it, it is plain that the statement of the one will correspond with reality and that of the other will not. For the predicate cannot both belong and not belong to the subject at one and the same time with regard to the future.

18^b   Thus, if it is true to say that a thing is white, it must necessarily be white; if the reverse proposition is true, it will of necessity not be white. Again, if it is white, the proposition stating that it is white was true; if it is not white, the proposition to the opposite effect was true. And if it is not white, the man who states that it is is making a false statement; and if the man who states that it is white is making a false statement, it follows that it is not white. It may therefore be argued that it is necessary that affirmations or denials must be either true or false.

5   Now if this be so, nothing is or takes place fortuitously, either in the present or in the future, and there are no real alternatives; everything takes place of necessity and is fixed. For either he that affirms that it will take place or he that denies this is in correspondence with fact, whereas if things did not take place of necessity, an event might just as easily not happen as happen; for the meaning of the word 'fortuitous' with regard to present or future events is that reality is so constituted that it may issue in either of two opposite directions.

10   Again, if a thing is white now, it was true before to say that it would be white, so that of anything that has taken place it was always true to say 'it is' or 'it will be'. But if it was always true to say that a thing is or will be, it is not possible that it should not be or not be about to be, and when a thing cannot not come to be, it is impossible that it should not come to be, and when it is impossible that it should not come to be, it must come to be.
15 All, then, that is about to be must of necessity take place. It results from this that nothing is uncertain or fortuitous, for if it were fortuitous it would not be necessary.

Again, to say that neither the affirmation nor the denial is true, maintaining, let us say, that an event neither will take place nor will not take place, is to take up a position impossible to defend. In the first place, though facts should prove the one proposition
20 false, the opposite would still be untrue. Secondly, if it was true to say that a thing was both white and large, both these qualities must

necessarily belong to it; and if they will belong to it the next day, they must necessarily belong to it the next day. But if an event is neither to take place nor not to take place the next day, the element of chance will be eliminated. For example, it would be necessary that a sea-fight should neither take place nor fail to take place on the 25 next day.

These awkward results and others of the same kind follow, if it is an irrefragable law that of every pair of contradictory propositions, whether they have regard to universals and are stated as universally applicable, or whether they have regard to individuals, one must be true and the other false, and that there are no real 30 alternatives, but that all that is or takes place is the outcome of necessity. There would be no need to deliberate or to take trouble, on the supposition that if we should adopt a certain course, a certain result would follow, while, if we did not, the result would not follow. For a man may predict an event ten thousand years beforehand, and another may predict the reverse; that which was truly predicted at the moment in the past will of necessity take place 35 in the fullness of time.

Further, it makes no difference whether people have or have not actually made the contradictory statements. For it is manifest that the circumstances are not influenced by the fact of an affirmation or denial on the part of anyone. For events will not take place or fail to take place because it was stated that they would or would not take place, nor is this any more the case if the prediction dates back ten thousand years or any other space of time. Wherefore, if through 19ª all time the nature of things was so constituted that a prediction about an event was true, then through all time it was necessary that that prediction should find fulfilment; and with regard to all events, circumstances have always been such that their occurrence is a matter of necessity. For that of which someone has said truly that it will be, cannot fail to take place; and of that which 5 takes place, it was always true to say that it would be.

Yet this view leads to an impossible conclusion; for we see that both deliberation and action are causative with regard to the future, and that, to speak more generally, in those things which are not continuously actual there is a potentiality in either direction. Such things may either be or not be; events also therefore may 10 either take place or not take place. There are many obvious instances of this. It is possible that this coat may be cut in half, and yet it may not be cut in half, but wear out first. In the same way, it is possible that it should not be cut in half; unless this were so, 15

it would not be possible that it should wear out first. So it is therefore with all other events which possess this kind of potentiality.
It is therefore plain that it is not of necessity that everything is
or takes place; but in some instances there are real alternatives, in
which case the affirmation is no more true and no more false than the
20 denial; while some exhibit a predisposition and general tendency
in one direction or the other, and yet can issue in the opposite
direction by exception.

Now that which is must needs be when it is, and that which is not
must needs not be when it is not. Yet it cannot be said without
qualification that all existence and non-existence is the outcome of
25 necessity. For there is a difference between saying that that which
is, when it is, must needs be, and simply saying that all that is
must needs be, and similarly in the case of that which is not.
In the case, also, of two contradictory propositions this holds good.
Everything must either be or not be, whether in the present or in
the future, but it is not always possible to distinguish and state
determinately which of these alternatives must necessarily come
about.

30 Let me illustrate. A sea-fight must either take place to-morrow or
not, but it is not necessary that it should take place to-morrow, neither
is it necessary that it should not take place, yet it is necessary
that it either should or should not take place to-morrow. Since
propositions correspond with facts, it is evident that when in future
events there is a real alternative, and a potentiality in contrary directions, the corresponding affirmation and denial have the same character.

35 This is the case with regard to that which is not always existent
or not always non-existent. One of the two propositions in such
instances must be true and the other false, but we cannot say determinately that this or that is false, but must leave the alternative
undecided. One may indeed be more likely to be true than the other,
but it cannot be either actually true or actually false. It is therefore
19ᵇ plain that it is not necessary that of an affirmation and a denial
one should be true and the other false. For in the case of that
which exists potentially, but not actually, the rule which applies
to that which exists actually does not hold good. The case is rather
as we have indicated.

5 10   An affirmation is the statement of a fact with regard to a subject, and this subject is either a noun or that which has no name;

the subject and predicate in an affirmation must each denote a single thing. I have already explained [5] what is meant by a noun and by that which has no name; for I stated that the expression 'not-man' was not a noun, in the proper sense of the word, but an indefinite noun, denoting as it does in a sense a single thing. Similarly the expression 'does not enjoy health' is not a verb proper, but an indefinite verb. Every affirmation, then, and every denial, will con- 10 sist of a noun and a verb, either definite or indefinite.

There can be no affirmation or denial without a verb; for the expressions 'is', 'will be', 'was', 'is coming to be', and the like are verbs according to our definition, since besides their specific mean- ing they convey the notion of time.

Thus the primary affirmation and denial are as follows: 'man is', 'man is not'. Next to these, there are the propositions: 'not-man is', 15 'not-man is not'. Again we have the propositions: 'every man is', 'every man is not', 'all that is not-man is', 'all that is not-man is not'. The same classification holds good with regard to such periods of time as lie outside the present.

When the verb 'is' is used as a third element in the sentence, there can be positive and negative propositions of two sorts. Thus in the sentence 'man is just' the verb 'is' is used as a third element, 20 call it verb or noun, which you will. Four propositions, therefore, instead of two can be formed with these materials. Two of the four, as regards their affirmation and denial, correspond in their logical sequence with the propositions which deal with a condition of privation; the other two do not correspond with these.

I mean that the verb 'is' is added either to the term 'just' or to the term ''not-just', and two negative propositions are formed in the 25 same way. Thus we have the four propositions. Reference to the sub- joined table will make matters clear:

A. Affirmation. Man is just.   B. Denial. Man is not just.

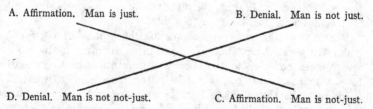

D. Denial. Man is not not-just.   C. Affirmation. Man is not-just.

Here 'is' and 'is not' are added either to 'just' or to 'not-just'. This then is the proper scheme for these propositions, as has been 30

---

[5] Cf. 16ª 19, 30.

said in the *Analytics*.[6] The same rule holds good, if the subject is distributed. Thus we have the table:

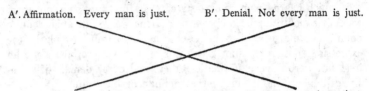

A'. Affirmation. Every man is just.   B'. Denial. Not every man is just.

D'. Denial. Not every man is not-just.   C'. Affirmation. Every man is not-just.

35 Yet here it is not possible, in the same way as in the former case, that the propositions joined in the table by a diagonal line should both be true; though under certain circumstances this is the case.

We have thus set out two pairs of opposite propositions; there are moreover two other pairs, if a term be conjoined with 'not-man', the latter forming a kind of subject. Thus:

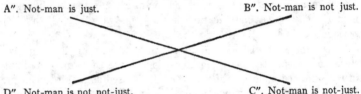

A". Not-man is just.   B". Not-man is not just.

D". Not-man is not not-just.   C". Not-man is not-just.

20ᵃ This is an exhaustive enumeration of all the pairs of opposite propositions that can possibly be framed. This last group should remain distinct from those which preceded it, since it employs as its subject the expression 'not-man'.

When the verb 'is' does not fit the structure of the sentence (for instance, when the verbs 'walks', 'enjoys health' are used), that scheme applies, which applied when the word 'is' was added.

5   Thus we have the propositions: 'every man enjoys health', 'every man does-not-enjoy-health', 'all that is not-man enjoys health', 'all that is not-man does-not-enjoy-health'.

We must not in these propositions use the expression 'not every man'. The negative must be attached to the word 'man', for the word 'every' does not give to the subject a universal significance, but

10 implies that, as a subject, it is distributed. This is plain from the following pairs: 'man enjoys health', 'man does not enjoy health'; 'not-man enjoys health', 'not-man does not enjoy health'. These propositions differ from the former in being indefinite and not universal in character. Thus the adjectives 'every' and 'no' have no

6 *Analytica Priora*, 51ᵇ 36–52ᵃ 17.

additional significance except that the subject, whether in a positive
or in a negative sentence, is distributed. The rest of the sentence,
therefore, will in each case be the same.   15

Since the contrary of the proposition 'every animal is just' is 'no
animal is just', it is plain that these two propositions will never both
be true at the same time or with reference to the same subject. Sometimes, however, the contradictories of these contraries will both be
true, as in the instance before us: the propositions 'not every animal
is just' and 'some animals are just' are both true.

Further, the proposition 'no man is just' follows from the proposi- 20
tion 'every man is not-just' and the proposition 'not every man is
not-just', which is the opposite of 'every man is not-just', follows
from the proposition 'some men are just'; for if this be true, there
must be some just men.

It is evident, also, that when the subject is individual, if a question is asked and the negative answer is the true one, a certain
positive proposition is also true. Thus, if the question were asked 25
'Is Socrates wise?' and the negative answer were the true one, the
positive inference 'Then Socrates is unwise' is correct. But no such
inference is correct in the case of universals, but rather a negative
proposition. For instance, if to the question 'Is every man wise?' the
answer is 'no', the inference 'Then every man is unwise' is false. But
under these circumstances the inference 'Not every man is wise' is 30
correct. This last is the contradictory, the former the contrary. Negative expressions, which consist of an indefinite noun or predicate,
such as 'not-man' or 'not-just', may seem to be denials containing
neither noun nor verb in the proper sense of the words. But they
are not. For a denial must always be either true or false, and he that 35
uses the expression 'not-man', if nothing more be added, is not nearer
but rather further from making a true or a false statement than he
who uses the expression 'man'.

The propositions 'everything that is not man is just', and the contradictory of this, are not equivalent to any of the other propositions;
on the other hand, the proposition 'everything that is not man is not
just' is equivalent to the proposition 'nothing that is not man is just'. 40

The conversion of the position of subject and predicate in a sen- 20ᵇ
tence involves no difference in its meaning. Thus we say 'man is
white' and 'white is man'. If these were not equivalent, there would
be more than one contradictory to the same proposition, whereas it
has been demonstrated [7] that each proposition has one proper contradictory and one only. For of the proposition 'man is white' the

[7] Cf. 17ᵇ 38.

5 appropriate contradictory is 'man is not white', and of the proposition 'white is man', if its meaning be different, the contradictory will
either be 'white is not not-man' or 'white is not man'. Now the
former of these is the contradictory of the proposition 'white is not-
man', and the latter of these is the contradictory of the proposition
'man is white'; thus there will be two contradictories to one proposition.

10 It is evident, therefore, that the inversion of the relative position of
subject and predicate does not affect the sense of affirmations and
denials.

11 There is no unity about an affirmation or denial which, either
positively or negatively, predicates one thing of many subjects, or
many things of the same subject, unless that which is indicated by
the many is really some one thing.

15 I do not apply this word 'one' to those things which, though they
have a single recognized name, yet do not combine to form a unity.
Thus, man may be an animal, and biped, and domesticated, but these
three predicates combine to form a unity. On the other hand, the
predicates 'white', 'man', and 'walking' do not thus combine. Neither,
therefore, if these three form the subject of an affirmation, nor if
20 they form its predicate, is there any unity about that affirmation.
In both cases the unity is linguistic, but not real.

If therefore the dialectical question is a request for an answer,
i. e. either for the admission of a premiss or for the admission of one
of two contradictories—and the premiss is itself always one of two
contradictories—the answer to such a question as contains the above
25 predicates cannot be a single proposition. For as I have explained
in the *Topics*,[8] the question is not a single one, even if the answer
asked for is true.

At the same time it is plain that a question of the form 'what is it?'
is not a dialectical question, for a dialectical questioner must by the
form of his question give his opponent the chance of announcing
one of two alternatives, whichever he wishes. He must therefore put
30 the question into a more definite form, and inquire, e. g. whether
man has such and such a characteristic or not.

Some combinations of predicates are such that the separate predicates unite to form a single predicate. Let us consider under what
conditions this is and is not possible. We may either state in two
separate propositions that man is an animal and that man is a biped,
or we may combine the two, and state that man is an animal with

[8] *Topica*, viii. 7.

two feet. Similarly we may use 'man' and 'white' as separate predicates, or unite them into one. Yet if a man is a shoemaker and is 35
also good, we cannot construct a composite proposition and say that
he is a good shoemaker. For if, whenever two separate predicates
truly belong to a subject, it follows that the predicate resulting from
their combination also truly belongs to the subject, many absurd
results ensue. For instance, a man is man and white. Therefore, if
predicates may always be combined, he is a white man. Again, if the
predicate 'white' belongs to him, then the combination of that predicate with the former composite predicate will be permissible. Thus it
will be right to say that he is a white white man and so on indefinitely. 40
Or, again, we may combine the predicates 'musical', 'white', and
'walking', and these may be combined many times. Similarly we 21ᵃ
may say that Socrates is Socrates and a man, and that therefore he is
the man Socrates, or that Socrates is a man and a biped, and that
therefore he is a two-footed man. Thus it is manifest that if a man 5
states unconditionally that predicates can always be combined, many
absurd consequences ensue.

We will now explain what ought to be laid down.

Those predicates, and terms forming the subject of predication,
which are accidental either to the same subject or to one another,
do not combine to form a unity. Take the proposition 'man is white 10
of complexion and musical'. Whiteness and being musical do not
coalesce to form a unity, for they belong only accidentally to the
same subject. Nor yet, if it were true to say that that which is white
is musical, would the terms 'musical' and 'white' form a unity, for it
is only incidentally that that which is musical is white; the combination of the two will, therefore, not form a unity.

Thus, again, whereas, if a man is both good and a shoemaker, we
cannot combine the two propositions and say simply that he is a good
shoemaker, we are, at the same time, able to combine the predicates
'animal' and 'biped' and say that a man is an animal with two feet, 15
for these predicates are not accidental.

Those predicates, again, cannot form a unity, of which the one is
implicit in the other: thus we cannot combine the predicate 'white'
again and again with that which already contains the notion 'white',
nor is it right to call a man an animal-man or a two-footed man; for
the notions 'animal' and 'biped' are implicit in the word 'man'. On
the other hand, it is possible to predicate a term simply of any one
instance, and to say that some one particular man is a man or that
some one white man is a white man.   20

Yet this is not always possible: indeed, when in the adjunct there

is some opposite which involves a contradiction, the predication of
the simple term is impossible. Thus it is not right to call a dead man a
man. When, however, this is not the case, it is not impossible.

Yet the facts of the case might rather be stated thus: when some
such opposite elements are present, resolution is never possible, but
25 when they are not present, resolution is nevertheless not always
possible. Take the proposition 'Homer is so-and-so', say 'a poet'; does
it follow that Homer is, or does it not? The verb 'is' is here used of
Homer only incidentally, the proposition being that Homer is a poet,
not that he is, in the independent sense of the word.

Thus, in the case of those predications which have within them no
30 contradiction when the nouns are expanded into definitions, and
wherein the predicates belong to the subject in their own proper
sense and not in any indirect way, the individual may be the subject
of the simple propositions as well as of the composite. But in the case
of that which is not, it is not true to say that because it is the object of
opinion, it is; for the opinion held about it is that it is not, not
that it is.

12   As these distinctions have been made, we must consider the
35 mutual relation of those affirmations and denials which assert or deny
possibility or contingency, impossibility or necessity: for the subject
is not without difficulty.

We admit that of composite expressions those are contradictory
each to each which have the verb 'to be' in its positive and negative
form respectively. Thus the contradictory of the proposition 'man is'
21ᵇ is 'man is not', not 'not-man is', and the contradictory of 'man is
white' is 'man is not white', not 'man is not-white'. For otherwise,
since either the positive or the negative proposition is true of any
subject, it will turn out true to say that a piece of wood is a man that
is not white.

5   Now if this is the case, in those propositions which do not contain
the verb 'to be' the verb which takes its place will exercise the same
function. Thus the contradictory of 'man walks' is 'man does not
walk', not 'not-man walks'; for to say 'man walks' is merely equivalent to saying 'man is walking'.

10   If then this rule is universal, the contradictory of 'it may be' is 'it
may *not* be', not 'it cannot be'.

Now it appears that the same thing both may and may not be;
for instance, everything that may be cut or may walk may also
escape cutting and refrain from walking; and the reason is that those
things that have potentiality in this sense are not always actual.

In such cases, both the positive and the negative propositions will be 15
true; for that which is capable of walking or of being seen has also a
potentiality in the opposite direction.

But since it is impossible that contradictory propositions should
both be true of the same subject, it follows that 'it may *not* be' is not
the contradictory of 'it may be'. For it is a logical consequence of
what we have said, either that the same predicate can be both applicable and inapplicable to one and the same subject at the same time, 20
or that it is not by the addition of the verbs 'be' and 'not be', respectively, that positive and negative propositions are formed. If the
former of these alternatives must be rejected, we must choose the
latter.

The contradictory, then, of 'it may be' is 'it cannot be'. The same
rule applies to the proposition 'it is contingent that it should be'; the
contradictory of this is 'it is not contingent that it should be'. The 25
similar propositions, such as 'it is necessary' and 'it is impossible',
may be dealt with in the same manner. For it comes about that just
as in the former instances the verbs 'is' and 'is not' were added to
the subject-matter of the sentence 'white' and 'man', so here 'that it
should be' and 'that it should not be' are the subject-matter and
'is possible', 'is contingent', are added. These indicate that a certain 30
thing is or is not possible, just as in the former instances 'is' and 'is
not' indicated that certain things were or were not the case.

The contradictory, then, of 'it may *not* be' is not 'it cannot be',
but 'it cannot not be', and the contradictory of 'it may be' is not 'it
may *not* be', but 'it cannot be'. Thus the propositions 'it may be' and 35
'it may *not* be' appear each to imply the other: for, since these two
propositions are not contradictory, the same thing both may and
may *not* be. But the propositions 'it may be' and 'it cannot be' can
never be true of the same subject at the same time, for they are
contradictory. Nor can the propositions 'it may not be' and 'it can- 22ᵃ
not not be' be at once true of the same subject.

The propositions which have to do with necessity are governed by
the same principle. The contradictory of 'it is necessary that it should
be' is not 'it is necessary that it should not be', but 'it is not necessary
that it should be', and the contradictory of 'it is necessary that it 5
should not be' is 'it is not necessary that it should not be'.

Again, the contradictory of 'it is impossible that it should be' is not
'it is impossible that it should not be' but 'it is not impossible that it
should be', and the contradictory of 'it is impossible that it should not
be' is 'it is not impossible that it should not be'.

To generalize, we must, as has been stated, define the clauses 'that

it should be' and 'that it should not be' as the subject-matter of the
propositions, and in making these terms into affirmations and denials
10 we must combine them with 'that it should be' and 'that it should not
be' respectively.

We must consider the following pairs as contradictory propositions:

It may be.	It cannot be.
It is contingent.	It is not contingent.
It is impossible.	It is not impossible.
It is necessary.	It is not necessary.
It is true.	It is not true.

13 Logical sequences follow in due course when we have arranged
15 the propositions thus. From the proposition 'it may be' it follows
that it is contingent, and the relation is reciprocal. It follows also that
it is not impossible and not necessary.

From the proposition 'it may *not* be' or 'it is contingent that it
should not be' it follows that it is not necessary that it should not be
and that it is not impossible that it should not be. From the proposition 'it cannot be' or 'it is not contingent' it follows that it is neces-
20 sary that it should not be and that it is impossible that it should be.
From the proposition 'it cannot not be' or 'it is not contingent that it
should not be' it follows that it is necessary that it should be and
that it is impossible that it should not be.

Let us consider these statements by the help of a table:

A. It may be.	B. It cannot be.
25 It is contingent.	It is not contingent.
It is not impossible that it should be.	It is impossible that it should be.
It is not necessary that it should be.	It is necessary that it should not be.
C. It may not be.	D. It cannot not be.
It is contingent that it should not be.	It is not contingent that it should not be.
30 It is not impossible that it should not be.	It is impossible that it should not be.
It is not necessary that it should not be.	It is necessary that it should be.

Now the propositions 'it is impossible that it should be' and 'it is
not impossible that it should be' are consequent upon the propositions
'it may be', 'it is contingent', and 'it cannot be', 'it is not contingent',
the contradictories upon the contradictories. But there is inversion.
The negative of the proposition 'it is impossible' is consequent upon

the proposition 'it may be' and the corresponding positive in the first 35
case upon the negative in the second. For 'it is impossible' is a positive
proposition and 'it is not impossible' is negative.

We must investigate the relation subsisting between these propositions and those which predicate necessity. That there is a distinction
is clear. In this case, contrary propositions follow respectively from
contradictory propositions, and the contradictory propositions belong
to separate sequences. For the proposition 'it is not necessary that it
should be' is not the negative of 'it is necessary that it should not be',
for both these propositions may be true of the same subject; for 22ᵇ
when it is necessary that a thing should not be, it is not necessary
that it should be. The reason why the propositions predicating necessity do not follow in the same kind of sequence as the rest, lies in the
fact that the proposition 'it is impossible' is equivalent, when used
with a contrary subject, to the proposition 'it is necessary'. For when
it is impossible that a thing should be, it is necessary, not that it 5
should be, but that it should not be, and when it is impossible that a
thing should not be, it is necessary that it should be. Thus, if the
propositions predicating impossibility or non-impossibility follow
without change of subject from those predicating possibility or non-
possibility, those predicating necessity must follow with the contrary subject; for the propositions 'it is impossible' and 'it is necessary' are not equivalent, but, as has been said, inversely connected.

Yet perhaps it is impossible that the contradictory propositions 10
predicating necessity should be thus arranged. For when it is necessary that a thing should be, it is possible that it should be. (For if not,
the opposite follows, since one or the other must follow; so, if it is not
possible, it is impossible, and it is thus impossible that a thing should
be, which must necessarily be; which is absurd.)

Yet from the proposition 'it may be' it follows that it is not impossible, and from that it follows that it is not necessary; it comes 15
about therefore that the thing which must necessarily be need not be;
which is absurd. But again, the proposition 'it is necessary that it
should be' does not follow from the proposition 'it may be', nor does
the proposition 'it is necessary that it should not be'. For the proposition 'it may be' implies a twofold possibility, while, if either of the
two former propositions is true, the twofold possibility vanishes. For
if a thing may be, it may also not be, but if it is necessary that it 20
should be or that it should not be, one of the two alternatives will be
excluded. It remains, therefore, that the proposition 'it is not necessary that it should not be' follows from the proposition 'it may be'.
For this is true also of that which must necessarily be.

Moreover the proposition 'it is not necessary that it should not be' is the contradictory of that which follows from the proposition 'it 25 cannot be'; for 'it cannot be' is followed by 'it is impossible that it should be' and by 'it is necessary that it should not be', and the contradictory of this is the proposition 'it is not necessary that it should not be'. Thus in this case also contradictory propositions follow contradictory in the way indicated, and no logical impossibilities occur when they are thus arranged.

It may be questioned whether the proposition 'it may be' follows from the proposition 'it is necessary that it should be'. If not, the 30 contradictory must follow, namely that it cannot be, or, if a man should maintain that this is not the contradictory, then the proposition 'it may not be'.

Now both of these are false of that which necessarily is. At the same time, it is thought that if a thing may be cut it may also not be cut, if a thing may be it may also not be, and thus it would follow that 35 a thing which must necessarily be may possibly not be; which is false. It is evident, then, that it is not always the case that that which may be or may walk possesses also a potentiality in the other direction. There are exceptions. In the first place we must except those things which possess a potentiality not in accordance with a rational principle, as fire possesses the potentiality of giving out heat, that is, an irrational capacity. Those potentialities which involve a rational principle are potentialities of more than one result, that is, of con- 23ᵃ trary results; those that are irrational are not always thus constituted. As I have said, fire cannot both heat and not heat, neither has anything that is always actual any twofold potentiality. Yet some even of those potentialities which are irrational admit of opposite results. 5 However, thus much has been said to emphasize the truth that it is not every potentiality which admits of opposite results, even where the word is used always in the same sense.

But in some cases the word is used equivocally. For the term 'possible' is ambiguous, being used in the one case with reference to facts, to that which is actualized, as when a man is said to find walking possible because he is actually walking, and generally when a capacity 10 is predicated because it is actually realized; in the other case, with reference to a state in which realization is conditionally practicable, as when a man is said to find walking possible because under certain conditions he would walk. This last sort of potentiality belongs only to that which can be in motion, the former can exist also in the case of that which has not this power. Both of that which is walking and is actual, and of that which has the capacity though not necessarily realized, it is true to say that it is not impossible that it should walk (or, in the other case, that it should be), but while we cannot predicate this latter kind of potentiality of that which is necessary 15 in the unqualified sense of the word, we can predicate the former.

Our conclusion, then, is this: that since the universal is consequent upon the particular, that which is necessary is also possible, though not in every sense in which the word may be used.

We may perhaps state that necessity and its absence are the initial principles of existence and non-existence, and that all else must be regarded as posterior to these.   20

It is plain from what has been said that that which is of necessity is actual. Thus, if that which is eternal is prior, actuality also is prior to potentiality. Some things are actualities without potentiality, namely, the primary substances; a second class consists of those things which are actual but also potential, whose actuality is in nature prior to their potentiality, though posterior in time; a third class comprises 25 those things which are never actualized, but are pure potentialities.

14   The question arises whether an affirmation finds its contrary in a denial or in another affirmation; whether the proposition 'every man is just' finds its contrary in the proposition 'no man is just', or in the proposition 'every man is unjust'. Take the propositions 'Callias is just', 'Callias is not just', 'Callias is unjust'; we have to 30 discover which of these form contraries.

Now if the spoken word corresponds with the judgement of the mind, and if, in thought, that judgement is the contrary of another, which pronounces a contrary fact, in the way, for instance, in which the judgement 'every man is just' pronounces a contrary to that pronounced by the judgement 'every man is unjust', the same must needs hold good with regard to spoken affirmations.   35

But if, in thought, it is not the judgement which pronounces a contrary fact that is the contrary of another, then one affirmation will not find its contrary in another, but rather in the corresponding denial. We must therefore consider which true judgement is the contrary of the false, that which forms the denial of the false judgement or that which affirms the contrary fact.

Let me illustrate. There is a true judgement concerning that which 40 is good, that it is good; another, a false judgement, that it is not good; and a third, which is distinct, that it is bad. Which of these two 23^b is contrary to the true? And if they are one and the same, which mode of expression forms the contrary?

It is an error to suppose that judgements are to be defined as contrary in virtue of the fact that they have contrary subjects; for the judgement concerning a good thing, that it is good, and that concerning a bad thing, that it is bad, may be one and the same, and whether they are so or not, they both represent the truth. Yet the subjects here are contrary. But judgements are not contrary because they have contrary subjects, but because they are to the contrary effect.

Now if we take the judgement that that which is good is good, and another that it is not good, and if there are at the same time other attributes, which do not and cannot belong to the good, we must nevertheless refuse to treat as the contraries of the true judgement those which opine that some other attribute subsists which does not subsist, as also those that opine that some other attribute does not subsist which does subsist, for both these classes of judgement are of unlimited content.

Those judgements must rather be termed contrary to the true judgements, in which error is present. Now these judgements are those which are concerned with the starting points of generation, and generation is the passing from one extreme to its opposite; therefore error is a like transition.

Now that which is good is both good and not bad. The first quality is part of its essence, the second accidental; for it is by accident that it is not bad. But if that true judgement is most really true, which concerns the subject's intrinsic nature, then that false judgement likewise is most really false, which concerns its intrinsic nature. Now the judgement that that which is good is not good is a false judgement concerning its intrinsic nature, the judgement that it is bad is one concerning that which is accidental. Thus the judgement which denies the truth of the true judgement is more really false than that which positively asserts the presence of the contrary quality. But it is the man who forms that judgement which is contrary to the true who is most thoroughly deceived, for contraries are among the things which differ most widely within the same class. If then of the two judgements one is contrary to the true judgement, but that which is contradictory is the more truly contrary, then the latter, it seems, is the real contrary. The judgement that that which is good is bad is composite. For presumably the man who forms that judgement must at the same time understand that that which is good is not good.

Further, the contradictory is either always the contrary or never; therefore, if it must necessarily be so in all other cases, our conclusion in the case just dealt with would seem to be correct. Now where terms have no contrary, that judgement is false, which forms the negative of the true; for instance, he who thinks a man is not a man forms a false judgement. If then in these cases the negative is the contrary, then the principle is universal in its application.

Again, the judgement that that which is not good is not good is parallel with the judgement that that which is good is good. Besides these there is the judgement that that which is good is not good, parallel with the judgement that that which is not good is good. Let 35 us consider, therefore, what would form the contrary of the true judgement that that which is not good is not good. The judgement that it is bad would, of course, fail to meet the case, since two true judgements are never contrary and this judgement might be true at the same time as that with which it is connected. For since some things which are not good are bad, both judgements may be true. Nor is the judgement that it is not bad the contrary, for this too might be true, since both qualities might be predicated of the same subject. It remains, therefore, that of the judgement concerning that which 40 is not good, that it is not good, the contrary judgement is that it is good; for this is false. In the same way, moreover, the judgement 24ᵃ concerning that which is good, that it is not good, is the contrary of the judgement that it is good.

It is evident that it will make no difference if we universalize the positive judgement, for the universal negative judgement will form the contrary. For instance, the contrary of the judgement that 5 everything that is good is good is that nothing that is good is good. For the judgement that that which is good is good, if the subject be understood in a universal sense, is equivalent to the judgement that whatever is good is good, and this is identical with the judgement that everything that is good is good. We may deal similarly with judgements concerning that which is not good.

If therefore this is the rule with judgements, and if spoken 24ᵇ affirmations and denials are judgements expressed in words, it is plain that the universal denial is the contrary of the affirmation about the same subject. Thus the propositions 'everything good is good', 'every man is good', have for their contraries the propositions 'nothing good is good', 'no man is good'. The contradictory propositions, on the 5 other hand, are 'not everything good is good', 'not every man is good'.

It is evident, also, that neither true judgements nor true propositions can be contrary the one to the other. For whereas, when two propositions are true, a man may state both at the same time without inconsistency, contrary propositions are those which state contrary conditions, and contrary conditions cannot subsist at one and the same time in the same subject.

ANALYTICA PRIORA

Translated by A. J. Jenkinson

CONTENTS

BOOK I

A. *Structure of the Syllogism.*

B. *Mode of discovery of arguments.*

1. GENERAL.

C. *Analysis (1) of arguments into figures and moods of syllogism.*

[Chapters 32-46 omitted.]

BOOK II

Properties and defects of syllogism; arguments akin to syllogism.

A. PROPERTIES.

[Chapters 1-15 omitted.]

B. DEFECTS.

C. ARGUMENTS AKIN TO SYLLOGISM.

ANALYTICA PRIORA

(*Prior Analytics*)

BOOK I

1 We must first state the subject of our inquiry and the faculty to 10
which it belongs: its subject is demonstration and the faculty that 24ᵃ
carries it out demonstrative science. We must next define a premiss, a
term, and a syllogism, and the nature of a perfect and of an imperfect
syllogism; and after that, the inclusion or non-inclusion of one term
in another as in a whole, and what we mean by predicating one term
of all, or none, of another.   15

A premiss then is a sentence affirming or denying one thing of another. This is either universal or particular or indefinite. By universal
I mean the statement that something belongs to all or none of something else; by particular that it belongs to some or not to some or not
to all; by indefinite that it does or does not belong, without any
mark to show whether it is universal or particular, e. g. 'contraries 20
are subjects of the same science', or 'pleasure is not good'. The
demonstrative premiss differs from the dialectical, because the demonstrative premiss is the assertion of one of two contradictory statements
(the demonstrator does not ask for his premiss, but lays it down),
whereas the dialectical premiss depends on the adversary's choice 25
between two contradictories. But this will make no difference to the
production of a syllogism in either case; for both the demonstrator
and the dialectician argue syllogistically after stating that something
does or does not belong to something else. Therefore a syllogistic
premiss without qualification will be an affirmation or denial of something concerning something else in the way we have described; it will
be demonstrative, if it is true and obtained through the first prin- 30
ciples of its science; while a dialectical premiss is the giving of a 24ᵇ
choice between two contradictories, when a man is proceeding by 10
question, but when he is syllogizing it is the assertion of that which
is apparent and generally admitted, as has been said in the *Topics*.[1]
The nature then of a premiss and the difference between syllogistic, demonstrative, and dialectical premisses, may be taken as suffi-

[1] 100ᵃ 29, 104ᵃ 8.

65

15 ciently defined by us in relation to our present need, but will be stated accurately in the sequel.[2]

I call that a term into which the premiss is resolved, i. e. both the predicate and that of which it is predicated, 'being' being added and 'not being' removed, or vice versa.

A syllogism is discourse in which, certain things being stated, something other than what is stated follows of necessity from their being 20 so. I mean by the last phrase that they produce the consequence, and by this, that no further term is required from without in order to make the consequence necessary.

I call that a perfect syllogism which needs nothing other than what has been stated to make plain what necessarily follows; a syllogism is imperfect, if it needs either one or more propositions, which 25 are indeed the necessary consequences of the terms set down, but have not been expressly stated as premisses.

That one term should be included in another as in a whole is the same as for the other to be predicated of all of the first. And we say that one term is predicated of all of another, whenever no instance of the subject can be found of which the other term cannot be 30 asserted: 'to be predicated of none' must be understood in the same way.

25ᵃ 2   Every premiss states that something either is or must be or may be the attribute of something else; of premisses of these three kinds some are affirmative, others negative, in respect of each of the three modes of attribution; again some affirmative and negative premisses 5 are universal, others particular, others indefinite. It is necessary then that in universal attribution the terms of the negative premiss should be convertible, e. g. if no pleasure is good, then no good will be pleasure; the terms of the affirmative must be convertible, not however universally, but in part, e. g. if every pleasure is good, some good must be pleasure; the particular affirmative must convert in part 10 (for if some pleasure is good, then some good will be pleasure); but the particular negative need not convert, for if some animal is not man, it does not follow that some man is not animal.

First then take a universal negative with the terms A and B. If no 15 B is A, neither can any A be B. For if some A (say C) were B, it would not be true that no B is A; for C is a B. But if every B is A, then some A is B. For if no A were B, then no B could be A. But we 20 assumed that every B is A. Similarly too, if the premiss is particular.

2 The nature of demonstrative premisses is discussed in the *Post. An.;* that of dialectical premisses in the *Topics*.

For if some *B* is *A*, then some of the *A*s must be *B*. For if none were, then no *B* would be *A*. But if some *B* is not *A*, there is no necessity that some of the *A*s should not be *B*; e. g. let *B* stand for animal and *A* for man. Not every animal is a man: but every man is an animal. 25

3   The same manner of conversion will hold good also in respect of necessary premises. The universal negative converts universally; each of the affirmatives converts into a particular. If it is necessary that no *B* is *A*, it is necessary also that no *A* is *B*. For if it is possible 30 that some *A* is *B*, it would be possible also that some *B* is *A*. If all or some *B* is *A* of necessity, it is necessary also that some *A* is *B*: for if there were no necessity, neither would some of the *B*s be *A* neces- sarily. But the particular negative does not convert, for the same 35 reason which we have already stated.[3]

In respect of possible premises, since possibility is used in several senses (for we say that what is necessary and what is not necessary and what is potential is possible), affirmative statements will all con- vert in a manner similar to those described.[4] For if it is possible that 40 all or some *B* is *A*, it will be possible that some *A* is *B*. For if that 25ᵇ were not possible, then no *B* could possibly be *A*. This has been already proved.[5] But in negative statements the case is different. Whatever is said to be possible, either because *B* necessarily is *A*, or because *B* is not necessarily *A*, admits of conversion like other negative 5 statements, e. g. if one should say, it is possible that man is not horse, or that no garment is white. For in the former case the one term necessarily does not belong to the other; in the latter there is no neces- sity that it should: and the premiss converts like other negative statements. For if it is possible for no man to be a horse, it is also admissible for no horse to be a man; and if it is admissible for no gar- 10 ment to be white, it is also admissible for nothing white to be a garment. For if any white thing must be a garment, then some gar- ment will necessarily be white. This has been already proved.[6] The particular negative also must be treated like those dealt with above.[7] But if anything is said to be possible because it is the general rule and natural (and it is in this way we define the possible), the negative 15 premisses can no longer be converted like the simple negative; the universal negative premiss does not convert, and the particular does. This will be plain when we speak about the possible.[8] At present we may take this much as clear in addition to what has been said: the statement that it is possible that no *B* is *A* or some *B* is not *A* is 20

---

[3] ll. 12, 22–6.   [4] In ll. 7–13.   [5] ᵃ20–2.
[6] ᵃ 14–17.   [7] In ᵃ 12.   [8] cc. 13, 17.

affirmative in form: for the expression 'is possible' ranks along with 'is', and 'is' makes an affirmation always and in every case, whatever the terms to which it is added in predication, e. g. 'it is not-good' or 'it is not-white' or in a word 'it is not-this'. But this also will be proved 25 in the sequel.[9] In conversion these premisses will behave like the other affirmative propositions.

4   After these distinctions we now state by what means, when, and how every syllogism is produced; subsequently [10] we must speak of demonstration. Syllogism should be discussed before demonstration, 30 because syllogism is the more general: the demonstration is a sort of syllogism, but not every syllogism is a demonstration.

Whenever three terms are so related to one another that the last is contained in the middle as in a whole, and the middle is either contained in, or excluded from, the first as in or from a whole, the 35 extremes must be related by a perfect syllogism. I call that term middle which is itself contained in another and contains another in itself: in position also this comes in the middle. By extremes I mean both that term which is itself contained in another and that in which another is contained. If [11] *A* is predicated of all *B*, and *B* of all *C*, 40 *A* must be predicated of all *C*: we have already explained [12] what we 26ᵃ mean by 'predicated of all'. Similarly [13] also, if *A* is predicated of no *B*, and *B* of all *C*, it is necessary that no *C* will be *A*.

But [14] if the first term belongs to all the middle, but the middle to none of the last term, there will be no syllogism in respect of the extremes; for nothing necessary follows from the terms being so 5 related; for it is possible that the first should belong either to all or to none of the last, so that neither a particular nor a universal conclusion is necessary. But if there is no necessary consequence, there cannot be a syllogism by means of these premisses. As an example of a universal affirmative relation between the extremes we may take the terms animal, man, horse; of a universal negative relation, the terms animal, man, stone. Nor [15] again can a syllogism be formed 10 when neither the first term belongs to any of the middle, nor the middle to any of the last. As an example of a positive relation between the extremes take the terms science, line, medicine: of a negative relation science, line, unit.

If then the terms are universally related, it is clear in this figure when a syllogism will be possible and when not, and that if a syllo-

[9] c. 46.   [10] In the *Posterior Analytics*.
[11] Barbara, major *A*, minor *A*.   [12] 24ᵇ 28.
[13] Celarent, major *E*, minor *A*.   [14] Major *A*, minor *E*.
[15] Major *E*, minor *E*.

gism is possible the terms must be related as described, and if they 15
are so related there will be a syllogism.

But if one term is related universally, the other in part only, to
its subject, there must be a perfect syllogism whenever universality
is posited with reference to the major term either affirmatively or
negatively, and particularity with reference to the minor term affirma- 20
tively: but whenever the universality is posited in relation to the
minor term, or the terms are related in any other way, a syllogism
is impossible. I call that term the major in which the middle is contained and that term the minor which comes under the middle. Let [16]
all *B* be *A* and some *C* be *B*. Then if 'predicated of all' means what
was said above,[17] it is necessary that some *C* is *A*. And [18] if no *B* 25
is *A*, but some *C* is *B*, it is necessary that some *C* is not *A*. (The meaning of 'predicated of none' has also been defined.[19]) So there will be a
perfect syllogism. This holds good also if the premiss *BC* [20] should
be indefinite, provided that it is affirmative: for we shall have the
same syllogism whether the premiss is indefinite or particular.

But if the universality is posited with respect to the minor term 30
either affirmatively or negatively, a syllogism will not be possible,
whether the major premiss is positive or negative, indefinite or particular: e.g. [21] if some *B* is or is not *A*, and all *C* is *B*. As an example
of a positive relation between the extremes take the terms good, state, 35
wisdom: of a negative relation, good, state, ignorance. Again [22] if no
C is *B*, but some *B* is or is not *A*, or not every *B* is *A*, there cannot
be a syllogism. Take the terms white, horse, swan: white, horse, raven.
The same terms may be taken also if the premiss *BA* is indefinite.

Nor when the major premiss is universal, whether affirmative or 26ᵇ
negative, and the minor premiss is negative and particular, can there
be a syllogism, whether the minor premiss be indefinite or particular:
e. g.[23] if all *B* is *A*, and some *C* is not *B*, or if not all *C* is *B*. For the
major term may be predicable both of all and of none of the minor,
to some of which the middle term cannot be attributed. Suppose the 5
terms are animal, man, white: next take some of the white things
of which man is not predicated—swan and snow: animal is predicated of all of the one, but of none of the other. Consequently there
cannot be a syllogism. Again [24] let no *B* be *A*, but let some *C* not be 10

---

16 Darii.   17 24 ᵇ 28.   18 Ferio.   19 24 ᵇ 30.

20 The Aristotelian formula for the proposition, *AB*, in which *B* represents the
subject and *A* the predicate (*A* belongs to *B*), has been retained throughout,
because in most places this suits the context better than the modern formula in
which *A* represents the subject and *B* the predicate.

21 Major *I* or *O*, minor *A*.   22 Major *I* or *O*, minor *E*.
23 Major *A*, minor *O*.   24 Major *E*, minor *O*.

B. Take the terms inanimate, man, white: then take some white things of which man is not predicated—swan and snow: the term inanimate is predicated of all of the one, of none of the other.

Further since it is indefinite to say some *C* is not *B*, and it is true
15 that some *C* is not *B*, whether no *C* is *B*, or not all *C* is *B*, and since if terms are assumed such that no *C* is *B*, no syllogism follows (this has already been stated [25]), it is clear that this arrangement of terms [26] will not afford a syllogism: otherwise one would have been
20 possible with a *universal* negative minor premiss. A similar proof may also be given if the universal premiss [27] is negative.[28]

Nor can there in any way be a syllogism if both the relations of subject and predicate are particular, either positively or negatively, or the one negative and the other affirmative,[29] or one indefinite and the other definite, or both indefinite. Terms common to all the above
25 are animal, white, horse: animal, white, stone.

It is clear then from what has been said that if there is a syllogism in this figure with a particular conclusion, the terms must be related as we have stated: if they are related otherwise, no syllogism is possible anyhow. It is evident also that all the syllogisms in this figure
30 are perfect (for they are all completed by means of the premisses originally taken) and that all conclusions are proved by this figure, viz. universal and particular, affirmative and negative. Such a figure I call the first.

5 Whenever the same thing belongs to all of one subject, and to
35 none of another, or to all of each subject or to none of either, I call such a figure the second; by middle term in it I mean that which is predicated of both subjects, by extremes the terms of which this is said, by major extreme that which lies near the middle, by minor that which is further away from the middle. The middle term stands
27ᵃ outside the extremes, and is first in position. A syllogism cannot be perfect anyhow in this figure, but it may be valid whether the terms are related universally or not.

If then the terms are related universally a syllogism will be possible, whenever the middle belongs to all of one subject and to
5 none of another (it does not matter which has the negative relation), but in no other way. Let *M* be predicated of no *N*, but of all *O*. Since, then, the negative relation is convertible, *N* will belong to no *M*: but *M* was assumed to belong to all *O*: consequently *N* will

[25] a 2.
[26] Major *A*, minor *O*.
[27] i.e. the major premiss.
[28] Major *E*, minor *O*.
[29] *II, OO, IO, OI*.

belong to no O.[30] This has already been proved.[31] Again if M belongs to all N, but to no O, then N will belong to no O.[32] For if M belongs 10 to no O, O belongs to no M: but M (as was said) belongs to all N: O then will belong to no N: for the first figure has again been formed. But since the negative relation is convertible, N will belong to no O. Thus it will be the same syllogism that proves both conclusions.

It is possible to prove these results also by reduction *ad impossibile*. 15

It is clear then that a syllogism is formed when the terms are so related, but not a perfect syllogism; for necessity is not perfectly established merely from the original premisses; others also are needed.

But if M is predicated of every N and O, there cannot be a syllogism. Terms to illustrate a positive relation between the extremes are substance, animal, man; a negative relation, substance, animal, 20 number—substance being the middle term.

Nor is a syllogism possible when M is predicated neither of any N nor of any O. Terms to illustrate a positive relation are line, animal, man: a negative relation, line, animal, stone.

It is clear then that if a syllogism is formed when the terms are universally related, the terms must be related as we stated at the outset: [33] for if they are otherwise related no necessary consequence 25 follows.

If the middle term is related universally to one of the extremes, a particular negative syllogism must result whenever the middle term is related universally to the major whether positively or negatively, and particularly to the minor and in a manner opposite to that of the universal statement: by 'an opposite manner' I mean, if the universal statement is negative, the particular is affirmative: if the 30 universal is affirmative, the particular is negative. For if M belongs to no N, but to some O, it is necessary that N does not belong to some O.[34] For since the negative statement is convertible, N will belong to no M: but M was admitted to belong to some O: therefore N will not belong to some O: for the result is reached by means of 35 the first figure. Again if M belongs to all N, but not to some O, it is necessary that N does not belong to some O: [35] for if N belongs to all O, and M is predicated also of all N, M must belong to all O: but we assumed that M does not belong to some O. And if M belongs to 27^b all N but not to all O, we shall conclude that N does not belong to all O: the proof is the same as the above. But if M is predicated of all O, but not of all N, there will be no syllogism. Take the terms

---

[30] Cesare.   [31] 25 ᵇ 40.   [32] Camestres.
[33] l. 3.   [34] Festino.   [35] Baroco.

5 animal, substance, raven; animal, white, raven. Nor will there be
a conclusion when M is predicated of no O, but of some N. Terms
to illustrate a positive relation between the extremes are animal,
substance, unit: a negative relation, animal, substance, science.

If then the universal statement is opposed to the particular, we
10 have stated when a syllogism will be possible and when not: but if
the premisses are similar in form, I mean both negative or both
affirmative, a syllogism will not be possible anyhow. First let them be
negative, and let the major premiss be universal, e. g. let M belong
15 to no N, and not to some O. It is possible then for N to belong either
to all O or to no O. Terms to illustrate the negative relation are
black, snow, animal. But it is not possible to find terms of which the
extremes are related positively and universally, if M belongs to some
O, and does not belong to some O. For if N belonged to all O, but M
to no N, then M would belong to no O: but we assumed that it belongs
20 to some O. In this way then it is not admissible to take terms: our
point must be proved from the indefinite nature of the particular
statement. For since it is true that M does not belong to some O,
even if it belongs to no O, and since if it belongs to no O a syllogism is
(as we have seen [36]) not possible, clearly it will not be possible
now either.

Again let the premisses be affirmative, and let the major premiss as
before be universal, e. g. let M belong to all N and to some O. It
25 is possible then for N to belong to all O or to no O. Terms to illustrate the negative relation are white, swan, stone. But it is not
possible to take terms to illustrate the universal affirmative relation,
for the reason already stated: [37] the point must be proved from
the indefinite nature of the particular statement. But if the *minor*
30 premiss is universal, and M belongs to no O, and not to some N, it
is possible for N to belong either to all O or to no O. Terms for the
positive relation are white, animal, raven: for the negative relation,
white, stone, raven. If the premisses are affirmative, terms for the
negative relation are white, animal, snow; for the positive relation,
white, animal, swan. Evidently then, whenever the premisses are simi-
35 lar in form, and one is universal, the other particular, a syllogism cannot be formed anyhow. Nor is one possible if the middle term belongs
to some of each of the extremes, or does not belong to some of either,
or belongs to some of the one, not to some of the other, or belongs to
neither universally, or is related to them indefinitely. Common terms
for all the above are white, animal, man: white, animal, inanimate.
28ª   It is clear then from what has been said that if the terms arᵉ

[36] a 21.   [37] l. 18.

related to one another in the way stated, a syllogism results of necessity; and if there is a syllogism, the terms must be so related. But it is evident also that all the syllogisms in this figure are imperfect: for all are made perfect by certain supplementary statements, which [5] either are contained in the terms of necessity or are assumed as hypotheses, i. e. when we prove *per impossibile*. And it is evident that an affirmative conclusion is not attained by means of this figure, but all are negative, whether universal or particular.

6 But if one term belongs to all, and another to none, of a third, [10] or if both belong to all, or to none, of it, I call such a figure the third; by middle term in it I mean that of which both the predicates are predicated, by extremes I mean the predicates, by the major extreme that which is further from the middle, by the minor that which is nearer to it. The middle term stands outside the extremes, and is last [15] in position. A syllogism cannot be perfect in this figure either, but it may be valid whether the terms are related universally or not to the middle term.

If they are universal, whenever both P and R belong to all S, it follows that P will necessarily belong to some R.[38] For, since the affirmative statement is convertible, S will belong to some R: consequently since P belongs to all S, and S to some R, P must belong to [20] some R: for a syllogism in the first figure is produced. It is possible to demonstrate this also *per impossibile* and by exposition. For if both P and R belong to all S, should one of the Ss, e. g. N, be taken, both P and R will belong to this, and thus P will belong to some R. [25]

If R belongs to all S, and P to no S, there will be a syllogism to prove that P will necessarily not belong to some R.[39] This may be demonstrated in the same way as before by converting the premiss RS.[40] It might be proved also *per impossibile*, as in the [30] former cases. But if R belongs to no S, P to all S, there will be no syllogism. Terms for the positive relation are animal, horse, man: for the negative relation animal, inanimate, man.

Nor can there be a syllogism when both terms are asserted of no S. Terms for the positive relation are animal, horse, inanimate; for the negative relation man, horse, inanimate—inanimate being [35] the middle term.

It is clear then in this figure also when a syllogism will be possible and when not, if the terms are related universally. For whenever both the terms are affirmative, there will be a syllogism to prove that one extreme belongs to some of the other; but when they are nega-

[38] Darapti.   [39] Felapton.   [40] See note 20.

28ᵇ tive, no syllogism will be possible. But when one is negative, the
other affirmative, if the major is negative, the minor affirmative,
there will be a syllogism to prove that the one extreme does not
belong to some of the other: but if the relation is reversed, no syllogism will be possible.

5   If one term is related universally to the middle, the other in part
only, when both are affirmative there must be a syllogism, no
matter which of the premisses is universal. For if R belongs to all
S, P to some S, P must belong to some R.[41] For since the affirmative
10 statement is convertible S will belong to some P: consequently since
R belongs to all S, and S to some P, R must also belong to some P:
therefore P must belong to some R.

Again if R belongs to some S, and P to all S, P must belong to
some R.[42] This may be demonstrated in the same way as the preceding. And it is possible to demonstrate it also *per impossibile* and by
15 exposition, as in the former cases. But if one term is affirmative, the
other negative, and if the affirmative is universal, a syllogism will
be possible whenever the minor term is affirmative. For if R belongs
to all S, but P does not belong to some S, it is necessary that P does
not belong to some R.[43] For if P belongs to all R, and R belongs to
all S, then P will belong to all S: but we assumed that it did not.
20 Proof is possible also without reduction *ad impossibile*, if one of the
Ss be taken to which P does not belong.

But whenever the major is affirmative, no syllogism will be possible, e. g. if P belongs to all S, and R does not belong to some S.
Terms for the universal affirmative relation are animate, man, animal.
For the universal negative relation it is not possible to get terms,
25 if R belongs to some S, and does not belong to some S. For if P
belongs to all S, and R to some S, then P will belong to some R: but
we assumed that it belongs to no R. We must put the matter as before.[44] Since the expression 'it does not belong to some' is indefinite,
it may be used truly of that also which belongs to none. But if R
30 belongs to no S, no syllogism is possible, as has been shown.[45] Clearly
then no syllogism will be possible here.

But if the negative term is universal, whenever the major is negative and the minor affirmative there will be a syllogism. For if P belongs to no S, and R belongs to some S, P will not belong to some
35 R:[46] for we shall have the first figure again, if the premiss RS is
converted.

But when the minor is negative, there will be no syllogism. Terms

---

[41] Disamis.   [42] Datisi.   [43] Bocardo.
[44] 27ᵇ 20.   [45] 28ᵃ 30.   [46] Ferison.

for the positive relation are animal, man, wild: for the negative relation, animal, science, wild—the middle in both being the term wild.

Nor is a syllogism possible when both are stated in the negative, but one is universal, the other particular. When the *minor* is related universally to the middle, take the terms animal, science, wild; animal, man, wild. When the *major* is related universally to the middle, take as terms for a negative relation raven, snow, white. For a positive relation terms cannot be found, if R belongs to some S, and does not belong to some S. For if P belongs to all R, and R to some S, then P belongs to some S: but we assumed that it belongs to no S. Our point, then, must be proved from the indefinite nature of the particular statement.

Nor is a syllogism possible anyhow, if each of the extremes belongs to some of the middle, or does not belong, or one belongs and the other does not to some of the middle, or one belongs to some of the middle, the other not to all, or if the premisses are indefinite. Common terms for all are animal, man, white: animal, inanimate, white.

It is clear then in this figure also when a syllogism will be possible, and when not; and that if the terms are as stated, a syllogism results of necessity, and if there is a syllogism, the terms must be so related. It is clear also that all the syllogisms in this figure are imperfect (for all are made perfect by certain supplementary assumptions), and that it will not be possible to reach a universal conclusion by means of this figure, whether negative or affirmative.

7   It is evident also that in all the figures, whenever a proper syllogism does not result, if both the terms are affirmative or negative nothing necessary follows at all, but if one is affirmative, the other negative, and if the negative is stated universally, a syllogism always results relating the minor to the major term, e. g. if A belongs to all or some B, and B belongs to no C: for if the premisses are converted it is necessary that C does not belong to some A.[47] Similarly also in the other figures: a syllogism always results by means of conversion. It is evident also that the substitution of an indefinite for a particular affirmative will effect the same syllogism in all the figures.

It is clear too that all the imperfect syllogisms are made perfect by means of the first figure. For all are brought to a conclusion either ostensively or *per impossibile*. In both ways the first figure is formed: if they are made perfect ostensively, because (as we saw) all are

29ᵃ

5

10

15

20

25

30

⁴⁷ Fesapo, Fresison.

brought to a conclusion by means of conversion, and conversion
35 produces the first figure: if they are proved *per impossibile*, because
on the assumption of the false statement the syllogism comes about
by means of the first figure, e. g. in the last figure, if A and B belong
to all C, it follows that A belongs to some B: for if A belonged to
no B, and B belongs to all C, A would belong to no C: but (as we
stated) it belongs to all C. Similarly also with the rest.

29ᵇ   It is possible also to reduce all syllogisms to the *universal* syllogisms in the first figure. Those in the second figure are clearly made
perfect by these, though not all in the same way; the universal syllo-
5 gisms are made perfect by converting the negative premiss, each of
the particular syllogisms by reduction *ad impossibile*. In the first
figure particular syllogisms are indeed made perfect by themselves,
but it is possible also to prove them by means of the second figure,
reducing them *ad impossibile*, e. g. if A belongs to all B, and B to
some C, it follows that A belongs to some C. For if it belonged to
no C, and belongs to all B, then B will belong to no C: this we
10 know by means of the second figure. Similarly also demonstration
will be possible in the case of the negative. For if A belongs to no
B, and B belongs to some C, A will not belong to some C: for if it
belonged to all C, and belongs to no B, then B will belong to no C:
15 and this (as we saw) is the middle figure. Consequently, since all
syllogisms in the middle figure can be reduced to universal syllogisms in the first figure, and since particular syllogisms in the first
figure can be reduced to syllogisms in the middle figure, it is clear
that particular syllogisms [48] can be reduced to universal syllogisms
in the first figure. Syllogisms in the third figure, if the terms are
20 universal, are directly made perfect by means of those syllogisms; [49]
but, when one of the premisses is particular, by means of the *particular* syllogisms in the first figure: and these (we have seen) may
be reduced to the universal syllogisms in the first figure: consequently also the particular syllogisms in the third figure may be so
reduced. It is clear then that all syllogisms may be reduced to the
25 universal syllogisms in the first figure.

We have stated then how syllogisms which prove that something
belongs or does not belong to something else are constituted, both
how syllogisms of the same figure are constituted in themselves,
and how syllogisms of different figures are related to one another. . . .

[48] *sc.* in the first figure.
[49] viz. by reduction *per impossibile* to Celarent and Barbara.

13 Perhaps enough has been said about the proof of necessity, 15
how it comes about and how it differs from the proof of a simple 32ᵃ
statement. We proceed to discuss that which is possible, when and
how and by what means it can be proved. I use the terms 'to be
possible' and 'the possible' of that which is not necessary but,
being assumed, results in nothing impossible. We say indeed ambigu- 20
ously of the necessary that it is possible. But that my definition of the
possible is correct is clear from the phrases by which we deny or on
the contrary affirm possibility. For the expressions 'it is not possible
to belong', 'it is impossible to belong', and 'it is necessary not to
belong' are either identical or follow from one another; consequently
their opposites also, 'it is possible to belong', 'it is not impossible 25
to belong', and 'it is not necessary not to belong', will either be
identical or follow from one another. For of everything the affirmation or the denial holds good. That which is possible then will be
not necessary and that which is not necessary will be possible. It
results that all premisses in the mode of possibility are convertible 30
into one another. I mean not that the affirmative are convertible
into the negative, but that those which are affirmative in form admit
of conversion by opposition, e. g. 'it is possible to belong' may be
converted into 'it is possible not to belong', and 'it is possible
for *A* to belong to all *B*' into 'it is possible for *A* to belong to no *B*'
or 'not to all *B*', and 'it is possible for *A* to belong to some *B*' into 35
'it is possible for *A* not to belong to some *B*'. And similarly the
other propositions in this mode can be converted. For since that
which is possible is not necessary, and that which is not necessary
may possibly not belong, it is clear that if it is possible that *A* should
belong to *B*, it is possible also that it should not belong to *B*:
and if it is possible that it should belong to all, it is also possible
that it should not belong to all. The same holds good in the case of 40
particular affirmations: for the proof is identical. And such prem- 32ᵇ
isses are affirmative and not negative: for 'to be possible' is in the
same rank as 'to be', as was said above.[50]

Having made these distinctions we next point out that the expression 'to be possible' is used in two ways. In one it means to 5
happen generally and fall short of necessity, e. g. man's turning grey
or growing or decaying, or generally what naturally belongs to a
thing (for this has not its necessity unbroken, since man's existence
is not continuous for ever, although if a man does exist, it comes about
either necessarily or generally). In another sense the expression means 10
the indefinite, which can be both thus and not thus, e. g. an animal's

[50] 25ᵇ 21.

walking or an earthquake's taking place while it is walking, or generally what happens by chance: for none of these inclines by nature in the one way more than in the opposite.

That which is possible in each of its two senses is convertible into its
15 opposite, not however in the same way: but what is natural is convertible because it does not necessarily belong (for in this sense it is possible that a man should not grow grey) and what is indefinite is convertible because it inclines this way no more than that. Science and demonstrative syllogism are not concerned with things which are indefinite, because the middle term is uncertain; but they
20 are concerned with things that are natural, and as a rule arguments and inquiries are made about things which are possible in this sense. Syllogisms indeed can be made about the former, but it is unusual at any rate to inquire about them.

These matters will be treated more definitely in the sequel;[51] our business at present is to state the moods and nature of the syllogism made from possible premisses. The expression 'it is possible for this
25 to belong to that' may be understood in two senses: 'that' may mean either that to which 'that' belongs or that to which it may belong; for the expression 'A is possible of the subject of B' means that it is possible either of that of which B is stated or of that of which B may possibly be stated. It makes no difference whether we say, A is pos-
30 sible of the subject of B, or all B admits of A. It is clear then that the expression 'A may possibly belong to all B' might be used in two senses. First then we must state the nature and characteristics of the syllogism which arises if B is possible of the subject of C, and A is possible of the subject of B. For thus both premisses are as-
35 sumed in the mode of possibility; but whenever A is possible of that of which B is true, one premiss is a simple assertion, the other a problematic. Consequently we must start from premisses which are similar in form, as in the other cases. . . .

40ᵇ **23** It is clear from what has been said that the syllogisms in these figures are made perfect by means of universal syllogisms in the first
20 figure and are reduced to them. That every syllogism without qualification can be so treated, will be clear presently, when it has been proved that every syllogism is formed through one or other of these figures.

It is necessary that every demonstration and every syllogism should prove either that something belongs or that it does not, and
25 this either universally or in part, and further either ostensively or

51 *Post An.* i. 8.

hypothetically. One sort of hypothetical proof is the *reductio ad impossibile*. Let us speak first of ostensive syllogisms: for after these have been pointed out the truth of our contention will be clear with regard to those which are proved *per impossibile*, and in general hypothetically.

If then one wants to prove syllogistically A of B, either as an attribute of it or as not an attribute of it, one must assert something of something else. If now A should be asserted of B, the proposition originally in question will have been assumed. But if A should be asserted of C, but C should not be asserted of anything, nor anything of it, nor anything else of A, no syllogism will be possible. For nothing necessarily follows from the assertion of some one thing concerning some other single thing. Thus we must take another premiss as well. If then A be asserted of something else, or something else of A, or something different of C, nothing prevents a syllogism being formed, but it will not be in relation to B through the premisses taken. Nor when C belongs to something else, and that to something else and so on, no connexion however being made with B, will a syllogism be possible concerning A in its relation to B. For in general we stated [52] that no syllogism can establish the attribution of one thing to another, unless some middle term is taken, which is somehow related to each by way of predication. For the syllogism in general is made out of premisses, and a syllogism referring to *this* out of premisses with the same reference, and a syllogism relating *this* to *that* proceeds through premisses which relate this to that. But it is impossible to take a premiss in reference to B, if we neither affirm nor deny anything of it; or again to take a premiss relating A to B, if we take nothing common, but affirm or deny peculiar attributes of each. So we must take something midway between the two, which will connect the predications, if we are to have a syllogism relating this to that. If then we must take something common in relation to both, and this is possible in three ways (either by predicating A of C, and C of B, or C of both, or both of C), and these are the figures of which we have spoken, it is clear that every syllogism must be made in one or other of these figures. The argument is the same if several middle terms should be necessary to establish the relation to B; for the figure will be the same whether there is one middle term or many.

It is clear then that the ostensive syllogisms are effected by means of the aforesaid figures; these considerations will show that *reductiones ad impossibile* also are effected in the same way. For all who

[52] Cf. 25[b] 32.

effect an argument *per impossibile* infer syllogistically what is false,
25 and prove the original conclusion hypothetically when something impossible results from the assumption of its contradictory; e. g. that
the diagonal of the square is incommensurate with the side, because
odd numbers are equal to evens if it is supposed to be commensurate.
One infers syllogistically that odd numbers come out equal to evens,
and one proves hypothetically the incommensurability of the diag-
30 onal, since a falsehood results through contradicting this. For this
we found to be reasoning *per impossibile,* viz. proving something impossible by means of an hypothesis conceded at the beginning.
Consequently, since the falsehood is established in reductions *ad impossibile* by an ostensive syllogism, and the original conclusion is
35 proved hypothetically, and we have already stated that ostensive
syllogisms are effected by means of these figures, it is evident that
syllogisms *per impossibile* also will be made through these figures.
Likewise all the other hypothetical syllogisms: for in every case the
syllogism leads up to the proposition that is substituted for the
40 original thesis; but the original thesis is reached by means of a conces-
41ᵇ sion or some other hypothesis.[53] But if this is true, every demonstration and every syllogism must be formed by means of the three figures
mentioned above. But when this has been shown it is clear that every
syllogism is perfected by means of the first figure and is reducible to
5 the universal syllogisms in this figure.

24 Further in every syllogism one of the premisses must be affirmative, and universality must be present: unless one of the premisses
is universal either a syllogism will not be possible, or it will not
refer to the subject proposed, or the original position will be begged.
10 Suppose we have to prove that pleasure in music is good. If one
should claim as a premiss that pleasure is good without adding
'all', no syllogism will be possible; if one should claim that some
pleasure is good, then if it is different from pleasure in music, it is
not relevant to the subject proposed; if it is this very pleasure, one
is assuming that which was proposed at the outset to be proved.
This is more obvious in geometrical proofs, e. g. that the angles at
15 the base of an isosceles triangle are equal. Suppose the lines A and
B have been drawn to the centre. If then one should assume that the
angle AC is equal to the angle BD, without claiming generally that
angles of semicircles are equal; and again if one should assume that

[53] Aristotle is thinking of the method of establishing a proposition A is B by
inducing the opponent to agree that A is B if X is Y. All that remains then is to
establish syllogistically that X is Y. That A is B thus follows from the agreement.

the angle C is equal to the angle D, without the additional assumption that every angle of a segment is equal to every other angle of the same segment; and further if one should assume that when equal angles are taken from the whole angles, which are themselves equal, the remainders E and F are equal, he will beg the thing to 20 be proved, unless he also states that when equals are taken from equals the remainders are equal.[54]

It is clear then that in every syllogism there must be a universal premiss, and that a universal statement is proved only when all the premisses are universal, while a particular statement is proved both from two universal premisses and from one only: consequently if the conclusion is universal, the premisses also must be universal, 25 but if the premisses are universal it is possible that the conclusion may not be universal. And it is clear also that in every syllogism either both or one of the premisses must be like the conclusion. I mean not only in being affirmative or negative, but also in being necessary, pure, or problematic. We must consider also the other forms of 30 predication.

[54] The diagram Aristotle has in mind appears to be the following:

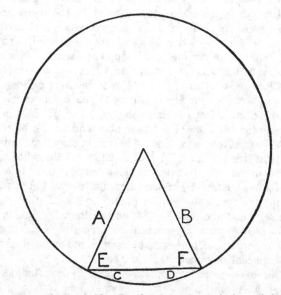

Here A and B are the equal sides, E and F the angles at the base of the isosceles triangle. C and D are the angles formed by the base with the circumference. The angles formed by the equal sides with the base are loosely called AC, BD.

It is clear also when a syllogism in general can be made and when it cannot; and when a valid,[55] when a perfect syllogism can be formed; and that if a syllogism is formed the terms must be 35 arranged in one of the ways that have been mentioned.

25 It is clear too that every demonstration will proceed through three terms and no more, unless the same conclusion is established by different pairs of propositions; e. g. the conclusion E may be established through the propositions A and B, and through the propositions C and D, or through the propositions A and B, or A and C, or 40 B and C. For nothing prevents there being several middles for the same terms. But in that case there is not one but several syllogisms. 42ᵃ Or again when each of the propositions A and B is obtained by syllo-gistic inference, e. g. A by means of D and E, and again B by means of F and G. Or one may be obtained by syllogistic, the other by inductive inference. But thus also the syllogisms are many; for the 5 conclusions are many, e. g. A and B and C. But if this can be called one syllogism, not many, the same conclusion may be reached by more than three terms in this way, but it cannot be reached as C is established by means of A and B. Suppose that the proposition E is inferred from the premisses A, B, C, and D. It is necessary then 10 that of these one should be related to another as whole to part: for it has already been proved that if a syllogism is formed some of its terms must be related in this way.[56] Suppose then that A stands in this relation to B. Some conclusion then follows from them. It must either be E or one or other of C and D, or something other than these. 15 (1) If it is E the syllogism will have A and B for its sole prem-isses. But if C and D are so related that one is whole, the other part, some conclusion will follow from them also; and it must be either E, or one or other of the propositions A and B, or something other than these. And if it is (i) E, or (ii) A or B, either (i) the syllogisms will be more than one, or (ii) the same thing happens to be inferred by means of several terms only in the sense which we saw to be possible.[57] 20 But if (iii) the conclusion is other than E or A or B, the syllogisms will be many, and unconnected with one another. But if C is not so related to D as to make a syllogism, the propositions will have been assumed to no purpose, unless for the sake of induction or of obscur-ing the argument or something of the sort.

(2) But if from the propositions A and B there follows not E 25 but some other conclusion, and if from C and D either A or B follows or something else, then there are several syllogisms, and

they do not establish the conclusion proposed: for we assumed that the syllogism proved *E*. And if no conclusion follows from *C* and *D*, it turns out that these propositions have been assumed to no purpose, and the syllogism does not prove the original proposition.   30

So it is clear that every demonstration and every syllogism will proceed through three terms only.

This being evident, it is clear that a syllogistic conclusion follows from two premisses and not from more than two. For the three terms make two premisses, unless a new premiss is assumed, as was said at the beginning,[58] to perfect the syllogisms. It is clear therefore that in whatever syllogistic argument the premisses 35 through which the main conclusion follows (for some of the preceding conclusions must be premisses) are not even in number, this argument either has not been drawn syllogistically or it has assumed more than was necessary to establish its thesis.   40

If then syllogisms are taken with respect to their main premisses, 42ᵇ every syllogism will consist of an even number of premisses and an odd number of terms (for the terms exceed the premisses by one), and the conclusions will be half the number of the premisses. But 5 whenever a conclusion is reached by means of prosyllogisms or by means of several continuous middle terms, e. g. the proposition *AB* by means of the middle terms *C* and *D*, the number of the terms will similarly exceed that of the premisses by one (for the extra term must either be added outside or inserted: but in either case it follows that the relations of predication are one fewer than the terms related), and the premisses will be equal in number to the 10 relations of predication. The premisses however will not always be even, the terms odd; but they will alternate—when the premisses are even, the terms must be odd; when the terms are even, the premisses must be odd: for along with one term one premiss is added, if a term is added from any quarter. Consequently since the premisses were (as we saw) even, and the terms odd, we must make them 15 alternately even and odd at each addition. But the conclusions will not follow the same arrangement either in respect to the terms or to the premisses. For if one term is added, conclusions will be added less by one than the pre-existing terms: for the conclusion is drawn not in relation to the single term last added, but in relation to all the 20 rest, e. g. if to *ABC* the term *D* is added, two conclusions are thereby added, one in relation to *A*, the other in relation to *B*. Similarly

---

[58] The reference is to the new premisses produced by conversion, when a syllogism in the second or third figure is being reduced to one in the first. Cf. 24ᵇ 24.

with any further additions. And similarly too if the term is inserted
in the middle: for in relation to one term only, a syllogism will not
25 be constructed. Consequently the conclusions will be much more
numerous than the terms or the premisses.

26 Since we understand the subjects with which syllogisms are concerned, what sort of conclusion is established in each figure, and
in how many moods this is done, it is evident to us both what sort
of problem is difficult and what sort is easy to prove. For that which
30 is concluded in many figures and through many moods is easier; that
which is concluded in few figures and through few moods is more
difficult to attempt. The universal affirmative is proved by means
of the first figure only and by this in only one mood; the universal
negative is proved both through the first figure and through the
35 second, through the first in one mood, through the second in two.
The particular affirmative is proved through the first and through
the last figure, in one mood through the first, in three moods through
the last. The particular negative is proved in all the figures, but
40 once in the first, in two moods in the second, in three moods in the
43ᵃ third. It is clear then that the universal affirmative is most difficult
to establish, most easy to overthrow. In general, universals are
easier game for the destroyer than particulars: for whether the predicate belongs to none or not to some, they are destroyed: and the
5 particular negative is proved in all the figures, the universal negative in two. Similarly with universal negatives: the original statement is destroyed, whether the predicate belongs to all or to some:
and this we found possible in two figures. But particular statements
can be refuted in one way only—by proving that the predicate
belongs either to all or to none. But particular statements are
easier to *establish*: for proof is possible in more figures and through
10 more moods. And in general we must not forget that it is possible
to refute statements by means of one another, I mean, universal
statements by means of particular, and particular statements by
means of universal: but it is not possible to establish universal
statements by means of particular, though it is possible to establish
particular statements by means of universal. At the same time it is
15 evident that it is easier to refute than to establish.

The manner in which every syllogism is produced, the number
of the terms and premisses through which it proceeds, the relation
of the premisses to one another, the character of the problem proved
in each figure, and the number of the figures appropriate to each
problem, all these matters are clear from what has been said.

27   We must now state how we may ourselves always have a supply 20
of syllogisms in reference to the problem proposed and by what road
we may reach the principles relative to the problem: for perhaps
we ought not only to investigate the construction of syllogisms,
but also to have the power of making them.

Of all the things which exist some are such that they cannot be 25
predicated of anything else truly and universally, e. g. Cleon and
Callias, i. e. the individual and sensible, but other things may be
predicated of them (for each of these is both man and animal); and
some things are themselves predicated of others, but nothing prior is 30
predicated of them; and some are predicated of others, and yet
others of them, e. g. man of Callias and animal of man. It is clear
then that some things are naturally not stated of anything: for as a
rule each sensible thing is such that it cannot be predicated of anything, save incidentally: for we sometimes say that that white object
is Socrates, or that that which approaches is Callias. We shall explain 35
in another place [59] that there is an upward limit also to the process
of predicating: for the present we must assume this. Of these ultimate predicates it is not possible to demonstrate another predicate,
save as a matter of opinion, but these may be predicated of other
things. Neither can individuals be predicated of other things, though 40
other things can be predicated of them. Whatever lies between these
limits can be spoken of in both ways: they may be stated of others,
and others stated of them. And as a rule arguments and inquiries
are concerned with these things.

We must select the premisses suitable to each problem in this 43ᵇ
manner: first we must lay down the subject and the definitions and
the properties of the thing; next we must lay down those attributes
which follow the thing, and again those which the thing follows,
and those which cannot belong to it. But those to which it cannot 5
belong need not be selected, because the negative statement implied
above is convertible. Of the attributes which follow we must distinguish those which fall within the definition, those which are predicated as properties, and those which are predicated as accidents, and
of the latter those which apparently and those which really belong.
The larger the supply a man has of these, the more quickly will he 10
reach a conclusion; and in proportion as he apprehends those which
are truer, the more cogently will he demonstrate. But he must select
not those which follow some particular but those which follow the
thing as a whole. e. g. not what follows a particular man but what

[59] *Post An.* i. 19–22.

follows every man: for the syllogism proceeds through universal
15 premisses. If the statement is indefinite, it is uncertain whether the
premiss is universal, but if the statement is definite, the matter is
clear. Similarly one must select those attributes which the subject
follows as wholes, for the reason given. But that which follows one
must not suppose to follow as a whole, e. g. that every animal follows
man or every science music, but only that it follows, without qualifi-
20 cation, as indeed we state it in a proposition: for the other statement
is useless and impossible, e. g. that every man is every animal or
justice is all good. But that which something follows receives the
mark 'every'. Whenever the subject, for which we must obtain the
attributes that follow, is contained by something else, what follows
or does not follow the highest term universally must not be selected
25 in dealing with the subordinate term (for these attributes have been
taken in dealing with the superior term; for what follows animal
also follows man, and what does not belong to animal does not
belong to man); but we must choose those attributes which are
peculiar to each subject. For some things are peculiar to the species
as distinct from the genus; for species being distinct there must be
attributes peculiar to each. Nor must we take as things which the
superior term follows, those things which the inferior term follows,
30 e. g. take as subjects of the predicate 'animal' what are really subjects of the predicate 'man'. It is necessary indeed, if animal follows
man, that it should follow all these also. But these belong more
properly to the choice of what concerns man. One must apprehend
also normal consequents and normal antecedents; for propositions
which obtain normally are established syllogistically from premisses
35 which obtain normally, some if not all of them having this character
of normality. For the conclusion of each syllogism resembles its principles. We must not however choose attributes which are consequent
upon all the terms: [60] for no syllogism can be made out of such
premisses. The reason why this is so will be clear in the sequel.[61]

28 If men wish to establish something about some whole, they must
40 look to the *subjects* of that which is being established (the subjects
of which it happens to be asserted), and the *attributes* which follow
that of which it is to be predicated. For if any of these subjects is
the same as any of these attributes, the attribute originally in ques-

---

[60] i. e. on the major and minor terms. Two affirmative premisses in the second
figure give no conclusion.

[61] 44b 20.

tion must belong to the subject originally in question.[62] But if the purpose is to establish not a universal but a particular proposition, they must look for the terms of which the terms in question are predicable: for if any of these are identical, the attribute in question 44ᵃ must belong to some of the subject in question.[63] Whenever the one term has to belong to none of the other, one must look to the consequents of the subject, and to those attributes which cannot possibly be present in the predicate in question: [64] or conversely to the attributes which cannot possibly be present in the subject, and to the consequents of the predicate.[65] If any members of these groups 5 are identical, one of the terms in question cannot possibly belong to any of the other. For sometimes a syllogism in the first figure results,[66] sometimes a syllogism in the second. But if the object is to establish a particular negative proposition, we must find antecedents of the subject in question and attributes which cannot possibly belong to the predicate in question.[67] If any members of these two 10 groups are identical, it follows that one of the terms in question does not belong to some of the other. Perhaps each of these statements will become clearer in the following way. Suppose the consequents of A are designated by B, the antecedents of A by C, attributes which cannot possibly belong to A by D. Suppose again that the attributes 15 of E are designated by F, the antecedents of E by G, and attributes which cannot belong to E by H. If then one of the Cs should be identical with one of the Fs, A must belong to all E: for F belongs to all E, and A to all C, consequently A belongs to all E. If C and G are identical, A must belong to some of the Es: for A follows C, and E 20 follows all G. If F and D are identical, A will belong to none of the Es by a prosyllogism: for since the negative proposition is convertible, and F is identical with D, A will belong to none of the Fs, but F belongs to all E. Again, if B and H are identical, A will belong to none of the Es: for B will belong to all A, but to no E: for 25 it was assumed to be identical with H, and H belonged to none of the Es. If D and G are identical, A will not belong to some of the Es: for it will not belong to G, because it does not belong to D: but G falls under E: consequently A will not belong to some of the Es. If 30 B is identical with G, there will be a converted syllogism: for E will belong to all A, since B belongs to A and E to B (for B was found to be identical with G): but that A should belong to all E is not

[62] We thus get a syllogism in Barbara.
[63] Darapti.   [64] Cesare.   [65] Camestres.
[66] By converting the major premiss of the Cesare syllogism or the minor premiss of the Camestres syllogism.   [67] Felapton, by conversion.

necessary, but it must belong to some *E* because it is possible to
35 convert the universal statement into a particular.

It is clear then that in every proposition which requires proof we
must look to the aforesaid relations of the subject and predicate in
question: for all syllogisms proceed through these. But if we are
seeking consequents and antecedents we must look for those which
40 are primary and most universal, e. g. in reference to *E* we must look
to *KF* rather than to *F* alone, and in reference to *A* we must look to
44ᵇ *KC* rather than to *C* alone. For if *A* belongs to *KF*, it belongs both
to *F* and to *E*: but if it does not follow *KF*, it may yet follow *F*.
Similarly we must consider the antecedents of *A* itself: for if a term
follows the primary antecedents, it will follow those also which are
5 subordinate, but if it does not follow the former, it may yet follow the
latter.

It is clear too that the inquiry proceeds through the three terms
and the two premisses, and that all the syllogisms proceed through
the aforesaid figures. For it is proved that *A* belongs to *all E*, whenever an identical term is found among the *C*s and *F*s. This will be
10 the middle term; *A* and *E* will be the extremes. So the first figure is
formed. And *A* will belong to *some E*, whenever *C* and *G* are apprehended to be the same. This is the last figure: for *G* becomes the middle term. And *A* will belong to *no E*, when *D* and *F* are identical.
Thus we have both the first figure and the middle figure; the first,
because *A* belongs to no *F*, since the negative statement is con-
15 vertible, and *F* belongs to all *E*; the middle figure because *D* belongs
to no *A*, and to all *E*. And *A* will *not* belong to *some E*, whenever
D and *G* are identical. This is the last figure: for *A* will belong to no
G, and *E* will belong to all *G*. Clearly then all syllogisms proceed
20 through the aforesaid figures, and we must not select consequents of
all the terms,[68] because no syllogism is produced from them. For
(as we saw)[69] it is not possible at all to establish a proposition
from consequents, and it is not possible to refute by means of a
consequent of both the terms in question: for the middle term must
belong to the one, and not belong to the other.

25   It is clear too that other methods of inquiry by selection of middle
terms are useless to produce a syllogism, e. g. if the consequents of
the terms in question are identical, or if the antecedents of *A* are
identical with those attributes which cannot possibly belong to *E*,
or if those attributes are identical which cannot belong to either
term: for no syllogism is produced by means of these. For if the con-
30 sequents are identical, e. g. *B* and *F*, we have the middle figure with

---

[68] i. e. the consequents of *A* and *E*.   [69] 27ᵃ 18–20, ᵇ 23–8.

both premisses affirmative: if the antecedents of *A* are identical with attributes which cannot belong to *E*, e. g. *C* with *H*, we have the first figure with its minor premiss negative. If attributes which cannot belong to either term are identical, e. g. *C* and *H*, both premisses 35 are negative, either in the first or in the middle figure. But no syllogism is possible in this way.

It is evident too that we must find out which terms in this inquiry are identical, not which are different or contrary, first because the object of our investigation is the middle term, and the middle 40 term must be not diverse but identical. Secondly, wherever it happens that a syllogism results from taking contraries or terms which 45ᵃ cannot belong to the same thing, all arguments can be reduced to the aforesaid moods, e. g. if *B* and *F* are contraries or cannot belong to the same thing. For if these are taken, a syllogism will be formed to 5 prove that *A* belongs to none of the *E*s, not however from the premisses taken but in the aforesaid mood. For *B* will belong to all *A* and to no *E*. Consequently *B* must be identical with one of the *H*s. Again, if *B* and *G* cannot belong to the same thing, it follows that *A* 10 will not belong to some of the *E*s: for then too we shall have the middle figure: for *B* will belong to all *A* and to no *G*. Consequently *B* must be identical with some of the *H*s. For the fact that *B* and *G* cannot belong to the same thing differs in no way from the fact that *B* is identical with some of the *H*s: for that includes everything which cannot belong to *E*. 15

It is clear then that from the inquiries taken by themselves no syllogism results; but if *B* and *F* are contraries *B* must be identical with one of the *H*s, and the syllogism results through these terms. 20 It turns out then that those who inquire in this manner are looking gratuitously for some other way than the necessary way because they have failed to observe the identity of the *B*s with the *H*s.

29 Syllogisms which lead to impossible conclusions are similar to ostensive syllogisms; they also are formed by means of the consequents and antecedents of the terms in question. In both cases the 25 same inquiry is involved. For what is proved ostensively may also be concluded syllogistically *per impossibile* by means of the same terms; and what is proved *per impossibile* may also be proved ostensively, e. g. that *A* belongs to none of the *E*s. For suppose *A* to belong to some *E*: then since *B* belongs to all *A* and *A* to some of the *E*s, *B* will belong to some of the *E*s: but it was assumed that it belongs to 30 none. Again we may prove that *A* belongs to some *E*: for if *A* belonged to none of the *E*s, and *E* belongs to all *G*, *A* will belong to none of the *G*s: but it was assumed to belong to all. Similarly with

the other propositions requiring proof. The proof *per impossibile*
35 will always and in all cases be from the consequents and antecedents
of the terms in question. Whatever the problem the same inquiry is
necessary whether one wishes to use an ostensive syllogism or a
reduction to impossibility. For both the demonstrations start from
the same terms, e. g. suppose it has been proved that *A* belongs to no
E, because it turns out that otherwise *B* belongs to some of the *E*s
40 and this is impossible—if now it is assumed that *B* belongs to no *E*
45^b and to all *A*, it is clear that *A* will belong to no *E*. Again if it has
been proved by an ostensive syllogism that *A* belongs to no *E*, assume
that *A* belongs to some *E* and it will be proved *per impossibile* to belong to no *E*. Similarly with the rest. In all cases it is necessary to find
5 some common term other than the subjects of inquiry, to which the
syllogism establishing the false conclusion may relate, so that if this
premiss is converted,[70] and the other remains as it is, the syllogism
will be ostensive by means of the same terms. For the ostensive syllogism differs from the *reductio ad impossibile* in this: in the ostensive syllogism both premisses are laid down in accordance with the
10 truth, in the *reductio ad impossibile* one of the premisses is assumed
falsely.

These points will be made clearer by the sequel,[71] when we discuss
the reduction to impossibility: at present this much must be clear,
that we must look to terms of the kinds mentioned whether we
15 wish to use an ostensive syllogism or a reduction to impossibility. In
the other hypothetical syllogisms, I mean those which proceed by
substitution,[72] or by positing a certain quality, the inquiry will be
directed to the terms of the problem to be proved—not the terms
of the original problem, but the new terms introduced; and the
method of the inquiry will be the same as before. But we must con-
20 sider and determine in how many ways hypothetical syllogisms are
possible.

Each of the problems then can be proved in the manner described;
but it is possible to establish some of them syllogistically in another
way, e. g. universal problems by the inquiry which leads up to a
particular conclusion, with the addition of an hypothesis. For if the
*C*s and the *G*s should be identical, but *E* should be assumed to belong
25 to the *G*s only, then *A* would belong to every *E*: and again if the
*D*s and the *G*s should be identical, but *E* should be predicated of
the *G*s only, it follows that *A* will belong to none of the *E*s. Clearly

---

[70] i. e. if this false conclusion is replaced by its contradictory and this is
treated as a premiss.

[71] ii. 14.   [72] Cf. 41^a 39.

then we must consider the matter in this way also. The method is the same whether the relation is necessary or possible. For the inquiry will be the same, and the syllogism will proceed through terms arranged in the same order whether a possible or a pure propo- 30 sition is proved. We must find in the case of possible relations, as well as terms that belong, terms which can belong though they actu- ally do not: for we have proved that the syllogism which establishes a possible relation proceeds through these terms as well. Similarly 35 also with the other modes of predication.

It is clear then from what has been said not only that all syllogisms can be formed in this way, but also that they cannot be formed in any other. For every syllogism has been proved to be formed through one of the aforementioned figures, and these cannot be 40 composed through other terms than the consequents and antecedents of the terms in question: for from these we obtain the premisses and 46^a find the middle term. Consequently a syllogism cannot be formed by means of other terms.

30   The method is the same in all cases, in philosophy, in any art or study. We must look for the attributes and the subjects of both our terms, and we must supply ourselves with as many of these as pos- 5 sible, and consider them by means of the three terms, refuting state- ments in one way, confirming them in another, in the pursuit of truth starting from premisses in which the arrangement of the terms is in accordance with truth, while if we look for dialectical syllogisms we must start from probable premisses. The principles of syllo- 10 gisms have been stated in general terms, both how they are charac- terized and how we must hunt for them, so as not to look to every- thing that is said about the terms of the problem or to the same points whether we are confirming or refuting, or again whether we are confirming of all or of some, and whether we are refuting of all 15 or some; we must look to fewer points and they must be definite. We have also stated how we must select with reference to every- thing that is, e. g. about good or knowledge. But in each science the principles which are peculiar are the most numerous. Consequently it is the business of experience to give the principles which belong to each subject. I mean for example that astronomical experience sup- plies the principles of astronomical science: for once the phenomena 20 were adequately apprehended, the demonstrations of astronomy were discovered. Similarly with any other art or science. Conse- quently, if the attributes of the thing are apprehended, our busi- ness will then be to exhibit readily the demonstrations. For if none

25 of the true attributes of things had been omitted in the historical
survey, we should be able to discover the proof and demonstrate
everything which admitted of proof, and to make that clear, whose
nature does not admit of proof.

In general then we have explained fairly well how we must select
30 premises: we have discussed the matter accurately in the treatise
concerning dialectic.[73]

31   It is easy to see that division into classes [74] is a small part of
the method we have described: for division is, so to speak, a weak
syllogism; for what it ought to prove, it begs, and it always establishes something more general than the attribute in question. First,
35 this very point had escaped all those who used the method of division; and they attempted to persuade men that it was possible to
make a demonstration of substance and essence. Consequently they
did not understand what it is possible to prove syllogistically by
division, nor did they understand that it was possible to prove syllogistically in the manner we have described.[75] In demonstrations,
40 when there is a need to prove a positive statement, the middle term
46^b through which the syllogism is formed must always be inferior to and
not comprehend the first of the extremes. But division has a contrary intention: for it takes the universal as middle. Let animal be
the term signified by A, mortal by B, and immortal by C, and let
5 man, whose definition is to be got, be signified by D. The man who
divides assumes that every animal is either mortal or immortal:
i. e. whatever is A is all either B or C. Again, always dividing, he lays
it down that man is an animal, so he assumes A of D as belonging
to it. Now the true conclusion is that every D is either B or C, con-
10 sequently man must be either mortal or immortal, but it is not
necessary that man should be a mortal animal—this is begged: and
this is what ought to have been proved syllogistically. And again,
taking A as mortal animal, B as footed, C as footless, and D as man,
15 he assumes in the same way that A inheres either in B or in C (for
every mortal animal is either footed or footless), and he assumes
A of D (for he assumed man, as we saw, to be a mortal animal);
consequently it is necessary that man should be either a footed or a
footless animal; but it is not necessary that man should be footed:
this he assumes: and it is just this again which he ought to have

---

73 *Topics*, especially i. 14.
74 Aristotle is thinking of Plato's establishment of definitions by means of
division by dichotomy.
75 In cc. 1-30.

demonstrated. Always dividing then in this way it turns out that 20
these logicians assume as middle the universal term, and as extremes
that which ought to have been the subject of demonstration and the
differentiae. In conclusion, they do not make it clear, and show it to
be necessary, that this is man or whatever the subject of inquiry
may be: for they pursue the other method altogether, never even
suspecting the presence of the rich supply of evidence which might 25
be used. It is clear that it is neither possible to refute a statement by
this method of division, nor to draw a conclusion about an accident
or property of a thing, nor about its genus, nor in cases in which
it is unknown whether it is thus or thus, e. g. whether the diagonal
is incommensurate. For if he assumes that every length is either com- 30
mensurate or incommensurate, and the diagonal is a length, he has
proved that the diagonal is either incommensurate or commensurate.
But if he should assume that it is incommensurate, he will have
assumed what he ought to have proved. He cannot then prove it: for
this is his method, but proof is not possible by this method. Let A
stand for 'incommensurate or commensurate', B for 'length', C for
'diagonal'. It is clear then that this method of investigation is not 35
suitable for every inquiry, nor is it useful in those cases in which it is
thought to be most suitable.

From what has been said it is clear from what elements demonstrations are formed and in what manner, and to what points we
must look in each problem. . . .

BOOK II

16   . . . To beg and assume the original question is a species of failure 64ᵇ
to demonstrate the problem proposed; but this happens in many
ways. A man may not reason syllogistically at all, or he may argue 30
from premisses which are less known or equally unknown, or he may
establish the antecedent by means of its consequents; for demonstration proceeds from what is more certain and is prior. Now begging the question is none of these: but since we get to know some
things naturally through themselves, and other things by means of
something else (the first principles through themselves, what is sub- 35
ordinate to them through something else), whenever a man tries to
prove what is not self-evident by means of itself, then he begs the
original question. This may be done by assuming what is in question
at once; it is also possible to make a transition to other things
which would naturally be proved through the thesis proposed, and 40

65ª demonstrate it through them, e. g. if *A* should be proved through *B*, and *B* through *C*, though it was natural that *C* should be proved through *A*: for it turns out that those who reason thus are proving *A* by means of itself. This is what those persons do who suppose
5 that they are constructing parallel straight lines: for they fail to see that they are assuming facts which it is impossible to demonstrate unless the parallels exist. So it turns out that those who reason thus merely say a particular thing is, if it is: in this way everything will be self-evident. But that is impossible.

10 If then it is uncertain whether *A* belongs to *C*, and also whether *A* belongs to *B*, and if one should assume that *A* does belong to *B*, it is not yet clear whether he begs the original question, but it is evident that he is not demonstrating: for what is as uncertain as the question to be answered cannot be a principle of a demonstration. If however *B* is so related to *C* that they are identical, or
15 if they are plainly convertible, or the one belongs to the other, the original question is begged. For one might equally well prove that *A* belongs to *B* through those terms if they are convertible. But if they are not convertible, it is the fact that they are not that prevents such a demonstration, not the method of demonstrating. But if one were to make the conversion, then he would be doing what we have described and effecting a reciprocal proof with three propositions.

Similarly if he should assume that *B* belongs to *C*, this being as
20 uncertain as the question whether *A* belongs to *C*, the question is not yet begged, but no demonstration is made. If however *A* and *B* are identical either because they are convertible or because *A* follows *B*, then the question is begged for the same reason as before. For we have explained the meaning of begging the question, viz. prov-
25 ing that which is not self-evident by means of itself.

If then begging the question is proving what is not self-evident by means of itself, in other words failing to prove when the failure is due to the thesis to be proved and the premiss through which it is proved being equally uncertain, either because predicates which are identical belong to the same subject, or because the same predicate belongs to subjects which are identical, the question may be begged
30 in the middle and third figures in both ways, though, if the syllogism is affirmative, only in the third and first figures. If the syllogism is negative, the question is begged when identical predicates are denied of the same subject; and both premisses do not beg the question indifferently (in a similar way the question may be begged in the middle figure), because the terms in negative syllogisms are

not convertible. In scientific demonstrations the question is begged 35
when the terms are really related in the manner described, in dialectical arguments when they are according to common opinion so
related.

17   The objection that 'this is not the reason why the result is false',
which we frequently make in argument, is made primarily in the case
of a *reductio ad impossibile*, to rebut the proposition which was 40
being proved by the reduction. For unless a man has contradicted 65ᵇ
this proposition he will not say, 'False cause', but urge that something false has been assumed in the earlier parts of the argument;
nor will he use the formula in the case of an ostensive proof; for
here what one denies is not assumed as a premiss. Further when anything is refuted ostensively by the terms *ABC*, it cannot be objected
that the syllogism does not depend on the assumption laid down. 5
For we use the expression 'false cause', when the syllogism is concluded in spite of the refutation of this position; but that is not
possible in ostensive proofs: since if an assumption is refuted, a syllogism can no longer be drawn in reference to it. It is clear then that
the expression 'false cause' can only be used in the case of a *reductio* 10
ad impossibile, and when the original hypothesis is so related to the
impossible conclusion, that the conclusion results indifferently
whether the hypothesis is made or not. The most obvious case of the
irrelevance of an assumption to a conclusion which is false is when a
syllogism drawn from middle terms to an impossible conclusion is
independent of the hypothesis, as we have explained in the *Topics*.[1] 15
For to put that which is not the cause as the cause, is just this:
e. g. if a man, wishing to prove that the diagonal of the square is
incommensurate with the side, should try to prove Zeno's theorem
that motion is impossible, and so establish a *reductio ad impossibile*:
for Zeno's false theorem has no connexion at all with the original 20
assumption. Another case is where the impossible conclusion is connected with the hypothesis, but does not result from it. This may
happen whether one traces the connexion upwards or downwards,
e. g. if it is laid down that *A* belongs to *B*, *B* to *C*, and *C* to *D*, and 25
it should be false that *B* belongs to *D*: for if we eliminated *A* and
assumed all the same that *B* belongs to *C* and *C* to *D*, the false conclusion would not depend on the original hypothesis. Or again trace
the connexion upwards; e. g. suppose that *A* belongs to *B*, *E* to *A*, 30
and *F* to *E*, it being false that *F* belongs to *A*. In this way too the
impossible conclusion would result, though the original hypothesis

[1] *Soph. El.* 167ᵇ 21–36.

were eliminated. But the impossible conclusion ought to be connected with the original terms: in this way it will depend on the hypothesis, e. g. when one traces the connexion downwards, the
35 impossible conclusion must be connected with that term which is predicate in the hypothesis: for if it is impossible that A should belong to D, the false conclusion will no longer result after A has been eliminated. If one traces the connexion upwards, the impossible conclusion must be connected with that term which is subject in the hypothesis: for if it is impossible that F should belong to B, the impossible conclusion will disappear if B is eliminated. Similarly
40 when the syllogisms are negative.

66ª   It is clear then that when the impossibility is not related to the original terms, the false conclusion does not result on account of the assumption. Or perhaps even so it may sometimes be independent. For if it were laid down that A belongs not to B but to K,
5 and that K belongs to C and C to D, the impossible conclusion would still stand. Similarly if one takes the terms in an ascending series. Consequently since the impossibility results whether the first assumption is suppressed or not, it would appear to be independent of that assumption. Or perhaps we ought not to understand the statement that the false conclusion results independently of the assumption, in the sense that if something else were supposed the
10 impossibility would result; but rather we mean that when the first assumption is eliminated, the same impossibility results through the remaining premises; since it is not perhaps absurd that the same false result should follow from several hypotheses, e. g. that parallels meet, both on the assumption that the interior angle is greater than the exterior and on the assumption that a triangle contains more
15 than two right angles.

18   A false argument depends on the first false statement in it. Every syllogism is made out of two or more premises. If then the false conclusion is drawn from two premises, one or both of them must be false: for (as was proved [2]) a false syllogism cannot be
20 drawn from true premises. But if the premises are more than two, e. g. if C is established through A and B, and these through D, E, F, and G, one of these higher propositions must be false, and on this the argument depends: for A and B are inferred by means of D, E, F, and G. Therefore the conclusion and the error results from one of them.

[2] 53ᵇ 11–25.

19   In order to avoid having a syllogism drawn against us, we must 25
take care, whenever an opponent asks us to admit the reason without
the conclusions, not to grant him the same term twice over in his
premises, since we know that a syllogism cannot be drawn without
a middle term, and that term which is stated more than once is the
middle. How we ought to watch the middle in reference to each conclusion, is evident from our knowing what kind of thesis is proved 30
in each figure. This will not escape us since we know how we are
maintaining the argument.

That which we urge men to beware of in their admissions, they
ought in attack to try to conceal. This will be possible first, if, instead
of drawing the conclusions of preliminary syllogisms, they take the 35
necessary premises and leave the conclusions in the dark; secondly
if instead of inviting assent to propositions which are closely connected they take as far as possible those that are not connected by
middle terms. For example suppose that A is to be inferred to be
true of F; B, C, D, and E being middle terms. One ought then to ask
whether A belongs to B, and next whether D belongs to E, instead
of asking whether B belongs to C; after that he may ask whether B 40
belongs to C, and so on. And if the syllogism is drawn through one 66ᵇ
middle term, he ought to begin with that: in this way he will most
likely deceive his opponent.

20   Since we know when a syllogism can be formed and how its
terms must be related, it is clear when refutation will be possible 5
and when impossible. A refutation is possible whether everything
is conceded, or the answers alternate (one, I mean, being affirmative,
the other negative). For as has been shown a syllogism is possible
whether the terms are related in affirmative propositions or one
proposition is affirmative, the other negative: consequently, if what is
laid down is contrary to the conclusion, a refutation must take 10
place: for a refutation is a syllogism which establishes the contradictory. But if nothing is conceded, a refutation is impossible: for no
syllogism is possible (as we saw [3]) when all the terms are negative:
therefore no refutation is possible. For if a refutation were possible, a syllogism must be possible; although if a syllogism is possible 15
it does not follow that a refutation is possible. Similarly refutation
is not possible if nothing is conceded universally: since the fields of
refutation and syllogism are defined in the same way.

[3] 41ᵇ 6.

21   It sometimes happens that just as we are deceived in the ar-
20 rangement of the terms,[4] so error may arise in our thought about
them, e. g. if it is possible that the same predicate should belong to
more than one subject immediately, but although knowing the one,
a man may forget the other and think the opposite true. Suppose that
A belongs to B and to C in virtue of their nature, and that B and C
belong to all D in the same way. If then a man thinks that A belongs
to all B, and B to D, but A to no C, and C to all D, he will both
25 know and not know the same thing [5] in respect of the same thing.[6]
Again if a man were to make a mistake about the members of a single
series; e. g. suppose A belongs to B, B to C, and C to D, but some one
thinks that A belongs to all B, but to no C: he will both know that
30 A belongs to D, and think that it does not. Does he then maintain
after this simply that what he knows, he does not think? For he
knows in a way that A belongs to C through B, since the part is
included in the whole; so that what he knows in a way, this he maintains he does not think at all: but that is impossible.

35   In the former case, where the middle term does not belong to the
same series, it is not possible to think both the premisses with
reference to each of the two middle terms: e. g. that A belongs to all
B, but to no C, and both B and C belong to all D. For it turns out
that the first premiss of the one syllogism is either wholly or partially
contrary to the first premiss of the other. For if he thinks that A be-
40 longs to everything to which B belongs, and he knows that B belongs
67ᵃ to D, then he knows that A belongs to D. Consequently if again he
:thinks that A belongs to nothing to which C belongs, he thinks that
A does not belong to some of that to which B belongs; but if he
thinks that A belongs to everything to which B belongs, and again
thinks that A does not belong to some of that to which B belongs,
5 these beliefs are wholly or partially contrary. In this way then it is
not possible to think; but nothing prevents a man thinking one
premiss of each syllogism or both premisses of one of the two syllogisms: e. g. A belongs to all B, and B to D, and again A belongs to
no C. An error of this kind is similar to the error into which we
fall concerning particulars: e. g. if A belongs to all B, and B to all
10 C, A will belong to all C. If then a man knows that A belongs to
everything to which B belongs, he knows that A belongs to C. But
nothing prevents his being ignorant that C exists; e. g. let A stand
for two right angles, B for triangle, C for a particular diagram of
a triangle. A man might think that C did not exist, though he

---

[4] Cf. i. 32 ff.
[5] i. e. subject.   [6] i. e. attribute.

knew that every triangle contains two right angles; consequently 15
he will know and not know the same thing at the same time. For
the expression 'to know that every triangle has its angles equal to two
right angles' is ambiguous, meaning to have the knowledge either of
the universal or of the particulars. Thus then he knows that C contains two right angles with a knowledge of the universal, but not with
a knowledge of the particulars; consequently his knowledge will 20
not be contrary to his ignorance. The argument in the *Meno* [7] that
learning is recollection may be criticized in a similar way. For it
never happens that a man starts with a foreknowledge of the particular, but along with the process of being led to see the general
principle he receives a knowledge of the particulars, by an act (as it
were) of recognition. For we know some things directly; e. g. that
the angles are equal to two right angles, if we know that the figure is 25
a triangle. Similarly in all other cases.

By a knowledge of the universal then we see the particulars, but
we do not know them by the kind of knowledge which is proper to
them; consequently it is possible that we may make mistakes about
them, but not that we should have the knowledge and error that
are contrary to one another: rather we have the knowledge of the
universal but make a mistake in apprehending the particular. Simi- 30
larly in the cases stated above.[8] The error in respect of the middle
term is not contrary to the knowledge obtained through the syllogism, nor is the thought in respect of one middle term contrary to
that in respect of the other. Nothing prevents a man who knows both
that A belongs to the whole of B, and that B again belongs to C,
thinking that A does not belong to C, e. g. knowing that every mule 35
is sterile and that this is a mule, and thinking that this animal is with
foal: for he does not know that A belongs to C, unless he considers
the two propositions together. So it is evident that if he knows the
one and does not know the other, he will fall into error. And this
is the relation of knowledge of the universal to knowledge of the particular. For we know no sensible thing, once it has passed beyond 67ᵇ
the range of our senses, even if we happen to have perceived it,
except by means of the universal *and* the possession of the knowledge
which is proper to the particular, but without the actual exercise of
that knowledge. For to know is used in three senses: it may mean
either to have knowledge of the universal or to have knowledge
proper to the matter in hand or to exercise such knowledge: conse- 5
quently three kinds of error also are possible. Nothing then prevents
a man both knowing and being mistaken about the same thing,

[7] 81.   [8] 66ᵇ 20–6, 26–30.

provided that his knowledge and his error are not contrary. And this
happens also to the man whose knowledge is limited to each of the
premisses and who has not previously considered the particular
question. For when he thinks that the mule is with foal he has
not the knowledge in the sense of its actual exercise, nor on the
10 other hand has his thought caused an error contrary to his knowledge: for the error contrary to the knowledge of the universal would
be a syllogism.

But he who thinks the essence of good is the essence of bad will
think the same thing to be the essence of good and the essence of
bad. Let A stand for the essence of good and B for the essence of bad,
15 and again C for the essence of good. Since then he thinks B and C
identical, he will think that C is B, and similarly that B is A, consequently that C is A. For just as we saw that if B is *true* of all of
which C is *true*, and A is true of all of which B is true, A is true of
C, similarly with the word 'think'. Similarly also with the word 'is';
20 for we saw that if C is the same as B, and B as A, C is the same as
A. Similarly therefore with 'opine'. Perhaps then this [9] is necessary
if a man will grant the first point.[10] But presumably that is false,
that any one could suppose the essence of good to be the essence of
25 bad, save incidentally. For it is possible to think this in many different
ways. But we must consider this matter better.[11]

22   Whenever the extremes are convertible it is necessary that the
middle should be convertible with both. For if A belongs to C through
B, then if A and C are convertible and C belongs to everything to
30 which A belongs, B is convertible with A, and B belongs to everything to which A belongs, through C as middle, and C is convertible
with B through A as middle. Similarly if the conclusion is negative,
e. g. if B belongs to C, but A does not belong to B, neither will A
belong to C. If then B is convertible with A, C will be convertible
35 with A. Suppose B does not belong to A; neither then will C: for
ex hypothesi B belonged to all C. And if C is convertible with B, B
is convertible also with A: for C is said of that of all of which B is
said. And if C is convertible in relation to A and to B, B also is convertible in relation to A. For C belongs to that to which B belongs:
68ᵃ but C does not belong to that to which A belongs. And this alone
starts from the conclusion; the preceding moods do not do so as in

---

9 That a man should think the same thing to be the essence of good and to
be the essence of bad.
10 That the essence of good is the essence of bad.
11 The reference may be to *Met*. iv. (Γ).

the affirmative syllogism. Again if A and B are convertible, and similarly C and D, and if A or C must belong to anything whatever, then B and D will be such that one or other belongs to anything whatever. For since B belongs to that to which A belongs, and D belongs to that to which C belongs, and since A or C belongs to everything, but not together, it is clear that B or D belongs to everything, but not together. For example if that which is uncreated is incorruptible and that which is incorruptible is uncreated, it is necessary that what is created should be corruptible and what is corruptible should have been created. For two syllogisms have been put together. Again if A or B belongs to everything and if C or D belongs to everything, but they cannot belong together, then when A and C are convertible B and D are convertible. For if B does not belong to something to which D belongs, it is clear that A belongs to it. But if A then C: for they are convertible. Therefore C and D belong together. But this is impossible. When A belongs to the whole of B and to C and is affirmed of nothing else, and B also belongs to all C, it is necessary that A and B should be convertible: for since A is said of B and C only, and B is affirmed both of itself and of C, it is clear that B will be said of everything of which A is said, except A itself. Again when A and B belong to the whole of C, and C is convertible with B, it is necessary that A should belong to all B: for since A belongs to all C, and C to B by conversion, A will belong to all B.

When, of two opposites A and B, A is preferable to B, and similarly D is preferable to C, then if A and C together are preferable to B and D together, A must be preferable to D. For A is an object of desire to the same extent as B is an object of aversion, since they are opposites: and C is similarly related to D, since they also are opposites. If then A is an object of desire to the same extent as D, B is an object of aversion to the same extent as C (since each is to the same extent as each—the one an object 'of aversion, the other an object of desire). Therefore both A and C together, and B and D together, will be equally objects of desire or aversion. But since A and C are preferable to B and D, A cannot be equally desirable with D; for then B along with D would be equally desirable with A along with C. But if D is preferable to A, then B must be less an object of aversion than C: for the less is opposed to the less. But the greater good and lesser evil are preferable to the lesser good and greater evil: the whole BD then is preferable to the whole AC. But *ex hypothesi* this is not so. A then is preferable to D, and C consequently is less an object of aversion than B. If then every lover in virtue of his love would prefer A, viz. that the beloved should be such as to grant a favour, and yet should not grant it (for which C stands), to the beloved's granting the favour (represented by D) 68^b without being such as to grant it (represented by B), it is clear that A (being of such a nature) is preferable to granting the favour. To receive affection then is preferable in love to sexual intercourse. Love then is more dependent on friendship than on intercourse. And if it is most dependent on receiving affection, then this is its 5 end. Intercourse then either is not an end at all or is an end relative to the further end, the receiving of affection. And indeed the same is true of the other desires and arts.

23   It is clear then how the terms are related in conversion, and in respect of being in a higher degree objects of aversion or of desire. 10 We must now state that not only dialectical and demonstrative syllogisms are formed by means of the aforesaid figures, but also rhetorical syllogisms and in general any form of persuasion, however it may be presented. For every belief comes either through syllogism or from induction.

15   Now induction, or rather the syllogism which springs out of induction, consists in establishing syllogistically a relation between one extreme and the middle by means of the other extreme, e. g. if B is the middle term between A and C, it consists in proving through C that A belongs to B. For this is the manner in which we make inductions. For example let A stand for long-lived, B for bile- 20 less, and C for the particular long-lived animals, e. g. man, horse, mule. A then belongs to the whole of C: for whatever is bileless is long-lived. But B also ('not possessing bile') belongs to all C. If then C is convertible with B, and the middle term is not wider in exten- sion, it is necessary that A should belong to B. For it has already been 25 proved that if two things belong to the same thing, and the extreme is convertible with one of them, then the other predicate will belong to the predicate that is converted. But we must apprehend C as made up of all the particulars. For induction proceeds through an enumera- tion of all the cases.

30   Such is the syllogism which establishes the first and immediate premiss: for where there is a middle term the syllogism proceeds through the middle term; when there is no middle term, through in- duction. And in a way induction is opposed to syllogism: for the latter proves the major term to belong to the third term by means of the mid- dle, the former proves the major to belong to the middle by means of 35 the third. In the order of nature, syllogism through the middle term is prior and better known, but syllogism through induction is clearer to *us*.

24 We have an 'example' when the major term is proved to belong
to the middle by means of a term which resembles the third. It ought
to be known both that the middle belongs to the third term, and that 40
the first belongs to that which resembles the third. For example let
A be evil, B making war against neighbours, C Athenians against 69ᵃ
Thebans, D Thebans against Phocians. If then we wish to prove that
to fight with the Thebans is an evil, we must assume that to fight
against neighbours is an evil. Evidence of this is obtained from similar
cases, e. g. that the war against the Phocians was an evil to the 5
Thebans. Since then to fight against neighbours is an evil, and to
fight against the Thebans is to fight against neighbours, it is clear
that to fight against the Thebans is an evil. Now it is clear that B
belongs to C and to D (for both are cases of making war upon one's
neighbours) and that A belongs to D (for the war against the Phocians
did not turn out well for the Thebans): but that A belongs to B 10
will be proved through D. Similarly if the belief in the relation of
the middle term to the extreme should be produced by several similar
cases. Clearly then to argue by example is neither like reasoning from
part to whole, nor like reasoning from whole to part, but rather
reasoning from part to part, when both particulars are subordinate 15
to the same term, and one of them is known. It differs from induction, because induction starting from all the particular cases proves
(as we saw [12]) that the major term belongs to the middle, and does
not apply the syllogistic conclusion to the minor term, whereas argument by example does make this application and does not draw its
proof from all the particular cases.

25 By reduction we mean an argument in which the first term clearly 20
belongs to the middle, but the relation of the middle to the last
term is uncertain though equally or more probable than the conclusion; or again an argument in which the terms intermediate between
the last term and the middle are few. For in any of these cases it turns
out that we approach more nearly to knowledge. For example let A
stand for what can be taught, B for knowledge, C for justice. Now it 25
is clear that knowledge can be taught: but it is uncertain whether
virtue is knowledge. If now the statement BC [13] is equally or more
probable than AC, we have a reduction: for we are nearer to knowledge, since we have taken a new term,[14] being so far without knowledge that A belongs to C. Or again suppose that the terms inter-

---

[12] ch. 23.   [13] See note 20.
[14] viz. B, thus obtaining a certain premiss AB, and a premiss BC, on which
the inquiry now turns.

30 mediate between *B* and *C* are few: for thus too we are nearer knowledge. For example let *D* stand for squaring, *E* for rectilinear figure,
F for circle. If there were only one term intermediate between *E*
and *F* (viz. that the circle is made equal to a rectilinear figure by
the help of lunules), we should be near to knowledge. But when
35 *BC* is not more probable than *AC*, and the intermediate terms are
not few, I do not call this reduction: nor again when the statement
BC is immediate: for such a statement is knowledge.

26 An objection is a premiss contrary to a premiss. It differs from
a premiss, because it may be particular, but a premiss either cannot
be particular at all or not in universal syllogisms. An objection is
69ᵇ brought in two ways and through two figures; in two ways because every objection is either universal or particular, by two figures
because objections are brought in opposition to the premiss, and
5 opposites can be proved only in the first and third figures. If a man
maintains a universal affirmative, we reply with a universal or a particular negative; the former is proved from the first figure, the latter
from the third. For example let *A* stand for there being a single
science, *B* for contraries. If a man premisses that contraries are sub-
10 jects of a single science, the objection may be either that opposites
are never subjects of a single science, and contraries are opposites, so
that we get the first figure, or that the knowable and the unknowable are not subjects of a single science: this proof is in the third
figure: for it is true of *C* (the knowable and the unknowable) that
they are contraries, and it is false that they are the subjects of a
single science.
15 Similarly if the premiss objected to is negative. For if a man maintains that contraries are not subjects of a single science, we reply
either that all opposites or that certain contraries, e. g. what is
healthy and what is sickly, are subjects of the same science: the
former argument issues from the first, the latter from the third figure.
In general if a man urges a universal objection he must frame
20 his contradiction with reference to the universal of the terms taken
by his opponent, e. g. if a man maintains that *contraries* are not
subjects of the same science, his opponent must reply that there is
a single science of all *opposites*. Thus we must have the first figure:
for the term which embraces the original subject becomes the middle
term.
If the objection is particular, the objector must frame his contradiction with reference to a term relatively to which the subject of
his opponent's premiss is universal, e. g. he will point out that

the knowable and the unknowable are not subjects of the same 25
science: 'contraries' is universal relatively to these. And we have
the third figure: for the particular term assumed is middle, e. g. the
knowable and the unknowable. Premisses from which it is possible
to draw the contrary conclusion are what we start from when we try
to make objections. Consequently we bring objections in these figures 30
only: for in them only are opposite syllogisms possible, since the
second figure cannot produce an affirmative conclusion.

Besides, an objection in the middle figure would require a fuller
argument, e. g. if it should not be granted that A belongs to B, because C does not follow B. This can be made clear only by other 35
premisses. But an objection ought not to turn off into other things,
but have its new premiss quite clear immediately. For this reason
also this is the only figure from which proof by signs cannot be
obtained.

We must consider later the other kinds of objection, namely the
objection from contraries, from similars, and from common opinion,
and inquire whether a particular objection cannot be elicited from 70ᵃ
the first figure or a negative objection from the second.

27   A probability and a sign are not identical, but a probability is a
generally approved proposition: what men know to happen or not
to happen, to be or not to be, for the most part thus and thus, is a 5
probability, e. g. 'the envious hate', 'the beloved show affection'. A
sign means a demonstrative proposition necessary or generally approved: for anything such that when it is another thing is, or when
it has come into being the other has come into being before or after,
is a sign of the other's being or having come into being. Now an
enthymeme is a syllogism starting from probabilities or signs, and a 10
sign may be taken in three ways, corresponding to the position of the
middle term in the figures. For it may be taken as in the first figure
or the second or the third. For example the proof that a woman is
with child because she has milk is in the first figure: for to have milk
is the middle term. Let A represent to be with child, B to have 15
milk, C woman. The proof that wise men are good, since Pittacus is
good, comes through the last figure. Let A stand for good, B for wise
men, C for Pittacus. It is true then to affirm both A and B of C:
only men do not say the latter, because they know it, though they
state the former. The proof that a woman is with child because she 20
is pale is meant to come through the middle figure: for since paleness follows women with child and is a concomitant of this woman,
people suppose it has been proved that she is with child. Let A stand

for paleness, *B* for being with child, *C* for woman. Now if the
25 one proposition is stated, we have only a sign, but if the other is
stated as well, a syllogism, e. g. 'Pittacus is generous, since ambitious
men are generous and Pittacus is ambitious'. Or again 'Wise men are
good, since Pittacus is not only good but wise'. In this way then
syllogisms are formed, only that which proceeds through the first
30 figure is irrefutable if it is true (for it is universal), that which proceeds through the last figure is refutable even if the conclusion is
true, since the syllogism is not universal nor correlative to the matter
in question: for though Pittacus is good, it is not therefore necessary
that all other wise men should be good. But the syllogism which proceeds through the middle figure is always refutable in any case: for
35 a syllogism can never be formed when the terms are related in this
way: for though a woman with child is pale, and this woman also is
pale, it is not necessary that she should be with child. Truth then may
be found in signs whatever their kind, but they have the differences
we have stated.

70^b   We must either divide signs in the way stated, and among them
designate the middle term as the index [15] (for people call that the
index which makes us know, and the middle term above all has this
character), or else we must call the arguments derived from the extremes signs, that derived from the middle term the index: for that
5 which is proved through the first figure is most generally accepted
and most true.

It is possible to infer character from features, if it is granted that
the body and the soul are changed together by the natural affections: I say 'natural', for though perhaps by learning music a man
10 has made some change in his soul, this is not one of those affections
which are natural to us; rather I refer to passions and desires when
I speak of natural motions. If then this were granted and also that
for each change there is a corresponding sign, and we could state
the affection and sign proper to each kind of animal, we shall be able
to infer character from features. For if there is an affection which
15 belongs properly to an individual kind, e. g. courage to lions, it is
necessary that there should be a sign of it: for *ex hypothesi* body and
soul are affected together. Suppose this sign is the possession of large
extremities: this may belong to other kinds also though not universally. For the sign is proper in the sense stated, because the affection
is proper to the whole kind, though not proper to it alone, according
20 to our usual manner of speaking. The same thing then will be found

15 This points to the argument in the first figure, whose middle term is a
genuine middle term.

in another kind, and man may be brave, and some other kinds of animal as well. They will then have the sign: for *ex hypothesi* there is one sign corresponding to each affection. If then this is so, and we can collect signs of this sort in these animals which have only one affection proper to them—but each affection has its sign, since it is necessary that it should have a single sign—we shall then be able to 25 infer character from features. But if the kind as a whole has two properties, e. g. if the lion is both brave and generous, how shall we know which of the signs which are its proper concomitants is the sign of a particular affection? Perhaps if both belong to some other kind though not to the whole of it, and if, in those kinds in which each is found though not in the whole of their members, some members possess one of the affections and not the other: e. g. if a man is brave but not generous, but possesses, of the two signs, large extremities, 30 it is clear that this is the sign of courage in the lion also. To judge character from features, then, is possible in the first figure if the middle term is convertible with the first extreme, but is wider than the third term and not convertible with it: e. g. let A stand for courage, B for large extremities, and C for lion. B then belongs to 35 everything to which C belongs, but also to others. But A belongs to everything to which B belongs, and to nothing besides, but is convertible with B: otherwise, there would not be a single sign correlative with each affection.

ANALYTICA POSTERIORA

Translated by G. R. G. Mure

CONTENTS
BOOK I

ANALYTICA POSTERIORA

(*Posterior Analytics*)

BOOK I

71ᵃ 1   All instruction given or received by way of argument proceeds
from pre-existent knowledge. This becomes evident upon a survey
of all the species of such instruction. The mathematical sciences and
all other speculative disciplines are acquired in this way, and so
5 are the two forms of dialectical reasoning, syllogistic and inductive:
for each of these latter makes use of old knowledge to impart new,
the syllogism assuming an audience that accepts its premises, induction exhibiting the universal as implicit in the clearly known particular. Again, the persuasion exerted by rhetorical arguments is in
principle the same, since they use either example, a kind of induc-
10 tion, or enthymeme, a form of syllogism.

The pre-existent knowledge required is of two kinds. In some
cases admission of the fact must be assumed, in others comprehension
of the meaning of the term used, and sometimes both assumptions
are essential. Thus, we assume that every predicate can be either truly
affirmed or truly denied of any subject, and that 'triangle' means so
and so; as regards 'unit' we have to make the double assumption of
15 the meaning of the word and the existence of the thing. The reason
is that these several objects are not equally obvious to us. Recognition
of a truth may in some cases contain as factors both previous knowledge and also knowledge acquired simultaneously with that recognition
—knowledge, this latter, of the particulars actually falling under the
universal and therein already virtually known. For example, the stu-
20 dent knew beforehand that the angles of every triangle are equal to two
right angles; but it was only at the actual moment at which he was
being led on to recognize this as true in the instance before him that
he came to know 'this figure inscribed in the semicircle' to be a
triangle. For some things (viz. the singulars finally reached which
are not predicable of anything else as subject) are only learnt in
this way, i. e. there is here no recognition through a middle of a minor
term as subject to a major. Before he was led on to recognition or be-

fore he actually drew a conclusion, we should perhaps say that in a 25 manner he knew, in a manner not.

If he did not in an unqualified sense of the term *know* the existence of this triangle, how could he *know* without qualification that its angles were equal to two right angles? No: clearly he *knows* not without qualification but only in the sense that he *knows* universally. If this distinction is not drawn, we are faced with the dilemma in the *Meno*: [1] either a man will learn nothing or what he already knows; for we cannot accept the solution which some people offer. A man is 30 asked, 'Do you, or do you not, know that every pair is even?' He says he does know it. The questioner then produces a particular pair, of the existence, and so *a fortiori* of the evenness, of which he was unaware. The solution which some people offer is to assert that they do not know that every pair is even, but only that everything which they know to be a pair is even: yet what they know to be even is 71ᵇ that of which they have demonstrated evenness, i. e. what they made the subject of their premiss, viz. not merely every triangle or number which they know to be such, but any and every number or triangle without reservation. For no premiss is ever couched in the form 'every number which you know to be such', or 'every rectilinear figure which you know to be such': the predicate is always construed as applicable to any and every instance of the thing. On the other hand, I imagine 5 there is nothing to prevent a man in one sense knowing what he is learning, in another not knowing it. The strange thing would be, not if in some sense he knew what he was learning, but if he were to know it in that precise sense and manner in which he was learning it. [2]

2 We suppose ourselves to possess unqualified scientific knowledge of a thing, as opposed to knowing it in the accidental way in which the sophist knows, when we think that we know the cause on 10 which the fact depends, as the cause of that fact and of no other, and, further, that the fact could not be other than it is. Now that scientific knowing is something of this sort is evident—witness both those who falsely claim it and those who actually possess it, since the former merely imagine themselves to be, while the latter are also actually, in the condition described. Consequently the proper object of unqualified scientific knowledge is something which cannot be 15 other than it is.

There may be another manner of knowing as well—that will be discussed later. [3] What I now assert is that at all events we do know

[1] Plato, *Meno*, 80 E.   [2] Cf. *An. Pr.* ii, ch. 21.
[3] Cf. the following chapter and more particularly ii, ch. 19.

by demonstration. By demonstration I mean a syllogism productive of scientific knowledge, a syllogism, that is, the grasp of which is *eo ipso* such knowledge. Assuming then that my thesis as to the nature
20 of scientific knowing is correct, the premisses of demonstrated knowledge must be true, primary, immediate, better known than and prior to the conclusion, which is further related to them as effect to cause. Unless these conditions are satisfied, the basic truths will not be 'appropriate' to the conclusion. Syllogism there may indeed be without these conditions, but such syllogism, not being productive of scientific knowledge, will not be demonstration. The premisses must
25 be true: for that which is non-existent cannot be known—we cannot know, e. g., that the diagonal of a square is commensurate with its side. The premisses must be primary and indemonstrable; otherwise they will require demonstration in order to be known, since to have knowledge, if it be not accidental knowledge, of things which are demonstrable, means precisely to have a demonstration of them. The premisses must be the causes of the conclusion, better known than it,
30 and prior to it; its causes, since we possess scientific knowledge of a thing only when we know its cause; prior, in order to be causes; antecedently known, this antecedent knowledge being not our mere understanding of the meaning, but knowledge of the fact as well. Now 'prior' and 'better known' are ambiguous terms, for there is a difference between what is prior and better known in the order of
72ª being and what is prior and better known to man. I mean that objects nearer to sense are prior and better known to man; objects without qualification prior and better known are those further from sense. Now the most universal causes are furthest from sense and particular
5 causes are nearest to sense, and they are thus exactly opposed to one another. In saying that the premisses of demonstrated knowledge must be primary, I mean that they must be the 'appropriate' basic truths, for I identify primary premiss and basic truth. A 'basic truth' in a demonstration is an immediate proposition. An immediate proposition is one which has no other proposition prior to it. A proposition is either part of an enunciation, i. e. it predicates a single attribute of a single subject. If a proposition is dialectical, it assumes either
10 part indifferently; if it is demonstrative, it lays down one part to the definite exclusion of the other because that part is true. The term 'enunciation' denotes either part of a contradiction indifferently. A contradiction is an opposition which of its own nature excludes a middle. The part of a contradiction which conjoins a predicate with a subject is an affirmation; the part disjoining them is a negation.
15 I call an immediate basic truth of syllogism a 'thesis' when, though

it is not susceptible of proof by the teacher, yet ignorance of it does not constitute a total bar to progress on the part of the pupil: one which the pupil must know if he is to learn anything whatever is an axiom. I call it an axiom because there are such truths and we give them the name of axioms *par excellence*. If a thesis assumes one part or the other of an enunciation, i. e. asserts either the existence or the 20 non-existence of a subject, it is a hypothesis; if it does not so assert, it is a definition. Definition *is* a 'thesis' or a 'laying something down', since the arithmetician lays it down that to be a unit is to be quantitatively indivisible; but it is not a hypothesis, for to define what a unit is is not the same as to affirm its existence.

Now since the required ground of our knowledge—i. e. of our 25 conviction—of a fact is the possession of such a syllogism as we call demonstration, and the ground of the syllogism is the facts constituting its premisses, we must not only know the primary premisses —some if not all of them—beforehand, but know them better than the conclusion: for the cause of an attribute's inherence in a subject always itself inheres in the subject more firmly than that attribute; e. g. the cause of our loving anything is dearer to us than the object of our love. So since the primary premisses are the cause of our 30 knowledge—i. e. of our conviction—it follows that we know them better—that is, are more convinced of them—than their consequences, precisely because our knowledge of the latter is the effect of our knowledge of the premisses. Now a man cannot believe in anything more than in the things he knows, unless he has either actual knowledge of it or something better than actual knowledge. But we are faced with this paradox if a student whose belief rests 35 on demonstration has not prior knowledge; a man must believe in some, if not in all, of the basic truths more than in the conclusion. Moreover, if a man sets out to acquire the scientific knowledge that comes through demonstration, he must not only have a better knowledge of the basic truths and a firmer conviction of them than of the connexion which is being demonstrated: more than this, nothing 72^b must be more certain or better known to him than these basic truths in their character as contradicting the fundamental premisses which lead to the opposed and erroneous conclusion. For indeed the conviction of pure science must be unshakable.

3 Some hold that, owing to the necessity of knowing the primary 5 premisses, there is no scientific knowledge. Others think there is, but that all truths are demonstrable. Neither doctrine is either true or a necessary deduction from the premisses. The first school,

assuming that there is no way of knowing other than by demonstration, maintain that an infinite regress is involved, on the ground that
if behind the prior stands no primary, we could not know the
10 posterior through the prior (wherein they are right, for one cannot
traverse an infinite series): if on the other hand—they say—the
series terminates and there are primary premisses, yet these are unknowable because incapable of demonstration, which according to
them is the only form of knowledge. And since thus one cannot know
the primary premisses, knowledge of the conclusions which follow
from them is not pure scientific knowledge nor properly knowing
at all, but rests on the mere supposition that the premisses are true.
15 The other party agree with them as regards knowing, holding that
it is only possible by demonstration, but they see no difficulty in
holding that all truths are demonstrated, on the ground that demonstration may be circular and reciprocal.

   Our own doctrine is that not all knowledge is demonstrative: on
the contrary, knowledge of the immediate premisses is independent
20 of demonstration. (The necessity of this is obvious; for since we
must know the prior premisses from which the demonstration is
drawn, and since the regress must end in immediate truths, those
truths must be indemonstrable.) Such, then, is our doctrine, and in
addition we maintain that besides scientific knowledge there is its
originative source which enables us to recognize the definitions.
25   Now demonstration must be based on premisses prior to and better
known than the conclusion; and the same things cannot simultaneously be both prior and posterior to one another: so circular
demonstration is clearly not possible in the unqualified sense of
'demonstration', but only possible if 'demonstration' be extended to
include that other method of argument which rests on a distinction
between truths prior to us and truths without qualification prior,
30 i. e. the method by which induction produces knowledge. But if we
accept this extension of its meaning, our definition of unqualified
knowledge will prove faulty; for there seem to be two kinds of it.
Perhaps, however, the second form of demonstration, that which proceeds from truths better known to us, is not demonstration in the
unqualified sense of the term.

   The advocates of circular demonstration are not only faced with
the difficulty we have just stated: in addition their theory reduces
to the mere statement that if a thing exists, then it does exist—an
35 easy way of proving anything. That this is so can be clearly shown
by taking three terms, for to constitute the circle it makes no difference whether many terms or few or even only two are taken.

Thus by direct proof, if A is, B must be; if B is, C must be; therefore if A is, C must be. Since then—by the circular proof—if A is, B 73ᵃ
must be, and if B is, A must be, A may be substituted for C above.
Then 'if B is, A must be' = 'if B is, C must be', which above gave
the conclusion 'if A is, C must be': but C and A have been identified.
Consequently the upholders of circular demonstration are in the
position of saying that if A is, A must be—a simple way of proving 5
anything. Moreover, even such circular demonstration is impossible
except in the case of attributes that imply one another, viz. 'peculiar'
properties.

Now, it has been shown that the positing of one thing—be it one
term or one premiss—never involves a necessary consequent: [4] two
premisses constitute the first and smallest foundation for drawing a 10
conclusion at all and therefore *a fortiori* for the demonstrative syllogism of science. If, then, A is implied in B and C, and B and C are
reciprocally implied in one another and in A, it is possible, as has
been shown in my writings on the syllogism,[5] to prove all the assumptions on which the original conclusion rested, by circular demonstration in the first figure. But it has also been shown that in the 15
other figures either no conclusion is possible, or at least none which
proves both the original premisses.[6] Propositions the terms of which
are not convertible cannot be circularly demonstrated at all, and
since convertible terms occur rarely in actual demonstrations, it is
clearly frivolous and impossible to say that demonstration is reciprocal
and that therefore everything can be demonstrated. 20

4   Since the object of pure scientific knowledge cannot be other than
it is, the truth obtained by demonstrative knowledge will be necessary. And since demonstrative knowledge is only present when we
have a demonstration, it follows that demonstration is an inference
from necessary premisses. So we must consider what are the premisses of demonstration—i. e. what is their character: and as a pre- 25
liminary, let us define what we mean by an attribute 'true in every
instance of its subject', an 'essential' attribute, and a 'commensurate
and universal' attribute. I call 'true in every instance' what is truly
predicable of all instances—not of one to the exclusion of others—
and at all times, not at this or that time only; e. g. if animal is truly
predicable of every instance of man, then if it be true to say 'this is 30
a man', 'this is an animal' is also true, and if the one be true now
the other is true now. A corresponding account holds if point is in
every instance predicable as contained in line. There is evidence for

[4] *An. Pr.* i, ch. 25.　　　[5] *Ibid.* ii, ch. 5.　　　[6] *Ibid.* ii, cc. 5 and 6.

this in the fact that the objection we raise against a proposition put
to us as true in every instance is either an instance in which, or an
occasion on which, it is not true. Essential attributes are (1) such as
35 belong to their subject as elements in its essential nature (e. g. line
thus belongs to triangle, point to line; for the very being or 'substance' of triangle and line is composed of these elements, which are
contained in the formulae defining triangle and line): (2) such that,
while they belong to certain subjects, the subjects to which they belong are contained in the attribute's own defining formula. Thus
straight and curved belong to line, odd and even, prime and com-
40 pound, square and oblong, to number; and also the formula defining
73ᵇ any one of these attributes contains its subject—e. g. line or number
as the case may be.

Extending this classification to all other attributes, I distinguish
those that answer the above description as belonging essentially to
their respective subjects; whereas attributes related in neither of these
two ways to their subjects I call accidents or 'coincidents'; e. g. musical or white is a 'coincident' of animal.

5   Further (a) that is essential which is not predicated of a subject
other than itself: e. g. 'the walking [thing]' walks and is white in
virtue of being something else besides; whereas substance, in the sense
of whatever signifies a 'this somewhat', is not what it is in virtue of
being something else besides. Things, then, not predicated of a subject I call essential; things predicated of a subject I call accidental or
'coincidental'.

10   In another sense again (b) a thing consequentially connected with
anything is essential; one not so connected is 'coincidental'. An example of the latter is 'While he was walking it lightened': the lightning
was not due to his walking; it was, we should say, a coincidence. If,
on the other hand, there is a consequential connexion, the predication is essential; e. g. if a beast dies when its throat is being cut, then
its death is also essentially connected with the cutting, because the
15 cutting was the cause of death, not death a 'coincident' of the cutting.

So far then as concerns the sphere of connexions scientifically
known in the unqualified sense of that term, all attributes which
(within that sphere) are essential either in the sense that their subjects
are contained in them, or in the sense that they are contained in their
subjects, are necessary as well as consequentially connected with their
subjects. For it is impossible for them not to inhere in their subjects—
either simply or in the qualified sense that one or other of a pair of
20 opposites must inhere in the subject; e. g. in line must be either
straightness or curvature, in number either oddness or evenness. For

within a single identical genus the contrary of a given attribute is either its privative or its contradictory; e. g. within number what is not odd is even, inasmuch as within this sphere even is a necessary consequent of not-odd. So, since any given predicate must be either affirmed or denied of any subject, essential attributes must inhere in their subjects of necessity.

Thus, then, we have established the distinction between the at- 25 tribute which is 'true in every instance' and the 'essential' attribute.

I term 'commensurately universal' an attribute which belongs to every instance of its subject, and to every instance essentially and as such; from which it clearly follows that all commensurate universals inhere *necessarily* in their subjects. The essential attribute, and the attribute that belongs to its subject as such, are identical. E. g. point and straight belong to line essentially, for they belong to line as such; 30 and triangle as such has two right angles, for it is *essentially* equal to two right angles.

An attribute belongs commensurately and universally to a subject when it can be shown to belong to any random instance of that subject and when the subject is the first thing to which it can be shown to belong. Thus, e. g., (1) the equality of its angles to two right angles is not a commensurately universal attribute of figure. For though it is possible to show that a figure has its angles equal to two right 35 angles, this attribute cannot be demonstrated of any figure selected at haphazard, nor in demonstrating does one take a figure at random—a square is a figure but its angles are not equal to two right angles. On the other hand, any isosceles triangle has its angles equal to two right angles, yet isosceles triangle is not the primary subject of this attribute but triangle is prior. So whatever can be shown to have its angles equal to two right angles, or to possess any other attribute, in 40 any random instance of itself and primarily—that is the first subject to which the predicate in question belongs commensurately and uni- 74ª versally, and the demonstration, in the essential sense, of any predicate is the proof of it as belonging to this first subject commensurately and universally: while the proof of it as belonging to the other subjects to which it attaches is demonstration only in a secondary and unessential sense. Nor again (2) is equality to two right angles a commensurately universal attribute of isosceles; it is of wider application.

5   We must not fail to observe that we often fall into error because our conclusion is not in fact primary and commensurately universal 5 in the sense in which we think we prove it so. We make this mistake (1) when the subject is an individual or individuals above which

there is no universal to be found: (2) when the subjects belong to
different species and there is a higher universal, but it has no name:
(3) when the subject which the demonstrator takes as a whole is
really only a part of a larger whole; for then the demonstration will
10 be true of the individual instances within the part and will hold in
every instance of it, yet the demonstration will not be true of this
subject primarily and commensurately and universally. When a demonstration is true of a subject primarily and commensurately and
universally, that is to be taken to mean that it is true of a given
subject primarily and as such. Case (3) may be thus exemplified. If a
proof were given that perpendiculars to the same line are parallel, it
might be supposed that *lines thus perpendicular* were the proper
subject of the demonstration because being parallel is true of every
15 instance of them. But it is not so, for the parallelism depends not on
these angles being equal to one another because each is a right angle,
but simply on their being equal to one another. An example of (1)
would be as follows: if isosceles were the only triangle, it would be
thought to have its angles equal to two right angles *qua* isosceles. An
instance of (2) would be the law that proportionals alternate. Alternation used to be demonstrated separately of numbers, lines, solids, and
20 durations, though it could have been proved of them all by a single
demonstration. Because there was no single name to denote that in
which numbers, lengths, durations, and solids are identical, and because they differed specifically from one another, this property was
proved of each of them separately. To-day, however, the proof is
commensurately universal, for they do not possess this attribute *qua*
lines or *qua* numbers, but *qua* manifesting this generic character
25 which they are postulated as possessing universally. Hence, even if one
prove of each kind of triangle that its angles are equal to two right
angles, whether by means of the same or different proofs; still, as long
as one treats separately equilateral, scalene, and isosceles, one does
not yet know, except sophistically, that triangle has its angles equal
to two right angles, nor does one yet know that triangle has this
property commensurately and universally, even if there is no other
30 species of triangle but these. For one does not know that triangle as
such has this property, nor even that 'all' triangles have it—unless
'all' means 'each taken singly': if 'all' means 'as a whole class', then,
though there be none in which one does not recognize this property,
one does not know it of 'all triangles'.

When, then, does our knowledge fail of commensurate universality,
and when is it unqualified knowledge? If triangle be identical in
essence with equilateral, i. e. with each or all equilaterals, then clearly

we have unqualified knowledge: if on the other hand it be not, and
the attribute belongs to equilateral *qua* triangle; then our knowledge fails of commensurate universality. 'But', it will be asked, 'does 35
this attribute belong to the subject of which it has been demonstrated
qua triangle or *qua* isosceles? What is the point at which the subject
to which it belongs is primary? (i. e. to what subject can it be demonstrated as belonging commensurately and universally?)' Clearly
this point is the first term in which it is found to inhere as the elimination of inferior *differentiae* proceeds. Thus the angles of a brazen
isosceles triangle are equal to two right angles: but eliminate brazen
and isosceles and the attribute remains. 'But'—you may say—'elimi- 74ᵇ
nate figure or limit, and the attribute vanishes'. True, but figure and
limit are not the first *differentiae* whose elimination destroys the
attribute. 'Then what is the first?' If it is triangle, it will be in virtue
of triangle that the attribute belongs to all the other subjects of which
it is predicable, and triangle is the subject to which it can be demonstrated as belonging commensurately and universally.

6 Demonstrative knowledge must rest on necessary basic truths; 5
for the object of scientific knowledge cannot be other than it is. Now
attributes attaching essentially to their subjects attach necessarily to
them: for essential attributes are either elements in the essential
nature of their subjects, or contain their subjects as elements in their
own essential nature. (The pairs of opposites which the latter class
includes are necessary because one member or the other necessarily
inheres.) It follows from this that premisses of the demonstrative syl- 10
logism must be connexions essential in the sense explained: for all
attributes must inhere essentially or else be accidental, and accidental
attributes are not necessary to their subjects.

We must either state the case thus, or else premise that the conclusion of demonstration is necessary and that a demonstrated conclusion cannot be other than it is, and then infer that the conclusion 15
must be developed from necessary premisses. For though you may
reason from true premisses without demonstrating, yet if your
premisses are necessary you will assuredly demonstrate—in such
necessity you have at once a distinctive character of demonstration.
That demonstration proceeds from necessary premisses is also indicated by the fact that the objection we raise against a professed
demonstration is that a premiss of it is not a necessary truth—whether 20
we think it altogether devoid of necessity, or at any rate so far as our
opponent's previous argument goes. This shows how naïve it is to
suppose one's basic truths rightly chosen if one starts with a proposi-

tion which is (1) popularly accepted and (2) true, such as the
sophists' assumption that to know is the same as to possess knowledge.[7] For (1) popular acceptance or rejection is no criterion of a
basic truth, which can only be the primary law of the genus consti-
25 tuting the subject matter of the demonstration; and (2) not *all*
truth is 'appropriate'.

A further proof that the conclusion must be the development of
necessary premises is as follows. Where demonstration is possible, one
who can give no account which includes the cause has no scientific
knowledge. If, then, we suppose a syllogism in which, though *A* necessarily inheres in *C*, yet *B*, the middle term of the demonstration, is
not necessarily connected with *A* and *C*, then the man who argues
30 thus has no reasoned knowledge of the conclusion, since this conclusion does not owe its necessity to the middle term; for though the
conclusion is necessary, the mediating link is a contingent fact. Or
again, if a man is without knowledge now, though he still retains the
steps of the argument, though there is no change in himself or in the
fact and no lapse of memory on his part; then neither had he knowledge previously. But the mediating link, not being necessary, may
35 have perished in the interval; and if so, though there be no change in
him nor in the fact, and though he will still retain the steps of the
argument, yet he has not knowledge, and therefore had not knowledge before. Even if the link has not actually perished but is liable
to perish, this situation is possible and might occur. But such a
condition cannot be knowledge.

75ᵃ   When the conclusion is necessary, the middle through which it was
proved may yet quite easily be non-necessary. You can in fact infer
the necessary even from a non-necessary premiss, just as you can
infer the true from the not true. On the other hand, when the middle
5 is necessary the conclusion must be necessary; just as true premisses
always give a true conclusion. Thus, if *A* is necessarily predicated of *B*
and *B* of *C*, then *A* is necessarily predicated of *C*. But when the conclusion is non-necessary the middle cannot be necessary either. Thus:
10 let *A* be predicated non-necessarily of *C* but necessarily of *B*, and
let *B* be a necessary predicate of *C*; then *A* too will be a necessary
predicate of *C*, which by hypothesis it is not.

To sum up, then: demonstrative knowledge must be knowledge of a
necessary nexus, and therefore must clearly be obtained through a
necessary middle term; otherwise its possessor will know neither the
15 cause nor the fact that his conclusion is a necessary connexion. Either
he will mistake the non-necessary for the necessary and believe the

---

[7] Plato, *Euthydemus*, 277 B.

necessity of the conclusion without knowing it, or else he will not even believe it—in which case he will be equally ignorant, whether he actually infers the mere fact through middle terms or the reasoned fact and from immediate premises.

Of accidents that are not essential according to our definition of essential there is no demonstrative knowledge; for since an accident, in the sense in which I here speak of it, may also not inhere, it 20 is impossible to prove its inherence as a necessary conclusion. A difficulty, however, might be raised as to why in dialectic, if the conclusion is not a necessary connexion, such and such determinate premisses should be proposed in order to deal with such and such determinate problems. Would not the result be the same if one asked any questions whatever and then merely stated one's conclusion? The solution is that determinate questions have to be put, not because the 25 replies to them affirm facts which necessitate facts affirmed by the conclusion, but because these answers are propositions which if the answerer affirm, he must affirm the conclusion—and affirm it with truth if they are true.

Since it is just those attributes within every genus which are essential and possessed by their respective subjects as such that are necessary, it is clear that both the conclusions and the premisses of demonstrations which produce scientific knowledge are essential. For 30 accidents are not necessary: and, further, since accidents are not necessary one does not necessarily have reasoned knowledge of a conclusion drawn from them (this is so even if the accidental premisses are invariable but not essential, as in proofs through signs; for though the conclusion be actually essential, one will not know it as essential nor know its reason); but to have reasoned knowledge of a conclusion 35 is to know it through its cause. We may conclude that the middle must be consequentially connected with the minor, and the major with the middle.

7   It follows that we cannot in demonstrating pass from one genus to another. We cannot, for instance, prove geometrical truths by arithmetic. For there are three elements in demonstration: (1) what is proved, the conclusion—an attribute inhering essentially in a genus; 40 (2) the axioms, i. e. axioms which are premisses of demonstration; 75b (3) the subject-genus whose attributes, i. e. essential properties, are revealed by the demonstration. The axioms which are premisses of demonstration may be identical in two or more sciences: but in the case of two different genera such as arithmetic and geometry you cannot apply arithmetical demonstration to the properties of mag- 5

nitudes unless the magnitudes in question are numbers.[8] How in certain cases transference is possible I will explain later.[9]

Arithmetical demonstration and the other sciences likewise possess, each of them, their own genera; so that if the demonstration is to pass from one sphere to another, the genus must be either absolutely 10 or to some extent the same. If this is not so, transference is clearly impossible, because the extreme and the middle terms must be drawn from the same genus: otherwise, as predicated, they will not be essential and will thus be accidents. That is why it cannot be proved by geometry that opposites fall under one science, nor even that the product of two cubes is a cube. Nor can the theorem of any one 15 science be demonstrated by means of another science, unless these theorems are related as subordinate to superior (e. g. as optical theorems to geometry or harmonic theorems to arithmetic). Geometry again cannot prove of lines any property which they do not possess *qua* lines, i. e. in virtue of the fundamental truths of their peculiar genus: it cannot show, for example, that the straight line is the most beautiful of lines or the contrary of the circle; for these qualities do not belong to lines in virtue of their peculiar genus, but through 20 some property which it shares with other genera.

8   It is also clear that if the premisses from which the syllogism proceeds are commensurately universal, the conclusion of such demonstration—demonstration, i. e., in the unqualified sense—must also be eternal. Therefore no attribute can be demonstrated nor known by strictly scientific knowledge to inhere in perishable things. The proof 25 can only be accidental, because the attribute's connexion with its perishable subject is not commensurately universal but temporary and special. If such a demonstration is made, one premiss must be perishable and not commensurately universal (perishable because only if it is perishable will the conclusion be perishable; not commensurately universal, because the predicate will be predicable of some instances of the subject and not of others); so that the conclusion can only be that a fact is true at the moment—not commensurately and uni- 30 versally. The same is true of definitions, since a definition is either a primary premiss or a conclusion of a demonstration, or else only differs from a demonstration in the order of its terms. Demonstration and science of merely frequent occurrences—e. g. of eclipse as happening to the moon—are, as such, clearly eternal: whereas so far as they are not eternal they are not fully commensurate. Other subjects

---

[8] Cf. *Met.* 1039ª 9.   [9] Cf. i, cc. 9 and 13.

too have properties attaching to them in the same way as eclipse 35 attaches to the moon.

9 It is clear that if the conclusion is to show an attribute inhering as such, nothing can be demonstrated except from its 'appropriate' basic truths. Consequently a proof even from true, indemonstrable, and immediate premises does not constitute knowledge. Such proofs 40 are like Bryson's method of squaring the circle; for they operate by taking as their middle a common character—a character, therefore, which the subject may share with another—and consequently they 76ᵃ apply equally to subjects different in kind. They therefore afford knowledge of an attribute only as inhering accidentally, not as belonging to its subject as such: otherwise they would not have been applicable to another genus.

Our knowledge of any attribute's connexion with a subject is accidental unless we know that connexion through the middle term in virtue of which it inheres, and as an inference from basic premises 5 essential and 'appropriate' to the subject—unless we know, e. g., the property of possessing angles equal to two right angles as belonging to that subject in which it inheres essentially, and as inferred from basic premises essential and 'appropriate' to that subject: so that if that middle term also belongs essentially to the minor, the middle must belong to the same kind as the major and minor terms. The only exceptions to this rule are such cases as theorems in harmonics which are demonstrable by arithmetic. Such theorems are proved by the 10 same middle terms as arithmetical properties, but with a qualification —the fact falls under a separate science (for the subject genus is separate), but the reasoned fact concerns the superior science, to which the attributes essentially belong. Thus, even these apparent exceptions show that no attribute is strictly demonstrable except from its 'appropriate' basic truths, which, however, in the case of these sciences 15 have the requisite identity of character.

It is no less evident that the peculiar basic truths of each inhering attribute are indemonstrable; for basic truths from which they might be deduced would be basic truths of all that is, and the science to which they belonged would possess universal sovereignty. This is so because he knows better whose knowledge is deduced from higher causes, for his knowledge is from prior premises when it derives from 20 causes themselves uncaused: hence, if he knows better than others or best of all, his knowledge would be science in a higher or the highest degree. But, as things are, demonstration is not transferable to another genus, with such exceptions as we have mentioned of the appli-

cation of geometrical demonstrations to theorems in mechanics or
25 optics, or of arithmetical demonstrations to those of harmonics.

It is hard to be sure whether one knows or not; for it is hard to be
sure whether one's knowledge is based on the basic truths appropriate
to each attribute—the differentia of true knowledge. We think we
have scientific knowledge if we have reasoned from true and primary
premisses. But that is not so: the conclusion must be homogeneous
30 with the basic facts of the science.

10 I call the basic truths of every genus those elements in it the
existence of which cannot be proved. As regards both these primary
truths and the attributes dependent on them the meaning of the name
is assumed. The fact of their existence as regards the primary truths
must be assumed; but it has to be proved of the remainder, the attributes. Thus we assume the meaning alike of unity, straight, and
35 triangular; but while as regards unity and magnitude we assume also
the fact of their existence, in the case of the remainder proof is
required.

Of the basic truths used in the demonstrative sciences some are
peculiar to each science, and some are common, but common only in
the sense of analogous, being of use only in so far as they fall within
the genus constituting the province of the science in question.
40 Peculiar truths are, e. g., the definitions of line and straight; common truths are such as 'take equals from equals and equals remain'.
Only so much of these common truths is required as falls within the
76ᵇ genus in question: for a truth of this kind will have the same force
even if not used generally but applied by the geometer only to magnitudes, or by the arithmetician only to numbers. Also peculiar to a
science are the subjects the existence as well as the meaning of which
it assumes, and the essential attributes of which it investigates, e. g.
5 in arithmetic units, in geometry points and lines. Both the existence
and the meaning of the subjects are assumed by these sciences; but
of their essential attributes only the meaning is assumed. For example
arithmetic assumes the meaning of odd and even, square and cube,
geometry that of incommensurable, or of deflection or verging of lines,
whereas the existence of these attributes is demonstrated by means
10 of the axioms and from previous conclusions as premisses. Astronomy
too proceeds in the same way. For indeed every demonstrative science
has three elements: (1) that which it posits, the subject genus whose
essential attributes it examines; (2) the so-called axioms, which are
15 primary premisses of its demonstration; (3) the attributes, the meaning of which it assumes. Yet some sciences may very well pass over

some of these elements; e. g. we might not expressly posit the existence of the genus if its existence were obvious (for instance, the existence of hot and cold is more evident than that of number); or we might omit to assume expressly the meaning of the attributes if it were well understood. In the same way the meaning of axioms, such as 'Take 20 equals from equals and equals remain', is well known and so not expressly assumed. Nevertheless in the nature of the case the essential elements of demonstration are three: the subject, the attributes, and the basic premisses.

That which expresses necessary self-grounded fact, and which we must necessarily believe,[10] is distinct both from the hypotheses of a science and from illegitimate postulate—I say 'must believe', because all syllogism, and therefore a fortiori demonstration, is addressed not to the spoken word, but to the discourse within the soul,[11] and 25 though we can always raise objections to the spoken word, to the inward discourse we cannot always object. That which is capable of proof but assumed by the teacher without proof is, if the pupil believes and accepts it, hypothesis, though only in a limited sense hypothesis— that is, relatively to the pupil; if the pupil has no opinion or a con- 30 trary opinion on the matter, the same assumption is an illegitimate postulate. Therein lies the distinction between hypothesis and illegiti-mate postulate: the latter is the contrary of the pupil's opinion, demonstrable, but assumed and used without demonstration.

The definitions—viz. those which are not expressed as statements 35 that anything is or is not—are not hypotheses: but it is in the premisses of a science that its hypotheses are contained. Definitions require only to be understood, and this is not hypothesis—unless it be contended that the pupil's hearing is also an hypothesis required by the teacher. Hypotheses, on the contrary, postulate facts on the being of which depends the being of the fact inferred. Nor are the geometer's hypotheses false, as some have held, urging that one must 40 not employ falsehood and that the geometer is uttering falsehood in stating that the line which he draws is a foot long or straight, when it is actually neither. The truth is that the geometer does not draw 77ᵃ any conclusion from the being of the particular line of which he speaks, but from what his diagrams symbolize. A further distinction is that all hypotheses and illegitimate postulates are either universal or particular, whereas a definition is neither.

11   So demonstration does not necessarily imply the being of Forms 5 nor a One beside a Many, but it does necessarily imply the possi-

10 sc. axioms.   11 Cf. Plato, Theaetetus, 189 E ff.

bility of truly predicating one of many; since without this possibility
we cannot save the universal, and if the universal goes, the middle
term goes with it, and so demonstration becomes impossible. We
conclude, then, that there must be a single identical term unequivo-
cally predicable of a number of individuals.

10   The law that it is impossible to affirm and deny simultaneously
the same predicate of the same subject is not expressly posited by any
demonstration except when the conclusion also has to be expressed
in that form; in which case the proof lays down as its major premiss
that the major is truly affirmed of the middle but falsely denied. It
makes no difference, however, if we add to the middle, or again to the
minor term, the corresponding negative. For grant a minor term of
15 which it is true to predicate man—even if it be also true to predicate
not-man of it—still grant simply that man is animal and not not-
animal, and the conclusion follows: for it will still be true to say that
Callias—even if it be also true to say that not-Callias—is animal and
not not-animal. The reason is that the major term is predicable not
only of the middle, but of something other than the middle as well,
20 being of wider application; so that the conclusion is not affected
even if the middle is extended to cover the original middle term and
also what is not the original middle term.[12]

The law that every predicate can be either truly affirmed or truly
denied of every subject is posited by such demonstration as uses
reductio ad impossibile, and then not always universally, but so far
as it is requisite; within the limits, that is, of the genus—the genus, I
25 mean (as I have already explained[13]), to which the man of science
applies his demonstrations. In virtue of the common elements of
demonstration—I mean the common axioms which are used as premisses of demonstration, not the subjects or the attributes demonstrated as belonging to them—all the sciences have communion
with one another, and in communion with them all is dialectic
and any science which might attempt a universal proof of axioms
30 such as the law of excluded middle, the law that the subtraction of equals from equals leaves equal remainders, or other axioms
of the same kind. Dialectic has no definite sphere of this kind,
not being confined to a single genus. Otherwise its method
would not be interrogative; for the interrogative method is barred

---

[12] Lit. 'even if the middle is itself and also what is not itself'; i. e. you may pass
from the middle term man to include not-man without affecting the conclusion.

[13] Cf. 75ᵃ 42 ff. and 76ᵇ 13.

to the demonstrator, who cannot use the opposite facts to prove the same *nexus*. This was shown in my work on the syllogism.[14] 35

12   If a syllogistic question [15] is equivalent to a proposition embodying one of the two sides of a contradiction, and if each science has its peculiar propositions from which its peculiar conclusion is developed, then there is such a thing as a distinctively scientific question, and it is the interrogative form of the premises from which the 'appropriate' conclusion of each science is developed. Hence it is 40 clear that not every question will be relevant to geometry, nor to medicine, nor to any other science: only those questions will be geometrical which form premises for the proof of the theorems of 77[b] geometry or of any other science, such as optics, which uses the same basic truths as geometry. Of the other sciences the like is true. Of these questions the geometer is bound to give his account, using the basic truths of geometry in conjunction with his previous conclusions; of the basic truths the geometer, as such, is not bound to give any 5 account. The like is true of the other sciences. There is a limit, then, to the questions which we may put to each man of science; nor is each man of science bound to answer all inquiries on each several subject, but only such as fall within the defined field of his own science. If, then, in controversy with a geometer *qua* geometer the disputant confines himself to geometry and proves anything from geometrical premises, he is clearly to be applauded; if he goes out- 10 side these he will be at fault, and obviously cannot even refute the geometer except accidentally. One should therefore not discuss geometry among those who are not geometers, for in such a company an unsound argument will pass unnoticed. This is correspondingly true in the other sciences.   15

Since there are 'geometrical' questions, does it follow that there are also distinctively 'ungeometrical' questions? Further, in each special science—geometry for instance—what kind of error is it that may vitiate questions, and yet not exclude them from that science? Again, is the erroneous conclusion one constructed from premises opposite to the true premises, or is it formal fallacy though drawn from 20 geometrical premises? Or, perhaps, the erroneous conclusion is due to the drawing of premises from another science; e. g. in a geometrical controversy a musical question is distinctively ungeometrical,

---

[14] *An. Pr.* i. 1. The 'opposite facts' are those which would be expressed in the alternatively possible answers to the dialectical question, the dialectician's aim being to refute his interlocutor whether the latter answers the question put to him affirmatively or in the negative.

[15] i. e. a premiss put in the form of a question.

whereas the notion that parallels meet is in one sense geometrical, being ungeometrical in a different fashion: the reason being that 'ungeo-metrical', like 'unrhythmical', is equivocal, meaning in the one case
25 not geometry at all, in the other bad geometry? It is this error, i. e. error based on premises of this kind—'of' the science but false—that is the contrary of science. In mathematics the formal fallacy is not so common, because it is the middle term in which the ambiguity lies, since the major is predicated of the whole of the middle and the
30 middle of the whole of the minor (the *predicate* of course never has the prefix 'all'); and in mathematics one can, so to speak, see these middle terms with an intellectual vision, while in dialectic the am-biguity may escape detection. E. g. 'Is every circle a figure?' A dia-gram shows that this is so, but the minor premiss 'Are epics circles?' is shown by the diagram to be false.

If a proof has an inductive minor premiss, one should not bring an
35 'objection' against it. For since every premiss must be applicable to a number of cases (otherwise it will not be true in every instance, which, since the syllogism proceeds from universals, it must be), then assuredly the same is true of an 'objection'; since premises and 'objections' are so far the same that anything which can be validly advanced as an 'objection' must be such that it could take the form
40 of a premiss, either demonstrative or dialectical. On the other hand arguments formally illogical do sometimes occur through taking as middles mere attributes of the major and minor terms. An instance
78a of this is Caeneus' proof that fire increases in geometrical proportion: 'Fire', he argues, 'increases rapidly, and so does geometrical propor-tion'. There is no syllogism so, but there is a syllogism if the most rapidly increasing proportion is geometrical and the most rapidly
5 increasing proportion is attributable to fire in its motion. Sometimes, no doubt, it is impossible to reason from premises predicating mere attributes: but sometimes it is possible, though the possibility is over-looked. If false premises could never give true conclusions 'resolu-tion' would be easy, for premises and conclusion would in that case inevitably reciprocate. I might then argue thus: let *A* be an existing fact; let the existence of *A* imply such and such facts actually known to me to exist, which we may call *B*. I can now, since they reciprocate, infer *A* from *B*.

10   Reciprocation of premises and conclusion is more frequent in mathematics, because mathematics takes definitions, but never an accident, for its premises—a second characteristic distinguishing mathematical reasoning from dialectical disputations.

A science expands not by the interposition of fresh middle terms, but by the apposition of fresh extreme terms. E. g. *A* is predicated of *B*, *B* of *C*, *C* of *D*, and so indefinitely. Or the expansion may be 15 lateral: e. g. one major, *A*, may be proved of two minors, *C* and *E*. Thus let *A* represent number—*a* number or *number* taken indeterminately; *B* determinate odd number; *C* any particular odd number. We can then predicate *A* of *C*. Next let *D* represent determinate even 20 number, and *E* even number. Then *A* is predicable of *E*.

13   Knowledge of the fact differs from knowledge of the reasoned fact. To begin with, they differ within the same science and in two ways: (1) when the premisses of the syllogism are not immediate (for then the proximate cause is not contained in them—a neces- 25 sary condition of knowledge of the reasoned fact): (2) when the premisses are immediate, but instead of the cause the better known of the two reciprocals is taken as the middle; for of two reciprocally predicable terms the one which is not the cause may quite easily be the better known and so become the middle term of the demonstration. Thus (2) (*a*) you might prove as follows that the planets are 30 near because they do not twinkle: let *C* be the planets, *B* not twinkling, *A* proximity. Then *B* is predicable of *C*; for the planets do not twinkle. But *A* is also predicable of *B*, since that which does not twinkle is near—we must take this truth as having been reached by induction or sense-perception. Therefore *A* is a necessary predicate of 35 *C*; so that we have demonstrated that the planets are near. This syllogism, then, proves not the reasoned fact but only the fact; since they are not near because they do not twinkle, but, because they are near, do not twinkle. The major and middle of the proof, however, may be reversed, and then the demonstration will be of the reasoned 40 fact. Thus: let *C* be the planets, *B* proximity, *A* not twinkling. Then 78ᵇ *B* is an attribute of *C*, and *A*—not twinkling—of *B*. Consequently *A* is predicable of *C*, and the syllogism proves the reasoned fact, since its middle term is the proximate cause. Another example is the inference that the moon is spherical from its manner of waxing. Thus: since that which so waxes is spherical, and since the moon so waxes, 5 clearly the moon is spherical. Put in this form, the syllogism turns out to be proof of the fact, but if the middle and major be reversed it is proof of the reasoned fact; since the moon is not spherical because it waxes in a certain manner, but waxes in such a manner because it is spherical. (Let *C* be the moon, *B* spherical, and *A* waxing.) Again 10 (*b*), in cases where the cause and the effect are not reciprocal and the effect is the better known, the fact is demonstrated but not

the reasoned fact. This also occurs (1) when the middle falls outside
the major and minor, for here too the strict cause is not given, and
so the demonstration is of the fact, not of the reasoned fact. For
15 example, the question 'Why does not a wall breathe?' might be answered, 'Because it is not an animal'; but that answer would not give
the strict cause, because if not being an animal causes the absence
of respiration, then being an animal should be the cause of respiration, according to the rule that if the negation of x causes the non-
20 inherence of y, the affirmation of x causes the inherence of y; e. g. if
the disproportion of the hot and cold elements is the cause of ill health,
their proportion is the cause of health; and conversely, if the assertion
of x causes the inherence of y, the negation of x must cause y's non-
inherence. But in the case given this consequence does not result;
for not every animal breathes. A syllogism with this kind of cause
takes place in the second figure. Thus: let A be animal, B respiration,
25 C wall. Then A is predicable of all B (for all that breathes is animal), but of no C; and consequently B is predicable of no C; that is,
the wall does not breathe. Such causes are like far-fetched explanations, which precisely consist in making the cause too remote, as in
30 Anacharsis' account of why the Scythians have no flute-players;
namely because they have no vines.

Thus, then, do the syllogism of the fact and the syllogism of the
reasoned fact differ within one science and according to the position
of the middle terms. But there is another way too in which the fact
and the reasoned fact differ, and that is when they are investigated
35 respectively by different sciences. This occurs in the case of
problems related to one another as subordinate and superior, as
when optical problems are subordinated to geometry, mechanical
40 problems to stereometry, harmonic problems to arithmetic, the data
79ᵃ of observation to astronomy. (Some of these sciences bear almost
the same name; e. g. mathematical and nautical astronomy, mathematical and acoustical harmonics.) Here it is the business of the
empirical observers to know the fact, of the mathematicians to
know the reasoned fact; for the latter are in possession of the
demonstrations giving the causes, and are often ignorant of the fact:
5 just as we have often a clear insight into a universal, but through lack
of observation are ignorant of some of its particular instances. These
connexions [16] have a perceptible existence though they are manifestations of forms. For the mathematical sciences concern forms: they do
not demonstrate properties of a substratum, since, even though the
geometrical subjects are predicable as properties of a perceptible

16 *sc.* 'which require two sciences for their proof'. Cf. 78ᵇ 35.

substratum, it is not as thus predicable that the mathematician demonstrates properties of them. As optics is related to geometry, 10 so another science is related to optics, namely the theory of the rainbow. Here knowledge of the fact is within the province of the natural philosopher, knowledge of the reasoned fact within that of the optician, either *qua* optician or *qua* mathematical optician. Many sciences not standing in this mutual relation enter into it at points; e. g. medicine and geometry: it is the physician's business to know that circular wounds heal more slowly, the geometer's to know the 15 reason why.

14 Of all the figures the most scientific is the first. Thus, it is the vehicle of the demonstrations of all the mathematical sciences, such as arithmetic, geometry, and optics, and practically of all sciences 20 that investigate causes: for the syllogism of the reasoned fact is either exclusively or generally speaking and in most cases in this figure—a second proof that this figure is the most scientific; for grasp of a reasoned conclusion is the primary condition of knowledge. Thirdly, the first is the only figure which enables us to pursue knowledge of the essence of a thing. In the second figure no affirmative conclusion 25 is possible, and knowledge of a thing's essence must be affirmative; while in the third figure the conclusion can be affirmative, but cannot be universal, and essence must have a universal character: e. g. man is not two-footed animal in any qualified sense, but universally. Finally, the first figure has no need of the others, while it is by 30 means of the first that the other two figures are developed, and have their intervals close-packed until immediate premisses are reached. Clearly, therefore, the first figure is the primary condition of knowledge.

15 Just as an attribute *A* may (as we saw) be atomically connected with a subject *B*, so its disconnexion may be atomic. I call 'atomic' connexions or disconnexions which involve no intermediate term; since in that case the connexion or disconnexion will not be mediated 35 by something other than the terms themselves. It follows that if either *A* or *B*, or both *A* and *B*, have a genus, their disconnexion cannot be primary. Thus: let *C* be the genus of *A*. Then, if *C* is not the genus of *B*—for *A* may well have a genus which is not the genus of *B*—there 40 will be a syllogism proving *A*'s disconnexion from *B* thus:

all *A* is *C*,   79ᵇ
no *B* is *C*,
∴ no *B* is *A*.

Or if it is *B* which has a genus *D*, we have

all *B* is *D*,
no *D* is *A*,
∴ no *B* is *A*, by syllogism;

5 and the proof will be similar if both *A* and *B* have a genus. That the genus of *A* need not be the genus of *B* and vice versa, is shown by the existence of mutually exclusive co-ordinate series of predication. If no term in the series *ACD* . . . is predicable of any term in the series *BEF* . . . , and if *G*—a term in the former series—is the genus 10 of *A*, clearly *G* will not be the genus of *B*; since, if it were, the series would not be mutually exclusive. So also if *B* has a genus, it will not be the genus of *A*. If, on the other hand, neither *A* nor *B* has a genus and *A* does not inhere in *B*, this disconnexion must be atomic. If there be a middle term, one or other of them is bound to have a 15 genus, for the syllogism will be either in the first or the second figure. If it is in the first, *B* will have a genus—for the premiss containing it must be affirmative;[17] if in the second, either *A* or *B* indifferently, since syllogism is possible if either is contained in a negative premiss,[18] 20 but not if both premisses are negative.

Hence it is clear that one thing may be atomically disconnected from another, and we have stated when and how this is possible.

16 Ignorance—defined not as the negation of knowledge but as a positive state of mind—is error produced by inference.

25   (1) Let us first consider propositions asserting a predicate's imme-diate connexion with or disconnexion from a subject. Here, it is true, positive error may befall one in alternative ways; for it may arise where one directly believes a connexion or disconnexion as well as where one's belief is acquired by inference. The error, however, that consists in a direct belief is without complication; but the error resulting from inference—which here concerns us—takes many forms. Thus, let *A* be atomically disconnected from all *B*: then the conclu-30 sion inferred through a middle term *C*, that all *B* is *A*, will be a case of error produced by syllogism. Now, two cases are possible. Either (*a*) both premisses, or (*b*) one premiss only, may be false. (*a*) If neither *A* is an attribute of any *C* nor *C* of any *B*, whereas the con-trary was posited in both cases, both premisses will be false. (*C* may 35 quite well be so related to *A* and *B* that *C* is neither subordinate to *A* nor a universal attribute of *B*: for *B*, since *A* was said to be primarily disconnected from *B*, cannot have a genus, and *A* need not

---

[17] i.e. in Celarent.   [18] i.e. in Cesare or Camestres.

necessarily be a universal attribute of all things. Consequently both premisses may be false.) On the other hand, (b) one of the premisses 40 may be true, though not either indifferently but only the major A–C; since, B having no genus, the premiss C–B will always be false, 80ᵃ while A–C may be true. This is the case if, for example, A is related atomically to both C and B; because when the same term is related atomically to more terms than one, neither of those terms will belong to the other. It is, of course, equally the case if A–C is not atomic. 5

Error of attribution, then, occurs through these causes and in this form only—for we found that no syllogism of universal attribution was possible in any figure but the first. On the other hand, an error of non-attribution may occur either in the first or in the second figure. Let us therefore first explain the various forms it takes in the first figure and the character of the premisses in each case.   10

(c) It may occur when both premisses are false; e. g. supposing A atomically connected with both C and B, if it be then assumed that no C is A, and all B is C, both premisses are false.

(d) It is also possible when one is false. This may be either premiss indifferently. A–C may be true, C–B false—A–C true because A is 15 not an attribute of all things, C–B false because C, which never has the attribute A, cannot be an attribute of B; for if C–B were true, the premiss A–C would no longer be true, and besides if both premisses were true, the conclusion would be true. Or again, C–B may be true 20 and A–C false; e. g. if both C and A contain B as genera, one of them must be subordinate to the other, so that if the premiss takes the form No C is A, it will be false. This makes it clear that whether 25 either or both premisses are false, the conclusion will equally be false.

In the second figure the premisses cannot both be wholly false; for if all B is A, no middle term can be with truth universally affirmed of one extreme and universally denied of the other: but premisses in 30 which the middle is affirmed of one extreme and denied of the other are the necessary condition if one is to get a valid inference at all. Therefore if, taken in this way, they are wholly false, their contraries conversely should be wholly true. But this is impossible. On the other hand, there is nothing to prevent both premisses being partially false; e. g. if actually some A is C and some B is C, then if it is premised 35 that all A is C and no B is C, both premisses are false, yet partially, not wholly, false. The same is true if the major is made negative instead of the minor. Or one premiss may be wholly false, and it may be either of them. Thus, supposing that actually an attribute of all A must also be an attribute of all B, then if C is yet taken to be a uni- 40 versal attribute of all A but universally non-attributable to B, C–A 80ᵇ

will be true but C–B false. Again, actually that which is an attribute
of no B will not be an attribute of all A either; for if it be an attribute
of all A, it will also be an attribute of all B, which is contrary to
supposition; but if C be nevertheless assumed to be a universal
5 attribute of A, but an attribute of no B, then the premiss C–B is true
but the major is false. The case is similar if the major is made the
negative premiss. For in fact what is an attribute of no A will not
be an attribute of any B either; and if it be yet assumed that C is
universally non-attributable to A, but a universal attribute of B,
10 the premiss C–A is true but the minor wholly false. Again, in fact it
is false to assume that that which is an attribute of all B is an attribute of no A, for if it be an attribute of all B, it must be an
attribute of some A. If then C is nevertheless assumed to be an
attribute of all B but of no A, C–B will be true but C–A false.

It is thus clear that in the case of atomic propositions erroneous
15 inference will be possible not only when both premisses are false
but also when only one is false.

17   (2) In the case of attributes not atomically connected with
or disconnected from their subjects, (a) (i) as long as the false
conclusion is inferred through the 'appropriate' middle, only the
20 major and not both premisses can be false. By 'appropriate middle'
I mean the middle term through which the contradictory—i. e. the
true—conclusion is inferrible. Thus, let A be attributable to B through
a middle term C: then, since to produce a conclusion the premiss
C–B must be taken affirmatively, it is clear that this premiss must
25 always be true, for its quality is not changed. But the major A–C is
false, for it is by a change in the quality of A–C that the conclusion becomes its contradictory—i. e. true. Similarly (ii) if the middle
is taken from another series of predication; e. g. suppose D to be
not only contained within A as a part within its whole but also
predicable of all B. Then the premiss D–B must remain unchanged,
30 but the quality of A–D must be changed; so that D–B is always true,
A–D always false. Such error is practically identical with that which
is inferred through the 'appropriate' middle. On the other hand,
(b) if the conclusion is not inferred through the 'appropriate'
middle—(i) when the middle is subordinate to A but is predicable of
35 no B, both premisses must be false, because if there is to be a conclusion both must be posited as asserting the contrary of what is
actually the fact, and so posited both become false: e. g. suppose that
actually all D is A but no B is D; then if these premisses are

changed in quality, a conclusion will follow and both of the new 40
premisses will be false. When, however, (ii) the middle D is not 81ᵃ
subordinate to A, A–D will be true, D–B false—A–D true because
A was not subordinate to D, D–B false because if it had been true,
the conclusion too would have been true; but it is *ex hypothesi* false.

When the erroneous inference is in the second figure, both prem- 5
isses cannot be entirely false; since if B is subordinate to A, there
can be no middle predicable of all of one extreme and of none of the
other as was stated before.[19] One premiss, however, may be false,
and it may be either of them. Thus, if C is actually an attribute
of both A and B, but is assumed to be an attribute of A only and 10
not of B, C–A will be true, C–B false: or again if C be assumed to
be attributable to B but to no A, C–B will be true, C–A false.

We have stated when and through what kinds of premisses error 15
will result in cases where the erroneous conclusion is negative. If
the conclusion is affirmative, (a) (i) it may be inferred through
the 'appropriate' middle term. In this case both premisses cannot
be false since, as we said before,[20] C–B must remain unchanged
if there is to be a conclusion, and consequently A–C, the quality of
which is changed, will always be false. This is equally true if (ii) the 20
middle is taken from another series of predication, as was stated to
be the case also with regard to negative error;[21] for D–B must remain
unchanged, while the quality of A–D must be converted, and the
type of error is the same as before.

(b) The middle may be inappropriate. Then (i) if D is subordi-' 25
nate to A, A–D will be true, but D–B false; since A may quite
well be predicable of several terms no one of which can be subordinated to another. If, however, (ii) D is not subordinate to A, obviously A–D, since it is affirmed, will always be false, while D–B
may be either true or false; for A may very well be an attribute of 30
no D, whereas all B is D, e. g. no science is animal, all music is
science. Equally well A may be an attribute of no D, and D of no
B. It emerges, then, that if the middle term is not subordinate to
the major, not only both premisses but either singly may be false.

Thus we have made it clear how many varieties of erroneous in- 35
ference are liable to happen and through what kinds of premisses
they occur, in the case both of immediate and of demonstrable truths.

18   It is also clear that the loss of any one of the senses entails the
loss of a corresponding portion of knowledge, and that, since we

---

[19] Cf. 80ᵃ 29.   [20] Cf. 80ᵇ 17–26.   [21] Cf. 80ᵇ 26–32.

learn either by induction or by demonstration, this knowledge can-
40 not be acquired. Thus demonstration develops from universals,
81ᵇ induction from particulars; but since it is possible to familiarize the
pupil with even the so-called mathematical abstractions only through
induction—i. e. only because each subject genus possesses, in virtue of
a determinate mathematical character, certain properties which can
be treated as separate even though they do not exist in isolation—
5 it is consequently impossible to come to grasp universals except
through induction. But induction is impossible for those who have
not sense-perception. For it is sense-perception alone which is adequate for grasping the particulars: they cannot be objects of scientific
knowledge, because neither can universals give us knowledge of them
without induction, nor can we get it through induction without sense-
perception.

10 **19** Every syllogism is effected by means of three terms. One kind
of syllogism serves to prove that A inheres in C by showing that
A inheres in B and B in C; the other is negative and one of its
premises asserts one term of another, while the other denies one
term of another. It is clear, then, that these are the fundamentals
15 and so-called hypotheses of syllogism. Assume them as they have
been stated, and proof is bound to follow—proof that A inheres in C
through B, and again that A inheres in B through some other middle
term, and similarly that B inheres in C. If our reasoning aims at
gaining credence and so is merely dialectical, it is obvious that we
have only to see that our inference is based on premises as credible
20 as possible: so that if a middle term between A and B is credible
though not real, one can reason through it and complete a dialectical
syllogism. If, however, one is aiming at truth, one must be guided
by the real connexions of subjects and attributes. Thus: since there
are attributes which are predicated of a subject essentially or natu-
25 rally and not coincidentally—not, that is, in a sense in which we
say 'That white (thing) is a man', which is not the same mode of
predication as when we say 'The man is white': the man is white not
because he is something else but because he is man, but the white is
man because 'being white' coincides with 'humanity' within one substratum—therefore there are terms such as are naturally subjects
30 of predicates. Suppose, then, C such a term not itself attributable to
anything else as to a subject, but the proximate subject of the attribute B—i. e. so that B–C is immediate; suppose further E related
immediately to F, and F to B. The first question is, must this series

terminate, or can it proceed to infinity? The second question is as
follows: Suppose nothing is essentially predicated of A, but A is
predicated primarily of H and of no intermediate prior term, and 35
suppose H similarly related to G and G to B; then must this series also
terminate, or can it too proceed to infinity? There is this much difference between the questions: the first is, is it possible to start from
that which is not itself attributable to anything else but is the subject
of attributes, and ascend to infinity? The second is the problem 40
whether one can start from that which is a predicate but not itself a 82ᵃ
subject of predicates, and descend to infinity? A third question is, if
the extreme terms are fixed, can there be an infinity of middles? I
mean this: suppose for example that A inheres in C and B is intermediate between them, but between B and A there are other middles, 5
and between these again fresh middles; can these proceed to infinity
or can they not? This is the equivalent of inquiring, do demonstrations
proceed to infinity, i. e. is everything demonstrable? Or do ultimate subject and primary attribute limit one another?

I hold that the same questions arise with regard to negative conclusions and premisses: viz. if A is attributable to no B, then either 10
this predication will be primary, or there will be an intermediate
term prior to B to which A is not attributable—G, let us say, which
is attributable to all B—and there may still be another term H prior
to G, which is attributable to all G. The same questions arise, I say,
because in these cases too either the series of prior terms to which A
is not attributable is infinite or it terminates.

One cannot ask the same questions in the case of reciprocating 15
terms, since when subject and predicate are convertible there is
neither primary nor ultimate subject, seeing that all the reciprocals
qua subjects stand in the same relation to one another, whether we
say that the subject has an infinity of attributes or that both subjects
and attributes—and we raised the question in both cases—are infinite
in number. These questions then cannot be asked—unless, indeed,
the terms can reciprocate by two different modes, by accidental
predication in one relation and natural predication in the other. 20

20   Now, it is clear that if the predications terminate in both the
upward and the downward direction (by 'upward' I mean the ascent
to the more universal, by 'downward' the descent to the more particular), the middle terms cannot be infinite in number. For suppose
that A is predicated of F, and that the intermediates—call them 25
$BB'B''$ . . . —are infinite, then clearly you might descend from A

and find one term predicated of another *ad infinitum,* since you have
an infinity of terms between you and F; and equally, if you ascend
from F, there are infinite terms between you and A. It follows that if
these processes are impossible there cannot be an infinity of inter-
30 mediates between A and F. Nor is it of any effect to urge that some
terms of the series AB . . . F are contiguous so as to exclude intermediates, while others cannot be taken into the argument at all:
whichever terms of the series B . . . I take, the number of intermediates in the direction either of A or of F must be finite or infinite: where
the infinite series starts, whether from the first term or from a later
35 one, is of no moment, for the succeeding terms in any case are infinite
in number.

21   Further, if in affirmative demonstration the series terminates
in both directions, clearly it will terminate too in negative demonstration. Let us assume that we cannot proceed to infinity either by ascending from the ultimate term (by 'ultimate term' I mean a term such
82ᵇ as F was, not itself attributable to a subject but itself the subject
of attributes), or by descending towards an ultimate from the primary
term (by 'primary term' I mean a term predicable of a subject but
not itself a subject [22]). If this assumption is justified, the series
will also terminate in the case of negation. For a negative conclusion
5 can be proved in all three figures. In the first figure it is proved thus:
no B is A, all C is B. In packing the interval B–C we must reach immediate propositions—as is always the case with the minor premiss—
since B–C is affirmative. As regards the other premiss it is plain that
if the major term is denied of a term D prior to B, D will have to be
10 predicable of all B, and if the major is denied of yet another term
prior to D, this term must be predicable of all D. Consequently,
since the ascending series is finite, the descent will also terminate
and there will be a subject of which A is primarily non-predicable.
In the second figure the syllogism is, all A is B, no C is B, .˙. no C is
A. If proof of this [23] is required, plainly it may be shown either in
15 the first figure as above, in the second as here, or in the third. The
first figure has been discussed, and we will proceed to display the
second, proof by which will be as follows: all B is D, no C is D . . . ,
since it is required that B should be a subject of which a predicate
is affirmed. Next, since D is to be proved not to belong to C, then D
has a further predicate which is denied of C. Therefore, since the

[22] *sc.* a predicate above which is no wider universal.   [23] *sc.* 'that no C is B'.

succession of predicates affirmed of an ever higher universal termi- 20
nates,[24] the succession of predicates denied terminates too.[25]

The third figure shows it as follows: all *B* is *A*, some *B* is not *C*,∴
some *A* is not *C*. This premiss, i. e. *C–B*, will be proved either in the
same figure or in one of the two figures discussed above. In the first 25
and second figures the series terminates. If we use the third figure,
we shall take as premisses, all *E* is *B*, some *E* is not *C*, and this premiss
again will be proved by a similar prosyllogism. But since it is assumed that the series of descending subjects also terminates, plainly
the series of more universal non-predicables will terminate also. Even
supposing that the proof is not confined to one method, but employs
them all and is now in the first figure, now in the second or third— 30
even so the regress will terminate, for the methods are finite in number, and if finite things are combined in a finite number of ways, the
result must be finite.

Thus it is plain that the regress of middles terminates in the case
of negative demonstration, if it does so also in the case of affirmative
demonstration. That in fact the regress terminates in both these cases
may be made clear by the following dialectical considerations. 35

22   In the case of predicates constituting the essential nature of a
thing, it clearly terminates, seeing that if definition is possible, or
in other words, if essential form is knowable, and an infinite series
cannot be traversed, predicates constituting a thing's essential nature
must be finite in number.[26] But as regards predicates generally we 83ᵃ
have the following prefatory remarks to make. (1) We can affirm
without falsehood 'the white (thing) is walking', and 'that big
(thing) is a log'; or again, 'the log is big', and 'the man walks'. But

---

[24] i. e. each of the successive prosyllogisms required to prove the negative
minors contains an affirmative major in which the middle is affirmed of a subject successively 'higher' or more universal than the subject of the first
syllogism. Thus:

Syllogism: All *B* is *D*	Prosyllogisms: All *D* is *E*	All *E* is *F*
No *C* is *D*	No *C* is *E*	No *C* is *F*
∴ No *C* is *B*	∴ No *C* is *D*	∴ No *C* is *E*

B, D, E, &c., are successively more universal subjects; and the series of affirmative
majors containing them must *ex hypothesi* terminate.

[25] Since the series of affirmative majors terminates and since an affirmative
major is required for each prosyllogism, we shall eventually reach a minor incapable of proof and therefore immediate.

[26] If the attributes in a series of predication such as we are discussing are substantial, they must be finite in number, because they are then the elements constituting the definition of a substance.

the affirmation differs in the two cases. When I affirm 'the white is a
5 log', I mean that something which happens to be white is a log—
not that white is the substratum in which log inheres, for it was not
qua white or *qua* a species of white that the white (thing) came to
be a log, and the white (thing) is consequently not a log except incidentally. On the other hand, when I affirm 'the log is white', I do
not mean that something else, which happens also to be a log, is
10 white (as I should if I said 'the musician is white', which would mean
'the man who happens also to be a musician is white'); on the contrary, log is here the substratum—the substratum which actually
came to be white, and did so *qua* wood or *qua* a species of wood and
qua nothing else.

If we must lay down a rule, let us entitle the latter kind of state-
15 ment predication, and the former not predication at all, or not strict
but accidental predication. 'White' and 'log' will thus serve as types
respectively of predicate and subject.

We shall assume, then, that the predicate is invariably predicated
20 strictly and not accidentally of the subject, for on such predication demonstrations depend for their force. It follows from this
that when a single attribute is predicated of a single subject, the
predicate must affirm of the subject either some element constituting
its essential nature, or that it is in some way qualified, quantified,
essentially related, active, passive, placed, or dated.[27]

(2) Predicates which signify substance signify that the subject
is identical with the predicate or with a species of the predicate.
25 Predicates not signifying substance which are predicated of a subject
not identical with themselves or with a species of themselves are
accidental or coincidental; e. g. white is a coincident of man, seeing
that man is not identical with white or a species of white, but rather
30 with animal, since man *is* identical with a species of animal. These
predicates which do not signify substance must be predicates of some
other subject, and nothing can be white which is not also other than
white. The Forms we can dispense with, for they are mere sound
without sense; and even if there are such things, they are not relevant

---

[27] The first of three statements preliminary to a proof that predicates which are
accidental—other than substantial—cannot be unlimited in number: Accidental
is to be distinguished from essential or natural predication [cf. i, ch. 4, 73^b 5 ff.
and *An. Pr.* i, ch. 25, 43^a 25–6]. The former is alien to demonstration: hence,
provided that a single attribute is predicated of a single subject, all genuine
predicates fall either under the category of substance or under one of the
adjectival categories.

to our discussion, since demonstrations are concerned with predicates such as we have defined.[28]   35

(3) If A is a quality of B, B cannot be a quality of A—a quality of a quality. Therefore A and B cannot be predicated reciprocally of one another in strict predication: they can be affirmed without falsehood of one another, but not genuinely predicated of each other.[29] For one alternative is that they should be substantially predicated of one another, i. e. B would become the genus or differentia of A—the predi-   83^{b} cate now become subject. But it has been shown that in these substantial predications neither the ascending predicates nor the descending subjects form an infinite series; e. g. neither the series, man is biped, biped is animal, &c., nor the series predicating animal of man, man of Callias, Callias of a further subject as an element of its essential nature, is infinite. For all such substance is definable, and an 5 infinite series cannot be traversed in thought: consequently neither the ascent nor the descent is infinite, since a substance whose predicates were infinite would not be definable. Hence they will not be predicated each as the genus of the other; for this would equate a genus with one of its own species. Nor (the other alternative) can a *quale* 10 be reciprocally predicated of a *quale*, nor any term belonging to an adjectival category of another such term, except by accidental predication; for all such predicates are coincidents and are predicated of substances.[30] On the other hand—in proof of the impossibility of an infinite ascending series—every predication displays the subject as somehow qualified or quantified or as characterized under one of the other adjectival categories, or else is an element in its substantial 15 nature: these latter are limited in number, and the number of the widest kinds under which predications fall is also limited, for every

[28] Second preliminary statement: The precise distinction of substantive from adjectival predication makes clear (implicitly) the two distinctions, (*a*) that between natural and accidental predication, (*b*) that between substantival and adjectival predication, which falls within natural predication. This enables us to reject the Platonic Forms.

[29] Third preliminary statement merging into the beginning of the proof proper: Reciprocal predication cannot produce an indefinite regress because it is not natural predication.

[30] Expansion of third preliminary statement: Reciprocals A and B might be predicated of one another (*a*) substantially; but it has been proved already that because a definition cannot contain an infinity of elements substantial predication cannot generate infinity; and it would disturb the relation of genus and species: (*b*) as *qualia* or *quanta* &c.; but this would be unnatural predication, because all such predicates are adjectival, i. e. accidents, or coincidents, of substances.

predication must exhibit its subject as somehow qualified, quantified, essentially related, acting or suffering, or in some place or at some time.[31]

I assume first that predication implies a single subject and a single attribute, and secondly that predicates which are not substantial are not predicated of one another. We assume this because such predicates are all coincidents, and though some are essential coinci-
20 dents, others of a different type, yet we maintain that all of them alike are predicated of some substratum and that a coincident is never a substratum—since we do not class as a coincident anything which does not owe its designation to its being something other than itself, but always hold that any coincident is predicated of some substratum other than itself, and that another group of coincidents may have a different substratum. Subject to these assumptions then,
25 neither the ascending nor the descending series of predication in which a single attribute is predicated of a single subject is infinite.[32] For the subjects of which coincidents are predicated are as many as the constitutive elements of each individual substance, and these we have seen are not infinite in number, while in the ascending series are contained those constitutive elements with their coincidents—both of which are finite.[33] We conclude that there is a given subject $<D>$ of which some attribute $<C>$ is primarily predicable; that there must be an attribute $<B>$ primarily predicable of the first
30 attribute, and that the series must end with a term $<A>$ not predic-

---

[31] The ascent of predicates is also finite; because all predicates fall under one or other of the categories, and (a) the series of predicates under each category terminates when the category is reached, and (b) the number of the categories is limited. [(a) seems to mean that an attribute as well as a substance is definable by genus and differentia, and the elements in its definition must terminate in an upward direction at the category, and can therefore no more form an infinite series than can the elements constituting the definition of a substance.]

[32] To reinforce this brief proof that descent and ascent are both finite we may repeat the premises on which it depends. These are (1) the assumption that predication means the predication of one attribute of one subject, and (2) our proof that accidents cannot be reciprocally predicated of one another, because that would be unnatural predication. It follows from these premises that both ascent and descent are finite. [Actually (2) only reinforces the proof that the *descent* terminates.]

[33] To repeat again the proof that both ascent and descent are finite: The subjects cannot be more in number than the constituents of a definable form, and these, we know, are not infinite in number: hence the descent is finite. The series regarded as an ascent contains subjects and ever more universal accidents, and neither subjects nor accidents are infinite in number.

able of any term prior to the last subject of which it was predicated
$<B>$, and of which no term prior to it is predicable.[34]

The argument we have given is one of the so-called proofs; an
alternative proof follows. Predicates so related to their subjects that
there are other predicates prior to them predicable of those subjects
are demonstrable; but of demonstrable propositions one cannot have
something better than knowledge, nor can one know them without 35
demonstration. Secondly, if a consequent is only known through an
antecedent (viz. premisses prior to it) and we neither know this antecedent nor have something better than knowledge of it, then we
shall not have scientific knowledge of the consequent. Therefore, if
it is possible through demonstration to know anything without qualification and not merely as dependent on the acceptance of certain
premisses—i. e. hypothetically—the series of intermediate predications must terminate. If it does not terminate, and beyond any predi- 84ᵃ
cate taken as higher than another there remains another still higher,
then every predicate is demonstrable. Consequently, since these
demonstrable predicates are infinite in number and therefore can-

[34] Formal restatement of the last conclusion. [This is obscure: apparently
Aristotle here contemplates a hybrid series: category, accident, further specified accident . . . substantial genus, subgenus . . . *infima species*, individual
substance.

If this interpretation of the first portion of the chapter is at all correct, Aristotle's first proof that the first two questions of ch. 19 must be answered in the
negative is roughly as follows: The ultimate subject of all judgement is an
individual substance, a concrete singular. Of such concrete singulars you can
predicate substantially only the elements constituting their *infima species*.
These are limited in number because they form an intelligible synthesis. So far,
then, as substantial predicates are concerned, the questions are answered.
But these elements are also the subjects of which accidents, or coincidents,
are predicated, and therefore as regards accidental predicates, at any rate,
the descending series of subjects terminates. The ascending series of attributes
also terminates, (1) because each higher attribute in the series can only be a
higher genus of the accident predicated of the ultimate subject of its genus,
and therefore an element in the accident's definition; (2) because the number
of the categories is limited.

We may note that the first argument seems to envisage a series which, viewed
as an ascent, starts with a concrete individual of which the elements of its
definition are predicated successively, specific differentia being followed by
proximate genus, which latter is the starting-point of a succession of ever more
universal attributes terminating in a category; and that the second argument
extends the scope of the dispute to the sum total of all the trains of accidental
predication which one concrete singular substance can beget. It is, as so often
in Aristotle, difficult to be sure whether he is regarding the *infima species* or the
concrete singular as the ultimate subject of judgement. I have assumed that he
means the latter.]

not be traversed, we shall *not* know them by demonstration. If,
therefore, we have not something better than knowledge of them,
5 we cannot through demonstration have unqualified but only hypothetical science of anything.[35]

As dialectical proofs of our contention these may carry conviction,
but an analytic process will show more briefly that neither the ascent
nor the descent of predication can be infinite in the demonstrative
10 sciences which are the object of our investigation. Demonstration
proves the inherence of essential attributes in things. Now attributes
may be essential for two reasons: either because they are elements
in the essential nature of their subjects, or because their subjects
are elements in their essential nature. An example of the latter is
15 odd as an attribute of number—though it is number's attribute, yet
number itself is an element in the definition of odd; of the former,
multiplicity or the indivisible, which are elements in the definition of
number. In neither kind of attribution can the terms be infinite. They
are not infinite where each is related to the term below it as odd
is to number, for this would mean the inherence in odd of another
20 attribute of odd in whose nature odd was an essential element: but
then number will be an ultimate subject of the whole infinite chain of
attributes, and be an element in the definition of each of them. Hence,
since an infinity of attributes such as contain their subject in their
definition cannot inhere in a single thing, the ascending series is
equally finite.[36] Note, moreover, that all such attributes must so
inhere in the ultimate subject—e. g. its attributes in number and
number in them—as to be commensurate with the subject and not
25 of wider extent. Attributes which are essential elements in the
nature of their subjects are equally finite: otherwise definition would

[35] The former proof was dialectical. So is that which follows in this paragraph. If a predicate inheres in a subject but is subordinate to a higher predicate also predicable of that subject [i. e. not to a wider predicate but to a middle
term giving logically prior premisses and in that sense higher], then the inherence
can be known by demonstration and only by demonstration. But that means that
it is known as the consequent of an antecedent. Therefore, if demonstration
gives genuine knowledge, the series must terminate; i. e. every predicate is
demonstrable and known only as a consequent and therefore hypothetically,
unless an antecedent known *per se* is reached.

[36] As regards type (2) [the opening of the chapter has disposed of type (1)]:
in any series of such predicates any given term will contain in its definition all
the lower terms, and the series will therefore terminate at the bottom in the
ultimate subject. But since every term down to and including the ultimate subject
is contained in the definition of any given term, if the series ascend infinitely
there must be a term containing an infinity of terms in its definition. But this
is impossible, and therefore the ascent terminates.

be impossible. Hence, if all the attributes predicated are essential and these cannot be infinite, the ascending series will terminate, and consequently the descending series too.[37]

If this is so, it follows that the intermediates between any two terms are also always limited in number.[38] An immediately obvious consequence of this is that demonstrations necessarily involve basic 30 truths, and that the contention of some—referred to at the outset— that all truths are demonstrable is mistaken. For if there are basic truths, (a) not all truths are demonstrable, and (b) an infinite regress is impossible; since if either (a) or (b) were not a fact, it would mean that no interval was immediate and indivisible, but that all intervals were divisible. This is true because a conclusion is 35 demonstrated by the interposition, not the apposition, of a fresh term. If such interposition could continue to infinity there might be an infinite number of terms between any two terms; but this is impossible if both the ascending and descending series of predication 84[b] terminate; and of this fact, which before was shown dialectically, analytic proof has now been given.[39]

23   It is an evident corollary of these conclusions that if the same attribute A inheres in two terms C and D predicable either not at all, or not of all instances, of one another, it does not always belong to 5 them in virtue of a common middle term. Isosceles and scalene possess the attribute of having their angles equal to two right angles in virtue of a common middle; for they possess it in so far as they are both a certain kind of figure, and not in so far as they differ from one another. But this is not always the case; for, were it so, if we take B as the common middle in virtue of which A inheres in C and D,

---

[37] Note too that either type of essential attribute must be commensurate with its subject, because the first defines, the second is defined by, its subject; and consequently no subject can possess an infinite number of essential predicates of either type, or definition would be impossible. Hence if the attributes predicated are all essential, the series terminates in both directions. [This passage merely displays the ground underlying the previous argument that the ascent of attributes of type (2) is finite, and notes in passing its more obvious and already stated application to attributes of type (1).]

[38] It follows that the intermediates between a given subject and a given attribute must also be limited in number.

[39] Corollary: (a) demonstrations necessarily involve basic truths, and therefore (b) not all truths, as we saw [84[a] 32] that some maintain, are demonstrable [cf. 72[b] 6]. If either (a) or (b) were not a fact, since conclusions are demonstrated by the interposition of a middle and not by the apposition of an extreme term [cf. note on 78[a] 15], no premiss would be an immediate indivisible interval. This closes the analytic argument.

10 clearly *B* would inhere in *C* and *D* through a second common middle,
and this in turn would inhere in *C* and *D* through a third, so that
between two terms an infinity of intermediates would fall—an impossibility. Thus it need not always be in virtue of a common middle
term that a single attribute inheres in several subjects, since there
15 must be immediate intervals. Yet if the attribute to be proved common
to two subjects is to be one of their essential attributes, the middle
terms involved must be within one subject genus and be derived from
the same group of immediate premises; for we have seen that
processes of proof cannot pass from one genus to another.[40]

It is also clear that when *A* inheres in *B*, this can be demonstrated
20 if there is a middle term. Further, the 'elements' of such a conclusion are the premises containing the middle in question, and they
are identical in number with the middle terms, seeing that the
immediate propositions—or at least such immediate propositions as are
universal—are the 'elements'. If, on the other hand, there is no
middle term, demonstration ceases to be possible: we are on the way
to the basic truths. Similarly if *A* does not inhere in *B*, this can be
25 demonstrated if there is a middle term or a term prior to *B* in which
A does not inhere: otherwise there is no demonstration and a basic
truth is reached. There are, moreover, as many 'elements' of the
demonstrated conclusion as there are middle terms, since it is propositions containing these middle terms that are the basic premises on
which the demonstration rests; and as there are some indemonstrable
basic truths asserting that 'this is that' or that 'this inheres in that',
30 so there are others denying that 'this is that' or that 'this inheres
in that'—in fact some basic truths will affirm and some will deny being.

When we are to prove a conclusion, we must take a primary essential predicate—suppose it *C*—of the subject *B*, and then suppose *A*
similarly predicable of *C*. If we proceed in this manner, no proposition or attribute which falls beyond *A* is admitted in the proof:
the interval is constantly condensed until subject and predicate
35 become indivisible, i. e. one. We have our unit when the premiss becomes immediate, since the immediate premiss alone is a single premiss in the unqualified sense of 'single'. And as in other spheres
the basic element is simple but not identical in all—in a system of
weight it is the mina, in music the quarter-tone, and so on—so in
85ᵃ syllogism the unit is an immediate premiss, and in the knowledge
that demonstration gives it is an intuition. In syllogisms, then, which
prove the inherence of an attribute, nothing falls outside the major
term. In the case of negative syllogisms on the other hand, (1) in

40 i, ch. 7.

the first figure nothing falls outside the major term whose inherence is in question; e. g. to prove through a middle C that A does not inhere in B the premises required are, all B is C, no C is A. Then if it has to be proved that no C is A, a middle must be found between A and C; and this procedure will never vary.

(2) If we have to show that E is not D by means of the premises, all D is C; no E, or not all E,[41] is C; then the middle will never fall beyond E, and E is the subject of which D is to be denied in the conclusion.

(3) In the third figure the middle will never fall beyond the limits of the subject and the attribute denied of it.

24 Since demonstrations may be either commensurately universal or particular,[42] and either affirmative or negative; the question arises, which form is the better? And the same question may be put in regard to so-called 'direct' demonstration and *reductio ad impossibile*. Let us first examine the commensurately universal and the particular forms, and when we have cleared up this problem proceed to discuss 'direct' demonstration and *reductio ad impossibile*.

The following considerations might lead some minds to prefer particular demonstration.

(1) The superior demonstration is the demonstration which gives us greater knowledge (for this is the ideal of demonstration), and we have greater knowledge of a particular individual when we know it in itself than when we know it through something else; e. g. we know Coriscus the musician better when we know that Coriscus is musical than when we know only that man is musical, and a like argument holds in all other cases. But commensurately universal demonstration, instead of proving that the subject itself actually is x, proves only that something else is x—e. g. in attempting to prove that isosceles is x, it proves not that isosceles but only that triangle is x—whereas particular demonstration proves that the subject itself is x. The demonstration, then, that a subject, as such, possesses an attribute is superior. If this is so, and if the particular rather than the commensurately universal form so demonstrates, particular demonstration is superior.

(2) The universal has not a separate being over against groups of singulars. Demonstration nevertheless creates the opinion that its function is conditioned by something like this—some separate entity

[41] Second figure, Camestres or Baroco.

[42] The distinction is that of whole and part, genus and species; not that of universal and singular.

belonging to the real world; that, for instance, of triangle or of
35 figure or number, over against particular triangles, figures, and
numbers. But demonstration which touches the real and will not mislead is superior to that which moves among unrealities and is delu-
sory. Now commensurately universal demonstration is of the latter
kind: if we engage in it we find ourselves reasoning after a fashion
well illustrated by the argument that the proportionate is what answers
to the definition of some entity which is neither line, number, solid,
85ᵇ nor plane, but a proportionate apart from all these. Since, then, such
a proof is characteristically commensurate and universal, and less
touches reality than does particular demonstration, and creates a
false opinion, it will follow that commensurate and universal is inferior to particular demonstration.

We may retort thus. (1) The first argument applies no more to
commensurate and universal than to particular demonstration. If
5 equality to two right angles is attributable to its subject not *qua*
isosceles but *qua* triangle, he who knows that isosceles possesses that
attribute knows the subject as *qua* itself possessing the attribute, to
a less degree than he who knows that triangle has that attribute.
To sum up the whole matter: if a subject is proved to possess *qua*
triangle an attribute which it does not in fact possess *qua* triangle,
that is not demonstration: but if it does possess it *qua* triangle, the
rule applies that the greater knowledge is his who knows the subject
as possessing its attribute *qua* that in virtue of which it actually does
10 possess it. Since, then, triangle is the wider term, and there is one
identical definition of triangle—i. e. the term is not equivocal—and
since equality to two right angles belongs to all triangles, it is
isosceles *qua* triangle and not triangle *qua* isosceles which has its
angles so related. It follows that he who knows a connexion universally
has greater knowledge of it as it in fact is than he who knows the
particular; and the inference is that commensurate and universal is
15 superior to particular demonstration. (2) If there is a single identical
definition—i. e. if the commensurate universal is unequivocal—then
the universal will possess being not less but more than some of the
particulars, inasmuch as it is universals which comprise the imperishable, particulars that tend to perish.

(3) Because the universal has a single meaning, we are not therefore compelled to suppose that in these examples it has being as
a substance apart from its particulars—any more than we need make
a similar supposition in the other cases of unequivocal universal
predication, viz. where the predicate signifies not substance but

quality, essential relatedness, or action. If such a supposition is enter- 20
tained, the blame rests not with the demonstration but with the
hearer.

(4) Demonstration is syllogism that proves the cause, i. e. the
reasoned fact, and it is rather the commensurate universal than the
particular which is causative (as may be shown thus: that which
possesses an attribute through its own essential nature is itself the 25
cause of the inherence, and the commensurate universal is primary; [43]
hence the commensurate universal is the cause). Consequently commensurately universal demonstration is superior as more especially
proving the cause, that is the reasoned fact.

(5) Our search for the reason ceases, and we think that we know,
when the coming to be or existence of the fact before us is not due to
the coming to be or existence of some other fact, for the last step of a
search thus conducted is *eo ipso* the end and limit of the problem. 30
Thus: 'Why did he come?' 'To get the money—wherewith to pay a
debt—that he might thereby do what was right.' When in this regress
we can no longer find an efficient or final cause, we regard the last
step of it as the end of the coming—or being or coming to be—and
we regard ourselves as then only having full knowledge of the reason
why he came.

If, then, all causes and reasons are alike in this respect, and if this 35
is the means to full knowledge in the case of final causes such as
we have exemplified, it follows that in the case of the other causes
also full knowledge is attained when an attribute no longer inheres
because of something else. Thus, when we learn that exterior angles
are equal to four right angles because they are the exterior angles of
an isosceles, there still remains the question 'Why has isosceles this
attribute?' and its answer 'Because it is a triangle, and a triangle has 86ᵃ
it because a triangle is a rectilinear figure.' If rectilinear figure possesses the property for no further reason,[44] at this point we have full
knowledge—but at this point our knowledge has become commensurately universal, and so we conclude that commensurately
universal demonstration is superior.

(6) The more demonstration becomes particular the more it sinks
into an indeterminate manifold, while universal demonstration tends
to the simple and determinate. But objects so far as they are an 5
indeterminate manifold are unintelligible, so far as they are determinate, intelligible: they are therefore intelligible rather in so far as
they are universal than in so far as they are particular. From this it

---

[43] And therefore also essential; cf. i, ch. 4, 73ᵇ 26 ff.
[44] i. e. for no reason other than its own nature.

follows that universals are more demonstrable: but since relative and correlative increase concomitantly, of the more demonstrable there will be fuller demonstration. Hence the commensurate and universal
10 form, being more truly demonstration, is the superior.

(7) Demonstration which teaches two things is preferable to demonstration which teaches only one. He who possesses commensurately universal demonstration knows the particular as well, but he who possesses particular demonstration does not know the universal. So that this is an additional reason for preferring commensurately universal demonstration. And there is yet this further argument:

(8) Proof becomes more and more proof of the commensurate universal as its middle term approaches nearer to the basic truth, and
15 nothing is so near as the immediate premiss which is itself the basic truth. If, then, proof from the basic truth is more accurate than proof not so derived, demonstration which depends more closely on it is more accurate than demonstration which is less closely dependent. But commensurately universal demonstration is characterized by this closer dependence, and is therefore superior. Thus, if A had to be proved to inhere in D, and the middles were B and C, B being the
20 higher term would render the demonstration which it mediated the more universal.

Some of these arguments, however, are dialectical. The clearest indication of the precedence of commensurately universal demonstration is as follows: if of two propositions, a prior and a posterior, we have a grasp of the prior, we have a kind of knowledge—a potential grasp—of the posterior as well. For example, if one knows that
25 the angles of all triangles are equal to two right angles, one knows in a sense—potentially—that the isosceles' angles also are equal to two right angles, even if one does not know that the isosceles is a triangle; but to grasp this posterior proposition is by no means to know the commensurate universal either potentially or actually. Moreover, commensurately universal demonstration is through and through intelligible; particular demonstration issues in sense-perception.
30

25 The preceding arguments constitute our defence of the superiority of commensurately universal to particular demonstration. That affirmative demonstration excels negative may be shown as follows.

(1) We may assume the superiority *ceteris paribus* of the demonstration which derives from fewer postulates or hypotheses—in short
35 from fewer premisses; for, given that all these are equally well known, where they are fewer knowledge will be more speedily acquired, and that is a desideratum. The argument implied in our contention that

demonstration from fewer assumptions is superior may be set out in universal form as follows. Assuming that in both cases alike the middle terms are known, and that middles which are prior are better known than such as are posterior, we may suppose two demonstrations of the inherence of A in E, the one proving it through the middles 86ᵇ B, C and D, the other through F and G. Then $A-D$ is known to the same degree as $A-E$ (in the second proof), but $A-D$ is better known than and prior to $A-E$ (in the first proof); since $A-E$ is proved through $A-D$, and the ground is more certain than the conclusion.

Hence demonstration by fewer premisses is *ceteris paribus* supe- 5 rior. Now both affirmative and negative demonstration operate through three terms and two premisses, but whereas the former assumes only that something is, the latter assumes both that something is and that something else is not, and thus operating through more kinds of premiss is inferior.

(2) It has been proved [45] that no conclusion follows if both prem- 10 isses are negative, but that one must be negative, the other affirmative. So we are compelled to lay down the following additional rule: as the demonstration expands, the affirmative premisses must increase in number, but there cannot be more than one negative premiss in 15 each complete proof.[46] Thus, suppose no B is A, and all C is B. Then, if both the premisses are to be again expanded, a middle must be interposed. Let us interpose D between A and B, and E between B and C. Then clearly E is affirmatively related to B and C, while D is 20 affirmatively related to B but negatively to A; for all B is D, but there must be no D which is A. Thus there proves to be a single negative premiss, $A-D$. In the further prosyllogisms too it is the same, because in the terms of an affirmative syllogism the middle is always related affirmatively to both extremes; in a negative syllogism it must be negatively related only to one of them, and so this negation 25 comes to be a single negative premiss, the other premisses being affirmative. If, then, that through which a truth is proved is a better known and more certain truth, and if the negative proposition is proved through the affirmative and not vice versa, affirmative demonstration, being prior and better known and more certain, will be superior.

(3) The basic truth of demonstrative syllogism is the universal 30 immediate premiss, and the universal premiss asserts in affirmative demonstration and in negative denies: and the affirmative proposition is prior to and better known than the negative (since affirmation

[45] *An. Pr.* i, ch. 7.
[46] i. e. in one syllogism and two prosyllogisms proving its premisses.

35 explains denial and is prior to denial, just as being is prior to not-being). It follows that the basic premiss of affirmative demonstration is superior to that of negative demonstration, and the demonstration which uses superior basic premisses is superior.

(4) Affirmative demonstration is more of the nature of a basic form of proof, because it is a *sine qua non* of negative demonstration.

87ᵃ 26 Since affirmative demonstration is superior to negative, it is clearly superior also to *reductio ad impossibile*. We must first make certain what is the difference between negative demonstration and *reductio ad impossibile*. Let us suppose that no B is A, and that all 5 C is B: the conclusion necessarily follows that no C is A. If these premisses are assumed, therefore, the negative demonstration that no C is A is direct. *Reductio ad impossibile*, on the other hand, proceeds as follows: Supposing we are to prove that A does not inhere in B, we have to assume that it does inhere, and further that B inheres in C, with the resulting inference that A inheres in C. This we have 10 to suppose a known and admitted impossibility; and we then infer that A cannot inhere in B. Thus if the inherence of B in C is not questioned, A's inherence in B is impossible.

The order of the terms is the same in both proofs: they differ according to which of the negative propositions is the better known, the one denying A of B or the one denying A of C. When the falsity 15 of the conclusion ⁴⁷ is the better known, we use *reductio ad impossibile*; when the major premiss of the syllogism is the more obvious, we use direct demonstration. All the same the proposition denying A of B is, in the order of being, prior to that denying A of C; for premisses are prior to the conclusion which follows from them, and 'no C is A' is the conclusion, 'no B is A' one of its premisses. For the 20 destructive result of *reductio ad impossibile* is not a proper conclusion, nor are its antecedents proper premisses. On the contrary: the constituents of syllogism are premisses related to one another as whole to part or part to whole, whereas the premisses A–C and A–B are not 25 thus related to one another. Now the superior demonstration is that which proceeds from better known and prior premisses, and while both these forms depend for credence on the not-being of something, yet the source of the one is prior to that of the other. Therefore negative demonstration will have an unqualified superiority to *reductio ad impossibile*, and affirmative demonstration, being superior to 30 negative, will consequently be superior also to *reductio ad impossibile*.

⁴⁷ i. e. the impossibility of A–C, the conclusion of the hypothetical syllogism.

27   The science which is knowledge at once of the fact and of the reasoned fact, not of the fact by itself without the reasoned fact, is the more exact and the prior science.

A science such as arithmetic, which is not a science of properties *qua* inhering in a substratum, is more exact than and prior to a science like harmonics, which is a science of properties inhering in a substratum; and similarly a science like arithmetic, which is constituted of fewer basic elements, is more exact than and prior to geometry, which requires additional elements. What I mean by 'additional ele- 35 ments' is this: a unit is substance without position, while a point is substance with position; the latter contains an additional element.

28   A single science is one whose domain is a single genus, viz. all the subjects constituted out of the primary entities of the genus—i. e. the parts of this total subject—and their essential properties.

One science differs from another when their basic truths have neither a common source nor are derived those of the one science from those of the other. This is verified when we reach the indemonstrable 87ᵇ premisses of a science, for they must be within one genus with its conclusions: and this again is verified if the conclusions proved by means of them fall within one genus—i. e. are homogeneous.

29   One can have several demonstrations of the same connexion 5 not only by taking from the same series of predication middles which are other than the immediately cohering term—e. g. by taking $C, D,$ and F severally to prove $A–B$—but also by taking a middle from another series. Thus let A be change, D alteration of a property, B feeling pleasure, and G relaxation. We can then without falsehood predicate D of B and A of D, for he who is pleased suffers alteration 10 of a property, and that which alters a property changes. Again, we can predicate A of G without falsehood, and G of B; for to feel pleasure is to relax, and to relax is to change. So the conclusion can be drawn through middles which are different, i. e. not in the same series—yet not so that neither of these middles is predicable of the other, for they must both be attributable to some one subject.   15

A further point worth investigating is how many ways of proving the same conclusion can be obtained by varying the figure.

30   There is no knowledge by demonstration of chance conjunctions; for chance conjunctions exist neither by necessity nor as general con- 20 nexions but comprise what comes to be as something distinct from these. Now demonstration is concerned only with one or other of

these two; for all reasoning proceeds from necessary or general premisses, the conclusion being necessary if the premises are necessary
25 and general if the premises are general. Consequently, if chance
conjunctions are neither general nor necessary, they are not demonstrable.

31 Scientific knowledge is not possible through the act of perception. Even if perception as a faculty is of 'the such' and not merely
of a 'this somewhat', yet one must at any rate actually perceive a
30 'this somewhat', and at a definite present place and time: but that
which is commensurately universal and true in all cases one cannot
perceive, since it is not 'this' and it is not 'now'; if it were, it would
not be commensurately universal—the term we apply to what is
always and everywhere. Seeing, therefore, that demonstrations are
commensurately universal and universals imperceptible, we clearly
cannot obtain scientific knowledge by the act of perception: nay, it
35 is obvious that even if it were possible to perceive that a triangle has
its angles equal to two right angles, we should still be looking for a
demonstration—we should not (as some [48] say) possess knowledge
of it; for perception must be of a particular, whereas scientific
knowledge involves the recognition of the commensurate universal.
So if we were on the moon, and saw the earth shutting out the sun's
40 light, we should not know the cause of the eclipse: we should per-
88ᵃ ceive the present fact of the eclipse, but not the reasoned fact at all,
since the act of perception is not of the commensurate universal. I
do not, of course, deny that by watching the frequent recurrence of
this event we might, after tracking the commensurate universal, possess a demonstration, for the commensurate universal is elicited from
the several groups of singulars.
5 The commensurate universal is precious because it makes clear
the cause; so that in the case of facts like these which have a cause
other than themselves universal knowledge [49] is more precious than
sense-perceptions and than intuition. (As regards primary truths there
is of course a different account to be given.[50]) Hence it is clear that
knowledge of things demonstrable cannot be acquired by percep-
10 tion, unless the term perception is applied to the possession of scientific knowledge through demonstration. Nevertheless certain points
do arise with regard to connexions to be proved which are referred
for their explanation to a failure in sense-perception: there are cases

[48] Protagoras is perhaps referred to.
[49] i. e. demonstration through the commensurate universal.
[50] Cf. e. g. 100ᵇ 12.

when an act of vision would terminate our inquiry, not because in seeing we should be knowing, but because we should have elicited the universal from seeing; if, for example, we saw the pores in the glass and the light passing through, the reason of the kindling would be 15 clear to us [51] because we should at the same time see it in each instance and intuit that it must be so in all instances.

32   All syllogisms cannot have the same basic truths. This may be shown first of all by the following dialectical considerations. (1) Some syllogisms are true and some false: for though a true inference 20 is possible from false premises, yet this occurs once only—I mean if A, for instance, is truly predicable of C, but B, the middle, is false, both A–B and B–C being false; nevertheless, if middles are taken to prove these premises, they will be false because every conclusion which is a falsehood has false premises, while true conclusions have 25 true premises, and false and true differ in kind. Then again, (2) falsehoods are not all derived from a single identical set of principles: there are falsehoods which are the contraries of one another and cannot coexist, e. g. 'justice is injustice', and 'justice is cowardice'; 'man is horse', and 'man is ox'; 'the equal is greater', and 'the equal is less'. From our established principles we may argue the case as follows, 30 confining ourselves therefore to true conclusions. Not even all these are inferred from the same basic truths; many of them in fact have basic truths which differ generically and are not transferable; units, for instance, which are without position, cannot take the place of points, which have position. The transferred terms could only fit in as middle terms or as major or minor terms, or else have some of the 35 other terms between them, others outside them.

Nor can any of the common axioms—such, I mean, as the law of excluded middle—serve as premises for the proof of all conclusions. For the kinds of being are different, and some attributes attach to 88^b quanta and some to qualia only; and proof is achieved by means of the common axioms taken in conjunction with these several kinds and their attributes.

Again, it is not true that the basic truths are much fewer than the conclusions, for the basic truths are the premises, and the premises 5 are formed by the apposition of a fresh extreme term or the interposition of a fresh middle. Moreover, the number of conclusions is indefinite, though the number of middle terms is finite; and lastly some of the basic truths are necessary, others variable.

[51] A theory of the concentration of rays through a burning-glass which was not Aristotle's.

Looking at it in this way we see that, since the number of conclusions is indefinite, the basic truth cannot be identical or limited in
10 number. If, on the other hand, identity is used in another sense, and it is said, e. g., 'these and no other are the fundamental truths of geometry, these the fundamentals of calculation, these again of medicine'; would the statement mean anything except that the sciences have basic truths? To call them identical because they are self-identical is absurd, since everything can be identified with every-
15 thing in that sense of identity. Nor again can the contention that all conclusions have the same basic truths mean that from the mass of all possible premises any conclusion may be drawn. That would be exceedingly naïve, for it is not the case in the clearly evident mathematical sciences, nor is it possible in analysis, since it is the immediate premises which are the basic truths, and a fresh conclusion is only
20 formed by the addition of a new immediate premiss: but if it be admitted that it is these primary immediate premises which are basic truths, each subject-genus will provide one basic truth. If, however, it is not argued that from the mass of all possible premises any conclusion may be proved, nor yet admitted that basic truths differ so as to be generically different for each science, it remains to consider the possibility that, while the basic truths of all knowledge are within one genus, special premises are required to prove special conclusions.
25 But that this cannot be the case has been shown by our proof that the basic truths of things generically different themselves differ generically. For fundamental truths are of two kinds, those which are premisses of demonstration and the subject-genus; and though the former are common, the latter—number, for instance, and magnitude—-are peculiar.

30 **33** Scientific knowledge and its object differ from opinion and the object of opinion in that scientific knowledge is commensurately universal and proceeds by necessary connexions, and that which is necessary cannot be otherwise. So though there are things which are true and real and yet can be otherwise, *scientific knowledge* clearly does not concern them; if it did, things which can be otherwise would be
35 incapable of being otherwise. Nor are they any concern of *rational intuition*—by rational intuition I mean an originative source of scientific knowledge—nor of indemonstrable knowledge, which is the
89ᵃ grasping of the immediate premiss. Since then rational intuition, science, and opinion, and what is revealed by these terms, are the only things that can be 'true', it follows that it is *opinion* that is concerned with that which may be true or false, and can be otherwise:

opinion in fact is the grasp of a premiss which is immediate but
not necessary. This view also fits the observed facts, for opinion is 5
unstable, and so is the kind of being we have described as its object.
Besides, when a man thinks a truth incapable of being otherwise he
always thinks that he knows it, never that he opines it. He thinks that
he opines when he thinks that a connexion, though actually so, may
quite easily be otherwise; for he believes that such is the proper
object of opinion, while the necessary is the object of knowledge.   10

In what sense, then, can the same thing be the object of both opinion and knowledge? And if any one chooses to maintain that all that
he knows he can also opine, why should not opinion be knowledge?
For he that knows and he that opines will follow the same train of
thought through the same middle terms until the immediate premisses
are reached; because it is possible to opine not only the fact but also 15
the reasoned fact, and the reason is the middle term; so that, since the
former knows, he that opines also has knowledge.

The truth perhaps is that if a man grasp truths that cannot be
other than they are, in the way in which he grasps the definitions
through which demonstrations take place, he will have not opinion
but knowledge: if on the other hand he apprehends these attributes
as inhering in their subjects, but not in virtue of the subjects' substance and essential nature, he possesses opinion and not genuine 20
knowledge; and his opinion, if obtained through immediate premisses,
will be both of the fact and of the reasoned fact; if not so obtained,
of the fact alone. The object of opinion and knowledge is not quite
identical; it is only in a sense identical, just as the object of true and
false opinion is in a sense identical. The sense in which some main- 25
tain that true and false opinion can have the same object leads them
to embrace many strange doctrines, particularly the doctrine that what
a man opines falsely he does not opine at all. There are really many
senses of 'identical', and in one sense the object of true and false
opinion can be the same, in another it cannot. Thus, to have a true
opinion that the diagonal is commensurate with the side would be 30
absurd: but because the diagonal with which they are both concerned
is the same, the two opinions have objects so far the same: on the
other hand, as regards their essential definable nature these objects
differ. The identity of the objects of knowledge and opinion is similar.
Knowledge is the apprehension of, e. g. the attribute 'animal' as
incapable of being otherwise, opinion the apprehension of 'animal'
as capable of being otherwise—e. g. the apprehension that animal is 35
an element in the essential nature of man is knowledge; the apprehension of animal as predicable of man but not as an element in

man's essential nature is opinion: man is the subject in both judgments, but the mode of inherence differs.

This also shows that one cannot opine and know the same thing simultaneously; for then one would apprehend the same thing as both capable and incapable of being otherwise—an impossibility. 89ᵇ Knowledge and opinion of the same thing can coexist in two different people in the sense we have explained, but not simultaneously in the same person. That would involve a man's simultaneously apprehending, e.g., (1) that man is essentially animal—i.e. cannot be other than animal—and (2) that man is not essentially animal, that 5 is, we may assume, may be other than animal.

Further consideration of modes of thinking and their distribution under the heads of discursive thought, intuition, science, art, practical wisdom, and metaphysical thinking, belongs rather partly to natural science, partly to moral philosophy.

10 **34**   Quick wit is a faculty of hitting upon the middle term instantaneously. It would be exemplified by a man who saw that the moon has her bright side always turned towards the sun, and quickly grasped the cause of this, namely that she borrows her light from him; or observed somebody in conversation with a man of wealth and divined that he was borrowing money, or that the friendship of these people sprang from a common enmity. In all these instances he has 15 seen the major and minor terms and then grasped the causes, the middle terms.

Let A represent 'bright side turned sunward', B 'lighted from the sun', C the moon. Then B, 'lighted from the sun', is predicable of C, the moon, and A, 'having her bright side towards the source of her 20 light', is predicable of B. So A is predicable of C through B.

BOOK II

1   The kinds of question we ask are as many as the kinds of things which we know. They are in fact four:—(1) whether the connexion of an attribute with a thing is a fact, (2) what is the reason of the 25 connexion, (3) whether a thing exists, (4) what is the nature of the thing. Thus, when our question concerns a complex of thing and attribute and we ask whether the thing is thus or otherwise qualified—whether, e.g., the sun suffers eclipse or not—then we are asking as to the fact of a connexion. That our inquiry ceases with the discovery that the sun does suffer eclipse is an indication of this; and if we know from the start that the sun suffers eclipse, we do not inquire whether it does so or not. On the other hand, when we know the fact we ask the reason; as, for example, when we know that the sun is being eclipsed and that an earthquake is in progress, it is the reason of eclipse or earthquake into which we inquire. 30

Where a complex is concerned, then, those are the two questions we ask; but for some objects of inquiry we have a different kind of question to ask, such as whether there is or is not a centaur or a God. (By 'is or is not' I mean 'is or is not, without further qualification'; as opposed to 'is or is not (e.g.) white'.) On the other hand, when we have ascertained the thing's existence, we inquire as to its nature, asking, for instance, 'what, then, is God?' or 'what is man?' 35

2   These, then, are the four kinds of question we ask, and it is in the answers to these questions that our knowledge consists.

Now when we ask whether a connexion is a fact, or whether a thing without qualification *is*, we are really asking whether the connexion or the thing has a 'middle'; and when we have ascertained either that the connexion is a fact or that the thing *is*—i. e. ascertained either the partial or the unqualified being of the thing—and are proceeding 90ᵃ to ask the reason of the connexion or the nature of the thing, then we are asking what the 'middle' is.

(By distinguishing the fact of the connexion and the existence of the thing as respectively the partial and the unqualified being of the thing, I mean that if we ask 'does the moon suffer eclipse?', or 'does the moon wax?', the question concerns a part of the thing's being; for what we are asking in such questions is whether a thing is this or that, i. e. has or has not this or that attribute: whereas, if we ask whether the moon or night exists, the question concerns the unqualified being of a thing.)

We conclude that in all our inquiries we are asking either whether 5 there is a 'middle' or what the 'middle' is: for the 'middle' here is precisely the cause, and it is the cause that we seek in all our inquiries. Thus, 'Does the moon suffer eclipse?' means 'Is there or is there not a cause producing eclipse of the moon?', and when we have learnt that there is, our next question is, 'What, then, is this cause?'; for the cause through which a thing *is*—not *is this or that*, i. e. has this or that attribute, but without qualification *is*—and the cause through which 10 it is—not *is* without qualification, but *is this or that* as having some essential attribute or some accident—are both alike the 'middle'. By that which *is* without qualification I mean the subject, e. g. moon or earth or sun or triangle; by that which a subject *is* (in the partial sense) I mean a property, e. g. eclipse, equality or inequality, inter-

position or non-interposition. For in all these examples it is clear
15 that the nature of the thing and the reason of the fact are identical:
the question 'What is eclipse?' and its answer 'The privation of the
moon's light by the interposition of the earth' are identical with the
question 'What is the reason of eclipse?' or 'Why does the moon suffer
eclipse?' and the reply 'Because of the failure of light through the
earth's shutting it out'. Again, for 'What is a concord? A commensurate numerical ratio of a high and a low note', we may substitute
20 'What reason makes a high and a low note concordant? Their relation
according to a commensurate numerical ratio.' 'Are the high and the
low note concordant?' is equivalent to 'Is their ratio commensurate?';
and when we find that it is commensurate, we ask 'What, then, is
their ratio?'.

Cases in which the 'middle' is sensible show that the object of our
25 inquiry is always the 'middle': we inquire, because we have not perceived it, whether there is or is not a 'middle' causing e. g. an eclipse.
On the other hand, if we were on the moon we should not be inquiring either as to the fact or the reason, but both fact and reason
would be obvious simultaneously. For the act of perception would
have enabled us to know the universal too; since, the present fact of
an eclipse being evident, perception would then at the same time
30 give us the present fact of the earth's screening the sun's light, and
from this would arise the universal.

Thus, as we maintain, to know a thing's nature is to know the
reason why it is; and this is equally true of things in so far as they
are said without qualification to *be* as opposed to being possessed of
some attribute, and in so far as they are said to be possessed of some
attribute such as equal to two right angles, or greater or less.

35 **3**   It is clear, then, that all questions are a search for a 'middle'.
Let us now state how essential nature is revealed, and in what way it
can be reduced to demonstration;[1] what definition is, and what
things are definable. And let us first discuss certain difficulties which
90b these questions raise, beginning what we have to say with a point
most intimately connected with our immediately preceding remarks,
namely the doubt that might be felt as to whether or not it is possible
to know the same thing in the same relation, both by definition and
by demonstration. It might, I mean, be urged that definition is held
to concern essential nature and is in every case universal and affirma-
5 tive; whereas, on the other hand, some conclusions are negative and
some are not universal; e. g. all in the second figure are negative, none

------

[1] Cf. 94a 11–14.

in the third are universal. And again, not even all affirmative conclusions in the first figure are definable, e. g. 'every triangle has
its angles equal to two right angles'. An argument proving this difference between demonstration and definition is that to have scientific
knowledge of the demonstrable is identical with possessing a demon- 10
stration of it: hence if demonstration of such conclusions as these is
possible, there clearly cannot also be definition of them. If there could,
one might know such a conclusion also in virtue of its definition without possessing the demonstration of it; for there is nothing to stop
our having the one without the other.

Induction too will sufficiently convince us of this difference; for
never yet by defining anything—essential attribute or accident—did 15
we get knowledge of it. Again, if to define is to acquire knowledge of a
substance, at any rate such attributes are not substances.

It is evident, then, that not everything demonstrable can be defined.
What then? Can everything definable be demonstrated, or not? There
is one of our previous arguments which covers this too. Of a single 20
thing *qua* single there is a single scientific knowledge. Hence, since to
know the demonstrable scientifically is to possess the demonstration
of it, an impossible consequence will follow:—possession of its definition without its demonstration will give knowledge of the demonstrable.

Moreover, the basic premisses of demonstrations are definitions,
and it has already been shown [2] that these will be found indemonstrable; either the basic premisses will be demonstrable and will 25
depend on prior premisses, and the regress will be endless; or the
primary truths will be indemonstrable definitions.

But if the definable and the demonstrable are not wholly the same,
may they yet be partially the same? Or is that impossible, because
there can be no demonstration of the definable? There can be none,
because definition is of the essential nature or being of something, 30
and all demonstrations evidently posit and assume the essential
nature—mathematical demonstrations, for example, the nature of
unity and the odd, and all the other sciences likewise. Moreover,
every demonstration proves a predicate of a subject as attaching or as
not attaching to it, but in definition one thing is not predicated of 35
another; we do not, e. g., predicate animal of biped nor biped of
animal, nor yet figure of plane—plane not being figure nor figure
plane. Again, to prove essential nature is not the same as to prove the
fact of a connexion. Now definition reveals essential nature, demon- 91ᵃ
stration reveals that a given attribute attaches or does not attach to a

2 Cf. 72ᵇ 18–25 and 84ᵃ 30–ᵇ 2.

given subject; but different things require different demonstrations—
unless the one demonstration is related to the other as part to whole.
I add this because if all triangles have been proved to possess angles
equal to two right angles, then this attribute has been proved to
attach to isosceles; for isosceles is a part of which all triangles consti-
5 tute the whole. But in the case before us the fact and the essential
nature are not so related to one another, since the one is not a part
of the other.

So it emerges that not all the definable is demonstrable nor all the
demonstrable definable; and we may draw the general conclusion that
there is no identical object of which it is possible to possess both a
10 definition and a demonstration. It follows obviously that definition
and demonstration are neither identical nor contained either within
the other: if they were, their objects would be related either as
identical or as whole and part.

4 So much, then, for the first stage of our problem. The next step is
to raise the question whether syllogism—i. e. demonstration—of the
definable nature is possible or, as our recent argument assumed,
impossible.

We might argue it impossible on the following grounds:—(*a*) syllogism proves an attribute of a subject through the middle term; on the
15 other hand (*b*) its definable nature is both 'peculiar' to a subject
and predicated of it as belonging to its essence. But in that case
(1) the subject, its definition, and the middle term connecting them
must be reciprocally predicable of one another; for if A is 'peculiar'
to C, obviously A is 'peculiar' to B and B to C—in fact all three
terms are 'peculiar' to one another: and further (2) if A inheres in
the essence of all B and B is predicated universally of all C as belong-
20 ing to C's essence, A also must be predicated of C as belonging to its
essence.

If one does not take this relation as thus duplicated—if, that is,
A is predicated as being of the essence of B, but B is not of the essence
of the subjects of which it is predicated—A will not necessarily be
predicated of C as belonging to its essence. So both premisses *will*
predicate essence, and consequently B also will be predicated of C as
25 its essence. Since, therefore, both premisses do predicate essence—
i. e. definable form—C's definable form will appear in the middle
term before the conclusion is drawn.

We may generalize by supposing that it is possible to prove the
essential nature of man. Let C be man, A man's essential nature—
two-footed animal, or aught else it may be. Then, if we are to syllogize,

A must be predicated of all *B*. But this premiss will be mediated by
a fresh definition, which consequently will also be the essential nature 30
of man.³ Therefore the argument assumes what it has to prove, since
B too is the essential nature of man. It is, however, the case in which
there are only the two premisses—i. e. in which the premisses are
primary and immediate—which we ought to investigate, because it
best illustrates the point under discussion.

Thus they who prove the essential nature of soul or man or any- 35
thing else through reciprocating terms beg the question. It would be
begging the question, for example, to contend that the soul is that
which causes its own life, and that what causes its own life is a self-
moving number; for one would have to postulate that the soul is a
self-moving number in the sense of being identical with it. For if *A* 91ᵇ
is predicable as a mere consequent of *B* and *B* of *C*, *A* will not on that
account be the definable form of *C*: *A* will merely be what it was true
to say of *C*. Even if *A* is predicated of all *B* inasmuch as *B* is identical
with a species of *A*, still it will not follow: being an animal is predicated of being a man—since it is true that in all instances to be human 5
is to be animal, just as it is also true that every man is an animal—
but not as identical with being man.

We conclude, then, that unless one takes both the premisses as
predicating essence, one cannot infer that *A* is the definable form and
essence of *C*: but if one does so take them, in assuming *B* one will have
assumed, before drawing the conclusion, what the definable form of
C is; so that there has been no inference, for one has begged the 10
question.

5   Nor, as was said in my formal logic, is the method of division a
process of inference at all, since at no point does the characterization
of the subject follow necessarily from the premising of certain other
facts: division demonstrates as little as does induction. For in a genu- 15
ine demonstration the conclusion must not be put as a question nor
depend on a concession, but must follow necessarily from its premisses,
even if the respondent deny it. The definer asks 'Is man animal or
inanimate?' and then assumes—he has not inferred—that man is
animal. Next, when presented with an exhaustive division of animal
into terrestrial and aquatic, he assumes that man is terrestrial. More- 20
over, that man is the complete formula, terrestrial-animal, does not
follow necessarily from the premisses: this too is an assumption, and

³ *sc.* 'and an indefinite regress occurs'. This argument is a corollary of the
proof in 91ᵃ 15–26 that if the proposition predicating *A*—its definition—
of *C* can be a conclusion, there must be a middle term, *B*, and since *A*, *B*, and
C are reciprocally predicable, *B* too, as well as *A*, will be a definition of *C*.

equally an assumption whether the division comprises many differentiae or few. (Indeed as this method of division is used by those who
proceed by it, even truths that can be inferred actually fail to appear
25 as such.) For why should not the whole of this formula be true of
man, and yet not exhibit his essential nature or definable form?
Again, what guarantee is there against an unessential addition, or
against the omission of the final or of an intermediate determinant
of the substantial being?

The champion of division might here urge that though these lapses
do occur, yet we can solve that difficulty if all the attributes we
assume are constituents of the definable form, and if, postulating the
genus, we produce by division the requisite uninterrupted sequence
30 of terms, and omit nothing; and that indeed we cannot fail to fulfil
these conditions if what is to be divided falls whole into the division
at each stage, and none of it is omitted; and that this—the dividendum—must without further question be (ultimately) incapable of
fresh specific division. Nevertheless, we reply, division does not involve inference; if it gives knowledge, it gives it in another way. Nor
is there any absurdity in this: induction, perhaps, is not demonstration any more than is division, yet it does make evident some truth.
35 Yet to state a definition reached by division is not to state a conclusion: as, when conclusions are drawn without their appropriate
middles, the alleged necessity by which the inference follows from
the premisses is open to a question as to the reason for it, so definitions
reached by division invite the same question. Thus to the question
92ᵃ 'What is the essential nature of man?' the divider replies 'Animal,
mortal, footed, biped, wingless'; and when at each step he is asked
'Why?', he will say, and, as he thinks, prove by division, that all animal is mortal or immortal: but such a formula taken in its entirety
is not definition; so that even if division does demonstrate its
5 formula, definition at any rate does not turn out to be a conclusion of
inference.

6   Can we nevertheless actually demonstrate what a thing essentially
and substantially is, but hypothetically, i. e. by premising (1) that its
definable form is constituted by the 'peculiar' attributes of its essential nature; (2) that such and such are the only attributes of its
essential nature, and that the complete synthesis of them is peculiar
to the thing; and thus—since in this synthesis consists the being of
the thing—obtaining our conclusion? Or is the truth that, since proof
10 must be through the middle term, the definable form is once more
assumed in this minor premiss too?

Further, just as in syllogizing we do not premise what syllogistic inference is (since the premisses from which we conclude must be related as whole and part),[4] so the definable form must not fall within the syllogism but remain outside the premisses posited. It is only against a doubt as to its having been a syllogistic inference at all that 15 we have to defend our argument as conforming to the definition of syllogism. It is only when some one doubts whether the conclusion proved is the definable form that we have to defend it as conforming to the definition of definable form which we assumed. Hence syllogistic inference must be possible even without the express statement of what syllogism is or what definable form is.

The following type of hypothetical proof also begs the question. 20 If evil is definable as the divisible, and the definition of a thing's contrary—if it has one—is the contrary of the thing's definition; then, if good is the contrary of evil and the indivisible of the divisible, we conclude that to be good is essentially to be indivisible. The question is begged because definable form is assumed as a premiss, and as a premiss which is to prove definable form. 'But not the same definable form', you may object. That I admit, for in demonstrations also we 25 premise that 'this' is predicable of 'that'; but in this premiss the term we assert of the minor is neither the major itself nor a term identical in definition, or convertible, with the major.

Again, both proof by division and the syllogism just described are open to the question why man should be animal-biped-terrestrial and not merely animal *and* terrestrial, since what they premise does not 30 ensure that the predicates shall constitute a genuine unity and not merely belong to a single subject as do musical and grammatical when predicated of the same man.

7   How then by definition shall we *prove* substance or essential nature? We cannot show it as a fresh fact necessarily following from 35 the assumption of premisses admitted to be facts—the method of demonstration: we may not proceed as by induction to establish a universal on the evidence of groups of particulars which offer no exception, because induction proves not what the essential nature of a thing is but that it has or has not some attribute. Therefore, since 92[b] presumably one cannot prove essential nature by an appeal to sense perception or by pointing with the finger, what other method remains?

[4] A reminder of a necessary condition of syllogism. If the definition of syllogism is premised the conclusion would have to affirm some subject to be of the nature of syllogism.

To put it another way: how shall we by definition prove *essential nature*? He who knows what human—or any other—nature is, must
5 know also that man exists; for no one knows the nature of what does not exist—one can know the meaning of the phrase or name 'goat-stag' but not what the essential nature of a goat-stag is. But further, if definition can prove what is the essential nature of a thing, can it also prove that it exists? And how will it prove them both by the same process, since definition exhibits one single thing and dem-
10 onstration another single thing, and what human nature is and the fact that man exists are not the same thing? Then too we hold that it is by *demonstration* that the being of everything must be proved— unless indeed to be were its essence; and, since being is not a genus, it is not the essence of anything. Hence the being of anything as fact
15 is matter for demonstration; and this is the actual procedure of the sciences, for the geometer assumes the meaning of the word triangle, but that it is possessed of some attribute he proves. What is it, then, that we shall prove in defining essential nature? Triangle? In that case a man will know by definition what a thing's nature is without knowing whether it exists. But that is impossible.

Moreover it is clear, if we consider the methods of defining actually in use, that definition does not prove that the thing defined exists:
20 since even if there does actually exist something which is equidistant from a centre, yet *why* should the thing named in the definition exist? Why, in other words, should this be the formula defining circle? One might equally well call it the definition of mountain copper. For definitions do not carry a further guarantee that the
25 thing defined can exist or that it is what they claim to define: one can always ask why.

Since, therefore, to define is to prove either a thing's essential nature or the meaning of its name, we may conclude that definition, if it in no sense proves essential nature, is a set of words signifying pre- cisely what a name signifies. But that were a strange consequence; for (1) both what is not substance and what does not exist at all would be definable, since even non-existents can be signified by a
30 name: (2) all sets of words or sentences would be definitions, since any kind of sentence could be given a name; so that we should all be talking in definitions, and even the *Iliad* would be a definition: (3) no demonstration can prove that any particular name means any particular thing: neither, therefore, do definitions, in addition to revealing the meaning of a name, also reveal that the name has *this*
35 meaning. It appears then from these considerations that neither definition and syllogism nor their objects are identical, and further

that definition neither demonstrates nor proves anything, and that knowledge of essential nature is not to be obtained either by definition or by demonstration.

8 We must now start afresh and consider which of these conclu- 93ᵃ
sions are sound and which are not, and what is the nature of definition, and whether essential nature is in any sense demonstrable and definable or in none.

Now to know its essential nature is, as we said, the same as to know the cause of a thing's existence, and the proof of this depends 5 on the fact that a thing must have a cause. Moreover, this cause is either identical with the essential nature of the thing or distinct from it; [5] and if its cause is distinct from it, the essential nature of the thing is either demonstrable or indemonstrable. Consequently, if the cause is distinct from the thing's essential nature and demonstration is possible, the cause must be the middle term, and, the conclusion proved being universal and affirmative, the proof is in the first figure. So the method just examined of proving it through another essential nature would be one way of proving essential nature, be- 10 cause a conclusion containing essential nature must be inferred through a middle which is an essential nature just as a 'peculiar' property must be inferred through a middle which is a 'peculiar' property; so that of the two definable natures of a single thing this method will prove one and not the other.[6]

Now it was said before[7] that this method could not amount to demonstration of essential nature—it is actually a dialectical proof 15 of it—so let us begin again and explain by what method it can be demonstrated. When we are aware of a fact we seek its reason, and though sometimes the fact and the reason dawn on us simultaneously, yet we cannot apprehend the reason a moment sooner than the fact; and clearly in just the same way we cannot apprehend a thing's definable form without apprehending that it exists, since while we are ignorant whether it exists we cannot know its essen- 20 tial nature. Moreover we are aware whether a thing exists or not

[5] 'distinct from it'; i. e. in the case of *properties,* with the definition of which Aristotle is alone concerned in this chapter. The being of a property consists in its inherence in a substance through a middle which defines it. Cf. the following chapter.

[6] Aristotle speaks of two moments of the definable form as two essential natures. His argument amounts to this: that if the conclusion contains the whole definition, the question has been begged in the premisses (cf. ii, ch. 4). Hence syllogism—and even so merely dialectical syllogism—is only possible if premisses and conclusion each contain a part of the definition.   [7] ii, ch. 2.

sometimes through apprehending an element in its character, and
sometimes accidentally,[8] as, for example, when we are aware of
thunder as a noise in the clouds, of eclipse as a privation of light, or
of man as some species of animal, or of the soul as a self-moving
thing. As often as we have accidental knowledge that the thing
25 exists, we must be in a wholly negative state as regards awareness
of its essential nature; for we have not got genuine knowledge even
of its existence, and to search for a thing's essential nature when
we are unaware that it exists is to search for nothing. On the other
hand, whenever we apprehend an element in the thing's character
there is less difficulty. Thus it follows that the degree of our knowledge of a thing's essential nature is determined by the sense in
which we are aware that it exists. Let us then take the following
as our first instance of being aware of an element in the essential
30 nature. Let A be eclipse, C the moon, B the earth's acting as a screen.
Now to ask whether the moon is eclipsed or not is to ask whether
or not B has occurred. But that is precisely the same as asking
whether A has a defining condition; and if this condition actually
exists, we assert that A also actually exists. Or again we may ask
which side of a contradiction the defining condition necessitates: does
it make the angles of a triangle equal or not equal to two right
angles? When we have found the answer, if the premisses are imme-
35 diate, we know fact and reason together; if they are not immediate, we know the fact without the reason, as in the following example: let C be the moon, A eclipse, B the fact that the moon fails
to produce shadows [9] though she is full and though no visible body
intervenes between us and her. Then if B, failure to produce shadows
93b in spite of the absence of an intervening body, is attributable to
C, and A, eclipse, is attributable to B, it is clear that the moon is
eclipsed, but the reason why is not yet clear, and we know that
eclipse exists, but we do not know what its essential nature is. But
when it is clear that A is attributable to C and we proceed to ask
5 the reason of this fact, we are inquiring what is the nature of B:
is it the earth's acting as a screen, or the moon's rotation or her
extinction? But B is the definition of the other term, viz., in these
examples, of the major term A; for eclipse is constituted by the earth
acting as a screen. Thus, (1) 'What is thunder?' 'The quenching of
fire in cloud', and (2) 'Why does it thunder?' 'Because fire is

---

[8] The distinction is that between genuine knowledge of a connexion through
its cause and accidental knowledge of it through a middle not the cause.
[9] i. e. that there is no moonlight casting shadows on the earth on a clear
night at full moon.

quenched in the cloud', are equivalent. Let C be cloud, A thunder, B the quenching of fire. Then B is attributable to C, cloud, since fire 10 is quenched in it; and A, noise, is attributable to B; and B is assuredly the definition of the major term A. If there be a further mediating cause of B, it will be one of the remaining partial definitions of A.

We have stated then how essential nature is discovered and be- 15 comes known, and we see that, while there is no syllogism—i. e. no demonstrative syllogism—of essential nature, yet it is through syllogism, viz. demonstrative syllogism, that essential nature is exhibited. So we conclude that neither can the essential nature of anything which has a cause distinct from itself be known without demonstration, nor can it be demonstrated; and this is what we contended in 20 our preliminary discussions.[10]

9   Now while some things have a cause distinct from themselves, others have not. Hence it is evident that there are essential natures which are immediate, that is, are basic premisses; and of these not only *that* they are but also *what* they are must be assumed or revealed in some other way. This too is the actual procedure of the arithmetician, who assumes both the nature and the existence of unit. 25 On the other hand, it is possible (in the manner explained) to exhibit through demonstration the essential nature of things which have a 'middle',[11] i. e. a cause of their substantial being other than that being itself; but we do not thereby demonstrate it.

10   Since definition is said to be the statement of a thing's nature, obviously one kind of definition will be a statement of the meaning of the name, or of an equivalent nominal formula. A definition in 30 this sense tells you, e. g. the meaning of the phrase 'triangular character'.[12] When we are aware that triangle exists, we inquire the reason why it exists. But it is difficult thus to learn the definition of things the existence of which we do not genuinely know—the cause of this difficulty being, as we said before,[13] that we only know accidentally whether or not the thing exises. Moreover, a statement may 35 be a unity in either of two ways, by conjunction, like the *Iliad,* or because it exhibits a single predicate as inhering not accidentally in a single subject.[14]

[10] ii, ch. 3.   [11] Cf., however, ii, ch. 2.
[12] i. e. as treated by geometry; that is, as abstracted *a materia* and treated as a subject. Cf. 81^b 25.   [13] Cf. 93^a 16–27.
[14] Presumably a reason for there being a kind of definition other than nominal. The reference is obviously to 92^b 32.

That then is one way of defining definition. Another kind of definition is a formula exhibiting the cause of a thing's existence. Thus 94ᵃ the former signifies without proving, but the latter will clearly be a *quasi*-demonstration of essential‧ nature, differing from demonstration in the arrangement of its terms. For there is a difference between stating why it thunders, and stating what is the essential nature of thunder; since the first statement will be 'Because fire is quenched in the clouds', while the statement of what the nature of thunder is 5 will be 'The noise of fire being quenched in the clouds'. Thus the same statement takes a different form: in one form it is continuous [15] demonstration, in the other definition. Again, thunder can be defined as noise in the clouds, which is the conclusion of the demonstration embodying essential nature. On the other hand the definition 10 of immediates is an indemonstrable positing of essential nature. We conclude then that definition is (*a*) an indemonstrable statement of essential nature, or (*b*) a syllogism of essential nature differing from demonstration in grammatical form, or (*c*) the conclusion of a demonstration giving essential nature.

Our discussion has therefore made plain (1) in what sense and of what things the essential nature is demonstrable, and in what 15 sense and of what things it is not; (2) what are the various meanings of the term definition, and in what sense and of what things it proves the essential nature, and in what sense and of what things it does not; (3) what is the relation of definition to demonstration, and how far the same thing is both definable and demonstrable and how far it is not.

20 **11** We think we have scientific knowledge when we know the cause, and there are four causes: (1) the definable form, (2) an antecedent which necessitates a consequent,[16] (3) the efficient cause, (4) the final cause. Hence each of these can be the middle term of a proof,‧for [17] (*a*) though the inference from antecedent to neces- 25 sary consequent does not hold if only one premiss is assumed—two is the minimum—still when there are two it holds on condition that they have a single common middle term. So it is from the assump-

---

[15] Demonstration, like a line, is continuous because its premisses are parts which are conterminous (as linked by middle terms), and there is a movement from premisses to conclusion. Definition resembles rather the indivisible simplicity of a point.

[16] By this Aristotle appears to mean the material cause; cf. *Physics* ii, 195ᵃ 18, 19, where the premisses of a syllogism are said to be the material cause of the conclusion.

[17] *sc.* 'lest you should suppose that (2) could not be a middle'.

tion of this single middle term that the conclusion follows necessarily. The following example will also show this.[18] Why is the angle in a semicircle a right angle?—or from what assumption does it follow that it is a right angle? Thus, let A be right angle, B the half of two right angles, C the angle in a semicircle. Then B is the cause in 30 virtue of which A, right angle, is attributable to C, the angle in a semicircle, since $B = A$ and the other, viz. C, $=B$, for C is half of two right angles. Therefore it *is* the assumption of B, the half of two right angles, from which it follows that A is attributable to C, i. e. that the angle in a semicircle is a right angle. Moreover, B is identical with (b) the defining form of A, since it is what A's definition [19] signifies. Moreover, the formal cause has already been shown 35 to be the middle.[20] (c) 'Why did the Athenians become involved in the Persian war?' means 'What cause originated the waging of war against the Athenians?' and the answer is, 'Because they raided Sardis with the Eretrians', since this originated the war. Let A be 94ᵇ war, B unprovoked raiding, C the Athenians. Then B, unprovoked raiding, is true of C, the Athenians, and A is true of B, since men make war on the unjust aggressor. So A, having war waged upon 5 them, is true of B, the initial aggressors, and B is true of C, the Athenians, who were the aggressors. Hence here too the cause— in this case the efficient cause—is the middle term. (d) This is no less true where the cause is the final cause. E. g. why does one take a walk after supper? For the sake of one's health. Why does a house exist? For the preservation of one's goods. The end in view is in 10 the one case health, in the other preservation. To ask the reason why one must walk after supper is precisely to ask to what end one must do it. Let C be walking after supper, B the non-regurgitation of food, A health. Then let walking after supper possess the property of preventing food from rising to the orifice of the stomach, and let 15 this condition be healthy; since it seems that B, the non-regurgitation of food, is attributable to C, taking a walk, and that A, health, is attributable to B. What, then, is the cause through which A, the final cause, inheres in C? It is B, the non-regurgitation of food; but B is a kind of definition of A, for A will be explained by it. Why is B 20 the cause of A's belonging to C? Because to be in a condition such as B is to be in health. The definitions must be transposed, and then

---

[18] sc. 'that (2) can appear as a middle'.

[19] Cf. Euclid, *Elem.* i, Def. x, but Aristotle may be referring to some earlier definition. The proof here given that the angle in a semicircle is a right angle is not that of Euclid iii. 31; cf. Heath, *Greek Mathematics,* i. pp. 339, 340.

[20] The reference is to 93ᵃ 3 ff., and other passages such as 94ᵃ 5 ff., where the middle is shown to define the major.

the detail will become clearer. Incidentally, here the order of coming to be is the reverse of what it is in proof through the efficient cause: in the efficient order the middle term must come to be first, whereas 25 in the teleological order the minor, C, must first take place, and the end in view comes last in time.

The same thing may exist for an end and be necessitated as well. For example, light shines through a lantern (1) because that which consists of relatively small particles necessarily passes through pores 30 larger than those particles—assuming that light does issue by penetration—and (2) for an end, namely to save us from stumbling. If, then, a thing can exist through two causes, can it come to be through two causes—as for instance if thunder be a hiss and a roar necessarily produced by the quenching of fire, and also designed, as the Pythagoreans say, for a threat to terrify those that lie in Tartarus? 35 Indeed, there are very many such cases, mostly among the processes and products of the natural world; for nature, in different senses of the term 'nature', produces now for an end, now by necessity.

Necessity too is of two kinds. It may work in accordance with a 95ᵃ thing's natural tendency, or by constraint and in opposition to it; as, for instance, by necessity a stone is borne both upwards and downwards, but not by the same necessity.

Of the products of man's intelligence some are never due to chance or necessity but always to an end, as for example a house or 5 a statue; others, such as health or safety, may result from chance as well.

It is mostly in cases where the issue is indeterminate (though only where the production does not originate in chance, and the end is consequently good), that a result is due to an end, and this is true alike in nature or in art. By chance, on the other hand, nothing comes to be for an end.

10 **12**   The effect may be still coming to be, or its occurrence may be past or future, yet the cause will be the same as when it is actually existent—for it is the middle which is the cause—except that if the effect actually exists the cause is actually existent, if it is coming to be so is the cause, if its occurrence is past the cause is past, if future the cause is future. For example, the moon was eclipsed because the earth intervened, is becoming eclipsed because the earth is in process 15 of intervening, will be eclipsed because the earth will intervene, is eclipsed because the earth intervenes.

To take a second example: assuming that the definition of ice is solidified water, let C be water, A solidified, B the middle, which is the cause, namely total failure of heat. Then B is attributed to C, and A, solidification, to B: ice forms when B is occurring, has formed 20 when B has occurred, and will form when B shall occur.

This sort of cause, then, and its effect come to be simultaneously when they are in process of becoming, and exist simultaneously when they actually exist; and the same holds good when they are past and when they are future. But what of cases where they are not simultaneous? Can causes and effects different from one another form, as they seem to us to form, a continuous succession, a past effect result- 25 ing from a past cause different from itself, a future effect from a future cause different from it, and an effect which is coming-to-be from a cause different from and prior to it? Now on this theory it is from the posterior event that we reason (and this though these later events actually have their source of origin in previous events —a fact which shows that also when the effect is coming-to-be we still reason from the posterior event), and from the prior event we cannot reason (we cannot argue that because an event A has oc- 30 curred, therefore an event B has occurred subsequently to A but still in the past—and the same holds good if the occurrence is future)— cannot reason because, be the time interval definite or indefinite, it will never be possible to infer that because it is true to say that A occurred, therefore it is true to say that B, the subsequent event, occurred; for in the interval between the events, though A has already occurred, the latter statement will be false. And the same 35 argument applies also to future events; i. e. one cannot infer from an event which occurred in the past that a future event will occur. The reason of this is that the middle must be homogeneous, past when the extremes are past, future when they are future, coming to be when they are coming-to-be, actually existent when they are actually existent; and there cannot be a middle term homogeneous with extremes respectively past and future. And it is a further difficulty in this theory that the time interval can be neither indefinite nor defi- 40 nite, since during it the inference will be false. We have also to inquire 95ᵇ what it is that holds events together so that the coming-to-be now occurring in actual things follows upon a past event. It is evident, we may suggest, that a past event and a present process cannot be 'contiguous', for not even two past events can be 'contiguous'. For past events are limits and atomic; so just as points are not 'contiguous' 5 neither are past events, since both are indivisible. For the same reason a past event and a present process cannot be 'contiguous', for the process is divisible, the event indivisible. Thus the relation of present process to past event is analogous to that of line to point, since a

10 process contains an infinity of past events. These questions, however, must receive a more explicit treatment in our general theory of change.[21]

The following must suffice as an account of the manner in which the middle would be identical with the cause on the supposition that coming-to-be is a series of consecutive events: for [22] in the terms of 15 such a series too the middle and major terms must form an immediate premiss; e. g. we argue that, since C has occurred, therefore A occurred: and C's occurrence was posterior, A's prior; but C is the source of the inference because it is nearer to the present moment, and the starting-point of time is the present. We next argue that, since D has occurred, therefore C occurred. Then we conclude that, 20 since D has occurred, therefore A must have occurred; and the cause is C, for since D has occurred C must have occurred, and since C has occurred A must previously have occurred.

If we get our middle term in this way, will the series terminate in an immediate premiss, or since, as we said, no two events are 'contiguous', will a fresh middle term always intervene because there is an infinity of middles? No: though no two events are 'contiguous', yet we must start from a premiss consisting of a middle and the pres-25 ent event as major. The like is true of future events too, since if it is true to say that D will exist, it must be a prior truth to say that A will exist, and the cause of this conclusion is C; for if D will exist, C will exist prior to D, and if C will exist, A will exist prior to it. And here too the same infinite divisibility might be urged, since 30 future events are not 'contiguous'. But here too an immediate basic premiss must be assumed. And in the world of fact this is so: if a house has been built, then blocks must have been quarried and shaped. The reason is that a house having been built necessitates a foundation having been laid, and if a foundation has been laid blocks must 35 have been shaped beforehand. Again, if a house will be built, blocks will similarly be shaped beforehand; and proof is through the middle in the same way, for the foundation will exist before the house.

Now we observe in Nature a certain kind of circular process of coming-to-be; and this is possible only if the middle and extreme

---

[21] Cf. *Physics* vi.

[22] i. e. Aristotle has had in this chapter to explain (1) how syllogisms concerning a process of events can be brought into line with other demonstrations equally derivable from immediate primary premisses, and (2) in what sense the middle term contains the cause. He has in fact had (1) to show that in these syllogisms inference must find its primary premiss in the effect, and (2) to imply that the 'cause' which appears as middle when cause and effect are not simultaneous is a *causa cognoscendi* and not *essendi*.

terms are reciprocal, since conversion is conditioned by reciprocity in 40
the terms of the proof. This—the convertibility of conclusions and 96ᵃ
premisses—has been proved in our early chapters,[23] and the circular
process is an instance of this. In actual fact it is exemplified thus:
when the earth had been moistened an exhalation was bound to rise,
and when an exhalation had risen cloud was bound to form, and
from the formation of cloud rain necessarily resulted, and by the
fall of rain the earth was necessarily moistened: but this was the 5
starting-point, so that a circle is completed; for posit any one of the
terms and another follows from it, and from that another, and from
that again the first.

Some occurrences are universal (for they are, or come-to-be what
they are, always and in every case); others again are not always
what they are but only as a general rule: for instance, not every man 10
can grow a beard, but it is the general rule. In the case of such
connexions the middle term too must be a general rule. For if *A* is
predicated universally of *B* and *B* of *C*, *A* too must be predicated
always and in every instance of *C*, since to hold in every instance
and always is of the nature of the universal. But we have assumed 15
a connexion which is a general rule; consequently the middle term
B must also be a general rule. So connexions which embody a general rule—i. e. which exist or come to be as a general rule—will also
derive from immediate basic premisses.

13 [24]   We have already explained how essential nature is set out in 20
the terms of a demonstration, and the sense in which it is or is not
demonstrable or definable; so let us now discuss the method to be
adopted in tracing the elements predicated as constituting the definable form.

Now of the attributes which inhere always in each several thing
there are some which are wider in extent than it but not wider than 25
its genus (by attributes of wider extent I mean all such as are universal attributes of each several subject, but in their application
are not confined to that subject). I. e. while an attribute may inhere
in every triad, yet also in a subject not a triad—as being inheres in
triad but also in subjects not numbers at all—odd on the other
hand is an attribute inhering in every triad and of wider application
(inhering as it does also in pentad), but which does not extend 30
beyond the genus of triad; for pentad is a number, but nothing outside number is odd. It is such attributes which we have to select, up

---

[23] i, ch. 3 and *An. Pr.* ii, cc. 3–5, 8–10.
[24] This chapter treats only the definition of substances.

to the exact point at which they are severally of wider extent than
the subject but collectively coextensive with it; for this synthesis
must be the substance of the thing. For example every triad possesses
35 the attributes number, odd, and prime in both senses, i. e. not only as
possessing no divisors, but also as not being a sum of numbers. This,
then, is precisely what triad is, viz. a number, odd, and prime in the
former and also the latter sense of the term: for these attributes taken
96ᵇ severally apply, the first two to all odd numbers, the last to the dyad
also as well as to the triad, but, taken collectively, to no other subject. Now since we have shown above ²⁵ that attributes predicated
as belonging to the essential nature are necessary and that universals
are necessary, and since the attributes which we select as inhering in
triad, or in any other subject whose attributes we select in this
5 way, are predicated as belonging to its essential nature, triad will
thus possess these attributes necessarily. Further, that the synthesis
of them constitutes the substance of triad is shown by the following
argument. If it is not identical with the being of triad, it must be related to triad as a genus named or nameless. It will then be of wider
extent than triad—assuming that wider potential extent is the char-
10 acter of a genus. If on the other hand this synthesis is applicable
to no subject other than the individual triads, it will be identical with
the being of triad, because we make the further assumption that the
substance of each subject is the predication of elements in its essential nature down to the last differentia characterizing the individuals.
It follows that any other synthesis thus exhibited will likewise be
identical with the being of the subject.

15   The author of a hand-book ²⁶ on a subject that is a generic whole
should divide the genus into its first *infimae species*—number e. g.
into triad and dyad—and then endeavour to seize their definitions
by the method we have described—the definition, for example, of
straight line or circle or right angle. After that, having established
what the category is to which the subaltern genus belongs—quantity
20 or quality, for instance—he should examine the properties 'peculiar'
to the species, working through the proximate common differentiae.
He should proceed thus because the attributes of the genera compounded of the *infimae species* will be clearly given by the definitions
of the species; since the basic element of them all ²⁷ is the definition,

²⁵ i, ch. 4.
²⁶ With the remainder of the chapter compare *An. Pr.* i, ch. 25, where the
treatment covers all syllogism.
²⁷ *sc.* genera and species.

i. e. the simple *infima species,* and the attributes inhere essentially in the simple *infimae species,* in the genera only in virtue of these.

Divisions according to differentiae are a useful accessory to this method. What force they have as proofs we did, indeed, explain above,[28] but that merely towards collecting the essential nature they may be of use we will proceed to show. They might, indeed, seem to be of no use at all, but rather to assume everything at the start and to be no better than an initial assumption made without division. But, in fact, the order in which the attributes are predicated does make a difference—it matters whether we say animal—tame—biped, or biped—animal—tame. For if every definable thing consists of two elements and 'animal-tame' forms a unity, and again out of this and the further differentia man (or whatever else is the unity under construction) is constituted, then the elements we assume have necessarily been reached by division. Again, division is the only possible method of avoiding the omission of any element of the essential nature. Thus, if the primary genus is assumed and we then take one of the lower divisions, the dividendum will not fall whole into this division: e. g. it is not all animal which is either whole-winged or split-winged but all winged animal, for it is winged animal to which this differentiation belongs. The primary differentiation of animal is that within which all animal falls. The like is true of every other genus, whether outside animal or a subaltern genus of animal; e. g. the primary differentiation of bird is that within which falls every bird, of fish that within which falls every fish. So, if we proceed in this way, we can be sure that nothing has been omitted: by any other method one is bound to omit something without knowing it.

To define and divide one need not know the whole of existence. Yet some hold it impossible to know the differentiae distinguishing each thing from every single other thing without knowing every single other thing; and one cannot, they say, know each thing without knowing its differentiae, since everything is identical with that from which it does not differ, and other than that from which it differs. Now first of all this is a fallacy: not every differentia precludes identity, since many differentiae inhere in things specifically identical, though not in the substance of these nor essentially. Secondly, when one has taken one's differing pair of opposites and assumed that the two sides exhaust the genus, and that the subject one seeks to define is present in one or other of them, and one has further verified its presence in one of them; then it does not matter whether or not one knows all the other subjects of which the differentiae are also

---

[28] ii, ch. 5 and *An. Pr.* i, ch. 31.

predicated. For it is obvious that when by this process one reaches subjects incapable of further differentiation one will possess the formula defining the substance. Moreover, to postulate that the divi-
20 sion exhausts the genus is not illegitimate if the opposites exclude a middle; since if it is the differentia of that genus, anything contained in the genus must lie on one of the two sides.

In establishing a definition by division one should keep three ob-jects in view: (1) the admission only of elements in the definable form, (2) the arrangement of these in the right order, (3) the omis-
25 sion of no such elements. The first is feasible because one can estab-lish genus and differentia through the topic of the genus,[29] just as one can conclude the inherence of an accident through the topic of the accident.[30] The right order will be achieved if the right term is assumed as primary, and this will be ensured if the term selected is
30 predicable of all the others but not all they of it; since there must be one such term. Having assumed this we at once proceed in the same way with the lower terms; for our second term will be the first of the remainder, our third the first of those which follow the second in a 'contiguous' series, since when the higher term is excluded, that term of the remainder which is 'contiguous' to it will be primary, and so on. Our procedure makes it clear that no elements in the de-
35 finable form have been omitted: we have taken the differentia that comes first in the order of division, pointing out that animal e. g. is divisible exhaustively into A and B, and that the subject accepts one of the two as its predicate. Next we have taken the differentia of the whole thus reached, and shown that the whole we finally reach is not further divisible—i. e. that as soon as we have taken the last differentia to form the concrete totality, this totality admits of no
97ᵇ division into species. For it is clear that there is no superfluous addi-tion, since all these terms we have selected are elements in the defin-able form; and nothing lacking, since any omission would have to be a genus or a differentia. Now the primary term is a genus, and this term taken in conjunction with its differentiae is a genus: moreover the differentiae are all included, because there is now no further
5 differentia; if there were, the final concrete would admit of division into species, which, we said, is not the case.

To resume our account of the right method of investigation: We must start by observing a set of similar—i. e. specifically identical —individuals, and consider what element they have in common. We must then apply the same process to another set of individuals which belong to one species and are generically but not specifically

²⁹ Cf. *Topics* iv.   ³⁰ Cf. *Topics* ii.

identical with the former set. When we have established what the 10
common element is in all members of this second species, and likewise in members of further species, we should again consider whether
the results established possess any identity, and persevere until we
reach a single formula, since this will be the definition of the thing.
But if we reach not one formula but two or more, evidently the
definiendum cannot be one thing but must be more than one. I may 15
illustrate my meaning as follows. If we were inquiring what the essential nature of pride is, we should examine instances of proud men we
know of to see what, as such, they have in common; e. g. if Alcibiades
was proud, or Achilles and Ajax were proud, we should find, on inquiring what they all had in common, that it was intolerance of insult; it was this which drove Alcibiades to war, Achilles to wrath, and 20
Ajax to suicide. We should next examine other cases, Lysander, for
example, or Socrates, and then if these have in common indifference
alike to good and ill fortune, I take these two results and inquire what
common element have equanimity amid the vicissitudes of life and
impatience of dishonour. If they have none, there will be two genera 25
of pride. Besides, every definition is always universal and commensurate: the physician does not prescribe what is healthy for a single
eye, but for all eyes or for a determinate species of eye. It is also
easier by this method to define the single species than the universal,
and that is why our procedure should be from the several species to
the universal genera—this for the further reason too that equivoca- 30
tion is less readily detected in genera than in *infimae species*. Indeed,
perspicuity is essential in definitions, just as inferential movement is
the minimum required in demonstrations; and we shall attain perspicuity if we can collect separately the definition of each species
through the group of singulars which we have established—e. g. the
definition of similarity not unqualified but restricted to colours and 35
to figures; the definition of acuteness, but only of sound—and so proceed to the common universal with a careful avoidance of equivocation. We may add that if dialectical disputation must not employ
metaphors, clearly metaphors and metaphorical expressions are pre-
cluded in definition: otherwise dialectic would involve metaphors.

14 In order to formulate the connexions we wish to prove we have 98ᵃ
to select our analyses and divisions. The method of selection consists in laying down the common genus of all our subjects of investigation—if e. g. they are animals, we lay down what the properties
are which inhere in every animal. These established, we next lay down
the properties essentially connected with the first of the remaining 5

classes—e. g. if this first subgenus is bird, the essential properties of every bird—and so on, always characterizing the proximate subgenus. This will clearly at once enable us to say in virtue of what character the subgenera—man, e. g., or horse—possess their proper-
10 ties. Let A be animal, B the properties of every animal, $C, D, E,$ various species of animal. Then it is clear in virtue of what character B inheres in D—namely A—and that it inheres in C and E for the same reason: and throughout the remaining subgenera always the same rule applies.

We are now taking our examples from the traditional class-names, but we must not confine ourselves to considering these. We must
15 collect any other common character which we observe, and then consider with what species it is connected and what properties belong to it. For example, as the common properties of horned animals we collect the possession of a third stomach and only one row of teeth. Then since it is clear in virtue of what character they possess these attributes—namely their horned character—the next question is, to what species does the possession of horns attach?
20 Yet a further method of selection is by analogy: for we cannot find a single identical name to give to a squid's pounce, a fish's spine, and an animal's bone, although these too possess common properties as if there were a single osseous nature.

15 Some connexions that require proof are identical in that they possess an identical 'middle'—e. g. a whole group might be proved
25 through 'reciprocal replacement'—and of these one class are identical in genus, namely all those whose difference consists in their concerning different subjects or in their mode of manifestation. This latter class may be exemplified by the questions as to the causes respectively of echo, of reflection, and of the rainbow: the connexions to be proved which these questions embody are identical generically, because all three are forms of repercussion; but specifically they are different.

Other connexions that require proof only differ in that the 'middle'
30 of the one is subordinate to the 'middle' of the other. For example: Why does the Nile rise towards the end of the month? Because towards its close the month is more stormy. Why is the month more stormy towards its close? Because the moon is waning. Here the one cause is subordinate to the other.

35 **16** The question might be raised with regard to cause and effect whether when the effect is present the cause also is present; whether, for instance, if a plant sheds its leaves or the moon is eclipsed, there

is present also the cause of the eclipse or of the fall of the leaves—
the possession of broad leaves, let us say, in the latter case, in the 98^b
former the earth's interposition. For, one might argue, if this cause
is not present, these phenomena will have some other cause: if it
is present, its effect will be at once implied by it—the eclipse by the
earth's interposition, the fall of the leaves by the possession of broad
leaves; but if so, they will be logically coincident and each capable
of proof through the other. Let me illustrate: Let A be deciduous char- 5
acter, B the possession of broad leaves, C vine. Now if A inheres
in B (for every broad-leaved plant is deciduous), and B in C (every
vine possessing broad leaves); then A inheres in C (every vine is
deciduous), and the middle term B is the cause. But we can also 10
demonstrate that the vine has broad leaves because it is deciduous.
Thus, let D be broad-leaved, E deciduous, F vine. Then E inheres
in F (since every vine is deciduous), and D in E (for every deciduous
plant has broad leaves): therefore every vine has broad leaves, and 15
the cause is its deciduous character. If,[31] however, they cannot each
be the cause of the other (for cause is prior to effect, and the earth's
interposition is the cause of the moon's eclipse and not the eclipse of the
interposition)—if, then, demonstration through the cause is of the
reasoned fact and demonstration not through the cause is of the bare 20
fact, one who knows it through the eclipse knows the fact of the
earth's interposition but not the reasoned fact. Moreover, that the
eclipse is not the cause of the interposition, but the interposition of the
eclipse, is obvious because the interposition is an element in the definition of eclipse, which shows that the eclipse is known through the
interposition and not vice versa.

On the other hand, can a single effect have more than one cause? 25
One might argue as follows: if the same attribute is predicable of
more than one thing as its primary subject, let B be a primary subject
in which A inheres, and C another primary subject of A, and D and
E primary subjects of B and C respectively. A will then inhere in D
and E, and B will be the cause of A's inherence in D, C of A's inherence in E. The presence of the cause thus necessitates that of the
effect, but the presence of the effect necessitates the presence not of all 30
that may cause it but only of *a* cause which yet need not be the whole
cause. We may, however, suggest [32] that if the connexion to be proved
is always universal and commensurate, not only will the cause be a
whole but also the effect will be universal and commensurate. For
instance, deciduous character will belong exclusively to a subject
which is a whole, and, if this whole has species, universally and com-

---

[31] Here begins Aristotle's answer.   [32] Here begins Aristotle's answer.

mensurately to those species—i. e. either to all species of plant or to
35 a single species. So in these universal and commensurate connexions
the 'middle' and its effect must reciprocate, i. e. be convertible.
Supposing, for example, that the reason why trees are deciduous is
the coagulation of sap, then if a tree is deciduous, coagulation must
be present, and if coagulation is present—not in *any* subject but in
a tree—then that tree must be deciduous.

99ᵃ 17   Can the cause of an identical effect be not identical in every
instance of the effect but different? Or is that impossible? Perhaps it
is impossible if the effect is demonstrated as essential and not as inhering in virtue of a symptom or an accident—because the middle is
then the definition of the major term—though possible if the demonstration is not essential. Now it is possible to consider the effect and
5 its subject as an accidental conjunction, though such conjunctions
would not be regarded as connexions demanding scientific proof. But
if they are accepted as such, the middle will correspond to the extremes, and be equivocal if they are equivocal, generically one if they
are generically one. Take the question why proportionals alternate.
The cause when they are lines, and when they are numbers, is both
different and identical; different in so far as lines are lines and not
10 numbers, identical as involving a given determinate increment. In
all proportionals this is so. Again, the cause of likeness between
colour and colour is other than that between figure and figure; for
likeness here is equivocal, meaning perhaps in the latter case equality
of the ratios of the sides and equality of the angles, in the case of
15 colours identity of the act of perceiving them, or something else of
the sort. Again, connexions requiring proof which are identical by
analogy have middles also analogous.
   The truth is that cause, effect, and subject are reciprocally predicable in the following way. If the species are taken severally, the effect
is wider than the subject (e. g. the possession of external angles equal
to four right angles is an attribute wider than triangle or square),
20 but it is coextensive with the species taken collectively (in this instance with all figures whose external angles are equal to four right
angles). And the middle likewise reciprocates, for the middle is a
definition of the major; which is incidentally the reason why all the
sciences are built up through definition.
   We may illustrate as follows. Deciduous is a universal attribute
of vine, and is at the same time of wider extent than vine; and of
fig, and is of wider extent than fig: but it is not wider than but co-
25 extensive with the totality of the species. Then if you take the middle

which is proximate, it is a definition of deciduous. I say that, because you will first reach a middle [33] next the subject,[34] and a premiss asserting it of the whole subject, and after that a middle—the coagulation of sap or something of the sort—proving the connexion of the first middle with the major: [35] but it is the coagulation of sap at the junction of leaf-stalk and stem which defines deciduous.[36]

If an explanation in formal terms of the inter-relation of cause 30 and effect is demanded, we shall offer the following. Let A be an attribute of all B, and B of every species of D, but so that both A and B are wider than their respective subjects. Then B will be a universal attribute of each species of D (since I call such an attribute universal even if it is not commensurate, and I call an attribute primary universal if it is commensurate,[37] not with each species severally but with their totality), and it extends beyond each of them taken separately. Thus, B is the cause of A's inherence in the species of D: 35 consequently A must be of wider extent than B; otherwise why should B be the cause of A's inherence in D any more than A the cause of B's inherence in D? Now if A is an attribute of all the species of E, all the species of E will be united by possessing some common cause other than B: otherwise how shall we be able to say that A is predicable of all of which E is predicable, while E is not predicable of all 99ᵇ of which A can be predicated? I mean how can there fail to be some special cause of A's inherence in E, as there was of A's inherence in all the species of D? Then are the species of E, too, united by possessing some common cause? This cause we must look for. Let us call it C.[38]

[33] *sc.* broad-leaved.   [34] Vine, fig, &c.   [35] Broad-leaved with deciduous.
[36] Aristotle contemplates four terms: (1) deciduous, (2) coagulation, (3) broad-leaved, (4) vine, fig, &c.

If we get the middle proximate to (1) it is a definition of (1). But in investigating vines, figs, &c. according to the method of chapter 13, we shall first find a common character of them in broad-leaved, and, taking this as a middle, we shall prove that vine, fig, &c., *qua* broad-leaved, are deciduous. But this proof is not demonstration, because broad-leaved is not a definition of deciduous. So our next step will be to find a middle—coagulation—mediating the major premiss of this proof, and demonstrate that broad-leaved plants, *qua* liable to coagulation, are deciduous. This is strict demonstration, because coagulation defines deciduous.   [37] But cf. i, ch. 4, 73ᵇ 21–74ᵃ 3.
[38] The schema of Aristotle's argument in this paragraph is:

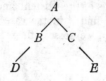

We conclude, then, that the same effect may have more than one cause, but not in subjects specifically identical. For instance, the 5 cause of longevity in quadrupeds is lack of bile, in birds a dry constitution—or certainly something different.

18 If immediate premises are not reached at once, and there is not merely one middle but several middles, i. e. several causes; is the cause of the property's inherence in the several species the middle 10 which is proximate to the primary universal,[39] or the middle which is proximate to the species? [40] Clearly the cause is that nearest to each species severally in which it is manifested, for that is the cause of the subject's falling under the universal. To illustrate formally: C is the cause of B's inherence in D; hence C is the cause of A's inherence in D, B of A's inherence in C, while the cause of A's inherence in B is B itself.

15 **19** As regards syllogism and demonstration, the definition of, and the conditions required to produce each of them, are now clear, and with that also the definition of, and the conditions required to produce, demonstrative knowledge, since it is the same as demonstration. As to the basic premises, how they become known and what is the developed state of knowledge of them is made clear by raising some preliminary problems.

20   We have already said [41] that scientific knowledge through demonstration is impossible unless a man knows the primary immediate premises. But there are questions which might be raised in respect of the apprehension of these immediate premises: one might not only ask whether it is of the same kind as the apprehension of the conclusions, but also whether there is or is not scientific knowledge of both; or scientific knowledge of the latter, and of the former a different kind of knowledge; and, further, whether the developed 25 states of knowledge are not innate but come to be in us, or are innate but at first unnoticed. Now it is strange if we possess them from birth; for it means that we possess apprehensions more accurate than demonstration and fail to notice them. If on the other hand we acquire them and do not previously possess them, how could we apprehend and learn without a basis of pre-existent knowledge? For that is impossible, as we used to find [42] in the case of demonstration. So it 30 emerges that neither can we possess them from birth, nor can they

[39] i. e. the property.
[41] i, ch. 2.

[40] the subject
[42] i, ch. 1.

come to be in us if we are without knowledge of them to the extent
of having no such developed state at all. Therefore we must possess
a capacity of some sort, but not such as to rank higher in accuracy
than these developed states. And this at least is an obvious characteristic of all animals, for they possess a congenital discriminative 35
capacity which is called sense-perception. But though sense-perception
is innate in all animals, in some the sense-impression comes to persist, in others it does not. So animals in which this persistence does
not come to be have either no knowledge at all outside the act of
perceiving, or no knowledge of objects of which no impression persists; animals in which it does come into being have perception and
can continue to retain the sense-impression in the soul: and when 100ᵃ
such persistence is frequently repeated a further distinction at once
arises between those which out of the persistence of such sense-
impressions develop a power of systematizing them and those which
do not. So out of sense-perception comes to be what we call memory,
and out of frequently repeated memories of the same thing develops 5
experience; for a number of memories constitute a single experience.[43]
From experience again—i. e. from the universal now stabilized in its
entirety within the soul, the one beside the many which is a single
identity within them all—originate the skill of the craftsman and
the knowledge of the man of science, skill in the sphere of coming
to be and science in the sphere of being.

We conclude that these states of knowledge are neither innate in
a determinate form, nor developed from other higher states of knowl- 10
edge, but from sense-perception. It is like a rout in battle stopped
by first one man making a stand and then another, until the original
formation has been restored. The soul is so constituted as to be
capable of this process.

Let us now restate the account given already, though with insufficient clearness. When one of a number of logically indiscriminable 15
particulars has made a stand, the earliest universal is present in the
soul: for though the act of sense-perception is of the particular, its
content is universal—is man, for example, not the man Callias. A 100ᵇ
fresh stand is made among these rudimentary universals, and the
process does not cease until the indivisible concepts, the true universals, are established: e. g. such and such a species of animal is a
step towards the genus animal, which by the same process is a step
towards a further generalization.

Thus it is clear that we must get to know the primary premisses
by induction; for the method by which even sense-perception im-

[43] Cf. *Met.* A 980ᵃ 28. *Met.* A I should be compared with this chapter.

5 plants the universal is inductive. Now of the thinking states by which we grasp truth, some are unfailingly true, others admit of error—opinion, for instance, and calculation, whereas scientific knowing and intuition are always true: further, no other kind of thought except intuition is more accurate than scientific knowledge, whereas primary premisses are more knowable than demonstrations, and all 10 scientific knowledge is discursive. From these considerations it follows that there will be no scientific knowledge of the primary premisses, and since except intuition nothing can be truer than scientific knowledge, it will be intuition that apprehends the primary premisses—a result which also follows from the fact that demonstration cannot be the originative source of demonstration, nor, consequently, scientific knowledge of scientific knowledge. If, therefore, it is the only other kind of true thinking except scientific knowing, intuition will 15 be the originative source of scientific knowledge. And the originative source of science grasps the original basic premiss, while science as a whole is similarly related as originative source to the whole body of fact.

TOPICA

Translated by W. A. Pickard-Cambridge

CONTENTS

BOOK I

INTRODUCTORY

[Books II-VIII omitted.]

TOPICA

(*Topics*)

BOOK I

18 1 Our treatise proposes to find a line of inquiry whereby we shall be able to reason from opinions that are generally accepted about
20 every problem propounded to us, and also shall ourselves, when standing up to an argument, avoid saying anything that will obstruct us. First, then, we must say what reasoning is, and what its varieties are, in order to grasp dialectical reasoning: for this is the object of our search in the treatise before us.

25 Now reasoning is an argument in which, certain things being laid down, something other than these necessarily comes about through them. (*a*) It is a 'demonstration', when the premisses from which the reasoning starts are true and primary, or are such that our knowledge of them has originally come through premisses which are
30 primary and true: (*b*) reasoning, on the other hand, is 'dialectical', if it reasons from opinions that are generally accepted. Things are
100ᵇ 'true' and 'primary' which are believed on the strength not of any-
18 thing else but of themselves: for in regard to the first principles of science it is improper to ask any further for the why and wherefore
20 of them; each of the first principles should command belief in and by itself. On the other hand, those opinions are 'generally accepted' which are accepted by every one or by the majority or by the philosophers—i. e. by all, or by the majority, or by the most notable and illustrious of them. Again (*c*), reasoning is 'contentious' if it starts from opinions that seem to be generally accepted, but are not really
25 such, or again if it merely seems to reason from opinions that are or seem to be generally accepted. For not every opinion that seems to be generally accepted actually is generally accepted. For in none of the opinions which we call generally accepted is the illusion entirely on the surface, as happens in the case of the principles of contentious arguments; for the nature of the fallacy in these is obvious immedi-
30 ately, and as a rule even to persons with little power of comprehen-
101ª sion. So then, of the contentious reasonings mentioned, the former really deserves to be called 'reasoning' as well, but the other should

be called 'contentious reasoning', but not 'reasoning', since it appears to reason, but does not really do so.

Further (d), besides all the reasonings we have mentioned there 5 are the mis-reasonings that start from the premisses peculiar to the special sciences, as happens (for example) in the case of geometry and her sister sciences. For this form of reasoning appears to differ from the reasonings mentioned above; the man who draws a false figure reasons from things that are neither true and primary, nor yet gen- 10 erally accepted. For he does not fall within the definition; he does not assume opinions that are received either by every one or by the majority or by philosophers—that is to say, by all, or by most, or by the most illustrious of them—but he conducts his reasoning upon assumptions which, though appropriate to the science in question, are not true; for he effects his mis-reasoning either by describing 15 the semicircles wrongly or by drawing certain lines in a way in which they could not be drawn.

The foregoing must stand for an outline survey of the species of reasoning. In general, in regard both to all that we have already discussed and to those which we shall discuss later, we may remark 20 that that amount of distinction between them may serve, because it is not our purpose to give the exact definition of any of them; we merely want to describe them in outline; we consider it quite enough from the point of view of the line of inquiry before us to be able to recognize each of them in some sort of way.

2   Next in order after the foregoing, we must say for how many and 25 for what purposes the treatise is useful. They are three—intellectual training, casual encounters, and the philosophical sciences. That it is useful as a training is obvious on the face of it. The possession of a plan of inquiry will enable us more easily to argue about the sub- 30 ject proposed. For purposes of casual encounters, it is useful because when we have counted up the opinions held by most people, we shall meet them on the ground not of other people's convictions but of their own, while we shift the ground of any argument that they appear to us to state unsoundly. For the study of the philosophical sciences · it is useful, because the ability to raise searching difficulties on both 35 sides of a subject will make us detect more easily the truth and error about the several points that arise. It has a further use in rela- tion to the ultimate bases of the principles used in the several sciences. For it is impossible to discuss them at all from the principles proper to the particular science in hand, seeing that the principles are the

101ᵇ *prius* of everything else: it is through the opinions generally held on
the particular points that these have to be discussed, and this task
belongs properly, or most appropriately, to dialectic: for dialectic is
a process of criticism wherein lies the path to the principles of all
inquiries.

5 3   We shall be in perfect possession of the way to proceed when
we are in a position like that which we occupy in regard to rhetoric
and medicine and faculties of that kind: this means the doing of that
which we choose with the materials that are available. For it is not
every method that the rhetorician will employ to persuade, or the
doctor to heal: still, if he omits none of the available means, we shall
10 say that his grasp of the science is adequate.

4   First, then, we must see of what parts our inquiry consists. Now
if we were to grasp (*a*) with reference to how many, and what kind of,
things arguments take place, and with what materials they start,
and (*b*) how we are to become well supplied with these, we should
have sufficiently won our goal. Now the materials with which arguments start are equal in number, and are identical, with the subjects
15 on which reasonings take place. For arguments start with 'propositions', while the subjects on which reasonings take place are 'problems'. Now every proposition and every problem indicates either a
genus or a peculiarity or an accident—for the differentia too, applying as it does to a class (or genus), should be ranked together with the
genus. Since, however, of what is peculiar to anything part signifies
20 its essence, while part does not, let us divide the 'peculiar' into both
the aforesaid parts, and call that part which indicates the essence a
'definition', while of the remainder let us adopt the terminology
which is generally current about these things, and speak of it as a
'property'. What we have said, then, makes it clear that according
to our present division, the elements turn out to be four, all told,
25 namely either property or definition or genus or accident. Do not let
any one suppose us to mean that each of these enunciated by itself
constitutes a proposition or problem, but only that it is from these
that both problems and propositions are formed. The difference between a problem and a proposition is a difference in the turn of the
30 phrase. For if it be put in this way, ' "An animal that walks on
two feet" is the definition of man, is it not?' or ' "Animal" is the
genus of man, is it not?' the result is a proposition: but if thus, 'Is
"an animal that walks on two feet" a definition of man or no?' [or

'Is "animal" his genus or no?'] the result is a problem. Similarly too
in other cases. Naturally, then, problems and propositions are equal in 35
number: for out of every proposition you will make a problem if you
change the turn of the phrase.

5　We must now say what are 'definition', 'property', 'genus', and
'accident'. A 'definition' is a phrase signifying a thing's essence. It is
rendered in the form either of a phrase in lieu of a term, or of a phrase 102ᵃ
in lieu of another phrase; for it is sometimes possible to define the
meaning of a phrase as well. People whose rendering consists of a
term only, try it as they may, clearly do not render the definition of
the thing in question, because a definition is always a phrase of a
certain kind. One may, however, use the word 'definitory' also of such 5
a remark as 'The "becoming" is "beautiful",' and likewise also of
the question, 'Are sensation and knowledge the same or different?',
for argument about definitions is mostly concerned with questions of
sameness and difference. In a word we may call 'definitory' everything that falls under the same branch of inquiry as definitions; and
that all the above-mentioned examples are of this character is clear 10
on the face of them. For if we are able to argue that two things are
the same or are different, we shall be well supplied by the same turn
of argument with lines of attack upon their definitions as well: for
when we have shown that they are not the same we shall have demolished the definition. Observe, please, that the converse of this last
statement does not hold: for to show that they are the same is not 15
enough to establish a definition. To show, however, that they are not
the same is enough of itself to overthrow it.

A 'property' is a predicate which does not indicate the essence of a
thing, but yet belongs to that thing alone, and is predicated convertibly of it. Thus it is a property of man to be capable of learning
grammar: for if A be a man, then he is capable of learning gram- 20
mar, and if he be capable of learning grammar, he is a man. For no
one calls anything a 'property' which may possibly belong to something
else, e. g. 'sleep' in the case of man, even though at a certain time it
may happen to belong to him alone. That is to say, if any such thing
were actually to be called a property, it will be called not a 'prop- 25
erty' absolutely, but a 'temporary' or a 'relative' property: for 'being
on the right hand side' is a temporary property, while 'two-footed'
is in point of fact ascribed as a property in certain relations; e. g.
it is a property of man relatively to a horse and a dog. That nothing
which may belong to anything else than A is a convertible predicate

30 of A is clear: for it does not necessarily follow that if something is asleep it is a man.

A 'genus' is what is predicated in the category of essence of a number of things exhibiting differences in kind. We should treat as predicates in the category of essence all such things as it would be appropriate to mention in reply to the question, 'What is the object 35 before you?'; as, for example, in the case of man, if asked that question, it is appropriate to say 'He is an animal'. The question, 'Is one thing in the same genus as another or in a different one?' is also a 'generic' question; for a question of that kind as well falls under the same branch of inquiry as the genus: for having argued that 'animal' is the genus of man, and likewise also of ox, we shall have argued that 102ᵇ they are in the same genus; whereas if we show that it is the genus of the one but not of the other, we shall have argued that these things are not in the same genus.

An 'accident' is (1) something which, though it is none of the 5 foregoing—i. e. neither a definition nor a property nor a genus—yet belongs to the thing: (2) something which may possibly either belong or not belong to any one and the self-same thing, as (e. g.) the 'sitting posture' may belong or not belong to some self-same thing. Likewise also 'whiteness', for there is nothing to prevent the same thing being at one time white, and at another not white. Of the defini-10 tions of accident the second is the better: for if he adopts the first, any one is bound, if he is to understand it, to know already what 'definition' and 'genus' and 'property' are, whereas the second is suf-ficient of itself to tell us the essential meaning of the term in question.
15 To Accident are to be attached also all comparisons of things to-gether, when expressed in language that is drawn in any kind of way from what happens (*accidit*) to be true of them; such as, for example, the question, 'Is the honourable or the expedient preferable?' and 'Is the life of virtue or the life of self-indulgence the pleasanter?', and any other problem which may happen to be phrased in terms like these. For in all such cases the question is 'to which of the two 20 does the predicate in question happen (*accidit*) to belong more closely?' It is clear on the face of it that there is nothing to prevent an accident from becoming a temporary or a relative property. Thus the sitting posture is an accident, but will be a temporary property, whenever a man is the only person sitting, while if he be not the only one sitting, it is still a property relatively to those who are not 25 sitting. So then, there is nothing to prevent an accident from becom-ing both a relative and a temporary property; but a property abso-lutely it will never be.

6 We must not fail to observe that all remarks made in criticism of a 'property' and 'genus' and 'accident' will be applicable to 'definitions' as well. For when we have shown that the attribute in question fails to belong only to the term defined, as we do also in the case of a 30 property, or that the genus rendered in the definition is not the true genus, or that any of the things mentioned in the phrase used does not belong, as would be remarked also in the case of an accident, we shall have demolished the definition; so that, to use the phrase previously employed,[1] all the points we have enumerated might in a certain sense be called 'definitory'. But we must not on this account 35 expect to find a single line of inquiry which will apply universally to them all: for this is not an easy thing to find, and, even were one found, it would be very obscure indeed, and of little service for the treatise before us. Rather, a special plan of inquiry must be laid down for each of the classes we have distinguished, and then, starting from the rules that are appropriate in each case, it will probably be easier to make our way right through the task before us. So then, as was 103ᵃ said before,[2] we must outline a division of our subject, and other questions we must relegate each to the particular branch to which it most naturally belongs, speaking of them as 'definitory' and 'generic' questions. The questions I mean have practically been already assigned to their several branches. 5

7 First of all we must define the number of senses borne by the term 'Sameness'. Sameness would be generally regarded as falling, roughly speaking, into three divisions. We generally apply the term numerically or specifically or generically—numerically in cases where there is more than one name but only one thing, e. g. 'doublet' 10 and 'cloak'; specifically, where there is more than one thing, but they present no differences in respect of their species, as one man and another, or one horse and another: for things like this that fall under the same species are said to be 'specifically the same'. Similarly, too, those things are called generically the same which fall under the same genus, such as a horse and a man. It might appear that the sense in which water from the same spring is called 'the same water' 15 is somehow different and unlike the senses mentioned above: but really such a case as this ought to be ranked in the same class with the things that in one way or another are called 'the same' in view of unity of species. For all such things seem to be of one family and to resemble one another. For the reason why all water is said to be specifically the same as all other water is because of a certain likeness 20

---

[1] ᵃ 9.　　　　　　　　　　　　　　[2] 101ᵃ 22.

it bears to it, and the only difference in the case of water drawn
from the same spring is this, that the likeness is more emphatic: that
is why we do not distinguish it from the things that in one way or
another are called 'the same' in view of unity of species. It is generally supposed that the term 'the same' is most used in a sense agreed
25 on by every one when applied to what is numerically one. But even
so, it is apt to be rendered in more than one sense; its most literal
and primary use is found whenever the sameness is rendered in reference to an alternative name or definition, as when a cloak is said to
be the same as a doublet, or an animal that walks on two feet is said
to be the same as a man: a second sense is when it is rendered in
reference to a property, as when what can acquire knowledge is
called the same as a man, and what naturally travels upward the
same as fire: while a third use is found when it is rendered in refer-
30 ence to some term drawn from Accident, as when the creature who is
sitting, or who is musical, is called the same as Socrates. For all these
uses mean to signify numerical unity. That what I have just said is
true may be best seen where one form of appellation is substituted
for another. For often when we give the order to call one of the
people who are sitting down, indicating him by name, we change our
35 description, whenever the person to whom we give the order happens
not to understand us; he will, we think, understand better from some
accidental feature; so we bid him call to us 'the man who is sitting'
or 'who is conversing over there'—clearly supposing ourselves to be
indicating the same object by its name and by its accident.

103ᵇ 8 Of 'sameness' then, as has been said,[3] three senses are to be distinguished. Now one way to confirm that the elements mentioned
above are those out of which and through which and to which arguments proceed, is by induction: for if any one were to survey propositions and problems one by one, it would be seen that each was
5 formed either from the definition of something or from its property or from its genus or from its accident. Another way to confirm
it is through reasoning. For every predicate of a subject must of necessity be either convertible with its subject or not: and if it is convertible, it would be its definition or property, for if it signifies the
10 essence, it is the definition; if not, it is a property: for this was [4] what
a property is, viz. what is predicated convertibly, but does not signify
the essence. If, on the other hand, it is not predicated convertibly
of the thing, it either is or is not one of the terms contained in the
definition of the subject: and if it be one of those terms, then it will

² ᵃ7.   ⁴ 102ᵃ 18.

be the genus or the differentia, inasmuch as the definition consists 15
of genus and differentiae; whereas, if it be not one of those terms,
clearly it would be an accident, for accident was said [5] to be what
belongs as an attribute to a subject without being either its definition
or its genus or a property.

9 Next, then, we must distinguish between the classes of predicates 20
in which the four orders in question are found. These are ten in
number: Essence, Quantity, Quality, Relation, Place, Time, Position,
State, Activity, Passivity. For the accident and genus and property
and definition of anything will always be in one of these categories: 25
for all the propositions found through these signify either something's
essence or its quality or quantity or some one of the other types of
predicate. It is clear, too, on the face of it that the man who signifies
something's essence signifies sometimes a substance, sometimes a
quality, sometimes some one of the other types of predicate. For
when a man is set before him and he says that what is set there is 'a 30
man' or 'an animal', he states its essence and signifies a substance;
but when a white colour is set before him and he says that what is
set there is 'white' or is 'a colour', he states its essence and signifies a
quality. Likewise, also, if a magnitude of a cubit be set before him
and he says that what is set there is a magnitude of a cubit, he will
be describing its essence and signifying a quantity. Likewise, also, in 35
the other cases: for each of these kinds of predicate, if either it be
asserted of itself, or its genus be asserted of it, signifies an essence:
if, on the other hand, one kind of predicate is asserted of another
kind, it does not signify an essence, but a quantity or a quality or
one of the other kinds of predicate. Such, then, and so many, are
the subjects on which arguments take place, and the materials with 104ᵃ
which they start. How we are to acquire them, and by what means
we are to become well supplied with them, falls next to be told.

10   First, then, a definition must be given of a 'dialectical proposition' and a 'dialectical problem'. For it is not every proposition nor yet
every problem that is to be set down as dialectical: for no one in his 5
senses would make a proposition of what no one holds, nor yet make
a problem of what is obvious to everybody or to most people: for
the latter admits of no doubt, while to the former no one would assent.
Now a dialectical proposition consists in asking something that is
held by all men or by most men or by the philosophers, i. e. either
by all, or by most, or by the most notable of these, provided it be not 10

[5] 102ᵇ 4.

contrary to the general opinion; for a man would probably assent to the view of the philosophers, if it be not contrary to the opinions of most men. Dialectical propositions also include views which are like those generally accepted; also propositions which contradict the contraries of opinions that are taken to be generally accepted, and
15 also all opinions that are in accordance with the recognized arts. Thus, supposing it to be a general opinion that the knowledge of contraries is the same, it might probably pass for a general opinion also that the perception of contraries is the same: also, supposing it to be a general opinion that there is but one single science of grammar, it might pass for a general opinion that there is but one science of flute-playing as well, whereas, if it be a general opinion that there is more than one science of grammar, it might pass for a general opinion that there is more than
20 one science of flute-playing as well: for all these seem to be alike and akin. Likewise, also, propositions contradicting the contraries of general opinions will pass as general opinions: for if it be a general opinion that one ought to do good to one's friends, it will also be a general opinion that one ought not to do them harm. Here, that one ought to do harm to one's friends is contrary to the general view, and that one ought not to do them harm is the contradictory of that contrary.
25 Likewise also, if one ought to do good to one's friends, one ought not to do good to one's enemies: this too is the contradictory of the view contrary to the general view; the contrary being that one ought to do good to one's enemies. Likewise, also, in other cases. Also, on comparison, it will look like a general opinion that the contrary predicate belongs to the contrary subject: e. g. if one ought to do good to one's
30 friends, one ought also to do evil to one's enemies. It might appear also as if doing good to one's friends were a contrary to doing evil to one's enemies: but whether this is or is not so in reality as well will be stated in the course of the discussion upon contraries.[6] Clearly also, all opinions that are in accordance with the arts are dialectical propositions; for people are likely to assent to the views held by those
35 who have made a study of these things, e. g. on a question of medicine they will agree with the doctor, and on a question of geometry with the geometrician; and likewise also in other cases.

104ᵇ 11   A dialectical problem is a subject of inquiry that contributes either to choice and avoidance, or to truth and knowledge, and that either by itself, or as a help to the solution of some other such problem. It must, moreover, be something on which either people hold no opinion either way, or the masses hold a contrary opinion to the

[6] ii. 7.

philosophers, or the philosophers to the masses, or each of them 5
among themselves. For some problems it is useful to know with a
view to choice or avoidance, e. g. whether pleasure is to be chosen or
not, while some it is useful to know merely with a view to knowledge,
e. g. whether the universe is eternal or not: others, again, are not
useful in and by themselves for either of these purposes, but yet help
us in regard to some such problems; for there are many things which 10
we do not wish to know in and by themselves, but for the sake of
other things, in order that through them we may come to know something else. Problems also include questions in regard to which reasonings conflict (the difficulty then being whether so-and-so is so or not,
there being convincing arguments for both views); others also in
regard to which we have no argument because they are so vast, and 15
we find it difficult to give our reasons, e. g. the question whether the
universe is eternal or no: for into questions of that kind too it is
possible to inquire.

Problems, then, and propositions are to be defined as aforesaid.[7]
A 'thesis' is a supposition of some eminent philosopher that conflicts with the general opinion; e. g. the view that contradiction is 20
impossible, as Antisthenes said; or the view of Heraclitus that all
things are in motion; or that Being is one, as Melissus says: for to
take notice when any ordinary person expresses views contrary to
men's usual opinions would be silly. Or it may be a view about
which we have a reasoned theory contrary to men's usual opinions,
e. g. the view maintained by the sophists that what is need not in every 25
case either have come to be or be eternal: for a musician who is a
grammarian 'is' so without ever having 'come to be' so, or being so
eternally. For even if a man does not accept this view, he might do
so on the ground that it is reasonable.

Now a 'thesis' also is a problem, though a problem is not always
a thesis, inasmuch as some problems are such that we have no 30
opinion about them either way. That a thesis, however, also forms
a problem, is clear: for it follows of necessity from what has been
said that either the mass of men disagree with the philosophers about
the thesis, or that the one or the other class disagree among themselves, seeing that the thesis is a supposition in conflict with general
opinion. Practically all dialectical problems indeed are now called 35
'theses'. But it should make no difference whichever description is
used; for our object in thus distinguishing them has not been to create
a terminology, but to recognize what differences happen to be found
between them.   105ᵃ

7 ᵇ 1, ᵃ 8.

Not every problem, nor every thesis, should be examined, but only one which might puzzle one of those who need argument, not pun-
5 ishment or perception. For people who are puzzled to know whether one ought to honour the gods and love one's parents or not need punishment, while those who are puzzled to know whether snow is white or not need perception. The subjects should not border too closely upon the sphere of demonstration, nor yet be too far removed from it: for the former cases admit of no doubt, while the latter in-volve difficulties too great for the art of the trainer.

10 **12**   Having drawn these definitions, we must distinguish how many species there are of dialectical arguments. There is on the one hand Induction, on the other Reasoning. Now what reasoning is has been said before:[8] induction is a passage from individuals to universals, e. g. the argument that supposing the skilled pilot is the most effec-
15 tive, and likewise the skilled charioteer, then in general the skilled man is the best at his particular task. Induction is the more convinc-ing and clear: it is more readily learnt by the use of the senses, and is applicable generally to the mass of men, though Reasoning is more forcible and effective against contradictious people.

20 **13**   The classes, then, of things about which, and of things out of which, arguments are constructed, are to be distinguished in the way we have said before. The means whereby we are to become well sup-plied with reasonings are four: (1) the securing of propositions; (2) the power to distinguish in how many senses a particular expres-sion is used; (3) the discovery of the differences of things; (4) the
25 investigation of likeness. The last three, as well, are in a certain sense propositions: for it is possible to make a proposition corresponding to each of them, e. g. (1) 'The desirable may mean either the hon-ourable or the pleasant or the expedient'; and (2) 'Sensation differs from knowledge in that the latter may be recovered again after it has
30 been lost, while the former cannot'; and (3) 'The relation of the healthy to health is like that of the vigorous to vigour'. The first proposition depends upon the use of one term in several senses, the second upon the differences of things, the third upon their likenesses.

14   Propositions should be selected in a number of ways correspond-ing to the number of distinctions drawn in regard to the proposition:
35 thus one may first take in hand the opinions held by all or by most men or by the philosophers, i. e. by all, or most, or the most notable

[8] 100ᵃ 25.

of them; or opinions contrary to those that seem to be generally held; 105ᵇ
and, again, all opinions that are in accordance with the arts. We must
make propositions also of the contradictories of opinions contrary to
those that seem to be generally held, as was laid down before. It is
useful also to make them by selecting not only those opinions that
actually are accepted, but also those that are like these, e. g. 'The 5
perception of contraries is the same'—the knowledge of them being so
—and 'we see by admission of something into ourselves, not by an
emission'; for so it is, too, in the case of the other senses; for in hearing we admit something into ourselves; we do not emit; and we taste
in the same way. Likewise also in the other cases. Moreover, all statements that seem to be true in all or in most cases, should be taken as 10
a principle or accepted position; for they are posited by those who
do not also see what exception there may be. We should select also
from the written handbooks of argument, and should draw up sketch-
lists of them upon each several kind of subject, putting them down
under separate headings, e. g. 'On Good', or 'On Life'—and that 'On 15
Good' should deal with every form of good, beginning with the category of essence. In the margin, too, one should indicate also the opinions of individual thinkers, e. g. 'Empedocles said that the elements
of bodies were four': for any one might assent to the saying of some
generally accepted authority.

Of propositions and problems there are—to comprehend the matter
in outline—three divisions: for some are ethical propositions, some 20
are on natural philosophy, while some are logical. Propositions such as
the following are ethical, e. g. 'Ought one rather to obey one's parents
or the laws, if they disagree?'; such as this are logical, e. g. 'Is the
knowledge of opposites the same or not?'; while such as this are on
natural philosophy, e. g. 'Is the universe eternal or not?' Likewise 25
also with problems. The nature of each of the aforesaid kinds of proposition is not easily rendered in a definition, but we have to try to
recognize each of them by means of the familiarity attained through
induction, examining them in the light of the illustrations given above.

For purposes of philosophy we must treat of these things accord- 30
ing to their truth, but for dialectic only with an eye to general
opinion. All propositions should be taken in their most universal
form; then, the one should be made into many. E. g. 'The knowledge
of opposites is the same'; next, 'The knowledge of contraries is the
same', and that 'of relative terms'. In the same way these two should
again be divided, as long as division is possible, e. g. the knowledge 35
of 'good and evil', of 'white and black', or 'cold and hot'. Likewise
also in other cases.

106ᵃ **15**   On the formation, then, of propositions, the above remarks
are enough. As regards the number of senses a term bears, we must
not only treat of those terms which bear different senses, but we
must also try to render their definitions; e. g. we must not merely
5   say that justice and courage are called 'good' in one sense, and that
what conduces to vigour and what conduces to health are called so
in another, but also that the former are so called because of a certain intrinsic quality they themselves have, the latter because they
are productive of a certain result and not because of any intrinsic
quality in themselves. Similarly also in other cases.

Whether a term bears a number of specific meanings or one only,
10   may be considered by the following means. First, look and see if its
contrary bears a number of meanings, whether the discrepancy between them be one of kind or one of names. For in some cases a
difference is at once displayed even in the names; e. g. the contrary
of 'sharp' in the case of a note is 'flat', while in the case of a solid
edge it is 'dull'. Clearly, then, the contrary of 'sharp' bears several
15   meanings, and if so, so also does 'sharp'; for corresponding to each
of the former terms the meaning of its contrary will be different. For
'sharp' will not be the same when contrary to 'dull' and to 'flat', though
'sharp' is the contrary of each. Again *baru* ('flat', 'heavy') in the case
of a note has 'sharp' as its contrary, but in the case of a solid mass
'light', so that *baru* is used with a number of meanings, inasmuch as
20   its contrary also is so used. Likewise, also, 'fine' as applied to a picture has 'ugly' as its contrary, but, as applied to a house, 'ramshackle';
so that 'fine' is an ambiguous term.

In some cases there is no discrepancy of any sort in the names
used, but a difference of kind between the meanings is at once
obvious: e. g. in the case of 'clear' and 'obscure': for sound is called
25   'clear' and 'obscure', just as 'colour' is too. As regards the names,
then, there is no discrepancy, but the difference in kind between the
meanings is at once obvious: for colour is not called 'clear' in a like
sense to sound. This is plain also through sensation: for of things
that are the same in kind we have the same sensation, whereas we
30   do not judge clearness by the same sensation in the case of sound and
of colour, but in the latter case we judge by sight, in the former by
hearing. Likewise also with 'sharp' and 'dull' in regard to flavours
and solid edges: here in the latter case we judge by touch, but in the
former by taste. For here again there is no discrepancy in the names
35   used, in the case either of the original terms or of their contraries:
for the contrary also of sharp in either sense is 'dull'.

Moreover, see if one sense of a term has a contrary, while another has absolutely none; e. g. the pleasure of drinking has a contrary in the pain of thirst, whereas the pleasure of seeing that the
diagonal is incommensurate with the side has none, so that 'pleasure' 106ᵇ
is used in more than one sense. To 'love' also, used of the frame of
mind, has to 'hate' as its contrary, while as used of the physical
activity (kissing) it has none: clearly, therefore, to 'love' is an ambiguous term. Further, see in regard to their intermediates, if some
meanings and their contraries have an intermediate, while others
have none, or if both have one but not the same one, as e. g. 'clear' 5
and 'obscure' in the case of colours have 'grey' as an intermediate,
whereas in the case of sound they have none, or, if they have, it is
'harsh', as some people say that a harsh sound is intermediate. 'Clear',
then, is an ambiguous term, and likewise also 'obscure'. See, moreover, if some of them have more than one intermediate, while others 10
have but one, as is the case with 'clear' and 'obscure', for in the case
of colours there are numbers of intermediates, whereas in regard to
sound there is but one, viz. 'harsh'.

Again, in the case of the contradictory opposite, look and see if it
bears more than one meaning. For if this bears more than one meaning, then the opposite of it also will be used in more than one mean- 15
ing; e. g. 'to fail to see' is a phrase with more than one meaning,
viz. (1) to fail to possess the power of sight, (2) to fail to put that
power to active use. But if this has more than one meaning, it follows necessarily that 'to see' also has more than one meaning: for
there will be an opposite to each sense of 'to fail to see'; e. g. the
opposite of 'not to possess the power of sight' is to possess it, while
of 'not to put the power of sight to active use', the opposite is to put 20
it to active use.

Moreover, examine the case of terms that denote the privation or
presence of a certain state: for if the one term bears more than one
meaning, then so will the remaining term: e. g. if 'to have sense' be
used with more than one meaning, as applied to the soul and to the
body, then 'to be wanting in sense' too will be used with more than
one meaning, as applied to the soul and to the body. That the oppo- 25
sition between the terms now in question depends upon the privation
or presence of a certain state is clear, since animals naturally possess
each kind of 'sense', both as applied to the soul and as applied to
the body.

Moreover, examine the inflected forms. For if 'justly' has more
than one meaning, then 'just', also, will be used with more than one 30
meaning; for there will be a meaning of 'just' corresponding to each

of the meanings of 'justly'; e. g. if the word 'justly' be used of judging according to one's own opinion, and also of judging as one ought, then 'just' also will be used in like manner. In the same way also, if 'healthy' has more than one meaning, then 'healthily' also will be
35 used with more than one meaning: e. g. if 'healthy' describes both what produces health and what preserves health and what betokens health, then 'healthily' also will be used to mean 'in such a way as to produce' or 'preserve' or 'betoken' health. Likewise also in other cases, whenever the original term bears more than one meaning, the
107ª inflexion also that is formed from it will be used with more than one meaning, and vice versa.

Look also at the classes of the predicates signified by the term, and see if they are the same in all cases. For if they are not the same,
5 then clearly the term is ambiguous: e. g. 'good' in the case of food means 'productive of pleasure', and in the case of medicine 'productive of health', whereas as applied to the soul it means to be of a certain quality, e. g. temperate or courageous or just: and likewise also, as applied to 'man'. Sometimes it signifies what happens at a certain time, as (e. g.) the good that happens at the right time: for what happens at the right time is called good. Often it signifies what
10 is of a certain quantity, e. g. as applied to the proper amount: for the proper amount too is called good. So then the term 'good' is ambiguous. In the same way also 'clear', as applied to a body, signifies a colour, but in regard to a note it denotes what is 'easy to hear'. 'Sharp', too, is in a closely similar case: for the same term does not
15 bear the same meaning in all its applications: for a sharp note is a swift note, as the mathematical theorists of harmony tell us, whereas a sharp (acute) angle is one that is less than a right angle, while a sharp dagger is one containing a sharp angle (point).

Look also at the genera of the objects denoted by the same term, and see if they are different without being subaltern, as (e. g.) 'donkey', which denotes both the animal and the engine. For the
20 definition of them that corresponds to the name is different: for the one will be declared to be an animal of a certain kind, and the other to be an engine of a certain kind. If, however, the genera be subaltern, there is no necessity for the definitions to be different. Thus (e. g.) 'animal' is the genus of 'raven', and so is 'bird'. Whenever therefore we say that the raven is a bird, we also say that it is
25 a certain kind of animal, so that both the genera are predicated of it. Likewise also whenever we call the raven a 'flying biped animal', we declare it to be a bird: in this way, then, as well, both the genera are predicated of raven, and also their definition. But in the case of genera

that are not subaltern this does not happen, for whenever we call a 30
thing an 'engine', we do not call it an animal, nor vice versa.

Look also and see not only if the genera of the term before you are
different without being subaltern, but also in the case of its contrary: for if its contrary bears several senses, clearly the term 35
before you does so as well.

It is useful also to look at the definition that arises from the use of
the term in combination, e. g. of a 'clear (*lit*. white) body' and of a
'clear note'. For then if what is peculiar in each case be abstracted,
the same expression ought to remain over. This does not happen in
the case of ambiguous terms, e. g. in the cases just mentioned. For 107ᵇ
the former will be 'a body possessing such and such a colour', while
the latter will be 'a note easy to hear'. Abstract, then, 'a body' and
'a note', and the remainder in each case is not the same. It should,
however, have been had the meaning of 'clear' in each case been 5
synonymous.

Often in the actual definitions as well ambiguity creeps in un-
awares, and for this reason the definitions also should be examined.
If (e. g.) any one describes what betokens and what produces health
as 'related commensurably to health', we must not desist but go
on to examine in what sense he has used the term 'commensurably' 10
in each case, e. g. if in the latter case it means that 'it is of the right
amount to produce health', whereas in the former it means that 'it
is such as to betoken what kind of state prevails'.

Moreover, see if the terms cannot be compared as 'more or less'
or as 'in like manner', as is the case (e. g.) with a 'clear' (*lit*. white)
sound and a 'clear' garment, and a 'sharp' flavour and a 'sharp' note. 15
For neither are these things said to be clear or sharp 'in a like degree',
nor yet is the one said to be clearer or sharper than the other. 'Clear',
then, and 'sharp' are ambiguous. For synonyms are always comparable; for they will always be used either in like manner, or else
in a greater degree in one case.

Now since of genera that are different without being subaltern 20
the differentiae also are different in kind, e. g. those of 'animal' and
'knowledge' (for the differentiae of these are different), look and see
if the meanings comprised under the same term are differentiae of
genera that are different without being subaltern, as e. g. 'sharp' is
of a 'note' and a 'solid'. For being 'sharp' differentiates note from
note, and likewise also one solid from another. 'Sharp', then, is an
ambiguous term: for it forms differentiae of genera that are different 25
without being subaltern.

Again, see if the actual meanings included under the same term

themselves have different differentiae, e. g. 'colour' in bodies and 'colour' in tunes: for the differentiae of 'colour' in bodies are 'sight-
30 piercing' and 'sight-compressing', whereas 'colour' in melodies has not the same differentiae. Colour, then, is an ambiguous term; for things that are the same have the same differentiae.

Moreover, since the species is never the differentia of anything, look and see if one of the meanings included under the same term be a species and another a differentia, as (e. g.) 'clear' (*lit.* white) as ap-
35 plied to a body is a species of colour, whereas in the case of a note it is a differentia; for one note is differentiated from another by being 'clear'.

16 The presence, then, of a number of meanings in a term may be investigated by these and like means. The differences which things present to each other should be examined within the same genera, e. g.
108ᵃ 'Wherein does justice differ from courage, and wisdom from temperance?'—for all these belong to the same genus; and also from one genus to another, provided they be not very much too far apart, e. g. 'Wherein does sensation differ from knowledge?': for in the
5 case of genera that are very far apart, the differences are entirely obvious.

17 Likeness should be studied, first, in the case of things belonging to different genera, the formulae being 'A : B = C : D' (e. g. as knowledge stands to the object of knowledge, so is sensation related to the object of sensation), and 'As A is in B, so is C in D' (e. g. as
10 sight is in the eye, so is reason in the soul, and as is a calm in the sea, so is windlessness in the air). Practice is more especially needed in regard to terms that are far apart; for in the case of the rest, we shall be more easily able to see in one glance the points of likeness. We should also look at things which belong to the same genus,
15 to see if any identical attribute belongs to them all, e. g. to a man and a horse and a dog; for in so far as they have any identical attribute, in so far they are alike.

18 It is useful to have examined the number of meanings of a term both for clearness' sake (for a man is more likely to know what it is he asserts, if it has been made clear to him how many meanings it
20 may have), and also with a view to ensuring that our reasonings shall be in accordance with the actual facts and not addressed merely to the term used. For as long as it is not clear in how many senses a term is used, it is possible that the answerer and the questioner

are not directing their minds upon the same thing: whereas when once it has been made clear how many meanings there are, and also upon which of them the former directs his mind when he makes his 25 assertion, the questioner would then look ridiculous if he failed to address his argument to this. It helps us also both to avoid being misled and to mislead by false reasoning: for if we know the number of meanings of a term, we shall certainly never be misled by false reasoning, but shall know if the questioner fails to address his argument to the same point; and when we ourselves put the questions we shall be able to mislead him, if our answerer happens not to know 30 the number of meanings of our terms. This, however, is not possible in all cases, but only when of the many senses some are true and others are false. This manner of argument, however, does not belong properly to dialectic; dialecticians should therefore by all means beware of this kind of verbal discussion, unless any one is absolutely 35 unable to discuss the subject before him in any other way.

The discovery of the differences of things helps us both in reasonings about sameness and difference, and also in recognizing what any 108^b particular thing is. That it helps us in reasoning about sameness and difference is clear: for when we have discovered a difference of any kind whatever between the objects before us, we shall already have shown that they are not the same: while it helps us in recognizing what a thing is, because we usually distinguish the expression that is 5 proper to the essence of each particular thing by means of the differentiae that are proper to it.

The examination of likeness is useful with a view both to inductive arguments and to hypothetical reasonings, and also with a view to the rendering of definitions. It is useful for inductive arguments, 10 because it is by means of an induction of individuals in cases that are alike that we claim to bring the universal in evidence: for it is not easy to do this if we do not know the points of likeness. It is useful for hypothetical reasonings because it is a general opinion that among similars what is true of one is true also of the rest. If, then, with regard to any of them we are well supplied with matter for a discussion, we shall secure a preliminary admission that however it is in these 15 cases, so it is also in the case before us: then when we have shown the former we shall have shown, on the strength of the hypothesis, the matter before us as well: for we have first made the hypothesis that however it is in these cases, so it is also in the case before us, and have then proved the point as regards these cases. It is useful for the rendering of definitions because, if we are able to see in one glance what is the same in each individual case of it, 20

we shall be at no loss into what genus we ought to put the object
before us when we define it: for of the common predicates that which
is most definitely in the category of essence is likely to be the genus.
Likewise, also, in the case of objects widely divergent, the examination of likeness is useful for purposes of definition, e. g. the sameness
25 of a calm at sea, and windlessness in the air (each being a form of
rest), and of a point on a line and the unit in number—each being a
starting point. If, then, we render as the genus what is common to
all the cases, we shall get the credit of defining not inappropriately.
Definition-mongers too nearly always render them in this way: for
30 they declare the unit to be the starting-point of number, and the
point the starting-point of a line. It is clear, then, that they place
them in that which is common to both as their genus.

The means, then, whereby reasonings are effected, are these: the
commonplace rules, for the observance of which the aforesaid means
are useful, are as follows.

[Books II-VIII omitted.]

DE SOPHISTICIS ELENCHIS

Translated by W. A. Pickard-Cambridge

CONTENTS

INTRODUCTORY (CHAPTERS 1-2)

PERPETRATION OF FALLACIES (CHAPTERS 3-15)

[Chapters 4-33 omitted.]

EPILOGUE

DE SOPHISTICIS ELENCHIS

(On Sophistical Refutations)

20 **1** Let us now discuss sophistic refutations, i. e. what appear to be refutations but are really fallacies instead. We will begin in the natural order with the first.

That some reasonings are genuine, while others seem to be so but are not, is evident. This happens with arguments, as also elsewhere, 25 through a certain likeness between the genuine and the sham. For 164^b physically some people are in a vigorous condition, while others 20 merely seem to be so by blowing and rigging themselves out as the tribesmen do their victims for sacrifice; and some people are beautiful thanks to their beauty, while others seem to be so, by dint of embellishing themselves. So it is, too, with inanimate things; for of these, too, some are really silver and others gold, while others are not and merely seem to be such to our sense; e. g. things made of litharge and tin seem to be of silver, while those made of yellow 25 metal look golden. In the same way both reasoning and refutation are sometimes genuine, sometimes not, though inexperience may make them appear so: for inexperienced people obtain only, as it 165^a were, a distant view of these things. For reasoning rests on certain statements such that they involve necessarily the assertion of something other than what has been stated, through what has been stated: refutation is reasoning involving the contradictory of the given conclusion. Now some of them do not really achieve this, though they seem to do so for a number of reasons; and of these the most prolific 5 and usual domain is the argument that turns upon names only. It is impossible in a discussion to bring in the actual things discussed: we use their names as symbols instead of them; and therefore we suppose that what follows in the names, follows in the things as well, just as people who calculate suppose in regard to their counters. 10 But the two cases (names and things) are not alike. For names are finite and so is the sum-total of formulae, while things are infinite in number. Inevitably, then, the same formulae, and a single name, have a number of meanings. Accordingly just as, in counting, those who are not clever in manipulating their counters are taken in by 15 the experts, in the same way in arguments too those who are not well acquainted with the force of names misreason both in their own discussions and when they listen to others. For this reason, then, and for others to be mentioned later, there exists both reasoning and refutation that is apparent but not real. Now for some people it is better worth while to seem to be wise, than to be wise without 20 seeming to be (for the art of the sophist is the semblance of wisdom without the reality, and the sophist is one who makes money from an apparent but unreal wisdom); for them, then, it is clearly essential also to seem to accomplish the task of a wise man rather than to accomplish it without seeming to do so. To reduce it to a single point of contrast it is the business of one who knows a thing, himself 25 to avoid fallacies in the subjects which he knows and to be able to show up the man who makes them; and of these accomplishments the one depends on the faculty to render an answer, and the other upon the securing of one. Those, then, who would be sophists are bound to study the class of arguments aforesaid: for it is worth their while: for a faculty of this kind will make a man seem to be wise, 30 and this is the purpose they happen to have in view.

Clearly, then, there exists a class of arguments of this kind, and it is at this kind of ability that those aim whom we call sophists. Let us now go on to discuss how many kinds there are of sophistical arguments, and how many in number are the elements of which this 35 faculty is composed, and how many branches there happen to be of this inquiry, and the other factors that contribute to this art.

2 Of arguments in dialogue form there are four classes:

Didactic, Dialectical, Examination-arguments, and Contentious arguments. Didactic arguments are those that reason from the prin- 165^b ciples appropriate to each subject and not from the opinions held by the answerer (for the learner should take things on trust): dialectical arguments are those that reason from premisses generally accepted, to the contradictory of a given thesis: examination-arguments are those that reason from premisses which are accepted by the answerer 5 and which any one who pretends to possess knowledge of the subject is bound to know—in what manner, has been defined in another treatise: contentious arguments are those that reason or appear to reason to a conclusion from premisses that appear to be generally accepted but are not so. The subject, then, of demonstrative arguments has been discussed in the *Analytics*, while that of dialectic arguments and examination-arguments has been discussed elsewhere: let us 10 now proceed to speak of the arguments used in competitions and contests.

3   First we must grasp the number of aims entertained by those who argue as competitors and rivals to the death. These are five in number, refutation, fallacy, paradox, solecism, and fifthly to re-
15 duce the opponent in the discussion to babbling—i. e. to constrain him to repeat himself a number of times: or it is to produce the appearance of each of these things without the reality. For they choose if possible plainly to refute the other party, or as the second best to show that he is committing some fallacy, or as a third best to lead him into paradox, or fourthly to reduce him to solecism, i. e. to make
20 the answerer, in consequence of the argument, to use an ungrammatical expression; or, as a last resort, to make him repeat himself. . . .

182ᵃ 34   As to the number, then, and kind of sources whence fallacies arise in discussion, and how we are to show that our opponent is committing a fallacy and make him utter paradoxes; moreover, by the use of what materials solecism is brought about, and how to question
30 and what is the way to arrange the questions; moreover, as to the question what use is served by all arguments of this kind, and concerning the answerer's part, both as a whole in general, and in particular how to solve arguments and solecisms—on all these things let the foregoing discussion suffice. It remains to recall our original
35 proposal and to bring our discussion to a close with a few words upon it.

Our programme was, then, to discover some faculty of reasoning about any theme put before us from the most generally accepted premises that there are. For that is the essential task of the art of discussion (dialectic) and of examination (peirastic). Inasmuch,
183ᵇ however, as it is annexed to it, on account of the near presence of the art of sophistry (sophistic), not only to be able to conduct an examination dialectically but also with a show of knowledge, we therefore proposed for our treatise not only the aforesaid aim of being able to exact an account of any view, but also the aim of
5 ensuring that in standing up to an argument we shall defend our thesis in the same manner by means of views as generally held as possible. The reason of this we have explained; [1] for this, too, was why Socrates used to ask questions and not to answer them; for he used to confess that he did not know. We have made clear, in the course of what precedes, the number both of the points with reference to which, and of the materials from which, this will be ac-
10 complished, and also from what sources we can become well supplied

[1] 165ᵃ 19–27.

with these: we have shown, moreover, how to question or arrange the questioning as a whole, and the problems concerning the answers and solutions to be used against the reasonings of the questioner. We have also cleared up the problems concerning all other matters that belong to the same inquiry into arguments. In addition to this we have been through the subject of Fallacies, as we have already stated above.[2]

That our programme, then, has been adequately completed is clear. But we must not omit to notice what has happened in regard to this inquiry. For in the case of all discoveries the results of previous labours that have been handed down from others have been advanced bit by bit by those who have taken them on, whereas the original discoveries generally make an advance that is small at first though much more useful than the development which later springs out of them. For it may be that in everything, as the saying is, 'the first start is the main part': and for this reason also it is the most difficult; for in proportion as it is most potent in its influence, so it is smallest in its compass and therefore most difficult to see: whereas when this is once discovered, it is easier to add and develop the remainder in connexion with it. This is in fact what has happened in regard to rhetorical speeches and to practically all the other arts: for those who discovered the beginnings of them advanced them in all only a little way, whereas the celebrities of to-day are the heirs (so to speak) of a long succession of men who have advanced them bit by bit, and so have developed them to their present form, Tisias coming next after the first founders, then Thrasymachus after Tisias, and Theodorus next to him, while several people have made their several contributions to it: and therefore it is not to be wondered at that the art has attained considerable dimensions. Of this inquiry, on the other hand, it was not the case that part of the work had been thoroughly done before, while part had not. Nothing existed at all. For the training given by the paid professors of contentious arguments was like the treatment of the matter by Gorgias. For they used to hand out speeches to be learned by heart, some rhetorical, others in the form of question and answer, each side supposing that their arguments on either side generally fall among them. And therefore the teaching they gave their pupils was ready but rough. For they used to suppose that they trained people by imparting to them not the art but its products, as though any one professing that he would impart a form of knowledge to obviate any pain in the feet, were then not to teach a man the art of shoe-making or the sources whence he can acquire

2 183ᵃ 27.

anything of the kind, but were to present him with several kinds of shoes of all sorts: for he has helped him to meet his need, but has not imparted an art to him. Moreover, on the subject of Rhetoric there 184ᵇ exists much that has been said long ago, whereas on the subject of reasoning we had nothing else of an earlier date to speak of at all, but were kept at work for a long time in experimental researches. If, then, it seems to you after inspection that, such being the situation as it existed at the start, our investigation is in a satisfactory 5 condition compared with the other inquiries that have been developed by tradition, there must remain for all of you, or for our students, the task of extending us your pardon for the shortcomings of the inquiry, and for the discoveries thereof your warm thanks.

Physica

Translated by R. P. Hardie and R. K. Gaye

CONTENTS

BOOK I

BOOK II

A.

B.

C. *The conditions of change.*

D. *Proof in natural philosophy.*

BOOK III

A. *Motion.*

B. *The infinite.*

BOOK IV

A. *Place.*

B. *The void.*

C. *Time.*

BOOK V

BOOK VI

BOOK VII

BOOK VIII

PHYSICA[1]

(*Physics*)

BOOK I

184ᵃ 1 When the objects of an inquiry, in any department, have prin-
10 ciples, conditions, or elements, it is through acquaintance with these
that knowledge, that is to say scientific knowledge, is attained. For
we do not think that we know a thing until we are acquainted with
its primary conditions or first principles, and have carried our analysis as far as its simplest elements. Plainly therefore in the science of
15 Nature, as in other branches of study, our first task will be to try to
determine what relates to its principles.

The natural way of doing this is to start from the things which are
more knowable and obvious to us and proceed towards those which
are clearer and more knowable by nature; for the same things are
not 'knowable relatively to us' and 'knowable' without qualification.
So in the present inquiry we must follow this method and advance
20 from what is more obscure by nature, but clearer to us, towards what
is more clear and more knowable by nature.

Now what is to us plain and obvious at first is rather confused
masses, the elements and principles of which become known to us
later by analysis. Thus we must advance from generalities to particu-
25 lars; for it is a whole that is best known to sense-perception, and a
generality is a kind of whole, comprehending many things within it,
184ᵇ like parts. Much the same thing happens in the relation of the name
10 to the formula. A name, e. g. 'round', means vaguely a sort of whole:
its definition analyses this into its particular senses. Similarly a child
begins by calling all men 'father', and all women 'mother', but later
on distinguishes each of them.

---

[1] The present treatise, usually called the *Physics*, deals with natural body in
general: the special kinds are discussed in Aristotle's other physical works, the
De Caelo, &c. The first book is concerned with the elements of a natural body
(matter and form) : the second mainly with the different types of cause studied by
the physicist. Books III–VII deal with movement, and the notions implied in it.
The subject of VIII is the prime mover, which, though not itself a natural body,
is the cause of movement in natural bodies.

2　The principles in question must be either (a) one or (b) more 15
than one.

If (a) one, it must be either (i) motionless, as Parmenides and
Melissus assert, or (ii) in motion, as the physicists hold, some declaring air to be the first principle, others water.

If (b) more than one, then either (i) a finite or (ii) an infinite
plurality. If (i) finite (but more than one), then either two or three or 20
four or some other number. If (ii) infinite, then either as Democritus
believed one in kind, but differing in shape or form; or different in
kind and even contrary.

A similar inquiry is made by those who inquire into the number of
existents: for they inquire whether the ultimate constituents of
existing things are one or many, and if many, whether a finite or an
infinite plurality. So they too are inquiring whether the principle
or element is one or many.

Now to investigate whether Being is one and motionless is not a 25
contribution to the science of Nature. For just as the geometer has 185ᵃ
nothing more to say to one who denies the principles of his science—
this being a question for a different science or for one common to
all—so a man investigating *principles* cannot argue with one who
denies their existence. For if Being is just one, and one in the way
mentioned, there is a principle no longer, since a principle must be
the principle of some thing or things.

To inquire therefore whether Being is one in this sense would be 5
like arguing against any other position maintained for the sake of
argument (such as the Heraclitean thesis, or such a thesis as that
Being is one man) or like refuting a merely contentious argument—
a description which applies to the arguments both of Melissus and of
Parmenides: their premisses are false and their conclusions do not 10
follow. Or rather the argument of Melissus is gross and palpable and
offers no difficulty at all: accept one ridiculous proposition and the
rest follows—a simple enough proceeding.

We physicists, on the other hand, must take for granted that the
things that exist by nature are, either all or some of them, in motion
—which is indeed made plain by induction. Moreover, no man of
science is bound to solve every kind of difficulty that may be raised, 15
but only as many as are drawn falsely from the principles of the
science: it is not our business to refute those that do not arise in this
way: just as it is the duty of the geometer to refute the squaring of
the circle by means of segments, but it is not his duty to refute Anti-

phon's proof.[2] At the same time the holders of the theory of which we are speaking do incidentally raise physical questions, though Nature is not their subject: so it will perhaps be as well to spend a few words on them, especially as the inquiry is not without scientific interest.

20 The most pertinent question with which to begin will be this: In what sense is it asserted that all things *are* one? For 'is' is used in many senses. Do they mean that all things 'are' *substance* or *quantities* or *qualities*? And, further, are all things *one* substance—one

25 man, one horse, or one soul—or quality and that one and the same—white or hot or something of the kind? These are all very different doctrines and all impossible to maintain.

For if *both* substance and quantity and quality are, then, whether these exist independently of each other or not, Being will be many.

If on the other hand it is asserted that all things are quality or quantity, then, whether substance exists or not, an absurdity re-

30 sults, if indeed the impossible can properly be called absurd. For none of the others can exist independently: substance alone is independent: for everything is predicated of substance as subject. Now Melissus says that Being is infinite. It is then a quantity. For the infinite is in the category of quantity, whereas substance or quality or affection cannot be infinite except through a concomitant at-

185ᵇ tribute, that is, if at the same time they are also quantities. For to define the infinite you must use quantity in your formula, but not substance or quality. If then Being is both substance and quantity, it is two, not one: if only substance, it is not infinite and has no magnitude; for to have that it will have to be a quantity.

5 Again, 'one' itself, no less than 'being', is used in many senses, so we must consider in what sense the word is used when it is said that the All is one.

Now we say that (*a*) the continuous is one or that (*b*) the indivisible is one, or (*c*) things are said to be 'one', when their essence is one and the same, as 'liquor' and 'drink'.

If (*a.*) their One is one in the sense of continuous, it is many, for

10 the continuous is divisible *ad infinitum*.

---

2 The former method was suggested by Hippocrates of Chios, and rested on the rather obvious *geometrical* fallacy of supposing that if a particular kind of lunule can be squared, another kind can be squared also. Antiphon's method was that of exhaustion. He drew a square in the circle, and then isosceles triangles on its sides, and so on, and inferred that ultimately the inscribed polygon was equal in area to the circle. This involves a denial of the geometrical *principle* that every geometrical magnitude can be divided *ad infinitum*, and gives only an approximate result.

There is, indeed, a difficulty about part and whole, perhaps not relevant to the present argument, yet deserving consideration on its own account—namely, whether the part and the whole are one or more than one, and how they can be one or many, and, if they are more than one, in what sense they are more than one. (Similarly with the parts of wholes which are not continuous.) 15 Further, if each of the two parts is indivisibly one with the whole, the difficulty arises that they will be indivisibly one with each other also.

But to proceed: If (*b*) their One is one as indivisible, nothing will have quantity or quality, and so the one will not be infinite, as Melissus says—nor, indeed, limited, as Parmenides says, for though the limit is indivisible, the limited is not.³

But if (*c*) all things are one in the sense of having the same definition, like 'raiment' and 'dress', then it turns out that they are 20 maintaining the Heraclitean doctrine, for it will be the same thing 'to be good' and 'to be bad', and 'to be good' and 'to be not good', and so the same thing will be 'good' and 'not good', and man and horse; in fact, their view will be, not that all things are one, but that they are nothing; and that 'to be of such-and-such a quality' is the same as 'to be of such-and-such a size'.

Even the more recent of the ancient thinkers were in a pother lest 25 the same thing should turn out in their hands both one and many. So some, like Lycophron,⁴ were led to omit 'is', others to change the mode of expression and say 'the man has been whitened' instead of 'is white', and 'walks' instead of 'is walking', for fear that if they added 30 the word 'is' they should be making the one to *be* many—as if 'one' and 'being' were always used in one and the same sense. What 'is' may be many either in definition (for example 'to be white' is one thing, 'to be musical' another, yet the same thing may be both, so the one is many) or by division, as the whole and its parts. On this 186ᵃ point, indeed, they were already getting into difficulties and admitted that the one was many—as if there was any difficulty about the same thing being both one and many, provided that these are not opposites; for 'one' may mean either 'potentially one' or 'actually one'.

3   If, then, we approach the thesis in this way it seems impossible for all things to be one. Further, the arguments they use to prove 5 their position are not difficult to expose. For both of them reason contentiously—I mean both Melissus and Parmenides. Their prem-

³ e. g. a point which terminates a line is indivisible, though the line is not.
⁴ An orator and a pupil of Gorgias.

isses are false and their conclusions do not follow. Or rather the argument of Melissus is gross and palpable and offers no difficulty at all: admit one ridiculous proposition and the rest follows—a simple enough proceeding.

10   The fallacy of Melissus is obvious. For he supposes that the assumption 'what has come into being always has a beginning' justifies the assumption 'what has not come into being has no beginning'. Then this also is absurd, that in every case there should be a beginning of the *thing*—not of the time and not only in the case of coming to be in the full sense but also in the case of coming to have a quality
15 —as if change never took place suddenly. Again, does it follow that Being, if one, is motionless? Why should it not move, the whole of it within itself, as parts of it do which are unities, e. g. this water? Again, why is qualitative change impossible? But, further, Being
20 cannot be one in form, though it may be in what it is made of. (Even some of the physicists hold it to be one in the latter way, though not in the former.) Man obviously differs from horse in form, and contraries from each other.

    The same kind of argument holds good against Parmenides also, besides any that may apply specially to his view: the answer to him being that '*this* is not true' and '*that* does not follow'. His assumption that one is used in a single sense only is false, because it
25 is used in several. His conclusion does not follow, because if we take only white things, and if 'white' has a single meaning, none the less what is white will be many and not one. For what is white will not be one either in the sense that it is continuous or in the sense that it must be defined in only one way. 'Whiteness' will be different from 'what has whiteness'. Nor does this mean that there is anything that
30 can exist separately, over and above what is white. For 'whiteness' and 'that which is white' differ in definition, not in the sense that they are things which can exist apart from each other. But Parmenides had not come in sight of this distinction.

    It is necessary for him, then, to assume not only that 'being' has the same meaning, of whatever it is predicated, but further that it means (1) what *just is* and (2) what is *just one*.

    It must be so, for (1) an attribute is predicated of some subject,
35 so that the subject to which 'being' is attributed will not be, as it is
186ᵇ something different from 'being'. Something, therefore, which is not will be. Hence 'substance' will not be a predicate of anything else. For the subject cannot be a *being*, unless 'being' means several things, in such a way that each *is* something. But *ex hypothesi* 'being' means only one thing.

If, then, 'substance' is not attributed to anything, but other things are attributed to it, how does 'substance' mean what is rather than 5 what is not? For suppose that 'substance' is also 'white'. Since the definition of the latter is different (for being cannot even be attributed to white, as nothing is which is not 'substance'), it follows that 'white' is not-being—and that not in the sense of a particular not-being, but in the sense that it is not at all. Hence 'substance' is 10 not; for it is true to say that it is white, which we found to mean not-being. If to avoid this we say that even 'white' means substance, it follows that 'being' has more than one meaning.

In particular, then, Being will not have magnitude, if it is substance. For each of the two parts must *be* in a different sense.

(2) Substance is plainly divisible into other substances, if we consider the mere nature of a definition. For instance, if 'man' is a sub- 15 stance, 'animal' and 'biped' must also be substances. For if not substances, they must be attributes—and if attributes, attributes either of (a) man or of (b) some other subject. But neither is possible.

(a) An attribute is either that which may or may not belong to the subject or that in whose definition the subject of which it is an 20 attribute is involved. Thus 'sitting' is an example of a separable attribute, while 'snubness' contains the definition of 'nose', to which we attribute snubness. Further, the definition of the whole is not contained in the definitions of the contents or elements of the definitory formula; that of 'man' for instance in 'biped', or that of 'white man' in 'white'. If then this is so, and if 'biped' is supposed to be 25 an attribute of 'man', it must be either separable, so that 'man' might possibly not be 'biped', or the definition of 'man' must come into the definition of 'biped'—which is impossible, as the converse is the case. 30

(b) If, on the other hand, we suppose that 'biped' and 'animal' are attributes not of man but of something else, and are not each of them a substance, then 'man' too will be an attribute of something else. But we must assume that substance is *not* the attribute of anything, and that the subject of which both 'biped' and 'animal' and each separately are predicated is the subject also of the complex 'biped animal'.

Are we then to say that the All is composed of indivisible sub- 35 stances? Some thinkers did, in point of fact, give way to both argu- 187ᵃ ments. To the argument that all things are one if being means one thing, they conceded that not-being is; to that from bisection, they yielded by positing atomic magnitudes. But obviously it is not true that if being means one thing, and cannot at the same time

5 mean the contradictory of this, there will be nothing which is not, for even if what is not cannot *be* without qualification, there is no reason why it should not be a particular not-being. To say that all things will be one, if there is nothing besides Being itself, is absurd. For who understands 'being itself' to be anything but a particular substance? But if this is so, there is nothing to prevent there being many beings, as has been said.

10   It is, then, clearly impossible for Being to be one in this sense.

4   The physicists on the other hand have two modes of explanation.

The first set make the underlying body one—either one of the three [5] or something else which is denser than fire and rarer than air—then generate everything else from this, and obtain multiplicity by condensation and rarefaction. Now these are contraries, which may be generalized into 'excess and defect'. (Compare Plato's 'Great and Small'—except that he makes these his matter, the one his form, while the others treat the one which underlies as matter and the contraries as differentiae, i. e. forms.)

20   The second set assert that the contrarieties are contained in the one and emerge from it by segregation, for example Anaximander and also all those who assert that 'what is' is one and many, like Empedocles and Anaxagoras; for they too produce other things from their mixture by segregation. These differ, however, from each other in that the former imagines a cycle of such changes, the latter a single series. Anaxagoras again made both his 'homœomerous' substances and his contraries infinite in multitude, whereas Empedocles posits only the so-called elements.

The theory of Anaxagoras that the principles are infinite in multitude was probably due to his acceptance of the common opinion of the physicists that nothing comes into being from not-being. For this is the reason why they use the phrase 'all things were together' and the coming into being of such and such a kind of thing is reduced to change of quality, while some spoke of combination and separation. Moreover, the fact that the contraries proceed from each other led them to the conclusion. The one, they reasoned, must have already existed in the other; for since everything that comes into being must arise either from what is or from what is not, and it is impossible for it to arise from what is not (on this point all the physicists agree), they thought that the truth of the alternative necessarily followed, namely that things come into being out of existent things, i. e. out

[5] Water, air, or fire. Aristotle points out elsewhere (*Met*. A. 988ᵇ 30) that no one made earth the substratum.

of things already present, but imperceptible to our senses because of the smallness of their bulk. So they assert that everything has been 187ᵇ mixed in everything, because they saw everything arising out of everything. But things, as they say, appear different from one another and receive different names according to the nature of the particles which are numerically predominant among the innumerable constituents of the mixture. For nothing, they say, is purely and entirely white or black or sweet, bone or flesh, but the nature of a 5 thing is held to be that of which it contains the most.

Now (1) the infinite *qua* infinite is unknowable, so that what is infinite in multitude or size is unknowable in quantity, and what is infinite in variety of kind is unknowable in quality. But the principles 10 in question are infinite both in multitude and in kind. Therefore it is impossible to know things which are composed of them; for it is when we know the nature and quantity of its components that we suppose we know a complex.

Further (2) if the parts of a whole may be of any size in the direction either of greatness or of smallness (by 'parts' I mean components into which a whole can be divided and which are actually 15 present in it), it is necessary that the whole thing itself may be of any size. Clearly, therefore, since it is impossible for an animal or plant to be indefinitely big or small, neither can its parts be such, or the whole will be the same. But flesh, bone, and the like are the parts of animals, and the fruits are the parts of plants. Hence it is obvious 20 that neither flesh, bone, nor any such thing can be of indefinite size in the direction either of the greater or of the less.

Again (3) according to the theory all such things are already present in one another and do not come into being but are constituents which are separated out, and a thing receives its designation from its chief constituent. Further, anything may come out of anything— water by segregation from flesh and flesh from water. Hence, since 25 every finite body is exhausted by the repeated abstraction of a finite body, it seems obviously to follow that everything *cannot* subsist in everything else. For let flesh be extracted from water and again more flesh be produced from the remainder by repeating the process of separation: then, even though the quantity separated out will continually decrease, still it will not fall below a certain magnitude. If, 30 therefore, the process comes to an end, everything will not be in everything else (for there will be no flesh in the remaining water); if on the other hand it does not, and further extraction is always possible, there will be an infinite multitude of finite equal particles in a finite quantity—which is impossible. Another proof may be added: 35

Since every body must diminish in size when something is taken from it, and flesh is quantitatively definite in respect both of greatness and smallness, it is clear that from the minimum quantity of 188ᵃ flesh no body can be separated out; for the flesh left would be less than the minimum of flesh.

Lastly (4) in each of his infinite bodies there would be already present infinite flesh and blood and brain—having a distinct existence, however, from one another, and no less real than the infinite bodies, and each infinite: which is contrary to reason.

5 The statement that complete separation never will take place is correct enough, though Anaxagoras is not fully aware of what it means. For affections are indeed inseparable. If then colours and states had entered into the mixture, and if separation took place, there would be a 'white' or a 'healthy' which was nothing *but* white or healthy, i. e. was not the predicate of a subject. So his 'Mind' is an absurd 10 person aiming at the impossible, if he is supposed to wish to separate them, and it is impossible to do so, both in respect of quantity and of quality—of quantity, because there is no minimum magnitude, and of quality, because affections are inseparable.

Nor is Anaxagoras right about the coming to be of homogeneous bodies. It is true there is a sense in which clay is divided into pieces 15 of clay, but there is another in which it is not. Water and air are, and are generated, 'from' each other, but not in the way in which bricks come 'from' a house and again a house 'from' bricks; and it is better to assume a smaller and finite number of principles, as Empedocles does.

5 All thinkers then agree in making the contraries principles, both those who describe the All as one and unmoved (for even Par-20 menides treats hot and cold as principles under the names of fire and earth) and those too who use the rare and the dense. The same is true of Democritus also, with his plenum and void, both of which exist, he says, the one as being, the other as not-being. Again he speaks of differences in position, shape, and order, and these are genera of which the species are contraries, namely, of position, above 25 and below, before and behind; of shape, angular and angle-less, straight and round.

It is plain then that they all in one way or another identify the contraries with the principles. And with good reason. For first principles must not be derived from one another nor from anything else, while everything has to be derived from them. But these conditions are fulfilled by the primary contraries, which are not derived from anything else because they are primary, nor from each other because they are contraries.

But we must see how this can be arrived at as a reasoned result, 30 as well as in the way just indicated.

Our first presupposition must be that in nature nothing acts on, or is acted on by, any other thing at random, nor may anything come from anything else, unless we mean that it does so in virtue of a concomitant attribute. For how could 'white' come from 'musical', 35 unless 'musical' happened to be an attribute of the not-white or of the black? No, 'white' comes from 'not-white'—and not from *any* 'not-white', but from black or some intermediate colour. Similarly, 188ᵇ 'musical' comes to be from 'not-musical', but not from *any* thing other than musical, but from 'unmusical' or any intermediate state there may be.

Nor again do things pass into the first chance thing; 'white' does not pass into 'musical' (except, it may be, in virtue of a concomitant attribute), but into 'not-white'—and not into any chance thing which is not white, but into black or an intermediate colour; 'musical' passes into 'not-musical'—and not into any chance thing other than 5 musical, but into 'unmusical' or any intermediate state there may be.

The same holds of other things also: even things which are not simple but complex follow the same principle, but the opposite state 10 has not received a name, so we fail to notice the fact. What is in tune must come from what is not in tune, and *vice versa*; the tuned passes into untunedness—and not into *any* untunedness, but into the corresponding opposite. It does not matter whether we take attunement, 15 order, or composition for our illustration; the principle is obviously the same in all, and in fact applies equally to the production of a house, a statue, or any other complex. A house comes from certain things in a certain state of separation instead of conjunction, a statue (or any other thing that has been shaped) from shapelessness— 20 each of these objects being partly order and partly composition.

If then this is true, everything that comes to be or passes away comes from, or passes into, its contrary or an intermediate state. But the intermediates are derived from the contraries—colours, for instance, from black and white. Everything, therefore, that comes to 25 be by a natural process is either a contrary or a product of contraries.

Up to this point we have practically had most of the other writers on the subject with us, as I have said already [6]: for all of them identify their elements, and what they call their principles, with the con-

[6] ᵃ 19–30.

traries, giving no reason indeed for the theory, but constrained as it
30 were by the truth itself. They differ, however, from one another in
that some assume contraries which are more primary, others contraries which are less so: some those more knowable in the order of
explanation, others those more familiar to sense. For some make hot
and cold, or again moist and dry, the conditions of becoming; while
35 others make odd and even, or again Love and Strife; and these differ
from each other in the way mentioned.

Hence their principles are in one sense the same, in another different; different certainly, as indeed most people think, but the same
189ᵃ inasmuch as they are analogous; for all are taken from the same table
of columns,[7] some of the pairs being wider, others narrower in extent.
In this way then their theories are both the same and different, some
better, some worse; some, as I have said, take as their contraries
what is more knowable in the order of explanation, others what is
5 more familiar to sense. (The universal is more knowable in the
order of explanation, the particular in the order of sense: for explanation has to do with the universal, sense with the particular.) 'The
great and the small', for example, belong to the former class, 'the
dense and the rare' to the latter.
10   It is clear then that our principles must be contraries.

6   The next question is whether the principles are two or three or
more in number.

One they cannot be, for there cannot be one contrary. Nor can they
be innumerable, because, if so, Being will not be knowable: and in
any one genus there is only one contrariety, and substance is one
15 genus: also a finite number is sufficient, and a finite number, such as
the principles of Empedocles, is better than an infinite multitude;
for Empedocles professes to obtain from his principles all that Anaxagoras obtains from his innumerable principles. Lastly, some
contraries are more primary than others, and some arise from others
—for example sweet and bitter, white and black—whereas the principles must always remain principles.
20   This will suffice to show that the principles are neither one nor
innumerable.

Granted, then, that they are a limited number, it is plausible to
suppose them more than two. For it is difficult to see how either density
should be of such a nature as to act in any way on rarity or rarity
on density. The same is true of any other pair of contraries; for Love
25 does not gather Strife together and make things out of it, nor does

[7] The table is given in *Met.* A. 986 ᵃ 23.

Strife make anything out of Love, but both act on a third thing different from both. Some indeed assume more than one such thing from which they construct the world of nature.

Other objections to the view that it is not necessary to assume a third principle as a substratum may be added. (1) We do not find that the contraries constitute the *substance* of any thing. But what is a first principle ought not to be the *predicate* of any subject. If it were, there would be a principle of the supposed principle: for the subject is a principle, and prior presumably to what is predicated of it. Again (2) we hold that a substance is not contrary to another substance. How then can substance be derived from what are not substances? Or how can non-substance be prior to substance?

If then we accept both the former argument [8] and this one,[9] we must, to preserve both, assume a third somewhat as the substratum of the contraries, such as is spoken of by those who describe the All as one nature—water or fire or what is intermediate between them. What is intermediate seems preferable; for fire, earth, air, and water are already involved with pairs of contraries. There is, therefore, much to be said for those who make the underlying substance different from these four; of the rest, the next best choice is air, as presenting sensible differences in a less degree than the others; and after air, water. All, however, agree in this, that they differentiate their One by means of the contraries, such as density and rarity and more and less, which may of course be generalized, as has already been said,[10] into excess and defect. Indeed this doctrine too (that the One and excess and defect are the principles of things) would appear to be of old standing, though in different forms; for the early thinkers made the two the active and the one the passive principle, whereas some of the more recent maintain the reverse.

To suppose then that the elements are three in number would seem, from these and similar considerations, a plausible view, as I said before.[11] On the other hand, the view that they are more than three in number would seem to be untenable.

For the one substratum is sufficient to be acted on; but if we have four contraries, there will be two contrarieties, and we shall have to suppose an intermediate nature for each pair separately. If, on the other hand, the contrarieties, being two, can generate from each other, the second contrariety will be superfluous. Moreover, it is impossible that there should be more than one *primary* contrariety. For substance is a single genus of being, so that the principles can differ only

---

[8] That the contraries are principles (ch. 5).   [10] 187[a] 16.
[9] That the contraries need a substratum (ll. 21–34).   [11] [a]21.

25 as prior and posterior, *not* in genus; in a single genus there is always a single contrariety, all the other contrarieties in it being held to be reducible to one.

It is clear then that the number of elements is neither one nor more than two or three; but whether two or three is, as I said, a question of considerable difficulty.

30 7   We will now give our own account, approaching the question first with reference to becoming in its widest sense: for we shall be following the natural order of inquiry if we speak first of common characteristics, and then investigate the characteristics of special cases.

We say that one thing comes to be from another thing, and one sort of thing from another sort of thing, both in the case of simple and of complex things. I mean the following. We can say (1) the 35 'man becomes musical', (2) what is 'not-musical becomes musical', 190ᵃ or (3) the 'not-musical man becomes a musical man'. Now what becomes in (1) and (2)—'man' and 'not musical'—I call *simple*, and what each becomes—'musical'—simple also. But when (3) we say the 'not-musical man becomes a musical man', both what becomes and what it becomes are *complex*.

5   As regards one of these simple 'things that become' we say not only 'this becomes so-and-so', but also 'from being this, comes to be so-and-so', as 'from being not-musical comes to be musical'; as regards the other we do not say this in all cases, as we do not say (1) 'from being a man he came to be musical' but only 'the man became musical'.

When a 'simple' thing is said to become something, in one case (1) it survives through the process, in the other (2) it does not. For 10 the man remains a man and is such even when he becomes musical, whereas what is not musical or is unmusical does not continue to exist, either simply or combined with the subject.

These distinctions drawn, one can gather from surveying the various cases of becoming in the way we are describing that, as we say, there must always be an underlying something, namely that which 15 becomes, and that this, though always one numerically, in form at least is not one. (By that I mean that it can be described in different ways.) For 'to be man' is not the same as 'to be unmusical'. One part survives, the other does not: what is not an opposite survives (for 'man' survives), but 'not-musical' or 'unmusical' does not sur-20 vive, nor does the compound of the two, namely 'unmusical man'.

We speak of 'becoming that from this' instead of 'this becoming that' more in the case of what does not survive the change—'becoming musical from unmusical', not 'from man'—but there are exceptions, as we sometimes use the latter form of expression even of what survives; we speak of 'a statue coming to be from bronze', not of the 'bronze becoming a statue'. The change, however, from an opposite which does not survive is described indifferently in both ways, 'becoming that from this' or 'this becoming that'. We say both that 'the unmusical becomes musical', and that 'from unmusical he becomes musical'. And so both forms are used of the complex, 'becoming a musical man from an unmusical man', and 'an unmusical man becoming a musical man'.

But there are different senses of 'coming to be'. In some cases we do not use the expression 'come to be', but 'come to be so-and-so'. Only substances are said to 'come to be' in the unqualified sense.

Now in all cases other than substance it is plain that there must be some subject, namely, that which becomes. For we know that when a thing comes to be of such a quantity or quality or in such a relation, time, or place, a subject is always presupposed, since substance alone is not predicated of another subject, but everything else of substance.

But that substances too, and anything else that can be said 'to be' without qualification, come to be from some substratum, will appear on examination. For we find in every case something that underlies from which proceeds that which comes to be; for instance, animals and plants from seed.

Generally things which come to be, come to be in different ways: (1) by change of shape, as a statue; (2) by addition, as things which grow; (3) by taking away, as the Hermes from the stone; (4) by putting together, as a house; (5) by alteration, as things which 'turn' in respect of their material substance.

It is plain that these are all cases of coming to be from a substratum.

Thus, clearly, from what has been said, whatever comes to be is always complex. There is, on the one hand, (a) something which comes into existence, and again (b) something which becomes that—the latter (b) in two senses, either the subject or the opposite. By the 'opposite' I mean the 'unmusical', by the 'subject' 'man', and similarly I call the absence of shape or form or order the 'opposite', and the bronze or stone or gold the 'subject'.

Plainly then, if there are conditions and principles which constitute natural objects and from which they primarily are or have come to be—have come to be, I mean, what each is said to be in its essential

nature, not what each is in respect of a concomitant attribute—plainly,
20 I say, everything comes to be from both subject and form. For 'musical
man' is composed (in a way) of 'man' and 'musical': you can analyse
it into the definitions of its elements. It is clear then that what
comes to be will come to be from these elements.

Now the subject is one numerically, though it is two in form. (For
it is the man, the gold—the 'matter' generally—that is counted, for
25 it is more of the nature of a 'this', and what comes to be does not
come from it in virtue of a concomitant attribute; the privation,
on the other hand, and the contrary *are* incidental in the process.)
And the positive form is one—the order, the acquired art of music,
or any similar predicate.

There is a sense, therefore, in which we must declare the principles
to be two, and a sense in which they are three; a sense in which the
30 contraries are the principles—say for example the musical and the
unmusical, the hot and the cold, the tuned and the untuned—and a
sense in which they are not, since it is impossible for the contraries to
be acted on by each other. But this difficulty also is solved by the
fact that the substratum is different from the contraries, for it is
35 itself not a contrary. The principles therefore are, in a way, not
more in number than the contraries, but as it were two, nor yet pre-
191ᵃ cisely two, since there is a difference of essential nature, but three.
For 'to be man' is different from 'to be unmusical', and 'to be un-
formed' from 'to be bronze'.

We have now stated the number of the principles of natural objects
which are subject to generation, and how the number is reached: and
it is clear that there must be a substratum for the contraries, and
5 that the contraries must be two. (Yet in another way of putting it
this is not necessary, as one of the contraries will serve to effect the
change by its successive absence and presence.)

The underlying nature is an object of scientific knowledge, by an
analogy. For as the bronze is to the statue, the wood to the bed, or
10 the matter and the formless before receiving form to any thing which
has form, so is the underlying nature to substance, i. e. the 'this' or
existent.

This then is one principle (though not one or existent in the same
sense as the 'this'), and the definition was one as we agreed; then
further there is its contrary, the privation. In what sense these are
15 two, and in what sense more, has been stated above. Briefly, we
explained first [12] that only the contraries were principles, and later [13]

12 Ch. 5.   13 Ch. 6.

that a substratum was indispensable, and that the principles were three; our last statement [14] has elucidated the difference between the contraries, the mutual relation of the principles, and the nature of the substratum. Whether the form or the substratum is the essential nature of a physical object is not yet clear.[15] But that the principles 20 are three, and in what sense, and the way in which each is a principle, is clear.

So much then for the question of the number and the nature of the principles.

8 We will now proceed to show that the difficulty of the early thinkers, as well as our own, is solved in this way alone.

The first of those who studied science were misled in their search for truth and the nature of things by their inexperience, which as it 25 were thrust them into another path. So they say that none of the things that are either comes to be or passes out of existence, because what comes to be must do so either from what is or from what is not, both of which are impossible. For what is cannot come to be 30 (because it *is* already), and from what is not nothing could have come to be (because something must be present as a substratum). So too they exaggerated the consequence of this, and went so far as to deny even the *existence* of a plurality of things, maintaining that only Being itself is. Such then was their opinion, and such the reason for its adoption.

Our explanation on the other hand is that the phrases 'something comes to be from what is or from what is not', 'what is not or what is does something or has something done to it or becomes some par- 35 ticular thing', are to be taken (in the first way of putting our explanation) in the same sense as 'a doctor does something or has some- 191ᵇ thing done to him', 'is or becomes something from being a doctor'. These expressions may be taken in two senses, and so too, clearly, may 'from being', and 'being acts or is acted on'. A doctor builds a house, not *qua* doctor, but *qua* housebuilder, and turns gray, not 5 *qua* doctor, but *qua* dark-haired. On the other hand he doctors or fails to doctor *qua* doctor. But we are using words most appropriately when we say that a doctor does something or undergoes something, or becomes something from being a doctor, if he does, undergoes, or becomes *qua* doctor. Clearly then also 'to come to be so-and-so from not-being' means '*qua* not-being'.

It was through failure to make this distinction that those thinkers 10 gave the matter up, and through this error that they went so much

[14] Ch. 7.   [15] This is discussed below, Bk. II, Ch. 1.

farther astray as to suppose that nothing else comes to be or exists apart from Being itself, thus doing away with all becoming.

We ourselves are in agreement with them in holding that nothing can be said without qualification to come from what is not. But nevertheless we maintain that a thing may 'come to be from what is not'—that is, in a qualified sense. For a thing comes to be from the privation, which in its own nature is not-being—this not surviving as a constituent of the result. Yet this causes surprise, and it is thought impossible that something should come to be in the way described from what is not.

In the same way we maintain that nothing comes to be from being, and that being does not come to be except in a qualified sense. In that way, however, it does, just as animal might come to be from animal, and an animal of a certain kind from an animal of a certain kind. Thus, suppose a dog to come to be from a horse. The dog would then, it is true, come to be from animal (as well as from an animal of a certain kind) but not as *animal,* for that is already there. But if anything is to become an animal, *not* in a qualified sense, it will not be from animal: and if being, not from being—nor from not-being either, for it has been explained [16] that by 'from not-being' we mean from not-being *qua* not-being.

Note further that we do not subvert the principle that everything either is or is not.

This then is one way of solving the difficulty. Another consists in pointing out that the same things can be explained in terms of potentiality and actuality. But this has been done with greater precision elsewhere.[17]

So as we said, the difficulties which constrain people to deny the existence of some of the things we mentioned are now solved. For it was this reason which also caused some of the earlier thinkers to turn so far aside from the road which leads to coming to be and passing away and change generally. If they had come in sight of this nature, all their ignorance would have been dispelled.

9   Others,[18] indeed, have apprehended the nature in question, but not adequately.

In the first place they allow that a thing may come to be without qualification from not-being, accepting on this point the statement [19]

[16] l. 9.   [17] *Met.* Bk. ix, and v. 1017^a 35–^{b} 9.   [18] The Platonists.
[19] That if a thing does not come to be from being, it must come to be from not-being.

of Parmenides. Secondly, they think that if the substratum is one 192ᵃ
numerically, it must have also only a single potentiality—which is a
very different thing.

Now we distinguish matter and privation, and hold that one of
these, namely the matter, is not-being only in virtue of an attribute which it has, while the privation in its own nature is not-being;
and that the matter is nearly, in a sense *is*, substance, while the priva- 5
tion in no sense is. They, on the other hand, identify their Great and
Small alike with not-being, and that whether they are taken together
as one or separately. Their triad is therefore of quite a different kind
from ours. For they got so far as to see that there must be some under- 10
lying nature, but they make it one—for even if one philosopher [20]
makes a dyad of it, which he calls Great and Small, the effect is the
same, for he overlooked the other nature.[21] For the one which persists is a joint cause, with the form, of what comes to be—a mother,
as it were.[22] But the negative part of the contrariety may often seem, 15
if you concentrate your attention on it as an evil agent, not to exist
at all.

For admitting with them that there is something divine, good, and
desirable, we hold that there are two other principles, the one contrary
to it, the other such as of its own nature to desire and yearn for it.
But the consequence of their view is that the contrary desires its
own extinction. Yet the form cannot desire itself, for it is not defec- 20
tive; nor can the contrary desire it, for contraries are mutually destructive. The truth is that what desires the form is matter, as the
female desires the male and the ugly the beautiful—only the ugly or
the female not *per se* but *per accidens*.

The matter comes to be and ceases to be in one sense, while in 25
another it does not. As that which contains the privation, it ceases to
be in its own nature, for what ceases to be—the privation—is contained within it. But as potentiality it does not cease to be in its own
nature, but is necessarily outside the sphere of becoming and ceasing
to be. For if it came to be, something must have existed as a primary
substratum from which it should come and which should persist in
it; but this is its own special nature, so that it will be before coming 30
to be. (For my definition of matter is just this—the primary substratum of each thing, from which it comes to be without qualification, and which persists in the result.) And if it ceases to be it will
pass into that at the last, so it will have ceased to be before ceasing
to be.

The accurate determination of the first principle in respect of

[20] Plato.   [21] The privation.   [22] Cf. *Tim.* 50 D, 51. A.

form, whether it is one or many and what it is or what they are, is
35 the province of the primary type of science;[23] so these questions may
192ᵇ stand over till then.[24] But of the natural, i. e. perishable, forms we
shall speak in the expositions which follow.

The above, then, may be taken as sufficient to establish that there
are principles and what they are and how many there are. Now let us
make a fresh start and proceed.

BOOK II

1　Of things that exist, some exist by nature, some from other causes.
'By nature' the animals and their parts exist, and the plants and
10 the simple bodies (earth, fire, air, water)—for we say that these
and the like exist 'by nature'.

All the things mentioned present a feature in which they differ from
things which are *not* constituted by nature. Each of them has *within
15 itself* a principle of motion and of stationariness (in respect of place,
or of growth and decrease, or by way of alteration). On the other
hand, a bed and a coat and anything else of that sort, *qua* receiving
these designations—i. e. in so far as they are products of art—have
no innate impulse to change. But in so far as they happen to be
20 composed of stone or of earth or of a mixture of the two, they *do*
have such an impulse, and just to that extent—which seems to indicate that *nature is a source or cause of being moved and of being at
rest in that to which it belongs primarily,* in virtue of itself and not
in virtue of a concomitant attribute.

I say 'not in virtue of a concomitant attribute', because (for instance) a man who is a doctor might cure himself. Nevertheless it is
25 not in so far as he is a patient that he possesses the art of medicine: it
merely has happened that the same man is doctor and patient—and
that is why these attributes are not always found together. So it is
with all other artificial products. None of them has in itself the source
of its own production. But while in some cases (for instance houses
and the other products of manual labour) that principle is in some-
30 thing else external to the thing, in others—those which may cause a
change in themselves in virtue of a concomitant attribute—it lies in
the things themselves (but not in virtue of what they are).

'Nature' then is what has been stated. Things 'have a nature' which
have a principle of this kind. Each of them is a substance; for it is a
subject, and nature always implies a subject in which it inheres.

35　The term 'according to nature' is applied to all these things and

23 Metaphysics or 'First philosophy' as it is often called.　　24 *Met.* xii 7–9.

also to the attributes which belong to them in virtue of what they are, for instance the property of fire to be carried upwards—which is not a 'nature' nor 'has a nature' but is 'by nature' or 'according to nature'.

What nature is, then, and the meaning of the terms 'by nature' 193ᵃ and 'according to nature', has been stated. *That* nature exists, it would be absurd to try to prove; for it is obvious that there are many things of this kind, and to prove what is obvious by what is not is the mark 5 of a man who is unable to distinguish what is self-evident from what is not. (This state of mind is clearly possible. A man blind from birth might reason about colours. Presumably therefore such persons must be talking about words without any thought to correspond.)

Some identify the nature or substance of a natural object with that immediate constituent of it which taken by itself is without arrange- 10 ment, e. g. the wood is the 'nature' of the bed, and the bronze the 'nature' of the statue.

As an indication of this Antiphon points out that if you planted a bed and the rotting wood acquired the power of sending up a shoot, it would not be a bed that would come up, but *wood*—which shows that the arrangement in accordance with the rules of the art is merely 15 an incidental attribute, whereas the real nature is the other, which, further, persists continuously through the process of making.

But if the material of each of these objects has itself the same relation to something else, say bronze (or gold) to water, bones (or wood) to earth and so on, *that* (they say) would be their nature and essence. 20 Consequently some assert earth, others fire or air or water or some or all of these, to be the nature of the things that are. For whatever any one of them supposed to have this character—whether one thing or more than one thing—this or these he declared to be the whole of 25 substance, all else being its affections, states, or dispositions. Every such thing they held to be eternal (for it could not pass into anything else), but other things to come into being and cease to be times without number.

This then is one account of 'nature', namely that it is the immediate material substratum of things which have in themselves a principle of motion or change.

Another account is that 'nature' is the shape or form which is 30 specified in the definition of the thing.

For the word 'nature' is applied to what is according to nature and the natural in the same way as 'art' is applied to what is artistic or a work of art. We should not say in the latter case that there is anything artistic about a thing, if it is a bed only potentially, not yet

35 having the form of a bed; nor should we call it a work of art. The
same is true of natural compounds. What is potentially flesh or bone
has not yet its own 'nature', and does not exist 'by nature', until it
193ᵇ receives the form specified in the definition, which we name in defining what flesh or bone is. Thus in the second sense of 'nature' it
would be the shape or form (not separable except in statement) of
5 things which have in themselves a source of motion. (The combination of the two, e. g. man, is not 'nature' but 'by nature' or
'natural'.)

The form indeed is 'nature' rather than the matter; for a thing is
more properly said to be what it is when it has attained to fulfilment
than when it exists potentially. Again man is born from man, but
not bed from bed. That is why people say that the figure is not the
10 nature of a bed, but the wood is—if the bed sprouted not a bed but
wood would come up. But even if the figure *is* art, then on the same
principle the shape of man is his nature. For man is born from man.

We also speak of a thing's nature as being exhibited in the process
of growth by which its nature is attained. The 'nature' in this sense
15 is not like 'doctoring', which leads not to the art of doctoring but to
health. Doctoring must start from the art, not lead to it. But it is
not in this way that nature (in the one sense) is related to nature
(in the other). What grows *qua* growing grows from something into
something. Into what then does it grow? Not into that from which
it arose but into that to which it tends. The shape then is nature.

'Shape' and 'nature', it should be added, are used in two senses.
20 For the privation too is in a way form. But whether in unqualified
coming to be there is privation, i. e. a contrary to what comes to be,
we must consider later.[1]

2   We have distinguished, then, the different ways in which the term
'nature' is used.

The next point to consider is how the mathematician differs from
the physicist. Obviously physical bodies contain surfaces and volumes,
lines and points, and these are the subject-matter of mathematics.
25   Further, is astronomy different from physics or a department of it?
It seems absurd that the physicist should be supposed to know the
nature of sun or moon, but not to know any of their essential attributes, particularly as the writers on physics obviously do discuss
30 their shape also and whether the earth and the world are spherical
or not.

Now the mathematician, though he too treats of these things,

[1] *De Gen. et Corr.* i. 3.

nevertheless does not treat of them as the limits of a physical body;
nor does he consider the attributes indicated as the attributes of such
bodies. That is why he separates them; for in thought they are separable from motion, and it makes no difference, nor does any falsity
result, if they are separated. The holders of the theory of Forms do 35
the same, though they are not aware of it; for they separate the
objects of physics, which are less separable than those of mathematics. This becomes plain if one tries to state in each of the two 194ᵃ
cases the definitions of the things and of their attributes. 'Odd' and
'even', 'straight' and 'curved', and likewise 'number', 'line', and
'figure', do not involve motion; not so 'flesh' and 'bone' and 'man'— 5
these are defined like 'snub nose', not like 'curved'.

Similar evidence is supplied by the more physical of the branches
of mathematics, such as optics, harmonics, and astronomy. These
are in a way the converse of geometry. While geometry investigates
physical lines but not *qua* physical, optics investigates mathematical 10
lines, but *qua* physical, not *qua* mathematical.

Since 'nature' has two senses, the form and the matter, we must
investigate its objects as we would the essence of snubness. That is,
such things are neither independent of matter nor can be defined in
terms of matter only. Here too indeed one might raise a difficulty. 15
Since there are two natures, with which is the physicist concerned?
Or should he investigate the combination of the two? But if the combination of the two, then also each severally. Does it belong then
to the same or to different sciences to know each severally?

If we look at the ancients, physics would seem to be concerned
with the *matter*. (It was only very slightly that Empedocles and 20
Democritus touched on the forms and the essence.)

But if on the other hand art imitates nature, and it is the part of
the same discipline to know the form and the matter up to a point
(e. g. the doctor has a knowledge of health and also of bile and
phlegm, in which health is realized, and the builder both of the form
of the house and of the matter, namely that it is bricks and beams, 25
and so forth): if this is so, it would be the part of physics also to know
nature in both its senses.

Again, 'that for the sake of which', or the end, belongs to the same
department of knowledge as the means. But the nature is the end or
'that for the sake of which'. For if a thing undergoes a continuous
change and there is a stage which is last, this stage is the end or 'that
for the sake of which'. (That is why the poet was carried away into 30
making an absurd statement when he said 'he has the end ² for the

² i. e. death.

sake of which he was born'. For not every stage that is last claims to be an end, but only that which is best.)

For the arts make their material (some simply 'make' it, others make it serviceable), and we use everything as if it was there for our 35 sake. (We also are in a sense an end. 'That for the sake of which' has two senses: the distinction is made in our work *On Philosophy*.[3])
194ᵇ The arts, therefore, which govern the matter and have knowledge are two, namely the art which uses the product and the art which directs the production of it. That is why the using art also is in a sense directive; but it differs in that it knows the form, whereas the art which is directive as being concerned with production knows the 5 matter. For the helmsman knows and prescribes what sort of form a helm should have, the other from what wood it should be made and by means of what operations. In the products of art, however, we make the material with a view to the function, whereas in the products of nature the matter is there all along.

Again, matter is a relative term: to each form there corresponds a 10 special matter. How far then must the physicist know the form or essence? Up to a point, perhaps, as the doctor must know sinew or the smith bronze (i. e. until he understands the purpose of each): and the physicist is concerned only with things whose forms are separable indeed, but do not exist apart from matter. Man is begotten by man and by the sun as well. The mode of existence and essence of the 15 separable it is the business of the primary type of philosophy to define.

3   Now that we have established these distinctions, we must proceed to consider causes, their character and number. Knowledge is the object of our inquiry, and men do not think they know a thing till 20 they have grasped the 'why' of it (which is to grasp its primary cause). So clearly we too must do this as regards both coming to be and passing away and every kind of physical change, in order that, knowing their principles, we may try to refer to these principles each of our problems.

In one sense, then, (1) that out of which a thing comes to be and which persists, is called 'cause', e. g. the bronze of the statue, the 25 silver of the bowl, and the genera of which the bronze and the silver are species.

In another sense (2) the form or the archetype, i. e. the statement of the essence, and its genera, are called 'causes' (e. g. of the octave the relation of 2 : 1, and generally number), and the parts in the definition.

─────────
[3] i. e. in the dialogue *De Philosophia*.

Again (3) the primary source of the change or coming to rest; e. g. the man who gave advice is a cause, the father is cause of the 30 child, and generally what makes of what is made and what causes change of what is changed.

Again (4) in the sense of end or 'that for the sake of which' a thing is done, e. g. health is the cause of walking about. ('Why is he walking about?' we say. 'To be healthy', and, having said that, we think we have assigned the cause.) The same is true also of all the intermedi- 35 ate steps which are brought about through the action of something else as means towards the end, e. g. reduction of flesh, purging, drugs, or surgical instruments are means towards health. All these things are 195ᵃ 'for the sake of' the end, though they differ from one another in that some are activities, others instruments.

This then perhaps exhausts the number of ways in which the term 'cause' is used.

As the word has several senses, it follows that there are several causes of the same thing (not merely in virtue of a concomitant attri- bute), e. g. both the art of the sculptor and the bronze are causes of the 5 statue. These are causes of the statue *qua* statue, not in virtue of anything else that it may be—only not in the same way, the one being the material cause, the other the cause whence the motion comes. Some things cause each other reciprocally, e. g. hard work causes fit- ness and *vice versa,* but again not in the same way, but the one as 10 end, the other as the origin of change. Further the same thing is the cause of contrary results. For that which by its presence brings about one result is sometimes blamed for bringing about the contrary by its absence. Thus we ascribe the wreck of a ship to the absence of the pilot whose presence was the cause of its safety.

All the causes now mentioned fall into four familiar divisions. The 15 letters are the causes of syllables, the material of artificial products, fire, &c., of bodies, the parts of the whole, and the premisses of the conclusion, in the sense of 'that from which'. Of these pairs the one set are causes in the sense of substratum, e. g. the parts, the other set 20 in the sense of essence—the whole and the combination and the form. But the seed and the doctor and the adviser, and generally the maker, are all sources whence the change or stationariness originates, while the others are causes in the sense of the end or the good of the rest; for 'that for the sake of which' means what is best and the end of the things that lead up to it. (Whether we say the 'good itself' or 25 the 'apparent good' makes no difference.)

Such then is the number and nature of the kinds of cause.

Now the modes of causation are many, though when brought under

heads they too can be reduced in number. For 'cause' is used in
30 many senses and even within the same kind one may be prior to another (e. g. the doctor and the expert are causes of health, the relation
2 : 1 and number of the octave), and always what is inclusive to what
is particular. Another mode of causation is the incidental and its
genera, e. g. in one way 'Polyclitus', in another 'sculptor' is the cause
35 of a statue, because 'being Polyclitus' and 'sculptor' are incidentally
conjoined. Also the classes in which the incidental attribute is included; thus 'a man' could be said to be the cause of a statue or,
195b generally, 'a living creature'. An incidental attribute too may be
more or less remote, e. g. suppose that 'a pale man' or 'a musical man'
were said to be the cause of the statue.

All causes, both proper and incidental, may be spoken of either as
5 potential or as actual; e. g. the cause of a house being built is either
'house-builder' or 'house-builder building'.

Similar distinctions can be made in the things of which the causes
are causes, e. g. of 'this statue' or of 'statue' or of 'image' generally,
of 'this bronze' or of 'bronze' or of 'material' generally. So too with
10 the incidental attributes. Again we may use a complex expression
for either and say, e. g., neither 'Polyclitus' nor 'sculptor' but 'Polyclitus, sculptor'.

All these various uses, however, come to six in number, under each
of which again the usage is twofold. Cause means either what is par-
15 ticular or a genus, or an incidental attribute or a genus of that, and
these either as a complex or each by itself; and all six either as actual
or as potential. The difference is this much, that causes which are
actually at work and particular exist and cease to exist simultaneously
with their effect, e. g. this healing person with this being-healed person and that housebuilding man with that being-built house; but this
20 is not always true of potential causes—the house and the housebuilder
do not pass away simultaneously.

In investigating the cause of each thing it is always necessary to
seek what is most precise (as also in other things): thus man builds
because he is a builder, and a builder builds in virtue of his art of
building. This last cause then is prior: and so generally.
25 Further, generic effects should be assigned to generic causes, particular effects to particular causes, e. g. statue to sculptor, this statue
to this sculptor; and powers are relative to possible effects, actually
operating causes to things which are actually being effected.

This must suffice for our account of the number of causes and the
30 modes of causation.

4   But chance also and spontaneity are reckoned among causes:
many things are said both to be and to come to be as a result of
chance and spontaneity. We must inquire therefore in what manner
chance and spontaneity are present among the causes enumerated, and
whether they are the same or different, and generally what chance and 35
spontaneity are.

Some people [4] even question whether they are real or not. They say
that nothing happens by chance, but that everything which we ascribe 196ᵃ
to chance or spontaneity has some definite cause, e. g. coming 'by
chance' into the market and finding there a man whom one wanted
but did not expect to meet is due to one's wish to go and buy in the
market. Similarly in other cases of chance it is always possible, they 5
maintain, to find something which is the cause; but not chance, for if
chance were real, it would seem strange indeed, and the question
might be raised, why on earth none of the wise men of old in speaking
of the causes of generation and decay took account of chance; whence
it would seem that they too did not believe that anything is by 10
chance. But there is a further circumstance that is surprising. Many
things both come to be and are by chance and spontaneity, and although all know that each of them can be ascribed to some cause
(as the old argument said which denied chance), nevertheless they 15
speak of some of these things as happening by chance and others
not. For this reason also they ought to have at least referred to the
matter in some way or other.

Certainly the early physicists found no place for chance among
the causes which they recognized—love, strife, mind, fire, or the like.
This is strange, whether they supposed that there is no such thing
as chance or whether they thought there is but omitted to mention 20
it—and that too when they sometimes used it, as Empedocles does
when he says that the air is not always separated into the highest
region, but 'as it may chance'. At any rate he says in his cosmogony
that 'it happened to run that way at that time, but it often ran otherwise.' He tells us also that most of the parts of animals came to be
by chance.

There are some [5] too who ascribe this heavenly sphere and all the 25
worlds to spontaneity. They say that the vortex arose spontaneously, ·
i. e. the motion that separated and arranged in its present order all
that exists. This statement might well cause surprise. For they are
asserting that chance is not responsible for the existence or generation of animals and plants, nature or mind or something of the kind 30

---

[4] Apparently Democritus is meant.
[5] Apparently Democritus is meant.

being the cause of them (for it is not any chance thing that comes from a given seed but an olive from one kind and a man from another); and yet at the same time they assert that the heavenly sphere and the divinest of visible things arose spontaneously, having 35 no such cause as is assigned to animals and plants. Yet if this is so, it is a fact which deserves to be dwelt upon, and something might 196ᵇ well have been said about it. For besides the other absurdities of the statement, it is the more absurd that people should make it when they see nothing coming to be spontaneously in the heavens, but much happening by chance among the things which as they say are not due to chance; whereas we should have expected exactly the opposite.

5   Others [6] there are who, indeed, believe that chance is a cause, but that it is inscrutable to human intelligence, as being a divine thing and full of mystery.

Thus we must inquire what chance and spontaneity are, whether they are the same or different, and how they fit into our division of causes.

10 **5**   First then we observe that some things always come to pass in the same way, and others for the most part. It is clearly of neither of these that chance is said to be the cause, nor can the 'effect of chance' be identified with any of the things that come to pass by necessity and always, or for the most part. But as there is a third class of events besides these two—events which all say are 'by chance'—it is plain that there is such a thing as chance and spontaneity; for we know 15 that things of this kind are due to chance and that things due to chance are of this kind.

But, secondly, some events are for the sake of something, others not. Again, some of the former class are in accordance with deliberate intention, others not, but both are in the class of things which 20 are for the sake of something. Hence it is clear that even among the things which are outside the necessary and the normal, there are some in connexion with which the phrase 'for the sake of something' is applicable. (Events that are for the sake of something include whatever may be done as a result of thought or of nature.) Things of this kind, then, when they come to pass incidentally are said to be 'by chance'. 25 For just as a thing is something either in virtue of itself or incidentally, so may it be a cause. For instance, the housebuilding faculty is in virtue of itself the cause of a house, whereas the pale or the musical [7]

[6] Democritus.   [7] Incidental attributes of the housebuilder.

is the incidental cause. That which is *per se* cause of the effect is determinate, but the incidental cause is indeterminable, for the possible attributes of an individual are innumerable. To resume then; when a thing of this kind comes to pass among events which are for 30 the sake of something, it is said to be spontaneous or by chance. (The distinction between the two must be made later [8]—for the present it is sufficient if it is plain that both are in the sphere of things done for the sake of something.)

Example: A man is engaged in collecting subscriptions for a feast. He would have gone to such and such a place for the purpose of getting the money, if he had known. He actually went there for an- 35 other purpose, and it was only incidentally that he got his money by going there; and this was not due to the fact that he went there as a rule or necessarily, nor is the end effected (getting the money) a 197ᵃ cause present in himself—it belongs to the class of things that are intentional and the result of intelligent deliberation. It is when these conditions are satisfied that the man is said to have gone 'by chance'. If he had gone of deliberate purpose and for the sake of this—if he always or normally went there when he was collecting payments— he would not be said to have gone 'by chance'.

It is clear then that chance is an incidental cause in the sphere of 5 those actions for the sake of something which involve purpose. Intelligent reflection, then, and chance are in the same sphere, for purpose implies intelligent reflection.

It is necessary, no doubt, that the causes of what comes to pass by chance be indefinite; and that is why chance is supposed to belong to the class of the indefinite and to be inscrutable to man, and why 10 it might be thought that, in a way, nothing occurs by chance. For all these statements are correct, because they are well grounded. Things *do*, in a way, occur by chance, for they occur incidentally and chance is an *incidental cause*. But strictly it is not the *cause*—without qualification—of anything; for instance, a housebuilder is the cause of a house; incidentally, a flute-player may be so.

And the causes of the man's coming and getting the money (when 15 he did not come for the sake of that) are innumerable. He may have wished to see somebody or been following somebody or avoiding somebody, or may have gone to see a spectacle. Thus to say that chance is a thing contrary to rule is correct. For 'rule' applies to what is always true or true for the most part, whereas chance belongs to a third type of event. Hence, to conclude, since causes of this kind are indefinite, 20 chance too is indefinite. (Yet in some cases one might raise the ques-

[8] In ch. 6.

tion whether *any* incidental fact might be the cause of the chance occurrence, e. g. of health the fresh air or the sun's heat may be the cause, but having had one's hair cut *cannot*; for some incidental causes are more relevant to the effect than others.)

25 Chance or fortune is called 'good' when the result is good, 'evil' when it is evil. The terms 'good fortune' and 'ill fortune' are used when either result is of considerable magnitude. Thus one who comes within an ace of some great evil or great good is said to be fortunate or unfortunate. The mind affirms the presence of the attribute, ignor-30 ing the hair's breadth of difference. Further, it is with reason that good fortune is regarded as unstable; for chance is unstable, as none of the things which result from it can be invariable or normal.

Both are then, as I have said, incidental causes—both chance and spontaneity—in the sphere of things which are capable of coming to pass not necessarily, nor normally, and with reference to such of 35 these as might come to pass for the sake of something.

6 They differ in that 'spontaneity' is the wider term. Every result of chance is from what is spontaneous, but not everything that is from what is spontaneous is from chance.

197ᵇ Chance and what results from chance are appropriate to agents that are capable of good fortune and of moral action generally. Therefore necessarily chance is in the sphere of moral actions. This is indicated by the fact that good fortune is thought to be the same, or nearly the same, as happiness, and happiness to be a kind of moral action, since 5 it is well-doing. Hence what is not capable of moral action cannot do anything by chance. Thus an inanimate thing or a lower animal or a child cannot do anything by chance, because it is incapable of deliberate intention; nor can 'good fortune' or 'ill fortune' be ascribed to them, except metaphorically, as Protarchus, for example, said that the stones of which altars are made are fortunate because they are 10 held in honour, while their fellows are trodden under foot. Even these things, however, can in a way be affected by chance, when one who is dealing with them does something to them by chance, but not otherwise.

The spontaneous on the other hand is found both in the lower 15 animals and in many inanimate objects. We say, for example, that the horse came 'spontaneously', because, though his coming saved him, he did not come for the sake of safety. Again, the tripod fell 'of itself', because, though when it fell it stood on its feet so as to serve for a seat, it did not fall for the sake of that.

Hence it is clear that events which (1) belong to the general class of things that may come to pass for the sake of something, (2) do not come to pass for the sake of what actually results, and (3) have an external cause, may be described by the phrase 'from spontaneity'. 20 These 'spontaneous' events are said to be 'from chance' if they have the further characteristics of being the objects of deliberate intention and due to agents capable of that mode of action. This is indicated by the phrase 'in vain', which is used when A, which is for the sake of B, does not result in B. For instance, taking a walk is for the sake of evacuation of the bowels; if this does not follow after walking, we say that we have walked 'in vain' and that the walking was 'vain'. This implies that what is naturally the means to an end 25 is 'in vain', when it does not effect the end towards which it was the natural means—for it would be absurd for a man to say that he had bathed in vain because the sun was not eclipsed, since the one was not done with a view to the other. Thus the spontaneous is even according to its derivation the case in which the thing itself happens in vain. The stone that struck the man did not fall for the purpose 30 of striking him; therefore it fell spontaneously, because it might have fallen by the action of an agent and for the purpose of striking. The difference between spontaneity and what results by chance is greatest in things that come to be by nature; for when anything comes to be contrary to nature, we do not say that it came to be by chance, but by spontaneity. Yet strictly this too is different from the spontane- 35 ous proper; for the cause of the latter is external, that of the former internal.

We have now explained what chance is and what spontaneity is, 198ᵃ and in what they differ from each other. Both belong to the mode of causation 'source of change', for either some natural or some intelligent agent is always the cause; but in this sort of causation the number of possible causes is infinite.

Spontaneity and chance are causes of effects which, though they 5 might result from intelligence or nature, have in fact been caused by something *incidentally*. Now since nothing which is incidental is prior to what is *per se*, it is clear that no incidental cause can be prior to a cause *per se*. Spontaneity and chance, therefore, are posterior to intelligence and nature. Hence, however true it may be that the 10 heavens are due to spontaneity, it will still be true that intelligence and nature will be prior causes of this All and of many things in it besides.

7 It is clear then that there are causes, and that the number of them is what we have stated. The number is the same as that of the 15

things comprehended under the question 'why'. The 'why' is referred ultimately either (1), in things which do not involve motion, e. g. in mathematics, to the 'what' (to the definition of 'straight line' or 'commensurable', &c.), or (2) to what initiated a motion, e. g. 'why did they go to war?—because there had been a raid'; or (3) we are in-
20 quiring 'for the sake of what?'—'that they may rule'; or (4), in the case of things that come into being, we are looking for the matter. The causes, therefore, are these and so many in number.

Now, the causes being four, it is the business of the physicist to know about them all, and if he refers his problems back to all of them, he will assign the 'why' in the way proper to his science—the matter,
25 the form, the mover, 'that for the sake of which'. The last three often coincide; for the 'what' and 'that for the sake of which' are one, while the primary source of motion is the same in species as these (for man generates man), and so too, in general, are all things which cause movement by being themselves moved; and such as are not of this kind are no longer inside the province of physics, for they cause motion not by possessing motion or a source of motion in themselves, but being themselves incapable of motion. Hence there are three
30 branches of study, one of things which are incapable of motion, the second of things in motion, but indestructible, the third of destructible things.

The question 'why', then, is answered by reference to the matter, to the form, and to the primary moving cause. For in respect of coming to be it is mostly in this last way that causes are investigated— 'what comes to be after what? what was the primary agent or patient?' and so at each step of the series.

35 Now the principles which cause motion in a physical way are two, of which one is not physical, as it has no principle of motion in itself.
198ᵇ Of this kind is whatever causes movement, not being itself moved, such as (1) that which is completely unchangeable, the primary reality, and (2) the essence of that which is coming to be, i. e. the form; for this is the end or 'that for the sake of which'. Hence since nature is for the sake of something, we must know this cause also. We must ex-
5 plain the 'why' in all the senses of the term, namely, (1) that from this that will necessarily result ('from this' either without qualification or in most cases); (2) that 'this must be so if that is to be so' (as the conclusion presupposes the premisses); (3) that this was the essence of the thing; and (4) because it is better thus (not without qualification, but with reference to the essential nature in each case).

8   We must explain then (1) that Nature belongs to the class of 10
causes which act for the sake of something; (2) about the necessary
and its place in physical problems, for all writers ascribe things to
this cause, arguing that since the hot and the cold, &c., are of such
and such a kind, therefore certain things *necessarily* are and come to
be—and if they mention any other cause (one [9] his 'friendship and 15
strife', another [10] his 'mind'), it is only to touch on it, and then good-
bye to it.

A difficulty presents itself: why should not nature work, not for
the sake of something, nor because it is better so, but just as the sky
rains, not in order to make the corn grow, but of necessity? What is
drawn up must cool, and what has been cooled must become water 20
and descend, the result of this being that the corn grows. Similarly if a
man's crop is spoiled on the threshing-floor, the rain did not fall for
the sake of this—in order that the crop might be spoiled—but that
result just followed. Why then should it not be the same with the
parts in nature, e. g. that our teeth should come up *of necessity*—the
front teeth sharp, fitted for tearing, the molars broad and useful for 25
grinding down the food—since they did not arise for this end, but it
was merely a coincident result; and so with all other parts in which we
suppose that there is purpose? Wherever then all the parts came about
just what they would have been if they had come to be for an end, 30
such things survived, being organized spontaneously in a fitting way;
whereas those which grew otherwise perished and continue to perish,
as Empedocles says his 'man-faced ox-progeny' did.

Such are the arguments (and others of the kind) which may cause
difficulty on this point. Yet it is impossible that this should be the true
view. For teeth and all other natural things either invariably or 35
normally come about in a given way; but of not one of the results of
chance or spontaneity is this true. We do not ascribe to chance or
mere coincidence the frequency of rain in winter, but frequent rain 199ᵃ
in summer we do; nor heat in the dog-days, but only if we have it
in winter. If then, it is agreed that things are either the result of coincidence or for an end, and these cannot be the result of coincidence
or spontaneity, it follows that they must be for an end; and that 5
such things are all due to nature even the champions of the theory
which is before us would agree. Therefore action for an end is present
in things which come to be and are by nature.

Further, where a series has a completion, all the preceding steps
are for the sake of that. Now surely as in intelligent action, so in na- 10
ture; and as in nature, so it is in each action, if nothing interferes.

[9] Empedocles.   [10] Anaxagoras.

Now intelligent action is for the sake of an end; therefore the nature
of things also is so. Thus if a house, e. g., had been a thing made by
nature, it would have been made in the same way as it is now by art;
and if things made by nature were made also by art, they would
15 come to be in the same way as by nature. Each step then in the series
is for the sake of the next; and generally art partly completes what
nature cannot bring to a finish, and partly imitates her. If, therefore,
artificial products are for the sake of an end, so clearly also are
natural products. The relation of the later to the earlier terms of the
series is the same in both.

20   This is most obvious in the animals other than man: they make
things neither by art nor after inquiry or deliberation. Wherefore
people discuss whether it is by intelligence or by some other faculty
that these creatures work,—spiders, ants, and the like. By gradual
advance in this direction we come to see clearly that in plants too
25 that is produced which is conducive to the end—leaves, e. g. grow
to provide shade for the fruit. If then it is both by nature and for an
end that the swallow makes its nest and the spider its web, and plants
grow leaves for the sake of the fruit and send their roots down (not
up) for the sake of nourishment, it is plain that this kind of cause is
30 operative in things which come to be and are by nature. And since
'nature' means two things, the matter and the form, of which the latter
is the end, and since all the rest is for the sake of the end, the form
must be the cause in the sense of 'that for the sake of which'.

Now mistakes come to pass even in the operations of art: the grammarian makes a mistake in writing and the doctor pours out the wrong
35 dose. Hence clearly mistakes are possible in the operations of nature
199ᵇ also. If then in art there are cases in which what is rightly produced
serves a purpose, and if where mistakes occur there was a purpose
in what was attempted, only it was not attained, so must it be also
in natural products, and monstrosities will be failures in the pur-
5 posive effort. Thus in the original combinations the 'ox-progeny' if
they failed to reach a determinate end must have arisen through the
corruption of some principle corresponding to what is now the seed.

Further, seed must have come into being first, and not straightway the animals: the words 'whole-natured first . . .' [11] must have
meant seed.

Again, in plants too we find the relation of means to end, though
10 the degree of organization is less. Were there then in plants also
'olive-headed vine-progeny', like the 'man-headed ox-progeny', or

[11] Empedocles, Fr. 62. 4.

not? An absurd suggestion; yet there must have been, if there were such things among animals.

Moreover, among the seeds anything must have come to be at random. But the person who asserts this entirely does away with 'nature' and what exists 'by nature'. For those things are natural 15 which, by a continuous movement originated from an internal principle, arrive at some completion: the same completion is not reached from every principle; nor any chance completion, but always the tendency in each is towards the same end, if there is no impediment.

The end and the means towards it may come about by chance. We say, for instance, that a stranger has come by chance, paid 20 the ransom, and gone away, when he does so as if he had come for that purpose, though it was not for that that he came. This is incidental, for chance is an incidental cause, as I remarked before.[12] But when an event takes place always or for the most part, it is not incidental or by chance. In natural products the sequence is invariable, 25 if there is no impediment.

It is absurd to suppose that purpose is not present because we do not observe the agent deliberating. Art does not deliberate. If the ship-building art were in the wood, it would produce the same results *by nature*. If, therefore, purpose is present in art, it is present also in nature. The best illustration is a doctor doctoring himself: 30 nature is like that.

It is plain then that nature is a cause, a cause that operates for a purpose.

9   As regards what is 'of necessity', we must ask whether the necessity is 'hypothetical', or 'simple' as well. The current view places 35 what is of necessity in the process of production, just as if one were to 200ᵃ suppose that the wall of a house necessarily comes to be because what is heavy is naturally carried downwards and what is light to the top, wherefore the stones and foundations take the lowest place, with earth above because it is lighter, and wood at the top of all as being the lightest. Whereas, though the wall does not come to be *without* these, 5 it is not *due* to these, except as its material cause: it comes to be for the sake of sheltering and guarding certain things. Similarly in all other things which involve production for an end; the product cannot come to be without things which have a necessary nature, but it is not due to these (except as its material); it comes to be for 10 an end. For instance, why is a saw such as it is? To effect so-and-so

[12] 196ᵇ 23-7.

and for the sake of so-and-so. This end, however, cannot be realized unless the saw is made of iron. It is, therefore, necessary for it to be of iron, *if* we are to have a saw and perform the operation of sawing. What is necessary then, is necessary *on a hypothesis*; it is not a result necessarily determined by antecedents. Necessity is in the matter, while 'that for the sake of which' is in the definition.

15   Necessity in mathematics is in a way similar to necessity in things which come to be through the operation of nature. Since a straight line is what it is, it is necessary that the angles of a triangle should equal two right angles. But not conversely; though if the angles are *not* equal to two right angles, then the straight line is not what it is either. But in things which come to be for an end, the reverse is true. If the
20 end is to exist or does exist, that also which precedes it will exist or does exist; otherwise just as there, if the conclusion is not true, the premiss will not be true, so here the end or 'that for the sake of which' will not exist. For this too is itself a starting-point, but of the reasoning, not of the action; while in mathematics the starting-point is the starting point of the reasoning only, as there is no action. If then there
25 is to be a house, such-and-such things must be made or be there already or exist, or generally the matter relative to the end, bricks and stones if it is a house. But the end is not due to these except as the matter, nor will it come to exist because of them. Yet if they do not exist at all, neither will the house, or the saw—the former in the absence of stones, the latter in the absence of iron—just as in the other case the premisses will not be true, if the angles of the triangle are not equal to two right angles.

30   The necessary in nature, then, is plainly what we call by the name of matter, and the changes in it. Both causes must be stated by the physicist, but especially the end; for that is the cause of the matter, not *vice versa*; and the end is 'that for the sake of which', and the
35 beginning starts from the definition or essence; as in artificial products,
200ᵇ since a house is of such-and-such a kind, certain things must *necessarily* come to be or be there already, or since health is this, these things must necessarily come to be or be there already. Similarly if man is this, then these; if these, then those. Perhaps the necessary is
5   present also in the definition. For if one defines the operation of sawing as being a certain kind of dividing, then this cannot come about unless the saw has teeth of a certain kind; and these cannot be unless it is of iron. For in the definition too there are some parts that are, as it were, its matter.

BOOK III

1 Nature has been defined as a 'principle of motion and change', 12
and it is the subject of our inquiry. We must therefore see that we
understand the meaning of 'motion'; for if it were unknown, the
meaning of 'nature' too would be unknown.

When we have determined the nature of motion, our next task 15
will be to attack in the same way the terms which are involved in it.
Now motion is supposed to belong to the class of things which are
continuous; and the *infinite* presents itself first in the continuous—
that is how it comes about that 'infinite' is often used in definitions of
the continuous ('what is infinitely divisible is continuous'). Besides
these, *place, void,* and *time* are thought to be necessary conditions of 20
motion.

Clearly, then, for these reasons and also because the attributes mentioned are common to, and coextensive with, all the objects of our
science, we must first take each of them in hand and discuss it.
For the investigation of special attributes comes after that of the
common attributes.

To begin then, as we said, with motion. 25

We may start by distinguishing (1) what exists in a state of fulfilment only, (2) what exists as potential, (3) what exists as potential
and also in fulfilment—one being a 'this', another 'so much', a third
'such', and similarly in each of the other modes of the predication of
being.

Further, the word 'relative' is used with reference to (1) excess and
defect, (2) agent and patient and generally what can move and 30
what can be moved. For 'what can cause movement' is relative to
'what can be moved', and *vice versa*.

Again, there is no such thing as motion *over and above* the things.
It is always with respect to substance or to quantity or to quality
or to place that what changes changes. But it is impossible, as we
assert, to find anything *common* to these which is neither 'this' nor 35
quantum nor *quale* nor any of the other predicates. Hence neither 201ᵇ
will motion and change have reference to something over and above
the things mentioned, for there *is* nothing over and above them.

Now each of these belongs to all its subjects in either of two ways:
namely (1) substance—the one is positive form, the other privation; 5
(2) in quality, white and black; (3) in quantity, complete and incomplete; (4) in respect of locomotion, upwards and downwards or
light and heavy. Hence there are as many types of motion or change
as there are meanings of the word 'is'.

We have now before us the distinctions in the various classes of being between what is fully real and what is potential.

10   Def. *The fulfilment of what exists potentially, in so far as it exists potentially, is motion*—namely, of what is alterable *qua* alterable, *alteration*: of what can be increased and its opposite what can be decreased (there is no common name), *increase* and *decrease*: of what can come to be and can pass away, *coming to be* and *passing away*: of what can be carried along, *locomotion.*

15   Examples will elucidate this definition of motion. When the buildable, in so far as it is just *that,* is fully real, it is *being built,* and this is build*ing*. Similarly, learning, doctoring, rolling, leaping, ripening, ageing.

The same thing, if it is of a certain kind, can be both potential and 20 fully real, not indeed at the same time or not in the same respect, but e. g. potentially hot and actually cold. Hence at once such things will act and be acted on by one another in many ways: each of them will be capable at the same time of causing alteration and of being altered. Hence, too, what effects motion as a physical agent can be moved: when a thing of this kind causes motion, it is itself also moved. This, 25 indeed, has led some people to suppose that every mover is moved. But this question depends on another set of arguments, and the truth will be made clear later.[1] It *is* possible for a thing to cause motion, though it is itself incapable of being moved.

It is the fulfilment of what is potential when it is already fully real and operates not as *itself* but as *movable,* that is motion. What I 30 mean by 'as' is this: Bronze is potentially a statue. But it is not the fulfilment of bronze as *bronze* which is motion. For 'to be bronze' and 'to be a certain potentiality' are not the same. If they were identical without qualification, i. e. in *definition,* the fulfilment of bronze as bronze *would* have been motion. But they are not the same, as has been said. (This is obvious in contraries. To be capable of health' 35 and 'to be capable of illness' are not the same, for if they were 201ᵇ there would be no difference between being ill and being well. Yet the *subject* both of health and of sickness—whether it is humour or blood —is one and the same.)

We can distinguish, then, between the two—just as, to give another example, 'colour' and 'visible' are different—and clearly it is the 5 fulfilment of what is potential *as* potential that is motion. So this, precisely, is motion.

Further it is evident that motion is an attribute of a thing just *when* it is fully real in this way, and neither before nor after. For each

----

[1] viii. 5.

thing of this kind is capable of being at one time actual, at another
not. Take for instance the buildable as buildable. The actuality of
the buildable as buildable is the process of building. For the actuality 10
of the buildable must be either this or the house. But when there
is a house, the buildable is no longer buildable. On the other hand,
it *is* the buildable which is *being* built. The process then of being built
must be the kind of actuality required. But building is a kind of motion, and the same account will apply to the other kinds also.   15

2   The soundness of this definition is evident both when we consider the accounts of motion that the others have given, and also
from the difficulty of defining it otherwise.

One could not easily put motion and change in another genus—this
is plain if we consider where some people put it; they identify motion 20
with 'difference' or 'inequality' [2] or 'not being'; but such things are
not necessarily moved, whether they are 'different' or 'unequal' or
'non-existent': Nor is change either *to* or from *these* rather than to or
from their opposites.

The reason why they put motion into these genera is that it is
thought to be something indefinite, and the principles in the second 25
column are indefinite because they are privative: none of them is
either 'this' or 'such' or comes under any of the other modes of
predication. The reason in turn why motion is thought to be indefinite is that it cannot be classed simply as a potentiality or as an
actuality—a thing that is merely *capable* of having a certain size
is not undergoing change, nor yet a thing that is *actually* of a certain 30
size, and motion is thought to be a sort of *actuality,* but incomplete,
the reason for this view being that the potential whose actuality it is
is incomplete. This is why it is hard to grasp what motion is. It is
necessary to class it with privation or with potentiality or with sheer
actuality, yet none of these seems possible. There remains then the 35
suggested mode of definition, namely that it is a sort of actuality, or 202ᵃ
actuality of the kind described, hard to grasp, but not incapable of
existing.

The mover too is moved, as has been said—every mover, that is,
which is capable of motion, and whose immobility is rest—when a
thing is subject to motion its immobility is rest. For to act on the
movable as such is just to *move* it. But this it does by *contact,* so that 5
at the same time it is also acted on. Hence we can define motion as
the fulfilment of the movable qua *movable, the cause of the attribute
being contact with what can move,* so that the mover is also acted on.

2 Plato in the *Timaeus* (52 ᴇ, 57 ᴇ, 58 ᴀ) makes motion depend on inequality.

The mover or agent will always be the vehicle of a form, either a 'this'
10 or a 'such,' which, when it acts, will be the source and cause of the
change, e. g. the full-formed man begets man from what is potentially
man.

3   The solution of the difficulty that is raised about the motion—
whether it is in the *movable*—is plain. It is the fulfilment of this
potentiality, and by the action of that which has the power of causing
motion; and the actuality of that which has the power of causing mo-
15 tion is not other than the actuality of the movable, for it must be the
fulfilment of *both*. A thing is capable of causing motion because it
can do this, it is a mover because it actually *does* it. But it is on the
movable that it is capable of acting. Hence there is a single actuality
of both alike, just as one to two and two to one are the same interval,
20 and the steep ascent and the steep descent are one—for these are
one and the same, although they can be described in different ways.
So it is with the mover and the moved.

This view has a dialectical difficulty. Perhaps it is necessary that
the actuality of the agent and that of the patient should not be the
same. The one is 'agency' and the other 'patiency'; and the outcome
and completion of the one is an 'action', that of the other a 'passion'.
25 Since then they are both motions, we may ask: *in* what are they, if
they are different? Either (*a*) both are in what is acted on and
moved, or (*b*) the agency is in the agent and the patiency in the
patient. (If we ought to call the latter also 'agency', the word would
be used in two senses.)

Now, in alternative (*b*) the motion will be in the mover, for the
same statement will hold of 'mover' and 'moved'.[3] Hence either
30 *every* mover will be moved, or, though having motion, it will not be
moved.

If on the other hand (*a*) both are in what is moved and acted on—
both the agency and the patiency (e. g. both teaching and learning,
though they are *two,* in the *learner*), then, first, the actuality of
each will not be present *in* each, and, a second absurdity, a thing
35 will have two motions at the same time. How will there be two alterations of quality in *one* subject towards *one* definite quality? The
thing is impossible: the actualization will be one.
202ᵇ   But (some one will say) it is contrary to reason to suppose that
there should be one identical actualization of two things which are
different in kind. Yet there will be, if teaching and learning are the

---

³ i. e. we can substitute 'mover' and 'moved' for 'agent' and 'patient' in the
formulation of the hypothesis.

same, and agency and patiency. To teach will be the same as to learn, and to act the same as to be acted on—the teacher will necessarily be learning everything that he teaches, and the agent will be acted on.

One may reply: 5

(1) It is *not* absurd that the actualization of one thing should be in another. Teaching is the activity of a person who can teach, yet the operation is performed *on* some patient—it is not cut adrift from a subject, but is of *A* on *B*.

(2) There is nothing to prevent two things having one and the same actualization, provided the actualizations are not *described* in the same way, but are related as what can act to what is acting.

(3) Nor is it necessary that the teacher should learn, even if to act 10 and to be acted on are one and the same, provided they are not the same in *definition* (as 'raiment' and 'dress'), but are the same merely in the sense in which the road from Thebes to Athens and the road from Athens to Thebes are the same, as has been explained above.[4] For it is not things which are in a way the same that have all their attributes the same, but only such as have the same definition. But 15 indeed it by no means follows from the fact that teaching is the same as learning, that to learn is the same as to teach, any more than it follows from the fact that there is one *distance* between two things which are at a distance from each other, that the two *vectors AB* and *BA* are one and the same. To generalize, teaching is not the same as learning, or agency as patiency, in the full sense, though they belong 20 to the same *subject*, the motion; for the 'actualization of *X* in *Y*' and the 'actualization of *Y* through the action of *X*' differ in *definition*.

What then Motion is, has been stated both generally and particularly. It is not difficult to see how each of its types will be defined 25 —alteration is the fulfilment of the alterable *qua* alterable (or, more scientifically, the fulfilment of what can act and what can be acted on, as such)—generally and again in each particular case, building, healing, &c. A similar definition will apply to each of the other kinds of motion.

4   The science of nature is concerned with spatial magnitudes and 30 motion and time, and each of these at least is necessarily infinite or finite, even if some things dealt with by the science are not, e. g. a quality or a point—it is not necessary perhaps that such things should be put under either head. Hence it is incumbent on the person who specializes in physics to discuss the infinite and to inquire whether 35 there *is* such a thing or not, and, if there is, *what* it is.

---

[4] Cf. [a]18–20.

The appropriateness to the science of this problem is clearly
203ᵃ indicated. All who have touched on this kind of science in a way
worth considering have formulated views about the infinite, and indeed, to a man, make it a principle of things.

(1) Some, as the Pythagoreans and Plato, make the infinite a
5 principle in the sense of a self-subsistent substance, and not as a mere
attribute of some other thing. Only the Pythagoreans place the infinite among the objects of sense (they do not regard number as
separable from these), and assert that what is outside the heaven
is infinite. Plato, on the other hand, holds that there is no body outside
(the Forms are not outside, because they are nowhere), yet that the
infinite is present not only in the objects of sense but in the Forms also.
10 Further, the Pythagoreans identify the infinite with the even. For
this, they say, when it is cut off and shut in by the odd, provides things
with the element of infinity. An indication of this is what happens
with numbers. If the gnomons are placed round the one, and without
the one,⁵ in the one construction the figure that results is always
15 different, in the other it is always the same. But Plato has two infinites, the Great and the Small.

The physicists, on the other hand, all of them, always regard the
infinite as an attribute of a substance which is different from it and
belongs to the class of the so-called elements ⁶—water or air or what
is intermediate between them. Those who make them limited in number never make them infinite in amount. But those who make the
20 elements' infinite in number, as Anaxagoras and Democritus do, say
that the infinite is continuous by contact—compounded of the homogeneous parts according to the one, of the seed-mass of the atomic
shapes according to the other.

Further, Anaxagoras held that any part is a mixture in the same
way as the All, on the ground of the observed fact that anything comes
out of anything. For it is probably for this reason that he maintains
25 that once upon a time all things were together. (*This* flesh and *this*
bone were together, and so of *any* thing: therefore *all* things: and at
the same time too.) For there is a beginning of separation, not only
for each thing, but for all. Each thing that comes to be comes to be
from a similar body, and there is a coming to be of all things, though
30 not, it is true, at the same time. Hence there must also be an origin of
coming to be. One such source there is which he calls Mind, and Mind

⁵ Aristotle's general meaning is fairly plain. He is describing *two* constructions:
in the one *odd* gnomons are placed round the *one,* in the other *even* gnomons
are placed round the *two.*
⁶ Aristotle does not regard them as elements.

begins its work of thinking from some starting-point. So necessarily all things must have been together at a certain time, and must have begun to be moved at a certain time.

Democritus, for his part, asserts the contrary, namely that no element arises from another element. Nevertheless for him the common body is a source of all things, differing from part to part in size and 203ᵇ in shape.

It is clear then from these considerations that the inquiry concerns the physicist. Nor is it without reason that they all make it a principle or source. We cannot say that the infinite has no effect, and the only 5 effectiveness which we can ascribe to it is that of a principle. Everything is either a source or derived from a source. But there cannot be a source of the infinite or limitless, for that would be a limit of it. Further, as it is a beginning, it is both uncreatable and indestructible. For there must be a point at which what has come to be reaches completion, and also a termination of all passing away. That is why, 10 as we say, there is no principle of *this*, but it is this which is held to be the principle of other things, and to encompass all and to steer all, as those assert who do not recognize, alongside the infinite, other causes, such as Mind or Friendship. Further they identify it with the Divine, for it is 'deathless and imperishable' as Anaximander says, with the majority of the physicists.

Belief in the existence of the infinite comes mainly from five con- 15 siderations:

(1) From the nature of time—for it is infinite.
(2) From the division of magnitudes—for the mathematicians also use the notion of the infinite.
(3) If coming to be and passing away do not give out, it is only because that from which things come to be is infinite.
(4) Because the limited always finds its limit in something, so that 20 there must be *no* limit, if everything is *always* limited by something different from itself.
(5) Most of all, a reason which is peculiarly appropriate and presents the difficulty that is felt by everybody—not only number but also mathematical magnitudes and what is outside the heaven are supposed to be infinite because they never give out in our *thought*.

The last fact (that what is outside is infinite) leads people to sup- 25 pose that body also is infinite, and that there is an infinite number of worlds. Why should there be body in one part of the void rather than in another? Grant only that mass is anywhere and it follows that it must be everywhere. Also, if void and place are infinite, there must be infinite body too, for in the case of eternal things what may be must be.

30 But the problem of the infinite is difficult: many contradictions result whether we suppose it to exist or not to exist. If it exists, we have still to ask *how* it exists; as a substance or as the essential attribute of some entity? Or in neither way, yet none the less is there something which is infinite or some things which are infinitely many?

204ᵃ The problem, however, which specially belongs to the physicist is to investigate whether there is a sensible magnitude which is infinite.

We must begin by distinguishing the various senses in which the term 'infinite' is used.

(1) What is incapable of being gone through, because it is not its nature to be gone through (the sense in which the voice is 'invisible').

(2) What admits of being gone through, the process however having
5 no termination, or (3) what scarcely admits of being gone through.

(4) What naturally admits of being gone through, but is not actually gone through or does not actually reach an end.

Further, everything that is infinite may be so in respe t of addition or division or both.

5 Now it is impossible that the infinite should be a thing which is itself infinite, separable from sensible objects. If the infinite is
10 neither a magnitude nor an aggregate, but is itself a substance and not an attribute, it will be indivisible; for the divisible must be either a magnitude or an aggregate. But if indivisible, then not infinite, except in the sense (1) in which the voice is 'invisible'. But this is not the sense in which it is used by those who say that the infinite exists, nor that in which we are investigating it, namely as (2), 'that which cannot be gone through'. But if the infinite exists as an attribute,
15 it would not be, *qua* infinite, an element in substances, any more than the invisible would be an element of speech, though the voice is invisible.

Further, how can the infinite be itself any thing, unless both number and magnitude, of which it is an essential attribute, exist in that way? If *they* are not substances, *a fortiori* the infinite is not.

20 It is plain, too, that the infinite cannot be an actual thing and a substance and principle. For any part of it that is taken will be infinite, if it has parts: for 'to be infinite' and 'the infinite' are the same, if it is a substance and not predicated of a subject. Hence it

will be either indivisible or divisible into infinites. But the same thing 25
cannot be many infinites. (Yet just as part of air is air, so a part of
the infinite would be infinite, if it is supposed to be a substance and
principle.) Therefore the infinite must be without parts and indivisible. But this cannot be true of what is infinite in full completion:
for it must be a definite quantity.

Suppose then that infinity belongs to substance as an attribute.
But, if so, it cannot, as we have said, be described as a principle, but 30
rather that of which it is an attribute—the air or the even number.

Thus the view of those who speak after the manner of the Pythagoreans is absurd. With the same breath they treat the infinite as
substance, and divide it into parts.

This discussion, however, involves the more general question 35
whether the infinite can be present in mathematical objects and things
which are intelligible and do not have extension, as well as among 204ᵇ
sensible objects. Our inquiry (as physicists) is limited to its special
subject-matter, the objects of sense, and we have to ask whether there
is or is not among *them* a body which is infinite in the direction of
increase.

We may begin with a dialectical argument and show as follows that
there is no such thing.

If 'bounded by a surface' is the definition of body there cannot be 5
an infinite body either intelligible or sensible. Nor can number taken
in abstraction be infinite. for number or that which has number is
numerable. If then the numerable can be numbered, it would also be
possible to go through the infinite.

If, on the other hand, we investigate the question more in accord- 10
ance with principles appropriate to physics, we are led as follows to
the same result.

The infinite body must be either (1) compound, or (2) simple;
yet neither alternative is possible.

(1) Compound the infinite body will not be, if the elements are
finite in number. For they must be more than one, and the contraries
must always balance, and no *one* of them can be infinite. If one of
the bodies falls in any degree short of the other in potency—suppose 15
fire is finite in amount while air is infinite and a given quantity of
fire exceeds in power the same amount of air in any ratio provided
it is numerically definite—the infinite body will obviously prevail over
and annihilate the finite body. On the other hand, it is impossible that
each should be infinite. 'Body' is what has extension in all directions 20
and the infinite is what is boundlessly extended, so that the infinite
body would be extended in all directions *ad infinitum*.

Nor (2) can the infinite body be one and simple, whether it is, as some[7] hold, a thing over and above the elements (from which they generate the elements) or is not thus qualified.

(*a*) We must consider the former alternative; for there *are* some people who make this the infinite, and not air or water, in order that
25 the other elements may not be annihilated by the element which is infinite. They have contrariety with each other—air is cold, water moist, fire hot; if one were infinite, the others by now would have ceased to be. As it is, they say, the infinite is different from them and is their source.

It is impossible, however, that there should be such a body; not
30 because it is infinite—on that point a general proof can be given which applies equally to all, air, water, or anything else—but simply because there is, as a matter of fact, no such *sensible* body, alongside the so-called elements. Everything can be resolved into the elements of which it is composed. Hence the body in question would have been present in our world here, alongside air and fire and earth and water: but nothing of the kind is observed.

35   (*b*) Nor can fire or any other of the elements be infinite. For
205ᵃ generally, and apart from the question how any of them could be infinite, the All, even if it were limited, cannot either be or become one of them, as Heraclitus says that at some time all things become fire.
5 (The same argument applies also to the one which the physicists suppose to exist alongside the elements: for everything changes from contrary to contrary, e. g. from hot to cold).

The preceding consideration of the various cases serves to show us whether it is or is not possible that there should be an infinite sensible body. The following arguments give a general demonstration that it is not possible.

10   It is the nature of every kind of sensible body to be somewhere, and there is a place appropriate to each, the same for the part and for the whole, e. g. for the whole earth and for a single clod, and for fire and for a spark.

Suppose (*a*) that the infinite sensible body is homogeneous. Then each part will be either immovable or always being carried along. Yet neither is possible. For why downwards rather than upwards or in any other direction? I mean, e. g., if you take a clod, where will
15 it be moved or where will it be at rest? For *ex hypothesi* the place of the body akin to it is infinite. Will it occupy the whole place, then? And how? What then will be the nature of its rest and of its movement, or where will they be? It will either be at home everywhere—

---

[7] The reference is probably to Anaximander.

then it will not be moved; or it will be moved everywhere—then it will not come to rest.

But if (*b*) the All has dissimilar parts, the proper places of the parts will be dissimilar also, and the body of the All will have no unity except that of contact. Then, further, the parts will be either finite or infinite in variety of kind. (i) *Finite* they cannot be, for if the All is to be infinite, some of them would have to be infinite, while the others were not, e. g. fire or water will be infinite. But, as we have seen before, such an element would destroy what is contrary to it. (This indeed is the reason why none of the physicists made fire or earth the one infinite body, but either water or air or what is intermediate between them, because the abode of each of the two was plainly determinate, while the others have an ambiguous place between up and down.)

But (ii) if the parts are *infinite* in number and simple, their proper places too will be infinite in number, and the same will be true of the elements themselves. If that is impossible, and the places are finite, the whole too must be finite; for the place and the body cannot but fit each other. Neither is the whole place larger than what can be filled by the body (and then the body would no longer be infinite), nor is the body larger than the place; for either there would be an empty space or a body whose nature it is to be nowhere.

Anaxagoras gives an absurd account of why the infinite is at rest. 205ᵇ He says that the infinite itself is the cause of its being fixed. This because it is *in* itself, since nothing else contains it—on the assumption that wherever anything is, it is there by its own nature. But this is not true: a thing could be somewhere by compulsion, and not where it is its nature to be.

Even if it is true as true can be that the whole is not moved (for what is fixed by itself and is in itself must be immovable), yet we must explain *why* it is not its nature to be moved. It is not enough just to make this statement and then decamp. Anything else might be in a state of rest, but there is no reason why it should not be its nature to be moved. The earth is not carried along, and would not be carried along if it were infinite, provided it is held together by the centre. But it would not be because there was no other region in which it could be carried along that it would remain at the centre, but because this is its nature. Yet in this case also we may say that it fixes itself. If then in the case of the earth, supposed to be infinite, it is at rest, not because it is infinite, but because it has weight and what is heavy rests at the centre and the earth is at the centre,

similarly the infinite also would rest in itself, not because it is infinite and fixes itself, but owing to some other cause.

Another difficulty emerges at the same time. Any part of the infinite
body ought to remain at rest. Just as the infinite remains at rest in
20 itself because it fixes itself, so too any part of it you may take will
remain in itself. The appropriate places of the whole and of the part
are alike, e. g. of the whole earth and of a clod the appropriate place
is the lower region; of fire as a whole and of a spark, the upper region.
If, therefore, to be in itself is the place of the infinite, that also
will be appropriate to the part. Therefore it will remain in itself.

In general, the view that there is an infinite body is plainly in-
25 compatible with the doctrine that there is necessarily a proper place
for each kind of body, if every sensible body has either weight or
lightness, and if a body has a natural locomotion towards the centre
if it is heavy, and upwards if it is light. This would need to be true
of the infinite also. But neither character can belong to it: it cannot
be either as a whole, nor can it be half the one and half the other.
30 For how should you divide it? or how can the infinite have the one
part up and the other down, or an extremity and a centre?

Further, every sensible body is in place, and the kinds or differences
of place are up-down, before-behind, right-left; and these distinctions hold not only in relation to us and by arbitrary agreement, but
35 also in the whole itself. But in the infinite body they cannot exist. In
general, if it is impossible that there should be an infinite place, and
206ᵃ if every body is in place, there cannot be an infinite body.

Surely what is in a special place is in place, and what is in place is
in a special place. Just, then, as the infinite cannot be quantity—that
would imply that it has a particular quantity, e. g. two or three cubits;
5 quantity just means these—so a thing's being in place means that it
is *some*where, and that is either up or down or in some other of the
six differences of position: but each of these is a limit.

It is plain from these arguments that there is no body which is
actually infinite.

6   But on the other hand to suppose that the infinite does not exist
in any way leads obviously to many impossible consequences: there
10 will be a beginning and an end of time, a magnitude will not be
divisible into magnitudes, number will not be infinite. If, then, in
view of the above considerations, neither alternative seems possible,
an arbiter must be called in; and clearly there is a sense in which the
infinite exists and another in which it does not.

We must keep in mind that the word 'is' means either what *potentially* is or what *fully* is.

Further, a thing is infinite either by addition or by division.   15

Now, as we have seen, magnitude is not actually infinite. But by division it is infinite. (There is no difficulty in refuting the theory of indivisible lines.) The alternative then remains that the infinite has a potential existence.

But the phrase 'potential existence' is ambiguous. When we speak of the potential existence of a statue we mean that there will be an actual statue. It is not so with the infinite. There will not be an 20 actual infinite. The word 'is' has many senses, and we say that the infinite 'is' in the sense in which we say 'it is day' or 'it is the games', because one thing after another is always coming into existence. For of these things too the distinction between potential and actual existence holds. We say that there are Olympic games, both in the sense that they may occur and that they are actually occurring.

The infinite exhibits itself in different ways—in time, in the genera- 25 tions of man, and in the division of magnitudes. For generally the infinite has this mode of existence: one thing is always being taken after another, and each thing that is taken is always finite, but always different. Again, 'being' has more than one sense, so that we must 30 not regard the infinite as a 'this', such as a man or a horse, but must suppose it to exist in the sense in which we speak of the day or the games as existing—things whose being has not come to them like that of a substance, but consists in a process of coming to be or passing away; definite if you like at each stage, yet always different.

But when this takes place in spatial magnitudes, what is taken 206ᵇ persists, while in the succession of time and of men it takes place by the passing away of these in such a way that the source of supply never gives out.

In a way the infinite by addition is the same thing as the infinite by division. In a finite magnitude, the infinite by addition comes about in a way inverse to that of the other. For in proportion as we see division going on, in the same proportion we see addition being 5 made to what is already marked off. For if we take a determinate part of a finite magnitude and add another part *determined by the same ratio* (not taking in the same amount of the original whole), and so on, we shall not traverse the given magnitude. But if we 10 increase the ratio of the part, so as always to take in the same amount, we shall traverse the magnitude, for every finite magnitude is exhausted by means of any determinate quantity however small.

The infinite, then, exists in no other way, but in this way it does

exist, potentially and by reduction. It exists fully in the sense in
which we say 'it is day' or 'it is the games'; and potentially as matter
15 exists, not independently as what is finite does.

By addition then, also, there is potentially an infinite, namely,
what we have described as being in a sense the same as the infinite in
respect of division. For it will always be possible to take something *ab extra*. Yet the sum of the parts taken will not exceed every
determinate magnitude, just as in the direction of division every
determinate magnitude is surpassed in smallness and there will be
a smaller part.

20   But in respect of addition there cannot be an infinite which even
potentially exceeds every assignable magnitude, unless it has the
attribute of being actually infinite, as the physicists hold to be true of
the body which is outside the world, whose essential nature is air or
something of the kind. But if there cannot be in this way a sensible
25 body which is infinite in the full sense, evidently there can no more
be a body which is potentially infinite in respect of addition, except
as the inverse of the infinite by division, as we have said. It is for
this reason that Plato also made the infinites two in number, because
it is supposed to be possible to exceed all limits and to proceed
ad infinitum in the direction both of increase and of reduction. Yet
though he makes the infinites two, he does not use them. For in the
30 numbers the infinite in the direction of reduction is not present, as
the monad is the smallest; nor is the infinite in the direction of
increase, for the parts number only up to the decad.

The infinite turns out to be the contrary of what it is said to be.
207ᵃ It is not what has nothing outside it that is infinite, but what always
has something outside it. This is indicated by the fact that rings also
that have no bezel are described as 'endless', because it is always
possible to take a part which is outside a given part. The description
depends on a certain similarity, but it is not true in the full sense of
5 the word. This condition alone is not sufficient: it is necessary also
that the next part which is taken should never be the same. In the
circle, the latter condition is not satisfied: it is only the adjacent part
from which the new part is different.

Our definition then is as follows:

*A quantity is infinite if it is such that we can always take a part
outside what has been already taken.* On the other hand, what has
nothing outside it is complete and whole. For thus we define the
10 whole—that from which nothing is wanting, as a whole man or a
whole box. What is true of each particular is true of the whole as
such—the whole is that of which nothing is outside. On the other hand

that from which something is absent and outside, however small that may be, is not 'all'. 'Whole' and 'complete' are either quite identical or closely akin. Nothing is complete (teleion) which has no end (telos); and the end is a limit.

Hence Parmenides must be thought to have spoken better than 15 Melissus. The latter says that the whole is infinite, but the former describes it as limited, 'equally balanced from the middle'. For to connect the infinite with the all and the whole is not like joining two pieces of string; for it is from this they get the dignity they ascribe to the infinite—its containing all things and holding the all in itself 20 —from its having a certain similarity to the whole. It is in fact the matter of the completeness which belongs to size, and what is potentially a whole, though not in the full sense. It is divisible both in the direction of reduction and of the inverse addition. It is a whole and limited; not, however, in virtue of its own nature, but in virtue of what is other than it. It does not contain, but, in so far as it is infinite, is contained. Consequently, also, it is unknowable, *qua* infinite; for 25 the matter has no form. (Hence it is plain that the infinite stands in the relation of part rather than of whole. For the matter is part of the whole, as the bronze is of the bronze statue.) If it contains in the case of sensible things, in the case of intelligible things the great and the small ought to contain them. But it is absurd and impossible to 30 suppose that the unknowable and indeterminate should contain and determine.

7   It is reasonable that there should not be held to be an infinite in respect of addition such as to surpass every magnitude, but that there should be thought to be such an infinite in the direction of division. For the matter and the infinite are contained inside what 35 contains them, while it is the form which contains. It is natural too 207ᵇ to suppose that in number there is a limit in the direction of the minimum, and that in the other direction every assigned number is surpassed. In magnitude, on the contrary, every assigned magnitude is surpassed in the direction of smallness, while in the other direction there is no infinite magnitude. The reason is that what is one is indi- 5 visible whatever it may be, e. g. a man is one man, not many. Number on the other hand is a plurality of 'ones' and a certain quantity of them. Hence number must stop at the indivisible: for 'two' and 'three' are merely derivative terms, and so with each of the other numbers. But in the direction of largeness it is always possible to 10 think of a larger number: for the number of times a magnitude can be bisected is infinite. Hence this infinite is potential, never actual:

the number of parts that can be taken always surpasses any assigned number. But this number is not separable from the process of bisection, and its infinity is not a permanent actuality but consists in a process of coming to be, like time and the number of time.

15   With magnitudes the contrary holds. What is continuous is divided *ad infinitum,* but there is no infinite in the direction of increase. For the size which it can potentially be, it can also actually be. Hence since no sensible magnitude is infinite, it is impossible to exceed
20 every assigned magnitude; for if it were possible there would be something bigger than the heavens.

The infinite is not the same in magnitude and movement and time, in the sense of a single nature, but its secondary sense depends on its primary sense, i.e. movement is called infinite in virtue of the magnitude covered by the movement (or alteration or growth), and
25 time because of the movement. (I use these terms for the moment. Later I shall explain what each of them means, and also why every magnitude is divisible into magnitudes.)

Our account does not rob the mathematicians of their science, by disproving the actual existence of the infinite in the direction of increase, in the sense of the untraversable. In point of fact they do not
30 need the infinite and do not use it. They postulate only that the finite straight line may be produced as far as they wish. It is possible to have divided in the same ratio as the largest quantity another magnitude of any size you like. Hence, for the purposes of proof, it will make no difference to them to have such an infinite instead, while its existence will be in the sphere of real magnitudes.

35   In the four-fold scheme of causes, it is plain that the infinite is a cause in the sense of matter, and that its essence is privation, the
208ᵃ subject as such being what is continuous and sensible. All the other thinkers, too, evidently treat the infinite as matter—that is why it is inconsistent in them to make it what contains, and not what is contained.

5 **8**   It remains to dispose of the arguments [8] which are supposed to support the view that the infinite exists not only potentially but as a separate thing. Some have no cogency; others can be met by fresh objections that are valid.

(1) In order that coming to be should not fail, it is not necessary that there should be a sensible body which is actually infinite. The
10 passing away of one thing may be the coming to be of another, the All being limited.

[8] Cf. 203ᵇ 15-30.

(2) There is a difference between touching and being limited. The former is relative to something and is the touching of something (for everything that touches touches something), and further is an attribute of some one of the things which are limited. On the other hand, what is limited is not limited in relation to anything. Again, contact is not necessarily possible between any two things taken at random.

(3) To rely on mere thinking is absurd, for then the excess or 15 defect is not in the thing but in the thought. One might think that one of us is bigger than he is and magnify him *ad infinitum*. But it does not follow that he is bigger than the size we are, just because some one thinks he is, but only because he *is* the size he is. The thought is an accident.

(*a*) Time indeed and movement are infinite, and also thinking, 20 in the sense that each part that is taken passes in succession out of existence.

(*b*) Magnitude is not infinite either in the way of reduction or of magnification in thought.

This concludes my account of the way in which the infinite exists, and of the way in which it does not exist, and of what it is.

BOOK IV

1   The physicist must have a knowledge of Place, too, as well as of the infinite—namely, whether there is such a thing or not, and the manner of its existence and what it is—both because all suppose that things which exist are *somewhere* (the non-existent is nowhere— 30 where is the goat-stag or the sphinx?), and because 'motion' in its most general and primary sense is change of place, which we call 'locomotion'.

The question, what is place? presents many difficulties. An examination of all the relevant facts seems to lead to divergent conclusions. Moreover, we have inherited nothing from previous thinkers, 35 whether in the way of a statement of difficulties or of a solution.

The existence of place is held to be obvious from the fact of mutual 208ᵇ replacement. Where water now is, there in turn, when the water has gone out as from a vessel, air is present. When therefore another body occupies this same place, the place is thought to be different from 5 all the bodies which come to be in it and replace one another. What now contains air formerly contained water, so that clearly the place

or space into which and out of which they passed was something
different from both.

Further, the typical locomotions of the elementary natural bodies
—namely, fire, earth, and the like—show not only that place is
10 something, but also that it exerts a certain influence. Each is carried to its own place, if it is not hindered, the one up, the other
down. Now these are regions or kinds of place—up and down and
the rest of the six directions. Nor do such distinctions (up and down
and right and left, &c.) hold only in relation to us. To *us* they are not
15 always the same but change with the direction in which we are
turned: that is why the same thing may be both right *and* left, up
and down, before *and* behind. But in *nature* each is distinct, taken
apart by itself. It is not every chance direction which is 'up', but
20 where fire and what is light are carried; similarly, too, 'down' is
not any chance direction but where what has weight and what is
made of earth are carried—the implication being that these places do
not differ merely in relative position, but also as possessing distinct
potencies. This is made plain also by the objects studied by mathematics. Though they have no real place, they nevertheless, in respect
of their position relatively to us, have a right and left as attributes
ascribed to them only in consequence of their relative position, not
having by nature these various characteristics. Again, the theory
25 that the void exists involves the existence of place: for one would
define void as place bereft of body.

These considerations then would lead us to suppose that place is
something distinct from bodies, and that every sensible body is in
place. Hesiod too might be held to have given a correct account of it
30 when he made chaos first. At least he says:

First of all things came chaos to being, then broad-breasted earth,

implying that things need to have space first, because he thought,
with most people, that everything is somewhere and in place. If this
is its nature, the potency of place must be a marvellous thing, and
35 take precedence of all other things. For that without which nothing
else can exist, while it can exist without the others, must needs be
209ᵃ first; for place does not pass out of existence when the things in it
are annihilated.

True, but even if we suppose its existence settled, the question of
its *nature* presents difficulty—whether it is some sort of 'bulk' of
body or some entity other than that, for we must first determine its
genus.

5   (1) Now it has three dimensions, length, breadth, depth, the

dimensions by which all body also is bounded. But the place cannot *be* body; for if it were there would be two bodies in the same place.

(2) Further, if body has a place and space, clearly so too have surface and the other limits of body; for the same statement will apply to them: where the bounding planes of the water were, there in turn will be those of the air. But when we come to a point we cannot 10 make a distinction between it and its place. Hence if the place of a point is not different from the point, no more will that of any of the others be different, and place will not be something different from each of them.

(3) What in the world then are we to suppose place to be? If it has the sort of nature described, it cannot be an element or composed of elements, whether these be corporeal or incorporeal: for while it has 15 size, it has not body. But the elements of sensible bodies are bodies, while nothing that has size results from a combination of intelligible elements.

(4) Also we may ask: of what in things is space the cause? None of the four modes of causation can be ascribed to it. It is neither cause in the sense of the matter of existents (for nothing is com- 20 posed of it), nor as the form and definition of things, nor as end, nor does it move existents.

(5) Further, too, if it is itself an existent, *where* will it be? Zeno's difficulty demands an explanation: for if everything that exists has a 25 place, place too will have a place, and so on *ad infinitum*.

(6) Again, just as every body is in place, so, too, every place has a body in it. What then shall we say about *growing* things? It follows from these premises that their place must grow with them, if their place is neither less nor greater than they are.

By asking these questions, then, we must raise the whole problem about place—not only as to what it is, but even whether there is such 30 a thing.

2   We may distinguish generally between predicating B of A because it (A) is itself, and because it is something else; and particularly between place which is common and in which all bodies are, and the special place occupied primarily by each. I mean, for instance, that you are now in the heavens because you are in the air and it is in the heavens; and you are in the air because you are on the earth; and similarly on the earth because you are in this place which contains no 35 more than you.

Now if place is what *primarily* contains each body, it would be a 209^{b}

limit, so that the place would be the form or shape of each body by which the magnitude or the matter of the magnitude is defined: for this is the limit of each body.

5   If, then, we look at the question in this way the place of a thing is its form. But, if we regard the place as the *extension* of the magnitude, it is the matter. For this is different from the magnitude: it is what is contained and defined by the form, as by a bounding plane. Matter or the indeterminate is of this nature; when the boundary and attributes of a sphere are taken away, nothing but the matter is left.

This is why Plato in the *Timaeus* [1] says that matter and space are the same; for the 'participant' and space are identical. (It is true, indeed, that the account he gives there of the 'participant' is different from what he says in his so-called 'unwritten teaching'.[2] Nevertheless, he did identify place and space.) I mention Plato because, while all hold place to be something, he alone tried to say *what* it is.

In view of these facts we should naturally expect to find difficulty in determining what place is, if indeed it *is* one of these two things, matter or form. They demand a very close scrutiny, especially as it is not easy to recognize them apart.

But it is at any rate not difficult to see that place cannot be either of them. The form and the matter are not separate from the thing, whereas the place can be separated. As we pointed out,[3] where air was, water in turn comes to be, the one replacing the other; and similarly with other bodies. Hence the place of a thing is neither a part nor a state of it, but is separable from it. For place is supposed to be something like a vessel—the vessel being a transportable place. But the vessel is no part of the thing.

30   In so far then as it is separable from the thing, it is not the form: *qua* containing, it is different from the matter.

Also it is held that what is anywhere is both itself something and that there is a different thing outside it.[4] (Plato of course, if we may digress, ought to tell us why the form and the numbers are not in place, if 'what participates' is place—whether what participates is the Great and the Small or the matter, as he called it in writing in the *Timaeus*.)

Further, how could a body be carried to its own place, if place was the matter or the form? It is impossible that what has no reference to motion or the distinction of up and down can be place. So place

---

[1] 52.

[2] Where he apparently identified 'the participant' with 'the great and the small'; cf. l. 35.

[3] 208ᵇ 2.   [4] Cf.212ᵇ 14–16.

must be looked for among things which have these characteristics.

If the place is in the thing (it must be if it is either shape or 5 matter) place will have a place: for both the form and the indeterminate undergo change and motion along with the thing, and are not always in the same place, but are where the thing is. Hence the place will have a place.

Further, when water is produced from air, the place has been destroyed, for the resulting body is not in the same place. What sort 10 of destruction then is that?

This concludes my statement of the reasons why space must be something, and again of the difficulties that may be raised about its essential nature.

3   The next step we must take is to see in how many senses one thing is said to be 'in' another.

(1) As the finger is 'in' the hand and generally the part 'in' the whole. 15
(2) As the whole is 'in' the parts: for there is no whole over and above the parts.
(3) As man is 'in' animal and generally species 'in' genus.
(4) As the genus is 'in' the species and generally the part of the specific form 'in' the definition of the specific form.
(5) As health is 'in' the hot and the cold and generally the form 'in' 20 the matter.
(6) As the affairs of Greece centre 'in' the king, and generally events centre 'in' their primary motive agent.
(7) As the existence of a thing centres 'in' its good and generally 'in' its end, i. e. 'in that for the sake of which' it exists.
(8) In the strictest sense of all, as a thing is 'in' a vessel, and generally 'in' place.

One might raise the question whether a thing can be in itself, or 25 whether nothing can be in itself—everything being either *no*where or in something *else*.

The question is ambiguous; we may mean the thing *qua* itself or *qua* something else.

When there are parts of a whole—the one that in which a thing is, the other the thing which is in it—the whole will be described as being in itself. For a thing is described in terms of its parts, as well as in terms of the thing as a whole, e. g. a man is said to be white because the visible surface of him is white, or to be scientific because his thinking faculty has been trained. The jar then will not be in itself 30 and the wine will not be in itself. But the jar of wine will: for the contents and the container are both parts of the same whole.

In this sense then, but not primarily, a thing can be in itself, namely, as 'white' is in body (for the visible surface is in body), and science is in the mind.

210ᵇ   It is from these, which are 'parts' (in the sense at least of being 'in' the man), that the man is called white, &c. But the jar and the wine in separation are not parts of a whole, though together they are. So when there are parts, a thing will be in itself, as 'white' is in man because it is in body, and in body because it resides in the visible
5 surface. We cannot go further and say that it is in surface in virtue of something other than itself. (Yet it is not in itself: though these are in a way the same thing,) they differ in essence, each having a special nature and capacity, 'surface' and 'white'.

Thus if we look at the matter inductively we do not find anything to be 'in' itself in any of the senses that have been distinguished; and it can be seen by argument that it is impossible. For each of two
10 things will have to be both, e. g. the jar will have to be both vessel and wine, and the wine both wine and jar, if it is possible for a thing to be in itself; so that, however true it might be that they were in each other, the jar will receive the wine in virtue not of *its* being wine
15 but of the wine's being wine, and the wine will be in the jar in virtue not of *its* being a jar but of the jar's being a jar. Now that they are different in respect of their essence is evident; for 'that in which something is' and 'that which is in it' would be differently defined.

Nor is it possible for a thing to be in itself even incidentally: for two things would be at the same time in the same thing. The jar
20 would be in itself—if a thing whose nature it is to receive can be in itself; and that which it receives, namely (if wine) wine, will be in it. Obviously then a thing cannot be in itself *primarily*.

Zeno's problem—that if Place is something it must be in something —is not difficult to solve. There is nothing to prevent the first place
25 from being 'in' something else—not indeed in that as 'in' place, but as health is 'in' the hot as a positive determination of it or as the hot is 'in' body as an affection. So we escape the infinite regress.

Another thing is plain: since the vessel is no part of what is in it (what contains in the *strict* sense is different from what is contained), place could not be either the matter or the form of the thing
30 contained, but must be different—for the latter, both the matter and the shape, are parts of what is contained.

This then may serve as a critical statement of the difficulties involved.

4 What then after all is place? The answer to this question may be elucidated as follows.

Let us take for granted about it the various characteristics which are supposed correctly to belong to it essentially. We assume then—

(1) Place is what contains that of which it is the place.

(2) Place is no part of the thing.   211ª

(3) The immediate place of a thing is neither less nor greater than the thing.

(4) Place can be left behind by the thing and is separable.

In addition:

(5) All place admits of the distinction of up and down, and each of the bodies is naturally carried to its appropriate place and rests there, and this makes the place either up or down.   5

Having laid these foundations, we must complete the theory. We ought to try to make our investigation such as will render an account of place, and will not only solve the difficulties connected with it, but will also show that the attributes supposed to belong to it do really belong to it, and further will make clear the cause of the trouble and 10 of the difficulties about it. Such is the most satisfactory kind of exposition.

First then we must understand that place would not have been thought of, if there had not been a special kind of motion, namely that with respect to place. It is chiefly for this reason that we suppose the heaven also to be in place, because it is in constant movement. Of this kind of change there are two species—locomotion on the one 15 hand and, on the other, increase and diminution. For these too involve variation of place: what was then in this place has now in turn changed to what is larger or smaller.

Again, when we say a thing is 'moved', the predicate either (1) belongs to it actually, in virtue of its own nature, or (2) in virtue of something conjoined with it. In the latter case it may be either (a) something which by its own nature is capable of being moved, e. g. the 20 parts of the body or the nail in the ship, or (b) something which is not in itself capable of being moved, but is *always* moved through its conjunction with something else, as 'whiteness' or 'science'. These have changed their place only because the subjects to which they belong do so.

We say that a thing is in the world, in the sense of in place, because it is in the air, and the air is in the world; and when we say it is in 25 the air, we do not mean it is in every part of the air, but that it is in the air because of the outer surface of the air which surrounds it; for if all the air were its place, the place of a thing would not be equal to the thing—which it is supposed to be, and which the primary place in which a thing is actually is.

When what surrounds, then, is not separate from the thing, but is
30 in continuity with it, the thing is said to be in what surrounds it, not in the sense of in place, but as a part in a whole. But when the thing is separate and in contact, it is immediately 'in' the inner surface of the surrounding body, and this surface is neither a part of what is in it nor yet greater than its extension, but equal to it; for the extremities of things which touch are coincident.

Further, if one body is in continuity with another, it is not moved
35 *in* that but *with* that. On the other hand it is moved *in* that if it is separate. It makes no difference whether what contains is moved or not.

211ᵇ Again, when it is not separate it is described as a part in a whole, as the pupil in the eye or the hand in the body: when it is separate, as the water in the cask or the wine in the jar. For the hand is moved *with* the body and the water *in* the cask.

5   It will now be plain from these considerations what place is. There are just four things of which place must be one—the shape, or the matter, or some sort of extension between the bounding surfaces of the containing body, or this boundary itself if it contains no extension over and above the bulk of the body which comes to be in it.

Three of these it obviously cannot be:

10   (1) The shape is supposed to be place because it surrounds, for the extremities of what contains and of what is contained are coincident. Both the shape and the place, it is true, are boundaries. But not of the same thing: the form is the boundary of the thing, the place is the boundary of the body which contains it.

(2) The extension between the extremities is thought to be something, because what is contained and separate may often be changed while the container remains the same (as water may be poured from
15 a vessel)—the assumption being that the extension is something over and above the body displaced. But there is no such extension. One of the bodies which change places and are naturally capable of being in contact with the container falls in—whichever it may chance to be.

If there were an extension which were such as to exist independently
20 and be permanent, there would be an infinity of places in the same thing. For when the water and the air change places, all the portions of,the two together will play the same part in the whole which was

previously played by all the water in the vessel; at the same time the place too will be undergoing change; so that there will be another place which is the place of the place, and many places will be coinci- 25 dent. There is not a different place of the part, in which it is moved, when the whole vessel changes its place: it is always the same: for it is in the (proximate) place where they are that the air and the water (or the parts of the water) succeed each other, not in that place in which they come to be, which is part of the place which is the place of the whole world.

(3) The matter, too, might seem to be place, at least if we consider 30 it in what is at rest and is thus separate but in continuity. For just as in change of quality there is something which was formerly black and is now white, or formerly soft and now hard—this is just why we say that the matter exists—so place, because it presents a similar phenomenon, is thought to exist—only in the one case we say so be- 35 cause *what* was air is now water, in the other because *where* air formerly was there is now water. But the matter, as we said before,[5] 212ᵃ is neither separable from the thing nor contains it, whereas place has both characteristics.

Well, then, if place is none of the three—neither the form nor the matter nor an extension which is always there, different from, and over and above, the extension of the thing which is displaced—place necessarily is the one of the four which is left, namely, the boundary 5 of the containing body at which it is in contact with the contained body. (By the contained body is meant what can be moved by way of locomotion.)

Place is thought to be something important and hard to grasp, both because the matter and the shape present themselves along with it, and because the displacement of the body that is moved takes place in a stationary container, for it seems possible that there should be an 10 interval which is other than the bodies which are moved. The air, too, which is thought to be incorporeal, contributes something to the belief: it is not only the boundaries of the vessel which seem to be place, but also what is between them, regarded as empty. Just, in fact, as the vessel is transportable place, so place is a non-portable vessel. So when what is within a thing which is moved, is moved and 15 changes its place, as a boat on a river, what contains plays the part of a vessel rather than that of place. Place on the other hand is rather what is motionless: so it is rather the whole river that is place, because as a whole it is motionless.

⁵ 209ᵇ 22–32.

20   Hence we conclude that *the innermost motionless boundary of what contains is place.*

This explains why the middle of the heaven and the surface which faces us of the rotating system are held to be 'up' and 'down' in the strict and fullest sense for all men: for the one is always at rest, while the inner side of the rotating body remains always coincident with
25 itself. Hence since the light is what is naturally carried up, and the heavy what is carried down, the boundary which contains in the direction of the middle of the universe, and the middle itself, are down, and that which contains in the direction of the outermost part of the universe, and the outermost part itself, are up.

For this reason, too, place is thought to be a kind of surface, and as it were a vessel, i. e. a container of the thing.

30   Further, place is coincident with the thing, for boundaries are coincident with the bounded.

5   If then a body has another body outside it and containing it, it is in place, and if not, not. That is why, even if there were to be water which had not a container, the parts of it, on the one hand, will be moved (for one part is contained in another), while, on the other
35 hand, the whole will be moved in one sense, but not in another. For as a whole it does not simultaneously change its place, though it will
212ᵇ be moved in a circle: for this place is the place of its parts. (Some things are moved, not up and down, but in a circle; others up and down, such things namely as admit of condensation and rarefaction.)

As was explained,[6] some things are potentially in place, others actually. So, when you have a homogeneous substance which is
5 continuous, the parts are potentially in place: when the parts are separated, but in contact, like a heap, they are actually in place.

Again, (1) some things are *per se* in place, namely every body which is movable either by way of locomotion or by way of increase is *per se* somewhere, but the heaven, as has been said,[7] is not anywhere as a whole, nor in any place, if at least, as we must sup-
10 pose, no body contains it. On the line on which it is moved, its parts have place: for each is contiguous to the next.

But (2) other things are in place indirectly, through something conjoined with them, as the soul and the heaven. The latter is, in a way, in place, for all its parts are: for on the orb one part contains another. That is why the upper part is moved in a circle, while the All
15 is not anywhere. For what is somewhere is itself something, and

[6] 211ᵃ 17–ᵇ5.   [7] ᵃ32.

there must be alongside it some other thing wherein it is and which contains it. But alongside the All or the Whole there is nothing outside the All, and for this reason all things are in the heaven; for the heaven, we may say, is the All. Yet their place is not the same as the heaven. It is part of it, the innermost part of it, which is in contact with the movable body; and for this reason the earth is in water, and 20 this in the air, and the air in the aether, and the aether in heaven, but we cannot go on and say that the heaven is in anything else.

It is clear, too, from these considerations that all the problems which were raised [8] about place will be solved when it is explained in this way:

(1) There is no necessity that the place should grow with the body in it,

(2) Nor that a point should have a place,

(3) Nor that two bodies should be in the same place,   25

(4) Nor that place should be a corporeal interval: for what is between the boundaries of the place is any body which may chance to be there, not an interval in body.

Further, (5) place is also somewhere, not in the sense of being in a place, but as the limit is in the limited; for not everything that is is in place, but only movable body.

Also (6) it is reasonable that each kind of body should be carried to its own place. For a body which is next in the series and in con- 30 tact (not by compulsion) is akin, and bodies which are united do not affect each other, while those which are in contact interact on each other.

Nor (7) is it without reason that each should remain naturally in its proper place. For this part has the same relation to its place, as a 35 separable part to its whole, as when one moves a part of water or 213ᵃ air: so, too, air is related to water, for the one is like matter, the other form—water is the matter of air, air as it were the actuality of water, for water is potentially air, while air is potentially water, though in another way.

These distinctions will be drawn more carefully later.[9] On the pres- ent occasion it was necessary to refer to them: what has now been 5 stated obscurely will then be made more clear. If the matter and the fulfilment are the same thing (for water is both, the one potentially, the other completely), water will be related to air in a way as part to whole. That is why these have *contact*: it is *organic union* when both become actually one.

[8] 209ᵃ 2-30.   [9] *De Gen. et Corr.* i. 3.

10   This concludes my account of place—both of its existence and of its nature.

6   The investigation of similar questions about the void, also, must be held to belong to the physicist—namely whether it exists or not, and how it exists or what it is—just as about place. The views taken of it involve arguments both for and against, in much the same sort 15 of way. For those who hold that the void exists regard it as a sort of place or vessel which is supposed to be 'full' when it holds the bulk which it is capable of containing, 'void' when it is deprived of that— as if 'void' and 'full' and 'place' denoted the same thing, though the essence of the three is different.

20   We must begin the inquiry by putting down the account given by those who say that it exists, then the account of those who say that it does not exist, and third the current view on these questions.

Those who try to show that the void does not exist do not disprove what people really mean by it, but only their erroneous way of speaking; this is true of Anaxagoras and of those who refute the existence 25 of the void in this way. They merely give an ingenious demonstration that air is something—by straining wine-skins and showing the resistance of the air, and by cutting it off in clepsydras. But people really mean that there is an empty interval in which there is *no* sensible body. They hold that everything which is is body and say 30 that what has nothing in it at all is void (so what is full of air is void). It is not then the existence of air that needs to be proved, but the non-existence of an interval, different from the bodies, either separable or actual—an interval which divides the whole body so as to break its continuity, as Democritus and Leucippus hold, and 213ᵇ many other physicists—or even perhaps as something which is outside the whole body, which remains continuous.

These people, then, have not reached even the threshold of the problem, but rather those who say that the void exists.

(1) They argue, for one thing, that change in place (i. e. locomo- 5 tion and increase) would not be. For it is maintained that motion would seem not to exist, if there were no void, since what is full cannot contain anything more. If it could, and there were two bodies in the same place, it would also be true that any number of bodies could be together; for it is impossible to draw a line of division beyond which the statement would become untrue. If this were possible, it 10 would follow also that the smallest body would contain the greatest; for 'many a little makes a mickle': thus if many equal bodies can be together, so also can many unequal bodies.

Melissus, indeed, infers from these considerations that the All is immovable; for if it were moved there must, he says, be void, but void is not among the things that exist.

This argument, then, is one way in which they show that there is a void.

(2) They reason from the fact that some things are observed to contract and be compressed, as people say that a cask will hold the wine which formerly filled it, along with the skins into which the wine has been decanted, which implies that the compressed body contracts into the voids present in it.

Again (3) increase, too, is thought to take place always by means of void, for nutriment is body, and it is impossible for two bodies to be together. A proof of this they find also in what happens to ashes, which absorb as much water as the empty vessel.

The Pythagoreans, too, (4) held that void exists and that it enters the heaven itself, which as it were inhales it, from the infinite air. Further it is the void which distinguishes the natures of things, as if it were like what separates and distinguishes the terms of a series. This holds primarily in the numbers, for the void distinguishes their nature.

These, then, and so many, are the main grounds on which people have argued for and against the existence of the void.

7   As a step towards settling which view is true, we must determine the meaning of the name.

The void is thought to be place with nothing in it. The reason for this is that people take what exists to be body, and hold that while every body is in place, void is place in which there is no body, so that where there is no body, there must be void.

Every body, again, they suppose to be tangible; and of this nature is whatever has weight or lightness.

Hence, by a syllogism, what has nothing heavy or light in it, is void.

This result, then, as I have said, is reached by syllogism. It would be absurd to suppose that the point is void; for the void must be *place* which has in it an interval in tangible body.

But at all events we observe then that in one way the void is described as what is not full of body perceptible to touch; and what has heaviness and lightness is perceptible to touch. So we would raise the question: what would they say of an interval that has colour or sound—is it void or not? Clearly they would reply that if it *could* receive what is tangible it was void, and if not, not.

In another way void is that in which there is no 'this' or corporeal substance. So some say that the void is the matter of the body (they identify the place, too, with this), and in this they speak incor-
15 rectly; for the matter is not separable from the things, but they are inquiring about the void as about something separable.

Since we have determined the nature of place, and void must, if it exists, be place deprived of body, and we have stated both in what sense place exists and in what sense it does not, it is plain that on this showing void does not exist, either unseparated or separated;
20 for the void is meant to be, not body but rather an interval in body. This is why the void is thought to be something, viz. because place is, and for the same reasons. For the fact of motion in respect of place comes to the aid both of those who maintain that place is something over and above the bodies that come to occupy it, and of those who maintain that the void is something. They state that the void is the condition of movement in the sense of that in which movement
25 takes place; and this would be the kind of thing that some say place is.

But there is no necessity for there being a void if there is movement. It is not in the least needed as a condition of movement in general, for a reason which, incidentally, escaped Melissus; viz. that the full can suffer *qualitative* change.

But not even movement in respect of place involves a void; for bodies may simultaneously make room for one another, though
30 there is no interval separate and apart from the bodies that are in movement. And this is plain even in the rotation of continuous things, as in that of liquids.

And things can also be compressed not into a void but because they squeeze out what is contained in them (as, for instance, when water is compressed the air within it is squeezed out); and things
214^b can increase in size not only by the entrance of something but also by qualitative change; e. g. if water were to be transformed into air.

In general, both the argument about increase of size and that about the water poured on to the ashes get in their own way. For
5 either not any and every part of the body is increased, or bodies may be increased otherwise than by the addition of body, or there may be two bodies in the same place (in which case they are claiming to solve a quite general difficulty, but are not proving the existence of void), or the *whole* body must be void, if it is increased in every part and is increased by means of void. The same argument applies to the ashes.
10 It is evident, then, that it is easy to refute the arguments by which they prove the existence of the void.

8   Let us explain again that there is no void existing separately, as some maintain. If each of the simple bodies has a natural locomotion, e. g. fire upward and earth downward and towards the middle of 15 the universe, it is clear that it cannot be the void that is the condition of locomotion. What, then, *will* the void be the condition of? It is thought to be the condition of movement in respect of place, and it is not the condition of this.

Again, if void is a sort of place deprived of body, when there is a void where will a body placed in it move to? It certainly cannot move into the whole of the void. The same argument applies as against those who think that place is something separate, into which 20 things are carried; viz. how will what is placed in it move, or rest? Much the same argument will apply to the void as to the 'up' and 'down' in place, as is natural enough since those who maintain the existence of the void make it a place.

And in what way will things be present either in place or in the 25 void? For the expected [10] result does not take place when a body is placed as a whole in a place conceived of as separate and permanent; for a part of it, unless it be placed apart, will not be in a place but in the whole. Further, if separate place does not exist, neither will void.

If people say that the void must exist, as being necessary if there is to be movement, what rather turns out to be the case, if one studies the matter, is the opposite, that not a single thing can be moved if 30 there *is* a void; for as with those who for a like reason say the earth is at rest, so, too, in the void things must be at rest; for there is no place to which things can move more or less than to another; since the void in so far as it is void admits no difference.

The second reason is this: all movement is either compulsory or 215ᵃ according to nature, and if there is compulsory movement there must also be natural (for compulsory movement is contrary to nature, and movement contrary to nature is posterior to that according to nature, so that if each of the natural bodies has not a natural movement, none of the other movements can exist); but how can there 5 be natural movement if there is no difference throughout the void or the infinite? For in so far as it is infinite, there will be no up or down or middle, and in so far as it is a void, up differs no whit from down; for as there is no difference in what is nothing, there is none in the void (for the void seems to be a non-existent and a privation of being), 10 but natural locomotion seems to be differentiated, so that the things that exist by nature must be differentiated. Either, then, nothing has a natural locomotion, or else there is no void.

[10] Expected by those who believe in a separately existing place or void.

Further, in point of fact things that are thrown move though that
which gave them their impulse is not touching them, either by reason
15 of mutual replacement, as some maintain, or because the air that has
been pushed pushes them with a movement quicker than the natural
locomotion of the projectile wherewith it moves to its proper place.
But in a void none of these things can take place, nor can anything
be moved save as that which is carried is moved.

Further, no one could say why a thing once set in motion should
20 stop anywhere; for why should it stop *here* rather than *here*? So that
a thing will either be at rest or must be moved *ad infinitum*, unless
something more powerful get in its way.

Further, things are now thought to move into the void because
it yields; but in a void this quality is present equally everywhere,
so that things should move in all directions.

Further, the truth of what we assert is plain from the following
25 considerations. We see the same weight or body moving faster than
another for two reasons, either because there is a difference in what
it moves through, as between water, air, and earth, or because, other
things being equal, the moving body differs from the other owing to
excess of weight or of lightness.

Now the medium causes a difference because it impedes the moving thing, most of all if it is moving in the opposite direction, but in
30 a secondary degree even if it is at rest; and especially a medium
that is not easily divided, i. e. a medium that is somewhat dense.

215ᵇ   A, then, will move through B in time C, and through D, which is
thinner, in time E (if the length of B is equal to D), in proportion
to the density of the hindering body. For let B be water and D air;
5 then by so much as air is thinner and more incorporeal than water,
A will move through D faster than through B. Let the speed have the
same ratio to the speed, then, that air has to water. Then if air is
twice as thin, the body will traverse B in twice the time that it does D,
and the time C will be twice the time E. And always, by so much
10 as the medium is more incorporeal and less resistant and more easily
divided, the faster will be the movement.

Now there is no ratio in which the void is exceeded by body, as there
is no ratio of o to a number. For if 4 exceeds 3 by 1, and 2 by more
15 than 1, and 1 by still more than it exceeds 2, still there is no ratio
by which it exceeds o; for that which exceeds must be divisible into
the excess + that which is exceeded, so that 4 will be what it exceeds
o by + o. For this reason, too, a line does not exceed a point—unless
20 it is composed of points! Similarly the void can bear no ratio to the

full, and therefore neither can movement through the one to movement through the other, but if a thing moves through the thickest
medium such and such a distance in such and such a time, it moves
through the void with a speed beyond any ratio. For let F be void,
equal in magnitude to B and to D. Then if A is to traverse and move
through it in a certain time, G, a time less than E, however, the void 25
will bear this ratio to the full. But in a time equal to G, A will traverse
the part H of D. And it will surely also traverse in that time any
substance F which exceeds air in thickness in the ratio which the
time E bears to the time G. For if the body F be as much thinner than 30
D as E exceeds G, A, if it moves through F, will traverse it in a time
inverse to the speed of the movement, i. e. in a time equal to G. If, 216ᵃ
then, there is *no* body in F, A will traverse F still more quickly.
But we supposed that its traverse of F when F was void occupied
the time G. So that it will traverse F in an equal time whether F be
full or void. But this is impossible. It is plain, then, that if there is
a time in which it will move through any part of the void, this impossible result will follow: it will be found to traverse a certain dis- 5
tance, whether this be full or void, in an equal time; for there will
be some *body* which is in the same ratio to the other body as the
time is to the time.

To sum the matter up, the cause of this result is obvious, viz. that
between any two movements there is a ratio (for they occupy time,
and there is a ratio between any two times, so long as both are 10
finite), but there is no ratio of void to full.

These are the consequences that result from a difference in the
media; the following depend upon an excess of one moving body
over another. We see that bodies which have a greater impulse either
of weight or of lightness, if they are alike in other respects, move 15
faster over an equal space, and in the ratio which their magnitudes
bear to each other. Therefore they will also move through the void
with this ratio of speed. But that is impossible; for why should
one move faster? (In moving through *plena* it must be so; for the
greater divides them faster by its force. For a moving thing cleaves
the medium either by its shape, or by the impulse which the body
that is carried along or is projected possesses.) Therefore all will 20
possess equal velocity. But this is impossible.

It is evident from what has been said, then, that, if there is a void,
a result follows which is the very opposite of the reason for which
those who believe in a void set it up. They think that if movement
in respect of place is to exist, the void cannot exist, separated all

25 by itself; but this is the same as to say that place is a separate cavity; and this has already been stated to be impossible.[11]

But even if we consider it on its own merits the so-called vacuum will be found to be really vacuous. For as, if one puts a cube in water, an amount of water equal to the cube will be displaced; so too in air; but the effect is imperceptible to sense. And indeed always,

30 in the case of any body that can be displaced, it must, if it is not compressed, be displaced in the direction in which it is its nature to be displaced—always either down, if its locomotion is downwards as in the case of earth, or up, if it is fire, or in both directions—whatever be the nature of the inserted body. Now in the void this is impossible; for it is not body; the void must have penetrated the cube to a dis-

35 tance equal to that which this portion of void formerly occupied in

216[b] the void, just as if the water or air had not been displaced by the wooden cube, but had penetrated right through it.

But the cube also has a magnitude equal to that occupied by the void; a magnitude which, if it is also hot or cold, or heavy or light, is none the

5 less different in essence from all its attributes, even if it is not separable from them; I mean the *volume* of the wooden cube. So that even if it were separated from everything else and were neither heavy nor light, it will occupy an equal amount of void, and fill the same place, as the part of place or of the void equal to itself. How then will the body of the

10 cube differ from the void or place that is equal to it? And if there can be two such things, why cannot there be any number coinciding?

This, then, is one absurd and impossible implication of the theory. It is also evident that the cube will have this same volume even if it is displaced, which is an attribute possessed by all other bodies also. Therefore if this differs in no respect from its place, why need we assume a place for bodies over and above the volume of each, if

15 their volume be conceived of as free from attributes? It contributes nothing to the situation if there is an equal interval attached to it as well. Further, it ought to be clear by the study of moving things what sort of thing void is. But in fact it is found nowhere in the world. For air is something, though it does not *seem* to be so—nor, for that matter, would water, if fishes were made of iron; for the discrimination of the tangible is by touch.

20 It is clear, then, from these considerations that there is no separate void.

9   There are some who think that the existence of rarity and density shows that there is a void. If rarity and density do not exist, they

[11] 211[b] 19 sqq., 213[a] 31.

say, neither can things contract and be compressed. But if this were not to take place, either there would be no movement at all, or the universe would bulge, as Xuthus [12] said, or air and water must always change into equal amounts (e. g. if air has been made out of a cupful of water, at the same time out of an equal amount of air a cupful of water must have been made), or void must necessarily exist; for compression and expansion cannot take place otherwise.

Now, if they mean by the rare that which has many voids existing separately, it is plain that if void cannot exist separate any more than a place can exist with an extension all to itself, neither can the rare exist in this sense. But if they mean that there is void, not separately existent, but still present in the rare, this is less impossible, yet, first, the void turns out not to be a condition of *all* movement, but only of movement upwards (for the rare is light, which is the reason why they say fire is rare); second, the void turns out to be a condition of movement not as that in which it takes place, but in that the void carries things up as skins by being carried up themselves carry up what is continuous with them. Yet how can void have a local movement or a place? For thus that into which void moves is till then void of a void.

Again, how will they explain, in the case of what is heavy, its movement downwards? And it is plain that if the rarer and more void a thing is the quicker it will move upwards, if it were completely void it would move with a maximum speed! But perhaps even this is impossible, that it should move at all; the same reason which showed that in the void all things are incapable of moving shows that the void cannot move, viz., the fact that the speeds are incomparable.

Since we deny that a void exists, but for the rest the problem has been truly stated, that *either* there will be no movement, if there is not to be condensation and rarefaction, *or* the universe will bulge, *or* a transformation of water into air will always be balanced by an equal transformation of air into water (for it is clear that the air produced from water is bulkier than the water): it is necessary therefore, if compression does not exist, *either* that the next portion will be pushed outwards and make the outermost part bulge, *or* that somewhere else there must be an equal amount of water produced out of air, so that the entire bulk of the whole may be equal, *or* that nothing moves. For when anything is displaced this will always happen, unless it comes round in a circle; but locomotion is not always circular, but sometimes in a straight line.

These then are the reasons for which they might say that there is a void; *our* statement is based on the assumption that there is a

[12] A Pythagorean of Croton.

single matter for contraries, hot and cold and the other natural contrarieties, and that what exists actually is produced from a potential
existent, and that matter is not separable from the contraries but its
25 being is different, and that a single matter may serve for colour and
heat and cold.

The same matter also serves for both a large and a small body.
This is evident; for when air is produced from water, the same
matter has become something different, not by acquiring an addition
to it, but has become actually what it was potentially, and, again,
30 water is produced from air in the same way, the change being sometimes from smallness to greatness, and sometimes from greatness to
smallness. Similarly, therefore, if air which is large in extent comes
to have a smaller volume, or becomes greater from being smaller, it
is the matter which is potentially both that comes to be each of the two.

For as the same matter becomes hot from being cold, and cold
from being hot, because it was potentially both, so too from hot it
217ᵇ can become more hot, though nothing in the matter has become hot
that was not hot when the thing was less hot; just as, if the arc or
curve of a greater circle becomes that of a smaller, whether it remains
the same or becomes a different curve, convexity has not come to
5 exist in anything that was not convex but straight (for differences of
degree do not depend on an intermission of the quality); nor can we
get any portion of a flame, in which both heat and whiteness are not
present. So too, then, is the earlier heat related to the later. So that
the greatness and smallness, also, of the sensible volume are extended,
not by the matter's acquiring anything new, but because the matter
10 is potentially matter for both states; so that the same thing is dense
and rare, and the two qualities have one matter.

The dense is heavy, and the rare is light. Again, as the arc of a
circle when contracted into a smaller space does not acquire a new
part which is convex, but what was there has been contracted; and as
any part of fire that one takes will be hot; so, too, it is all a question
15 of contraction and expansion of the same matter. There are two types
in each case, both in the dense and in the rare; for both the heavy and
the hard are thought to be dense, and contrariwise both the light and
the soft are rare; and weight and hardness fail to coincide in the case
of lead and iron.

20   From what has been said it is evident, then, that void does not
exist either separate (either absolutely separate or as a separate element in the rare) or potentially, unless one is willing to call the condition of movement void, whatever it may be. At that rate the matter
of the heavy and the light, *qua* matter of them, would be the void;

for the dense and the rare are productive of locomotion in virtue of *this* contrariety, and in virtue of their hardness and softness produc- 25 tive of passivity and impassivity, i. e. not of locomotion but rather of qualitative change.

So much, then, for the discussion of the void, and of the sense in which it exists and the sense in which it does not exist.

10   Next for discussion after the subjects mentioned is Time.

The best plan will be to begin by working out the difficulties 30 connected with it, making use of the current arguments. First, does it belong to the class of things that exist or to that of things that do not exist? Then secondly, what is its nature? To start, then: the following considerations would make one suspect that it either does not exist at all or barely, and in an obscure way. One part of it has been and is not, while the other is going to be and is not yet. Yet time 218 —both infinite time and any time you like to take—is made up of these. One would naturally suppose that what is made up of things which do not exist could have no share in reality.

Further, if a divisible thing is to exist, it is necessary that, when it exists, all or some of its parts must exist. But of time some parts have 5 been, while others have to be, and no part of it *is*, though it is divisible. For what is 'now' is not a part: a part is a measure of the whole, which must be made up of parts. Time, on the other hand, is not held to be made up of 'nows'.

Again, the 'now' which seems to bound the past and the future— does it always remain one and the same or is it always other and other? It is hard to say.   10

(1) If it is always different and different, and if none of the *parts* in time which are other and other are simultaneous (unless the one contains and the other is contained, as the shorter time is by the longer), and if the 'now' which is not, but formerly was, must have ceased-to-be at some time, the *'nows'* too cannot be simultaneous with 15 one another, but the prior 'now' must always have ceased-to-be. But the prior 'now' cannot have ceased-to-be in [13] itself (since it then existed); yet it cannot have ceased-to-be in another 'now'. For we may lay it down that one 'now' cannot be next to another, any more than point to point. If then it did not cease-to-be in the next 'now' but in another, it would exist simultaneously with the innumerable 20 'nows' between the two—which is impossible.

Yes, but (2) neither is it possible for the 'now' to remain always

[13] The argument would be clearer if we could say 'during' itself. If the existent perished 'in' itself, it would never exist without perishing.

the same. No determinate divisible thing has a single termination, whether it is continuously extended in one or in more than one dimension: but the 'now' is a termination, and it is possible to cut off a
25 determinate time. Further, if coincidence in time (i. e. being neither prior nor posterior) means to be 'in one and the same "now"', then, if both what is before and what is after are in this same 'now', things which happened ten thousand years ago would be simultaneous with what has happened to-day, and nothing would be before or after anything else.

30   This may serve as a statement of the difficulties about the attributes of time.

      As to what time is or what is its nature, the traditional accounts give us as little light as the preliminary problems which we have worked through.

      Some assert that it is (1) the movement of the whole, others that
218ᵇ it is (2) the sphere itself.¹⁴

      (1) Yet part, too, of the revolution is a time, but it certainly is not a revolution: for what is taken is part of a revolution, not a revolution. Besides, if there were more heavens than one, the movement of any of them equally would be time, so that there would be many times at the same time.

5   (2) Those who said that time is the sphere of the whole thought so, no doubt, on the ground that all things are in time and all things are in the sphere of the whole. The view is too naive for it to be worth while to consider the impossibilities implied in it.

      But as time is most usually supposed to be (3) motion and a kind of change, we must consider this view.

10   Now (a) the change or movement of each thing is only *in* the thing which changes or *where* the thing itself which moves or changes may chance to be. But time is present equally everywhere and with all things.

      Again, (b) change is always faster or slower, whereas time is not:
15 for 'fast' and 'slow' are defined by time—'fast' is what moves much in a short time, 'slow' what moves little in a long time; but time is not defined by time, by being either a certain amount or a certain kind of it.

      Clearly then it is not movement. (We need not distinguish at
20 present between 'movement' and 'change'.)

11   But neither does time exist without change; for when the state of our own minds does not change at all, or we have not noticed

¹⁴ Aristotle is probably referring to Plato and the Pythagoreans respectively.

its changing, we do not realize that time has elapsed, any more than those who are fabled to sleep among the heroes in Sardinia do when 25 they are awakened; for they connect the earlier 'now' with the later and make them one, cutting out the interval because of their failure to notice it. So, just as, if the 'now' were not different but one and the same, there would not have been time, so too when its difference escapes our notice the interval does not seem to be time. If, then, the non-realization of the existence of time happens to us when we do not 30 distinguish any change, but the soul seems to stay in one indivisible state, and when we perceive and distinguish we say time has elapsed, evidently time is not independent of movement and change. It is evident, then, that time is neither movement nor independent of 219ᵃ movement.

We must take this as our starting-point and try to discover—since we wish to know what time is—what exactly it has to do with movement.

Now we perceive movement and time together: for even when it is dark and we are not being affected through the body, if any move- 5 ment takes place in the mind we at once suppose that some time also has elapsed; and not only that but also, when some time is thought to have passed, some movement also along with it seems to have taken place. Hence time is either movement or something that belongs to movement. Since then it is not movement, it must be the other.

But what is moved is moved from something to something, and 10 all magnitude is continuous. Therefore the movement goes with the magnitude. Because the magnitude is continuous, the movement too must be continuous, and if the movement, then the time; for the time that has passed is always thought to be in proportion to the movement.

The distinction of 'before' and 'after' holds primarily then, in place; and there in virtue of relative position. Since then 'before' and 'after' hold in magnitude, they must hold also in movement, these 15 corresponding to those. But also in time the distinction of 'before' and 'after' must hold, for time and movement always correspond with each other. The 'before' and 'after' in motion identical in substratum with motion yet differs from it in definition, and is not 20 identical with motion.

But we apprehend time only when we have marked motion, marking it by 'before' and 'after'; and it is only when we have perceived 'before' and 'after' in motion that we say that time has elapsed. Now 25 we mark them by judging that A and B are different, and that some third thing is intermediate to them. When we think of the extremes as different from the middle and the mind pronounces that the 'nows' are two, one before and one after, it is then that we say that there is time, and this that we say is time. For what is bounded by the 'now' is thought to be time—we may assume this.

30   When, therefore, we perceive the 'now' as one, and neither as before and after in a motion nor as an identity but in relation to a 'before' and an 'after', no time is thought to have elapsed, because there has been no motion either. On the other hand, when we do per-
219ᵇ ceive a 'before' and an 'after', then we say that there is time. For time is just this—number of motion in respect of 'before' and 'after'.

Hence time is not movement, but only movement in so far as it admits of enumeration. A proof of this: we discriminate the more or the less by number, but more or less movement by time. Time then is
5 a kind of number. (Number, we must note, is used in two senses—both of what is counted or the countable and also of that with which we count. Time obviously is what is counted, not that with which we count: these are different kinds of thing.)

Just as motion is a perpetual succession, so also is time. But every
10 simultaneous time is self-identical; for the 'now' as a subject is an identity, but it accepts different attributes.[15] The 'now' measures time, in so far as time involves the 'before and after'.

The 'now' in one sense is the same, in another it is not the same. In so far as it is in succession, it is different (which is just what its being now was supposed to mean), but its substratum is an identity:
15 for motion, as was said, goes with magnitude, and time, as we maintain, with motion. Similarly, then, there corresponds to the point the body which is carried along, and by which we are aware of the motion and of the 'before and after' involved in it. This is an identical *substratum* (whether a point or a stone or something else of the
20 kind), but it has different *attributes*—as the sophists assume that Coriscus' being in the Lyceum is a different thing from Coriscus' being in the market-place. And the body which is carried along is different, in so far as it is at one time here and at another there. But the 'now' corresponds to the body that is carried along, as time corresponds to the motion. For it is by means of the body that is carried along that
25 we become aware of the 'before and after' in the motion, and if we regard these as countable we get the 'now'. Hence in these also the 'now' as substratum remains the same (for it is what is before and after in movement), but what is predicated of it is different; for it is

[15] E. g. if you come in when I go out, the time of your coming in is in fact the time of my going out, though for it to be the one and to be the other are different things.

in so far as the 'before and after' is numerable that we get the 'now'.
This is what is most knowable: for, similarly, motion is known because of that which is moved, locomotion because of that which is
carried. For what is carried is a real thing, the movement is not. 30
Thus what is called 'now' in one sense is always the same; in another
it is not the same: for this is true also of what is carried.

Clearly, too, if there were no time, there would be no 'now', and
vice versa. Just as the moving body and its locomotion involve each 220ᵃ
other mutually, so too do the number of the moving body and the
number of its locomotion. For the number of the locomotion is time,
while the 'now' corresponds to the moving body, and is like the unit
of number.

Time, then, also is both made continuous by the 'now' and divided 5
at it. For here too there is a correspondence with the locomotion and
the moving body. For the motion or locomotion is made one by the
thing which is moved, because *it* is one—not because it is one in its
own nature (for there might be pauses in the movement of such a
thing)—but because it is one in definition: for this determines the
movement as 'before' and 'after'. Here, too, there is a correspondence
with the point; for the point also both connects and terminates the 10
length—it is the beginning of one and the end of another. But when
you take it in this way, using the one point as two, a pause is necessary, if the same point is to be the beginning and the end. The 'now' on
the other hand, since the body carried is moving, is always different.

Hence time is not number in the sense in which there is 'number'
of the same point because it is beginning and end, but rather as the
extremities of a line form a number, and not as the parts of the line 15
do so, both for the reason given (for we can use the middle point as
two, so that on that analogy time might stand still), and further because obviously the 'now' is no *part* of time nor the section any part
of the movement, any more than the points are parts of the line—
for it is two *lines* that are *parts* of one line.　　　　　　　　　　　20

In so far then as the 'now' is a boundary, it is not time, but an
attribute of it; in so far as it numbers, it is number; for boundaries
belong only to that which they bound, but number (*e. g.* ten) is the
number of these horses, and belongs also elsewhere.

It is clear, then, that time is 'number of movement in respect of
the before and after', and is continuous since it is an attribute of what 25
is continuous.

12　The smallest number, in the strict sense of the word 'number',
is two. But of number as concrete, sometimes there is a minimum,

sometimes not: e. g. of a 'line', the smallest in respect of *multiplicity*
is two (or, if you like, one), but in respect of *size* there is no mini-
30 mum; for every line is divided *ad infinitum*. Hence it is so with time.
In respect of number the minimum is one (or two); in point of extent
there is no minimum.

It is clear, too, that time is not described as fast or slow, but as
220ᵇ many or few[16] and as long or short. For as continuous it is long or
short and as a number many or few, but it is not fast or slow—any
more than any number with which we number is fast or slow.

5   Further, there is the same time everywhere at once, but not the
same time before and after, for while the present change is one, the
change which has happened and that which will happen are different.
Time is not number with which we count, but the number of things
which are counted, and this according as it occurs before or after is
10 always different, for the 'nows' are different. And the number of a
hundred horses and a hundred men is the same, but the things numbered are different—the horses from the men. Further, as a movement
can be one and the same again and again, so too can time, e. g. a
year or a spring or an autumn.

15   Not only do we measure the movement by the time, but also the
time by the movement, because they define each other. The time marks
the movement, since it is its number, and the movement the time.
We describe the time as much or little, measuring it by the movement, just as we know the number by what is numbered, e. g. the
20 number of the horses by one horse as the unit. For we know how
many horses there are by the use of the number; and again by using
the one horse as unit we know the number of the horses itself. So it is
with the time and the movement; for we measure the movement by the
time and vice versa. It is natural that this should happen; for the
25 movement goes with the distance and the time with the movement,
because they are quanta and continuous and divisible. The movement has these attributes because the distance is of this nature, and
the time has them because of the movement. And we measure both
the distance by the movement and the movement by the distance; for
we say that the road is long, if the journey is long, and that this is long,
30 if the road is long—the time, too, if the movement, and the movement, if the time.

221ᵃ   Time is a measure of motion and of being moved, and it measures
the motion by determining a motion which will measure exactly the
whole motion, as the cubit does the length by determining an amount
which will measure out the whole. Further 'to be in time' means, for

---

16 e. g. 'many years'.

movement, that both it and its essence are measured by time (for simultaneously it measures both the movement and its essence, and 5 this is what being in time means for it, that its essence should be measured).

Clearly then 'to be in time' has the same meaning for other things also, namely, that their being should be measured by time. 'To be in time' is one of two things: (1) to exist when time exists, (2) as we say 10 of some things that they are 'in number'. The latter means either what is a part or mode of number—in general, something which belongs to number—or that things have a number.

Now, since time is number, the 'now' and the 'before' and the like are in time, just as 'unit' and 'odd' and 'even' are in number, i. e. in 15 the sense that the one set belongs to number, the other to time. But things are in time as they are in number. If this is so, they are contained by time as things in place are contained by place.

Plainly, too, to be in time does not mean to coexist with time, any more than to be in motion or in place means to coexist with motion 20 or place. For if 'to be in something' is to mean this, then all things will be in anything, and the heaven will be in a grain; for when the grain is, then also is the heaven. But this is a merely incidental conjunction, whereas the other is necessarily involved: that which is in time necessarily involves that there is time when *it* is, and that which 25 is in motion that there is motion when *it* is.

Since what is 'in time' is so in the same sense as what is in number is so, a time greater than everything in time can be found. So it is necessary that all the things in time should be contained by time, just like other things also which are 'in anything', e. g. the things 'in place' by place.

A thing, then, will be affected by time, just as we are accustomed 30 to say that time wastes things away, and that all things grow old through time, and that there is oblivion owing to the lapse of time, but we do not say the same of getting to know or of becoming young or fair. For time is by its nature the cause rather of decay, since it 221^b is the number of change, and change removes what is.

Hence, plainly, things which are always are not, as such, in time, for they are not contained by time, nor is their being measured by time. A proof of this is that none of them is *affected* by time, which 5 indicates that they are not in time.

Since time is the measure of motion, it will be the measure of rest too—indirectly. For all rest is in time. For it does not follow that what is in time is moved, though what is in motion is necessarily moved. 10 For time is not motion, but 'number of motion': and what is at rest, also, can be in the number of motion. Not everything that is not in motion can be said to be 'at rest'—but only that which can be moved, though it actually is not moved, as was said above.[17]

'To be in number' means that there is a number of the thing, and that its being is measured by the number in which it is. Hence if a thing is 'in time' it will be measured by time. But time will measure what is moved and what is at rest, the one *qua* moved, the other *qua* at rest; for it will measure their motion and rest respectively.

Hence what is moved will not be measurable by the time simply in so far as it has quantity, but in so far as its *motion* has quantity. Thus none of the things which are neither moved nor at rest are in time: for 'to be in time' is 'to be measured by time', while time is the measure of motion and rest.

Plainly, then, neither will everything that does not exist be in time, i. e. those non-existent things that cannot exist, as the diagonal cannot be commensurate with the side.

Generally, if time is directly the measure of motion and indirectly of other things, it is clear that a thing whose existence is measured by it will have its existence in rest or motion. Those things therefore which are subject to perishing and becoming—generally, those which at one time exist, at another do not—are necessarily in time: for there is a greater time which will extend both beyond their existence and beyond the time which measures their existence. Of things which do not exist but are contained by time some were, e. g. Homer once was, some will be, e. g. a future event; this depends on the direction in which time contains them; if on both, they have both modes of existence. As to such things as it does not contain in any way, they neither were nor are nor will be. These are those non-existents whose opposites always are, as the incommensurability of the diagonal always is—and this will not be in time. Nor will the commensurability, therefore; hence this eternally is not, because it is contrary to what eternally is. A thing whose contrary is not eternal can be and not be, and it is of such things that there is coming to be and passing away.

13   The 'now' is the link of time, as has been said [18] (for it connects past and future time), and it is a limit of time (for it is the beginning of the one and the end of the other). But this is not obvious as it is with the point, which is fixed. It divides potentially, and in so far as it is dividing the 'now' is always different, but in so far as it connects it is always the same, as it is with mathematical lines. For the

[17] 202[a] 4.   [18] 220[a] 5.

intellect it is not always one and the same point, since it is other and other when one divides the line; but in so far as it is one, it is the same in every respect.

So the 'now' also is in one way a potential dividing of time, in another the termination of both parts, and their unity. And the dividing and the uniting are the same thing and in the same reference, but in essence they are not the same.

So one kind of 'now' is described in this way: another is when the 20 time is *near* this kind of 'now'. 'He will come now' because he will come to-day; 'he has come now' because he came to-day. But the things in the *Iliad* have not happened 'now', nor is the flood 'now'— not that the time from now to them is not continuous, but because they are not near.

'At some time' means a time determined in relation to the first of the two types of 'now', e. g. 'at some time' Troy was taken, and 'at 25 some time' there will be a flood; for it must be determined with reference to the 'now'. There *will* thus be a determinate time from this 'now' to that, and there *was* such in reference to the past event. But if there be no time which is not 'sometime', every time will be determined.

Will time then fail? Surely not, if motion always exists. Is time then always different or does the same time recur? Clearly time is, in 30 the same way as motion is. For if one and the same motion sometimes recurs, it will be one and the same time, and if not, not.

Since the 'now' is an end and a beginning of time, not of the same 222^{b} time however, but the end of that which is past and the beginning of that which is to come, it follows that, as the circle has its convexity and its concavity, in a sense, in the same thing, so time is always at a beginning and at an end. And for this reason it seems to be always different; for the 'now' is not the beginning and the end of the same 5 thing; if it were, it would be at the same time and in the same respect two opposites. And time will not fail; for it is always at a beginning.

'Presently' or 'just' refers to the part of future time which is near the indivisible present 'now' ('When do you walk?' 'Presently', be- 10 cause the time in which he is going to do so is near), and to the part of past time which is not far from the 'now' ('When do you walk?' 'I have just been walking'). But to say that Troy has just been taken —we do not say that, because it is too far from the 'now'. 'Lately', too, refers to the part of past time which is near the present 'now'. 'When did you go?' 'Lately', if the time is near the existing now. 'Long ago' refers to the distant past.

'Suddenly' refers to what has departed from its former condition in 15

a time imperceptible because of its smallness; but it is the nature of *all* change to alter things from their former condition. In time all things come into being and pass away; for which reason some called it the wisest of all things, but the Pythagorean Paron called it the most stupid, because in it we also forget; and his was the truer view. It is clear then that it must be in itself, as we said before [19]
20 the condition of destruction rather than of coming into being (for change, in itself, makes things depart from their former condition), and only incidentally of coming into being, and of being. A sufficient evidence of this is that nothing comes into being without itself moving somehow and acting, but a thing can be destroyed even if it does not move at all. And this is what, as a rule, we chiefly mean by a
25 thing's being destroyed by time. Still, time does not work even this change; even this sort of change takes place *incidentally* in time.

We have stated, then, that time exists and what it is, and in how many senses we speak of the 'now', and what 'at some time', 'lately', 'presently' or 'just', 'long ago', and 'suddenly' mean.

30 14   These distinctions having been drawn, it is evident that every change and everything that moves is in time; for the distinction of faster and slower exists in reference to all change, since it is found in every instance. In the phrase 'moving faster' I refer to that which
223ᵃ changes before another into the condition in question, when it moves over the same interval and with a regular movement; e. g. in the case of locomotion, if both things move along the circumference of a circle, or both along a straight line; and similarly in all other cases. But
5 what is *before* is in time; for we say 'before' and 'after' with reference to the distance from the 'now', and the 'now' is the boundary of the past and the future; so that since 'nows' are in time, the before and the after will be in time too; for in that in which the 'now' is, the distance from the 'now' will also be. But 'before' is used contrariwise
10 with reference to past and to future time; for in the past we call 'before' what is farther from the 'now', and 'after' what is nearer, but in the future we call the nearer 'before' and the farther 'after'. So that since the 'before' is in time, and every movement involves a
15 'before', evidently every change and every movement is in time.

It is also worth considering how time can be related to the soul; and why time is thought to be in everything, both in earth and in sea and in heaven. Is it because it is an attribute, or state, of movement (since it is the number of movement) and all these things are

[19] 221ᵇ 1.

movable (for they are all in place), and time and movement are to- 20 gether, both in respect of potentiality and in respect of actuality?

Whether if soul did not exist time would exist or not, is a question that may fairly be asked; for if there cannot be some one to count there cannot be anything that can be counted, so that evidently there cannot be number; for number is either what has been, or what can be, counted. But if nothing but soul, or in soul reason, is qualified to 25 count, there would not be time unless there were soul, but only that of which time is an attribute, i. e. if *movement* can exist without soul, and the before and after are attributes of movement, and time is these *qua* numerable.

One might also raise the question what sort of movement time is the number of. Must we not say 'of *any* kind'? For things both come 30 into being in time and pass away, and grow, and are altered in time, and are moved locally; thus it is of each movement *qua* movement that time is the number. And so it is simply the number of continuous movement, not of any particular kind of it.

But other things as well may have been moved now, and there 223ᵇ would be a number of each of the two movements. Is there another time, then, and will there be two equal times at once? Surely not. For a time that is both equal and simultaneous is one and the same time, and even those that are not simultaneous are one in kind; for if there were dogs, and horses, and seven of each, it would be the same 5 number. So, too, movements that have simultaneous limits have the same time, yet the one may in fact be fast and the other not, and one may be locomotion and the other alteration; still the time of the two changes is the same if their number also is equal and simulta- neous; and for this reason, while the movements are different and 10 separate, the time is everywhere the same, because the number of equal and simultaneous movements is everywhere one and the same.

Now there is such a thing as locomotion, and in locomotion there is included circular movement, and everything is measured by some one thing homogeneous with it, units by a unit, horses by a horse, and similarly times by some definite time, and, as we said,[20] time is 15 measured by motion as well as motion by time (this being so because by a motion definite in time the quantity both of the motion and of the time is measured): if, then, what is first is the measure of everything homogeneous with it, regular circular motion is above all else the measure, because the number of this is the best known. Now 20 neither alteration nor increase nor coming into being can be regular, but locomotion can be. This also is why time is thought to be the

[20] 220ᵇ 28.

movement of the sphere, viz. because the other movements are measured by this, and time by this movement.

This also explains the common saying that human affairs form a 25 circle, and that there is a circle in all other things that have a natural movement and coming into being and passing away. This is because all other things are discriminated by time, and end and begin as though conforming to a cycle; for even time itself is thought to be 30 a circle. And this opinion again is held because time is the measure of this kind of locomotion and is itself measured by such. So that to say that the things that come into being form a circle is to say that there is a circle of time; and this is to say that it is measured by the circular movement; for apart from the measure nothing else to be 224ᵃ measured is observed; the whole is just a plurality of measures.

It is said rightly, too, that the number of the sheep and of the dogs is the same *number* if the two numbers are equal, but not the same *decad* or the same *ten*; just as the equilateral and the scalene 5 are not the same *triangle*, yet they are the same *figure*, because they are both triangles. For things are called the same so-and-so if they do not differ by a differentia of that thing, but not if they do; e. g. triangle differs from triangle by a differentia of triangle, therefore they are different triangles; but they do not differ by a differentia of figure, but are in one and the same division of it. For a figure of one 10 kind is a circle and a figure of another kind a triangle, and a triangle of one kind is equilateral and a triangle of another kind scalene. They are the same figure, then, and that, triangle, but not the same triangle. Therefore the number of two groups also is the same number (for their number does not differ by a differentia of number), but it is not the same decad; for the things of which it is asserted differ; one group are dogs, and the other horses.

15   We have now discussed time—both time itself and the matters appropriate to the consideration of it.

BOOK V

21 **1** Everything with changes does so in one of three senses. It may change (i) *accidentally,* as for instance when we say that something musical walks, that which walks being something in which aptitude for music is an *accident*. Again (2) a thing is said without qualification to change because *something belonging to it* changes, i. e. in state- 25 ments which refer to part of the thing in question: thus the body is restored to health because the eye or the chest, that is to say a *part* of the whole body, is restored to health. And above all there is (3) the case of a thing which is in motion neither accidentally nor in

respect of something else belonging to it, but in virtue of being *itself*
directly in motion. Here we have a thing which is *essentially* movable:
and that which is so is a different thing according to the particular
variety of motion: for instance it may be a thing capable of alteration: and within the sphere of alteration it is again a different thing
according as it is capable of being restored to health or capable of 30
being heated. And there are the same distinctions in the case of the
mover: (1) one thing causes motion accidentally, (2) another partially
(because something belonging to it causes motion), (3) another
of itself directly, as, for instance, the physician heals, the hand strikes.
We have, then, the following factors: (*a*) on the one hand that
which directly causes motion, and (*b*) on the other hand that which
is in motion: further, we have (*c*) that in which motion takes place, 35
namely time, and (distinct from these three) (*d*) that from which
and (*e*) that to which it proceeds: for every motion proceeds from 224ᵇ
something and to something, that which is directly in motion being
distinct from that to which it is in motion and that from which it
is in motion: for instance, we may take the three things 'wood', 'hot',
and 'cold', of which the first is that which is in motion, the second is
that to which the motion proceeds, and the third is that from which
it proceeds. This being so, it is clear that the motion is in the wood,
not in its form: for the motion is neither caused nor experienced 5
by the form or the place or the quantity. So we are left with a mover,
a moved, and a goal of motion. I do not include the starting-point of
motion: for it is the goal rather than the starting-point of motion that
gives its name to a particular process of change. Thus 'perishing'
is change *to not-being,* though it is also true that that which perishes
changes *from being*: and 'becoming' is change *to being,* though it
is also change *from not-being.*

Now a definition of motion has been given above,[1a] from which it 10
will be seen that every goal of motion, whether it be a form, an
affection, or a place, is immovable, as, for instance, knowledge and
heat. Here, however, a difficulty may be raised. Affections, it may be
said, are motions, and whiteness is an affection: thus there may be
change *to* a motion. To this we may reply that it ıs not whiteness 15
but whitening that is a motion. Here also the same distinctions are
to be observed: a goal of motion may be so accidentally, or partially
and with reference to something other than itself, or directly and with
no reference to anything else: for instance, a thing which is becoming
white changes accidentally to an object of thought, the *colour* being
only accidentally the object of thought; it changes to colour, be- 20

[1a] 201ᵃ 10.

cause white is a part of colour, or to Europe, because Athens is a part of Europe; but it changes essentially to white colour. It is now clear in what sense a thing is in motion essentially, accidentally, or in respect of something other than itself, and in what sense the phrase 'itself directly' is used in the case both of the mover and of
25 the moved: and it is also clear that the motion is not in the form but in that which is in motion, that is to say 'the movable in activity'. Now accidental change we may leave out of account: for it is to be found in everything, at any time, and in any respect. Change which is not accidental on the other hand is not to be found in everything, but only in contraries, in things intermediate between contraries, and
30 in contradictories, as may be proved by induction. An intermediate may be a starting-point of change, since for the purposes of the change it serves as contrary to either of two contraries: for the intermediate is in a sense the extremes. Hence we speak of the intermediate as in a sense a contrary relatively to the extremes and of either extreme as a contrary relatively to the intermediate: for instance, the central note is low relatively to the highest and high relatively to the lowest, and grey is light relatively to black and dark relatively to white.

35 And since every change is *from* something *to* something—as the word
225ᵃ itself *metabole* indicates, implying something 'after' (*meta*) something else, that is to say something earlier and something later— that which changes must change in one of four ways: from subject
5 to subject, from subject to non-subject, from non-subject to subject, or from non-subject to non-subject, where by 'subject' I mean what is affirmatively expressed. So it follows necessarily from what has been said above that there are only three kinds of change, that from subject to subject, that from subject to non-subject, and that
10 from non-subject to subject: for the fourth conceivable kind, that from non-subject to non-subject, is not change, as in that case there is no opposition either of contraries or of contradictories.

Now change from non-subject to subject, the relation being that of contradiction, is 'coming to be'—'unqualified coming to be' when the change takes place in an unqualified way, 'particular coming to be' when the change is change in a particular character: for instance, a change from not-white to white is a coming to be of the
15 particular thing, white, while change from unqualified not-being to being is coming to be in an unqualified way, in respect of which we say that a thing 'comes to be' without qualification, not that it 'comes to be' some particular thing. Change from subject to non-subject is 'perishing'—'unqualified perishing' when the change is from being to

not-being, 'particular perishing' when the change is to the opposite
negation, the distinction being the same as that made in the case of
coming to be.

Now the expression 'not-being' is used in several senses: and there 20
can be motion neither of that which 'is not' in respect of the affirmation or negation of a predicate, nor of that which 'is not' in the sense
that it only *potentially* 'is', that is to say the opposite of that which
actually 'is' in an unqualified sense: for although that which is 'not-
white' or 'not-good' may nevertheless be in motion *accidentally* (for
example that which is 'not-white' might be a man), yet that which
is without qualification 'not-so-and-so' cannot in any sense be in
motion: Therefore it is impossible for that which *is not* to be in 25
motion. This being so, it follows that 'becoming' cannot be a motion:
for it is that which 'is not' that 'becomes'. For however true it may
be that it *accidentally* 'becomes', it is nevertheless correct to say that
it is that which 'is not' that in an unqualified sense 'becomes'. And
similarly it is impossible for that which 'is not' to be at rest.

There are these difficulties, then, in the way of the assumption that 30
that which 'is not' can be in motion: and it may be further objected
that, whereas everything which is in motion is in space, that which 'is
not' is not in space: for then it would be *somewhere*.

So, too, 'perishing' is not a motion: for a motion has for its contrary either another motion or rest, whereas 'perishing' is the
contrary of 'becoming'.

Since, then, every motion is a kind of change, and there are only the
three kinds of change mentioned above; and since of these three those 35
which take the form of 'becoming' and 'perishing', that is to say those
which imply a relation of contradiction, are not motions: it neces- 225ᵇ
sarily follows that only change from subject to subject is motion.
And every such subject is either a contrary or an intermediate (for a
privation may be allowed to rank as a contrary) and can be affirmatively expressed, as naked, toothless, or black. If, then, the categories 5
are severally distinguished as Being, Quality, Place, Time, Relation,
Quantity, and Activity or Passivity, it necessarily follows that there
are three kinds of motion—qualitative, quantitative, and local.

2   In respect of Substance there is no motion, because Substance 10
has no contrary among things that are. Nor is there motion in respect
of Relation: for it may happen that when one correlative changes,
the other, although this does not itself change, is no longer applicable,
so that in these cases the motion is accidental. Nor is there motion
in respect of Agent and Patient—in fact there can never be motion of

¹⁵ mover and moved, because there cannot be motion of motion or becoming of becoming or in general change of change.

For in the first place there are two senses in which motion of
motion is conceivable. (1) The motion of which there is motion
might be conceived as subject; e. g. a man is in motion because he
changes from fair to dark. Can it be that in this sense motion grows
²⁰ hot or cold, or changes place, or increases or decreases? Impossible:
for change is not a subject. Or (2) can there be motion of motion in
the sense that some other subject changes from a change to another
mode of being, as e. g. a man changes from falling ill to getting well?
Even this is possible only in an accidental sense. For, whatever the
subject may be, movement is change from one form to another. (And
²⁵ the same holds good of becoming and perishing, except that in these
processes we have a change to a particular ¹ kind of opposite, while the
other, motion, is a change to a different ² kind.) So, if there is to be
motion of motion, that which is changing from health to sickness
must simultaneously be changing from this very change to another.
It is clear, then, that by the time that it has become sick, it must
also have changed to whatever may be the other change concerned
(for that it should be at rest, though logically possible, is excluded
by the theory). Moreover this other can never be any casual change,
³⁰ but must be a change from something definite to some other definite
thing. So in this case it must be the opposite change, viz. convalescence. It is only accidentally that there can be change of change,
e. g. there is a change from remembering to forgetting only because
the subject of this change changes at one time to knowledge, at
another to ignorance.

In the second place, if there is to be change of change and becoming of becoming, we shall have an infinite regress. Thus if one of a
³⁵ series of changes is to be a change of change, the preceding change
226ᵃ must also be so: e. g. if simple becoming was ever in process of becoming, then that which was becoming simple becoming was also in
process of becoming, so that we should not yet have arrived at what
was in process of simple becoming but only at what was already in
process of becoming in process of becoming. And this again was
sometime in process of becoming, so that even then we should not
have arrived at what was in process of simple becoming. And since in
an infinite series there is no first term, here there will be no first stage
⁵ and therefore no following stage either. On this hypothesis, then,
nothing can become or be moved or change.

Thirdly, if a thing is capable of any particular motion, it is also

¹ *sc.* a contradictory.   ² *sc.* a contrary.

capable of the corresponding contrary motion or the corresponding coming to rest, and a thing that is capable of becoming is also capable of perishing: consequently, if there be becoming of becoming, that which is in process of becoming is in process of perishing at the very moment when it has reached the stage of becoming: since it cannot be in process of perishing when it is just beginning to become or after it has ceased to become: for that which is in process of perishing must be in existence.

Fourthly, there must be a substrate underlying all processes of becoming and changing. What can this be in the present case? It is either the body or the soul that undergoes alteration: what is it that correspondingly becomes motion or becoming? And again what is the goal of their motion? It must be the motion or becoming of something from something to something else. But in what sense can this be so? For the becoming of learning cannot be learning: so neither can the becoming of becoming be becoming, nor can the becoming of any process be that process.

Finally, since there are three kinds of motion, the substratum and the goal of motion must be one or other of these, e. g. locomotion will have to be altered or to be locally moved.

To sum up, then, since everything that is moved is moved in one of three ways, either accidentally, or partially, or essentially, change can change only accidentally, as e. g. when a man who is being restored to health runs or learns: and accidental change we have long ago [3] decided to leave out of account.

Since, then, motion can belong neither to Being nor to Relation nor to Agent and Patient, it remains that there can be motion only in respect of Quality, Quantity, and Place: for with each of these we have a pair of contraries. Motion in respect of Quality let us call alteration, a general designation that is used to include both contraries: and by Quality I do not here mean a property of substance (in that sense that which constitutes a specific distinction is a quality) but a passive quality in virtue of which a thing is said to be acted on or to be incapable of being acted on. Motion in respect of Quantity has no name that includes both contraries, but it is called increase or decrease according as one or the other is designated: that is to say motion in the direction of complete magnitude is increase, motion in the contrary direction is decrease. Motion in respect of Place has no name either general or particular: but we may designate it by the general name of locomotion, though strictly the term 'locomotion' is applicable to things that change their place only when they have not the

35 power to come to a stand, and to things that do not move *themselves* locally.

226ᵇ   Change within the same kind from a lesser to a greater or from a greater to a lesser degree is alteration: for it is motion either from a contrary or to a contrary, whether in an unqualified or in a qualified sense: for change to a lesser degree of a quality will be called change to the contrary of that quality, and change to a greater

5 degree of a quality will be regarded as change from the contrary of that quality to the quality itself. It makes no difference whether the change be qualified or unqualified, except that in the former case the contraries will have to be contrary to one another only in a qualified sense: and a thing's possessing a quality in a greater or in a lesser degree means the presence or absence in it of more or less of the opposite quality. It is now clear, then, that there are only these three kinds of motion.

10   The term 'immovable' we apply in the first place to that which is absolutely incapable of being moved (just as we correspondingly apply the term invisible to sound); in the second place to that which is moved with difficulty after a long time or whose movement is slow at the start—in fact, what we describe as hard to move; and in the third place to that which is naturally designed for and capable of motion, but is not in motion when, where, and as it naturally would be so. This last is the only kind of immovable thing of which I use

15 the term 'being at rest': for rest is contrary to motion, so that rest will be negation of motion in that which is capable of admitting motion.

The foregoing remarks are sufficient to explain the essential nature of motion and rest, the number of kinds of change, and the different varieties of motion.

3   Let us now proceed to define the terms 'together' and 'apart', 'in contact', 'between', 'in succession', 'contiguous', and 'continuous',

20 and to show in what circumstances each of these terms is naturally applicable.

Things are said to be together in place when they are in one place (in the strictest sense of the word 'place') and to be apart when they are in different places.

Things are said to be in contact when their extremities are together.

That which a changing thing, if it changes continuously in a natu-

25 ral manner, naturally reaches before it reaches that to which it changes last, is between. Thus 'between' implies the presence of at least three things: for in a process of change it is the contrary that is 'last': and a thing is moved continuously if it leaves no gap or only

the smallest possible gap in the material—not in the time (for a gap in the time does not prevent things having a 'between', while, on the other hand, there is nothing to prevent the highest note sounding immediately after the lowest) but in the material in which the motion 30 takes place. This is manifestly true not only in local changes but in every other kind as well. <Now every change implies a pair of oppo- 7 227ᵃ sites, and opposites may be either contraries or contradictories; since then contradiction admits of no mean term, it is obvious that 'between' must imply a pair of contraries.>³ᵃ That is locally contrary which is most distant in a straight line: for the shortest line is definitely 32 226ᵇ limited, and that which is definitely limited constitutes a measure.

A thing is 'in succession' when it is after the beginning in position or in form or in some other respect in which it is definitely so re- 35 garded, and when further there is nothing of the *same* kind as itself 227ᵃ between it and that to which it is in succession, e. g. a line or lines if it is a line, a unit or units if it is a unit, a house if it is a house (there is nothing to prevent something of a *different* kind being between). For that which is in succession is in succession to a particular thing, and is something posterior: for one is not 'in succession' to two, nor is the first day of the month to the second: in each case the latter is 5 'in succession' to the former.

A thing that is in succession and touches is 'contiguous'.

The 'continuous' is a subdivision of the contiguous: things are 10 called continuous when the touching limits of each become one and the same and are, as the word implies, contained in each other: continuity is impossible if these extremities are two. This definition makes it plain that continuity belongs to things that naturally in virtue of their mutual contact form a unity. And in whatever way that which 15 holds them together is one, so too will the whole be one, e. g. by a rivet or glue or contact or organic union.

It is obvious that of these terms 'in succession' is first in order of analysis: for that which touches is necessarily in succession, but not everything that is in succession touches: and so succession is a property of things prior in definition, e. g. numbers, while contact is not. 20 And if there is continuity there is necessarily contact, but if there is contact, that alone does not imply continuity: for the extremities of things may be *'together'* without necessarily being *one*: but they cannot be one without being necessarily together. So natural junction is last in coming to be: for the extremities must necessarily come into contact if they are to be naturally joined: but things that are in con- 25

³ᵃ This sentence has been transposed from its place in the next paragraph in the interest of sense.—Ed.

tact are not all naturally joined, while where there is no contact
clearly there is no natural junction either. Hence, if as some say
'point' and 'unit' have an independent existence of their own, it is
impossible for the two to be identical: for points can touch while
30 units can only be in succession. Moreover, there can always be something between points (for all lines are intermediate between points),
whereas it is not necessary that there should possibly be anything
between units: for there can be nothing between the numbers one
and two.

We have now defined what is meant by 'together' and 'apart',
227ᵇ 'contact', 'between' and 'in succession', 'contiguous' and 'continuous':
and we have shown in what circumstances each of these terms is
applicable.

4   There are many senses in which motion is said to be 'one': for
we use the term 'one' in many senses.

Motion is one *generically* according to the different categories to
5 which it may be assigned: thus any locomotion is one generically with
any other locomotion, whereas alteration is different generically from
locomotion.

Motion is one specifically when besides being one generically it
also takes place in a species incapable of subdivision: e. g. colour has
specific differences: therefore blackening and whitening differ specifically; but at all events every whitening will be specifically the same
10 with every other whitening and every blackening with every other
blackening. But whiteness is not further subdivided by specific differences: hence any whitening is specifically one with any other whitening. Where it happens that the genus is at the same time a species, it
is clear that the motion will then in a sense be one specifically though
not in an unqualified sense: learning is an example of this, knowledge being on the one hand a species of apprehension and on the
other hand a genus including the various knowledges. A difficulty,
however, may be raised as to whether a motion is specifically one
15 when the same thing changes from the same to the same, e. g. when
one point changes again and again from a particular place to a particular place: if this motion is specifically one, circular motion will be the
same as rectilinear motion, and rolling the same as walking. But is
not this difficulty removed by the principle already laid down that if
that in which the motion takes place is specifically different (as in
the present instance the circular path is specifically different from
20 the straight) the motion itself is also different? We have explained,

then, what is meant by saying that motion is one generically or one specifically.

Motion is one in an unqualified sense when it is one essentially or numerically: and the following distinctions will make clear what this kind of motion is. There are three classes of things in connexion with which we speak of motion, the 'that which', the 'that in which', and the 'that during which'. I mean that there must *be* something that is in motion, e. g. a man or gold, and it must be in motion *in* some- 25 thing, e. g. a place or an affection, and *during* something, for all motion takes place during a time. Of these three it is the thing in which the motion takes place that makes it one generically or specifically, it is the thing moved that makes the motion one in subject, and it is the time that makes it consecutive: but it is the three together that make it one without qualification: to effect this, that in which the motion 30 takes place (the species) must be one and incapable of subdivision, that during which it takes place (the time) must be one and unintermittent, and that which is in motion must be one—not in an accidental sense (i. e. it must be one as the white that blackens is one or Coriscus who walks is one, not in the accidental sense in which Coriscus and 228ᵃ white may be one), nor merely in virtue of community of nature (for there might be a case of two men being restored to health at the same time in the same way, e. g. from inflammation of the eye, yet this motion is not really one, but only specifically one).

Suppose, however, that Socrates undergoes an alteration specifically the same but at one time and again at another: in this case if it is possible for that which ceased to be again to come into being and remain numerically the same, then this motion too will be one: otherwise it 5 will be the same but not one. And akin to this difficulty there is another; viz. is health one? and generally are the states and affections in bodies severally one in essence although (as is clear) the things that contain them are obviously in motion and in flux? Thus if a person's health at daybreak and at the present moment is one and the same,10 why should not this health be numerically one with that which he recovers after an interval? The same argument applies in each case. There is, however, we may answer, this difference: that if the states are two then it follows simply from this fact that the activities must also in point of number be two (for only that which is numerically one can give rise to an activity that is numerically one), but if the state is 15 one, this is not in itself enough to make us regard the activity also as one: for when a man ceases walking, the walking no longer is, but it will again be if he begins to walk again. But, be this as it may, if in the above instance the health is one and the same, then it must be possible for that which is one and the same to come to be and to cease to be many times. However, these difficulties lie outside our present inquiry.

20   Since every motion is continuous, a motion that is one in an un-qualified sense must (since every motion is divisible) be continuous, and a continuous motion must be one. There will not be continuity between any motion and any other indiscriminately any more than there is between any two things chosen at random in any other sphere: there can be continuity only when the extremities of the two things are one. Now some things have no extremities at all: and the extremities

25 of others differ specifically although we give them the same name of 'end': how should e. g. the 'end' of a line and the 'end' of walking touch or come to be one? Motions that are not the same either specifi-cally or generically may, it is true, be *consecutive* (e. g. a man may run and then at once fall ill of a fever), and again, in the torch-race we have consecutive but not continuous locomotion: for according to our definition there can be continuity only when the ends of the two

30 things are one. Hence motions may be consecutive or successive in virtue of the time being continuous, but there can be continuity only in virtue of the motions themselves being continuous, that is when the end of each is one with the end of the other. Motion, therefore,

228ᵇ that is in an unqualified sense continuous and one must be specifi-cally the same, of one thing, and in one time. Unity is required in respect of time in order that there may be no interval of immobility, for where there is intermission of motion there must be rest, and a motion that includes intervals of rest will be not one but many, so

5 that a motion that is interrupted by stationariness is not one or con-tinuous, and it is so interrupted if there is an interval of time. And though of a motion that is not specifically one (even if the time is unintermittent) the time is one, the motion is specifically different, and so cannot really be one, for motion that is one must be specifically

10 one, though motion that is specifically one is not necessarily one in an unqualified sense. We have now explained what we mean when we call a motion one without qualification.

Further, a motion is also said to be one generically, specifically, or essentially when it is complete, just as in other cases completeness and wholeness are characteristics of what is one: and sometimes a motion even if incomplete is said to be one, provided only that it is continuous.

15   And besides the cases already mentioned there is another in which a motion is said to be one, viz. when it is regular: for in a sense a motion that is irregular is not regarded as one, that title belonging rather to that which is regular, as a straight line is regular, the irregu-

lar being as such divisible. But the difference would seem to be one of degree. In every kind of motion we may have regularity or irregularity: thus there may be regular alteration, and locomotion in a regular 20 path, e. g. in a circle or on a straight line, and it is the same with regard to increase and decrease. The difference that makes a motion irregular is sometimes to be found in its path: thus a motion cannot be regular if its path is an irregular magnitude, e. g. a broken line, a spiral, or any other magnitude that is not such that any part of it taken at random fits on to any other that may be chosen. Sometimes it is found neither 25 in the place nor in the time nor in the goal but in the manner of the motion: for in some cases the motion is differentiated by quickness and slowness: thus if its velocity is uniform a motion is regular, if not it is irregular. So quickness and slowness are not species of motion nor do they constitute specific differences of motion, because this distinction occurs in connexion with all the distinct species of motion. The same is true of heaviness and lightness when they refer to the same 30 thing: e. g. they do not specifically distinguish earth from itself or fire from itself. Irregular motion, therefore, while in virtue of being 229ᵃ continuous it is one, is so in a lesser degree, as is the case with locomotion in a broken line: and a lesser degree of something always means an admixture of its contrary. And since every motion that is one can be both regular and irregular, motions that are consecutive but not specifically the same cannot be one and continuous: for how should 5 a motion composed of alteration and locomotion be regular? If a motion is to be regular its parts ought to fit one another.

5   We have further to determine what motions are contrary to each other, and to determine similarly how it is with rest. And we have first to decide whether contrary motions are motions respectively from and to the same thing, e. g. a motion from health and a motion to 10 health (where the opposition, it would seem, is of the same kind as that between coming to be and ceasing to be); or motions respectively from contraries, e. g. a motion from health and a motion from disease; or motions respectively to contraries, e. g. a motion to health and a motion to disease; or motions respectively from a contrary and to the opposite contrary, e. g. a motion from health and a motion to disease; or motions respectively from a contrary to the opposite contrary and from the latter to the former, e. g. a motion from health to disease and a motion from disease to health: for motions must be contrary to one another in one or more of these ways, as there is no 15 other way in which they can be opposed.

Now motions respectively from a contrary and to the opposite contrary, e. g. a motion from health and a motion to disease, are not contrary motions: for they are one and the same. (Yet their essence is not the same, just as changing from health is different from changing to disease.) Nor are motions respectively from a contrary and from the opposite contrary contrary motions, for a motion from a contrary is at the same time a motion to a contrary or to an intermediate (of this, however, we shall speak later),[4] but changing to a contrary rather than changing from a contrary would seem to be the cause of the contrariety of motions, the latter being the loss, the former the gain, of contrariness. Moreover, each several motion takes its name rather from the goal than from the starting-point of change, e. g. motion to health we call convalescence, motion to disease sickening. Thus we are left with motions respectively to contraries, and motions respectively to contraries from the opposite contraries. Now it would seem that motions to contraries are at the same time motions from contraries (though their essence may not be the same; 'to health' is distinct, I mean, from 'from disease', and 'from health' from 'to disease').

Since then change differs from motion (motion being change from a particular subject to a particular subject), it follows that contrary motions are motions respectively from a contrary to the opposite contrary and from the latter to the former, e. g. a motion from health to disease and a motion from disease to health. Moreover, the consideration of particular examples will also show what kinds of processes are generally recognized as contrary: thus falling ill is regarded as contrary to recovering one's health, these processes having contrary goals, and being taught as contrary to being led into error by another, it being possible to acquire error, like knowledge, either by one's own agency or by that of another. Similarly we have upward locomotion and downward locomotion, which are contrary lengthwise, locomotion to the right and locomotion to the left, which are contrary breadthwise, and forward locomotion and backward locomotion, which too are contraries.

On the other hand, a process simply to a contrary, e. g. that denoted by the expression 'becoming white', where no starting-point is specified, is a change but not a motion. And in all cases of a thing that has no contrary we have as contraries change from and change to the same thing. Thus coming to be is contrary to ceasing to be, and losing to gaining. But these are changes and not motions. And wherever a pair of contraries admit of an intermediate, motions to that intermediate must be held to be in a sense motions to one or other of the

[4] l. 28 sqq.

contraries: for the intermediate serves as a contrary for the purposes
of the motion, in whichever direction the change may be, e. g. grey in
a motion from grey to white takes the place of black as starting-point,
in a motion from white to grey it takes the place of black as goal,
and in a motion from black to grey it takes the place of white as goal:
for the middle is opposed in a sense to either of the extremes, as has 20
been said above.[5] Thus we see that two motions are contrary to each
other only when one is a motion from a contrary to the opposite contrary and the other is a motion from the latter to the former.

6   But since a motion appears to have contrary to it not only another motion but also a state of rest, we must determine how this is so.
A motion has for its contrary in the strict sense of the term another
motion, but it also has for an opposite a state of rest (for rest is the
privation of motion and the privation of anything may be called its 25
contrary), and motion of one kind has for its opposite rest of that kind,
e. g. local motion has local rest. This statement, however, needs further qualification: there remains the question, is the opposite of remaining at a particular place motion from or motion to that place?
It is surely clear that since there are two subjects between which
motion takes place, motion from one of these (A) to its contrary 30
(B) has for its opposite remaining in A, while the reverse motion
has for its opposite remaining in B. At the same time these two are
also contrary to each other: for it would be absurd to suppose that
there are contrary motions and not opposite states of rest. States of 230ᵃ
rest in contraries *are* opposed. To take an example, a state of rest in
health is (1) contrary to a state of rest in disease, and (2) the motion
to which it is contrary is that from health to disease. For (2) it would
be absurd that its contrary motion should be that from disease to
health, since motion to that in which a thing is at rest is rather a
coming to rest, the coming to rest being found to come into being 5
simultaneously with the motion; and one of these two motions it must
be. And (1) rest in *whiteness* is of course not contrary to rest in health.
   Of all things that have no contraries there are opposite *changes*
(viz. change from the thing and change to the thing, e. g. change from
being and change to being), but no *motion*. So, too, of such things
there is no remaining though there is absence of change. Should there 10
be a particular subject, absence of change in its being will be contrary to absence of change in its not-being. And here a difficulty may
be raised: if not-being is not a particular something, what is it, it may
be asked, that is contrary to absence of change in a thing's being?

[5] 224ᵇ 32 sqq.

and is this absence of change a state of rest? If it is, then either it is not true that every state of rest is contrary to a motion or else coming to be and ceasing to be are motion. It is clear then that, since we exclude these from among motions, we must not say that this absence of change is a state of rest: we must say that it is similar to a state of rest and call it absence of change. And it will have for its contrary either nothing or absence of change in the thing's not-being, or the ceasing to be of the thing: for such ceasing to be is change from it and the thing's coming to be is change to it.

Again, a further difficulty may be raised. How is it, it may be asked, that whereas in local change both remaining and moving may be natural or unnatural, in the other changes this is not so? e. g. alteration is not now natural and now unnatural, for convalescence is no more natural or unnatural than falling ill, whitening no more natural or unnatural than blackening; so, too, with increase and decrease: these are not contrary to each other in the sense that either of them is natural while the other is unnatural, nor is one increase contrary to another in this sense; and the same account may be given of becoming and perishing: it is not true that becoming is natural and perishing unnatural (for growing old is natural), nor do we observe one becoming to be natural and another unnatural. We answer that if what happens under violence is unnatural, then violent perishing is unnatural and as such contrary to natural perishing. Are there then also some becomings that are violent and not the result of natural necessity, and are therefore contrary to natural becomings, and violent increases and decreases, e. g. the rapid growth to maturity of profligates and the rapid ripening of seeds even when not packed close in the earth? And how is it with alterations? Surely just the same: we may say that some alterations are violent while others are natural, e. g. patients alter naturally or unnaturally according as they throw off fevers on the critical days or not. But, it may be objected, then we shall have perishings contrary to one another, not to becoming. Certainly: and why should not this in a sense be so? Thus it is so if one perishing is pleasant and another painful: and so one perishing will be contrary to another not in an unqualified sense, but in so far as one has this quality and the other that.

Now motions and states of rest universally exhibit contrariety in the manner described above,[6] e. g. upward motion and rest above are respectively contrary to downward motion and rest below, these being instances of local contrariety; and upward locomotion belongs naturally to fire and downward to earth, i. e. the locomotions of the

[6] In chapter 5.

two are contrary to each other. And again, fire moves up naturally and down unnaturally: and its natural motion is certainly contrary to its unnatural motion. Similarly with remaining: remaining above is con- 15 trary to motion from above downwards, and to earth this remaining comes unnaturally, this motion naturally. So the unnatural remaining of a thing is contrary to its natural motion, just as we find a similar contrariety in the motion of the same thing: one of its motions, the 20 upward or the downward, will be natural, the other unnatural.

Here, however, the question arises, has every state of rest that is not permanent a becoming, and is this becoming a coming to a standstill? If so, there must be a becoming of that which is at rest unnaturally, e. g. of earth at rest above: and therefore this earth during the time that it was being carried violently upward was coming to a standstill. But whereas the velocity of that which comes to a standstill seems always to increase, the velocity of that which is carried violently seems always to decrease: so it will *be* in a state of rest without having 25 *become* so. Moreover 'coming to a standstill' is generally recognized to be identical or at least concomitant with the locomotion of a thing to its proper place.

There is also another difficulty involved in the view that remaining in a particular place is contrary to motion from that place. For when a thing is moving from or discarding something, it still appears to have that which is being discarded, so that if a state of rest is itself con- 30 trary to the motion from the state of rest to its contrary, the contraries rest and motion will be simultaneously predicable of the same thing. May we not say, however, that in so far as the thing is still stationary it is in a state of rest in a qualified sense? For, in fact, whenever a thing is in motion, part of it is at the starting-point while part is at the goal to which it is changing: and consequently a motion finds its true 231ᵃ contrary rather in another motion than in a state of rest.

With regard to motion and rest, then, we have now explained in what sense each of them is one and under what conditions they exhibit contrariety.

With regard to coming to a standstill the question may be raised 5 whether there is an opposite state of rest to unnatural as well as to natural motions. It would be absurd if this were not the case: for a thing may remain still merely under violence: thus we shall have a thing being in a non-permanent state of rest without having become so. But it is clear that it must be the case: for just as there is unnatural motion, so, too, a thing may be in an unnatural state of rest. Further, some things have a natural and an unnatural motion, e. g. fire 10 has a natural upward motion and an unnatural downward motion:

is it, then, this unnatural downward motion or is it the natural
downward motion of earth that is contrary to the natural upward
motion? Surely it is clear that both are contrary to it though not in
the same sense: the natural motion of earth is contrary inasmuch as
15 the motion of fire is also natural, whereas the upward motion of fire as
being natural is contrary to the downward motion of fire as being unnatural. The same is true of the corresponding cases of remaining. But
there would seem to be a sense in which a state of rest and a motion
are opposites.

BOOK VI

21 1   Now if the terms 'continuous', 'in contact', and 'in succession' are
understood as defined above [1]—things being 'continuous' if their extremities are one, 'in contact' if their extremities are together, and
'in succession' if there is nothing of their own kind intermediate
between them—nothing that is continuous can be composed of indi-
25 visibles: e. g. a line cannot be composed of points, the line being continuous and the point indivisible. For the extremities of two points
can neither be *one* (since of an indivisible there can be no extremity
as distinct from some other part) nor *together* (since that which has
no parts can have no extremity, the extremity and the thing of which
it is the extremity being distinct).

Moreover, if that which is continuous is composed of points, these
30 points must be either *continuous* or *in contact* with one another: and
231ᵇ the same reasoning applies in the case of all indivisibles. Now for
the reason given above they cannot be continuous: and one thing
can be in contact with another only if whole is in contact with
whole or part with part or part with whole. But since indivisibles
have no parts, they must be in contact with one another as whole with
whole. And if they are in contact with one another as whole with whole,
they will not be continuous: for that which is continuous has distinct
5 parts: and these parts into which it is divisible are different in this
way, i. e. spatially separate.

Nor, again, can a point be *in succession* to a point or a moment to
a moment in such a way that length can be composed of points or
time of moments: for things are in succession if there is nothing of
their own kind intermediate between them, whereas that which is
intermediate between points is always a line and that which is intermediate between moments is always a period of time.

10   Again, if length and time could thus be composed of indivisibles,

[1] v. 3.

they could be divided into indivisibles, since each is divisible into the parts of which it is composed. But, as we saw, no continuous thing is divisible into things without parts. Nor can there be anything of any other kind intermediate between the parts or between the moments: for if there could be any such thing it is clear that it must be either indivisible or divisible, and if it is divisible, it must be divisible either into indivisibles or into divisibles that are infinitely divisible, in which case it is continuous.

Moreover, it is plain that everything continuous is divisible into 15 divisibles that are infinitely divisible: for if it were divisible into indivisibles, we should have an indivisible in contact with an indivisible, since the extremities of things that are continuous with one another are one and are in contact.

The same reasoning applies equally to magnitude, to time, and to motion: either all of these are composed of indivisibles and are divisible into indivisibles, or none. This may be made clear as follows. If a 20 magnitude is composed of indivisibles, the motion over that magnitude must be composed of corresponding indivisible motions: e. g. if the magnitude ABC is composed of the indivisibles A, B, C, each corresponding part of the motion DEF of Z over ABC is indivisible. Therefore, since where there is motion there must be something that 25 is in motion, and where there is something in motion there must be motion, therefore the being-moved will also be composed of indivisibles. So Z traversed A when its motion was D, B when its motion was E, and C similarly when its motion was F. Now a thing that is in motion from one place to another cannot at the moment when it was in motion both be in motion and at the same time have completed its motion at the place to which it was in motion: e. g. if a man is walking to Thebes, he cannot be walking to Thebes and at the same time have completed his walk to Thebes: and, as we saw, Z traverses the 30 partless section A in virtue of the presence of the motion D. Conse- 232ᵃ quently, if Z actually passed through A *after* being in process of passing through, the motion must be divisible: for at the time when Z was passing through, it neither was at rest nor had completed its passage but was in an intermediate state: while if it is passing through and has completed its passage *at the same moment,* then that which is walking will at the moment when it is walking have completed its 5 walk and will be in the place to which it is walking; that is to say, it will have completed its motion at the place to which it is in motion.[2] And if a thing is in motion over the whole ABC and its motion is the three D, E, and F, and if it is not in motion at all over the partless

---

[2] Which is *ex hypothesi* impossible (231ᵇ 28–30).

section A but has completed its motion over it, then the motion will
consist not of motions but of starts, and will take place by a thing's
having completed a motion without being in motion: for on this
assumption it has completed its passage through A without passing
10 through it. So it will be possible for a thing to have completed a
walk without ever walking: for on this assumption it has completed
a walk over a particular distance without walking over that distance.
Since, then, everything must be either at rest or in motion, and Z is
therefore at rest in each of the sections A, B, and C, it follows that a
thing can be continuously at rest and at the same time in motion:
for, as we saw, Z is in motion over the whole ABC and at rest in any
15 part (and consequently in the whole) of it. Moreover, if the indivisibles composing DEF are motions, it would be possible for a thing
in spite of the presence in it of motion to be not in motion but at rest,
while if they are not motions, it would be possible for motion to be
composed of something other than motions.

And if length and motion are thus indivisible, it is neither more nor
less necessary that time also be similarly indivisible, that is to say be
20 composed of indivisible moments: for if the whole distance is divisible
and an equal velocity will cause a thing to pass through less of it in
less time, the time must also be divisible, and conversely, if the time
in which a thing is carried over the section Λ is divisible, this section
A must also be divisible.

2   And since every magnitude is divisible into magnitudes—for we
have shown that it is impossible for anything continuous to be composed of indivisible parts, and every magnitude is continuous—it
25 necessarily follows that the quicker of two things traverses a greater
magnitude in an equal time, an equal magnitude in less time, and a
greater magnitude in less time, in conformity with the definition
sometimes given of 'the quicker'. Suppose that A is quicker than B.
Now since of two things that which changes sooner is quicker, in the
30 time FG, in which A has changed from C to D, B will not yet have
arrived at D but will be short of it: so that in an equal time the
quicker will pass over a greater magnitude. More than this, it will pass
over a greater magnitude in less time: for in the time in which A has
arrived at D, B being the slower has arrived, let us say, at E. Then
232ᵇ since A has occupied the whole time FG in arriving at D, it will have
arrived at H in less time than this, say FJ. Now the magnitude CH
that A has passed over is greater than the magnitude CE, and the time
FJ is less than the whole time FG: so that the quicker will pass over a
5 greater magnitude in less time. And from this it is also clear that the

quicker will pass over an equal magnitude in less time than the slower. For since it passes over the greater magnitude in less time than the slower, and (regarded by itself) passes over KL the greater in more time than KN the lesser, the time PQ in which it passes over KL will be more than the time PR in which it passes over KN: so that, the 10 time PQ being less than the time PV in which the slower passes over KN, the time PR will also be less than the time PV: for it is less than the time PQ, and that which is less than something else that is less than a thing is also itself less than that thing. Hence it follows that the quicker will traverse an equal magnitude in less time than the slower. Again, since the motion of anything must always occupy either 15 an equal time or less or more time in comparison with that of another thing, and since, whereas a thing is slower if its motion occupies more time and of equal velocity if its motion occupies an equal time, the quicker is neither of equal velocity nor slower, it follows that the motion of the quicker can occupy neither an equal time nor more time. It can only be, then, that it occupies less time, and thus we get the necessary consequence that the quicker will pass over an equal magnitude (as well as a greater) in less time than the slower.   20

And since every motion is in time and a motion may occupy any time, and the motion of everything that is in motion may be either quicker or slower, both quicker motion and slower motion may occupy any time: and this being so, it necessarily follows that time also is continuous. By continuous I mean that which is divisible into divisibles that are infinitely divisible: and if we take this as the definition 25 of continuous, it follows necessarily that time is continuous. For since it has been shown that the quicker will pass over an equal magnitude in less time than the slower, suppose that A is quicker and B slower, and that the slower has traversed the magnitude CD in the time FG. 30 Now it is clear that the quicker will traverse the same magnitude in less time than this: let us say in the time FH. Again, since the quicker has passed over the whole CD in the time FH, the slower will in the same time pass over CJ, say, which is less than CD. And since B, 233ᵃ the slower, has passed over CJ in the time FH, the quicker will pass over it in less time: so that the time FH will again be divided. And if this is divided the magnitude CJ will also be divided just as CD was: and again, if the magnitude is divided, the time will also be divided. And we can carry on this process for ever, taking the slower 5 after the quicker and the quicker after the slower alternately, and using what has been demonstrated at each stage as a new point of departure: for the quicker will divide the time and the slower will divide the length. If, then, this alternation always holds good, and at

10 every turn involves a division, it is evident that all time must be
continuous. And at the same time it is clear that all magnitude is also
continuous; for the divisions of which time and magnitude respectively are susceptible are the same and equal.

Moreover, the current popular arguments make it plain that, if time
is continuous, magnitude is continuous also, inasmuch as a thing
15 passes over half a given magnitude in half the time taken to cover the
whole: in fact without qualification it passes over a less magnitude in
less time; for the divisions of time and of magnitude will be the same.
And if either is infinite, so is the other, and the one is so in the
same way as the other; i. e. if time is infinite in respect of its
extremities, length is also infinite in respect of its extremities: if
time is infinite in respect of divisibility, length is also infinite in
20 respect of divisibility: and if time is infinite in both respects, magnitude is also infinite in both respects.

Hence Zeno's argument makes a false assumption in asserting that
it is impossible for a thing to pass over or severally to come in contact
with infinite things in a finite time. For there are two senses in which
length and time and generally anything continuous are called 'in-
25 finite': they are called so either in respect of divisibility or in respect
of their extremities. So while a thing in a finite time cannot come in
contact with things quantitatively infinite, it can come in contact
with things infinite in respect of divisibility: for in this sense the time
itself is also infinite: and so we find that the time occupied by the
30 passage over the infinite is not a finite but an infinite time, and the
contact with the infinites is made by means of moments not finite
but infinite in number.

The passage over the infinite, then, cannot occupy a finite time,
and the passage over the finite cannot occupy an infinite time: if
the time is infinite the magnitude must be infinite also, and if the
magnitude is infinite, so also is the time. This may be shown as
follows. Let AB be a finite magnitude, and let us suppose that it
35 is traversed in infinite time C, and let a finite period CD of the
233ᵇ time be taken. Now in this period the thing in motion will pass
over a certain segment of the magnitude: let BE be the segment
that it has thus passed over. (This will be either an exact measure
of AB or less or greater than an exact measure: it makes no difference which it is.) Then, since a magnitude equal to BE will al-
5 ways be passed over in an equal time, and BE measures the whole
magnitude, the whole time occupied in passing over AB will be
finite: for it will be divisible into periods equal in number to the segments into which the magnitude is divisible. Moreover, if it is the

case that infinite time is not occupied in passing over every magnitude, but it is possible to pass over some magnitude, say BE, in a finite time, and if this BE measures the whole of which it is a part, and if 10 an equal magnitude is passed over in an equal time, then it follows that the time like the magnitude is finite. That infinite time will not be occupied in passing over BE is evident if the time be taken as limited in one direction: for as the part will be passed over in less time than the whole, the time occupied in traversing this part must be finite, the limit in one direction being given. The same reasoning will also show the falsity of the assumption that infinite length can be traversed in a finite time. It is evident, then, from what has been said 15 that neither a line nor a surface nor in fact anything continuous can be indivisible.

This conclusion follows not only from the present argument but from the consideration that the opposite assumption implies the divisibility of the indivisible. For since the distinction of quicker and slower may apply to motions occupying any period of time and in an equal 20 time the quicker passes over a greater length, it may happen that it will pass over a length twice, or one and a half times, as great as that passed over by the slower: for their respective velocities may stand to one another in this proportion. Suppose, then, that the quicker has in the same time been carried over a length one and a half times as great as that traversed by the slower, and that the respective magnitudes are divided, that of the quicker, the magnitude ABCD, into three indivisibles, and that of the slower into the two indivisibles EF, FG. Then the time may also be divided into three indivisibles, for an equal 25 magnitude will be passed over in an equal time. Suppose then that it is thus divided into JK, KL, LM. Again, since in the same time the slower has been carried over EF, FG, the time may also be similarly divided into two. Thus the indivisible will be divisible, and that which has no parts will be passed over not in an indivisible but in a greater 30 time.[3] It is evident, therefore, that nothing continuous is without parts.

3   The present also is necessarily indivisible—the present, that is, not in the sense in which the word is applied to one thing in virtue of another,[4] but in its proper and primary sense; in which sense it is in- 35 herent in all time. For the present is something that is an extremity of 234ᵃ the past (no part of the future being on this side of it) and also of the

[3] The slower will traverse EF in a greater time than the indivisible time in which the quicker traverses JK.

[4] i. e. in which it means a period of time including the present proper.

future (no part of the past being on the other side of it): it is, as we have said,[5] a limit of both. And if it is once shown that it is essentially of this character and one and the same, it will at once be evident also that it is indivisible.

5   Now the present that is the extremity of both times must be one and the same: for if each extremity were different, the one could not be in succession to the other, because nothing continuous can be composed of things having no parts: and if the one is apart from the other, there will be time intermediate between them, because everything continuous is such that there is something intermediate between its limits and described by the same name as itself. But if
10 the intermediate thing is time, it will be divisible: for all time has been shown [6] to be divisible. Thus on this assumption the present is divisible. But if the present is divisible, there will be part of the past in the future and part of the future in the past: for past time will be marked off from future time at the actual point of division. Also the present will be a present not in the proper sense but in virtue of
15 something else: for the division which yields it will not be a division proper.[7] Furthermore, there will be a part of the present that is past and a part that is future, and it will not always be the same part that is past or future: in fact one and the same present will not be simultaneous: for the time may be divided at many points. If, therefore, the present cannot possibly have these characteristics, it follows that it must be the same present that belongs to each of the two times.
20 But if this is so it is evident that the present is also indivisible: for if it is divisible it will be involved in the same implications as before. It is clear, then, from what has been said that time contains something indivisible, and this is what we call a present.

      We will now show that nothing can be in motion in a present. For
25 if this is possible, there can be both quicker and slower motion in the present. Suppose then that in the present M the quicker has traversed the distance AB. That being so, the slower will in the same present traverse a distance less than AB, say AC. But since the slower will have occupied the whole present in traversing AC, the quicker will
30 occupy less than this in traversing it. Thus we shall have a division of the present, whereas we found it to be indivisible. It is impossible, therefore, for anything to be in motion in a present.

      Nor can anything be at rest in a present: for, as we were saying,[8] that only can be at rest which is naturally designed to be in motion

---

[5] 222[a] 12.   [6] Chapter 2.

[7] i.e. it will not be a *point* of division but merely something intermediate between past and future.   [8] 226[b] 12 sqq.

but is not in motion when, where, or as it would naturally be so: since, therefore, nothing is naturally designed to be in motion in a present, it is clear that nothing can be at rest in a present either.

Moreover, inasmuch as it is the same present that belongs to both the times,[9] and it is possible for a thing to be in motion throughout 35 one time and to be at rest throughout the other, and that which is in 234b motion or at rest for the whole of a time will be in motion or at rest as the case may be in any part of it in which it is naturally designed to be in motion or at rest: this being so, the assumption that there can be motion or rest in a present will carry with it the implication that the same thing can at the same time be at rest and in motion: for both the times have the same extremity, viz. the present.

Again, when we say that a thing is at rest, we imply that its con- 5 dition in whole and in part is at the time of speaking uniform with what it was previously: but the present contains no 'previously': consequently, there can be no rest in it.

It follows then that the motion of that which is in motion and the rest of that which is at rest must occupy time.

4 Further, everything that changes must be divisible. For since 10 every change is from something to something, and when a thing is at the goal of its change it is no longer changing, and when both it itself and all its parts are at the starting-point of its change it is not changing (for that which is in whole and in part in an unvarying condition is not in a state of change); it follows, therefore, that part of that 15 which is changing must be at the starting-point and part at the goal: for as a whole it cannot be in both or in neither. (Here by 'goal of change' I mean that which comes first in the process of change: e. g. in a process of change from white the goal in question will be grey, not black: for it is not necessary that that which is changing should be at either of the extremes.) It is evident, therefore, that everything that 20 changes must be divisible.

Now motion is divisible in two senses. In the first place it is divisible in virtue of the time that it occupies. In the second place it is divisible according to the motions of the several parts of that which is in motion: e. g. if the whole AC is in motion, there will be a motion of AB and a motion of BC. That being so, let DE be the motion of the part AB and EF the motion of the part BC. Then the whole DF 25 must be the motion of AC: for DF must constitute the motion of AC inasmuch as DE and EF severally constitute the motions of each of its parts. But the motion of a thing can never be constituted by

9 viz. past and future.

the motion or something else: consequently the whole motion is the motion of the whole magnitude.

Again, since every motion is a motion of something, and the whole motion DF is not the motion of either of the parts (for each of the parts DE, EF is the motion of one of the parts AB, BC) or of any-
30 thing else (for, the whole motion being the motion of a whole, the parts of the motion are the motions of the parts of that whole: and the parts of DF are the motions of AB, BC and of nothing else: for, as we saw,[10] a motion that is one cannot be the motion of more things than one): since this is so, the whole motion will be the motion of the magnitude ABC.

Again, if there is a motion of the whole other than DF, say HI, the motion of each of the parts may be subtracted from it: and these
35 motions will be equal to DE, EF respectively: for the motion of that
235ᵃ which is one must be one. So if the whole motion HI may be divided into the motions of the parts, HI will be equal to DF: if on the other hand there is any remainder, say JI, this will be a motion of noth-
5 ing: for it can be the motion neither of the whole nor of the parts (as the motion of that which is one must be one) nor of anything else: for a motion that is continuous must be the motion of things that are continuous. And the same result follows if the division of HI reveals a surplus on the side of the motions of the parts. Conse-quently, if this is impossible, the whole motion must be the same as and equal to DF.

This then is what is meant by the division of motion according to the motions of the parts: and it must be applicable to everything that is divisible into parts.
10   Motion is also susceptible of another kind of division, that accord-ing to time. For since all motion is in time and all time is divisible, and in less time the motion is less, it follows that every motion must be divisible according to time. And since everything that is in motion is in motion in a certain sphere and for a certain time and has a
15 motion belonging to it, it follows that the time, the motion, the being-in-motion, the thing that is in motion, and the sphere of the motion must all be susceptible of the same divisions (though spheres of motion are not all divisible in a like manner: thus quantity is essentially, quality accidentally divisible). For suppose that A is the
20 time occupied by the motion B. Then if all the time has been occu-pied by the whole motion, it will take less of the motion to occupy half the time, less again to occupy a further subdivision of the time, and so on to infinity. Again, the time will be divisible similarly to the

10 223ᵇ 1 sqq.

motion: for if the whole motion occupies all the time half the motion will occupy half the time, and less of the motion again will occupy less of the time.

In the same way the being-in-motion will also be divisible. For let 25 C be the whole being-in-motion. Then the being-in-motion that corresponds to half the motion will be less than the whole being-in-motion, that which corresponds to a quarter of the motion will be less again, and so on to infinity. Moreover by setting out successively the being-in-motion corresponding to each of the two motions DC (say) and CE, we may argue that the whole being-in-motion will correspond to the whole motion (for if it were some other being-in-motion that 30 corresponded to the whole motion, there would be more than one being-in-motion corresponding to the same motion), the argument being the same as that whereby we showed [11] that the motion of a thing is divisible into the motions of the parts of the thing: for if we take separately the being-in-motion corresponding to each of the two motions, we shall see that the whole being-in-motion is continuous.

The same reasoning will show the divisibility of the length, and in fact of everything that forms a sphere of change (though some of these 35 are only accidentally divisible because that which changes is so): for the division of one term will involve the division of all. So, too, in the matter of their being finite or infinite, they will all alike be either the one or the other. And we now see that in most cases the fact that all 235ᵇ the terms are divisible or infinite is a direct consequence of the fact that the thing that changes is divisible or infinite: for the attributes 'divisible' and 'infinite' belong in the first instance to the thing that changes. That divisibility does so we have already [12] shown; that 5 infinity does so will be made clear in what follows.[13]

5 Since everything that changes changes from something to something, that which has changed must at the moment when it has first changed be in that to which it has changed. For that which changes retires from or leaves that from which it changes: and leaving, if not identical with changing, is at any rate a consequence of it. And if 10 leaving is a consequence of changing, having left is a consequence of having changed: for there is a like relation between the two in each case.

One kind of change, then, being change in a relation of contradiction, where a thing has changed from not-being to being it has left 15 not-being. Therefore it will be in being: for everything must either be

[11] 234ᵇ 24 sqq., especially 234ᵇ 34 sqq.

[12] 234ᵇ 10-20.

[13] Chapter 7.

or not be. It is evident, then, that in contradictory change that which
has changed must be in that to which it has changed. And if this is
true in this kind of change, it will be true in all other kinds as well:
for in this matter what holds good in the case of one will hold good
likewise in the case of the rest.

Moreover, if we take each kind of change separately, the truth of
our conclusion will be equally evident, on the ground that that which
20 has changed must be somewhere or in something. For, since it has
left that from which it has changed and must be somewhere, it must
be either in that to which it has changed or in something else. If, then,
that which has changed to B is in something other than B, say C, it
must again be changing from C to B: for it cannot be assumed that
25 there is no interval between C and B, since change is continuous.
Thus we have the result that the thing that has changed, at the moment
when it has changed, is changing to that to which it has changed,
which is impossible: that which has changed, therefore, must be in
that to which it has changed. So it is evident likewise that that which
has come to be, at the moment when it has come to be, will *be,* and
that which has ceased to be will *not-be*: for what we have said
applies universally to every kind of change, and its truth is most
30 obvious in the case of contradictory change. It is clear, then, that that
which has changed, at the moment when it has first changed, is in
that to which it has changed.

We will now show that the 'primary when' in which that which has
changed effected the completion of its change must be indivisible,
where by 'primary' I mean possessing the characteristics in question
of itself and not in virtue of the possession of them by something
else belonging to it. For let AC be divisible, and let it be divided at
35 B. If then the completion of change has been effected in AB or again
in BC, AC cannot be the primary thing in which the completion of
change has been effected. If, on the other hand, it has been changing
in both AB and BC (for it must either have changed or be changing
236ᵃ in each of them), it must have been changing in the whole AC: but
our assumption was that AC contains only the *completion* of the
change. It is equally impossible to suppose that one part of AC contains the process and the other the completion of the change: for
then we shall have something prior to what is primary.[14] So that
in which the completion of change has been effected must be indivis-
5 ible. It is also evident, therefore, that that in which that which

[14] *sc.* BC will have more right than AC to be regarded as that in which the
change has been completed.

has ceased to be has ceased to be and that in which that which has come to be has come to be are indivisible.

But there are two senses of the expression 'the primary when in which something has changed'. On the one hand it may mean the primary when containing the *completion* of the process of change—the moment when it is correct to say 'it has changed': on the other hand it may mean the primary when containing the *beginning* of the process of change. Now the primary when that has reference to the end of the change is something really existent: for a change may really be completed, and there is such a thing as an end of change, which we have in fact shown to be indivisible because it is a limit. But that which has reference to the beginning is not existent at all: for there is no such thing as a beginning of a process of change, and the time occupied by the change does not contain any primary when in which the change began. For suppose that AD is such a primary when. Then it cannot be indivisible: for, if it were, the moment immediately preceding the change and the moment in which the change begins would be consecutive (and moments cannot be consecutive). Again, if the changing thing is at rest in the whole preceding time CA (for we may suppose that it is at rest), it is at rest in A also: so if AD is without parts, it will simultaneously be at rest and have changed: for it is at rest in A and has changed in D. Since then AD is not without parts, it must be divisible, and the changing thing must have changed in every part of it (for if it has changed in neither of the two parts into which AD is divided, it has not changed in the whole either: if, on the other hand, it is in process of change in both parts, it is likewise in process of change in the whole: and if, again, it has changed in one of the two parts, the whole is not the primary when in which it has changed: it must therefore have changed in every part). It is evident, then, that with reference to the beginning of change there is no primary when in which change has been effected: for the divisions are infinite.

So, too, of that which has changed there is no primary part that has changed. For suppose that of DE the primary part that has changed is DF (everything that changes having been shown [15] to be divisible): and let HI be the time in which DF has changed. If, then, in the whole time DF has changed, in half the time there will be a part that has changed, less than and therefore prior to DF: and again there will be another part prior to this, and yet another, and so on to infinity. Thus of that which changes there cannot be any primary part that has changed. It is evident, then, from what has

[15] 234^{b} 10 sqq.

35 been said, that neither of that which changes nor of the time in which
it changes is there any primary part.

236ᵇ   With regard, however, to the actual subject of change—that is to
say that in respect of which a thing changes—there is a difference
to be observed. For in a process of change we may distinguish three
terms—that which changes, that in which it changes, and the actual
subject of change, e. g. the man, the time, and the fair complexion.
5 Of these the man and the time are divisible: but with the fair complexion it is otherwise (though they are all divisible accidentally, for
that in which the fair complexion or any other quality is an accident
is divisible). For of actual subjects of change it will be seen that
those which are classed as essentially, not accidentally, divisible have
10 no primary part. Take the case of magnitudes: let AB be a magnitude, and suppose that it has moved from B to a primary 'where' C.
Then if BC is taken to be indivisible, two things without parts will
have to be contiguous (which is impossible): if on the other hand it
is taken to be divisible, there will be something prior to C to which the
magnitude has changed, and something else again prior to that,
and so on to infinity, because the process of division may be con-
15 tinued without end. Thus there can be no primary 'where' to which
a thing has changed. And if we take the case of quantitative change,
we shall get a like result, for here too the change is in something
continuous. It is evident, then, that only in qualitative motion can
there be anything essentially indivisible.

20 6   Now everything that changes changes in time, and that in two
senses: for the time in which a thing is said to change may be the
primary time, or on the other hand it may have an extended reference, as e. g. when we say that a thing changes in a particular year
because it changes in a particular day. That being so, that which
changes must be changing in any part of the primary time in which it
changes. This is clear from our definition of 'primary',[16] in which
the word is said to express just this: it may also, however, be made
25 evident by the following argument. Let VQ be the primary time in
which that which is in motion is in motion: and (as all time is
divisible) let it be divided at J. Now in the time VJ it either is in
motion or is not in motion, and the same is likewise true of the time
JQ. Then if it is in motion in neither of the two parts, it will be at
rest in the whole: for it is impossible that it should be in motion in

[16] 235ᵇ 33. The 'primary time' is the irreducible minimum: thus the very terms
of the definition make it clear that a thing must be changing in the *whole* of
the 'primary time' in which it changes.

a time in no part of which it is in motion. If on the other hand it is 30 in motion in only one of the two parts of the time, VQ cannot be the primary time in which it is in motion: for its motion will have reference to a time other than VQ. It must, then, have been in motion in any part of VQ.

And now that this has been proved, it is evident that everything that is in motion must have been in motion before. For if that which is in motion has traversed the distance JK in the primary time VQ, 35 in half the time a thing that is in motion with equal velocity and began its motion at the same time will have traversed half the distance. But if this second thing whose velocity is equal has traversed a certain distance in a certain time, the original thing that is in mo- 237ᵃ tion must have traversed the same distance in the same time. Hence that which is in motion must have been in motion before.

Again, if by taking the extreme moment of the time—for it is the moment that defines the time, and time is that which is inter- 5 mediate between moments—we are enabled to say that motion has taken place in the whole time VQ or in fact in any period of it, motion may likewise be said to have taken place in every other such period. But half the time finds an extreme in the point of division. Therefore motion will have taken place in half the time and in fact in any part of it: for as soon as any division is made there is always a time defined by moments. If, then, all time is divisible, and that which 10 is intermediate between moments is time, everything that is changing must have completed an infinite number of changes.

Again, since a thing that changes continuously and has not perished or ceased from its change must either be changing or have changed in any part of the time of its change, and since it cannot be changing in a moment, it follows that it must have changed at every moment in the time: consequently, since the moments are in- 15 finite in number, everything that is changing must have completed an infinite number of changes.

And not only must that which is changing have changed, but that which has changed must also previously have been changing, since everything that has changed from something to something has changed in a period of time. For suppose that a thing has changed 20 from A to B in a moment. Now the moment in which it has changed cannot be the same as that in which it is at A (since in that case it would be in A and B at once): for we have shown above [17] that that which has changed, when it has changed, is not in that from which it has changed. If, on the other hand, it is a different moment, there

[17] 235ᵇ 6 sqq.

will be a period of time intermediate between the two: for, as we
25 saw,[18] moments are not consecutive. Since, then, it has changed in a
period of time, and all time is divisible, in half the time it will have
completed another change, in a quarter another, and so on to infinity:
consequently when it has changed, it must have previously been
changing.

Moreover, the truth of what has been said is more evident in
the case of magnitude, because the magnitude over which what is
30 changing changes is continuous. For suppose that a thing has changed
from C to D. Then if CD is indivisible, two things without parts will
be consecutive. But since this is impossible, that which is intermediate
between them must be a magnitude and divisible into an infinite
number of segments: consequently, before the change is completed,
the thing changes to those segments. Everything that has changed,
35 therefore, must previously have been changing: for the same proof
237[b] also holds good of change with respect to what is not continuous,
changes, that is to say, between contraries and between contradictories. In such cases we have only to take the time in which a thing
has changed and again apply the same reasoning. So that which has
changed must have been changing and that which is changing must
have changed, and a process of change is preceded by a completion
5 of change and a completion by a process: and we can never take any
stage and say that it is absolutely the first. The reason of this is that
no two things without parts can be contiguous, and therefore in
change the process of division is infinite, just as lines may be infinitely divided so that one part is continually increasing and the other
continually decreasing.[19]

10   So it is evident also that that which has become must previously
have been in process of becoming, and that which is in process of
becoming must previously have become, everything (that is) that is
divisible and continuous: though it is not always the actual thing
that is in process of becoming of which this is true: sometimes it is
something else, that is to say, some part of the thing in question,
e. g. the foundation-stone of a house. So, too, in the case of that
which is perishing and that which has perished: for that which becomes and that which perishes must contain an element of infinite-
15 ness as an immediate consequence of the fact that they are continuous things: and so a thing cannot be in process of becoming with-

[18] 231[b] 6 sqq.
[19] i. e. you may begin by cutting off half the line, then half of what remains,
and so on, the part cut off thus continuously increasing and the part remaining
continually decreasing.

out having become or have become without having been in process of becoming. So, too, in the case of perishing and having perished: perishing must be preceded by having perished, and having perished must be preceded by perishing. It is evident, then, that that which has become must previously have been in process of becoming, and that which is in process of becoming must previously have become: 20 for all magnitudes and all periods of time are infinitely divisible.

Consequently no absolutely first stage of change can be represented by any particular part of space or time which the changing thing may occupy.

7   Now since the motion of everything that is in motion occupies a period of time, and a greater magnitude is traversed in a longer time, it is impossible that a thing should undergo a finite motion in an 25 infinite time, if this is understood to mean not that the same motion or a part of it is continually repeated, but that the whole infinite time is occupied by the whole finite motion. In all cases where a thing is in motion with uniform velocity it is clear that the finite magnitude is traversed in a finite time. For if we take a part of the motion which shall be a measure of the whole, the whole motion is completed in as many equal periods of the time as there are parts of 30 the motion. Consequently, since these parts are finite, both in size individually and in number collectively, the whole time must also be finite: for it will be a multiple of the portion, equal to the time occupied in completing the aforesaid part multiplied by the number of the parts.

But it makes no difference even if the velocity is not uniform. For let us suppose that the line AB represents a finite stretch over which a 35 thing has been moved in the given time, and let CD be the infinite time. Now if one part of the stretch must have been traversed before 238ᵃ another part (this is clear, that in the earlier and in the later part of the time a different part of the stretch has been traversed: for as the time lengthens a different part of the motion will always be completed in it, whether the thing in motion changes with uniform velocity or 5 not: and whether the rate of motion increases or diminishes or remains stationary this is none the less so), let us then take AE a part of the whole stretch of motion AB which shall be a measure of AB. Now this part of the motion occupies a certain period of the infinite time: it cannot itself occupy an infinite time, for we are assuming that that is occupied by the whole AB. And if again I take another part equal to AE, that also must occupy a finite time in consequence of 10 the same assumption. And if I go on taking parts in this way, on the

one hand there is no part which will be a measure of the infinite time (for the infinite cannot be composed of finite parts whether equal or unequal, because there must be some unity which will be a measure
15 of things finite in multitude or in magnitude, which, whether they are equal or unequal, are none the less limited in magnitude); while on the other hand the finite stretch of motion AB is a certain multiple of AE: consequently the motion AB must be accomplished in a finite time. Moreover it is the same with coming to rest as with motion. And so it is impossible for one and the same thing to be infinitely in process of becoming or of perishing.
20   The same reasoning will prove that in a finite time there cannot be an infinite extent of motion or of coming to rest, whether the motion is regular or irregular. For if we take a part which shall be a measure of the whole time, in this part a certain fraction, not the whole, of the magnitude will be traversed, because we assume that the traversing of the whole occupies all the time. Again, in another equal part of the time another part of the magnitude will be traversed:
25 and similarly in each part of the time that we take, whether equal or unequal to the part originally taken. It makes no difference whether the parts are equal or not, if only each is finite: for it is clear that while the time is exhausted by the subtraction of its parts, the infinite magnitude will not be thus exhausted, since the process of subtraction is finite both in respect of the quantity subtracted and of the number of times a subtraction is made. Consequently the infinite magnitude will not be traversed in a finite time:
30 and it makes no difference whether the magnitude is infinite in only one direction or in both: for the same reasoning will hold good.
    This having been proved, it is evident that neither can a finite magnitude traverse an infinite magnitude in a finite time, the reason being the same as that given above: in part of the time it will traverse
35 a finite magnitude and in each several part likewise, so that in the whole time it will traverse a finite magnitude.
    And since a finite magnitude will not traverse an infinite in a
238ᵇ finite time, it is clear that neither will an infinite traverse a finite in a finite time. For if the infinite could traverse the finite, the finite could traverse the infinite; for it makes no difference which of the two is the thing in motion: either case involves the traversing of the
5 infinite by the finite. For when the infinite magnitude A is in motion a part of it, say CD, will occupy the finite B, and then another, and then another, and so on to infinity. Thus the two results will coincide: the infinite will have completed a motion over the finite and the finite will have traversed the infinite: for it would seem to be

impossible for the motion of the infinite over the finite to occur in 10
any way other than by the finite traversing the infinite either by locomotion over it or by measuring it. Therefore, since this is impossible,
the infinite cannot traverse the finite.

Nor again will the infinite traverse the infinite in a finite time.
Otherwise it would also traverse the finite, for the infinite includes the 15
finite. We can further prove this in the same way by taking the time
as our starting-point.

Since, then, it is established that in a finite time neither will the
finite traverse the infinite, nor the infinite the finite, nor the infinite
the infinite, it is evident also that in a finite time there cannot be in- 20
finite motion: for what difference does it make whether we take the
motion or the magnitude to be infinite? If either of the two is infinite,
the other must be so likewise: for all locomotion is in space.

8 Since everything to which motion or rest is natural is in motion
or at rest in the natural time, place, and manner, that which is coming to a stand, when it is coming to a stand, must be in motion: for 25
if it is not in motion it must be at rest: but that which is at rest cannot be coming to rest. From this it evidently follows that coming to
a stand must occupy a period of time: for the motion of that which
is in motion occupies a period of time, and that which is coming
to a stand has been shown to be in motion: consequently coming to
a stand must occupy a period of time.

Again, since the terms 'quicker' and 'slower' are used only of that
which occupies a period of time, and the process of coming to a 30
stand may be quicker or slower, the same conclusion follows.

And that which is coming to a stand must be coming to a stand in
any part of the primary time in which it is coming to a stand. For if
it is coming to a stand in neither of two parts into which the time may
be divided, it cannot be coming to a stand in the whole time, with the
result that that which is coming to a stand will not be coming to a
stand. If on the other hand it is coming to a stand in only one of the
two parts of the time, the whole cannot be the primary time in which
it is coming to a stand: for it is coming to a stand in the whole time not 35
primarily but in virtue of something distinct from itself, the argument
being the same as that which we used above about things in motion.[20]

And just as there is no primary time in which that which is in
motion is in motion, so too there is no primary time in which that 239ᵃ
which is coming to a stand is coming to a stand, there being no primary stage either of being in motion or of coming to a stand. For

[20] Ch. 6.

let AB be the primary time in which a thing is coming to a stand.
Now AB cannot be without parts: for there cannot be motion in
that which is without parts, because the moving thing would necessarily have been already moved for part of the time of its move-
5 ment: and that which is coming to a stand has been shown to be
in motion. But since AB is therefore divisible, the thing is coming
to a stand in every one of the parts of AB: for we have shown above [21]
that it is coming to a stand in every one of the parts in which it is
primarily coming to a stand. Since, then, that in which primarily a
thing is coming to a stand must be a period of time and not something
indivisible, and since all time is infinitely divisible, there cannot be
anything in which primarily it is coming to a stand.

10   Nor again can there be a primary time at which the being at rest
of that which is at rest occurred: for it cannot have occurred in
that which has no parts, because there cannot be motion in that
which is indivisible, and that in which rest takes place is the same
as that in which motion takes place: for we defined [22] a state of rest
to be the state of a thing to which motion is natural but which is not
in motion when (that is to say in that [23] in which) motion would
be natural to it. Again, our use of the phrase 'being at rest' also im-
15 plies that the previous state of a thing is still unaltered, not one
point only but two at least being thus needed to determine its presence: consequently that in which a thing is at rest cannot be without
parts. Since, then, it is divisible, it must be a period of time, and
the thing must be at rest in every one of its parts, as may be shown
by the same method as that used above in similar demonstrations.
20   So there can be no primary part of the time: and the reason is
that rest and motion are always in a period of time, and a period of
time has no primary part any more than a magnitude or in fact anything continuous: for everything continuous is divisible into an
infinite number of parts.

And since everything that is in motion is in motion in a period
of time and changes from something to something, when its motion
is comprised within a particular period of time essentially—that is
25 to say when it fills the whole and not merely a part of the time in
question—it is impossible that in that time that which is in motion
should be over against some particular thing primarily.[24] For if a
thing—itself and each of its parts—occupies the same space for a
definite period of time, it is at rest: for it is in just these circum-

[21] 238^b 31 sqq.   [22] 226^b 12 sqq.   [23] sc. time.
[24] i. e. a space only just large enough to contain it, not a larger space of which
only part is occupied.

stances that we use the term 'being at rest'—when at one moment
after another it can be said with truth that a thing, itself and its
parts, occupies the same space. So if this is being at rest it is impossible for that which is changing to be as a whole, at the time when it 30
is primarily changing, over against any particular thing (for the
whole period of time is divisible), so that in one part of it after another it will be true to say that the thing, itself and its parts, occupies the same space. If this is not so and the aforesaid proposition
is true only at a single moment, then the thing will be over against
a particular thing not for any period of time but only at a moment
that limits the time. It is true that at any moment it is always over 35
against something stationary: but it is not at rest: for at a moment 239^b
it is not possible for anything to be either in motion or at rest. So
while it is true to say that that which is in motion is at a moment
not in motion and is opposite some particular thing, it cannot in a
period of time be over against that which is at rest: for that would
involve the conclusion that that which is in locomotion is at rest.

9   Zeno's reasoning, however, is fallacious, when he says that if 5
everything when it occupies an equal space is at rest, and if that
which is in locomotion is always occupying such a space at any
moment, the flying arrow is therefore motionless. This is false, for
time is not composed of indivisible moments any more than any other
magnitude is composed of indivisibles.

Zeno's arguments about motion, which cause so much disquietude 10
to those who try to solve the problems that they present, are four
in number. The first asserts the non-existence of motion on the
ground that that which is in locomotion must arrive at the half-way
stage before it arrives at the goal. This we have discussed above.[25]

The second is the so-called 'Achilles', and it amounts to this, that
in a race the quickest runner can never overtake the slowest, since 15
the pursuer must first reach the point whence the pursued started,
so that the slower must always hold a lead. This argument is the
same in principle as that which depends on bisection,[26] though it
differs from it in that the spaces with which we successively have to
deal are not divided into halves. The result of the argument is that 20
the slower is not overtaken: but it proceeds along the same lines as
the bisection-argument (for in both a division of the space in a certain way leads to the result that the goal is not reached, though the
'Achilles' goes further in that it affirms that even the quickest runner
in legendary tradition must fail in his pursuit of the slowest), so

[25] 233^a 13 sqq.   [26] viz. the first argument given above, ll. 11–14.

25 that the solution must be the same. And the axiom that that which holds a lead is never overtaken is false: it is not overtaken, it is true, while it holds a lead: but it is overtaken nevertheless if it is granted that it traverses the finite distance prescribed. These then are two of his arguments.

30   The third is that already given above, to the effect that the flying arrow is at rest, which result follows from the assumption that time is composed of moments: if this assumption is not granted, the conclusion will not follow.

The fourth argument is that concerning the two rows of bodies, each row being composed of an equal number of bodies of equal size, passing each other on a race-course as they proceed with equal velocity in opposite directions, the one row originally occupying the space between the goal and the middle point of the course and the

35 other that between the middle point and the starting-post. This, he thinks, involves the conclusion that half a given time is equal to

240ᵃ double that time. The fallacy of the reasoning lies in the assumption that a body occupies an equal time in passing with equal velocity a body that is in motion and a body of equal size that is at rest; which is false. For instance (so runs the argument), let A, A . . . be the

5 stationary bodies of equal size, B, B . . . the bodies, equal in number and in size to A, A . . ., originally occupying the half of the course from the starting-post to the middle of the A's, and C, C, . . . those originally occupying the other half from the goal to the middle of the A's, equal in number, size, and velocity to B, B. . . . Then three consequences follow:

First, as the B's and the C's pass one another, the first B reaches

10 the last C at the same moment as the first C reaches the last B. Secondly, at this moment the first C has passed all the A's, whereas the first B has passed only half the A's, and has consequently occupied only half the time occupied by the first C, since each of the two occupies an equal time in passing each A. Thirdly, at the same moment all the B's have passed all the C's: for the first C and the first B will simultaneously reach the opposite ends of the course,

15 since (so says Zeno) the time occupied by the first C in passing each of the B's is equal to that occupied by it in passing each of the A's, because an equal time is occupied by both the first B and the first C in passing all the A's. This is the argument, but it presupposed the aforesaid fallacious assumption.

Nor in reference to contradictory change shall we find anything

20 unanswerable in the argument that if a thing is changing from not-white, say, to white, and is in neither condition, then it will be

neither white nor not-white: for the fact that it is not *wholly* in either condition will not preclude us from calling it white or not-white. We call a thing white or not-white not necessarily because it is wholly either one or the other, but because most of its parts or the most essential parts of it are so: not being in a certain condition is different 25 from not being wholly in that condition. So, too, in the case of being and not-being and all other conditions which stand in a contradictory relation: while the changing thing must of necessity be in one of the two opposites, it is never wholly in either.

Again, in the case of circles and spheres and everything whose motion is confined within the space that it occupies, it is not true to say that the motion can be nothing but rest, on the ground that such 30 things in motion, themselves and their parts, will occupy the same position for a period of time, and that therefore they will be at once at rest and in motion. For in the first place the parts do not occupy the same position for any period of time: and in the second place the whole also is always changing to a different position: for if we take the orbit as described from a point A on a circumference, it will not 240ᵇ be the same as the orbit as described from B or C or any other point on the same circumference except in an accidental sense, the sense that is to say in which a musical man is the same as a man. Thus one 5 orbit is always changing into another, and the thing will never be at rest. And it is the same with the sphere and everything else whose motion is confined within the space that it occupies.

10   Our next point is that that which is without parts cannot be in motion except accidentally: i. e. it can be in motion only in so far as the body or the magnitude is in motion and the partless is in mo- 10 tion by inclusion therein, just as that which is in a boat may be in motion in consequence of the locomotion of the boat, or a part may be in motion in virtue of the motion of the whole. (It must be remembered, however, that by 'that which is without parts' I mean that which is quantitatively indivisible (and that the case of the motion of a part is not exactly parallel): for parts have motions belonging essentially and severally to themselves distinct from the motion of 15 the whole. The distinction may be seen most clearly in the case of a revolving sphere, in which the velocities of the parts near the centre and of those on the surface are different from one another and from that of the whole; this implies that there is not one motion but many.) As we have said, then, that which is without parts can be in motion in the sense in which a man sitting in a boat is in motion when the boat is travelling, but it cannot be in motion of itself. For 20

suppose that it is changing from AB to BC—either from one magnitude to another, or from one form to another, or from some state to
its contradictory—and let D be the primary time in which it undergoes the change. Then in the time in which it is changing it must be
either in AB or in BC or partly in one and partly in the other: for
25 this, as we saw,[27] is true of everything that is changing. Now it cannot be partly in each of the two: for then it would be divisible into
parts. Nor again can it be in BC: for then it will have completed the
change, whereas the assumption is that the change is in process. It
remains, then, that in the time in which it is changing, it is in AB.
That being so, it will be at rest: for, as we saw,[28] to be in the same
30 condition for a period of time is to be at rest. So it is not possible for
that which has no parts to be in motion or to change in any way:
for only one condition could have made it possible for it to have
motion, viz. that time should be composed of moments, in which case
at any moment it would have completed a motion or a change, so
241ᵃ that it would never be in motion, but would always have been in
motion. But this we have already shown above[29] to be impossible:
time is not composed of moments, just as a line is not composed of
points, and motion is not composed of starts: for this theory simply
5 makes motion consist of indivisibles in exactly the same way as
time is made to consist of moments or a length of points.

Again, it may be shown in the following way that there can be no
motion of a point or of any other indivisible. That which is in motion
can never traverse a space greater than itself without first traversing a space equal to or less than itself. That being so, it is evident
10 that the point also must first traverse a space equal to or less than
itself. But since it is indivisible, there can be no space less than itself
for it to traverse first: so it will have to traverse a distance equal
to itself. Thus the line will be composed of points, for the point, as
it continually traverses a distance equal to itself, will be a measure
of the whole line. But since this is impossible, it is likewise impossible
for the indivisible to be in motion.

15 Again, since motion is always in a period of time and never in a
moment, and all time is divisible, for everything that is in motion
there must be a time less than that in which it traverses a distance as
great as itself. For that in which it is in motion will be a time, because all motion is in a period of time; and all time has been shown
above[30] to be divisible. Therefore, if a point is in motion, there must
be a time less than that in which it has itself traversed any distance.

[27] 234ᵇ 10 sqq.   [28] 239ᵃ 27.
[29] 231ᵇ 18 sqq.   [30] 232ᵇ 23 sqq.

But this is impossible, for in less time it must traverse less distance, 20 and thus the indivisible will be divisible into something less than itself, just as the time is so divisible: the fact being that the only condition under which that which is without parts and indivisible could be in motion would have been the possibility of the infinitely small being in motion in a moment: for in the two questions—that 25 of motion in a moment and that of motion of something indivisible— the same principle is involved.

Our next point is that no process of change is infinite: for every change, whether between contradictories or between contraries, is a change from something to something. Thus in contradictory changes the positive or the negative, as the case may be, is the limit, e. g. being is the limit of coming to be and not-being is the limit of ceasing to be: and in contrary changes the particular contraries are the limits, since these are the extreme points of any such process of change, 30 and consequently of every process of alteration: for alteration is always dependent upon some contraries. Similarly contraries are the extreme points of processes of increase and decrease: the limit of increase is to be found in the complete magnitude proper to the peculiar nature of the thing that is increasing, while the limit of decrease is 241ᵇ the complete loss of such magnitude. Locomotion, it is true, we cannot show to be finite in this way, since it is not always between contraries. But since that which cannot be cut (in the sense that it is inconceivable that it should be cut, the term 'cannot' being used in several senses)—since it is inconceivable that that which in this 5 sense cannot be cut should be in process of being cut, and generally that that which cannot come to be should be in process of coming to be, it follows that it is inconceivable that that which cannot complete a change should be in process of changing to that to which it cannot complete a change. If, then, it is to be assumed that that which is in locomotion is in process of changing, it must be capable of completing the change. Consequently its motion is not infinite, and it will not be in locomotion over an infinite distance, for it cannot 10 traverse such a distance.

It is evident, then, that a process of change cannot be infinite in the sense that it is not defined by limits. But it remains to be considered whether it is possible in the sense that one and the same process of change may be infinite in respect of the time which it occupies. If it is not one process, it would seem that there is nothing to prevent its being infinite in this sense; e. g. if a process of locomo- 15 tion be succeeded by a process of alteration and that by a process of increase and that again by a process of coming to be: in this way there

may be motion for ever so far as the time is concerned, but it will not be one motion, because all these motions do not compose one. If it is to be one process, no motion can be infinite in respect of the
20 time that it occupies, with the single exception of rotatory locomotion.

BOOK VII

1 Everything that is in motion must be moved by something.
25 For if it has not the source of its motion in itself it is evident that it is moved by something other than itself, for there must be something else that moves it. If on the other hand it has the source of its motion in itself, let AB be taken to represent that which is in motion essentially of itself and not in virtue of the fact that something belonging to it is in motion. Now in the first place to assume that AB, because
30 it is in motion as a whole and is not moved by anything external to itself, is therefore moved by itself—this is just as if, supposing that JK is moving KL and is also itself in motion, we were to deny that JL is moved by anything on the ground that it is not evident which is the part that is moving it and which the part that is moved. In the second place that which is in motion without being moved by anything does not necessarily cease from its motion because something
242ᵃ else is at rest, but a thing must be moved by something if the fact of something else having ceased from its motion causes it to be at rest. Thus, if this is accepted, everything that is in motion must be moved
5 by something. For AB, which has been taken to represent that which is in motion, must be divisible, since everything that is in motion is divisible. Let it be divided, then, at C. Now if CB is not in motion, then AB will not be in motion: for if it is, it is clear that AC would be
10 in motion while BC is at rest, and thus AB cannot be in motion essentially and primarily. But *ex hypothesi* AB is in motion essentially and primarily. Therefore if CB is not in motion AB will be at rest. But we have agreed that that which is at rest if something else is not in motion must be moved by something. Consequently, everything that is in motion must be moved by something: for that which is in
15 motion will always be divisible, and if a part of it is not in motion the whole must be at rest.

Since everything that is in motion must be moved by something, let us take the case in which a thing is in locomotion and is moved by something that is itself in motion, and that again is moved by something else that is in motion, and that by something else, and so
20 on continually: then the series cannot go on to infinity, but there must be some first movent. For let us suppose that this is not so

and take the series to be infinite. Let A then be moved by B, B by C, C by D, and so on, each member of the series being moved by that which comes next to it. Then since *ex hypothesi* the movent while causing motion is also itself in motion, and the motion of the moved and the motion of the movent must proceed simultaneously (for the movent is causing motion and the moved is being moved simul- 25 taneously) it is evident that the respective motions of A, B, C, and each of the other moved movents are simultaneous. Let us take the motion of each separately and let E be the motion of A, F of B, and G and H respectively the motions of C and D: for though they are all moved severally one by another, yet we may still take the motion of each as numerically one, since every motion is from 30 something to something and is not infinite in respect of its extreme points. By a motion that is numerically one I mean a motion that proceeds from something numerically one and the same to something numerically one and the same in a period of time numerically one and the same: for a motion may be the same generically, specifically, 35 or numerically: it is generically the same if it belongs to the same category, e. g. substance or quality: it is specifically the same if it proceeds from something specifically the same to something specifically the same, e. g. from white to black or from good to bad, which is not of a kind specifically distinct: it is numerically the same if it proceeds from something numerically one to something numerically one in the same period of time, e. g. from a particular white to a 242$^\text{b}$ particular black, or from a particular place to a particular place, in a particular period of time: for if the period of time were not one and the same, the motion would no longer be numerically one though it would still be specifically one. We have dealt with this question 4 above.[1] Now let us further take the time in which A has completed 8 its motion, and let it be represented by J. Then since the motion of A is finite the time will also be finite. But since the movents and the things moved are infinite, the motion EFGH, i. e. the motion that is composed of all the individual motions, must be infinite. For the 15 motions of A, B, and the others may be equal, or the motions of the others may be greater: but assuming what is conceivable, we find that whether they are equal or some are greater, in both cases the whole motion is infinite. And since the motion of A and that of each of the others are simultaneous, the whole motion must occupy the same time as the motion of A: but the time occupied by the motion of A is finite: consequently the motion will be infinite in a finite time, which is impossible.

[1] v. 4. 227$^\text{b}$ 3 sqq.

20 It might be thought that what we set out to prove has thus been shown, but our argument so far does not prove it, because it does not yet prove that anything impossible results from the contrary supposition: for in a finite time there may be an infinite motion, though not of one thing, but of many: and in the case that we are considering this is so: for each thing accomplishes its own motion, and there is no impossibility in many things being in motion simultaneously. But if (as we see to be universally the case) that which 25 primarily is moved locally and corporeally must be either in contact with or continuous with that which moves it, the things moved and the movents must be continuous or in contact with one another, so that together they all form a single unity: whether this unity is finite or infinite makes no difference to our present argument; for in any case since the things in motion are infinite in number the whole motion will be infinite, if, as is theoretically possible, each motion is either equal to or greater than that which follows it in the series: for we shall take as actual that which is theoretically possible. If, 30 then, A, B, C, D form an infinite magnitude that passes through the motion EFGH in the finite time J, this involves the conclusion that an infinite motion is passed through in a finite time: and whether the magnitude in question is finite or infinite this is in either case impossible. Therefore the series must come to an end, and there must be a first movent and a first moved: for the fact that this impossi-243ᵃ bility results only from the assumption of a particular case is immaterial, since the case assumed is theoretically possible, and the assumption of a theoretically possible case ought not to give rise to any impossible result.

2   That which is the first movent of a thing—in the sense that it supplies not 'that for the sake of which' but the source of the motion—is always together with that which is moved by it (by 'together' I mean that there is nothing intermediate between them). 5 This is universally true wherever one thing is moved by another. And since there are three kinds of motion, local, qualitative, and quantitative, there must also be three kinds of movent, that which causes locomotion, that which causes alteration, and that which causes increase or decrease.

10   Let us begin with locomotion, for this is the primary motion. Everything that is in locomotion is moved either by itself or by something else. In the case of things that are moved by themselves it is evident that the moved and the movent are together: for they contain within themselves their first movent, so that there is nothing

in between. The motion of things that are moved by something else 15
must proceed in one of four ways: for there are four kinds of locomotion caused by something other than that which is in motion, viz. pulling, pushing, carrying, and twirling. All forms of locomotion are reducible to these. Thus pushing on is a form of pushing in which that
which is causing motion away from itself follows up that which it
pushes and continues to push it: pushing off occurs when the movent
does not follow up the thing that it has moved: throwing when the 20
movent causes a motion away from itself more violent than the 243ᵇ
natural locomotion of the thing moved, which continues its course
so long as it is controlled by the motion imparted to it. Again, pushing apart and pushing together are forms respectively of pushing off
and pulling: pushing apart is pushing off, which may be a motion
either away from the pusher or away from something else, while
pushing together is pulling, which may be a motion towards some- 5
thing else as well as towards the puller. We may similarly classify
all the varieties of these last two, e. g. packing and combing: the
former is a form of pushing together, the latter a form of pushing
apart. The same is true of the other processes of combination and
separation (they will all be found to be forms of pushing apart
or of pushing together), except such as are involved in the processes
of becoming and perishing. (At the same time it is evident that there 10
is no other kind of motion but combination and separation: for they
may all be apportioned to one or other of those already mentioned.)
Again, inhaling is a form of pulling, exhaling a form of pushing: and
the same is true of spitting and of all other motions that proceed
through the body, whether secretive or assimilative, the assimilative being forms of pulling, the secretive of pushing off. All other 15
kinds of locomotion must be similarly reduced, for they all fall under
one or other of our four heads. And again, of these four, carrying
and twirling are reducible to pulling and pushing. For carrying
always follows one of the other three methods, for that which is
carried is in motion accidentally, because it is in or upon something
that is in motion, and that which carries it is in doing so being either 20
pulled or pushed or twirled; thus carrying belongs to all the other 244ᵃ
three kinds of motion in common. And twirling is a compound of
pulling and pushing, for that which is twirling a thing must be
pulling one part of the thing and pushing another part, since it
impels one part away from itself and another part towards itself.
If, therefore, it can be shown that that which is pushing and that
which is pulling are adjacent respectively to that which is being
pushed and that which is being pulled, it will be evident that in all 5

locomotion there is nothing intermediate between moved and movent. But the former fact is clear even from the definitions of pushing and pulling, for pushing is motion to something else from oneself or from something else, and pulling is motion from something else to oneself or to something else, when the motion of that which is
10 pulling is quicker than the motion that would separate from one another the two things that are continuous:[2] for it is this that causes one thing to be pulled on along with the other. (It might indeed be thought that there is a form of pulling that arises in another way: that wood, e. g. pulls fire in a manner different from that described above. But it makes no difference whether that which pulls is in motion or is stationary when it is pulling: in the latter case it pulls to the place where it is, while in the former it pulls to the place where it was.) Now it is impossible to move anything either
15 from oneself to something else or from something else to oneself without being in contact with it: it is evident, therefore, that in all
244^b locomotion there is nothing intermediate between moved and movent.

Nor again is there anything intermediate between that which undergoes and that which causes alteration: this can be proved by induction: for in every case we find that the respective extremities of that which causes and that which undergoes alteration are adjacent. For our assumption is that things that are undergoing alteration are altered in virtue of their being affected in respect of their so-called affective qualities, since that which is of a certain quality is altered in so far as it is sensible, and the characteristics in which bodies differ from one another are sensible characteristics: for every body differs from another in possessing a greater or lesser number of sensible characteristics or in possessing the same sensible characteristics in a greater or lesser degree. But the alteration of that which undergoes alteration is also caused by the above-men-
5 tioned characteristics, which are affections of some particular underlying quality. Thus we say that a thing is altered by becoming hot or sweet or thick or dry or white: and we make these assertions alike of what is inanimate and of what is animate, and further, where animate things are in question, we make them both of the
10 parts that have no power of sense-perception and of the senses themselves. For in a way even the senses undergo alteration, since the active sense is a motion through the body in the course of which the sense is affected in a certain way. We see, then, that the ani-

---

[2] i. e. the thing pulling and the thing pulled. The second motion is the natural resistance of the thing pulled, which seeks to disconnect itself from that which is pulling it.

mate is capable of every kind of alteration of which the inanimate
is capable: but the inanimate is not capable of every kind of alteration of which the animate is capable, since it is not capable of
alteration in respect of the senses: moreover the inanimate is uncon- 15
scious of being affected by alteration, whereas the animate is conscious 245ᵃ
of it, though there is nothing to prevent the animate also being unconscious of it when the process of the alteration does not concern
the senses. Since, then, the alteration of that which undergoes alteration is caused by sensible things, in every case of such alteration it
is evident that the respective extremities of that which causes and
that which undergoes alteration are adjacent. Thus the air is con- 5
tinuous with that which causes the alteration, and the body that
undergoes alteration is continuous with the air. Again, the colour is
continuous with the light and the light with the sight. And the same
is true of hearing and smelling: for the primary movent in respect
to the moved is the air. Similarly, in the case of tasting, the flavour
is adjacent to the sense of taste. And it is just the same in the case 10
of things that are inanimate and incapable of sense-perception. Thus
there can be nothing intermediate between that which undergoes
and that which causes alteration.

Nor, again, can there be anything intermediate between that which
suffers and that which causes increase: for the part of the latter that
starts the increase does so by becoming attached in such a way to
the former that the whole becomes one. Again, the decrease of that
which suffers decrease is caused by a part of the thing becoming
detached. So that which causes increase and that which causes de- 15
crease must be continuous with that which suffers increase and
that which suffers decrease respectively: and if two things are continuous with one another there can be nothing intermediate between
them.

It is evident, therefore, that between the extremities of the moved
and the movent that are respectively first and last in reference to the 245ᵇ
moved there is nothing intermediate.

3   Everything, we say, that undergoes alteration is altered by sensible causes, and there is alteration only in things that are said to
be essentially affected by sensible things. The truth of this is to be
seen from the following considerations. Of all other things it would 5
be most natural to suppose that there is alteration in figures and
shapes, and in acquired states and in the processes of acquiring and
losing these: but as a matter of fact in neither of these two classes
of things is there alteration.

In the first place, when a particular formation of a thing is com-
10 pleted, we do not call it by the name of its material: e. g. we do not
call the statue 'bronze' or the pyramid [3] 'wax' or the bed 'wood', but
we use a derived expression and call them 'of bronze', 'waxen', and
'wooden' respectively. But when a thing has been affected and
altered in any way we still call it by the original name: thus we
speak of the bronze or the wax being dry or fluid or hard or hot.
15 And not only so: we also speak of the particular fluid or hot substance as being bronze, giving the material the same name as that
which we use to describe the affection.
246ᵃ   Since, therefore, having regard to the figure or shape of a thing
we no longer call that which has become of a certain figure by the
name of the material that exhibits the figure, whereas having regard
to a thing's affections or alterations we still call it by the name of its
material, it is evident that becomings of the former kind cannot be
alterations.

Moreover it would seem absurd even to speak in *this* way, to speak,
5 that is to say, of a man or house or anything else that has come into
existence as having been altered. Though it may be true that every
such becoming is necessarily the result of something's being altered,
the result, e. g. of the material's being condensed or rarefied or heated
or cooled, nevertheless it is not the things that are coming into
existence that are altered, and their becoming is not an alteration.
10   Again, acquired states, whether of the body or of the soul, are not
alterations. For some are excellences and others are defects, and
neither excellence nor defect is an alteration: excellence is a perfection (for when anything acquires its proper excellence we call it per-
15 fect, since it is then if ever that we have a thing in its natural state:
e. g. we have a perfect circle when we have one as good as possible),
while defect is a perishing of or departure from this condition. So
just as when speaking of a house we do not call its arrival at perfection an alteration (for it would be absurd to suppose that the
20 coping or the tiling is an alteration or that in receiving its coping
or its tiling a house is altered and not perfected), the same also
holds good in the case of excellences and defects and of the persons
246ᵇ or things that possess or acquire them: for excellences are perfections of a thing's nature and defects are departures from it: consequently they are not alterations.

Further, we say that all excellences depend upon particular relations. Thus bodily excellences such as health and a good state of body
5 we regard as consisting in a blending of hot and cold elements within

3 *sc.* candle.

the body in due proportion, in relation either to one another or to the surrounding atmosphere: and in like manner we regard beauty, strength, and all the other bodily excellences and defects. Each of them exists in virtue of a particular relation and puts that which possesses it in a good or bad condition with regard to its proper affections, where by 'proper' affections I mean those influences that from the natural constitution of a thing tend to promote or destroy its existence. Since, then, relatives are neither themselves alterations 10 nor the subjects of alteration or of becoming or in fact of any change whatever, it is evident that neither states nor the processes of losing and acquiring states are alterations, though it may be true that their becoming or perishing is necessarily, like the becoming or 15 perishing of a specific character or form, the result of the alteration of certain other things, e. g. hot and cold or dry and wet elements or the elements, whatever they may be, on which the states primarily depend. For each several bodily defect or excellence involves a relation with those things from which the possessor of the defect or excellence is naturally subject to alteration: thus excellence disposes its possessor to be unaffected by these influences or to be affected by those of them that ought to be admitted, while defect disposes its possessor to be affected by them or to be unaffected by those of them that ought to be admitted.

And the case is similar in regard to the states of the soul, all of 20 which (like those of body) exist in virtue of particular relations, the 247ᵃ excellences being perfections of nature and the defects departures from it: moreover, excellence puts its possessor in good condition, while defect puts its possessor in a bad condition, to meet his proper affections. Consequently these cannot any more than the bodily states 5 be alterations, nor can the processes of losing and acquiring them be so, though their becoming is necessarily the result of an alteration of the sensitive part of the soul, and this is altered by sensible objects: for all moral excellence is concerned with bodily pleasures and pains, which again depend either upon acting or upon remembering or upon anticipating. Now those that depend upon action are determined by sense-perception, i. e. they are stimulated by something 10 sensible: and those that depend upon memory or anticipation are likewise to be traced to sense-perception, for in these cases pleasure is felt either in remembering what one has experienced or in anticipating what one is going to experience. Thus all pleasure of this kind must be produced by sensible things: and since the presence in any one of moral defect or excellence involves the presence in him of pleasure or pain (with which moral excellence and defect are always 15 concerned), and these pleasures and pains are alterations of the sensitive part, it is evident that the loss and acquisition of these states no less than the loss and acquisition of the states of the body must be the result of the alteration of something else. Consequently, though their becoming is accompanied by an alteration, they are not themselves alterations.

247^b   Again, the states of the intellectual part of the soul are not alterations, nor is there any becoming of them. In the first place it is much more true of the possession of knowledge that it depends upon a particular relation. And further, it is evident that there is no becoming of these states. For that which is potentially possessed of knowledge becomes actually possessed of it not by being set in motion at all
5   itself but by reason of the presence of something else: i. e. it is when it meets with the particular object that it knows in a manner the particular through its knowledge of the universal. (Again, there is no becoming of the actual use and activity of these states, unless it is thought that there is a becoming of vision and touching and that the activity in question is similar to these.) And the original acquisi-
10 tion of knowledge is not a becoming or an alteration: for the terms 'knowing' and 'understanding' imply that the intellect has reached a state of rest and come to a standstill,[4] and there is no becoming that leads to a state of rest, since, as we have said above,[5] no change at all can have a becoming. Moreover, just as to say, when any one has passed from a state of intoxication or sleep or disease to the con-
15 trary state, that he has become possessed of knowledge again is incorrect in spite of the fact that he was previously incapable of using his knowledge, so, too, when any one originally acquires the state, it is incorrect to say that he becomes possessed of knowledge: for the possession of understanding and knowledge is produced by the soul's settling down[6] out of the restlessness natural to it. Hence, too, in learning and in forming judgements on matters relating to their sense-
248^a perceptions children are inferior to adults owing to the great amount of restlessness and motion in their souls. Nature itself causes the soul to settle down and come to a state of rest for the performance of some of its functions, while for the performance of others other things do so: but in either case the result is brought about through the alteration of something in the body, as we see in the case of the use and
5   activity of the intellect arising from a man's becoming sober or being

---

[4] The etymological connexion between *episteme* and *stenai* can hardly be adequately given in translation.

[5] v. 2. 225^b 15 sqq.

[6] The same etymological connexion is here present to Aristotle's mind as that noted above.

awakened. It is evident, then, from the preceding argument that alteration and being altered occur in sensible things and in the sensitive
part of the soul and, except accidentally, in nothing else.

4   A difficulty may be raised as to whether every motion is com- 10
mensurable with every other or not. Now if they are all commensurable and if two things to have the same velocity must accomplish
an equal motion in an equal time, then we may have a circumference
equal to a straight line, or, of course, the one may be greater or less
than the other. Further, if one thing alters and another accomplishes
a locomotion in an equal time, we may have an alteration and a locomotion equal to one another: thus an affection will be equal to a length, 15
which is impossible. But is it not only when an equal motion is
accomplished by two things in an equal time that the velocities of
the two are equal? Now an affection cannot be equal to a length.
Therefore there cannot be an alteration equal to or less than a locomotion: and consequently it is not the case that every motion is
commensurable with every other.

But how will our conclusion work out in the case of the circle and
the straight line? It would be absurd to suppose that the motion of
one thing in a circle and of another in a straight line cannot be simi- 20
lar, but that the one must inevitably move more quickly or more
slowly than the other, just as if the course of one were downhill and
of the other uphill. Moreover it does not as a matter of fact make
any difference to the argument to say that the one motion must inevitably be quicker or slower than the other: for then the circumference can be greater or less than the straight line; and if so it is
possible for the two to be equal. For if in the time A the quicker (B) 25
passes over the distance B′ and the slower (C) passes over the distance C′, B′ will be greater than C′: for this is what we [7] took 248ᵇ
'quicker' to mean: and so quicker motion also implies that one thing
traverses an equal distance in less time than another: consequently
there will be a part of A in which B will pass over a part of the circle
equal to C′, while C will occupy the whole of A in passing over C′.
None the less, if the two motions are commensurable, we are con- 5
fronted with the consequence stated above, viz. that there may be a
straight line equal to a circle. But these are not commensurable: and
so the corresponding motions are not commensurable either.

But may we say that things are always commensurable if the same
terms are applied to them without equivocation? e. g. a pen, a wine,
and the highest note in a scale are not commensurable: we cannot say

[7] vi. 2. 232ᵃ 25 sqq.

whether any one of them is sharper than any other: and why is this? they are incommensurable because it is only equivocally that the same term 'sharp' is applied to them: whereas the highest note in a scale is commensurable with the leading-note, because the term
10 'sharp' has the same meaning as applied to both. Can it be, then, that the term 'quick' has not the same meaning as applied to straight motion and to circular motion respectively? If so, far less will it have the same meaning as applied to alteration and to locomotion.

Or shall we in the first place deny that things are always commensurable if the same terms are applied to them without equivocation? For the term 'much' has the same meaning whether applied to water or to air, yet water and air are not commensurable in respect of it: or, if this illustration is not considered satisfactory, 'double' at any rate would seem to have the same meaning as applied to each (denoting in each case the proportion of two to one), yet water and air are not commensurable in respect of it. But here again may we
15 not take up the same position and say that the term 'much' is equivocal? In fact there are some terms of which even the definitions are equivocal; e. g. if 'much' were defined as 'so much and more', 'so much' would mean something different in different cases: 'equal' is similarly equivocal; and 'one' again is perhaps inevitably an equivo-
20 cal term; and if 'one' is equivocal, so is 'two'. Otherwise why is it that some things are commensurable while others are not, if the nature of the attribute in the two cases is really one and the same?

Can it be that the incommensurability of two things in respect of any attribute is due to a difference in that which is primarily capable of carrying the attribute? Thus horse and dog are so commensurable that we may say which is the whiter, since that which primarily contains the whiteness is the same in both, viz. the surface: and similarly they are commensurable in respect of size. But water and speech are not commensurable in respect of clearness, since that which primarily contains the attribute is different in the two cases.
25 It would seem, however, that we must reject this solution, since clearly we could thus make all equivocal attributes univocal and say merely that that which contains each of them is different in different cases:
249ª thus 'equality', 'sweetness', and 'whiteness'' will severally always be the same, though that which contains them is different in different cases. Moreover, it is not any casual thing that is capable of carrying any attribute: each single attribute can be carried primarily only by one single thing.

Must we then say that, if two things are to be commensurable in respect of any attribute, not only must the attribute in question be

applicable to both without equivocation, but there must also be no
specific differences either in the attribute itself or in that which contains the attribute—that these, I mean, must not be divisible in the 5
way in which colour is divided into kinds? Thus in this respect one
thing will not be commensurable with another, i. e. we cannot say
that one is more coloured than the other where only colour in general
and not any particular colour is meant; but they are commensurable
in respect of whiteness.

Similarly in the case of motion: two things are of the same velocity
if they occupy an equal time in accomplishing a certain equal amount
of motion. Suppose, then, that in a certain time an alteration is undergone by one half of a body's length and a locomotion is accomplished
by the other half: can we say that in this case the alteration is equal 10
to the locomotion and of the same velocity? That would be absurd,
and the reason is that there are different species of motion. And if in
consequence of this we must say that two things are of equal velocity
if they accomplish locomotion over an equal distance in an equal time,
we have to admit the equality of a straight line and a circumference.
What, then, is the reason of this? Is it that locomotion is a genus or
that line is a genus? (We may leave the time out of account, since 15
that is one and the same.) If the lines are specifically different, the
locomotions also differ specifically from one another: for locomotion is
specifically differentiated according to the specific differentiation of
that over which it takes place. (It is also similarly differentiated, it
would seem, accordingly as the instrument of the locomotion is different: thus if feet are the instrument, it is walking, if wings it is flying;
but perhaps we should rather say that this is not so, and that in this
case the differences in the locomotion are merely differences of posture in that which is in motion.) We may say, therefore, that things
are of equal velocity if in an equal time they traverse the same mag- 20
nitude: and when I call it 'the same' I mean that it contains no specific
difference and therefore no difference in the motion that takes place
over it. So we have now to consider how motion is differentiated: and
this discussion serves to show that the genus is not a unity but contains a plurality latent in it and distinct from it, and that in the case
of equivocal terms sometimes the different senses in which they are
used are far removed from one another, while sometimes there is a
certain likeness between them, and sometimes again they are nearly
related either generically or analogically, with the result that they
seem not to be equivocal though they really are.

When, then, is there a difference of species? Is an attribute specifi- 25
cally different if the subject is different while the attribute is the

same, or must the attribute itself be different as well? And how are we to define the limits of a species? What will enable us to decide that particular instances of whiteness or sweetness are the same or different? Is it enough that it appears different in one subject from what it appears in another? Or must there be no sameness at all? And further, where alteration is in question, how is one alteration to be of equal velocity with another? One person may be cured quickly and
30 another slowly, and cures may also be simultaneous: so that, recovery of health being an alteration, we have here alterations of equal
249ᵇ velocity, since each alteration occupies an equal time. But what alteration? We cannot here speak of an 'equal' alteration: what corresponds in the category of quality to equality in the category of quantity is 'likeness'. However, let us say that there is equal velocity
5 where *the same* change is accomplished in an equal time. Are we, then, to find the commensurability in the subject of the affection or in the affection itself? In the case that we have just been considering it is the fact that health is one and the same that enables us to arrive at the conclusion that the one alteration is neither more nor less than the other, but that both are alike. If on the other hand the affection is different in the two cases, e. g. when the alterations take the form of becoming white and becoming healthy respectively, here there is no sameness or equality or likeness inasmuch as the difference in the
10 affections at once makes the alterations specifically different, and there is no unity of alteration any more than there would be unity of locomotion under like conditions.⁸ So we must find out how many species there are of alteration and of locomotion respectively. Now if the things that are in motion—that is to say, the things to which the motions belong essentially and not accidentally—differ specifically, then their respective motions will also differ specifically: if on the other hand they differ generically or numerically, the motions also will differ generically or numerically as the case may be. But there still
15 remains the question whether, supposing that two alterations are of equal velocity, we ought to look for this equality in the sameness (or likeness) of the affections, or in the things altered, to see e. g. whether a certain quantity of each has become white. Or ought we not rather to look for it in both? That is to say, the alterations are the same or different according as the affections are the same or different, while they are equal or unequal according as the things altered are equal or unequal.

And now we must consider the same question in the case of becom-
20 ing and perishing: how is one becoming of equal velocity with an-

⁸ *sc.* if there are two locomotions of different species.

other? They are of equal velocity if in an equal time there are produced two things that are the same and specifically inseparable,
e. g. two men (not merely generically inseparable as e. g. two animals). Similarly one is quicker than the other if in an equal time the
product is different in the two cases. I state it thus because we have
no pair of terms that will convey this 'difference' in the way in which
unlikeness is conveyed. If we adopt the theory that it is number that
constitutes being, we may indeed speak of a 'greater number' and a
'lesser number' within the same species, but there is no common term
that will include both relations, nor are there terms to express each
of them separately in the same way as we indicate a higher degree or 25
preponderance of an affection by 'more', of a quantity by 'greater'.

5   Now since wherever there is a movent, its motion always acts
upon something, is always in something, and always extends to something (by 'is always in something' I mean that it occupies a time:
and by 'extends to something' I mean that it involves the traversing
of a certain amount of distance: for at any moment when a thing is
causing motion, it also has caused motion, so that there must always
be a certain amount of distance that has been traversed and a certain
amount of time that has been occupied). If, then, A the movent have 30
moved B a distance C in a time D, then in the same time the same 250ᵃ
force A will move ½ B twice the distance C, and in ½ D it will
move ½ B the whole distance C: for thus the rules of proportion will
be observed. Again if a given force move a given weight a certain distance in a certain time and half the distance in half the time, half the 5
motive power will move half the weight the same distance in the same
time. Let E represent half the motive power A and F half the weight
B: then the ratio between the motive power and the weight in the one
case is similar and proportionate to the ratio in the other, so that
each force will cause the same distance to be traversed in the same
time.

But if E move F a distance C in a time D, it does not necessarily 10
follow that E can move twice F half the distance C in the same time.
If, then, A move B a distance C in a time D, it does not follow that E,
being half of A, will in the time D or in any fraction of it cause B
to traverse a part of C the ratio between which and the whole of C is
proportionate to that between A and E (whatever fraction of A E may
be): in fact it might well be that it will cause no motion at all; for it 15
does not follow that, if a given motive power causes a certain amount
of motion, half that power will cause motion either of any particular
amount or in any length of time: otherwise one man might move a

ship, since both the motive power of the shiphaulers and the distance
that they all cause the ship to traverse are divisible into as many
20 parts as there are men. Hence Zeno's reasoning is false when he
argues that there is no part of the millet that does not make a sound:
for there is no reason why any such part should not in any length of
time fail to move the air that the whole bushel moves in falling. In
fact it does not of itself move even such a quantity of the air as it
would move if this part were by itself: for no part even exists otherwise than potentially.

25 If on the other hand we have two forces each of which separately
moves one of two weights a given distance in a given time, then the
forces in combination will move the combined weights an equal distance in an equal time: for in this case the rules of proportion apply.

Then does this hold good of alteration and of increase also?
Surely it does, for in any given case we have a definite thing that
30 causes increase and a definite thing that suffers increase, and the one
causes and the other suffers a certain amount of increase in a certain
amount of time. Similarly we have a definite thing that causes alteration and a definite thing that undergoes alteration, and a certain amount, or rather degree, of alteration is completed in a certain
250ᵇ amount of time: thus in twice as much time twice as much alteration
will be completed and conversely twice as much alteration will occupy
twice as much time: and the alteration of half of its object will occupy
half as much time and in half as much time half of the object will
be altered: or again, in the same amount of time it will be altered
twice as much.

On the other hand if that which causes alteration or increase causes
a certain amount of increase or alteration respectively in a certain
5 amount of time, it does not necessarily follow that half the force will
occupy twice the time in altering or increasing the object, or that in
twice the time the alteration or increase will be completed by it: it
may happen that there will be no alteration or increase at all, the
case being the same as with the weight.

BOOK VIII

11 1 It remains to consider the following question. Was there ever a
becoming of motion before which it had no being, and is it perishing
again so as to leave nothing in motion? Or are we to say that it never
had any becoming and is not perishing, but always was and always
will be? Is it in fact an immortal never-failing property of things that
are, a sort of life as it were to all naturally constituted things?

Now the *existence* of motion is asserted by all who have anything 15
to say about nature, because they all concern themselves with the
construction of the world and study the question of becoming and perishing, which processes could not come about without the existence of
motion. But those who say that there is an infinite number of worlds,
some of which are in process of becoming while others are in process
of perishing, assert that there is always motion (for these processes of 20
becoming and perishing of the worlds necessarily involve motion),
whereas those who hold that there is only one world, whether everlasting or not, make corresponding assumptions in regard to motion.
If then it is possible that at any time nothing should be in motion,
this must come about in one of two ways: either in the manner described by Anaxagoras, who says that all things were together and at 25
rest for an infinite period of time, and that then Mind introduced
motion and separated them; or in the manner described by Empedocles, according to whom the universe is alternately in motion and at
rest—in motion, when Love is making the one out of many, or Strife
is making many out of one, and at rest in the intermediate periods of
time—his account being as follows:

> 'Since One hath learned to spring from Manifold,   30
> And One disjoined makes Manifold arise,
> Thus they Become, nor stable is their life: 251ᵃ
> But since their motion must alternate be,
> Thus have they ever Rest upon their round':

for we must suppose that he means by this that they alternate from
the one motion to the other. We must consider, then, how this matter 5
stands, for the discovery of the truth about it is of importance, not
only for the study of nature, but also for the investigation of the
First Principle.

Let us take our start from what we have already [1] laid down in our
course on Physics. Motion, we say, is the fulfilment of the movable
in so far as it is movable. Each kind of motion, therefore, necessarily 10
involves the presence of the things that are capable of that motion.
In fact, even apart from the definition of motion, every one would
admit that in each kind of motion it is that which is capable of that
motion that is in motion: thus it is that which is capable of alteration
that is altered, and that which is capable of local change that is in 15
locomotion: and so there must be something capable of being burned
before there can be a process of being burned, and something capable
of burning before there can be a process of burning. Moreover, these

---

[1] iii. 1.

things also must either have a beginning before which they had no being, or they must be eternal. Now if there was a becoming of every movable thing, it follows that before the motion in question another change or motion must have taken place in which that which was capable of being moved or of causing motion had its becoming. To suppose, on the other hand, that these things were in being throughout all previous time without there being any motion appears unreasonable on a moment's thought, and still more unreasonable, we shall find, on further consideration. For if we are to say that, while there are on the one hand things that are movable, and on the other hand things that are motive, there is a time when there is a first movent and a first moved, and another time when there is no such thing but only something that is at rest, then this thing that is at rest must previously have been in process of change: for there must have been some cause of its rest, rest being the privation of motion. Therefore, before this first change there will be a previous change. For some things cause motion in only one way, while others can produce either of two contrary motions: thus fire causes heating but not cooling, whereas it would seem that knowledge may be directed to two contrary ends while remaining one and the same. Even in the former class, however, there seems to be something similar, for a cold thing in a sense causes heating by turning away and retiring, just as one possessed of knowledge voluntarily makes an error when he uses his knowledge in the reverse way.[2] But at any rate all things that are capable respectively of affecting and being affected, or of causing motion and being moved, are capable of it not under all conditions, but only when they are in a particular condition and approach one another: so it is on the approach of one thing to another that the one causes motion and the other is moved, and when they are present under such conditions as rendered the one motive and the other movable. So if the motion was not always in process, it is clear that they must have been in a condition not such as to render them capable respectively of being moved and of causing motion, and one or other of them must have been in process of change: for in what is relative this is a necessary consequence: e. g. if one thing is double another when before it was not so, one or other of them, if not both, must have been in process of change. It follows, then, that there will be a process of change previous to the first.

(Further, how can there be any 'before' and 'after' without the existence of time? Or how can there be any time without the exist-

---

[2] i. e. by means of his knowledge he can be sure of giving a wrong opinion and thus deceiving some one.

ence of motion? If, then, time is the number of motion or itself a kind
of motion, it follows that, if there is always time, motion must also be
eternal. But so far as time is concerned we see that all with one exception are in agreement in saying that it is uncreated: in fact, it is just
this that enables Democritus to show that all things cannot have had 15
a becoming: for time, he says, is uncreated. Plato alone asserts the
creation of time, saying ³ that it had a becoming together with the
universe, the universe according to him having had a becoming. Now
since time cannot exist and is unthinkable apart from the moment,
and the moment is a kind of middle-point, uniting as it does in itself 20
both a beginning and an end, a beginning of future time and an end
of past time, it follows that there must always be time: for the
extremity of the last period of time that we take must be found in
some moment, since time contains no point of contact for us except
the moment. Therefore, since the moment is both a beginning and an 25
end, there must always be time on both sides of it. But if this is true
of time, it is evident that it must also be true of motion, time being a
kind of affection of motion.)

The same reasoning will also serve to show the imperishability of
motion: just as a becoming of motion would involve, as we saw, the 30
existence of a process of change previous to the first, in the same way
a perishing of motion would involve the existence of a process of
change subsequent to the last: for when a thing ceases to be moved, it
does not therefore at the same time cease to be movable—e. g. the
cessation of the process of being burned does not involve the cessation
of the capacity of being burned, since a thing may be capable of
being burned without being in process of being burned—nor, when a
thing ceases to be movent, does it therefore at the same time cease to
be motive. Again, the destructive agent will have to be destroyed, after 252ᵃ
what it destroys has been destroyed, and then that which has the
capacity of destroying *it* will have to be destroyed afterwards, (so
that there will be a process of change subsequent to the last,) for
being destroyed also is a kind of change. If, then, the view which we
are criticizing involves these impossible consequences, it is clear that
motion is eternal and cannot have existed at one time and not at
another: in fact, such a view can hardly be described as anything
else than fantastic.

And much the same may be said of the view that such is the ordi- 5
nance of nature and that this must be regarded as a principle, as
would seem to be the view of Empedocles when he says that the constitution of the world is of necessity such that Love and Strife alter-

³ Aristotle is thinking of a passage in the *Timaeus* (38 ʙ).

nately predominate and cause motion, while in the intermediate period
10 of time there is a state of rest. Probably also those who, like Anaxagoras, assert a single principle (of motion) would hold this view. But
that which is produced or directed by nature can never be anything
disorderly: for nature is everywhere the cause of order. Moreover,
there is no ratio in the relation of the infinite to the infinite, whereas
order always means ratio. But if we say that there is first a state of
rest for an infinite time, and then motion is started at some moment,
15 and that the fact that it is this rather than a previous moment is of
no importance, and involves no order, then we can no longer say that
it is nature's work: for if anything is of a certain character *naturally*, it either is so invariably and is not sometimes of this and sometimes of another character (e. g. fire, which travels upwards naturally,
does not sometimes do so and sometimes not) or there is a ratio in
20 the variation. It would be better, therefore, to say with Empedocles
and any one else who may have maintained such a theory as his that
the universe is alternately at rest and in motion: for in a system of
this kind we have at once a certain order. But even here the holder
of the theory ought not only to assert the fact: he ought also to
explain the cause of it: i. e. he should not make any mere assumption
or lay down any gratuitous axiom, but should employ either induc-
25 tive or demonstrative reasoning. The Love and Strife postulated by
Empedocles are not in themselves causes of the fact in question, nor
is it of the essence of either that it should be so, the essential function
of the former being to unite, of the latter to separate. If he is to go
on to explain this alternate predominance, he should adduce cases
where such a state of things exists, as he points to the fact that
among mankind we have something that unites men, namely Love,
30 while on the other hand enemies avoid one another: thus from the
observed fact that this occurs in certain cases comes the assumption that it occurs also in the universe. Then, again, some argument is
needed to explain why the predominance of each of the two forces
lasts for an equal period of time. But it is a wrong assumption to
suppose universally that we have an adequate first principle in virtue
of the fact that something always is so or always happens so. Thus
Democritus reduces the causes that explain nature to the fact that
things happened in the past in the same way as they happen now:
35 but he does not think fit to seek for a first principle to explain this
252ᵇ 'always': so, while his theory is right in so far as it is applied to
certain individual cases, he is wrong in making it of universal application. Thus, a triangle always has its angles equal to two right angles,
but there is nevertheless an ulterior cause of the eternity of this truth,

whereas first principles are eternal and have no ulterior cause. Let
this conclude what we have to say in support of our contention that 5
there never was a time when there was not motion, and never will be a
time when there will not be motion.

2   The arguments that may be advanced against this position are not
difficult to dispose of. The chief considerations that might be thought
to indicate that motion may exist though at one time it had not existed at all are the following:

First, it may be said that no process of change is eternal: for the
nature of all change is such that it proceeds *from* something *to* some- 10
thing, so that every process of change must be bounded by the contraries that mark its course, and no motion can go on to infinity.

Secondly, we see that a thing that neither is in motion nor contains
any motion within itself can be set in motion; e. g. inanimate things
that are (whether the whole or some part is in question) not in motion
but at rest, are at some moment set in motion: whereas, if motion 15
cannot have a becoming before which it had no being, these things
ought to be either always or never in motion.

Thirdly, the fact is evident above all in the case of animate beings:
for it sometimes happens that there is no motion in us and we are
quite still, and that nevertheless we are then at some moment set in
motion, that is to say it sometimes happens that we produce a beginning of motion in ourselves spontaneously without anything having 20
set us in motion from without. We see nothing like this in the case of
inanimate things, which are always set in motion by something else
from without: the animal, on the other hand, we say, moves itself:
therefore, if an animal is ever in a state of absolute rest, we have a
motionless thing in which motion can be produced from the thing
itself, and not from without. Now if this can occur in an animal, why
should not the same be true also of the universe as a whole? If it can 25
occur in a small world it could also occur in a great one: and if it
can occur in the world, it could also occur in the infinite; that is, if
the infinite could as a whole possibly be in motion or at rest.

Of these objections, then, the first-mentioned—that motion to
opposites is not always the same and numerically one—is a correct 30
statement; in fact, this may be said to be a necessary conclusion,
provided that it is possible for the motion of that which is one and
the same to be not always one and the same. (I mean that e. g. we
may question whether the note given by a single string is one and the
same, or is different each time the string is struck, although the string
is in the same condition and is moved in the same way.) But still,

³⁵ however this may be, there is nothing to prevent there being a motion
253ᵃ that is the same in virtue of being continuous and eternal: we shall
have something to say later ⁴ that will make this point clearer.

As regards the second objection, no absurdity is involved in the
fact that something not in motion may be set in motion, that which
caused the motion from without being at one time present, and at
another absent. Nevertheless, how this can be so remains matter for
inquiry; how it comes about, I mean, that the same motive force at
one time causes a thing to be in motion, and at another does not do
⁵ so: for the difficulty raised by our objector really amounts to this—
why is it that some things are not always at rest, and the rest always
in motion?

The third objection may be thought to present more difficulty
than the others, namely, that which alleges that motion arises in
things in which it did not exist before, and adduces in proof the case
¹⁰ of animate things: thus an animal is first at rest and afterwards
walks, not having been set in motion apparently by anything from
without. This, however, is false: for we observe that there is always
some part of the animal's organism in motion, and the cause of the
motion of this part is not the animal itself, but, it may be, its environment. Moreover, we say that the animal itself originates not all of its
¹⁵ motions but its locomotion. So it may well be the case—or rather we
may perhaps say that it must necessarily be the case—that many
motions are produced in the body by its environment, and some of
these set in motion the intellect or the appetite, and this again then
sets the whole animal in motion: this is what happens when animals
are asleep: though there is then no perceptive motion in them, there
²⁰ is some motion that causes them to wake up again. But we will leave
this point also to be elucidated at a later ⁵ stage in our discussion.

3   Our enquiry will resolve itself at the outset into a consideration
of the above-mentioned problem—what can be the reason why some
things in the world at one time are in motion and at another are at
rest again? Now one of three things must be true: either all things
²⁵ are always at rest, or all things are always in motion, or some things
are in motion and others at rest: and in this last case again either the
things that are in motion are always in motion and the things that are
at rest are always at rest, or they are all constituted so as to be
capable alike of motion and of rest; or there is yet a third possibility
remaining—it may be that some things in the world are always motionless, others always in motion, while others again admit of both

⁴ Chapter 8.   ⁵ Chapter 6.

conditions. This last is the account of the matter that we must give: 30
for herein lies the solution of all the difficulties raised and the conclusion of the investigation upon which we are engaged.

To maintain that all things are at rest, and to disregard sense-
perception in an attempt to show the theory to be reasonable, would
be an instance of intellectual weakness: it would call in question a
whole system, not a particular detail: moreover, it would be an attack 35
not only on the physicist but on almost all sciences and all received
opinions, since motion plays a part in all of them. Further, just as in 253ᵇ
arguments about mathematics objections that involve first principles
do not affect the mathematician—and the other sciences are in similar
case—so, too, objections involving the point that we have just raised
do not affect the physicist: for it is a fundamental assumption with 5
him that motion is ultimately referable to nature herself.

The assertion that all things are in motion we may fairly regard as
equally false, though it is less subversive of physical science: for
though in our course on physics ⁶ it was laid down that rest no less
than motion is ultimately referable to nature herself, nevertheless
motion is the characteristic fact of nature: moreover, the view is actually held by some that not merely some things but all things in the 10
world are in motion and always in motion, though we cannot apprehend the fact by sense-perception. Although the supporters of this
theory do not state clearly what kind of motion they mean, or whether
they mean all kinds, it is no hard matter to reply to them: thus we
may point out that there cannot be a continuous process either of
increase or of decrease: that which comes between the two has to be
included. The theory resembles that about the stone being worn 15
away by the drop of water or split by plants growing out of it: if so
much has been extruded or removed by the drop, it does not follow
that half the amount has previously been extruded or removed in half
the time: the case of the hauled ship is exactly comparable: here we
have so many drops setting so much in motion, but a part of them will
not set as much in motion in any period of time. The amount removed
is, it is true, divisible into a number of parts, but no one of these was 20
set in motion separately: they were all set in motion together. It is
evident, then, that from the fact that the decrease is divisible into
an infinite number of parts it does not follow that some part must
always be passing away: it all passes away at a particular moment.
Similarly, too, in the case of any alteration whatever if that which
suffers alteration is infinitely divisible it does not follow from this that
the same is true of the alteration itself, which often occurs all at once, 25

⁶ ii. 1. 192ᵇ 21.

as in freezing. Again, when any one has fallen ill, there must follow a period of time in which his restoration to health is in the future: the process of change cannot take place in an instant: yet the change cannot be a change to anything else but health. The assertion, therefore, that alteration is continuous is an extravagant calling into ques-
30 tion of the obvious: for alteration is a change from one contrary to another. Moreover, we notice that a stone becomes neither harder nor softer. Again, in the matter of locomotion, it would be a strange thing if a stone could be falling or resting on the ground without our being able to perceive the fact. Further, it is a law of nature that earth and all other bodies should remain in their proper places and be moved
35 from them only by violence: from the fact then that some of them are in their proper places it follows that in respect of place also all
254ᵃ things cannot be in motion. These and other similar arguments, then, should convince us that it is impossible either that all things are always in motion or that all things are always at rest.

Nor again can it be that some things are always at rest, others always in motion, and nothing sometimes at rest and sometimes in
5 motion. This theory must be pronounced impossible on the same grounds as those previously mentioned: viz. that we see the above-mentioned changes occurring in the case of the same things. We may further point out that the defender of this position is fighting against the obvious, for on this theory there can be no such thing as increase: nor can there be any such thing as compulsory motion, if it is
10 impossible that a thing can be at rest before being set in motion unnaturally. This theory, then, does away with becoming and perishing. Moreover, motion, it would seem, is generally thought to be a sort of becoming and perishing, for that to which a thing changes comes to be, or occupancy of it comes to be, and that from which a thing changes ceases to be, or there ceases to be occupancy of it. It is clear, therefore, that there are cases of occasional motion and occasional rest.
15 We have now to take the assertion that all things are sometimes at rest and sometimes in motion and to confront it with the arguments previously advanced. We must take our start as before from the possibilities that we distinguished just above. Either all things are at rest, or all things are in motion, or some things are at rest and others in motion. And if some things are at rest and others in motion, then it
20 must be that either all things are sometimes at rest and sometimes in motion, or some things are always at rest and the remainder always in motion, or some of the things are always at rest and others always in motion while others again are sometimes at rest and sometimes in motion. Now we have said before that it is impossible that all things

should be at rest: nevertheless we may now repeat that assertion. We
may point out that, even if it is really the case, as certain persons 25
assert,[7] that the existent is infinite and motionless, it certainly does
not appear to be so if we follow sense-perception: many things that
exist appear to be in motion. Now if there is such a thing as false opinion at all, there is also motion: and similarly if there is such a thing
as imagination, or if it is the case that anything seems to be different
at different times: for imagination and opinion are thought to be
motions of a kind.[8] But to investigate this question at all—to see a 30
reasoned justification of a belief with regard to which we are too well
off to require reasoned justification—implies bad judgment of what
is better and what is worse, what commends itself to belief and what
does not, what is ultimate and what is not. It is likewise impossible
that all things should be in motion or that some things should be
always in motion and the remainder always at rest. We have sufficient 35
ground for rejecting all these theories in the single fact that we *see*
some things that are sometimes in motion and sometimes at rest. It 254[b]
is evident, therefore, that it is no less impossible that some things
should be always in motion and the remainder always at rest than
that all things should be at rest or that all things should be in motion
continuously. It remains, then, to consider whether all things are so
constituted as to be capable both of being in motion and of being at
rest, or whether, while some things are so constituted, some are always 5
at rest and some are always in motion: for it is this last view that we
have to show to be true.

4　Now of things that cause motion or suffer motion, to some the
motion is accidental, to others essential: thus it is accidental to
what merely belongs to or contains as a part a thing that causes
motion or suffers motion, essential to a thing that causes motion or 10
suffers motion not merely by belonging to such a thing or containing
it as a part.

Of things to which the motion is essential some derive their motion
from themselves, others from something else: and in some cases their
motion is natural, in others violent and unnatural. Thus in things that
derive their motion from themselves, e. g. all animals, the motion is 15
natural (for when an animal is in motion its motion is derived from
itself): and whenever the source of the motion of a thing is in the
thing itself we say that the motion of that thing is natural. Therefore
the animal as a whole moves itself naturally: but the body of the
animal may be in motion unnaturally as well as naturally: it depends

[7] Melissus is meant; cf. 185[a] 32.　　　[8] Cf. *De An.* iii. 3. 428[b] 11.

upon the kind of motion that it may chance to be suffering and the
20 kind of element [9] of which it is composed. And the motion of things
that derive their motion from something else is in some cases natural,
in others unnatural: e. g. upward motion of earthy things and downward motion of fire are unnatural. Moreover the parts of animals are
often in motion in an unnatural way, their positions and the character
of the motion being abnormal. The fact that a thing that is in motion
25 derives its motion from something is most evident in things that are
in motion unnaturally, because in such cases it is clear that the
motion is derived from something other than the thing itself. Next
to things that are in motion unnaturally those whose motion while
natural is derived from themselves—e. g. animals—make this fact
clear: for here the uncertainty is not as to whether the motion is derived from something but as to how we ought to distinguish in the
30 thing between the movent and the moved. It would seem that in animals, just as in ships and things not naturally organized, that which
causes motion is separate from that which suffers motion, and that it
is only in this sense that the animal as a whole causes its own motion.

The greatest difficulty, however, is presented by the remaining
case of those that we last distinguished. Where things derive their
35 motion from something else we distinguished the cases in which the
motion is unnatural: we are left with those that are to be contrasted
255ᵃ with the others by reason of the fact that the motion is natural. It is
in these cases that difficulty would be experienced in deciding whence
the motion is derived, e. g. in the case of light and heavy things.
When these things are in motion to positions the reverse of those
they would properly occupy, their motion is violent: when they are in
motion to their proper positions—the light thing up and the heavy
thing down—their motion is natural; but in this latter case it is no
longer evident, as it is when the motion is unnatural, whence their
5 motion is derived. It is impossible to say that their motion is derived
from themselves: this is a characteristic of life and peculiar to living
things. Further, if it were, it would have been in their power to stop
themselves (I mean that if e. g. a thing can cause itself to walk it can
also cause itself not to walk), and so, since on this supposition fire
itself possesses the power of upward locomotion, it is clear that it
10 should also possess the power of downward locomotion. Moreover
if things move themselves, it would be unreasonable to suppose that
in only one kind of motion is their motion derived from themselves.
Again, how can anything of continuous and naturally connected sub-

---

[9] i.e. the material of which a body is composed may be so light as naturally
to have an upward tendency.

stance move itself? In so far as a thing is one and continuous not merely in virtue of contact, it is impassive: it is only in so far as a thing is divided that one part of it is by nature active and another passive. Therefore none of the things that we are now considering 15 move themselves (for they are of naturally connected substance), nor does anything else that is continuous: in each case the movent must be separate from the moved, as we see to be the case with inanimate things when an animate thing moves them. It is the fact that these things also always derive their motion from something: what it is would become evident if we were to distinguish the different kinds of cause.

The above-mentioned distinctions can also be made in the case of 20 things that cause motion: some of them are capable of causing motion unnaturally (e. g. the lever is not naturally capable of moving the weight), others naturally (e. g. what is actually hot is naturally capable of moving [10] what is potentially hot): and similarly in the case of all other things of this kind.

In the same way, too, what is potentially of a certain quality or of a certain quantity or in a certain place is naturally movable when it contains the corresponding principle in itself and not accidentally 25 (for the same thing may be both of a certain quality and of a certain quantity, but the one is an accidental, not an essential property of the other). So when fire or earth is moved by something the motion is violent when it is unnatural, and natural when it brings to actuality the proper activities [11] that they potentially possess. But the fact that 30 the term 'potentially' is used in more than one sense is the reason why it is not evident whence such motions as the upward motion of fire and the downward motion of earth are derived. One who is learning a science potentially knows it in a different sense from one who while already possessing the knowledge is not actually exercising it. Wherever we have something capable of acting and something capable of being correspondingly acted on, in the event of any such pair being in contact what is potential becomes at times actual: e. g. the learner 35 becomes from one potential something another potential something: 255ᵇ for one who possesses knowledge of a science but is not actually exercising it knows the science potentially in a sense, though not in the same sense as he knew it potentially before he learnt it. And when he is in this condition, if something does not prevent him, he actively exercises his knowledge: otherwise he would be in the contradictory state of not knowing. In regard to natural bodies also the 5

[10] i. e. causing to become hot.

[11] *sc.* upward motion and downward motion respectively.

case is similar. Thus what is cold is potentially hot: then a change takes place and it is fire, and it burns, unless something prevents and hinders it. So, too, with heavy and light: light is generated from heavy, e. g. air from water (for water is the first thing that is poten-
10 tially light), and air is actually light, and will at once realize its proper activity as such unless something prevents it. The activity of lightness consists in the light thing being in a certain situation, namely high up: when it is in the contrary situation, it is being prevented from rising. The case is similar also in regard to quantity and quality. But, be it noted, this is the question we are trying to answer —how can we account for the motion of light things and heavy things
15 to their proper situations? The reason for it is that they have a natural tendency respectively towards a certain position: and this constitutes the essence of lightness and heaviness, the former being determined by an upward, the latter by a downward, tendency. As we have said, a thing may be potentially light or heavy in more senses than one. Thus not only when a thing is water is it in a sense potentially light, but when it has become air it may be still potentially light: for it may be that through some hindrance it does not
20 occupy an upper position, whereas, if what hinders it is removed, it realizes its activity and continues to rise higher. The process whereby what is of a certain quality changes to a condition of active existence is similar: thus the exercise of knowledge follows at once upon the possession of it unless something prevents it. So, too, what is of a certain quantity extends itself over a certain space unless something prevents it. The thing in a sense is and in a sense is not moved by one who moves what is obstructing and preventing its motion
25 (e. g. one who pulls away a pillar from under a roof or one who removes a stone from a wine-skin in the water is the accidental cause of motion): [12] and in the same way the real cause of the motion of a ball rebounding from a wall is not the wall but the thrower. So it is clear that in all these cases the thing does not move itself, but it
30 contains within itself the source of motion—not of moving something or of causing motion, but of suffering it.

    If then the motion of all things that are in motion is either natural or unnatural and violent, and all things whose motion is violent and unnatural are moved by something, and something other than themselves, and again all things whose motion is natural are moved by something—both those that are moved by themselves and those that
35 are not moved by themselves (e. g. light things and heavy things,
256ª which are moved either by that which brought the thing into exist-

[12] The real cause here is the upward or downward tendency.

ence as such and made it light and heavy, or by that which released what was hindering and preventing it); then all things that are in motion must be moved by something.

5 Now this may come about in either of two ways. Either the movent is not itself responsible for the motion, which is to be referred to something else which moves the movent, or the movent is itself re- 5 sponsible for the motion. Further, in the latter case, either the movent immediately precedes the last thing in the series,[13] or there may be one or more intermediate links: e. g. the stick moves the stone and is moved by the hand, which again is moved by the man: in the man, however, we have reached a movent that is not so in virtue of being moved by something else. Now we say that the thing is moved both by the last and by the first movent in the series, but more strictly by the first, since the first movent moves the last, whereas the last does not 10 move the first, and the first will move the thing without the last, but the last will not move it without the first: e. g. the stick will not move anything unless it is itself moved by the man. If then everything that is in motion must be moved by something, and the movent must either itself be moved by something else or not, and in the former case there 15 must be some first movent that is not itself moved by anything else, while in the case of the immediate movent being of this kind there is no need of an intermediate movent that is also moved (for it is impossible that there should be an infinite series of movents, each of which is itself moved by something else, since in an infinite series there is no first term)—if then everything that is in motion is moved by something, and the first movent is moved but not by anything else, it must 20 be moved by itself.

This same argument may also be stated in another way as follows. Every movent moves something and moves it with something, either with itself or with something else: e. g. a man moves a thing either himself or with a stick, and a thing is knocked down either by the wind itself or by a stone propelled by the wind. But it is impossible for 25 that with which a thing is moved to move it without being moved by that which imparts motion by its own agency: on the other hand, if a thing imparts motion by its own agency, it is not necessary that there should be anything else with which it imparts motion, whereas if there is a different thing with which it imparts motion, there must be something that imparts motion not with something else but with itself, or else there will be an infinite series. If, then, anything is a movent while being itself moved, the series must stop somewhere and 30

13 i. e. the thing that is moved.

not be infinite. Thus, if the stick moves something in virtue of being moved by the hand, the hand moves the stick: and if something else moves with the *hand*, the hand also is moved by something different from itself. So when motion by means of an instrument is at each stage caused by something different from the instrument, this must always be preceded by something else which imparts motion with itself. Therefore, if this last movent is in motion and there is nothing

256ᵇ else that moves it, it must move itself. So this reasoning also shows that, when a thing is moved, if it is not moved immediately by something that moves itself, the series brings us at some time or other to a movent of this kind.

And if we consider the matter in yet a third way we shall get this same result as follows: If everything that is in motion is moved by
5 something that is in motion, either this being in motion is an accidental attribute of the movents in question, so that each of them moves something while being itself in motion, but not always because it is itself in motion, or it is not an accidental but an essential attribute. Let us consider the former alternative. If then it is an accidental attribute, it is not necessary that that which is in motion should be in motion: and if this is so it is clear that there may be a time when nothing that exists is in motion, since the accidental is not necessary
10 but contingent. Now if we assume the existence of a possibility, any conclusion that we thereby reach will not be an impossibility, though it may be contrary to fact. But the non-existence of motion is an impossibility: for we have shown above ¹⁴ that there must always be motion.

Moreover, the conclusion to which we have been led is a reason-
15 able one. For there must be three things—the moved, the movent, and the instrument of motion. Now the moved must be in motion, but it need not move anything else: the instrument of motion must both move something else and be itself in motion (for it changes together with the moved, with which it is in contact and continuous, as is clear in the case of things that move other things locally, in which case the two things must up to a certain point ¹⁵ be in contact): and the movent—that is to say, that which causes motion in such a manner that it is not merely the instrument of motion—
20 must be unmoved. Now we have visual experience of the last term in this series, namely that which has the capacity of being in motion, but does not contain a motive principle, and also of that which is

---

¹⁴ Chapter ɪ.
¹⁵ i. e. not necessarily continuously: e. g. a thing thrown continues its course after contact with the thrower has ceased.

in motion but is moved by itself and not by anything else: it is
reasonable, therefore, not to say necessary, to suppose the existence
of the third term also, that which causes motion but is itself unmoved. So, too, Anaxagoras is right when he says that Mind is 25
impassive and unmixed, since he makes it the principle of motion:
for it could cause motion in this sense only by being itself unmoved,
and have supreme control only by being unmixed.

We will now take the second alternative. If the movent is not
accidentally but necessarily in motion—so that, if it were not in
motion, it would not move anything—then the movent, in so far as
it is in motion, must be in motion in one of two ways: it is moved 30
either as that is which is moved with the same kind of motion, or
with a different kind—either that which is heating, I mean, is itself
in process of becoming hot, that which is making healthy in process
of becoming healthy, and that which is causing locomotion in process
of locomotion, or else that which is making healthy is, let us say, in
process of locomotion, and that which is causing locomotion in process
of, say, increase. But it is evident that this is impossible. For if we
adopt the first assumption we have to make it apply within each of
the very lowest species into which motion can be divided: e. g. we 257ª
must say that if some one is teaching some lesson in geometry, he
is also in process of being taught that same lesson in geometry, and
that if he is throwing he is in process of being thrown in just the
same manner. Or if we reject this assumption we must say that one
kind of motion is derived from another; e. g. that that which is causing locomotion is in process of increase, that which is causing this' in- 5
crease is in process of being altered by something else, and that
which is causing this alteration is in process of suffering some different
kind of motion. But the series must stop somewhere, since the kinds
of motion are limited; and if we say that the process is reversible,
and that that which is causing alteration is in process of locomotion,
we do no more than if we had said at the outset that that which is
causing locomotion is in process of locomotion, and that one who is 10
teaching is in process of being taught: for it is clear that everything
that is moved is moved by the movent that is further back in
the series as well as by that which immediately moves it: in fact
the earlier movent is that which more strictly moves it. But this is
of course impossible: for it involves the consequence that one who is
teaching is in process of learning what he is teaching, whereas teaching necessarily implies possessing knowledge, and learning not possessing it. Still more unreasonable is the consequence involved that,
since everything that is moved is moved by something that is itself 15

moved by something else, everything that has a capacity for causing
motion has as such a corresponding capacity for being moved: i. e. it
will have a capacity for being moved in the sense in which one might
say that everything that has a capacity for making healthy, and exercises that capacity, has as such a capacity for being made healthy,
and that which has a capacity for building has as such a capacity for
being built. It will have the capacity for being thus moved either
immediately or through one or more links (as it will if, while everything that has a capacity for causing motion has as such a capacity for
20 being moved by something else, the motion that it has the capacity
for suffering is not that with which it affects what is next to it, but
a motion of a different kind; e. g. that which has a capacity for
making healthy might as such have a capacity for learning: the series,
however, could be traced back, as we said before, until at some time
or other we arrived at the same kind of motion). Now the first
alternative is impossible, and the second is fantastic: it is absurd
that that which has a capacity for causing alteration should as such
25 necessarily have a capacity, let us say, for increase. It is not necessary, therefore, that that which is moved should always be moved
by something else that is itself moved by something else: so there
will be an end to the series. Consequently the first thing that is in
motion will derive its motion either from something that is at rest or
from itself. But if there *were* any need to consider which of the two,
that which moves itself or that which is moved by something else,
30 is the cause and principle of motion, every one would decide for
the former: for that which is itself independently a cause is always
prior as a cause to that which is so only in virtue of being itself
dependent upon something else that makes it so.

We must therefore make a fresh start and consider the question;
if a thing moves itself, in what sense and in what manner does it do
so? Now everything that is in motion must be infinitely divisible,
257ᵇ for it has been shown already [16] in our general course on Physics,
that everything that is essentially in motion is continuous. Now it
is impossible that that which moves itself should in its entirety move
itself: for then, while being specifically one and indivisible, it would
as a whole both undergo and cause the same locomotion or altera-
5 tion: thus it would at the same time be both teaching and being
taught (the same thing), or both restoring to and being restored to
the same health. Moreover, we have [17] established the fact that it is
the movable that is moved; and this is potentially, not actually, in

[16] The reference is apparently to vi. 4. 234ᵇ 10 sqq.
[17] Ch. I. 251ᵃ 9 sqq.

motion, but the potential is in process to actuality, and motion is an incomplete actuality of the movable. The movent on the other hand is already in activity: e. g. it is that which is hot that produces heat: in fact, that which produces the form [18] is always something that possesses it. Consequently (if a thing can move itself as a whole), 10 the same thing in respect of the same thing [19] may be at the same time both hot and not hot. So, too, in every other case where the movent must be described by the same name in the same sense as the moved. Therefore when a thing moves itself it is one part of it that is the movent and another part that is moved. But it is not self-moving in the sense that each of the two parts is moved by the other part: the following considerations make this evident. In the first place, if each of the two parts is to move the other, there will be no 15 first movent. If a thing is moved by a series of movents, that which is earlier in the series is more the cause of its being moved than that which comes next, and will be more truly the movent: for we found that there are two kinds of movent, that which is itself moved by something else and that which derives its motion from itself: and that which is further from the thing that is moved is nearer to the principle of motion than that which is intermediate. In the second 20 place, there is no necessity for the movent part to be moved by anything but itself: so it can only be accidentally that the other part moves it in return. I take then the possible case of its not moving it: then there will be a part that is moved and a part that is an unmoved movent. In the third place, there is no necessity for the movent to be moved in return: on the contrary the necessity that there should always be motion makes it necessary that there should be some movent that is either unmoved or moved by itself. In the fourth place we should then have a thing undergoing the same motion 25 that it is causing—that which is producing heat, therefore, being heated. But as a matter of fact that which primarily moves itself cannot contain either a single part that moves itself or a number of parts each of which moves itself. For, if the whole is moved by itself, it must be moved either by some part of itself or as a whole by itself as a whole. If, then, it is moved in virtue of some part of it 30 being moved by that part itself, it is this part that will be the primary self-movent, since, if this part is separated from the whole, the part will still move itself, but the whole will do so no longer. If on the other hand the whole is moved by itself as a whole, it must be accidentally

---

[18] i. e. any particular characteristic such as heat.

[19] i. e. the whole of itself: there is no question of one *part* of a thing heating another part.

that the parts move themselves: and therefore, their self-motion
not being necessary, we may take the case of their not being moved
258ᵃ by themselves. Therefore in the whole of the thing we may distinguish that which imparts motion without itself being moved and
that which is moved: for only in this way is it possible for a thing
to be self-moved. Further, if the whole moves itself we may distinguish
in it that which imparts the motion and that which is moved: so while
5 we say that AB is moved by itself, we may also say that it is moved
by A. And since that which imparts motion may be either a thing
that is moved by something else or a thing that is unmoved, and
that which is moved may be either a thing that imparts motion to
something else or a thing that does not, that which moves itself must
be composed of something that is unmoved but imparts motion and
also of something that is moved but does not necessarily impart motion but may or may not do so. Thus let A be something
that imparts motion but is unmoved, B something that is moved by
10 A and moves C, C something that is moved by B but moves nothing (granted that we eventually arrive at C we may take it that
there is only one intermediate term, though there may be more). Then
the whole ABC moves itself. But if I take away C, AB will move
itself, A imparting motion and B being moved, whereas C will not
15 move itself or in fact be moved at all. Nor again will BC move itself
apart from A: for B imparts motion only through being moved by
something else, not through being moved by any part of itself. So
only AB moves itself. That which moves itself, therefore, must comprise something that imparts motion but is unmoved and something
that is moved but does not necessarily move anything else: and each
20 of these two things, or at any rate one of them, must be in contact
with the other. If, then, that which imparts motion is a continuous
substance—that which is moved must of course be so—it is clear that
it is not through some part of the whole being of such a nature
as to be capable of moving itself that the whole moves itself: it moves
itself as a whole, both being moved and imparting motion through
25 containing a part that imparts motion and a part that is moved. It
does not impart motion as a whole nor is it moved as a whole: it is
A alone that imparts motion and B alone that is moved. It is not
true, further, that C is moved by A, which is impossible.

Here a difficulty arises: if something is taken away from A (supposing that that which imparts motion but is unmoved is a continuous
substance), or from B the part that is moved, will the remainder
of A continue to impart motion or the remainder of B continue to
30 be moved? If so, it will not be AB primarily that is moved by itself,

since, when something is taken away from AB, the remainder of
AB will still continue to move itself. Perhaps we may state the case
thus: there is nothing to prevent each of the two parts, or at any 258ᵇ
rate one of them, that which is moved, being divisible though actually
undivided, so that if it is divided it will not continue in the possession
of the same capacity: and so there is nothing to prevent self-
motion residing primarily in things that are potentially divisible.

From what has been said, then, it is evident that that which
primarily imparts motion is unmoved: for, whether the series is 5
closed at once by that which is in motion but moved by something
else deriving its motion directly from the first unmoved, or whether
the motion is derived from what is in motion but moves itself and
stops its own motion, on both suppositions we have the result that in
all cases of things being in motion that which primarily imparts
motion is unmoved.

6 Since there must always be motion without intermission, there 10
must necessarily be something, one thing or it may be a plurality,
that first imparts motion, and this first movent must be unmoved.
Now the question whether each of the things that are unmoved but
impart motion [20] is eternal is irrelevant to our present argument:
but the following considerations will make it clear that there must
necessarily be some such thing, which, while it has the capacity of
moving something else, is itself unmoved and exempt from all change, 15
which can affect it neither in an unqualified nor in an accidental
sense. Let us suppose, if any one likes, that in the case of certain
things it is possible for them at different times to be and not to be,
without any process of becoming and perishing (in fact it would seem
to be necessary, if a thing that has not parts at one time is and at
another time is not, that any such thing should without undergoing
any process of change at one time be and at another time not be).
And let us further suppose it possible that some principles that are 20
unmoved but capable of imparting motion at one time are and at
another time are not. Even so, this cannot be true of *all* such principles, since there must clearly be something that *causes* things that
move themselves at one time to be and at another not to be. For,
since nothing that has not parts can be in motion, that which moves
itself must as a whole have magnitude, though nothing that we have 25
said makes this necessarily true of every movent. So the fact that
some things become and others perish, and that this is so continuously, cannot be caused by any one of those things that, though they

[20] e.g. individual souls.

are unmoved, do not always exist: nor again can it be caused by any of those which move certain particular things, while others move other things. The eternity and continuity of the process cannot be caused either by any one of them singly or by the sum of them,

30 because this causal relation must be eternal and necessary, whereas the sum of these movents is infinite and they do not all exist together. It is clear, then, that though there may be countless instances

259ᵃ of the perishing of some principles that are unmoved but impart motion, and though many things that move themselves perish and are succeeded by others that come into being, and though one thing that is unmoved moves one thing while another moves another, nevertheless there is something that comprehends them all, and that as something apart from each one of them, and this it is that is the cause of the fact that some things are and others are not and of

5 the continuous process of change: and this causes the motion of the other movents, while they are the causes of the motion of other things. Motion, then, being eternal, the first movent, if there is but one, will be eternal also: if there are more than one, there will be a plurality of such eternal movents. We ought, however, to suppose that there is one rather than many, and a finite rather than an infinite number. When the consequences of either assumption are the same, we should always assume that things are finite rather than

10 infinite in number, since in things constituted by nature that which is finite and that which is better ought, if possible, to be present rather than the reverse: and here it is sufficient to assume only one movent, the first of unmoved things, which being eternal will be the principle of motion to everything else.

The following argument also makes it evident that the first movent

15 must be something that is one and eternal. We have shown [21] that there must always be motion. That being so, motion must also be continuous, because what is always is continuous, whereas what is merely in succession is not continuous. But further, if motion is continuous, it is one: and it is one only if the movent and the moved that constitute it are each of them one, since in the event of a thing's being moved now by one thing and now by another the whole motion will not be continuous but successive.

20 Moreover a conviction that there is a first unmoved something may be reached not only from the foregoing arguments, but also by considering again the principles operative in movents. Now it is evident that among existing things there are some that are sometimes in motion and sometimes at rest. This fact has served above [22]

[21] Chapter 1.   [22] Chapter 3.

to make it clear that it is not true either that all things are in motion
or that all things are at rest or that some things are always at rest
and the remainder always in motion: on this matter proof is supplied 25
by things that fluctuate between the two and have the capacity of
being sometimes in motion and sometimes at rest. The existence of
things of this kind is clear to all: but we wish to explain also the
nature of each of the other two kinds and show that there are some
things that are always unmoved and some things that are always
in motion. In the course of our argument directed to this end we established the fact that everything that is in motion is moved by some- 30
thing,[23] and that the movent is either unmoved or in motion, and that,
if it is in motion, it is moved either by itself or by something else and so
on throughout the series: and so we proceeded to the position [24] that
the first principle that directly causes things that are in motion to be
moved is that which moves itself, and the first principle of the whole
series is the unmoved. Further it is evident from actual observation that 259[b]
there are things that have the characteristic of moving themselves,
e. g. the animal kingdom and the whole class of living things. This
being so, then, the view was suggested [25] that perhaps it may be
possible for motion to come to be in a thing without having been in
existence at all before, because we see this actually occurring in 5
animals: they are unmoved at one time and then again they are in
motion, as it seems. We must grasp the fact, therefore, that animals
move themselves only with one kind of motion,[26] and that this is
not strictly originated by them. The cause of it is not derived from
the animal itself: it is connected with other natural motions in
animals, which they do not experience through their own instru-
mentality, e. g. increase, decrease, and respiration: these are experienced by every animal while it is at rest and not in motion in respect 10
of the motion set up by its own agency: [27] here the motion is caused
by the atmosphere and by many things that enter into the animal:
thus in some cases the cause is nourishment: when it is being digested
animals sleep, and when it is being distributed through the system
they awake and move themselves, the first principle of this motion
being thus originally derived from outside. Therefore animals are
not always in continuous motion by their own agency: it is something 15
else that moves them, itself being in motion and changing as it
comes into relation with each several thing that moves itself. (Moreover in all these self-moving things the first movent and cause of
their self-motion is itself moved by itself, though in an accidental

[23] Chapter 4.   [24] Chapter 5.   [25] 253[a] 7 sqq.
[26] sc. locomotion.   [27] sc. locomotion.

sense: that is to say, the body changes its place, so that that which
is in the body changes its place also and is a self-movent through
20 its exercise of leverage.) Hence we may confidently conclude that if
a thing belongs to the class of unmoved movents that are also themselves moved accidentally, it is impossible that it should cause continuous motion. So the necessity that there should be motion continuously requires that there should be a first movent that is unmoved even accidentally, if, as we have said,[28] there is to be in the
25 world of things an unceasing and undying motion, and the world is
to remain permanently self-contained and within the same limits:
for if the first principle is permanent, the universe must also be permanent, since it is continuous with the first principle. (We must
distinguish, however, between accidental motion of a thing by itself
and such motion by something else, the former being confined to
perishable things, whereas the latter belongs also to certain first
30 principles of heavenly bodies, of all those, that is to say, that experience more than one locomotion.[29])

And further, if there is always something of this nature, a movent
260ᵃ that is itself unmoved and eternal, then that which is first moved
by it must be eternal. Indeed this is clear also from the consideration that there would otherwise be no becoming and perishing and
no change of any kind in other things, which require something that
is in motion to move them: for the motion imparted by the unmoved
will always be imparted in the same way and be one and the same,
since the unmoved does not itself change in relation to that which
5 is moved by it. But that[30] which is moved by something that,
though it is in motion, is moved directly by the unmoved stands
in varying relations to the things that it moves, so that the motion
that it causes will not be always the same: by reason of the fact
that it occupies contrary positions or assumes contrary forms at
different times it will produce contrary motions in each several
10 thing that it moves and will cause it to be at one time at rest and at
another time in motion.

The foregoing argument, then, has served to clear up the point
about which we raised a difficulty at the outset[31]—why is it that
instead of all things being either in motion or at rest, or some things
being always in motion and the remainder always at rest, there are
things that are sometimes in motion and sometimes not? The cause
of this is now plain: it is because, while some things are moved by
an eternal unmoved movent and are therefore always in motion,

[28] Chapter 1.
[30] e. g. any one of the heavenly bodies.
[29] *sc.* the planets.
[31] Chapter 3.

other things are moved by a movent that is in motion and changing, 15
so that they too must change. But the unmoved movent, as has been
said, since it remains permanently simple and unvarying and in the
same state, will cause motion that is one and simple

7   This matter will be made clearer, however, if we start afresh 20
from another point. We must consider whether it is or is not possible
that there should be a continuous motion, and, if it is possible,
which motion this is, and which is the primary motion: for it is plain
that if there must always be motion, and a particular motion is
primary and continuous, then it is this motion that is imparted by 25
the first movent, and so it is necessarily one and the same and continuous and primary.

Now of the three kinds of motion that there are—motion in respect of magnitude, motion in respect of affection, and motion in
respect of place—it is this last, which we call locomotion, that must
be primary. This may be shown as follows. It is impossible that there
should be increase without the previous occurrence of alteration: 30
for that which is increased, although in a sense it is increased by
what is like itself, is in a sense increased by what is unlike itself:
thus it is said that contrary is nourishment to contrary: [32] but
growth is effected only by things becoming like to like. There must be
alteration, then, in that there is this change from contrary to contrary. 260ᵇ
But the fact that a thing is altered requires that there should be
something that alters it, something e. g. that makes the potentially
hot into the actually hot: so it is plain that the movent does not
maintain a uniform relation to it but is at one time nearer to and at
another farther from that which is altered: and we cannot have this 5
without locomotion. If, therefore, there must always be motion, there
must also always be locomotion as the primary motion, and, if there
is a primary as distinguished from a secondary form of locomotion,
it must be the primary form. Again, all affections have their origin
in condensation and rarefaction: thus heavy and light, soft and hard, 10
hot and cold, are considered to be forms of density and rarity. But
condensation and rarefaction are nothing more than combination and
separation, processes in accordance with which substances are said
to become and perish: and in being combined and separated things
must change in respect of place. And further, when a thing is increased or decreased its magnitude changes in respect of place.

Again, there is another point of view from which it will be clearly 15
seen that locomotion is primary. As in the case of other things so

32 Cf. *De An.* ii. 4. 416ᵃ 21 sqq.

too in the case of motion the word 'primary' may be used in several senses. A thing is said to be prior to other things when, if it does not exist, the others will not exist, whereas it can exist without the others: and there is also priority in time and priority in perfection of existence. Let us begin, then, with the first sense. Now there must be
20 motion continuously, and there may be continuously either continuous motion or successive motion, the former, however, in a higher degree than the latter: moreover it is better that it should be continuous rather than successive motion, and we always assume the presence in nature of the better, if it be possible: since, then, continuous motion is possible (this will be proved later: [33] for the present let us take it for granted), and no other motion can be continuous
25 except locomotion, locomotion must be primary. For there is no necessity for the subject of locomotion to be the subject either of increase or of alteration, nor need it become or perish: on the other hand there cannot be any one of these processes without the existence of the continuous motion imparted by the first movent.

Secondly, locomotion must be primary in time: for this is the only
30 motion possible for eternal things. It is true indeed that, in the case of any individual thing that has a becoming, locomotion must be the last of its motions: for after its becoming it first experiences alteration and increase, and locomotion is a motion that belongs to such
261ᵃ things only when they are perfected. But there must previously be something else that is in process of locomotion to be the cause even of the becoming of things that become, without itself being in process of becoming, as e. g. the begotten is preceded by what begot it: otherwise becoming might be thought to be the primary motion on the
5 ground that the thing must first become. But though this is so in the case of any individual thing that becomes, nevertheless before anything becomes, something else must be in motion, not itself becoming but being, and before this there must again be something else. And since becoming cannot be primary—for, if it were, everything that is in motion would be perishable—it is plain that no one
10 of the motions next in order can be prior to locomotion. By the motions next in order I mean increase and then alteration, decrease, and perishing. All these are posterior to becoming: consequently, if not even becoming is prior to locomotion, then no one of the other processes of change is so either.

Thirdly, that which is in process of becoming appears universally as something imperfect and proceeding to a first principle: and so what is posterior in the order of becoming is prior in the order of

[33] Chapter 8.

nature. Now all things that go through the process of becoming acquire locomotion last. It is this that accounts for the fact that some 15
living things, e. g. plants and many kinds of animals, owing to lack
of the requisite organ, are entirely without motion, whereas others
acquire it in the course of their being perfected. Therefore, if the
degree in which things possess locomotion corresponds to the degree
in which they have realized their natural development, then this motion must be prior to all others in respect of perfection of existence: 20
and not only for this reason but also because a thing that is in
motion loses its essential character less in the process of locomotion
than in any other kind of motion: it is the only motion that does
not involve a change of being in the sense in which there is a change
in quality when a thing is altered and a change in quantity when a
thing is increased or decreased. Above all it is plain that this motion,
motion in respect of place, is what is in the strictest sense produced
by that which moves itself; but it is the self-movent that we declare 25
to be the first principle of things that are moved and impart motion
and the primary source to which things that are in motion are to be
referred.

It is clear, then, from the foregoing arguments that locomotion is
the primary motion. We have now to show which kind of locomotion is primary. The same process of reasoning will also make clear
at the same time the truth of the assumption we have made both now
and at a previous stage [34] that it is possible that there should be 30
a motion that is continuous and eternal. Now it is clear from the
following considerations that no other than locomotion can be continuous. Every other motion and change is from an opposite to an
opposite: thus for the processes of becoming and perishing the limits
are the existent and the non-existent, for alteration the various pairs
of contrary affections, and for increase and decrease either greatness 35
and smallness or perfection and imperfection of magnitude: and
changes to the respective contraries are contrary changes. Now a
thing that is undergoing any particular kind of motion, but though 261[b]
previously existent has not always undergone it, must previously have
been at rest so far as that motion is concerned. It is clear, then, that
for the changing thing the contraries will be states of rest. And
we have a similar result in the case of changes that are not motions:
for becoming and perishing, whether regarded simply as such without
qualification or as affecting something in particular, are opposites:
therefore provided it is impossible for a thing to undergo opposite 5
changes at the same time, the change will not be continuous, but

[34] 253[a] 29.

a period of time will intervene between the opposite processes. The
question whether these contradictory changes are contraries or not
makes no difference, provided only it is impossible for them both to
be present to the same thing at the same time: the point is of no
10 importance to the argument. Nor does it matter if the thing need not
rest in the contradictory state, or if there is no state of rest as a
contrary to the process of change: it may be true that the non-
existent is not at rest, and that perishing is a process to the non-
existent. All that matters is the intervention of a time: it is this
that prevents the change from being continuous: so, too, in our
previous instances the important thing was not the relation of contrariety but the impossibility of the two processes being present to
15 a thing at the same time. And there is no need to be disturbed by
the fact that on this showing there may be more than one contrary
to the same thing, that a particular motion will be contrary both to
rest and to motion in the contrary direction. We have only to grasp
the fact that a particular motion is in a sense the opposite both of
a state of rest and of the contrary motion, in the same way as that
which is of equal or standard measure is the opposite both of that
20 which surpasses it and of that which it surpasses, and that it is
impossible for the opposite motions or changes to be present to a
thing at the same time. Furthermore, in the case of becoming and
perishing it would seem to be an utterly absurd thing if as soon as
anything has become it must necessarily perish and cannot continue
to exist for any time: and, if this is true of becoming and perishing,
25 we have fair grounds for inferring the same to be true of the other
kinds of change, since it would be in the natural order of things that
they should be uniform in this respect.

8   Let us now proceed to maintain that it is possible that there should
be an infinite motion that is single and continuous, and that this
motion is rotatory motion. The motion of everything that is in
process of locomotion is either rotatory or rectilinear or a compound
of the two: consequently, if one of the former two is not continuous,
30 that which is composed of them both cannot be continuous either.
Now it is plain that if the locomotion of a thing is rectilinear and
finite it is not continuous locomotion: for the thing must turn back,
and that which turns back in a straight line undergoes two contrary
locomotions, since, so far as motion in respect of place is concerned,
upward motion is the contrary of downward motion, forward motion.
35 of backward motion, and motion to the left of motion to the right,
these being the pairs of contraries in the sphere of place. But we have

already [35] defined single and continuous motion to be motion of a 262ᵃ
single thing in a single period of time and operating within a sphere
admitting of no further specific differentiation (for we have three
things to consider, first that which is in motion, e. g. a man or a god,
secondly the 'when' of the motion, that is to say, the time, and
thirdly the sphere within which it operates, which may be either
place or affection or essential form or magnitude): and contraries
are specifically not one and the same but distinct: and within the 5
sphere of place we have the above-mentioned distinctions. Moreover
we have an indication that motion from A to B is the contrary of
motion from B to A in the fact that, if they occur at the same time,
they arrest and stop each other. And the same is true in the case of a
circle: the motion from A towards B is the contrary of the motion
from A towards C: for even if they are continuous and there is no 10
turning back they arrest each other, because contraries annihilate or
obstruct one another. On the other hand lateral motion is not the
contrary of upward motion. But what shows most clearly that rectilinear motion cannot be continuous is the fact that turning back
necessarily implies coming to a stand, not only when it is a straight
line that is traversed, but also in the case of locomotion in a circle 15
(which is not the same thing as rotatory locomotion: for, when a
thing merely traverses a circle, it may either proceed on its course
without a break or turn back again when it has reached the same
point from which it started). We may assure ourselves of the necessity
of this coming to a stand not only on the strength of observation,
but also on theoretical grounds. We may start as follows: we have
three points, starting-point, middle-point, and finishing-point, of
which the middle-point in virtue of the relations in which it stands 20
severally to the other two is both a starting-point and a finishing-
point, and though numerically one is theoretically two. We have further the distinction between the potential and the actual. So in the
straight line in question any one of the points lying between the
two extremes is potentially a middle-point: but it is not actually so
unless that which is in motion divides the line by coming to a stand
at that point and beginning its motion again: thus the middle-point 25
becomes both a starting-point and a goal, the starting-point of the
latter part and the finishing-point of the first part of the motion.
This is the case e. g. when A in the course of its locomotion comes
to a stand at B and starts again towards C: but when its motion is
continuous A cannot either have come to be or have ceased to be at
the point B: it can only have been there at the moment of passing, 30

[35] v. 4.

its passage not being contained within any period of time except the whole of which the particular moment is a dividing-point. To maintain that it has come to be and ceased to be there will involve the consequence that A in the course of its locomotion will always be 262ᵇ coming to a stand: for it is impossible that A should simultaneously have come to be at B and ceased to be there, so that the two things must have happened at different points of time, and therefore there will be the intervening period of time: consequently A will be in a state of rest at B, and similarly at all other points, since the same 5 reasoning holds good in every case. When to A, that which is in process of locomotion, B, the middle-point, serves both as a finishing-point and as a starting-point for its motion, A must come to a stand at B, because it makes it two just as one might do in thought. However, the point A is the real starting-point at which the moving body has ceased to be, and it is at C that it has really come to be when its course is finished and it comes to a stand. So this is how we must 10 meet the difficulty that then arises, which is as follows. Suppose the line E is equal to the line F, that A proceeds in continuous locomotion from the extreme point of E to C, and that, at the moment when A is at the point B, D is proceeding in uniform locomotion and with the same velocity as A from the extremity of F to G: then, says the argument, D will have reached G before A has reached C: for that which makes an earlier start and departure must make an earlier 15 arrival: the reason, then, for the late arrival of A is that it has not simultaneously come to be and ceased to be at B: otherwise it will not arrive later: for this to happen it will be necessary that it should come to a stand there. Therefore we must not hold that there was a moment when A came to be at B and that at the same moment D was in motion from the extremity of F: for the fact of A's having 20 come to be at B will involve the fact of its also ceasing to be there, and the two events will not be simultaneous, whereas the truth is that A is at B at a sectional point of time and does not occupy time there. In this case, therefore, where the motion of a thing is continuous, it is impossible to use this form of expression. On the other hand in the case of a thing that turns back in its course we must do so. For suppose G in the course of its locomotion proceeds to D and then turns back and proceeds downwards again: then the extreme point D has served as finishing-point and as starting-point for it, one 25 point thus serving as two: therefore G must have come to a stand there: it cannot have come to be at D and departed from D simultaneously, for in that case it would simultaneously be there and not be there at the same moment. And here we cannot apply the argu-

ment used to solve the difficulty stated above: we cannot argue that
G is at D at a sectional point of time and has not come to be or
ceased to be there. For here the goal that is reached is necessarily 30
one that is actually, not potentially, existent. Now the point in the
middle is potential: but this one is actual, and regarded from below
it is a finishing-point, while regarded from above it is a starting-point,
so that it stands in these same two respective relations to the two 263ᵃ
motions. Therefore that which turns back in traversing a rectilinear
course must in so doing come to a stand. Consequently there cannot
be a continuous rectilinear motion that is eternal.

The same method should also be adopted in replying to those who
ask, in the terms of Zeno's argument, whether we admit that before 5
any distance can be traversed half the distance must be traversed,
that these half-distances are infinite in number, and that it is impossible to traverse distances infinite in number—or some on the
lines of this same argument put the questions in another form, and
would have us grant that in the time during which a motion is in
progress it should be possible to reckon a half-motion before the whole
for every half-distance that we get, so that we have the result that
when the whole distance is traversed we have reckoned an infinite 10
number, which is admittedly impossible. Now when we first discussed
the question of motion we put forward a solution [36] of this difficulty
turning on the fact that the period of time occupied in traversing
the distance contains within itself an infinite number of units: there
is no absurdity, we said, in supposing the traversing of infinite distances in infinite time, and the element of infinity is present in the
time no less than in the distance. But, although this solution is ade- 15
quate as a reply to the questioner (the question asked being whether
it is possible in a finite time to traverse or reckon an infinite number
of units), nevertheless as an account of the fact and explanation of
its true nature it is inadequate. For suppose the distance to be left
out of account and the question asked to be no longer whether it is
possible in a finite time to traverse an infinite number of distances, 20
and suppose that the inquiry is made to refer to the time taken by
itself (for the time contains an infinite number of divisions): then
this solution will no longer be adequate, and we must apply the truth
that we enunciated in our recent discussion, stating it in the following way. In the act of dividing the continuous distance into two
halves one point is treated as two, since we make it a starting-point
and a finishing-point: and this same result is also produced by the 25
act of reckoning halves as well as by the act of dividing into halves.

[36] vi. 2. 233ᵃ 21 sqq., and vi. 9.

But if divisions are made in this way, neither the distance nor the motion will be continuous: for motion if it is to be continuous must relate to what is continuous: and though what is continuous contains an infinite number of halves, they are not actual but potential halves. If the halves are made actual, we shall get not a continuous

30 but an intermittent motion. In the case of reckoning the halves, it is

263ᵇ clear that this result follows: for then one point must be reckoned as two: it will be the finishing-point of the one half and the starting-point of the other, if we reckon not the one continuous whole but the two halves. Therefore to the question whether it is possible to pass through an infinite number of units either of time or of distance we must reply that in a sense it is and in a sense it is not. If

5 the units are actual, it is not possible: if they are potential, it is possible. For in the course of a continuous motion the traveller has traversed an infinite number of units in an accidental sense but not in an unqualified sense: for though it is an accidental characteristic of the distance to be an infinite number of half-distances, this is not its real and essential character. It is also plain that unless we

10 hold that the point of time that divides earlier from later always belongs only to the later so far as the thing is concerned, we shall be involved in the consequence that the same thing is at the same moment existent and not existent, and that a thing is not existent at the moment when it has become. It is true that the point is common to both times, the earlier as well as the later, and that, while numerically one and the same, it is theoretically not so, being the finishing-point of the one and the starting-point of the other: but so

15 far as the thing is concerned it belongs to the later stage of what happens to it. Let us suppose a time KBC and a thing D, D being white in the time A and not-white in the time B. Then D is at the moment C white and not-white: for if we were right in saying that it is white during the whole time A, it is true to call it white at any moment of A, and not-white in B, and C is in both A and B. We must

20 not allow, therefore, that it is white in the whole of A, but must say that it is so in all of it except the last moment C. C belongs already to the later period, and if in the whole of A not-white was in process of becoming and white of perishing, at C the process is complete. And so C is the first moment at which it is true to call the thing white or not-white respectively. Otherwise a thing may be non-existent at the moment when it has become and existent at the moment when it

25 has perished: or else it must be possible for a thing at the same time to be white and not white and in fact to be existent and non-existent. Further, if anything that exists after having been previously non-

existent must become existent and does not exist when it is becoming,
time cannot be divisible into time-atoms. For suppose that D was becoming white in the time A and that at another time B, a time-atom
consecutive with the last atom of A, D has already become white and
so is white at that moment: then, inasmuch as in the time A it was 30
becoming white and so was not white and at the moment B it is white,
there must have been a becoming between A and B and therefore also
a time in which the becoming took place. On the other hand, those
who deny atoms of time (as we do) are not affected by this argu-264ᵃ
ment: according to them D has become and so is white at the last
point of the actual time in which it was becoming white: and this
point has no other point consecutive with or in succession to it, whereas
time-atoms are conceived as successive. Moreover it is clear that if
D was becoming white in the whole time A, the time occupied by it
in having become white in addition to having been in process of 5
becoming white is no more than all that it occupied in the mere
process of becoming white.

These and such-like, then, are the arguments for our conclusion
that derive cogency from the fact that they have a special bearing
on the point at issue. If we look at the question from the point of
view of general theory, the same result would also appear to be
indicated by the following arguments. Everything whose motion is
continuous must, on arriving at any point in the course of its locomo- 10
tion, have been previously also in process of locomotion to that point,
if it is not forced out of its path by anything: e. g. on arriving at
B a thing must also have been in process of locomotion to B, and that
not merely when it was near to B, but from the moment of its
starting on its course, since there can be no reason for its being so
at any particular stage rather than at an earlier one. So, too, in the
case of the other kinds of motion. Now we are to suppose that a thing
proceeds in locomotion from A to C and that at the moment of its
arrival at C the continuity of its motion is unbroken and will remain 15
so until it has arrived back at A. Then when it is undergoing locomotion from A to C it is at the same time undergoing also its locomotion to A from C: consequently it is simultaneously undergoing two
contrary motions, since the two motions that follow the same straight
line are contrary to each other. With this consequence there also follows another: we have a thing that is in process of change from a
position in which it has not yet been: so, inasmuch as this is impossible, the thing must come to a stand at C. Therefore the motion is not 20
a single motion, since motion that is interrupted by stationariness
is not single.

Further, the following argument will serve better to make this point clear universally in respect of every kind of motion. If the motion undergone by that which is in motion is always one of those already enumerated, and the state of rest that it undergoes is one of those that are the opposites of the motions (for we found [37] that there could be no other besides these), and moreover that which is undergoing but does not always undergo a particular motion (by 25 this I mean one of the various specifically distinct motions, not some particular part of the whole motion) must have been previously undergoing the state of rest that is the opposite of the motion, the state of rest being privation of motion; then, inasmuch as the two motions that follow the same straight line are contrary motions, and it is impossible for a thing to undergo simultaneously two con-30 trary motions, that which is undergoing locomotion from A to C cannot also simultaneously be undergoing locomotion from C to A: and since the latter locomotion is not simultaneous with the former but is still to be undergone, before it is undergone there must occur a state of rest at C: for this, as we found,[38] is the state of rest that is the opposite of the motion from C. The foregoing argument, then, makes it plain that the motion in question is not continuous.

264[b] Our next argument has a more special bearing than the foregoing on the point at issue. We will suppose that there has occurred in something simultaneously a perishing of not-white and a becoming of white. Then if the alteration to white and from white is a con-5 tinuous process and the white does not remain any time, there must have occurred simultaneously a perishing of not-white, a becoming of white, and a becoming of not-white: for the time of the three will be the same.

Again, from the continuity of the time in which the motion takes place we cannot infer continuity in the motion, but only successiveness: in fact, how could contraries, e. g. whiteness and blackness, meet in the same extreme point?

On the other hand, in motion on a circular line we shall find singleness and continuity: for here we are met by no impossible conse-10 quence: that which is in motion from A will in virtue of the same direction of energy be simultaneously in motion to A (since it is in motion to the point at which it will finally arrive), and yet will not be undergoing two contrary or opposite motions: for a motion to a point and a motion from that point are not always contraries or opposites: they are contraries only if they are on the same straight 15 line (for then they are contrary to one another in respect of place,

37 v. 2.   38 v. 6. 229[b] 28 sqq.

as e. g. the two motions along the diameter of the circle, since the ends of this are at the greatest possible distance from one another), and they are opposites only if they are along the same line. Therefore in the case we are now considering there is nothing to prevent the motion being continuous and free from all intermission: for rotatory motion is motion of a thing from its place to its place, whereas recti- 20 linear motion is motion from its place to another place.

Moreover the progress of rotatory motion is never localized within certain fixed limits, whereas that of rectilinear motion repeatedly is so. Now a motion that is always shifting its ground from moment to moment can be continuous: but a motion that is repeatedly localized within certain fixed limits cannot be so, since then the same thing would have to undergo simultaneously two opposite motions. So, too, there cannot be continuous motion in a semicircle or in any other arc 25 of a circle, since here also the same ground must be traversed repeatedly and two contrary processes of change must occur. The reason is that in these motions the starting-point and the termination do not coincide, whereas in motion over a circle they do coincide, and so this is the only perfect motion.[39]

This differentiation also provides another means of showing that the other kinds of motion cannot be continuous either: for in all of them we find that there is the same ground to be traversed repeatedly: 30 thus in alteration there are the intermediate stages of the process, and in quantitative change there are the intervening degrees of magnitude: and in becoming and perishing the same thing is true. It makes no difference whether we take the intermediate stages of the process to be few or many, or whether we add or subtract one: for in either 265ᵃ case we find that there is still the same ground to be traversed repeatedly. Moreover it is plain from what has been said that those physicists who assert that all sensible things are always in motion are wrong: for their motion must be one or other of the motions just 5 mentioned: in fact they mostly conceive it as alteration (things are always in flux and decay, they say), and they go so far as to speak even of becoming and perishing as a process of alteration. On the other hand, our argument has enabled us to assert the fact, applying universally to all motions, that no motion admits of continuity except rotatory motion: consequently neither alteration nor increase admits 10 of continuity. We need now say no more in support of the position that there is no process of change that admits of infinity or continuity except rotatory locomotion.

[39] Because finite lines may be extended, whereas a circle is once for all complete.

9   It can now be shown plainly that rotation is the primary locomotion. Every locomotion, as we said before,[40] is either rotatory or
15 rectilinear or a compound of the two: and the two former must be
prior to the last, since they are the elements of which the latter consists. Moreover rotatory locomotion is prior to rectilinear locomotion,
because it is more simple and complete, which may be shown as
follows. The straight line traversed in rectilinear motion cannot be
infinite: for there is no such thing as an infinite straight line; and
even if there were, it would not be traversed by anything in motion:
for the impossible does not happen and it is impossible to traverse
20 an infinite distance. On the other hand rectilinear motion on a finite
straight line is if it turns back a composite motion, in fact two motions, while if it does not turn back it is incomplete and perishable:
and in the order of nature, of definition, and of time alike the complete
is prior to the incomplete and the imperishable to the perishable.
Again, a motion that admits of being eternal is prior to one that does
25 not. Now rotatory motion can be eternal: but no other motion,
whether locomotion or motion of any other kind, can be so, since in
all of them rest must occur, and with the occurrence of rest the
motion has perished. Moreover the result at which we have arrived,
that rotatory motion is single and continuous, and rectilinear motion
is not, is a reasonable one. In rectilinear motion we have a definite
starting-point, finishing-point, and middle-point, which all have their
30 place in it in such a way that there is a point from which that which
is in motion can be said to start and a point at which it can be said
to finish its course (for when anything is at the limits of its course,
whether at the starting-point or at the finishing-point, it must be in a
state of rest [41]). On the other hand in circular motion there are no
such definite points: for why should any one point on the line be a
limit rather than any other? Any one point as much as any other is
alike starting-point, middle-point, and finishing-point, so that we can
say of certain things both that they are always and that they never
265ᵇ are at a starting-point and at a finishing-point (so that a revolving
sphere, while it is in motion, is also in a sense at rest, for it continues to occupy the same place). The reason of this is that in this
case all these characteristics belong to the centre: that is to say, the
centre is alike starting-point, middle-point, and finishing-point of the
5 space traversed; consequently since this point is not a point on the
circular line, there is no point at which that which is in process of
locomotion can be in a state of rest as having traversed its course,

[40] Ch. 8. 261ᵇ 28.
[41] And therefore the motion must have limits.

because in its locomotion it is proceeding always about a central
point and not to an extreme point: therefore it remains still, and the
whole is in a sense always at rest as well as continuously in motion.
Our next point gives a convertible result: on the one hand, because
rotation is the measure of motions it must be the primary motion
(for all things are measured by what is primary): on the other hand, 10
because rotation is the primary motion it is the measure of all other
motions. Again, rotatory motion is also the only motion that admits
of being regular. In rectilinear locomotion the motion of things in
leaving the starting-point is not uniform with their motion in approaching the finishing-point, since the velocity of a thing always
increases proportionately as it removes itself farther from its position of rest: on the other hand rotatory motion is the only motion
whose course is naturally such that it has no starting-point or 15
finishing-point in itself but is determined from elsewhere.

As to locomotion being the primary motion, this is a truth that is
attested by all who have ever made mention of motion in their theories: they all assign their first principles of motion to things that
impart motion of this kind. Thus 'separation' and 'combination' are
motions in respect of place, and the motion imparted by 'Love' and 20
'Strife' [42] takes these forms, the latter 'separating' and the former
'combining'. Anaxagoras, too, says that 'Mind', his first movent,
'separates'. Similarly those [43] who assert no cause of this kind but say
that 'void' accounts for motion—they also hold that the motion of 25
natural substance is motion in respect of place: for their motion
that is accounted for by 'void' is locomotion, and its sphere of operation may be said to be place. Moreover they are of opinion that
the primary substances are not subject to any of the other motions,
though the things that are compounds of these substances are so
subject: the processes of increase and decrease and alteration,
they say, are effects of the 'combination' and 'separation' of 'atoms'. 30
It is the same, too, with those who make out that the becoming or
perishing of a thing is accounted for by 'density' or 'rarity': [44] for it
is by 'combination' and 'separation' that the place of these things
in their systems is determined. Moreover to these we may add
those who make Soul the cause of motion: [45] for they say that things
that undergo motion have as their first principle 'that which moves

[42] The motive forces in the system of Empedocles.

[43] Leucippus and Democritus.

[44] The early Ionian school: Thales, Anaximenes, and Heraclitus, the last two
of whom are known to have employed these terms.

[45] Plato and the Platonists.

itself': and when animals and all living things move themselves,
266ᵃ the motion is motion in respect of place. Finally it is to be noted
that we say that a thing 'is in motion' in the strictest sense of the
term only when its motion is motion in respect of place: if a thing
is in process of increase or decrease or is undergoing some alteration while remaining at rest in the same place, we say that it is in
motion in some particular respect: we do not say that it 'is in motion'
5 without qualification.

Our present position, then, is this: We have argued that there
always was motion and always will be motion throughout all time,
and we have explained what is the first principle of this eternal
motion: we have explained further which is the primary motion and
which is the only motion that can be eternal: and we have pronounced the first movent to be unmoved.

10 **10**   We have now to assert that the first movent must be without
parts and without magnitude, beginning with the establishment of
the premises on which this conclusion depends.

One of these premises is that nothing finite can cause motion
during an infinite time. We have three things, the movent, the
moved, and thirdly that in which the motion takes place, namely
the time: and these are either all infinite or all finite or partly—that
15 is to say two of them or one of them—finite and partly infinite. Let
A be the movent, B the moved, and C the infinite time. Now let us
suppose that D [46] moves E, a part of B. Then the time occupied
by this motion cannot be equal to C: for the greater the amount
moved, the longer the time occupied.[47] It follows that the time F [48]
is not infinite. Now we see that by continuing to add to D, I shall
20 use up A, and by continuing to add to E, I shall use up B: but I
shall not use up the time by continually subtracting a corresponding
amount from it, because it is infinite. Consequently the duration of
the part of C which is occupied by all A in moving the whole of B,
will be finite. Therefore a finite thing cannot impart to anything
an infinite motion. It is clear, then, that it is impossible for the finite
to cause motion during an infinite time.

25   It has now to be shown that in no case is it possible for an infinite
force to reside in a finite magnitude. This can be shown as follows:
we take it for granted that the greater force is always that which in
less time than another does an equal amount of work when engaged

[46] *sc.* a part of A.
[47] Clearly D must be a larger fraction of A than E is of B.
[48] The time occupied by D in moving E to the same extent as B is moved by A.

in any activity—in heating, for example, or sweetening or throwing; in fact, in causing any kind of motion. Then that on which the forces act must be affected to some extent by our supposed finite magnitude possessing an infinite force as well as by anything else, in fact to a greater extent than by anything else, since the infinite force is greater than any other. But then there cannot be any time 30 in which its action could take place. Suppose that A is the time occupied by the infinite power in the performance of an act of heating or pushing, and that AB is the time occupied by a finite power in the performance of the same act: then by adding to the latter another finite power and continually increasing the magnitude of 266ᵇ the power so added I shall at some time or other reach a point at which the finite power has completed the motive act in the time A: for by continual addition to a finite magnitude I must arrive at a magnitude that exceeds any assigned limit, and in the same way by continual subtraction I must arrive at one that falls short of any assigned limit. So we get the result that the finite force will occupy the same amount of time in performing the motive act as the infinite force. But this is impossible. Therefore nothing finite can 5 possess an infinite force. So it is also impossible for a finite force to reside in an infinite magnitude. It is true that a greater force can reside in a lesser magnitude: but the superiority of any such greater force can be still greater if the magnitude in which it resides is greater. Now let AB be an infinite magnitude. Then BC ⁴⁹ possesses a certain force that occupies a certain time, let us say the time EF ⁵⁰ in moving D. Now if I take a magnitude twice as great as BC, the 10 time occupied by this magnitude in moving D will be half of EF (assuming this to be the proportion ⁵¹): so we may call this time FG. That being so, by continually taking a greater magnitude in this way I shall never arrive at the full AB, whereas I shall always be getting a lesser fraction of the time originally given. Therefore the force must be infinite, since it exceeds any finite force. More- 15 over the time occupied by the action of any finite force must also be finite: for if a given force moves something in a certain time, a greater force will do so in a lesser time, but still a definite time, in inverse proportion. But a force must always be infinite—just as a number or a magnitude is—if it exceeds all definite limits. This 20

---

⁴⁹ *sc.* a part of AB.

⁵⁰ E being presumably the time occupied by AB in moving D.

⁵¹ He assumes that the force increases proportionately to the magnitude, so that the time decreases proportionately. This simplifies the argument, though of course it is not essential to it.

point may also be proved in another way—by taking a finite
magnitude in which there resides a force the same in kind as that
which resides in the infinite magnitude, so that this force will be a
measure of the finite force residing in the infinite magnitude.

25   It is plain, then, from the foregoing arguments that it is impossible for an infinite force to reside in a finite magnitude or for a
finite force to reside in an infinite magnitude. But before proceeding to our conclusion it will be well to discuss a difficulty that arises
in connexion with locomotion. If everything that is in motion with
the exception of things that move themselves is moved by something else, how is it that some things, e. g. things thrown, continue to be in motion when their movent is no longer in contact
30 with them? If we say that the movent in such cases moves something else at the same time, that the thrower e. g. also moves the air,
and that this in being moved is also a movent, then it would be no
more possible for this second thing than for the original thing to
be in motion when the original movent is not in contact with it or
moving it: all the things moved would have to be in motion simultaneously and also to have ceased simultaneously to be in motion
267ᵃ when the original movent ceases to move them, even if, like the magnet, it makes that which it has moved capable of being a movent.
Therefore, while we must accept this explanation to the extent of
saying that the original movent gives the power of being a movent
either to air or to water or to something else of the kind, naturally
5 adapted for imparting and undergoing motion, we must say further
that this thing does not cease simultaneously to impart motion and
to undergo motion: it ceases to be in motion at the moment when
its movent ceases to move it, but it still remains a movent, and so
it causes something else consecutive with it to be in motion, and of
this again the same may be said. The motion begins to cease when
the motive force produced in one member of the consecutive series
is at each stage less than that possessed by the preceding member,
and it finally ceases when one member no longer causes the next
10 member to be a movent but only causes it to be in motion. The
motion of these last two—of the one as movent and of the other as
moved—must cease simultaneously, and with this the whole motion
ceases. Now the things in which this motion is produced are things
that admit of being sometimes in motion and sometimes at rest, and
the motion is not continuous but only appears so: for it is motion
of things that are either successive or in contact, there being not one
15 movent but a number of movents consecutive with one another: and

so motion of this kind takes place in air and water. Some say [52] that
it is 'mutual replacement': but we must recognize that the difficulty
raised cannot be solved otherwise than in the way we have described.
So far as they are affected by 'mutual replacement', all the members of the series are moved and impart motion simultaneously, so
that their motions also cease simultaneously: but our present problem concerns the appearance of continuous motion in a single thing, 20
and therefore, since it cannot be moved throughout its motion by
the same movent, the question is, what moves it?

Resuming our main argument, we proceed from the positions
that there must be continuous motion in the world of things, that
this is a single motion, that a single motion must be a motion of a
magnitude (for that which is without magnitude cannot be in
motion), and that the magnitude must be a single magnitude moved
by a single movent (for otherwise there will not be continuous
motion but a consecutive series of separate motions), and that if
the movent is a single thing, it is either itself in motion or itself
unmoved: if, then, it is in motion, it will have to be subject to the 25
same conditions as that which it moves, that is to say it will itself be
in process of change and in being so will also have to be moved by 267^b
something: so we have a series that must come to an end, and a
point will be reached at which motion is imparted by something
that is unmoved. Thus we have a movent that has no need to change
along with that which it moves but will be able to cause motion
always (for the causing of motion under these conditions involves
no effort): and this motion alone is regular, or at least it is so in a
higher degree than any other, since the movent is never subject to
any change. So, too, in order that the motion may continue to be 5
of the same character, the moved must not be subject to change in
respect of its relation to the movent. Moreover the movent must
occupy either the centre or the circumference, since these are the
first principles from which a sphere is derived. But the things nearest
the movent are those whose motion is quickest, and in this case it is
the motion of the circumference that is the quickest: therefore the
movent occupies the circumference.

There is a further difficulty in supposing it to be possible for
anything that is in motion to cause motion continuously and not
merely in the way in which it is caused by something repeatedly 10
pushing (in which case the continuity amounts to no more than successiveness). Such a movent must either itself continue to push or
pull or perform both these actions, or else the action must be taken

---

[52] Cf. Pl. *Tim.* 59 A, 79 B, C, E, 80 C.

up by something else and be passed on from one movent to another
(the process that we described before as occurring in the case of
things thrown, since the air or the water, being divisible, is a movent
only in virtue of the fact that different parts of the air are moved
15 one after another): and in either case the motion cannot be a single
motion, but only a consecutive series of motions. The only continuous motion, then, is that which is caused by the unmoved movent:
and this motion is continuous because the movent remains always
invariable, so that its relation to that which it moves remains also
invariable and continuous.

Now that these points are settled, it is clear that the first unmoved
movent cannot have any magnitude. For if it has magnitude, this
must be either a finite or an infinite magnitude. Now we have
20 already [53] proved in our course on Physics that there cannot be an
infinite magnitude: and we have now proved that it is impossible
for a finite magnitude to have an infinite force, and also that it is
impossible for a thing to be moved by a finite magnitude during
an infinite time. But the first movent causes a motion that is eternal
25 and does cause it during an infinite time. It is clear, therefore, that
the first movent is indivisible and is without parts and without
magnitude.

[53] iii. 5.

De Caelo

Translated by J. L. Stocks

CONTENTS

BOOK I. OF THE HEAVENLY BODIES

BOOK II. OF THE HEAVENLY BODIES *(Continued)*

[Chapters 1-12 omitted.]

BOOK III. OF THE SUBLUNARY BODIES

DE CAELO

(*On the Heavens*)

BOOK I

1 The science which has to do with nature clearly concerns itself for the most part with bodies and magnitudes and their properties and movements, but also with the principles of this sort of substance, 5 as many as they may be. For of things constituted by nature some are bodies and magnitudes, some possess body and magnitude,[1] and some are principles of things which possess these.[2] Now a continuum is that which is divisible into parts always capable of subdivision, and a body is that which is every way divisible. A magnitude if divisible one way is a line, if two ways a surface, and if three a body. 10 Beyond these there is no other magnitude, because the three dimensions are all that there are, and that which is divisible in three directions is divisible in all. For, as the Pythagoreans say, the world and all that is in it is determined by the number three, since beginning and middle and end give the number of an 'all', and the number they give is the triad. And so, having taken these three[3] from nature as 15 (so to speak) laws of it, we make further use of the number three in the worship of the Gods. Further, we use the terms in practice in this way. Of two things, or men, we say 'both', but not 'all': three is the first number to which the term 'all' has been appropriated. And 20 in this, as we have said, we do but follow the lead which nature gives. Therefore, since 'every' and 'all' and 'complete' do not differ from one another in respect of form, but only, if at all, in their matter and in that to which they are applied, body alone among magnitudes can be complete. For it alone is determined by the three dimensions, that is, is an 'all'. But if it is divisible in three dimensions it is every way 25 divisible, while the other magnitudes are divisible in one dimension or in two alone: for the divisibility and continuity of magnitudes depend upon the number of the dimensions, one sort being continuous in one direction, another in two, another in all. All magnitudes, then, which are divisible are also continuous. Whether we can also say that

---

[1] i.e. animate things, such as plants and animals.

[2] e. g. matter and form, movement, or, in the case of living things, soul.

[3] viz. beginning, middle, and end.

whatever is continuous is divisible does not yet, on our present 30
grounds, appear. One thing, however, is clear. We cannot pass beyond body to a further kind, as we passed from length to surface, 268ᵇ
and from surface to body. For if we could, it would cease to be true
that body is complete magnitude. We could pass beyond it only in
virtue of a defect in it; and that which is complete cannot be
defective, since it has being in every respect. Now bodies which are 5
classed as parts of the whole [4] are each complete according to our
formula, since each possesses every dimension. But each is determined relatively to that part which is next to it by contact, for
which reason each of them is in a sense many bodies. But the whole
of which they are parts must necessarily be complete, and thus, in
accordance with the meaning of the word, have being, not in some 10
respects only, but in every respect.

2   The question as to the nature of the whole, whether it is infinite
in size or limited in its total mass, is a matter for subsequent inquiry.[5] We will now speak of those parts of the whole which are
specifically distinct. Let us take this as our starting-point. All natu- 15
ral bodies and magnitudes we hold to be, as such, capable of locomotion; for nature, we say, is their principle of movement. But all
movement that is in place, all locomotion, as we term it, is either
straight or circular or a combination of these two, which are the only
simple movements. And the reason of this is that these two, the
straight and the circular line, are the only simple magnitudes. Now 20
revolution about the centre is circular motion, while the upward and
downward movements are in a straight line, 'upward' meaning motion
away from the centre, and 'downward' motion towards it. All simple
motion, then, must be motion either away from or towards or about
the centre. This seems to be in exact accord with what we said 25
above: as body found its completion in three dimensions, so its movement completes itself in three forms.

Bodies are either simple or compounded of such; and by simple
bodies I mean those which possess a principle of movement in their
own nature, such as fire and earth with their kinds, and whatever is
akin to them. Necessarily, then, movements also will be either simple 30
or in some sort compound—simple in the case of the simple bodies, 269ᵃ
compound in that of the composite—and in the latter case the motion
will be that of the simple body which prevails in the composition.
Supposing, then, that there is such a thing as simple movement, and
that circular movement is an instance of it, and that both movement

---

[4] i. e. the elements.   [5] See c. vii.

of a simple body is simple and simple movement is of a simple body
5 (for if it is movement of a compound it will be in virtue of a prevailing simple element), then there must necessarily be some simple
body which revolves naturally and in virtue of its own nature with a
circular movement. By constraint, of course, it may be brought to
move with the motion of something else different from itself, but it
cannot so move naturally, since there is one sort of movement natural
to each of the simple bodies. Again, if the unnatural movement is the
10 contrary of the natural and a thing can have no more than one contrary, it will follow that circular movement, being a simple motion,
must be unnatural, if it is not natural, to the body moved. If then
(1) the body, whose movement is circular, is fire or some other element, its natural motion must be the contrary of the circular motion.
But a single thing has a single contrary; and upward and downward
15 motion are the contraries of one another. If, on the other hand, (2)
the body moving with this circular motion which is unnatural to it is
something different from the elements, there will be some other motion
which is natural to it. But this cannot be. For if the natural motion is
upward, it will be fire or air, and if downward, water or earth. Further, this circular motion is necessarily primary. For the perfect is
20 naturally prior to the imperfect, and the circle is a perfect thing. This
cannot be said of any straight line:—not of an infinite line; for, if it
were perfect, it would have a limit and an end: nor of any finite line;
for in every case there is something beyond it, since any finite line can
be extended. And so, since the prior movement belongs to the body
25 which is naturally prior, and circular movement is prior to straight,
and movement in a straight line belongs to simple bodies—fire moving
straight upward and earthy bodies straight downward towards the
centre—since this is so, it follows that circular movement also must
be the movement of some simple body. For the movement of composite bodies is, as we said, determined by that simple body which
30 preponderates in the composition. These premises clearly give the
conclusion that there is in nature some bodily substance other than
the formations we know, prior to them all and more divine than they.
But it may also be proved as follows. We may take it that all movement is either natural or unnatural, and that the movement which is
unnatural to one body is natural to another—as, for instance, is the
35 case with the upward and downward movements, which are natural
269ᵇ and unnatural to fire and earth respectively. It necessarily follows that
circular movement, being unnatural to these bodies, is the natural
movement of some other. Further, if, on the one hand, circular movement is *natural* to something, it must surely be some simple and pri-

mary body which is ordained to move with a natural circular motion, 5
as fire is ordained to fly up and earth down. If, on the other hand, the
movement of the rotating bodies about the centre is *unnatural*, it
would be remarkable and indeed quite inconceivable that this movement alone should be continuous and eternal, being nevertheless contrary to nature. At any rate the evidence of all other cases goes to
show that it is the unnatural which quickest passes away. And so, 10
if, as some say, the body so moved is fire, this movement is just as
unnatural to it as downward movement; for any one can see that fire
moves in a straight line away from the centre. On all these grounds,
therefore, we may infer with confidence that there is something 15
beyond the bodies that are about us on this earth, different and separate from them; and that the superior glory of its nature is proportionate to its distance from this world of ours.

3   In consequence of what has been said, in part by way of assumption and in part by way of proof, it is clear that not every body either
possesses lightness or heaviness. As a preliminary we must explain in 20
what sense we are using the words 'heavy' and 'light', sufficiently, at
least, for our present purpose: we can examine the terms more closely
later, when we come to consider their essential nature.[6] Let us then
apply the term 'heavy' to that which naturally moves towards the
centre, and 'light' to that which moves naturally away from the
centre. The heaviest thing will be that which sinks to the bottom of all 25
things that move downward, and the lightest that which rises to the
surface of everything that moves upward. Now, necessarily, everything which moves either up or down possesses lightness or heaviness
or both—but not both relatively to the same thing: for things are
heavy and light relatively to one another; air, for instance, is light
relatively to water, and water light relatively to earth. The body, 30
then, which moves in a circle cannot possibly possess either heaviness
or lightness. For neither naturally nor unnaturally can it move
either towards or away from the centre. Movement in a straight line
certainly does not belong to it *naturally*, since one sort of movement
is, as we saw, appropriate to each simple body, and so we should be
compelled to identify it with one of the bodies which move in this 35
way. Suppose, then, that the movement is *unnatural*. In that case, if it
is the downward movement which is unnatural, the upward move- 270ª
ment will be natural; and if it is the upward which is unnatural, the
downward will be natural. For we decided that of contrary movements, if the one is unnatural to anything, the other will be natural

[6] Below, Bk. IV, cc. 1-4.

to it. But since the natural movement of the whole and of its part—of
5 earth, for instance, as a whole and of a small clod—have one and the
same direction, it results, in the first place, that this body can possess
no lightness or heaviness at all (for that would mean that it could
move by its own nature either from or towards the centre, which, as
we know, is impossible); and, secondly, that it cannot possibly move
in the way of locomotion by being forced violently aside in an upward
10 or downward direction. For neither naturally nor unnaturally can it
move with any other motion but its own, either itself or any part of it,
since the reasoning which applies to the whole applies also to the
part.

It is equally reasonable to assume that this body will be ungenerated and indestructible and exempt from increase and alteration, since
15 everything that comes to be comes into being from its contrary and in
some substrate, and passes away likewise in a substrate by the action
of the contrary into the contrary, as we explained in our opening discussions.[7] Now the motions of contraries are contrary. If then this
body can have no contrary, because there can be no contrary mo-
20 tion to the circular, nature seems justly to have exempted from contraries the body which was to be ungenerated and indestructible. For
it is in contraries that generation and decay subsist. Again, that which
is subject to increase increases upon contact with a kindred body,
25 which is resolved into its matter. But there is nothing out of which
this body can have been generated. And if it is exempt from increase
and diminution, the same reasoning leads us to suppose that it is also
unalterable. For alteration is movement in respect of quality; and
qualitative states and dispositions, such as health and disease, do not
come into being without changes of properties. But all natural bodies
30 which change their properties we see to be subject without exception
to increase and diminution. This is the case, for instance, with the
bodies of animals and their parts and with vegetable bodies, and similarly also with those of the elements. And so, if the body which
moves with a circular motion cannot admit of increase or diminu-
35 tion, it is reasonable to suppose that it is also unalterable.

270^b The reasons why the primary body is eternal and not subject to
increase or diminution, but unaging and unalterable and unmodified,
will be clear from what has been said to any one who believes in our
5 assumptions. Our theory seems to confirm experience and to be confirmed by it. For all men have some conception of the nature of the
gods, and all who believe in the existence of gods at all, whether barbarian or Greek, agree in allotting the highest place to the deity,

7 *Phys.* i. 7-9.

surely because they suppose that immortal is linked with immortal
and regard any other supposition as inconceivable. If then there is,
as there certainly is, anything divine, what we have just said about 10
the primary bodily substance was well said. The mere evidence of
the senses is enough to convince us of this, at least with human certainty. For in the whole range of time past, so far as our inherited
records reach, no change appears to have taken place either in the 15
whole scheme of the outermost heaven or in any of its proper parts.
The common name, too, which has been handed down from our distant ancestors even to our own day, seems to show that they conceived
of it in the fashion which we have been expressing. The same ideas,
one must believe, recur in men's minds not once or twice but again 20
and again. And so, implying that the primary body is something else
beyond earth, fire, air, and water, they gave the highest place a name
of its own, *aither*, derived from the fact that it 'runs always' [8] for an
eternity of time. Anaxagoras, however, scandalously misuses this 25
name, taking *aither* as equivalent to fire.[9]

It is also clear from what has been said why the number of what
we call simple bodies cannot be greater than it is. The motion of a
simple body must itself be simple, and we assert that there are only
these two simple motions, the circular and the straight, the latter 30
being subdivided into motion away from and motion towards the
centre.

4   That there is no other form of motion opposed as contrary to the
circular may be proved in various ways. In the first place, there is an
obvious tendency to oppose the straight line to the circular. For con- 35
cave and convex are not only regarded as opposed to one another, 271ᵃ
but they are also coupled together and treated as a unity in opposition to the straight. And so, if there is a contrary to circular motion,
motion in a straight line must be recognized as having the best claim
to that name. But the two forms of rectilinear motion are opposed to
one another by reason of their places; for up and down is a differ- 5
ence and a contrary opposition in place. Secondly, it may be thought
that the same reasoning which holds good of the rectilinear path
applies also to the circular, movement from *A* to *B* being opposed as
contrary to movement from *B* to *A*. But what is meant is still rectilinear motion. For that is limited to a single path, while the circular 10
paths which pass through the same two points are infinite in number.
Even if we are confined to the single semicircle and the opposition is
between movement from *C* to *D* and from *D* to *C* along that semicircle,

---

[8] i. e. *aither* from *aei thein*.   [9] i. e. deriving *aither* from *aithein*.

the case is no better. For the motion is the same as that along the diameter, since we invariably regard the distance between two points as the length of the straight line which joins them. It is no more satis-
15 factory to construct a circle and treat motion along one semicircle as contrary to motion along the other. For example, taking a complete circle, motion from E to F on the semicircle G may be opposed to motion from F to E on the semicircle H. But even supposing these are contraries, it in no way follows that the reverse motions on the com-
20 plete circumference are contraries. Nor again can motion along the circle from A to B be regarded as the contrary of motion from A to C: for the motion goes from the same point towards the same point, and contrary motion was distinguished as motion from a contrary to its contrary.[10] And even if the motion round a circle is the contrary of the reverse motion, one of the two would be ineffective: for both move
25 to the same point, because that which moves in a circle, at whatever point it begins, must necessarily pass through all the contrary places alike. (By contrarieties of place I mean up and down, back and front, and right and left; and the contrary oppositions of movements are determined by those of places.) One of the motions, then, would be ineffective, for if the two motions were of equal strength, there would
30 be no movement either way, and if one of the two were preponderant, the other would be inoperative. So that if both bodies were there, one of them, inasmuch as it would not be moving with its own move-ment, would be useless, in the sense in which a shoe is useless when it is not worn. But God and nature create nothing that has not its use.

271ᵇ 5   This being clear, we must go on to consider the questions which remain. First, is there an infinite body, as the majority of the ancient philosophers thought, or is this an impossibility? The decision of this
5 question, either way, is not unimportant, but rather all-important, to our search for the truth. It is this problem which has practically always been the source of the differences of those who have written about nature as a whole. So it has been and so it must be; since the least
10 initial deviation from the truth is multiplied later a thousandfold. Admit, for instance, the existence of a minimum magnitude, and you will find that the minimum which you have introduced, small as it is, causes the greatest truths of mathematics to totter. The reason is that a principle is great rather in power than in extent; hence that which was small at the start turns out a giant at the end. Now the con-ception of the infinite possesses this power of principles, and indeed
15 in the sphere of quantity possesses it in a higher degree than any other

[10] *Phys.* v. 5. 229ᵇ 21.

conception; so that it is in no way absurd or unreasonable that the assumption that an infinite body exists should be of peculiar moment to our inquiry. The infinite, then, we must now discuss, opening the whole matter from the beginning.

Every body is necessarily to be classed either as simple or as composite; the infinite body, therefore, will be either simple or composite. But it is clear, further, that if the simple bodies are finite, the composite must also be finite, since that which is composed of bodies finite both in number and in magnitude is itself finite in respect of number and magnitude: its quantity is in fact the same as that of the bodies which compose it. What remains for us to consider, then, is whether any of the simple bodies can be infinite in magnitude, or whether this is impossible. Let us try the primary body first, and then go on to consider the others.

The body which moves in a circle must necessarily be finite in every respect, for the following reasons. (1) If the body so moving is infinite, the radii drawn from the centre will be infinite. But the space between infinite radii is infinite: and by the space between the radii I mean the area outside which no magnitude which is in contact with the two lines can be conceived as falling. This, I say, will be infinite: first, because in the case of finite radii it is always finite; and secondly, because in it one can always go on to a width greater than any given width; thus the reasoning which forces us to believe in infinite number, because there is no maximum, applies also to the space between the radii. Now the infinite cannot be traversed, and if the body is infinite the interval between the radii is necessarily infinite: circular motion therefore is an impossibility. Yet our eyes tell us that the heavens revolve in a circle, and by argument also we have determined that there is something to which circular movement belongs.

(2) Again, if from a finite time a finite time be subtracted, what remains must be finite and have a beginning. And if the time of a journey has a beginning, there must be a beginning also of the movement, and consequently also of the distance traversed. This applies universally. Take a line, *ACE,* infinite in one direction, *E,* and another line, *BB,* infinite in both directions. Let *ACE* describe a circle, revolving upon *C* as centre. In its movement it will cut *BB* continuously for a certain time. This will be a finite time, since the total time is finite in which the heavens complete their circular orbit, and consequently the time subtracted from it, during which the one line in its motion cuts the other, is also finite. Therefore there will be a point at which *ACE* began for the first time to cut *BB*. This, however, is

20 impossible. The infinite, then, cannot revolve in a circle; nor could the world, if it were infinite.

(3) That the infinite cannot move may also be shown as follows. Let *A* be a finite line moving past the finite line, *B*. Of necessity *A* will pass clear of *B* and *B* of *A* at the same moment; for each over-
25 laps the other to precisely the same extent. Now if the two were both moving, and moving in contrary directions, they would pass clear of one another more rapidly; if one were still and the other moving past it, less rapidly; provided that the speed of the latter were the same in both cases. This, however, is clear: that it is impossible to traverse an
30 infinite line in a finite time. Infinite time, then, would be required. (This we demonstrated above in the discussion of movement.[11])
272ᵇ And it makes no difference whether a finite is passing by an infinite or an infinite by a finite. For when *A* is passing *B*, then *B* overlaps *A*, and it makes no difference whether *B* is moved or unmoved, except that, if both move, they pass clear of one another more quickly. It is, however, quite possible that a moving line should in certain cases pass one which is stationary quicker than it passes one moving in an
5 opposite direction. One has only to imagine the movement to be slow where both move and much faster where one is stationary. To suppose one line stationary, then, makes no difficulty for our argument, since it is quite possible for *A* to pass *B* at a slower rate when both
10 are moving than when only one is. If, therefore, the time which the finite moving line takes to pass the other is infinite, then necessarily the time occupied by the motion of the infinite past the finite is also infinite. For the infinite to move at all is thus absolutely impossible; since the very smallest movement conceivable must take an infinity of time. Moreover the heavens certainly revolve, and they complete
15 their circular orbit in a finite time; so that they pass round the whole extent of any line within their orbit, such as the finite line *AB*. The revolving body, therefore, cannot be infinite.

(4) Again, as a line which has a limit cannot be infinite, or, if it is infinite, is so only in length, so a surface cannot be infinite in that respect in which it has a limit; or, indeed, if it is completely determi-
20 nate, in any respect whatever. Whether it be a square or a circle or a sphere, it cannot be infinite, any more than a foot-rule can. There is then no such thing as an infinite sphere or square or circle, and where there is no circle there can be no circular movement, and similarly where there is no infinite at all there can be no infinite movement;

---

[11] Aristotle refers to the *Physics*, here and elsewhere, as continuous with the *De Caelo*. Different parts of the *Physics* are referred to by different names.

and from this it follows that, an infinite circle being itself an impossibility, there can be no circular motion of an infinite body.

(5) Again, take a centre C, an infinite line, AB, another infinite 25 line at right angles to it, E, and a moving radius, CD. CD will never cease contact with E, but the position will always be something like CE, CD cutting E at F. The infinite line, therefore. refuses to complete the circle.

(6) Again, if the heaven is infinite and moves in a circle, we shall 30 have to admit that in a finite time it has traversed the infinite. For suppose the fixed heaven infinite, and that which moves within it equal to it. It results that when the infinite body has completed its revolution, it has traversed an infinite equal to itself in a finite time. But 273ᵃ that we know to be impossible.

(7) It can also be shown, conversely, that if the time of revolution is finite, the area traversed must also be finite; but the area traversed was equal to itself; therefore, it is itself finite.

We have now shown that the body which moves in a circle is not 5 endless or infinite, but has its limit.

6   Further, neither that which moves towards nor that which moves away from the centre can be infinite. For the upward and downward motions are contraries and are therefore motions towards contrary places. But if one of a pair of contraries is determinate, the other must 10 be determinate also. Now the centre is determined; for, from whatever point the body which sinks to the bottom starts its downward motion, it cannot go farther than the centre. The centre, therefore, being determinate, the upper place must also be determinate. But if these two places are determined and finite, the corresponding bodies 15 must also be finite. Further, if up and down are determinate, the intermediate place is also necessarily determinate. For, if it is indeterminate, the movement within it will be infinite; and that we have already shown to be an impossibility.[12] The middle region then is determinate, and consequently any body which either is in it, or might be in it, is determinate. But the bodies which move up and down 20 may be in it, since the one moves naturally away from the centre and the other towards it.

From this alone it is clear that an infinite body is an impossibility; but there is a further point. If there is no such thing as infinite weight, then it follows that none of these bodies can be infinite. For the supposed infinite body would have to be infinite in weight. (The same 25 argument applies to lightness: for as the one supposition involves in-

12 *Phys.* viii. 8.

finite weight, so the infinity of the body which rises to the surface
involves infinite lightness.) This is proved as follows. Assume the
weight to be finite, and take an infinite body, *AB*, of the weight *C*.
30 Subtract from the infinite body a finite mass, *BD*, the weight of which
shall be *E*. *E* then is less than *C*, since it is the weight of a lesser mass.
Suppose then that the smaller goes into the greater a certain number
273ᵇ of times, and take *BF* bearing the same proportion to *BD* which the
greater weight bears to the smaller. For you may subtract as much as
you please from an infinite. If now the masses are proportionate to
the weights, and the lesser weight is that of the lesser mass, the greater
5 must be that of the greater. The weights, therefore, of the finite and
of the infinite body are equal. Again, if the weight of a greater body
is greater than that of a less, the weight of *GB* will be greater than that
of *FB*; and thus the weight of the finite body is greater than that of
the infinite. And, further, the weight of unequal masses will be the
10 same, since the infinite and the finite cannot be equal. It does not
matter whether the weights are commensurable or not. If (*a*) they are
incommensurable the same reasoning holds. For instance, suppose *E*
multiplied by three is rather more than *C*: the weight of three masses
15 of the full size of *BD* will be greater than *C*. We thus arrive at the
same impossibility as before. Again (*b*) we may assume weights which
are *commensurate*; for it makes no difference whether we begin with
the weight or with the mass. For example, assume the weight *E* to be
commensurate with *C*, and take from the infinite mass a part *BD* of
20 weight *E*. Then let a mass *BF* be taken having the same proportion
to *BD* which the two weights have to one another. (For the mass
being infinite you may subtract from it as much as you please.) These
assumed bodies will be commensurate in mass and in weight alike. Nor
again does it make any difference to our demonstration whether the
total mass has its weight equally or unequally distributed. For it must
25 always be possible to take from the infinite mass a body of equal
weight to *BD* by diminishing or increasing the size of the section to
the necessary extent.

From what we have said, then, it is clear that the weight of the
infinite body cannot be finite. It must then be infinite. We have therefore only to show this to be impossible in order to prove an infinite
30 body impossible. But the impossibility of infinite weight can be shown
in the following way. A given weight moves a given distance in a given
time; a weight which is as great and more moves the same distance
in a less time, the times being in inverse proportion to the weights.
274ᵃ For instance, if one weight is twice another, it will take half as long
over a given movement. Further, a finite weight traverses any finite

distance in a finite time. It necessarily follows from this that infinite weight, if there is such a thing, being, on the one hand, as great and more than as great as the finite, will move accordingly, but being, 5 on the other hand, compelled to move in a time inversely proportionate to its greatness, cannot move at all. The time should be less in proportion as the weight is greater. But there is no proportion between the infinite and the finite: proportion can only hold between a less and a greater *finite* time. And though you may say that the time of the movement can be continually diminished, yet there is no minimum. Nor, if there were, would it help us. For some finite 10 body could have been found greater than the given finite in the same proportion which is supposed to hold between the infinite and the given finite; so that an infinite and a finite weight must have traversed an equal distance in equal time. But that is impossible. Again, whatever the time, so long as it is finite, in which the infinite per-15 forms the motion, a finite weight must necessarily move a certain finite distance in that same time. Infinite weight is therefore impossible, and the same reasoning applies also to infinite lightness. Bodies then of infinite weight and of infinite lightness are equally impossible.

That there is no infinite body may be shown, as we have shown it, by a detailed consideration of the various cases. But it may also be 20 shown universally, not only by such reasoning as we advanced in our discussion of principles [13] (though in that passage we have already determined universally the sense in which the existence of an infinite is to be asserted or denied), but also suitably to our present purpose in the following way. That will lead us to a further question. Even if the total mass is not infinite, it may yet be great enough to admit a 25 plurality of universes. The question might possibly be raised whether there is any obstacle to our believing that there are other universes composed on the pattern of our own, more than one, though stopping short of infinity. First, however, let us treat of the infinite universally.

7   Every body must necessarily be either finite or infinite, and if 30 infinite, either of similar or of dissimilar parts. If its parts are *dissimilar*, they must represent either a finite or an infinite number of kinds. That the kinds cannot be *infinite* is evident, if our original presuppositions remain unchallenged. For the primary movements 274[b] being finite in number, the kinds of simple body are necessarily also finite, since the movement of a simple body is simple, and the simple movements are finite, and every natural body must always have its proper motion. Now if the infinite body is to be composed of a *finite* 5

<hr>

[13] *Phys.* iii. 4-8.

number of kinds, then each of its parts must necessarily be infinite in quantity, that is to say, the water, fire, &c., which compose it. But this is impossible, because, as we have already shown, infinite weight and lightness do not exist. Moreover it would be necessary also that their 10 places should be infinite in extent, so that the movements too of all these bodies would be infinite. But this is not possible, if we are to hold to the truth of our original presuppositions and to the view that neither that which moves downward, nor, by the same reasoning, that which moves upward, can prolong its movement to infinity. For it is true in regard to quality, quantity, and place alike that any process 15 of change is impossible which can have no end. I mean that if it is impossible for a thing to have come to be white, or a cubit long, or in Egypt, it is also impossible for it to be in process of coming to be any of these. It is thus impossible for a thing to be moving to a place at which in its motion it can never by any possibility arrive. Again, suppose the body to exist in dispersion, it may be maintained none the less that the total of all these scattered particles, say, of fire, is 20 infinite. But body we saw to be that which has extension every way. How can there be several dissimilar elements, each infinite? Each would have to be infinitely extended every way.

It is no more conceivable, again, that the infinite should exist as a whole of *similar* parts. For, in the first place, there is no other [straight] movement beyond those mentioned: we must therefore 25 give it one of them. And if so, we shall have to admit either infinite weight or infinite lightness. Nor, secondly, could the body whose movement is circular be infinite, since it is impossible for the infinite to move in a circle. This, indeed, would be as good as saying that the heavens are infinite, which we have shown to be impossible.

30 Moreover, in general, it is impossible that the infinite should move at all. If it did, it would move either naturally or by constraint: and if by constraint, it possesses also a natural motion, that is to say, there is another place, infinite like itself, to which it will move. But that is impossible.

That in general it is impossible for the infinite to be acted upon by the finite or to act upon it may be shown as follows.

275ᵃ <I. *The infinite cannot be acted upon by the finite.*> Let A be an infinite, B a finite, C the time of a given movement produced by one in the other. Suppose, then, that A was heated, or impelled, or modified in any way, or caused to undergo any sort of movement whatever, by B in the time C. Let D be less than B; and, assuming that a 5 lesser agent moves a lesser patient in an equal time, call the quantity thus modified by D, E. Then, as D is to B, so is E to some finite

quantum. We assume that the alteration of equal by equal takes equal
time, and the alteration of less by less or of greater by greater takes
the same time, if the quantity of the patient is such as to keep the
proportion which obtains between the agents, greater and less. If so, 10
no movement can be caused in the infinite by any finite agent in any
time whatever. For a less agent will produce that movement in a less
patient in an equal time, and the proportionate equivalent of that
patient will be a finite quantity, since no proportion holds between
finite and infinite.

<2. *The infinite cannot act upon the finite.*> Nor, again, can the
infinite produce a movement in the finite in any time whatever. Let 15
A be an infinite, B [14] a finite, C the time of action. In the time C, D
will produce that motion in a patient less than B, say F. Then take E,
bearing the same proportion to D as the whole BF bears to F. E will
produce the motion in BF in the time C. Thus the finite and the
infinite effect the same alteration in equal times. But this is impos- 20
sible; for the assumption is that the greater effects it in a shorter
time. It will be the same with any time that can be taken, so that
there will be no time in which the infinite can effect this movement.
And, as to infinite time, in that nothing can move another or be
moved by it. For such time has no limit, while the action and reaction
have.

<3. *There is no interaction between infinites.*> Nor can infinite be
acted upon in any way by infinite. Let A and B be infinites, CD being 25
the time of the action of A upon B. Now the whole B was modified
in a certain time, and the part of this infinite, E, cannot be so modified
in the same time, since we assume that a less quantity makes the
movement in a less time. Let E then, when acted upon by A, complete the movement in the time D. Then, as D is to CD, so is E to some 30
finite part of B. This part will necessarily be moved by A in the time
CD. For we suppose that the same agent produces a given effect on
a greater and a smaller mass in longer and shorter times, the times 275^b
and masses varying proportionately. There is thus no finite time in
which infinites can move one another. Is their time then infinite?
No, for infinite time has no end, but the movement communicated
has.

If therefore every perceptible body possesses the power of acting 5
or of being acted upon, or both of these, it is impossible that an
infinite body should be perceptible. All bodies, however, that occupy
place are perceptible. There is therefore no infinite body beyond the
heaven. Nor again is there anything of limited extent beyond it.

---

[14] Called BF a few lines below.

And so beyond the heaven there is no body at all. For if you suppose
10 it an object of intelligence, it will be in a place—since place is what
'within' and 'beyond' denote—and therefore an object of perception.
But nothing that is not in a place is perceptible.

The question may also be examined in the light of more general
considerations as follows. The infinite, considered as a whole of similar parts, cannot, on the one hand, move in a circle. For there is no
15 centre of the infinite, and that which moves in a circle moves about
the centre. Nor again can the infinite move in a straight line. For
there would have to be another place infinite like itself to be the goal
of its natural movement and another, equally great, for the goal of
its unnatural movement. Moreover, whether its rectilinear movement is natural or constrained, in either case the force which causes
20 its motion will have to be infinite. For infinite force is force of an
infinite body, and of an infinite body the force is infinite. So the
motive body also will be infinite. (The proof of this is given in our
discussion of movement,[15] where it is shown that no finite thing possesses infinite power, and no infinite thing finite power.) If then
that which moves naturally can also move unnaturally, there will be
25 two infinites, one which causes, and another which exhibits the latter
motion. Again, what is it that moves the infinite? If it moves itself,
it must be animate. But how can it possibly be conceived as an infinite animal? And if there is something else that moves it, there will
be two infinites, that which moves and that which is moved, differing in their form and power.

30   If the whole is not continuous, but exists, as Democritus and
Leucippus think, in the form of parts separated by void, there must
necessarily be one movement of all the multitude. They are dis-
276ª tinguished, we are told, from one another by their figures; but their
nature is one, like many pieces of gold separated from one another.
But each piece must, as we assert, have the same motion. For a single
clod moves to the same place as the whole mass of earth, and a spark
to the same place as the whole mass of fire. So that if it be weight
5 that all possess, no body is, strictly speaking, light; and if lightness
be universal, none is heavy. Moreover, whatever possesses weight or
lightness will have its place either at one of the extremes or in the
middle region. But this is impossible while the world is conceived as
infinite. And, generally, that which has no centre or extreme limit,
10 no up or down, gives the bodies no place for their motion; and without that movement is impossible. A thing must move either naturally
or unnaturally, and the two movements are determined by the proper

[15] *Phys.* viii. 10.

and alien places. Again, a place in which a thing rests or to which it moves unnaturally, must be the natural place for some other body, 15 as experience shows. Necessarily, therefore, not everything possesses weight or lightness, but some things do and some do not. From these arguments then it is clear that the body of the universe is not infinite.

8 We must now proceed to explain why there cannot be more than one heaven—the further question mentioned above. For it may be thought that we have not proved universally of bodies that none 20 whatever can exist outside our universe, and that our argument applied only to those of indeterminate extent.

Now all things rest and move naturally and by constraint. A thing moves naturally to a place in which it rests without constraint, and rests naturally in a place to which it moves without constraint. On the other hand, a thing moves by constraint to a 25 place in which it rests by constraint, and rests by constraint in a place to which it moves by constraint. Further, if a given movement is due to constraint, its contrary is natural. If, then, it is by constraint that earth moves from a certain place to the centre here, its movement from here to there will be natural, and if earth from there rests here without constraint, its movement hither will be natural. And the natural movement in each case is one. Further, 30 these worlds, being similar in nature to ours, must all be composed of the same bodies as it. Moreover each of the bodies, fire, I mean, and earth and their intermediates, must have the same power 276^b as in our world. For if these names are used equivocally, if the identity of name does not rest upon an identity of form in those elements and ours, then the whole to which they belong can only be called a world by equivocation. Clearly, then, one of the bodies will move naturally away from the centre and another towards the centre, 5 since fire must be identical with fire, earth with earth, and so on, as the fragments of each are identical in this world. That this must be the case is evident from the principles laid down in our discussion of the movements; [16] for these are limited in number, and the distinction of the elements depends upon the distinction of the movements. Therefore, since the movements are the same, the elements 10 must also be the same everywhere. The particles of earth, then, in another world move naturally also to our centre and its fire to our circumference. This, however, is impossible, since, if it were true, earth must, in its own world, move upwards, and fire to the centre; 15

[16] Above, cc. 2-4.

in the same way the earth of our world must move naturally away
from the centre when it moves towards the centre of another universe.
This follows from the supposed juxtaposition of the worlds. For
either we must refuse to admit the identical nature of the simple
20 bodies in the various universes, or, admitting this, we must make the
centre and the extremity one as suggested. This being so, it follows
that there cannot be more worlds than one.

To postulate a difference of nature in the simple bodies according
as they are more or less distant from their proper places is unreasonable. For what difference can it make whether we say that a thing
25 is this distance away or that? One would have to suppose a difference
proportionate to the distance and increasing with it, but the form is
in fact the same. Moreover, the bodies must have some movement,
since the fact that they move is quite evident. Are we to say then that
all their movements, even those which are mutually contrary, are
due to constraint? No, for a body which has no natural movement at
30 all cannot be moved by constraint. If then the bodies have a natural
movement, the movement of the particular instances of each form must
necessarily have for goal a place numerically one, i. e. a particular
centre or a particular extremity. If it be suggested that the goal in each
277ᵃ case is one in form but numerically more than one, on the analogy of
particulars which are many though each undifferentiated in form, we
reply that the variety of goal cannot be limited to this portion or that
but must extend to all alike. For all are equally undifferentiated in form,
5 but any one is different numerically from any other. What I mean is
this: if the portions in this world behave similarly both to one another
and to those in another world, then the portion which is taken hence
will not behave differently either from the portions in another world
or from those in the same world, but similarly to them, since in form
no portion differs from another. The result is that we must either
10 abandon our present assumptions or assert that the centre and the
extremity are each numerically one. But this being so, the heaven, by
the same evidence and the same necessary inferences, must be one
only and no more.

A consideration of the other kinds of movement also makes it plain
that there is some point to which earth and fire move naturally. For
15 in general that which is moved changes from something into something, the starting-point and the goal being different in form, and
always it is a finite change. For instance, to recover health is to change
from disease to health, to increase is to change from smallness to
greatness. Locomotion must be similar: for it also has its goal and
starting-point—and therefore the starting-point and the goal of the

natural movement must differ in form—just as the movement of coming to health does not take any direction which chance or the wishes 20 of the mover may select. Thus, too, fire and earth move not to infinity but to opposite points; and since the opposition in place is between above and below, these will be the limits of their movement. (Even in circular movement there is a sort of opposition between the ends of the diameter, though the movement as a whole has no contrary: so that here too the movement has in a sense an opposed and 25 finite goal.) There must therefore be same end to locomotion: it cannot continue to infinity.

This conclusion that local movement is not continued to infinity is corroborated by the fact that earth moves more quickly the nearer it is to the centre, and fire the nearer it is to the upper place. But 30 if movement were infinite speed would be infinite also; and if speed then weight and lightness. For as superior speed in downward movement implies superior weight, so infinite increase of weight necessitates infinite increase of speed.

Further, it is not the action of another body that makes one of 277ᵇ these bodies move up and the other down; nor is it constraint, like the 'extrusion' of some writers.[17] For in that case the larger the mass of fire or earth the slower would be the upward or downward movement; but the fact is the reverse: the greater the mass of fire or earth the quicker always is its movement towards its own place. Again, the 5 speed of the movement would not increase towards the end if it were due to constraint or extrusion; for a constrained movement always diminishes in speed as the source of constraint becomes more distant, and a body moves without constraint to the place whence it was moved by constraint.

A consideration of these points, then, gives adequate assurance of the truth of our contentions. The same could also be shown with the aid of the discussions which fall under First Philosophy,[18] as well as 10 from the nature of the circular movement, which must be eternal both here and in the other worlds. It is plain, too, from the following considerations that the universe must be one.

The bodily elements are three, and therefore the places of the elements will be three also; the place, first, of the body which sinks 15 to the bottom, namely the region about the centre; the place, secondly, of the revolving body, namely the outermost place, and thirdly, the intermediate place, belonging to the intermediate body. Here in this third place will be the body which rises to the surface;

17 The atomists, Leucippus and Democritus.
18 i. e. Metaphysics, Cf. *Met.* v. 8.

since, if not here, it will be elsewhere, and it cannot be elsewhere:
for we have two bodies, one weightless, one endowed with weight, and
20 below is the place of the body endowed with weight, since the region
about the centre has been given to the heavy body. And its position
cannot be unnatural to it, for it would have to be natural to something else, and there is nothing else. It must then occupy the intermediate place. What distinctions there are within· the intermediate
itself we will explain later on.

We have now said enough to make plain the character and number
of the bodily elements, the place of each, and further, in general,
25 how many in number the various places are.

9 We must show not only that the heaven is one, but also that
more than one heaven is impossible, and, further, that, as exempt
from decay and generation, the heaven is eternal. We may begin by
30 raising a difficulty. From one point of view it might seem impossible
that the heaven should be one and unique, since in all formations and
products whether of nature or of art we can distinguish the shape in
278ª itself and the shape in combination with matter. For instance, the
form of the sphere is one thing and the gold or bronze sphere another;
the shape of the circle again is one thing, the bronze or wooden circle
another. For when we state the essential nature of the sphere or circle
we do not include in the formula gold or bronze, because they do not
5 belong to the essence, but if we are speaking of the copper or gold
sphere we do include them. We still make the distinction even if we
cannot conceive or apprehend any other example beside the particular
thing. This may, of course, sometimes be the case: it might be, for
instance, that only one circle could be found; yet none the less the
difference will remain between the being of circle and of this par-
10 ticular circle, the one being form, the other form in ,matter, i. e. a
particular thing. Now since the universe is perceptible it must be regarded as a particular; for everything that is perceptible subsists, as
we know, in matter. But if it is a particular, there will be a distinction between the being of 'this universe' and of 'universe' unqualified.
There is a difference, then, between 'this universe' and simple 'uni-
15 verse'; the second is form and shape, the first form in combination
with matter; and any shape or form has, or may have, more than one
particular instance.

On the supposition of Forms such as some assert, this must be the
case, and equally on the view that no such entity has a separate
existence. For in every case in which the essence is in matter it is
a fact of observation that the particulars of like form are several or

infinite in number. Hence there either are, or may be, more heavens 20
than one. On these grounds, then, it might be inferred either that
there are or that there might be several heavens. We must, however, return and ask how much of this argument is correct and how much not.

Now it is quite right to say that the formula of the shape apart
from the matter must be different from that of the shape in the
matter, and we may allow this to be true. We are not, however, there- 25
fore compelled to assert a plurality of worlds. Such a plurality is in
fact impossible if this world contains the entirety of matter, as in
fact it does. But perhaps our contention can be made clearer in this
way. Suppose 'aquilinity' to be curvature in the nose or flesh, and
flesh to be the matter of aquilinity. Suppose, further, that all flesh 30
came together into a single whole of flesh endowed with this aquiline
quality. Then neither would there be, nor could there arise, any
other thing that was aquiline. Similarly, suppose flesh and bones
to be the matter of man, and suppose a man to be created of all
flesh and all bones in indissoluble union. The possibility of another 35
man would be removed. Whatever case you took it would be the same.
The general rule is this: a thing whose essence resides in a substratum 278^b
of matter can never come into being in the absence of all matter.
Now the universe is certainly a particular and a material thing: if
however it is composed not of a part but of the whole of matter,
then though the being of 'universe' and of 'this universe' are still dis- 5
tinct, yet there is no other universe, and no possibility of others being
made, because all the matter is already included in this. It remains,
then, only to prove that it is composed of all natural perceptible body.

First, however, we must explain what we mean by 'heaven' and in 10
how many senses we use the word, in order to make clearer the
object of our inquiry. (a) In one sense, then, we call 'heaven' the
substance of the extreme circumference of the whole, or that natural body whose place is at the extreme circumference. We recognize
habitually a special right to the name 'heaven' in the extremity or 15
upper region, which we take to be the seat of all that is divine. (b)
In another sense, we use this name for the body continuous with the
extreme circumference, which contains the moon, the sun, and some
of the stars; these we say are 'in the heaven'. (c) In yet another
sense we give the name to all body included within the extreme cir- 20
cumference, since we habitually call the whole or totality 'the heaven'.
The word, then, is used in three senses.

Now the whole included within the extreme circumference must
be composed of *all* physical and sensible body, because there neither
is, nor can come into being, any body outside the heaven. For if 25

there is a natural body outside the extreme circumference it must be
either a simple or a composite body, and its position must be either
natural or unnatural. But it cannot be any of the simple bodies. For,
first, it has been shown [19] that that which moves in a circle cannot
30 change its place. And, secondly, it cannot be that which moves from
the centre or that which lies lowest. *Naturally* they could not be there,
since their proper places are elsewhere; and if these are there *unnaturally,* the exterior place will be natural to some other body, since a
place which is unnatural to one body must be natural to another: but
35 we saw that there is no other body besides these. Then it is not pos-
279ª sible that any simple body should be outside the heaven. But, if no
simple body, neither can any mixed body be there: for the presence of
the simple body is involved in the presence of the mixture. Further
neither can any body come into that place: for it will do so either
5 naturally or unnaturally, and will be either simple or composite; so
that the same argument will apply, since it makes no difference
whether the question is 'does *A* exist?' or 'could *A* come to exist?'
From our arguments then it is evident not only that there is not,
but also that there could never come to be, any bodily mass whatever outside the circumference. The world as a whole, therefore, includes *all* its appropriate matter, which is, as we saw, natural perceptible body. So that neither are there now, nor have there ever been,
10 nor can there ever be formed more heavens than one, but this heaven
of ours is one and unique and complete.

It is therefore evident that there is also no place or void or time
outside the heaven. For in every place body can be present; and void
is said to be that in which the presence of body, though not actual, is
15 possible; and time is the number of movement. But in the absence of
natural body there is no movement, and outside the heaven, as we
have shown, body neither exists nor can come to exist. It is clear
then that there is neither place, nor void, nor time, outside the heaven.
Hence whatever is there, is of such a nature as not to occupy any
20 place, nor does time age it; nor is there any change in any of the
things which lie beyond the outermost motion; they continue through
their entire duration unalterable and unmodified, living the best and
most self-sufficient of lives. As a matter of fact, this word 'duration'
possessed a divine significance for the ancients, for the fulfilment which
includes the period of life of any creature, outside of which no natural
25 development can fall, has been called its duration. On the same principle the fulfilment of the whole heaven, the fulfilment which includes
all time and infinity, is 'duration'—a name based upon the fact that

[19] The reference is to cc. 2 and 3 above.

it *is always* [20]—duration immortal and divine. From it derive the being and life which other things, some more or less articulately but others feebly, enjoy. So, too, in its discussions concerning the divine, popular philosophy often propounds the view that whatever is divine, whatever is primary and supreme, is necessarily unchangeable. This fact confirms what we have said. For there is nothing else stronger than it to move it—since that would mean more divine—and it has no defect and lacks none of its proper excellences. Its unceasing movement, then, is also reasonable, since everything ceases to move when it comes to its proper place, but the body whose path is the circle has one and the same place for starting-point and goal.

10 Having established these distinctions, we may now proceed to the question whether the heaven is ungenerated or generated, indestructible or destructible. Let us start with a review of the theories of other thinkers; for the proofs of a theory are difficulties for the contrary theory. Besides, those who have first heard the pleas of our adversaries will be more likely to credit the assertions which we are going to make. We shall be less open to the charge of procuring judgement by default. To give a satisfactory decision as to the truth it is necessary to be rather an arbitrator than a party to the dispute.

That the world was generated all are agreed, but, generation over, some say that it is eternal, others say that it is destructible like any other natural formation.[21] Others again, with Empedocles of Acragas and Heraclitus of Ephesus, believe that there is alteration in the destructive process, which takes now this direction, now that, and continues without end.

Now to assert that it was generated and yet is eternal is to assert the impossible; for we cannot reasonably attribute to anything any characteristics but those which observation detects in many or all instances. But in this case the facts point the other way: generated things are seen always to be destroyed. Further, a thing whose present state had no beginning and which could not have been other than it was at any previous moment throughout its entire duration, cannot possibly be changed. For there will have to be some cause of change, and if this had been present earlier it would have made possible another condition of that to which any other condition was impossible. Suppose that the world was formed out of elements which were formerly otherwise conditioned than as they are now. Then (1)

[20] i. e. *aion* is derived from *aei on*.
[21] The former view is that of Orpheus (i. e. of Orphic cosmogony), Hesiod, and Plato, while the latter is that of Democritus and his school.

if their condition was always so and could not have been otherwise, the world could never have come into being. And (2) if the world did come into being, then, clearly, their condition must have been capable of change and not eternal: after combination therefore they will be dispersed, just as in the past after dispersion they came into combination, and this process either has been, or could have been,
30 indefinitely repeated. But if this is so, the world cannot be indestructible, and it does not matter whether the change of condition has actually occurred or remains a possibility.

Some of those who hold that the world, though indestructible, was yet generated, try to support their case by a parallel which is illusory.[22] They say that in their statements about its generation they
35 are doing what geometricians do when they construct their figures, not implying that the universe really had a beginning, but for didactic
280ᵃ reasons facilitating understanding by exhibiting the object, like the figure, as in course of formation. The two cases, as we said, are not parallel; for, in the construction of the figure, when the various steps are completed the required figure forthwith results; but in these other
5 demonstrations what results is not that which was required. Indeed it cannot be so; for antecedent and consequent, as assumed, are in contradiction. The ordered, it is said,[23] arose out of the unordered; and the same thing cannot be at the same time both ordered and unordered; there must be a process and a lapse of time separating the
10 two states. In the figure, on the other hand, there is no temporal separation. It is clear then that the universe cannot be at once eternal and generated.

To say that the universe alternately combines and dissolves is no more paradoxical than to make it eternal but varying in shape.
15 It is as if one were to think that there was now destruction and now existence when from a child a man is generated, and from a man a child. For it is clear that when the elements come together the result is not a chance system and combination, but the very same as before —especially on the view of those who hold this theory, since they say that the contrary is the cause of each state.[24] So that if the totality of
20 body, which is a continuum, is now in this order or disposition and now in that, and if the combination of the whole is a world or heaven,

[22] Simpl. refers the following argument to Xenocrates and the Platonists.
[23] Cp. Plato, *Timaeus* 30ᴀ.
[24] Here Aristotle clearly refers to Empedocles, rather than to Heraclitus. The two causes of Empedocles are Love and Strife and since these are two it follows, Aristotle argues, that the world would merely oscillate between two arrangements or dispositions.

then it will not be the world that comes into being and is destroyed, but only its dispositions.

If the world is believed to be one, it is impossible to suppose that it should be, as a whole, first generated and then destroyed, never to reappear; since before it came into being there was always present 25 the combination prior to it, and that, we hold, could never change if it was never generated. If, on the other hand, the worlds are infinite in number the view is more plausible. But whether this is, or is not, impossible will be clear from what follows. For there are some who think it possible both for the ungenerated to be destroyed and for the generated to persist undestroyed. (This is held in the *Timaeus*,[25] 30 where Plato says that the heaven, though it was generated, will none the less exist to eternity.) So far as the heaven is concerned we have answered this view with arguments appropriate to the nature of the heaven: on the general question we shall attain clearness when we examine the matter universally.

11 We must first distinguish the senses in which we use the words 280^b 'ungenerated' and 'generated', 'destructible' and 'indestructible'. These have many meanings, and though it may make no difference to the argument, yet some confusion of mind must result from treating as uniform in its use a word which has several distinct applications. 5 The character which is the ground of the predication will always remain obscure.

The word 'ungenerated' then is used (*a*) in one sense whenever something now is which formerly was not, no process of becoming or change being involved. Such is the case, according to some, with contact and motion, since there is no process of coming to be in contact or in motion. (*b*) It is used in another sense, when something which is capable of coming to be, with or without process, does not exist; 10 such a thing is ungenerated in the sense that its generation is not a fact but a possibility. (*c*) It is also applied where there is general impossibility of any generation such that the thing now is which then was not. And 'impossibility' has two uses: first, where it is untrue to say that the thing can ever come into being, and secondly, where it cannot do so easily, quickly, or well. In the same way the word 'gener- 15 ated' is used, (*a*) first, where what formerly was not afterwards is, whether a process of becoming was or was not involved, so long as that which then was not, now is; (*b*) secondly, of anything capable

---

[25] The reference is to Plato, *Timaeus* 31. Plato is quoted as authority for the indestructible-generated not for the ungenerated-destructible, as the context shows.

of existing, 'capable' being defined with reference either to truth
or to facility; (c) thirdly, of anything to which the passage from not
being to being belongs, whether already actual, if its existence is
20 due to a past process of becoming, or not yet actual but only possible.
The uses of the words 'destructible' and 'indestructible' are similar.
'Destructible' is applied (a) to that which formerly was and afterwards either is not or might not be, whether a period of being destroyed and changed intervenes or not; and (b) sometimes we apply
the word to that which a process of destruction may cause not to be;
and also (c) in a third sense, to that which is easily destructible, to
25 the 'easily-destroyed', so to speak. Of the indestructible the same account holds good. It is either (a) that which now is and now is not,
without any process of destruction, like contact, which without being
destroyed afterwards is not, though formerly it was; or (b) that
which is but might not be, or which will at some time not be, though
30 it now is. For you exist now and so does the contact; yet both are
destructible, because a time will come when it will not be true of you
that you exist, nor of these things that they are in contact. Thirdly
(c) in its most proper use, it is that which is, but is incapable of
any destruction such that the thing which now is later ceases to be
or might cease to be; or again, that which has not yet been destroyed,
281ᵃ but in the future may cease to be. For indestructible is also used of
that which is destroyed with difficulty.

This being so, we must ask what we mean by 'possible' and 'impossible'. For in its most proper use the predicate 'indestructible'
is given because it is impossible that the thing should be destroyed,
5 i. e. exist at one time and not at another. And 'ungenerated' also involves impossibility when used for that which cannot be generated,
in such fashion that, while formerly it was not, later it is. An instance
is a commensurable diagonal. Now when we speak of a power to move
or to lift weights, we refer always to the maximum. We speak, for
instance, of a power to lift a hundred talents or walk a hundred stades
—though a power to effect the maximum is also a power to effect any
10 part of the maximum—since we feel obliged in defining the power
to give the limit or maximum. A thing, then, which is capable of a
certain amount as maximum must also be capable of that which lies
within it. If, for example, a man can lift a hundred talents, he can also
lift two, and if he can walk a hundred stades, he can also walk two.
15 But the power is of the maximum, and a thing said, with reference
to its maximum, to be incapable of so much is also incapable of any
greater amount. It is, for instance, clear that a person who cannot
walk a thousand stades will also be unable to walk a thousand and

one. This point need not trouble us, for we may take it as settled that
what is, in the strict sense, possible is determined by a limiting
maximum. Now perhaps the objection might be raised that there is 20
no necessity in this, since he who sees a stade need not see the smaller
measures contained in it, while, on the contrary, he who can see a dot
or hear a small sound will perceive what is greater. This, however,
does not touch our argument. The maximum may be determined
either in the power or in its object. The application of this is plain. 25
Superior sight is sight of the smaller body, but superior speed is that
of the greater body.

12   Having established these distinctions we can now proceed to the
sequel. If there are things capable both of being and of not being,
there must be some definite maximum time of their being and not
being; a time, I mean, during which continued existence is possible to 30
them and a time during which continued non-existence is possible.
And this is true in every category, whether the thing is, for example,
'man', or 'white', or 'three cubits long', or whatever it may be. For if
the time is not definite in quantity, but longer than any that can be
suggested and shorter than none, then it will be possible for one and
the same thing to exist for infinite time and not to exist for another in- 281^b
finity. This, however, is impossible.

Let us take our start from this point. The impossible and the false
have not the same significance. One use of 'impossible' and 'possible',
and 'false' and 'true', is hypothetical. It is impossible, for instance, 5
on a certain hypothesis that the triangle should have its angles equal
to two right angles, and on another the diagonal is commensurable.
But there are also things possible and impossible, false and true,
absolutely. Now it is one thing to be absolutely false, and another
thing to be absolutely impossible. To say that you are standing when
you are not standing is to assert a falsehood, but not an impossi- 10
bility. Similarly to say that a man who is playing the harp, but not
singing, is singing, is to say what is false but not impossible. To say,
however, that you are at once standing and sitting, or that the diagonal
is commensurable, is to say what is not only false but also impossible.
Thus it is not the same thing to make a false and to make an impossible hypothesis; and from the impossible hypothesis impossible re- 15
sults follow. A man has, it is true, the capacity at once of sitting and
of standing, because when he possesses the one he also possesses the
other; but it does not follow that he can at once sit and stand, only
that at another time he can do the other also. But if a thing has for
infinite time more than one capacity, another time is impossible and

20 the times must coincide. Thus if anything which exists for infinite time is destructible, it will have the capacity of not being. Now if it exists for infinite time let this capacity be actualized; and it will be in actuality at once existent and non-existent. Thus a false conclusion would follow because a false assumption was made, but if what
25 was assumed had not been impossible its consequence would not have been impossible.

Anything then which always exists is absolutely imperishable. It is also ungenerated, since if it was generated it will have the power for some time of not being. For as that which formerly was, but now is not, or is capable at some future time of not being, is destructible, so that which is capable of formerly not having been is generated. But in the case of that which always is, there is no time for such
30 a capacity of not being, whether the supposed time is finite or infinite; for its capacity of being must include the finite time since it covers infinite time.

It is therefore impossible that one and the same thing should be capable of always existing and of always not-existing. And 'not always existing', the contradictory, is also excluded. Thus it is impossible
282ᵃ for a thing always to exist and yet to be destructible. Nor, similarly, can it be generated. For of two attributes if B cannot be present without A, the impossibility of A proves the impossibility of B. What always is, then, since it is incapable of ever not being, cannot possibly be generated. But since the contradictory of 'that which is
5 always capable of being' is 'that which is not always capable of being'; while 'that which is always capable of not being' is the contrary, whose contradictory in turn is 'that which is not always capable of not being', it is necessary that the contradictories of both terms should be predicable of one and the same thing, and thus that, intermediate between what always is and what always is not, there should be that
10 to which being and not-being are both possible; for the contradictory of each will at times be true of it unless it always exists. Hence that which not always is not will sometimes be and sometimes not be; and it is clear that this is true also of that which cannot always be but sometimes is and therefore sometimes is not. One thing, then, will have the power of being and of not being, and will thus be intermediate between the other two.

Expressed universally our argument is as follows. Let there be
15 two attributes, A and B, not capable of being present in any one thing together, while either A or C and either B or D are capable of being present in everything. Then C and D must be predicated of everything of which neither A nor B is predicated. Let E lie between

A and *B*; for that which is neither of two contraries is a mean between them. In *E* both *C* and *D* must be present, for either *A* or *C* is present everywhere and therefore in *E*. Since then *A* is impossible, 20 *C* must be present, and the same argument holds of *D*.[26]

Neither that which always is, therefore, nor that which always is not is either generated or destructible. And clearly whatever is generated or destructible is not eternal. If it were, it would be at once capable of always being and capable of not always being, but it has 25 already been shown [27] that this is impossible. Surely then whatever is ungenerated and in being must be eternal, and whatever is indestructible and in being must equally be so. (I use the words 'ungenerated' and 'indestructible' in their proper sense, 'ungenerated' for that which now is and could not at any previous time have been truly said not to be; 'indestructible' for that which now is and cannot at any future time be truly said not to be.) If, again, the two terms are 30 coincident, if the ungenerated is indestructible, and the indestructible ungenerated, then each of them is coincident with 'eternal'; anything ungenerated is eternal and anything indestructible is eternal. This is 282^b clear too from the definition of the terms. Whatever is destructible must be generated; for it is either ungenerated or generated, but, if ungenerated, it is by hypothesis indestructible. Whatever, further, is generated must be destructible. For it is either destructible or indestructible, but, if indestructible, it is by hypothesis ungenerated. 5 If, however, 'indestructible' and 'ungenerated' are not coincident, there is no necessity that either the ungenerated or the indestructible should be eternal. But they must be coincident, for the following reasons. The terms 'generated' and 'destructible' are coincident; this is obvious from our former remarks, since between what always is and 10 what always is not there is an intermediate which is neither, and that intermediate is the generated and destructible. For whatever is either of these is capable both of being and of not being for a definite time: in either case, I mean, there is a certain period of time during which the thing is and another during which it is not. Anything therefore which is generated or destructible must be intermedi- 15 ate. Now let *A* be that which always is and *B* that which always is not, *C* the generated, and *D* the destructible. Then *C* must be inter-

---

[26] The four letters *ABCD* are to be allotted as follows: *A* is 'that which is always capable of being' = 'what always is', *B* is its contrary, 'that which is always capable of not being' = 'what always is not', *C* is its contradictory, 'that which is not always capable of being', and *D* is the contradictory of *B*, 'that which is not always capable of not being'. *C* and *D* might also be described by the terms 'what not always is' and 'what not always is not' respectively.

[27] 281^b 18 ff.

mediate between A and B. For in their case there is no time in the
direction of either limit, in which either A is not or B is. But for the
20 generated there must be such a time either actually or potentially,
though not for A and B in either way. C then will be, and also not
be, for a limited length of time, and this is true also of D, the destructible. Therefore each is both generated and destructible. Therefore 'generated' and 'destructible' are coincident. Now let E stand
25 for the ungenerated, F for the generated, G for the indestructible,
and H for the destructible. As for F and H, it has been shown that
they are coincident. But when terms stand to one another as these
do, F and H coincident, E and F never predicated of the same thing
30 but one or other of everything, and G and H likewise, then E and
G must needs be coincident. For suppose that E is not coincident
with G, then F will be, since either E or F is predicable of everything.
But of that of which F is predicated H will be predicable also. H will
283ᵃ then be coincident with G, but this we saw to be impossible. And the
same argument shows that G is coincident with E.

Now the relation of the ungenerated (E) to the generated (F) is
the same as that of the indestructible (G) to the destructible (H).
To say then that there is no reason why anything should not be gener-
5 ated and yet indestructible or ungenerated and yet destroyed, to
imagine that in the one case generation and in the other case destruction occurs once for all, is to destroy part of the data.[28] For (1)
everything is capable of acting or being acted upon, of being or not
being, either for an infinite, or for a definitely limited space of time;
and the infinite time is only a possible alternative because it is after
10 a fashion defined, as a length of time which cannot be exceeded. But
infinity in one direction is neither infinite nor finite. (2) Further,
why, after always existing, was the thing destroyed, why, after an
infinity of not being, was it generated, at one moment rather than
another? If every moment is alike and the moments are infinite in
number, it is clear that a generated or destructible thing existed for
an infinite time. It has therefore for an infinite time the capacity of
15 not being (since the capacity of being and the capacity of not being
will be present together), if destructible, in the time before destruction, if generated, in the time after generation. If then we assume the
two capacities to be actualized, opposites will be present together. (3)

---

[28] Aristotle now proceeds to apply his results to the refutation of the view
attributed in 280ᵃ 30 to Plato's *Timaeus*. He there promised to give a clearer
demonstration of its absurdity when the terms 'generated', 'ungenerated', &c.
should be investigated on their own account and apart from the special case
of the heaven.

Further, this second capacity will be present like the first at every moment, so that the thing will have for an infinite time the capacity both of being and of not being; but this has been shown to be impossible. (4) Again, if the capacity is present prior to the activity, 20 it will be present for all time, even while the thing was as yet ungenerated and non-existent, throughout the infinite time in which it was capable of being generated. At the time, then, when it was not, at that same time it had the capacity of being, both of being then and of being thereafter, and therefore for an infinity of time.

It is clear also on other grounds that it is impossible that the 25 destructible should not at some time be destroyed. For otherwise it will always be at once destructible and in actuality indestructible, so that it will be at the same time capable of always existing and of not always existing. Thus the destructible is at some time actually destroyed. The generable, similarly, has been generated, for it is capable of having been generated and thus also of not always existing.

We may also see in the following way how impossible it is either 30 for a thing which is generated to be thenceforward indestructible, or for a thing which is ungenerated and has always hitherto existed to be destroyed. Nothing that is by chance can be indestructible or ungenerated, since the products of chance and fortune are opposed to what is, or comes to be, always or usually, while anything which 283ᵇ exists for a time infinite either absolutely or in one direction, is in existence either always or usually. That which is by chance, then, is by nature such as to exist at one time and not at another. But in things of that character the contradictory states proceed from one and the same capacity, the matter of the thing being the cause 5 equally of its existence and of its non-existence. Hence contradictories would be present together in actuality.

Further, it cannot truly be said of a thing now that it exists last year, nor could it be said last year that it exists now. It is therefore impossible for what once did not exist later to be eternal. For in its later state it will possess the capacity of not existing, only not of not existing at a time when it exists—since then it exists in actuality— 10 but of not existing last year or in the past. Now suppose it to be in actuality what it is capable of being. It will then be true to say now that it does not exist last year. But this is impossible. No capacity relates to being in the past, but always to being in the present or future. It is the same with the notion of an eternity of existence followed later by non-existence. In the later state the capacity will be 15 present for that which is not there in actuality. Actualize, then, the capacity. It will be true to say now that this exists last year or in the past generally.

Considerations also not general like these but proper to the subject show it to be impossible that what was formerly eternal should later be destroyed or that what formerly was not should later be 20 eternal. Whatever is destructible or generated is always alterable. Now alteration is due to contraries, and the things which compose the natural body are the very same that destroy it. . . .

BOOK II

293ᵃ 15 13 It remains to speak of the earth, of its position, of the question whether it is at rest or in motion, and of its shape.

I. As to its *position* there is some difference of opinion. Most people —all, in fact, who regard the whole heaven as finite—say it lies 20 at the centre. But the Italian philosophers known as Pythagoreans take the contrary view. At the centre, they say, is fire, and the earth is one of the stars, creating night and day by its circular motion about the centre. They further construct another earth in opposition to ours 25 to which they give the name counter-earth. In all this they are not seeking for theories and causes to account for observed facts, but rather forcing their observations and trying to accommodate them to certain theories and opinions of their own. But there are many others who would agree that it is wrong to give the earth the central 30 position, looking for confirmation rather to theory than to the facts of observation. Their view is that the most precious place befits the most precious thing: but fire, they say, is more precious than earth, and the limit than the intermediate, and the circumference and the centre are limits. Reasoning on this basis they take the view that it 293ᵇ is not earth that lies at the centre of the sphere, but rather fire. The Pythagoreans have a further reason. They hold that the most important part of the world, which is the centre, should be most strictly guarded, and name it, or rather the fire which occupies that place, the 'Guard-house of Zeus', as if the word 'centre' were 5 quite unequivocal, and the centre of the mathematical figure were always the same with that of the thing or the natural centre. But it is better to conceive of the case of the whole heaven as analogous to that of animals, in which the centre of the animal and that of the body are different. For this reason they have no need to be so dis- 10 turbed about the world, or to call in a guard for its centre: rather let them look for the centre in the other sense and tell us what it is like and where nature has set it. That centre will be something primary and precious; but to the mere position we should give the last place rather than the first. For the middle is what is defined, and what defines it is the limit, and that which contains or limits is more precious than that which is limited, seeing that the latter is the matter 15 and the former the essence of the system.

II. As to the position of the earth, then, this is the view which some advance, and the views advanced concerning its *rest or motion* are similar. For here too there is no general agreement. All who deny that the earth lies at the centre think that it revolves about the centre, and not the earth only but, as we said before, the counter-earth as 20 well. Some of them even consider it possible that there are several bodies so moving, which are invisible to us owing to the interposition of the earth. This, they say, accounts for the fact that eclipses of the moon are more frequent than eclipses of the sun: for in addition to the earth each of these moving bodies can obstruct it. Indeed, as in 25 any case the surface of the earth is not actually a centre but distant from it a full hemisphere, there is no more difficulty, they think, in accounting for the observed facts on their view that we do not dwell at the centre, than on the common view that the earth is in the middle. Even as it is, there is nothing in the observations to suggest that we are removed from the centre by half the diameter of the 30 earth. Others, again, say that the earth, which lies at the centre, is 'rolled', and thus in motion, about the axis of the whole heaven. So it stands written in the *Timaeus*.[1]

III. There are similar disputes about the *shape* of the earth. Some think it is spherical, others that it is flat and drum-shaped. For evidence they bring the fact that, as the sun rises and sets, the part con- 294ª cealed by the earth shows a straight and not a curved edge, whereas if the earth were spherical the line of section would have to be circular. In this they leave out of account the great distance of the sun 5 from the earth and the great size of the circumference, which, seen from a distance on these apparently small circles appears straight. Such an appearance ought not to make them doubt the circular shape of the earth. But they have another argument. They say that because it is at rest, the earth must necessarily have this shape. For there are 10 many different ways in which the movement or rest of the earth has been conceived.

The difficulty must have occurred to every one. It would indeed be a complacent mind that felt no surprise that, while a little bit of earth, let loose in mid-air, moves and will not stay still, and the more there 15

_____
[1] *Timaeus*, 40 B.

is of it the faster it moves, the whole earth, free in mid-air, should
show no movement at all. Yet here is this great weight of earth,
and it is at rest. And again, from beneath one of these moving
fragments of earth, before it falls, take away the earth, and it will
continue its downward movement with nothing to stop it. The diffi-
20 culty then, has naturally passed into a commonplace of philosophy;
and one may well wonder that the solutions offered are not seen
to involve greater absurdities than the problem itself.

By these considerations some have been led to assert that the earth
below us is infinite, saying, with Xenophanes of Colophon, that it
has 'pushed its roots to infinity',—in order to save the trouble of
25 seeking for the cause. Hence the sharp rebuke of Empedocles, in the
words 'if the deeps of the earth are endless and endless the ample
ether—such is the vain tale told by many a tongue, poured from the
mouths of those who have seen but little of the whole'. Others say the
earth rests upon water. This, indeed, is the oldest theory that has
30 been preserved, and is attributed to Thales of Miletus. It was supposed to stay still because it floated like wood and other similar substances, which are so constituted as to rest upon water but not upon
air. As if the same account had not to be given of the water which
carries the earth as of the earth itself! It is not the nature of water,
any more than of earth, to stay in mid-air: it must have something
294ᵇ to rest upon. Again, as air is lighter than water, so is water than earth:
how then can they think that the naturally lighter substance lies below
the heavier? Again, if the earth as a whole is capable of floating upon
water, that must obviously be the case with any part of it. But
5 observation shows that this is not the case. Any piece of earth goes
to the bottom, the quicker the larger it is. These thinkers seem to
push their inquiries some way into the problem, but not so far as they
might. It is what we are all inclined to do, to direct our inquiry not
by the matter itself, but by the views of our opponents: and even
10 when interrogating oneself one pushes the inquiry only to the point
at which one can no longer offer any opposition. Hence a good inquirer will be one who is ready in bringing forward the objections
proper to the genus, and that he will be when he has gained an understanding of all the differences.

Anaximenes and Anaxagoras and Democritus give the flatness of
15 the earth as the cause of its staying still. Thus, they say, it does not
cut, but covers like a lid, the air beneath it. This seems to be the way
of flat-shaped bodies: for even the wind can scarcely move them
because of their power of resistance. The same immobility, they say,
is produced by the flatness of the surface which the earth presents to

the air which underlies it; while the air, not having room enough to change its place because it is underneath the earth, stays there in a 20 mass, like the water in the case of the water-clock. And they adduce an amount of evidence to prove that air, when cut off and at rest, can bear a considerable weight.

Now, first, if the shape of the earth is not flat, its flatness cannot be the cause of its immobility. But in their own account it is rather the size of the earth than its flatness that causes it to remain at rest. For 25 the reason why the air is so closely confined that it cannot find a passage, and therefore stays where it is, is its great amount: and this amount is great because the body which isolates it, the earth, is very large. This result, then, will follow, even if the earth is spherical, so long as it retains its size. So far as their arguments go, the earth will 30 still be at rest.

In general, our quarrel with those who speak of movement in this way cannot be confined to the parts [2]; it concerns the whole universe. One must decide at the outset whether bodies have a natural movement or not, whether there is no natural but only constrained movement. Seeing, however, that we have already decided this mat- 295ᵃ ter to the best of our ability, we are entitled to treat our results as representing fact. Bodies, we say, which have no natural movement, have no constrained movement; and where there is no natural and no constrained movement there will be no movement at all. This is a con- 5 clusion, the necessity of which we have already decided,[3] and we have seen further that rest also will be inconceivable, since rest, like movement, is either natural or constrained. But if there is any natural movement, constraint will not be the sole principle of motion or of rest. If, then, it is by constraint that the earth now keeps its place, the so-called 'whirling' movement by which its parts came together at 10 the centre was also constrained. (The form of causation supposed they all borrow from observations of liquids and of air, in which the larger and heavier bodies always move to the centre of the whirl. This is thought by all those who try to generate the heavens to explain why the earth came together at the centre. They then seek a reason for its 15 staying there; and some say, in the manner explained, that the reason is its size and flatness, others, with Empedocles, that the motion of the heavens, moving about it at a higher speed, prevents movement of the earth, as the water in a cup, when the cup is given a circu- 20 lar motion, though it is often underneath the bronze, is for this same reason prevented from moving with the downward movement which is

[2] i. e. to the single element earth or to earth and air.
[3] i. 2-4.

natural to it.) But suppose both the 'whirl' and its flatness (the air beneath being withdrawn) cease to prevent the earth's motion, where will the earth move to then? Its movement to the centre was constrained and its rest at the centre is due to constraint; but there
25 must be some motion which is natural to it. Will this be upward motion or downward or what? It must have some motion; and if upward and downward motion are alike to it, and the air above the earth does not prevent upward movement, then no more could air below it prevent downward movement. For the same cause must necessarily have the same effect on the same thing.

30   Further, against Empedocles there is another point which might be made. When the elements were separated off by Hate, what caused the earth to keep its place? Surely the 'whirl' cannot have been then also the cause. It is absurd too not to perceive that, while the whirling movement may have been responsible for the original coming together of the parts of earth at the centre, the question remains, why *now*
35 do all heavy bodies move to the earth? For the whirl surely does not
295ᵇ come near us. Why, again, does fire move upward? Not, surely, because of the whirl. But if fire is naturally such as to move in a certain direction, clearly the same may be supposed to hold of earth. Again, it cannot be the whirl which determines the heavy and the light.
5 Rather that movement caused the pre-existent heavy and light things to go to the middle and stay on the surface respectively. Thus, before ever the whirl began, heavy and light existed; and what can have been the ground of their distinction, or the manner and direction of their natural movements? In the infinite chaos there can have been neither above nor below, and it is by these that heavy and light are determined.

10   It is to these causes that most writers pay attention: but there are some, Anaximander, for instance, among the ancients, who say that the earth keeps its place because of its indifference. Motion upward and downward and sideways were all, they thought, equally inappropriate to that which is set at the centre and indifferently
15 related to every extreme point; and to move in contrary directions at the same time was impossible: so it must needs remain still. This view is ingenious but not true. The argument would prove that everything, whatever it be, which is put at the centre, must stay there. Fire, then, will rest at the centre: for the proof turns on no peculiar
20 property of earth. But this does not follow. The observed facts about earth are not only that it remains at the centre, but also that it moves to the centre. The place to which any fragment of earth moves must necessarily be the place to which the whole moves; and in the place to

which a thing naturally moves, it will naturally rest. The reason then is not in the fact that the earth is indifferently related to every extreme point: for this would apply to any body, whereas movement to the centre is peculiar to earth. Again it is absurd to look for a reason why the earth remains at the centre and not for a reason why fire remains at the extremity. If the extremity is the natural place of fire, clearly earth must also have a natural place. But suppose that the centre is not its place, and that the reason of its remaining there is this necessity of indifference—on the analogy of the hair which, it is said, however great the tension, will not break under it, if it be evenly distributed, or of the man who, though exceedingly hungry and thirsty, and both equally, yet being equidistant from food and drink, is therefore bound to stay where he is—even so, it still remains to explain why fire stays at the extremities. It is strange, too, to ask about things staying still but not about their motion—why, I mean, one thing, if nothing stops it, moves up, and another thing to the centre. Again, their statements are not true. It happens, indeed, to be the case that a thing to which movement this way and that is equally inappropriate is obliged to remain at the centre.[4] But so far as their argument goes, instead of remaining there, it will move, only not as a mass but in fragments. For the argument applies equally to fire. Fire, if set at the centre, should stay there, like earth, since it will be indifferently related to every point on the extremity. Nevertheless it will move, as in fact it always does move when nothing stops it, away from the centre to the extremity. It will not, however, move in a mass to a single point on the circumference—the only possible result on the lines of the indifference theory—but rather each corresponding portion of fire to the corresponding part of the extremity, each fourth part, for instance, to a fourth part of the circumference. For since no body is a point, it will have parts. The expansion, when the body increased the place occupied, would be on the same principle as the contraction, in which the place was diminished. Thus, for all the indifference theory shows to the contrary, earth also would have moved in this manner away from the centre, unless the centre had been its natural place.

We have now outlined the views held as to the shape, position, and rest or movement of the earth.

14   Let us first decide the question whether the earth moves or is at rest. For, as we said, there are some who make it one of the stars,

---

[4] The principle is in fact true, if it is properly understood, i. e. seen to apply, as explained in what follows, only to indivisible bodies.

and others who, setting it at the centre, suppose it to be 'rolled' and in motion about the pole as axis. That both views are untenable will be clear if we take as our starting-point the fact that the earth's motion, whether the earth be at the centre or away from it, must
30 needs be a constrained motion. It cannot be the movement of the earth itself. If it were, any portion of it would have this movement; but in fact every part moves in a straight line to the centre. Being, then, constrained and unnatural, the movement could not be eternal. But the order of the universe is eternal. Again, everything that moves
35 with the circular movement, except the first sphere, is observed to
296ᵇ be passed, and to move with more than one motion. The earth, then, also, whether it move about the centre or as stationary at it, must necessarily move with two motions. But if this were so, there would
5 have to be passings and turnings of the fixed stars. Yet no such thing is observed. The same stars always rise and set in the same parts of the earth.

Further, the natural movement of the earth, part and whole alike, is to the centre of the whole—whence the fact that it is now actually
10 situated at the centre—but it might be questioned, since both centres are the same, which centre it is that portions of earth and other heavy things move to. Is this their goal because it is the centre of the earth or because it is the centre of the whole? The goal, surely, must be the centre of the whole. For fire and other light things move to the
15 extremity of the area which contains the centre. It happens, however, that the centre of the earth and of the whole is the same. Thus they do move to the centre of the earth, but accidentally, in virtue of the fact that the earth's centre lies at the centre of the whole. That the centre of the earth is the goal of their movement is indicated by the fact that
20 heavy bodies moving towards the earth do not move parallel but so as to make equal angles,[5] and thus to a single centre, that of the earth. It is clear, then, that the earth must be at the centre and im-movable, not only for the reasons already given, but also because heavy bodies forcibly thrown quite straight upward return to the point
25 from which they started, even if they are thrown to an infinite dis-tance. From these considerations then it is clear that the earth does not move and does not lie elsewhere than at the centre.

From what we have said the explanation of the earth's immobility is also apparent. If it is the nature of earth, as observation shows, to move from any point to the centre, as of fire contrariwise to move
30 from the centre to the extremity, it is impossible that any portion of

---

[5] i. e. at right angles to a tangent: if it fell otherwise than at right angles, the angles on each side of the line of fall would be unequal.

earth should move away from the centre except by constraint. For a single thing has a single movement, and a simple thing a simple: contrary movements cannot belong to the same thing, and movement away from the centre is the contrary of movement to it. If then no portion of earth can move away from the centre, obviously still less can the earth as a whole so move. For it is the nature of the whole to 35 move to the point to which the part naturally moves. Since, then, it 297ᵃ would require a force greater than itself to move it, it must needs stay at the centre. This view is further supported by the contributions of mathematicians to astronomy, since the observations made as the 5 shapes change by which the order of the stars is determined, are fully accounted for on the hypothesis that the earth lies at the centre. Of the position of the earth and of the manner of its rest or movement, our discussion may here end.

Its shape must necessarily be spherical. For every portion of earth has weight until it reaches the centre, and the jostling of parts greater 10 and smaller would bring about not a waved surface, but rather compression and convergence of part and part until the centre is reached. The process should be conceived by supposing the earth to come into being in the way that some of the natural philosophers describe.⁶ Only they attribute the downward movement to constraint, and it is 15 better to keep to the truth and say that the reason of this motion is that a thing which possesses weight is naturally endowed with a centripetal movement. When the mixture, then, was merely potential, the things that were separated off moved similarly from every side towards the centre. Whether the parts which came together at the centre were distributed at the extremities evenly, or in some other 20 way, makes no difference. If, on the one hand, there were a similar movement from each quarter of the extremity to the single centre, it is obvious that the resulting mass would be similar on every side. For if an equal amount is added on every side the extremity of the mass will be everywhere equidistant from its centre, i. e. the figure will be 25 spherical. But neither will it in any way affect the argument if there is not a similar accession of concurrent fragments from every side. For the greater quantity, finding a lesser in front of it, must necessarily drive it on, both having an impulse whose goal is the centre, and the greater weight driving the lesser forward till this goal is 30 reached. In this we have also the solution of a possible difficulty. The earth, it might be argued, is at the centre and spherical in shape: if, then, a weight many times that of the earth were added to one hemisphere, the centre of the earth and of the whole will no longer be coin-

⁶ The cosmogony which follows is in principle that of Anaxagoras.

cident. So that either the earth will not stay still at the centre, or if it
297ᵇ does, it will be at rest without having its centre at the place to which
it is still its nature to move. Such is the difficulty. A short consideration will give us an easy answer, if we first give precision to our
postulate that any body endowed with weight, of whatever size,
5 moves towards the centre. Clearly it will not stop when its edge
touches the centre. The greater quantity must prevail until the body's
centre occupies the centre. For that is the goal of its impulse. Now
it makes no difference whether we apply this to a clod or common
fragment of earth or to the earth as a whole. The fact indicated
10 does not depend upon degrees of size but applies universally to
everything that has the centripetal impulse. Therefore earth in motion,
whether in a mass or in fragments, necessarily continues to move
until it occupies the centre equally every way, the less being forced to
equalize itself by the greater owing to the forward drive of the
impulse.[7]

If the earth was generated, then, it must have been formed in this
15 way, and so clearly its generation was spherical; and if it is ungenerated and has remained so always, its character must be that which
the initial generation, if it had occurred, would have given it. But the
spherical shape, necessitated by this argument, follows also from the
fact that the motions of heavy bodies always make equal angles,
20 and are not parallel. This would be the natural form of movement
towards what is naturally spherical. Either then the earth is spherical
or it is at least naturally spherical. And it is right to call anything
that which nature intends it to be, and which belongs to it, rather than
that which it is by constraint and contrary to nature. The evidence of
the senses further corroborates this. How else would eclipses of the
25 moon show segments shaped as we see them? As it is, the shapes
which the moon itself each month shows are of every kind—
straight, gibbous, and concave—but in eclipses the outline is always
curved: and, since it is the interposition of the earth that makes the
30 eclipse, the form of this line will be caused by the form of the earth's
surface, which is therefore spherical. Again, our observations of the
stars make it evident, not only that the earth is circular, but also that

[7] The argument is quite clear if it is understood that 'greater' and 'less' here
and in ᵃ 30 and in ᵇ 5 stand for greater and smaller portions of one body, the
line of division passing through the centre which is the goal. Suppose the earth so
placed in regard to the centre. The larger and heavier division would 'drive the
lesser forward', i. e. beyond the centre (ᵃ 30); it would 'prevail until the body's
centre occupied the centre' (ᵇ 5); it would 'force the less to equalize itself', i. e.
to move on until the line passing through the central goal divided the body
equally.

it is a circle of no great size. For quite a small change of position to south or north causes a manifest alteration of the horizon. There is much change, I mean, in the stars which are overhead, and the stars 298ᵃ seen are different, as one moves northward or southward. Indeed there are some stars seen in Egypt and in the neighbourhood of Cyprus which are not seen in the northerly regions; and stars, which in the 5 north are never beyond the range of observation, in those regions rise and set. All of which goes to show not only that the earth is circular in shape, but also that it is a sphere of no great size: for otherwise the effect of so slight a change of place would not be so quickly apparent. Hence one should not be too sure of the incredibility of the 10 view of those who conceive that there is continuity between the parts about the pillars of Hercules and the parts about India, and that in this way the ocean is one. As further evidence in favour of this they quote the case of elephants, a species occurring in each of these extreme regions, suggesting that the common characteristic of these extremes is explained by their continuity. Also, those mathemati- 15 cians who try to calculate the size of the earth's circumference arrive at the figure 400,000 stades.⁸ This indicates not only that the earth's mass is spherical in shape, but also that as compared with the stars it is not of great size.   20

BOOK III

1 We have already discussed the first heaven and its parts, the moving stars within it, the matter of which these are composed and 25 their bodily constitution, and we have also shown that they are un-generated and indestructible. Now things that we call natural are either substances or functions and attributes of substances. As sub-stances I class the simple bodies—fire, earth, and the other terms of 30 the series—and all things composed of them; for example, the heaven as a whole and its parts, animals, again, and plants and their parts. By attributes and functions I mean the movements of these and of all other things in which they have power in themselves to cause move-ment, and also their alterations and reciprocal transformations. It is 298ᵇ obvious, then, that the greater part of the inquiry into nature con-cerns bodies: for a natural substance is either a body or a thing which cannot come into existence without body and magnitude. This ap-pears plainly from an analysis of the character of natural things, and 5

⁸ This appears to be the oldest recorded estimate of the size of the earth. 400,000 stades = 9,987 geographical miles. Other estimates (in miles) are: Archimedes, 7,495; Eratosthenes and Hipparchus, 6,292; Posidonius, 5,992 or 4,494; present day, 5,400.

equally from an inspection of the instances of inquiry into nature. Since, then, we have spoken of the primary element, of its bodily constitution, and of its freedom from destruction and generation, it remains to speak of the other two.[1] In speaking of them we shall be obliged also to inquire into generation and destruction. For if there is generation anywhere, it must be in these elements and things composed of them.

This is indeed the first question we have to ask: is generation a fact or not? Earlier speculation was at variance both with itself and with the views here put forward as to the true answer to this question. Some removed generation and destruction from the world altogether. Nothing that is, they said, is generated or destroyed, and our conviction to the contrary is an illusion. So maintained the school of Melissus and Parmenides. But however excellent their theories may otherwise be, anyhow they cannot be held to speak as students of nature. There may be things not subject to generation or any kind of movement, but if so they belong to another and a higher inquiry than the study of nature. They, however, had no idea of any form of being other than the substance of things perceived; and when they saw, what no one previously had seen, that there could be no knowledge or wisdom without some such unchanging entities, they naturally transferred what was true of them to things perceived. Others, perhaps intentionally, maintain precisely the contrary opinion to this. It had been asserted that everything in the world was subject to generation and nothing was ungenerated, but that after being generated some things remained indestructible while the rest were again destroyed. This had been asserted in the first instance by Hesiod and his followers, but afterwards outside his circle by the earliest natural philosophers.[2] But what these thinkers maintained was that all else has been generated and, as they said, 'is flowing away', nothing having any solidity, except one single thing which persists as the basis of all these transformations. So we may interpret the statements of Heraclitus of Ephesus and many others.[3] And some [4] subject all bodies whatever

---

[1] Aristotle speaks of the four sublunary elements as two, because generically they are two. Two are heavy, two light: two move up and two down. Books III and IV of this treatise deal solely with these elements.

[2] The reference, according to Simplicius, is to Orphic writings ('the school of Orpheus and Musaeus').

[3] e.g. Thales, Anaximander, Anaximenes.

[4] The theory criticized is certainly that advanced in the *Timaeus*, and is usually attributed to Plato, but Aristotle probably has also in mind certain members of the Academy, particularly Xenocrates.

to generation, by means of the composition and separation of 299ᵃ planes.

Discussion of the other views may be postponed. But this last theory which composes every body of planes is, as the most superficial observation shows, in many respects in plain contradiction with mathematics. It is, however, wrong to remove the foundations of a science 5 unless you can replace them with others more convincing. And, secondly, the same theory which composes solids of planes clearly composes planes of lines and lines of points, so that a part of a line need not be a line. This matter has been already considered in our discussion of movement, where we have shown that an indivisible length 10 is impossible. But with respect to natural bodies there are impossibilities involved in the view which asserts indivisible lines, which we may briefly consider at this point. For the impossible consequences which result from this view in the mathematical sphere will reproduce themselves when it is applied to physical bodies, but there will be difficulties in physics which are not present in mathematics; for mathe- 15 matics deals with an abstract and physics with a more concrete object. There are many attributes necessarily present in physical bodies which are necessarily excluded by indivisibility; all attributes, in fact, which are divisible. There can be nothing divisible in an indivisible thing, but the attributes of bodies are all divisible in one of two ways. They are divisible into kinds, as colour is divided into white and black, 20 and they are divisible *per accidens* when that which has them is divisible. In this latter sense attributes which are simple are nevertheless divisible. Attributes of this kind will serve, therefore, to illustrate the impossibility of the view. It is impossible, if two parts of a thing have no weight, that the two together should have weight. But either 25 all perceptible bodies or some, such as earth and water, have weight, as these thinkers would themselves admit. Now if the point has no weight, clearly the lines have not either, and, if they have not, neither have the planes. Therefore no body has weight. It is, further, manifest that the point cannot have weight. For while a heavy thing 30 may always be heavier than something and a light thing lighter than 299ᵇ something, a thing which is heavier or lighter than something need not be itself heavy or light, just as a large thing is larger than others, but what is larger is not always large. A thing which, judged absolutely, is small may none the less be larger than other things. What- 5 ever, then, is heavy and also heavier than something else, must exceed this by something which is heavy. A heavy thing therefore is always divisible. But it is common ground that a point is indivisible. Again, suppose that what is heavy is a dense body, and what is light rare.

Dense differs from rare in containing more matter in the same cubic
10 area. A point, then, if it may be heavy or light, may be dense or rare.
But the dense is divisible while a point is indivisible. And if what is
heavy must be either hard or soft, an impossible consequence is easy
to draw. For a thing is soft if its surface can be pressed in, hard if it
cannot; and if it can be pressed in it is divisible.

15   Moreover, no weight can consist of parts not possessing weight.
For how, except by the merest fiction, can they specify the number
and character of the parts which will produce weight? And, further,
when one weight is greater than another, the difference is a third
weight; from which it will follow that every indivisible part possesses
weight. For suppose that a body of four points possesses weight. A
body composed of more than four points will be superior in weight
20 to it, a thing which has weight. But the difference between weight and
weight must be a weight, as the difference between white and whiter is
white. Here the difference which makes the superior weight heavier
is the single point which remains when the common number, four,
is subtracted. A single point, therefore, has weight.

Further, to assume, on the one hand, that the planes can only be
25 put in linear contact would be ridiculous. For just as there are two
ways of putting lines together, namely, end to end and side by side, so
there must be two ways of putting planes together. Lines can be put
together so that contact is linear by laying one along the other,
though not by putting them end to end. But if, similarly, in putting
the planes together, superficial contact is allowed as an alternative to
30 linear, that method will give them bodies which are not any element
nor composed of elements. Again, if it is the number of planes in a
300ᵃ body that makes one heavier than another, as the *Timaeus* explains,
clearly the line and the point will have weight. For the three cases are,
as we said before, analogous. But if the reason of differences of
5 weight is not this, but rather the heaviness of earth and the lightness
of fire, then some of the planes will be light and others heavy (which
involves a similar distinction in the lines and the points); the earth-
plane, I mean, will be heavier than the fire-plane. In general, the result
is either that there is no magnitude at all, or that all magnitude could
10 be done away with. For a point is to a line as a line is to a plane and
as a plane is to a body. Now the various forms in passing into one
another will each be resolved into its ultimate constituents. It might
happen therefore that nothing existed except points, and that there
was no body at all. A further consideration is that if time is similarly
constituted, there would be, or might be, a time at which it was done
15 away with. For the indivisible now is like a point in a line. The same

consequences follow from composing the heaven of numbers, as some of the Pythagoreans do who make all nature out of numbers. For natural bodies are manifestly endowed with weight and lightness, but an assemblage of units can neither be composed to form a body nor possess weight.

2   The necessity that each of the simple bodies should have a natural 20 movement may be shown as follows. They manifestly move, and if they have no proper movement they must move by constraint: and the constrained is the same as the unnatural. Now an unnatural movement presupposes a natural movement which it contravenes, 25 and which, however many the unnatural movements, is always one. For naturally a thing moves in one way, while its unnatural movements are manifold. The same may be shown from the fact of rest. Rest, also, must either be constrained or natural, constrained in a place to which movement was constrained, natural in a place movement to which was natural. Now manifestly there is a body which is at rest at 30 the centre. If then this rest is natural to it, clearly motion to this place is natural to it. If, on the other hand, its rest is constrained, what is hindering its motion? Something, perhaps, which is at rest: but if so, we shall simply repeat the same argument; and either we shall come to an ultimate something to which rest where it is is natural, or we 300ᵇ shall have an infinite process, which is impossible. The hindrance to its movement, then, we will suppose, is a moving thing—as Empedocles says that it is the vortex which keeps the earth still—: but in that case we ask, where would it have moved to but for the vortex? It could not move infinitely; for to traverse an infinite is impossible, 5 and impossibilities do not happen. So the moving thing must stop somewhere, and there rest not by constraint but naturally. But a natural rest proves a natural movement to the place of rest. Hence Leucippus and Democritus, who say that the primary bodies are in perpetual movement in the void or infinite, may be asked to explain 10 the manner of their motion and the kind of movement which is natural to them. For if the various elements are constrained by one another to move as they do, each must still have a natural movement which the constrained contravenes, and the prime mover must cause motion not by constraint but naturally. If there is no ultimate natural cause 15 of movement and each preceding term in the series is always moved by constraint, we shall have an infinite process. The same difficulty is involved even if it is supposed, as we read in the *Timaeus*,⁵ that before the ordered world was made the elements moved without order. Their

⁵ Plato, *Tim.* 30 a.

movement must have been due either to constraint or to their nature.
20 And if their movement was natural, a moment's consideration shows
that there was already an ordered world. For the prime mover must
cause motion in virtue of its own natural movement, and the other
bodies, moving without constraint, as they came to rest in their proper
places, would fall into the order in which they now stand, the heavy
25 bodies moving towards the centre and the light bodies away from it.
But that is the order of their distribution in our world. There is a
further question, too, which might be asked. Is it possible or impossible that bodies in unordered movement should combine in some
cases into combinations like those of which bodies of nature's composing are composed, such, I mean, as bones and flesh? Yet this is
30 what Empedocles asserts to have occurred under Love. 'Many a head',
says he, 'came to birth without a neck'. The answer to the view that
there are infinite bodies moving in an infinite is that, if the cause of
movement is single, they must move with a single motion, and there-
301ᵃ fore not without order; and if, on the other hand, the causes are of
infinite variety, their motions too must be infinitely varied. For a
finite number of causes would produce a kind of order, since absence
of order is not proved by diversity of direction in motions: indeed, in
the world we know, not all bodies, but only bodies of the same kind,
5 have a common goal of movement. Again, disorderly movement means
in reality unnatural movement, since the order proper to perceptible
things is their nature. And there is also absurdity and impossibility
in the notion that the disorderly movement is infinitely continued.
For the nature of things is the nature which most of them possess
for most of the time. Thus their view brings them into the con-
10 trary position that disorder is natural, and order or system unnatural.
But no natural fact can originate in chance. This is a point which
Anaxagoras seems to have thoroughly grasped; for he starts his cosmogony from unmoved things. The others, it is true, make things
collect together somehow before they try to produce motion and
separation. But there is no sense in starting generation from an origi-
15 nal state in which bodies are separated and in movement. Hence
Empedocles begins after the process ruled by Love: for he could not
have constructed the heaven by building it up out of bodies in
separation, making them to combine by the power of Love, since
our world has its constituent elements in separation, and therefore
20 presupposes a previous state of unity and combination.

These arguments make it plain that every body has its natural
movement, which is not constrained or contrary to its nature. We go
on to show that there are certain bodies whose necessary impetus is

that of weight and lightness. Of necessity, we assert, they must move, and a moved thing which has no natural impetus cannot move either towards or away from the centre. Suppose a body A without weight, and a body B endowed with weight. Suppose the weightless body to move the distance CD, while B in the same time moves the distance CE, which will be greater since the heavy thing must move further. Let the heavy body then be divided in the proportion $CE:CD$ (for there is no reason why a part of B should not stand in this relation to the whole). Now if the whole moves the whole distance CE, the part must in the same time move the distance CD. A weightless body, therefore, and one which has weight will move the same distance, which is impossible. And the same argument would fit the case of lightness. Again, a body which is in motion but has neither weight nor lightness, must be moved by constraint, and must continue its constrained movement infinitely. For there will be a force which moves it, and the smaller and lighter a body is the further will a given force move it. Now let A, the weightless body, be moved the distance CE, and B, which has weight, be moved in the same time the distance CD. Dividing the heavy body in the proportion $CE:CD$, we subtract from the heavy body a part which will in the same time move the distance CE, since the whole moved CD: for the relative speeds of the two bodies will be in inverse ratio to their respective sizes. Thus the weightless body will move the same distance as the heavy in the same time. But this is impossible. Hence, since the motion of the weightless body will cover a greater distance than any that is suggested, it will continue infinitely. It is therefore obvious that every body must have a definite [6] weight or lightness. But since 'nature' means a source of movement within the thing itself, while a force is a source of movement in something other than it or in itself *quâ* other, and since movement is always due either to nature or to constraint, movement which is natural, as downward movement is to a stone, will be merely accelerated by an external force, while an unnatural movement will be due to the force alone. In either case the air is as it were instrumental to the force. For air is both light and heavy, and thus *quâ* light produces upward motion, being propelled and set in motion by the force, and *quâ* heavy produces a downward motion. In either case the force transmits the movement to the body by first, as it were, impregnating the air. That is why a body moved by constraint continues to move when that which gave the impulse ceases to accompany it. Otherwise, i. e. if the air were not endowed with this function, constrained movement would be impossible. And the natural movement of a body

25

30

301^{b}

5

10

15

20

25

30

[6] i. e. not infinite.

may be helped on in the same way. This discussion suffices to show (1) that all bodies are either light or heavy, and (2) how unnatural movement takes place.

From what has been said earlier it is plain that there cannot be generation either of everything or in an absolute sense of anything. It 302ᵃ is impossible that everything should be generated, unless an extra-corporeal [7] void is possible. For, assuming generation, the place which is to be occupied by that which is coming to be, must have been previously occupied by void in which no body was. Now it is quite possible for one body to be generated out of another, air for instance out of fire, 5 but in the absence of any pre-existing mass generation is impossible. That which is potentially a certain kind of body may, it is true, become such in actuality. But if the potential body was not already in actuality some other kind of body, the existence of an extra-corporeal void must be admitted.

10 **3** It remains to say what bodies are subject to generation, and why. Since in every case knowledge depends on what is primary, and the elements are the primary constituents of bodies, we must ask which of such bodies [8] are elements, and why; and after that what is their 15 number and character. The answer will be plain if we first explain what kind of substance an element is. An element, we take it, is a body into which other bodies may be analysed, present in them potentially or in actuality (which of these, is still disputable), and not itself divisible into bodies different in form. That, or something like it, is what all men in every case mean by element. Now if what we 20 have described is an element, clearly there must be such bodies. For flesh and wood and all other similar bodies contain potentially fire and earth, since one sees these elements exuded from them; and, on the other hand, neither in potentiality nor in actuality does fire con-25 tain flesh or wood, or it would exude them. Similarly, even if there were only one elementary body, it would not contain them. For though it will be either flesh or bone or something else, that does not at once show that it contained these in potentiality: the further question remains, in what manner it becomes them. Now Anaxagoras opposes Empedocles' view of the elements. Empedocles says that fire and 30 earth and the related bodies are elementary bodies of which all things are composed; but this Anaxagoras denies. His elements are

[7] i. e. a void outside bodies, as distinct from the fragments of void which are supposed to be distributed throughout the texture of every body.
[8] viz. bodies subject to generation.

the homoeomerous things, [9] viz. flesh, bone, and the like. Earth and 302ᵇ
fire are mixtures, composed of them and all the other seeds, each
consisting of a collection of all the homoeomerous bodies, separately
invisible; and that explains why from these two bodies all others are
generated. (To him fire and *aither* are the same thing.) But since 5
every natural body has its proper movement, and movements are
either simple or mixed, mixed in mixed bodies and simple in simple,
there must obviously be simple bodies; for there are simple movements. It is plain, then, that there are elements, and why.

4   The next question to consider is whether the elements are finite 10
or infinite in number, and, if finite, what their number is. Let us first
show reason for denying that their number is infinite, as some suppose. We begin with the view of Anaxagoras that all the homoeomerous
bodies are elements. Any one who adopts this view misapprehends 15
the meaning of element. Observation shows that even mixed bodies
are often divisible into homoeomerous parts; examples are flesh, bone,
wood, and stone. Since then the composite cannot be an element, not
every homoeomerous body can be an element; only, as we said before,[10] that which is not divisible into bodies different in form. But 20
even taking 'element' as they do, they need not assert an infinity of
elements, since the hypothesis of a finite number will give identical
results. Indeed even two or three such bodies serve the purpose as well,
as Empedocles' attempt shows. Again, even on their view it turns out
that all things are not composed of homoeomerous bodies. They do 25
not pretend that a face is composed of faces, or that any other natural conformation is composed of parts like itself. Obviously then it
would be better to assume a finite number of principles. They should,
in fact, be as few as possible, consistently with proving what has to be
proved. This is the common demand of mathematicians, who always 30
assume as principles things finite either in kind or in number. Again,
if body is distinguished from body by the appropriate qualitative difference, and there is a limit to the number of differences (for the dif- 303ᵃ
ference lies in qualities apprehended by sense, which are in fact finite
in number, though this requires proof), then manifestly there is necessarily a limit to the number of elements.

There is, further, another view—that of Leucippus and Democritus
of Abdera—the implications of which are also unacceptable. The
primary masses, according to them, are infinite in number and indi- 5

[9] 'Homoeomerous' means 'having parts like one another and like the whole of
which they are parts'.
[10] Above, 302ᵃ 18.

visible in mass: one cannot turn into many nor many into one; and all things are generated by their combination and involution. Now this view in a sense makes things out to be numbers or composed of
10 numbers.[11] The exposition is not clear, but this is its real meaning. And further, they say that since the atomic bodies differ in shape, and there is an infinity of shapes, there is an infinity of simple bodies. But they have never explained in detail the shapes
15 of the various elements, except so far as to allot the sphere to fire. Air, water, and the rest they distinguished by the relative size of the atom, assuming that the atomic substance was a sort of master-seed for each and every element. Now, in the first place, they make the mistake already noticed. The principles which they assume are not limited in number, though such limitation would necessitate no other alteration in their theory. Further, if the differences of bodies
20 are not infinite, plainly the elements will not be an infinity. Besides, a view which asserts atomic bodies must needs come into conflict with the mathematical sciences, in addition to invalidating many common opinions and apparent data of sense perception. But of these things we have already spoken in our discussion of time and movement.[12]
25 They are also bound to contradict themselves. For if the elements are atomic, air, earth, and water cannot be differentiated by the relative sizes of their atoms, since then they could not be generated out of one another. The extrusion of the largest atoms is a process that will in time exhaust the supply; and it is by such a process that they account for the generation of water, air, and earth from one
30 another. Again, even on their own presuppositions it does not seem as if the elements would be infinite in number. The atoms differ in
303[b] figure, and all figures are composed of pyramids, rectilinear in the case of rectilinear figures, while the sphere has eight pyramidal parts.[13] The figures must have their principles,[14] and, whether these are one or two or more, the simple bodies must be the same in number as they. Again, if every element has its proper movement, and a
5 simple body has a simple movement, and the number of simple movements is not infinite, because the simple motions are only two

[11] Because the atom is practically a mathematical unit, out of which bodies are formed by simple addition. Cp. *Met.* vii. 13. 1039[a] 3 ff.

[12] Esp. *Phys.* vi. 1–2 (231[a] 18 ff.).

[13] The pyramids are tetrahedrons; and those produced by triple section of a sphere are irregular, having a spherical base.

[14] i. e. there must be a limited number of primary figures to which all other figures are reducible.

and the number of places is not infinite,[15] on these grounds also we
should have to deny that the number of elements is infinite.

5   Since the number of the elements must be limited, it remains to
inquire whether there is more than one element. Some assume one [10]
only, which is according to some [16] water, to others [17] air, to others [18]
fire, to others [19] again something finer than water and denser than air,
an infinite body—so they say—embracing all the heavens.

Now those who decide for a single element, which is either water
or air or a body finer than water and denser than air, and proceed
to generate other things out of it by use of the attributes density [15]
and rarity, all alike fail to observe the fact that they are depriving
the element of its priority. Generation out of the elements is, as they
say, synthesis, and generation into the elements is analysis, so that
the body with the finer parts must have priority in the order of
nature. But they say that fire is of all bodies the finest. Hence fire [20]
will be first in the natural order. And whether the finest body is fire
or not makes no difference; anyhow it must be one of the other
bodies that is primary and not that which is intermediate. Again,
density and rarity, as instruments of generation, are equivalent to
fineness and coarseness, since the fine is rare, and coarse in their use
means dense. But fineness and coarseness, again, are equivalent to [25]
greatness and smallness, since a thing with small parts is fine and a
thing with large parts coarse. For that which spreads itself out widely
is fine, and a thing composed of small parts is so spread out. In the
end, then, they distinguish the various other substances from the
element by the greatness and smallness of their parts. This method [30]
of distinction makes all judgment relative. There will be no absolute distinction between fire, water, and air, but one and the same
body will be relatively to this fire, relatively to something else air. [304ᵃ]
The same difficulty is involved equally in the view which recognizes
several elements and distinguishes them by their greatness and smallness. The principle of distinction between bodies being quantity,
the various sizes will be in a definite ratio, and whatever bodies
are in this ratio to one another must be air, fire, earth, and water [5]

[15] There are only two places to which movement can be directed, viz. the
circumference and the centre. By the two simple motions Aristotle probably here
means motions towards these two places, motion up and motion down. Circular
motion is not possible beneath the moon.

[16] Thales and Hippon.   [17] Anaximenes and Diogenes of Apollonia.
[18] Heraclitus and Hippasus.
[19] Anaximander. This identification has been rejected by many modern
scholars.

respectively. For the ratios of smaller bodies may be repeated among greater bodies.

Those who start from fire as the single element, while avoiding this difficulty, involve themselves in many others. Some of them give fire a particular shape, like those who make it a pyramid, and this on one of two grounds. The reason given may be—more crudely—that the pyramid is the most piercing of figures as fire is of bodies, or—more ingeniously—the position may be supported by the following argument. As all bodies are composed of that which has the finest parts, so all solid figures are composed of pyramids: but the finest body is fire, while among figures the pyramid is primary and has the smallest parts; and the primary body must have the primary figure: therefore fire will be a pyramid. Others, again, express no opinion on the subject of its figure, but simply regard it as the body of the finest parts, which in combination will form other bodies, as the fusing of gold-dust produces solid gold. Both of these views involve the same difficulties. For (1) if, on the one hand, they make the primary body an atom, the view will be open to the objections already advanced against the atomic theory. And further the theory is inconsistent with a regard for the facts of nature. For if all bodies are quantitatively commensurable, and the relative size of the various homoeomerous masses and of their several elements are in the same ratio, so that the total mass of water, for instance, is related to the total mass of air as the elements of each are to one another, and so on, and if there is more air than water and, generally, more of the finer body than of the coarser, obviously the element of water will be smaller than that of air. But the lesser quantity is contained in the greater. Therefore the air element is divisible. And the same could be shown of fire and of all bodies whose parts are relatively fine. (2) If, on the other hand, the primary body is divisible, then (a) those who give fire a special shape will have to say that a part of fire is not fire, because a pyramid is not composed of pyramids,[20] and also that not every body is either an element or composed of elements, since a part of fire will be neither fire nor any other element. And (b) those whose ground of distinction is size will have to recognize an element prior to the element, a regress which continues infinitely, since every body is divisible and that which has the smallest parts is the element. Further, they too will have to say that the same body is relatively to this fire and relatively to that air, to others again water and earth.

The common error of all views which assume a single element is

[20] i. e. a pyramid cannot be divided so that *every* part is a pyramid.

that they allow only one natural movement, which is the same for every body. For it is a matter of observation that a natural body possesses a principle of movement. If then all bodies are one, all will have one movement. With this motion the greater their quantity 15 the more they will move, just as fire, in proportion as its quantity is greater, moves faster with the upward motion which belongs to it. But the fact is that increase of quantity makes many things move the faster downward. For these reasons, then, as well as from the 20 distinction already established [21] of a plurality of natural movements, it is impossible that there should be only one element. But if the elements are not an infinity and not reducible to one, they must be several and finite in number.

6 First we must inquire whether the elements are eternal or subject to generation and destruction; for when this question has been 25 answered their number and character will be manifest. In the first place, they cannot be eternal. It is a matter of observation that fire, water, and every simple body undergo a process of analysis, which must either continue infinitely or stop somewhere. (1) Suppose it infinite. Then the time occupied by the process will be infinite, and also that occupied by the reverse process of synthesis. For the 30 processes of analysis and synthesis succeed one another in the various parts. It will follow that there are two infinite times which are mutually exclusive, the time occupied by the synthesis, which is infinite, being preceded by the period of analysis. There are thus two mutually exclusive infinites, which is impossible. (2) Suppose, on 305ᵃ the other hand, that the analysis stops somewhere. Then the body at which it stops will be either atomic or, as Empedocles seems to have intended, a divisible body which will yet never be divided. The foregoing arguments [22] show that it cannot be an atom; but neither can 5 it be a divisible body which analysis will never reach. For a smaller body is more easily destroyed than a larger; and a destructive process which succeeds in destroying, that is, in resolving into smaller bodies, a body of some size, cannot reasonably be expected to fail with the smaller body. Now in fire we observe a destruction of two kinds: 10 it is destroyed by its contrary when it is quenched, and by itself when it dies out. But the effect is produced by a greater quantity upon a lesser, and the more quickly the smaller it is. The elements of bodies must therefore be subject to destruction and generation.

Since they are generated, they must be generated either from something incorporeal or from a body, and if from a body, either from 15

21 Book I, c. 2.   22 c. 4.

one another or from something else. The theory which generates them from something incorporeal requires an extra-corporeal void. For everything that comes to be comes to be in something, and that in which the generation takes place must either be incorporeal or possess body; and if it has body, there will be two bodies in the same place at the same time, viz. that which is coming to be and that which was 20 previously there, while if it is incorporeal, there must be an extra-corporeal void. But we have already shown [23] that this is impossible. But, on the other hand, it is equally impossible that the elements should be generated from some kind of body. That would involve a body distinct from the elements and prior to them. But if this body 25 possesses weight or lightness, it will be one of the elements; and if it has no tendency to movement, it will be an immovable or mathematical entity, and therefore not in a place at all. A place in which a thing is at rest is a place in which it might move, either by constraint, i. e. unnaturally, or in the absence of constraint, i. e. naturally. If, then, it is in a place and somewhere, it will be one of the 30 elements; and if it is not a place, nothing can come from it, since that which comes into being and that out of which it comes must needs be together. The elements therefore cannot be generated from something incorporeal nor from a body which is not an element, and the only remaining alternative is that they are generated from one another.

7 We must, therefore, turn to the question, what is the manner of their generation from one another? Is it as Empedocles and 35 Democritus say, or as those who resolve bodies into planes say, 305ᵇ or is there yet another possibility? (1) What the followers of Empedocles do, though without observing it themselves, is to reduce the generation of elements out of one another to an illusion. They make it a process of excretion from a body of what was in it all the time—as though generation required a vessel rather than a material 5 —so that it involves no change of anything. And even if this were accepted, there are other implications equally unsatisfactory. We do not expect a mass of matter to be made heavier by compression. But they will be bound to maintain this, if they say that water is a body present in air and excreted from air, since air becomes heavier 10 when it turns into water. Again, when the mixed body is divided, they can show no reason why one of the constituents must by itself take up more room than the body did: but when water turns into air, the room occupied is increased. The fact is that the finer body takes up more room, as is obvious in any case of transformation. As the

[23] *Phys.* iv. 8.

liquid is converted into vapour or air the vessel which contains it is 15 often burst because it does not contain room enough. Now, if there is no void at all, and if, as those who take this view say, there is no expansion of bodies, the impossibility of this is manifest: and if there is void and expansion, there is no accounting for the fact that the body which results from division occupies of necessity a greater 20 space. It is inevitable, too, that generation of one out of another should come to a stop, since a finite quantum cannot contain an infinity of finite quanta. When earth produces water something is taken away from the earth, for the process is one of excretion. The same thing happens again when the residue produces water. But this can only go on for ever, if the finite body contains an infinity, which is im- 25 possible. Therefore the generation of elements out of one another will not always continue.

(2) We have now explained that the mutual transformations of the elements cannot take place by means of excretion. The remaining alternative is that they should be generated by changing into one another. And this in one of two ways, either by change of shape, as 30 the same wax takes the shape both of a sphere and of a cube, or, as some assert, by resolution into planes. (a) Generation by change of shape would necessarily involve the assertion of atomic bodies. For if the particles were divisible there would be a part of fire which was not fire and a part of earth which was not earth, for the reason that 35 not every part of a pyramid is a pyramid nor of a cube a cube. 306ª But if (b) the process is resolution into planes, the first difficulty is that the elements cannot all be generated out of one another. This they are obliged to assert, and do assert. It is absurd, because it is unreasonable that one element alone should have no part in the transformations, and also contrary to the observed data of sense, according to 5 which all alike change into one another. In fact their explanation of the observations is not consistent with the observations. And the reason is that their ultimate principles are wrongly assumed: they had certain predetermined views, and were resolved to bring everything into line with them. It seems that perceptible things require perceptible principles, eternal things eternal principles, corruptible things 10 corruptible principles; and, in general, every subject matter principles homogeneous with itself. But they, owing to their love for their principles, fall into the attitude of men who undertake the defence of a position in argument. In the confidence that the principles are true they are ready to accept any consequence of their application. As though some principles did not require to be judged from their results, 15 and particularly from their final issue! And that issue, which in the

case of productive knowledge [24] is the product, in the knowledge of nature is the unimpeachable evidence of the senses as to each fact.

20 The result of their view is that earth has the best right to the name element, and is alone indestructible; for that which is indissoluble is indestructible and elementary, and earth alone cannot be dissolved into any body but itself. Again, in the case of those elements which do suffer dissolution, the 'suspension' of the triangles is unsatisfactory. But this takes place whenever one is dissolved into another, because of the numerical inequality of the triangles which compose them. Further, those who hold these views must needs 25 suppose that generation does not start from a body. For what is generated out of planes cannot be said to have been generated from a body. And they must also assert that not all bodies are divisible, coming thus into conflict with our most accurate sciences, namely the mathematical, which assume that even the intelligible is divisible, while they, in their anxiety to save their hypothesis, cannot 30 even admit this of every perceptible thing. For any one who gives each element a shape of its own, and makes this the ground of distinction between the substances, has to attribute to them indivisibility; since division of a pyramid or a sphere must leave somewhere at least a residue which is not a sphere or a pyramid. Either, then, a part of 306[b] fire is not fire, so that there is a body prior to the element—for every body is either an element or composed of elements—or not every body is divisible.

8 In general, the attempt to give a shape to each of the simple bodies is unsound, for the reason, first, that they will not succeed in 5 filling the whole. It is agreed that there are only three plane figures which can fill a space, the triangle, the square, and the hexagon, and only two solids, the pyramid and the cube. But the theory needs more than these because the elements which it recognizes are more in number. Secondly, it is manifest that the simple bodies are often 10 given a shape by the place in which they are·included, particularly water and air. In such a case the shape of the element cannot persist; for, if it did, the contained mass would not be in continuous contact with the containing body; while, if its shape is changed, it will cease to be water, since the distinctive quality is shape. Clearly, then, 15 their shapes are not fixed. Indeed, nature itself seems to offer corroboration of this theoretical conclusion. Just as in other cases the substratum must be formless and unshapen—for thus the 'all-receptive', as we read in the *Timaeus*,[25] will be best for modelling—

---

[24] i. e. in the case of art.   [25] Plato, *Tim.* 51 A.

so the elements should be conceived as a material for composite 20
things; and that is why they can put off their qualitative distinctions and pass into one another. Further, how can they account for
the generation of flesh and bone or any other continuous body?
The elements alone cannot produce them because their collocation cannot produce a continuum. Nor can the composition of planes; for 25
this produces the elements themselves, not bodies made up of them.
Any one then who insists upon an exact statement of this kind of
theory, instead of assenting after a passing glance at it, will see that
it removes generation from the world.

Further, the very properties, powers, and motions, to which they
pay particular attention in allotting shapes, show the shapes not to 30
be in accord with the bodies. Because fire is mobile and productive
of heat and combustion, some made it a sphere, others a pyramid.
These shapes, they thought, were the most mobile because they
offer the fewest points of contact and are the least stable of any; 307[a]
they were also the most apt to produce warmth and combustion,
because the one is angular throughout while the other has the most
acute angles, and the angles, they say, produce warmth and combustion. Now, in the first place, with regard to movement both are
in error. These may be the figures best adapted to movement; they 5
are not, however, well adapted to the movement of fire, which is
an upward and rectilinear movement, but rather to that form of circular movement which we call rolling. Earth, again, they call a cube
because it is stable and at rest. But it rests only in its own place, not
anywhere; from any other it moves if nothing hinders, and fire and 10
the other bodies do the same. The obvious inference, therefore, is that
fire and each several element is in a foreign place a sphere or a pyramid,
but in its own a cube. Again, if the possession of angles makes a body
produce heat and combustion, every element produces heat, though 15
one may do so more than another. For they all possess angles, the
octahedron and dodecahedron as well as the pyramid; and Democritus makes even the sphere a kind of angle, which cuts things because
of its mobility. The difference, then, will be one of degree: and this is
plainly false. They must also accept the inference that the mathematical solids produce heat and combustion, since they too possess 20
angles and contain atomic spheres and pyramids, especially if there
are, as they allege, atomic figures.[26] Anyhow if these functions belong
to some of these things and not to others, they should explain the difference, instead of speaking in quite general terms as they do.
Again, combustion of a body produces fire, and fire is a sphere or a 25

[26] i. e. indivisible units of line, of which the geometrical figures are composed.

pyramid. The body, then, is turned into spheres or pyramids. Let us grant that these figures may reasonably be supposed to cut and break up bodies as fire does; still it remains quite inexplicable that a pyramid must needs produce pyramids or a sphere spheres. One might as well 30 postulate that a knife or a saw divides things into knives or saws. It is also ridiculous to think only of division when allotting fire its shape. Fire is generally thought of as combining and connecting 307ᵇ rather than as separating. For though it separates bodies different in kind, it combines those which are the same; and the combining is essential to it, the functions of connecting and uniting being a mark of fire, while the separating is incidental. For the expulsion of the foreign body is an incident in the compacting of the homogeneous. In 5 choosing the shape, then, they should have thought either of both functions or preferably of the combining function. In addition, since hot and cold are contrary powers, it is impossible to allot any shape to the cold. For the shape given must be the contrary of that given to the hot, but there is no contrariety between figures. That is why they have all 10 left the cold out, though properly either all or none should have their distinguishing figures. Some of them, however, do attempt to explain this power, and they contradict themselves. A body of large particles, they say, is cold because instead of penetrating through the passages it crushes. Clearly, then, that which is hot is that which penetrates these passages, or in other words that which has fine 15 particles. It results that hot and cold are distinguished not by the figure but by the size of the particles. Again, if the pyramids are unequal in size, the large ones will not be fire, and that figure will produce not combustion but its contrary.

From what has been said it is clear that the difference of the elements does not depend upon their shape. Now their most important 20 differences are those of property, function, and power; for every natural body has, we maintain, its own functions, properties, and powers. Our first business, then, will be to speak of these, and that inquiry will enable us to explain the differences of each from each.

BOOK IV

1   We have now to consider the terms 'heavy' and 'light.' We must ask 30 what the bodies so called are, how they are constituted, and what is the reason of their possessing these powers. The consideration of these questions is a proper part of the theory of movement, since we call things heavy and light because they have the power of being moved naturally in a certain way. The activities corresponding to these

powers have not been given any name, unless it is thought that 308ᵛ
'impetus' is such a name. But because the inquiry into nature is concerned with movement, and these things have in themselves some
spark (as it were) of movement, all inquirers avail themselves of these
powers, though in all but a few cases without exact discrimination.
We must then first look at whatever others have said, and formulate 5
the questions which require settlement in the interests of this inquiry,
before we go on to state our own view of the matter.

Language recognizes (*a*) an absolute, (*b*) a relative heavy and light.
Of two heavy things, such as wood and bronze, we say that the
one is relatively light, the other relatively heavy. Our predecessors 10
have not dealt at all with the absolute use of the terms, but only
with the relative. I mean, they do not explain what the heavy is
or what the light is, but only the relative heaviness and lightness of
things possessing weight. This can be made clearer as follows. There
are things whose constant nature it is to move away from the centre,
while others move constantly towards the centre; and of these move- 15
ments that which is away from the centre I call upward movement and
that which is towards it I call downward movement. (The view, urged
by some,[1] that there is no up and no down in the heaven, is absurd.
There can be, they say, no up and no down, since the universe is similar
every way, and from any point on the earth's surface a man by advanc- 20
ing far enough will come to stand foot to foot with himself. But the
extremity of the whole, which we call 'above', is in position above
and in nature primary. And since the universe has an extremity
and a centre, it must clearly have an up and down. Common usage is
thus correct, though inadequate. And the reason of its inadequacy is 25
that men think that the universe is not similar every way. They recognize only the hemisphere which is over us. But if they went on to think
of the world as formed on this pattern all round, with a centre
identically related to each point on the extremity, they would have to
admit that the extremity was above and the centre below.) By
absolutely light, then, we mean that which moves upward or to the
extremity, and by absolutely heavy that which moves downward 30
or to the centre. By lighter or relatively light we mean that one, of two
bodies endowed with weight and equal in bulk, which is exceeded
by the other in the speed of its natural downward movement.

2   Those of our predecessors who have entered upon this inquiry have
for the most part spoken of light and heavy things only in the sense 35

[1] The digression is directed against Plato, *Tim.* 62 ε; but the view was held
by others besides Timaeus.

308ᵇ in which one of two things both endowed with weight is said to
be the lighter. And this treatment they consider a sufficient analysis
also of the notions of absolute heaviness and absolute lightness, to
which their account does not apply. This, however, will become clearer
5 as we advance. One use of the terms 'lighter' and 'heavier' is that
which is set forth in writing in the *Timaeus*,[2] that the body which
is composed of the greater number of identical parts is relatively
heavy, while that which is composed of a smaller number is relatively
light. As a larger quantity of lead or of bronze is heavier than a smaller
—and this holds good of all homogeneous masses, the superior
10 weight always depending upon a numerical superiority of equal parts
—in precisely the same way, they assert, lead is heavier than wood.
For all bodies, in spite of the general opinion to the contrary, are composed of identical parts and of a single material. But this analysis says
nothing of the absolutely heavy and light. The facts are that fire is
always light and moves upward, while earth and all earthy things
15 move downwards or towards the centre. It cannot then be the fewness
of the triangles (of which, in their view, all these bodies are composed) which disposes fire to move upward. If it were, the greater the
quantity of fire the slower it would move, owing to the increase of
weight due to the increased number of triangles. But the palpable
fact, on the contrary, is that the greater the quantity, the lighter the
20 mass is and the quicker its upward movement: and, similarly, in the
reverse movement from above downward, the small mass will move
quicker and the large slower. Further, since to be lighter is to have
fewer of these homogeneous parts and to be heavier is to have more,
and air, water, and fire are composed of the same triangles, the only
25 difference being in the number of such parts, which must therefore
explain any distinction of relatively light and heavy between these
bodies, it follows that there must be a certain quantum of air which
is heavier than water. But the facts are directly opposed to this. The
larger the quantity of air the more readily it moves upward, and any
portion of air without exception will rise up out of the water.

So much for one view of the distinction between light and heavy.
30 To others [3] the analysis seems insufficient; and their views on the
subject, though they belong to an older generation than ours, have
an air of novelty. It is apparent that there are bodies which, when
smaller in bulk than others, yet exceed them in weight. It is therefore obviously insufficient to say that bodies of equal weight are
35 composed of an equal number of primary parts: for that would give
equality of bulk. Those who maintain that the primary or atomic

---

[2] 63 C.   [3] The atomists, Democritus and Leucippus.

parts, of which bodies endowed with weight are composed, are planes, cannot so speak without absurdity; [4] but those who regard them as solids are in a better position to assert that of such bodies the larger is the heavier. But since in composite bodies the weight obviously does not correspond in this way to the bulk, the lesser bulk being often superior in weight (as, for instance, if one be wool and the other bronze), there are some who think and say that the cause is to be found elsewhere. The void, they say, which is imprisoned in bodies, lightens them and sometimes makes the larger body the lighter. The reason is that there is more void. And this would also account for the fact that a body composed of a number of solid parts equal to, or even smaller than, that of another is sometimes larger in bulk than it. In short, generally and in every case a body is relatively light when it contains a relatively large amount of void. This is the way they put it themselves, but their account requires an addition. Relative lightness must depend not only on an excess of void, but also on a defect of solid: for if the ratio of solid to void exceeds a certain proportion, the relative lightness will disappear. Thus fire, they say, is the lightest of things just for this reason that it has the most void. But it would follow that a large mass of gold, as containing more void than a small mass of fire, is lighter than it, unless it also contains many times as much solid. The addition is therefore necessary.

Of those who deny the existence of a void some, like Anaxagoras and Empedocles, have not tried to analyse the notions of light and heavy at all; and those who, while still denying the existence of a void, have attempted this,[5] have failed to explain why there are bodies which are absolutely heavy and light, or in other words why some move upward and others downward. The fact, again, that the body of greater bulk is sometimes lighter than smaller bodies is one which they have passed over in silence, and what they have said gives no obvious suggestion for reconciling their views with the observed facts.

But those who attribute the lightness of fire to its containing so much void are necessarily involved in practically the same difficulties. For though fire be supposed to contain less solid than any other body, as well as more void, yet there will be a certain quantum of fire in which the amount of solid or plenum is in excess of the solids contained in some small quantity of earth. They may reply that there is an excess of void also. But the question is, how will they discriminate the absolutely heavy? Presumably, either by its excess of solid or by its defect of void. On the former view there could be 309^b

---

[4] For, since the planes have no weight, their number cannot affect the weight of a body.   [5] Plato, in the *Timaeus*.

an amount of earth so small as to contain less solid than a large mass
of fire. And similarly, if the distinction rests on the amount of void,
there will be a body, lighter than the absolutely light, which neverthe-
5 less moves downward as constantly as the other moves upward.
But that cannot be so, since the absolutely light is always lighter than
bodies which have weight and move downward, while, on the other
hand, that which is lighter need not be light, because in common
speech we distinguish a lighter and a heavier (viz. water and earth)
among bodies endowed with weight. Again, the suggestion of a certain ratio between the void and the solid in a body is no more equal
10 to solving the problem before us. This manner of speaking will issue
in a similar impossibility. For any two portions of fire, small or great,
will exhibit the same ratio of solid to void; but the upward movement of the greater is quicker than that of the less, just as the down-
15 ward movement of a mass of gold or lead, or of any other body
endowed with weight, is quicker in proportion to its size. This, however, should not be the case if the ratio is the ground of distinction
between heavy things and light. There is also an absurdity in attribut-
ing the upward movement of bodies to a void which does not itself
move. If, however, it is the nature of a void to move upward and
of a plenum to move downward, and therefore each causes a like
20 movement in other things, there was no need to raise the question why
composite bodies are some light and some heavy; they had only
to explain why these two things are themselves light and heavy respectively, and to give, further, the reason why the plenum and the void
are not eternally separated. It is also unreasonable to imagine a place
25 for the void, as if the void were not itself a kind of place. But
if the void is to move, it must have a place out of which and into
which the change carries it. Also what is the cause of its movement?
Not, surely, its voidness: for it is not the void only which is moved,
but also the solid.

   Similar difficulties are involved in all other methods of distinction,
30 whether they account for the relative lightness and heaviness of bodies
by distinctions of size, or proceed on any other principle, so long as
they attribute to each the same matter, or even if they recognize
more than one matter, so long as that means only a pair of contraries.
If there is a single matter, as with those who compose things of
triangles, nothing can be absolutely heavy or light: and if there is
310ᵃ one matter and its contrary—the void, for instance, and the plenum
—no reason can be given for the relative lightness and heaviness of
the bodies intermediate between the absolutely light and heavy when
compared either with one another or with these themselves. The view

which bases the distinction upon differences of size is more like a mere fiction than those previously mentioned, but, in that it is able to 5 make distinctions between the four elements, it is in a stronger position for meeting the foregoing difficulties. Since, however, it imagines that these bodies which differ in size are all made of one substance, it implies, equally with the view that there is but one matter, that there is nothing absolutely light and nothing which moves upward (except 10 as being passed by other things or forced up by them); and since a multitude of small atoms are heavier than a few large ones, it will follow that much air or fire is heavier than a little water or earth, which is impossible.

3   These, then, are the views which have been advanced by others and the terms in which they state them. We may begin our own state- 15 ment by settling a question which to some has been the main difficulty —the question why some bodies move always and naturally upward and others downward, while others again move both upward and downward. After that we will inquire into light and heavy and the explanation of the various phenomena connected with them. The 20 local movement of each body into its own place must be regarded as similar to what happens in connexion with other forms of generation and change. There are, in fact, three kinds of movement, affecting respectively the size, the form, and the place of a thing, and in each it is observable that change proceeds from a contrary to a contrary or 25 to something intermediate: it is never the change of any chance subject in any chance direction, nor, similarly, is the relation of the mover to its object fortuitous: the thing altered is different from the thing increased, and precisely the same difference holds between that which produces alteration and that which produces increase. In the same manner it must be thought that that which produces local 30 motion and that which is so moved are not fortuitously related. Now, that which produces upward and downward movement is that which produces weight and lightness, and that which is moved is that which is potentially heavy or light, and the movement of each body to its own place is motion towards its own form. (It is best to interpret in this sense the common statement of the older writers that 'like moves 310ᵇ to like'. For the words are not in every sense true to fact. If one were to remove the earth to where the moon now is, the various fragments of earth would each move not towards it but to the place in which it now is. In general, when a number of similar and undifferentiated 5 bodies are moved with the same motion this result is necessarily produced, viz. that the place which is the natural goal of the movement

of each single part is also that of the whole. But since the place
of a thing is the boundary of that which contains it, and the continent
of all things that move upward or downward is the extremity and the
10 centre, and this boundary comes to be, in a sense, the form of that
which is contained, it is to its like that a body moves when it moves to
its own place. For the successive members of the series are like one another: water, I mean, is like air and air like fire, and between intermediates the relation may be converted, though not between them and
the extremes; thus air is like water, but water is like earth: for
15 the relation of each outer body to that which is next within it is that
of form to matter.) Thus to ask why fire moves upward and earth
downward is the same as to ask why the healable, when moved and
changed *qua* healable, attains health and not whiteness; and similar
questions might be asked concerning any other subject of altera-
20 tion. Of course the subject of increase, when changed *qua* increasable,
attains not health but a superior size. The same applies in the other
cases. One thing changes in quality, another in quantity: and so in
place, a light thing goes upward, a heavy thing downward. The only
difference is that in the last case, viz. that of the heavy and the
25 light, the bodies are thought to have a spring of change within themselves, while the subjects of healing and increase are thought to be
moved purely from without. Sometimes, however, even they change
of themselves, i. e. in response to a slight external movement reach
health or increase, as the case may be. And since the same thing
30 which is healable is also receptive of disease, it depends on whether it
is moved *qua* healable or *qua* liable to disease whether the motion
is towards health or towards disease. But the reason why the heavy and
the light appear more than these things to contain within themselves
the source of their movements is that their matter is nearest to being.
This is indicated by the fact that locomotion belongs to bodies only
when isolated from other bodies, and is generated last of the several kinds of movement; in order of being then it will be first.
311ᵃ Now whenever air comes into being out of water, light out of heavy,
it goes to the upper place. It is forthwith light: becoming is at an end,
and in that place it has being. Obviously, then, it is a potentiality,
5 which, in its passage to actuality, comes into that place and quantity
and quality which belong to its actuality. And the same fact explains
why what is already actually fire or earth moves, when nothing ob-
structs it, towards its own place. For motion is equally immediate in
the case of nutriment, when nothing hinders, and in the case of the
thing healed, when nothing stays the healing. But the movement is also
10 due to the original creative force and to that which removes the

hindrance or off which the moving thing rebounded, as was explained in our opening discussions, where we tried to show how none of these things moves itself.[6] The reason of the various motions of the various bodies, and the meaning of the motion of a body to its own place, have now been explained.

4 We have now to speak of the distinctive properties of these bodies 15 and of the various phenomena connected with them. In accordance with general conviction we may distinguish the absolutely heavy, as that which sinks to the bottom of all things, from the absolutely light, which is that which rises to the surface of all things. I use the term 'absolutely', in view of the generic character of 'light' and 'heavy',[7] in order to confine the application to bodies which do not combine lightness and heaviness. It is apparent, I mean, that fire, in what- 20 ever quantity, so long as there is no external obstacle, moves upward, and earth downward; and, if the quantity is increased, the movement is the same, though swifter. But the heaviness and lightness of bodies which combine these qualities is different from this, since while they rise to the surface of some bodies they sink to the bottom of others. Such are air and water. Neither of them is absolutely either light or heavy. Both are lighter than earth—for any portion of either 25 rises to the surface of it—but heavier than fire, since a portion of either, whatever its quantity, sinks to the bottom of fire; compared together, however, the one has absolute weight, the other absolute lightness, since air in any quantity rises to the surface of water, while water in any quantity sinks to the bottom of air. Now other bodies are severally light and heavy, and evidently in them the attributes are 30 due to the difference of their uncompounded parts: that is to say, according as the one or the other happens to preponderate the bodies will be heavy and light respectively. Therefore we need only speak of these parts, since they are primary and all else consequential: and in 35 so doing we shall be following the advice which we gave [8] to those who attribute heaviness to the presence of plenum and lightness 311ᵇ to that of void. It is due to the properties of the elementary bodies that a body which is regarded as light in one place is regarded as heavy in another, and vice versa. In air, for instance, a talent's weight of wood is heavier than a mina of lead, but in water the wood is the lighter. The reason is that all the elements except fire have weight and all but 5

---

[6] *Phys.* vii. 1. 241ᵇ 24; viii. 4. 254ᵇ 7.

[7] i. e. because there are distinct species of light and heavy.

[8] Above, 309ᵇ 20: if they would only give an account of the simple bodies, their questions as to the composite would answer themselves.

earth lightness. Earth, then, and bodies in which earth preponderates, must needs have weight everywhere, while water is heavy anywhere but in earth, and air is heavy when not in water or earth. In its own place each of these bodies has weight except fire, even air. Of this we
10 have evidence in the fact that a bladder when inflated weighs more than when empty. A body, then, in which air preponderates over earth and water, may well be lighter than something in water and yet heavier than it in air, since such a body does not rise in air but rises to the surface in water.

15   The following account will make it plain that there is an absolutely light and an absolutely heavy body. And by absolutely light I mean one which of its own nature always moves upward, by absolutely heavy one which of its own nature always moves downward, if no obstacle is in the way. There are, I say, these two kinds of body, and it is not the case, as some [9] maintain, that all bodies have weight. Different views are in fact agreed that there is a heavy body, which
20 moves uniformly towards the centre. But there is also similarly a light body. For we see with our eyes, as we said before,[10] that earthy things sink to the bottom of all things and move towards the centre. But the centre is a fixed point. If therefore there is some body which rises to the surface of all things—and we observe fire to move upward even in air itself, while the air remains at rest—clearly this body is moving towards the extremity. It cannot then have any weight. If
25 it had, there would be another body in which it sank: and if that had weight, there would be yet another which moved to the extremity and thus rose to the surface of all moving things. In fact, however, we have no evidence of such a body. Fire, then, has no weight. Neither has earth any lightness, since it sinks to the bottom of all things, and that which sinks moves to the centre. That there is a centre towards
30 which the motion of heavy things, and away from which that of light things is directed, is manifest in many ways. First, because no movement can continue to infinity. For what cannot be can no more come-to-be than be, and movement is a coming-to-be in one place from another. Secondly, like the upward movement of fire, the downward
35 movement of earth and all heavy things makes equal angles on every side with the earth's surface: it must therefore be directed towards the
312ᵃ centre. Whether it is really the centre of the earth and not rather that of the whole to which it moves, may be left to another inquiry,

────────

[9] This view is maintained in its most unqualified form, by those (atomists, probably) who distinguish the four elements by the size of their particles (Cf. C. 2. 310ᵃ 9).
[10] Above, 311ᵃ 20.

since these are coincident.[11] But since that which sinks to the bottom of all things moves to the centre, necessarily that which rises to the surface moves to the extremity of the region in which the movement 5 of these bodies takes place. For the centre is opposed as contrary to the extremity, as that which sinks is opposed to that which rises to the surface. This also gives a reasonable ground for the duality of heavy and light in the spatial duality centre and extremity. Now there is also the intermediate region to which each name is given in opposition to the other extreme. For that which is intermediate be- 10 tween the two is in a sense both extremity and centre. For this reason there is another heavy and light; namely, water and air. But in our view the continent pertains to form and the contained to matter: and this distinction is present in every genus.[12] Alike in the sphere of quality and in that of quantity there is that which corre- 15 sponds rather to form and that which corresponds to matter. In the same way, among spatial distinctions, the above belongs to the determinate, the below to matter. The same holds, consequently, also of the matter itself of that which is heavy and light: as potentially possessing the one character, it is matter for the heavy, and as potentially possessing the other, for the light. It is the same matter, but its being is different, as that which is receptive of disease is the same as 20 that which is receptive of health, though in being different from it, and therefore diseasedness is different from healthiness.

5 A thing then which has the one kind of matter is light and always moves upward, while a thing which has the opposite matter is heavy and always moves downward. Bodies composed of kinds of matter different from these but having relatively to each other the character which these have absolutely, possess both the upward and 25 the downward motion. Hence air and water each have both lightness and weight, and water sinks to the bottom of all things except earth, while air rises to the surface of all things except fire. But since there is one body only which rises to the surface of all things and one only which sinks to the bottom of all things, there must needs be two other bodies which sink in some bodies and rise to the surface of others. 30 The kinds of matter, then, must be as numerous as these bodies, i. e. four, but though they are four there must be a common matter of all—particularly if they pass into one another—which in each is in being different. There is no reason why there should not be one or 312[b] more intermediates between the contraries, as in the case of colour;

[11] The question is discussed in ii. 14. 296[b] 9.
[12] i. e. in every category.

for 'intermediate' and 'mean' are capable of more than one application.

Now in its own place every body endowed with both weight and lightness has weight—whereas earth has weight everywhere—but
5 they only have lightness among bodies to whose surface they rise. Hence when a support is withdrawn such a body moves downward until it reaches the body next below it, air to the place of water and water to that of earth. But if the fire above air is removed, it will not move upward to the place of fire, except by constraint; and in that way water also may be drawn up, when the upward move-
10 ment of air which has had a common surface with it is swift enough to overpower the downward impulse of the water. Nor does water move upward to the place of air, except in the manner just described. Earth is not so affected at all, because a common surface is not possible to it. Hence water is drawn up into the vessel to which fire is applied, but not earth. As earth fails to move upward, so fire fails
15 to move downward when air is withdrawn from beneath it: for fire has no weight even in its own place, as earth has no lightness. The other two move downward when the body beneath is withdrawn because, while the absolutely heavy is that which sinks to the bottom of all things, the relatively heavy sinks to its own place or to the surface of the body in which it rises, since it is similar in matter to it.
20   It is plain that one must suppose as many distinct species of matter as there are bodies. For if, *first*, there is a single matter of all things, as, for instance, the void or the plenum or extension or the triangles, either all things will move upward or all things will move downward, and the second motion will be abolished. And so, either there will be no absolutely light body, if superiority of weight is due
25 to superior size or number of the constituent bodies or to the fullness of the body: but the contrary is a matter of observation, and it has been shown that the downward and upward movements are equally constant and universal: or, if the matter in question is the void or something similar, which moves uniformly upward, there will be nothing to move uniformly downward. Further, it will follow that the intermediate bodies move downward in some cases quicker than earth: for air in sufficiently large quantity will contain a larger number of triangles or solids or particles. It is, however, manifest
30 that no portion of air whatever moves downward.[13] And the same reasoning applies to lightness, if that is supposed to depend on supe-

13 *sc.* in earth.

riority of quantity of matter.[14] But if, *secondly*, the kinds of matter
are two, it will be difficult to make the intermediate bodies behave as
air and water behave. Suppose, for example, that the two asserted 313ᵃ
are void and plenum. Fire, then, as moving upward, will be void, earth,
as moving downward, plenum; and in air, it will be said, fire preponderates, in water, earth. There will then be a quantity of water
containing more fire than a little air, and a large amount of air will
contain more earth than a little water: consequently we shall have to 5
say that air in a certain quantity moves downward more quickly than
a little water. But such a thing has never been observed anywhere.
Necessarily, then, as fire goes up because it has something, e. g. void,
which other things do not have, and earth goes downward because it
has plenum, so air goes to its own place above water because it has 10
something else, and water goes downward because of some special
kind of body. But if the two bodies [15] are one matter, or two matters
both present in each, there will be a certain quantity of each at which
water will excel a little air in the upward movement and air excel
water in the downward movement, as we have already often said.

6 The shape of bodies will not account for their moving upward or 15
downward in general, though it will account for their moving faster or
slower. The reasons for this are not difficult to see. For the problem
thus raised is why a flat piece of iron or lead floats upon water, while
smaller and less heavy things, so long as they are round or long—a
needle, for instance—sink down; and sometimes a thing floats because it is small, as with gold dust and the various earthy and dusty 20
materials which throng the air. With regard to these questions, it is
wrong to accept the explanation offered by Democritus. He says that
the warm bodies moving up out of the water hold up heavy bodies
which are broad, while the narrow ones fall through, because the 313ᵇ
bodies which offer this resistance are not numerous. But this would
be even more likely to happen in air—an objection which he himself raises. His reply to the objection is feeble. In the air, he says,
the 'drive' (meaning by drive the movement of the upward moving 5
bodies) is not uniform in direction. But since some continua are
easily divided and others less easily, and things which produce division
differ similarly in the ease with which they produce it, the explanation
must be found in this fact. It is the easily bounded, in proportion as
it is easily bounded, which is easily divided; and air is more so than 10

---

[14] On the somewhat absurd theory that the universal 'matter' is void or
absolute lightness.
[15] viz. air and water.

water, water than earth. Further, the smaller the quantity in each kind, the more easily it is divided and disrupted. Thus the reason why broad things keep their place is because they cover so wide a surface and the greater quantity is less easily disrupted. Bodies of the oppo-
15 site shape sink down because they occupy so little of the surface, which is therefore easily parted. And these considerations apply with far greater force to air, since it is so much more easily divided than water. But since there are two factors, the force responsible for the downward motion of the heavy body and the disruption-resisting force of the continuous surface, there must be some ratio between the two. For in proportion as the force applied by the heavy thing
20 towards disruption and division exceeds that which resides in the continuum, the quicker will it force its way down; only if the force of the heavy thing is the weaker, will it ride upon the surface.

We have now finished our examination of the heavy and the light and of the phenomena connected with them.

De Generatione et Corruptione

Translated by Harold H. Joachim

CONTENTS

BOOK I

BOOK II

DE GENERATIONE ET CORRUPTIONE

(On Generation and Corruption)

BOOK I

314ª 1 Our next task is to study coming-to-be and passing-away. We are
to distinguish the causes, and to state the definitions, of these processes considered in general—as changes predicable uniformly of all
the things that come-to-be and pass-away by nature. Further, we
are to study growth and 'alteration'. We must inquire what each of
5 them is; and whether 'alteration' is to be identified with coming-to-
be, or whether to these different names there correspond two separate
processes with distinct natures.

On this question, indeed, the early philosophers are divided. Some
of them assert that the so-called 'unqualified coming-to-be' is 'alteration', while others maintain that 'alteration' and coming-to-be are distinct. For those who say that the universe is one something (i. e. those
who generate all things out of one thing) are bound to assert that
10 coming-to-be is 'alteration', and that whatever 'comes-to-be' in the
proper sense of the term is 'being altered': but those who make the
matter of things more than one must distinguish coming-to-be from
'alteration'. To this latter class belong Empedocles, Anaxagoras, and
Leucippus. And yet Anaxagoras himself failed to understand his own
utterance. He *says*, at all events, that coming-to-be and passing-away
15 are the same as 'being altered': yet, in common with other thinkers,
he affirms that the elements are many. Thus Empedocles holds that
the corporeal elements are four, while all the elements—including
those which initiate movement—are six in number; whereas Anaxagoras agrees with Leucippus and Democritus that the elements are
infinite.

(Anaxagoras posits as elements the 'homoeomeries', viz. bone, flesh,
20 marrow, and everything else which is such that part and whole are
the same in name and nature; while Democritus and Leucippus say
that there are indivisible bodies, infinite both in number and in the
varieties of their shapes, of which everything else is composed—the
470

compounds differing one from another according to the shapes, 'positions', and 'groupings' of their constituents.)

For the views of the school of Anaxagoras seem diametrically op- 25 posed to those of the followers of Empedocles. Empedocles says that Fire, Water, Air, and Earth are four elements, and are thus 'simple' rather than flesh, bone, and bodies which, like these, are 'homoeomeries'. But the followers of Anaxagoras regard the 'homoeomeries' as 'simple' and elements, whilst they affirm that Earth, Fire, Water, and Air are composite; for each of these is (according to them) a 'common seminary' of all the 'homoeomeries'. 314ᵇ

Those, then, who construct all things out of a single element, must maintain that coming-to-be and passing-away are 'alteration'. For they must affirm that the underlying something always remains identical and one; and change of such a *substratum* is what we call 'altering'. Those, on the other hand, who make the ultimate kinds of things more than one, must maintain that 'alteration' is distinct from com- 5 ing-to-be: for coming-to-be and passing-away result from the consilience and the dissolution of the many kinds. That is why Empedocles too [1] uses language to this effect, when he says 'There is no coming-to-be of anything, but only a mingling and a divorce of what has been mingled'. Thus it is clear (i) that to describe coming-to-be and passing-away in these terms is in accordance with their fundamental assumption, and (ii) that they do in fact so describe them: neverthe- 10 less, they too [2] must recognize 'alteration' as a fact distinct from coming-to-be, though it is impossible for them to do so consistently with what they say.

That we are right in this criticism is easy to perceive. For 'alteration' is a fact of observation. While the substance of the thing remains unchanged, we *see* it 'altering' just as we *see* in it the changes of mag- 15 nitude called 'growth' and 'diminution'. Nevertheless, the statements of those who posit more 'original reals' than one make 'alteration' impossible. For 'alteration', as we assert, takes place in respect to certain qualities: and these qualities (I mean, e. g., hot-cold, white-black, dry-moist, soft-hard, and so forth) are, all of them, differences 20 characterizing the 'elements'. The actual words of Empedocles may be quoted in illustration—

> The sun everywhere bright to see, and hot;
> The rain everywhere dark and cold;

and he distinctively characterizes his remaining elements in a similar

---

[1] i. e. as well as Anaxagoras: Cf. above, 314ª 13–15.
[2] i. e. as well as ordinary people: Cf. ᵇ 13 ff.

manner. Since, therefore, it is not possible[3] for Fire to become
Water, or Water to become Earth, neither will it be possible for
25 anything white to become black, or anything soft to become hard;
and the same argument applies to all the other qualities. Yet this is
what 'alteration' essentially is.

It follows, as an obvious corollary, that a single matter must
always be assumed as underlying the contrary 'poles' of any change
—whether change of place, or growth and diminution, or 'alteration';
further, that the being of this matter and the being of 'alteration'
315ᵃ stand and fall together. For if the change is 'alteration', then the
substratum is a single element; i. e. all things which admit of change
into one another have a single matter. And, conversely, if the *substratum* of the changing things is one, there is 'alteration'.

Empedocles, indeed, seems to contradict his own statements as
5 well as the observed facts. For he denies that any one of his elements
comes-to-be out of any other, insisting on the contrary that they are
the things out of which everything else comes-to-be; and yet (having brought the entirety of existing things, except Strife, together into
one) he maintains, simultaneously with this denial, that each thing
once more comes-to-be out of the One. Hence it was clearly out of a
One that *this* came-to-be Water, and *that* Fire, various portions of
10 it being separated off by certain characteristic differences or qualities
—as indeed he calls the sun 'white and hot', and the earth 'heavy
and hard'. If, therefore, these characteristic differences be taken away
(for they can be taken away, since they came-to-be), it will clearly
be inevitable for Earth to come-to-be out of Water and Water out of
Earth, and for each of the other elements to undergo a similar trans-
15 formation—not only *then*,[4] but also *now*—if, and because, they
change their qualities. And, to judge by what he says, the qualities
are such that they *can* be 'attached' to things and *can* again be
'separated' from them, especially since Strife and Love are still fighting with one another for the mastery. It was owing to this same conflict that the elements were generated from a One at the former
period. I say 'generated', for presumably Fire, Earth, and Water had
no distinctive existence at all while merged in one.

There is another obscurity in the theory of Empedocles. Are we to
20 regard the One as his 'original real'? Or is it the Many—i. e. Fire
and Earth, and the bodies co-ordinate with these? For the One is an
'element' in so far as it underlies the process as matter—as that out

---

[3] i. e. according to Empedocles.

[4] i. e. at the period when Empedocles himself appears to recognize that his 'elements' come-to-be.

of which Earth and Fire come-to-be through a change of qualities due to 'the motion'.[5] On the other hand, in so far as the One results from *composition* (by a consilience of the Many), whereas they result from *disintegration,* the Many are more 'elementary' than the One, and prior to it in their nature. 25

2 We have therefore to discuss the whole subject of 'unqualified' coming-to-be and passing-away; we have to inquire whether these changes do or do not occur and, if they occur, to explain the precise conditions of their occurrence. We must also discuss the remaining forms of change, viz. growth and 'alteration'. For though, no doubt, Plato investigated the conditions under which things come-to-be and pass-away, he confined his inquiry to these changes; and he dis- 30 cussed not *all* coming-to-be, but only that of the elements. He asked no questions as to how flesh or bones, or any of the other similar compound things, come-to-be; nor again did he examine the conditions under which 'alteration' or growth are attributable to things.

A similar criticism applies to all our predecessors with the single exception of Democritus. Not one of them penetrated below the sur- 35 face or made a thorough examination of a single one of the problems. Democritus, however, does seem not only to have thought carefully about all the problems, but also to be distinguished from the outset 315[b] by his method. For, as we are saying, none of the other philosophers made any definite statement about growth, except such as any amateur might have made. They said that things grow 'by the accession of like to like', but they did not proceed to explain the manner of this acces- sion. Nor did they give any account of 'combination': and they neg- lected almost every single one of the remaining problems, offering no explanation, e. g., of 'action' or 'passion'—how in physical actions one 5 thing acts and the other undergoes action. Democritus and Leucippus, however, postulate the 'figures', and make 'alteration' and coming-to- be result from them. They explain coming-to-be and passing-away by their 'dissociation' and 'association', but 'alteration' by their 'group- ing' and 'position'. And since they thought that the truth lay in the appearance, and the appearances are conflicting and infinitely many, 10 they made the 'figures' infinite in number. Hence—owing to the changes of the compound—*the same* thing seems different and con- flicting to different people: it is 'transposed' by a small additional in- gredient, and appears utterly other by the 'transposition' of a single constituent. For Tragedy and Comedy are both composed of *the same* 15 letters.

[5] i. e. the motion of dissociation initiated by Strife.

Since almost all our predecessors think (i) that coming-to-be is distinct from 'alteration', and (ii) that, whereas things 'alter' by change of their qualities, it is by 'association' and 'dissociation' that they come-to-be and pass-away, we must concentrate our attention on these theses. For they lead to many perplexing and well-grounded
20 dilemmas. If, on the one hand, coming-to-be *is* 'association', many impossible consequences result: and yet there are other arguments, not easy to unravel, which force the conclusion upon us that coming-to-be cannot possibly be anything else. If, on the other hand, coming-to-be *is not* 'association', either there is no such thing as coming-to-be at all or it is 'alteration': or else [6] we must endeavour to unravel this dilemma too—and a stubborn one we shall find it.

25   The fundamental question, in dealing with all these difficulties, is this: 'Do things come-to-be and "alter" and grow, and undergo the contrary changes, because the primary "reals" are indivisible magnitudes? Or is no magnitude indivisible?' For the answer we give to this question makes the greatest difference. And again, if the primary
30 'reals' are indivisible magnitudes, are these *bodies,* as Democritus and Leucippus maintain? Or are they *planes,* as is asserted in the *Timaeus*?

To resolve bodies into planes and no further—this, as we have also remarked elsewhere,[7] is in itself a paradox. Hence there is more to be said for the view that there are indivisible bodies. Yet even these involve much of paradox. Still, as we have said, it is possible to con-
35 struct 'alteration' and coming-to-be with them, if one 'transposes' *the*
316ᵃ *same* by 'turning' and 'intercontact', and by 'the varieties of the figures', as Democritus does. (His denial of the reality of colour is a corollary from this position: for, according to him, things get coloured by 'turning' of the 'figures'.) But the possibility of such a construction no longer exists for those who divide bodies into planes. For nothing except solids results from putting planes together: they do not even attempt to generate any quality from them.

5   Lack of experience diminishes our power of taking a comprehensive view of the admitted facts. Hence those who dwell in intimate association with nature and its phenomena grow more and more able to formulate, as the foundations of their theories, principles such as to admit of a wide and coherent development: while those whom devotion to abstract discussions has rendered unobservant of the facts are too
10 ready to dogmatize on the basis of a few observations. The rival treatments of the subject now before us will serve to illustrate how

---

[6] i. e. if we still wish to maintain that coming-to-be (though it actually occurs and is distinct from 'alteration') is not 'association'.

[7] Cf. e. g. *de Caelo* 299 ᵃ 6–11.

great is the difference between a 'scientific' and a 'dialectical' method of inquiry. For, whereas the Platonists argue that there must be atomic magnitudes 'because otherwise "The Triangle" will be more than one', Democritus would appear to have been convinced by arguments appropriate to the subject, i. e. drawn from the science of nature. Our meaning will become clear as we proceed.

For to suppose that a body (i. e. a magnitude) is divisible through 15 and through, and that this division is possible, involves a difficulty. What will there be in the body which escapes the division?

If it is divisible through and through, and if this division is possible, then it might *be*, at one and the same moment, *divided* through and through, even though the dividings had not been effected simultaneously: and the actual occurrence of this result would involve no impossibility. Hence the same principle will apply whenever a body is by 20 nature divisible through and through, whether by bisection,[8] or generally by any method whatever: nothing impossible will have resulted if it has actually been divided—not even if it has been divided into innumerable parts, themselves divided innumerable times. Nothing impossible will have resulted, though perhaps nobody in fact could so divide it.

Since, therefore, the body is divisible through and through, let it have been divided. What, then, will remain? A magnitude? No: that is impossible, since then there will be something not divided, whereas 25 *ex hypothesi* the body was divisible *through and through*. But if it be admitted that neither a body nor a magnitude will remain, and yet division[9] is to take place, the constituents of the body will *either* be points (i. e. without magnitude) *or* absolutely nothing. If its constituents are nothings, then it might both come-to-be out of nothings and exist as a composite of nothings: and thus presumably the whole body will be nothing but an appearance. But if it consists of points, a similar absurdity will result: it will not possess any magnitude. 30 For when the points were in contact and coincided to form a single magnitude, they did not make the whole any bigger (since, when the body was divided into two or more parts, the whole[10] was not a bit smaller or bigger than it was before the division): hence, even if all the points[11] be put together, they will not make any magnitude.

But suppose that, as the body is being divided, a minute section—

[8] i. e. by progressive bisection *ad infinitum*.

[9] i. e. 'through and through' division.

[10] i. e. the sum of the now separated parts.

[11] i. e. all the points into which the body has been dissolved by the 'through and through' division.

316ᵇ a piece of sawdust, as it were—is extracted, and that in this sense a body 'comes away' from the magnitude, evading the division. Even then the same [12] argument applies. For in what sense is that section divisible? But if what 'came away' was not a body but a separable form or quality, and if the magnitude *is* 'points or contacts thus
5 qualified': it is paradoxical that a magnitude should consist of elements which are not magnitudes. Moreover, *where* will the points be? And are they motionless or moving? And every contact is always a contact of two somethings, i. e. there is always something besides the contact or the division or the point.

These, then, are the difficulties resulting from the supposition that any and every body, whatever its size, is divisible through and through.
10 There is, besides, this further consideration. If, having divided a piece of wood or anything else, I put it together, it is again equal to what it was, and is one. Clearly this is so, whatever the point at which I cut the wood. The wood, therefore, has been divided *potentially* through and through. What, then, is there in the wood besides the division? For even if we suppose there is some quality, yet how is the wood dissolved into such constituents [13] and how does it come-to-be out of them? Or how are such constituents separated so as to exist apart from one another?

15 Since, therefore, it is impossible for magnitudes to consist of contacts or points, there must be indivisible bodies and magnitudes. Yet, if we *do* postulate the latter, we are confronted with equally impossible consequences, which we have examined in other works.[14] But we must try to disentangle these perplexities, and must therefore formulate the whole problem over again.

20 On the one hand, then, it is in no way paradoxical that every perceptible body should be indivisible as well as divisible at any and every point. For the second predicate will attach to it *potentially*, but the first *actually*. On the other hand, it would seem to be impossible for a body to be, even potentially, divisible at all points simultaneously. For if it were possible, then it might actually occur, with the result, not that the body would simultaneously be actually *both* (indivisible and divided), but that it would be simultaneously divided
25 at any and every point. Consequently, nothing will remain and the body will have passed-away into what is incorporeal: and so it might come-to-be again either out of points or absolutely out of nothing. And how is that possible?

---

¹² Cf. above, 316ᵃ 24–5.
¹³ i. e. points-of-division and quality.
¹⁴ Cf. *Physics* 231ᵃ 21 ff.; *de Caelo* 303ᵃ 3 ff.

But now it is obvious that a body is in fact divided into separable magnitudes which are smaller at each division—into magnitudes which fall apart from one another and are actually separated. Hence (it is urged) the process of dividing a body part by part is not a 'breaking 30 up' which could continue *ad infinitum*; nor can a body be simultaneously divided at every point, for that is not possible; but there is a limit, beyond which the 'breaking up' cannot proceed. The necessary consequence—especially if coming-to-be and passing-away are to take place by 'association' and 'dissociation' respectively—is that a body [15] must contain atomic magnitudes which are invisible.

Such is the argument which is believed to establish the necessity of 317ª atomic magnitudes: we must now show that it conceals a faulty inference, and exactly where it conceals it.

For, since point is not 'immediately-next' to point, magnitudes are 'divisible through and through' in one sense, and yet not in another. When, however, it is admitted that a magnitude is 'divisible through 5 and through', it is thought there is a point not only anywhere, but also everywhere, in it: hence it is supposed to follow, from the admission, that the magnitude must be divided away into nothing. For—it is supposed—there is a point everywhere within it, so that it consists either of contacts or of points. But it is only *in one sense* that the magnitude is 'divisible through and through', viz. in so far as there is one point *anywhere* within it and all its points are *everywhere* within it if you take them singly one by one. But there are not more points than one *anywhere* within it, for the points are not 'consecutive': hence it is not simultaneously 'divisible through and through'. For if it 10 were, then, if it be divisible at its centre, it will be divisible also at a point 'immediately-next' to its centre. But it is not so divisible: for position is not 'immediately-next' to position, nor point to point—in other words, division is not 'immediately-next' to division, nor composition to composition.

Hence there are both 'association' and 'dissociation', though neither (*a*) into, and out of, atomic magnitudes (for that involves many impossibilities), nor (*b*) so that division takes place through and 15 through—for this would have resulted only if point had been 'immediately-next' to point: but 'dissociation' takes place into small (i. e. relatively small) parts, and 'association' takes place out of relatively small parts.

It is wrong, however, to suppose, as some assert, that coming-to-be and passing-away in the unqualified and complete sense are distinctively defined by 'association' and 'dissociation', while the change that

[15] i. e. every perceptible body: Cf. above, 316ᵇ 21.

takes place in what is continuous is 'alteration'. On the contrary, this
20 is where the whole error lies. For unqualified coming-to-be and passing-away are not effected by 'association' and 'dissociation'. They
take place when a thing changes, from *this* to *that*, as a whole. But
the philosophers we are criticizing suppose that all such change [16] is
'alteration': whereas in fact there is a difference. For in that which
underlies the change there is a factor corresponding to the definition [17]
25 and there is a material factor. When, then, the change is in these
constitutive factors, there will be coming-to-be or passing-away: but
when it is in the thing's qualities, i. e. a change of the thing *per accidens*, there will be 'alteration'.

'Dissociation' and 'association' affect the thing's susceptibility to
passing-away. For if water has first been 'dissociated' into smallish
drops, air comes-to-be out of it more quickly: while, if drops of water
have first been 'associated', air comes-to-be more slowly. Our doc-
30 trine will become clearer in the sequel.[18] Meantime, so much may be
taken as established—viz. that coming-to-be cannot be 'association',
at least not the kind of 'association' some philosophers assert it to be.

3 Now that we have established the preceding distinctions, we must
first [19] consider whether there is anything which comes-to-be and
passes-away in the unqualified sense: or whether nothing comes-to-
be in this strict sense, but everything always comes-to-be *something*
35 and *out of something*—I mean, e. g., comes-to-be-healthy out of
being-ill and ill out of being-healthy, comes-to-be-small out of being-
317b big and big out of being-small, and so on in every other instance. For
if there is to be coming-to-be without qualification, 'something' must
—without qualification—'come-to-be out of not-being', so that it
would be true to say that 'not-being is an attribute of some things'.
For *qualified* coming-to-be is a process out of *qualified* not-being (e. g.
5 out of not-white or not-beautiful), but *unqualified* coming-to-be is a
process out of *unqualified* not-being.

Now 'unqualified' means either (i) the primary predication within
each Category, or (ii) the universal, i. e. the all-comprehensive, predication. Hence, if 'unqualified not-being' means the negation of 'being'
in the sense of the primary term of the Category in question, we shall
have, in 'unqualified coming-to-be', a coming-to-be of a substance

---

[16] i. e. all change 'in what is continuous'.

[17] i. e. a 'formal' factor.

[18] Cf. 328a 23 ff.

[19] The second main topic of investigation is formulated below, 317b 34-5.

out of not-substance. But that which is not a substance or a 'this' clearly cannot possess predicates drawn from any of the other Cate- 10 gories either—e. g. we cannot attribute to it any quality, quantity, or position. Otherwise, properties would admit of existence in separation from substances. If, on the other hand, 'unqualified not-being' means 'what is not in any sense at all', it will be a universal negation of all forms of being, so that what comes-to-be will have to come-to-be out of nothing.

Although we have dealt with these problems at greater length in another work,[20] where we have set forth the difficulties and established the distinguishing definitions, the following concise restatement of our 15 results must here be offered:—

In one sense things come-to-be out of that which has no 'being' without qualification: yet in another sense they come-to-be always out of 'what is'. For coming-to-be necessarily implies the pre-existence of something which *potentially* 'is', but *actually* 'is not'; and this something is spoken of both as 'being' and as 'not-being'.

These distinctions may be taken as established: but even then it is extraordinarily difficult to see how there can be 'unqualified coming-to-be' (whether we suppose it to occur out of what potentially 'is', or in some other way), and we must recall this problem for further 20 examination. For the question might be raised whether substance (i. e. the 'this') comes-to-be at all. Is it not rather the 'such', the 'so-great', or the 'somewhere', which comes-to-be? And the same question might be raised about 'passing-away' also. For if a substantial thing comes-to-be, it is clear that there will 'be' (not actually, but potentially) a substance, out of which its coming-to-be will proceed and into which the thing that is passing-away will necessarily change. Then will any predicate belonging to the remaining Categories attach 25 *actually* to this presupposed substance? In other words, will that which is only potentially a 'this' (which only potentially *is*), while without the qualification 'potentially' it is not a 'this' (i. e. *is not*), possess, e. g., any determinate size or quality or position? For (i) if it possesses none of these determinations actually, but all of them only potentially, the result is *first* that a being, which is not a determinate being, is capable of separate existence; and *in addition* that coming-to-be proceeds out of nothing pre-existing—a thesis which, more than any other, preoccupied and alarmed the earliest philoso- 30 phers. On the other hand (ii) if, although it is not a 'this somewhat' or a substance, it is to possess some of the remaining determinations

[20] *Physics* i. 6–9.

quoted above, then (as we said) [21] properties will be separable from substances.

We must therefore concentrate all our powers on the discussion of these difficulties and on the solution of a further question—viz.
35 What is the cause of the perpetuity of coming-to-be? Why is there always unqualified,[22] as well as *partial*,[23] coming-to-be?

318ᵃ 'Cause' in this connexion has two senses. It means (i) the source from which, as we say, the process 'originates', and (ii) the matter. It is the material cause that we have here to state. For, as to the other cause, we have already explained (in our treatise on Motion [24]) that it involves (*a*) something immovable through all time and (*b*) some-
5 thing always being moved. And the accurate treatment of the first of these—of the immovable 'originative source'—belongs to the province of the other, or 'prior', philosophy: while as regards 'that which sets everything else in motion by being itself continuously moved', we shall have to explain later [25] which amongst the so-called 'specific' causes exhibits this character. But at present we are to state the material cause—the cause classed under the head of matter—to
10 which it is due that passing-away and coming-to-be never fail to occur in Nature. For perhaps, if we succeed in clearing up this question, it will simultaneously become clear what account we ought to give of that which perplexed us just now, i. e. of *unqualified* passing-away and coming-to-be.

Our new question too—viz. 'what is the cause of the unbroken continuity of coming-to-be?'—is sufficiently perplexing, if in fact
15 what passes-away vanishes into 'what is not' and 'what is not' is noth-ing (since 'what is not' is neither a thing, nor possessed of a quality or quantity, nor in any place). If, then, some one of the things 'which are' is constantly disappearing, why has not the whole of 'what is' been used up long ago and vanished away—assuming of course that the material of all the several comings-to-be was finite? For, pre-sumably, the unfailing continuity of coming-to-be cannot be attributed
20 to the infinity of the material. That is impossible, for nothing is actually infinite. A thing is infinite only potentially, i. e. the dividing of it can continue indefinitely: so that we should have to suppose there is only one kind of coming-to-be in the world—viz. one which never fails,

---

21 Cf. above, 317ᵇ 10–11.

22 'Unqualified coming-to-be' = substantial change.

23 'Partial' = 'qualified' coming-to-be, i. e. change of quality, quantity, or place.

24 *Physics* viii. 3 ff., especially 258ᵇ 10 ff.

25 Cf. below, II. 10.

because it is such that what comes-to-be is on each successive occasion smaller than before. But in fact this is not what we see occurring.

Why, then, is this form of change necessarily ceaseless? Is it because the passing-away of *this* is a coming-to-be of *something else*, and the coming-to-be of *this* a passing-away of *something else?*

The cause implied in this solution [26] must no doubt be considered adequate to account for coming-to-be and passing-away in their general character as they occur in all existing things alike. Yet, if the same process is a coming-to-be of *this* but a passing-away of *that*, and a passing-away of *this* but a coming-to-be of *that*, why are some things said to come-to-be and pass-away without qualification, but others only with a qualification?

This distinction must be investigated once more, for it demands some explanation. <It is applied in a twofold manner.> For (i) we say 'it is now passing-away' without qualification, and not merely '*this* is passing-away': [27] and we call *this* change 'coming-to-be', and *that* 'passing-away', without qualification. And (ii) so-and-so 'comes-to-be-something', but does not 'come-to-be' without qualification; for we say that the student 'comes-to-be-learned', not 'comes-to-be' without qualification.

(i) Now we often divide terms into those which signify a 'this 318ᵇ somewhat' and those which do not. And <the first form of> the distinction, which we are investigating, results from a similar division of terms: for it makes a difference *into what* the changing thing changes. Perhaps, e. g., the passage into Fire is 'coming-to-be' *unqualified*, but 'passing-away-of-something' (e. g. of Earth): whilst the coming-to-be of Earth is *qualified* (not *unqualified*) 'coming-to-be', though *unqualified* 'passing-away' (e. g. of Fire). This would be the case on the theory set forth in Parmenides: [28] for he says that the things into which change takes place are two, and he asserts that these two, viz. *what is* and *what is not*, are Fire and Earth. Whether we postulate these,[29] or other things of a similar kind, makes no difference. For we are trying to discover not what undergoes these changes, but what is their characteristic manner. The passage, then, into what 'is not' except with a qualification is unqualified passing-away, while the passage into what 'is' without qualification is unqualified coming-to-be. Hence whatever the contrasted 'poles' of the changes may be—

---

[26] i. e. the material cause.

[27] i. e. not merely '*this* is passing-away and *that* is coming-to-be.'

[28] The theory is put forward by Parmenides as the prevalent, but erroneous, view.

[29] *sc.* as the things into which the unqualified changes take place.

whether Fire and Earth, or some other couple—the one of them will
be a 'being' and the other 'a not-being'.[30]

We have thus stated one characteristic manner in which *unqualified* will be distinguished from *qualified* coming-to-be and passing-
away; but they are also distinguished according to the special nature
15 of the material of the changing thing. For a material, whose constitutive differences signify more a 'this somewhat', is itself more 'substantial' or 'real': while a material, whose constitutive differences signify
privation, is 'not real'. (Suppose, e. g., that 'the hot' is a positive predication, i. e. a 'form', whereas 'cold' is a privation, and that Earth and
Fire differ from one another by these constitutive differences.)

The opinion, however, which most people are inclined to prefer, is
that the distinction [31] depends upon the difference between 'the per-
20 ceptible' and 'the imperceptible'. Thus, when there is a change into
perceptible material, people say there is 'coming-to-be'; but when
there is a change into invisible material, they call it 'passing-away'.
For they distinguish 'what is' and 'what is not' by their perceiving and
not-perceiving, just as what is knowable 'is' and what is unknowable 'is
not'—perception on their view having the force of knowledge. Hence,
25 just as they deem themselves to live and to 'be' in virtue of their perceiving or their capacity to perceive, so too they deem the things to 'be'
qua perceived or perceptible—and in this they are in a sense on the
track of the truth, though what they actually say is not true.

Thus unqualified coming-to-be and passing-away turn out to be
different according to common opinion from what they are in truth.[32]
For Wind and Air are in truth more real—more a 'this somewhat' or
a 'form'—than Earth. But they are less real to perception—which
30 explains why things are commonly said to 'pass-away' without qualification when they change into Wind and Air, and to 'come-to-be' [33]
when they change into what is tangible, i. e. into Earth.

We have now explained why there is 'unqualified coming-to-be'
(though it is a passing-away-of-something) and 'unqualified passing-
away' (though it is a coming-to-be-of-something). For this distinc-
35 tion of appellation depends upon a difference in the material out of
which, and into which, the changes are effected. It depends *either* upon
319ᵃ whether the material is or is not 'substantial', *or* upon whether it is more
or less 'substantial', *or* upon whether it is more or less perceptible.

(ii) But why are some things said to 'come-to-be' without qualifi-

---

[30] i. e. one will be 'a positive real' and the other 'a negative something'.

[31] *sc.* between the *unqualified* and the *qualified* changes.

[32] 'In truth', i. e. according to Aristotle's own view which he has just stated
(above, 318ᵇ 14–18).   [33] *sc.* without qualification.

cation, and others only to 'come-to-be-so-and-so', in cases different
from the one we have been considering where two things come-to-be
reciprocally out of one another? For at present we have explained
no more than this:—why, when two things change reciprocally into 5
one another, we do not attribute coming-to-be and passing-away *uniformly* to them both, although every coming-to-be is a passing-away
of something else and every passing-away some other thing's coming-
to-be. But the question subsequently formulated involves a different
problem—viz. why, although the learning thing is said to 'come-to-be-
learned' but not to 'come-to-be' without qualification, yet the grow- 10
ing thing *is* said to 'come-to-be'.

The distinction here turns upon the difference of the Categories.
For some things signify a *this somewhat*, others a *such*, and others a
so-much. Those things, then, which do not signify substance, are not
said to 'come-to-be' without qualification, but only to 'come-to-be-
so-and-so'. Nevertheless, in all changing things alike, we speak of
'coming-to-be' [34] when the thing comes-to-be something in *one* [35] of 15
the two Columns—e. g. in Substance, if it comes-to-be Fire but not
if it comes-to-be Earth; and in Quality, if it comes-to-be learned but
not when it comes-to-be ignorant.

We have explained why some things come-to-be without qualification, but not others—both in general, and also when the changing
things are substances and nothing else; and we have stated that the
substratum is the material cause of the continuous occurrence of
coming-to-be, because it is such as to change from contrary to con- 20
trary and because, in substances, the coming-to-be of one thing is always a passing-away of another, and the passing-away of one thing is
always another's coming-to-be. But there is no need even to discuss
the other question we raised—viz. why coming-to-be continues
though things are constantly being destroyed.[36] For just as people
speak of 'a passing-away' without qualification when a thing has
passed into what is imperceptible and what in that sense 'is not', so
also they speak of 'a coming-to-be out of a not-being' when a thing 25
emerges from an imperceptible. Whether, therefore, the *substratum*
is or is not something, what comes-to-be emerges out of a 'not-being': [37]
so that a thing 'comes-to-be out of a not-being' just as much as it
'passes-away into what is not'. Hence it is reasonable enough that

[34] i. e. without qualification.

[35] i. e. in the Column containing the positive terms: Cf. above, 318ᵇ 14–18.

[36] Cf. above, 318ª 13–23.

[37] A 'not-being' in the popular sense of the term, i. e. an 'imperceptible'. The
imperceptibility of the material is irrelevant to the question of its reality.

coming-to-be should never fail. For coming-to-be is a passing-away
of 'what is not' and passing-away is a coming-to-be of 'what is not'.[38]

But what about that which 'is' not except with a qualification?
30 Is it one of the two contrary poles of the change—e. g. is Earth (i. e.
the heavy) a 'not-being', but Fire (i. e. the light) a 'being'? Or, on
the contrary, does 'what is' include Earth as well as Fire, whereas
'what is not' is matter—the matter of Earth and Fire alike? And
again, is the matter of each different? Or is it the same, since other-
319ᵇ wise they would not come-to-be reciprocally out of one another, i. e.
contraries out of contraries? For these things—Fire, Earth, Water,
Air—are characterized by 'the contraries.' [39]

Perhaps the solution is that their matter is in one sense the same,
but in another sense different. For that which underlies them, whatever its nature may be *qua* underlying them, is the same: but its
actual being is not the same.

4 So much, then, on these topics. Next we must state what the
5 difference is between coming-to-be and 'alteration'—for we maintain
that these changes are distinct from one another.

Since, then, we must distinguish (*a*) the *substratum*, and (*b*)
the property whose nature it is to be predicated of the *substratum*;
10 and since change of each of these occurs; there is 'alteration' when
the *substratum* is perceptible and persists, but changes in its own
properties, the properties in question being opposed to one another
either as contraries or as intermediates. The body, e. g., although persisting as the same body, is now healthy and now ill; and the bronze
is now spherical and at another time angular, and yet remains the same
15 bronze. But when nothing perceptible persists in its identity as a *substratum*, and the thing changes as a whole (when e. g. the seed as a
whole is converted into blood, or water into air, or air as a whole
into water), such an occurrence is no longer 'alteration'. It is a
coming-to-be of one substance and a passing-away of the other—
especially if the change proceeds from an imperceptible something
to something perceptible (either to touch or to all the senses), as when
20 water comes-to-be out of, or passes-away into, air: for air is pretty
well imperceptible. If, however, in such cases, any property (being
one of a pair of contraries) persists, in the thing that has come-to-be,
the same as it was in the thing which has passed-away—if, e. g.,
when water comes-to-be out of air, both are transparent or cold [40]—

---

[38] 'what is not' = what is imperceptible.   [39] Cf. below, II. 1–3.
[40] Aristotle is not saying that water and air are in fact 'cold', but is only quoting a common view in illustration.

the *second* thing, into which the *first* changes, must not be a property of this persistent identical something. Otherwise the change will be 'alteration'.

Suppose, e. g., that *the musical man* passed-away and *an unmusical* 25 *man* came-to-be, and that *the man* persists as something identical. Now, if 'musicalness and unmusicalness' had not been a property essentially inhering in man, these changes would have been a coming-to-be of unmusicalness and a passing-away of musicalness: but in fact 'musicalness and unmusicalness' are a property of the persistent identity, viz. man. (Hence, as regards *man*, these changes are 'modifications'; though, as regards *musical man* and *unmusical man*, they 30 are a passing-away and a coming-to-be.) Consequently such changes are 'alteration'.

When the change from contrary to contrary is *in quantity*, it is 'growth and diminution'; when it is *in place*, it is 'motion'; when it is in property, i. e. *in quality*, it is 'alteration': but when nothing per- 320ᵃ sists, of which the resultant is a property (or an 'accident' in any sense of the term), it is 'coming-to-be', and the converse change is 'passing-away'.

'Matter', in the most proper sense of the term, is to be identified with the *substratum* which is receptive of coming-to-be and passing-away: but the *substratum* of the remaining kinds of change is also, in a certain sense, 'matter', because all these *substrata* are receptive of 5 'contrarieties' of some kind. So much, then, as an answer to the questions (i) whether coming-to-be 'is' or 'is not'—i. e. what are the precise conditions of its occurrence—and (ii) what 'alteration' is: but we have still to treat of growth.⁴¹

5 We must explain (i) wherein growth differs from coming-to-be and from 'alteration', and (ii) what is the process of growing and the 10 process of diminishing in each and all of the things that grow and diminish.

Hence our first question is this: Do these changes differ from one another solely because of a difference in their respective 'spheres'? In other words, do they differ because, while a change from *this* to *that* (viz. from potential to actual *substance*) is coming-to-be, a change in the sphere of *magnitude* is growth and one in the sphere of *quality* is 'alteration'—both growth and 'alteration' being changes from 15 what is-potentially to what is-actually magnitude and quality respectively? Or is there also a difference in the manner of the change, since it is evident that, whereas neither what is 'altering' nor what is coming-

⁴¹ Cf. above, 315ᵃ 26–28.

to-be necessarily changes its place, what is growing or diminishing changes its spatial position of necessity, though in a different manner from that in which the moving thing does so? For that which is
20 being moved changes its place as a whole: but the growing thing changes its place like a metal that is being beaten, retaining its position as a whole while its parts change their places. They change their places, but not in the same way as the parts of a revolving globe. For the parts of the globe change their places while the whole continues to occupy an equal place: but the parts of the growing thing
25 expand over an ever-increasing place and the parts of the diminishing
. thing contract within an ever-diminishing area.

It is clear, then, that these changes—the changes of that which is coming-to-be, of that which is 'altering', and of that which is growing—differ *in manner* as well as *in sphere*. But how are we to conceive the 'sphere' of the change which is growth and diminution? The 'sphere' of growing and diminishing is believed to be magnitude. Are we to suppose that body and magnitude come-to-be out of something
30 which, though potentially magnitude and body, is actually incorporeal and devoid of magnitude? And since this description may be understood in two different ways, in which of these two ways are we to apply it to the process of growth? Is the matter,[42] out of which growth takes place, (i) 'separate' and existing alone by itself, or (ii) 'separate' but contained in another body? [43]

Perhaps it is impossible for growth to take place in either of these
320ᵇ ways. For since the matter [44] is 'separate', either (*a*) it will occupy no place (as if it were a point), or (*b*) it will be a 'void', i. e. a non-perceptible body. But the first of these alternatives is impossible. For since what comes-to-be out of this incorporeal and sizeless something will always be 'somewhere', it too must be 'somewhere'—either
5 intrinsically or indirectly.[45] And the second alternative necessarily implies that the matter is contained in some other body. But if it is to be 'in' another body and yet remains 'separate' in such a way that it is in no sense a part of that body (neither a part of its substantial being nor an 'accident' of it), many impossibilities will result. It is as if we were to suppose that when, e. g., air comes-to-be out of water
10 the process were due not to a change of the water, but to the matter of

[42] i. e. the supposed incorporeal and sizeless matter.
[43] It is clear from what follows that the incorporeal and sizeless matter is assumed to be 'separate'—to be real independently of body—under both alternatives.
[44] i. e. the supposed incorporeal and sizeless matter.
[45] i. e. either as itself occupying a place, or as contained within a body which itself occupies a place.

the air being 'contained in' the water as in a vessel. This is impossible. For (i) there is nothing to prevent an indeterminate number of matters being thus 'contained in' the water, so that they might come-to-be actually an indeterminate quantity of air; and (ii) we do not in fact see air coming-to-be out of water in this fashion, viz. withdrawing out of it and leaving it unchanged.

It is therefore better to suppose that in all instances of coming-to-be the matter is inseparable,[46] being numerically identical and one with the 'containing' body, though isolable from it by definition. But the same reasons also forbid us to regard the matter, out of which the body comes-to-be, as points or lines. The matter is that of which 15 points and lines are limits, and it is something that can never exist without quality and without form.

Now it is no doubt true, as we have also established elsewhere,[47] that one thing 'comes-to-be' (in the unqualified sense) out of another thing: and further it is true that the efficient cause of its coming-to-be is either (i) an actual thing (which is the same as the effect either *generically*—for the efficient cause of the coming-to-be of a hard thing is not a hard thing[48]—or *specifically*, as e. g. fire is the 20 efficient cause of the coming-to-be of fire or one man of the birth of another), or (ii) an actuality.[49] Nevertheless, since there is also a matter out of which corporeal substance itself comes-to-be (corporeal substance, however, already characterized as such-and-such a determinate body, for there is no such thing as body in general), this same matter is also the matter of magnitude and quality—being separable from these matters by definition, but not separable in place unless Qualities are, in their turn, separable.[50]   25

It is evident, from the preceding[51] development and discussion of difficulties, that growth is not a change out of something which, though potentially a magnitude, actually possesses no magnitude. For, if it were, 'the void' would exist in separation; but we have explained in a former work[52] that this is impossible. Moreover, a change of that kind is not peculiarly distinctive of growth, but characterizes coming-to-be as such or in general. For growth is an increase, and diminution 30 is a lessening, of the magnitude which is there already—that, indeed,

---

[46] 'inseparable' from the actual body in which it is contained.

[47] Cf. *Physics* i. 7; *Metaph.* 1032ᵃ 12 ff.

[48] The efficient cause of the coming-to-be of a hard thing (e. g. of ice or terra-cotta) is something cold or hot (a freezing wind or a baking fire). Such efficient causes are only generically, not specifically, identical with their effects.

[49] An 'actuality' or 'form': Cf. *Metaph.* 1032ᵃ 25 ff.

[50] i. e. unless Qualities or Adjectivals are separable from Substances.

[51] Cf. above, 320ᵃ 27–ᵇ 12.   [52] Cf. *Physics* iv. 6–9.

is why the growing thing must possess some magnitude. Hence growth must not be regarded as a process from a matter without magnitude to an actuality of magnitude: for this would be a body's coming-to-be rather than its growth.

321ᵃ We must therefore come to closer quarters with the subject of our inquiry. We must 'grapple' with it (as it were) from its beginning, and determine the precise character of the growing and diminishing whose causes we are investigating.

It is evident (i) that any and every part of the growing thing has increased, and that similarly in diminution every part has become smaller: also (ii) that a thing grows by the accession, and diminishes
5 by the departure, of something. Hence it must grow by the accession either (a) of something incorporeal or (b) of a body. Now, if (a) it grows by the accession of something incorporeal, there will exist *separate* a void: but (as we have stated before) [53] it is impossible for *a matter of magnitude* to exist 'separate'. If, on the other hand, (b) it grows by the accession of a body, there will be two bodies—that which grows and that which increases it—in the same place: and this too is impossible.

10 But neither is it open to us to say that growth or diminution occurs in the way in which e. g. air is generated from water. For, although the volume has then become greater, the change will not be growth, but a coming-to-be of the one—viz. of that into which the change is taking place—and a passing-away of the contrasted body. It is not a *growth* of either. Nothing grows in the process; unless indeed there be something common to both things (to that which
15 is coming-to-be and to that which passed-away), e. g. 'body', and this grows. The water has not grown, nor has the air: but the former has passed-away and the latter has come-to-be, and—if anything has grown—there has been a growth of 'body'. Yet this too is impossible. For our account of growth must preserve the characteristics of that which is growing and diminishing. And these characteristics are three:
20 (i) any and every part of the growing magnitude is made bigger (e. g. if flesh grows, every particle of the flesh gets bigger), (ii) by the accession of something, and (iii) in such a way that the growing thing is preserved and persists. For whereas a thing does not persist in the processes of unqualified coming-to-be or passing-away, that which grows or 'alters' persists in its identity through the 'altering' and
25 through the growing or diminishing, though the quality (in 'alteration') and the size (in growth) do not remain the same. Now if the generation of air from water is to be regarded as growth, a thing

[53] Cf. above, 320ᵃ 27–ᵇ 25.

might grow without the accession (and without the persistence) of anything, and diminish without the departure of anything—and that which grows need not persist. But this characteristic [54] must be preserved: for the growth we are discussing has been assumed to be thus characterized.

One might raise a further difficulty. What is 'that which grows'? 30 Is it that to which something is added? If, e. g., a man grows in his shin, is it the shin which is greater [55]—but not that 'whereby' he grows, viz. not the food? Then why have not both 'grown'? For when A is added to B, both A and B are greater, as when you mix wine with water; for each ingredient is alike increased in volume. Perhaps the explanation is that the substance of the one [56] remains unchanged, but the substance of the other (viz. of the food) does not. For in- 35 deed, even in the mixture of wine and water, it is the prevailing in- 321ᵇ gredient which is said to have increased in volume. We say, e. g., that the wine has increased, because the whole mixture acts as wine but not as water. A similar principle applies also to 'alteration'. Flesh is said to have been 'altered' if, while its character and substance remain, some one of its essential properties, which was not there before, now qualifies it: on the other hand, that 'whereby' it has been 'altered' 5 may have undergone no change, though sometimes it too has been affected. The altering agent, however, and the originative source of the process are in the growing thing and in that which is being 'altered': for the efficient cause is in these.[57] No doubt the food, which has come in, may sometimes expand as well as the body that has consumed it (that is so, e. g., if, after having come in, a food is converted into wind), but when it has undergone this change it has passed-away: 10 and the efficient cause is not in the food.

We have now developed the difficulties sufficiently and must therefore try to find a solution of the problem. Our solution must preserve intact the three characteristics of growth—that the growing thing persists, that it grows by the accession (and diminishes by the departure) of something, and further that every perceptible particle of it has become either larger or smaller. We must recognize also (a) that the 15 growing body is not 'void' and that yet there are not two magnitudes in the same place, and (b) that it does not grow by the accession of something incorporeal.

Two preliminary distinctions will prepare us to grasp the cause

[54] viz. the third characteristic—that the growing thing 'persists'.
[55] i. e. has 'grown'.
[56] i. e. the substance of the shin.
[57] And therefore it is these which are said to grow or to be 'altered'.

of growth. We must note (i) that the organic parts grow by the growth
of the tissues (for every organ is composed of these as its constitu-
20 ents); and (ii) that flesh, bone, and every such part—like every other
thing which has its form immersed in matter—has a twofold nature:
for the form as well as the matter is called 'flesh' or 'bone'.

Now, that any and every part of the tissue *qua* form should grow
—and grow by the accession of something—is possible, but not that
any and every part of the tissue *qua* matter should do so. For we
25 must think of the tissue after the image of flowing water that is
measured by one and the same measure; particle after particle comes-
to-be, and each successive particle is different. And it is in this
sense that the matter of the flesh grows, some flowing out and some
flowing in fresh; not in the sense that fresh matter accedes to every
particle of it. There is, however, an accession to every part of its
figure or 'form'.

That growth has taken place proportionally,[58] is more manifest
in the organic parts—e. g. in the hand. For *there* the fact that the
30 matter is distinct from the form is more manifest than in flesh, i. e.
than in the tissues. That is why there is a greater tendency to suppose
that a corpse still possesses flesh and bone than that it still has a
hand or an arm.

Hence in one sense it is true that any and every part of the flesh
has grown; but in another sense it is false. For there has been an
accession to every part of the flesh in respect to its form, but not in
35 respect to its matter. The whole, however, has become larger. And this
increase is due (*a*) on the one hand to the accession of something,
322ᵃ which is called 'food' and is said to be 'contrary' to flesh, but (*b*) on
the other hand to the transformation of this food into the same form
as that of flesh—as if, e. g., 'moist' were to accede to 'dry' and, having
acceded, were to be transformed and to become 'dry'. For in one sense
'Like grows by Like', but in another sense 'Unlike grows by Unlike'.

One might discuss what must be the character of that 'whereby'
5 a thing grows. Clearly it must be potentially that which is growing
—potentially flesh, e. g., if it is flesh that is growing. Actually, therefore, it must be 'other' than the growing thing. This 'actual other',
then, has passed-away and come-to-be flesh. But it has not been transformed into flesh alone by itself (for that would have been a coming-
to-be, not a growth): on the contrary, it is the growing thing which
has come-to-be flesh <and grown> *by* the food. In what way, then,
has the food been modified by the growing thing?[59] Perhaps we should

---

[58] i. e. by an expansion of all parts of the 'form'.
[59] i. e. 'been modified' so as to be transformed into flesh.

say that it has been 'mixed' with it, as if one were to pour water
into wine and the wine were able to convert the new ingredient into 10
wine. And as fire lays hold of the inflammable,[60] so the active principle of growth, dwelling in the growing thing (i. e. in that which is
actually flesh), lays hold of an acceding food which is potentially flesh
and converts it into actual flesh. The acceding food, therefore, must
be *together with* the growing thing: [61] for if it were apart from it,
the change would be a coming-to-be.[62] For it is possible to produce
fire by piling logs on to the already burning fire. That is 'growth'. But 15
when the logs themselves are set on fire, that is 'coming-to-be'.

'Quantum-in-general' does not come-to-be any more than 'animal'
which is neither man nor any other of the specific forms of animal:
what 'animal-in-general' is in coming-to-be, that 'quantum-in-general'
is in growth. But what does come-to-be in growth is flesh or bone—
or a hand or arm (i. e. the tissues of these organic parts).[63] Such
things come-to-be, then, by the accession not of quantified-flesh but 20
of a quantified-something. In so far as this acceding food is potentially
the double result—e. g. is potentially so-much-flesh—it produces
growth: for it is bound to become actually both *so-much* and *flesh*.
But in so far as it is potentially flesh only, it nourishes: for it is thus
that 'nutrition' and 'growth' differ by their definition. That is why a
body's 'nutrition' continues so long as it is kept alive (even when it
is diminishing), though not its 'growth'; and why nutrition, though
'the same' as growth, is yet different from it in its actual being. For in 25
so far as that which accedes is potentially 'so-much-flesh' it tends to
increase flesh: whereas, in so far as it is potentially 'flesh' only, it is
nourishment.

The form of which we have spoken [64] is a kind of power immersed
in matter—a duct, as it were. If, then, a matter accedes—a matter, which is potentially a duct and also potentially possesses deter- 30
minate quantity—the ducts to which it accedes will become bigger.
But if it [65] is no longer able to act—if it has been weakened by the
continued influx of matter, just as water, continually mixed in greater
and greater quantity with wine, in the end makes the wine watery and

[60] i. e. 'lays hold' of it and converts it into fire.

[61] i. e. 'must be together with' it when this conversion takes place.

[62] i. e. an independent coming-to-be of flesh, not a growth of the already existing tissue.

[63] i. e. what comes-to-be in growth is so-much flesh or bone, or a hand or arm
of such and such a size: not 'quantum-in-general', but a 'quantified-something'.

[64] i. e. the form which grows in every part of itself: Cf. above, 321^b 22–34.

[65] i. e. this form or power immersed in matter.

converts it into water—then it will cause a diminution of the *quantum*; [66] though still the form persists.

322ᵇ 6   <In discussing the causes of coming-to-be> we must first investigate the *matter*, i. e. the so-called 'elements'. We must ask whether they really are elements or not, i. e. whether each of them is eternal or whether there is a sense in which they come-to-be: and, if they do come-to-be, whether all of them come-to-be in the same manner, reciprocally out of one another, or whether one amongst them is some-
5 thing primary. Hence we must begin by explaining certain preliminary matters, about which the statements now current are vague.

For all <the pluralist philosophers>—those who generate the 'elements' as well as those who generate the bodies that are compounded of the elements—make use of 'dissociation' and 'association', and of 'action' and 'passion'. Now 'association' is 'combination'; but the precise meaning of the process we call 'combining' has not been explained. Again, <all the monists make use of 'alteration'; but> with-
10 out an agent and a patient there cannot be 'altering' any more than there can be 'dissociating' and 'associating'. For not only those who postulate a plurality of elements employ their reciprocal action and passion to generate the compounds: those who derive things from a single element are equally compelled to introduce 'acting'. And in this respect Diogenes is right when he argues that 'unless all things were
15 derived from one, reciprocal action and passion could not have occurred'. The hot thing, e. g., would not be cooled and the cold thing in turn be warmed: for heat and cold do not change reciprocally into one another, but what changes (it is clear) is the *substratum*. Hence, whenever there is action and passion between two things, that which underlies them must be a single something. No doubt, it is not true
20 to say that *all* things are of this character: [67] but it is true of all things between which there is reciprocal action and passion.

But if we must investigate 'action-passion' and 'combination', we must also investigate 'contact'. For action and passion (in the proper sense of the terms) can only occur between things which are such as
25 to touch one another; nor can things enter into combination at all unless they have come into a certain kind of contact. Hence we must give a definite account of these three things—of 'contact', 'combination', and 'acting'.

Let us start as follows. All things which admit of 'combination'

[66] i. e. a diminution of the size of the tissue whose form it is.
[67] i. e. are transformations of a single *substratum,* or 'derived from one thing' as Diogenes maintained.

must be capable of reciprocal contact: and the same is true of any two things, of which one 'acts' and the other 'suffers action' in the proper sense of the terms. For this reason we must treat of 'contact' first.

Now every term which possesses a variety of meanings includes 30 those various meanings *either* owing to a mere coincidence of language, *or* owing to a real order of derivation in the different things to which it is applied: but, though this may be taken to hold of 'contact' as of all such terms, it is nevertheless true that 'contact' *in the proper sense* applies only to things which have 'position'. And 'position' belongs only to those things which also have a 'place': for in so far as we attribute 'contact' to the mathematical things, we must also at- 323ᵃ tribute 'place' to them, whether they exist in separation or in some other fashion. Assuming, therefore, that 'to touch' is—as we have defined it in a previous work [68]—'to have the extremes together', only those things will touch one another which, being separate magnitudes 5 and possessing position, have their extremes 'together'. And since position belongs only to those things which also have a 'place', while the primary differentiation of 'place' is 'the above' and 'the below' (and the similar pairs of opposites), all things which touch one another will have 'weight' or 'lightness'—*either* both these qualities *or* one or the other of them.[69] But bodies which are heavy or light are such as to 'act' and 'suffer action'. Hence it is clear that those things are 10 by nature such as to touch one another, which (being separate magnitudes) have their extremes 'together' and are able to move, and be moved by, one another.

The manner in which the 'mover' moves the 'moved' is not always the same: on the contrary, whereas one kind of 'mover' can only impart motion by being itself moved, another kind can do so though remaining itself unmoved. Clearly therefore we must recognize a 15 corresponding variety in speaking of the 'acting' thing too: for the 'mover' is said to 'act' (in a sense) and the 'acting' thing to 'impart motion'. Nevertheless there is a difference and we must draw a distinction. For not every 'mover' can 'act', if (*a*) the term 'agent' is to be used in contrast to 'patient' and (*b*) 'patient' is to be applied only to those things whose motion is a 'qualitative affection'—i. e. a quality, like 'white' or 'hot', in respect to which they are 'moved' 20 only in the sense that they are 'altered': on the contrary, to 'impart motion' is a wider term than to 'act'. Still, so much, at any rate,

[68] Cf. *Physics* 226ᵇ 21–23.
[69] i. e. if A and B are in reciprocal contact, *either* A must be heavy and B light, or A light and B heavy: *or* A and B must both be heavy, or both be light.

is clear: the things which are 'such as to impart motion', if that description be interpreted in one sense, will touch the things which are 'such as to be moved by them'—while they will not touch them, if the description be interpreted in a different sense. But the disjunctive definition of 'touching' must include and distinguish (*a*) 'contact in general' as the relation between two things which, having position, are such that one is able to impart motion and the other to be moved, and (*b*) 'reciprocal contact' as the relation between two things, one able to impart motion and the other able
25 to be moved in such a way that 'action and passion' are predictable of them.

As a rule, no doubt, if A touches B, B touches A. For indeed practically all the 'movers' within our ordinary experience impart motion by being moved: in their case, what touches inevitably must, and also evidently does, touch something which reciprocally touches it. Yet, if A moves B, it is possible—as we sometimes express it—for A 'merely to touch' B, and that which touches need
30 not touch a something which touches it. Nevertheless it is commonly supposed that 'touching' must be reciprocal. The reason of this belief is that 'movers' which belong to the same kind as the 'moved' impart motion by being moved. Hence if anything imparts motion without itself being moved, it may touch the 'moved' and yet itself be touched by nothing—for we say sometimes that the man who grieves us 'touches' us, but not that we 'touch' him.

The account just given may serve to distinguish and define the
323ᵇ 'contact' which occurs in the things of Nature. Next in order we must discuss 'action' and 'passion'.

7   The traditional theories on the subject are conflicting. For (i) most thinkers are unanimous in maintaining (*a*) that 'like' is always
5 unaffected by 'like', because (as they argue) neither of two 'likes' is more apt than the other either to act or to suffer action, since all the properties which belong to the one belong identically and in the same degree to the other; and (*b*) that 'unlikes', i. e. 'differents', are by nature such as to act and suffer action reciprocally. For even when the smaller fire is destroyed by the greater, it suffers this effect (they
10 say) owing to its 'contrariety'—since the great is contrary to the small. But (ii) Democritus dissented from all the other thinkers and maintained a theory peculiar to himself. He asserts that agent and patient are identical, i. e. 'like'. It is not possible (he says) that 'others', i. e. 'differents', should suffer action from one another: on the contrary,
15 even if two things, being 'others', do act in some way on one another,

this happens to them not *qua* 'others' but *qua* possessing an identical property.

Such, then, are the traditional theories, and it looks as if the statements of their advocates were in manifest conflict. But the reason of this conflict is that each group is in fact stating *a part*, whereas they ought to have taken a comprehensive view of the subject *as a whole*. For (i) if A and B are 'like'—absolutely and in all respects without difference from one another—it is reasonable to infer that 20 neither is in any way affected by the other. Why, indeed, should either of them tend to act any more than the other? Moreover, if 'like' can be affected by 'like', a thing can also be affected by itself: and yet if that were so—if 'like' tended in fact to act *qua* 'like'— there would be nothing indestructible or immovable, for everything would move itself. And (ii) the same consequence follows if A and B are absolutely 'other', i. e. in no respect identical. *Whiteness* could 25 not be affected in any way by *line* nor *line* by *whiteness*—except perhaps 'coincidentally', viz. if the line happened to be white or black: for unless two things either are, or are composed of, 'contraries', neither drives the other out of its natural condition. But (iii) since 30 only those things which either involve a 'contrariety' or are 'contraries'—and not any things selected at random—are such as to suffer action and to act, agent and patient must be 'like' (i. e. identical) in kind and yet 'unlike' (i. e. contrary) in species. (For it is a law of nature that body is affected by body, flavour by flavour, colour by colour, and so in general what belongs to any kind by a mem- 324ᵃ ber of the same kind—the reason being that 'contraries' are in every case within a single identical kind, and it is 'contraries' which reciprocally act and suffer action.) Hence agent and patient must be in one sense identical, but in another sense other than (i. e. 5 'unlike') one another. And since (*a*) patient and agent are generically identical (i. e. 'like') but specifically 'unlike', while (*b*) it is 'contraries' that exhibit this character: it is clear that 'contraries' and their 'intermediates' are such as to suffer action and to act reciprocally —for indeed it is these that constitute the entire sphere of passing-away and coming-to-be.

We can now understand why fire heats and the cold thing cools, 10 and in general why the active thing assimilates to itself the patient. For agent and patient are contrary to one another, and coming-to-be is a process into the contrary: hence the patient *must* change into the agent, since it is only thus that coming-to-be will be a process into the contrary. And, again, it is intelligible that the advocates of both views, although their theories are not the same, are yet in con-

15 tact with the nature of the facts. For sometimes we speak of the *substratum* as suffering action (e. g. of 'the man' as being healed, being warmed and chilled, and similarly in all the other cases), but at other times we say 'what is cold is being warmed', 'what is sick is being healed': and in both these ways of speaking we express the truth, since in one sense it is the 'matter', while in another sense it is the 'contrary', which suffers action. (We make the same distinction in
20 speaking of the agent: for sometimes we say that 'the man', but at other times that 'what is hot', produces heat.) Now the one group of thinkers supposed that agent and patient must possess something identical, because they fastened their attention on the *substratum*: while the other group maintained the opposite because their attention was concentrated on the 'contraries.'

25   We must conceive the same account to hold of action and passion as that which is true of 'being moved' and 'imparting motion'. For the 'mover', like the 'agent', has two meanings. Both (*a*) that which contains the originative source of the motion is thought to 'impart motion' (for the originative source is first amongst the causes), and also (*b*) that which is last, i. e. immediately next to the moved thing and to the coming-to-be. A similar distinction holds also of the
30 agent: for we speak not only (*a*) of the doctor, but also (*b*) of the wine, as healing. Now, in motion, there is nothing to prevent *the first mover* being unmoved (indeed, as regards some 'first movers' this is actually necessary) although *the last mover* always imparts motion by being itself moved: and, in action, there is nothing to prevent *the first agent* being unaffected, while *the last agent* only acts by suffering action itself. For (*a*) if agent and patient have not the same matter,
35 agent acts without being affected: thus the art of healing produces
324ᵇ health without itself being acted upon in any way by that which is being healed. But (*b*) the food, in acting, is itself in some way acted upon: for, in acting, it is simultaneously heated or cooled or otherwise affected. Now the art of healing corresponds to an 'originative source', while the food corresponds to 'the last' (i. e. 'contiguous') mover.

5   Those active powers, then, whose forms are not embodied in matter, are unaffected: but those whose forms are in matter are such as to be affected in acting. For we maintain that one and the same 'matter' is *equally*, so to say, the basis of either of the two opposed things—being as it were a 'kind';⁷⁰ and that *that which can be hot* must be made hot, provided the heating agent is there, i. e. comes
10 near. Hence (as we have said) some of the active powers are unaffected while others are such as to be affected; and what holds of

⁷⁰ i. e. a kind, of which the two opposed things are contrasted species.

motion is true also of the active powers. For as in motion 'the first mover' is moved, so among the active powers 'the first agent' is unaffected.

The active power is a 'cause' in the sense of that from which the process originates: but the end, for the sake of which it takes place, is not 'active'. (That is why *health* is not 'active', except metaphorically.) For when the agent is there, the patient *becomes* something: but when 'states' [71] are there, the patient no longer *becomes* but already *is*—and 'forms' (i. e. 'ends') are a kind of 'state'. As to the matter', it (*qua* matter) is passive. Now fire contains 'the hot' embodied in matter: but a 'hot' separate from matter (if such a thing existed) could not suffer any action. Perhaps, indeed, it is impossible that 'the hot' should exist in separation from matter: but if there are any entities thus separable, what we are saying would be true of them.

We have thus explained what action and passion are, what things exhibit them, why they do so, and in what manner.

8   We must go on to discuss how it is possible for action and passion to take place.

Some philosophers think that the 'last' agent—the 'agent' in the strictest sense—enters in through certain pores, and so the patient suffers action. It is in this way, they assert, that we see and hear and exercise all our other senses. Moreover, according to them, things are seen through air and water and other transparent bodies, because such bodies possess pores, invisible indeed owing to their minuteness, but close-set and arranged in rows: and the more transparent the body, the more frequent and serial they suppose its pores to be.

Such was the theory which some philosophers (including Empedocles) advanced in regard to the structure of certain bodies. They do not restrict it to the bodies which act and suffer action: but 'combination' too, they say, takes place 'only between bodies whose pores are in reciprocal symmetry'. The most systematic and consistent theory, however, and one that applied to all bodies, was advanced by Leucippus and Democritus: and, in maintaining it, they took as their starting-point what naturally comes first.

For some of the older philosophers [72] thought that 'what is' must of necessity be 'one' and immovable. The void, they argue, 'is not': but unless there is a void with a separate being of its own, 'what is' cannot be moved—nor again can it be 'many', since there is nothing to keep things apart. And in *this* respect,[73] they insist, the view

---

[71] i. e. like 'health'.

[72] The reference is to Parmenides, Melissus, and (probably) Zeno.

[73] i. e. for rendering intelligible the being of a 'many'.

that the universe is not 'continuous' but 'discretes-in-contact'[74] is
no better than the view that there are 'many' (and not 'one') and a
void.[75] For <suppose that the universe is discretes-in-contact. Then>,
if it is divisible through and through, there is no 'one', and therefore no
'many' either, but the Whole is void; while to maintain that it is
10 divisible at some points, but not at others, looks like an arbitrary
fiction. For up to what limit is it divisible? And for what reason is
part of the Whole indivisible, i. e. a *plenum,* and part divided?
Further, they maintain, it is equally [76] necessary to deny the existence
of motion.

Reasoning in this way, therefore, they were led to transcend
sense-perception, and to disregard it on the ground that 'one ought
to follow the argument': and so they assert that the universe is
15 'one' and immovable. Some of them add that it is 'infinite', since
the limit (if it had one) would be a limit against the void.

There were, then, certain thinkers who, for the reasons we have
stated, enunciated views of this kind as their theory of 'The Truth'.[77]
. . . Moreover, although these opinions appear to follow logically in
a dialectical discussion, yet to believe them seems next door to mad-
20 ness when one considers the facts. For indeed no lunatic seems to be
so far out of his senses as to suppose that fire and ice are 'one': it is
only between what *is* right, and what *seems* right from habit, that
some people are mad enough to see no difference.

Leucippus, however, thought he had a theory which harmonized
25 with sense-perception and would not abolish either coming-to-be and
passing-away or motion and the multiplicity of things. He made
these concessions to the facts of perception: on the other hand, he
conceded to the Monists that there could be no motion without a void.
The result is a theory which he states as follows: 'The void is a "not-
being", and no part of "what is" is a "not-being"; for what "is" in
the strict sense of the term is an absolute *plenum.* This *plenum,*
30 however, is not "one": on the contrary, it is a "many" infinite in
number and invisible owing to the minuteness of their bulk. The
"many" move in the void (for there is a void): and by coming
together they produce "coming-to-be", while by separating they
produce "passing-away". Moreover, they act and suffer action where-

[74] This appears to be the view of Empedocles, as Aristotle here expresses it:
Cf. below, 325^b 5–10.

[75] This appears to be the view of the Pythagoreans: Cf. *Physics* 213^b 22–7.

[76] i. e. the existence of motion is just as impossible on the hypothesis of
Empedocles as on that of the Pythagoreans.

[77] These words seem to be intended to suggest 'The Way of Truth' in the poem
of Parmenides.

ever they chance to be in contact (for *there* they are not "one"),
and they generate by being put together and becoming intertwined.
From the genuinely-one, on the other hand, there never could have 35
come-to-be a multiplicity, nor from the genuinely-many a "one":
that is impossible. But (just as Empedocles and some of the other 325ᵇ
philosophers say that things suffer action through their pores, so)
all "alteration" and all "passion" take place in the way that has
been explained: breaking-up (i. e. passing-away) is effected by means
of the void, and so too is growth—solids creeping in to fill the void 5
places.'

Empedocles too is practically bound to adopt the same theory as
Leucippus. For he must say that there are certain solids which,
however, are indivisible—unless there are continuous pores all through
the body. But this last alternative is impossible: for *then* there will
be nothing solid in the body (nothing beside the pores) but all of it
will be void. It is necessary, therefore, for his 'contiguous discretes'
to be indivisible, while the intervals between them—which he calls 10
'pores'—must be void. But this is precisely Leucippus's theory of
action and passion.

Such, approximately, are the current explanations of the manner in
which some things 'act' while others 'suffer action'. And as regards the
Atomists, it is not only clear what their explanation is: it is also
obvious that it follows with tolerable consistency from the assump- 15
tions they employ. But there is less obvious consistency in the explanation offered by the other thinkers. It is not clear, for instance,
how, on the theory of Empedocles, there is to be 'passing-away' as
well as 'alteration'. For the primary bodies of the Atomists—the
primary constituents of which bodies are composed, and the ultimate
elements into which they are dissolved—are indivisible, differing from
one another only in figure. In the philosophy of Empedocles, on the
other hand, it is evident that all the other bodies down to the 'ele- 20
ments' have their coming-to-be and their passing-away: but it is not
clear how the 'elements' themselves, severally in their aggregated
masses, come-to-be and pass-away. Nor is it possible for Empedocles
to explain how they do so, since he does not assert that Fire too [78]
(and similarly every one of his other 'elements') possesses 'elementary
constituents' of itself.

Such an assertion would commit him to doctrines like those which
Plato has set forth in the *Timaeus*.[79] For although both Plato and 25
Leucippus postulate elementary constituents that are indivisible and
distinctively characterized by figures, there is this great difference be-

[78] i. e. as well as the composite bodies.   [79] Cf. *Timaeus* 53 c ff.

tween the two theories: the 'indivisibles' of Leucippus (i) are solids,
while those of Plato are planes, and (ii) are characterized by an infinite
variety of figures, while the characterizing figures employed by Plato
30 are limited in number. Thus the 'comings-to-be' and the 'dissociations'
result from the 'indivisibles' (a) *according to Leucippus* through the
void and through contact (for it is at the point of contact that each of
the composite bodies is divisible), but (b) *according to Plato* in virtue
of contact alone, since he denies there is a void.

Now we have discussed 'indivisible planes' in the preceding
35 treatise.[80] But with regard to the assumption of 'indivisible solids',
although we must not now enter upon a detailed study of its consequences, the following criticisms fall within the compass of a short
digression:—

326ᵃ   (I) The Atomists are committed to the view that every 'indivisible'
is incapable alike of receiving a sensible property (for nothing can
'suffer action' except through the void) and of producing one—no
'indivisible' can be, e. g., either hard or cold. Yet it is surely a
5 paradox that an exception is made of 'the hot'—'the hot' being assigned
as peculiar to the spherical figure: for, that being so, its 'contrary' also ('the cold') is bound to belong to another of the figures.
If, however, these properties (heat and cold) do belong to the 'indivisibles', it is a further paradox that they should not possess heavi-
10 ness and lightness, and hardness and softness. And yet Democritus says
'the more any indivisible exceeds, the heavier it is'—to which we must
clearly add 'and the hotter it is'. But if *that* is their character, it is
impossible they should not be affected by one another: the 'slightly-
hot indivisible', e. g., will inevitably suffer action from one which far
exceeds it in heat. Again, if any 'indivisible' is 'hard', there must also
be one which is 'soft': but 'the soft' derives its very name from the fact
that it suffers a certain action—for 'soft' is that which yields to pressure. (II) But further, not only is it paradoxical (i) that no property
15 except figure should belong to the 'indivisibles': it is also paradoxical
(ii) that, if other properties do belong to them, one only of these additional properties should attach to each—e. g. that *this* 'indivisible'
should be cold and *that* 'indivisible' hot. For, on that supposition,
their substance would not even be uniform.[81] And it is equally impossible (iii) that more than one of these additional properties should
belong to the single 'indivisible'. For, being *indivisible*, it will possess

80 Cf. *de Caelo* iii. 1, especially 298ᵇ 33 ff., iii. 7 and iv. 2.
81 The uniformity of the substance or 'stuff' of the atoms was a fundamental
doctrine in the theory.

these properties in the same point [82]—so that, if it 'suffers action' by being chilled, it will also, *qua* chilled, 'act' or 'suffer action' in some 20 other way. And the same line of argument applies to all the other properties too: for the difficulty we have just raised confronts, as a necessary consequence, all who advocate 'indivisibles' (whether solids or planes), since their 'indivisibles' cannot become either 'rarer' or 'denser' inasmuch as there is no void in them. (III) It is a further paradox that there should be small 'indivisibles', but not large ones. 25 For it is natural enough, from the ordinary point of view, that the larger bodies should be more liable to fracture than the small ones, since they (viz. the large bodies) are easily broken up because they collide with many other bodies. But why should indivisibility *as such* be the property of small, rather than of large, bodies? (IV) Again, is the substance of all those solids uniform, or do they fall into sets 30 which differ from one another—as if, e. g., some of them, in their aggregated bulk, were 'fiery', others 'earthy'? For (i) if all of them are uniform in substance, what is it that separated one from another? Or why, when they come into contact, do they not coalesce into one, as drops of water run together when drop touches drop (for the two cases are precisely parallel)? On the other hand (ii) if they fall into differing sets, how are these characterized? It is clear, too, that 35 *these*,[83] rather than the 'figures', ought to be postulated as 'original 326^b reals', i. e causes from which the phenomena result. Moreover, if they differed in substance, they would both act and suffer action on coming into reciprocal contact. (V) Again, what is it which sets them moving? For if their 'mover' is other than themselves, they are such as to 'suffer action'. If, on the other hand, each of them sets itself in motion, either (*a*) it will be divisible ('imparting motion' *qua this,* 'being moved' *qua that*), or (*b*) contrary properties will attach to it 5 in the same respect—i. e. 'matter' will be identical-in-potentiality as well as numerically-identical.[84]

As to the thinkers who explain modification of property through the movement facilitated by the pores, if this is supposed to occur notwithstanding the fact that the pores are filled, their postulate of pores is superfluous. For if the whole body suffers action under these conditions, it would suffer action in the same way even if it 10 had no pores but were just its own continuous self. Moreover, how can their account of 'vision through a *medium*' be correct? It is impossible

---

[82] i. e. in its single, indivisible, undifferentiated identity.

[83] i. e. these qualitatively-distinct sets of atoms.

[84] For the doctrine implied in this argument, Cf. *Physics* 190^b 24, 192^a 1 ff.

for <the visual ray> to penetrate the transparent bodies at their 'contacts'; and impossible for it to pass through their pores if every pore
be full. For how will that [85] differ from having no pores at all? The
15 body will be uniformly 'full' throughout. But, further, even if these
passages, though they must *contain* bodies, are 'void', the same consequence will follow once more.[86] And if they are 'too minute to
admit any body', it is absurd to suppose there is a 'minute' void and
yet to deny the existence of a 'big' one (no matter how small the
'big' may be [87]), or to imagine 'the void' means anything else than
20 a body's place—whence it clearly follows that to every body there
will correspond a void of equal cubic capacity.

As a general criticism we must urge that to postulate pores is
superfluous. For if the agent produces no effect by touching the
patient, neither will it produce any by passing through its pores.
On the other hand, if it acts by contact, then—even without pores
—some things will 'suffer action' and others will 'act', provided they
are by nature adapted for reciprocal action and passion. Our argu-
25 ments have shown that it is either false or futile to advocate pores
in the sense in which some thinkers conceive them. But since
bodies are divisible through and through, the postulate of pores is
ridiculous: for, *qua* divisible, a body can fall into separate parts.

9 Let us explain the way in which things in fact possess the power
30 of generating, and of acting and suffering action: and let us start from
the principle we have often enunciated. For, assuming the distinction
between (*a*) that which is *potentially* and (*b*) that which is *actually*
such-and-such, it is the nature of the first, precisely in so far as it is
what it is, to suffer action *through and through,* not merely to be
susceptible in some parts while insusceptible in others. But its susceptibility varies in degree, according as it is more or less such-and-
such, and one would be more justified in speaking of 'pores' in this
35 connexion [88]: for instance, in the metals there are veins of 'the sus-
327ª ceptible' stretching continuously through the substance.

So long, indeed, as any body is naturally coherent and one, it is

[85] *sc.* having pores, all of which are 'full'.

[86] i. e. the body will still be impenetrable, even if the pores as such (as
channels) are distinguished in thought from what fills them. For *in fact* the pores
are always 'full' and the body is a *plenum* throughout—though perhaps not a
'uniform' *plenum*.

[87] 'Big' is a relative term and may include a void in any degree bigger than the
infinitesimal.

[88] viz. to express such lines of greater susceptibility.

insusceptible. So, too, bodies are insusceptible so long as they are not in contact either with one another or with other bodies which are by nature such as to act and suffer action. (To illustrate my meaning: Fire heats not only when in contact, but also from a distance. For the fire heats the air, and the air—being by nature such as both 5 to act and suffer action—heats the body.) But the supposition that a body is 'susceptible in some parts, but insusceptible in others' <is only possible for those who hold an erroneous view concerning the divisibility of magnitudes. For us> the following account results from the distinctions we established at the beginning.[89] For (i) if magnitudes are not divisible through and through—if, on the contrary, there are indivisible solids or planes—then indeed no body would be susceptible through and through: but neither would any be continuous. Since, however, (ii) this is false, i. e. since every 10 body is divisible, there is no difference between 'having been divided into parts which remain in contact' and 'being divisible'. For if a body *'can* be separated at the contacts' (as some thinkers express it), then, even though it has not yet been divided, it will be in a state of dividedness—since, as it *can* be divided, nothing inconceivable results.[90] And (iii) the supposition is open to this general objection—it is a paradox that 'passion' should occur in this manner 15 *only,* viz. by the bodies being split. For this theory abolishes 'alteration': but we see the same body *liquid* at one time and *solid* at another, without losing its continuity. It has suffered this change not by 'division' and 'composition', nor yet by 'turning' and 'intercontact' as Democritus asserts; for it has passed from the liquid to 20 the solid state without any change of 'grouping' or 'position' in the constituents of its substance. Nor are there contained within it those 'hard' (i. e. congealed) particles 'indivisible in their bulk': on the contrary, it is liquid—and again, solid and congealed— uniformly all through. This theory, it must be added, makes growth and diminution impossible also. For if there is to be *apposition* (instead of the growing thing having changed as a whole, either by the admixture of something or by its own transformation), increase 25 of size will not have resulted in any and every part.

So much, then, to establish that things generate and are generated, act and suffer action, reciprocally; and to distinguish the way in which these processes *can* occur from the (impossible) way in which some thinkers say they occur.

[89] Cf. above, 316ᵃ 14—317ᵃ 17.
[90] i. e. if this potentiality be realized: Cf. 316ᵃ 19.

10 But we have still to explain 'combination', for that was the third
30 of the subjects we originally [91] proposed to discuss. Our explanation
will proceed on the same method as before. We must inquire: What
is 'combination', and what is that which can 'combine'? Of what things,
and under what conditions, is 'combination' a property? And, further,
does 'combination' exist in fact, or is it false to assert its existence?
35 For, according to some thinkers, it is impossible for one thing
to be combined with another. They argue that (i) if *both* the 'com-
327ᵇ bined' constituents persist unaltered, they are no more 'combined'
now than they were before, but are in the same condition: while
(ii) if *one* has been destroyed, the constituents have not been 'combined'—on the contrary, one constituent *is* and the other *is not*,
whereas 'combination' demands uniformity of condition in them
5 both: and on the same principle (iii) even if *both* the combining
constituents have been destroyed as the result of their coalescence,
they cannot 'have been combined' since *they* have no being at all.

What we have in this argument is, it would seem, a demand for
the precise distinction of 'combination' from coming-to-be and passing-away (for it is obvious that 'combination', if it exists, must
differ from these processes) and for the precise distinction of the
'combinable' from that which is such as to come-to-be and pass-away.
10 As soon, therefore, as these distinctions are clear, the difficulties raised
by the argument would be solved.

Now (i) we do not speak of the wood as 'combined' with the
fire, nor of its burning as a 'combining' either of its particles with
one another or of itself with the fire: what we say is that 'the fire
is coming-to-be, but the wood is passing-away'. Similarly, we speak
15 neither (ii) of the food as 'combining' with the body, nor (iii) of the
shape as 'combining' with the wax and thus fashioning the lump.
Nor can body 'combine' with white, nor (to generalize) 'properties'
and 'states' with 'things': for we *see* them persisting unaltered.[92]
But again (iv) white and knowledge cannot be 'combined' either,
20 nor any other of the 'adjectivals'. (Indeed, this is a blemish in the
theory of those who assert that 'once upon a time all things were together and combined'. For not everything can 'combine' with everything. On the contrary, both of the constituents that are combined
in the compound must originally have existed in separation: but
no property can have separate existence.)

Since, however, some things *are-potentially* while others *are-
actually*, the constituents combined in a compound can 'be' in a sense

[91] Cf. above, 322ᵇ 5 ff.
[92] *sc.* in the resulting complex (e. g. 'white-body' or 'learned-man').

and yet 'not-be'. The compound may *be-actually* other than the con- 25 stituents from which it has resulted; nevertheless each of them may still *be-potentially* what it was before they were combined, and both of them may survive undestroyed. (For this was the difficulty that emerged in the previous argument: and it is evident that the combining constituents not only coalesce, having formerly existed in separation, but also can again be separated out from the compound.) The constituents, therefore, neither (*a*) *persist actually*, as 'body' 30 and 'white' persist: nor (*b*) are they *destroyed* (either one of them or both), for their 'power of action' is preserved. Hence these difficulties may be dismissed: but the problem immediately connected with them—'whether combination is something relative to perception'—must be set out and discussed.

When the combining constituents have been divided into parts so small, and have been juxtaposed in such a manner that perception fails to discriminate them one from another, have they then 'been 35 combined'? Or ought we to say 'No, not until any and every part of 328ᵃ one constituent is juxtaposed to a part of the other'? The term, no doubt, is applied in the former sense: we speak, e. g., of wheat having been 'combined' with barley when each *grain* of the one is juxtaposed to a *grain* of the other. But every body is divisible and therefore, since body 'combined' with body is uniform in texture throughout, *any and every part* of each constituent ought to be juxtaposed to a part 5 of the other.

No body, however, can be divided into its 'least' parts: and 'composition' is not identical with 'combination', but other than it. From these premises it clearly follows (i) that so long as the constituents are preserved in small particles, we must not speak of them as 'combined'. (For this will be a 'composition' instead of a 'blending' or 'combination': nor will every portion of the resultant exhibit the same ratio between its constituents as the whole. But we maintain 10 that, if 'combination' has taken place, the compound *must* be uniform in texture throughout—any part of such a compound being the same as the whole, just as any part of water is water: whereas, if 'combination' is 'composition of the small particles', nothing of the kind will happen. On the contrary, the constituents will only be 'combined' relatively to perception: and the same thing will be 'combined' to one percipient, if his sight is not sharp, <but not to another,> 15 while to the eye of Lynkeus nothing will be 'combined'.) It clearly follows (ii) that we must not speak of the constituents as 'combined' in virtue of a division such that *any and every part* of each is juxtaposed to a part of the other: for it is impossible for them to be thus divided. Either, then, there is no 'combination', or we have still to explain the manner in which it can take place.

Now, as we maintain,[93] some things are such as to act and others such as to suffer action from them. Moreover, some things—viz. those
20 which have the same matter—'reciprocate', i. e. are such as to act upon one another and to suffer action from one another; while other things, viz. agents which have not the same matter as their patients, act without themselves suffering action. Such agents cannot 'combine'—that is why neither the art of healing nor health produces health by 'combining' with the bodies of the patients. Amongst those things, however, which are reciprocally active and passive, some are easily-divisible. Now (i) if a great quantity (or a large bulk) of one
25 of these easily-divisible 'reciprocating' materials be brought together with a little (or with a small piece) of another, the effect produced is not 'combination', but increase of the dominant: for the other material is transformed into the dominant. (That is why a drop of wine does not 'combine' with ten thousand gallons of water: for its form is dissolved, and it [94] is changed so as to merge in the total volume of water.) On the other hand (ii) when there is a certain
30 equilibrium between their 'powers of action', then each of them changes out of its own nature towards the dominant: yet neither becomes the other, but both become an intermediate with properties common to both.[95]

Thus it is clear that only those agents are 'combinable' which involve a contrariety—for these are such as to suffer action reciprocally. And, further, they combine more freely if small pieces of each of them are juxtaposed. For in that condition they change
35 one another more easily and more quickly; whereas this effect takes a long time when agent and patient are present in bulk.
328[b]   Hence, amongst the divisible susceptible materials, those whose shape is readily adaptable have a tendency to combine: for they are easily divided into small particles, since that is precisely what 'being readily adaptable in shape' implies. For instance, liquids are the most 'combinable' of all bodies—because, of all divisible materials, the liquid is most readily adaptable in shape, unless it be viscous. Viscous
5 liquids, it is true, produce no effect except to increase the volume and bulk. But when one of the constituents is alone susceptible—or super-

---

[93] Cf. above, I. 7.

[94] *sc.* the drop of wine.

[95] Each of the constituents, *qua* acting on the other, is *relatively* 'dominant'. Neither of them is *absolutely* 'dominant', for each 'suffers action' from the other. Hence each meets the other half-way, and the resultant is a compromise between them.

latively susceptible, the other being susceptible in a very slight degree
—the compound resulting from their combination is either no greater
in volume or only a little greater. This is what happens when tin is
combined with bronze. For some things display a hesitating and ambiguous attitude towards one another—showing a slight tendency to
combine and also an inclination to behave as 'receptive matter' and 10
'form' respectively. The behaviour of these metals is a case in point.
For the tin almost vanishes, behaving as if it were an immaterial property of the bronze: having been combined, it disappears, leaving no
trace except the colour it has imparted to the bronze. The same phenomenon occurs in other instances too.

It is clear, then, from the foregoing account, that 'combination' 15
occurs, what it is, to what it is due, and what kind of thing is 'combinable'. The phenomenon depends upon the fact that some things are
such as to be (a) reciprocally susceptible and (b) readily adaptable
in shape, i. e. easily divisible. For such things can be 'combined' without its being necessary either that they should have been destroyed
or that they should survive absolutely unaltered: and their 'combination' need not be a 'composition', nor merely 'relative to perception'.
On the contrary: anything is 'combinable' which, being readily 20
adaptable in shape, is such as to suffer action and to act; and it is
'combinable with' another thing similarly characterized (for the
'combinable' is relative to the 'combinable'); and 'combination' is
unification of the 'combinables', resulting from their 'alteration'.

BOOK II

1 We have explained under what conditions 'combination', 'contact', and 'action-passion' are attributable to the things which undergo natural change. Further, we have discussed 'unqualified' coming-
to-be and passing-away, and explained under what conditions they
are predicable, of what subject, and owing to what cause. Similarly, 3r'
we have also discussed 'alteration', and explained what 'altering' is
and how it differs from coming-to-be and passing-away. But we have
still to investigate the so-called 'elements' of bodies.

For the complex substances whose formation and maintenance are
due to natural processes all presuppose the perceptible bodies as the
condition of their coming-to-be and passing-away: but philosophers
disagree in regard to the matter which underlies these perceptible
bodies. Some maintain it is single, supposing it to be, e. g., Air or Fire,
or an 'intermediate' between these two (but still a body with a 35
separate existence). Others, on the contrary, postulate two or more 329ᵃ

materials—ascribing to their 'association' and 'dissociation', or to their 'alteration', the coming-to-be and passing-away of things. (Some, for instance, postulate Fire and Earth: some add Air, making three: and some, like Empedocles, reckon Water as well, thus postulating four.)

5 Now we may agree that the primary materials, whose change (whether it be 'association and dissociation' or a process of another kind) results in coming-to-be and passing-away, are rightly described as 'originative sources, i.e. elements'. But (i) those thinkers are in error who postulate, beside the bodies we have mentioned, a single 10 matter—and that a corporeal and separable matter. For this 'body' of theirs cannot possibly exist without a 'perceptible contrariety': this 'Boundless', which some thinkers identify with the 'original real', must be either light or heavy, either cold or hot.[1] And (ii) what Plato has written in the Timaeus is not based on any precisely-articulated 15 conception. For he has not stated clearly whether his 'Omnirecipient'[2] exists in separation from the 'elements'; nor does he make any use of it. He says, indeed, that it is a substratum prior to the so-called 'elements'—underlying them, as gold underlies the things that are fashioned of gold. (And yet this comparison, if thus ex- 20 pressed, is itself open to criticism. Things which come-to-be, and pass-away cannot be called by the name of the material out of which they have come-to-be: it is only the results of 'alteration' which retain the name of the substratum whose 'alterations' they are. However, he actually says[3] that 'far the truest account is to affirm that each of them[4] is "gold"'.) Nevertheless he carries his analysis of the 'elements'—solids though they are—back to 'planes',[5] and it is impossible for 'the Nurse'[6] (i. e. the primary matter) to be identical with the 'planes'.

Our own doctrine is that although there is a matter of the per- 25 ceptible bodies (a matter out of which the so-called 'elements' come-to-be), it has no separate existence, but is always bound up with a contrariety. A more precise account of these presuppositions has been given in another work[7]: we must, however, give a detailed explanation of the primary bodies as well, since they too are 30 similarly derived from the matter. We must reckon as an 'originative source' and as 'primary' the matter which underlies, though it is

---

[1] Cf. below, 332ª 20–6.   [2] Cf. Timaeus 51 A.
[3] Cf. Timaeus 49 D–50 C.
[4] i. e. each of the things that are 'fashioned of gold'.
[5] Cf. Timaeus 53 C ff.   [6] Cf. Timaeus, e. g. 49 A, 52 D.
[7] Cf. Physics i. 6–9.

inseparable from, the contrary qualities: for 'the hot' is not matter for 'the cold' nor 'the cold' for 'the hot', but the *substratum* is matter for them both. We therefore have to recognize three 'originative sources': *firstly* that which is potentially perceptible body, *secondly* the contrarieties (I mean, e. g., heat and cold), and *thirdly* Fire, 35 Water, and the like. *Only* 'thirdly', however: for these bodies change into one another (they are not immutable as Empedocles and other 329ᵇ thinkers assert, since 'alteration' would then have been impossible), whereas the contrarieties do not change.

Nevertheless, even so [8] the question remains: What sorts of contrarieties, and how many of them, are to be accounted 'originative sources' of body? For all the other thinkers assume and use them with- 5 out explaining why they are *these* or why they are just so *many*.

2   Since, then, we are looking for 'originative sources' of perceptible body; and since 'perceptible' is equivalent [9] to 'tangible', and 'tangible' is that of which the perception is touch; it is clear that not all the contrarieties constitute 'forms' and 'originative sources' of body, but only those which correspond to touch. For it is in accordance 10 with a contrariety—a contrariety, moreover, of *tangible* qualities— that the primary bodies are differentiated. That is why neither whiteness (and blackness), nor sweetness (and bitterness), nor (similarly) any quality belonging to the other [10] perceptible contrarieties either, constitutes an 'element'. And yet vision is prior to touch, so that its object also is prior to the object of touch. The object of vision, 15 however, is a quality of tangible body not *qua* tangible, but *qua* something else—*qua* something which may well be naturally prior to the object of touch.

Accordingly, we must segregate the tangible differences and contrarieties, and distinguish which amongst them are primary. Contrarieties correlative to touch are the following: hot-cold, dry-moist, heavy-light, hard-soft, viscous-brittle, rough-smooth, coarse-fine. Of 20 these (i) heavy and light are neither active nor susceptible. Things are not called 'heavy' and 'light' because they act upon, or suffer action from, other things. But the 'elements' must be reciprocally active and susceptible, since they 'combine' and are transformed into one another. On the other hand (ii) hot and cold, and dry and moist, 25 are terms, of which the first pair implies *power to act* and the second

[8] i. e. notwithstanding the sketch Aristotle has just given.

[9] *sc.* in this connexion: the tangible qualities are the only qualities which characterize *all* perceptible bodies.

[10] *sc.* the other *non-tangible* perceptible contrarieties.

pair *susceptibility*. 'Hot' is that which 'associates' things of the same
kind (for 'dissociating', which people attribute to Fire as its function,
is 'associating' things of the same class, since its effect is to eliminate
30 what is foreign), while 'cold' is that which brings together, i. e. 'associates', homogeneous and heterogeneous things alike. And 'moist' is
that which, being readily adaptable in shape, is not determinable by
any limit of its own: while 'dry' is that which is readily determinable
by its own limit, but not readily adaptable in shape.

From moist and dry are derived (iii) the fine and coarse, viscous
and brittle, hard and soft, and the remaining tangible differences.
35 For (*a*) since the moist has no determinate shape, but is readily adapt-
330ᵃ able and follows the outline of that which is in contact with it, it is
characteristic of it to be 'such as to fill up'. Now 'the fine' is 'such as
to fill up.' For 'the fine' consists of subtle particles; but that which
consists of small particles is 'such as to fill up', inasmuch as it is in
contact ¹¹ whole with whole—and 'the fine' exhibits this character ¹²
in a superlative degree. Hence it is evident that the fine derives from
the moist, while the coarse derives from the dry. Again (*b*) 'the
5 viscous' derives from the moist: for 'the viscous' (e. g. oil) is a 'moist'
modified in a certain way. 'The brittle', on the other hand, derives from
the dry: for 'brittle' is that which is *completely* dry—so completely,
that its solidification has actually been due to failure of moisture.
Further (*c*) 'the soft' derives from the moist. For 'soft' is that
which yields to pressure by retiring into itself, though it does not
10 yield by total displacement as the moist does—which explains why
the moist is not 'soft', although 'the soft' derives from the moist.
'The hard', on the other hand, derives from the dry: for 'hard' is
that which is solidified, and the solidified is dry.

The terms 'dry' and 'moist' have more senses than one. For 'the
damp', as well as the moist, is opposed to the dry: and again 'the
solidified', as well as the dry, is opposed to the moist. But all these
15 qualities derive from the dry and moist we mentioned first.¹³ For (i)
the dry is opposed to the damp: i. e. 'damp' is that which has foreign
moisture on its surface ('sodden' being that which is penetrated to its
core ¹⁴), while 'dry' ¹⁵ is that which has lost foreign moisture. Hence
it is evident that the damp will derive from the moist, and 'the dry'
20 which is opposed to it will derive from the primary dry. Again (ii)

¹¹ 'in contact' with the vessel which contains it.
¹² The fine, owing to the subtlety (= the smallness) of its particles, leaves no
corner of its containing receptacle unfilled.
¹³ Cf. above, 329ᵇ 30–2.
¹⁴ *sc.* by foreign moisture: Cf. below, ᵃ 22.
¹⁵ i. e. the 'dry' which is contrasted with the damp: the 'dried'.

the 'moist' and the solidified derive in the same way from the primary pair. For 'moist'[16] is that which contains moisture *of its own* deep within it ('sodden' being that which is deeply penetrated by *foreign* moisture), whereas 'solidified' is that which has lost this inner moisture. Hence these too derive from the primary pair, the 'solidified' from the dry and the 'liquefiable' from the moist.

It is clear, then, that all the other differences reduce to the first 25 four, but that these admit of no further reduction. For the hot is not *essentially* moist or dry, nor the moist *essentially* hot or cold: nor are the cold and the dry derivative forms, either of one another or of the hot and the moist. Hence these must be four.

3   The elementary qualities are four, and any four terms can be 30 combined in six couples. Contraries, however, refuse to be coupled: for it is impossible for the same thing to be hot and cold, or moist and dry. Hence it is evident that the 'couplings' of the elementary qualities will be four: hot with dry and moist with hot, and again 330ᵇ cold with dry and cold with moist. And these four couples have attached themselves to the *apparently* 'simple' bodies (Fire, Air, Water, and Earth) in a manner consonant with theory. For Fire is hot and dry, whereas Air is hot and moist (Air being a sort of aqueous 5 vapour); and Water is cold and moist, while Earth is cold and dry. Thus the differences are reasonably distributed among the primary bodies, and the number of the latter is consonant with theory. For all who make the simple bodies 'elements' postulate either one, or two, or three, or four. Now (i) those who assert there is *one* 10 only, and then generate everything else by condensation and rarefaction, are in effect making their 'originative sources' two, viz. the rare and the dense, or rather the hot and the cold: for it is these which are the moulding forces, while the 'one' underlies them as a 'matter'. But (ii) those who postulate *two* from the start—as Parmenides postulated Fire and Earth—make the intermediates (e. g. Air and 15 Water) blends of these. The same course is followed (iii) by those who advocate *three*. (We may compare what Plato does in 'The Divisions': for he makes 'the middle' a blend.) Indeed, there is practically no difference between those who postulate *two* and those who postulate *three,* except that the former split the middle 'element' into two, while the latter treat it as only one. But (iv) some advocate *four* 20 from the start, e. g. Empedocles: yet he too draws them together so as to reduce them to *the two,* for he opposes all the others to Fire.

[16] i. e. the 'moist' which is contrasted with the solidified: the 'liquefiable'.

In fact, however, fire and air, and each of the bodies we have mentioned, are not simple, but blended. The 'simple' bodies are indeed
similar in nature to them, but not identical with them. Thus the
'simple' body corresponding to fire is 'such-as-fire', not fire: that
25 which corresponds to air is 'such-as-air': and so on with the rest of
them. But fire is an excess of heat, just as ice is an excess of cold.
For freezing and boiling are excesses of heat and cold respectively.
Assuming, therefore, that ice is a freezing of moist and cold, fire
analogously will be a boiling of dry and hot: a fact, by the way,
30 which explains why nothing comes-to-be either out of ice or out of fire.

The 'simple' bodies, since they are four, fall into two pairs which
belong to the two regions, each to each: for Fire and Air are forms
of the body moving towards the 'limit', while Earth and Water are
forms of the body which moves towards the 'centre'. Fire and Earth,
331ᵃ moreover, are extremes and purest: Water and Air, on the contrary,
are intermediates and more like blends. And, further, the members
of either pair are contrary to those of the other, Water being contrary
to Fire and Earth to Air; for the qualities constituting Water and
Earth are contrary to those that constitute Fire and Air. Nevertheless, since they are four, each of them is characterized *par excellence*
by a single quality: Earth by dry rather than by cold, Water by
5 cold rather than by moist, Air by moist rather than by hot, and
Fire by hot rather than by dry.

4 It has been established before [17] that the coming-to-be of the
'simple' bodies is reciprocal. At the same time, it is manifest, even
on the evidence of perception, that they *do* come-to-be: for otherwise
10 there would not have been 'alteration', since 'alteration' is change in
respect to the qualities of the objects of touch. Consequently, we
must explain (i) what is the manner of their reciprocal transformation, and (ii) whether every one of them can come-to-be out of every
one—or whether some can do so, but not others.

Now it is evident that all of them are by nature such as to change
15 into one another: for coming-to-be is a change into contraries and
out of contraries, and the 'elements' all involve a contrariety in
their mutual relations because their distinctive qualities are contrary.
For in some of them *both* qualities are contrary—e. g. in Fire and
Water, the first of these being dry and hot, and the second moist
and cold: while in others *one* of the qualities (though only one) is contrary—e. g. in Air and Water, the first being moist and hot, and

[17] The reference is probably neither to 314ᵇ 15–26 nor to 329ᵃ 35, but to
de Caelo 304ᵇ 23 ff.

the second moist and cold. It is evident, therefore, if we consider 20
them in general, that every one is by nature such as to come-to-
be out of every one: and when we come to consider them severally,
it is not difficult to see the manner in which their transformation
is effected. For, though all will result from all, both the speed and
the facility of their conversion will differ in degree.

Thus (i) the process of conversion will be quick between those 25
which have interchangeable 'complementary factors', but slow between
those which have none. The reason is that it is easier for a single
thing to change than for many. Air, e. g., will result from Fire if a
single quality changes: for Fire, as we saw, is hot and dry while Air
is hot and moist, so that there will be Air if the dry be overcome by
the moist. Again, Water will result from Air if the hot be over- 30
come by the cold: for Air, as we saw, is hot and moist while Water
is cold and moist, so that, if the hot changes, there will be Water.
So too, in the same manner, Earth will result from Water and Fire
from Earth, since the two 'elements' in both these couples have interchangeable 'complementary factors'. For Water is moist and cold
while Earth is cold and dry—so that, if the moist be overcome, 35
there will be Earth: and again, since Fire is dry and hot while Earth
is cold and dry, Fire will result from Earth, if the cold pass-away. 331^b

It is evident, therefore, that the coming-to-be of the 'simple' bodies
will be cyclical; and that this cyclical method of transformation is
the easiest, because the *consecutive* 'elements' contain interchangeable
'complementary factors'.[18] On the other hand (ii) the transformation
of Fire into Water and of Air into Earth, and again of Water and 5
Earth into Fire and Air respectively, though possible, is more difficult
because it involves the change of more qualities. For if Fire is
to result from Water, both the cold and the moist must pass-away:
and again, both the cold and the dry must pass-away if Air is to
result from Earth. So, too, if Water and Earth are to result from Fire 10
and Air respectively—both qualities must change.

This second method of coming-to-be, then, takes a longer time.
But (iii) if one quality in each of two 'elements' pass-away, the
transformation, though easier, is not reciprocal. Still, from Fire
plus Water there will result Earth and [19] Air, and from Air *plus*
Earth, Fire and [20] Water. For there will be Air, when the cold of the 15

---

[18] Aristotle has shown that, by the conversion of a single quality in each case,
Fire is transformed into Air, Air into Water, Water into Earth, and Earth into
Fire. This is a *cycle* of transformations. Moreover, the 'elements' have been taken
in their natural consecutive series, according to their order in the Cosmos.

[19] *sc.* alternatively.   [20] *sc.* alternatively.

Water and the dry of the Fire have passed-away (since the hot of the latter and the moist of the former are left): whereas, when the hot of the Fire and the moist of the Water have passed-away, there will be Earth, owing to the survival of the dry of the Fire and the cold of the Water. So, too in the same way, Fire and Water will result from
20 Air *plus* Earth. For there will be Water, when the hot of the Air and the dry of the Earth have passed-away (since the moist of the former and the cold of the latter are left): whereas, when the moist of the Air and the cold of the Earth have passed-away, there will be Fire, owing to the survival of the hot of the Air and the dry of the Earth—qualities essentially constitutive of Fire. Moreover, this
25 mode of Fire's coming-to-be is confirmed by perception. For flame is *par excellence* Fire: but flame is burning smoke, and smoke consists of Air and Earth.

No transformation, however, into any of the 'simple' bodies can result from the passing-away of one elementary quality in each of two 'elements' when they are taken in their consecutive order, because
30 either *identical* or *contrary* qualities are left in the pair: but no 'simple' body can be formed either out of identical, or out of contrary, qualities. Thus no 'simple' body would result, if the dry of Fire and the moist of Air were to pass-away: for the hot is left in both. On the other hand, if the hot pass-away out of both, the contraries—dry and moist—are left. A similar result will occur in all the others too: for all the *consecutive* 'elements' contain one identical, and one con-
35 trary, quality.[21] Hence, too, it clearly follows that, when one of the *consecutive* 'elements' is transformed into one, the coming-to-be is effected by the passing-away of a single quality: whereas, when two of them are transformed into a third, more than one quality must have passed-away.[22]

332ᵃ   We have stated that all the 'elements' come-to-be out of any one of them; and we have explained the manner in which their mutual conversion takes place.

[21] If the 'elements' are taken in their natural order, Water (e. g.) is 'consecutive' to Earth, and Air to Water. Water is moist and cold. It shares its 'cold' with Earth and its 'moist' with Air: its 'moist' is contrary to Earth's 'dry', and its 'cold' is contrary to Air's 'hot'.

[22] If, e. g., Fire *plus* Air are to be transformed into Water or into Earth, it is not enough that a single quality should be eliminated from each of the generating pair: for this would leave either two 'hots' or a 'dry' and a 'moist' (Cf. 331ᵇ 26–33). Either Fire's 'dry' or Air's 'moist' must be eliminated: and, *in addition*, the 'hot' of one must be eliminated and the 'hot' of the other be converted into 'cold'.

5   Let us nevertheless supplement our theory by the following speculations concerning them.

If Water, Air, and the like are a 'matter' of which the natural 5 bodies consist, as some thinkers in fact believe, these 'elements' must be either one, or two, or more. Now they cannot all of them be *one*—they cannot, e. g., all be Air or Water or Fire or Earth— because 'Change is into contraries'. For if they all were Air, then (assuming Air to persist) there will be 'alteration' instead of coming-to-be. Besides, nobody supposes a single 'element' to persist, as the basis of all, in such a way that it is Water as well as Air (or any 10 other 'element') *at the same time*. So there will be a certain contrariety, i. e. a differentiating quality:[23] and the other member of this contrariety, e. g. heat, will belong to some other 'element', e. g. to Fire. But Fire will certainly not be 'hot Air'. For a change of that kind [24] (*a*) is 'alteration', and (*b*) is not what is observed. Moreover (*c*) if Air is again to result out of the Fire, it will do so by the conversion of the hot into its contrary: this contrary, 15 therefore, will belong to Air, and Air will be a cold something: hence it is impossible for Fire to be 'hot Air', since in that case the same thing will be simultaneously hot and cold. Both Fire and Air, therefore, will be something else which is the same; i. e. there will be some 'matter', other than either, common to both.

The same argument applies to all the 'elements', proving that there is no single one of them out of which they all originate. 20 But neither is there, beside these four, some other body from which they originate—a something intermediate, e. g., between Air and Water (coarser than Air, but finer than Water), or between Air and Fire (coarser than Fire, but finer than Air). For the supposed 'intermediate' will be Air and Fire when a pair of contrasted qualities is added to it: but, since one of every two contrary qualities is a 'privation', the 'intermediate' never can exist— as some thinkers assert the 'Boundless' or the 'Environing' exists 25 —in isolation.[25] It is, therefore, equally and indifferently any one of the 'elements', or else it is nothing.

Since, then, there is nothing—at least, nothing *perceptible*—prior to these,[26] they must be all.[27] That being so, either they must always persist and not be transformable into one another: or they

---

[23] If Air is to 'alter' into (e. g.) Fire, we must assume a pair of contrasted differentiating qualities, and assign one to Fire and the other to Air.

[24] i. e. Air becoming Fire by being heated.

[25] i. e. bare of all qualities.   [26] *sc.* Earth, Air, Fire, and Water.

[27] i. e. all the 'simple' bodies there are.

must undergo transformation—either all of them, or some only
30 (as Plato wrote in the *Timaeus*).[28] Now it has been proved before [29]
that they must undergo reciprocal transformation. It has also been
proved [30] that the speed with which they come-to-be, one out of
another, is not uniform—since the process of reciprocal transformation is relatively *quick* between the 'elements' with a 'complementary
factor', but relatively *slow* between those which possess no such factor. Assuming, then, that the contrariety, in respect to which they
35 are transformed, is *one*, the 'elements' will inevitably be two: for it
is 'matter' that is the 'mean' between the two contraries, and mat-
332ᵇ ter is imperceptible and inseparable from them. Since, however, the
'elements' are seen to be more than two, the contrarieties must at the
least be two. But the contrarieties being two, the 'elements' must
be four (as they evidently are) and cannot be three: for the 'couplings' are four, since, though six are possible,[31] the two in which the
5 qualities are contrary to one another cannot occur.

These subjects have been discussed before: [32] but the following
arguments will make it clear that, since the 'elements' are transformed into one another, it is impossible for any one of them—
—whether it be at the end or in the middle [33]—to be an 'originative source' of the rest. There can be no such 'originative element'
at the ends: for all of them would then be Fire or Earth, and this
theory amounts to the assertion that all things are made of Fire
10 or Earth. Nor can a 'middle-element' be such an 'originative source'
—as some thinkers suppose that Air is transformed both into Fire
and into Water, and Water both into Air and into Earth, while the
'end-elements' are not further transformed into one another. For the
process must come to a stop, and cannot continue *ad infinitum* in a
straight line in either direction, since otherwise an infinite number
15 of contrarieties would attach to the single 'element'. Let E stand for
Earth, W for Water, A for Air, and F for Fire. Then (i) since A is
transformed into F and W, there will be a contrariety belonging to
A F. Let these contraries be whiteness and blackness. Again (ii)
since A is transformed into W, there will be another contrariety [34] :
for W is not the same as F. Let this second contrariety be dryness
20 and moistness, D being dryness and M moistness. Now if, when A
is transformed into W, the 'white' persists, Water will be moist

---

28 Cf. *Timaeus* 54 b–d.   29 Cf. above, 331ᵃ 12–20.
30 Cf. above, 331ᵃ 22 ff.   31 i. e. *mathematically* 'possible.'
32 Cf. above, II. 2 and 3.
33 i. e. at either end, or in the middle, of the 'natural series' of the 'elements'.
34 *sc.* belonging to AW.

and white: but if it does not persist, Water will be black since change is into contraries. Water, therefore, must be either white or black. Let it then be the first. On similar grounds, therefore, D (dryness) will also belong to F. Consequently F (Fire) as well as Air will be able to be transformed into Water: for it has qualities contrary 25 to those of Water, since Fire was *first* taken to be black and *then* to be dry, while Water was moist and *then* showed itself white. Thus it is evident that all the 'elements' will be able to be transformed out of one another; and that, in the instances we have taken, E (Earth) also will contain the remaining two 'complementary factors', viz. the black and the moist (for these have not yet been coupled). 30

We have dealt with this last topic before the thesis we set out to prove.[35] That thesis—viz. that the process cannot continue *ad infinitum*—will be clear from the following considerations. If Fire (which is represented by F) is not to revert, but is to be transformed in turn into some other 'element' (e. g. into Q), a new contrariety, other than those mentioned, will belong to Fire and Q: for it has 35 been assumed that Q is not the same as any of the four, E W A and 333[a] F. Let K, then, belong to F and Y to Q. Then K will belong to all four, E W A and F: for they are transformed into one another. This last point, however, we may admit, has not yet been proved: but at any rate it is clear that if Q is to be transformed in turn into yet another 'element', yet another contrariety will belong not only to 5 Q but also to F (Fire). And, similarly, every addition of a new 'element' will carry with it the attachment of a new contrariety to the preceding 'elements'. Consequently, if the 'elements' are infinitely many, there will also belong *to the single 'element'* an infinite number of contrarieties. But if that be so, it will be impossible to define any 'element': impossible also for any to come-to-be. For if one is to result from another, it will have to pass through such a vast num- 10 ber of contrarieties—and indeed even more than any determinate number. Consequently (i) into some 'elements' transformation will never be effected—viz. if the intermediates are infinite in number, as they must be if the 'elements' are infinitely many: further (ii) there will not even be a transformation of Air into Fire, if the contrarieties are infinitely many: moreover (iii) all the 'elements' become one. For all the contrarieties of the 'elements' above F must belong to those below F, and *vice versa*: hence they will all be one. 15

6   As for those who agree with Empedocles that the 'elements' of body are more than one, so that they are not transformed into one

[35] Cf. above, 332[b] 12–13.

another [36]—one may well wonder in what sense it is open to them to maintain that the 'elements' are comparable. Yet Empedocles says
20 'For these are all not only equal . . .'

If (i) it is meant that they are comparable in their amount, all the 'comparables' must possess an identical something whereby they are measured. If, e. g., one pint of Water yields ten of Air, both are measured by the same unit; and therefore both were from the first an identical something. On the other hand, suppose (ii) they are not 'comparable in their amount' in the sense that so-much of the one yields so-much of the other, but comparable in 'power of action' (a
25 pint of Water, e. g., having a power of cooling equal to that of ten pints of Air); even so, they *are* 'comparable in their amount', though not *qua* 'amount' but *qua* 'so-much power'.[37] There is also (iii) a third possibility. Instead of comparing their powers by the measure of their amount, they might be compared as terms in a 'correspondence': e. g., 'as x is hot, so correspondingly y is white'. But
30 'correspondence', though it means equality in the *quantum,* means similarity [38] in a *quale*. Thus it is manifestly absurd that the 'simple' bodies, though they are not transformable, are comparable not merely as 'corresponding', but by a measure of their powers; i. e. that so-much Fire is comparable with many-times-that-amount of Air, as being 'equally' or 'similarly' hot. For the same thing, if it be greater in amount, will, since it belongs to the same kind,[39] have its *ratio* correspondingly increased.

35   A further objection to the theory of Empedocles is that it makes even *growth* impossible, unless it be increase by addition. For his Fire
333ᵇ increases by Fire: 'And Earth increases its own frame and Ether increases Ether.' These, however, are cases of addition: but it is not by addition that growing things are believed to increase. And it is far more difficult for him to account for the *coming-to-be* which
5 occurs in nature. For the things which come-to-be by natural process all exhibit, in their coming-to-be, a uniformity either absolute or highly regular: while any exceptions—any results which are in accordance neither with the invariable nor with the general rule—are products of chance and luck. Then what is the cause determining that man comes-to-be from man, that wheat (instead of an olive) comes-to-be

---

[36] i. e. so that the 'elements' are genuinely or irreducibly 'many'.

[37] i. e. we are comparing the *amounts of cooling energy* possessed by one pint of Water and ten pints of Air respectively.

[38] i. e. *only* 'similarity'. Empedocles might have said the 'elements' were all *analogous* or *similar* without inconsistency: but he asserts that they are *equal,* i. e. quantitatively comparable (and therefore, ultimately, transformable).

[39] *sc.* as the thing of less amount with which it is being compared.

from wheat, either invariably or generally? Are we to say 'Bone comes-to-be if the "elements" be put together in such-and-such a manner'? For, according to his own statements, nothing comes-to-be 10 from their 'fortuitous consilience', but only from their 'consilience' in a certain proportion. What, then, is the cause of this proportional consilience? Presumably not Fire or Earth. But neither is it Love and Strife: for the former is a cause of 'association' only, and the latter only of 'dissociation'. No: the cause in question is the essential nature of each thing—not merely (to quote his words) 'a mingling and a divorce of what has been mingled'. And *chance*, not *proportion*, 15 'is the name given to these occurrences': for things can be 'mingled' fortuitously.

The cause, therefore, of the coming-to-be of the things which owe their existence to nature is that they are in such-and-such a determinate condition: [40] and it is *this* which constitutes the 'nature' of each thing—a 'nature' about which he says nothing. What he says, therefore, is no explanation of 'nature'. Moreover, it is *this* which is both 'the excellence' of each thing and its 'good': whereas he assigns the whole credit to the 'mingling'. (And yet the *'elements'* at all 20 events are 'dissociated' not by Strife, but by Love: since the 'elements' are by nature prior to the Deity, and they too are Deities.)

Again, his account of motion is vague. For it is not an adequate explanation to say that 'Love and Strife set things moving', unless the very nature of Love is a movement of *this* kind and the very nature of Strife a movement of *that* kind. He ought, then, either to have defined or to have postulated these characteristic movements, 25 or to have demonstrated them—whether strictly or laxly or in some other fashion. Moreover, since (*a*) the 'simple' bodies *appear* to move 'naturally' as well as by compulsion, i. e. in a manner contrary to nature (fire, e. g., appears to move upwards without compulsion, though it appears to move by compulsion downwards); and since (*b*) what is 'natural' is contrary to that which is due to compulsion, and movement by compulsion actually occurs; [41] it follows that 'natural movement' can also occur in fact. Is *this*, then, the movement that Love sets going? No: for, on the contrary, the 30 'natural movement' moves Earth downwards and resembles 'dissociation', and Strife rather than Love is its cause—so that in general, too, Love rather than Strife would seem to be contrary to nature. And unless Love or Strife is actually setting them in motion, the 'simple'

[40] i. e. that they are compounds produced by the consilience of their constituents in a certain proportion.

[41] i. e. according to Empedocles himself.

35 bodies themselves have absolutely no movement or rest. But this is paradoxical: and what is more, they do in fact obviously move.[42]
334ᵃ For though Strife 'dissociated',[43] it was not by Strife that the 'Ether' was borne upwards. On the contrary, sometimes he attributes its movement to something like *chance* ('For *thus,* as it ran, it *happened* to meet them then, though often otherwise'), while at other times he says it is the *nature* of Fire to be borne upwards, but 'the Ether'
5 (to quote his words) 'sank down upon the Earth with long roots'. With such statements, too, he combines the assertion that the Order of the World is the same *now,* in the reign of Strife, as it was *formerly* in the reign of Love. What, then, is the 'first mover' of the 'elements'? What causes their motion? Presumably not Love and Strife: on the contrary, these are causes of a *particular* motion, if at least we assume that 'first mover' to be an 'originative source'. [44]

10   An additional paradox is that the soul should consist of the 'elements', or that it should be one of them. How are the soul's 'alterations' to take place? How, e. g., is the change from being musical to being unmusical, or how is memory or forgetting, to occur? For clearly, if the soul be Fire, only such modifications will happen to it as characterize Fire *qua* Fire: while if it be compounded out of the 'elements', only the corporeal modifications will occur in it. But the
15 changes we have mentioned are none of them corporeal.

7   The discussion of these difficulties, however, is a task appropriate to a different investigation: [45] let us return to the 'elements' of which bodies are composed. The theories that 'there is something common to all the "elements" ', and that 'they are reciprocally transformed', are so related that those who accept *either* are bound to accept *the other* as well. Those, on the other hand, who do not make their coming-to-be reciprocal—who refuse to suppose that any one of the 'elements' comes-to-be out of any other *taken singly*, except in the sense
20 in which bricks come-to-be out of a wall—are faced with a paradox. How, on their theory, are flesh and bones or any of the other compounds to result from the 'elements' *taken together*?

Indeed, the point we have raised constitutes a problem even for those who generate the 'elements' out of one another. In what manner does anything other than, and beside, the 'elements' come-to-be out of them? Let me illustrate my meaning. Water can come-to-be out of

---

42 i. e. according to Empedocles' own statements.
43 i. e. though Strife initiated the disintegration of the Sphere.
44 *sc.* a first cause of motion in general.
45 Cf. *de Anima*, i. 4 and 5.

Fire and Fire out of Water; for their *substratum* is something common
to them both. But flesh too, presumably, and marrow come-to-be 25
out of them. How, then, do such things come-to-be? For (*a*) how
is the manner of their coming-to-be to be conceived by those who
maintain a theory like that of Empedocles? They must conceive
it as *composition*—just as a wall comes-to-be out of bricks and stones:
and the 'Mixture', of which they speak, will be composed of the 'elements', these being preserved in it unaltered but with their small particles juxtaposed each to each. That will be the manner, presumably, 30
in which flesh and every other compound results from the 'elements'.
Consequently, it follows that Fire and Water do not come-to-be 'out
of any and every part of flesh'. For instance, although a sphere might
come-to-be out of *this* part of a lump of wax and a pyramid out of
some other part, it was nevertheless possible for either figure to have
come-to-be out of either part indifferently: *that* is the manner of 35
coming-to-be when 'both Fire and Water come-to-be out of any and
every part of flesh'. Those, however, who maintain the theory in ques- 334ᵇ
tion, are not at liberty to conceive that 'both come-to-be out of
flesh' in that manner, but only as a stone and a brick 'both come-to-be
out of a wall'—viz. each out of a different place or part. Similarly
(*b*) even for those who postulate a single matter of their 'elements'
there is a certain difficulty in explaining how anything is to result
from two of them taken together—e. g. from 'cold' and 'hot', or from
Fire and Earth. For if flesh consists of both and is neither of them, 5
nor again is a 'composition' of them in which they are preserved
unaltered, what alternative is left except to identify the resultant of
the two 'elements' with their matter? For the passing-away of either
'element' produces *either* the other *or* the matter.

Perhaps we may suggest the following solution. (i) There are
differences of degree in hot and cold. Although, therefore, when either
is fully real without qualification, the other will exist potentially;
yet, when neither exists in the full completeness of its being, but both 10
by combining destroy one another's excesses so that there exist instead
a hot which (for a 'hot') is cold and a cold which (for a 'cold') is
hot; then what results from these two contraries will be neither
their matter, nor either of them existing in its full reality without
qualification. There will result instead an 'intermediate': and this
'intermediate', according as it is potentially more hot than cold or 15
vice versa, will possess a power-of-heating that is double or triple its
power-of-cooling, or otherwise related thereto in some similar ratio.
Thus all the other bodies will result from the contraries, or rather
from the 'elements', in so far as these have been 'combined': while the

'elements' will result from the contraries, in so far as these 'exist potentially' in a special sense—not as matter 'exists potentially', but in
the sense explained above. And when a thing comes-to-be in *this*
20 manner, the process is 'combination'; whereas what comes-to-be in
the other manner [46] is matter. Moreover (ii) contraries also 'suffer
action', in accordance with the disjunctively-articulated definition
established in the early part of this work.[47] For the actually-hot is
potentially-cold and the actually-cold potentially-hot; so that hot
and cold, unless they are equally balanced, are transformed into
one another (and all the other contraries behave in a similar way). It
25 is thus, then, that *in the first place* the 'elements' are transformed;
and that <*in the second place*>[48] out of the 'elements' there come-
to-be flesh and bones and the like—the hot becoming cold and the
cold becoming hot when they have been brought to the 'mean'. For at
the 'mean' is neither hot nor cold. The 'mean', however, is of considerable extent and not indivisible.[49] Similarly, it is *qua* reduced
to a 'mean' condition that the dry and the moist, as well as the con-
30 traries we have used as examples, produce flesh and bone and the
remaining compounds.

8   All the compound bodies—all of which exist in the region belonging to the central body—are composed of all the 'simple' bodies.
For they all contain Earth because every 'simple' body is to be found
specially and most abundantly in its own place. And they all contain
35 Water because (*a*) the compound must possess a definite outline
335ᵃ and Water, alone of the 'simple' bodies, is readily adaptable in shape:
moreover (*b*) Earth has no power of cohesion without the moist. On
the contrary, the moist is what holds it together; for it would fall to
pieces if the moist were eliminated from it completely.

They contain Earth and Water, then, for the reasons we have
given: and they contain Air and Fire, because these are contrary
5 to Earth and Water (Earth being contrary to Air and Water
to Fire, in so far as one Substance can be 'contrary' to another). Now
all compounds presuppose in their coming-to-be constituents which
are contrary to one another: and in all compounds there is contained one set of the contrasted extremes.[50] Hence the other set [51]

[46] *sc.* in the only manner which was taken into account in the formulation of
the problem at 334ᵇ 6–7.
[47] Cf. above, I. 7.
[48] *sc.* these extremes, the completely-hot and the completely-cold.
[49] i. e. the 'mean' is a *stretch*, not a *point*.
[50] i. e. cold-dry (Earth) and cold-moist (Water).
[51] i. e. hot-moist (Air) and hot-dry (Fire).

must be contained in them also, so that every compound will include all the 'simple' bodies.

Additional evidence seems to be furnished by the food each compound takes. For all of them are fed by substances which are the same as their constituents, and all of them are fed by more substances than one. Indeed, even the plants, though it might be thought they are fed by one substance only, viz. by Water, are fed by more than one: for Earth has been mixed with the Water. That is why farmers too endeavour to mix before watering.[52]

Although food is akin to the matter, that which is fed is the 'figure' —i. e. the 'form'—taken along with the matter. This fact enables us to understand why, whereas all the 'simple' bodies come-to-be out of one another, Fire is the only one of them which (as our predecessors also assert) 'is fed'. For Fire alone—or more than all the rest—is akin to the 'form' because it tends by nature to be borne towards the limit. Now each of them naturally tends to be borne towards its own place: but the 'figure'—i. e the 'form'—of them all is at the limits.

Thus we have explained that all the compound bodies are composed of all the 'simple' bodies.

9 Since some things are such as to come-to-be and pass-away, and since coming-to-be in fact occurs in the region about the centre, we must explain the *number* and the *nature* of the 'originative sources' of all coming-to-be alike: for a grasp of the true theory of any universal facilitates the understanding of its specific forms.

The 'originative sources', then, of the things which come-to-be are equal in number to, and identical in kind with, those in the sphere of the eternal and primary things. For there is *one* in the sense of 'matter', and a *second* in the sense of 'form': and, in addition, the *third* 'originative source' must be present as well. For the two first are not sufficient to bring things into being, any more than they are adequate to account for the primary things.

Now cause, in the sense of material origin, for the things which are such as to come-to-be is 'that which can be-and-not-be': and this is identical with 'that which can come-to-be-and-pass-away', since the latter, while it *is* at one time, at another time *is not*. (For whereas some things *are* of necessity, viz. the eternal things, others of necessity *are not*. And of these two sets of things, since they cannot diverge from the necessity of their nature, it is impossible for the first *not to be* and impossible for the second *to be*. Other things, however, can both

---

[52] Plants are nourished *naturally* by water impregnated with earth and *artificially* by water mixed with manure, which is a kind of earth.

be and *not be*.) Hence coming-to-be and passing-away must occur
5 within the field of 'that which can be-and-not-be'. This, therefore,
is cause in the sense of material origin for the things which are such
as to come-to-be; while cause, in the sense of their 'end', is their
'figure' or 'form'—and that is the formula expressing the essential
nature of each of them.

But the third 'originative source' must be present as well—the
cause vaguely dreamed of by all our predecessors, definitely stated
by none of them. On the contrary (*a*) some amongst them thought the
10 nature of 'the Forms' was adequate to account for coming-to-be. Thus
Socrates in the *Phaedo* first blames everybody else for having given
no explanation; [53] and then lays it down that 'some things are Forms,
others Participants in the Forms', and that 'while a thing is said to
"be" in virtue of the Form, it is said to "come-to-be" *qua* "sharing
in", to "pass-away" *qua* "losing", the Form'. Hence he thinks that
15 'assuming the truth of these theses, the Forms *must* be causes both
of coming-to-be and of passing-away'.[54] On the other hand (*b*) there
were others who thought 'the matter' was adequate by itself to account
for coming-to-be, since 'the movement originates from the matter'.

Neither of these theories, however, is sound. For (*a*) if the Forms
are causes, why is their generating activity intermittent instead of
20 perpetual and continuous—since there always *are* Participants as well
as Forms? Besides, in some instances we *see* that the cause is other
than the Form. For it is the doctor who implants health and the man
of science who implants science, although 'Health itself' and 'Science
itself' *are* as well as the Participants: and the same principle applies
to everything else that is produced in accordance with an art. On the
25 other hand (*b*) to say that 'matter generates owing to its movement'
would be, no doubt, more scientific than to make such statements as
are made by the thinkers we have been criticizing. For what 'alters'
and transfigures plays a greater part [55] in bringing things into being;
and we are everywhere accustomed, in the products of nature and of
art alike, to look upon that which can initiate movement as the
producing cause. Nevertheless this second theory is not right either.
30 For, to begin with, it is characteristic of matter to suffer action,
i.e. to be moved: but to move, i.e. to act, belongs to a different
'power'. This is obvious both in the things that come-to-be by art and
in those that come-to-be by nature. Water does not of itself produce
out of itself an animal: and it is the art, not the wood, that makes
35 a bed. Nor is this their only error. They make a second mistake in

[53] Cf. Plato, *Phaedo* 96 A–99 C.   [54] Cf. Plato, *Phaedo* 100 B–101 E.
[55] *sc.* than the Forms.

omitting the more controlling cause: for they eliminate the essen- 336ᵃ
tial nature, i. e. the 'form'. And what is more, since they remove the
formal cause, they invest the forces they assign to the 'simple' bodies
—the forces which enable these bodies to bring things into being—
with too instrumental a character. For 'since' (as they say) 'it is the
nature of the hot to dissociate, of the cold to bring together, and of
each remaining contrary either to act or to suffer action', it is out 5
of such materials and by their agency (so they maintain) that everything else comes-to-be and passes-away. Yet (a) it is evident that
even Fire is itself moved, i. e. suffers action. Moreover (b) their procedure is virtually the same as if one were to treat the saw (and
the various instruments of carpentry) as 'the cause' of the things
that come-to-be: for the wood *must* be divided if a man saws, *must* 10
become smooth if he planes, and so on with the remaining tools.
Hence, however true it may be that Fire is active, i.e. sets things moving, there is a further point they fail to observe—viz. that Fire is
inferior to the tools or instruments in the manner in which it
sets things moving.

As to our own theory—we have given a general account of the
causes in an earlier work,[56] and we have now explained and distinguished the 'matter' and the 'form'.[57]

10   Further, since the change which is motion has been proved [58] to 15
be eternal, the continuity of the occurrence of coming-to-be follows
necessarily from what we have established: for the eternal motion,
by causing 'the generator' [59] to approach and retire, will produce
coming-to-be uninterruptedly. At the same time it is clear that we
were also right when, in an earlier work,[60] we called motion (not 20
coming-to-be) 'the primary form of change'. For it is far more reasonable that *what is* should cause the coming-to-be of *what is not,* than
that *what is not* should cause the being of *what is.* Now that which is
being moved *is,* but that which is coming-to-be *is not:* hence, also,
motion is prior to coming-to-be.

We have assumed, and have proved,[61] that coming-to-be and passing-away happen to things continuously; and we assert that motion 25
causes coming-to-be. That being so, it is evident that, if the motion be
single, *both* processes cannot occur since they are contrary to one another: for it is a law of nature that the same cause, provided it remain in
the same condition, always produces the same effect, so that, from a

[56] Cf. *Physics* ii. 3–9.   [57] Cf. above, 335ᵃ 32–ᵇ 7.
[58] Cf. *Physics* viii. 7–9.   [59] i. e. the sun, as will appear presently.
[60] Cf. *Physics* 260ᵃ 26–261ᵃ 26.   [61] Cf. above, 317ᵇ 33 ff.

single motion, either coming-to-be or passing-away will always result.
The movements must, on the contrary, be more than one, and
30 they must be contrasted with one another either by the sense of their
motion [62] or by its irregularity: [63] for contrary effects demand contraries as their causes.

This explains why it is not the primary motion that causes coming-to-be and passing-away, but the motion along the inclined
circle: [64] for this motion not only possesses the necessary continuity, but includes a duality of movements as well.. For if coming-
336ᵇ to-be and passing-away are always to be continuous, there must be
some body always being moved (in order that these changes may
not fail) and moved with a duality of movements (in order that both
changes, not one only, may result). Now the continuity of this movement is caused by the motion of the whole: but the approaching and
retreating of the moving body are caused by the inclination.[65] For the
5 consequence of the inclination is that the body becomes alternately
remote and near; and since its distance is thus unequal, its movement
will be irregular. Therefore, if it generates by approaching and by its
proximity, it—this very same body—destroys by retreating and
becoming remote: and if it generates by many successive approaches,
its also destroys by many successive retirements. For contrary effects
10 demand contraries as their causes; and the natural processes of
passing-away and coming-to-be occupy equal periods of time. Hence,
too, the times—i. e the lives—of the several kinds of living things
have a number by which they are distinguished: for there is an Order
controlling all things, and every time (i. e. every life) is measured by a
period. Not all of them, however, are measured by the same period,
but some by a smaller and others by a greater one: for to some of
15 them the period, which is their measure, is a year, while to some it is
longer and to others shorter.

And there are facts of observation in manifest agreement with our
theories. Thus we see that coming-to-be occurs as the sun approaches
and decay as it retreats; and we see that the two processes occupy
equal times. For the durations of the natural processes of passing-away
20 and coming-to-be are equal. Nevertheless it often happens that things
pass-away in too short a time. This is due to the 'intermingling' by
which the things that come-to-be and pass-away are implicated with

[82] Cf. *de Caelo* 270ᵇ 32—271ᵃ 33.

[63] Cf. *de Caelo* 288ᵃ 13–27; Physics 228ᵇ 15—229ᵃ 6.

[64] i. e. the annual movement of the sun in the ecliptic or zodiac circle.

[65] i. e. the inclination of the ecliptic to the equator of the outermost sphere,
which (on Aristotle's theory) is the equator of the universe and is in the same
plane as the terrestrial equator.

one another. For their matter is 'irregular', i. e. is not everywhere the same: hence the processes by which they come-to-be must be 'irregular' too, i. e. some too quick and others too slow. Consequently the phenomenon in question occurs, because the 'irregular' coming-to-be of these things is the passing-away of other things.

Coming-to-be and passing-away will, as we have said, always be 25 continuous, and will never fail owing to the cause we stated.[66] And this continuity has a sufficient reason on our theory. For in all things, as we affirm, Nature always strives after 'the better'. Now 'being' (we have explained elsewhere [67] the exact variety of meanings we recognize in this term) is better than 'not-being': but not all 30 things can possess 'being', since they are too far removed from the 'originative source'. God therefore adopted the remaining alternative, and fulfilled the perfection of the universe by making coming-to-be uninterrupted: for the greatest possible coherence would thus be secured to existence, because that 'coming-to-be should itself come-to-be perpetually' is the closest approximation to eternal being.

The cause of this perpetuity of coming-to-be, as we have often said, is circular motion: for that is the only motion which is con- 337ᵃ tinuous. That, too, is why all the other things—the things, I mean, which are reciprocally transformed in virtue of their 'passions' and their 'powers of action', e. g. the 'simple' bodies—imitate circular motion. For when Water is transformed into Air, Air into Fire, and 5 the Fire back into Water, we say the coming-to-be 'has completed the circle', because it reverts again to the beginning. Hence it is by imitating circular motion that rectilinear motion too is continuous.

These considerations serve at the same time to explain what is to some people a baffling problem—viz. why the 'simple' bodies, since each of them is travelling towards its own place, have not become dissevered from one another in the infinite lapse of time. 10 The reason is their reciprocal transformation. For, had each of them persisted in its own place instead of being transformed by its neighbour, they would have got dissevered long ago. They are transformed, however, owing to the motion with its dual character: [68] and because they are transformed, none of them is able to persist in any place allotted to it by the Order.[69]   15

It is clear from what has been said (i) that coming-to-be and

<hr>

[66] Cf. above, 318ᵃ 9 ff.   [67] Cf. e. g. *Metaph.* 1017ᵃ 7 ff.

[68] The sun's annual movement, by which it alternately approaches and retreats, causes the alternate ascent and descent of Water, Air, and Fire. They are thus brought into contact, with the result that their constitutive contrary qualities act and suffer action reciprocally, and the 'simple' bodies themselves are transformed.   [69] Cf. above, 336ᵇ 12.

passing-away actually occur, (ii) what causes them, and (iii) what subject undergoes them. But (*a*) if there is to be movement (as we have explained elsewhere, in an earlier work [70]) there must be something which initiates it; if there is to be movement always, there must always be something which initiates it; if the move-
20 ment is to be continuous, what initiates it must be single, unmoved, ungenerated, and incapable of 'alteration'; and if the circular [71] movements are more than one, their initiating causes must all of them, in spite of their plurality, be in some way subordinated to a single 'originative source'. Further (*b*) since time is continuous, movement must be continuous, inasmuch as there can be no time without movement. Time, therefore, is a 'number' [72] of some con-
25 tinuous movement—a 'number', therefore, of the circular move-ment, as was established in the discussions at the beginning.[73] But (*c*) is movement continuous because of the continuity of that which is moved, or because that in which the movement occurs (I mean, e. g., the place or the quality) is continuous? The answer must clearly be 'because that which is moved is continuous'. (For how can the quality be continuous except in virtue of the continuity of the thing to which it belongs? But if the continuity of 'that in which'
30 contributes to make the movement continuous, this is true only of 'the place in which'; for that has 'magnitude' in a sense.) But (*d*) amongst continuous bodies which are moved, only that which is moved in a circle is 'continuous' in such a way that it preserves its continuity with itself throughout the movement. The conclusion therefore is that *this* is what produces continuous movement, viz. the body which is being moved in a circle; and its movement makes time continuous.

11 Wherever there is continuity in any process (coming-to-be or
35 'alteration' or any kind of change whatever) we observe 'consecu-
337b tiveness', i. e. *this* coming-to-be after *that* without any interval. Hence we must investigate whether, amongst the consecutive mem-bers, there is any whose future being is necessary; or whether, on the contrary, every one of them may fail to come-to-be. For that some of them may fail to occur, is clear. (*a*) We need only appeal to the

---

[70] *Physics* 255[b] 31—260[a] 10. Cf. also *Metaph.* 1072[a] 19—1074[b] 14.

[71] i. e. the supposed continuous movements which, *qua* continuous, must be circular.

[72] i. e. time is that which is *numerable* in continuous movement: Cf. *Physics* 219[b] 1–8.

[73] *sc.* at the beginning of Aristotle's 'Philosophy of Nature': cf. *Physics* 217[b] 29—224[a] 17.

distinction between the statements '*x* will be' and '*x* is about to
. . .', which depends upon this fact. For if it be true to say of *x* that
it 'will be', it must at some time be true to say of it that 'it is': 5
whereas, though it be true to say of *x* *now* that 'it is about to occur',
it is quite possible for it not to come-to-be—thus a man might not
walk, though he is now 'about to' walk. And (*b*) since (to appeal to
a general principle) amongst the things which 'are' some are capable
also of 'not-being', it is clear that the same ambiguous character will
attach to them no less when they are coming-to-be: in other words,
their coming-to-be will not be necessary.

Then are all the things that come-to-be of this contingent charac- 10
ter? Or, on the contrary, is it absolutely necessary for some of them
to come-to-be? Is there, in fact, a distinction in the field of 'coming-
to-be' corresponding to the distinction, within the field of 'being',
between things that cannot possibly 'not-be' and things that can 'not-
be'? For instance, is it necessary that solstices shall come-to-be,
i. e. impossible that they should fail to be able to occur?

Assuming that the antecedent must have come-to-be if the consequent is to be (e. g. that foundations must have come-to-be if 15
there is to be a house: clay, if there are to be foundations), is the
converse also true? If foundations have come-to-be, must a house
come-to-be? The answer seems to be that the necessary *nexus* no
longer holds, unless it is 'necessary' for the consequent (as well as for
the antecedent) [74] to come-to-be—'necessary' *absolutely*. If that be
the case, however, 'a house must come-to-be if foundations have
come-to-be', as well as *vice versa*. For the antecedent was assumed to
be so related to the consequent that, if the latter is to be, the antecedent must have come-to-be before it. If, therefore, it is necessary 20
that the consequent should come-to-be, the antecedent also must
have come-to-be: and if the antecedent has come-to-be, then the
consequent also must come-to-be—not, however, because of the antecedent, but because the future being of the consequent was assumed
as necessary. Hence, in any sequence, when the being of the consequent
is necessary, the *nexus* is reciprocal—in other words, when the antecedent has come-to-be the consequent must always come-to-be too. 25

Now (i) if the sequence of occurrences is to proceed *ad infinitum*
'downwards',[75] the coming-to-be of any determinate 'this' amongst
the later members of the sequence will not be *absolutely*, but only
conditionally, necessary. For it will always be necessary that some

---

[74] Cf. above, ^b 14–15: the coming-to-be of the antecedent was *conditionally*
necessary, i. e. necessarily presupposed in the being of the consequent.

[75] i. e. so that effect *will* succeed effect endlessly.

other [76] member shall have come-to-be before 'this' as the presupposed condition of the necessity that 'this' should come-to-be: consequently, since what is 'infinite' has no 'originative source', neither will there be in the infinite sequence any 'primary' member which will make it 'necessary' for the remaining members to come-to-be.

30   Nor again (ii) will it be possible to say with truth, even in regard to the members of a limited sequence, that it is 'absolutely necessary' for any one of them to come-to-be. We cannot truly say, e. g., that 'it is absolutely necessary for a house to come-to-be when foundations have been laid': for (unless it is *always* necessary for a house to be coming-to-be) we should be faced with the consequence that, when foundations have been laid, a thing which need not always be, must always be. No: if its coming-to-be is to be 'necessary', it must
35 be 'always' in its coming-to-be. For what is 'of necessity' coincides
338ᵃ with what is 'always', since that which 'must be' cannot possibly 'not-be'. Hence a thing is eternal if its 'being' is necessary: and if it is eternal, its 'being' is necessary. And if, therefore, the 'coming-to-be' of a thing is necessary, its 'coming-to-be' is eternal; and if eternal, necessary.

It follows that the coming-to-be of anything, if it is absolutely
5 necessary, must be cyclical—i. e. must return upon itself. For coming-to-be must either be limited or not limited: and if not limited, it must be either rectilinear or cyclical. But the first of these last two alternatives is impossible if coming-to-be is to be eternal, because there could not be any 'originative source' whatever in an infinite rectilinear sequence, whether its members be taken 'downwards' (as future events) or 'upwards' (as past events). Yet coming-to-be must have an 'originative source' <if it is to be necessary and therefore
10 eternal>, nor can it be eternal if it is limited. Consequently it must be cyclical. Hence the *nexus* must be reciprocal. By this I mean that the necessary occurrence of 'this' involves the necessary occurrence of its antecedent: and conversely that, given the antecedent, it is also necessary for the consequent to come-to-be. And this reciprocal *nexus* will hold continuously throughout the sequence: for it makes no difference whether the reciprocal *nexus*, of which we are speaking, is mediated by two, or by many, members.

15   It is in circular movement, therefore, and in cyclical coming-to-be that the 'absolutely necessary' is to be found. In other words, if the coming-to-be of any things is cyclical, it is 'necessary' that each of them is coming-to-be and has come-to-be: and if the coming-to-be of any things is 'necessary', their coming-to-be is cyclical.

        [76] i. e. some other *still later* member of the sequence.

The result we have reached is logically concordant with the eternity of circular motion, i.e. the eternity of the revolution of the heavens (a fact which approved itself on other and independent evidence),[77] since precisely those movements which belong to, and depend upon, this eternal revolution 'come-to-be' of necessity, and of necessity 'will be'. For since the revolving body is always setting something else in motion, the movement of the things it moves must also be circular. Thus, from the being of the 'upper revolution' it follows that the sun revolves in this determinate manner; and since the sun revolves *thus*, the seasons in consequence come-to-be in a cycle, i.e. return upon themselves; and since they come-to-be-cyclically, so in their turn do the things whose coming-to-be the seasons initiate.

Then why do some things manifestly come-to-be in this cyclical fashion (as, e.g., showers and air, so that it must rain if there is to be a cloud and, conversely, there must be a cloud if it is to rain), while men and animals do not 'return upon themselves' so that the same individual comes-to-be a second time (for though your coming-to-be presupposes your father's, his coming-to-be does not presuppose yours)? Why, on the contrary, does this coming-to-be seem to constitute a rectilinear sequence?

In discussing this new problem, we must begin by inquiring whether all things 'return upon themselves' in a uniform manner; or whether, on the contrary, though in some sequences what recurs is *numerically* the same, in other sequences it is the same *only in species*.[78] In consequence of this distinction, it is evident that those things, whose 'substance'—that which is undergoing the process—is imperishable, will be numerically, as well as specifically, the same in their recurrence: for the character of the process is determined by the character of that which undergoes it. Those things, on the other hand, whose 'substance' is perishable (not imperishable) must 'return upon themselves' in the sense that what recurs, though specifically the same, is not the same numerically. That is why, when Water comes-to-be from Air and Air from Water, the Air is the same 'specifically', not 'numerically': and if these too recur numerically the same,[79] at any rate this does not happen with things whose 'substance' comes-to-be—whose 'substance' is such that it is essentially capable of not-being.

[77] Cf. *Physics* viii. 7–9.

[78] i.e. in some cycles the same individual eternally recurs: in others the same *species* or *specific form* is eternally represented in the succession of its perishing individual embodiments.

[79] As, e.g., a follower of Empedocles would maintain.

De Anima

Translated by J. A. Smith

CONTENTS

BOOK I

DE ANIMA

(*On the Soul*)

BOOK I

1 Holding as we do that, while knowledge of any kind is a thing 402ᵃ
to be honoured and prized, one kind of it may, either by reason of
its greater exactness or of a higher dignity and greater wonderful-
ness in its objects, be more honourable and precious than another,
on both accounts we should naturally be led to place in the front rank
the study of the soul. The knowledge of the soul admittedly contributes greatly to the advance of truth in general, and, above all, to 5
our understanding of Nature, for the soul is in some sense the principle of animal life. Our aim is to grasp and understand, first its
essential nature, and secondly its properties; of these some are
thought to be affections proper to the soul itself, while others are
considered to attach to the animal¹ owing to the presence within it
of soul.

To attain any assured knowledge about the soul is one of the 10
most difficult things in the world. As the form of question which
here presents itself, viz. the question 'What is it?', recurs in other
fields, it might be supposed that there was some single method of
inquiry applicable to all objects whose essential nature we are 15
endeavouring to ascertain (as there *is* for derived properties the single
method of demonstration); in that case what we should have to seek
for would be this unique method. But if there is no such single and
general method for solving the question of essence, our task becomes still more difficult; in the case of each different subject we
shall have to determine the appropriate process of investigation. If
to this there be a clear answer, e. g. that the process is demonstration
or division, or some other known method, difficulties and hesitations 20
still beset us—with what facts shall we begin the inquiry? For the
facts which form the starting-points in different subjects must be different, as e. g. in the case of numbers and surfaces.

First, no doubt, it is necessary to determine in which of the
summa genera soul lies, what it *is*; is it 'a this-somewhat', a sub-

¹ i. e. the complex of soul and body.

535

stance, or is it a quale or a quantum, or some other of the remaining
25 kinds of predicates which we have distinguished? Further, does soul
belong to the class of potential existents, or is it not rather an actuality? Our answer to this question is of the greatest importance.

402ᵇ   We must consider also whether soul is divisible or is without parts,
and whether it is everywhere homogeneous or not; and if not homogeneous, whether its various forms are different specifically or generically: up to the present time those who have discussed and investi-
5 gated soul seem to have confined themselves to the human soul. We
must be careful not to ignore the question whether soul can be defined in a single unambiguous formula, as is the case with animal, or
whether we must not give a separate formula for each sort of it, as
we do for horse, dog, man, god (in the latter case the 'universal'
animal—and so too every other 'common predicate'—being treated
either as nothing at all or as a later product[2]). Further, if what
exists is not a plurality of souls, but a plurality of parts of one soul,
10 which ought we to investigate first, the whole soul or its parts? (It is
also a difficult problem to decide which of these parts are in nature distinct from one another.) Again, which ought we to investigate first,
these parts or their functions, mind or thinking, the faculty or the act
of sensation, and so on? If the investigation of the functions precedes that of the parts, the further question suggests itself: ought we
15 not before either to consider the correlative objects, e. g. of sense or
thought? It seems not only useful for the discovery of the causes of
the derived properties of substances to be acquainted with the essential nature of those substances (as in mathematics it is useful for the
understanding of the property of the equality of the interior angles of
20 a triangle to two right angles to know the essential nature of the
straight and the curved or of the line and the plane) but also conversely, for the knowledge of the essential nature of a substance is
largely promoted by an acquaintance with its properties: for, when
we are able to give an account conformable to experience of all or
most of the properties of a substance, we shall be in the most favourable position to say something worth saying about the essential nature
25 of that subject; in all demonstration a definition of the essence is
required as a starting-point, so that definitions which do not enable
403ᵃ us to discover the derived properties, or which fail to facilitate even
a conjecture about them, must obviously, one and all, be dialectical
and futile.

A further problem presented by the affections of soul is this: are
they all affections of the complex of body and soul, or is there any one

[2] i. e. as presupposing the various sorts instead of being presupposed by them.

among them peculiar to the soul by itself? To determine this is indispensable but difficult. If we consider the majority of them, there seems to be no case in which the soul can act or be acted upon without involving the body; e. g. anger, courage, appetite, and sensation generally. Thinking seems the most probable exception; but if this too proves to be a form of imagination or to be impossible without imagination, it too requires a body as a condition of its existence. If there is any way of acting or being acted upon proper to soul, soul will be capable of separate existence; if there is none, its separate existence is impossible. In the latter case, it will be like what is straight, which has many properties arising from the straightness in it, e. g. that of touching a bronze sphere at a point, though straightness divorced from the other constituents of the straight thing cannot touch it in this way; it cannot be so divorced at all, since it is always found in a body. It therefore seems that all the affections of soul involve a body—passion, gentleness, fear, pity, courage, joy, loving, and hating; in all these there is a concurrent affection of the body. In support of this we may point to the fact that, while sometimes on the occasion of violent and striking occurrences there is no excitement or fear felt, on others faint and feeble stimulations produce these emotions, viz. when the body is already in a state of tension resembling its condition when we are angry. Here is a still clearer case: in the absence of any external cause of terror we find ourselves experiencing the feelings of a man in terror. From all this it is obvious that the affections of soul are enmattered formulable essences.

Consequently their definitions ought to correspond, e. g. anger should be defined as a certain mode of movement of such and such a body (or part or faculty of a body) by this or that cause and for this or that end. That is precisely why the study of the soul must fall within the science of Nature, at least so far as in its affections it manifests this double character. Hence a physicist would define an affection of soul differently from a dialectician; the latter would define e. g. anger as the appetite for returning pain for pain, or something like that, while the former would define it as a boiling of the blood or warm substance surrounding the heart. The latter assigns the material conditions, the former the form or formulable essence; for what he states is the formulable essence of the fact, though for its actual existence there must be embodiment of it in a material such as is described by the other. Thus the essence of a house is assigned in such a formula as 'a shelter against destruction by wind, rain, and heat'; the physicist would describe it as 'stones, bricks, and timbers'; but there is a third possible description which would say that it was that form in that material with that purpose or end. Which, then, among these is entitled to be regarded as the genuine physicist? The one who confines himself to the material, or the one who restricts himself to the formulable essence alone? Is it not rather the one who combines both in a single formula? If this is so, how are we to characterize the other two? Must we not say that there is no type of thinker who concerns himself with those qualities or attributes of the material which are in fact inseparable from the material, 10 and without attempting even in thought to separate them? The physicist is he who concerns himself with all the properties active and passive of bodies or materials thus or thus defined; attributes not considered as being of this character he leaves to others, in certain cases it may be to a specialist, e. g. a carpenter or a physician, in others (*a*) where they are inseparable in fact, but are separable 15 from any particular kind of body by an effort of abstraction, to the mathematician, (*b*) where they are separate both in fact and in thought from body altogether, to the First Philosopher or metaphysician. But we must return from this digression, and repeat that the affections of soul are inseparable from the material substratum of animal life, to which we have seen that such affections, e. g. passion and fear, attach, and have not the same mode of being as a line or a plane.

20 2   For our study of soul it is necessary, while formulating the problems of which in our further advance we are to find the solutions, to call into council the views of those of our predecessors who have declared any opinion on this subject, in order that we may profit by whatever is sound in their suggestions and avoid their errors.

The starting-point of our inquiry is an exposition of those characteristics which have chiefly been held to belong to soul in its very 25 nature. Two characteristic marks have above all others been recognized as distinguishing that which has soul in it from that which has not—movement and sensation. It may be said that these two are what our predecessors have fixed upon as characteristic of soul.

Some say that what originates movement is both pre-eminently and primarily soul; believing that what is not itself moved cannot 30 originate movement in another, they arrived at the view that soul belongs to the class of things in movement. This is what led 404ᵃ Democritus to say that soul is a sort of fire or hot substance; his 'forms' or atoms are infinite in number; those which are spherical he calls fire and soul, and compares them to the motes in the air which we see in shafts of light coming through windows; the mixture of

seeds of all sorts he calls the elements of the whole of Nature (Leucippus gives a similar account); the spherical atoms are identified 5
with soul because atoms of that shape are most adapted to permeate
everywhere, and to set all the others moving by being themselves in
movement. This implies the view that soul is identical with what
produces movement in animals. That is why, further, they regard
respiration as the characteristic mark of life; as the environment 10
compresses the bodies of animals, and tends to extrude those atoms
which impart movement to them, because they themselves are never at
rest, there must be a reinforcement of these by similar atoms coming
in from without in the act of respiration; for they prevent the extrusion of those which are already within by counteracting the compressing and consolidating force of the environment; and animals continue 15
to live only as long as they are able to maintain this resistance.

The doctrine of the Pythagoreans seems to rest upon the same
ideas; some of them declared the motes in air, others what moved
them, to be soul. These motes were referred to because they are seen
always in movement, even in a complete calm.

The same tendency is shown by those who define soul as that which 20
moves itself; all seem to hold the view that movement is what is
closest to the nature of soul, and that while all else is moved by soul,
it alone moves itself. This belief arises from their never seeing anything originating movement which is not first itself moved.

Similarly also Anaxagoras (and whoever agrees with him in say- 25
ing that mind set the whole in movement) declares the moving cause
of things to be soul. His position must, however, be distinguished from
that of Democritus. Democritus roundly identifies soul and mind, for
he identifies what appears with what is true—that is why he commends Homer for the phrase 'Hector lay with thought distraught' [3];
he does not employ mind as a special faculty dealing with truth, but 30
identifies soul and mind. What Anaxagoras says about them is more 404ᵇ
obscure; in many places he tells us that the cause of beauty and order
is mind, elsewhere that it is soul; it is found, he says, in all animals,
great and small, high and low, but mind (in the sense of intelli- 5
gence) appears not to belong alike to all animals, and indeed not
even to all human beings.

All those, then, who had special regard to the fact that what has
soul in it is moved, adopted the view that soul is to be identified with
what is eminently originative of movement. All, on the other hand,
who looked to the fact that what has soul in it knows or perceives
what is, identify soul with the principle or principles of Nature, 10

[3] II. xxiii. 698.

according as they admit several such principles or one only. Thus Empedocles declares that it is formed out of all his elements, each of them also being soul; his words are:

> For 'tis by Earth we see Earth, by Water Water,
> By Ether Ether divine, by Fire destructive Fire,
15   By Love Love, and Hate by cruel Hate.

In the same way Plato in the *Timaeus* [4] fashions the soul out of his elements; for like, he holds, is known by like, and things are formed out of the principles or elements, so that soul must be so too. Simi-
20 larly also in his lectures 'On Philosophy' it was set forth that the Animal-itself is compounded of the Idea itself of the One together with the primary length, breadth, and depth, everything else, the objects of its perception, being similarly constituted. Again he puts his view in yet other terms: Mind is the monad, science or knowl-edge the dyad (because [5] it goes undeviatingly from one point to another), opinion the number of the plane,[6] sensation the number of the solid [7]; the numbers are by him expressly identified with the Forms themselves or principles, and are formed out of the elements;
25 now things are apprehended either by mind or science or opinion or sensation, and these same numbers are the Forms of things.

Some thinkers, accepting both premisses, viz. that the soul is both originative of movement and cognitive, have compounded it of both and declared the soul to be a self-moving number.

30   As to the nature and number of the first principles opinions dif-fer. The difference is greatest between those who regard them as corporeal and those who regard them as incorporeal, and from both
405ᵃ dissent those who make a blend and draw their principles from both sources. The number of principles is also in dispute; some admit one only, others assert several. There is a consequent diversity in their several accounts of soul; they assume, naturally enough, that what
5 is in its own nature originative of movement must be among what is primordial. That has led some to regard it as fire, for fire is the subtlest of the elements and nearest to incorporeality; further, in the most primary sense, fire both is moved and originates movement in all the others.

Democritus has expressed himself more ingeniously than the rest on the grounds for ascribing each of these two characters to soul;
10 soul and mind are, he says, one and the same thing, and this thing must be one of the primary and indivisible bodies, and its power of

---

[4] 35 A ff.   [5] Like the straight line, whose number is the dyad.
[6] The triad.   [7] The tetrad.

originating movement must be due to its fineness of grain and the shape of its atoms; he says that of all the shapes the spherical is the most mobile, and that this is the shape of the particles of both fire and mind.

Anaxagoras, as we said above,[8] seems to distinguish between soul and mind, but in practice he treats them as a single substance, except that it is mind that he specially posits as the principle of 15 all things; at any rate what he says is that mind alone of all that is is simple, unmixed, and pure. He assigns both characteristics, knowing and origination of movement, to the same principle, when he says that it was mind that set the whole in movement.

Thales, too, to judge from what is recorded about him, seems 20 to have held soul to be a motive force, since he said that the magnet has a soul in it because it moves the iron.

Diogenes (and others) held the soul to be air because he believed air to be finest in grain and a first principle; therein lay the grounds of the soul's powers of knowing and originating movement. As the primordial principle from which all other things are derived, it is cognitive; as finest in grain, it has the power to originate movement.

Heraclitus too says that the first principle—the 'warm exhalation' 25 of which, according to him, everything else is composed—is soul; further, that this exhalation is most incorporeal and in ceaseless flux; that what is in movement requires that what knows it should be in movement; and that all that is has its being essentially in movement (herein agreeing with the majority).

Alcmaeon also seems to have held a similar view about soul; he says that it is immortal because it resembles 'the immortals', and that 30 this immortality belongs to it in virtue of its ceaseless movement; for all the 'things divine', moon, sun, the planets, and the whole heavens, are in perpetual movement.

Of more superficial writers, some, e. g. Hippo, have pronounced 405[b] it to be water; they seem to have argued from the fact that the seed of all animals is fluid, for Hippo tries to refute those who say that the soul is blood, on the ground that the seed, which is the primordial soul, is not blood.

Another group (Critias, for example) did hold it to be blood; they 5 take perception to be the most characteristic attribute of soul, and hold that perceptiveness is due to the nature of blood.

Each of the elements has thus found its partisan, except earth— earth has found no supporter unless we count as such those who have declared soul to be, or to be compounded of, *all* the elements. All, 10

_____
[8] 404[b] 1–6.

then, it may be said, characterize the soul by three marks, Movement, Sensation, Incorporeality, and each of these is traced back to the first principles. That is why (with one exception) all those who define the soul by its power of knowing make it either an element or constructed out of the elements. The language they all use is simi-
15 lar; like, they say, is known by like; as the soul knows everything, they construct it out of all the principles. Hence all those who admit but one cause or element, make the soul also one (e.g. fire or air), while those who admit a multiplicity of principles make the soul also
20 multiple. The exception is Anaxagoras; he alone says that mind is impassible and has nothing in common with anything else. But, if this is so, how or in virtue of what cause can it know? That Anaxagoras has not explained, nor can any answer be inferred from his words. All who acknowledge pairs of opposites among their principles, construct the soul also out of these contraries, while those who
25 admit as principles only one contrary of each pair, e.g. either hot or cold, likewise make the soul some one of these. That is why, also, they allow themselves to be guided by the names; those who identify soul with the hot argue that *zen* (to live) is derived from *zein* (to boil), while those who identify it with the cold say that soul (*psyche*) is so called from the process of respiration and refrigeration (*katapsyxis*).
30 Such are the traditional opinions concerning soul, together with the grounds on which they are maintained.

3 We must begin our examination with movement; for, doubtless, not only is it false that the essence of soul is correctly described
406ª by those who say that it is what moves (or is capable of moving) itself, but it is an impossibility that movement should be even an attribute of it.

We have already [9] pointed out that there is no necessity that what originates movement should itself be moved. There are two senses in which anything may be moved—either (*a*) indirectly, owing to some-
5 thing other than itself, or (*b*) directly, owing to itself. Things are 'indirectly moved' which are moved as being contained in something which is moved, e.g. sailors in a ship, for they are moved in a different sense from that in which the ship is moved; the ship is 'directly moved', they are 'indirectly moved', because they are in a moving vessel. This is clear if we consider their limbs; the movement proper to the legs (and so to man) is walking, and in this case the sailors
10 are not walking. Recognizing the double sense of 'being moved', what

[9] *Phys.* viii. 5, esp. 257ª 31–258ᵇ 9.

we have to consider now is whether the soul is 'directly moved' and participates in such direct movement.

There are four species of movement—locomotion, alteration, diminution, growth; consequently if the soul is moved, it must be moved with one or several or all of these species of movement. Now if its movement is not incidental, there must be a movement natural 15 to it, and, if so, as all the species enumerated involve place, place must be natural to it. But if the essence of soul be to move itself, its being moved cannot be incidental to it, as it is to what is white or three cubits long; they too can be moved, but only incidentally—what is moved is that of which 'white' and 'three cubits long' are the attributes, the body in which they inhere; hence *they* have no place: but 20 if the soul naturally partakes in movement, it follows that it must have a place.

Further, if there be a movement natural to the soul, there must be a counter-movement unnatural to it, and conversely. The same applies to rest as well as to movement; for the *terminus ad quem* of a thing's natural movement is the place of its natural rest, and similarly 25 the *terminus ad quem* of its enforced movement is the place of its enforced rest. But what meaning can be attached to enforced movements or rests of the soul, it is difficult even to imagine.

Further, if the natural movement of the soul be upward, the soul must be fire; if downward, it must be earth; for upward and downward movements are the definitory characteristics of these bodies. The same reasoning applies to the intermediate movements, *termini*, and bodies. Further, since the soul is observed to originate move- 30 ment in the body, it is reasonable to suppose that it transmits to the body the movements by which it itself is moved, and so, reversing the order, we may infer from the movements of the body back to similar movements of the soul. Now the body is moved from place to place 406ᵇ with movements of locomotion. Hence it would follow that the soul too must in accordance with the body change either its place as a whole or the relative places of its parts. This carries with it the possibility that the soul might even quit its body and re-enter it, and with this would be involved the possibility of a resurrection of animals from the dead. But, it may be contended, the soul can be 5 moved indirectly by something else; for an animal can be pushed out of its course. Yes, but that to whose *essence* belongs the power of being moved by itself, cannot be moved by something else except incidentally,[10] just as what is good by or in itself cannot owe its good-

10 i. e. so that what is moved is not it but something which 'goes along with it', e. g. a vehicle in which it is contained.

ness to something external to it or to some end to which it is a means.

10 If the soul *is* moved, the most probable view is that what moves it is sensible things.[11]

We must note also that, if the soul moves itself, it must be the mover itself that is moved, so that it follows that if movement is in every case a displacement of that which is in movement, in that respect in which it is said to be moved, the movement of the soul must be a departure from its essential nature, at least if its self-movement is essential to it, not incidental.

15 Some go so far as to hold that the movements which the soul imparts to the body in which it is are the same in kind as those with which it itself is moved. An example of this is Democritus, who uses language like that of the comic dramatist Philippus, who accounts for the movements that Daedalus imparted to his wooden Aphrodite by saying that he poured quicksilver into it; similarly Democritus

20 says that the spherical atoms which according to him constitute soul, owing to their own ceaseless movements draw the whole body after them and so produce its movements. We must urge the question whether it is these very same atoms which produce rest also—how they could do so, it is difficult and even impossible to say. And, in general, we may object that it is not in this way that the soul appears

25 to originate movement in animals—it is through intention or process of thinking.

It is in the same fashion that the *Timaeus*[12] also tries to give a physical account of how the soul moves its body; the soul, it is here said, is in movement, and so owing to their mutual implication moves the body also. After compounding the soul-substance out of the elements and dividing it in accordance with the harmonic numbers, in order

30 that it may possess a connate sensibility for 'harmony' and that the whole may move in movements well attuned, the Demiurge bent the straight line into a circle; this single circle he divided into two circles

407ᵃ united at two common points; one of these he subdivided into seven circles. All this implies that the movements of the soul are identified with the local movements of the heavens.

Now, in the first place, it is a mistake to say that the soul is a spatial magnitude. It is evident that Plato means the soul of the whole

5 to be like the sort of soul which is called mind—not like the sensitive or the desiderative soul, for the movements of neither of these are circular. Now mind is one and continuous in the sense in which the

[11] *sc.* in which case the movement can only be 'incidental'; for, as we shall see later, it is really the bodily organ of sensation that then is 'moved'.

[12] 35 ᴀ ff.

process of thinking is so, and thinking is identical with the thoughts which are its parts; these have a serial unity like that of number, not a unity like that of a spatial magnitude. Hence mind cannot have that kind of unity either; mind is either without parts or is continuous in some other way than that which characterizes a spatial magnitude. How, indeed, if it were a spatial magnitude, could mind possibly 10 think? Will it think with any one indifferently of its parts? In this case, the 'part' must be understood either in the sense of a spatial magnitude or in the sense of a point (if a point *can* be called a part of a spatial magnitude). If we accept the latter alternative, the points being infinite in number, obviously the mind can never exhaustively traverse them; if the former, the mind must think the same thing over and over again, indeed an infinite number of times (whereas it is manifestly possible to think a thing once only). If contact of any part 15 whatsoever of itself with the object is all that is required, why need mind move in a circle, or indeed possess magnitude at all? On the other hand, if contact with the whole circle is necessary, what meaning can be given to the contact of the parts? Further, how could what has no parts think what has parts, or what has parts think what has none? [13] We must identify the circle referred to with mind; for it is mind whose movement is thinking, and it is the circle whose 20 movement is revolution, so that if thinking is a movement of revolution, the circle which has this characteristic movement must be mind.

If the circular movement is eternal, there must be something which mind is always thinking—what *can* this be? For all practical processes of thinking have limits—they all go on for the sake of something outside the process, and all theoretical processes come to a close in the same way as the phrases in speech which express processes and results of thinking. Every such linguistic phrase is either definitory or 25 demonstrative. Demonstration has both a starting-point and may be said to end in a conclusion or inferred result; even if the process never reaches final completion, at any rate it never returns upon itself again to its starting-point, it goes on assuming a fresh middle term or a fresh extreme, and moves straight forward, but circular movement returns to its starting-point. Definitions, too, are closed groups of terms.　30

Further, if the same revolution is repeated, mind must repeatedly think the same object.

Further, thinking has more resemblance to a coming to rest or arrest than to a movement; the same may be said of inferring.

It might also be urged that what is difficult and enforced is incompatible with blessedness; if the movement of the soul is not of its 407ᵇ

13 *sc.* but mind in fact thinks or cognizes both.

essence, movement of the soul must be contrary to its nature.[14] It must also be painful for the soul to be inextricably bound up with the body; nay more, if, as is frequently said and widely accepted, it is better for mind not to be embodied, the union must be for it undesirable.

5   Further, the cause of the revolution of the heavens is left obscure. It is not the essence of soul which is the cause of this circular movement—that movement is only incidental to soul—nor is, a fortiori, the body its cause. Again, it is not even asserted that it is better that soul should be so moved; and yet the reason for which God caused the soul to move in a circle can only have been that movement was better for it than rest, and movement of this kind better than any other. But since this sort of consideration is more appropriate to another field of speculation, let us dismiss it for the present.

The view we have just been examining, in company with most theories about the soul, involves the following absurdity: they all join the soul to a body, or place it in a body, without adding any specification of the reason of their union, or of the bodily conditions required for it. Yet such explanation can scarcely be omitted; for some community of nature is presupposed by the fact that the one acts and the other is acted upon, the one moves and the other is moved; interaction always implies a *special* nature in the two interagents. All, however, that these thinkers do is to describe the specific characteristics of the soul; they do not try to determine anything about the body which is to contain it, as if it were possible, as in the Pythagorean myths, that any soul could be clothed upon with any body—an absurd view, for each body seems to have a form and shape of its own. It is as absurd as to say that the art of carpentry could embody itself in flutes; each art must use its tools, each soul its body.

4   There is yet another theory about soul, which has commended itself to many as no less probable than any of those we have hitherto mentioned, and has rendered public account of itself in the court of popular discussion. Its supporters say that the soul is a kind of harmony, for (a) harmony is a blend or composition of contraries, and (b) the body is compounded out of contraries. Harmony, however, is a certain proportion or composition of the constituents blended, and soul can be neither the one nor the other of these. Further, the power of originating movement cannot belong to a harmony, while almost all concur in regarding this as a principal attribute of soul. It 408ᵃ is more appropriate to call health (or generally one of the good

14 *sc.* 'and so a hindrance to its bliss'.

states of the body) a harmony than to predicate it of the soul. The absurdity becomes most apparent when we try to attribute the active and passive affections of the soul to a harmony; the necessary readjustment of their conceptions is difficult. Further, in using the word 'harmony' we have one or other of two cases in our mind; the most proper sense is in relation to spatial magnitudes which have motion and position, where harmony means the disposition and cohesion of their parts in such a manner as to prevent the introduction into the whole of anything homogeneous with it, and the secondary sense, derived from the former, is that in which it means the ratio between the constituents so blended; in neither of these senses is it plausible to predicate it of soul. That soul is a harmony in the sense of the mode of composition of the parts of the body is a view easily refutable; for there are many composite parts and those variously compounded; of what bodily part is mind or the sensitive or the appetitive faculty the mode of composition? And what *is* the mode of composition which constitutes each of them? It is equally absurd to identify the soul with the ratio of the mixture; for the mixture which makes flesh has a different ratio between the elements from that which makes bone. The consequence of this view will therefore be that distributed throughout the whole body there will be many souls, since every one of the bodily parts is a different mixture of the elements, and the ratio of mixture is in each case a harmony, i. e. a soul.

From Empedocles at any rate we might demand an answer to the following question—for he says that each of the parts of the body is what it is in virtue of a ratio between the elements: is the soul identical with this ratio, or is it not rather something over and above this which is formed in the parts? Is love the cause of any and every mixture, or only of those that are in the right ratio? Is love this ratio itself, or is love something over and above this? Such are the problems raised by this account. But, on the other hand, if the soul is different from the mixture, why does it disappear at one and the same moment with that relation between the elements which constitutes flesh or the other parts of the animal body? Further, if the soul is not identical with the ratio of mixture, and it is consequently not the case that each of the parts has a soul, what is that which perishes when the soul quits the body?

That the soul cannot either be a harmony, or be moved in a circle, is clear from what we have said. Yet that it can be moved incidentally is, as we said above,[15] possible, and even that in a sense it can move itself, i. e. in the sense that *the vehicle* in which it is can be moved,

[15] 406ᵃ 30 ff., ᵇ5–8.

and moved by it; in no other sense can the soul be moved in space. More legitimate doubts might remain as to its movement in view of 408ᵇ the following facts. We speak of the soul as being pained or pleased, being bold or fearful, being angry, perceiving, thinking. All these are regarded as modes of movement, and hence it might be inferred that the soul is moved. This, however, does not necessarily follow. We may 5 admit to the full that being pained or pleased, or thinking, are movements (each of them a 'being moved'), and that the movement is originated by the soul. For example we may regard anger or fear as such and such movements of the heart, and thinking as such and such another movement of that organ, or of some other; these modifications may arise either from changes of place in certain parts or from 10 qualitative alterations (the special nature of the parts and the special modes of their changes being for our present purpose irrelevant). Yet to say that it is *the soul* which is angry is as inexact as it would be to say that it is the soul that weaves webs or builds houses. It is doubtless better to avoid saying that the soul pities or learns or thinks, and 15 rather to say that it is the man who does this with his soul. What we mean is not that the movement is in the soul, but that sometimes it terminates in the soul and sometimes starts from it, sensation e. g. coming from without inwards, and reminiscence starting from the soul and terminating with the movements, actual or residual, in the sense organs.

The case of mind is different; it seems to be an independent substance implanted within the soul and to be incapable of being destroyed. If it could be destroyed at all, it would be under the blunting 20 influence of old age. What really happens in respect of mind in old age is, however, exactly parallel to what happens in the case of the sense organs; if the old man could recover the proper kind of eye, he would see just as well as the young man. The incapacity of old age is due to an affection not of the soul but of its vehicle, as occurs in drunkenness or disease. Thus it is that in old age the activity of mind or intellectual apprehension declines only through the decay of some 25 other inward part; mind itself is impassible. Thinking, loving, and hating are affections not of mind, but of that which has mind, so far as it has it. That is why, when this vehicle decays, memory and love cease; they were activities not of mind, but of the composite which has perished; mind is, no doubt, something more divine and impassible. 30 That the soul cannot be moved is therefore clear from what we have said, and if it cannot be moved at all, manifestly it cannot be moved by itself.

Of all the opinions we have enumerated, by far the most unrea-

sonable is that which declares the soul to be a self-moving number; it
involves in the first place all the impossibilities which follow from regarding the soul as moved, and in the second special absurdities 409^a
which follow from calling it a number. How are we to imagine a unit
being moved? By what agency? What sort of movement can be
attributed to what is without parts or internal differences? If the unit
is both originative of movement and itself capable of being moved, it
must contain difference.[16]

Further, since they say a moving line generates a surface and a
moving point a line, the movements of the psychic units must be 5
lines (for a point is a unit having position, and the number of the
soul is, of course, somewhere and has position).

Again, if from a number a number or a unit is subtracted, the remainder is another number; but plants and many animals when
divided continue to live, and each segment is thought to retain the
same kind of soul.

It must be all the same whether we speak of units or corpuscles; 10
for if the spherical atoms of Democritus became points, nothing being
retained but their being a quantum, there must remain in each a moving and a moved part, just as there is in what is continuous; what happens has nothing to do with the size of the atoms, it depends solely
upon their being a quantum. That is why there must be something to 15
originate movement in the units. If in the animal what originates
movement is the soul, so also must it be in the case of the number,
so that not the mover and the moved together, but the mover only,
will be the soul. But how is it possible for one of the units to fulfil this
function of originating movement? There must be *some* difference
between such a unit and all the other units, and what difference can 20
there be between one placed unit and another except a difference of
position? If then, on the other hand, these psychic units within the
body are different from the points *of* the body, there will be two sets
of units both occupying the same place; for each unit will occupy a
point. And yet, if there can be two, why cannot there be an infinite
number? For if things can occupy an indivisible place, they must
themselves be indivisible. If, on the other hand, the points of the 25
body are identical with the units whose number is the soul, or if the
number of the points in the body is the soul, why have not all bodies
souls? For all bodies contain points or an infinity of points.

Further, how is it possible for these points to be isolated or separated from their bodies, seeing that lines cannot be resolved into 30
points?

[16] *sc.* 'and so, be no unit'.

5 The result is, as we have said,[17] that this view, while on the one side identical with that of those who maintain that soul is a subtle kind of body,[18] is on the other entangled in the absurdity peculiar to Democritus' way of describing the manner in which movement is originated by soul. For if the soul is present throughout the whole percipient body, there must, if the soul be a kind of body, be two bodies in the same place; and for those who call it a number, there must be many points at one point, or every body must have a soul, unless the soul be a different sort of number—other, that is, than the sum of the points existing in a body. Another consequence that follows is that the animal must be moved by its number precisely in the way that Democritus explained its being moved by his spherical psychic atoms. What difference does it make whether we speak of small spheres or of large [19] units, or, quite simply, of units in movement? One way or another, the movements of the animal must be due to their movements. Hence those who combine movement and number in the same subject lay themselves open to these and many other similar absurdities. It is impossible not only that these characters should give the definition of soul—it is impossible that they should even be attributes of it. The point is clear if the attempt be made to start from this as the account of soul and explain from it the affections and actions of the soul, e. g. reasoning, sensation, pleasure, pain, &c. For, to repeat what we have said earlier,[20] movement and number do not facilitate even conjecture about the derivative properties of soul.

Such are the three ways in which soul has traditionally been defined; one group of thinkers declared it to be that which is most originative of movement because it moves itself, another group to be the subtlest and most nearly incorporeal of all kinds of body. We have now sufficiently set forth the difficulties and inconsistencies to which these theories are exposed. It remains now to examine the doctrine that soul is composed of the elements.

The reason assigned for this doctrine is that thus the soul may perceive or come to know everything that is, but the theory necessarily involves itself in many impossibilities. Its upholders assume that like is known only by like, and imagine that by declaring the soul to be composed of the elements they succeed in identifying the soul with all the things it is capable of apprehending. But the elements are not the only things it knows; there are many others, or, more exactly, an infinite number of others, formed out of the elements. Let us admit that the soul knows or perceives the elements out of which

409ᵇ

---

[17] 408ᵇ 33 ff.
[18] e. g. Heraclitus, and Diogenes of Apollonia.
[19] i. e. extended.
[20] 402ᵇ 25–403ᵃ 2.

each of these composites is made up; but by what means will it know
or perceive the composite whole, e. g. what God, man, flesh, bone (or
any other compound) is? For each *is*, not merely the elements of 410ᵃ
which it is composed, but those elements combined in a determinate
mode or ratio, as Empedocles himself says of bone,

> The kindly Earth in its broad-bosomed moulds
> Won of clear Water two parts out of eight   5
> And four of Fire; and so white bones were formed.

Nothing, therefore, will be gained by the presence of the elements
in the soul, unless there be also present there the various formulae of
proportion and the various compositions in accordance with them.
Each element will indeed know its fellow outside, but there will be no
knowledge of bone or man, unless they too are present in the constitution of the soul. The impossibility of this needs no pointing out; for 10
who would suggest that stone or man could enter into the constitution
of the soul? The same applies to 'the good' and 'the not-good', and so
on.

Further, the word 'is' has many meanings: it may be used of a 'this'
or substance, or of a quantum, or of a quale, or of any other of the
kinds of predicates we have distinguished. Does the soul consist of
all of these or not? It does not appear that all have common ele- 15
ments. Is the soul formed out of those elements alone which enter into
substances? If so, how will it be able to know each of the other kinds
of thing? Will it be said that each kind of thing has elements or principles of its own, and that the soul is formed out of the whole of these?
In that case, the soul must be a quantum *and* a quale *and* a substance. 20
But all that can be made out of the elements of a quantum is a quantum,
not a substance. These (and others like them) are the consequences of
the view that the soul is composed of all the elements.

It is absurd, also, to say both (*a*) that like is not capable of
being affected by like, and (*b*) that like is perceived or known by
like, for perceiving, and also both thinking and knowing, are, on 25
their own assumption, ways of being affected or moved.

There are many puzzles and difficulties raised by saying, as Empedocles does, that each set of things is known by means of its corporeal
elements and by reference to something in soul which is like them,
and additional testimony is furnished by this new consideration; 30
for all the parts of the animal body which consist wholly of earth such
as bones, sinews, and hair seem to be wholly insensitive and conse- 410ᵇ
quently not perceptive even of objects earthy like themselves, as
they ought to have been.

Further, each of the principles will have far more ignorance than knowledge, for though each of them will know one thing, there will be many of which it will be ignorant. Empedocles at any rate
5 must conclude that his God is the least intelligent of· all beings, for of him alone is it true that there is one thing, Strife, which he does not know, while there is nothing which mortal beings do not know, for there is nothing which does not enter into their composition.

In general, we may ask, Why has not everything a soul, since everything either is an element, or is formed out of one or several or all of the elements? Each must certainly know one or several or all.
10   The problem might also be raised, What is that which unifies the elements into a soul? The elements correspond, it would appear, to the matter; what unites them, whatever it is, is the supremely important factor. But it is impossible that there should be something superior to, and dominant over, the soul (and *a fortiori* over the mind); it is reasonable to hold that mind is by nature most primordial and
15 dominant, while their statement is that it is the elements which are first of all that is.

All, both those who assert that the soul, because of its knowledge or perception of what is, is compounded out of the elements, and those who assert that it is of all things the most originative of movement, fail to take into consideration all kinds of soul. In fact (1) not all beings that perceive can originate movement; there appear to be
20 certain animals which are stationary, and yet local movement is the only one, so it seems, which the soul originates in animals. And (2) the same objection holds against all those who construct mind and the perceptive faculty out of the elements; for it appears that plants live, and yet are not endowed with locomotion or perception, while a large number of animals are without discourse of reason. Even if these points were waived and mind admitted to be a part of the soul (and
25 so too the perceptive faculty), still, even so, there would be kinds and parts of soul of which they had failed to give any account.

The same objection lies against the view expressed in the 'Orphic' poems: there it is said that the soul comes in from the whole when
30 breathing takes place, being borne in upon the winds. Now this cannot take place in the case of plants, nor indeed in the case of cer-
411ᵃ tain classes of animal, for not all classes of animal breathe. This fact has escaped the notice of the holders of this view.

If we must construct the soul out of the elements, there is no necessity to suppose that *all* the elements enter into its construction; one element in each pair of contraries will suffice to enable it to know

both that element itself and its contrary. By means of the straight line
we know both itself and the curved—the carpenter's rule enables 5
us to test both—but what is curved does not enable us to distinguish
either itself or the straight.

Certain thinkers say that soul is intermingled in the whole universe,
and it is perhaps for that reason that Thales came to the opinion
that all things are full of gods. This presents some difficulties: Why
does the soul when it resides in air or fire not form an animal, while it 10
does so when it resides in mixtures of the elements, and that although
it is held to be of higher quality when contained in the former?
(One might add the question, why the soul in air is maintained to be
higher and more immortal than that in animals.) Both possible ways
of replying to the former question lead to absurdity or paradox;
for it is beyond paradox to say that fire or air is an animal, and it is 15
absurd to refuse the name of animal to what has soul in it. The opinion
that the elements have soul in them seems to have arisen from the
doctrine that a whole must be homogeneous with its parts. If it is true
that animals become animate by drawing into themselves a portion of
what surrounds them, the partisans of this view are bound to say
that the soul of the Whole too is homogeneous with all its parts. If the
air sucked in is homogeneous, but soul heterogeneous, clearly while 20
some part of soul will exist in the inbreathed air, some other part will
not. The soul must either be homogeneous, or such that there are
some parts of the Whole in which it is not to be found.

From what has been said it is now clear that knowing as an attribute of soul cannot be explained by soul's being composed of the elements, and that it is neither sound nor true to speak of soul as moved. 25
But since (a) knowing, perceiving, opining, and further (b) desiring,
wishing, and generally all other modes of appetition, belong to soul,
and (c) the local movements of animals, and (d) growth, maturity, 30
and decay are produced by the soul, we must ask whether each of
these is an attribute of the soul as a whole, i. e. whether it is with 411ᵇ
the whole soul we think, perceive, move ourselves, act or are acted
upon, or whether each of them requires a different part of the soul?
So too with regard to life. Does it depend on one of the parts of
soul? Or is it dependent on more than one? Or on all? Or has it some
quite other cause?

Some hold that the soul is divisible, and that one part thinks, 5
another desires. If, then, its nature admits of its being divided, what
can it be that holds the parts together? Surely not the body; on the
contrary it seems rather to be the soul that holds the body together;

at any rate when the soul departs the body disintegrates and decays.
If, then, there is something else which makes the soul one, this unify-
10 ing agency would have the best right to the name of soul, and we shall
have to repeat for it the question: Is *it* one or multipartite? If it is one,
why not at once admit that 'the soul' is one? If it has parts, once
more the question must be put: What holds *its* parts together, and so
ad infinitum?

The question might also be raised about the parts of the soul: What
is the separate rôle of each in relation to the body? For, if the whole
15 soul holds together the whole body, we should expect each part of the
soul to hold together a part of the body. But this seems an impossibility; it is difficult even to imagine what sort of bodily part
mind will hold together, or how it will do this.

It is a fact of observation that plants and certain insects go on liv-
20 ing when divided into segments; this means that each of the segments
has a soul in it identical in species, though not numerically identical
in the different segments, for both of the segments for a time possess
the power of sensation and local movement. That this does not last
is not surprising, for they no longer possess the organs necessary for
self-maintenance. But, all the same, in each of the bodily parts there
25 are present all the parts of soul, and the souls so present are homogeneous with one another and with the whole; this means that the
several parts of the soul are indisseverable from one another, although
the whole soul is [21] divisible. It seems also that the principle found in
plants is also a kind of soul; for this is the only principle which is
common to both animals and plants; and this exists in isolation
30 from the principle of sensation, though there is nothing which has the
latter without the former.

BOOK II

412ª 1   Let the foregoing suffice as our account of the views concerning the
soul which have been handed on by our predecessors; let us now dismiss them and make as it were a completely fresh start, endeavouring
5 to give a precise answer to the question, What is soul? i. e. to formulate the most general possible definition of it.

We are in the habit of recognizing, as one determinate kind of
what is, substance, and that in several senses, (*a*) in the sense of matter or that which in itself is not 'a this', and (*b*) in the sense of form
or essence, which is that precisely in virtue of which a thing is called
'a this', and thirdly (*c*) in the sense of that which is compounded of

[21] *sc.* 'in a sense, i. e. so as to preserve its homogeneity in even its smallest part'.

both (*a*) and (*b*). Now matter is potentiality, form actuality; of the 10 latter there are two grades related to one another as e. g. knowledge to the exercise of knowledge.

Among substances are by general consent reckoned bodies and especially natural bodies; for they are the principles of all other bodies. Of natural bodies some have life in them, others not; by life we mean self-nutrition and growth (with its correlative decay). It 15 follows that every natural body which has life in it is a substance in the sense of a composite.

But since it is also a *body* of such and such a kind, viz. having life, the *body* cannot be soul; the body is the subject or matter, not what is attributed to it. Hence the soul must be a substance in the 20 sense of the form of a natural body having life potentially within it. But substance [1] is actuality, and thus soul is the actuality of a body as above characterized. Now the word actuality has two senses corresponding respectively to the possession of knowledge and the actual exercise of knowledge. It is obvious that the soul is actuality in the first sense, viz. that of knowledge as possessed, for both sleeping and waking presuppose the existence of soul, and of these waking corre- 25 sponds to actual knowing, sleeping to knowledge possessed but not employed, and, in the history of the individual, knowledge comes before its employment or exercise.

That is why the soul is the first grade of actuality of a natural body having life potentially in it. The body so described is a body which is organized. The parts of plants in spite of their extreme simplicity 412ᵇ are 'organs'; e. g. the leaf serves to shelter the pericarp, the pericarp to shelter the fruit, while the roots of plants are analogous to the mouth of animals, both serving for the absorption of food. If, then, we have to give a general formula applicable to all kinds of soul, we must describe it as the first grade of actuality of a 5 natural organized body. That is why we can wholly dismiss as unnecessary the question whether the soul and the body are one: it is as meaningless as to ask whether the wax and the shape given to it by the stamp are one, or generally the matter of a thing and that of which it is the matter. Unity has many senses (as many as 'is' has), but the most proper and fundamental sense of both is the relation of an actuality to that of which it is the actuality.

We have now given an answer to the question, What is soul?—an 10 answer which applies to it in its full extent. It is substance in the sense which corresponds to the definitive formula of a thing's essence. That means that it is 'the essential whatness' of a body of the character just

---

[1] *sc.* in the sense of form.

assigned.[2] Suppose that what is literally an 'organ',[3] like an axe, were a *natural* body, its 'essential whatness', would have been its essence, and so its soul; if this disappeared from it, it would have ceased to
15 be an axe, except in name. As it is,[4] it is just an axe; it wants the character which is required to make its whatness or formulable essence a soul; for that, it would have had to be a *natural* body of a particular kind, viz. one having *in itself* the power of setting itself in movement and arresting itself. Next, apply this doctrine in the case of the 'parts' of the living body. Suppose that the eye were an animal—sight would have been its soul, for sight is the substance
20 or essence of the eye which corresponds to the formula,[5] the eye being merely the matter of seeing; when seeing is removed the eye is no longer an eye, except in name—it is no more a real eye than the eye of a statue or of a painted figure. We must now extend our consideration from the 'parts' to the whole living body; for what the departmental sense is to the bodily part which is its organ, that the whole faculty of sense is to the whole sensitive body as such.

25 We must not understand by that which is 'potentially capable of living' what has lost the soul it had, but only what still retains it; but seeds and fruits are bodies which possess the qualification.[6] Consequently, while waking is actuality in a sense corresponding to
413ᵃ the cutting and the seeing,[7] the soul is actuality in the sense corresponding to the power of sight and the power in the tool;[8] the body corresponds to what exists in potentiality; as the pupil *plus* the power of sight constitutes the eye, so the soul *plus* the body constitutes the animal.

From this it indubitably follows that the soul is inseparable from its body, or at any rate that certain parts of it are (if it has parts)—
5 for the actuality of some of them is nothing but the actualities of their bodily parts. Yet some may be separable because they are not the actualities of any body at all. Further, we have no light on the problem whether the soul may not be the actuality of its body in the sense in which the sailor is the actuality[9] of the ship.

This must suffice as our sketch or outline determination of the
10 nature of soul.

---

[2] viz. organized, or possessed potentially of life.   [3] i. e. instrument.
[4] Being an artificial, not a natural, body.
[5] i. e. which states what it is to be an eye.
[6] Though only potentially, i. e. they are at a further remove from actuality than the fully formed and organized body.
[7] i. e. to the second grade of actuality.   [8] i. e. to the first grade of actuality.
[9] i. e. actuator.

2   Since what is clear or logically more evident emerges from what
in itself is confused but more observable by us, we must reconsider
our results from this point of view. For it is not enough for a definitive
formula to express as most now do the mere fact; it must include 15
and exhibit the ground also. At present definitions are given in a
form analogous to the conclusion of a syllogism; e. g. What is squaring? The construction of an equilateral rectangle equal to a given
oblong rectangle. Such a definition is in form equivalent to a conclusion.[10] One that tells us that squaring is the discovery of a line
which is a mean proportional between the two unequal sides of the
given rectangle discloses the ground of what is defined.

We resume our inquiry from a fresh starting-point by calling 20
attention to the fact that what has soul in it differs from what has
not in that the former displays life. Now this word has more than
one sense, and provided any one alone of these is found in a thing we
say that thing is living. Living, that is, may mean thinking or perception or local movement and rest, or movement in the sense of
nutrition, decay and growth. Hence we think of plants also as liv- 25
ing, for they are observed to possess in themselves an originative
power through which they increase or decrease in all spatial directions; they grow up *and* down, and everything that grows increases
its bulk alike in both directions or indeed in all, and continues to
live so long as it can absorb nutriment.   30

This power of self-nutrition can be isolated from the other powers
mentioned, but not they from it—in mortal beings at least. The
fact is obvious in plants; for it is the only psychic power they possess.

This is the originative power the possession of which leads us to 413ᵇ
speak of things as *living* at all, but it is the possession of sensation
that leads us for the first time to speak of living things as animals;
for even those beings which possess no power of local movement
but do possess the power of sensation we call animals and not merely
living things.

The primary form of sense is touch, which belongs to all animals.
Just as the power of self-nutrition can be isolated from touch and 5
sensation generally, so touch can be isolated from all other forms of
sense. (By the power of self-nutrition we mean that departmental
power of the soul which is common to plants and animals: all
animals whatsoever are observed to have the sense of touch.) What
the explanation of these two facts is, we must discuss later.[11] At 10
present we must confine ourselves to saying that soul is the source

10 i. e. it has nothing in it corresponding to a middle term.
11 iii. 12, esp. 434ᵃ 22–30, ᵇ10 ff.

of these phenomena and is characterized by them, viz. by the powers of self-nutrition, sensation, thinking, and motivity.

Is each of these a soul or a part of a soul? And if a part, a part in what sense? A part merely distinguishable by definition or a part
15 distinct in local situation as well? In the case of certain of these powers, the answers to these questions are easy, in the case of others we are puzzled what to say. Just as in the case of plants which when divided are observed to continue to live though removed to a distance from one another (thus showing that in *their* case the soul of each individual plant before division was actually one, potentially many), so we notice a similar result in other varieties of soul, i. e. in insects
20 which have been cut in two; each of the segments possesses both sensation and local movement; and if sensation, necessarily also imagination and appetition; for, where there is sensation, there is also pleasure and pain, and, where these, necessarily also desire.

We have no evidence as yet about mind or the power to think;
25 it seems to be a widely different kind of soul, differing as what is eternal from what is perishable; it alone is capable of existence in isolation from all other psychic powers. All the other parts of soul, it is evident from what we have said, are, in spite of certain statements to the contrary, incapable of separate existence though, of course, distinguishable by definition. If opining is distinct from
30 perceiving, to be capable of opining and to be capable of perceiving must be distinct, and so with all the other forms of living above enumerated. Further, some animals possess all these parts of soul, some certain of them only, others one only (this is what enables us to
414ª classify animals); the cause must be considered later.¹² A similar arrangement is found also within the field of the senses; some classes of animals have all the senses, some only certain of them, others only one, the most indispensable, touch.

Since the expression 'that whereby we live and perceive' has two
5 meanings, just like the expression 'that whereby we know'—that may mean either (*a*) knowledge or (*b*) the soul, for we can speak of knowing *by* or *with* either, and similarly that whereby we are in health may be either (*a*) health or (*b*) the body or some part of the body; and since of the two terms thus contrasted knowledge or health is the name of a form, essence, or ratio, or if we so express it
10 an actuality of a recipient matter—knowledge of what is capable of knowing, health of what is capable of being made healthy (for the operation of that which is capable of originating change terminates and has its seat in what is changed or altered); further, since it is the

¹² iii. 12, 13.

soul by or with which primarily we live, perceive, and think:—it
follows that the soul must be a ratio or formulable essence, not a
matter or subject. For, as we said,[13] the word substance has three
meanings—form, matter, and the complex of both—and of these 15
three what is called matter is potentiality, what is called form actuality. Since then the complex here is the living thing, the body cannot be the actuality of the soul; it is the soul which is the actuality
of a certain kind of body. Hence the rightness of the view that the
soul cannot be without a body, while it cannot *be* a body; it is not a 20
body but something relative to a body. That is why it is *in* a body,
and a body of a definite kind. It was a mistake, therefore, to do as
former thinkers did, merely to fit it into a body without adding a definite specification of the kind or character of that body. Reflection
confirms the observed fact; the actuality of any given thing can only 25
be realized in what is already potentially that thing, i. e. in a matter
of its own appropriate to it. From all this it follows that soul is an
actuality or formulable essence of something that possesses a potentiality of being besouled.

3   Of the psychic powers above enumerated [14] some kinds of living
things, as we have said,[15] possess all, some less than all, others one
only. Those we have mentioned are the nutritive, the appetitive, the 30
sensory, the locomotive, and the power of thinking. Plants have none
but the first, the nutritive, while another order of living things has
this *plus* the sensory. If any order of living things has the sensory, it 414ᵇ
must also have the appetitive; for appetite is the genus of which desire, passion, and wish are the species; now all animals have one sense
at least, viz. touch, and whatever has a sense has the capacity for
pleasure and pain and therefore has pleasant and painful objects
present to it, and wherever these are present, there is desire, for
desire is just appetition of what is pleasant. Further, all animals have 5
the sense for food (for touch is the sense for food); the food of all
living things consists of what is dry, moist, hot, cold, and these are
the qualities apprehended by touch; all other sensible qualities are
apprehended by touch only indirectly. Sounds, colours, and odours 10
contribute nothing to nutriment; flavours fall within the field of
tangible qualities. Hunger and thirst are forms of desire, hunger a
desire for what is dry and hot, thirst a desire for what is cold and
moist; flavour is a sort of seasoning added to both. We must later [16]
clear up these points, but at present it may be enough to say that all 15

[13] 412ᵃ 7.   [14] 413ᵃ 23–5, ᵇ11–13, 21–4.   [15] 413ᵇ 32–414ᵃ 1.
[16] c. ii. iii. 12. 434ᵇ 18–21.

animals that possess the sense of touch have also appetition. The case of imagination is obscure; we must examine it later.[17] Certain kinds of animals possess in addition the power of locomotion, and still another order of animate beings, i. e. man and possibly another order like man or superior to him, the power of thinking, i. e. mind. It is now evident that a single definition can be given of soul only in the same sense as one can be given of figure. For, as in that case there is no figure distinguishable and apart from triangle, &c., so here there is no soul apart from the forms of soul just enumerated. It is true that a highly general definition can be given for figure which will fit all figures without expressing the peculiar nature of any figure. So here in the case of soul and its specific forms. Hence it is absurd in this and similar cases to demand an absolutely general definition, which will fail to express the peculiar nature of anything that *is*, or again, omitting this, to look for separate definitions corresponding to each *infima species*. The cases of figure and soul are exactly parallel; for the particulars subsumed under the common name in both cases—figures and living beings—constitute a series, each successive term of which potentially contains its predecessor, e. g. the square the triangle, the sensory power the self-nutritive. Hence we must ask in the case of each order of living things, What is its soul, i. e. What is the soul of plant, animal, man? Why the terms are related in this serial way must form the subject of later examination.[18] But the facts are that the power of perception is never found apart from the power of self-nutrition, while—in plants—the latter is found isolated from the former. Again, no sense is found apart from that of touch, while touch *is* found by itself; many animals have neither sight, hearing, nor smell. Again, among living things that possess sense some have the power of locomotion, some not. Lastly, certain living beings—a small minority—possess calculation and thought, for (among mortal beings) those which possess calculation have all the other powers above mentioned, while the converse does not hold—indeed some live by imagination alone, while others have not even imagination. The mind that knows with immediate intuition presents a different problem.[19]

It is evident that the way to give the most adequate definition of soul is to seek in the case of *each* of its forms for the most appropriate definition.

4   It is necessary for the student of these forms of soul first to find a definition of each, expressive of what it is, and then to investigate its derivative properties, &c. But if we are to express what each is,

---

[17] iii. 3, 11. 433^b 31–434^a 7.   [18] iii. 12, 13.   [19] Cf. iii. 4–8.

viz. what the thinking power is, or the perceptive, or the nutritive, we must go farther back and first give an account of thinking or perceiving, for in the order of investigation the question of what an agent does precedes the question, what enables it to do what it does. If this is correct, we must on the same ground go yet another step 20 farther back and have some clear view of the objects of each; thus we must *start* with these objects, e. g. with food, with what is perceptible, or with what is intelligible.

It follows that first of all we must treat of nutrition and reproduction,[20] for the nutritive soul is found along with all the others and is the most primitive and widely distributed power of soul, being indeed that one in virtue of which all are said to have life. The acts in which 25 it manifests itself are reproduction and the use of food—reproduction, I say, because for any living thing that has reached its normal development and which is unmutilated, and whose mode of generation is not spontaneous, the most natural act is the production of another like itself, an animal producing an animal, a plant a plant, in order that, as far as its nature allows, it may partake in the eternal 415^b and divine. That is the goal towards which all things strive, that for the sake of which they do whatsoever their nature renders possible. The phrase 'for the sake of which' is ambiguous; it may mean either (*a*) the end to achieve which, or (*b*) the being in whose interest, the act is done. Since then no living thing is able to partake in what is eternal and divine by uninterrupted continuance (for nothing perishable can for ever remain one and the same), it tries to achieve that 5 end in the only way possible to it, and success is possible in varying degrees; so it remains not indeed as the self-same individual but continues its existence in something *like* itself—not numerically but specifically one.[21]

The soul is the cause or source of the living body. The terms cause and source have many senses. But the soul is the cause of its body alike in all three senses which we explicitly recognize. It is (*a*) the 10 source or origin of movement, it is (*b*) the end, it is (*c*) the essence of the whole living body.

That it is the last, is clear; for in everything the essence is identical with the ground of its being, and here, in the case of living things, their being is to live, and of their being and their living the soul in them is the cause or source. Further, the actuality of whatever is potential is identical with its formulable essence.

---

[20] *sc.* 'which we shall see to be inseparable from nutrition'.

[21] There is an unbroken current of the same specific life flowing through a discontinuous series of individual beings of the same species united by descent.

15 It is manifest that the soul is also the final cause of its body. For Nature, like mind, always does whatever it does for the sake of something, which something is its end. To that something corresponds in the case of animals the soul and in this it follows the order of nature; all natural bodies are organs of the soul. This is true of those that enter into the constitution of plants as well as of those which enter into that of animals. This shows that that for the sake 20 of which they are is soul. We must here recall the two senses of 'that for the sake of which', viz. (a) the end to achieve which, and (b) the being in whose interest, anything is or is done.

We must maintain, further, that the soul is also the cause of the living body as the original source of local movement. The power of locomotion is not found, however, in all living things. But change of quality and change of quantity are also due to the soul. Sensation is held to be a qualitative alteration, and nothing except what has 25 soul in it is capable of sensation. The same holds of the quantitative changes which constitute growth and decay; nothing grows or decays naturally [22] except what feeds itself, and nothing feeds itself except what has a share of soul in it.

Empedocles is wrong in adding that growth in plants is to be explained, the downward rooting by the natural tendency of earth 416ª to travel downwards, and the upward branching by the similar natural tendency of fire to travel upwards. For he misinterprets up and down; up and down are not for all things what they are for the whole Cosmos: if we are to distinguish and identify organs according 5 to their *functions*, the roots of plants are analogous to the head in animals. Further, we must ask what is the force that holds together the earth and the fire which tend to travel in contrary directions; if there is no counteracting force, they will be torn asunder; if there is, this must be the soul and the cause of nutrition and growth. By some the element of fire is held to be *the* cause of nutrition and 10 growth, for it alone of the primary bodies or elements is observed to feed and increase *itself*. Hence the suggestion that in both plants and animals it is it which is the operative force. A concurrent cause in a sense it certainly is, but not the principal cause; that is rather the 15 soul; for while the growth of fire goes on without limit so long as there is a supply of fuel, in the case of all complex wholes formed in the course of nature there is a limit or ratio which determines their size and increase, and limit and ratio are marks of soul but not of fire, and belong to the side of formulable essence rather than that of matter.

Nutrition and reproduction are due to one and the same psychic

[22] i. e. of itself.

power. It is necessary first to give precision to our account of food, for it is by this function of absorbing food that this psychic power is distinguished from all the others. The current view is that what serves as food to a living thing is what is contrary to it—not that in every pair of contraries each is food to the other: to be food a contrary must not only be transformable into the other and vice versa, it must also in so doing increase the bulk of the other. Many a contrary is transformed into its other and vice versa, where neither is even a quantum and so cannot increase in bulk, e. g. an invalid into a healthy subject. It is clear that not even those contraries which satisfy both the conditions mentioned above are food to one another in precisely the same sense; water may be said to feed fire, but not fire water. Where the members of the pair are elementary bodies only one of the contraries, it would appear, can be said to feed the other. But there is a difficulty here. One set of thinkers assert that like is fed, as well as increased in amount, by like. Another set, as we have said, maintain the very reverse, viz. that what feeds and what is fed are contrary to one another; like, they argue, is incapable of being affected by like; but food is changed in the process of digestion, and change is always *to* what is opposite or to what is intermediate. Further, food is acted upon by what is nourished by it, not the other way round, as timber is worked by a carpenter and not conversely; there is a change in the carpenter but it is merely a change from not-working to working. In answering this problem it makes all the difference whether we mean by 'the food' the 'finished' or the 'raw' product. If we use the word food of both, viz. of the completely undigested and the completely digested matter, we can justify both the rival accounts of it; taking food in the sense of undigested matter, it is the contrary of what is fed by it, taking it as digested it is like what is fed by it. Consequently it is clear that in a certain sense we may say that both parties are right, both wrong.

Since nothing except what is alive can be fed, what is fed is the besouled body and just because it has soul in it. Hence food is essentially related to what has soul in it. Food has a power which is other than the power to increase the bulk of what is fed by it; so far forth as what has soul in it is a quantum, food may increase its quantity, but it is only so far as what has soul in it is a 'this-somewhat' or substance that food acts *as* food; in that case it maintains the being of what is fed, and that continues to be what it is so long as the process of nutrition continues. Further, it is the agent in generation, i. e. not the generation of the individual fed but the reproduction of another like it; the substance of the individual fed is already in existence; the existence of no substance is a self-generation but only a self-maintenance.

Hence the psychic power which we are now studying may be described as that which tends to maintain whatever has this power in it of continuing such as it was, and food helps it to do its work. That is why, if deprived of food, it must cease to be.

20   The process of nutrition involves three factors, (a) what is fed, (b) that wherewith it is fed, (c) what does the feeding; of these (c) is the first soul,[23] (a) the body which has that soul in it, (b) the food. But since it is right to call things after the ends they realize, and the end of this soul is to generate another being like that in 25 which it is, the first soul ought to be named the reproductive soul. The expression (b) 'wherewith it is fed' is ambiguous just as is the expression 'wherewith the ship is steered'; that may mean either (i) the hand or (ii) the rudder, i. e. either (i) what is moved and sets in movement, or (ii) what is merely moved. We can apply this analogy here if we recall that all food must be capable of being digested, and that what produces digestion is warmth; that is why everything that has soul in it possesses warmth.

30   We have now given an outline account of the nature of food; further details must be given in the appropriate place.

5 Having made these distinctions let us now speak of sensation in the widest sense. Sensation depends, as we have said,[24] on a process of movement or affection from without, for it is held to be some sort 35 of change of quality. Now some thinkers assert that like is affected 417ª only by like; in what sense this is possible and in what sense impossible, we have explained in our general discussion of acting and being acted upon.[25]

Here arises a problem: why do we not perceive the senses themselves as well as the external objects of sense, or why without the stimulation of external objects do they not produce sensation, seeing 5 that they contain in themselves fire, earth, and all the other elements, which are the direct or indirect objects of sense? It is clear that what is sensitive is so only potentially, not actually. The power of sense is parallel to what is combustible, for that never ignites itself spontaneously, but requires an agent which has the power of starting ignition; otherwise it could have set itself on fire, and would not have needed actual fire to set it ablaze.

In reply we must recall that we use the word 'perceive' in two

[23] i. e. the earliest and most indispensable kind of soul.
[24] 415ᵇ 24, cf. 410ª 25.   [25] De Gen. et Corr. 323ᵇ 18 ff.

ways, for we say (*a*) that what has the power to hear or see, 'sees' 10
or 'hears', even though it is at the moment asleep, and also (*b*) that
what is actually seeing or hearing, 'sees' or 'hears'. Hence 'sense' too
must have two meanings, sense potential, and sense actual. Similarly
'to be a sentient' means either (*a*) to have a certain power or (*b*) to
manifest a certain activity. To begin with, for a time, let us speak as
if there were no difference between (i) being moved or affected, and 15
(ii) being active, for movement is a kind of activity—an imperfect
kind, as has elsewhere been explained.²⁶ Everything that is acted
upon or moved is acted upon by an agent which is actually at work.
Hence it is that in one sense, as has already been stated,²⁷ what acts
and what is acted upon are like, in another unlike, i. e. prior to and 20
during the change the two factors are unlike, after it like.

But we must now distinguish not only *between* what is potential
and what is actual but also different senses in which things can be
said to be potential or actual; up to now we have been speaking as if
each of these phrases had only one sense. We can speak of something as 'a knower' either (*a*) as when we say that man is a knower,
meaning that man falls within the class of beings that know or have
knowledge, or (*b*) as when we are speaking of a man who possesses 25
a knowledge of grammar; each of these is so called as having in him
a certain potentiality, but there is a difference between their respective potentialities, the one (*a*) being a potential knower, because his
kind or matter is such and such, the other (*b*), because he can in the
absence of any external counteracting cause realize his knowledge in
actual knowing at will. This implies a third meaning of 'a knower'
(*c*), one who is already realizing his knowledge—he is a knower in
actuality and in the most proper sense is knowing, e. g. this A. Both 30
the former are potential knowers, who realize their respective potentialities, the one (*a*) by change of quality, i. e. repeated transitions
from one state to its opposite ²⁸ under instruction, the other (*b*) by
the transition from the inactive possession of sense or grammar to 417ᵇ
their active exercise. The two kinds of transition are distinct.

Also the expression 'to be acted upon' has more than one meaning;
it may mean either (*a*) the extinction of one of two contraries by
the other, or (*b*) the maintenance of what is potential by the agency
of what is actual and already like what is acted upon, with such likeness as is compatible with one's being actual and the other potential. 5
For what possesses knowledge becomes an actual knower by a transition which is either not an alteration of it at all (being in reality a

---

²⁶ *Phys.* 201ᵇ 31, 257ᵇ 8.   ²⁷ 416ᵃ 29–ᵇ9.
²⁸ viz. from ignorance or error to knowledge or truth.

development into its true self or actuality) or at least an alteration in a quite different sense from the usual meaning.

Hence it is wrong to speak of a wise man as being 'altered' when he uses his wisdom, just as it would be absurd to speak of a builder as being altered when he is using his skill in building a house.
10 What in the case of knowing or understanding leads from potentiality to actuality ought not to be called teaching but something else. That which starting with the power to know learns or acquires knowledge through the agency of one who actually knows and has the power of teaching either (a) ought not to be said 'to be acted
15 upon' at all or (b) we must recognize two senses of alteration, viz. (i) the substitution of one quality for another, the first being the contrary of the second, or (ii) the development of an existent quality from potentiality in the direction of fixity or nature.

In the case of what is to possess sense, the first transition is due to the action of the male parent and takes place before birth so that at birth the living thing is, in respect of sensation, at the stage which corresponds to the *possession* of knowledge. Actual sensation corresponds to the stage of the exercise of knowledge. But between the
20 two cases compared there is a difference; the objects that excite the sensory powers to activity, the seen, the heard, &c., are outside. The ground of this difference is that what actual sensation apprehends is individuals, while what knowledge apprehends is universals, and these are in a sense within the soul. That is why a man can exercise his knowledge when he wishes, but his sensation does not depend upon
25 himself—a sensible object must be there. A similar statement must be made about our *knowledge* of what is sensible—on the same ground, viz. that the sensible objects are individual and external.

A later more appropriate occasion may be found [29] thoroughly
30 to clear up all this. At present it must be enough to recognize the distinctions already drawn; a thing may be said to be potential in either of two senses, (a) in the sense in which we might say of a boy that he may become a general or (b) in the sense in which we might say the same of an adult, and there are two corresponding senses of
418ª the term 'a potential sentient'. There are no separate names for the two stages of potentiality; we have pointed out that they are different and how they are different. We cannot help using the incorrect terms 'being acted upon or altered' of the two transitions involved. As we have said,[30] what has the power of sensation is potentially like what the perceived object is actually; that is, while at the beginning
5 of the process of its being acted upon the two interacting factors are

29 iii. 4, 5.   30 417ª 12–20.

dissimilar, at the end the one acted upon is assimilated to the other and is identical in quality with it.

6   In dealing with each of the senses we shall have first to speak of the objects which are perceptible by each. The term 'object of sense' covers three kinds of objects, two kinds of which are, in our language, directly perceptible, while the remaining one is only incidentally perceptible. Of the first two kinds one (a) consists of what is perceptible by a single sense, the other (b) of what is perceptible by any and all 10 of the senses.³¹ I call by the name of special object of this or that sense that which cannot be perceived by any other sense than that one and in respect of which no error is possible; in this sense colour is the special object of sight, sound of hearing, flavour of taste. Touch, indeed, discriminates more than one set of different qualities. Each sense has one kind of object which it discerns, and never errs in 15 reporting that what is before it is colour or sound (though it may err as to what it is that is coloured or where that is, or what it is that is sounding or where that is). Such objects are what we propose to call the special objects of this or that sense.

'Common sensibles' are movement, rest, number, figure, magnitude; these are not peculiar to any one sense, but are common to all. There are at any rate certain kinds of movement which are perceptible both by touch and by sight.

We speak of an incidental object of sense where e. g. the white 20 object which we see is the son of Diares; here because 'being the son of Diares' is incidental to the directly visible white patch we speak of the son of Diares as being (incidentally) perceived or seen by us. Because this is only incidentally an object of sense, it in no way as such affects the senses. Of the two former kinds, both of which are in their own nature perceptible by sense, the first kind—that of special objects of the several senses—constitute *the* objects of sense in the strictest sense of the term and it is to them that in the nature 25 of things the structure of each several sense is adapted.

7   The object of sight is the visible, and what is visible is (a) colour and (b) a certain kind of object which can be described in words but which has no single name; what we mean by (b) will be abundantly clear as we proceed. Whatever is visible is colour and colour is what lies upon what is in its own nature visible; 'in its own nature' here 30 means not that visibility is involved in the definition of what thus underlies colour, but that that substratum contains in itself the cause of visibility. Every colour has in it the power to set in movement what is

³¹ Really, it is enough if it is perceptible by more than one sense.

418^b actually transparent; that power constitutes its very nature. That is why it is not visible except with the help of light; it is only in light that the colour of a thing is seen. Hence our first task is to explain what light is.

Now there clearly is something which is transparent, and by 5 'transparent' I mean what is visible, and yet not visible in itself, but rather owing its visibility to the colour *of something else*; of this character are air, water, and many solid bodies. Neither air nor water is transparent because it is air or water; they are transparent because each of them has contained in it a certain substance which is the same in both and is also found in the eternal body which constitutes the uppermost shell of the physical Cosmos. Of this substance light is the activity—the activity of what is transparent so far forth as it 10 has in it the determinate power of becoming transparent; where this power is present, there is also the potentiality of the contrary, viz. darkness. Light is as it were the proper colour of what is transparent, and exists whenever the potentially transparent is excited to actuality by the influence of fire or something resembling 'the uppermost body'; for fire too contains something which is one and the same with the substance in question.

We have now explained what the transparent is and what light is; light is neither fire nor any kind whatsoever of body nor an efflux 15 from any kind of body (if it were, it would again itself be a kind of body)—it is the presence of fire or something resembling fire in what is transparent. It is certainly not a body, for two bodies cannot be present in the same place. The opposite of light is darkness; darkness is the absence from what is tranparent of the corresponding positive state above characterized; clearly therefore, light is just the presence of that.

20 Empedocles (and with him all others who used the same forms of expression) was wrong in speaking of light as 'travelling' or being at a given moment between the earth and its envelope, its movement being unobservable by us; that view is contrary both to the clear evidence of argument and to the observed facts; if the distance 25 traversed were short, the movement might have been unobservable, but where the distance is from extreme East to extreme West, the draught upon our powers of belief is too great.

What is capable of taking on colour is what in itself is colourless, as what can take on sound is what is soundless; what is colourless includes (*a*) what is transparent and (*b*) what is invisible or scarcely visible, 30 i. e. what is 'dark'. The latter (*b*) is the same as what is transparent, when it is potentially, not of course when it is actually transparent; it is the same substance which is now darkness, now light.

Not everything that is visible depends upon light for its visibility. 419ª
This is only true of the 'proper' colour of things. Some objects of sight
which in light are invisible, in darkness stimulate the sense; that is,
things that appear fiery or shining. This class of objects has no simple
common name, but instances of it are fungi, flesh, heads, scales, and 5
eyes of fish. In none of these is what is seen their own 'proper'
colour. Why we see these at all is another question. At present what
is obvious is that what is seen in light is always colour. That is why
without the help of light colour remains invisible. Its being colour at
all means precisely its having in it the power to set in movement 10
what is already actually transparent, and, as we have seen, the actuality of what is transparent is just light.

The following experiment makes the necessity of a medium clear.
If what has colour is placed in immediate contact with the eye, it
cannot be seen. Colour sets in movement not the sense organ but
what is transparent, e. g. the air, and that, extending continuously
from the object of the organ, sets the latter in movement. Democritus 15
misrepresents the facts when he expresses the opinion that if the
interspace were empty one could distinctly see an ant on the vault of
the sky; that is an impossibility. Seeing is due to an affection or
change of what has the perceptive faculty, and it cannot be affected
by the seen colour itself; it remains that it must be affected by
what comes between. Hence it is indispensable that there be *something* in between—if there were nothing, so far from seeing with 20
greater distinctness, we should see nothing at all.

We have now explained the cause why colour cannot be seen otherwise than in light. Fire on the other hand is seen both in darkness and
in light; this double possibility follows necessarily from our theory,
for it is just fire that makes what is potentially transparent actually
transparent.

The same account holds also of sound and smell; if the object of 25
either of these senses is in immediate contact with the organ no sensation is produced. In both cases the object sets in movement only
what lies between, and this in turn sets the organ in movement: if
what sounds or smells is brought into immediate contact with the
organ, no sensation will be produced. The same, in spite of all appear- 30
ances, applies also to touch and taste; why there is this apparent difference will be clear later.[32] What comes between in the case of sounds
is air; the corresponding medium in the case of smell has no name.
But, corresponding to what is transparent in the case of colour, there
is a quality found both in air and water, which serves as a medium

[32] 422ᵇ 34 ff.

35 for what has smell—I say 'in water' because animals that live in water as well as those that live on land seem to possess the sense 419ᵇ of smell, and 'in air' because man and all other land animals that breathe, perceive smells only when they breathe air in. The explanation of this too will be given later.[33]

8 Now let us, to begin with, make certain distinctions about sound and hearing.

5 Sound may mean either of two things—(a) actual, and (b) potential, sound. There are certain things which, as we say, 'have no sound', e. g. sponges or wool, others which have, e. g. bronze and in general all things which are smooth and solid—the latter are said to have a sound because they can make a sound, i. e. can generate actual sound between themselves and the organ of hearing.

Actual sound requires for its occurrence (i, ii) two such bodies and 10 (iii) a space between them; for it is generated by an impact. Hence it is impossible for one body only to generate a sound—there must be a body impinging and a body impinged upon; what sounds does so by striking against something else, and this is impossible without a movement from place to place.

As we have said, not all bodies can by impact on one another produce sound; impact on wool makes no sound, while the impact on 15 bronze or any body which is smooth and hollow does. Bronze gives out a sound when struck because it is smooth; bodies which are hollow owing to reflection repeat the original impact over and over again, the body originally set in movement being unable to escape from the concavity.

Further, we must remark that sound is heard both in air and in water, though less distinctly in the latter. Yet neither air nor water 20 is the principal cause of sound. What is required for the production of sound is an impact of two solids against one another and against the air. The latter condition is satisfied when the air impinged upon does not retreat before the blow, i. e. is not dissipated by it.

That is why it must be struck with a sudden sharp blow, if it is to sound—the movement of the whip must outrun the dispersion of the air, just as one might get in a stroke at a heap or whirl of sand as it was travelling rapidly past.

25 An echo occurs, when, a mass of air having been unified, bounded, and prevented from dissipation by the containing walls of a vessel, the air originally struck by the impinging body and set in movement by it rebounds from this mass of air like a ball from a wall. It

[33] 421ᵇ 13–422ᵃ 6.

is probable that in all generation of sound echo takes place, though
it is frequently only indistinctly heard. What happens here must be
analogous to what happens in the case of light; light is *always*
reflected—otherwise it would not be diffused and outside what was 30
directly illuminated by the sun there would be blank darkness; but
this reflected light is not always strong enough, as it *is* when it is
reflected from water, bronze, and other smooth bodies, to cast a
shadow, which is the distinguishing mark by which we recognize light.

It is rightly said that an empty space plays the chief part in the
production of hearing, for what people mean by 'the vacuum' is
the air, which is what causes hearing, when that air is set in movement as one continuous mass; but owing to its friability it emits no 35
sound, being dissipated by impinging upon any surface which is not 420ᵃ
smooth. When the surface on which it impinges is quite smooth, what
is produced by the original impact is a united mass, a result due to
the smoothness of the surface with which the air is in contact at the
other end.

What has the power of producing sound is what has the power of
setting in movement a single mass of air which is continuous from the
impinging body up to the organ of hearing. The organ of hearing is
physically united with air,[34] and because it is *in* air, the air inside is
moved concurrently with the air outside. Hence animals do not hear 5
with all parts of their bodies, nor do all parts admit of the entrance
of air; for even the part which can be moved and can sound has not
air everywhere in it. Air in itself is, owing to its friability, quite
soundless; only when its dissipation is prevented is its movement
sound. The air in the ear is built into a chamber just to prevent this
dissipating movement, in order that the animal may accurately 10
apprehend all varieties of the movements of the air outside. That is
why we hear also in water, viz. because the water cannot get into
the air chamber or even, owing to the spirals, into the outer ear. If
this does happen, hearing ceases, as it also does if the tympanic
membrane is damaged, just as sight ceases if the membrane covering the pupil is damaged. It is also a test of deafness whether the 15
ear does or does not reverberate like a horn; the air inside the ear
has always a movement of its own, but the sound we hear is always
the sounding of something else, not of the organ itself. That is why
we say that we hear with what is empty and echoes, viz. because
what we hear with is a chamber which contains a bounded mass of air.

Which is it that 'sounds', the striking body or the struck? Is not
the answer 'it is both, but each in a different way'? Sound is a 20

[34] i. e. it has air incorporated in its structure.

movement of what can rebound from a smooth surface when struck
against it. As we have explained [35] not everything sounds when it
strikes or is struck, e. g. if one needle is struck against another,
25 neither emits any sound. In order, therefore, that sound may be
generated, what is struck must be smooth, to enable the air to rebound and be shaken off from it in one piece.

The distinctions between different sounding bodies show themselves only in actual sound; [36] as without the help of light colours
remain invisible, so without the help of actual sound the distinctions
between acute and grave sounds remain inaudible. Acute and grave
are here metaphors, transferred from their proper sphere, viz. that of
30 touch, where they mean respectively (a) what moves the sense much
in a short time, (b) what moves the sense little in a long time. Not
that what is sharp really moves fast, and what is grave, slowly, but
that the difference in the qualities of the one and the other movement
420ᵇ is due to their respective speeds. There seems to be a sort of parallelism between what is acute or grave to hearing and what is sharp or
blunt to touch; what is sharp as it were stabs, while what is blunt
pushes, the one producing its effect in a short, the other in a long time,
so that the one is quick, the other slow.

5　　Let the foregoing suffice as an analysis of sound. Voice is a kind
of sound characteristic of what has soul in it; nothing that is without soul utters voice, it being only by a metaphor that we speak of
the voice of the flute or the lyre or generally of what (being without
soul) possesses the power of producing a succession of notes which
differ in length and pitch and timbre. The metaphor is based on the
fact that all these differences are found also in voice. Many animals
are voiceless, e. g. all non-sanguineous animals and among san-
10 guineous animals fish. This is just what we should expect, since voice
is a certain movement of air. The fish, like those in the Achelous,
which are said to have voice, really make the sounds with their gills
or some similar organ. Voice is the sound made by an animal, and that
with a special organ. As we saw, everything that makes a sound does
so by the impact of something (a) against something else, (b)
15 across a space, (c) filled with air; hence it is only to be expected that
no animals utter voice except those which take in air. Once air is
inbreathed, Nature uses it for two different purposes, as the tongue is
used both for tasting and for articulating; in that case of the two
functions tasting is necessary for the animal's existence (hence it is
found more widely distributed), while articulate speech is a luxury

---

[35] 419ᵇ 6, 13.
[36] i. e. when these bodies, e. g. the strings of a lyre, are actually sounding.

subserving its possessor's well-being; similarly in the former case [20] Nature employs the breath both as an indispensable means to the regulation of the inner temperature of the living body and also as the matter of articulate voice, in the interests of its possessor's well-being. Why its former use is indispensable must be discussed elsewhere.[37]

The organ of respiration is the windpipe, and the organ to which this is related as means to end is the lungs. The latter is the part of the body by which the temperature of land animals is raised above that of all others. But what primarily requires the air drawn in by [25] respiration is not only this but the region surrounding the heart. That is why when animals breathe the air must penetrate inwards.

Voice then is the impact of the inbreathed air against the 'windpipe', and the agent that produces the impact is the soul resident in these parts of the body. Not every sound, as we said, made by an [30] animal is voice (even with the tongue we may merely make a sound which is not voice, or without the tongue as in coughing); what produces the impact must have soul in it and must be accompanied by an act of imagination, for voice is a sound *with a meaning,* and is not *merely* the result of any impact of the breath as in coughing; in voice the breath in the windpipe is used as an instrument to knock with against the walls of the windpipe. This is confirmed by our [421ª] inability to speak when we are breathing either out or in—we can only do so by holding our breath; we make the movements with the breath so checked. It is clear also why fish are voiceless; they have no windpipe. And they have no windpipe because they do not breathe [5] or take in air. Why they do not is a question belonging to another inquiry.[38]

9 Smell and its object are much less easy to determine than what we have hitherto discussed; the distinguishing characteristic of the object of smell is less obvious than those of sound or colour. The ground of this is that our power of smell is less discriminating and in general inferior to that of many species of animals; men have a poor [10] sense of smell and our apprehension of its proper objects is inseparably bound up with and so confused by pleasure and pain, which shows that in us the organ is inaccurate. It is probable that there is a parallel failure in the perception of colour by animals that have hard eyes: probably they discriminate differences of colour only by the presence or absence of what excites fear, and that it is thus that [15]

[37] De Resp. 478ª 28; P. A. 642ª 31–b4.
[38] Cf. De Resp. 474b 25–9, 476ª 6–15; P. A. 669ª 2–5.

human beings distinguish smells. It seems that there is an analogy between smell and taste, and that the species of tastes run parallel to those of smells—the only difference being that our sense of taste is more discriminating than our sense of smell, because the former is a modification of touch, which reaches in man the maximum of dis-
20 criminative accuracy. While in respect of all the other senses we fall below many species of animals, in respect of touch we far excel all other species in exactness of discrimination. That is why man is the most intelligent of all animals. This is confirmed by the fact that it is to differences in the organ of touch and to nothing else that the differences between man and man in respect of natural endowment
25 are due; men whose flesh is hard are ill-endowed by nature, men whose flesh is soft, well-endowed.

As flavours may be divided into (a) sweet, (b) bitter, so with smells. In some things the flavour and the smell have the same quality, i. e. both are sweet or both bitter, in others they diverge. Similarly
30 a smell, like a flavour, may be pungent, astringent, acid, or succulent. But, as we said, because smells are much less easy to discriminate than flavours, the names of these varieties are applied to smells
421ᵇ only metaphorically; for example 'sweet' is extended from the taste to the smell of saffron or honey, 'pungent' to that of thyme, and so on.³⁹

In the same sense in which hearing has for its object both the
5 audible and the inaudible, sight both the visible and the invisible, smell has for its object both the odorous and the inodorous. 'Inodorous' may be either (a) what has no smell at all, or (b) what has a small or feeble smell. The same ambiguity lurks in the word 'tasteless'.

Smelling, like the operation of the senses previously examined, takes place through a medium, i. e. through air or water—I add water,
10 because water-animals too (both sanguineous and non-sanguineous) seem to smell just as much as land-animals; at any rate some of them make directly for their food from a distance if it has any scent. That is why the following facts constitute a problem for us. All animals smell in the same way, but man smells only when he inhales; if he
15 exhales or holds his breath, he ceases to smell, no difference being made whether the odorous object is distant or near, or even placed inside the nose and actually on the wall of the nostril; it is a disability common to all the senses not to perceive what is in immediate contact with the organ of sense, but our failure to apprehend what is

³⁹ Because of the felt likeness between the respective smells and the really sweet or pungent tastes of the same herbs, &c.

odorous without the help of inhalation is peculiar (the fact is obvious on making the experiment). Now since bloodless animals do not breathe, they must, it might be argued, have some novel sense not 20 reckoned among the usual five. Our reply must be that this is impossible, since it is scent that is perceived; a sense that apprehends what is odorous and what has a good or bad odour cannot be anything but smell. Further, they are observed to be deleteriously affected by the same strong odours as man is, e. g. bitumen, sulphur, and the like. 25 These animals must be able to smell without being able to breathe. The probable explanation is that in man the organ of smell has a certain superiority over that in all other animals just as his eyes have over those of hard-eyed animals. Man's eyes have in the eyelids a kind of shelter or envelope, which must be shifted or drawn back in order that we may see, while hard-eyed animals have nothing of 30 the kind, but at once see whatever presents itself in the transparent medium. Similarly in certain species of animals the organ of smell is like the eye of hard-eyed animals, uncurtained, while in others which 422ᵃ take in air it probably has a curtain over it, which is drawn back in inhalation, owing to the dilating of the veins or pores. That explains also why such animals cannot smell under water; to smell they must 5 first inhale, and that they cannot do under water.

Smells come from what is dry as flavours from what is moist. Consequently the organ of smell is potentially dry.

10 What can be tasted is always something that can be touched, and just for that reason it cannot be perceived *through* an interposed foreign body, for touch means the absence of any intervening body. 10 Further, the flavoured and tasteable body is suspended in a liquid matter, and this is tangible. Hence, if we lived in water, we should perceive a sweet object introduced into the water, but the water would not be the medium *through* which we perceived; our perception would be due to the solution of the sweet substance in what we imbibed, just as if it were mixed with some drink. There is no parallel here to the perception of colour, which is due neither to any blending of anything with anything, nor to any efflux of anything from anything. In the case of taste, there is nothing corresponding to the 15 medium in the case of the senses previously discussed; but as the object of sight is colour, so the object of taste is flavour. But nothing excites a perception of flavour without the help of liquid; what acts upon the sense of taste must be either actually or potentially liquid like what is saline; it must be both (*a*) itself easily dissolved, and (*b*) capable of dissolving along with itself the tongue. Taste appre- 20

hends both (*a*) what has taste and (*b*) what has no taste, if we mean by (*b*) what has only a slight or feeble flavour or what tends to destroy the sense of taste. In this it is exactly parallel to sight, which apprehends both what is visible and what is invisible (for darkness is invisible and yet is discriminated by sight; so is, in a different way, what is over-brilliant), and to hearing, which apprehends both sound and silence, of which the one is audible and the
25 other inaudible, and also over-loud sound. This corresponds in the case of hearing to over-bright light in the case of sight. As a faint sound is 'inaudible', so in a sense is a loud or violent sound. The word 'invisible' and similar privative terms cover not only (*a*) what is simply without some power, but also (*b*) what is adapted by nature to have it but has not it or has it only in a very low degree, as when we say that a species of swallow is 'footless' or that a variety of fruit is 'stoneless'. So too taste has as its object both what can be tasted
30 and the tasteless—the latter in the sense of what has little flavour or a bad flavour or one destructive of taste. The difference between what is tasteless and what is not seems to rest ultimately on that between what is drinkable and what is undrinkable—both are tasteable, but the latter is bad and tends to destroy taste, while the former is the normal stimulus of taste. What is drinkable is the common object of both touch and taste.

422ᵇ   Since what can be tasted is liquid, the organ for its perception cannot be either (*a*) actually liquid or (*b*) incapable of becoming liquid. Tasting means a being affected by ⁴⁰ what can be tasted as such; hence the organ of taste must be liquefied, and so to start with must be non-liquid but capable of liquefaction without loss of its
5 distinctive nature. This is confirmed by the fact that the tongue cannot taste either when it is too dry or when it is too moist; in the latter case what occurs is due to a contact with the pre-existent moisture in the tongue itself, when after a foretaste of some strong flavour we try to taste another flavour; it is in this way that sick persons find everything they taste bitter, viz. because, when they taste, their tongues are overflowing with bitter moisture.
10   The species of flavour are, as in the case of colour, (*a*) simple, i. e. the two contraries, the sweet and the bitter, (*b*) secondary, viz. (i) on the side of the sweet, the succulent, (ii) on the side of the bitter, the saline, (iii) between these come the pungent, the harsh, the astringent, and the acid; these pretty well exhaust the varieties of
15 flavour. It follows that what has the power of tasting is what is po-

---

⁴⁰ *sc.* 'and so, as we have seen, a being assimilated to'.

tentially of that kind, and that what is tasteable is what has the power of making it actually what it itself already is.

11   Whatever can be said of what is tangible, can be said of touch, and vice versa; if touch is not a single sense but a group of senses, there must be several kinds of what is tangible. It is a problem whether touch is a single sense or a group of senses. It is also a prob- 20 lem, what is the organ of touch; is it or is it not the flesh (including what in certain animals is homologous with flesh)? On the second view, flesh is 'the medium' of touch, the real organ being situated farther inward. The problem arises because the field of each sense is according to the accepted view determined as the range between a single pair of contraries, white and black for sight, acute and grave for hearing, bitter and sweet for taste; but in the field of what is 25 tangible we find several such pairs, hot cold, dry moist, hard soft, &c. This problem finds a partial solution, when it is recalled that in the case of the other senses more than one pair of contraries are to be met with, e. g. in sound not only acute and grave but loud and soft, 30 smooth and rough, &c.; there are similar contrasts in the field of colour. Nevertheless we are unable clearly to detect in the case of touch what the single subject is which underlies the contrasted qualities and corresponds to sound in the case of hearing.

To the question whether the organ of touch lies inward or not (i. e. whether we need look any farther than the flesh), no indication in favour of the second answer can be drawn from the fact that if the 423ᵃ object comes into contact with the flesh it is at once perceived. For even under present conditions if the experiment is made of making a web and stretching it tight over the flesh, as soon as this web is touched the sensation is reported in the same manner as before, yet it is clear that the organ is not in this membrane. If the membrane could be *grown* on to the flesh, the report would travel still quicker. 5 The flesh plays in touch very much the same part as would be played in the other senses by an air-envelope growing round our body; had we such an envelope attached to us we should have supposed that it was by a single organ that we perceived sounds, colours, and smells, and we should have taken sight, hearing, and smell to be a single sense. But as it is, because that through which the different move- 10 ments are transmitted is not naturally attached to our bodies, the difference of the various sense-organs is too plain to miss. But in the case of touch the obscurity remains.

There must be such a naturally attached 'medium' as flesh, for no living body could be constructed of air or water; it must be some-

thing solid. Consequently it must be composed of earth along with
these, which is just what flesh and its analogue in animals which
15 have no true flesh tend to be. Hence of necessity the medium
through which are transmitted the manifoldly contrasted tactual
qualities must be a body naturally attached to the organism. That
they are manifold is clear when we consider touching with the tongue;
we apprehend at the tongue all tangible qualities as well as flavour.
Suppose all the rest of our flesh was, like the tongue, sensitive to
20 flavour, we should have identified the sense of taste and the sense of
touch; what saves us from this identification is the fact that touch and
taste are not always found together in the same part of the body. The
following problem might be raised. Let us assume that every body has
depth, i. e. has three dimensions, and that if two bodies have a third
body between them they cannot be in contact with one another; let
25 us remember that what is liquid is a body and must be or contain water,
and that if two bodies touch one another under water, their touching
surfaces cannot be dry, but must have water between, viz. the water
which wets their bounding surfaces; from all this it follows that in
water two bodies cannot be in contact with one another. The same
holds of two bodies in air—air being to bodies in air precisely what
30 water is to bodies in water—but the facts are not so evident to our
observation, because we live in air, just as animals that live in water
423ᵇ would not notice that the things which touch one another in water
have wet surfaces. The problem, then, is: does the perception of all
objects of sense take place in the same way, or does it not, e. g. taste
and touch requiring contact (as they are commonly thought to
do), while all other senses perceive over a distance? The distinction
5 is unsound; we perceive what is hard or soft, as well as the objects of
hearing, sight, and smell, through a 'medium', only that the latter
are perceived over a *greater* distance than the former; that is why the
facts escape our notice. For we do perceive everything through a
medium; but in these cases the fact escapes us. Yet, to repeat what
we said before, if the medium for touch were a membrane separating
us from the object without our observing its existence, we should be
10 relatively to it in the same condition as we are now to air or water in
which we are immersed; in their case we fancy we can touch objects,
nothing coming in between us and them. But there remains this difference between what can be touched and what can be seen or can
sound; in the latter two cases we perceive because the medium produces a certain effect upon us, whereas in the perception of objects
15 of touch we are affected not *by* but *along with* the medium; it is as
if a man were struck through his shield, where the shock is not first

given to the shield and passed on to the man, but the concussion of both is simultaneous.

In general, flesh and the tongue are related to the real organs of touch and taste, as air and water are to those of sight, hearing, and smell. Hence in neither the one case nor the other can there be any 20 perception of an object if it is placed immediately upon the organ, e. g. if a white object is placed on the surface of the eye. This again shows that what has the power of perceiving the tangible is seated inside. Only so would there be a complete analogy with all the other senses. In their case if you place the object on the *organ* it is not perceived, here if you place it on the flesh it *is* perceived; therefore flesh 23 is not the organ but the *medium* of touch.

What can be touched are distinctive qualities of body *as* body; by such differences I mean those which characterize the elements, viz. hot cold, dry moist, of which we have spoken earlier in our treatise on the elements.[41] The organ for the perception of these is that of 30 touch—that part of the body in which primarily the sense of touch resides. This is that part which is potentially such as its object is actually: for all sense-perception is a process of being so affected; so that that which makes something such as it itself actually is makes 424ᵛ the other such because the other is already potentially such. That is why when an object of touch is equally hot and cold or hard and soft we cannot perceive; what we perceive must have a degree of the sensible quality lying beyond the neutral point. This implies that the sense itself is a 'mean' between any two opposite qualities which determine the field of that sense. It is to this that it owes its power of 5 discerning the objects in that field. What is 'in the middle' is fitted to discern; relatively to either extreme it can put itself in the place of the other. As what is to perceive *both* white and black must, to begin with, be actually neither but potentially either (and so with all the other sense-organs), so the organ of touch must be neither hot nor cold.

Further, as in a sense sight had[42] for its object both what was 10 visible and what was invisible (and there was a parallel truth about all the other senses discussed),[43] so touch has for its object both what is tangible and what is intangible. Here by 'intangible' is meant (*a*) what like air possesses some quality of tangible things in a very slight degree and (*b*) what possesses it in an excessive degree, as destructive things do.

We have now given an outline account of each of the several senses. 15

---

[41] *De Gen. et Corr.* ii. 2, 3.　　　[42] 422ᵃ 20 ff.　　　[43] 421ᵇ 3–6, 422ᵃ 29.

12   The following results applying to any and every sense may now be formulated.

(A) By a 'sense' is meant what has the power of receiving into itself the sensible forms of things without the matter. This must be conceived of as taking place in the way in which a piece of wax takes on
20 the impress of a signet-ring without the iron or gold; we say that what produces the impression is a signet of bronze or gold, but its particular metallic constitution makes no difference: in a similar way the sense is affected by what is coloured or flavoured or sounding, but it is indifferent what in each case the *substance* is; what alone matters is what *quality* it has, i. e. in what *ratio* its constituents are combined.

(B) By 'an organ of sense' is meant that in which ultimately such a power is seated.

25   The sense and its organ are the same in fact, but their essence is not the same. What perceives is, of course, a spatial magnitude, but we must not admit that either the having the power to perceive or the sense itself is a magnitude; what they are is a certain ratio or power *in* a magnitude. This enables us to explain why objects of sense which possess one of two opposite sensible qualities in a degree largely in excess of the other opposite destroy the organs of sense; if the move-
30 ment set up by an object is too strong for the organ, the equipoise of contrary qualities in the organ, which just *is* its sensory power, is disturbed; it is precisely as concord and tone are destroyed by too violently twanging the strings of a lyre. This explains also why plants cannot perceive, in spite of their having a portion of soul in them and obviously being affected by tangible objects themselves; for undoubtedly their temperature can be lowered or raised. The explana-
424b tion is that they have no mean of contrary qualities, and so no principle in them capable of taking on the forms of sensible objects without their matter; in the case of plants the affection is an affection by form-and-matter together. The problem might be raised: Can what cannot smell be said to be affected by smells or what cannot see by
5 colours, and so on? It might be said that a smell is just what can be smelt, and if it produces any effect it can only be so as to make something smell it, and it might be argued that what cannot smell cannot be affected by smells and further that what can smell can be affected by it only in so far as it has in it the power to smell (similarly with the proper objects of all the other senses). Indeed that this *is* so is made quite evident as follows. Light or darkness, sounds and
10 smells leave *bodies* quite unaffected; what does affect bodies is not these but the bodies which are their vehicles, e. g. what splits the

trunk of a tree is not the sound of the thunder but the air which accompanies thunder. Yes, but, it may be objected, bodies are affected by what is tangible and by flavours. If not, by what are things that are without soul affected, i. e. altered in quality? Must we not, then, admit that the objects of the other senses also may affect them? Is not the true account this, that all bodies *are* capable of being affected by smells and sounds, but that some on being acted upon, having no 15 boundaries of their own, disintegrate, as in the instance of air, which does become odorous, showing that *some* effect is produced on it by what is odorous? But smelling is more than such an affection by what is odorous—*what* more? Is not the answer that, while the air owing to the momentary duration of the action upon it of what is odorous does itself become perceptible to the sense of smell, smelling is an *observing* of the result produced?

BOOK III

1　That there is no sixth sense in addition to the five enumerated— 20 sight, hearing, smell, taste, touch—may be established by the following considerations:

If we have actually sensation of everything of which touch can give us sensation (for all the qualities of the tangible *qua* tangible 25 are perceived by us through touch); and if absence of a sense necessarily involves absence of a sense-organ; and if (1) all objects that we perceive by immediate contact with them are perceptible by touch, which sense we actually possess, and (2) all objects that we perceive through media, i. e. without immediate contact, are perceptible by 30 or through the simple elements, e. g. air and water (and this is so arranged that (*a*) if more than one kind of sensible object is perceivable through a single medium, the possessor of a sense-organ homogeneous with that medium has the power of perceiving both kinds of objects; for example, if the sense-organ is made of air, and air is a medium both for sound and for colour; and that (*b*) if more than one medium can transmit the same kind of sensible objects, as 425ᵃ e. g. water as well as air can transmit colour, both being transparent, then the possessor of either alone will be able to perceive the kind of objects transmissible through both); and if of the simple elements two only, air and water, go to form sense-organs (for the pupil is made of water, the organ of hearing is made of air, and the organ of smell of one or other of these two, while fire is found either in none or in all—warmth being an essential condition of all sensibility—and 5 earth either in none or, if anywhere, specially mingled with the com-

ponents of the organ of touch; wherefore it would remain that there can be no sense-organ formed of anything except water and air); and if these sense-organs are actually found in certain animals;—then all the possible senses are possessed by those animals that are not im-
10 perfect or mutilated (for even the mole is observed to have eyes beneath its skin); so that, if there is no fifth element and no property other than those which belong to the four elements of our world, no sense can be wanting to such animals.

Further, there cannot be a special sense-organ for the common
15 sensibles either, i. e. the objects which we perceive incidentally through this or that special sense, e. g. movement, rest, figure, magnitude, number, unity; for all these we perceive by movement, e. g. magnitude by movement, and therefore also figure (for figure is a species of magnitude), what is at rest by the absence of movement: number is perceived by the negation of continuity, and by the special sensibles; for each sense perceives one class of sensible objects. So
20 that it is clearly impossible that there should be a special sense for any one of the common sensibles, e. g. movement; for, if that were so, our perception of it would be exactly parallel to our present perception of what is sweet by vision. *That* is so because we have a sense for each of the two qualities, in virtue of which when they happen to meet in one sensible object we are aware of both contemporaneously.
25 If it were not like this our perception of the common qualities would always be incidental, i. e. as is the perception of Cleon's son, where we perceive him not as Cleon's son but as white, and the white thing which we really perceive happens to be Cleon's son.

But in the case of the common sensibles there is already in us a general sensibility which enables us to perceive them directly; there is therefore no special sense required for their perception: if there were, our perception of them would have been exactly like what has been above described.

30 The senses perceive each other's special objects incidentally; not because the percipient sense is this or that special sense, but because all form a unity: this incidental perception takes place whenever sense is directed at one and the same moment to two disparate qualities
425ᵇ in one and the same object, e. g. to the bitterness and the yellowness of bile; the assertion of the identity of both cannot be the act of either of the senses; hence the illusion of sense, e. g. the belief that if a thing is yellow it is bile.

It might be asked why we have more senses than one. Is it to pre-
5 vent a failure to apprehend the common sensibles, e. g. movement, magnitude, and number, which go along with the special sensibles?

Had we no sense but sight, and that sense no object but white, they would have tended to escape our notice and everything would have merged for us into an indistinguishable identity because of the concomitance of colour and magnitude. As it is, the fact that the common sensibles are given in the objects of more than one sense reveals their distinction from each and all of the special sensibles.   10

2   Since it is through sense that we are aware that we are seeing or hearing, it must be either by sight that we are aware of seeing, or by some sense other than sight. But the sense that gives us this new sensation must perceive both sight and its object, viz. colour: so that either (1) there will be two senses both percipient of the same sensible object, or (2) the sense must be percipient of itself. Further, even if 15 the sense which perceives sight were different from sight, we must either fall into an infinite regress, or we must somewhere assume a sense which is aware of itself. If so, we ought to do this in the first case.

This presents a difficulty: if to perceive by sight is just to see, and what is seen is colour (or the coloured), then if we are to *see* that which sees, that which sees originally must be coloured. It is clear therefore that 'to perceive by sight' has more than one meaning; 20 for even when we are not *seeing,* it is by sight that we discriminate darkness from light, though not in the same way as we distinguish one colour from another. Further, in a sense even that which sees *is* coloured; for in each case the sense-organ is capable of receiving the sensible object without its matter. That is why even when the sensible objects are gone the sensings and imaginings continue to 25 exist in the sense-organs.

The activity of the sensible object and that of the percipient sense is one and the same activity, and yet the distinction between their being remains. Take as illustration actual sound and actual hearing: a man may have hearing and yet not be hearing, and that which has a sound is not always sounding. But when that which can hear is actively hearing and that which can sound is sounding, then the 30 actual hearing and the actual sound are merged in one (these one 426ᵃ might call respectively hearkening and sounding).

If it is true that the movement, both the acting and the being acted upon, is to be found in that which is acted upon,[1] both the sound and the hearing so far as it is actual must be found in that which has the faculty of hearing; for it is in the passive factor that the actuality of the active or motive factor is realized; that is why that which 5

---

[1] Cf. *Phys.* iii. 3.

causes movement may be at rest. Now the actuality of that which can sound is just sound or sounding, and the actuality of that which can hear is hearing or hearkening; 'sound' and 'hearing' are both ambiguous. The same account applies to the other senses and their objects.
10 For as the-acting-and-being-acted-upon is to be found in the passive, not in the active factor, so also the actuality of the sensible object and that of the sensitive subject are both realized in the latter. But while in some cases each aspect of the total actuality has a distinct name, e. g. sounding and hearkening, in some one or other is nameless, e. g. the actuality of sight is called seeing, but the actuality of colour has no name: the actuality of the faculty of taste is called
15 tasting, but the actuality of flavour has no name. Since the actualities of the sensible object and of the sensitive faculty are *one* actuality in spite of the difference between their modes of being, actual hearing and actual sounding appear and disappear from existence at one and the same moment, and so actual savour and actual tasting, &c., while
20 as potentialities one of them may exist without the other. The earlier students of nature were mistaken in their view that without sight there was no white or black, without taste no savour. This statement of theirs is partly true, partly false: 'sense' and 'the sensible object' are ambiguous terms, i. e. may denote either potentialities or actuali-
25 ties: the statement is true of the latter, false of the former. This ambiguity they wholly failed to notice.

If voice always implies a concord, and if the voice and the hearing of it are in one sense one and the same, and if concord always implies a ratio, hearing as well as what is heard must be a ratio. That
30 is why the excess of either the sharp or the flat destroys the hearing. (So also in the case of savours excess destroys the sense of taste,
426ᵇ and in the case of colours excessive brightness or darkness destroys the sight, and in the case of smell excess of strength whether in the direction of sweetness or bitterness is destructive.) This shows that the sense is a ratio.

That is also why the objects of sense are (1) pleasant when the sensible extremes such as acid or sweet or salt being pure and unmixed are brought into the proper ratio; [2] then they are pleasant:
5 and in general what is blended is more pleasant than the sharp or the flat alone; or, to touch, that which is capable of being either warmed or chilled: the sense and the ratio are identical: while (2) in excess the sensible extremes are painful or destructive.

Each sense then is relative to its particular group of sensible

[2] i. e. that which is involved in the structure of the sense-organ.

qualities: it is found in a sense-organ as such [3] and discriminates the differences which exist within that group; e. g. sight discriminates white and black, taste sweet and bitter, and so in all cases. Since we 10 also discriminate white from sweet, and indeed each sensible quality from every other, with what do we perceive that they are different? It must be by sense; for what is before us is sensible objects. (Hence it is also obvious that the flesh cannot be the ultimate sense-organ: 15 if it were, the discriminating power could not do its work without immediate contact with the object.)

Therefore (1) discrimination between white and sweet cannot be effected by two agencies which remain separate; both the qualities discriminated must be present to something that is one and single. On any other supposition even if I perceived sweet and you perceived white, the difference between them would be apparent. What says 20 that two things are different must be one; for sweet is different from white. Therefore what asserts this difference must be self-identical, and as what asserts, so also what thinks or perceives. That it is not possible by means of two agencies which remain separate to discriminate two objects which are separate is therefore obvious; and that (2) it is not possible to do this in separate moments of time may be seen if we look at it as follows. For as what asserts the difference between the good and the bad is one and the same, so also the time at which 25 it asserts the one to be different and the other to be different is not accidental to the assertion (as it is for instance when I now assert a difference but do not assert that there is now a difference); it asserts thus—both now and that the objects are different now; the objects therefore must be present at one and the same moment. Both the discriminating power and the time of its exercise must be one and undivided.

But, it may be objected, it is impossible that what is self-identical should be moved at one and the same time with contrary movements 30 in so far as it is undivided, and in an undivided moment of time. For if what is sweet be the quality perceived, it moves the sense or thought in this determinate way, while what is bitter moves it in a 427ᵃ contrary way, and what is white in a different way. Is it the case then that what discriminates, though both numerically one and indivisible, is at the same time divided in its being? In one sense, it is what is divided that perceives two separate objects at once, but in another sense it does so *qua* undivided; for it is divisible in its being, but spatially and numerically undivided.

[3] The qualification appears to mean that the sense-organ may in other respects have other qualities. Thus the tongue can touch as well as taste.

5   But is not this impossible? For while it is true that what is self-identical and undivided may be both contraries at once *potentially*, it cannot be self-identical in its being—it must lose its unity by being put into activity. It is not possible to be at once white and black, and therefore it must also be impossible for a thing to be affected at one and the same moment by the forms of both, assuming it to be the case that sensation and thinking are properly so described.[4]

10   The answer is that just as what is called a 'point' is, as being at once one and two, properly said to be divisible, so here, that which discriminates is *qua* undivided one, and active in a single moment of time, while so far forth as it is divisible it twice over uses the same dot at one and the same time. So far forth then as it takes the limit as two, it discriminates two separate objects with what in a sense is divided: while so far as it takes it as one, it does so with what is one and occupies in its activity a single moment of time.

About the principle in virtue of which we say that animals are 15 percipient, let this discussion suffice.

3   There are two distinctive peculiarities by reference to which we characterize the soul—(1) local movement and (2) thinking, discriminating, and perceiving. Thinking, both speculative and practical, is regarded as akin to a form of perceiving; for in the one as well as 20 the other the soul discriminates and is cognizant of something which *is*. Indeed the ancients go so far as to identify thinking and perceiving; e. g. Empedocles says 'For 'tis in respect of what is present that man's wit is increased', and again 'whence it befalls them from time to time to think diverse thoughts', and Homer's phrase [5] 'For 25 suchlike is man's mind' means the same. They all look upon thinking as a bodily process like perceiving, and hold that like is *known* as well as *perceived* by like, as I explained at the beginning of our discussion.[6] Yet they ought at the same time to have accounted for

427ᵇ error also; for it is more intimately connected with animal existence and the soul continues longer in the state of error than in that of truth. They cannot escape the dilemma: either (1) whatever seems is true (and there are some who accept this) or (2) error is contact with the unlike; for that is the opposite of the knowing of like by like.

5   But it is a received principle that error as well as knowledge in respect to contraries is one and the same.

That perceiving and practical thinking are not identical is therefore obvious; for the former is universal in the animal world, the

---

[4] i. e. as the being affected by the forms of sensible qualities.
[5] *Od*. xviii. 136.   [6] 404ᵇ 8–18.

latter is found in only a small division of it. Further, speculative thinking is also distinct from perceiving—I mean that in which we find rightness and wrongness—rightness in prudence, knowledge, true 10 opinion, wrongness in their opposites; for perception of the special objects of sense is always free from error, and is found in all animals, while it is possible to think falsely as well as truly, and thought is found only where there is discourse of reason as well as sensibility. For imagination is different from either perceiving or dis- 15 cursive thinking, though it is not found without sensation, or judgement without it. That this activity is not the same kind of thinking as judgement is obvious. For imagining lies within our own power whenever we wish (e. g. we can call up a picture, as in the practice of mnemonics by the use of mental images), but in forming opinions we 20 are not free: we cannot escape the alternative of falsehood or truth. Further, when we think something to be fearful or threatening, emotion is immediately produced, and so too with what is encouraging; but when we merely imagine we remain as unaffected as persons who are looking at a painting of some dreadful or encouraging scene. Again within the field of judgement itself we find varieties—knowledge, opinion, prudence, and their opposites; of the differences between these I must speak elsewhere.[7]

Thinking is different from perceiving and is held to be in part imagination, in part judgement: we must therefore first mark off the sphere of imagination and then speak of judgement. If then imagina- 428ᵃ tion is that in virtue of which an image arises for us, excluding metaphorical uses of the term, is it a single faculty or disposition relative to images, in virtue of which we discriminate and are either in error or not? The faculties in virtue of which we do this are sense, opinion, science, intelligence.

That imagination is not sense is clear from the following consider- 5 ations: (1) Sense is either a faculty or an activity, e. g. sight or seeing: imagination takes place in the absence of both, as e. g. in dreams. (2) Again, sense is always present, imagination not. If actual imagination and actual sensation were the same, imagination would be found in all the brutes: this is held not to be the case; e. g. it is not found 10 in ants or bees or grubs. (3) Again, sensations are always true, imaginations are for the most part false. (4) Once more, even in ordinary speech, we do not, when sense functions precisely with regard to its object, say that we imagine it to be a man, but rather when there is some failure of accuracy in its exercise. And (5), as we were 15 saying before, visions appear to us even when our eyes are shut.

---

[7] The reference is perhaps to *E. N.* 1139ᵇ 15 ff.

Neither is imagination *any* of the things that are never in error: e. g. knowledge or intelligence; for imagination may be false.

It remains therefore to see if it is opinion, for opinion may be either true or false.

20　But opinion involves belief (for without belief in what we opine we cannot have an opinion), and in the brutes though we often find imagination we never find belief. Further, every opinion is accompanied by belief, belief by conviction, and conviction by discourse of reason: while there are some of the brutes in which we find imagination, without discourse of reason. It is clear then that imagination 25 cannot, again, be (1) opinion *plus* sensation, or (2) opinion mediated by sensation, or (3) a blend of opinion and sensation; [8] this is impossible both for these reasons and because the content of the supposed opinion cannot be different from that of the sensation (I mean that imagination must be the blending of the perception of white 30 with the opinion that it is white: it could scarcely be a blend of the opinion that it is good with the perception that it is white): to 428b imagine is therefore (on this view) identical with the thinking of exactly the same as what one in the strictest sense perceives. But what we imagine is sometimes false though our contemporaneous judgement about it is true; e. g. we imagine the sun to be a foot in diameter though we are convinced that it is larger than the inhabited part of the earth, and the following dilemma presents itself. Either (*a*) while the fact has not changed and the observer has neither forgotten 5 nor lost belief in the true opinion which he had, that opinion has disappeared, or (*b*) if he retains it then his opinion is at once true and false. A true opinion, however, becomes false only when the fact alters without being noticed.

Imagination is therefore neither any one of the states enumerated, nor compounded out of them.

10　But since when one thing has been set in motion another thing may be moved by it, and imagination is held to be a movement and to be impossible without sensation, i. e. to occur in beings that are percipient and to have for its content what can be perceived, and since movement may be produced by actual sensation and that movement is necessarily similar in character to the sensation itself, this move- 15 ment must be (1) necessarily (*a*) incapable of existing apart from sensation, (*b*) incapable of existing except when we perceive, (2) such that in virtue of its possession that in which it is found may present various phenomena both active and passive, and (3) such that it may be either true or false.

[8] For these three views Cf. Pl. *Tim.* 52 A, *Soph.* A, B, *Phil.* 39 B.

The reason of the last characteristic is as follows. Perception (1) of the special objects of sense is never in error or admits the least possible amount of falsehood. (2) That of the concomitance of the objects concomitant with the sensible qualities comes next: in this case certainly we may be deceived; for while the perception that there is white before us cannot be false, the perception that what is white is this or that may be false. (3) Third comes the perception of the universal attributes which accompany the concomitant objects to which the special sensibles attach (I mean e. g. of movement and magnitude); it is in respect of these that the greatest amount of sense-illusion is possible.

The motion which is due to the activity of sense in these three modes of its exercise will differ from the activity of sense; (1) the first kind of derived motion is free from error while the sensation is present; (2) and (3) the others may be erroneous whether it is present or absent, especially when the object of perception is far off. If then imagination presents no other features than those enumerated and is what we have described, then imagination must be a movement resulting from an actual exercise of a power of sense.

As sight is the most highly developed sense, the name *phantasia* (imagination) has been formed from *phaos* (light) because it is not possible to see without light.

And because imaginations remain in the organs of sense and resemble sensations, animals in their actions are largely guided by them, some (i. e. the brutes) because of the non-existence in them of mind, others (i. e. men) because of the temporary eclipse in them of mind by feeling or disease or sleep.

About imagination, what it is and why it exists, let so much suffice.

4 Turning now to the part of the soul with which the soul knows and thinks (whether this is separable from the others in definition only, or spatially as well) we have to inquire (1) what differentiates this part, and (2) how thinking can take place.

If thinking is like perceiving, it must be either a process in which the soul is acted upon by what is capable of being thought, or a process different from but analogous to that. The thinking part of the soul must therefore be, while impassible, capable of receiving the form of an object; that is, must be potentially identical in character with its object without being the object. Mind must be related to what is thinkable, as sense is to what is sensible.

Therefore, since everything is a possible object of thought, mind

in order, as Anaxagoras says, to dominate, that is, to know, must be
20 pure from all admixture; for the co-presence of what is alien to its
nature is a hindrance and a block: it follows that it too, like the
sensitive part, can have no nature of its own, other than that of
having a certain capacity. Thus that in the soul which is called
mind (by mind I mean that whereby the soul thinks and judges) is,
before it thinks, not actually any real thing. For this reason it cannot
25 reasonably be regarded as blended with the body: if so, it would acquire some quality, e. g. warmth or cold, or even have an organ like the
sensitive faculty: as it is, it has none. It was a good idea to call the soul
'the place of forms', though (1) this description holds only of the intellective soul, and (2) even this is the forms only potentially, not actually.

Observation of the sense-organs and their employment reveals a
30 distinction between the impassibility of the sensitive and that of
the intellective faculty. After strong stimulation of a sense we are
429ᵇ less able to exercise it than before, as e. g. in the case of a loud sound
we cannot hear easily immediately after, or in the case of a bright
colour or a powerful odour we cannot see or smell, but in the case
of mind, thought about an object that is highly intelligible renders it
more and not less able afterwards to think objects that are less intelligible: the reason is that while the faculty of sensation is dependent upon the body, mind is separable from it.

5   Once the mind has become each set of its possible objects, as a
man of science has, when this phrase is used of one who is actually
a man of science (this happens when he is now able to exercise the
power on his own initiative), its condition is still one of potentiality,
but in a different sense from the potentiality which preceded the
acquisition of knowledge by learning or discovery: the mind too is then
able to think *itself*.

10   Since we can distinguish between a spatial magnitude and what it is
to be such, and between water and what it is to be water, and so in
many other cases (though not in all; for in certain cases the thing
and its form are identical), flesh and what it is to be flesh are discriminated either by different faculties, or by the same faculty in two
different states: for flesh necessarily involves matter and is like what
is snub-nosed, a *this* in a *this*.⁹ Now it is by means of the sensitive
faculty that we discriminate the hot and the cold, i. e. the factors
15 which combined in a certain ratio constitute flesh: the essential character of flesh is apprehended by something different either wholly
separate from the sensitive faculty or related to it as a bent line to
the same line when it has been straightened out.

⁹ i. e. a particular form in a particular matter.

Again in the case of abstract objects what is straight is analogous to what is snub-nosed; for it necessarily implies a continuum as its matter: its constitutive essence is different, if we may distinguish between straightness and what is straight: let us take it to be two-ness. 20 It must be apprehended, therefore, by a different power or by the same power in a different state. To sum up, in so far as the realities it knows are capable of being separated from their matter, so it is also with the powers of mind.

The problem might be suggested: if thinking is a passive affection, then if mind is simple and impassible and has nothing in common with anything else, as Anaxagoras says, how can it come to think at all? For interaction between two factors is held to require a precedent community of nature between the factors. Again it might be asked, is mind a possible object of thought to itself? For if mind is thinkable *per se* and what is thinkable is in kind one and the same, then either (*a*) mind will belong to everything, or (b) mind will contain some element common to it with all other realities which makes them all thinkable.

(1) Have not we already disposed of the difficulty about inter-action involving a common element, when we said [10] that mind is 30 in a sense potentially whatever is thinkable, though actually it is nothing until it has thought? What it thinks must be in it just as characters may be said to be on a writing-tablet on which as yet 430ª nothing actually stands written: this is exactly what happens with mind.

(2) Mind is itself thinkable in exactly the same way as its objects are. For (*a*) in the case of objects which involve no matter, what thinks and what is thought are identical; for speculative knowledge and its object are identical. (Why mind is not always thinking we 5 must consider later.) [11] (*b*) In the case of those which contain matter each of the objects of thought is only potentially present. It follows that while *they* will not have mind in them (for mind is a potentiality of them only in so far as they are capable of being disengaged from matter) mind may yet be thinkable.

5　Since in every class of things, as in nature as a whole, we find 10 two factors involved, (1) a matter which is potentially all the particulars included in the class, (2) a cause which is productive in the sense that it makes them all (the latter standing to the former, as e. g. an art to its material), these distinct elements must likewise be found within the soul.

10 ª15–24.

11 Ch. 5.

And in fact mind as we have described it [12] is what it is by virtue
15 of becoming all things, while there is another which is what it is by
virtue of making all things: this is a sort of positive state like light;
for in a sense light makes potential colours into actual colours.

Mind in this sense of it is separable, impassible, unmixed, since it
is in its essential nature activity (for always the active is superior
to the passive factor, the originating force to the matter which it
forms).

20   Actual knowledge is identical with its object: in the individual, potential knowledge is in time prior to actual knowledge, but in the universe as a whole it is not prior even in time. Mind is not at one time
knowing and at another not. When mind is set free from its present
conditions it appears as just what it is and nothing more: this alone is
immortal and eternal (we do not, however, remember its former
activity because, while mind in this sense is impassible, mind as pas-
25 sive is destructible), and without it nothing thinks.

6   The thinking then of the simple objects of thought is found in
those cases where falsehood is impossible: where the alternative of
true or false applies, there we always find a putting together of objects of thought in a quasi-unity. As Empedocles said that 'where
heads of many a creature sprouted without necks' they afterwards by
30 Love's power were combined, so here too objects of thought which
were given separate are combined, e. g. 'incommensurate' and
'diagonal': if the combination be of objects past or future the combination of thought includes in its content the date. For falsehood al-
430ᵇ ways involves a synthesis; for even if you assert that what is white is
not white you have included not-white in a synthesis. It is possible also
to call all these cases division as well as combination. However that
may be, there is not only the true or false assertion that Cleon is white
but also the true or false assertion that he *was* or *will be* white. In
5 each and every case that which unifies is mind.

Since the word 'simple' has two senses, i. e. may mean either (*a*)
'not capable of being divided' or (*b*) 'not actually divided', there is
nothing to prevent mind from knowing what is undivided, e. g. when
it apprehends a length (which is actually undivided) and that in an
undivided time; for the time is divided or undivided in the same
10 manner as the line. It is not possible, then, to tell what part of the line
it was apprehending in each half of the time: the object has no actual
parts until it has been divided: if in thought you think each half
separately, then by the same act you divide the time also, the half-

---

[12] In ch. 4.

lines becoming as it were new wholes of length. But if you think it as a whole consisting of these two possible parts, then also you think it in a time which corresponds to both parts together. (But what is not quantitatively but qualitatively simple is thought in a simple 15 time and by a simple act of the soul.)

But that which mind thinks and the time in which it thinks are in this case divisible only incidentally and not as such. For in them too there is something indivisible (though, it may be, not isolable) which gives unity to the time and the whole of length; and this is found equally in every continuum whether temporal or spatial.

Points and similar instances of things that divide, themselves being 20 indivisible, are realized in consciousness in the same manner as privations.

A similar account may be given of all other cases, e. g. how evil or black is cognized; they are cognized, in a sense, by means of their contraries. That which cognizes must have an element of potentiality in its being, and one of the contraries must be in it.[13] But if there is anything that has no contrary, then it knows itself and is actually and 25 possesses independent existence.

Assertion is the saying of something concerning something, e. g. affirmation, and is in every case either true or false: this is not always the case with mind: the thinking of the definition in the sense of the constitutive essence is never in error nor is it the assertion of something concerning something, but, just as while the seeing of the special object of sight can never be in error, the belief that the white object seen is a man may be mistaken, so too in the case of objects which are 30 without matter.

7   Actual knowledge is identical with its object: potential knowledge 431ᵃ in the individual is in time prior to actual knowledge but in the universe it has no priority even in time; for all things that come into being arise from what actually is. In the case of sense clearly the sensitive faculty already was potentially what the object makes it to be 5 actually; the faculty is not affected or altered. This must therefore be a different kind from movement; for movement is, as we saw,[14] an activity of what is imperfect, activity in the unqualified sense, i. e. that of what has been perfected, is different from movement.

To perceive then is like bare asserting or knowing; but when the object is pleasant or painful, the soul makes a quasi-affirmation or

negation, and pursues or avoids the object. To feel pleasure or pain is
10 to act with the sensitive mean towards what is good or bad as such.
Both avoidance and appetite when actual are identical with this: the
faculty of appetite and avoidance are not different, either from one another or from the faculty of sense-perception; but their being *is*
different.

To the thinking soul images serve as if they were contents of per-
15 ception (and when it asserts or denies them to be good or bad it avoids
or pursues them). That is why the soul never thinks without an
image. The process is like that in which the air modifies the pupil in
this or that way and the pupil transmits the modification to some third
thing (and similarly in hearing), while the ultimate point of arrival is
one, a single mean, with different manners of being.

20 With what part of itself the soul discriminates sweet from hot [15]
I have explained before [16] and must now describe again as follows:
That with which it does so is a sort of unity, but in the way just mentioned,[17] i. e. as a connecting term. And the two faculties it connects,[18] being one by analogy and numerically, are each to each as
the qualities discerned are to one another (for what difference does
it make whether we raise the problem of discrimination between dis-
25 parates or between contraries, e. g. white and black?). Let then C be
to D as A is to B: [19] it follows *alternando* that $C:A::D:B$. If then
C and D belong to one subject, the case will be the same with them
as with A and B; A and B form a single identity with different modes
431ᵇ of being; so too will the former pair. The same reasoning holds
if A be sweet and B white.

The faculty of thinking then thinks the forms in the images, and as
in the former case [20] what is to be pursued or avoided is marked out for
it, so where there is no sensation and it is engaged upon the images it is
5 moved to pursuit or avoidance. E. g. perceiving by sense thɑt the
beacon is fire, it recognizes in virtue of the general faculty of sense
that it signifies an enemy, because it sees it moving; but sometimes by
means of the images or thoughts which are within the soul, just as if
it were seeing, it calculates and deliberates what is to come by reference to what is present; and when it makes a pronouncement, as in the
case of sensation it pronounces the object to be pleasant or painful,

---

[15] i. e. the sweetness and the heat in a sweet-hot object.
[16] 426ᵇ 12–427ᵃ 14.   [17] i. e. as one thing with two aspects; cf. l. 19.
[18] i. e. the faculty by which we discern sweet and that by which we discern hot.
[19] i. e. let the faculty that discerns sweet be to that which discerns hot as
sweet is to hot.   [20] i. e. that of sense-data.

in this case it avoids or pursues; and so generally in cases of action.

That too which involves no action, i. e. that which is true or false, is [10] in the same province with what is good or bad: yet they differ in this, that the one set imply and the other do not a reference to a particular person.

The so-called abstract objects the mind thinks just as, if one had thought of the snub-nosed not as snub-nosed but as hollow, one would have thought of an actuality without the flesh in which it is embodied: [15] it is thus that the mind when it is thinking the objects of Mathematics thinks as separate, elements which do not exist separate. In every case the mind which is actively thinking is the objects which it thinks. Whether it is possible for it while not existing separate from spatial conditions to think anything that is separate, or not, we must consider later.[21]

8   Let us now summarize our results about soul, and repeat that the [20] soul is in a way all existing things; for existing things are either sensible or thinkable, and knowledge is in a way what is knowable, and sensation is in a way what is sensible: in *what* way we must inquire.

Knowledge and sensation are divided to correspond with the realities, potential knowledge and sensation answering to potentialities, [25] actual knowledge and sensation to actualities. Within the soul the faculties of knowledge and sensation are *potentially* these objects, the one what is knowable, the other what is sensible. They must be either the things themselves or their forms. The former alternative is of course impossible: it is not the stone which is present in the soul but its form.

It follows that the soul is analogous to the hand; for as the hand [432^a] is a tool of tools,[22] so the mind is the form of forms and sense the form of sensible things.

Since according to common agreement there is nothing outside and separate in existence from sensible spatial magnitudes, the objects of thought are in the sensible forms, viz. both the abstract objects [5] and all the states and affections of sensible things. Hence (1) no one can learn or understand anything in the absence of sense, and (2) when the mind is actively aware of anything it is necessarily aware of it along with an image; for images are like sensuous contents except in that they contain no matter.

Imagination is different from assertion and denial; for what is true or false involves a synthesis of concepts. In what will the primary [10]

21 This promise does not seem to have been fulfilled.
22 i. e. a tool for using tools.

concepts differ from images? Must we not say that neither these nor even our other concepts are images, though they necessarily involve them?

15 9 The soul of animals is characterized by two faculties, (*a*) the faculty of discrimination which is the work of thought and sense, and (*b*) the faculty of originating local movement. Sense and mind we have now sufficiently examined. Let us next consider what it is in the soul which originates movement. Is it a single part of the soul 20 separate either spatially or in definition? Or is it the soul as a whole? If it is a part, is that part different from those usually distinguished or already mentioned by us, or is it one of them? The problem at once presents itself, in what sense we are to speak of parts of the soul, or how many we should distinguish. For in a sense there is an in-25 finity of parts: it is not enough to distinguish, with some thinkers,[23] the calculative, the passionate, and the desiderative, or with others [24] the rational and the irrational; for if we take the dividing lines fol-lowed by these thinkers we shall find parts far more distinctly separated from one another than these, namely those we have just mentioned: (1) the nutritive, which belongs both to plants and to 30 all animals, and (2) the sensitive, which cannot easily be classed as either irrational or rational; further (3) the imaginative, which is, 432ᵇ in its being, different from all, while it is very hard to say with which of the others it is the same or not the same, supposing we determine to posit *separate* parts in the soul; and lastly (4) the appetitive, which would seem to be distinct both in definition and in power from all hitherto enumerated.

5 It is absurd to break up the last-mentioned faculty: as these thinkers do, for wish is found in the calculative part and desire and passion in the irrational;[25] and if the soul is tripartite appetite will be found in all three parts. Turning our attention to the present object of discussion, let us ask what that is which originates local movement of the animal.

The movement of growth and decay, being found in all living 10 things, must be attributed to the faculty of reproduction and nutri-tion, which is common to all: inspiration and expiration, sleep and waking, we must consider later:[26] these too present much difficulty: at present we must consider local movement, asking what it is that originates forward movement in the animal.

---

[23] Pl. *Rep.* 435-41. [24] A popular view, Cf. *E. N.* 1102ᵃ 26-8.
[25] All three being forms of appetite.
[26] Cf. *De Respiratione, De Somno.*

That it is not the nutritive faculty is obvious; for this kind of ¹⁵ movement is always for an end and is accompanied either by imagination or by appetite; for no animal moves except by compulsion unless it has an impulse towards or away from an object. Further, if it were the nutritive faculty, even plants would have been capable of originating such movement and would have possessed the organs necessary to carry it out. Similarly it cannot be the sensitive faculty either; for there are many animals which have sensibility but remain fast and immovable throughout their lives. ²⁰

If then Nature never makes anything without a purpose and never leaves out what is necessary (except in the case of mutilated or imperfect growths; and that here we have neither mutilation nor imperfection may be argued from the facts that such animals (*a*) can reproduce their species and (*b*) rise to completeness of nature and decay to an end), it follows that, had they been capable of originat- ²⁵ ing forward movement, they would have possessed the organs necessary for that purpose. Further, neither can the calculative faculty or what is called 'mind' be the cause of such movement; for mind as speculative never thinks what is practicable, it never says anything about an object to be avoided or pursued, while this movement is always in something which is avoiding or pursuing an object. No, not even when it is aware of such an object does it at once enjoin pursuit ³⁰ or avoidance of it; e. g. the mind often thinks of something terrifying or pleasant without enjoining the emotion of fear. It is the heart that is moved (or in the case of a pleasant object some other part). Fur- 433ᵃ ther, even when the mind does command and thought bids us pursue or avoid something, sometimes no movement is produced; we act in accordance with desire, as in the case of moral weakness. And, generally, we observe that the possessor of medical knowledge is not necessarily healing, which shows that something else is required to produce action in accordance with knowledge; the knowledge alone is ⁵ not the cause. Lastly, appetite too is incompetent to account fully for movement; for those who successfully resist temptation have appetite and desire and yet follow mind and refuse to enact that for which they have appetite.

10   These two at all events appear to be sources of movement: appetite and mind (if one may venture to regard imagination as a kind of ¹⁰ thinking; for many men follow their imaginations contrary to knowledge, and in all animals other than man there is no thinking or calculation but only imagination).

Both of these then are capable of originating local movement, mind and appetite: (1) mind, that is, which calculates means to an end,
15 i. e. mind practical (it differs from mind speculative in the character of its end); while (2) appetite is in every form of it relative to an end: for that which is the object of appetite is the stimulant of mind practical; and that which is last in the process of thinking is the beginning of the action. It follows that there is a justification for regarding these two as the sources of movement, i. e. appetite and practical thought; for the object of appetite starts a movement and as a result of that thought gives rise to movement, the object of
20 appetite being to it a source of stimulation. So too when imagination originates movement, it necessarily involves appetite.

That which moves therefore is a single faculty and the faculty of appetite; for if there had been two sources of movement—mind and appetite—they would have produced movement in virtue of some common character. As it is, mind is never found producing movement without appetite (for wish is a form of appetite; and when movement is produced according to calculation it is also according to
25 wish), but appetite can originate movement contrary to calculation, for desire is a form of appetite. Now mind is always right, but appetite and imagination may be either right or wrong. That is why, though in any case it is the object of appetite which originates movement, this object may be either the real or the apparent good. To produce movement the object must be more than this: it must be good that can be brought into being by action; and only what can
30 be otherwise than as it is can thus be brought into being. That then such a power in the soul as has been described, i. e. that called appe-
433ᵇ tite, originates movement is clear. Those who distinguish parts in the soul, if they distinguish and divide in accordance with differences of power, find themselves with a very large number of parts, a nutritive, a sensitive, an intellective, a deliberative, and now an appetitive part; for these are more different from one another than the faculties of desire and passion.

Since appetites run counter to one another, which happens when a principle of reason and a desire are contrary and is possible only in beings with a sense of time (for while mind bids us hold back because of what is future, desire is influenced by what is just at hand: a pleasant object which is just at hand presents itself as both pleasant and good, without condition in either case, because of want
10 of foresight into what is farther away in time), it follows that while that which originates movement must be specifically one, viz. the

faculty of appetite as such (or rather farthest back of all the object of that faculty; for it is it that itself remaining unmoved originates the movement by being apprehended in thought or imagination), the things that originate movement are numerically many.

All movement involves three factors, (1) that which originates the movement, (2) that by means of which it originates it, and (3) that which is moved. The expression 'that which originates the movement' is ambiguous: it may mean either (a) something which itself is unmoved or (b) that which at once moves and is moved. 15 Here that which moves without itself being moved is the realizable good, that which at once moves and is moved is the faculty of appetite (for that which is influenced by appetite so far as it is actually so influenced is set in movement, and appetite in the sense of actual appetite *is* a kind of movement), while that which is in motion is the animal. The instrument which appetite employs to produce movement is no longer psychical but bodily: hence the examination of it 20 falls within the province of the functions common to body and soul.[27] To state the matter summarily at present, that which is the instrument in the production of movement is to be found where a beginning and an end coincide as e. g. in a ball and socket joint; for there the convex and the concave sides are respectively an end and a beginning (that is why while the one remains at rest, the other is moved): they are separate in definition but not separable spatially. For everything is moved by pushing and pulling. Hence just as in the 25 case of a wheel, so here there must be a point which remains at rest, and from that point the movement must originate.

To sum up, then, and repeat what I have said, inasmuch as an animal is capable of appetite it is capable of self-movement; it is not capable of appetite without possessing imagination; and all imagination is either (1) calculative or (2) sensitive. In the latter all ani- 30 mals, and not only man, partake.

11   We must consider also in the case of imperfect animals, sc. those which have no sense but touch, what it is that in them originates movement. Can they have imagination or not? or desire? Clearly 434ᵃ they have feelings of pleasure and pain, and if they have these they must have desire. But how can they have imagination? Must not we say that, as their movements are indefinite, they have imagination and desire, but indefinitely?

Sensitive imagination, as we have said,[28] is found in all animals, 5

<hr />

[27] Cf. *De Motu An.* 702ᵃ 21–703ᵃ 22.   [28] 433ᵇ 29.

deliberative imagination only in those that are calculative: for whether this or that shall be enacted is already a task requiring calculation; and there must be a single standard to measure by, for that is pursued which is *greater*. It follows that what acts in this way must be able to make a unity out of several images.

10   This is the reason why imagination is held not to involve opinion, in that it does not involve opinion based on inference, though opinion involves imagination. Hence appetite contains no deliberative element. Sometimes it overpowers wish and sets it in movement: at times wish acts thus upon appetite, like one sphere imparting its movement to another, or appetite acts thus upon appetite, i. e. in the condition of moral weakness (though by *nature* the higher faculty is *always* more authoritative and gives rise to movement). Thus *three* 15 modes of movement are possible.

The faculty of knowing is never moved but remains at rest. Since the one premiss or judgement is universal and the other deals with the particular (for the first tells us that such and such a kind of man should do such and such a kind of act, and the second that *this* is an act of the kind meant, and I a person of the type intended), it is the 20 latter opinion that really originates movement, not the universal; or rather it is both, but the one does so while it remains in a state more like rest, while the other partakes in movement.

12   The nutritive soul then must be possessed by everything that is alive, and every such thing is endowed with soul from its birth to its death. For what has been born must grow, reach maturity, and decay 25 —all of which are impossible without nutrition. Therefore the nutritive faculty must be found in everything that grows and decays.

But sensation need not be found in all things that live. For it is impossible for touch to belong either (1) to those whose body is uncompounded or (2) to those which are incapable of taking in the forms without their matter.

30   But animals must be endowed with sensation, since Nature does nothing in vain. For all things that exist by Nature are means to an end, or will be concomitants of means to an end. Every body capable of forward movement would, if unendowed with sensation, perish 434ᵇ and fail to reach its end, which is the aim of Nature; for how could it obtain nutriment? Stationary living things, it is true, have as their nutriment that from which they have arisen; but it is not possible that a body which is not stationary but produced by generation should have a soul and a discerning mind without also having sensa-

tion. (Nor yet even if it were not produced by generation. Why should it not have sensation? Because it were better so either for the body or for the soul? But clearly it would not be better for either: the absence of sensation will not enable the one to think better or the other to exist better.) Therefore no body which is not stationary has soul without sensation.

But if a body *has* sensation, it must be either simple or compound. And simple it cannot be; for then it could not have touch, which is indispensable. This is clear from what follows. An animal is a body with soul in it: every body is tangible, i. e. perceptible by touch; hence necessarily, if an animal is to survive, its body must have tactual sensation. All the other senses, e. g. smell, sight, hearing, apprehend through media; but where there is immediate contact the animal, if it has no sensation, will be unable to avoid some things and take others, and so will find it impossible to survive. That is why taste also is a sort of touch; it is relative to nutriment, which is just tangible body; whereas sound, colour, and odour are innutritious, and further neither grow nor decay. Hence it is that taste also must be a sort of touch, because it is the sense for what is tangible and nutritious.

Both these senses, then, are indispensable to the animal, and it is clear that without touch it is impossible for an animal to be. All the other senses subserve well-being and for that very reason belong not to any and every kind of animal, but only to some, e. g. those capable of forward movement must have them; for, if they are to survive, they must perceive not only by immediate contact but also at a distance from the object. This will be possible if they can perceive through a medium, the medium being affected and moved by the perceptible object, and the animal by the medium. Just as that which produces local movement causes a change extending to a certain point, and that which gave an impulse causes another to produce a new impulse so that the movement traverses a medium—the first mover impelling without being impelled, the last moved being impelled without impelling, while the medium (or media, for there are many) is both—so is it also in the case of alteration, except that the agent produces it without the patient's changing its place. Thus if an object is dipped into wax, the movement goes on until submersion has taken place, and in stone it goes no distance at all, while in water the disturbance goes far beyond the object dipped: in air the disturbance is propagated farthest of all, the air acting and being acted upon, so long as it maintains an unbroken unity. That is why in the case of

5 reflection it is better, instead of saying that the sight issues from the eye and is reflected, to say that the air, so long as it remains one, is affected by the shape and colour. On a smooth surface the air possesses unity; hence it is that it in turn sets the sight in motion, just 10 as if the impression on the wax were transmitted as far as the wax extends.

13   It is clear that the body of an animal cannot be simple, i. e. consist of one element such as fire or air. For without touch it is impossible to have any other sense; for every body that has soul in it must, as we have said,[29] be capable of touch. All the other elements with 15 the exception of earth can constitute organs of sense, but all of them bring about perception only through something else, viz. through the media. Touch takes place by direct contact with its objects, whence also its name. All the other organs of sense, no doubt, perceive by contact, only the contact is mediate: touch alone perceives by immediate contact. Consequently no animal body can consist of these other elements.

20   Nor can it consist solely of earth. For touch is as it were a mean between all tangible qualities, and its organ is capable of receiving not only all the specific qualities which characterize earth, but also the hot and the cold and all other tangible qualities whatsoever. 25 That is why we have no sensation by means of bones, hair, &c., 435b because they consist of earth. So too plants, because they consist of earth, have no sensation. Without touch there can be no other sense, and the organ of touch cannot consist of earth or of any other single element.

It is evident, therefore, that the loss of this one sense alone must 5 bring about the death of an animal. For as on the one hand nothing which is not an animal can have this sense, so on the other it is the only one which is indispensably necessary to what is an animal. This explains, further, the following difference between the other senses and touch. In the case of all the others excess of intensity in the qualities which they apprehend, i. e. excess of intensity in colour, sound, and smell, destroys not the animal but only the organs of 10 the sense (except incidentally, as when the sound is accompanied by an impact or shock, or where through the objects of sight or of smell certain other things are set in motion, which destroy by contact); flavour also destroys only in so far as it is at the same time tangible. But excess of intensity in tangible qualities, e. g. heat, cold, or hard- 15 ness, destroys the animal itself. As in the case of every sensible qual-

29 434b 10-24.

ity excess destroys the organ, so here what is tangible destroys touch, which is the essential mark of life; for it has been shown that without touch it is impossible for an animal to be. That is why excess in intensity of tangible qualities destroys not merely the organ, but the animal itself, because this is the only sense which it must have.

All the other senses are necessary to animals, as we have said,[30] not for their being, but for their well-being. Such, e. g., is sight, which, since it lives in air or water, or generally in what is pellucid, it must have in order to see, and taste because of what is pleasant or painful to it, in order that it may perceive these qualities in its nutriment and so may desire to be set in motion, and hearing that it may have communication made to it, and a tongue that it may communicate with its fellows.

[30] 434^{b} 24.

Parva Naturalia

(The Short Physical Treatises)

Translated by J. I. Beare

DE MEMORIA ET REMINISCENTIA

(On Memory and Reminiscence)

1 We have, in the next place, to treat of Memory and Remember- 449^b
ing, considering its nature, its cause, and the part of the soul to which
this experience, as well as that of Recollecting, belongs. For the per- 5
sons who possess a retentive memory are not identical with those who
excel in power of recollection; indeed, as a rule, slow people have a
good memory, whereas those who are quick-witted and clever are
better at recollecting.

We must first form a true conception of the objects of memory,
a point on which mistakes are often made. Now to remember the 10
future is not possible, but this is an object of opinion or expectation
(and indeed there might be actually a science of expectation, like
that of divination, in which some believe); nor is there memory of
the present, but only sense-perception. For by the latter we know
not the future, nor the past, but the present only. But memory relates 15
to the past. No one would say that he remembers the present, when
it is present, e. g. a given white object at the moment when he sees
it; nor would one say that he remembers an object of scientific contemplation at the moment when he is actually contemplating it, and
has it full before his mind;—of the former he would say only that he
perceives it, of the latter only that he knows it. But when one has
scientific knowledge, or perception, apart from the actualizations of
the faculty concerned, he thus 'remembers' [that the angles of a tri- 20
angle are together equal to two right angles]; as to the former, that
he learned it, or thought it out for himself, as to the latter, that he
heard, or saw, it, or had some such sensible experience of it. For
whenever one exercises the faculty of remembering, he must say
within himself, 'I formerly heard (or otherwise perceived) this,' or
'I formerly had this thought'.

Memory is, therefore, neither Perception nor Conception, but a
state or affection of one of these, conditioned by lapse of time. As 25
already observed, there is no such thing as memory of the present
while present, for the present is object only of perception, and the
future, of expectation, but the object of memory is the past. All memory, therefore, implies a time elapsed; consequently only those ani-

607

mals which perceive time remember, and the organ whereby they perceive time is also that whereby they remember.

30 The subject of 'presentation' has been already considered in our work *de Anima*.[1] Without a presentation intellectual activity is im-
450ᵃ possible. For there is in such activity an incidental affection identical with one also incidental in geometrical demonstrations. For in the latter case, though we do not for the purpose of the proof make any use of the fact that the quantity in the triangle [for example, which we have drawn] is determinate, we nevertheless draw it determinate in quantity. So likewise when one exerts the intellect [e. g. on the
5 subject of first principles], although the object may not be quantitative, one envisages it as quantitative, though he thinks it in abstraction from quantity; while, on the other hand, if the object of the intellect is essentially of the class of things that are quantitative, but indeterminate, one envisages it as if it had determinate quantity, though subsequently, in thinking it, he abstracts from its determinateness. Why we cannot exercise the intellect on any object absolutely apart from the continuous, or apply it even to non-temporal
10 things unless in connexion with time, is another question. Now, one must cognize magnitude and motion by means of the same faculty by which one cognizes time [i. e. by that which is also the faculty of memory], and the presentation [involved in such cognition] is an affection of the *sensus communis*; whence this follows, viz. that the cognition of these objects [magnitude, motion, time] is effected by the [said *sensus communis*, i. e. the] primary faculty of perception. Accordingly, memory [not merely of sensible, but] even of intellectual objects involves a presentation: hence we may conclude that it belongs to the faculty of intelligence only incidentally, while directly and essentially it belongs to the primary faculty of sense-perception.

15 Hence not only human beings and the beings which possess opinion or intelligence, but also certain other animals, possess memory. If memory were a function of [pure] intellect, it would not have been as it is an attribute of many of the lower animals, but probably, in that case, no mortal beings would have had memory; since, even as the case stands, it is not an attribute of them all, just because all have not the faculty of perceiving time. Whenever one actually
20 remembers having seen or heard, or learned, something, he includes in this act (as we have already observed) the consciousness of 'formerly'; and the distinction of 'former' and 'latter' is a distinction in time.

[1] Cf. 427ᵇ 29 seqq.

Accordingly, if asked, of which among the parts of the soul memory is a function, we reply: manifestly of that part to which 'presentation' appertains; and all objects capable of being presented [viz. sensibles] are immediately and properly objects of memory, while those [viz. intelligibles] which necessarily involve [but *only* involve] presentation are objects of memory incidentally.   25

One might ask how it is possible that though the affection [the presentation] alone is present, and the [related] fact absent, the latter—that which is not present—is remembered. [This question arises], because it is clear that we must conceive that which is generated through sense-perception in the sentient soul, and in the part of the body which is its seat—viz. that affection the state whereof we call memory—to be some such thing as a picture. The process of 30 movement [sensory stimulation] involved in the act of perception stamps in, as it were, a sort of impression of the percept, just as persons do who make an impression with a seal. This explains why, 450ᵇ in those who are strongly moved owing to passion, or time of life, no mnemonic impression is formed; just as no impression would be formed if the movement of the seal were to impinge on running water; while there are others in whom, owing to the receiving surface being frayed, as happens to [the stucco on] old [chamber] 5 walls, or owing to the hardness of the receiving surface, the requisite impression is not implanted at all. Hence both very young and very old persons are defective in memory; they are in a state of flux, the former because of their growth, the latter, owing to their decay. In like manner, also, both those who are too quick and those who are too slow have bad memories. The former are too soft, the latter too 10 hard [in the texture of their receiving organs], so that in the case of the former the presented image [though imprinted] does not remain in the soul, while on the latter it is not imprinted at all.

But then, if this truly describes what happens in the genesis of memory, [the question stated above arises:] when one remembers, is it this impressed affection that he remembers, or is it the objective thing from which this was derived? If the former, it would follow that we remember nothing which is absent; if the latter, how is it pos- 15 sible that, though perceiving directly only the impression, we remember that absent thing which we do not perceive? Granted that there is in us something like an impression or picture, why should the perception of the mere impression be memory of something else, instead of being related to this impression alone? For when one actually remembers, this impression is what he contemplates, and

this is what he perceives. How then does he remember what is not
present? One might as well suppose it possible also to see or hear that
20 which is not present. In reply, we suggest that this very thing is quite
conceivable, nay, actually occurs in experience. A picture painted on
a panel is at once a picture and a likeness: that is, while one and the
same, it is both of these, although the 'being' of both is not the same,
and one may contemplate it either as a picture, or as a likeness .Just
in the same way we have to conceive that the mnemonic presenta-
25 tion within us is something which by itself is merely an object of
contemplation, while, in relation to something else, it is also a presentation of that other thing. In so far as it is regarded in itself, it is
only an object of contemplation, or a presentation; but when considered as relative to something else, e. g., as its likeness, it is also a
mnemonic token. Hence, whenever the residual sensory process implied by it is actualized in consciousness, if the soul perceives this
in so far as it is something absolute, it appears to occur as a mere
thought or presentation; but if the soul perceives it *qua* related to
something else, then,—just as when one contemplates the painting in
30 the picture as being a likeness, and without having [at the moment]
seen the actual Coriscus, contemplates it as a likeness of Coriscus,
451ª and in that case the experience involved in this contemplation of it
[as relative] is different from what one has when he contemplates it
simply as a painted figure—[so in the case of memory we have the
analogous difference, for], of the objects in the soul, the one [the
unrelated object] presents itself simply as a thought, but the other
[the related object], just because, as in the painting, it is a likeness,
presents itself as a mnemonic token.

We can now understand why it is that sometimes, when we have
such processes, based on some former act of perception, occurring in
the soul, we do not know whether this really implies our having had
5 perceptions corresponding to them, and we doubt whether the case is
or is not one of memory. But occasionally it happens that [while
thus doubting] we get a sudden idea and recollect that we heard or
saw something formerly. This [occurrence of the 'sudden idea']
happens whenever, from contemplating a mental object as absolute,
one changes his point of view, and regards it as relative to something else.

The opposite [sc. to the case of those who at first do not recognize
their phantasms as mnemonic] also occurs, as happened in the cases
of Antipheron of Oreus and others suffering from mental derange-
10 ment; for they were accustomed to speak of their mere phantasms as

facts of their past experience, and as if remembering them. This takes place whenever one contemplates what is not a likeness as if it were a likeness.

Mnemonic exercises aim at preserving one's memory of something by repeatedly reminding him of it; which implies nothing else [on the learner's part] than the frequent contemplation of something [viz. the 'mnemonic', whatever it may be] as a likeness, and not as out of relation.

As regards the question, therefore, what memory or remembering 15 is, it has now been shown that it is the state of a presentation, related as a *likeness* to that of which it is a presentation; and as to the question of which of the faculties within us memory is a function, [it has been shown] that it is a function of the primary faculty of sense-perception, i. e. of that faculty whereby we perceive time.

2   Next comes the subject of Recollection, in dealing with which we must assume as fundamental the truths elicited above in our intro- 20 ductory discussions. For recollection is not the 'recovery' or 'acquisition' of memory; since at the instant when one at first learns [a fact of science] or experiences [a particular fact of sense], he does not thereby 'recover' a memory, inasmuch as none has preceded, nor does he acquire one *ab initio*. It is only at the instant when the aforesaid state or affection [of the perception or conception; see 449ᵇ 24] is implanted in the soul that memory exists, and therefore memory is not itself implanted concurrently with the continuous implanta- 25 tion of the [original] sensory experience.

Further: at the very individual and concluding instant when first [the sensory experience or scientific knowledge] has been completely implanted, there is then already established in the person affected the [sensory] affection, or the scientific knowledge (if one ought to apply the term 'scientific knowledge' to the [mnemonic] state or affection; and indeed one may well remember, in the 'incidental' sense, some of the things [i. e. universals] which are properly objects of scientific knowledge); but to remember, strictly and properly speaking, is an activity which will not be immanent until the 30 original experience has undergone lapse of time. For one remembers now what one saw or otherwise experienced formerly; the moment of the original experience and the moment of the memory of it are never identical.

Again, [even when time has elapsed, and one can be said really to have acquired memory, this is not necessarily recollection, for

451ᵇ firstly] it is obviously possible, without any present act of recollection, to remember as a continued consequence of the original perception or other experience; whereas when [after an interval of
obliviscence] one recovers some scientific knowledge which he had
before, or some perception, or some other experience, the state of
which we above declared to be memory, it is then, and then only, that
this recovery may amount to a recollection of any of the things afore-
5 said. But, [though, as observed above, remembering does not necessarily imply recollecting], recollecting always implies remembering,
and actualized memory follows [upon the successful act of recol-
lecting].

But secondly, even the assertion that recollection is the reinstate-
ment in consciousness of something which was there before but had
disappeared requires qualification. This assertion may be true, but
it may also be false; for the same person may twice learn [from
some teacher], or twice discover [i. e. excogitate], the same fact.
Accordingly, the act of recollecting ought [in its definition] to be
distinguished from these acts; i. e. recollecting must imply in those
who recollect the presence of some spring over and above that from
which they originally learn.

10   Acts of recollection, as they occur in experience, are due to the
fact that one movement has by nature another that succeeds it in
regular order.

If this order be necessary, whenever a subject experiences the
former of two movements thus connected, it will [invariably] experience the latter; if, however, the order be not necessary, but customary, only in the majority of cases will the subject experience the
latter of the two movements. But it is a fact that there are some
movements, by a single experience of which persons take the impress
15 of custom more deeply than they do by experiencing others many
times; hence upon seeing some things but once we remember them
better than others which we may have seen frequently.

Whenever, therefore, we are recollecting, we are experiencing certain of the antecedent movements until finally we experience the one
after which customarily comes that which we seek. This explains
why we hunt up the series [of movements], having started in thought
either from a present intuition or some other, and from something
either similar, or contrary, to what we seek, or else from that which
20 is contiguous with it. Such is the empirical ground of the process of
recollection; for the mnemonic movements involved in these starting-
points are in some cases identical, in others, again, simultaneous,
with those of the idea we seek, while in others they comprise a portion

of them, so that the remnant which one experienced after that portion [and which still requires to be excited in memory] is comparatively small.

Thus, then, it is that persons seek to recollect, and thus, too, it is that they recollect even without the effort of seeking to do so, viz. when the movement implied in recollection has supervened on some other which is its condition. For, as a rule, it is when antecedent 25 movements of the classes here described have first been excited, that the particular movement implied in recollection follows. We need not examine a series of which the beginning and end lie far apart, in order to see how [by recollection] we remember; one in which they lie near one another will serve equally well. For it is clear that the method is in each case the same, that is, one hunts up the objective series, without any previous search or previous recollection. For [there is, besides the natural order, viz. the order of the things, or events of the primary experience, also a customary order, and] by the effect of custom the mnemonic movements tend to succeed one another in a certain order. Accordingly, therefore, when one wishes to 30 recollect, this is what he will do: he will try to obtain a beginning of movement whose sequel shall be the movement which he desires to reawaken. This explains why attempts at recollection succeed soonest and best when they start from a beginning [of some objective series]. 452ᵃ For, in order of succession, the mnemonic movements are to one another as the objective facts [from which they are derived]. Accordingly, things arranged in a fixed order, like the successive demonstrations in geometry, are easy to remember [or recollect], while badly arranged subjects are remembered with difficulty.

Recollecting differs also in this respect from relearning, that one who recollects will be able, somehow, to move, solely by his own 5 effort, to the term next after the starting-point. When one cannot do this of himself, but only by external assistance, he no longer remembers [i. e. he has totally forgotten, and therefore of course cannot recollect]. It often happens that, though a person cannot recollect at the moment, yet by seeking he can do so, and discovers what he seeks. This he succeeds in doing by setting up many movements, until finally he excites one of a kind which will have for its sequel the fact he wishes to recollect. For remembering [which is the *condicio* 10 *sine qua non* of recollecting] is the existence, potentially, in the mind of a movement capable of stimulating it to the desired movement, and this, as has been said, in such a way that the person should be moved [prompted to recollection] from within himself, i. e. in consequence of movements wholly contained within himself.

But one must get hold of a starting-point. This explains why it is that persons are supposed to recollect sometimes by starting from mnemonic *loci*. The cause is that they pass swiftly in thought from 15 one point to another, e. g. from milk to white, from white to mist, and thence to moist, from which one remembers Autumn [the 'season of mists'], if this be the season he is trying to recollect.

It seems true in general that the middle point also among all things is a good mnemonic starting-point from which to reach any of them. For if one does not recollect before, he will do so when he has come to this, or, if not, nothing can help him; as, e. g. if one were to have 20 in mind the numerical series denoted by the symbols 1, 2, 3, 4, 5, 6, 7, 8, 9. For, if he does not remember what he wants at 5, then at 5 he remembers 9; because from 5 movement in either direction is possible, to 4 or to 6. But, if it is not for one of these that he is searching, he will remember [what he *is* searching for] when he has come to 3, if he is searching for 8 or 7. But if [it is] not [for 8 or 7 that he is searching, but for one of the terms that remain], he will remember by going to 1, and so in all cases [in which one starts from 25 a middle point]. The cause of one's sometimes recollecting and sometimes not, though starting from the same point, is, that from the same starting-point a movement can be made in several directions, as, for instance, from 3 to 7 or to 4. If, then, the mind has not [when starting from 5] moved in an old path [i. e. one in which it moved when first having the objective experience, and that, therefore, in which un-'ethized' nature would have it again move], it tends to move to the more customary; for [the mind having, by chance or otherwise, *missed* moving in the 'old' way] Custom now assumes the rôle of Nature. Hence the rapidity with which we recollect what we frequently think about. For as regular sequence of events is in accordance with nature, so, too, regular sequence is observed in the actualization of movements [in consciousness], and 30 here frequency tends to produce [the regularity of] nature. And 452^b since in the realm of nature occurrences take place which are even contrary to nature, or fortuitous, the same happens *a fortiori* in the sphere swayed by custom, since in this sphere natural law is not similarly established. Hence it is that [from the same starting-point] the mind receives an impulse to move sometimes in the required direction, and at other times otherwise, [doing the latter] particularly when something else somehow deflects the mind from the right direction and attracts it to itself. This last consideration explains 5 too how it happens that, when we want to remember a name, we remember one somewhat like it, indeed, but blunder in reference to [i. e. in pronouncing] the one we intended.

Thus, then, recollection takes place.

But the point of capital importance is that [for the purpose of recollection] one should cognize, determinately or indeterminately, the time-relation [of that which he wishes to recollect]. There is—let it be taken as a fact—something by which one distinguishes a greater and a smaller time; and it is reasonable to think that one does this in a way analogous to that in which one discerns [spatial] magni- 10 tudes. For it is not by the mind's reaching out towards them, as some say a visual ray from the eye does [in seeing], that one thinks of large things at a distance in space (for even if they are not there, one may similarly think them); but one does so by a proportionate mental movement. For there are in the mind the like figures and movements [i. e. 'like' to those of objects and events]. Therefore, when one thinks the greater objects, in what will his thinking those differ from his thinking the smaller? [In nothing,] because all the internal though smaller are as it were proportional to the external. Now, as we may assume within a person something proportional to 15 the forms [of distant magnitudes], so, too, we may doubtless assume also something else proportional to their distances. As, therefore, if one has [psychically] the movement in AB, BE, he constructs in thought [i. e. knows objectively] CD, since AC and CD bear equal ratios respectively [to AB and BE], [so he who recollects also proceeds]. Why then does he construct CD rather than FG? Is it not because as AC is to AB, so is H to I? These movements therefore [sc. in AB, BE, *and* in H:I] he has si- 20 multaneously. But if he wishes to construct to thought FG, he has in mind BE in like manner as before [when constructing CD], but now, instead of [the movements of the ratio] H:I, he has in mind [those of the ratio] J:K; for J:K::FA: BA.

When, therefore, the 'movement' corresponding to the object and that corresponding to its time concur, then one actually remembers. If one supposes [himself to move in these different but concurrent ways] without really doing so, he supposes himself to remember. For 25 one may be mistaken, and think that he remembers when he really does not. But it is not possible, conversely, that when one actually remembers he should not suppose himself to remember, but should remember unconsciously. For remembering, as we have conceived it, essentially implies consciousness of itself. If, however, the movement corresponding to the objective fact takes place without that corresponding to the time, or, if the latter takes place without the former, one does not remember.

30   The movement answering to the time is of two kinds. Sometimes in remembering a fact one has no determinate time-notion of it, no 453ª such notion as that, e. g., he did something or other on the day before yesterday; while in other cases he has a determinate notion of the time. Still, even though one does not remember with actual determination of the time, he genuinely remembers, none the less. Persons are wont to say that they remember [something], but yet do not know when [it occurred, as happens] whenever they do not know determinately the exact length of time implied in the 'when'.

5   It has been already stated that those who have a good memory are not identical with those who are quick at recollecting. But the act of recollecting differs from that of remembering, not only chronologically, but also in this, that many also of the other animals [as well as man] have memory, but, of all that we are acquainted with, none, we venture to say, except man, shares in the faculty of recollection. 10 The cause of this is that recollection is, as it were, a mode of inference. For he who endeavours to recollect *infers* that he formerly saw, or heard, or had some such experience, and the process [by which he succeeds in recollecting] is, as it were, a sort of investigation. But to investigate in this way belongs naturally to those animals alone which are also endowed with the faculty of deliberation; [which proves what was said above], for deliberation is a form of inference.

15   That the affection is corporeal, i. e. that recollection is a searching for an 'image' in a corporeal substrate, is proved by the fact that in some persons, when, despite the most strenuous application of thought, they have been unable to recollect, it [viz. the effort at recollection] excites a feeling of discomfort, which, even though they abandon the effort at recollection, persists in them none the less; and especially in persons of melancholic temperament. For these are most 20 powerfully moved by presentations. The reason why the effort of recollection is not under the control of their will is that, as those who throw a stone cannot stop it at their will when thrown, so he who tries to recollect and 'hunts' [after an idea] sets up a process in a material part, [that] in which resides the affection. Those who have moisture around that part which is the centre of sense-perception suffer most

discomfort of this kind. For when once the moisture has been set in motion it is not easily brought to rest, until the idea which was sought 25 for has again presented itself, and thus the movement has found a straight course. For a similar reason bursts of anger or fits of terror, when once they have excited such motions, are not at once allayed, even though the angry or terrified persons [by efforts of will] set up counter motions, but the passions continue to move them on, in the same direction as at first, in opposition to such counter motions. The affection resembles also that in the case of words, tunes, or sayings, whenever one of them has become inveterate on the lips. People give them up and resolve to avoid them; yet again and again they 30 find themselves humming the forbidden air, or using the prohibited word.

Those whose upper parts are abnormally large, as is the case with 453b dwarfs, have abnormally weak memory, as compared with their opposites, because of the great weight which they have resting upon the organ of perception, and because their mnemonic movements are, from the very first, not able to keep true to a course, but are dispersed, and because, in the effort at recollection, these movements do 5 not easily find a direct onward path. Infants and very old persons have bad memories, owing to the amount of movement going on within them; for the latter are in process of rapid decay, the former in process of vigorous growth; and we may add that children, until considerably advanced in years, are dwarf-like in their bodily structure. Such then is our theory as regards memory and remembering— their nature, and the particular organ of the soul by which animals remember; also as regards recollection, its formal definition, and the 10 manner and causes of its performance.

DE SOMNIIS

(On Dreams)

We must, in the next place, investigate the subject of the dream,
and first inquire to which of the faculties of the soul it presents itself,
i. e. whether the affection is one which pertains to the faculty of intelligence or to that of sense-perception; for these are the only faculties within us by which we acquire knowledge.

If, then, the exercise of the faculty of sight is actual seeing, that of
the auditory faculty, hearing, and, in general that of the faculty of
sense-perception, perceiving; and if there are some perceptions com-
5 mon to the senses, such as figure, magnitude, motion, &c., while there
are others, as colour, sound, taste, peculiar [each to its own sense];
and further, if all creatures, when the eyes are closed in sleep, are
unable to see, and the analogous statement is true of the other senses,
so that manifestly we perceive nothing when asleep; we may conclude
that it is not by sense-perception we perceive a dream.

But neither is it by opinion that we do so. For [in dreams] we not
10 only assert, e. g., that some object approaching is a man or a horse
[which would be an exercise of opinion], but that the object is
white or beautiful, points on which opinion without sense-perception
asserts nothing either truly or falsely. It is, however, a fact that the
soul makes such assertions in sleep. We seem to see equally well that
the approaching figure is a man, and that it is white. [In dreams],
15 too, we think something else, over and above the dream presentation,
just as we do in waking moments when we perceive something; for
we often also reason about that which we perceive. So, too, in sleep
we sometimes have thoughts other than the mere phantasms immediately before our minds. This would be manifest to any one who
should attend and try, immediately on arising from sleep, to re-
20 member [his dreaming experiences]. There are cases of persons who
have seen such dreams, those, for example, who believe themselves
to be mentally arranging a given list of subjects according to the
mnemonic rule. They frequently find themselves engaged in something else besides the dream, viz. in setting a phantasm which they
envisage into its mnemonic position. Hence it is plain that not every
25 'phantasm' in sleep is a mere dream-image, and that the further think-

ing which we perform then is due to an exercise of the faculty of opinion.

So much at least is plain on all these points, viz. that the faculty by which, in waking hours, we are subject to illusion when affected by disease, is identical with that which produces illusory effects in sleep. So, even when persons are in excellent health, and know the facts of the case perfectly well, the sun, nevertheless, appears to them to be only a foot wide. Now, whether the presentative faculty of the soul be identical with, or different from, the faculty of sense-percep- 30 tion, in either case the illusion does not occur without our actually seeing or [otherwise] perceiving something. Even to see wrongly or to hear wrongly can happen only to one who sees or hears something real, though not exactly what he supposes. But we have assumed that in sleep one neither sees, nor hears, nor exercises any sense whatever. 459ᵃ Perhaps we may regard it as true that the dreamer sees nothing, yet as false that his faculty of sense-perception is unaffected, the fact being that the sense of seeing and the other senses may possibly be then in a certain way affected, while each of these affections, as duly as when he is awake, gives its impulse in a certain manner to his 5 [primary] faculty of sense, though not in precisely the same manner as when he is awake. Sometimes, too, opinion says [to dreamers] just as to those who are awake, that the object seen is an illusion; at other times it is inhibited, and becomes a mere follower of the phantasm.

It is plain therefore that this affection, which we name 'dreaming', is no mere exercise of opinion or intelligence, but yet is not an affection 10 of the faculty of perception in the simple sense. If it were the latter it would be possible [when asleep] to hear and see in the simple sense.

How then, and in what manner, it takes place, is what we have to examine. Let us assume, what is indeed clear enough, that the affection [of dreaming] pertains to sense-perception as surely as sleep itself does. For sleep does not pertain to one organ in animals and dreaming to another; both pertain to the same organ.

But since we have, in our work on the Soul,[1] treated of presenta- 15 tion, and the faculty of presentation is identical with that of sense-perception, though the essential notion of a faculty of presentation is different from that of a faculty of sense-perception; and since presentation is the movement set up by a sensory faculty when actually discharging its function, while a dream appears to be a presentation (for a presentation which occurs in sleep—whether simply or in 20 some particular way—is what we call a dream): it manifestly follows

¹ 427ᵇ 27–429ᵃ 9.

that dreaming is an activity of the faculty of sense-perception, but belongs to this faculty *qua* presentative.

2   We can best obtain a scientific view of the nature of the dream and the manner in which it originates by regarding it in the light of 25 the circumstances attending sleep. The objects of sense-perception corresponding to each sensory organ produce sense-perception in us, and the affection due to their operation is present in the organs of sense not only when the perceptions are actualized, but even when they have departed.

What happens in these cases may be compared with what happens in the case of projectiles moving in space. For in the case of these the movement continues even when that which set up the movement 30 is no longer in contact [with the things that are moved]. For that which set them in motion moves a certain portion of air, and this, in turn, being moved excites motion in another portion; and so, accordingly, it is in this way that [the bodies], whether in air or in liquids, continue moving, until they come to a standstill.

459ᵇ   This we must likewise assume to happen in the case of qualitative change,[2] for that part which [for example] has been heated by something hot, heats [in turn] the part next to it, and this propagates the affection continuously onwards until the process has come round to its 5 point of origination. This must also happen in the organ wherein the exercise of sense-perception takes place, since sense-perception, as realized in actual perceiving, is a mode of qualitative change. This explains why the affection continues in the sensory organs, both in their deeper and in their more superficial parts, not merely while they are actually engaged in perceiving, but even after they have ceased to do so. That they do this, indeed, is obvious in cases where we continue for some time engaged in a particular form of perception, for then, when we shift the scene of our perceptive activity, the previous affection remains; for instance, when we have turned our gaze from sunlight into darkness. For the result of this is that one 10 sees nothing, owing to the motion excited by the light still subsisting in our eyes. Also, when we have looked steadily for a long while at one colour, e. g. at white or green, that to which we next transfer our gaze appears to be of the same colour. Again if, after having looked at the sun or some other brilliant object, we close the eyes, then, if we 15 watch carefully, it appears in a right line with the direction of vision (whatever this may be), at first in its own colour; then it changes to crimson, next to purple, until it becomes black and disappears. And

2 Not merely, as with projectiles, in change of place.

also when persons turn away from looking at objects in motion, e. g.
rivers, and especially those which flow very rapidly, they find that the
visual stimulations still present themselves, for the things really at 20
rest are then seen moving: persons become very deaf after hearing
loud noises, and after smelling very strong odours their power of
smelling is impaired; and similarly in other cases. These phenomena
manifestly take place in the way above described. . . .

From this therefore it is plain that stimulatory motion is set up 460[a]
even by slight differences, and that sense-perception is quick to re-
spond to it; and further that the organ which perceives colour is
not only affected by its object, but also reacts upon it. Further evi- 25
dence to the same point is afforded by what takes place in wines, and
in the manufacture of unguents. For both oil, when prepared, and wine
become rapidly infected by the odours of the things near them; they
not only acquire the odours of the things thrown into or mixed with 30
them, but also those of the things which are placed, or which grow,
near the vessels containing them.

In order to answer our original question, let us now, therefore,
assume one proposition, which is clear from what precedes, viz. that 460[b]
even when the external object of perception has departed, the impressions it has made persist, and are themselves objects of perception;
and [let us assume], besides, that we are easily deceived respecting
the operations of sense-perception when we are excited by emotions,
and different persons according to their different emotions; for example, the coward when excited by fear, the amorous person by 5
amorous desire; so that, with but little resemblance to go upon, the
former thinks he sees his foes approaching, the latter, that he sees the
object of his desire; and the more deeply one is under the influence
of the emotion, the less similarity is required to give rise to these
illusory impressions. Thus too, both in fits of anger, and also in all
states of appetite, all men become easily deceived, and more so the 10
more their emotions are excited. This is the reason too why persons
in the delirium of fever sometimes think they see animals on their
chamber walls, an illusion arising from the faint resemblance to animals of the markings thereon when put together in patterns; and this
sometimes corresponds with the emotional states of the sufferers, in
such a way that, if the latter be not very ill, they know well enough
that it is an illusion; but if the illness is more severe they actually 15
move according to the appearances. The cause of these occurrences
is that the faculty in virtue of which the controlling sense judges is
not identical with that in virtue of which presentations come before
the mind. A proof of this is, that the sun presents itself as only a foot

in diameter, though often something else gainsays the presentation.
20 Again, when the fingers are crossed, the one object [placed between
them] is felt [by the touch] as two; but yet we deny that it is two;
for sight is more authoritative than touch. Yet, if touch stood alone,
we should actually have pronounced the one object to be two. The
ground of such false judgments is that any appearances whatever
present themselves, not only when its object stimulates a sense, but
also when the sense by itself alone is stimulated, provided only it
25 be stimulated in the same manner as it is by the object. For example,
to persons sailing past the land seems to move, when it is really the
eye that is being moved by something else [the moving ship].

3   From this it is manifest that the stimulatory movements based
upon sensory impressions, whether the latter are derived from external
objects or from causes within the body, present themselves not only
30 when persons are awake, but also then, when this affection which is
called sleep has come upon them, with even greater impressiveness.
For by day, while the senses and the intellect are working together,
461ᵃ they (i. e. such movements) are extruded from consciousness or obscured, just as a smaller is beside a larger fire, or as small beside great
pains or pleasures, though, as soon as the latter have ceased, even
those which are trifling emerge into notice. But by night [i. e. in
sleep] owing to the inaction of the particular senses, and their power-
lessness to realize themselves, which arises from the reflux of the hot
5 from the exterior parts to the interior, they [i. e. the above 'movements'] are borne in to the head quarters of sense-perception, and
there display themselves as the disturbance (of waking life) subsides.
We must suppose that, like the little eddies which are being ever
formed in rivers, so the sensory movements are each a continuous
10 process, often remaining like what they were when first started, but
often, too, broken into other forms by collisions with obstacles. This
[last mentioned point], moreover, gives the reason why no dreams
occur in sleep immediately after meals, or to sleepers who are extremely young, e. g. to infants. The internal movement in such cases
is excessive, owing to the heat generated from the food. Hence, just as
15 in a liquid, if one vehemently disturbs it, sometimes no reflected image
appears, while at other times one appears, indeed, but utterly distorted, so as to seem quite unlike its original; while, when once the
motion has ceased, the reflected images are clear and plain; in the same
manner during sleep the phantasms, or residuary movements, which
are based upon the sensory impressions, become sometimes quite
20 obliterated by the above described motion when too violent; while at

other times the sights are indeed seen, but confused and weird, and the dreams [which then appear] are unhealthy, like those of persons who are atrabilious, or feverish, or intoxicated with wine. For all such affections, being spirituous, cause much commotion and disturbance. In sanguineous animals, in proportion as the blood becomes calm, and 25 as its purer are separated from its less pure elements, the fact that the movement, based on impressions derived from each of the organs of sense, is preserved in its integrity, renders the dreams healthy, causes a [clear] image to present itself, and makes the dreamer think, owing to the effects borne in from the organ of sight, that he actually sees, and owing to those which come from the organ of hearing, that he really hears; and so on with those also which proceed from the 30 other sensory organs. For it is owing to the fact that the movement which reaches the primary organ of sense comes from them, that one even when awake believes himself to see, or hear, or otherwise per- 461ᵇ ceive; just as it is from a belief that the organ of sight is being stimulated,³ though in reality not so stimulated, that we sometimes erroneously declare ourselves to see, or that, from the fact that touch announces two movements, we think that the one object is two. For, as a rule, the governing sense affirms the report of each particular sense, unless another particular sense, more authoritative, makes a 5 contradictory report. In every case an appearance presents itself, but what appears does not in every case seem real, unless when the deciding faculty is inhibited, or does not move with its proper motion. Moreover, as we said that different men are subject to illusions, each according to the different emotion present in him, so it is that the sleeper, owing to sleep, and to the movements then going on in his sensory organs, as well as to the other facts of the sensory process, [is liable to illusion], so that the dream presentation, though but little 10 like it, appears as some actual given thing. For when one is asleep, in proportion as most of the blood sinks inwards to its fountain [the heart], the internal [sensory] movements, some potential, others actual ⁴ accompany it inwards. They are so related [in general] that, if anything move the blood, some one sensory movement will emerge from it, while if this perishes another will take its place; while to one another also they are related in the same way as the artificial frogs 15 in water which severally rise [in fixed succession] to the surface in the order in which the salt [which keeps them down] becomes dissolved. The residuary movements are like these: they are within

³ By objective visual impressions.
⁴ The 'actual' are those in consciousness at the time when one is falling asleep: the potential, those which had before that subsided into latency. Cf. 461ᵃ 1.

the soul potentially, but actualize themselves only when the impediment to their doing so has been relaxed; and according as they are
thus set free, they begin to move in the blood which remains in the
sensory organs, and which is now but scanty, while they possess veri-
20 similitude after the manner of cloud-shapes, which in their rapid
metamorphoses one compares now to human beings and a moment
afterwards to centaurs. Each of them is however, as has been said, the
remnant of a sensory impression taken when sense was actualizing
itself; and when this, the true impression, has departed, its remnant
is still immanent, and it is correct to say of it, that though not
25 actually Coriscus, it is like Coriscus. For when the person was actually perceiving, his controlling and judging sensory faculty did not
call it [5] Coriscus, but, prompted by this [impression], called the
genuine person yonder Coriscus. Accordingly, this sensory impulse,
which, when actually perceiving, it [the controlling faculty] so describes (unless completely inhibited by the blood), it now [in
dreams], when quasi-perceiving, receives from the movements persisting in the sense-organs, and mistakes it—an impulse that is
merely like the true [objective] impression—for the true impression
30 itself, while the effect of sleep is so great that it causes this mistake to
pass unnoticed. Accordingly, just as if a finger be inserted beneath the
462[a] eyeball without being observed, one object will not only present two
visual images, but will create an opinion of its being two objects;
while if it [the finger] be observed, the presentation will be the
same, but the same opinion will not be formed of it; exactly so it is in
states of sleep: if the sleeper perceives that he is asleep, and is conscious of the sleeping state during which the perception comes before
5 his mind, it presents itself still, but something within him speaks to
this effect: 'the image of Coriscus presents itself, but the real
Coriscus is not present'; for often, when one is asleep, there is something in consciousness which declares that what then presents itself
is but a dream. If, however, he is not aware of being asleep, there is
nothing which will contradict the testimony of the bare presentation.

That what we here urge is true, i. e. that there are such presentative movements in the sensory organs, any one may convince himself,
10 if he attends to and tries to remember the affections we experience
when sinking into slumber or when being awakened. He will sometimes, in the moment of awakening, surprise the images which present themselves to him in sleep, and find that they are really but
movements lurking in the organs of sense. And indeed some very young
persons, if it is dark, though looking with wide open eyes, see multi-

[5] The impression synchronous with actual perception.

tudes of phantom figures moving before them, so that they often cover up their heads in terror.

From all this, then, the conclusion to be drawn is, that the dream is a sort of presentation, and, more particularly, one which occurs in sleep; since the phantoms just mentioned are not dreams, nor is any other a dream which presents itself when the sense-perceptions are in a state of freedom. Nor is every presentation which occurs in sleep necessarily a dream. For in the first place, some persons [when asleep] actually, in a certain way, perceive sounds, light, savour, and contact; feebly, however, and, as it were, remotely. For there have been cases in which persons while asleep, but with the eyes partly open, saw faintly in their sleep (as they supposed) the light of a lamp, and afterwards, on being awakened, straightway recognized it as the actual light of a real lamp; while, in other cases, persons who faintly heard the crowing of cocks or the barking of dogs identified these clearly with the real sounds as soon as they awoke. Some persons, too, return answers to questions put to them in sleep. For it is quite possible that, of waking or sleeping, while the one is present in the ordinary sense, the other also should be present in a certain way. But none of these occurrences [6] should be called a dream. Nor should the true thoughts, as distinct from the mere presentations, which occur in sleep [be called dreams]. The dream proper is a presentation based on the movement of sense impressions, when such presentation occurs during sleep, taking sleep in the strict sense of the term.

There are cases of persons who in their whole lives have never had a dream, while others dream when considerably advanced in years, 462^{b} having never dreamed before. The cause of their not having dreams appears somewhat like that which operates in the case of infants, and [that which operates] immediately after meals. It is intelligible enough that no dream-presentation should occur to persons whose natural constitution is such that in them copious evaporation is borne upwards, which, when borne back downwards, causes a large quantity of motion. But it is not surprising that, as age advances, a dream should at length appear to them. Indeed, it is inevitable that, as a change is wrought in them in proportion to age or emotional experience, this reversal [from non-dreaming to dreaming] should occur also.

[6] Those due to this ambiguous condition.

DE DIVINATIONE PER SOMNUM

(*On Prophesying by Dreams*)

462^b 1 As to the divination which takes place in sleep, and is said to be based on dreams, we cannot lightly either dismiss it with contempt or give it implicit confidence. The fact that all persons, or many, suppose dreams to possess a special significance, tends to inspire us 15 with belief in it [such divination], as founded on the testimony of experience; and indeed that divination in dreams should, as regards some subjects, be genuine, is not incredible, for it has a show of reason; from which one might form a like opinion also respecting all other dreams. Yet the fact of our seeing no probable cause to account for 20 such divination tends to inspire us with distrust. For, in addition to its further unreasonableness, it is absurd to combine the idea that the sender of such dreams should be God with the fact that those to whom he sends them are not the best and wisest, but merely commonplace persons. If, however, we abstract from the causality of God, none of the other causes assigned appears probable. For that, certain persons should have foresight in dreams concerning things destined to take 25 place at the Pillars of Hercules, or on the banks of the Borysthenes, seems to be something to discover the explanation of which surpasses the wit of man. Well then, the dreams in question must be regarded either as *causes*, or as *tokens*, of the events, or else as *coincidences*; either as all, or some, of these, or as one only. I use the word 'cause' in the sense in which the moon is [the cause] of an eclipse of the sun, 30 or in which fatigue is [a cause] of fever; 'token [in the sense in which] the entrance of a star [into the shadow] is a token of the eclipse, or [in which] roughness of the tongue [is a token] of fever; while by 'coincidence' I mean, for example, the occurrence of an eclipse of the sun while some one is taking a walk; for the walking is neither a 463^a token nor a cause of the eclipse, nor the eclipse [a cause or token] of the walking. For this reason no coincidence takes place according to a universal or general rule. Are we then to say that some dreams are causes, others tokens, e. g. of events taking place in the bodily organism? At all events, even scientific physicians tell us that one should 5 pay diligent attention to dreams, and to hold this view is reasonable also for those who are not practitioners, but speculative philosophers. For the movements which occur in the daytime [within the body] are,

626

unless very great and violent, lost sight of in contrast with the waking movements, which are more impressive. In sleep the opposite takes 10 place, for then even trifling movements seem considerable. This is plain in what often happens during sleep; for example, dreamers fancy that they are affected by thunder and lightning, when in fact there are only faint ringings in their ears; or that they are enjoying honey or other sweet savours, when only a tiny drop of phlegm is flowing down [the oesophagus]; or that they are walking through fire, and 15 feeling intense heat, when there is only a slight warmth affecting certain parts of the body. When they are awakened, these things appear to them in this their true character. But since the beginnings of all events are small, so, it is clear, are those also of the diseases or other affections about to occur in our bodies. In conclusion, it is mani- 20 fest that these beginnings must be more evident in sleeping than in waking moments.

Nay, indeed, it is not improbable that some of the presentations which come before the mind in sleep may even be causes of the actions cognate to each of them. For as when we are about to act [in waking hours], or are engaged in any course of action, or have already performed certain actions, we often find ourselves concerned with these 25 actions, or performing them, in a vivid dream; the cause whereof is that the dream-movement has had a way paved for it from the original movements set up in the daytime; exactly so, but conversely, it must happen that the movements set up first in sleep should also prove to be starting-points of actions to be performed in the daytime, since the recurrence by day of the thought of these actions also has had its way paved for it in the images before the mind at night. Thus then 30 it is quite conceivable that some dreams may be tokens and causes [of future events].

Most [so-called prophetic] dreams are, however, to be classed as mere coincidences, especially all such as are extravagant, and those 463^b in the fulfilment of which the dreamers have no initiative, such as in the case of a sea-fight, or of things taking place far away. As regards these it is natural that the fact should stand as it does whenever a person, on mentioning something, finds the very thing mentioned 5 come to pass. Why, indeed, should this not happen also in sleep? The probability is, rather, that many such things should happen. As, then, one's mentioning a particular person is neither token nor cause of this person's presenting himself, so, in the parallel instance, the dream is, to him who has seen it, neither token nor cause of its [so-called] fulfilment, but a mere coincidence. Hence the fact that many dreams

10 have no 'fulfilment', for coincidences do not occur according to any universal or general law.

2   On the whole, forasmuch as certain of the lower animals also dream, it may be concluded that dreams are not sent by God, nor are they designed for this purpose [to reveal the future]. They have a divine aspect, however, for Nature [their cause] is divinely planned, though 15 not itself divine. A special proof [of their not being sent by God] is this: the power of foreseeing the future and of having vivid dreams is found in persons of inferior type, which implies that God does not send their dreams; but merely that all those whose physical temperament is, as it were, garrulous and excitable, see sights of all descriptions; for, inasmuch as they experience many movements of every kind, they just chance to have visions resembling objective facts, their 20 luck in these matters being merely like that of persons who play at even and odd. For the principle which is expressed in the gambler's maxim: 'If you make many throws your luck must change,' holds good in their case also.

That many dreams have no fulfilment is not strange, for it is so too with many bodily symptoms and weather-signs, e. g., those of 25 rain or wind. For if another movement occurs more influential than that from which, while [the event to which it was pointed was] still future, the given token was derived, the event [to which such token pointed] does not take place. So, of the things which ought to be accomplished by human agency, many, though well-planned, are by the operation of other principles more powerful [than man's agency] brought to nought. For, speaking generally, that which *was* about to happen is not in every case what now is *happening*; nor is that which *shall* hereafter *be* identical with that which *is* now *going to* be. Still, 30 however, we must hold that the beginnings from which, as we said, no consummation follows, are *real* beginnings, and these constitute natural tokens of certain events, even though the events do not come to pass.

As for [prophetic] dreams which involve not such beginnings [sc. of future events] as we have here described, but such as are extrava-
464ᵃ gant in times, or places, or magnitudes; or those involving beginnings which are not extravagant in any of these respects, while yet the persons who see the dream hold not in their own hands the beginnings [of the event to which it points]: unless the foresight which such dreams give is the result of pure coincidence, the following would be a better explanation of it than that proposed by Democritus, who 5 alleges 'images' and 'emanations' as its cause. As, when something

has caused motion in water or air, this [the portion moved] moves another [portion of water or air], and, though the cause has ceased to
operate, such motion propagates itself to a certain point, though there
the prime movent is not present; just so it may well be that a
movement and a consequent sense-perception should reach sleeping
souls from the objects from which Democritus represents 'images' 10
and 'emanations' as coming; that such movements, in whatever way
they arrive, should be more perceptible at night [than by day],
because when proceeding thus in the daytime they are more liable to
dissolution (since at night the air is less disturbed, there being then
less wind); and that they shall be perceived within the body owing 15
to sleep, since persons are more sensitive even to slight sensory movements when asleep than when awake. It is these movements then that
cause 'presentations', as a result of which sleepers foresee the future
even relatively to such events as those referred to above. These considerations also explain why this experience befalls commonplace per- 20
sons and not the most intelligent. For it would have regularly occurred
both in the daytime and to the wise had it been God who sent it;
but, as we have explained the matter, it is quite natural that commonplace persons should be those who have foresight [in dreams]. For
the mind of such persons is not given to thinking, but, as it were,
derelict, or totally vacant, and, when once set moving, is borne
passively on in the direction taken by that which moves it. With regard to the fact that some persons who are liable to derangement have 25
this foresight, its explanation is that their normal mental movements
do not impede [the alien movements], but are beaten off by the
latter. Therefore it is that they have an especially keen perception of
the alien movements.

That certain persons in particular should have vivid dreams, e. g.
that familiar friends should thus have foresight in a special degree
respecting one another, is due to the fact that such friends are most
solicitous on one another's behalf. For as acquaintances in particular 30
recognize and perceive one another a long way off, so also they do as
regards the sensory movements respecting one another; for sensory
movements which refer to persons familiarly known are themselves
more familiar. Atrabilious persons, owing to their impetuosity, are,
when they, as it were, shoot from a distance, expert at hitting; while,
owing to their mutability, the series of movements deploys quickly 464^b
before their minds. For even as the insane recite, or con over in
thought, the poems of Philaegides, e. g. the Aphrodite, whose parts
succeed in order of similitude, just so do they [the 'atrabilious'] go
on and on stringing sensory movements together. Moreover, owing

5 to their aforesaid impetuosity, one movement within them is not liable to be knocked out of its course by some other movement.

The most skilful interpreter of dreams is he who has the faculty of observing resemblances. Any one may interpret dreams which are vivid and plain. But, speaking of 'resemblances', I mean that dream presentations are analogous to the forms reflected in water, as in-10 deed we have already stated. In the latter case, if the motion in the water be great, the reflexion has no resemblance to its original, nor do the forms resemble the real objects. Skilful, indeed, would he be in interpreting such reflexions who could rapidly discern, and at a glance comprehend, the scattered and distorted fragments of such forms, so as to perceive that one of them represents a man, or a horse, 15 or anything whatever. Accordingly, in the other case also, in a similar way, some such thing as this [blurred image] is all that a dream amounts to; for the internal movement effaces the clearness of the dream.

The questions, therefore, which we proposed as to the nature of sleep and the dream, and the cause to which each of them is due, and also as to divination as a result of dreams, in every form of it, have now been discussed.

Historia Animalium

Translated by D'Arcy Wentworth Thompson

CONTENTS

[Books I-IV omitted.]

632

HISTORIA ANIMALIUM

(*The History of Animals*)

BOOK V

1   As to the parts internal and external that all animals are furnished 538^b
withal, and further as to the senses, to voice, and sleep, and the duality 30
of sex, all these topics have now been touched upon. It now remains 539^a
for us to discuss, duly and in order, their several modes of propagation.

These modes are many and diverse, and in some respects are alike,
and in other respects are unlike to one another. As we carried on our
previous discussion genus by genus, so we must attempt to follow 5
the same divisions in our present argument; only that whereas in the
former case we started with a consideration of the parts of man, in the
present case it behooves us to treat of man last of all because he involves most discussion. We shall commence, then, with testaceans, 10
and then proceed to crustaceans, and then to the other genera in due
order; and these other genera are, severally, molluscs, and insects,
then fishes viviparous and fishes oviparous, and next birds; and afterwards we shall treat of animals provided with feet, both such as
are oviparous and such as are viviparous; and we may observe that
some quadrupeds are viviparous, but that the only viviparous biped 15
is man.

Now there is one property that animals are found to have in common with plants. For some plants are generated from the seed
of plants, whilst other plants are self-generated through the formation of some elemental principle similar to a seed; and of these latter
plants some derive their nutriment from the ground, whilst others grow
inside other plants, as is mentioned, by the way, in my treatise on 20
Botany. So with animals, some spring from parent animals according
to their kind, whilst others grow spontaneously and not from kindred
stock; and of these instances of spontaneous generation some come
from putrefying earth or vegetable matter, as is the case with a
number of insects, while others are spontaneously generated in the
inside of animals out of the secretions of their several organs. 25

In animals where generation goes by heredity, wherever there is
duality of sex generation is due to copulation. In the group of fishes,

633

however, there are some that are neither male nor female, and these, while they are identical generically with other fish, differ from them specifically; but there are others that stand altogether isolated and apart by themselves. Other fishes there are that are always female 30 and never male, and from them are conceived what correspond to the wind-eggs in birds. Such eggs, by the way, in birds are all unfruitful; but it is their nature to be independently capable of generation up 539ᵇ to the egg-stage, unless indeed there be some other mode than the one familiar to us of intercourse with the male; but concerning these topics we shall treat more precisely later on. In the case of certain fishes, however, after they have spontaneously generated eggs, these eggs develop into living animals; only that in certain of these cases development is spontaneous, and in others is not independent of 5 the male; and the method of proceeding in regard to these matters will be set forth by and by, for the method is somewhat like to the method followed in the case of birds. But whensoever creatures are spontaneously generated, either in other animals, in the soil, or on plants, or in the parts of these, and when such are generated male and female, then from the copulation of such spontaneously generated 10 males and females there is generated a something—a something never identical in shape with the parents, but a something imperfect. For instance, the issue of copulation in lice is nits; in flies, grubs; in fleas, grubs egg-like in shape; and from these issues the parent-species is never reproduced, nor is any animal produced at all, but the like nondescripts only.

First, then, we must proceed to treat of 'covering' in regard to such animals as cover and are covered; and then after this to treat in due 15 order of other matters, both the exceptional and those of general occurrence. [Chapters 2-34 of Book V and Books VI and VII omitted.]

BOOK VIII

588ᵃ 1 We have now discussed the physical characteristics of animals and their methods of generation. Their habits and their modes of living vary according to their character and their food.

In the great majority of animals there are traces of psychical quali- ties or attitudes, which qualities are more markedly differentiated 20 in the case of human beings. For just as we pointed out resemblances in the physical organs, so in a number of animals we observe gentle- ness or fierceness, mildness or cross temper, courage or timidity, fear or confidence, high spirit or low cunning, and, with regard to intelli- gence, something equivalent to sagacity. Some of these qualities in

man, as compared with the corresponding qualities in animals, differ 25
only quantitatively: that is to say, a man has more or less of this
quality, and an animal has more or less of some other; other qualities in man are represented by analogous and not identical qualities:
for instance, just as in man we find knowledge, wisdom, and sagacity,
so in certain animals there exists some other natural potentiality 30
akin to these. The truth of this statement will be the more clearly
apprehended if we have regard to the phenomena of childhood: for in
children may be observed the traces and seeds of what will one day
be settled psychological habits, though psychologically a child hardly 588ᵇ
differs for the time being from an animal; so that one is quite justified in saying that, as regards man and animals, certain psychical
qualities are identical with one another, whilst others resemble, and
others are analogous to, each other.

Nature proceeds little by little from things lifeless to animal life
in such a way that it is impossible to determine the exact line of de- 5
marcation, nor on which side thereof an intermediate form should lie.
Thus, next after lifeless things in the upward scale comes the plant,
and of plants one will differ from another as to its amount of apparent
vitality; and, in a word, the whole genus of plants, whilst it is devoid
of life as compared with an animal, is endowed with life as compared 10
with other corporeal entities. Indeed, as we just remarked, there is
observed in plants a continuous scale of ascent towards the animal.
So, in the sea, there are certain objects concerning which one would
be at a loss to determine whether they be animal or vegetable. For
instance, certain of these objects are fairly rooted, and in several cases
perish if detached; thus the pinna is rooted to a particular spot, and 15
the solen (or razor-shell) cannot survive withdrawal from its burrow.
Indeed, broadly speaking, the entire genus of testaceans have a resemblance to vegetables, if they be contrasted with such animals
as are capable of progression.

In regard to sensibility, some animals give no indication whatsoever of it, whilst others indicate it but indistinctly. Further, the
substance of some of these intermediate creatures is fleshlike, as is
the case with the so-called tethya (or ascidians) and the acalephae 20
(or sea-anemones); but the sponge is in every respect like a vegetable. And so throughout the entire animal scale there is a graduated
differentiation in amount of vitality and in capacity for motion.

A similar statement holds good with regard to habits of life. Thus
of plants that spring from seed the one function seems to be the
reproduction of their own particular species, and the sphere of action 25
with certain animals is similarly limited. The faculty of reproduction,

then, is common to all alike. If sensibility be superadded, then their
lives will differ from one another in respect to sexual intercourse
through the varying amount of pleasure derived therefrom, and also
30 in regard to modes of parturition and ways of rearing their young.
Some animals, like plants, simply procreate their own species at definite seasons; other animals busy themselves also in procuring food for
their young, and after they are reared quit them and have no further
589ᵃ dealings with them; other animals are more intelligent and endowed
with memory, and they live with their offspring for a longer period and
on a more social footing.

The life of animals, then, may be divided into two acts—procreation and feeding; for on these two acts all their interests and life
5 concentrate. Their food depends chiefly on the substance of which
they are severally constituted; for the source of their growth in all
cases will be this substance. And whatsoever is in conformity with
nature is pleasant, and all animals pursue pleasure in keeping with
their nature. [Chapters 2-30 of Book VIII omitted.]

BOOK IX

608ᵃ 1   Of the animals that are comparatively obscure and short-lived
the characters or dispositions are not so obvious to recognition as are
those of animals that are longer-lived. These latter animals appear to
15 have a natural capacity corresponding to each of the passions: to
cunning or simplicity, courage or timidity, to good temper or to bad,
and to other similar dispositions of mind.

Some also are capable of giving or receiving instruction—of receiving it from one another or from man: those that have the faculty of
hearing, for instance; and, not to limit the matter to audible sound,
20 such as can differentiate the suggested meanings of word and gesture.

In all genera in which the distinction of male and female is found,
Nature makes a similar differentiation in the mental characteristics of
the two sexes. This differentiation is the most obvious in the case of
human kind and in that of the larger animals and the viviparous quad-
25 rupeds. In the case of these latter the female is softer in character,
is the sooner tamed, admits more readily of caressing, is more apt in
the way of learning; as, for instance, in the Laconian breed of dogs the
female is cleverer than the male. Of the Molossian breed of dogs, such
as are employed in the chase are pretty much the same as those else-
30 where; but the sheep-dogs of this breed are superior to the others in
size, and in the courage with which they face the attacks of wild
animals.

Dogs that are born of a mixed breed between these two kinds are remarkable for courage and endurance of hard labour.

In all cases, excepting those of the bear and leopard, the female is less spirited than the male; in regard to the two exceptional cases, the superiority in courage rests with the female. With all other animals the female is softer in disposition than the male, is more 608ᵇ mischievous, less simple, more impulsive, and more attentive to the nurture of the young; the male, on the other hand, is more spirited than the female, more savage, more simple and less cunning. The traces of these differentiated characteristics are more or less visible everywhere, but they are especially visible where character is the more 5 developed, and most of all in man.

The fact is, the nature of man is the most rounded off and complete, and consequently in man the qualities or capacities above referred to are found in their perfection. Hence woman is more compassionate than man, more easily moved to tears, at the same time is more jealous, more querulous, more apt to scold and to strike. She is, 10 furthermore, more prone to despondency and less hopeful than the man, more void of shame or self-respect, more false of speech, more deceptive, and of more retentive memory. She is also more wakeful, more shrinking, more difficult to rouse to action, and requires a smaller quantity of nutriment.

As was previously stated, the male is more courageous than the 15 female, and more sympathetic in the way of standing by to help. Even in the case of molluscs, when the cuttle-fish is struck with the trident the male stands by to help the female; but when the male is struck the female runs away.[1]

There is enmity between such animals as dwell in the same localities or subsist on the same food. If the means of subsistence run short, 20 creatures of like kind will fight together. Thus it is said that seals which inhabit one and the same district will fight, male with male, and female with female, until one combatant kills the other, or one is driven away by the other; and their young do even in like manner. 25

All creatures are at enmity with the carnivores, and the carnivores with all the rest, for they all subsist on living creatures. Soothsayers take notice of cases where animals keep apart from one another, and cases where they congregate together; calling those that live at war with one another 'dissociates', and those that dwell in peace with one another 'associates'. One may go so far as to say that if there 30 were no lack or stint of food, then those animals that are now afraid of man or are wild by nature would be tame and familiar with him,

[1] Arist. *ap*. Athen. vii. 323 c.

and in like manner with one another. This is shown by the way
animals are treated in Egypt, for owing to the fact that food is constantly supplied to them the very fiercest creatures live peaceably together. The fact is they are tamed by kindness, and in some places
609ª crocodiles are tame to their priestly keeper from being fed by him.
And elsewhere also the same phenomenon is to be observd.

The eagle and the snake are enemies, for the eagle lives on snakes;
5 so are the ichneumon and the venom-spider, for the ichneumon preys
upon the latter. In the case of birds, there is mutual enmity between
the poecilis, the crested lark, the woodpecker (?), and the chloreus,
for they devour one another's eggs; so also between the crow and the
owl; for, owing to the fact that the owl is dim-sighted by day, the
10 crow at midday preys upon the owl's eggs, and the owl at night upon
the crow's, each having the whip-hand of the other, turn and turn
about, night and day.

There is enmity also between the owl and the wren; for the latter also devours the owl's eggs. In the daytime all other little birds
flutter round the owl—a practice which is popularly termed 'admir-
15 ing him'—buffet him, and pluck out his feathers; in consequence of
this habit, bird-catchers use the owl as a decoy for catching little birds
of all kinds.

The so-called presbys or 'old man' is at war with the weasel and the
crow, for they prey on her eggs and her brood; and so the turtle-dove
with the pyrallis, for they live in the same districts and on the same
food; and so with the green woodpecker and the libyus; and so with
20 the kite and the raven, for, owing to his having the advantage from
stronger talons and more rapid flight the former can steal whatever
the latter is holding, so that it is food also that makes enemies of
these. In like manner there is war between birds that get their living
from the sea, as between the brenthus, the gull, and the harpe; and
so between the buzzard on one side and the toad and snake on the
other, for the buzzard preys upon the eggs of the two others; and so
25 between the turtle-dove and the chloreus; the chloreus kills the dove,
and the crow kills the so-called drummer-bird.

The aegolius, and birds of prey in general, prey upon the calaris,
and consequently there is war between it and them; and so is there
war between the gecko-lizard and the spider, for the former preys
30 upon the latter; and so between the woodpecker and the heron, for
the former preys upon the eggs and brood of the latter. And so
between the aegithus and the ass, owing to the fact that the ass, in
passing a furze-bush, rubs its sore and itching parts against the
prickles; by so doing, and all the more if it brays, it topples the eggs

and the brood out of the nest, the young ones tumble out in fright, and the mother-bird, to avenge this wrong, flies at the beast and pecks at his sore places.

The wolf is at war with the ass, the bull, and the fox, for as being 609^b a carnivore, he attacks these other animals; and so for the same reason with the fox and the circus, for the circus, being carnivorous and furnished with crooked talons, attacks and maims the animal. And so the raven is at war with the bull and the ass, for it flies at 5 them, and strikes them, and pecks at their eyes; and so with the eagle and the heron, for the former, having crooked talons, attacks the latter, and the latter usually succumbs to the attack; and so the merlin with the vulture; and the crex with the eleus-owl, the blackbird, and the oriole (of this latter bird, by the way, the story goes that he was 10 originally born out of a funeral pyre): the cause of warfare is that the crex injures both them and their young. The nuthatch and the wren are at war with the eagle; the nuthatch breaks the eagle's eggs, so the eagle is at war with it on special grounds, though, as a bird of prey, it carries on a general war all round. The horse and the anthus are enemies, and the horse will drive the bird out of the field 15 where he is grazing: the bird feeds on grass, and sees too dimly to foresee an attack; it mimics the whinnying of the horse, flies at him, and tries to frighten him away; but the horse drives the bird away, and whenever he catches it he kills it: this bird lives beside rivers or on marsh ground; it has pretty plumage, and finds its food without trouble. The ass is at enmity with the lizard, for the lizard sleeps in 20 his manger, gets into his nostril, and prevents his eating.

Of herons there are three kinds: the ash-coloured, the white, and the starry heron (or bittern). Of these the first mentioned submits with reluctance to the duties of incubation, or to union of the sexes; in fact, it screams during the union, and it is said drips blood from its eyes; it lays its eggs also in an awkward manner, not un- 25 attended with pain. It is at war with certain creatures that do it injury: with the eagle for robbing it, with the fox for worrying it at night, and with the lark for stealing its eggs.

The snake is at war with the weasel and the pig; with the weasel when they are both at home, for they live on the same food; with the pig for preying on her kind. The merlin is at war with the fox; it 30 strikes and claws it, and, as it has crooked talons, it kills the animal's young. The raven and the fox are good friends, for the raven is at enmity with the merlin; and so when the merlin assails the fox the raven comes and helps the animal. The vulture and the merlin are mutual enemies, as being both furnished with crooked talons. The

610ª vulture fights with the eagle, and so, by the way, does the swan; and the swan is often victorious: moreover, of all birds swans are most prone to the killing of one another.

In regard to wild creatures, some sets are at enmity with other sets at all times and under all circumstances; others, as in the case of man and man, at special times and under incidental circumstances. 5 The ass and the acanthis are enemies; for the bird lives on thistles, and the ass browses on thistles when they are young and tender. The anthus, the acanthis, and the aegithus are at enemity with one another; it is said that the blood of the anthus will not intercommingle with the blood of the aegithus. The crow and the heron are friends, as also are the sedge-bird and lark, the laedus and the celeus or green woodpecker; the woodpecker lives on the banks of 10 rivers and beside brakes, the laedus lives on rocks and hills, and is greatly attached to its nesting-place. The piphinx, the harpe, and the kite are friends; as are the fox and the snake, for both burrow underground; so also are the blackbird and the turtle-dove. The lion and the thos or civet are enemies, for both are carnivorous and live on the same food.

15   Elephants fight fiercely with one another, and stab one another with their tusks; of two combatants the beaten one gets completely cowed, and dreads the sound of his conqueror's voice. These animals differ from one another to an extraordinary extent in the way of courage. Indians employ these animals for war purposes, irrespective 20 of sex; the females, however, are less in size and much inferior in point of spirit. An elephant by pushing with his big tusks can batter down a wall, and will butt with his forehead at a palm until he brings it down, when he stamps on it and lays it in orderly fashion on the ground. Men hunt the elephant in the following way: they mount 25 tame elephants of approved spirit and proceed in quest of wild animals; when they come up with these they bid the tame brutes to beat the wild ones until they tire the latter completely. Hereupon the driver mounts a wild brute and guides him with the application of his metal prong; after this the creature soon becomes tame, and 30 obeys guidance. Now when the driver is on their back they are all tractable, but after he has dismounted, some are tame and others vicious; in the case of these latter, they tie their front-legs with ropes to keep them quiet. The animal is hunted whether young or full grown.

Thus we see that in the case of the creatures above mentioned their mutual friendship or enmity is due to the food they feed on and the life they lead. [Chapters 2-50 of Book IX omitted.]

De Partibus Animalium

Translated by William Ogle

CONTENTS

BOOK I

DE PARTIBUS ANIMALIUM

(*On the Parts of Animals*)

BOOK I

1 Every systematic science, the humblest and the noblest alike, 639ª
seems to admit of two distinct kinds of proficiency; one of which may
be properly called scientific knowledge of the subject, while the other
is a kind of educational acquaintance with it. For an educated man 5
should be able to form a fair off-hand judgement as to the goodness or
badness of the method used by a professor in his exposition. To be
educated is in fact to be able to do this; and even the man of universal
education we deem to be such in virtue of his having this ability. It
will, however, of course, be understood that we only ascribe universal
education to one who in his own individual person is thus critical in 10
all or nearly all branches of knowledge, and not to one who has a like
ability merely in some special subject. For it is possible for a man to
have this competence in some one branch of knowledge without having it in all.

It is plain then that, as in other sciences, so in that which inquires
into nature, there must be certain canons, by reference to which a
hearer shall be able to criticize the method of a professed exposition,
quite independently of the question whether the statements made be
true or false. Ought we, for instance (to give an illustration of what 15
I mean), to begin by discussing each separate species—man, lion, ox,
and the like—taking each kind in hand independently of the rest, or
ought we rather to deal first with the attributes which they have in
common in virtue of some common element of their nature, and proceed from this as a basis for the consideration of them separately? For 20
genera that are quite distinct yet oftentimes present many identical
phenomena, sleep, for instance, respiration, growth, decay, death, and
other similar affections and conditions, which may be passed over for the
present, as we are not yet prepared to treat of them with clearness and
precision. Now it is plain that if we deal with each species independently of the rest, we shall frequently be obliged to repeat the same
statements over and over again; for horse and dog and man present, 25
each and all, every one of the phenomena just enumerated. A discus-

643

sion therefore of the attributes of each such species separately would necessarily involve frequent repetitions as to characters, themselves identi-
30 cal but recurring in animals specifically distinct. (Very possibly also
there may be other characters which, though they present specific
639ᵇ differences, yet come under one and the same category. For instance,
flying, swimming, walking, creeping, are plainly specifically distinct,
but yet are all forms of animal progression.) We must, then, have
some clear understanding as to the manner in which our investigation
5 is to be conducted; whether, I mean, we are first to deal with the common or generic characters, and afterwards to take into consideration
special peculiarities; or whether we are to start straight off with the
ultimate species. For as yet no definite rule has been laid down in this
matter. So also there is a like uncertainty as to another point now to
be mentioned. Ought the writer who deals with the works of nature to
follow the plan adopted by the mathematicians in their astronomical
demonstrations, and after considering the phenomena presented by
10 animals, and their several parts, proceed subsequently to treat of the
causes and the reason why; or ought he to follow some other method?
And when these questions are answered, there yet remains another.
The causes concerned in the generation of the works of nature are,
as we see, more than one. There is the final cause and there is the
motor cause. Now we must decide which of these two causes comes
first, which second. Plainly, however, that cause is the first which we
15 call the final one. For this is the Reason, and the Reason forms the
starting-point, alike in the works of art and in works of nature. For
consider how the physician or how the builder sets about his work. He
starts by forming for himself a definite picture, in the one case perceptible to mind, in the other to sense, of his end—the physician of health,
the builder of a house—and this he holds forward as the reason and
explanation of each subsequent step that he takes, and of his acting in
20 this or that way as the case may be. Now in the works of nature the
good end and the final cause is still more dominant than in works of
art such as these, nor is necessity a factor with the same significance
in them all; though almost all writers, while they try to refer their
origin to this cause, do so without distinguishing the various senses in
which the term necessity is used. For there is absolute necessity, mani-
25 fested in eternal phenomena; and there is hypothetical necessity,
manifested in everything that is generated by nature as in everything
that is produced by art, be it a house or what it may. For if a house
or other such final object is to be realized, it is necessary that such and
such material shall exist; and it is necessary that first this and then
that shall be produced, and first this and then that set in motion, and

so on in continuous succession, until the end and final result is 30
reached, for the sake of which each prior thing is produced and exists.
As with these productions of art, so also is it with the productions of
nature. The mode of necessity, however, and the mode of ratiocination
are different in natural science from what they are in the theoretical 640ᵃ
sciences; of which we have spoken elsewhere. For in the latter the
starting-point is that which is; in the former that which is to be. For
it is that which is yet to be—health, let us say, or a man—that, owing 5
to its being of such and such characters, necessitates the pre-existence
or previous production of this and that antecedent; and not this or
that antecedent which, because it exists or has been generated, makes
it necessary that health or a man is in, or shall come into, existence.
Nor is it possible to trace back the series of necessary antecedents to a
starting-point, of which you can say that, existing itself from eternity,
it has determined their existence as its consequent. These however,
again, are matters that have been dealt with in another treatise. 10
There too it was stated in what cases absolute and hypothetical necessity exist; in what cases also the proposition expressing hypothetical
necessity is simply convertible, and what cause it is that determines
this convertibility.

Another matter which must not be passed over without consideration is, whether the proper subject of our exposition is that with which
the ancient writers concerned themselves, namely, what is the process
of formation of each animal; or whether it is not rather, what are the
characters of a given creature when formed. For there is no small
difference between these two views. The best course appears to be that
we should follow the method already mentioned, and begin with the
phenomena presented by each group of animals, and, when this is 15
done, proceed afterwards to state the causes of those phenomena, and
to deal with their evolution. For elsewhere, as for instance in house
building, this is the true sequence. The plan of the house, or the house,
has this and that form; and because it has this and that form, therefore is its construction carried out in this or that manner. For the
process of evolution is for the sake of the thing finally evolved, and
not this for the sake of the process. Empedocles, then, was in error
when he said that many of the characters presented by animals were
merely the results of incidental occurrences during their development; 20
for instance, that the backbone was divided as it is into vertebrae,
because it happened to be broken owing to the contorted position of
the foetus in the womb. In so saying he overlooked the fact that propagation implies a creative seed endowed with certain formative properties. Secondly, he neglected another fact, namely, that the parent

²⁵ animal pre-exists, not only in idea, but actually in time. For man is generated from man; and thus it is the possession of certain characters by the parent that determines the development of like characters in the child. The same statement holds good also for the operations of art, and even for those which are apparently spontaneous. For the same result as is produced by art may occur spontaneously. Spontaneity, for instance, may bring about the restoration of health. The ³⁰ products of art, however, require the pre-existence of an efficient cause homogeneous with themselves, such as the statuary's art, which must necessarily precede the statue; for this cannot possibly be produced spontaneously. Art indeed consists in the conception of the result to be produced before its realization in the material. As with spontaneity, so with chance; for this also produces the same result as art, and by the same process.

The fittest mode, then, of treatment is to say, a man has such and such parts, because the conception of a man includes their presence, and because they are necessary conditions of his existence, or, if we ³⁵ cannot quite say this, which would be best of all, then the next thing to it, namely, that it is either quite impossible for him to exist without them, or, at any rate, that it is better for him that they should be there; and their existence involves the existence of other antecedents. 640ᵇ This we should say, because man is an animal with such and such characters, therefore is the process of his development necessarily such as it is; and therefore is it accomplished in such and such an order, this part being formed first, that next, and so on in succession; and after a like fashion should we explain the evolution of all other works of nature.

⁵   Now that with which the ancient writers, who first philosophized about Nature, busied themselves, was the material principle and the material cause. They inquired what this is, and what its character; how the universe is generated out of it, and by what motor influence, whether, for instance, by antagonism or friendship, whether by intelligence or spontaneous action, the substratum of matter being assumed to have certain inseparable properties; fire, for instance, to have a hot ¹⁰ nature, earth a cold one; the former to be light, the latter heavy. For even the genesis of the universe is thus explained by them. After a like fashion do they deal also with the development of plants and of animals. They say, for instance, that the water contained in the body causes by its currents the formation of the stomach and the other receptacles of food or of excretion; and that the breath by its passage ¹⁵ breaks open the outlets of the nostrils; air and water being the

materials of which bodies are made; for all represent nature as composed of such or similar substances.

But if men and animals and their several parts are natural phenomena, then the natural philosopher must take into consideration not merely the ultimate substances of which they are made, but also flesh, bone, blood, and all the other homogeneous parts; not only these, 20 but also the heterogeneous parts, such as face, hand, foot; and must examine how each of these comes to be what it is, and in virtue of what force. For to say what are the ultimate substances out of which an animal is formed, to state, for instance, that it is made of fire or earth, is no more sufficient than would be a similar account in the case of a couch or the like. For we should not be content with saying that the couch was made of bronze or wood or whatever it might be, but should try to describe its design or mode of composition in prefer- 25 ence to the material; or, if we did deal with the material, it would at any rate be with the concretion of material and form. For a couch is such and such a form embodied in this or that matter, or such and such a matter with this or that form; so that its shape and structure must be included in our description. For the formal nature is of greater importance than the material nature.

Does, then, configuration and colour constitute the essence of the 30 various animals and of their several parts? For if so, what Democritus says will be strictly correct. For such appears to have been his notion. At any rate he says that it is evident to every one what form it is that makes the man, seeing that he is recognizable by his shape and colour. And yet a dead body has exactly the same configuration as a living 35 one; but for all that is not a man. So also no hand of bronze or wood or constituted in any but the appropriate way can possibly be a hand in more than name. For like a physician in a painting, or like a flute 641ᵃ in a sculpture, in spite of its name it will be unable to do the office which that name implies. Precisely in the same way no part of a dead body, such I mean as its eye or its hand, is really an eye or a hand. To say, then, that shape and colour constitute the animal is an 5 inadequate statement, and is much the same as if a woodcarver were to insist that the hand he had cut out was really a hand. Yet the physiologists, when they give an account of the development and causes of the animal form, speak very much like such a craftsman. What, however, I would ask, are the forces by which the hand or the body was fashioned into its shape? The woodcarver will perhaps say, by the axe or the auger; the physiologist, by air and by earth. Of 10 these two answers the artificer's is the better, but it is nevertheless insufficient. For it is not enough for him to say that by the stroke of his tool this part was formed into a concavity, that into a flat surface; but he must state the reasons why he struck his blow in such a way as to effect this, and what his final object was; namely, that the piece of wood should develop eventually into this or that shape. It is plain, then, that the teaching of the old physiologists is inadequate, 15 and that the true method is to state what the definitive characters are that distinguish the animal as a whole; to explain what it is both in substance and in form, and to deal after the same fashion with its several organs; in fact, to proceed in exactly the same way as we should do, were we giving a complete description of a couch.

If now this something that constitutes the form of the living being be the soul, or part of the soul, or something that without the soul cannot exist; as would seem to be the case, seeing at any rate that when the soul departs, what is left is no longer a living animal, and that none 20 of the parts remain what they were before, excepting in mere config-uration, like the animals that in the fable are turned into stone; if, I say, this be so, then it will come within the province of the natural philosopher to inform himself concerning the soul, and to treat of it, either in its entirety, or, at any rate, of that part of it which consti-tutes the essential character of an animal; and it will be his duty to say what this soul or this part of a soul is; and to discuss the attributes 25 that attach to this essential character, especially as nature is spoken of in two senses, and the nature of a thing is either its matter or its essence; nature as essence including both the motor cause and the final cause. Now it is in the latter of these two senses that either the whole soul or some part of it constitutes the nature of an animal; and inasmuch as it is the presence of the soul that enables matter to con-stitute the animal nature, much more than it is the presence of matter 30 which so enables the soul, the inquirer into nature is bound on every ground to treat of the soul rather than of the matter. For though the wood of which they are made constitutes the couch and the tripod, it only does so because it is capable of receiving such and such a form.

What has been said suggests the question, whether it is the whole soul or only some part of it, the consideration of which comes within 35 the province of natural science. Now if it be of the whole soul that this should treat, then there is no place for any other philosophy 641ᵇ beside it. For as it belongs in all cases to one and the same science to deal with correlated subjects—one and the same science, for in-stance, deals with sensation and with the objects of sense—and as therefore the intelligent soul and the objects of intellect, being corre-lated, must belong to one and the same science, it follows that natural 5 science will have to include the whole universe in its province. But perhaps it is not the whole soul, nor all its parts collectively, that constitutes the source of motion; but there may be one part, identical with that in plants, which is the source of growth, another, namely the sensory part, which is the source of change of quality, while still another, and this not the intellectual part, is the source of locomotion. I say not the intellectual part; for other animals than man have the power of locomotion, but in none but him is there intellect. Thus then it is plain that it is not of the whole soul that we have to treat. For it is not the whole soul that constitutes the animal nature, but only some part or parts of it. Moreover, it is impossible that any abstraction 10 can form a subject of natural science, seeing that everything that Nature makes is means to an end. For just as human creations are the products of art, so living objects are manifestly the products of an analogous cause or principle, not external but internal, derived like 15 the hot and the cold from the environing universe. And that the heaven, if it had an origin, was evolved and is maintained by such a cause, there is therefore even more reason to believe, than that mortal animals so originated. For order and definiteness are much more plainly manifest in the celestial bodies than in our own frame; while change and chance are characteristic of the perishable things of earth. 20 Yet there are some who, while they allow that every animal exists and was generated by nature, nevertheless hold that the heaven was constructed to be what it is by chance and spontaneity; the heaven, in which not the faintest sign of hap-hazard or of disorder is discernible! Again, whenever there is plainly some final end, to which a motion tends should nothing stand in the way, we always say that such final 25 end is the aim or purpose of the motion; and from this it is evident that there must be a something or other really existing, corresponding to what we call by the name of Nature. For a given germ does not give rise to any chance living being, nor spring from any chance one; but each germ springs from a definite parent and gives rise to a definite progeny. And thus it is the germ that is the ruling influence and fabricator of the offspring. For these it is by nature, the offspring being at 30 any rate that which in nature will spring from it. At the same time the offspring is anterior to the germ; for germ and perfected progeny are related as the developmental process and the result. Anterior, however, to both germ and product is the organism from which the germ was derived. For every germ implies two organisms, the parent and the progeny. For germ or seed is both the seed of the organism from which it came, of the horse, for instance, from which it was de- 35 rived, and the seed of the organism that will eventually arise from it, of the mule, for example, which is developed from the seed of the horse. The same seed then is the seed both of the horse and of the mule, though in different ways as here set forth. Moreover, the seed is potentially that which will spring from it, and the relation of potentiality to actuality we know.

642ª   There are then two causes, namely, necessity and the final end. For many things are produced, simply as the results of necessity. It may, however, be asked, of what mode of necessity are we speaking when 5 we say this. For it can be of neither of those two modes which are set forth in the philosophical treatises. There is, however, the third mode, in such things at any rate as are generated. For instance, we say that food is necessary; because an animal cannot possibly do without it. This third mode is what may be called hypothetical necessity. Here 10 is another example of it. If a piece of wood is to be split with an axe, the axe must of necessity be hard; and, if hard, must of necessity be made of bronze or iron. Now exactly in the same way the body, which like the axe is an instrument—for both the body as a whole and its several parts individually have definite operations for which they are made—just in the same way, I say, the body, if it is to do its work, must of necessity be of such and such a character, and made of such and such materials.

It is plain then that there are two modes of causation, and that 15 both of these must, so far as possible, be taken into account in explaining the works of nature, or that at any rate an attempt must be made to include them both; and that those who fail in this tell us in reality nothing about nature. For primary cause constitutes the nature of an animal much more than does its matter. There are indeed passages in which even Empedocles hits upon this, and following the 20 guidance of fact, finds himself constrained to speak of the ratio as constituting the essence and real nature of things. Such, for instance, is the case when he explains what is a bone. For he does not merely describe its material, and say it is this one element, or those two or three elements, or a compound of all the elements, but states the ratio of their combination. As with a bone, so manifestly is it with the flesh and all other similar parts.

25   The reason why our predecessors failed in hitting upon this method of treatment was, that they were not in possession of the notion of essence, nor of any definition of substance. The first who came near it was Democritus, and he was far from adopting it as a necessary method in natural science, but was merely brought to it, spite of himself, by constraint of facts. In the time of Socrates a nearer approach was made to the method. But at this period men gave up inquiring into the works of nature, and philosophers diverted their

attention to political science and to the virtues which benefit mankind. 30

Of the method itself the following is an example. In dealing with respiration we must show that it takes place for such or such a final object; and we must also show that this and that part of the process is necessitated by this and that other stage of it. By necessity we shall sometimes mean hypothetical necessity, the necessity, that is, that the requisite antecedents shall be there, if the final end is to be reached; and sometimes absolute necessity, such necessity as that which connects substances and their inherent properties and characters. For the alternate discharge and re-entrance of heat and the inflow 35 of air are necessary if we are to live. Here we have at once a necessity in the former of the two senses. But the alternation of heat and refrig- 642ᵇ eration produces of necessity an alternate admission and discharge of the outer air, and this is a necessity of the second kind.

In the foregoing we have an example of the method which we must adopt, and also an example of the kind of phenomena, the causes of which we have to investigate.

2 Some writers propose to reach the definitions of the ultimate 5 forms of animal life by bipartite division. But this method is often difficult, and often impracticable.

Sometimes the final differentia of the subdivision is sufficient by itself, and the antecedent differentiae are mere surplusage. Thus in the series Footed, Two-footed, Cleft-footed, the last term is all-expressive by itself, and to append the higher terms is only an idle iteration.

Again it is not permissible to break up a natural group, Birds for 10 instance, by putting its members under different bifurcations, as is done in the published dichotomies, where some birds are ranked with animals of the water, and others placed in a different class. The group Birds and the group Fishes happen to be named, while other natural groups have no popular names; for instance, the groups that we may 15 call Sanguineous and Bloodless are not known popularly by any designations. If such natural groups are not to be broken up, the method of Dichotomy cannot be employed, for it necessarily involves such breaking up and dislocation. The group of the Many-footed, for instance, would, under this method, have to be dismembered, and some of its kinds distributed among land animals, others among water 20 animals.

3 Again, privative terms inevitably form one branch of dichotomous division, as we see in the proposed dichotomies. But privative terms

in their character of privatives admit of no subdivision. For there can
be no specific forms of a negation, of Featherless for instance or of
Footless, as there are of Feathered and of Footed. Yet a generic dif-
25 ferentia must be subdivisible; for otherwise what is there that makes it
generic rather than specific? There are to be found generic, that is
specifically subdivisible, differentiae; Feathered for instance and
Footed. For feathers are divisible into Barbed and Unbarbed, and
feet into Manycleft, and Twocleft, like those of animals with bifid
hoofs, and Uncleft or Undivided, like those of animals with solid
30 hoofs. Now even with differentiae capable of this specific subdivision
it is difficult enough so to make the classification, as that each animal
shall be comprehended in some one subdivision and in not more than
one; but far more difficult, nay impossible, is it to do this, if we start
35 with a dichotomy into two contradictories. (Suppose for instance we
start with the two contradictories, Feathered and Unfeathered; we
shall find that the ant, the glow-worm, and some other animals fall
under both divisions.) For each differentia must be presented by some
species. There must be some species, therefore, under the privative
643ᵃ heading. Now specifically distinct animals cannot present in their
essence a common undifferentiated element, but any apparently common element must really be differentiated. (Bird and Man for instance are both Two-footed, but their two-footedness is diverse and
differentiated. So any two sanguineous groups must have some difference in their blood, if their blood is part of their essence.) From this
it follows that a privative term, being insusceptible of differentiation,
5 cannot be a generic differentia; for, if it were, there would be a common undifferentiated element in two different groups.

Again, if the species are ultimate indivisible groups, that is, are
groups with indivisible differentiae, and if no differentia be common
to several groups, the number of differentiae must be equal to the
number of species. If a differentia though not divisible could yet be
10 common to several groups, then it is plain that in virtue of that common differentia specifically distinct animals would fall into the same
division. It is necessary then, if the differentiae, under which are
ranged all the ultimate and indivisible groups, are specific characters,
that none of them shall be common; for otherwise, as already said,
specifically distinct animals will come into one and the same division.
But this would violate one of the requisite conditions, which are as
follows. No ultimate group must be included in more than a single
15 division; different groups must not be included in the same division;
and every group must be found in some division. It is plain then that
we cannot get at the ultimate specific forms of the animal, or any

other, kingdom by bifurcate division. If we could, the number of ultimate differentiae would equal the number of ultimate animal 20 forms. For assume an order of beings whose prime differentiae are White and Black. Each of these branches will bifurcate, and their branches again, and so on till we reach the ultimate differentiae, whose number will be four or some other power of two, and will also be the number of the ultimate species comprehended in the order.

(A species is constituted by the combination of differentia and matter. For no part of an animal is purely material or purely imma- 25 terial; nor can a body, independently of its condition, constitute an animal or any of its parts, as has repeatedly been observed.)

Further, the differentiae must be elements of the essence, and not merely essential attributes. Thus if Figure is the term to be divided, it must not be divided into figures whose angles are equal to two right angles, and figures whose angles are together greater than two right angles. For it is only an attribute of a triangle and not part of 30 its essence that its angles are equal to two right angles.

Again, the bifurcations must be opposites, like White and Black, Straight and Bent; and if we characterize one branch by either term, we must characterize the other by its opposite, and not, for example, characterize one branch by a colour, the other by a mode of progression, swimming for instance.

Furthermore, living beings cannot be divided by the functions com- 35 mon to body and soul, by Flying, for instance, and Walking, as we see them divided in the dichotomies already referred to. For some 643ᵇ groups, Ants for instance, fall under both divisions, some ants flying while others do not. Similarly as regards the division into Wild and Tame; for it also would involve the disruption of a species into differ- ent groups. For in almost all species in which some members are 5 tame, there are other members that are wild. Such, for example, is the case with Men, Horses, Oxen, Dogs in India, Pigs, Goats, Sheep; groups which, if double, ought to have what they have not, namely, different appellations; and which, if single, prove that Wildness and Tameness do not amount to specific differences. And whatever single element we take as a basis of division the same difficulty will occur.

The method then that we must adopt is to attempt to recognize 10 the natural groups, following the indications afforded by the instincts of mankind, which led them for instance to form the class of Birds and the class of Fishes, each of which groups combines a multitude of differentiae, and is not defined by a single one as in dichotomy. The method of dichotomy is either impossible (for it would put a single group under different divisions or contrary groups under the same

15 division), or it only furnishes a single ultimate differentia for each
species, which either alone or with its series of antecedents has to
constitute the ultimate species.

If, again, a new differential character be introduced at any stage
into the division, the necessary result is that the continuity of the
division becomes merely a unity and continuity of agglomeration, like
the unity and continuity of a series of sentences coupled together by
conjunctive particles. For instance, suppose we have the bifurcation
20 Feathered and Featherless, and then divide Feathered into Wild and
Tame, or into White and Black. Tame and White are not a differentiation of Feathered, but are the commencement of an independent
bifurcation, and are foreign to the series at the end of which they are
introduced.

As we said then, we must define at the outset by a multiplicity of
25 differentiae. If we do so, privative terms will be available, which are
unavailable to the dichotomist.

The impossibility of reaching the definition of any of the ultimate
forms by dichotomy of the larger group, as some propose, is manifest
also from the following considerations. It is impossible that a single
30 differentia, either by itself or with its antecedents, shall express the
whole essence of a species. (In saying a single differentia by itself I
mean such an isolated differentia as Cleft-footed; in saying a single
differentia with antecedent I mean, to give an instance, Many-cleft-
footed preceded by Cleft-footed. The very continuity of a series of
successive differentiae in a division is intended to show that it is their
combination that expresses the character of the resulting unit, or ulti-
35 mate group. But one is misled by the usages of language into imagining that it is merely the final term of the series, Many-cleft-footed for
instance, that constitutes the whole differentia, and that the antece-
644ᵃ dent terms, Footed, Cleft-footed, are superfluous. Now it is evident
that such a series cannot consist of many terms. For if one divides
and subdivides, one soon reaches the final differential term, but for
all that will not have got to the ultimate division, that is, to the
species.) No single differentia, I repeat, either by itself or with its
5 antecedents, can possibly express the essence of a species. Suppose, for
example, Man to be the animal to be defined; the single differentia
will be Cleft-footed, either by itself or with its antecedents, Footed and
Two-footed. Now if man was nothing more than a Cleft-footed
animal, this single differentia would duly represent his essence. But
seeing that this is not the case, more differentiae than this one will
necessarily be required to define him; and these cannot come under
one division; for each single branch of a dichotomy ends in a single

differentia, and cannot possibly include several differentiae belonging to one and the same animal.

It is impossible then to reach any of the ultimate animal forms by dichotomous division.   10

4   It deserves inquiry why a single name denoting a higher group was not invented by mankind, as an appellation to comprehend the two groups of Water animals and Winged animals. For even these have certain attributes in common. However, the present nomenclature 15 is just. Groups that only differ in degree, and in the more or less of an identical element that they possess, are aggregated under a single class; groups whose attributes are not identical but analogous are separated. For instance, bird differs from bird by gradation, or by 20 excess and defect; some birds have long feathers, others short ones, but all are feathered. Bird and Fish are more remote and only agree in having analogous organs; for what in the bird is feather, in the fish is scale. Such analogies can scarcely, however, serve universally as indications for the formation of groups, for almost all animals present analogies in their corresponding parts.

The individuals comprised within a species, such as Socrates and Coriscus, are the real existences; but inasmuch as these individuals possess one common specific form, it will suffice to state the universal 25 attributes of the species, that is, the attributes common to all its individuals, once for all, as otherwise there will be endless reiteration, as has already been pointed out.[1]

But as regards the larger groups—such as Birds—which comprehend many species, there may be a question. For on the one hand it may be urged that as the ultimate species represent the real existences, it will be well, if practicable, to examine these ultimate species 30 separately, just as we examine the species Man separately; to examine, that is, not the whole class Birds collectively, but the Ostrich, the Crane, and the other indivisible groups or species belonging to the class.

On the other hand, however, this course would involve repeated mention of the same attribute, as the same attribute is common to 35 many species, and so far would be somewhat irrational and tedious. 644^b Perhaps, then, it will be best to treat generically the universal attributes of the groups that have a common nature and contain closely. allied subordinate forms, whether they are groups recognized by a true instinct of mankind, such as Birds and Fishes, or groups not popu- 5 larly known by a common appellation, but withal composed of closely allied subordinate groups; and only to deal individually with the

[1] Cf. i. 1. 639^a 27.

attributes of a single species, when such species—man, for instance, and any other such, if such there be—stands apart from others, and does not constitute with them a larger natural group.

It is generally similarity in the shape of particular organs, or of the whole body, that has determined the formation of the larger groups.
10 It is in virtue of such a similarity that Birds, Fishes, Cephalopoda, and Testacea have been made to form each a separate class. For within the limits of each such class, the parts do not differ in that they have no nearer resemblance than that of analogy—such as exists between the bone of man and the spine of fish—but differ merely in respect of such corporeal conditions as largeness smallness, softness hardness,
15 smoothness roughness, and other similar oppositions, or, in one word, in respect of degree.

We have now touched upon the canons for criticizing the method of natural science, and have considered what is the most systematic and easy course of investigation; we have also dealt with division, and the mode of conducting it so as best to attain the ends of science, and have shown why dichotomy is either impracticable or inefficacious for its professed purposes.
20   Having laid this foundation, let us pass on to our next topic.

5   Of things constituted by nature some are ungenerated, imperishable, and eternal, while others are subject to generation and decay.
25 The former are excellent beyond compare and divine, but less accessible to knowledge. The evidence that might throw light on them, and on the problems which we long to solve respecting them, is furnished but scantily by sensation; whereas respecting perishable plants and animals we have abundant information, living as we do in their midst,
30 and ample data may be collected concerning all their various kinds, if only we are willing to take sufficient pains. Both departments, however, have their special charm. The scanty conceptions to which we can attain of celestial things give us, from their excellence, more pleasure than all our knowledge of the world in which we live; just
35 as a half glimpse of persons that we love is more delightful than a
645ª leisurely view of other things, whatever their number and dimensions. On the other hand, in certitude and in completeness our knowledge of terrestrial things has the advantage. Moreover, their greater nearness and affinity to us balances somewhat the loftier interest of the heavenly things that are the objects of the higher philosophy. Having
5 already treated of the celestial world, as far as our conjectures could reach, we proceed to treat of animals, without omitting, to the best of our ability, any member of the kingdom, however ignoble. For if some

have no graces to charm the sense, yet even these, by disclosing to
intellectual perception the artistic spirit that designed them, give
immense pleasure to all who can trace links of causation, and are 10
inclined to philosophy. Indeed, it would be strange if mimic representations of them were attractive, because they disclose the mimetic
skill of the painter or sculptor, and the original realities themselves
were not more interesting, to all at any rate who have eyes to discern
the reasons that determined their formation. We therefore must not 15
recoil with childish aversion from the examination of the humbler
animals. Every realm of nature is marvellous: and as Heraclitus,
when the strangers who came to visit him found him warming himself
at the furnace in the kitchen and hesitated to go in, is reported to
have bidden them not to be afraid to enter, as even in that kitchen 20
divinities were present, so we should venture on the study of every
kind of animal without distaste; for each and all will reveal to us
something natural and something beautiful. Absence of haphazard
and conduciveness of everything to an end are to be found in Nature's
works in the highest degree, and the resultant end of her generations 25
and combinations is a form of the beautiful.

   If any person thinks the examination of the rest of the animal
kingdom an unworthy task, he must hold in like disesteem the study
of man. For no one can look at the primordia of the human frame—
blood, flesh, bones, vessels, and the like—without much repugnance. 30
Moreover, when any one of the parts or structures, be it which it may,
is under discussion, it must not be supposed that it is its material
composition to which attention is being directed or which is the object
of the discussion, but the relation of such part to the total form.
Similarly, the true object of architecture is not bricks, mortar, or
timber, but the house; and so the principal object of natural philoso- 35
phy is not the material elements, but their composition, and the totality
of the form, independently of which they have no existence.

   The course of exposition must be first to state the attributes com- 645ᵇ
mon to whole groups of animals, and then to attempt to give their
explanation. Many groups, as already noticed,[2] present common attributes, that is to say, in some cases absolutely identical affections, and 5
absolutely identical organs—feet, feathers, scales, and the like; while
in other groups the affections and organs are only so far identical
as that they are analogous. For instance, some groups have lungs,
others have no lung, but an organ analogous to a lung in its place;
some have blood, others have no blood, but a fluid analogous to blood,
and with the same office. To treat of the common attributes in con- 10

----

[2] Cf. i. 1. 639ᵃ 18 and 27.

nexion with each individual group would involve, as already suggested, useless iteration. For many groups have common attributes. So much for this topic.

As every instrument and every bodily member subserves some
15 partial end, that is to say, some special action, so the whole body must be destined to minister to some plenary sphere of action. Thus the saw is made for sawing, for sawing is a function, and not sawing for the saw. Similarly, the body too must somehow or other be made for the soul, and each part of it for some subordinate function, to which it is adapted.

20   We have, then, first to describe the common functions, common, that is, to the whole animal kingdom, or to certain large groups, or to the members of a species. In other words, we have to describe the attributes common to all animals, or to assemblages, like the class of
25 Birds, of closely allied groups differentiated by gradation, or to groups like Man not differentiated into subordinate groups. In the first case the common attributes may be called analogous, in the second generic, in the third specific.

When a function is ancillary to another, a like relation manifestly obtains between the organs which discharge these functions; and
30 similarly, if one function is prior to and the end of another, their respective organs will stand to each other in the same relation. Thirdly, the existence of these parts involves that of other things as their necessary consequents.

Instances of what I mean by functions and affections are Repro-
35 duction, Growth, Copulation, Waking, Sleep, Locomotion, and other similar vital actions. Instances of what I mean by parts are Nose, Eye,
646ᵃ Face, and other so-called members or limbs, and also the more elementary parts of which these are made. So much for the method to be pursued. Let us now try to set forth the causes of all vital phenomena, whether universal or particular, and in so doing let us
5 follow that order of exposition which conforms, as we have indicated, to the order of nature.

BOOK II

1   The nature and the number of the parts of which animals are severally composed are matters which have already been set forth in
10 detail in the book of Researches about Animals. We have now to inquire what are the causes that in each case have determined this composition, a subject quite distinct from that dealt with in the Researches.

Now there are three degrees of composition; and of these the first in order, as all will allow, is composition out of what some call the elements, such as earth, air, water, fire. Perhaps, however, it would be more accurate to say composition out of the elementary forces; nor indeed out of all of these, but out of a limited number of them, as defined in previous treatises. For fluid and solid, hot and cold, form the material of all composite bodies; and all other differences are secondary to these, such differences, that is, as heaviness or lightness, density or rarity, roughness or smoothness, and any other such properties of matter as there may be. The second degree of composition is that by which the homogeneous parts of animals, such as bone, flesh, and the like, are constituted out of the primary substances. The third and last stage is the composition which forms the heterogeneous parts, such as face, hand, and the rest.

Now the order of actual development and the order of logical existence are always the inverse of each other. For that which is posterior in the order of development is antecedent in the order of nature, and that is genetically last which in nature is first.

(That this is so is manifest by induction; for a house does not exist for the sake of bricks and stones, but these materials for the sake of the house; and the same is the case with the materials of other bodies. Nor is induction required to show this. It is included in our conception of generation. For generation is a process from a something to a something; that which is generated having a cause in which it originates and a cause in which it ends. The originating cause is the primary efficient cause, which is something already endowed with tangible existence, while the final cause is some definite form or similar end; for man generates man, and plant generates plant, in each case out of the underlying material.)

In order of time, then, the material and the generative process must necessarily be anterior to the being that is generated; but in logical order the definitive character and form of each being precedes the material. This is evident if one only tries to define the process of formation. For the definition of house-building includes and presupposes that of the house; but the definition of the house does not include nor presuppose that of house-building; and the same is true of all other productions. So that it must necessarily be that the elementary material exists for the sake of the homogeneous parts, seeing that these are genetically posterior to it, just as the heterogeneous parts are posterior genetically to them. For these heterogeneous parts have reached the end and goal, having the third degree of composition, in which degree generation or development often attains its final term.

Animals, then, are composed of homogeneous parts, and are also composed of heterogeneous parts. The former, however, exist for the sake of the latter. For the active functions and operations of the body are carried on by these; that is, by the heterogeneous parts, such as the eye, the nostril, the whole face, the fingers, the hand, and
15 the whole arm. But inasmuch as there is a great variety in the functions and motions not only of aggregate animals but also of the individual organs, it is necessary that the substances out of which these are composed shall present a diversity of properties. For some purposes softness is advantageous, for others hardness; some parts must be capable of extension, others of flexion. Such properties, then, are
20 distributed separately to the different homogeneous parts, one being soft another hard, one fluid another solid, one viscous another brittle; whereas each of the heterogeneous parts presents a combination of multifarious properties. For the hand, to take an example, requires one property to enable it to effect pressure, and another and differ-
25 ent property for simple prehension. For this reason the active or executive parts of the body are compounded out of bones, sinews, flesh, and the like, but not these latter out of the former.

So far, then, as has yet been stated, the relations between these two orders of parts are determined by a final cause. We have, however, to inquire whether necessity may not also have a share in the
30 matter; and it must be admitted that these mutual relations could not from the very beginning have possibly been other than they are. For heterogeneous parts can be made up out of homogeneous parts, either from a plurality of them, or from a single one, as is the case with some of the viscera which, varying in configuration, are yet, to
35 speak broadly, formed from a single homogeneous substance; but that homogeneous substances should be formed out of a combination of
647ª heterogeneous parts is clearly an impossibility. For these causes, then, some parts of animals are simple and homogeneous, while others are composite and heterogeneous; and dividing the parts into the active or executive and the sensitive, each one of the
5 former is, as before said, heterogeneous, and each one of the latter homogeneous. For it is in homogeneous parts alone that sensation can occur, as the following considerations show.

Each sense is confined to a single order of sensibles, and its organ must be such as to admit the action of that kind or order. But it is only that which is endowed with a property *in posse* that is acted on by that which has the like property *in esse*, so that the two are the
10 same in kind, and if the latter is single so also is the former. Thus it is that while no physiologists ever dream of saying of the hand or face

or other such part that one is earth, another water, another fire, they couple each separate sense-organ with a separate element, asserting this one to be air and that other to be fire.

Sensation, then, is confined to the simple or homogeneous parts. 15 But, as might reasonably be expected, the organ of touch, though still homogeneous, is yet the least simple of all the sense-organs. For touch more than any other sense appears to be correlated to several distinct kinds of objects, and to recognize more than one category of contrasts, heat and cold, for instance, solidity and fluidity, and other similar oppositions. Accordingly, the organ which deals with these varied objects is of all the sense-organs the most corporeal, being 20 either the flesh, or the substance which in some animals takes the place of flesh.

Now as there cannot possibly be an animal without sensation, it follows as a necessary consequence that every animal must have some homogeneous parts; for these alone are capable of sensation, the heterogeneous p rts serving for the active functions. Again, as the sensory faculty, the motor faculty, and the nutritive faculty are all 25 lodged in one and the same part of the body, as was stated in a former treatise, it is necessary that the part which is the primary seat of these principles shall on the one hand, in its character of general sensory recipient, be one of the simple parts; and on the other hand shall, in its motor and active character, be one of the heterogeneous 30 parts. For this reason it is the heart which in sanguineous animals constitutes this central part, and in bloodless animals it is that which takes the place of a heart. For the heart, like the other viscera, is one of the homogeneous parts; for, if cut up, its pieces are homogeneous in substance with each other. But it is at the same time heterogeneous in virtue of its definite configuration. And the same is true of the other 35 so-called viscera, which are indeed formed from the same material as the heart. For all these viscera have a sanguineous character owing 647^b to their being situated upon vascular ducts and branches. For just as a stream of water deposits mud, so the various viscera, the heart excepted, are, as it were, deposits from the stream of blood in the vessels. And as to the heart, the very starting-point of the vessels, 5 and the actual seat of the force by which the blood is first fabricated, it is but what one would naturally expect, that out of the selfsame nutriment of which it is the recipient its own proper substance shall be formed. Such, then, are the reasons why the viscera are of sanguineous aspect; and why in one point of view they are homogeneous, in another heterogeneous. [Chapters 2-17 of Book II and Books III and IV omitted.]

De Generatione Animalium

Translated by Arthur Platt

CONTENTS

BOOK I

DE GENERATIONE ANIMALIUM

(*On the Generation of Animals*)

1   We have now discussed the other parts of animals, both generally 715ᵃ
and with reference to the peculiarities of each kind, explaining how
each part exists on account of such a cause, and I mean by this the
final cause.

There are four causes underlying everything: first, the final cause,
that for the sake of which a thing exists; secondly, the formal cause,
the definition of its essence (and these two we may regard pretty
much as one and the same); thirdly, the material; and fourthly, the 5
moving principle or efficient cause.

We have then already discussed the other three causes, for the
definition and the final cause are the same, and the material of animals is their parts—of the whole animal the non-homogeneous parts, 10
of these again the homogeneous, and of these last the so-called elements of all matter. It remains to speak of those parts which contribute
to the generation of animals and of which nothing definite has yet
been said, and to explain what is the moving or efficient cause. To
inquire into this last and to inquire into the generation of each animal is in a way the same thing; and, therefore, my plan has united 15
them together, arranging the discussion of these parts last, and the
beginning of the question of generation next to them.

Now some animals come into being from the union of male and
female, i. e. all those kinds of animal which possess the two sexes. 20
This is not the case with all of them; though in the sanguinea with
few exceptions the creature, when its growth is complete, is either male
or female, and though some bloodless animals have sexes so that they
generate offspring of the same kind, yet other bloodless animals generate indeed, but not offspring of the same kind; such are all that come
into being not from a union of the sexes, but from decaying earth and 25
excrements. To speak generally, if we take all animals which change
their locality, some by swimming, others by flying, others by walking, we find in these the two sexes, not only in the sanguinea but also
in some of the bloodless animals; and this applies in the case of the

715^b latter sometimes to the whole class, as the cephalopoda and crustacea, but in the class of insects only to the majority. Of these, all which are produced by union of animals of the same kind generate also after their kind, but all of which are not produced by animals, but from

5 decaying matter, generate indeed, but produce another kind, and the offspring is neither male nor female; such are some of the insects. This is what might have been expected, for if those animals which are not produced by parents had themselves united and produced others, then their offspring must have been either like or unlike to

10 themselves. If like, then their parents ought to have come into being in the same way; this is only a reasonable postulate to make, for it is plainly the case with other animals. If unlike, and yet able to copulate, then there would have come into being again from them another kind of creature and again another from these, and this would have gone

15 on to infinity. But Nature flies from the infinite, for the infinite is unending or imperfect, and Nature ever seeks amend.

But all those creatures which do not move, as the testacea and animals that live by clinging to something else, inasmuch as their nature resembles that of plants, have no sex any more than plants

20 have, but as applied to them the word is only used in virtue of a similarity and analogy. For there is a slight distinction of this sort, since even in plants we find in the same kind some trees which bear fruit and others which, while bearing none themselves, yet contribute

25 to the ripening of the fruits of those which do, as in the case of the fig-tree and caprifig.

The same holds good also in plants, some coming into being from seed and others, as it were, by the spontaneous action of Nature, arising either from decomposition of the earth or of some parts in other plants, for some are not formed by themselves separately but are

716^a produced upon other trees, as the mistletoe. Plants, however, must be investigated separately. [Chapters 2-16 omitted.]

721^a 17   Some animals manifestly emit semen, as all the sanguinea, but

30 whether the insects and cephalopoda do so is uncertain. Therefore this is a question to be considered, whether all males do so, or not all; and if not all, why some do and some not; and whether the

721^b female also contributes any semen or not; and, if not semen, whether she does not contribute anything else either, or whether she contributes something else which is not semen. We must also inquire what those animals which emit semen contribute by means of it to

5 generation, and generally what is the nature of semen, and of the so-called catamenia in all animals which discharge this liquid.

Now it is thought that all animals are generated out of semen, and that the semen comes from the parents. Wherefore it is part of the same inquiry to ask whether both male and female produce it or only one of them, and to ask whether it comes from the whole of the body or not from the whole; for if the latter is true it is reasonable 10 to suppose that it does not come from both parents either. Accordingly, since some say that it comes from the whole of the body, we must investigate this question first.

The proofs from which it can be argued that the semen comes from each and every part of the body may be reduced to four. First, the intensity of the pleasure of coition; for the same state of feel- 15 ing is more pleasant if multiplied, and that which affects all the parts is multiplied as compared with that which affects only one or a few. Secondly, the alleged fact that mutilations are inherited, for they argue that since the parent is deficient in this part the semen does not come from thence, and the result is that the corresponding part is not 20 formed in the offspring. Thirdly, the resemblances to the parents, for the young are born like them part for part as well as in the whole body; if then the coming of the semen from the whole body is cause of the resemblance of the whole, so the parts would be like because it comes from each of the parts. Fourthly, it would seem to be reason- able to say that as there is some first thing from which the whole 25 arises, so it is also with each of the parts, and therefore if semen or seed is cause of the whole so each of the parts would have a seed peculiar to itself. And these opinions are plausibly supported by such evidence as that children are born with a likeness to their parents, not only in 30 congenital but also in acquired characteristics; for before now, when the parents have had scars, the children have been born with a mark in the form of the scar in the same place, and there was a case at Chalcedon where the father had a brand on his arm and the letter was marked on the child, only confused and not clearly articulated. That is pretty much the evidence on which some believe that the semen comes from all the body.   722ᵃ

18   On examining the question, however, the opposite appears more likely, for it is not hard to refute the above arguments and the view involves impossibilities. First, then, the resemblance of children to parents is no proof that the semen comes from the whole body, be- 5 cause the resemblance is found also in voice, nails, hair, and way of moving, from which nothing comes. And men generate before they yet have certain characters, such as a beard or grey hair. Further, chil- dren are like their more remote ancestors from whom nothing has

come, for the resemblances recur at an interval of many generations,
10 as in the case of the woman in Elis who had intercourse with the
Aethiop; her daughter was not an Aethiop but the son of that
daughter was. The same thing applies also to plants, for it is clear
that if this theory were true the seed would come from all parts of
plants also; but often a plant does not possess one part, and another
part may be removed, and a third grows afterwards. Besides, the
15 seed does not come from the pericarp, and yet this also comes into
being with the same form as in the parent plant.

We may also ask whether the semen comes from each of the homogeneous parts only, such as flesh and bone and sinew, or also from
the heterogeneous, such as face and hands. For if (1) from the former
20 only, we object that the resemblance exists rather in the heterogeneous parts, such as face and hands and feet; if then it is not because of the semen coming from all parts that children resemble their
parents in *these*, what is there to stop the homogeneous parts also from
being like for some other reason than this? If (2) the semen comes
from the heterogeneous alone, then it does not come from all parts;
25 but it is more fitting that it should come from the homogeneous parts,
for they are prior to the heterogeneous which are composed of them;
and as children are born like their parents in face and hands, so they
are, necessarily, in flesh and nails. If (3) the semen comes from both,
what would be the manner of generation? For the heterogeneous parts
30 are composed of the homogeneous, so that to come from the former
would be to come from the latter and from their composition. To
make this clearer by an illustration, take a written name; if anything came from the whole of it, it would be from each of the syllables, and if from these, from the letters and their composition. So
that if really flesh and bones are composed of fire and the like elements, the semen would come rather from the elements than anything else, for how can it come from their composition? Yet with-
722ᵇ out this composition there would be no resemblance. If again
something creates this composition later, it would be *this* that would
be the cause of the resemblance, not the coming of the semen from
every part of the body.

Further, if the parts of the future animal are separated in the
semen, how do they live? and if they are connected, they would form
a small animal.

5 And what about the generative parts? For that which comes from
the male is not similar to what comes from the female.

Again, if the semen comes from all parts of both parents alike,
the result is *two* animals, for the offspring will have all the parts of

both. Wherefore Empedocles seems to say what agrees pretty well with this view (if we are to adopt it), to a certain extent at any rate, but to be wrong if we think otherwise. What he says agrees with it when he declares that there is a sort of tally in the male and female, and that the whole offspring does not come from either, 'but sundered is the fashion of limbs, some in man's . . .' For why does not the female generate from herself if the semen comes from all parts alike and she has a receptacle ready in the uterus? But, it seems, either it does not come from all the parts, or if it does it is in the way Empedocles says, not the same parts coming from each parent, which is why they need intercourse with each other.

Yet this also is impossible, just as much as it is impossible for the parts when full grown to survive and have life in them when torn apart, as Empedocles accounts for the creation of animals; in the time of his 'Reign of Love', says he, 'many heads sprang up without necks,' and later on these isolated parts combined into animals. Now that *this* is impossible is plain, for neither would the separate parts be able to survive without having any soul or life in them, nor if they were living things, so to say, could several of them combine so as to become one animal again. Yet those who say that semen comes from the whole of the body really have to talk in that way, and as it happened then in the earth during the 'Reign of Love', so it happens according to them in the body. Now it is impossible that the parts should be united together when they come into being and should come from different parts of the parent, meeting together in one place. Then how can the upper and lower, right and left, front and back parts have been 'sundered'? All these points are unintelligible. Further, some parts are distinguished by possessing a faculty, others by being in certain states or conditions; the heterogeneous, as tongue and hand, by the faculty of doing something, the homogeneous by hardness and softness and the other similar states. Blood, then, will not to be blood, nor flesh flesh, in any and every state. It is clear, then, that that which comes from any part, as blood from blood or flesh from flesh, will not be identical with that part. But if it is something different from which the blood of the offspring comes, the coming of the semen from all the parts will not be the cause of the resemblance, as is held by the supporters of this theory. For if blood is formed from something which is not blood, it is enough that the semen come from one part only, for why should not all the other parts of the offspring as well as blood be formed from one part of the parent? Indeed, this theory seems to be the same as that of Anaxagoras, that none of the homogeneous parts come into being, except that these theorists assume, in the case of the generation of animals, what he assumed of the universe.

Then, again, how will these parts that came from all the body of the parent be increased or grow? It is true that Anaxagoras plausibly says that particles of flesh out of the food are added to the flesh. But if we do not say this (while saying that semen comes from all parts of the body), how will the foetus become greater by the addition of something else if that which is added remain unchanged? But if that which is added *can* change, then why not say that the semen from the very first is of such a kind that blood and flesh can be made out of it, instead of saying that it itself *is* blood and flesh? Nor is there any other alternative, for surely we cannot say that it is increased later by a process of mixing, as wine when water is poured into it. For in that case each element of the mixture would be itself *at first* while still unmixed, but the fact rather is that flesh and bone and each of the other parts *is* such *later*. And to say that some part of the semen is sinew and bone is quite above us, as the saying is.

Besides all this there is a difficulty if the sex is determined in conception (as Empedocles says: 'it is shed in clean vessels; some wax female, if they fall in with cold'). Anyhow, it is plain that both men and women change not only from infertile to fertile, but also from bearing female to bearing male offspring, which looks as if the cause does not lie in the semen coming from all the parent or not, but in the mutual proportion or disproportion of that which comes from the woman and the man, or in something of this kind. It is clear, then, if we are to put this down as being so, that the female sex is not determined by the semen coming from any particular part, and consequently neither is the special sexual part so determined (if really the same semen can become either a male or female child, which shows that the sexual part does not exist in the semen). Why, then, should we assert this of *this* part any more than of the others? 723ᵇ For if semen does not come from this part, the uterus, the same account may be given of the others.

Again, some creatures come into being neither from parents of the same kind nor from parents of a different kind, as flies and the various kinds of what are called fleas; from these are produced animals indeed, but not in this case of similar nature, but a kind of scolex. It is plain in this case that the young of a different kind are not produced by semen coming from all parts of the parent, for they would then resemble them, if indeed resemblance is a sign of its coming from all parts.

Further, even among animals some produce many young from a single coition (and something like this is universal among plants, for it is plain that they bear all the fruit of a whole season from a single movement). And yet how would this be possible if the semen were secreted from all the body? For from a single coition and a single segregation of the semen scattered throughout the body must needs follow only a single secretion. Nor is it possible for it to be separated in the uterus, for this would no longer be a mere separation of semen, but, as it were, a severance from a new plant or animal.

Again, the cuttings from a plant bear seed; clearly, therefore, even before they were cut from the parent plant, they bore their fruit from their own mass alone, and the seed did not come from *all* the plant.

But the greatest proof of all is derived from observations we have sufficiently established on insects. For, if not in all, at least in most of these, the female in the act of copulation inserts a part of herself into the male. This, as we said before, is the way they copulate, for the females manifestly insert this from below into the males above, not in all cases, but in most of those observed. Hence it seems clear that, when the males do emit semen, then also the cause of the generation is not its coming from all the body, but something else which must be investigated hereafter. For even if it were true that it comes from all the *body*, as they say, they ought not to claim that it comes from all *parts* of it, but only from the creative part—from the workman, so to say, not the material he works in. Instead of that, they talk as if one were to say that the semen comes from the shoes, for, generally speaking, if a son is like his father, the shoes he wears are like his father's shoes.

As to the vehemence of pleasure in sexual intercourse, it is not because the semen comes from all the body, but because there is a strong friction (wherefore if this intercourse is often repeated the pleasure is diminished in the persons concerned). Moreover, the pleasure is at the end of the act, but it ought, on the theory, to be in each of the parts, and not at the same time, but sooner in some and later in others.

If mutilated young are born of mutilated parents, it is for the same reason as that for which they are like them. And the young of mutilated parents are not always mutilated, just as they are not always like their parents; the cause of this must be inquired into later, for this problem is the same as that.

Again, if the female does not produce semen, it is reasonable to suppose it does not come from all the body of the male either. Conversely, if it does not come from all the male it is not unreasonable

10 to suppose that it does not come from the female, but that the female is cause of the generation in some other way. Into this we must next inquire, since it is plain that the semen is not secreted from all the parts.

In this investigation and those which follow from it, the first thing to 15 do is to understand what semen is, for then it will be easier to inquire into its operations and the phenomena connected with it. Now the object of semen is to be of such a nature that from it as their origin come into being those things which are naturally formed, not because there is any agent which makes them from it as . . . but simply 20 because this is the semen. Now we speak of one thing coming *from* another in many senses; it is one thing when we say that night comes *from* day or a man becomes man *from* boy, meaning that A follows B; it is another if we say that a statute is made *from* bronze and a bed *from* wood, and so on in all the other cases where we say that the thing 25 made is made *from* a material, meaning that the whole is formed from something pre-existing which is only put into shape. In a third sense a man becomes unmusical *from* being musical, sick *from* being well, and generally in this sense contraries arise from contraries. Fourthly, as in the 'climax' of Epicharmus; thus *from* slander comes railing and *from* 30 this fighting, and all these are *from* something in the sense that it is the efficient cause. In this last class sometimes the efficient cause is in the things themselves, as in the last mentioned (for the slander is a part of the whole trouble), and sometimes external, as the art is 35 external to the work of art or the torch to the burning house.

Now the offspring comes *from* the semen, and it is plainly in one of the two following senses that it does so—either the semen is the material from which it is made, or it is the first efficient cause. For 724ᵇ assuredly it is not in the sense of A being *after* B, as the voyage comes *from*, i. e. after, the Panathenaea; nor yet as contraries come from contraries, for then one of the two contraries ceases to be, and a third substance must exist as an immediate underlying basis from which 5 the new thing comes into being. We must discover, then, in which of the two other classes the semen is to be put, whether it is to be regarded as matter, and therefore acted upon by something else, or as a form, and therefore acting upon something else, or as both at once. For perhaps at the same time we shall see clearly also how all the products of semen come into being from contraries, since coming into being from contraries is also a natural process, for some animals do so, i. e. 10 from male and female, others from only one parent, as is the case with plants and all those animals in which male and female are not separately differentiated. Now that which comes from the generating parent is called the seminal fluid, being that which first has in it a principle of generation, in the case of all animals whose nature it is to unite; semen is that which has in it the principles from *both* united parents, as the first mixture which arises from the union of 15 male and female, be it a foetus or an ovum, for these already have in them that which comes from both. (Semen, or seed, and grain differ only in the one being earlier and the other later, grain in that it comes from something else, i. e. the seed, and seed in that something else, 20 the grain, comes from *it*, for both are really the same thing.)

We must again take up the question what the primary nature of what is called semen is. Needs must everything which we find in the body either be (1) one of the natural parts, whether homogeneous or heterogeneous, or (2) an unnatural part such as a growth, or 25 (3) a secretion or excretion, or (4) waste-product, or (5) nutriment. (By secretion or excretion I mean the residue of the nutriment, by waste-product that which is given off from the tissues by an unnatural decomposition.)

Now that semen cannot be a part of the body is plain, for it is homogeneous, and from the homogeneous nothing is composed, e. g. from only sinew or only flesh; nor is it separated as are all the other 30 parts. But neither is it contrary to Nature nor a defect, for it exists in all alike, and the development of the young animal comes from it. Nutriment, again, is obviously introduced from without.

It remains, then, that it must be either a waste-product or a 35 secretion or excretion. Now the ancients seem to think that it is a waste-product, for when they say that it comes from all the body by reason of the heat of the movement of the body in copulation, they 725ᵃ imply that it is a kind of waste-product. But these are contrary to Nature, and from such arises nothing according to Nature. So then it must be a secretion or excretion.

But, to go further into it, every secretion or excretion is either of 5 useless or useful nutriment; by 'useless' I mean that from which nothing further is contributed to natural growth, but which is particularly mischievous to the body if too much of it is consumed; by 'useful' I mean the opposite. Now it is evident that it cannot be of the former character, for such is most abundant in persons of the worst condition of body through age or sickness; semen, on the contrary, is least abundant in them, for either they have none at all or it is not 10 fertile, because a useless and morbid secretion is mingled with it.

Semen, then, is part of a useful secretion. But the *most* useful is the last and that from which finally is formed each of the parts of the

body. For secretions are either earlier or later; of the nutriment in the
15 first stage the secretion is phlegm and the like, for phlegm also is a
secretion of the useful nutriment, an indication of this being that if it
is mixed with pure nutriment it is nourishing, and that it is used up in
cases of illness. The final secretion is the smallest in proportion to the
quantity of nutriment. But we must reflect that the daily nutriment
20 by which animals and plants grow is but small, for if a very little be
added continually to the same thing the size of it will become excessive.

So we must say the opposite of what the ancients said. For whereas
they said that semen is that which comes *from* all the body, *we* shall
say it is that whose nature is to go *to* all of it, and what they thought
a waste-product seems rather to be a secretion. For it is more reason-
25 able to suppose that the last extract of the nutriment which goes to all
parts resembles that which is left over from it, just as part of a
painter's colour is often left over resembling that which he has used
up. Waste-products, on the contrary, are always due to corruption or
decay and to a departure from Nature.

A further proof that it is not a waste-product, but rather a secretion, is the fact that the large animals have few young, the small
30 many. For the large must have more waste and less secretion, since
the great size of the body causes most of the nutriment to be used up,
so that the residue or secretion is small.

Again, no place has been set apart by Nature for waste-products
but they flow wherever they can find an easy passage in the body,
but a place has been set apart for all the natural secretions; thus
725ᵇ the lower intestine serves for the excretion of the solid nutriment, the
bladder for that of the liquid; for the useful part of the nutriment we
have the upper intestine, for the spermatic secretions the uterus and
pudenda and breasts, for it is collected and flows together into them.
5 And the resulting phenomena are evidence that semen is what we
have said, and these result because such is the nature of the secretion. For the exhaustion consequent on the loss of even a very little of
the semen is conspicuous because the body is deprived of the ultimate gain drawn from the nutriment. With some few persons, it is
true, during a short time in the flower of their youth the loss of it,
10 if it be excessive in quantity, is an alleviation (just as in the case of
the nutriment in its first stage, if too much have been taken, since getting rid of this also makes the body more comfortable), and so it may
be also when other secretions come away with it, for in that case it is
not only semen that is lost but also other influences come away
15 mingled with it, and these are morbid. Wherefore, with some men at

least, that which comes from them proves sometimes incapable of procreation because the seminal element in it is so small. But still in most men and as a general rule the result of intercourse is exhaustion and weakness rather than relief, for the reason given. Moreover, semen does not exist in them either in childhood or in old age or in 20 sickness—in the last case because of weakness, in old age because they do not sufficiently concoct their food, and in childhood because they are growing and so all the nutriment is used up too soon, for in about five years, in the case of human beings at any rate, the body seems to gain half the height that is gained in all the rest of life. 25

In many animals and plants we find a difference in this connexion not only between kinds as compared with kinds, but also between similar individuals of the same kind as compared with each other, e. g. man with man or vine with vine. Some have much semen, others little, others again none at all, not through weakness but the contrary, at any 30 rate in some cases. This is because the nutriment is used up to form the body, as with some human beings, who, being in good condition and developing much flesh or getting rather too fat, produce less semen and are less desirous of intercourse. Like this is what happens with those vines which 'play the goat', that is, luxuriate wantonly through too much nutrition, for he-goats when fat are less inclined to mount 726ª the female; for which reason they thin them before breeding from them, and say that the vines 'play the goat', so calling it from the condition of the goats. And fat people, women as well as men, appear to be less fertile than others from the fact that the secretion when in process of concoction turns to fat with those who are too well- 5 nourished. For fat also is a healthy secretion due to good living.

In some cases no semen is produced at all, as by the willow and poplar. This condition is due to each of the two causes, weakness and strength; the former prevents concoction of the nutriment, the latter causes it to be all consumed, as said above. In like manner other animals produce much semen through weakness as well as through 10 strength, when a great quantity of a useless secretion is mixed with it; this sometimes results in actual disease when a passage is not found to carry off the impurity, and though some recover of this, others actually die of it. For corrupt humours collect here as in the urine, 15 which also has been known to cause disease. . . .

From what has been said, it is clear that semen is a secretion of use- 26 ful nutriment, and that in its last stage, whether it is produced by all or no. [Chapter 19 and most of chapter 20 omitted.]

. . . That, then, the female does not contribute semen to generation, 22 but does contribute something, and that this is the matter of the 729ª

catamenia, or that which is analogous to it in bloodless animals, is
clear from what has been said, and also from a general and abstract
25 survey of the question. For there must needs be that which generates
and that from which it generates; even if these be one, still they must
be distinct in form and their essence must be different; and in
those animals that have these powers separate in two sexes the body
and nature of the active and the passive sex must also differ. If, then,
the male stands for the effective and active, and the female, con-
30 sidered as female, for the passive, it follows that what the female
would contribute to the semen of the male would not be semen but
material for the semen to work upon. This is just what we find to be
the case, for the catamenia have in their nature an affinity to the
primitive matter.

21   So much for the discussion of this question. At the same time
the answer to the next question we have to investigate is clear from
729ᵇ these considerations, I mean how it is that the male contributes to
generation and how it is that the semen from the male is the cause of
the offspring. Does it exist in the body of the embryo as a part of it
from the first, mingling with the material which comes from the
5 female? Or does the semen communicate nothing to the material
body of the embryo but only to the power and movement in it? For
this power is that which acts and makes, while that which is made and
receives the form is the residue of the secretion in the female. Now
the latter alternative appears to be the right one both *a priori* and
in view of the facts. For, if we consider the question on general
10 grounds, we find that, whenever one thing is made from two of which
one is active and the other passive, the active agent does not exist
in that which is made; and, still more generally, the same applies
when one thing moves and another is moved; the moving thing does
not exist in that which is moved. But the female, as female, is passive, and the male, as male, is active, and the principle of the movement comes from him. Therefore, if we take the highest genera under
15 which they each fall, the one being active and motive and the other
passive and moved, that one thing which is produced comes from
them only in the sense in which a bed comes into being from the carpenter and the wood, or in which a ball comes into being from the
wax and the form. It is plain then that it is not necessary that anything at all should come away from the male, and if anything does
come away it does not follow that this gives rise to the embryo as
being in the embryo, but only as that which imparts the motion and
20 as the form; so the medical art cures the patient.

This *a priori* argument is confirmed by the facts. For it is for this reason that some males which unite with the female do not, it appears, insert any part of themselves into the female, but on the contrary the female inserts a part of herself into the male; this occurs in some 25 insects. For the effect produced by the semen in the female (in the case of those animals whose males do insert a part) is produced in the case of these insects by the heat and power in the male animal itself when the female inserts that part of herself which receives the secretion. And therefore such animals remain united a long time, and when they are separated the young are produced quickly. For the 30 union lasts until that which is analogous to the semen has done its work, and when they separate the female produces the embryo quickly; for the young is imperfect inasmuch as all such creatures give birth to scoleces.

What occurs in birds and oviparous fishes is the greatest proof that neither does the semen come from all parts of the male nor does he emit anything of such a nature as to exist within that which is 730ᵃ generated, as part of the material embryo, but that he only makes a living creature by the power which resides in the semen (as we said in the case of those insects whose females insert a part of themselves into the male). For if a hen-bird is in process of producing wind-eggs and is then trodden by the cock before the egg has begun to whiten 5 and while it is all still yellow, then they become fertile instead of being wind-eggs. And if while it is still yellow she be trodden by another cock, the whole brood of chicks turn out like the second cock. Hence some of those who are anxious to rear fine birds act thus; they 10 change the cocks for the first and second treading, not as if they thought that the semen is mingled with the egg or exists in it, or that it comes from all parts of the cock; for if it did it would have come from both cocks, so that the chick would have all its parts doubled. But it is by its force that the semen of the male gives a certain quality to the material and the nutriment in the female, for the sec- 15 ond semen added to the first can produce this effect by heat and concoction, as the egg acquires nutriment so long as it is growing.

The same conclusion is to be drawn from the generation of oviparous fishes. When the female has laid her eggs, the male sprinkles 20 the milt over them, and those eggs are fertilized which it reaches, but not the others; this shows that the male does not contribute anything to the quantity but only to the quality of the embryo.

From what has been said it is plain that the semen does not come from the whole of the body of the male in those animals which emit it, 25 and that the contribution of the female to the generative product is

not the same as that of the male, but the male contributes the principle of movement and the female the material. This is why the female does not produce offspring by herself, for she needs a principle, i. e. something to begin the movement in the embryo and
30 to define the form it is to assume. Yet in some animals, as birds, the nature of the female unassisted can generate to a certain extent, for they do form something, only it is incomplete; I mean the so-called wind-eggs.

22   For the same reason the development of the embryo takes place in the female; neither the male himself nor the female emits semen into the male, but the female receives within herself the share con-
730ᵇ tributed by both, because in the female is the material from which is made the resulting product. Not only must the mass of material exist there from which the embryo is formed in the first instance, but further material must constantly be added that it may increase in
5 size. Therefore the birth must take place in the female. For the carpenter must keep in close connexion with his timber and the potter with his clay, and generally all workmanship and the ultimate movement imparted to matter must be connected with the material concerned, as, for instance, architecture is *in* the buildings it makes.

From these considerations we may also gather how it is that the
10 male contributes to generation. The male does not emit semen at all in some animals, and where he does this is no part of the resulting embryo; just so no material part comes from the carpenter to the material, i. e. the wood in which he works, nor does any part of the carpenter's art exist within what he makes, but the shape and the
15 form are imparted from him to the material by means of the motion he sets up. It is his hands that move his tools, his tools that move the material; it is his knowledge of his art, and his soul, in which is the form, that move his hands or any other part of him with a motion of some definite kind, a motion varying with the varying nature of the object made. In like manner, in the male of those animals which
20 emit semen, Nature uses the semen as a tool and as possessing motion in actuality, just as tools are used in the products of any art, for in them lies in a certain sense the motion of the art. Such, then, is the way in which these males contribute to generation. But when the male
25 does not emit semen, but the female inserts some part of herself into the male, this is parallel to a case in which a man should carry the material to the workman. For by reason of weakness in such males Nature is not able to do anything by any secondary means, but the movements imparted to the material are scarcely strong enough

when Nature herself watches over them. Thus here she resembles a modeller in clay rather than a carpenter, for she does not touch the ³⁰ work she is forming by means of tools, but, as it were, with her own hands.

23 In all animals which can move about, the sexes are separated, one individual being male and one female, though both are the same in species, as with man and horse. But in plants these powers are 731ᵃ mingled, female not being separated from male. Wherefore they generate out of themselves, and do not emit semen but produce an embryo, what is called the seed. Empedocles puts this well in the line: 'and thus the tall trees oviposit; first olives . . .' For as the egg is an embryo, a certain part of it giving rise to the animal and the rest 5 being nutriment, so also from a part of the seed springs the growing plant, and the rest is nutriment for the shoot and the first root.

In a certain sense the same thing happens also in those animals which have the sexes separate. For when there is need for them to 10 generate the sexes are no longer separated any more than in plants, their nature desiring that they shall become one; and this is plain to view when they copulate and are united, that one animal is made out of both.

It is the nature of those creatures which do not emit semen to 15 remain united a long time until the male element has formed the embryo, as with those insects which copulate. The others so remain only until the male has discharged from the parts of himself introduced something which will form the embryo in a longer time, as among the sanguinea. For the former remain paired some part of a day, while the semen forms the embryo in several days. And after 20 emitting this they cease their union.

And animals seem literally to be like divided plants, as though one should separate and divide them, when they bear seed, into the male and female existing in them.

In all this Nature acts like an intelligent workman. For to the essence of plants belongs no other function or business than the 25 production of seed; since, then, this is brought about by the union of male and female, Nature has mixed these and set them together in plants, so that the sexes are not divided in them. Plants, however, have been investigated elsewhere. But the function of the animal is 30 not only to generate (which is common to all living things), but they all of them participate also in a kind of knowledge, some more and some less, and some very little indeed. For they have sense-perception, and this is a kind of knowledge. (If we consider the value of

this we find that it is of great importance compared with the class
of lifeless objects, but of little compared with the use of the intel-
731ᵇ lect. For against the latter the mere participation in touch and taste
seems to be practically nothing, but beside absolute insensibility it
seems most excellent; for it would seem a treasure to gain even this
kind of knowledge rather than to lie in a state of death and non-
existence.) Now it is by sense-perception that an animal differs from
5 those organisms which have only life. But since, if it is a living animal, it must also live; therefore, when it is necessary for it to accomplish the function of that which has life, it unites and copulates,
becoming like a plant, as we said before.

Testaceous animals, being intermediate between animals and plants,
perform the function of neither class as belonging to both. As plants
10 they have no sexes, and one does not generate in another; as animals
they do not bear fruit from themselves like plants; but they are
formed and generated from a liquid and earthy concretion. However,
we must speak later of the generation of these animals.

[Books II-V omitted.]

Metaphysica

Translated by W. D. Ross

CONTENTS

A. (I)

a. (II)

B. (III)

Γ. (IV)

Δ. (V)

Philosophical Lexicon.

E. (VI)

Z. (VII)

Λ. (XII)

M. (XIII)

N. (XIV)

METAPHYSICA

(*Metaphysics*)

BOOK A (I)

1   All men by nature desire to know. An indication of this is the 980ᵃ
delight we take in our senses; for even apart from their usefulness
they are loved for themselves; and above all others the sense of sight.
For not only with a view to action, but even when we are not going 25
to do anything, we prefer seeing (one might say) to everything else.
The reason is that this, most of all the senses, makes us know and
brings to light many differences between things.

By nature animals are born with the faculty of sensation, and
from sensation memory is produced in some of them, though not in
others. And therefore the former are more intelligent and apt at learn- 980ᵇ
ing than those which cannot remember; those which are incapable
of hearing sounds are intelligent though they cannot be taught, e. g.
the bee, and any other race of animals that may be like it; and
those which besides memory have this sense of hearing can be taught.

The animals other than man live by appearances and memories, 25
and have but little of connected experience; but the human race lives
also by art and reasonings. Now from memory experience is produced in men; for the several memories of the same thing produce
finally the capacity for a single experience. And experience seems 981ᵃ
pretty much like science and art, but really science and art come to
men *through* experience; for 'experience made art', as Polus says,[1]
'but inexperience luck'. Now art arises when from many notions 5
gained by experience one universal judgement about a class of objects
is produced. For to have a judgement that when Callias was ill of this
disease this did him good, and similarly in the case of Socrates and
in many individual cases, is a matter of experience; but to judge that
it has done good to all persons of a certain constitution, marked off 10
in one class, when they were ill of this disease, e. g. to phlegmatic or
bilious people when burning with fever—this is a matter of art.

With a view to action experience seems in no respect inferior to
art, and men of experience succeed even better than those who have

---

[1] Cf. Pl. *Gorg.* 448 c, 462 BC.

689

15 theory without experience. (The reason is that experience is knowledge of individuals, art of universals, and actions and productions are
all concerned with the individual; for the physician does not cure
man, except in an incidental way, but Callias or Socrates or some
other called by some such individual name, who happens to be a
20 man. If, then, a man has the theory without the experience, and
recognizes the universal but does not know the individual included
in this, he will often fail to cure; for it is the individual that is to
be cured.) But yet we think that *knowledge* and *understanding* be-
25 long to art rather than to experience, and we suppose artists to be
wiser than men of experience (which implies that Wisdom depends in
all cases rather on knowledge); and this because the former know the
cause, but the latter do not. For men of experience know that the
30 thing is so, but do not know why, while the others know the 'why'
and the cause. Hence we think also that the master-workers in each
craft are more honourable and know in a truer sense and are wiser
981ᵇ than the manual workers, because they know the causes of the
things that are done (we think the manual workers are like certain
lifeless things which act indeed, but act without knowing what they
do, as fire burns—but while the lifeless things perform each of their
5 functions by a natural tendency, the labourers perform them through
habit); thus we view them as being wiser not in virtue of being able
to act, but of having the theory for themselves and knowing the
causes. And in general it is a sign of the man who knows and of the
man who does not know, that the former can teach, and therefore we
think art more truly knowledge than experience is; for artists can
teach, and men of mere experience cannot.

10   Again, we do not regard any of the senses as Wisdom; yet surely
these give the most authoritative knowledge of particulars. But they
do not tell us the 'why' of anything—e. g. why fire is hot; they only
say *that* it is hot.

At first he who invented any art whatever that went beyond the
common perceptions of man was naturally admired by men, not
15 only because there was something useful in the inventions, but
because he was thought wise and superior to the rest. But as more
arts were invented, and some were directed to the necessities of life,
others to recreation, the inventors of the latter were naturally always
regarded as wiser than the inventors of the former, because their
branches of knowledge did not aim at utility. Hence when all such
20 inventions were already established, the sciences which do not aim
at giving pleasure or at the necessities of life were discovered, and
first in the places where men first began to have leisure. This is why

the mathematical arts were founded in Egypt; for there the priestly caste was allowed to be at leisure.

We have said in the *Ethics* [2] what the difference is between art 25 and science and the other kindred faculties; but the point of our present discussion is this, that all men suppose what is called Wisdom to deal with the first causes and the principles of things; so that, as has been said before, the man of experience is thought to be wiser 30 than the possessors of any sense-perception whatever, the artist wiser than the men of experience, the master-worker than the mechanic, and the theoretical kinds of knowledge to be more of the nature of Wisdom than the productive. Clearly then Wisdom is knowledge 982ª about certain principles and causes.

2 Since we are seeking this knowledge, we must inquire of what 5 kind are the causes and the principles, the knowledge of which is Wisdom. If one were to take the notions we have about the wise man, this might perhaps make the answer more evident. We suppose first, then, that the wise man knows all things, as far as possible, although he has not knowledge of each of them in detail; secondly, 10 that he who can learn things that are difficult, and not easy for man to know, is wise (sense-perception is common to all, and therefore easy and no mark of Wisdom); again, that he who is more exact and more capable of teaching the causes is wiser, in every branch of knowledge; and that of the sciences, also, that which is desirable on 15 its own account and for the sake of knowing it is more of the nature of Wisdom than that which is desirable on account of its results, and the superior science is more of the nature of Wisdom than the ancillary; for the wise man must not be ordered but must order, and he must not obey another, but the less wise must obey *him*.

Such and so many are the notions, then, which we have about 20 Wisdom and the wise. Now of these characteristics that of knowing all things must belong to him who has in the highest degree universal knowledge; for he knows in a sense all the instances that fall under the universal. And these things, the most universal, are on the whole the hardest for men to know; for they are farthest from the senses. And the most exact of the sciences are those which deal 25 most with first principles; for those which involve fewer principles are more exact than those which involve additional principles, e. g. arithmetic than geometry. But the science which investigates causes is also *instructive*, in a higher degree, for the people who instruct us are those who tell the causes of each thing. And understanding and 30

[2] 1139ᵇ 14–1141ᵇ 8.

knowledge pursued for their own sake are found most in the knowledge of that which is most knowable (for he who chooses to know for the sake of knowing will choose most readily that which is most 982ᵇ truly knowledge, and such is the knowledge of that which is most knowable); and the first principles and the causes are most knowable; for by reason of these, and from these, all other things come to be known, and not these by means of the things subordinate to them. And the science which knows to what end each thing must be done 5 is the most authoritative of the sciences, and more authoritative than any ancillary science; and this end is the good of that thing, and in general the supreme good in the whole of nature. Judged by all the tests we have mentioned, then, the name in question falls to the same science; this must be a science that investigates the first principles 10 and causes; for the good, i. e. the end, is one of the causes.

That it is not a science of production is clear even from the history of the earliest philosophers. For it is owing to their wonder that men both now begin and at first began to philosophize; they wondered originally at the obvious difficulties, then advanced little by little 15 and stated difficulties about the greater matters, e. g. about the phenomena of the moon and those of the sun and of the stars, and about the genesis of the universe. And a man who is puzzled and wonders thinks himself ignorant (whence even the lover of myth is in a sense a lover of Wisdom, for the myth is composed of wonders); 20 therefore since they philosophized in order to escape from ignorance, evidently they were pursuing science in order to know, and not for any utilitarian end. And this is confirmed by the facts; for it was when almost all the necessities of life and the things that make for comfort and recreation had been secured, that such knowledge began to be sought. Evidently then we do not seek it for the sake of 25 any other advantage; but as the man is free, we say, who exists for his own sake and not for another's, so we pursue this as the only free science, for it alone exists for its own sake.

Hence also the possession of it might be justly regarded as beyond human power; for in many ways human nature is in bondage, so 30 that according to Simonides 'God alone can have this privilege', and it is unfitting that man should not be content to seek the knowledge that is suited to him. If, then, there is something in what the poets 983ᵃ say, and jealousy is natural to the divine power, it would probably occur in this case above all, and all who excelled in this knowledge would be unfortunate. But the divine power cannot be jealous (nay, according to the proverb, 'bards tell many a lie'), nor should 5 any other science be thought more honourable than one of this sort.

For the most divine science is also most honourable; and this science alone must be, in two ways, most divine. For the science which it would be most meet for God to have is a divine science, and so is any science that deals with divine objects; and this science alone has both these qualities; for (1) God is thought to be among the causes of all things and to be a first principle, and (2) such a science either God alone can have, or God above all others. All the sciences, 10 indeed, are more necessary than this, but none is better.

Yet the acquisition of it must in a sense end in something which is the opposite of our original inquiries. For all men begin, as we said, by wondering that things are as they are, as they do about self- 15 moving marionettes, or about the solstices or the incommensurability of the diagonal of a square with the side; for it seems wonderful to all who have not yet seen the reason, that there is a thing which cannot be measured even by the smallest unit. But we must end in the contrary and, according to the proverb, the better state, as is the case in these instances too when men learn the cause; for there is nothing which would surprise a geometer so much as if the diagonal turned 20 out to be commensurable.

We have stated, then, what is the nature of the science we are searching for, and what is the mark which our search and our whole investigation must reach.

3 Evidently we have to acquire knowledge of the original causes (for we say we know each thing only when we think we recognize its 25 first cause), and causes are spoken of in four senses. In one of these we mean the substance, i. e. the essence (for the 'why' is reducible finally to the definition, and the ultimate 'why' is a cause and principle); in another the matter or substratum, in a third the source of 30 the change, and in a fourth the cause opposed to this, the purpose and the good (for this is the end of all generation and change). We 983ᵇ have studied these causes sufficiently in our work on nature,[3] but yet let us call to our aid those who have attacked the investigation of being and philosophized about reality before us. For obviously they too speak of certain principles and causes; to go over their views, then, will be of profit to the present inquiry, for we shall either find 5 another kind of cause, or be more convinced of the correctness of those which we now maintain.

Of the first philosophers, then, most thought the principles which were of the nature of matter were the only principles of all things. That of which all things that are consist, the first from which they

[3] *Phys.* ii. 3, 7.

come to be, the last into which they are resolved (the substance
10 remaining, but changing in its modifications), this they say is the
element and this the principle of things, and therefore they think
nothing is either generated or destroyed, since this sort of entity is
always conserved, as we say Socrates neither comes to be absolutely
when he comes to be beautiful or musical, nor ceases to be when he
15 loses these characteristics, because the substratum, Socrates himself,
remains. Just so they say nothing else comes to be or ceases to be;
for there must be some entity—either one or more than one—from
which all other things come to be, it being conserved.

Yet they do not all agree as to the number and the nature of these
20 principles. Thales, the founder of this type of philosophy, says the
principle is water (for which reason he declared that the earth rests
on water), getting the notion perhaps from seeing that the nutriment of all things is moist, and that heat itself is generated from
the moist and kept alive by it (and that from which they come to be
25 is a principle of all things). He got his notion from this fact, and
from the fact that the seeds of all things have a moist nature, and
that water is the origin of the nature of moist things.

Some [4] think that even the ancients who lived long before the present generation, and first framed accounts of the gods, had a similar
30 view of nature; for they made Ocean and Tethys the parents of creation,[5] and described the oath of the gods as being by water,[6] to
which they give the name of Styx; for what is oldest is most honourable, and the most honourable thing is that by which one swears.
984a It may perhaps be uncertain whether this opinion about nature is
primitive and ancient, but Thales at any rate is said to have declared himself thus about the first cause. Hippo no one would think
fit to include among these thinkers, because of the paltriness of his
thought.

5   Anaximenes and Diogenes make air prior to water, and the most
primary of the simple bodies, while Hippasus of Metapontium and
Heraclitus of Ephesus say this of fire, and Empedocles says it of the
four elements (adding a fourth—earth—to those which have been
named); for these, he says, always remain and do not come to be,
10 except that they come to be more or fewer, being aggregated into
one and segregated out of one.

Anaxagoras of Clazomenae, who, though older than Empedocles,
was later in his philosophical activity, says the principles are infinite in number; for he says almost all the things that are made of

---

[4] The reference is probably to Plato (*Crat.* 402 b, *Theaet.* 152 e, 162 d, 180 c).
[5] Hom. *Il.* xiv, 201, 246.   [6] *Ibid.* ii. 755, xiv. 271, xv. 37.

parts like themselves, in the manner of water or fire, are generated
and destroyed in this way, only by aggregation and segregation, and 15
are not in any other sense generated or destroyed, but remain
eternally.

From these facts one might think that the only cause is the so-
called material cause; but as men thus advanced, the very facts
opened the way for them and joined in forcing them to investigate
the subject. However true it may be that all generation and destruc- 20
tion proceed from some one or (for that matter) from more elements,
why does this happen and what is the cause? For at least the substratum itself does not make itself change; e. g. neither the wood nor
the bronze causes the change of either of them, nor does the wood
manufacture a bed and the bronze a statue, but something else is 25
the cause of the change. And to seek this is to seek the second cause,
as *we* should say—that from which comes the beginning of the
movement. Now those who at the very beginning set themselves to
this kind of inquiry, and said the substratum was one,[7] were not at
all dissatisfied with themselves; but some at least of those who maintain it to be one[8]—as though defeated by this search for the second 30
cause—say the one and nature as a whole is unchangeable not only
in respect of generation and destruction (for this is a primitive belief, and all agreed in it), but also of all other change; and this view
is peculiar to them. Of those who said the universe was one, then, 984ᵇ
none succeeded in discovering a cause of this sort, except perhaps
Parmenides, and he only inasmuch as he supposes that there is not
only one but also in some sense two causes. But for those who make
more elements[9] it is more possible to state the second cause, e. g. for 5
those who make hot and cold, or fire and earth, the elements; for they
treat fire as having a nature which fits it to move things, and water
and earth and such things they treat in the contrary way.

When these men and the principles of this kind had had their day,
as the latter were found inadequate to generate the nature of things
men were again forced by the truth itself, as we said,[10] to inquire 10
into the next kind of cause. For it is not likely either that fire or earth
or any such element should be the reason why things manifest goodness and beauty both in their being and in their coming to be, or that
those thinkers should have supposed it was; nor again could it be
right to entrust so great a matter to spontaneity and chance. When
one man[11] said, then, that reason was present—as in animals, so 15

[7] Thales, Anaximenes, and Heraclitus.   [8] The Eleatics.
[9] The reference is probably to Empedocles.   [10] ᵃ18.
[11] Anaxagoras.

throughout nature—as the cause of order and of all arrangement, he seemed like a sober man in contrast with the random talk of his predecessors. We know that Anaxagoras certainly adopted these views, but Hermotimus of Clazomenae is credited with expressing them earlier. 20 Those who thought thus stated that there is a principle of things which is at the same time the cause of beauty, and that sort of cause from which things acquire movement.

4   One might suspect that Hesiod was the first to look for such a thing—or some one else who put love or desire among existing things 25 as a principle, as Parmenides, too, does; for he, in constructing the genesis of the universe, says:—

> Love first of all the Gods she planned.

And Hesiod says:—

> First of all things was chaos made, and then
> Broad-breasted earth, . . .
> And love, 'mid all the gods pre-eminent,

30 which implies that among existing things there must be from the first a cause which will move things and bring them together. How these thinkers should be arranged with regard to priority of discovery let us be allowed to decide later; [12] but since the contraries of the various forms of good were also perceived to be present in nature—not only order and the beautiful, but also disorder and the ugly, and 985ᵃ bad things in greater number than good, and ignoble things than beautiful—therefore another thinker introduced friendship and strife, each of the two the cause of one of these two sets of qualities. For if we were to follow out the view of Empedocles, and interpret it 5 according to its meaning and not to its lisping expression, we should find that friendship is the cause of good things, and strife of bad. Therefore, if we said that Empedocles in a sense both mentions, and is the first to mention, the bad and the good as principles, we should perhaps be right, since the cause of all goods is the good itself. 10   These thinkers, as we say, evidently grasped, and to this extent, two of the causes which we distinguished in our work on nature [13]— the matter and the source of the movement—vaguely, however, and with no clearness, but as untrained men behave in fights; for they go 15 round their opponents and often strike fine blows, but they do not

---

[12] The promise is not fulfilled.   [13] *Phys.* ii. 3, 7.

fight on scientific principles, and so too these thinkers do not seem to know what they say; for it is evident that, as a rule, they make no use of their causes except to a small extent. For Anaxagoras uses reason as a *deus ex machina* for the making of the world, and when he is at a loss to tell from what cause something necessarily is, then 20 he drags reason in, but in all other cases ascribes events to anything rather than to reason.[14] And Empedocles, though he uses the causes to a greater extent than this, neither does so sufficiently nor attains consistency in their use. At least, in many cases he makes love segregate things, and strife aggregate them. For whenever the universe is 25 dissolved into its elements by strife, fire is aggregated into one, and so is each of the other elements; but whenever again under the influence of love they come together into one, the parts must again be segregated out of each element.

Empedocles, then, in contrast with his predecessors, was the first to introduce the dividing of this cause, not positing one source of 30 movement, but different and contrary sources. Again, he was the first to speak of four material elements; yet he does not *use* four, but 985ᵇ treats them as two only; he treats fire by itself, and its opposites— earth, air, and water—as one kind of thing. We may learn this by study of his verses.

This philosopher then, as we say, has spoken of the principles in this way, and made them of this number. Leucippus and his associate Democritus say that the full and the empty are the elements, 5 calling the one being and the other non-being—the full and solid being being, the empty non-being (whence they say being no more is than non-being, because the solid no more is than the empty); and they make these the material causes of things. And as those who make 10 the underlying substance one generate all other things by its modifications, supposing the rare and the dense to be the sources of the modifications, in the same way these philosophers say the differences in the elements are the causes of all other qualities. These differences, they say, are three—shape and order and position. For they say the 15 real is differentiated only by 'rhythm' and 'inter-contact' and 'turning'; and of these rhythm is shape, inter-contact is order, and turning is position; for A differs from N in shape, AN from NA in order, ⊨ from H in position. The question of movement—whence or how it is to belong to things—these thinkers, like the others, lazily neglected.

Regarding the two causes, then, as we say, the inquiry seems to 20 have been pushed thus far by the early philosophers.

[14] Cf. Pl. *Phaedo*, 98 BC, *Laws*, 967 B–D.

5 Contemporaneously with these philosophers and before them, the so-called Pythagoreans, who were the first to take up mathematics, 25 not only advanced this study, but also having been brought up in it they thought its principles were the principles of all things. Since of these principles numbers are by nature the first, and in numbers they seemed to see many resemblances to the things that exist and come into being—more than in fire and earth and water (such and such a modification of numbers being justice, another being soul 30 and reason, another being opportunity—and similarly almost all other things being numerically expressible); since, again, they saw that the modifications and the ratios of the musical scales were expressible in numbers;—since, then, all other things seemed in their whole nature to be modelled on numbers, and numbers seemed to be 986ᵃ the first things in the whole of nature, they supposed the elements of numbers to be the elements of all things, and the whole heaven to be a musical scale and a number. And all the properties of numbers and scales which they could show to agree with the attributes and parts 5 and the whole arrangement of the heavens, they collected and fitted into their scheme; and if there was a gap anywhere, they readily made additions so as to make their whole theory coherent. E. g. as the number 10 is thought to be perfect and to comprise the whole nature of numbers, they say that the bodies which move through the heavens are ten, but as the visible bodies are only nine, to meet this they invent a tenth—the 'counter-earth'. We have discussed these matters more exactly elsewhere.[15]

But the object of our review is that we may learn from these philosophers also what they suppose to be the principles and how 15 these fall under the causes we have named. Evidently, then, these thinkers also consider that number is the principle both as matter for things and as forming both their modifications and their permanent states, and hold that the elements of number are the even and the odd, and that of these the latter is limited, and the former unlimited; and that the One proceeds from both of these (for it is both even and 20 odd), and number from the One; and that the whole heaven, as has been said, is numbers.

Other members of this same school say there are ten principles, which they arrange in two columns of cognates—limit and unlimited, 25 odd and even, one and plurality, right and left, male and female, resting and moving, straight and curved, light and darkness, good and bad, square and oblong. In this way Alcmaeon of Croton seems also to have conceived the matter, and either he got this view from them

[15] *De Caelo,* ii. 13.

or they got it from him; for he expressed himself similarly to them. 30
For he says most human affairs go in pairs, meaning not definite
contrarieties such as the Pythagoreans speak of, but any chance contrarieties, e. g. white and black, sweet and bitter, good and bad,
great and small. He threw out indefinite suggestions about the other
contrarieties, but the Pythagoreans declared both how many and 986^b
which their contrarieties are.

From both these schools, then, we can learn this much, that the contraries are the principles of things; and how many these principles are
and which they are, we can learn from one of the two schools. But how
these principles can be brought together under the causes we have 5
named has not been clearly and articulately stated by them; they seem,
however, to range the elements under the head of matter; for out of
these as immanent parts they say substance is composed and moulded.

From these facts we may sufficiently perceive the meaning of the
ancients who said the elements of nature were more than one; but
there are some who spoke of the universe as if it were one entity, 10
though they were not all alike either in the excellence of their statement or in its conformity to the facts of nature. The discussion of
them is in no way appropriate to our present investigation of causes,
for they do not, like some of the natural philosophers, assume being
to be one and yet generate it out of the one as out of matter, but they 15
speak in another way; those others add change, since they generate
the universe, but these thinkers say the universe is unchangeable. Yet
this much is germane to the present inquiry: Parmenides seems to
fasten on that which is one in definition, Melissus on that which is
one in matter, for which reason the former says that it is limited, 20
the latter that it is unlimited; while Xenophanes, the first of these
partisans of the One (for Parmenides is said to have been his pupil),
gave no clear statement, nor does he seem to have grasped the nature
of either of these causes, but with reference to the whole material
universe he says the One is God. Now these thinkers, as we said, 25
must be neglected for the purposes of the present inquiry—two of
them entirely, as being a little too naïve, viz. Xenophanes and Melissus; but Parmenides seems in places to speak with more insight.
For, claiming that, besides the existent, nothing non-existent exists,
he thinks that of necessity one thing exists, viz. the existent and nothing else (on this we have spoken more clearly in our work on na- 30
ture),[16] but being forced to follow the observed facts, and supposing
the existence of that which is one in definition, but more than one
according to our sensations, he now posits two causes and two prin-

[16] *Phys.* i. 3.

ciples, calling them hot and cold, i. e. fire and earth; and of these
987ᵃ he ranges the hot with the existent, and the other with the non-
existent.

From what has been said, then, and from the wise men who have
now sat in council with us, we have got thus much—on the one
hand from the earliest philosophers, who regard the first principle as
5 corporeal (for water and fire and such things are bodies), and of
whom some suppose that there is one corporeal principle, others
that there are more than one, but both put these under the head of
matter; and on the other hand from some who posit both this cause
and besides this the source of movement, which we have got from
some as single and from others as twofold.

Down to the Italian school, then, and apart from it, philosophers
10 have treated these subjects rather obscurely, except that, as we said,
they have in fact used two kinds of cause, and one of these—the
source of movement—some treat as one and others as two. But the
Pythagoreans have said in the same way that there are two principles,
15 but added this much, which is peculiar to them, that they thought
that finitude and infinity were not attributes of certain other things,
e. g. of fire or earth or anything else of this kind, but that infinity
itself and unity itself were the substance of the things of which they
are predicated. This is why number was the substance of all things.
20 On this subject, then, they expressed themselves thus; and regarding the question of essence they began to make statements and definitions, but treated the matter too simply. For they both defined
superficially and thought that the first subject of which a given
definition was predicable was the substance of the thing defined, as
if one supposed that 'double' and '2' were the same, because 2 is the
25 first thing of which 'double' is predicable. But surely to be double and
to be 2 are not the same; if they are, one thing will be many [17]—a
consequence which they actually drew.[18] From the earlier philosophers, then, and from their successors we can learn thus much.

6 After the systems we have named came the philosophy of Plato,
30 which in most respects followed these thinkers, but had peculiarities
that distinguished it from the philosophy of the Italians. For, having
in his youth first become familiar with Cratylus and with the Heraclitean doctrines (that all sensible things are ever in a state of flux and
there is no knowledge about them), these views he held even in
987ᵇ later years. Socrates, however, was busying himself about ethical

[17] i. e. 2 will be each of several things whose definition is predicable of it.
[18] e. g. 2 was identified both with opinion and with daring.

matters and neglecting the world of nature as a whole but seeking the universal in these ethical matters, and fixed thought for the first time on definitions; Plato accepted his teaching, but held that the problem applied not to sensible things but to entities of another 5 kind—for this reason, that the common definition could not be a definition of any sensible thing, as they were always changing. Things of this other sort, then, he called Ideas, and sensible things, he said, were all named after these, and in virtue of a relation to these; for the many existed by participation in the Ideas that have the same name as they. Only the name 'participation' was new; for 10 the Pythagoreans say that things exist by 'imitation' of numbers, and Plato says they exist by participation, changing the name. But what the participation or the imitation of the Forms could be they left an open question.

Further, besides sensible things and Forms he says there are the objects of mathematics, which occupy an intermediate position, dif- 15 fering from sensible things in being eternal and unchangeable, from Forms in that there are many alike, while the Form itself is in each case unique.

Since the Forms were the causes of all other things, he thought their elements were the elements of all things. As matter, the great 20 and the small were principles; as essential reality, the One; for from the great and the small, by participation in the One, come the Numbers.

But he agreed with the Pythagoreans in saying that the One is substance and not a predicate of something else; and in saying that the Numbers are the causes of the reality of other things he agreed 25 with them; but positing a dyad and constructing the infinite out of great and small, instead of treating the infinite as one, is peculiar to him; and so is his view that the Numbers exist apart from sensible things, while *they* say that the things themselves are Numbers, and do not place the objects of mathematics between Forms and sensible things. His divergence from the Pythagoreans in making the One and 30 the Numbers separate from things, and his introduction of the Forms, were due to his inquiries in the region of definitions (for the earlier thinkers had no tincture of dialectic), and his making the other entity besides the One a dyad was due to the belief that the numbers, except those which were prime, could be neatly produced out of the dyad as out of some plastic material.

Yet what *happens* is the contrary; the theory is not a reasonable 988ᵃ one. For they make many things out of the matter, and the form generates only once, but what we observe is that one table is made

from one matter, while the man who applies the form, though he is
5 one, makes many tables. And the relation of the male to the female
is similar; for the latter is impregnated by one copulation, but the
male impregnates many females; yet these are analogues of those first
principles.

Plato, then, declared himself thus on the points in question; it is
evident from what has been said that he has used only two causes,
that of the essence and the material cause (for the Forms are the
10 causes of the essence of all other things, and the One is the cause
of the essence of the Forms); and it is evident what the underlying matter is, of which the Forms are predicated in the case of
sensible things, and the One in the case of Forms, viz. that this is a
dyad, the great and the small. Further, he has assigned the cause of
good and that of evil to the elements, one to each of the two, as we
15 say [19] some of his predecessors sought to do, e. g. Empedocles and
Anaxagoras.

7 Our review of those who have spoken about first principles and
reality and of the way in which they have spoken, has been concise
20 and summary; but yet we have learnt *this* much from them, that of
those who speak about 'principle' and 'cause' no one has mentioned
any principle except those which have been distinguished in our work
on nature,[20] but all evidently have some inkling of *them,* though only
vaguely. For some speak of the first principle as matter, whether
they suppose one or more first principles, and whether they sup-
25 pose this to be a body or to be incorporeal; e. g. Plato spoke of the
great and the small, the Italians of the infinite, Empedocles of fire,
earth, water, and air, Anaxagoras of the infinity of things composed
of similar parts. These, then, have all had a notion of this kind of
30 cause, and so have all who speak of air or fire or water, or something denser than fire and rarer than air; for some have said the
prime element is of this kind.

These thinkers grasped this cause only; but certain others have
mentioned the source of movement, e. g. those who make friendship
and strife, or reason, or love, a principle.

The essence, i. e. the substantial reality, no one has expressed
35 distinctly. It is hinted at chiefly by those who believe in the Forms;
988^b for they do not suppose either that the Forms are the matter of
sensible things, and the One the matter of the Forms, or that they
are the source of movement (for they say these are causes rather of
immobility and of being at rest), but they furnish the Forms as the

---

[19] Cf. 984^b 15–19, 32–^{b} 10.   [20] *Phys.* ii. 3, 7.

essence of every other thing, and the One as the essence of the Forms. 5

That for whose sake actions and changes and movements take place, they assert to be a cause in a way, but not in this way, i. e. not in the way in which it is its *nature* to be a cause. For those who speak of reason or friendship class these causes as goods; they do not speak, however, as if anything that exists either existed or came into being for the sake of these, but as if movements started from these. In 10 the same way those who say the One or the existent is the good, say that it is the cause of substance, but not that substance either is or comes to be for the sake of this. Therefore it turns out that in a sense they both say and do not say the good is a cause; for they do not 15 call it a cause *qua* good but only incidentally.

All these thinkers, then, as they cannot pitch on another cause, seem to testify that we have determined rightly both how many and of what sort the causes are. Besides this it is plain that when the causes are being looked for, either all four must be sought thus or they must be sought in one of these four ways. Let us next discuss the possible 20 difficulties with regard to the way in which each of these thinkers has spoken, and with regard to his situation relatively to the first principles.

8   Those, then, who say the universe is one and posit one kind of thing as matter, and as corporeal matter which has spatial magnitude, evidently go astray in many ways. For they posit the elements of bodies only, not of incorporeal things, though there are also in- 25 corporeal things. And in trying to state the causes of generation and destruction, and in giving a physical account of all things, they do away with the cause of movement. Further, they err in not positing the substance, i. e. the essence, as the cause of anything, and besides this in lightly calling any of the simple bodies except earth the first 30 principle, without inquiring how they are produced out of one another, —I mean fire, water, earth, and air. For some things are produced out of each other by combination, others by separation, and this makes the greatest difference to their priority and posteriority. For (1) in a way the property of being most elementary of all 35 would seem to belong to the first thing from which they are pro- duced by combination, and *this* property would belong to the most 989ᵃ fine-grained and subtle of bodies. For this reason those who make fire the principle would be most in agreement with this argument. But each of the other thinkers agrees that the element of corporeal things 5 is of this sort. At least none of those who named one element claimed that earth was the element, evidently because of the coarse-

ness of its grain. (Of the other three elements each has found some
judge on its side; for some maintain that fire, others that water,
others that air is the element. Yet why, after all, do they not name
earth also, as most men do? For people say all things are earth.
10 And Hesiod says earth was produced first of corporeal things; so
primitive and popular has the opinion been.) According to this argument, then, no one would be right who either says the first principle
is any of the elements other than fire, or supposes it to be denser
15 than air but rarer than water. But (2) if that which is later in generation is prior in nature, and that which is concocted and compounded
is later in generation, the contrary of what we have been saying must
be true—water must be prior to air, and earth to water.

So much, then, for those who posit one cause such as we men-
20 tioned; but the same is true if one supposes more of these, as Empedocles says the matter of things is four bodies. For he too is confronted by consequences some of which are the same as have been
mentioned, while others are peculiar to him. For we see these bodies
produced from one another, which implies that the same body does
not always remain fire or earth (we have spoken about this in our
25 works on nature [21]); and regarding the cause of movement and the
question whether we must posit one or two, he must be thought to
have spoken neither correctly nor altogether plausibly. And in
general, change of quality is necessarily done away with for those who
speak thus, for on their view cold will not come from hot nor hot from
cold. For if it did there would be something that accepted the contraries themselves, and there would be some one entity that became fire
and water, which Empedocles denies.

30   As regards Anaxagoras, if one were to suppose that he said there
were two elements, the supposition would accord thoroughly with an
argument which Anaxagoras himself did not state articulately, but
which he must have accepted if any one had led him on to it. True, to
say that in the beginning all things were mixed is absurd both on other
grounds and because it follows that they must have existed before in an
989ᵇ unmixed form, and because nature does not allow any chance thing to
be mixed with any chance thing, and also because on this view modifications and accidents could be separated from substances (for the same
things which are mixed can be separated); yet if one were to follow him
5 up, piecing together what he means, he would perhaps be seen to be
somewhat modern in his views. For when nothing was separated out,
evidently nothing could be truly asserted of the substance that then existed. I mean, e. g., that it was neither white nor black, nor grey nor any

[21] *De Caelo*, iii. 7.

other colour, but of necessity colourless; for if it had been coloured, it would have had one of these colours. And similarly, by this same argu- 10 ment, it was flavourless, nor had it any similar attribute; for it could not be either of any quality or of any size, nor could it be any definite kind of thing. For if it were, one of the particular forms would have belonged to it, and this is impossible, since all were mixed together; for the particular form would necessarily have been already separated out, but he says all were mixed except reason, and this alone was un- 15 mixed and pure. From this it follows, then, that he must say the principles are the One (for this is simple and unmixed) and the Other, which is of such a nature as we suppose the indefinite to be before it is defined and partakes of some form. Therefore, while expressing himself neither rightly nor clearly, he means something like what the later thinkers say and what is now more clearly seen to be the case.   20

But these thinkers are, after all, at home only in arguments about generation and destruction and movement; for it is practically only of this sort of substance that they seek the principles and the causes. But those who extend their vision to all things that exist, and 25 of existing things suppose some to be perceptible and others not perceptible evidently study both classes, which is all the more reason why one should devote some time to seeing what is good in their views and what bad from the standpoint of the inquiry we have now before us.

The 'Pythagoreans' treat of principles and elements stranger than those of the physical philosophers (the reason is that they got the 30 principles from non-sensible things, for the objects of mathematics, except those of astronomy, are of the class of things without movement); yet their discussions and investigations are all about nature; for they generate the heavens, and with regard to their parts and 990ᵃ attributes and functions they observe the phenomena, and use up the principles and the causes in explaining these, which implies that they agree with the others, the physical philosophers, that the *real* is just all that which is perceptible and contained by the so-called 'heavens'. 5 But the causes and the principles which they mention are, as we said, sufficient to act as steps even up to the higher realms of reality, and are more suited to these than to theories about nature. They do not tell us at all, however, how there can be movement if limit and unlimited and odd and even are the only things assumed, or how without move- 10 ment and change there can be generation and destruction, or the bodies that move through the heavens can do what they do.

Further, if one either granted them that spatial magnitude consists of these elements, or this were proved, still how would some

bodies be light and others have weight? To judge from what they as-
15 sume and maintain they are speaking no more of mathematical
bodies than of perceptible; hence they have said nothing whatever about fire or earth or the other bodies of this sort, I suppose
because they have nothing to say which applies *peculiarly* to perceptible things.

Further, how are we to combine the beliefs that the attributes of
20 number, and number itself, are causes of what exists and happens in
the heavens both from the beginning and now, and that there is no
other number than this number out of which the world is composed?
When in one particular region they place opinion and opportunity,
and, a little above or below, injustice and decision or mixture, and
allege, as proof, that each of these is a number, and that there hap-
25 pens to be already in this place a plurality of the extended bodies composed of numbers, because these attributes of number attach to the
various places—this being so, is this number, which we must suppose
each of these abstractions to be, the same number which is exhibited
in the material universe, or is it another than this? Plato says it is
30 different; yet even he thinks that both these bodies and their causes
are numbers, but that the *intelligible* numbers are causes, while the
others are *sensible*.

9   Let us leave the Pythagoreans for the present; for it is enough to
have touched on them as much as we have done. But as for those
990ᵇ who posit the Ideas as causes, firstly, in seeking to grasp the causes
of the things around us, they introduced others equal in number to
these, as if a man who wanted to count things thought he would
not be able to do it while they were few, but tried to count them when
he had added to their number. For the Forms are practically equal to
5 —or not fewer than—the things, in trying to explain which these
thinkers proceeded from them to the Forms. For to each thing there
answers an entity which has the same name and exists apart from the
substances, and so also in the case of all other groups there is a one
over many, whether the many are in this world or are eternal.

Further, of the ways in which we prove that the Forms exist, none
10 is convincing; for from some no inference necessarily follows, and
from some arise Forms even of things of which we think there are no
Forms. For according to the arguments from the existence of the sciences there will be Forms of all things of which there are sciences, and
according to the 'one over many' argument there will be Forms even of
negations, and according to the argument that there is an object for
thought even when the thing has perished, there will be Forms of per-

ishable things; for we have an image of these. Further, of the more [15] accurate arguments, some lead to Ideas of relations, of which we say there is no independent class, and others introduce the 'third man'.

And in general the arguments for the Forms destroy the things for whose existence we are more zealous than for the existence of the Ideas; for it follows that not the dyad but number is first, i. e. that the relative is prior to the absolute—besides all the other points [20] on which certain people by following out the opinions held about the Ideas have come into conflict with the principles of the theory.

Further, according to the assumption on which our belief in the Ideas rests, there will be Forms not only of substances but also of many other things (for the concept is single not only in the case of [25] substances but also in the other cases, and there are sciences not only of substance but also of other things, and a thousand other such difficulties confront them). But according to the necessities of the case and the opinions held about the Forms, if Forms can be shared in there must be Ideas of substances only. For they are not shared in incidentally, but a thing must share in its Form as in some- [30] thing not predicated of a subject (by 'being shared in incidentally' I mean that e. g. if a thing shares in 'double itself', it shares also in 'eternal', but incidentally; for 'eternal' happens to be predicable of the 'double'). Therefore the Forms will be substance; but the same terms indicate substance in this and in the ideal world (or what will be the meaning of saying that there is something apart from the par- [991ª] ticulars—the one over many?). And if the Ideas and the particulars that share in them have the same form, there will be something common to these; for why should '2' be one and the same in the perishable 2's or in those which are many but eternal, and not the same in the '2 itself' as in the particular 2? But if they have not the same [5] form, they must have only the name in common, and it is as if one were to call both Callias ánd a wooden image a 'man', without observing any community between them.[22]

Above all one might discuss the question what on earth the Forms contribute to sensible things, either to those that are eternal or to those that come into being and cease to be. For they cause neither [10] movement nor any change in them. But again they help in no wise either towards the knowledge of the other things (for they are not even the substance of these, else they would have been in them), or towards their being, if they are not *in* the particulars which share in them; though if they were, they might be thought to be causes, as white causes whiteness in a white object by entering into its composi- [15]

[22] With 990ᵇ 2–991ª 8 Cf. xiii. 1078ᵇ 34–1079ᵇ 3.

tion. But this argument, which first Anaxagoras and later Eudoxus and certain others used, is very easily upset; for it is not difficult to collect many insuperable objections to such a view.

But, further, all other things cannot come from the Forms in any of 20 the usual senses of 'from'. And to say that they are patterns and the other things share in them is to use empty words and poetical metaphors. For what is it that works, looking to the Ideas? And anything can either be, or become, like another without being copied from it, 25 so that whether Socrates exists or not a man like Socrates might come to be; and evidently this might be so even if Socrates were eternal. And there will be several patterns of the same thing, and therefore several Forms; e. g. 'animal' and 'two-footed' and also 'man himself' will be Forms of man. Again, the Forms are patterns not only of 30 sensible things, but of Forms themselves also; i. e. the genus, as genus of various species, will be so; therefore the same thing will be pattern and copy.

991ᵇ   Again, it would seem impossible that the substance and that of which it is the substance should exist apart; how, therefore, could the Ideas, being the substances of things, exist apart? In the *Phaedo* [23] the case is stated in this way—that the Forms are causes both of being and of becoming; yet when the Forms exist, still the things 5 that share in them do not come into being, unless there is something to originate movement; and many other things come into being (e. g. a house or a ring) of which we say there are no Forms. Clearly, therefore, even the other things can both be and come into being owing to such causes as produce the things just mentioned.[24]

Again, if the Forms are numbers, how can they be causes? Is it 10 because existing things are other numbers, e. g. one number is man, another is Socrates, another Callias? Why then are the one set of numbers causes of the other set? It will not make any difference even if the former are eternal and the latter are not. But if it is because things in this sensible world (e. g. harmony) are ratios of numbers, evidently the things between which they are ratios are some one 15 class of things. If, then, this—the matter—is some definite thing, evidently the numbers themselves too will be ratios of something to something else. E. g. if Callias is a numerical ratio between fire and earth and water and air, his Idea also will be a number of certain other underlying things; and man-himself, whether it is a number in a sense or not, will still be a numerical ratio of certain things and not 20 a number proper, nor will it be a kind of number merely because it is a numerical ratio.

[23] 100 c–e.   [24] With 991ª 8–ᵇ 9 Cf. xiii. 1079ᵇ 12–1080ª 8.

Again, from many numbers one number is produced, but how can one Form come from many Forms? And if the number comes not from the many numbers themselves but from the units in them, e. g. in 10,000, how is it with the units? If they are specifically alike, numerous absurdities will follow, and also if they are not alike 25 (neither the units in one number being themselves like one another nor those in other numbers being all like to all); for in what will they differ, as they are without quality? This is not a plausible view, nor is it consistent with our thought on the matter.

Further, they must set up a second kind of number (with which arithmetic deals), and all the objects which are called 'intermediate' by some thinkers; and how do these exist or from what principles do they proceed? Or why must they be intermediate between the 30 things in this sensible world and the things-themselves?

Further, the units in 2 must each come from a prior 2; but this is impossible.

Further, why is a number, when taken all together, one?   992ᵃ

Again, besides what has been said, if the units are *diverse* the Platonists should have spoken like those who say there are four, or two, elements; for each of these thinkers gives the name of element not to that which is common, e. g. to body, but to fire and earth, 5 whether there is something common to them, viz. body, or not. But in fact the Platonists speak as if the One were *homogeneous* like fire or water; and if this is so, the numbers will not be substances. Evidently, if there is a One-itself and this is a first principle, 'one' is being used in more than one sense; for otherwise the theory is impossible.

When we wish to reduce substances to their principles, we state 10 that lines come from the short and long (i. e. from a kind of small and great), and the plane from the broad and narrow, and body from the deep and shallow. Yet how then can either the plane contain a line, or the solid a line or a plane? For the broad and narrow is a different class from the deep and shallow. Therefore, just as number is not 15 present in these, because the many and few are different from these, evidently no other of the higher classes will be present in the lower. But again the broad is not a genus which includes the deep, for then the solid would have been a species of plane.²⁵ Further, from what principle will the presence of the *points* in the line be derived? Plato even used to object to this class of things as being a geometrical 20 fiction. He gave the name of principle of the line—and this he often posited—to the indivisible lines. Yet these must have a limit; there-

²⁵ With 992ᵃ 10–19 Cf. xiii. 1085ᵃ 9–19.

fore the argument from which the existence of the line follows proves also the existence of the point.

In general, though philosophy seeks the cause of perceptible things,
25 we have given this up (for we say nothing of the cause from which change takes its start), but while we fancy we are stating the substance of perceptible things, we assert the existence of a second class of substances, while our account of the way in which they are the substances of perceptible things is empty talk; for 'sharing', as we said before,[26] means nothing.

Nor have the Forms any connexion with what we see to be the
30 cause in the case of the arts, that for whose sake both all mind and the whole of nature are operative [27]—with this cause which we assert to be one of the first principles; but mathematics has come to be identical with philosophy for modern thinkers, though they say that it should be studied for the sake of other things.[28]

Further, one might suppose that the substance which accord-
992b ing to them underlies as matter is too mathematical, and is a predicate and differentia of the substance, i. e. of the matter, rather than than matter itself; i. e. the great and the small are like the rare and
5 the dense which the physical philosophers speak of, calling these the primary differentiae of the substratum; for these are a kind of excess and defect. And regarding movement, if the great and the small are to *be* movement, evidently the Forms will be moved; but if they are not to be movement, whence did movement come? The whole study of nature has been annihilated.

And what is thought to be easy—to show that all things are one—
10 is not done; for what is proved by the method of setting out instances [29] is not that all things are one but that there is a One-itself,—if we grant all the assumptions. And not even this follows, if we do not grant that the universal is a genus; and this in some cases it cannot be.

Nor can it be explained either how the lines and planes and solids that come after the numbers exist or can exist, or what significance
15 they have; for these can neither be Forms (for they are not numbers), nor the intermediates (for those are the objects of mathematics), nor the perishable things. This is evidently a distinct fourth class.

In general, if we search for the elements of existing things without distinguishing the many senses in which things are said to exist,

[26] 991ᵃ 20–22.   [27] *sc.* the final cause.
[28] Cf. Plato, *Rep.* vii. 531 D, 533 B–E.
[29] For this Platonic method Cf. vii. 1031ᵇ 21, xiii. 1086ᵇ 9, xiv. 1090ᵃ 17.

we cannot find them, especially if the search for the elements of which things are made is conducted in this manner. For it is surely 20 impossible to discover what 'acting' or 'being acted on', or 'the straight', is made of, but if elements can be discovered at all, it is only the elements of substances; therefore either to seek the elements of all existing things or to think one has them is incorrect.

And how could we *learn* the elements of all things? Evidently we cannot start by knowing anything before. For as he who is learning 25 geometry, though he may know other things before, knows none of the things with which the science deals and about which he is to learn, so is it in all other cases. Therefore if there is a science of all things, such as some assert to exist, he who is learning this will know nothing before. Yet all learning is by means of premises which are 30 (either all or some of them) known before—whether the learning be by demonstration or by definitions; for the elements of the definition must be known before and be familiar; and learning by induction proceeds similarly. But again, if the science were actually innate, it 993ᵃ were strange that we are unaware of our possession of the greatest of sciences.

Again, how is one to *come to know* what all things are made of, and how is this to be made *evident*? This also affords a difficulty; for there might be a conflict of opinion, as there is about certain 5 syllables; some say *za* is made out of *s* and *d* and *a*, while others say it is a distinct sound and none of those that are familiar.

Further, how could we know the objects of sense without having the sense in question? Yet we ought to, if the elements of which all things consist, as complex sounds consist of the elements proper to 10 sound, are the same.

10   It is evident, then, even from what we have said before, that all men seem to seek the causes named in the *Physics*,³⁰ and that we cannot name any beyond these; but they seek these vaguely; and though in a sense they have all been described before, in a sense they have not been described at all. For the earliest philosophy is, on all 15 subjects, like one who lisps, since it is young and in its beginnings. For even Empedocles says bone exists by virtue of the ratio in it. Now this is the essence and the substance of the thing. But it is similarly necessary that flesh and each of the other tissues should be the ratio of its elements, or that not one of them should; for it is on account 20 of this that both flesh and bone and everything else will exist, and not on account of the matter, which *he* names—fire and earth and water

³⁰ ii. 3, 7.

and air. But while he would necessarily have agreed if another had said this, he has not said it clearly. .

On these questions our views have been expressed before; but let
25 us return to enumerate the difficulties that might be raised on these same points;[31] for perhaps we may get from them some help towards our later difficulties.

BOOK α (II)

30 1 The investigation of the truth is in one way hard, in another easy. An indication of this is found in the fact that no one is able to attain
993b the truth adequately, while, on the other hand, we do not collectively fail, but every one says something true about the nature of things, and while individually we contribute little or nothing to the truth, by the union of all a considerable amount is amassed. Therefore, since the truth seems to be like the proverbial door, which no one can fail
5 to hit, in this respect it must be easy, but the fact that we can have a whole truth and not the particular part we aim at shows the difficulty of it.

Perhaps, too, as difficulties are of two kinds, the cause of the present difficulty is not in the facts but in us. For as the eyes of bats are
10 to the blaze of day, so is the reason in our soul to the things which are by nature most evident of all.

It is just that we should be grateful, not only to those with whose views we may agree, but also to those who have expressed more superficial views; for these also contributed something, by developing before
15 us the powers of thought. It is true that if there had been no Timotheus we should have been without much of our lyric poetry; but if there had been no Phrynis there would have been no Timotheus. The same holds good of those who have expressed views about the truth; for from some thinkers we have inherited certain opinions, while the others have been responsible for the appearance of the former.

It is right also that philosophy should be called knowledge of the
20 truth. For the end of theoretical knowledge is truth, while that of practical knowledge is action (for even if they consider how things are, practical men do not study the eternal, but what is relative and in the present). Now we do not know a truth without its cause; and a thing has a quality in a higher degree than other things if in virtue of it the similar quality belongs to the other things as well (e. g. fire

[31] The reference is to Bk. iii.

is the hottest of things; for it is the cause of the heat of all other 25 things); so that that which causes derivative truths to be true is most true. Hence the principles of eternal things must be always most true (for they are not merely sometimes true, nor is there any cause of their being, but they themselves are the cause of the being of other things), so that as each thing is in respect of being, so is it in respect 30 of truth.

2 But evidently there *is* a first principle, and the causes of things 994ᵃ are neither an infinite series nor infinitely various in kind. For (1) neither can one thing proceed from another, as from matter, *ad in-finitum* (e. g. flesh from earth, earth from air, air from fire, and so on 5 without stopping), nor can the sources of movement form an endless series (man for instance being acted on by air, air by the sun, the sun by Strife,[1] and so on without limit). Similarly the final causes cannot go on *ad infinitum*—walking being for the sake of health, this for the sake of happiness, happiness for the sake of something else, and so one thing always for the sake of another. And the case of the 10 essence is similar. For in the case of intermediates, which have a last term and a term prior to them, the prior must be the cause of the later terms. For if we had to say which of the three is the cause, we should say the first; surely not the last, for the final term is the cause of none; nor even the intermediate, for it is the cause only of 15 one. (It makes no difference whether there is one intermediate or more, nor whether they are infinite or finite in number.) But of series which are infinite in this way, and of the infinite in general, all the parts down to that now present are alike intermediates; so that if there *is* no first there is no cause at all.

Nor can there be an infinite process downwards, with a beginning in the upward direction, so that water should proceed from fire, earth 20 from water, and so always some other kind should be produced. For one thing comes *from* another in two ways—not in the sense in which 'from' means 'after' (as we say 'from the Isthmian games come the Olympian'), but either (i) as the man comes from the boy, by the boy's changing, or (ii) as air comes from water. By 'as the man comes 25 from the boy' we mean 'as that which has come to be from that which is coming to be, or as that which is finished from that which is being achieved' (for as becoming is between being and not being, so that which is becoming is always between that which is and that which is not; for the learner is a man of science in the making, and this is what is meant when we say that *from* a learner a man of science is being 30

---

[1] The illustration is taken from the cosmology of Empedocles.

made); on the other hand, coming from another thing as water comes from air implies the destruction of the other thing. This is why changes of the former kind are not reversible, and the boy does not come from the man (for it is not that which comes to be something that 994ᵇ comes to be as a result of coming to be, but that which exists after the coming to be; for it is thus that the day, too, comes from the morning—in the sense that it comes after the morning; which is the reason why the morning cannot come from the day); but changes of the other kind are reversible. But in both cases it is impossible that the number of terms should be infinite. For terms of the former kind, 5 being intermediates, must have an end, and terms of the latter kind change back into *one another*; for the destruction of either is the generation of the other.

At the same time it is impossible that the first cause, being eternal, should be destroyed; for since the process of becoming is not infinite in the upward direction, that which is the first thing by whose destruction something came to be must be non-eternal.

Further, the *final cause* is an end, and that sort of end which is not for the sake of something else, but for whose sake everything else 10 is; so that if there is to be a last term of this sort, the process will not be infinite; but if there is no such term, there will be no final cause, but those who maintain the infinite series eliminate the Good without knowing it (yet no one would try to do anything if he were not going to come to a limit); nor would there be reason in the world; 15 the reasonable man, at least, always acts for a purpose, and this is a limit; for the end is a limit.

But the *essence*, also, cannot be reduced to another definition which is fuller in expression.² For the original definition is always more of a definition, and not the later one; and in a series in which the first term 20 has not the required character, the next has not it either.—Further, those who speak thus destroy science; for it is not possible to have this till one comes to the unanalysable terms. And knowledge becomes impossible; for how can one apprehend things that are infinite in this way?³ For this is not like the case of the line, to whose divisibility there is no stop, but which we cannot think if we do not make a stop, (for which reason one who is tracing the infinitely divisible line 25 cannot be counting the possibilities of section), but the whole line also must be apprehended by something in us that does not move from

---

² i. e. one can reduce the definition of man as 'rational animal' to 'rational sensitive living substance', but one cannot carry on this process *ad infinitum*.

³ i. e. *actually* infinite.

part to part.—Again, nothing infinite can exist; and if it could, at least the notion of infinity is not infinite.[4]

But (2) if the *kinds* of causes had been infinite in number, then also knowledge would have been impossible; for we think we know, only when we have ascertained the causes, but that which is infinite by addition cannot be gone through in a finite time.   30

3   The effect which lectures produce on a hearer depends on his habits; for we demand the language we are accustomed to, and that which is different from this seems not in keeping but somewhat un- 995ᵃ intelligible and foreign because of its unwontedness. For it is the customary that is intelligible. The force of habit is shown by the laws, in which the legendary and childish elements prevail over our knowl- 5 edge about them, owing to habit. Thus some people do not listen to a speaker unless he speaks mathematically, others unless he gives instances, while others expect him to cite a poet as witness. And some want to have everything done accurately, while others are annoyed by accuracy, either because they cannot follow the connexion of thought or because they regard it as pettifoggery. For accuracy has 10 something of this character, so that as in trade so in argument some people think it mean. Hence one must be already trained to know how to take each sort of argument, since it is absurd to seek at the same time knowledge and the way of attaining knowledge; and it is not easy to get even one of the two.

The minute accuracy of mathematics is not to be demanded in all 15 cases, but only in the case of things which have no matter. Hence its method is not that of natural science; for presumably the whole of nature has matter. Hence we must inquire first what nature is: for thus we shall also see what natural science treats of [and whether it belongs to one science or to more to investigate the causes and the principles of things].   20

BOOK B (III)

1   We must, with a view to the science which we are seeking, first recount the subjects that should be first discussed. These include both the other opinions that some have held on the first principles, and 25 any point besides these that happens to have been overlooked. For those who wish to get clear of difficulties it is advantageous to discuss the difficulties well; for the subsequent free play of thought implies

[4] i. e. does not contain an infinite number of marks.

the solution of the previous difficulties, and it is not possible to untie
30 a knot of which one does not know. But the difficulty of our thinking
points to a 'knot' in the object; for in so far as our thought is in
difficulties, it is in like case with those who are bound; for in either
case it is impossible to go forward. Hence one should have surveyed
all the difficulties beforehand, both for the purposes we have stated
and because people who inquire without first stating the difficulties
35 are like those who do not know where they have to go; besides, a man
does not otherwise know even whether he has at any given time found
995ᵇ what he is looking for or not; for the end is not clear to such a man,
while to him who has first discussed the difficulties it is clear. Further,
he who has heard all the contending arguments, as if they were the
parties to a case, must be in a better position for judging.

The first problem concerns the subject[1] which we discussed in our
5 prefatory remarks. It is this—(1) whether the investigation of the
causes belongs to one or to more sciences,[2] and (2) whether such a
science should survey only the first principles of substance, or also the
principles on which all men base their proofs, e. g. whether it is
possible at the same time to assert and deny one and the same thing
10 or not, and all other such questions;[3] and (3) if the science in question deals with substance, whether *one* science deals with all substances,
or more than one,[4] and if more, whether all are akin, or some of them
must be called forms of Wisdom and the others something else. And
(4) this itself is also one of the things that must be discussed—
whether sensible substances alone should be said to exist or others
15 also besides them, and whether these others are of one kind or there
are several classes of substances, as is supposed by those who believe
both in Form and in mathematical objects intermediate between these
and sensible things.[5] Into these questions, then, as we say, we must
inquire, and also (5) whether our investigation is concerned only with
substances or also with the essential attributes of substances.[6]
20 Further, with regard to the same and other and like and unlike and
contrariety, and with regard to prior and posterior and all other such
terms about which the dialecticians try to inquire, starting their investigation from probable premises only—whose business is it to
25 inquire into all these? Further, we must discuss the essential attributes
of these themselves; and we must ask not only what each of these
is, but also whether one thing always has one contrary.[7] Again (6),

---

[1] *sc.* the four causes.   [2] Cf. 996ᵃ 18–ᵇ 26.
[3] Cf. 996ᵇ 26–997ᵃ 15.   [4] Cf. 997ᵃ 15–25.
[5] Cf. 997ᵃ 34–998ᵃ 19. The reference is to Plato.
[6] Cf. 997ᵃ 25–34.   [7] Cf. iv. 1003ᵇ 22–1005ᵃ 18.

are the principles and elements of things the *genera,* or the parts
present in each thing, into which it is divided;[8] and (7) if they are
the genera, are they the genera that are predicated proximately of
the individuals, or the highest genera, e. g. is animal or man the first 30
principle and the more independent of the individual instance?[9] And
(8) we must inquire and discuss especially whether there is, besides
the matter, any thing that is a cause in itself or not, and whether this
can exist apart or not, and whether it is one or more in number, and
whether there is something apart from the concrete thing (by the 35
concrete thing I mean the matter with something already predicated
of it), or there is nothing apart, or there is something in some cases
though not in others, and what sort of cases these are.[10] Again (9)
we ask whether the principles are limited in number or in kind, both 996ᵃ
those in the definitions and those in the substratum;[11] and (10)
whether the principles of perishable and of imperishable things are the
same or different; and whether they are all imperishable or those of
perishable things are perishable.[12] Further (11) there is the question
which is hardest of all and most perplexing, whether unity and being, 5
as the Pythagoreans and Plato said, are not attributes of something
else but the substance of existing things, or this is not the case, but
the substratum is something else—as Empedocles says, love; as some
one else[13] says, fire; while another[14] says water or air.[15] Again (12)
we ask whether the principles are universal or like individual things,[16]
and (13) whether they exist potentially or actually,[17] and further, 10
whether they are potential or actual in any other sense than in reference to movement;[18] for these questions also would present much
difficulty. Further (14), are numbers and lines and figures and points
a kind of substance or not, and if they are substances are they separate from sensible things or present in them?[19] With regard to all 15
these matters not only is it hard to get possession of the truth, but
it is not easy even to think out the difficulties well.

2 (1) First then with regard to what we mentioned first, does it
belong to one or to more sciences to investigate all the kinds of causes?
How could it belong to one science to recognize the principles if these 20
are not contrary?

[8] Cf. 998ᵃ 20–ᵇ 14.   [9] Cf. 998ᵇ 14–999ᵃ 23.
[10] Cf. 999ᵃ 24–ᵇ 24.   [11] Cf. 999ᵇ 24–1000ᵃ 4.
[12] Cf. 1000ᵃ 5–1001ᵃ 3.   [13] Hippasus and Heraclitus.
[14] Thales (water); Anaximenes and Diogenes of Apollonia (air).
[15] Cf. 1001ᵃ 4–ᵇ 25.   [16] Cf. 1003ᵃ 5–17.
[17] Cf. 1002ᵇ 32–1003ᵃ 5.   [18] Cf. ix. 6.
[19] Cf. 1001ᵇ 26–1002ᵇ 11.

Further, there are many things to which not all the principles pertain. For how can a principle of change or the nature of the good exist for unchangeable things, since everything that in itself and by
25 its own nature is good is an end, and a cause in the sense that for its sake the other things both come to be and are, and since an end or purpose is the end of some action, and all actions imply change? So in the case of unchangeable things this principle could not exist, nor could there be a good-itself. This is why in mathematics nothing
30 is proved by means of this kind of cause, nor is there any demonstration of this kind—'because it is better, or worse'; indeed no one even mentions anything of the kind. And so for this reason some of the Sophists, e. g. Aristippus, used to ridicule mathematics; for in the arts (he maintained), even in the industrial arts, e. g. in carpentry and
35 cobbling, the reason always given is 'because it is better, or worse', but the mathematical sciences take no account of goods and evils.

996ᵇ   But if there are *several* sciences of the causes, and a different science for each different principle, which of these sciences should be said to be that which we seek, or which of the people who possess them has
5 the most scientific knowledge of the object in question? The same thing may have all the kinds of causes, e. g. the moving cause of a house is the art or the builder, the final cause is the function it fulfils, the matter is earth and stones, and the form is the definition. To judge from our previous discussion [20] of the question which of the sciences should be called Wisdom, there is reason for applying the
10 name to each of them. For inasmuch as it is most architectonic and authoritative and the other sciences, like slave-women, may not even contradict it, the science of the *end* and of the *good* is of the nature of Wisdom (for the other things are for the sake of the end). But inasmuch as it was described [21] as dealing with the first causes and that which is in the highest sense object of knowledge, the science of *substance* [22] must be of the nature of Wisdom. For since men may
15 know the same thing in many ways, we say that he who recognizes what a thing is by its being so and so knows more fully than he who recognizes it by its not being so and so, and in the former class itself one knows more fully than another, and he knows most fully who knows what a thing is, not he who knows its quantity or quality or what it can by nature do or have done to it. And further in all other cases also we think that the knowledge of each even of the things of which demonstration is possible is present only when we know what
20 the thing is, e. g. what squaring a rectangle is, viz. that it is the finding of a mean; and similarly in all other cases. And we know about becom-

[20] Cf. i. 982ᵃ 8–19.   [21] ib. 30–ᵇ 2.   [22] i. e. essence.

ings and actions and about every change when we know the *source
of the movement*; and this is other than and opposed to the end.
Therefore it would seem to belong to different sciences to investigate 25
these causes severally.[23]

But (2), taking the starting-points of demonstration as well as the
causes, it is a disputable question whether they are the object of one
science or of more (by the starting-points of demonstration I mean
the common beliefs, on which all men base their proofs); e. g. that
everything must be either affirmed or denied, and that a thing cannot
at the same time be and not be, and all other such premisses:—the 30
question is whether the same science deals with them as with substance, or a different science, and if it is not one science, which of the
two must be identified with that which we now seek.—It is not reasonable that these topics should be the object of one science; for why
should it be peculiarly appropriate to geometry or to any other science
to understand these matters? If then it belongs to every science alike, 35
and cannot belong to all, it is not peculiar to the science which investi-   997ᵃ
gates substances, any more than to any other science, to know about
these topics.—And, at the same time, in what way can there be a *science*
of the first principles? For we are aware even now what each of them
in fact is (at least even other sciences use them as familiar); but if 5
there is a demonstrative science which deals with them, there will have
to be an underlying kind, and some of them must be demonstrable
attributes and others must be axioms (for it is impossible that there
should be demonstration about all of them); for the demonstration
must start from certain premisses and be about a certain subject and
prove certain attributes. Therefore it follows that all attributes that
are proved must belong to a single class; for all demonstrative sciences 10
use the axioms.

But if the science of substance and the science which deals with the
axioms are different, which of them is by nature more authoritative
and prior? The *axioms* are most universal and are principles of all
things. And if it is not the business of the philosopher, to whom else
will it belong to inquire what is true and what is untrue about them? [24]

(3) In general, do all substances fall under one science or under 15
more than one? If the latter, to what sort of substance is the present
science to be assigned?—On the other hand, it is not reasonable that
one science should deal with all. For then there would be one demonstrative science dealing with all attributes. For every demonstrative

²³ With 996ᵃ 18–ᵇ 26 Cf. 995ᵇ 4–6, xi. 1059ᵃ 20–23 (with 996ᵃ 21–ᵇ 1 Cf. 1059ᵃ
34–8).

²⁴ With 996ᵇ 26–997ᵃ 15 Cf. 995ᵇ 6–10, 1059ᵃ 23–6. For the answer Cf. iv. 3.

20 science investigates with regard to some subject its essential attributes, starting from the common beliefs.[25] Therefore to investigate the essential attributes of one class of things, starting from one set of beliefs, is the business of one science. For the subject belongs to one science, and the premisses belong to one, whether to the same or to another; so that the attributes do so too, whether they are investigated by these sciences or by one compounded out of them.[26]

25   (4)[27] Further, does our investigation deal with substances alone or also with their attributes? I mean for instance, if the solid is a substance and so are lines and planes, is it the business of the same science to know these and to know the attributes of each of these classes (the attributes about which the mathematical sciences offer proofs), or of a different

30 science? If of the *same*, the science of substance also must be a demonstrative science; but it is thought that there is *no* demonstration of the essence of things. And if of *another*, what will be the science that investigates the attributes of substance? This is a very difficult question.[28]

   (5) Further, must we say that sensible substances alone exist, or

35 that there are others besides these? And are substances of one kind or

997ᵇ are there in fact several kinds of substances, as those say who assert the existence both of the Forms and of the intermediates, with which they say the mathematical sciences deal?—The sense in which we say the Forms are both causes and self-dependent substances has been explained in our first remarks about them;[29] while the theory presents

5 difficulties in many ways, the most paradoxical thing of all is the statement that there are certain things besides those in the material universe, and that these are the same as sensible things except that they are eternal while the latter are perishable. For they say there is a man-himself and a horse-itself and health-itself, with no further qualifica-

10 tion—a procedure like that of the people who said there are gods, but in human form. For they were positing nothing but eternal men, nor are the Platonists making the Forms anything other than eternal sensible things.

   Further, if we are to posit besides the Forms and the sensibles the intermediates between them, we shall have many difficulties. For clearly on the same principle there will be lines besides the lines-them-

---

25 Cf. 996ᵇ 28.

26 With 997ᵃ 15–25 Cf. 995ᵇ 10–13, 1059ᵃ 26–9. For the answer Cf. iv. 1004ᵃ 2–9, vi. 1.

27 I number the problems as in ch. 1.

28 With 997ᵃ 25–34 Cf. 995ᵇ 18–20, 1059ᵃ 29–34. For the answer Cf. iv. 1003ᵇ 22–1005ᵃ 18.

29 Cf. i. 6 and 9.

selves and the sensible lines, and so with each of the other classes of 15
things; so that since astronomy is one of these mathematical sciences
there will also be a heaven besides the sensible heaven, and a sun and
a moon (and so with the other heavenly bodies) besides the sensible.
Yet how are we to believe in these things? It is not reasonable even to
suppose such a body immovable, but to suppose it *moving* is quite
impossible.—And similarly with the things of which optics and 20
mathematical harmonics treat; for these also cannot exist apart from
the sensible things, for the same reasons. For if there are sensible
things and sensations intermediate between Form and individual,
evidently there will also be animals intermediate between animals-
themselves and the perishable animals.—We might also raise the ques- 25
tion, with reference to *which kind* of existing things we must look for
these sciences of intermediates. If geometry is to differ from mensuration only in this, that the latter deals with things that we perceive,
and the former with things that are not perceptible, evidently there
will also be a science other than medicine, intermediate between
medical-science-itself and this individual medical science, and so with
each of the other sciences. Yet how is this possible? There would 30
have to be also healthy things besides the perceptible healthy things
and the healthy-itself.—And at the same time not even this is true,
that mensuration deals with perceptible and perishable magnitudes;
for then it would have perished when they perished.

But on the other hand astronomy cannot be dealing with perceptible magnitudes nor with this heaven above us. For ɴeither are per- 35
ceptible lines such lines as the geometer speaks of (for no perceptible 998ᵃ
thing is straight or round in the way in which ʜᴇ defines 'straight'
and 'round'; for a hoop touches a straight edge not at a point, but
as Protagoras used to say it did, in his refutation of the geometers),
nor are the movements and spiral orbits in the heavens like those of 5
which astronomy treats, nor have geometrical points the same nature
as the actual stars.—Now there are some who say that these so-called
intermediates between the Forms and the perceptible things exist, not
apart from the perceptible things, however, but in these; the impossible results of this view would take too long to enumerate, but it is 10
enough to consider even such points as the following:—It is not
reasonable that this should be so only in the case of these *intermediates*, but clearly the *Forms* also might be in the perceptible things;
for both statements are parts of the same theory. Further, it follows
from this theory that there are two solids in the same place, and that
the intermediates are not immovable, since they are in the moving
perceptible things. And in general to what purpose would one suppose 15

them to *exist* indeed, but to exist *in* perceptible things? For the same paradoxical results will follow which we have already mentioned; there will be a heaven besides *the* heaven, only it will be not apart but in the same place; which is still more impossible.[30]

20 **3**   (6) Apart from the great difficulty of stating the case truly with regard to these matters, it is very hard to say, with regard to the first principles, whether it is the genera that should be taken as elements and principles, or rather the primary constituents of a thing; e. g. it is the primary parts of which articulate sounds consist that are thought to be elements and principles of articulate sound, not the common 25 genus—articulate sound; and we give the name of 'elements' to those geometrical propositions, the proofs of which are implied in the proofs of the others, either of all or of most. Further, both those who say there are several elements of corporeal things and those who say there is one, say the parts of which bodies are compounded and consist are 30 principles; e. g. Empedocles says fire and water and the rest are the constituent elements of things, but does not describe these as genera of existing things. Besides this, if we want to examine the nature of 998ᵇ anything else, we examine the parts of which, e. g., a bed consists and how they are put together, and then we know its nature.

To, judge from these arguments, then, the principles of things would not be the genera; but if we know each thing by its definition, 5 and the genera are the principles or starting-points of definitions, the genera must also be the principles of definable things. And if to get the knowledge of the species according to which things are named is to get the knowledge of things, the genera are at least starting-points of the *species*. And some also of those who say unity or being,[31] 10 or the great and the small,[32] are elements of things, seem to treat them as genera.

But, again, it is not possible to describe the principles in *both* ways. For the formula of the essence is one; but definition by genera will be different from that which states the constituent parts of a thing.[33]

(7) Besides this, even if the genera are in the highest degree prin- 15 ciples, should one regard the first of the genera as principles, or those which are predicated directly of the individuals? This also admits of dispute. For if the universals are always more of the nature of prin-

---

[30] With 997ᵃ 34–998ᵃ 19 Cf. 995ᵇ 13–18, 1059ᵃ 38–ᵇ 21. For the answer Cf. xii. 6–10, xiii, xiv.

[31] The reference is to the Pythagoreans and Plato (Cf. 996ᵃ 6).

[32] The reference is to Plato (Cf. i. 987ᵇ 20).

[33] With 998ᵃ 20–ᵇ 14 Cf. 995ᵇ 27–9. For the answer Cf. vii. 10, 13.

ciples, evidently the uppermost of the genera are the principles; for
these are predicated of all things. There will, then, be as many principles of things as there are primary genera, so that both being and
unity will be principles and substances; for these are most of all 20
predicated of all existing things. But it is not possible that either unity
or being should be a single genus of things; for the differentiae of any
genus must each of them both have being and be one, but it is not
possible for the genus taken apart from its species (any more than
for the species of the genus) to be predicated of its proper differentiae; 25
so that if unity or being is a genus, no differentia will either have being
or be one. But if unity and being are not genera, neither will they
be principles, if the genera are the principles.—Again, the intermediate
kinds, in whose nature the differentiae are included, will on this theory
be genera, down to the indivisible species; but as it is, some are
thought to be genera and others are not thought to be so. Besides this, 30
the differentiae are principles even more than the genera; and if
these also are principles, there comes to be practically an infinite
number of principles, especially if we suppose the highest genus to
be a principle.—But again, if unity *is* more of the nature of a prin- 999ª
ciple, and the indivisible is one, and everything indivisible is so either
in quantity or in species, and that which is so in species is the prior,
and genera are divisible into species (for man is not the *genus* of
individual men), that which is predicated directly of the individuals 5
will have more unity.—Further, in the case of things in which the
distinction of prior and posterior is present, that which is predicable
of these things cannot be something apart from them (e. g. if two is
the first of numbers, there will not be a Number apart from the kinds
of numbers; and similarly there will not be a Figure apart from the
kinds of figures; and if the genera of these things do not exist apart 10
from the species, the genera of *other* things will scarcely do so; for
genera of these things are thought to exist if any do). But among the
individuals one is not prior and another posterior. Further, where one
thing is better and another worse, the better is always prior; so that
of these also no genus can exist.

From these considerations, then, the species predicated of indi- 15
viduals seem to be principles rather than the genera. But again, it is
not easy to say in what sense these are to be taken as principles. For
the principle, and must be capable of existing in separation from
the principle, and must be capable of existing in separation from
them; but for what reason should we suppose any such thing to exist
alongside of the individual, except that it is predicated universally 20
and of all? But if this is the reason, the things that are more universal

must be supposed to be more of the nature of principles; so that the highest genera would be the principles.[34]

4 (8) There is a difficulty connected with these, the hardest of all
25 and the most necessary to examine, and of this the discussion now awaits us. If, on the one hand, there is nothing apart from individual things, and the individuals are infinite in number, how then is it possible to get knowledge of the infinite individuals? For all things that we come to know, we come to know in so far as they have some unity and identity, and in so far as some attribute belongs to them universally.

But if this is necessary, and there must be something apart from
30 the individuals, it will be necessary that the genera exist apart from the individuals—either the lowest or the highest genera; but we found by discussion just now that this is impossible.[35]

Further, if we admit in the fullest sense that something exists apart from the concrete thing, whenever something is predicated of the matter, must there, if there is something apart, be something apart
999b from each set of individuals, or from some and not from others, or from none? (A) If there is nothing apart from individuals, there will be no object of thought, but all things will be objects of sense, and there will not be knowledge of anything, unless we say that sensation is knowledge.[36] Further, nothing will be eternal or unmovable; for all
5 perceptible things perish and are in movement. But if there is nothing eternal, neither can there be a process of coming to be; for there must be something that comes to be, i. e. from which something comes to be, and the ultimate term in this series cannot have come to be, since the series has a limit and since nothing can come to be out of that which is not. Further, if generation and movement exist there must
10 also be a limit; for no movement is infinite, but every movement has an end, and that which is incapable of completing its coming to be cannot be in process of coming to be; and that which has completed its coming to be must *be* as soon as it has come to be.[37] Further, since the matter exists, because it is ungenerated, it is *a fortiori* reasonable that the substance or essence, that which the matter is at any time coming to be, should exist; for if neither essence nor matter is to be,
15 nothing will be at all, and since this is impossible there must be something besides the concrete thing, viz. the shape or form.

---

[34] With 998b 14–999a 23 Cf. 995b 29–31. For the answer Cf. vii. 12. 1038a 19, and 13. With this and the previous problem Cf. 1059b 21–1060a 1.
[35] Ch. 3.
[36] The reference is to Protagoras (Cf. Pl. *Theaet.* 152–E–153 A).
[37] *sc.* and thus there is a limit to its coming to be.

But again (B) if we are to suppose this, it is hard to say in which cases we are to suppose it and in which not. For evidently it is not possible to suppose it in all cases; we could not suppose that there is a house besides the particular houses.—Besides this, will the sub- 20 stance of all the individuals, e. g. of all men, be one? This is paradoxical, for all the things whose substance is one are one. But are the substances many and different? This also is unreasonable.—At the same time, how does the matter become each of the individuals, and how *is* the concrete thing these two elements? [38]

(9) Again, one might ask the following question also about the first principles. If they are one *in kind* only, nothing will be numerically 25 one, not even unity-itself and being-itself; and how will knowing exist, if there is not to be something common to a whole set of individuals?

But if there is a common element which is *numerically* one, and each of the principles is one, and the principles are not as in the case of perceptible things different for different things (e. g. since this particular syllable is the same in kind whenever it occurs, the elements of it are also the same in kind; only in kind, for these also, like the 30 syllable, are numerically different in different contexts),—if it is not like this but the principles of things are numerically one, there will be nothing else besides the elements (for there is no difference of meaning between 'numerically one' and 'individual'; for this is just what we mean by the individual—the numerically one, and by the universal we mean that which is predicable of the individuals). Therefore it will 1000ᵃ be just as if the elements of articulate sound were limited in number; all the language in the world would be confined to the ABC, since there could not be two or more letters of the same kind. [39]

(10) One difficulty which is as great as any has been neglected both 5 by modern philosophers and by their predecessors—whether the principles of perishable and those of imperishable things are the same or different. If they are the same, how are some things perishable and others imperishable, and for what reason? The school of Hesiod and all the theologians thought only of what was plausible to themselves, and had no regard to us. For, asserting the first principles to be gods 10 and born of gods, they say that the beings which did not taste of nectar and ambrosia became mortal; and clearly they are using words which are familiar to themselves, yet what they have said about the very application of these causes is above our comprehension. For

[38] With 999ᵃ 24–ᵇ 24 Cf. 995ᵇ 31–6, 1060ᵃ 3–27, ᵇ 23–8. For the answer Cf. vii. 8, 13, 14, xii. 6–10, xiii. 10.

[39] With 999ᵇ 24–1000ᵃ 4 Cf. 996ᵃ 1–2, 1060 ᵇ 28–30. For the answer Cf. vii. 14, xii. 4, 5, xiii. 10.

15 if the gods taste of nectar and ambrosia for their pleasure, these are in no wise the causes of their existence; and if they taste them to maintain their existence, how can gods who need food be eternal?— But into the subtleties of the mythologists it is not worth our while to inquire seriously; those, however, who use the language of proof
20 we must cross-examine and ask why, after all, things which consist of the same elements are, some of them, eternal in nature, while others perish. Since these philosophers mention no cause, and it is unreasonable that things should be as they say, evidently the principles or causes of things cannot be the same. Even the man whom one might
25 suppose to speak most consistently—Empedocles—even he has made the same mistake; for he maintains that strife is a principle that causes *destruction,* but even strife would seem no less to *produce* everything, except the One; for all things excepting God proceed from strife. At least he says:—

> From which all that was and is and will be hereafter—
30 > Trees, and men and women, took their growth,
> And beasts and birds and water-nourished fish,
> And long-aged gods.

The implication is evident even apart from these words; for if strife
1000ᵇ had not been present in things, all things would have been one, according to him; for when they have come together, 'then strife stood outermost.' Hence it also follows on his theory that God most blessed is
5 less wise than all others; for he does not know all the elements; for he has in him no strife, and knowledge is of the like by the like. 'For by earth,' he says,

> we see earth, by water water,
> By ether godlike ether, by fire wasting fire,
> Love by love, and strife by gloomy strife.

But—and this is the point we started from—this at least is evident,
10 that on his theory it follows that strife is as much the cause of existence as of destruction. And similarly love is not specially the cause of existence; for in collecting things into the One it destroys all other things. And at the same time Empedocles mentions no cause of the change itself, except that things are so by nature.

> But when strife at last waxed great in the limbs of the Sphere,
> And sprang to assert its rights as the time was fulfilled
15 > Which is fixed for them in turn by a mighty oath.

This implies that change was necessary; but he shows no cause of the necessity. But yet so far at least he alone speaks consistently; for he does not make 'some things perishable and others imperishable, but makes all perishable except the elements. The difficulty we are speak- 20 ing of now is, why some things are perishable and others are not, if they consist of the same principles.

Let this suffice as proof of the fact that the principles cannot be the same. But if there are different principles, one difficulty is whether these also will be imperishable or perishable. For if they are *perishable,* evidently these also must consist of certain elements (for 25 all things that perish, perish by being resolved into the elements of which they consist); so that it follows that prior to the principles there are other principles. But this is impossible, whether the process has a limit or proceeds to infinity. Further, how will perishable things exist, if their principles are to be annulled? But if the principles are *imperishable,* why will things composed of *some* imperishable principles be perishable, while those composed of the others are imperish- 30 able? This is not probable, but is either impossible or needs much proof. Further, no one has even tried to maintain different principles; they maintain the same principles for all things. But they swallow the difficulty we stated first [40] as if they took it to be something 1001ᵃ trifling.[41]

(11) The inquiry that is both the hardest of all and the most necessary for knowledge of the truth is whether being and unity are 5 the substances of things, and whether each of them, without being anything else, is being or unity respectively, *or* we must inquire what being and unity are, with the implication that they have some other underlying nature. For some people think they are of the former, others think they are of the latter character. Plato and the Pythagoreans thought being and unity were nothing else, but this was their 10 nature, their essence being just unity and being. But the natural philosophers take a different line; e. g. Empedocles—as though reducing it to something more intelligible—says what unity is; for he would seem to say it is love: at least, this is for all things the cause of their being one. Others say this unity and being, of which things 15 consist and have been made, is fire,[42] and others say it is air.[43] A similar view is expressed by those who make the elements more than one; for these also must say that unity and being are precisely all the things which they say are principles.

(A) If we do not suppose unity and being to be substances, it

[40] 1000ᵃ 5–ᵇ 21.

[41] With 1000ᵃ 5–1001ᵃ 3 Cf. 996ᵃ 2–4, 1060ᵃ 27–36. For the answer Cf. vii. 7–10.

[42] Hippasus and Heraclitus.

[43] Anaximenes and Diogenes of Apollonia.

20 follows that none of the other universals is a substance; for these are most universal of all, and if there is no unity-itself or being-itself, there will scarcely be in any *other* case anything apart from what are called
25 the individuals. Further, if unity is not a substance, evidently number also will not exist as an entity separate from the individual things; for number is units, and the unit is precisely a certain kind of one.

But (B) if there is a unity-itself and a being-itself, unity and being must be their substance; for it is not something else that is predicated universally of the things that are and are one, but just unity and being.
30 But if there *is* to be a being-itself and a unity-itself, there is much difficulty in seeing how there will be anything else besides these—I mean, how things will be more than one in number. For what is different from being does not exist, so that it necessarily follows, according to the argument of Parmenides, that all things that are are one and this is being.

1001ᵇ   There are objections to both views. For whether unity is not a substance or there *is* a unity-itself, number cannot be a substance. We have already [44] said why this result follows if unity is not a substance; and if it is, the same difficulty arises as arose [45] with regard
5 to being. For whence is there to be another one besides unity-itself? It must be not-one; but all things are either one or many, and of the many each is one.

Further, if unity-itself is indivisible, according to Zeno's postulate it will be nothing. For that which neither when added makes a thing greater nor when subtracted makes it less, he asserts to have no
10 being, evidently assuming that whatever has being is a spatial magnitude. And if it is a magnitude, it is corporeal; for the corporeal has being in every dimension, while the other objects of mathematics, e. g. a plane or a line, added in one way will increase what they are added to, but in another way will not do so,[46] and a point or a unit does so in no way. But, since his theory is of a low order, and an
15 indivisible thing *can* exist in such a way as to have a defence even against him (for the indivisible when added will make the number, though not the size, greater)—yet how can a *magnitude* proceed from one such indivisible or from many? It is like saying that the line is made out of points.
20   But even if one supposes the case to be such that, as some say, number proceeds from unity-itself and something else which is not one, none the less we must inquire why and how the product will be

[44] ᵃ 24–27.
[45] ᵃ 31–ᵇ 1.
[46] e. g. a line added to another at the end makes it longer, but one which lies beside another makes it no broader.

sometimes a number and sometimes a magnitude, if the not-one was inequality [47] and was the same principle in either case. For it is not evident how magnitudes could proceed either from the one and this principle, or from some number and this principle.[48]   25

5 (14) A question connected with these is whether numbers and bodies and planes and points are substances of a kind, or not. If they are not, it baffles us to say what being is and what the substances of things are. For modifications and movements and relations and 30 dispositions and ratios do not seem to indicate the substance of anything; for all are predicated of a subject, and none is a 'this'. And as to the things which might seem most of all to indicate substance, water and earth and fire and air, of which composite bodies consist, heat and cold and the like are modifications of these, not substances, 1002ᵃ and the body which is thus modified alone persists as something real and as a substance. But, on the other hand, the body is surely less of a substance than the surface, and the surface than the line, and the 5 line than the unit and the point. For the body is bounded by these; and they are thought to be capable of existing without body, but body incapable of existing without these. This is why, while most of the philosophers and the earlier among them thought that substance and being were identical with *body,* and that all other things were modifications of this, so that the first principles of bodies were the 10 first principles of being, the more recent and those who were held to be wiser thought *numbers* were the first principles. As we said, then, if these are not substance, there is no substance and no being at all; for the *accidents* of these it cannot be right to call beings.

But if this is admitted, that lines and points are substance more 15 than bodies, but we do not see to what sort of bodies these could belong (for they cannot be in perceptible bodies), there can be no substance.—Further, these are all evidently divisions of body—one in breadth, another in depth, another in length.—Besides this, no sort 20 of shape is present in the solid more than any other; so that if the Hermes is not in the stone, neither is the half of the cube in the cube as something determinate; therefore the surface is not in it either; for if any sort of surface were in it, the surface which marks off the half of the cube would be in it too. And the same account applies to 25 the line and to the point and the unit. Therefore, if on the one hand body is in the highest degree substance, and on the other hand these things are so more than body, but these are not even instances of

---

[47] The reference is to Plato's theory (Cf. xiii. 1081ᵃ 24).
[48] With 1001ᵃ 4–ᵇ 25 Cf. 996ᵃ 4–9. For the answer Cf. vii. 1040ᵇ 16–24, I. 2.

substance,⁴⁹ it baffles us to say what being is and what the substance of things is.—For besides what has been said, the questions
30 of generation and destruction confront us with further paradoxes.
For if substance, not having existed before, now exists, or having
existed before, afterwards does not exist, this change is thought to be
accompanied by a process of becoming or perishing; but points and
lines and surfaces cannot be in process either of becoming or of
perishing, when they at one time exist and at another do not. For
1002ᵇ when bodies come into contact or are divided, their boundaries simultaneously become one in the one case—when they touch, and two
in the other—when they are divided; so that when they have been
put together one boundary does not exist but has perished, and when
they have been divided the boundaries exist which before did not
exist (for it cannot be said that the point, which is indivisible, was
divided into two). And if the boundaries come into being and cease
5 to be, from what do they come into being? A similar account may
also be given of the 'now' in time; for this also cannot be in process of
coming into being or of ceasing to be, but yet seems to be always
different, which shows that it is not a substance. And evidently the
same is true of points and lines and planes; for the same argu-
10 ment applies, since they are all alike either limits or divisions.⁵⁰

6 In general one might raise the question why after all, besides perceptible things and the intermediates,⁵¹ we have to look for another
class of things, i. e. the Forms which we posit. If it is for this reason,
because the objects of mathematics, while they differ from the
15 things in this world in some other respect, differ not at all in that
there are many of the same kind, so that their first principles cannot
be limited in number (just as the elements of all the language in this
sensible world are not limited in number, but in kind, unless one
20 takes the elements of this individual syllable or of this individual
articulate sound—whose elements will be limited even in number;
so is it also in the case of the intermediates; for there also the members of the same kind are infinite in number), so that if there are
not—besides perceptible and mathematical objects—others such as
some maintain the Forms to be, there will be no substance which
is one in number, but only in kind, nor will the first principles of
25 things be determinate in number, but only in kind:—if then this
must be so, the Forms also must therefore be held to exist. Even

⁴⁹ sc. not to speak of their being the most real substances.
⁵⁰ For the answer Cf. xiii. 1–3 (esp. 1090ᵇ 5–13), 6–9, xiv. 1–3, 5, 6. With problems (11), (14) Cf. 1060ᵃ 36–ᵇ 19.
⁵¹ For these Cf. i. 987ᵇ 14–18.

if those who support this view do not express it articulately, still this is what they mean, and they must be maintaining the Forms just because each of the Forms is a substance and none is by accident.

But if we *are* to suppose both that the Forms exist and that the 30 principles are one in number, not in kind, we have mentioned [52] the impossible results that necessarily follow.[53]

(13) Closely connected with this is the question whether the elements exist potentially or in some other manner. If in some other way, there will be something else prior to the first principles; for the potency is prior to the actual cause, and it is not necessary 1003ᵃ for everything potential to be actual.—But if the elements exist potentially, it is possible that everything that is should not be. For even that which is not yet is capable of being; for that which is not comes to be, but nothing that is incapable of being comes to be.[54]

(12) We must not only raise these questions about the first principles, but also ask whether they are universal or what we call individuals. If they are universal, they will not be substances; for everything that is common indicates not a 'this' but a 'such', but substance is a 'this'. And if we are to be allowed to lay it down that a common predicate is a 'this' and a single thing, Socrates will be 10 several animals—himself and 'man' and 'animal', if each of these indicates a 'this' and a single thing.

If, then, the principles are universals, these results follow; if they are not universals but of the nature of individuals, they will not be knowable; for the knowledge of anything is universal. Therefore if there is to be knowledge of the principles there must be other 15 principles prior to them, namely those that are universally predicated of them.[55]

BOOK Γ (IV)

1   There is a science which investigates being as being and the attributes which belong to this in virtue of its own nature. Now this is not the same as any of the so-called special sciences; for none of these others treats universally of being as being. They cut off a part of being and investigate the attribute of this part; this is what 25 the mathematical sciences for instance do. Now since we are seeking the first principles and the highest causes, clearly there must be some

[52] 999ᵇ 27–1000ᵃ 4.
[53] (15) is a question not raised in ch. 1 but akin to problems (4), (8), (14).
[54] With 1002ᵇ 32–1003ᵃ 5 Cf. 996ᵃ 10–11. For the answer Cf. ix. 8, xii. 6, 7.
[55] With 1003ᵃ 5–17 Cf. 996ᵃ 9–10, 1060ᵇ 19–23. For the answer Cf. vii. 13, 15, xiii. 10.

thing to which these belong in virtue of its own nature. If then those who sought the elements of existing things were seeking these same
30 principles, it is necessary that the elements must be elements of being not by accident but just because it *is* being. Therefore it is of being as being that we also must grasp the first causes.

2   There are many senses in which a thing may be said to 'be', but all that 'is' is related to one central point, one definite kind of thing, and is not said to 'be' by a mere ambiguity. Everything which
35 is healthy is related to health, one thing in the sense that it pre- serves health, another in the sense that it produces it, another in the sense that it is a symptom of health, another because it is capable
1003ᵇ of it. And that which is medical is relative to the medical art, one thing being called medical because it possesses it, another because it is naturally adapted to it, another because it is a function of the
5 medical art. And we shall find other words used similarly to these. So, too, there are many senses in which a thing is said to be, but all refer to one starting-point; some things are said to be because they are substances, others because they are affections of substance, others because they are a process towards substance, or destructions or privations or qualities of substance, or productive or generative of substance, or of things which are relative to substance, or negations
10 of one of these things or of substance itself. It is for this reason that we say even of non-being that it *is* non-being. As, then, there is one science which deals with all healthy things, the same applies in the other cases also. For not only in the case of things which have one common notion does the investigation belong to one science, but also in the case of things which are related to one common nature;
15 for even these in a sense have one common notion. It is clear then that it is the work of one science also to study the things that are, *qua* being.—But everywhere science deals chiefly with that which is primary, and on which the other things depend, and in virtue of which they get their names. If, then, this is substance, it will be of substances that the philosopher must grasp the principles and the causes.

Now for each one class of things, as there is one perception, so
20 there is one science, as for instance grammar, being one science, investigates all articulate sounds. Hence to investigate all the species of being *qua* being is the work of a science which is generically one, and to investigate the several species is the work of the specific parts of the science.

If, now, being and unity are the same and are one thing in the

sense that they are implied in one another as principle and cause are,
not in the sense that they are explained by the same definition
(though it makes no difference even if we suppose them to be like 25
that—in fact this would even strengthen our case); for 'one man'
and 'man' are the same thing, and so are 'existent man' and 'man',
and the doubling of the words in 'one man and one *existent* man' does
not express anything different (it is clear that the two things are
not separated either in coming to be or in ceasing to be); and
similarly '*one* existent man' adds nothing to 'existent man', so that it 30
is obvious that the addition in these cases means the same thing, and
unity is nothing apart from being; and if, further, the substance of
each thing is one in no merely accidental way, and similarly is from
its very nature something that *is*:—all this being so, there must be
exactly as many species of being as of unity. And to investigate the
essence of these is the work of a science which is generically one— 35
I mean, for instance, the discussion of the same and the similar and
the other concepts of this sort; and nearly all contraries may be
referred to this origin; let us take them as having been investigated 1004ᵃ
in the 'Selection of Contraries'.

And there are as many parts of philosophy as there are kinds of
substance, so that there must necessarily be among them a first
philosophy and one which follows this. For being falls immediately
into genera; for which reason the sciences too will correspond to 5
these genera. For the philosopher is like the mathematician, as that
word is used; for mathematics also has parts, and there is a first and
a second science and other successive ones within the sphere of
mathematics.[1]

Now since it is the work of one science to investigate opposites,
and plurality is opposed to unity—and it belongs to one science to 10
investigate the negation and the privation because in both cases we
are really investigating the one thing of which the negation or the
privation is a negation or privation (for we either say simply that that
thing is not present, or that it is not present in some particular class;
in the latter case difference is present over and above what is implied
in negation; for negation means just the absence of the thing in ques- 15
tion, while in privation there is also employed an underlying nature
of which the privation is asserted):—in view of all these facts, the
contraries of the concepts we named above, the other and the dissimilar and the unequal, and everything else which is derived either
from these or from plurality and unity, must fall within the province
of the science above named. And contrariety is one of these concepts; 20

[1] With 1004ᵃ 2–9 Cf. iii. 995ᵇ 10–13, 997ᵃ 15–25, vi. 1.

for contrariety is a kind of difference, and difference is a kind of otherness. Therefore, since there are many senses in which a thing is said to be one, these terms also will have many senses, but yet it belongs to one science to know them all; for a term belongs to different sciences not if it has different senses, but if it has not one meaning *and*
25 its definitions cannot be referred to one central meaning. And since all things are referred to that which is primary, as for instance all things which are called one are referred to the primary one, we must say that this holds good also of the same and the other and of contraries in general; so that after distinguishing the various senses of each, we must then explain by reference to what is primary in the case of each of the predicates in question, saying how they are
30 related to it; for some will be called what they are called because they possess it, others because they produce it, and others in other such ways.

It is evident, then, that it belongs to one science to be able to give an account of these concepts as well as of substance (this was one of the questions in our book of problems),[2] and that it is the function
1004ᵇ of the philosopher to be able to investigate all things. For if it is not the function of the philosopher, who is it who will inquire whether Socrates and Socrates seated are the same thing, or whether one thing has one contrary, or what contrariety is, or how many meanings it has? And similarly with all other such questions. Since,
5 then, these are essential modifications of unity *qua* unity and of being *qua* being, not *qua* numbers or lines or fire, it is clear that it belongs to this science to investigate both the essence of these concepts and their properties. And those who study these properties err not by leaving the sphere of philosophy,[3] but by forgetting that substance, of which they have no correct idea, is prior to these other
10 things. For number *qua* number has peculiar attributes, such as oddness and evenness, commensurability and equality, excess and defect, and these belong to numbers either in themselves or in relation to one another. And similarly the solid and the motionless and that which is in motion and the weightless and that which has weight have other
15 peculiar properties. So too there are certain properties peculiar to being as such, and it is about these that the philosopher has to investigate the truth.—An indication of this may be mentioned:— dialecticians and sophists assume the same guise as the philosopher, for sophistic is Wisdom which exists only in semblance, and dialec-
20 ticians embrace all things in their dialectic, and being is common to all things; but evidently their dialectic embraces these subjects be-

[2] i. e. iii. 995ᵇ 18–27, 997ᵃ 25–34.   [3] *sc.* which they do not do.

cause these are proper to philosophy.—For sophistic and dialectic turn on the same class of things as philosophy, but this differs from dialectic in the nature of the faculty required and from sophistic in respect of the purpose of the philosophic life. Dialectic is merely 25 critical where philosophy claims to know, and sophistic is what appears to be philosophy but is not.

Again, in the list of contraries one of the two columns is privative, and all contraries are reducible to being and non-being, and to unity and plurality, as for instance rest belongs to unity and movement to plurality. And nearly all thinkers agree that being and substance 30 are composed of contraries; at least all name contraries as their first principles—some name odd and even,[4] some hot and cold,[5] some limit and the unlimited,[6] some love and strife.[7] And all the others as well are evidently reducible to unity and plurality (this reduction 1005ᵃ we must take for granted), and the principles stated by other thinkers fall entirely under these as their genera. It is obvious then from these considerations too that it belongs to one science to examine being *qua* being. For all things are either contraries or composed of contraries, and unity and plurality are the starting-points of all contraries. And these belong to one science, whether they have or 5 have not one single meaning. Probably the truth is that they have not; yet even if 'one' has several meanings, the other meanings will be related to the primary meaning (and similarly in the case of the contraries), even if being or unity is not a universal and the same in every instance or is not separable from the particular instances (as in fact it probably is not; the unity is in some cases that 10 of common reference, in some cases that of serial succession). And for this reason it does not belong to the geometer to inquire what is contrariety or completeness or unity or being or the same or the other, but only to presuppose these concepts and reason from this starting-point.—Obviously then it is the work of one science to examine being *qua* being, and the attributes which belong to it *qua* being, and the same science will examine not only substances but also their attri- 15 butes, both those above named and the concepts 'prior' and 'posterior', 'genus' and 'species', 'whole' and 'part', and the others of this sort.[8]

3   We must state whether it belongs to one or to different sciences to inquire into the truths which are in mathematics called axioms, and into substance. Evidently, the inquiry into these also belongs to 20

---

[4] The Pythagoreans.   [5] Parmenides in the 'Way of Opinion'.
[6] The Platonists.   [7] Empedocles.
[8] With 1003ᵇ 22–1005ᵃ 18 Cf. iii. 995ᵇ 18–27, 997ᵃ 25–34. With the whole ch. Cf. xi. 3.

one science, and that the science of the philosopher; for these truths hold good for everything that is, and not for some special genus apart from others. And all men use them, because they are true of
25 being *qua* being and each genus has being. But men use them just so far as to satisfy their purposes; that is, as far as the genus to which their demonstrations refer extends. Therefore since these truths clearly hold good for all things *qua* being (for this is what is common to them), to him who studies being *qua* being belongs the inquiry into these as well. And for this reason no one who is conducting a
30 special inquiry tries to say anything about their truth or falsity— neither the geometer nor the arithmetician. Some natural philosophers indeed have done so, and their procedure was intelligible enough; for they thought that they alone were inquiring about the whole of nature and about being. But since there is one kind of thinker who is above even the natural philosopher (for nature is only one particular genus
35 of being), the discussion of these truths also will belong to him whose
1005ᵇ inquiry is universal and deals with primary substance. Physics also is a kind of Wisdom, but it is not the first kind.[9]—And the attempts of some of those who discuss the terms on which truth should be accepted,[10] are due to a want of training in logic; for they should know these things already when they come to a special study, and not be inquiring
5 into them while they are listening to lectures on it.

Evidently then it belongs to the philosopher, i. e. to him who is studying the nature of all substance, to inquire also into the principles of syllogism. But he who knows best about each genus must be able to state the most certain principles of his subject, so that he whose subject
10 is existing things *qua* existing must be able to state the most certain principles of all things. This is the philosopher, and the most certain principle of all is that regarding which it is impossible to be mistaken; for such a principle must be both the best known (for all men may be mistaken about things which they do not know), and non-hypothet-
15 ical. For a principle which every one must have who understands anything that is, is not a hypothesis; and that which every one must know who knows anything, he must already have when he comes to a special study. Evidently then such a principle is the most certain of all; which principle this is, let us proceed to say. It is, that the same attribute cannot at the same time belong and not belong to the same subject
20 and in the same respect; we must presuppose, to guard against dia- lectical objections, any further qualifications which might be added. This, then, is the most certain of all principles, since it answers to the

---

⁹ With 1005ᵃ 19–ᵇ2 Cf. xi. 4.   ¹⁰ The reference may be to Antisthenes.

definition given above. For it is impossible for any one to believe the same thing to be and not to be, as some think Heraclitus says. For what a man says, he does not necessarily believe; and if it is impossible that 25 contrary attributes should belong at the same time to the same subject (the usual qualifications must be presupposed in this premiss too), and if an opinion which contradicts another is contrary to it, obviously it is impossible for the same man at the same time to believe the same thing to be and not to be; for if a man were mistaken on this point he would 30 have contrary opinions at the same time. It is for this reason that all who are carrying out a demonstration reduce it to this as an ultimate belief; for this is naturally the starting-point even for all the other axioms.[11]

4   There are some who, as we said,[12] both themselves assert that it 35 is possible for the same thing to be and not to be, and say that people can judge this to be the case.[13] And among others many writers about 1006ᵃ nature use this language. But we have now posited that it is impossible for anything at the same time to be and not to be, and by this means have shown that this is the most indisputable of all principles.—Some indeed demand that even this shall be demonstrated, but this they do 5 through want of education, for not to know of what things one should demand demonstration, and of what one should not, argues want of education. For it is impossible that there should be demonstration of absolutely everything (there would be an infinite regress, so that there would still be no demonstration); but if there are things of which one 10 should not demand demonstration, these persons could not say what principle they maintain to be more self-evident than the present one.

We can, however, demonstrate negatively even that this view is impossible, if our opponent will only say something; and if he says nothing, it is absurd to seek to give an account of our views to one who cannot give an account of anything, in so far as he cannot do so. For such a man, as such, is from the start no better than a vegetable. Now 15 negative demonstration I distinguish from demonstration proper, because in a demonstration one might be thought to be begging the question, but if another person is responsible for the assumption we shall have negative proof, not demonstration.[14] The starting-point for all such arguments is not the demand that our opponent shall say that something either is or is not (for this one might perhaps take to be a 20

---

11 With ch. 3 Cf. iii. 995ᵇ 6–10, 996ᵇ 26–997ᵃ 15. With 1005ᵇ 8–34 Cf. xi. 1061ᵇ 34–1062ᵃ 2 (with 1005ᵇ 23–6 Cf. 1062ᵃ 31–5).
12 Apparently a loose reference to 1005ᵇ 23–5.
13 The Megaric school may be referred to.
14 With ll. 5–18 Cf. xi. 1062ᵃ 2–5.

begging of the question), but that he shall say something which is *significant* both for himself and for another; for this is necessary, if he really is to say anything. For, if he means nothing, such a man will not be capable of reasoning, either with himself or with another. But if any one grants this, demonstration will be possible; for we shall already
25 have something definite. The person responsible for the proof, however, is not he who demonstrates but he who listens; for while disowning reason he listens to reason. And again he who admits this has admitted that something is true apart from demonstration [so that not everything will be 'so and not so'].

First then this at least is obviously true, that the word 'be' or 'not be'
30 has a definite meaning, so that not everything will be 'so and not so'.[15]—Again, if 'man' has one meaning, let this be 'two-footed animal'; by having one meaning I understand this:—if 'man' means 'X', then if A is a man 'X' will be what 'being a man' means for him. (It makes no difference even if one were to say a word has several meanings, if only
1006[b] they are limited in number; for to each definition there might be assigned a different word. For instance, we might say that 'man' has not one meaning but several, one of which would have one definition, viz. 'two-footed animal', while there might be also several other definitions if only they were limited in number; for a peculiar name might be
5 assigned to each of the definitions. If, however, they were not limited but one were to say that the word has an infinite number of meanings, obviously reasoning would be impossible; for not to have one meaning is to have no meaning, and if words have no meaning our reasoning with one another, and indeed with ourselves, has been annihilated;
10 for it is impossible to think of anything if we do not think of one thing; but if this *is* possible, one name might be assigned to this thing.)

Let it be assumed then, as was said at the beginning,[16] that the name has a meaning and has one meaning; it is impossible, then, that 'being a man' should mean precisely 'not being a man', if 'man'
15 not only signifies something about one subject but also has one significance (for we do not identify 'having one significance' with 'signifying something about one subject', since on *that* assumption even 'musical' and 'white' and 'man' would have had one significance, so that all things would have been one; for they would all have had the same significance).

And it will not be possible to be and not to be the same thing, except in virtue of an ambiguity, just as if one whom we call 'man',
20 others were to call 'not-man'; but the point in question is not this,

15 For 'so and not so' Cf. Pl. *Theaet.* 183 A.   16 a21, 31.

whether the same thing can at the same time be and not be a man in
name, but whether it can in fact.—Now if 'man' and 'not-man' mean
nothing different, obviously 'not being a man' will mean nothing different from 'being a man'; so that 'being a man' will be 'not being
a man'; for they will be one. For being one means this—being related 25
as 'raiment' and 'dress' are, if their definition is one. And if 'being a
man' and 'being a not-man' are to be one, they must mean one thing.
But it was shown earlier [17] that they mean different things.—Therefore, if it is true to say of anything that it is a man, it must be a
two-footed animal (for this was what 'man' meant [18]); and if this is
necessary, it is impossible that the same thing should not at that time 30
be a two-footed animal; for this is what 'being necessary' means—
that it is impossible for the thing not to be. It is, then, impossible
that it should be at the same time true to say the same thing is a
man and is not a man.

The same account holds good with regard to 'not being a man',
for 'being a man' and 'being a not-man' mean different things, since 1007[a]
even 'being white' and 'being a man' are different; for the former
terms are much more opposed, so that they must *a fortiori* mean
different things. And if any one says that *'white'* means one and the
same thing as 'man', again we shall say the same as what was said 5
before,[19] that it would follow that *all* things are one, and not only
opposites. But if this is impossible, then what we have maintained will
follow, if our opponent will only answer our question.

And if, when one asks the question simply, he adds the contradictories, he is not answering the question. For there is nothing to 10
prevent the same thing from being both a man and white and countless other things: but still, if one asks whether it is or is not true to say
that this is a man, our opponent must give an answer which means
one thing, and not add that 'it is also white and large'. For, besides
other reasons, it is impossible to enumerate its accidental attributes, 15
which are infinite in number; let him, then, enumerate either all or
none. Similarly, therefore, even if the same thing is a thousand times
a man and a not-man, he must not, in answering the question whether
this is a man, add that it is also at the same time a not-man, unless
he is bound to add also all the other accidents, all that the subject
is or is not; and if he does this, he is not observing the rules of argument.[20]

And in general those who say this do away with substance and 20
essence. For they must say that all attributes are accidents, and that

[17] ll. 11–15.   [18] in [a] 31 f.   [19] 1006[b] 17.
[20] With 1006[a] 18–1007[a] Cf. xi. 1062[a] 5–20 (with 1006[b] 28–34 Cf. 1062[a] 20–3).

there is no such thing as 'being essentially a man' or 'an animal'. For if there is to be any such thing as 'being essentially a man' this will not be 'being a not-man' or 'not being a man' (yet these are negations
25 of it [21]); for there was one thing which it meant, and this was the substance of something. And denoting the substance of a thing means that the essence of the thing is nothing else. But if its being essentially a man is to be the same as either being essentially a not-man or essentially not being a man, then its essence *will* be something else. Therefore our opponents must say that there cannot be such a defini-
30 tion of anything, but that all attributes are accidental; for this is the distinction between substance and accident—'white' is accidental to man, because though he is white, whiteness is not his essence. But if *all* statements are accidental, there will be nothing primary about
35 which they are made, if the accidental always implies predication
1007b about a subject. The predication, then, must go on *ad infinitum*. But this is impossible; for not even more than two terms can be combined in accidental predication. For (1) an accident is not an accident of an accident, unless it be because both are accidents of the same subject. I mean, for instance, that the white is musical and the latter
5 is white, only because both are accidental to man. But (2) Socrates is musical, not in this sense, that both terms are accidental to something else. Since then some predicates are accidental in this and some in that sense, (*a*) those which are accidental in the latter sense, in which white is accidental to Socrates, cannot form an infinite series in the upward direction;[22] e. g. Socrates the white has not yet another
10 accident; for no unity can be got out of such a sum. Nor again (*b*) will 'white' have another term accidental to it, e. g. 'musical'. For this is no more accidental to that than that is to this; and at the same time we have drawn the distinction, that while some predicates are accidental in this sense, others are so in the sense in which 'musical' is accidental to Socrates; and the accident is an accident of
15 an accident not in cases of the latter kind, but only in cases of the other kind, so that not *all* terms will be accidental.[23] There must, then, even so be something which denotes substance. And if this is so, it has been shown that contradictories cannot be predicated at the same time.

Again, if all contradictory statements are true of the same subject

---

[21] *sc.* and hence (on the view attacked) should be compatible with it.

[22] i. e. in the direction of predicates, which are naturally wider or higher than the subject.

[23] Sense (1) reduces to sense (2), and in this an infinite number of accidents combined together is impossible; there must be substance somewhere.

at the same time, evidently all things will be one. For the same thing
will be a trireme, a wall, and a man, if of everything it is possible 20
either to affirm or to deny anything (and this premiss must be
accepted by those who share the views of Protagoras). For if any one
thinks that the man is not a trireme, evidently he is not a trireme; so
that he also *is* a trireme, if, as they say, contradictory statements 25
are both true. And we thus get the doctrine of Anaxagoras, that all
things are mixed together; so that nothing really exists. They seem,
then, to be speaking of the indeterminate, and, while fancying themselves to be speaking of being, they are speaking about non-being;
for it is that which exists potentially and not in complete reality that
is indeterminate. But they *must* predicate of every subject the affirmation or the negation of every attribute. For it is absurd if of each 30
subject its own negation is to be predicable, while the negation of
something else which cannot be predicated of it is not to be predicable
of it; for instance, if it is true to say of a man that he is not a man,
evidently it is also true to say that he is either a trireme or not a
trireme. If, then, the affirmative [24] can be predicated, the negative
must be predicable too; and if the affirmative is not predicable, the 35
negative, at least, will be more predicable than the negative of the 1008ᵃ
subject itself. If, then, even the latter negative is predicable, the
negative of 'trireme' will be also predicable; and, if this is predicable,
the affirmative will be so too.[25]

Those, then, who maintain this view are driven to this conclusion,
and to the further conclusion that it is not necessary either to assert
or to deny. For if it is true that a thing is a man and a not-man, evi- 5
dently also it will be neither a man nor a not-man. For to the two
assertions there answer two negations, and if the former [26] is treated as
a single proposition compounded out of two, the latter also is a single
proposition opposite to the former.[27]

Again, either the theory is true in all cases, and a thing is both white
and not-white, and existent and non-existent, and all other assertions.
and negations are similarly compatible, or the theory is true of some 10
statements and not of others. And if not of all, the exceptions will be
contradictories of which admittedly only one is true; but if of all,
again either the negation will be true wherever the assertion is, and the
assertion true wherever the negation is, or the negation will be true
where the assertion is, but the assertion not always true where the 15
negation is. And (*a*) in the latter case there will be something which

[24] *sc.* 'trireme'.   [25] With 1007ᵇ 18–1008ᵃ 2 Cf. xi. 1062ᵃ 23–30.
[26] *sc.* that the thing is a man and a not-man.
[27] With ll. 6–7 Cf. xi. 1062ᵃ 36–ᵇ 7.

fixedly *is not*, and this will be an indisputable belief; and if non-being is something indisputable and knowable, the opposite assertion will be more knowable. But (*b*) if it is equally possible also to assert all that it is possible to deny, one must either be saying what is true when one separates the predicates (and says, for instance, that a thing is
20 white, and again that it is not-white), or not. And if (i) it is not true to apply the predicates separately, our opponent is not saying what he professes to say, and also nothing at all exists, but how could non-existent things speak or walk, as he does? Also all things would on this view be one, as has been already said,[28] and man and God and trireme
25 and their contradictories will be the same. For if contradictories can be predicated alike of each subject, one thing will in no wise differ from another; for if it differ, this difference will be something true and peculiar to it. And (ii) if one may with truth apply the predicates separately, the above-mentioned result follows none the less, and, further, it follows that all would then be right and all would Le in error, and our opponent himself confesses himself to be in error.—And
30 at the same time our discussion with him is evidently about nothing at all; for he says nothing. For he says neither 'yes' nor 'no', but 'yes and no'; and again he denies both of these and says 'neither yes nor no'; for otherwise there would already be something definite.

Again, if when the assertion is true, the negation is false, and when
35 this is true, the affirmation is false, it will not be possible to assert and deny the same thing truly at the same time. But perhaps they might say this was the very question at issue.
1008ᵇ

Again, is he in error who judges either that the thing is so or that it is not so, and is he right who judges both? If he is right, what can
5 they mean by saying that the nature of existing things is of this kind? And if he is not right, but more right than he who judges in the other way, being will already be of a definite nature, and this will be true, and not at the same time also not true. But if all are alike both wrong and right, one who is in this condition will not be able either to speak
10 or to say anything intelligible; for he says at the same time both 'yes' and 'no'. And if he makes no judgement but 'thinks' and 'does not think', indifferently, what difference will there be between him and a vegetable?—Thus, then, it is in the highest degree evident that neither any one of those who maintain this view nor any one else is really in this position. For why does a man walk to Megara and not
15 stay at home, when he thinks he ought to be walking there? Why does he not walk early some morning into a well or over a precipice, if one happens to be in his way? Why do we observe him guarding against

[28] 1006ᵇ 17, 1007ᵃ 6.

this, evidently because he does not think that falling in is alike good
and not good? Evidently, then, he judges one thing to be better and
another worse. And if this is so, he must also judge one thing to be
a man and another to be not-a-man, one thing to be sweet and another 20
to be not-sweet. For he does not aim at and judge all things alike,
when, thinking it desirable to drink water or to see a man, he proceeds
to aim at these things; yet he *ought*, if the same thing were alike a
man and not-a-man. But, as was said, there is no one who does not
obviously avoid some things and not others. Therefore, as it seems, 25
all men make unqualified judgements, if not about all things, still
about what is better and worse.[29] And if this is not knowledge but
opinion, they should be all the more anxious about the truth, as a sick
man should be more anxious about his health than one who is healthy; 30
for he who has opinions is, in comparison with the man who knows,
not in a healthy state as far as the truth is concerned.

Again, however much all things may be 'so and not so', still there is a
more and a less in the nature of things; for we should not say that two
and three are equally even, nor is he who thinks four things are five
equally wrong with him who thinks they are a thousand. If then they 35
are not equally wrong, obviously one is less wrong and therefore more
right. If then that which has more of any quality is nearer the norm,
there must be some truth to which the more true is nearer. And even 1009ᵃ
if there is not, still there is already something better founded and liker
the truth, and we shall have got rid of the unqualified doctrine which
would prevent us from determining anything in our thought.   5

5   From the same opinion proceeds the doctrine of Protagoras, and
both doctrines must be alike true or alike untrue. For on the one hand,
if all opinions and appearances are true, all statements must be at
the same time true and false. For many men hold beliefs in which they
conflict with one another, and think those mistaken who have not the 10
same opinions as themselves; so that the same thing must both be and
not be. And on the other hand, if this is so, all opinions must be true;
for those who are mistaken and those who are right are opposed to one
another in their opinions; if, then, reality is such as the view in question supposes, all will be right in their beliefs.

Evidently, then, both doctrines proceed from the same way of think- 15
ing. But the same method of discussion must not be used with all
opponents; for some need persuasion, and others compulsion. Those
who have been driven to this position by difficulties in their thinking
can easily be cured of their ignorance; for it is not their expressed

29 With ll. 12–27 Cf. xi. 1063ᵃ 28–35.

20 argument but their thought that one has to meet. But those who argue
for the sake of argument can be cured only by refuting the argument
as expressed in speech and in words.[30]

Those who really feel the difficulties have been led to this opinion
by observation of the sensible world. (1) They think that contradictories or contraries are true at the same time, because they see con-
25 traries coming into existence out of the same thing. If, then, that which
is not cannot come to be, the thing must have existed before as both
contraries alike, as Anaxagoras says all is mixed in all, and Democritus
too; for *he* says the void and the full exist alike in every part, and yet
30 one of these is being, and the other non-being.[31] To those, then, whose
belief rests on these grounds, we shall say that in a sense they speak
rightly and in a sense they err. For 'that which is' has two meanings,
so that in some sense a thing can come to be out of that which is not,
while in some sense it cannot, and the same thing can at the same
time be in being and not in being—but not in the same respect. For
35 the same thing can be potentially at the same time two contraries, but
it cannot actually.[32] And again we shall ask them to believe that among
existing things there is also another kind of substance to which neither
movement nor destruction nor generation at all belongs.

1009ᵇ   And (2) similarly some have inferred from observation of the sensible world the truth of appearances. For they think that the truth
should not be determined by the large or small number of those who
hold a belief, and that the same thing is thought sweet by some when
5 they taste it, and bitter by others; so that if all were ill or all were
mad, and only two or three were well or sane, these would be thought
ill and mad, and not the others.

And again, they say that many of the other animals receive impressions contrary to ours; and that even to the senses of each individual,
things do not always seem the same. Which, then, of these impressions
10 are true and which are false is not obvious; for the one set is no more
true than the other, but both are alike. And this is why Democritus,
at any rate, says that either there is no truth or to us at least it is not
evident.

And in general it is because these thinkers suppose knowledge to
be sensation, and this to be a physical alteration, that they say that
15 what appears to our senses must be true; for it is for these reasons
that both Empedocles and Democritus and, one may almost say, all
the others have fallen victims to opinions of this sort. For Empedocles

[30] With ll. 16–22 Cf. xi. 1063ᵇ 7–16.
[31] With ll. 6–16, 22–30 Cf. xi. 1062ᵇ 12–24.
[32] With ll. 30–6 Cf. xi. 1062ᵇ 24–33.

says that when men change their condition they change their knowledge;

For wisdom increases in men according to what is before them.

And elsewhere he says that

So far as their nature changed, so far to them always   20
Came changed thoughts into mind.

And Parmenides also expresses himself in the same way:

For as at each time the much-bent limbs are composed,
So is the mind of men; for in each and all men
'Tis one thing thinks—the substance of their limbs:
For that of which there is more is thought.

A saying of Anaxagoras to some of his friends is also related—that 25
things would be for them such as they supposed them to be. And they
say that Homer also evidently had this opinion, because he made
Hector, when he was unconscious from the blow, lie 'thinking other
thoughts'—which implies that even those who are bereft of thought 30
have thoughts, though not the same thoughts. Evidently, then, if both
are forms of knowledge, the real things also are at the same time 'both
so and not so'.[33] And it is in this direction that the consequences are
most difficult. For if those who have seen most of such truth as is
possible for us (and these are those who seek and love it most)—if 35
these have such opinions and express these views about the truth, is
it not natural that beginners in philosophy should lose heart? For to
seek the truth would be to follow flying game.

But the reason why these thinkers held this opinion is that while 1010ᵃ
they were inquiring into the truth of that which is, they thought 'that
which is' was identical with the sensible world; in this, however, there
is largely present the nature of the indeterminate—of that which exists
in the peculiar sense which we have explained;[34] and therefore, while
they speak plausibly, they do not say what is true (for it is fitting to
put the matter so rather than as Epicharmus put it against Xenoph- 5
anes [35]). And again, because they saw that all this world of nature
is in movement, and that about that which changes no true statement
can be made, they said that of course, regarding that which everywhere
in every respect is changing, nothing could truly be affirmed. It was
this belief that blossomed into the most extreme of the views above 10
mentioned, that of the professed Heracliteans, such as was held by
Cratylus, who finally did not think it right to say anything but only

[33] With ᵃ38–ᵇ 33 Cf. xi. 1063ᵃ 35–ᵇ 7.   [34] Cf. 1009ᵃ 32.
[35] Epicharmus may have said that Xenophanes' views were 'neither plausible
nor true', or that they were 'true but not plausible'.

moved his finger, and criticized Heraclitus for saying that it is impossible to step twice into the same river; for *he* thought one could not do it even once.

15 But we shall say in answer to this argument also, that while there is some justification for their thinking that the changing, when it is changing, does not exist, yet it is after all disputable; for that which is losing a quality has something of that which is being lost, and of that which is coming to be, something must already be. And in general if a thing is perishing, there will be present something that exists; and if 20 a thing is coming to be, there must be something from which it comes to be and something by which it is generated, and this process cannot go on *ad infinitum*.—But, leaving these arguments, let us insist on this, that it is not the same thing to change in quantity and in quality. Grant that in quantity a thing is not constant; still it is in respect of 25 its form that we know each thing.[36]—And again, it would be fair to criticize those who hold this view for asserting about the whole material universe what they saw only in a minority even of sensible things. For only that region of the sensible world which immediately surrounds 30 us is always in process of destruction and generation; but this is—so to speak—not even a fraction of the whole, so that it would have been juster to acquit this part of the world because of the other part, than to condemn the other because of this.[37]—And again, obviously we shall make to them also the same reply that we made long ago;[38] we must show them and persuade them that there is something whose nature 35 is changeless. Indeed, those who say that things at the same time are and are not, should in consequence say that all things are at rest rather than that they are in movement; for there is nothing into which they can change, since all attributes belong already to all subjects.

1010ᵇ Regarding the nature of truth, we must maintain that not everything which appears is true; firstly, because even if sensation—at least of the object peculiar to the sense in question—is not false, still appearance is not the same as sensation.—Again, it is fair to express surprise at our opponents' raising the question whether magnitudes are as great, 5 and colours are of such a nature, as they appear to people at a distance, or as they appear to those close at hand, and whether they are such as they appear to the healthy or to the sick, and whether those things are heavy which appear so to the weak or those which appear so to the strong, and those things true which appear to the sleeping or to the waking. For obviously they do not think these to be open questions; 10 no one, at least, if when he is in Libya he has fancied one night that

---

36 With ll. 22–5 Cf. xi. 1063ᵃ 22–8.
37 With ll. 25–32 Cf. xi. 1063ᵃ 10–17.   38 Cf. 1009ᵃ 36–8.

he is in Athens, starts for the concert hall.—And again with regard to the future, as Plato says,[39] surely the opinion of the physician and that of the ignorant man are not equally weighty, for instance, on the question whether a man will get well or not.—And again, among sensa- tions themselves the sensation of a foreign object and that of the 15 appropriate object, or that of a kindred object and that of the object of the sense in question,[40] are not equally authoritative, but in the case of colour sight, not taste, has the authority, and in the case of flavour taste, not sight; each of which senses never says at the same time of the same object that it simultaneously is 'so and not so'.—But not even at different times does one sense disagree about the quality, but only 20 about that to which the quality belongs. I mean, for instance, that the same wine might seem, if either it or one's body changed, at one time sweet and at another time not sweet; but at least the sweet, such as it is when it exists, has never yet changed, but one is always right about 25 it, and that which is to be sweet is of necessity of such and such a nature.[41] Yet all these views destroy this necessity, leaving nothing to be of necessity, as they leave no essence of anything; for the neces- sary cannot be in this way and also in that, so that if anything is of necessity, it will not be 'both so and not so'.

And, in general, if only the sensible exists, there would be nothing 30 if animate things were not; for there would be no faculty of sense. Now the view that neither the sensible qualities nor the sensations would exist is doubtless true (for they are affections of the perceiver), but that the substrata which cause the sensation should not exist even apart from sensation is impossible. For sensation is surely not the 35 sensation of itself, but there is something beyond the sensation, which must be prior to the sensation; for that which moves is prior in nature to that which is moved, and if they are correlative terms, this is no 1011ᵃ less the case.

6   There are, both among those who have these convictions and among those who merely profess these views, some who raise a difficulty by asking, who is to be the judge of the healthy man, and in general 5 who is likely to judge rightly on each class of questions. But such inquiries are like puzzling over the question whether we are now asleep or awake. And all such questions have the same meaning. These people demand that a reason shall be given for everything;[42] for they seek a starting-point, and they seek to get this by demonstration, while it 10

---

[39] Cf. *Theaetetus* 178 B–179 A.
[40] e. g. the awareness which smell gives us of savour and of odour respectively.
[41] With ll. 1–26 Cf. xi. 1062ᵇ 33–1063ᵃ 10.
[42] The reference may be to Antisthenes.

is obvious from their actions that they have no conviction. But their mistake is what we have stated it to be; they seek a reason for things for which no reason can be given; for the starting-point of demonstration is not demonstration.

These, then, might be easily persuaded of this truth, for it is not
15 difficult to grasp; but those who seek merely compulsion in argument seek what is impossible; for they demand to be allowed to contradict themselves—a claim which contradicts itself from the very first.[43]— But if not all things are relative, but some are self-existent, not everything that appears will be true; for that which appears is apparent to some one; so that he who says all things that appear are true, makes
20 all things relative. And, therefore, those who ask for an irresistible argument, and at the same time demand to be called to account for their views, must guard themselves by saying that the truth is not that what appears exists, but that what appears exists *for him to whom* it appears, and *when*, and *to the sense to which*, and *under the conditions under which* it appears. And if they give an account of their view, but do not give it in this way, they will soon find themselves
25 contradicting themselves. For it is possible that the same thing may appear to be honey to the sight, but not to the taste, and that, since we have two eyes, things may not appear the same to each, if their sight is unlike. For to those who for the reasons named some time ago [44]
30 say that what appears is true, and therefore that all things are alike false and true, for things do not appear either the same to all men or always the same to the same man, but often have contrary appearances at the same time (for touch says there are two objects when we cross our fingers, while sight says there is one),[45]—to these we shall say 'yes,
35 but not to the same sense and in the same part of it and under the same conditions and at the same time', so that what appears will be
1011b with these qualifications true. But perhaps for this reason those who argue thus not because they feel a difficulty but for the sake of argument, should say that this is not true, but true for this man. And as has been said [46] before, they must make everything relative—relative
5 to opinion and perception, so that nothing either has come to be or will be without some one's first thinking so. But if things *have* come to be or will be,[47] evidently not all things will be relative to opinion.—Again, if a thing is one, it is in relation to one thing or to a definite number of things; and if the same thing is both half and equal, it is not to the

---

[43] With ll. 3–16 Cf. xi. 1063b 7–16.   [44] Cf. 1009a 38–1010a 15.

[45] With ll. 31–4 Cf. xi. 1062b 33–1063a 10.   [46] a 19 f.

[47] *sc.* without some one's first thinking **so.**

double that the equal is correlative.[48] If, then, in relation to that which thinks, man and that which is thought are the same, man will not be 10 that which thinks, but only that which is thought. And if each thing is to be relative to that which thinks, that which thinks will be relative to an infinity of specifically different things.

Let this, then, suffice to show (1) that the most indisputable of all beliefs is that contradictory statements are not at the same time true, and (2) what consequences follow from the assertion that they are, and (3) why people do assert this. Now since it is impossible that 15 contradictories should be at the same time true of the same thing, obviously contraries also cannot belong at the same time to the same thing. For of contraries, one is a privation no less than it is a contrary —and a privation of the essential nature; and privation is the denial of a predicate to a determinate genus. If, then, it is impossible to affirm 20 and deny truly at the same time, it is also impossible that contraries should belong to a subject at the same time, unless both belong to it in particular relations, or one in a particular relation and one without qualification.[49]

7   But on the other hand there cannot be an intermediate between contradictories, but of one subject we must either affirm or deny any one predicate. This is clear, in the first place, if we define what the true 25 and the false are. To say of what is that it is not, or of what is not that it is, is false, while to say of what is that it is, and of what is not that it is not, is true; so that he who says of anything that it is, or that it is not, will say either what is true or what is false; but neither what is nor what is not is said to be or not to be.[50]—Again, the intermediate between the contradictories will be so either in the way in which grey 30 is between black and white,[51] or as that which is neither man nor horse is between man and horse. (a) If it were of the latter kind, it could not change into the extremes (for change is from not-good to good, or from good to not-good), but as a matter of fact when there is an intermediate it is always observed to change into the extremes. For there is no change except to opposites [52] and to their intermediates. 35 (b) But if it is really intermediate,[53] in this way too there would have

---

[48] sc. but the equal to the equal, the half to the double.

[49] With ll. 17–22 Cf. xi. 1063^b 17–19.

[50] sc. by those who say there is an intermediate between contradictories. Hence such a statement is neither true nor false, which is absurd.

[51] Though of course it differs from this case in being between contradictories, not contraries.

[52] sc. contrary, not contradictory opposites.

[53] sc. as grey is between black and white.

to be a change to white, which was not from not-white; but as it is,
1012ᵃ this is never seen.—Again, every object of understanding or reason the
understanding either affirms or denies—this is obvious from the definition—whenever it says what is true or false. When it connects in
one way by assertion or negation, it says what is true, and when it does
5 so in another way, what is false.—Again, there must be an intermediate
between *all* contradictories, if one is not arguing merely for the sake
of argument; so that it will be possible for a man to say what is neither
true nor untrue, and there will be a middle between that which is and
that which is not, so that there will also be a kind of change intermediate
between generation and destruction.—Again, in all classes in which the
negation of an attribute involves the assertion of its contrary, even in
10 these there will be an intermediate; for instance, in the sphere of numbers there will be number which is neither odd nor not-odd. But this
is impossible, as is obvious from the definition.—Again, the process
will go on *ad infinitum*, and the number of realities will be not only
half as great again, but even greater. For again it will be possible to
deny this intermediate with reference both to its assertion and to its
negation,⁵⁴ and this new term will be some definite thing; for its
15 essence is something different.—Again, when a man, on being asked
whether a thing is white, says 'no', he has denied nothing except that
it is; and its not being is a negation.

Some people have acquired this opinion as other paradoxical opinions
have been acquired; when men cannot refute eristical arguments, they
20 give in to the argument and agree that the conclusion is true. This,
then, is why some express this view; others do so because they demand
a reason for everything.⁵⁵ And the starting-point in dealing with all
such people is definition. Now the definition rests on the necessity of
their meaning something; for the form of words of which the word is a
sign will be its definition.⁵⁶—While the doctrine of Heraclitus, that
25 all things are and are not, seems to make everything true, that of
Anaxagoras, that there is an intermediate between the terms of a
contradiction, seems to make everything false; for when things are
mixed, the mixture is neither good nor not-good, so that one cannot
say anything that is true.

8   In view of these distinctions it is obvious that the one-sided theories
30 which some people express about all things cannot be valid—on the
one hand the theory that nothing is true (for, say they, there is nothing

⁵⁴ i. e. if there is a term *B* which is neither *A* nor not-*A*, there will be a new
term *C* which is neither *B* nor not-*B*.
⁵⁵ The reference may be to Antisthenes.
⁵⁶ With 1011ᵇ 23–1012ᵃ 24 Cf. xi. 1063ᵇ 19–24.

to prevent every statement from being like the statement 'the diagonal of a square is commensurate with the side'), on the other hand the theory that everything is true. These views are practically the same as that of Heraclitus; for he who says that 'all things are true and all are 35 false' also makes each of these statements separately, so that since 1012ᵇ they are impossible, the double statement must be impossible too. —Again, there are obviously contradictories which cannot be at the same time true—nor on the other hand can all statements be false; yet this would *seem* more possible in the light of what has been said. —But against all such views we must postulate, as we said above,[57] 5 not that something is or is not, but that something has a meaning, so that we must argue from a definition, viz. by assuming what falsity or truth means. If that which it is true to affirm is nothing other than that which it is false to deny, it is impossible that all statements should be false; for one side of the contradiction must be true. Again, 10 if it is necessary with regard to everything either to assert or to deny it, it is impossible that both should be false; for it is *one* side of the contradiction that is false.—Therefore all such views are also exposed to the often expressed objection, that they destroy themselves. For he who says that everything is true makes even the statement con- 15 trary to his own true, and therefore his own not true (for the contrary statement denies that it is true), while he who says everything is false makes himself also false.[58]—And if the former person excepts the contrary statement, saying it alone is not true, while the latter excepts his own as being not false, none the less they are driven to postulate 20 the truth or falsity of an infinite number of statements; for that which says the true statement is true is true, and this process will go on to infinity.

Evidently, again, those who say all things are at rest are not right, nor are those who say all things are in movement. For if all things are at rest, the same statements will always be true and the same always false—but this obviously changes; for he who makes 25 a statement, himself at one time was not and again will not be. And if all things are in motion, nothing will be true; everything therefore will be false. But it has been shown that this is impossible. Again, it must be that which is that changes; for change is from something to something. But again it is not the case that all things are at rest or in motion *sometimes,* and nothing *for ever*; for there is something 30 which always moves the things that are in motion, and the first mover is itself unmoved.

---

[57] Cf. 1006ᵃ 18–22.
[58] With ᵃ 24–ᵇ 18 Cf. xi. 1063ᵇ 24–35 (with ᵇ 13–18 Cf. 1062ᵇ 7–9).

BOOK △ (*V*)

1 'Beginning' means (1) that part of a thing from which one would
35 start first, e. g. a line or a road has a beginning in either of the con-
1013ª trary directions. (2) That from which each thing would best be
originated, e. g. even in learning we must sometimes begin not from
the first point and the beginning of the subject, but from the point
from which we should learn most easily. (3) That from which, as an
immanent part, a thing first comes to be, e. g. as the keel of a ship
5 and the foundation of a house, while in animals some suppose the
heart, others the brain, others some other part, to be of this nature.
(4) That from which, *not* as an immanent part, a thing first comes
to be, and from which the movement or the change naturally first
begins, as a child comes from its father and its mother, and a fight
10 from abusive language. (5) That at whose will that which is moved
is moved and that which changes changes, e. g. the magistracies in cities,
and oligarchies and monarchies and tyrannies, are called *archai* and so
are the arts, and of these especially the architectonic arts. (6) That
15 from which a thing can first be known—this also is called the beginning of the thing, e. g. the hypotheses are the beginnings of
demonstrations. (Causes are spoken of in an equal number of
senses; for all causes are beginnings.) It is common, then, to all
beginnings to be the first point from which a thing either is or comes
to be or is known; but of these some are immanent in the thing
20 and others are outside. Hence the nature of a thing is a beginning,
and so is the element of a thing, and thought and will, and essence,
and the final cause—for the good and the beautiful are the beginning
both of the knowledge and of the movement of many things.

2 'Cause' means (1) that from which, as immanent material, a
25 thing comes into being, e. g. the bronze is the cause of the statue and
the silver of the saucer, and so are the classes which include these.
(2) The form or pattern, i. e. the definition of the essence, and the
classes which include this (e. g. the ratio 2:1 and number in general are causes of the octave), and the parts included in the definition. (3) That from which the change or the resting from change first
30 begins; e. g. the adviser is a cause of the action, and the father a
cause of the child, and in general the maker a cause of the thing
made and the change-producing of the changing. (4) The end, i. e.
that for the sake of which a thing is; e. g. health is the cause of
walking. For 'Why does one walk?' we say; 'that one may be
35 healthy'; and in speaking thus we think we have given the cause.

The same is true of all the means that intervene before the end, when something else has put the process in motion, as e. g. thinning or purging or drugs or instruments intervene before health is reached; 1013ᵇ for all these are for the sake of the end, though they differ from one another in that some are instruments and others are actions.

These, then, are practically all the senses in which causes are spoken of, and as they are spoken of in several senses it follows both that there are several causes of the same thing, and in no accidental 5 sense (e. g. both the art of sculpture and the bronze are causes of the statue not in respect of anything else but *qua* statue; not, however, in the same way, but the one as matter and the other as source of the movement), and that things can be causes of one another (e. g. exercise of good condition, and the latter of exercise; not, however, in the same way, but the one as end and the other as source of move- 10 ment).—Again, the same thing is the cause of contraries; for that which when present causes a particular thing, we sometimes charge, when absent, with the contrary, e. g. we impute the shipwreck to the absence of the steersman, whose presence was the cause of safety; and both—the presence and the privation—are causes as sources of 15 movement.

All the causes now mentioned fall under four senses which are the most obvious. For the letters are the cause of syllables, and the material is the cause of manufactured things, and fire and earth and all such things are the causes of bodies, and the parts are causes of the whole, and the hypotheses are causes of the conclusion, 20 in the sense that they are that out of which these respectively are made; but of these some are cause as the *substratum* (e. g. the parts), others as the *essence* (the whole, the synthesis, and the form). The semen, the physician, the adviser, and in general the agent, are all *sources of change* or of rest. The remainder are causes as the *end* 25 and the good of the other things; for that for the sake of which other things are tends to be the best and the end of the other things; let us take it as making no difference whether we call it good or apparent good.

These, then, are the causes, and this is the number of their kinds, but the *varieties* of causes are many in number, though when summarized these also are comparatively few. Causes are spoken of in 30 many senses, and even of those which are of the same kind some are causes in a prior and others in a posterior sense, e. g. both 'the physician' and 'the professional man' are causes of health, and both 'the ratio 2 : 1' and 'number' are causes of the octave, and the classes that include any particular cause are always causes of the particular

effect. Again, there are accidental causes and the classes which in-
35 clude these; e. g. while in one sense 'the sculptor' causes the statue,
in another sense 'Polyclitus' causes it, because the sculptor happens
1014ᵃ to be Polyclitus; and the classes that include the accidental cause
are also causes, e. g. 'man'—or in general 'animal'—is the cause of the
statue, because Polyclitus is a man, and man is an animal. Of acci-
5 dental causes also some are more remote or nearer than others, as,
for instance, if 'the white' and 'the musical' were called causes of
the statue, and not only 'Polyclitus' or 'man'. But besides all these
varieties of causes, whether proper or accidental, some are called
causes as being able to act, others as acting; e. g. the cause of the
house's being built is a builder, or a builder who is building.—
10 The same variety of language will be found with regard to the
effects of causes; e. g. a thing may be called the cause of this statue
or of a statue or in general of an image, and of this bronze or of
bronze or of matter in general; and similarly in the case of accidental
effects. Again, both accidental and proper causes may be spoken of in
combination; e. g. we may say not 'Polyclitus' nor 'the sculptor', but
'Polyclitus the sculptor'.
15   Yet all these are but six in number, while each is spoken of in two
ways; for (A) they are causes either as the individual, or as the
genus, or as the accidental, or as the genus that includes the accidental, and these either as combined, or as taken simply; and (B)
20 all may be taken as acting or as having a capacity. But they differ
inasmuch as the acting causes, i. e. the individuals, exist, or do not
exist, simultaneously with the things of which they are causes, e. g.
this particular man who is healing, with this particular man who is
recovering health, and this particular builder with this particular
thing that is being built; but the potential causes are not always in
25 this case; for the house does not perish at the same time as the
builder.

3   'Element' means (1) the primary component immanent in a thing,
and indivisible in kind into other kinds; e. g. the elements of speech
are the parts of which speech consists and into which it is ultimately
divided, while *they* are no longer divided into other forms of speech dif-
30 ferent in kind from them. If they *are* divided, their parts are of the same
kind, as a part of water is water (while a part of the syllable is not
a syllable). Similarly those who speak of the elements of bodies mean
the things into which bodies are ultimately divided, while *they* are no
longer divided into other things differing in kind; and whether the
35 things of this sort are one or more, they call these elements. The so-

called elements of geometrical proofs, and in general the elements of demonstrations, have a similar character; for the primary demonstrations, each of which is implied in many demonstrations, are called 1014ᵇ elements of demonstrations; and the primary syllogisms, which have three terms and proceed by means of one middle, are of this nature. (2) People also transfer the word 'element' from this meaning and apply it to that which, being one and small, is useful for many purposes; for which reason what is small and simple and indivisible 5 is called an element. Hence come the facts that the most universal things are elements (because each of them being one and simple is present in a plurality of things, either in all or in as many as possible), and that unity and the point are thought by some to be first principles. Now, since the so-called genera are universal and indivisible (for there is no definition of them), some say the genera are 10 elements, and more so than the differentia, because the genus is more universal; for where the differentia is present, the genus accompanies it, but where the genus is present, the differentia is not always so. It is common to all the meanings that the element of each thing is 15 the first component immanent in each.

4 'Nature' means (1) the genesis of growing things—the meaning which would be suggested if one were to pronounce the *y* in *physis* long.[1] (2) That immanent part of a growing thing, from which its growth first proceeds. (3) The source from which the primary movement in each natural object is present in it in virtue of its own 20 essence. Those things are said to grow which derive increase from something else by contact and either by organic unity, or by organic adhesion as in the case of embryos. Organic unity differs from contact; for in the latter case there need not be anything besides the contact, but in organic unities there is something identical in both parts, which makes them grow together instead of merely touching, and 25 be one in respect of continuity and quantity, though not of quality. —(4) 'Nature' means the primary material of which any natural object consists or out of which it is made, which is relatively unshaped and cannot be changed from its own potency, as e. g. bronze is said to be the nature of a statue and of bronze utensils, and wood the nature of wooden things; and so in all other cases; for when a 30 product is made out of these materials, the first matter is preserved throughout. For it is in this way that people call the elements of

---

[1] This (i. e. 'growth') is the etymological sense of *physis. Phuesthai,* 'to grow', has *u* long in most of its forms.

natural objects also their nature, some naming fire, others earth, others air, others water, others something else of the sort, and some
35 naming more than one of these, and others all of them.—(5) 'Nature' means the *essence* of natural objects, as with those who say the nature is the primary mode of composition, or as Empedocles says:—

1015ª

> Nothing that is has a nature,
> But only mixing and parting of the mixed,
> And nature is but a name given them by men.

Hence as regards the things that are or come to be by nature, though that *from which* they naturally come to be or are is already present, we say they have not their nature yet, unless they have
5 their form or shape. That which comprises both of these[2] exists *by* nature, e. g. the animals and their parts; and not only is the first matter nature (and this in two senses, either the first, counting from the thing, or the first in general; e. g. in the case of works in bronze, bronze is first with reference to them, but in general perhaps water is first, if all things that can be melted are water), but also the
10 form or essence, which is the end of the process of becoming.—(6) By an extension of meaning from this sense of 'nature' every essence in general has come to be called a 'nature', because the nature of a thing is one kind of essence.

From what has been said, then, it is plain that nature in the primary and strict sense is the essence of things which have in themselves, as
15 such, a source of movement; for the matter is called the nature because it is qualified to receive this, and processes of becoming and growing are called nature because they are movements proceeding from this. And nature in this sense is the source of the movement of natural objects, being present in them somehow, either potentially or in complete reality.

20 **5** We call 'necessary' (1) (*a*) that without which, as a condition, a thing cannot live; e. g. breathing and food are necessary for an animal; for it is incapable of existing without these; (*b*) the conditions without which good cannot be or come to be, or without which we cannot get rid or be freed of evil; e. g. drinking the medicine is necessary in
25 order that we may be cured of disease, and a man's sailing to Aegina is necessary in order that he may get his money.—(2) The compulsory and compulsion, i. e. that which impedes and tends to hinder, contrary

---

[2] Matter and form.

to impulse and purpose. For the compulsory is called necessary (whence the necessary is painful, as Evenus says: 'For every necessary thing is ever irksome'), and compulsion is a form of necessity, as Sophocles 30 says: 'But force necessitates me to this act.' And necessity is held to be something that cannot be persuaded—and rightly, for it is contrary to the movement which accords with purpose and with reasoning.—(3) We say that that which cannot be otherwise is necessarily as it is. And from this sense of 'necessary' all the others are somehow derived; for 35 a thing is said to do or suffer what is necessary in the sense of compulsory, only when it cannot act according to its impulse because of 1015ᵇ the compelling force—which implies that necessity is that because of which a thing cannot be otherwise; and similarly as regards the conditions of life and of good; for when in the one case good, in the other life and being, are not possible without certain conditions, these are 5 necessary, and this kind of cause is a sort of necessity. Again, demonstration is a necessary thing because the conclusion cannot be otherwise, if there has been demonstration in the unqualified sense; and the causes of this necessity are the first premisses, i. e. the fact that the propositions from which the syllogism proceeds cannot be otherwise.

Now some things owe their necessity to something other than themselves; others do not, but are themselves the source of necessity in 10 other things. Therefore the necessary in the primary and strict sense is the simple; for this does not admit of more states than one, so that it cannot even be in one state and also in another; for if it did it would already be in more than one. If, then, there are any things that are eternal and unmovable, nothing compulsory or against their nature 15 attaches to them.

6 'One' means (1) that which is one by accident, (2) that which is one by its own nature. (1) Instances of the accidentally one are 'Coriscus and what is musical', and 'musical Coriscus' (for it is the same thing to say 'Coriscus and what is musical', and 'musical Coriscus'); and 'what is musical and what is just', and 'musical Coriscus and just Coriscus'. For all of these are called one by virtue of an accident, 'what 20 is just and what is musical' because they are accidents of one substance, 'what is musical and Coriscus' because the one is an accident of the other; and similarly in a sense 'musical Coriscus' is one with 'Coriscus' because one of the parts of the phrase is an accident of the other, i. e. 25 'musical' is an accident of Coriscus; and 'musical Coriscus' is one with 'just Coriscus' because one part of each is an accident of one and the same subject. The case is similar if the accident is predicated of a genus or of any universal name, e. g. if one says that man is the same as 30

'musical man'; for this is either because 'musical' is an accident of man, which is one substance, or because both are accidents of some individual, e. g. Coriscus. Both, however, do not belong to him in the same way, but one presumably as genus and included in his substance, the other as a state or affection of the substance.

35 The things, then, that are called one in virtue of an accident, are called so in this way. (2) Of things that are called one in virtue of their own nature some (a) are so called because they are continuous, 1016ᵃ e. g. a bundle is made one by a band, and pieces of wood are made one by glue; and a line, even if it is bent, is called one if it is continuous, as each part of the body is, e. g. the leg or the arm. Of these themselves, the continuous by nature are more one than the continuous 5 by art. A thing is called continuous which has by its own nature one movement and cannot have any other; and the movement is one when it is indivisible, and it is indivisible in respect of time. Those things are continuous by their own nature which are one not merely by contact; for if you put pieces of wood touching one another, you will not say these are one piece of wood or one body or one *continuum* of any other sort. Things, then, that are continuous in any way are called one, 10 even if they admit of being bent, and still more those which cannot be bent; e. g. the shin or the thigh is more one than the leg, because the movement of the leg need not be one. And the straight line is more one than the bent; but that which is bent and has an angle we call both one and not one, because its movement may be either simultaneous 15 or not simultaneous; but that of the straight line is always simultaneous, and no part of it which has magnitude rests while another moves, as in the bent line.

(*b*) (i) Things are called one in another sense because their substratum does not differ in kind; it does not differ in the case of things whose kind is indivisible to sense. The substratum meant is either the 20 nearest to, or the farthest from, the final state. For, on the one hand, wine is said to be one and water is said to be one, *qua* indivisible in kind; and, on the other hand, *all* juices, e. g. oil and wine, are said to be one, and so are all things that can be melted, because the ultimate substratum of all is the same; for all of these are water or air.

(ii) Those things also are called one whose genus is one though 25 distinguished by opposite differentiae—these too are all called one because the genus which underlies the differentiae is one (e. g. horse, man, and dog form a unity, because all are animals), and indeed in a way similar to that in which the matter is one. These are sometimes called one in this way, but sometimes it is the higher genus that is said to be the same (if they are *infimae species* of their genus)—the genus above the proximate genera; e. g. the isosceles and the equilateral are ³⁰ one and the same *figure* because both are triangles; but they are not the same triangles.

(*c*) Two things are called one, when the definition which states the essence of one is indivisible from another definition which shows us the other (though *in itself* every definition is divisible). Thus even that ³⁵ which has increased or is diminishing is one, because its definition is one, as, in the case of plane figures, is the definition of their form. In 1016ᵇ general those things the thought of whose essence is indivisible, and cannot separate them either in time or in place or in definition, are most of all one, and of these especially those which are substances. For in general those things that do not admit of division are called one in so far as they do not admit of it; e. g. if two things are indistinguish- ⁵ able *qua* man, they are one kind of man; if *qua* animal, one kind of animal; if *qua* magnitude, one kind of magnitude.—Now most things are called one because they either do or have or suffer or are related to something else that is one, but the things that are primarily called one are those whose substance is one—and one either in continuity or in form or in definition; for we count as more than one either things that are not continuous, or those whose form is not one, or those whose ¹⁰ definition is not one.

While in a sense we call anything one if it is a quantity and continuous, in a sense we do not unless it is a whole, i. e. unless it has unity of form; e. g. if we saw the parts of a shoe put together anyhow we should not call them one all the same (unless because of their ¹⁵ continuity); we do this only if they are put together so as to be a shoe and to have already a certain single form. This is why the circle is of all lines most truly one, because it is whole and complete.

(3) The *essence* of what is one is to be some kind of beginning of number; for the first measure is the beginning, since that by which we first know each class is the first measure of the class; the one, then, ²⁰ is the beginning of the knowable regarding each class. But the one is not the same in all classes. For here it is a quarter-tone, and there it is the vowel or the consonant; and there is another unit of weight and another of movement. But everywhere the one is indivisible either in quantity or in kind. Now that which is indivisible in quantity is called ²⁵ a unit if it is not divisible in any dimension and is without position, a point if it is not divisible in any dimension, and has position, a line if it is divisible in one dimension, a plane if in two, a body if divisible in quantity in all—i. e. in three—dimensions. And, reversing the order, that which is divisible in two dimensions is a plane, that which is divisible in one a line, that which is in no way divisible in quantity is a ³⁰

point or a unit—that which has not position a unit, that which has position a point.

Again, some things are one in number, others in species, others in genus, others by analogy; in number those whose matter is one, in species those whose definition is one, in genus those to which the same figure of predication applies,³ by analogy those which are related as 35 a third thing is to a fourth. The latter kinds of unity are always found when the former are; e. g. things that are one in number are also one in species, while things that are one in species are not all one in num-1017ᵃ ber; but things that are one in species are all one in genus, while things that are so in genus are not all one in species but are all one by analogy; while things that are one by analogy are not all one in genus.

Evidently 'many' will have meanings opposite to those of 'one'; some things are many because they are not continuous, others because 5 their matter—either the proximate matter or the ultimate—is divisible in kind, others because the definitions which state their essence are more than one.

7   Things are said to 'be' (1) in an accidental sense, (2) by their own nature.

(1) In an accidental sense, e. g., we say 'the righteous doer is musical', and 'the man is musical', and 'the musician is a man', just 10 as we say 'the musician builds', because the builder happens to be musical or the musician to be a builder; for here 'one thing is another' means 'one is an accident of another'. So in the cases we have mentioned; for when we say 'the man is musical' and 'the musician is a 15 man', or 'he who is pale is musical' or 'the musician is pale', the last two mean that both attributes are accidents of the same thing; the first that the attribute is an accident of that which *is*; while 'the musical is a man' means that 'musical' is an accident of a man. (In this sense, too, the not-pale is said to *be*, because that of which it is an accident *is*.) Thus when one thing is said in an accidental sense to be 20 another, this is either because both belong to the same thing, and this *is*, or because that to which the attribute belongs *is*, or because the subject which has as an attribute that of which it is itself predicated, itself *is*.

(2) The kinds of essential being are precisely those that are indicated by the figures of predication;⁴ for the senses of 'being' are just 25 as many as these figures. Since, then, some predicates indicate what the subject is, others its quality, others quantity, others relation, others

---

³ *sc.* the same category.   ⁴ i. e. the categories.

activity or passivity, others its 'where', others its 'when', 'being' has a meaning answering to each of these. For there is no difference between 'the man is recovering' and 'the man recovers', nor between 'the man is walking' or 'cutting' and 'the man walks' or 'cuts'; and similarly in all other cases.

(3) Again, 'being' and 'is' mean that a statement is true, 'not being' that it is not true but false—and this alike in the case of affirmation and of negation; e. g. 'Socrates *is* 'musical' means that this is true, or 'Socrates *is* not-pale' means that this is true; but 'the diagonal of the square *is not* commensurate with the side' means that it is false to say it is.

(4) Again, 'being' and 'that which is' mean that some of the things we have mentioned 'are' potentially, others in complete reality. For we say both of that which sees potentially and of that which sees actually, that it is 'seeing', and both of that which can actualize its knowledge and of that which is actualizing it, that it knows, and both of that to which rest is already present and of that which can rest, that it rests. And similarly in the case of substances; we say the Hermes is in the stone, and the half of the line is in the line, and we say of that which is not yet ripe that it is corn. *When* a thing is potential and when it is not yet potential must be explained elsewhere.[5]

8   We call 'substance' (1) the simple bodies, i. e. earth and fire and water and everything of the sort, and in general bodies and the things composed of them, both animals and divine beings, and the parts of these. All these are called substance because they are not predicated of a subject but everything else is predicated of them.—(2) That which, being present in such things as are not predicated of a subject, is the cause of their being, as the soul is of the being of an animal.—(3) The parts which are present in such things, limiting them and marking them as individuals, and by whose destruction the whole is destroyed, as the body is by the destruction of the plane, as some [6] say, and the plane by the destruction of the line; and in general number is thought by some [6] to be of this nature; for if it is destroyed, they say, nothing exists, and it limits all things.—(4) The essence, the formula of which is a definition, is also called the substance of each thing.

It follows, then, that 'substance' has two senses, (A) the ultimate substratum, which is no longer predicated of anything else, and (B) that which, being a 'this', is also separable [7]—and of this nature is the shape or form of each thing.

---

[5] ix. 7.   [6] The Pythagoreans and Plato.   [7] Cf. viii. 1042ᵃ 29.

9 'The same' means (1) that which is the same in an accidental sense, e. g. 'the pale' and 'the musical' are the same because they are accidents of the same thing, and 'a man' and 'musical' because the one is an accident of the other; and 'the musical' is 'a man' because it is
30 an accident of the man. (The complex entity is the same as either of the simple ones and each of these is the same as it; for both 'the man' and 'the musical' are said to be the same as 'the musical man', and this the same as they.) This is why all of these statements are made
35 not universally; for it is not true to say that *every* man is the same as 'the musical' (for universal attributes belong to things in virtue of their own nature, but accidents do not belong to them in virtue of their
1018ᵃ own nature); but of the individuals the statements are made without qualification. For 'Socrates' and 'musical Socrates' are thought to be the same; but 'Socrates' is not predicable of more than one subject, and therefore we do not say 'every Socrates' as we say 'every man'.

Some things are said to be the same in this sense, others (2) are the
5 same by their own nature, in as many senses as that which is one by its own nature is so; for both the things whose matter is one either in kind or in number, and those whose essence is one, are said to be the same. Clearly, therefore, sameness is a unity of the being either of more than one thing or of one thing when it is treated as more than one, i. e. when we say a thing is the same as itself; for we treat it as two.
10 Things are called 'other' if either their kinds or their matters or the definitions of their essence are more than one; and in general 'other' has meanings opposite to those of 'the same'.

'Different' is applied (1) to those things which though other are the same in some respect, only not in number but either in species or in genus or by analogy; (2) to those whose genus is other, and to contraries, and to all things that have their otherness in their essence.
15 Those things are called 'like' which have the same attributes in every respect, and those which have more attributes the same than different, and those whose quality is one; and that which shares with another thing the greater number or the more important of the attributes (each of them one of two contraries) in respect of which things are capable of altering, is like that other thing.[8] The senses of 'unlike' are opposite to those of 'like'.

20 10 The term 'opposite' is applied to contradictories, and to contraries, and to relative terms, and to privation and possession, and to the ex-

---

[8] Such attributes are hot and cold, wet and dry, rough and smooth, hard and soft, white and black, sweet and bitter. The more important pairs of contraries, in Aristotle's view, are the first two.

tremes from which and into which generation and dissolution take place; and the attributes that cannot be present at the same time in that which is receptive of both, are said to be opposed—either themselves or their constituents. Grey and white colour do not belong at the same time to the same thing; hence their constituents are opposed.[9]

The term 'contrary' is applied (1) to those attributes differing in 25 genus which cannot belong at the same time to the same subject, (2) to the most different of the things in the same genus, (3) to the most different of the attributes in the same recipient subject, (4) to the most different of the things that fall under the same faculty, (5) to the 30 things whose difference is greatest either absolutely or in genus or in species. The other things that are called contrary are so called, some because they possess contraries of the above kind, some because they are receptive of such, some because they are productive of or susceptible to such, or are producing or suffering them, or are losses or acquisitions, or possessions or privations, of such. Since 'one' and 'being' have 35 many senses, the other terms which are derived from these, and therefore 'same', 'other', and 'contrary', must correspond, so that they must be different for each category.

The term 'other in species' is applied to things which being of the same genus are not subordinate the one to the other, or which being in the same genus have a difference,[10] or which have a contrariety in 1018^{b} their substance; and contraries are other than one another in species (either all contraries or those which are so called in the primary sense [11]), and so are those things whose definitions differ in the *infima species* of the genus (e. g. man and horse are indivisible in genus but 5 their definitions are different), and those which being in the same substance have a difference. 'The same in species' has the various meanings opposite to these.

11   The words 'prior' and 'posterior' are applied (1) to some things (on the assumption that there is a first, i. e. a beginning, in each class) because they are nearer some beginning determined either absolutely 10 and by nature, or by reference to something or in some place or by certain people; e. g. things are prior in place because they are nearer either to some place determined by nature (e. g. the middle or the last place), or to some chance object; and that which is farther is posterior.

---

[9] We cannot say grey and white are opposites, but we say the constituents of grey (black and white) are opposites.

[10] This definition is wider than the previous one, since it includes species subordinate one to the other.

[11] Cf. ^{a} 25–31 in distinction from 31–35.

15 —Other things are prior in time; some by being farther from the present, i. e. in the case of past events (for the Trojan war is prior to the Persian, because it is farther from the present), others by being nearer the present, i. e. in the case of future events (for the Nemean games are prior to the Pythian, if we treat the present as beginning and first point, because they are nearer the present).—Other things are prior

20 in movement; for that which is nearer the first mover is prior (e. g. the boy is prior to the man); and the prime mover also is a beginning absolutely.—Others are prior in power; for that which exceeds in power, i. e. the more powerful, is prior; and such is that according to whose will the other—i. e. the posterior—must follow, so that if the prior does not set it in motion the other does not move, and if it sets

25 it in motion it does move; and here will is a beginning.—Others are prior in arrangement; these are the things that are placed at intervals in reference to some one definite thing according to some rule, e. g. in the chorus the second man is prior to the third, and in the lyre the second lowest string is prior to the lowest; for in the one case the leader and in the other the middle string is the beginning.

30 These, then, are called prior in this sense, but (2) in another sense that which is prior for knowledge is treated as also absolutely prior; of these, the things that are prior in definition do not coincide with those that are prior in relation to perception. For in definition universals are prior, in relation to perception individuals. And in definition also the accident is prior to the whole, e. g. 'musical' to 'musical man',

35 for the definition cannot exist as a whole without the part; yet musicalness cannot exist unless there is some one who is musical.

(3) The attributes of prior things are called prior, e. g. straightness is prior to smoothness; for one is an attribute of a line as such, and the other of a surface.

1019ª Some things then are called prior and posterior in this sense, others (4) in respect of nature and substance, i. e. those which can be without other things, while the others cannot be without *them*—a distinction

5 which Plato used. (If we consider the various senses of 'being', firstly the subject is prior, so that substance is prior; secondly, according as potency or complete reality is taken into account, different things are prior, for some things are prior in respect of potency, others in respect of complete reality, e. g. in potency the half line is prior to the whole line, and the part to the whole, and the matter to the concrete substance, but in complete reality these are posterior; for it is only when

10 the whole has been dissolved that they will exist in complete reality.) In a sense, therefore, all things that are called prior and posterior are so called with reference to this fourth sense; for some things can exist

without others in respect of generation, e. g. the whole without the
parts, and others in respect of dissolution, e. g. the part without the
whole. And the same is true in all other cases.

12 'Potency' means (1) a source of movement or change, which is 15
in another thing than the thing moved or in the same thing *qua* other;
e. g. the art of building is a potency which is not in the thing built,
while the art of healing, which is a potency, may be in the man healed,
but not in him *qua* healed. 'Potency' then means the source, in general,
of change or movement in another thing or in the same thing *qua*
other, and also (2) the source of a thing's being moved by another 20
thing or by itself *qua* other. For in virtue of that principle, in virtue
of which a patient suffers anything, we call it 'capable' of suffering;
and this we do sometimes if it suffers anything at all, sometimes not
in respect of everything it suffers, but only if it suffers a change for
the better.—(3) The capacity of performing this well or according to
intention; for sometimes we say of those who merely can walk or
speak but not well or not as they intend, that they cannot speak or 25
walk. So too (4) in the case of passivity.—(5) The states in virtue of
which things are absolutely impassive or unchangeable, or not easily
changed for the worse, are called potencies; for things are broken and
crushed and bent and in general destroyed not by having a potency 30
but by not having one and by lacking something, and things are impassive with respect to such processes if they are scarcely and slightly
affected by them, because of a 'potency' and because they 'can' do
something and are in some positive state.

  'Potency' having this variety of meanings, so too the 'potent' or
'capable' in one sense will mean that which can begin a movement (or
a change in general, for even that which can bring things to rest is a
'potent' thing) in another thing or in itself *qua* other; and in one sense 35
that over which something else has such a potency; and in one sense 1019^b
that which has a potency of changing into something, whether for the
worse or for the better (for even that which perishes is thought to be
'capable' of perishing, for it would not have perished if it had not been
capable of it; but, as a matter of fact, it has a certain disposition and
cause and principle which fits it to suffer this; sometimes it is thought 5
to be of this sort because it has something, sometimes because it is
deprived of something; but if privation is in a sense 'having' or 'habit',
everything will be capable by having something, so that things are
capable both by having a positive habit and principle, and by having
the privation of this, if it is possible to *have* a privation; and if privation is *not* in a sense 'habit', 'capable' is used in two distinct senses); 10

and a thing is capable in another sense because neither any other thing, nor itself *qua* other, has a potency or principle which can destroy it. Again, all of these are capable either merely because the thing might chance to happen or not to happen, or because it might do so *well*. This sort of potency is found even in lifeless things, e. g. in instruments; for we say one lyre can speak, and another cannot speak at all, if it has not a good tone.

15   Incapacity is privation of capacity—i. e. of such a principle as has been described—either in general or in the case of something that would naturally have the capacity, or even at the time when it would naturally already have it; for the senses in which we should call a boy and a man and a eunuch 'incapable of begetting' are distinct.—Again, to either kind of capacity there is an opposite incapacity—both to that 20 which only *can* produce movement and to that which can produce it well.

Some things, then, are called *adunata* in virtue of this kind of incapacity, while others are so in another sense; i. e. both *dunaton* and *adunaton* are used as follows. The impossible is that of which the contrary is of necessity true, e. g. that the diagonal of a square is com-25 mensurate with the side is impossible, because such a statement is a falsity of which the contrary is not only true but also necessary; that it is commensurate, then, is not only false but also of necessity false. The contrary of this, the possible, is found when it is not necessary that the contrary is false, e. g. that a man should be seated is possible; 30 for that he is not seated is not of necessity false. The possible, then, in one sense, as has been said, means that which is not of necessity false; in one, that which is true; in one, that which may be true.—A 'potency' or 'power' [12] in geometry is so called by a change of meaning. 35 —These senses of 'capable' or 'possible' involve no reference to potency. But the senses which involve a reference to potency all refer to the 1020ᵃ primary kind of potency; and this is a source of change in another thing or in the same thing *qua* other. For other things are called 'capable', some because something else has such a potency over them, some because it has not, some because it has it in a particular way. The same is true of the things that are incapable. Therefore the proper definition 5 of the primary kind of potency will be 'a source of change in another thing or in the same thing *qua* other'.

13   'Quantum' means that which is divisible into two or more constituent parts of which each is by nature a 'one' and a 'this'. A quan-10 tum is a plurality if it is numerable, a magnitude if it is measurable.

---

[12] The reference is to squares and cubes.

'Plurality' means that which is divisible potentially into non-continu-
ous parts, 'magnitude' that which is divisible into continuous parts;
of magnitude, that which is continuous in one dimension is length, in
two breadth, in three depth. Of these, limited plurality is number, limited length is a line, breadth a surface, depth a solid.

Again, some things are called quanta in virtue of their own nature,
others incidentally; e. g. the line is a quantum by its own nature, the 15
musical is one incidentally. Of the things that are quanta by their own
nature some are so as substances, e. g. the line is a quantum (for 'a
certain kind of quantum' is present in the definition which states what
it is), and others are modifications and states of this kind of substance,
e. g. much and little, long and short, broad and narrow, deep and 20
shallow, heavy and light, and all other such attributes. And also great
and small, and greater and smaller, both in themselves and when taken
relatively to each other, are by their own nature attributes of what is
quantitative; but these names are transferred to other things also. Of 25
things that are quanta incidentally, some are so called in the sense
in which it was said that the musical and the white were quanta, viz.
because that to which musicalness and whiteness belong is a quantum,
and some are quanta in the way in which movement and time are so;
for these also are called quanta of a sort and continuous because the 30
things of which these are attributes are divisible. I mean not that which
is moved, but the space through which it is moved; for because that
is a quantum movement also is a quantum, and because this is a
quantum time is one.

14 'Quality' means (1) the differentia of the essence, e. g. man is an
animal of a certain quality because he is two-footed, and the horse is
so because it is four-footed; and a circle is a figure of particular quality 35
because it is without angles—which shows that the essential differentia 1020ᵇ
is a quality.—This, then, is one meaning of quality—the differentia of
the essence, but (2) there is another sense in which it applies to the
unmovable objects of mathematics, the sense in which the numbers
have a certain quality, e. g. the composite numbers which are not in
one dimension only, but of which the plane and the solid are copies 5
(these are those which have two or three factors); and in general that
which exists in the essence of numbers besides quantity is quality; for
the essence of each is what it is once, e. g. that of 6 is not what it is
twice or thrice, but what it is once; for 6 is once 6.

(3) All the modifications of substances that move (e. g. heat and
cold, whiteness and blackness, heaviness and lightness, and the others 10
of the sort) in virtue of which, when they change, bodies are said to

alter. (4) Quality in respect of virtue and vice and, in general, of evil and good.

Quality, then, seems to have practically two meanings, and one of these is the more proper. The primary quality is the differentia of the essence, and of this the quality in numbers is a part; for it is a differentia of essences, but either not of things that move or not of them *qua* moving. Secondly, there are the modifications of things that move, *qua* moving, and the differentiae of movements. Virtue and vice fall among these modifications; for they indicate differentiae of the movement or activity, according to which the things in motion act or are acted on well or badly; for that which can be moved or act in one way is good, and that which can do so in another—the contrary—way is vicious. Good and evil indicate quality especially in living things, and among these especially in those which have purpose.

15 Things are 'relative' (1) as double to half, and treble to a third, and in general that which contains something else many times to that which is contained many times in something else, and that which exceeds to that which is exceeded; (2) as that which can heat to that which can be heated, and that which can cut to that which can be cut, and in general the active to the passive; (3) as the measurable to the measure, and the knowable to knowledge, and the perceptible to perception.

(1) Relative terms of the first kind are numerically related either indefinitely or definitely, to numbers themselves or to 1. E. g. the double is in a definite numerical relation to 1, and that which is 'many times as great' is in a numerical, but not a definite, relation to 1, i. e. not in this or in that numerical relation to it; the relation of that which is half as big again as something else to that something is a definite numerical relation to a number; that which is $\dfrac{n+1}{n}$ times something else is in an indefinite relation to that something, as that which is 'many times as great' is in an indefinite relation to 1; the relation of that which exceeds to that which is exceeded is numerically quite indefinite; for number is always commensurate, and 'number' is not predicated of that which is not commensurate, but that which exceeds is, in relation to that which is exceeded, so much and something more; and this something is indefinite; for it can, indifferently, be either equal or not equal to that which is exceeded.—All these relations, then, are numerically expressed and are determinations of number, and so in another way are the equal and the like and the same. For all refer to unity. Those

things are the same whose substance is one; those are like whose quality is one; those are equal whose quantity is one; and 1 is the beginning and measure of number, so that all these relations imply number, though not in the same way.

(2) Things that are active or passive imply an active or a passive potency and the actualizations of the potencies; e. g. that which is capable of heating is related to that which is capable of being heated, because it *can* heat it, and, again, that which heats is related to that which is heated and that which cuts to that which is cut, in the sense that they actually do these things. But *numerical* relations are not actualized except in the sense which has been elsewhere stated; actualizations in the sense of movement they have not. Of relations which imply potency some further imply particular periods of time, e. g. that which has made is relative to that which has been made, and that which will make to that which will be made. For it is in this way that a father is called the father of his son; for the one has acted and the other has been acted on in a certain way. Further, some relative terms imply *privation* of potency, i. e. 'incapable' and terms of this sort, e. g. 'invisible'.

Relative terms which imply number or potency, therefore, are all relative because their very essence includes in its nature a reference to something else, not because something else involves a reference to *it*; but (3) that which is measurable or knowable or thinkable is called relative because something else involves a reference to it. For 'that which is thinkable' implies that the thought of it is possible, but the thought is not relative to 'that of which it is the thought'; for we should then have said the same thing twice. Similarly sight is the sight of something, not 'of that of which it is the sight' (though of course it is true to say this); in fact it is relative to colour or to something else of the sort. But according to the other way of speaking the same thing would be said twice—'the sight is of that of which it is.'

Things that are by their own nature called relative are called so sometimes in these senses, sometimes if the classes that include them are of this sort; e. g. medicine is a relative term because its genus, science, is thought to be a relative term. Further, there are the properties in virtue of which the things that have them are called relative, e. g. equality is relative because the equal is, and likeness because the like is. Other things are relative by accident; e. g. a man is relative because he happens to be double of something and double is a relative term; or the white is relative, if the same thing happens to be double and white.

16   What is called 'complete' is (1) that outside which it is not possible to find any, even one, of its parts; e. g. the complete time of each thing is that outside which it is not possible to find any time which is
15 a part proper to it.—(2) That which in respect of excellence and goodness cannot be excelled in its kind; e. g. we have a complete doctor or a complete flute-player, when they lack nothing in respect of the form of their proper excellence. And thus, transferring the word to bad things, we speak of a complete scandal-monger and a complete thief;
20 indeed we even call them *good*, i. e. a good thief and a good scandal-monger. And excellence is a completion; for each thing is complete and every substance is complete, when in respect of the form of its proper excellence it lacks no part of its natural magnitude.—(3) The things which have attained their end, this being good, are called complete; for
25 things are complete in virtue of having attained their end. Therefore, since the end is something ultimate, we transfer the word to bad things and say a thing has been completely spoilt, and completely destroyed, when it in no wise falls short of destruction and badness, but is at its last point. This is why death, too, is by a figure of speech called the end, because both are last things. But the ultimate purpose is also an
30 end.—Things, then, that are called complete in virtue of their *own* nature are so called in all these senses, some because in respect of goodness they lack nothing and cannot be excelled and no part proper to them can be found outside them, others in general because they cannot be exceeded in their several classes and no part proper to them is outside
1022ª them; the *others* presuppose these first two kinds, and are called complete because they either make or have something of the sort or are adapted to it or in some way or other involve a reference to the things that are called complete in the primary sense.

17   'Limit' means (1) the last point of each thing, i. e. the first point beyond which it is not possible to find any part, and the first point
5 within which every part is; (2) the form, whatever it may be, of a spatial magnitude or of a thing that has magnitude; (3) the end of each thing (and of this nature is that towards which the movement and the action are, not that from which they are—though sometimes it is both, that from which and that to which the movement is, i. e. the final cause); (4) the substance of each thing, and the essence of each; for
10 this is the limit of knowledge; and if of knowledge, of the object also. Evidently, therefore, 'limit' has as many senses as 'beginning', and yet more; for the beginning is a limit, but not every limit is a beginning.

18 'That in virtue of which' has several meanings:—(1) the form
or substance of each thing, e. g. that in virtue of which a man is good 15
is the good itself, (2) the proximate subject in which it is the nature
of an attribute to be found, e. g. colour in a surface. 'That in virtue of
which', then, in the primary sense is the form, and in a secondary sense
the matter of each thing and the proximate substratum of each.—In
general 'that in virtue of which' will be found in the same number of
senses as 'cause'; for we say indifferently (3) 'in virtue of what has 20
he come?' or 'for what end has he come?'; and (4) 'in virtue of what
has he inferred wrongly, or inferred?' or 'what is the cause of the inference, or of the wrong inference?'—Further (5) *kath'ho* is used in
reference to position, e. g. 'at which he stands' or 'along which he
walks'; for all such phrases indicate place and position.

Therefore 'in virtue of itself' must likewise have several meanings.
The following belong to a thing in virtue of itself:—(1) the essence 25
of each thing, e. g. Callias is in virtue of himself Callias and what it
was to be Callias; (2) whatever is present in the 'what', e. g. Callias
is in virtue of himself an animal. For 'animal' is present in his definition; Callias is a particular animal.—(3) Whatever attribute a
thing receives in itself directly or in one of its parts; e. g. a surface
is white in virtue of itself, and a man is alive in virtue of himself; 30
for the soul, in which life directly resides, is a part of the man.—
(4) That which has no cause other than itself; man has more than
one cause—animal, two-footed—but yet man is man in virtue of
himself.—(5) Whatever attributes belong to a thing alone, and in so 35
far as they belong to it merely by virtue of itself considered apart by
itself.

19 'Disposition' means the arrangement of that which has parts, in 1022ᵇ
respect either of place or of potency or of kind; for there must be a
certain position, as even the *word* 'disposition' shows.

20 'Having' means (1) a kind of activity of the haver and of what
he has—something like an action or movement. For when one thing
makes and one is made, between them there is a making; so too 5
between him who has a garment and the garment which he has there
is a having. This sort of having, then, evidently we cannot *have*; for
the process will go on to infinity, if it is to be possible to have the
having of what we have.—(2) 'Having' or 'habit' means a disposition 10
according to which that which is disposed is either well or ill disposed,
and either in itself or with reference to something else; e. g. health

is a 'habit'; for it is such a disposition.—(3) We speak of a 'habit' if there is a portion of such a disposition; and so even the excellence of the parts is a 'habit' of the whole thing.

15 **21** 'Affection' means (1) a quality in respect of which a thing can be altered, e. g. white and black, sweet and bitter, heaviness and lightness, and all others of the kind.—(2) The actualization of these —the already accomplished alterations.—(3) Especially, injurious 20 alterations and movements, and, above all, painful injuries.—(4) Misfortunes and painful experiences when on a large scale are called affections.

22 We speak of 'privation' (1) if something has not one of the attributes which a thing might naturally have, even if this thing itself would not naturally have it; e. g. a plant is said to be 'deprived' of eyes.—(2) If, though either the thing itself or its genus would natu- 25 rally have an attribute, it has it not; e. g. a blind man and a mole are in different senses 'deprived' of sight; the latter in contrast with its genus,[13] the former in contrast with his own normal nature.—(3) If, though it would naturally have the attribute, and when it would naturally have it, it has it not; for blindness is a privation, but one is not 'blind' at any and every age, but only if one has not sight at the 30 age at which one would naturally have it. Similarly a thing is called blind if it has not sight in the medium in which, and in respect of the organ in respect of which, and with reference to the object with refer- ence to which, and in the circumstances in which, it would naturally have it.—(4) The violent taking away of anything is called privation.

Indeed there are just as many kinds of privations as there are of words with negative prefixes; for a thing is called unequal because it has not equality though it would naturally have it, and invisible either 35 because it has no colour at all or because it has a poor colour, and apodous either because it has no feet at all or because it has imperfect feet. Again, a privative term may be used because the thing has little 1023ᵃ of the attribute (and this means having it in a sense imperfectly), e. g. 'kernel-less'; or because it has it not easily or not well (e. g. we call a thing uncuttable not only if it cannot be cut but also if it cannot be cut easily or well); or because it has not the attribute at all; for it is not the one-eyed man but he who is sightless in both eyes 5 that is called blind. This is why not every man is 'good' or 'bad', 'just' or 'unjust', but there is also an intermediate state.

[13] i. e. 'animal'.

23   To 'have' or 'hold' means many things:—(1) to treat a thing
according to one's own nature or according to one's own impulse; so
that fever is said to have a man, and tyrants to have their cities, 10
and people to have the clothes they wear.—(2) That in which a thing is
present as in something receptive of it is said to have the thing; e. g.
the bronze has the form of the statue, and the body has the disease.—
(3) As that which contains holds the things contained; for a thing is
said to be held by that in which it is as in a container; e. g. we say 15
that the vessel holds the liquid and the city holds men and the ship
sailors; and so too that the whole holds the parts.—(4) That which
hinders a thing from moving or acting according to its own impulse
is said to hold it, as pillars hold the incumbent weights, and as the
poets make Atlas hold the heavens, implying that otherwise they would 20
collapse on the earth, as some of the natural philosophers also say.
In this way also that which holds things together is said to hold the
things it holds together, since they would otherwise separate, each
according to its own impulse.

'Being in something' has similar and corresponding meanings to
'holding' or 'having'.   25

24   'To come *from* something' means (1) to come from something
as from matter, and this in two senses, either in respect of the highest
genus or in respect of the lowest species; e. g. in a sense all things that
can be melted come from water, but in a sense the statue comes from
bronze.—(2) As from the first moving principle; e. g. 'what did the 30
fight come from?' From abusive language, because this was the origin
of the fight.—(3) From the compound of matter and shape, as the
parts come from the whole, and the verse from the *Iliad*, and the stones
from the house; [in every such case the whole is a compound of matter
and shape,] for the shape is the end, and only that which attains an
end is complete.—(4) As the form from its part, e. g. man from 'two- 35
footed' and syllable from 'letter'; for this is a different sense from that
in which the statue comes from bronze; for the composite substance 1023ᵇ
comes from the sensible matter, but the form also comes from the
matter of the form.—Some things, then, are said to come from something else in these senses; but (5) others are so described if one of
these senses is applicable to a part of that other thing; e. g. the child
comes from its father and mother, and plants come from the earth,
because they come from a part of those things.—(6) It means coming 5
after a thing in time, e. g. night comes from day and storm from fine
weather, because the one comes after the other. Of these things some
are so described because they admit of change into one another, as in

the cases now mentioned; some merely because they are successive
in time, e. g. the voyage took place 'from' the equinox, because it took
10 place after the equinox, and the festival of the Thargelia comes 'from'
the Dionysia, because after the Dionysia.

25 'Part' means (1) (a) that into which a quantum can in any way
be divided; for that which is taken from a quantum *qua* quantum is
15 always called a part of it, e. g. two is called in a sense a part of three.
It means (b), of the parts in the first sense, only those which measure
the whole; this is why two, though in one sense it is, in another is not,
called a part of three.—(2) The elements into which a kind might be
divided apart from the quantity are also called parts of it; for which
reason we say the species are parts of the genus.—(3) The elements
into which a whole is divided, or of which it consists—the 'whole' mean-
20 ing either the form or that which has the form; e. g. of the bronze
sphere or of the bronze cube both the bronze—i. e. the matter in which
the form is—and the characteristic angle are parts.—(4) The elements
in the definition which explains a thing are also parts of the whole;
this is why the genus is called a part of the species, though in another
25 sense the species is part of the genus.

26 'A whole' means (1) that from which is absent none of the parts
of which it is said to be naturally a whole, and (2) that which so contains the things it contains that they form a unity; and this in two
senses—either as being each severally one single thing, or as making
up the unity between them. For (a) that which is true of a whole class
and is said to hold good as a whole (which implies that it is a kind
30 of whole) is true of a whole in the sense that it contains many things
by being predicated of each, and by all of them, e. g. man, horse, god,
being severally one single thing, because all are living things. But (b)
the continuous and limited is a whole, when it is a unity consisting of
several parts, especially if they are present only potentially,[14] but,
failing this, even if they are present actually. Of these things themselves, those which are so by nature are wholes in a higher degree than
35 those which are so by art, as we said [15] in the case of unity also, wholeness being in fact a sort of oneness.
1024ᵃ   Again (3), of quanta that have a beginning and a middle and an
end, those to which the position does not make a difference are called
totals, and those to which it does, wholes. Those which admit of both

---

[14] i. e. if they are only distinguishable, not distinct.   [15] Cf. 1016ᵃ 4.

descriptions are both wholes and totals. These are the things whose nature remains the same after transposition, but whose form does not, e. g. wax or a coat; they are called both wholes and totals; for they 5 have both characteristics. Water and all liquids and number are called totals, but 'the whole number' or 'the whole water' one does not speak of, except by an extension of meaning. To things, to which *qua* one the term 'total' is applied, the term 'all' is applied when they are treated as separate; 'this total number', 'all these units.'   10

27   It is not any chance quantitative thing that can be said to be 'mutilated'; it must be a whole as well as divisible. For not only is two not 'mutilated' if one of the two ones is taken away (for the part removed by mutilation is never equal to the remainder), but in general no number is thus mutilated; for it is also necessary that the essence remain; if a cup is mutilated, it must still be a cup; but the number 15 is no longer the same. Further, even if things consist of unlike parts, not even these things can all be said to be mutilated, for in a sense a number has unlike parts (e. g. two and three) as well as like; but in general of the things to which their position makes no difference, e. g. water or fire, none can be mutilated; to be mutilated, things must be such as in virtue of their essence have a certain position. Again, they must be continuous; for a musical scale consists of unlike parts and 20 has position, but cannot become mutilated. Besides, not even the things that are wholes are mutilated by the privation of *any* part. For the parts removed must be neither those which determine the essence nor any chance parts, irrespective of their position; e. g. a cup is not mutilated if it is bored through, but only if the handle or a projecting part is 25 removed, and a man is mutilated not if the flesh or the spleen is removed, but if an extremity is, and that not every extremity but one which when completely removed cannot grow again. Therefore baldness is not a mutilation.

28   The term 'race' or 'genus' is used (1) if generation of things which have the same form is continuous, e. g. 'while the race of men 30 lasts' means 'while the generation of them goes on continuously'.— (2) It is used with reference to that which first brought things into existence; for it is thus that some are called Hellenes by race and others Ionians, because the former proceed from Hellen and the latter from Ion as their first begetter. And the word is used in reference to the begetter more than to the matter, though people also get a race- 35 name from the female, e. g. 'the descendants of Pyrrha'.—(3) There is genus in the sense in which 'plane' is the genus of plane figures and 1024ᵇ

'solid' of solids; for each of the figures is in the one case a plane of such and such a kind, and in the other a solid of such and such a kind; and this is what underlies the differentiae. Again (4), in definitions the 5 first constituent element, which is included in the 'what', is the genus, whose differentiae the qualities are said to be.—'Genus' then is used in all these ways, (1) in reference to continuous generation of the same kind, (2) in reference to the first mover which is of the same kind as the things it moves, (3) as matter; for that to which the differentia or quality belongs is the substratum, which we call matter.

10   Those things are said to be 'other in genus' whose proximate substratum is different, and which are not analysed the one into the other nor both into the same thing (e. g. form and matter are different in genus); and things which belong to different categories of being (for some of the things that are said to 'be' signify essence, others a quality, 15 others the other categories we have before distinguished [16]); these also are not analysed either into one another or into some one thing.

29   'The false' means (1) that which is false as a *thing*, and that (*a*) because it is not put together or cannot be put together, e. g. 'that 20 the diagonal of a square is commensurate with the side' or 'that you are sitting'; for one of these is false always, and the other sometimes; it is in these two senses that they are non-existent. (*b*) There are things which exist, but whose nature it is to appear either not to be such as they are or to be things that do not exist, e. g. a sketch or a dream; for these are something, but are not the things the appearance of which 25 they produce in us. We call things false in this way, then—either because they themselves do not exist, or because the appearance which results from them is that of something that does not exist.

    (2) A false *account* is the account of non-existent objects, in so far as it is false. Hence every account is false when applied to something other than that of which it is true; e. g. the account of a circle is false when applied to a triangle. In a sense there is one account of each thing, i. e. the account of its essence, but in a sense there are many, 30 since the thing itself and the thing itself with an attribute are in a sense the same, e. g. Socrates and musical Socrates (a false account is not the account of anything, except in a qualified sense). Hence Antisthenes was too simple-minded when he claimed that nothing could be described except by the account proper to it—one predicate to one subject; from which the conclusion used to be drawn that there could be no contradiction, and almost that there could be no error. But it is possible to 35 describe each thing not only by the account of itself, but also by that

----

[16] 1017[a] 24–27.

of something else. This may be done altogether falsely indeed, but there is also a way in which it may be done truly; e. g. eight may be described as a double number by the use of the definition of two.

These things, then, are called false in these senses, but (3) a false 1025a
man is one who is ready at and fond of such accounts, not for any other reason but for their own sake, and one who is good at impressing such accounts on other people, just as we say *things* are false, which produce a false appearance. This is why the proof in the *Hippias* that the same man is false and true is misleading. For it assumes that he is false who can deceive[17] (i. e. the man who knows and is wise); and further that he who is *willingly* bad is better.[18] This is a false result of induction—for a man who limps willingly is better than one who does so unwillingly—by 'limping' Plato means 'mimicking a limp', for if the man *were* lame willingly, he would presumably be worse in this case as in the corresponding case of moral character.

30 'Accident' means (1) that which attaches to something and can be truly asserted, but neither of necessity nor usually, e. g. if some one in digging a hole for a plant has found treasure. This—the finding of treasure—is for the man who dug the hole an accident; for neither does the one come of necessity from the other or after the other, nor, if a man plants, does he usually find treasure. And a musical man *might* be pale; but since this does not happen of necessity nor usually, we call it an accident. Therefore since there are attributes and they attach to subjects, and some of them attach to these only in a particular place and at a particular time, whatever attaches to a subject, but not because it was this subject, or the time this time, or the place this place, will be an accident. Therefore, too, there is no definite cause for an accident, but a chance cause, i. e. an indefinite one. Going to Aegina was an accident for a man, if he went not in order to get there, but because he was carried out of his way by a storm or captured by pirates. The accident has happened or exists—not in virtue of the subject's nature, however, but of something else; for the *storm* was the cause of his coming to a place for which he was not sailing, and this was Aegina.

'Accident' has also (2) another meaning, i. e. all that attaches to each thing in virtue of itself but is not in its essence, as having its angles equal to two right angles attaches to the triangle. And accidents of this sort may be eternal, but no accident of the other sort is. This is explained elsewhere.[19]

[17] *Hippias Minor* 365–9.
[18] Ib. 371–6.
[19] *An. Post.* i. 75a 18–22, 39–41, 76b 11–16.

BOOK E (VI)

1025ᵇ 1   We are seeking the principles and the causes of the things that are,
and obviously of them *qua* being. For, while there is a cause of health
and of good condition, and the objects of mathematics have first princi-
5 ples and elements and causes, and in general every science which is
ratiocinative or at all involves reasoning deals with causes and principles, more or less precise, all these sciences mark off some particular
10 being—some genus, and inquire into this, but not into being simply
nor *qua* being, nor do they offer any discussion of the essence of the
things of which they treat; but starting from the essence—some making
it plain to the senses, others assuming it as a hypothesis—they then
demonstrate, more or less cogently, the essential attributes of the genus
with which they deal. It is obvious, therefore, that such an induction
15 yields no demonstration of substance or of the essence, but some other
way of exhibiting it. And similarly the sciences omit the question
whether the genus with which they deal exists or does not exist, because
it belongs to the same kind of thinking to show what it is and that it is.

And since natural science, like other sciences, is in fact about one
20 class of being, i. e. to that sort of substance which has the principle of
its movement and rest present in itself, evidently it is neither practical
nor productive. For in the case of things made the principle is in the
maker—it is either reason or art or some faculty, while in the case of
things done it is in the doer—viz. will, for that which is done and that
25 which is willed are the same. Therefore, if all thought is either practical
or productive or theoretical, physics must be a theoretical science, but
it will theorize about such being as admits of being moved, and about
substance-as-defined for the most part only as not separable from
matter. Now, we must not fail to notice the mode of being of the
essence and of its definition, for, without this, inquiry is but idle. Of
30 things defined, i. e. of 'whats', some are like 'snub', and some like
'concave'. And these differ because 'snub' is bound up with matter (for
what is snub is a concave *nose*), while concavity is independent of
perceptible matter. If then all natural things are analogous to the snub
1026ᵃ in their nature—e. g. nose, eye, face, flesh, bone, and, in general,
animal; leaf, root, bark, and, in general, plant (for none of these can
be defined without reference to movement—they always have matter),
it is clear how we must seek and define the 'what' in the case of natural
5 objects, and also that it belongs to the student of nature to study even
soul in a certain sense, i. e. so much of it as is not independent of matter.

That physics, then, is a theoretical science, is plain from these considerations. Mathematics also, however, is theoretical; but whether its objects are immovable and separable from matter, is not at present clear; still, it is clear that *some* mathematical theorems *consider* them *qua* immovable and *qua* separable from matter. But if there is some- 10 thing which is eternal and immovable and separable, clearly the knowledge of it belongs to a theoretical science—not, however, to physics (for physics deals with certain movable things) nor to mathematics, but to a science prior to both. For physics deals with things which exist separately but are not immovable, and some parts of mathematics deal with things which are immovable but presumably do not exist separately, but as embodied in matter; while the first science deals with 15 things which both exist separately and are immovable. Now all causes must be eternal, but especially these; for they are the causes that operate on so much of the divine as appears to us.[1] There must, then, be three theoretical philosophies, mathematics, physics, and what we may call theology, since it is obvious that if the divine is present anywhere, it is present in things of this sort. And the highest science must 20 deal with the highest genus. Thus, while the theoretical sciences are more to be desired than the other sciences, this is more to be desired than the other theoretical sciences. For one might raise the question whether first philosophy is universal, or deals with one genus, i. e. some one kind of being; for not even the mathematical sciences are all alike in 25 this respect—geometry and astronomy deal with a certain particular kind of thing, while universal mathematics applies alike to all. We answer that if there is no substance other than those which are formed by nature, natural science will be the first science; but if there is an immovable substance, the science of this must be prior and must be 30 first philosophy, and universal in this way, because it is first. And it will belong to this to consider being *qua* being—both what it is and the attributes which belong to it *qua* being.[2]

2   But since the unqualified term 'being' has several meanings, of which one was seen [3] to be the accidental, and another the true ('non-being' being the false), while besides these there are the figures of 35 predication (e. g. the 'what', quality, quantity, place, time, and any similar meanings which 'being' may have), and again besides all these 1026ᵇ there is that which 'is' potentially or actually:—since 'being' has many meanings, we must first say regarding the *accidental*, that there can be no scientific treatment of it. This is confirmed by the fact that no 5

[1] i. e. produce the movements of the heavenly bodies.
[2] With ch. 1 Cf. iii. 955ᵇ 10–13, 997ᵃ 15–25, xi. 7.   [3] Cf. v. 7.

science—practical, productive, or theoretical—troubles itself about it. For on the one hand he who produces a house does not produce all the attributes that come into being along with the house; for these are innumerable; the house that has been made may quite well be pleasant for some people, hurtful to some, and useful to others, and different— to put it shortly—from all things that are; and the science of building 10 does not aim at producing any of these attributes. And in the same way the geometer does not consider the attributes which attach thus to figures, nor whether 'triangle' is different from 'triangle whose angles are equal to two right angles'.—And this happens naturally enough; for the accidental is practically a mere name. And so Plato [4] was in a 15 sense not wrong in ranking sophistic as dealing with that which is not. For the arguments of the sophists deal, we may say, above all with the accidental; e. g. the question whether 'musical' and 'lettered' are different or the same, and whether 'musical Coriscus' and 'Coriscus' are the same, and whether 'everything which is, but is not eternal, has come to be', with the paradoxical conclusion that if one who was musical has come to be lettered, he must also have been lettered and have come 20 to be musical—and all the other arguments of this sort; the accidental is obviously akin to non-being. And this is clear also from arguments such as the following: things which are in another sense come into being and pass out of being by a process, but things which are accidentally do not. But still we must, as far as we can, say further, regarding the 25 accidental, what its nature is and from what cause it proceeds; for it will perhaps at the same time become clear why there is no science of it.

Since, among things which are, some are always in the same state and are of necessity (not necessity in the sense of compulsion but that which we assert of things because they cannot be otherwise), and some 30 are not of necessity nor always, but for the most part, this is the prin- ciple and this the cause of the existence of the accidental; for that which is neither always nor for the most part, we call accidental. For instance, if in the dog-days there is wintry and cold weather, we say this is an accident, but not if there is sultry heat, because the latter is 35 always or for the most part so, but not the former. And it is an accident that a man is pale (for this is neither always nor for the most part so), but it is not by accident that he is an animal. And that the builder 1027ᵃ produces health is an accident, because it is the nature not of the builder but of the doctor to do this—but the builder happened to be a doctor. Again, a confectioner, aiming at giving pleasure, may make something wholesome, but not in virtue of the confectioner's art; and therefore

<hr>

[4] Cf. *Sophistes* 237 A, 254 A.

we say 'it was an accident', and while there is a sense in which he makes it, in the unqualified sense he does not. For to other things answer facul- 5 ties productive of them, but to accidental results there corresponds no determinate art nor faculty; for of things which are or come to be by accident, the cause also is accidental. Therefore, since not all things either are or come to be of necessity and always, but the majority of things are *for the most part*, the accidental must exist; for instance a 10 pale man is not always nor for the most part musical, but since this sometimes happens, it must be accidental (if not, everything will be of necessity). The matter, therefore, which is capable of being otherwise than as it usually is, must be the cause of the accidental. And we must 15 take as our starting-point the question whether there is nothing that is neither always nor for the most part. Surely this is impossible. There is, then, besides these something which is fortuitous and accidental. But while the usual exists, can nothing be said to be always, or are there eternal things? This must be considered later,[5] but that there is no science of the accidental is obvious; for all science is either of that 20 which is always or of that which is for the most part. (For how else is one to learn or to teach another? The thing must be determined as occurring either always or for the most part, e. g. that honey-water is useful for a patient in a fever is true for the most part.) But that which is contrary to the usual law science will be unable to state, i. e. when the thing does *not* happen, e. g. 'on the day of new moon'; for even that which happens on the day of new moon happens then either 25 always or for the most part; but the accidental is contrary to such laws. We have stated, then, what the accidental is, and from what cause it arises, and that there is no science which deals with it.

3   That there are principles and causes which are generable and destructible without ever being in course of being generated or de- 30 stroyed, is obvious. For otherwise all things will be of necessity, since that which is being generated or destroyed must have a cause which is not accidentally its cause. Will *A* exist or not? It will *if B* happens; and if not, not. And *B* will exist if *C* happens. And thus if time is constantly subtracted from a limited extent of time, one will obviously come to the present. This man, then, will die by violence, *if* he goes out; and he will 1027[b] do this if he gets thirsty; and he will get thirsty if something else happens; and thus we shall come to that which is now present, or to some past event. For instance, he will go out if he gets thirsty; and he will get thirsty if he is eating pungent food; and this is either the case

[5] Cf. xii. 6–8.

5 or not; so that he will of necessity die, or of necessity not die. And similarly if one jumps over to past events, the same account will hold good; for this—I mean the past condition—is already present in something. Everything, therefore, that will be, will be of necessity; e. g. it is necessary that he who lives shall one day die; for already some condition has come into existence, e. g. the presence of contraries in the same
10 body. But whether he is to die by disease or by violence is not yet determined, but depends on the happening of something else. Clearly then the process goes back to a certain starting-point, but this no longer points to something further. This then will be the starting-point for the fortuitous, and will have nothing else as cause of its coming to be.
15 But to what sort of starting-point and what sort of cause we thus refer the fortuitous—whether to matter or to the purpose or to the motive power, must be carefully considered.

4 Let us dismiss accidental being; for we have sufficiently determined its nature. But since that which *is* in the sense of being true, or *is not* in the sense of being false, depends on combination and separation, and truth and falsity together depend on the allocation of a pair
20 of contradictory judgements (for the true judgement affirms where the subject and predicate really are combined, and denies where they are separated, while the false judgement has the opposite of this allocation; it is another question, how it happens that we think things together or apart; by 'together' and 'apart' I mean thinking them so that there
25 is no succession in the thoughts but they become a unity); for falsity and truth are not in things—it is not as if the good were true, and the bad were in itself false—but in thought; while with regard to simple concepts and 'whats' falsity and truth do not exist even in thought:— this being so, we must consider later [6] what has to be discussed with regard to that which is or is not in this sense. But since the combina-
30 tion and the separation are in thought and not in the things, and that which is in this sense is a different sort of 'being' from the things that are in the full sense (for the thought attaches or removes either the subject's 'what' or its having a certain quality or quantity or something else), that which *is* accidentally and that which *is* in the sense of being true must be dismissed. For the cause of the former is indeterminate, and that of the latter is some affection of the thought, and
1028ᵃ both are related to the remaining genus of being, and do not indicate the existence of any separate class of being. Therefore let these be dismissed, and let us consider the causes and the principles of being

[6] Cf. ix. 10.

itself, *qua* being. [It was clear in our discussion of the various meanings of terms, that 'being' has several meanings.] [7]   5

BOOK Z (VII)

1   There are several senses in which a thing may be said to 'be', as   10
we pointed out previously in our book on the various senses of words; [1]
for in one sense the 'being' meant is 'what a thing is' or a 'this', and in
another sense it means a quality or quantity or one of the other things
that are predicated as these are. While 'being' has all these senses,
obviously that which 'is' primarily is the 'what', which indicates the
substance of the thing. For when we say of what quality a thing is,   15
we say that it is good or bad, not that it is three cubits long or that
it is a man; but when we say *what* it is, we do not say 'white' or 'hot'
or 'three cubits long', but 'a man' or 'a god'. And all other things are
said to be because they are, some of them, quantities of that which *is*
in this primary sense, others qualities of it, others affections of it, and
others some other determination of it. And so one might even raise   20
the question whether the words 'to walk', 'to be healthy', 'to sit' imply
that each of these things is existent, and similarly in any other case
of this sort; for none of them is either self-subsistent or capable of
being separated from substance, but rather, if anything, it is that which
walks or sits or is healthy that is an existent thing. Now these are   25
seen to be more real because there is something definite which underlies them (i. e. the substance or individual), which is implied in such a
predicate; for we never use the word 'good' or 'sitting' without implying this. Clearly then it is in virtue of this category that each of the
others also *is*. Therefore that which is primarily, i. e. not in a qualified
sense but without qualification, must be substance.   30

Now there are several senses in which a thing is said to be first;
yet substance is first in every sense—(1) in definition, (2) in order
of knowledge, (3) in time. For (3) of the other categories none can
exist independently, but only substance. And (1) in definition also   35
this is first; for in the definition of each term the definition of its
substance must be present. And (2) we think we know each thing
most fully, when we know what it is, e. g. what man is or what fire is,
rather than when we know its quality, its quantity, or its place; since
we know each of these predicates also, only when we know *what* the   1028ᵇ
quantity or the quality *is*.

And indeed the question which was raised of old and is raised now

[7] With chs. 2–4 Cf. xi. 1064ᵇ 15–1065ᵃ 26.   [1] Cf. v. 7.

and always, and is always the subject of doubt, viz. what being is, is just the question, what is substance? For it is this that some [2] assert to be one, others more than one, and that some [3] assert to be limited in number, others [4] unlimited. And so we also must consider chiefly and primarily and almost exclusively what that is which *is* in *this* sense.

2   Substance is thought to belong most obviously to bodies; and so we say that not only animals and plants and their parts are substances, but also natural bodies such as fire and water and earth and everything of the sort, and all things that are either parts of these or composed of these (either of parts or of the whole bodies), e. g. the physical universe and its parts, stars and moon and sun. But whether these alone are substances, or there are also others, or only some of these, or others as well, or none of these but only some other things, are substances, must be considered. Some [5] think the limits of body, i. e. surface, line, point, and unit, are substances, and more so than body or the solid.
   Further, some do not think there is anything substantial besides sensible things, but others think there are eternal substances which are more in number and more real; e. g. Plato posited two kinds of substance—the Forms and the objects of mathematics—as well as a third kind, viz. the substance of sensible bodies. And Speusippus made still more kinds of substance, beginning with the One, and assuming principles for each kind of substance, one for numbers, another for spatial magnitudes, and then another for the soul; and by going on in this way he multiplies the kinds of substance. And some [6] say Forms and numbers have the same nature, and the other things come after them—lines and planes—until we come to the substance of the material universe and to sensible bodies.
   Regarding these matters, then, we must inquire which of the common statements are right and which are not right, and what substances there are, and whether there are or are not any besides sensible substances, and how sensible substances exist, and whether there is a substance capable of separate existence (and if so why and how) or no such substance, apart from sensible substances; and we must first sketch the nature of substance.

3   The word 'substance' is applied, if not in more senses, still at least to four main objects; for both the essence and the universal and the genus are thought to be the substance of each thing, and fourthly the

---

[2] The schools of Miletus and Elea.
[3] The Pythagoreans and Empedocles.
[4] Anaxagoras and the Atomists.
[5] The Pythagoreans.
[6] The school of Xenocrates.

substratum. Now the substratum is that of which everything else is predicated, while it is itself not predicated of anything else. And so we must first determine the nature of this; for that which underlies 1029ᵃ a thing primarily is thought to be in the truest sense its substance. And in one sense matter is said to be of the nature of substratum, in another, shape, and in a third, the compound of these. (By the matter I mean, for instance, the bronze, by the shape the pattern of its form, and by the compound of these the statue, the concrete whole.) There- 5 fore if the form is prior to the matter and more real, it will be prior also to the compound of both, for the same reason.

We have now outlined the nature of substance, showing that it is that which is not predicated of a stratum, but of which all else is predicated. But we must not merely state the matter thus; for this is not enough. The statement itself is obscure, and further, on this view, *matter* becomes substance. For if this is not substance, it baffles us to 10 say what else is. When all else is stripped off evidently nothing but matter remains. For while the rest are affections, products, and potencies of bodies, length, breadth, and depth are quantities and not substances (for a quantity is not a substance), but the substance is 15 rather that to which these belong primarily. But when length and breadth and depth are taken away we see nothing left unless there is something that is bounded by these; so that to those who consider the question thus matter alone must seem to be substance. By matter I mean that which in itself is neither a particular thing nor of a certain 20 quantity nor assigned to any other of the categories by which being is determined. For there is something of which each of these is predicated, whose being is different from that of each of the predicates (for the predicates other than substance are predicated of substance, while substance is predicated of matter). Therefore the ultimate substratum is of itself neither a particular thing nor of a particular quantity nor otherwise positively characterized; nor yet is it the negations of these, 25 for negations also will belong to it only by accident.

If we adopt this point of view, then, it follows that matter is substance. But this is impossible; for both separability and 'thisness' are thought to belong chiefly to substance. And so form and the compound of form and matter would be thought to be substance, rather than 30 matter. The substance compounded of both, i. e. of matter and shape, may be dismissed; for it is posterior and its nature is obvious. And matter also is in a sense manifest. But we must inquire into the third kind of substance; for this is the most perplexing.

Some of the sensible substances are generally admitted to be substances, so that we must look first among these. For it is an advantage

1029^b 3 to advance to that which is more knowable. For learning proceeds for
all in this way—through that which is less knowable by nature to that
5 which is more knowable; and just as in conduct our task is to start
from what is good for each and make what is without qualification good
good for each, so it is our task to start from what is more knowable to
oneself and make what is knowable by nature knowable to oneself.
Now what is knowable and primary for particular sets of people is
often knowable to a very small extent, and has little or nothing of
10 reality. But yet one must start from that which is barely knowable but
knowable to oneself, and try to know what is knowable without qualification, passing, as has been said, by way of those very things which
one does know.

1 4   Since at the start [7] we distinguished the various marks by which
we determine substance, and one of these was thought to be the essence,
13 we must investigate this. And first let us make some linguistic remarks
about it. The essence of each thing is what it is said to be *propter se*.[8]
For being you is not being musical, since you are not by your very
15 nature musical. What, then, you are by your very nature is your essence.
Nor yet is the whole of this the essence of a thing; not that which
is *propter se* as white is to a surface, because being a surface is not
identical with being white. But again the combination of both—'being
a white surface'—is not the essence of surface, because 'surface' itself
is added. The formula, therefore, in which the term itself is not present
20 but its meaning is expressed, this is the formula of the essence of each
thing. Therefore if to be a white surface is to be a smooth surface,[9] to
be white and to be smooth are one and the same.[10]
But since there are also compounds answering to the other categories
25 (for there is a substratum for each category, e. g. for quality, quantity,
time, place, and motion), we must inquire whether there is a formula
of the essence of each of them, i. e. whether to these compounds also
there belongs an essence, e. g. to 'white man'. Let the compound be
denoted by 'cloak'. What is the essence of cloak? But, it may be said,
this also is not a *propter se* expression. We reply that there are just two
30 ways in which a predicate may fail to be true of a subject *propter se*,

[7] 1028^b 33–6.

[8] It seems convenient here to translate thus the phrase translated in v. 18 as 'in
virtue of itself'.

[9] i. e. this identification does not give the essence of 'surface' (for 'surface' is
repeated) but it gives the essence of 'white', since this is not repeated but replaced
by an equivalent.

[10] i. e. compounds of substance with the other categories.

and one of these results from the addition, and the other from the omission, of a determinant. *One* kind of predicate is not *propter se* because the term that is being defined is combined with another determinant, e. g. if in defining the essence of white one were to state the formula of white *man*; the *other* because in the subject another determinant is combined with that which is expressed in the formula, e. g. if 'cloak' meant 'white man', and one were to define cloak as white; white man is white indeed, but its essence is not to be white.   1030ʳ

But is being-a-cloak an essence at all? Probably not. For the essence is precisely what something *is*; but when an attribute is asserted of a subject other than itself, the complex is not precisely what some 'this' *is*, e. g. white man is not precisely what some 'this' *is*, since thisness 5 belongs only to substances. Therefore there is an essence only of those things whose formula is a definition. But we have a definition not where we have a word and a formula identical in meaning (for in that case all formulae or sets of words would be definitions; for there will be some name for any set of words whatever, so that even the *Iliad* will be a definition [11]), but where there is a formula of something primary; and primary things are those which do not imply the predica- 10 tion of one element in them of another element. Nothing, then, which is not a species of a genus will have an *essence*—only species will have it, for these are thought to imply not merely that the subject partici- pates in the attribute and has it as an affection, or has it by accident; but for everything else as well, if it has a name, there will be a *formula of its meaning*—viz. that this attribute belongs to this subject; or 15 instead of a simple formula we shall be able to give a more accurate one; but there will be no definition nor essence.

Or has 'definition', like 'what a thing is', several meanings? 'What a thing is' in one sense means substance and the 'this', in another one or other of the predicates, quantity, quality, and the like. For as 'is' 20 belongs to all things, not however in the same sense, but to one sort of thing primarily and to others in a secondary way, so too 'what a thing is' belongs in the simple sense to substance, but in a limited sense to the other categories. For even of a quality we might ask what it is, so that quality also is a 'what a thing is'—not in the simple sense, however, 25 but just as, in the case of that which is not, some say,[12] emphasizing the linguistic form, that that which is not *is*—not *is* simply, but *is* non- existent; so too with quality.

We must no doubt inquire how we should express ourselves on each point, but certainly not more than how the facts actually stand. And

[11] *sc.* of the word 'Iliad'.   [12] Cf. Pl. *Soph.* 237, 256 ff.

so now also, since it is evident what language we use, essence will belong, just as 'what a thing is' does, primarily and in the simple sense
30 to substance, and in a secondary way to the other categories also—not essence in the simple sense, but the essence of a quality or of a quantity. For it must be either by an equivocation that we say these *are*, or by adding to and taking from the meaning of 'are' (in the way in which that which is not known may be said to be known [13])—the truth being that we use the word neither ambiguously nor in the same sense, but
35 just as we apply the word 'medical' by virtue of a *reference* to one and
1030ᵇ the same thing, not *meaning* one and the same thing, nor yet speaking ambiguously; for a patient and an operation and an instrument are called medical neither by an ambiguity nor with a single meaning, but with reference to a common end. But it does not matter at all in which of the two ways one likes to describe the facts; this is evident, that
5 definition and essence in the primary and simple sense belong to substances. Still they belong to other things as well, only not in the primary sense. For if we suppose this it does not follow that there is a definition of every word which means the same as any formula; it must mean the same as a particular kind of formula; and this condition is satisfied if it is a formula of something which is one, not by continuity like the
10 *Iliad* or the things that are one by being bound together, but in one of the main senses of 'one', which answer to the senses of 'is'; now 'that which is' in one sense denotes a 'this', in another a quantity, in another a quality. And so there can be a formula or definition even of white man, but not in the sense in which there is a definition either of white or of a substance.

5   It is a difficult question, if one denies that a formula with an added
15 determinant is a definition, whether any of the terms that are not simple but coupled will be definable. For we *must* explain them by adding a determinant. E. g. there is the nose, and concavity, and snubness, which is compounded out of the two by the presence of the one in the other, and it is not by *accident* that the nose has the attribute either of concavity or of snubness, but in virtue of its nature; nor
20 do they attach to it as whiteness does to Callias, or to man (because Callias, who happens to be a man, is white), but as 'male' attaches to animal and 'equal' to quantity, and as all so-called 'attributes *propter se*' attach to their subjects. And such attributes are those in which is involved either the *formula* or the *name* of the subject of the particular attribute, and which cannot be explained without this;
25 e. g. white can be explained apart from man, but not female apart from

[13] i. e. it is known to be unknown.

animal. Therefore there is either no essence and definition of any of these things, or if there is, it is in another sense, as we have said.[14]

But there is also a second difficulty about them. For if snub nose and concave nose are the same thing, snub and concave will be the same thing; but if snub and concave are not the same (because it is 30 impossible to speak of snubness apart from the thing of which it is an attribute *propter se*, for snubness is concavity-*in-a-nose*), either it is impossible to say 'snub nose' or the same thing will have been said twice, concave-nose nose; for snub nose will be concave-nose nose. And so it is absurd that such things should have an essence; if they 35 have, there will be an infinite regress; for in snub-nose nose yet another 'nose' will be involved.

Clearly, then, only substance is definable. For if the other categories 1031[a] also are definable, it must be by addition of a determinant, e. g. the qualitative is defined thus, and so is the odd, for it cannot be defined apart from number; nor can female be defined apart from animal. (When I say 'by addition' I mean the expressions in which it turns out that we are saying the same thing twice, as in these instances.) And if this is true, coupled terms also, like 'odd number', will not be 5 definable (but this escapes our notice because our formulae are not accurate). But if these also are definable, either it is in some other way or, as we said,[15] definition and essence must be said to have more than one sense. Therefore in one sense nothing will have a definition 10 and nothing will have an essence, except substances, but in another sense other things will have them. Clearly, then, definition is the formula of the essence, and essence belongs to substances either alone or chiefly and primarily and in the unqualified sense.

6 We must inquire whether each thing and its essence are the same 15 or different. This is of some use for the inquiry concerning substance; for each thing is thought to be not different from its substance, and the essence is said to be the substance of each thing.

Now in the case of accidental unities the two would be generally thought to be different, e. g. white man would be thought to be different 20 from the essence of white man. For if they are the same, the essence of man and that of white man are also the same; for a man and a white man are the same thing, as people say, so that the essence of white man and that of man would be also the same. But perhaps it does not follow that the essence of accidental unities should be the same as that of the simple terms. For the extreme terms are not in the same way identical with the middle term. But perhaps *this* might 25

14 a 17–b13.   15 1030 a17–b13.

be thought to follow, that the extreme terms, the accidents, should turn out to be the same, e. g. the essence of white and that of musical; but this is not actually thought to be the case.

But in the case of so-called self-subsistent things, is a thing necessarily the same as its essence? E. g. if there are some substances which
30 have no other substances nor entities prior to them—substances such as some assert the Ideas to be?—If the essence of good is to be different from good-itself, and the essence of animal from animal-itself, and the
1031ᵇ essence of being from being-itself, there will, firstly, be other substances and entities and Ideas besides those which are asserted, and, secondly, these others will be prior substances, if essence is substance. And if the posterior substances and the prior are severed from each other, (a) there will be no knowledge of the former,[16] and (b) the latter [17] will
5 have no being. (By 'severed' I mean, if the good-itself has not the essence of good, and the latter has not the property of being good.) For (a) there is knowledge of each thing only when we know its essence. And (b) the case is the same for other things as for the good; so that if the essence of good is not good, neither is the essence of reality real,
10 nor the essence of unity one. And all essences alike exist or none of them does; so that if the essence of reality is not real, neither is any of the others. Again, that to which the essence of good does not belong [18] is not good.—The good, then, must be one with the essence of good, and the beautiful with the essence of beauty, and so with all things which do not depend on something else but are self-subsistent and primary. For it is enough if they are this, even if they are not
15 Forms; or rather, perhaps, even if they *are* Forms. (At the same time it is clear that if there are Ideas such as some people say there are, it will not be substratum that is substance; for these must be substances, but not predicable of a substratum; for if they were they would exist only by being participated in.[19])

Each thing itself, then, and its essence are one and the same in no merely accidental way, as is evident both from the preceding argu-
20 ments and because to *know* each thing, at least, is just to know its essence, so that even by the exhibition of instances it becomes clear that both must be one.

(But of an accidental term, e. g. 'the musical' or 'the white', since it has two meanings, it is not true to say that it itself is identical with its essence; for both that to which the accidental quality belongs, and
25 the accidental quality, are white, so that in a sense the accident and its essence are the same, and in a sense they are not; for the essence of

---

[16] The Ideas or things-themselves.　　　[17] The essences.
[18] i. e. the Idea of good (l. 5).　　　[19] i. e. as immanent in particulars.

white is not the same as the man [20] or the white man, but it is the same as the attribute white.)

The absurdity of the separation would appear also if one were to assign a name to each of the essences; for there would be yet another essence besides the original one, e. g. to the essence of horse there will belong a second essence.[21] Yet why should not some things be their essences from the start, since essence is substance? But indeed not only are a thing and its essence one, but the formula of them is also the same, as is clear even from what has been said; for it is not by accident that the essence of one, and the one, are one. Further, if they are to be different, the process will go on to infinity; for we shall have (1) the essence of one, and (2) the one, so that to terms of the former kind the same argument will be applicable.[22]

Clearly, then, each primary and self-subsistent thing is one and the same as its essence. The sophistical objections to this position, and the question whether Socrates and to be Socrates are the same thing, are obviously answered by the same solution; for there is no difference either in the standpoint from which the question would be asked, or in that from which one could answer it successfully. We have explained, then, in what sense each thing is the same as its essence and in what sense it is not.

7   Of things that come to be, some come to be by nature, some by art, some spontaneously. Now everything that comes to be comes to be by the agency of something and from something and comes to be something. And the something which I say it comes to be may be found in any category; it may come to be either a 'this' or of some size or of some quality or somewhere.

Now natural comings to be are the comings to be of those things which come to be by nature; and that out of which they come to be is what we call matter; and that by which they come to be is something which exists naturally; and the something which they come to be is a man or a plant or one of the things of this kind, which we say are substances if anything is—all things produced either by nature or by art have matter; for each of them is capable both of being and of not being, and this capacity is the matter in each—and, in general, both that from which they are produced is nature, and the type according

[20] *sc.* who is white.

[21] *sc.* and so *ad infinitum*. As an infinite process is absurd, why take the first step that commits you to it—why say that the essence of horse is separate from the horse?

[22] i. e. if the essence of one is different from the one, the essence of the essence of one is different from the essence of one.

to which they are produced is nature (for that which is produced, e. g.
a plant or an animal, has a nature), and so is that by which they are
produced—the so-called 'formal' nature, which is specifically the same
25 (though this is in another individual); for man begets man.

Thus, then, are natural products produced; all other productions
are called 'makings'. And all makings proceed either from art or from
a faculty or from thought.[23] Some of them happen also spontaneously
30 or by luck [24] just as natural products sometimes do; for there also the
same things sometimes are produced without seed as well as from seed.
Concerning these cases, then, we must inquire later,[25] but from art
proceed the things of which the form is in the soul of the artist. (By
1032ᵇ form I mean the essence of each thing and its primary substance.) For
even contraries have in a sense the same form; for the substance of a
privation is the opposite substance, e. g. health is the substance of
5 disease (for disease is the absence of health); and health is the formula
in the soul or the knowledge of it. The healthy subject is produced as
the result of the following train of thought:—since *this* is health, if
the subject is to be healthy *this* must first be present, e. g. a uniform
state of body, and if this is to be present, there must be heat; and the
physician goes on thinking thus until he reduces the matter to a final
something which he himself can produce. Then the process from this
10 point onward, i. e. the process towards health, is called a 'making'.
Therefore it follows that in a sense health comes from health and house
from house, that with matter from that without matter; for the medical
art and the building art are the form of health and of the house, and
when I speak of substance without matter I mean the essence.

15   Of the productions or processes one part is called thinking and the
other making—that which proceeds from the starting-point and the
form is thinking, and that which proceeds from the final step of the
thinking is making. And each of the other, intermediate, things is
produced in the same way. I mean, for instance, if the subject is to be
healthy his bodily state must be made uniform. What then does being
made uniform imply? This or that. And this depends on his being
20 made warm. What does this imply? Something else. And this something is present potentially; and what is present potentially is already
in the physician's power.

The active principle then and the starting-point for the process of
becoming healthy is, if it happens by art, the form in the soul, and
if spontaneously, it is that, whatever it is, which starts the making,[26]

---

[23] Cf. vi. 1025ᵇ 22.   [24] For the theory of these Cf. *Phys.* ii. 5, 6.
[25] Cf. ᵇ23–30, 1034ᵃ 9–21, ᵇ 4–7.
[26] *sc.* not the thinking, Cf. ll. 15–17.

for the man who makes by art, as in healing the starting-point is 25
perhaps the production of warmth (and this the physician produces
by rubbing). Warmth in the body, then, is either a part of health or is
followed (either directly or through several intermediate steps) by
something similar which is a part of health; and this, viz. that which
produces the part of health, is the limiting-point [27]—and so too with
a house (the stones are the limiting-point here) and in all other cases.

Therefore, as the saying goes, it is impossible that anything should 30
be produced if there were nothing existing before. Obviously then some
part of the result will pre-exist of necessity; for the matter is a part;
for this is present in the process and it is this that becomes something.
But is the matter an element even in the *formula*? We certainly describe 1033ª
in both ways [28] what brazen circles are; we describe both the matter
by saying it is brass, and the form by saying that it is such and such
a figure; and figure is the proximate genus in which it is placed. The
brazen circle, then, has its matter *in its formula*.

As for that out of which as matter they are produced, some things 5
are said, when they have been produced, to be not that but 'thaten';
e. g. the statue is not gold but golden. And a healthy man is not said
to be that from which he has come. The reason is that though a thing
comes both from its privation and from its substratum, which we
call its matter (e. g. what becomes healthy is both a man and an 10
invalid), it is said to come rather from its privation (e. g. it is from an
invalid rather than from a man that a healthy subject is produced).
And so the healthy subject is not said to *be* an invalid, but to be a man,
and the man is said to be healthy. But as for the things whose privation
is obscure and nameless, e. g. in brass the privation of a particular
shape or in bricks and timber the privation of arrangement as a house,
the thing is thought to be produced *from* these materials, as in the 15
former case the healthy man is produced *from* an invalid. And so, as
there also a thing is not said to be that from which it comes, here the
statue is not said to be wood but is said by a verbal change to be wooden,
not brass but brazen, not gold but golden, and the house is said to
be not bricks but bricken (though we should not say without qualifi- 20
cation, if we looked at the matter carefully, even that a statue is produced from wood or a house from bricks, because coming to be implies
change in that from which a thing comes to be, and not permanence).
It is for this reason, then, that we use this way of speaking.

[27] i. e. the minimum necessary basis.
[28] From the proportion established, warmth : health :: stones : house, and from
the next paragraph, it would appear that warmth is treated as the matter which
when specialized in a particular way becomes health.

8   Since anything which is produced is produced by something (and
this I call the starting-point of the production), and from something
25 (and let this be taken to be not the privation but the matter; for the
meaning we attach to this has already [29] been explained), and since
something is produced (and this is either a sphere or a circle or whatever else it may chance to be), just as we do not make the substratum
(the brass), so we do not make the sphere, except incidentally, because
30 the brazen sphere is a sphere and we make the former. For to make a
'this' is to make a 'this' out of the substratum in the full sense of the
word.[30] (I mean that to make the brass round is not to make the round
or the sphere, but something else, i. e. to produce this form in something
different from itself. For if we make the form, we must make it out of
1033ᵇ something else; for this was assumed.[31] E. g. we make a brazen sphere;
and that in the sense that out of this, which is brass, we make this
other, which is a sphere.) If, then, we also make the substratum itself,
clearly we shall make it in the same way, and the processes of making
5 will regress to infinity. Obviously then the form also,[32] or whatever
we ought to call the shape present in the sensible thing, is not produced,
nor is there any production of it, nor is the essence produced; for this
is that which is made to be in something else either by art or by nature
or by some faculty. But that there is a *brazen sphere*, this we make.
10 For we make it out of brass and the sphere; we bring the form into
this particular matter, and the result is a brazen sphere. But if the
essence of sphere in general is to be produced, something must be
produced out of something. For the product will always have to be
divisible, and one part must be this and another that; I mean the
one must be matter and the other form. If, then, a sphere is 'the figure
whose circumference is at all points equidistant from the centre', part
15 of this will be the medium in which the thing made will be, and part
will be in that medium, and the whole will be the thing produced,
which corresponds to the brazen sphere. It is obvious, then, from what
has been said, that that which is spoken of as form or substance is not
produced, but the concrete thing which gets its name from this is
produced, and that in everything which is generated matter is present,
and one part of the thing is matter and the other form.

Is there, then, a sphere apart from the individual spheres or a house
20 apart from the bricks? Rather we may say that no 'this' would ever
have been coming to be, if this had been so, but that the 'form' means
the 'such', and is not a 'this'—a definite thing; but the artist makes,

---

[29] Cf. 1032ᵃ 17.

[30] i. e. including form as well as matter (Cf. 1029ᵃ 3).

[31] ᵃ 25.   [32] *sc.* as well as the matter.

or the father begets, a 'such' out of a 'this'; and when it has been begotten, it is a 'this such'.[33] And the whole 'this', Callias or Socrates, is analogous to 'this brazen sphere', but man and animal to 'brazen sphere' in general. Obviously, then, the cause which consists of the Forms (taken in the sense in which some maintain the existence of the Forms, i. e. if they are something apart from the individuals) is useless, at least with regard to comings-to-be and to substances; and the Forms need not, for this reason at least, be self-subsistent substances. In some cases indeed it is even obvious that the begetter is of the same kind as the begotten (not, however, the *same* nor one in number, but in form), i. e. in the case of natural products (for man begets man), unless something happens contrary to nature, e. g. the production of a mule by a horse. (And even these cases are similar; for that which would be found to be common to horse and ass, the genus next above them, has not received a name, but it would doubtless be both, in fact 1034ᵃ something like a mule.) Obviously, therefore, it is quite unnecessary to set up a Form as a pattern (for we should have looked for Forms in these cases if in any; for these are substances if anything is so); the begetter is adequate to the making of the product and to the causing of the form in the matter. And when we have the whole, such and such a form in this flesh and in these bones, this is Callias or Socrates; and they are different in virtue of their matter (for that is different), but the same in form; for their form is indivisible.

9　The question might be raised, why some things are produced spontaneously as well as by art, e. g. health, while others are not, e. g. a house. The reason is that in some cases the matter which governs the production in the making and producing of any work of art, and in which a part of the product is present—some matter is such as to be set in motion by itself and some is not of this nature, and of the former kind some can move itself in the particular way required, while other matter is incapable of this; for many things can be set in motion by themselves but not in some particular way, e. g. that of dancing. The things, then, whose matter is of this sort, e. g. stones, cannot be moved in the particular way required,[34] except by something else, but in another way they can move themselves—and so it is with fire. Therefore some things will not exist apart from some one who has the art of making them, while others will; for motion will be started by these things which have not the art but can themselves

---

[33] i. e. the artist, or the father, turns a mere piece of matter into a qualified piece of matter.

[34] *sc.* for building.

be moved by other things which have not the art or with a motion starting from a part of the product.[35]

And it is clear also from what has been said that in a sense every product of art is produced from a thing which shares its name (as natural products are produced), or from a part of itself which shares its name (e. g. the house is produced from a house, *qua* produced by reason; for the art of building is the form of the house), or from something which contains a part of it—if we exclude things produced 25 by accident; for the cause of the thing's producing the product directly *per se* is a part of the product. The heat in the movement [36] caused heat in the body, and this is either health, or a part of health, or is followed by a part of health or by health itself. And so it is said to cause health, because it causes that to which health attaches as a consequence.

30   Therefore, as in syllogisms, substance [37] is the starting-point of everything. It is from 'what a thing is' that syllogisms start; and from it also we now find processes of production to start.

Things which are formed by nature are in the same case as these products of art. For the seed is productive in the same way as the things that work by art; for it has the form potentially, and that from 1034[b] which the seed comes has in a sense the same name as the offspring —only in a sense, for we must not expect parent and offspring always to have exactly the same name, as in the production of 'human being' from 'human being'; for a 'woman' also can be produced by a 'man'—unless the offspring be an imperfect form; which is the reason why the parent of a mule is not a mule.[38] The natural things 5 which (like the artificial objects previously considered [39]) can be produced spontaneously are those whose matter can be moved even by itself in the way in which the seed usually moves it; those things which have not such matter cannot be produced except from the parent animals themselves.

But not only regarding substance does our argument prove that its form does not come to be, but the argument applies to all the primary classes alike, i. e. quantity, quality, and the other categories. 10 For as the brazen sphere comes to be, but not the sphere nor the brass, and so too in the case of brass itself, if it comes to be, it is its concrete unity that comes to be (for the matter and the form must always exist before), so is it both in the case of substance and in that of quality and quantity and the other categories likewise; for

---

[35] i. e. an element of it pre-existing in the things themselves (Cf. 1032[b] 26–1033[a] I, 1034[a] 12).   [36] *sc.* of the rubber's hand.
[37] i. e. essence.   [38] Cf. 1033[b] 33.   [39] Cf. [a]9–32.

the quality does not come to be, but the wood of that quality, and the quantity does not come to be, but the wood or the animal of that 15 size. But we may learn from these instances a peculiarity of substance, that there must exist beforehand in complete reality another substance which produces it, e. g. an animal if an animal is produced; but it is not necessary that a quality or quantity should pre-exist otherwise than potentially.

10   Since a definition is a formula, and every formula has parts, and 20 as the formula is to the thing, so is the part of the formula to the part of the thing, the question is already being asked whether the formula of the parts must be present in the formula of the whole or not. For in some cases the formulae of the parts are seen to be present, and in some not. The formula of the circle does not include that of the segments, but that of the syllable includes that of the 25 letters; yet the circle is divided into segments as the syllable is into letters.—And further if the parts are prior to the whole, and the acute angle is a part of the right angle and the finger a part of the animal, the acute angle will be prior to the right angle and the finger 30 to the man. But the latter are thought to be prior; for in formula the parts are explained by reference to them, and in respect also of the power of existing apart from each other the wholes are prior to the parts.

Perhaps we should rather say that 'part' is used in several senses. One of these is 'that which measures another thing in respect of quantity'. But let this sense be set aside; let us inquire about the parts of which *substance* consists. If then matter is one thing, form 1035ᵃ another, the compound of these a third, and both the matter and the form and the compound are substance, even the matter is in a sense called part of a thing, while in a sense *it* is not, but only the elements of which the formula of the form consists. E. g. of concavity flesh (for this is the matter in which it is produced) is not a part, but of snubness it is a part; and the bronze is a part of the concrete 5 statue, but not of the statue when this is spoken of in the sense of the form. (For the form, or the thing as having form, should be said to be the thing, but the material element by itself must never be said to be so.) And so the formula of the circle does not include that of the segments, but the formula of the syllable includes that of the 10 letters; for the letters are parts of the formula of the form, and not matter, but the segments are parts in the sense of matter on which the form supervenes; yet they are nearer the form than the bronze is when roundness is produced in bronze. But in a sense not even

every kind of letter will be present in the formula of the syllable,
15 e. g. particular waxen letters or the letters as movements in the air;
for in these also we have already something that is part of the syllable only in the sense that it is its perceptible matter. For even if the
line when divided passes away into its halves, or the man into bones
and muscles and flesh, it does not follow that they are composed of
these as parts of their essence, but rather as matter; and these are
20 parts of the concrete thing, but not also of the form, i. e. of that to
which the formula refers; wherefore also they are not present in the
formulae. In one kind of formula, then, the formula of such parts
will be present, but in another it must not be present, where the
formula does not refer to the concrete object. For it is for this reason
that some things have as their constituent principles parts into which
they pass away, while some have not. Those things which are the
25 form and the matter taken together, e. g. the snub, or the bronze
circle, pass away into these materials, and the matter is a part of
them; but those things which do not involve matter but are without
matter, and whose formulae are formulae of the form only, do not
pass away—either not at all or at any rate not in this way. Therefore
30 these materials are principles and parts of the concrete things, while
of the form they are neither parts nor principles. And therefore the
clay statue is resolved into clay and the ball into bronze and Callias
into flesh and bones, and again the circle into its segments; for there
is a sense of 'circle' in which it involves matter. For 'circle' is used
1035ᵇ ambiguously, meaning both the circle, unqualified, and the individual
circle, because there is no name peculiar to the individuals.

The truth has indeed now been stated, but still let us state it yet
more clearly, taking up the question again. The parts of the formula,
5 into which the formula is divided, are prior to it, either all or some
of them. The formula of the right angle, however, does not include
the formula of the acute, but the formula of the acute includes that
of the right angle; for he who defines the acute uses the right angle;
for the acute is 'less than a right angle'. The circle and the semicircle
also are in a like relation; for the semicircle is defined by the circle;
10 and so is the finger by the whole body, for a finger is 'such and such
a part of a man'. Therefore the parts which are of the nature of
matter, and into which as its matter a thing is divided, are posterior;
but those which are of the nature of parts of the formula, and of the
substance according to its formula, are prior, either all or some of
them. And since the soul of animals (for this is the substance of a
15 living being) is their substance according to the formula, i. e. the
form and the essence of a body of a certain kind (at least we shall

define each part, if we define it well, not without reference to its
function, and this cannot belong to it without perception [40]), so that
the parts of soul are prior, either all or some of them, to the concrete
'animal', and so too with each individual animal; and the body and 20
its parts are posterior to this, the essential substance, and it is not
the substance but the concrete thing that is divided into these parts
as its matter:—this being so, to the concrete thing these are in a
sense prior, but in a sense they are not. For they cannot even exist
if severed from the whole; for it is not a finger in any and every state
that is the finger of a living thing, but a dead finger is a finger only 25
in name. Some parts are neither prior nor posterior to the whole,
i. e. those which are dominant and in which the formula, i. e. the
essential substance, is immediately present, e. g. perhaps the heart or
the brain; for it does not matter in the least which of the two has
this quality. But man and horse and terms which are thus applied
to individuals, but universally, are not substance but something composed of this particular formula and this particular matter treated 30
as universal; and as regards the individual, Socrates already includes
in him ultimate individual matter; and similarly in all other cases.
'A part' may be a part either of the form (i. e. of the essence), or
of the compound of the form and the matter, or of the matter itself.
But only the parts of the form are parts of the formula, and the
formula is of the universal; for 'being a circle' is the same as the 1036ᵃ
circle, and 'being a soul' the same as the soul. But when we come to
the concrete thing, e. g. *this* circle, i. e. one of the individual circles,
whether perceptible or intelligible (I mean by intelligible circles the
mathematical, and by perceptible circles those of bronze and of wood) 5
—of these there is no definition, but they are known by the aid of
intuitive thinking or of perception; and when they pass out of this
complete realization it is not clear whether they exist or not; but they
are always stated and recognized by means of the universal formula.
But matter is unknowable in itself. And some matter is perceptible
and some intelligible, perceptible matter being for instance bronze 10
and wood and all matter that is changeable, and intelligible matter
being that which is present in perceptible things not *qua* perceptible,
i. e. the objects of mathematics.

We have stated, then, how matters stand with regard to whole and
part, and their priority and posteriority. But when any one asks whether
the right angle and the circle and the animal are prior, or the things 15
into which they are divided and of which they consist, i. e. the parts, we
must meet the inquiry by saying that the question cannot be answered

[40] And therefore not without soul.

simply. For if even bare soul is the animal or [41] the living thing, or the soul of each individual is the individual itself, and 'being a circle' is the circle, and 'being a right angle' and the essence of the right angle is the right angle, then the whole in one sense must be called posterior to the part in one sense, i. e. to the parts included 20 in the formula and to the parts of the individual right angle (for both the material right angle which is made of bronze, and that which is formed by individual lines, are posterior to their parts); while the immaterial right angle is posterior to the parts included in the formula, but prior to those included in the particular instance, and the question must not be answered simply. If, however, the soul is something different and is not identical with the animal, even so 25 some parts must, as we have maintained, be called prior and others must not.

11 Another question is naturally raised, viz. what sort of parts belong to the form and what sort not to the form, but to the concrete thing. Yet if this is not plain it is not possible to define any thing; for definition is of the universal and of the form. If then it 30 is not evident what sort of parts are of the nature of matter and what sort are not, neither will the formula of the thing be evident. In the case of things which are found to occur in specifically different materials, as a circle may exist in bronze or stone or wood, it seems plain that these, the bronze or the stone, are no part of the essence of the circle, since it is found apart from them. Of things which are 35 *not* seen to exist apart, there is no reason why the same may not 1036ᵇ be true, just as if all circles that had ever been seen were of bronze; for none the less the bronze would be no part of the form; but it is hard to eliminate it in thought. E. g. the form of man is always found in flesh and bones and parts of this kind; are these then also parts 5 of the form and the formula? No, they are matter; but because man is not found also in other matters we are unable to perform the abstraction.

Since this is thought to be possible, but it is not clear *when* it is the case, some people,[42] already raise the question even in the case of the circle and the triangle, thinking that it is not right to define 10 these by reference to lines and to the continuous, but that all these are to the circle or the triangle as flesh and bones are to man, and bronze or stone to the statue; and they reduce all things to numbers, and they say the formula of 'line' is that of 'two'. And of those who

[41] *sc.* to put it more widely so as to include the vegetable world.
[42] Aristotle is thinking of Pythagoreans.

assert the Ideas some [43] make 'two' the line-itself, and others make
it the Form of the line; for in some cases they say the Form and [15]
that of which it is the Form are the same, e. g. 'two' and the Form
of two; but in the case of 'line' they say this is no longer so.

It follows then that there is one Form for many things whose form
is evidently different (a conclusion which confronted the Pythagoreans also); and it is possible to make one thing the Form-itself
of all, and to hold that the others are not Forms; but thus all things
will be one. [20]

We have pointed out, then, that the question of definitions contains
some difficulty, and why this is so. And so to reduce all things thus
to Forms and to eliminate the matter is useless labour; for some things
surely are a particular form in a particular matter, or particular
things in a particular state. And the comparison which Socrates the
younger [44] used to make in the case of 'animal' [45] is not sound; for [25]
it leads away from the truth, and makes one suppose that man can
possibly exist without his parts, as the circle can without the bronze.
But the case is not similar; for an animal is something perceptible,
and it is not possible to define it without reference to movement—
nor, therefore, without reference to the parts' being in a certain state.
For it is not a hand in any and every state that is a part of man, [30]
but only when it can fulfil its work, and therefore only when it is
alive; if it is not alive it is not a part.

Regarding the objects of mathematics, why are the formulae of
the parts not parts of the formulae of the wholes; e. g. why are not
the semicircles included in the formula of the circle? It cannot be
said, 'because these parts are perceptible things'; for they are not.
But perhaps this makes no difference; for even some things which [35]
are not perceptible must have matter; indeed there is some matter [1037ª]
in everything which is not an essence and a bare form but a 'this'.
The semicircles, then, will not be parts of the universal circle, but
will be parts of the individual circles, as has been said before [46]; for
while one kind of matter is perceptible, there is another which is
intelligible.

It is clear also that the soul is the primary substance and the [5]
body is matter, and man or animal is the compound of both taken
universally; and 'Socrates' or 'Coriscus', if even the soul of Socrates
may be called Socrates,[47] has two meanings (for some mean by such
a term the soul, and others mean the concrete thing), but if 'Socrates'

[43] This probably includes Plato himself.
[44] Cf. Pl. *Theaet.* 147 D; *Soph.* 218 B; *Pol.* 257 C; *Epp.* 358 D.
[45] Cf. ª 34–ᵇ 7.   [46] 1035ª 30–ᵇ 3.   [47] Cf. 1036ª 16–17, viii. 1043ᵇ 2–4.

or 'Coriscus' means simply this particular soul and this particular body, the individual is analogous to the universal in its composition.[48]

10 Whether there is, apart from the matter of such substances, another kind of matter, and one should look for some substance other than these, e. g. numbers or something of the sort, must be considered later.[49] For it is for the sake of this that we are trying to determine the nature of perceptible substances as well, since in a sense the 15 inquiry about perceptible substances is the work of physics, i. e. of second philosophy; for the physicist must come to know not only about the matter, but also about the substance expressed in the formula, and even more than about the other. And in the case of definitions, how the elements in the formula are parts of the definition, and why the definition is one formula (for clearly the thing is one, but in 20 virtue of *what* is the thing one, although it has parts?)—this must be considered later.[50]

What the essence is and in what sense it is independent, has been stated universally in a way which is true of every case,[51] and also why the formula of the essence of some things contains the parts of the thing defined, while that of others does not. And we have stated 25 that in the formula of the substance the material parts will not be present (for they are not even parts of the substance in that sense, but of the concrete substance; but of *this* there is in a sense a formula, and in a sense there is not; for there is no formula of it with its matter, for this is indefinite, but there is a formula of it with reference to its primary substance—e. g. in the case of man the formula of the soul—for the substance is the indwelling form, from which and the matter the so-called concrete substance is derived; [52] 30 e. g. concavity is a form of this sort, for from this and the nose arise 'snub nose' and 'snubness'); but in the concrete substance, e. g. a snub nose or Callias, the matter also will be present.[53] And we have stated that the essence and the thing itself are in some 1037ᵇ cases the same; i. e. in the case of primary substances, e. g. curvature and the essence of curvature, if this is primary. (By a 'primary' substance I mean one which does not imply the presence of something in something else, i. e. in something that underlies it which acts as matter.) But things which are of the nature of matter, or of wholes 5 that include matter, are not the same as their essences, nor are accidental unities like that of 'Socrates' and 'musical'; for these are the same only by accident.[54]

---

[48] i. e. as man = soul + body, Socrates = this soul + this body.
[49] Cf. xiii, xiv.   [50] Cf. vii. 12, viii. 6.   [51] Ch. 4.
[52] Chs. 10, 11.   [53] Ch. 5.   [54] Ch. 6.

12 Now let us treat first of definition, in so far as we have not treated of it in the *Analytics* [55]; for the problem stated in them [56] is useful for our inquiries concerning substance. I mean this problem: —wherein can consist the unity of that, the formula of which we 10 call a definition, as for instance, in the case of man, 'twofooted animal'; for let this be the formula of man. Why, then, is this one, and not many, viz. 'animal' *and* 'two-footed'? For in the case of 'man' and 'pale' there is a plurality when one term does not belong to the 15 other, but a unity when it does belong and the subject, man, has a certain attribute; for then a unity is produced and we have 'the pale man'. In the present case, on the other hand,[57] one does not share in the other; the genus is not thought to share in its differentiae (for then the same thing would share in contraries; for the differentiae by which the genus is divided are contrary). And even if the genus 20 does share in them, the same argument applies, since the differentiae present in man are many, e. g. endowed with feet, two-footed, feather-less. Why are these one and not many? Not because they are present in one thing; for on this principle a unity can be made out of *all* the attributes of a thing. But surely all the attributes in the definition 25 *must* be one; for the definition is a single formula and a formula of substance, so that it must be a formula of some one thing; for substance means a 'one' and a 'this', as we maintain.

We must first inquire about definitions reached by the method of divisions. There is nothing in the definition except the first-named genus and the differentiae. The other genera are the first genus and 30 along with this the differentiae that are taken with it, e. g. the first may be 'animal', the next 'animal which is two-footed', and again 'animal which is two-footed and featherless', and similarly if the definition includes more terms. And in general it makes no difference 1038ª whether it includes many or few terms—nor, therefore, whether it includes few or simply two; and of the two the one is differentia and the other genus; e. g. in 'two-footed animal' 'animal' is genus, and the other is differentia.

If then the genus absolutely does not exist apart from the species- 5 of-a-genus, or if it exists but exists as matter (for the voice is genus and matter, but its differentiae make the species, i. e. the letters, out of it), clearly the definition is the formula which comprises the differentiae.

But it is also necessary that the division be by the differentia *of the differentia*; e. g. 'endowed with feet' is a differentia of 'animal';

---

[55] Cf. *An. Post.* ii. 3–10, 13.   [56] Cf. *ib.* 97ª 29.
[57] That of 'animal' and 'two-footed'.

10 again the differentia of 'animal endowed with feet' must be of it *qua* endowed with feet. Therefore we must not say, if we are to speak rightly, that of that which is endowed with feet one part has feathers and one is featherless (if we do this we do it through incapacity); we must divide it only into cloven-footed and not-cloven; for these are differentiae in the foot; cloven-footedness is a form of footedness.
15 And the process wants always to go on so till it reaches the species that contain no differences. And then there will be as many kinds of foot as there are differentiae, and the kinds of animals endowed with feet will be equal in number to the differentiae. If then this is so, clearly the *last* differentia will be the substance of the thing and its
20 definition, since it is not right to state the same things more than once in our definitions; for it is superfluous. And this does happen; for when we say 'animal endowed with feet and two-footed' we have said nothing other than 'animal having feet, having two feet'; and if we divide this by the proper division, we shall be saying the same thing more than once—as many times as there are differentiae.

25   If then a differentia of a differentia be taken at each step, one differentia—the last—will be the form and the substance; but if we divide according to accidental qualities, e. g. if we were to divide that which is endowed with feet into the white and the black, there will be as many differentiae as there are cuts. Therefore it is plain that the definition is the formula which contains the differentiae, or,
30 according to the right method, the last of these. This would be evident, if we were to change the order of such definitions, e. g. of that of man, saying 'animal which is two-footed and endowed with feet'; for 'endowed with feet' is superfluous when 'two-footed' has been said. But there is no order in the substance; for how are we to think the one element posterior and the other prior? Regarding the definitions, then, which are reached by the method of divisions, let this suffice as
35 our first attempt at stating their nature.

1038ᵇ 13   Let us return to the subject of our inquiry, which is substance. As the substratum and the essence and the compound of these are called substance, so also is the universal. About two of these we have spoken; both about the essence [58] and about the substratum,[59] of
5 which we have said [60] that it underlies in two senses, either being a 'this'—which is the way in which an animal underlies its attributes— or as the matter underlies the complete reality. The universal also is thought by some to be in the fullest sense a cause, and a principle; therefore let us attack the discussion of this point also. For it seems

---

[58] Chs. 4–6, 10–12.   [59] Ch. 3.   [60] 1029ᵃ 2–3, 23–4.

impossible that any universal term should be the name of a substance.
For firstly the substance of each thing is that which is peculiar to
it, which does not belong to anything else; but the universal is com- 10
mon, since that is called universal which is such as to belong to more
than one thing. Of which individual then will this be the substance?
Either of all or of none; but it cannot be the substance of all. And
if it is to be the substance of one, this one will be the others also; for
things whose substance is one and whose essence is one are themselves also one.

Further, substance means that which is not predicable of a subject, 15
but the universal is predicable of some subject always.

But perhaps the universal, while it cannot be substance in the
way in which the essence is so, can be present in this; e. g. animal'
can be present in 'man' and 'horse'. Then clearly it is a formula of
the essence. And it makes no difference even if it is not a formula of
everything that is in the substance; for none the less the universal 20
will be the substance of something, as 'man' is the substance of the
individual man in whom it is present, so that the same result will
follow once more; for the universal, e. g. 'animal', will be the substance of that in which it is present as something peculiar to it. And
further it is impossible and absurd that the 'this', i. e. the substance,
if it consists of parts, should not consist of substances nor of what is 25
a 'this', but of quality; for that which is not substance, i. e. the
quality, will then be prior to substance and to the 'this'. Which is
impossible; for neither in formula nor in time nor in coming to be can
the modifications be prior to the substance; for then they will also be
separable from it. Further, Socrates will contain a substance present
in a substance, so that this will be the substance of two things. And
in general it follows, if man and such things are substance, that none 30
of the elements in their formulae is the substance of anything, nor
does it exist apart from the species or in anything else; I mean, for
instance, that no 'animal' exists apart from the particular kinds of
animal, nor does any other of the elements present in formulae exist
apart.

If, then, we view the matter from these standpoints, it is plain
that no universal attribute is a substance, and this is plain also from 35
the fact that no common predicate indicates a 'this', but rather a
'such'. If not, many difficulties follow and especially the 'third man'.[61] 1039ᵃ

The conclusion is evident also from the following consideration. A
substance cannot consist of substances present in it in complete
reality; for things that are thus in complete reality two are never in 5

61 Cf. i. 990ᵇ 17.

complete reality one, though if they are *potentially* two, they can be one (e. g. the double line consists of two halves—potentially; for the complete realization of the halves divides them from one another); therefore if the substance is one, it will not consist of substances present in it and present in this way, which Democritus describes rightly; he
10 says one thing cannot be made out of two nor two out of one; for he identifies substances with his indivisible magnitudes. It is clear therefore that the same will hold good of number, if number is a synthesis of units, as is said by some [62]; for two is either not one, or there is no unit present in it in complete reality.
15   But our result involves a difficulty. If no substance can consist of universals because a universal indicates a 'such', not a 'this', and if no substance can be composed of substances existing in complete reality, every substance would be incomposite, so that there would not even be a formula of any substance. But it is *thought* by all and was stated long ago [63] that it is either only, or primarily, substance
20 that can be defined; yet now it seems that not even substance can. There cannot, then, be a definition of anything; or in a sense there can be, and in a sense there cannot. And what we are saying will be plainer from what follows.[64]

   14   It is clear also from these very facts what consequence confronts those who say the Ideas are substances capable of separate existence,
25 and at the same time make the Form consist of the genus and the differentiae. For if the Forms exist and 'animal' is present in 'man' and 'horse', it is either one and the same in number, or different. (In formula it is clearly one; for he who states the formula will go through
30 the same formula in either case.) If then there is a 'man-in-himself' who is a 'this' and exists apart, the parts also of which he consists, e. g. 'animal' and 'two-footed', must indicate 'thises', and be capable of separate existence, and substances; therefore 'animal', as well as 'man', must be of this sort.
   Now (1) if the 'animal' in 'the horse' and in 'man' is one and the same, as you are with yourself, (a) how will the one in things that
1039ᵇ exist apart be one, and how will this 'animal' escape being divided even from itself?
   Further, (b) if it is to share in 'two-footed' and 'many-footed', an impossible conclusion follows; for contrary attributes will belong at the same time to it, although it is one and a 'this'. If it is not to share in them, what is the relation implied when one says the animal

---

[62] Thales is said to have defined number as 'a system of units'.
[63] Cf. 1031ª 11-14.   [64] Cf. vii. 15, viii. 6.

is two-footed or possessed of feet? But perhaps the two things are 5
'put together' and are 'in contact', or are 'mixed'. Yet all these expressions are absurd.

But (2) suppose the Form to be different in each species. Then
there will be practically an infinite number of things whose *substance*
is 'animal'; for it is not by accident that 'man' has 'animal' for one
of its elements. Further, many things will be 'animal-itself'. For (i)
the 'animal' in each species will be the substance of the species; for 10
it is after nothing else that the species is called; if it were, that other
would be an element in 'man', i. e. would be the genus of man. And
further, (ii) all the elements of which 'man' is composed will be Ideas.
None of them, then, will be the Idea of one thing and the substance
of another; this is impossible. The 'animal', then, present in each
species of animals will be animal-itself. Further, from what is this
'animal' in each species derived, and how will it be derived from
animal-itself? Or how can this 'animal', whose essence is simply 15
animality, exist apart from animal-itself?

Further, (3) in the case of sensible things both these consequences
and others still more absurd follow. If, then, these consequences are
impossible, clearly there are not Forms of sensible things in the sense
in which some maintain their existence.

15 Since substance is of two, kinds, the concrete thing and the 20
formula (I mean that one kind of substance is the formula taken with
the matter, while another kind is the formula in its generality), substances in the former sense are capable of destruction (for they are
capable also of generation), but there is no destruction of the formula
in the sense that it is ever in course of being destroyed (for there
is no generation of it either; the being of house is not generated, but
only the being of *this* house), but without generation and destruction 25
formulae are and are not; for it has been shown [65] that no one begets
nor makes these. For this reason, also, there is neither definition of
nor demonstration about sensible individual substances, because they
have matter whose nature is such that they are capable both of being
and of not being; for which reason all the individual instances of them 30
are destructible. If then demonstration is of necessary truths and
definition is a scientific process, and if, just as knowledge cannot be
sometimes knowledge and sometimes ignorance, but the state which
varies thus is opinion, so too demonstration and definition cannot
vary thus, but it is opinion that deals with that which can be otherwise than as it is, clearly there can neither be definition of nor 1040ᵃ

[65] Ch. 8.

demonstration about sensible individuals. For perishing things are obscure to those who have the relevant knowledge, when they have passed from our perception; and though the formulae remain in the soul unchanged, there will no longer be either definition or demon-
5 stration. And so when one of the definition-mongers defines any individual, he must recognize that his definition may always be overthrown; for it is not possible to define such things.

Nor is it possible to define any Idea. For the Idea is, as its supporters say, an individual, and can exist apart; and the formula must
10 consist of words; and he who defines must not invent a word (for it would be unknown), but the established words are common to all the members of a class; these then must apply to something besides the thing defined; e. g. if one were defining you, he would say 'an animal which is lean' or 'pale', or something else which will apply also to some one other than you. If any one were to say that perhaps all the attributes taken apart may belong to many subjects, but together
15 they belong only to this one, we must reply first that they belong also to both the elements; e. g. 'two-footed animal' belongs to animal and to the two-footed. (And in the case of eternal entities [66] this is even necessary, since the elements are prior to and parts of the compound; nay more, they can also exist apart, if 'man' can exist apart.
20 For either neither or both can. If, then, neither can, the genus will not exist apart from the various species; but if it does, the differentia will also.) Secondly, we must reply that 'animal' and 'two-footed' are prior in being to 'two-footed animal'; and things which are prior to others are not destroyed when the others are.

Again, if the Ideas consist of Ideas (as they must, since elements are simpler than the compound), it will be further necessary that the elements also of which the Idea consists, e. g. 'animal' and 'two-
25 footed', should be predicated of many subjects. If not, how will they come to be known? For there will then be an Idea which cannot be predicated of more subjects than one. But this is not thought possible —every Idea is thought to be capable of being shared.

As has been said,[67] then, the impossibility of defining individuals escapes notice in the case of eternal things, especially those which
30 are unique, like the sun or the moon. For people err not only by adding attributes whose removal the sun would survive, e. g. 'going round the earth' or 'night-hidden' (for from their view it follows that if it stands still or is visible,[68] it will no longer be the sun; but it is strange if this is so; for 'the sun' means a certain *substance*); but also by the mention of attributes which can belong to another subject;

---

[66] i. e. the Ideas.   [67] Cf. l. 17.   [68] *sc.* at night.

e. g. if another thing with the stated attributes comes into existence, clearly it will be a sun; the formula therefore is general. But the sun 1040 was supposed to be an individual, like Cleon or Socrates. After all, why does not one of the supporters of the Ideas produce a definition of an Idea? It would become clear, if they tried, that what has now been said is true.

16   Evidently even of the things that are thought to be substances, 5 most are only potencies—both the parts of animals (for none of them exists separately; and when they *are* separated, then too they exist, all of them, merely as matter) and earth and fire and air; for none of them is a unity, but as it were a mere heap, till they are worked up and some unity is made out of them. One might most readily 10 suppose the parts of living things and the parts of the soul nearly related to them to turn out to be both, i. e. existent in complete reality as well as in potency, because they have sources of movement in something in their joints; for which reason some animals live when divided. Yet all the parts must exist only potentially, when they are one and continuous by nature—not by force or by growing into one, 15 for such a phenomenon is an abnormality.

Since the term 'unity' is used like the term 'being', and the substance of that which is one is one, and things whose substance is numerically one are numerically one, evidently neither unity nor being can be the substance of things, just as being an element or a principle cannot be the substance, but we ask what, then, the prin- 20 ciple is, that we may reduce the thing to something more knowable. Now of these concepts 'being' and 'unity' are more substantial than 'principle' or 'element' or 'cause', but not even the former are substance, since in general nothing that is common is substance; for substance does not belong to anything but to itself and to that which has it, of which it is the substance. Further, that which is one cannot 25 be in many places at the same time, but that which is common is present in many places at the same time; so that clearly no universal exists apart from its individuals.

But those who say the Forms exist, in one respect are right, in giving the Forms separate existence, *if* they are substances; but in another respect they are not right, because they say the one over 30 many is a Form. The reason for their doing this is that they cannot declare what are the substances of this sort, the imperishable substances which exist apart from the individual and sensible substances. They make them, then, the same in kind as the perishable things (for this kind of substance we know)—'man-himself' and 'horse-itself', adding to the sensible things the word 'itself'. Yet even if we

1041ᵃ had not seen the stars, none the less, I suppose, would they have been
eternal substances apart from those which we knew; so that now
also if we do not know what non-sensible substances there are, yet it
is doubtless necessary that there should *be* some.—Clearly, then, no
5 universal term is the name of a substance, and no substance is composed of substances.

17 Let us state what, i. e. what kind of thing, substance should be
said to be, taking once more another starting-point; for perhaps from
this we shall get a clear view also of that substance which exists apart
from sensible substances. Since, then, substance is a principle and a
10 cause, let us pursue it from this starting-point. The 'why' is always
sought in this form—'why does one thing attach to some other?' For
to inquire why the musical man is a musical man, is either to inquire
—as we have said—why the man is musical, or it is something else.
15 Now 'why a thing is itself' is a meaningless inquiry (for [to give
meaning to the question 'why'] the fact or the existence of the thing
must already be evident—e. g. that the moon is eclipsed—but the fact
that a thing is itself is the single reason and the single cause to be
given in answer to all such questions as 'why the man is man, or the
musician musical',⁶⁹ unless one were to answer 'because each thing
is inseparable from itself, and its being one just meant this'; this,
however, is common to all things and is a short and easy way with
20 the question). But we *can* inquire why man is an animal of such and
such a nature. This, then, is plain, that we are not inquiring why he
who is a man is a man. We are inquiring, then, why something is
predicable of something (that it is predicable must be clear; for if
not, the inquiry is an inquiry into nothing). E. g. why does it thunder?
This is the same as 'why is sound produced in the clouds?' Thus the
25 inquiry is about the predication of one thing of another. And why
are these things, i. e. bricks and stones, a house? Plainly we are
seeking the cause. And this is the essence (to speak abstractly), which
in some cases is the end, e. g. perhaps in the case of a house or a bed,
30 and in some cases is the first mover; for this also is a cause. But
while the efficient cause is sought in the case of genesis and destruction, the final cause is sought in the case of being also.
The object of the inquiry is most easily overlooked where one term
is not expressly predicated of another (e. g. when we inquire 'what
1041ᵇ man is'), because we do not distinguish and do not say definitely
that certain elements make up a certain whole. But we must articulate

⁶⁹ *sc.* and therefore in this case, when the fact is known, there is no question as
to the 'why'.

our meaning before we begin to inquire; if not, the inquiry is on the border-line between being a search for something and a search for nothing. Since we must have the existence of the thing as something given, clearly the question is *why* the matter is some definite thing; e. g. why are these materials a house? Because that which was the essence of a house is present. And why is this individual thing, or 5 this body having this form, a man? Therefore what we seek is the cause, i. e. the form, by reason of which the matter is some definite thing; and this is the substance of the thing. Evidently, then, in the case of *simple* terms no inquiry nor teaching is possible; our 10 attitude towards such things is other than that of inquiry.

Since that which is compounded out of something so that the whole is one, not like a heap but like a syllable—now the syllable is not its elements, *ba* is not the same as *b* and *a*, nor is flesh fire and earth (for when these are separated the wholes, i. e. the flesh and the syllable, no longer exist, but the elements of the syllable exist, and so do fire and 15 earth); the syllable, then, is something—not only its elements (the vowel and the consonant) but also something else, and the flesh is not only fire and earth or the hot and the cold, but also something else:— if, then, that something must itself be either an element or composed of elements, (1) if it is an element the same argument will again apply; 20 for flesh will consist of this and fire and earth and something still further, so that the process will go on to infinity. But (2) if it is a compound, clearly it will be a compound not of one but of more than one (or else that one will be the thing itself), so that again in this case we can use the same argument as in the case of flesh or of the syllable. But it would seem that this 'other' is something, and not an element, 25 and that it is the *cause* which makes *this* thing flesh and *that* a syllable. And similarly in all other cases. And this is the *substance* of each thing (for this is the primary cause of its being); and since, while some things are not substances, as many as are substances are formed in accordance with a nature of their own and by a process of nature, their substance would seem to be this kind of 'nature',[70] which is not an 30 element but a principle. An *element*, on the other hand, is that into which a thing is divided and which is present in it as matter; e. g. *a* and *b* are the elements of the syllable.

BOOK H (VIII)

1   We must reckon up the results arising from what has been said, and 1042ᵃ compute the sum of them, and put the finishing touch to our inquiry.

[70] *sc.* the formal cause. Cf. v. 1014ᵇ 36 in contrast with ib. 27.

5 We have said that the causes, principles, and elements of substances
are the object of our search.[1] And some substances are recognized by
every one, but some have been advocated by particular schools. Those
generally recognized are the natural substances, i. e. fire, earth, water,
air, &c., the simple bodies; secondly, plants and their parts, and animals
10 and the parts of animals; and finally the physical universe and its
parts; while some particular schools say that Forms and the objects
of mathematics are substances.[2] But there are arguments which lead
to the conclusion that there are other substances, the essence and the
substratum. Again, in another way the genus seems more substantial
15 than the various species, and the universal than the particulars.[3] And
with the universal and the genus the Ideas are connected; it is in
virtue of the same argument that they are thought to be substances.
And since the essence is substance, and the definition is a formula
of the essence, for this reason we have discussed definition and essential
predication.[4] Since the definition is a formula, and a formula has parts,
20 we had to consider also with respect to the notion of 'part', what are
parts of the substance and what are not, and whether the parts of the
substance are also parts of the definition.[5] Further, too, neither the
universal nor the genus is a substance;[6] we must inquire later into
the Ideas and the objects of mathematics;[7] for some say these are
substances as well as the sensible substances.

But now let us resume the discussion of the generally recognized
25 substances. These are the sensible substances, and sensible substances
all have matter. The substratum is substance, and this is in one sense
the matter (and by matter I mean that which, not being a 'this' actually,
is potentially a 'this'), and in another sense the formula or shape (that
which being a 'this' can be separately formulated), and thirdly the
30 complex of these two, which alone is generated and destroyed, and is,
without qualification, capable of separate existence; for of substances
completely expressible in a formula some are separable and some are
not.

But clearly matter also is substance; for in all the opposite changes
that occur there is something which underlies the changes, e. g. in
respect of place that which is now here and again elsewhere, and in
35 respect of increase that which is now of one size and again less or
greater, and in respect of alteration that which is now healthy and
1042ᵇ again diseased; and similarly in respect of substance there is something
that is now being generated and again being destroyed, and now [8]

---

[1] Cf. vii. 1.   [2] Cf. vii. 2.   [3] Cf. vii. 3. 1028ᵇ 33–6.   [4] Cf. vii. 4–6, 12, 15.
[5] Cf. vii. 10, 11.   [6] Cf. vii. 13, 14, 16. 1040ᵇ 16–1041ª 5.
[7] Cf. xiii and xiv.   [8] *sc.* in the case of destruction.

underlies the process as a 'this' and again [9] underlies it in respect of
a privation of positive character. And in *this* change the others are
involved. But in either one or two of the others this is not involved; [5]
for it is not necessary if a thing has matter for change of place that
it should also have matter for generation and destruction.

The difference between becoming in the full sense and becoming
in a qualified sense has been stated in our physical works.[10]

2   Since the substance which exists as underlying and as matter is
generally recognized, and this is that which exists potentially, it [10]
remains for us to say what is the substance, in the sense of *actuality*,
of sensible things. Democritus seems to think there are three kinds of
difference between things; the underlying body, the matter, is one
and the same, but they differ either in rhythm, i. e. shape, or in turning, i. e. position, or in inter-contact, i. e. order.[11] But evidently there
are many differences; for instance, some things are characterized by [15]
the mode of composition of their matter, e. g. the things formed by
blending, such as honey-water; and others by being bound together,
e. g. a bundle; and others by being glued together, e. g. a book; and
others by being nailed together, e. g. a casket; and others in more
than one of these ways; and others by position, e. g. threshold and
lintel (for these differ by being placed in a certain way); and others [20]
by time, e. g. dinner and breakfast; and others by place, e. g. the
winds; and others by the affections proper to sensible things, e. g.
hardness and softness, density and rarity, dryness and wetness; and
some things by some of these qualities, others by them all, and in
general some by excess and some by defect. Clearly, then, the word
'is' has just as many meanings; a thing *is* a threshold because it lies [25]
in such and such a position, and its being means its lying in that position, while being ice means having been solidified in such and such
a way. And the being of some things will be defined by *all* these
qualities, because some parts of them are mixed, others are blended,
others are bound together, others are solidified, and others use the [30]
other differentiae; e. g. the hand or the foot requires such complex
definition. We must grasp, then, the kinds of differentiae (for these
will be the principles of the being of things), e. g. the things characterized by the more and the less, or by the dense and the rare, and
by other such qualities; for all these are forms of excess and defect.
And anything that is characterized by shape or by smoothness and [35]

---

[9] *sc.* in the case of generation.
[10] Cf. *Phys.* 225ᵃ 12–20, *De Gen. et Corr.* 317ᵃ 17–31.
[11] Cf. i. 985ᵇ 13–19.

roughness is characterized by the straight and the curved. And for
1043ᵃ other things their being will mean their being mixed, and their not
being will mean the opposite.

It is clear, then, from these facts that, since its substance is the
cause of each thing's being, we must seek in these differentiae what
is the cause of the being of each of these things. Now none of these
differentiae is substance, even when coupled with matter, yet it is
5 what is analogous to substance in each case; and as in substances
that which is predicated of the matter is the actuality itself, in all
other definitions also it is what most resembles full actuality. E. g. if
we had to define a threshold, we should say 'wood or stone in such
and such a position', and a house we should define as 'bricks and
timbers in such and such a position' (or a purpose may exist as well
in some cases), and if he had to define ice we should say 'water frozen
10 or solidified in such and such a way', and harmony is 'such and such
a blending of high and low'; and similarly in all other cases.

Obviously, then, the actuality or the formula is different when the
matter is different; for in some cases it is the composition, in others
the mixing, and in others some other of the attributes we have named.
And so, of the people who go in for defining, those who define a house
15 as stones, bricks, and timbers are speaking of the potential house, for
these are the matter; but those who propose 'a receptacle to shelter
chattels and living beings', or something of the sort, speak of the
actuality. Those who combine both of these speak of the third kind
of substance, which is composed of matter and form (for the formula
that gives the differentiae seems to be an account of the form or
20 actuality, while that which gives the components is rather an account
of the matter); and the same is true of the kind of definitions which
Archytas used to accept; they are accounts of the combined form and
matter. E. g. what is still weather? Absence of motion in a large expanse
of air; air is the matter, and absence of motion is the actuality and
25 substance. What is a calm? Smoothness of sea; the material substratum
is the sea, and the actuality or shape is smoothness. It is obvious then,
from what has been said, what sensible substance is and how it exists—
one kind of it as matter, another as form or actuality, while the third
kind is that which is composed of these two.

3 We must not fail to notice that sometimes it is not clear whether
30 a name means the composite substance, or the actuality or form, e. g.
whether 'house' is a sign for the composite thing, 'a covering consisting
of bricks and stones laid thus and thus', or for the actuality or form,
'a covering', and whether a line is 'twoness in length' or 'twoness', and

whether an animal is 'a soul in a body' or 'a soul'; for soul is the 35
substance or actuality of some body. 'Animal' might even be applied
to both, not as something definable by one formula, but as related to
a single thing. But this question,[12] while important for another purpose,
is of no importance for the inquiry into sensible substance; for the
essence certainly attaches to the form and the actuality. For 'soul' and 1043ᵇ
'to be soul' are the same, but 'to be man' and 'man' are not the same,
unless even the bare soul is to be called man; and thus on one interpretation the thing is the same as its essence, and on another it is not.

If we examine [13] we find that the syllable does not consist of the 5
letters + juxtaposition, nor is the house bricks + juxtaposition. And
this is right; for the juxtaposition or mixing does not consist of those
things of which it is the juxtaposition or mixing. And the same is true
in all other cases; e. g. if the threshold is characterized by its position,
the position is not constituted by the threshold, but rather the latter
is constituted by the former. Nor is man animal + biped, but there 10
must be something besides these, if these are matter—something
which is neither an element in the whole nor a compound, but is the
substance; but this people eliminate, and state only the matter. If,
then, this is the cause of the thing's being, and if the cause of its being
is its substance,[14] they will not be stating the substance itself.

(This, then, must either be eternal or it must be destructible with- 15
out being ever in course of being destroyed, and must have come to
be without ever being in course of coming to be. But it has been proved
and explained elsewhere [15] that no one makes or begets the form, but
it is the individual that is made, i. e. the complex of form and matter
that is generated. Whether the substances of destructible things can
exist apart, is not yet at all clear; except that obviously this is impossi- 20
ble in *some* cases—in the case of things which cannot exist apart from
the individual instances, e. g. house or utensil. Perhaps, indeed, neither
these things themselves, nor any of the other things which are not
formed by nature, are substances at all; for one might say that the
nature in natural objects is the only substance to be found in destructible things.)

Therefore the difficulty which used to be raised by the school of
Antisthenes and other such uneducated people has a certain timeliness.
They said that the 'what' cannot be defined (for the definition so called 25
is a 'long rigmarole' [16]) but of what *sort* a thing, e. g. silver, is, they

[12] *sc.* whether the name means the form or the concrete thing.
[13] Aristotle returns to the subject discussed in ch. 2.
[14] Cf. v. 1017ᵇ 14–15.
[15] Cf. vii. 8.   [16] *sc.* and therefore cannot give the essence, which is simple.

thought it possible actually to explain, not saying what it is, but that it is like tin. Therefore one kind of substance can be defined and formulated, i. e. the composite kind, whether it be perceptible or intelli-
30 gible; but the primary parts of which this consists cannot be defined, since a definitory formula predicates something of something, and one part of the definition must play the part of matter and the other that of form.

It is also obvious that, if substances are in a sense numbers, they are so in this sense and not, as some say,[17] as numbers of units. For a
35 definition is a sort of number; for (1) it is divisible, and into indivisible parts (for definitory formulae are not infinite), and number also is of this nature. And (2) as, when one of the parts of which a number consists has been taken from or added to the number, it is no longer the same number, but a different one, even if it is the very smallest
1044ᵃ part that has been taken away or added, so the definition and the essence will no longer remain when anything has been taken away or added. And (3) the number must be something in virtue of which it is one, and this these thinkers cannot state, what makes it one, if it is one (for either it is not one but a sort of heap, or if it is, we ought
5 to say what it is that makes one out of many); and the definition is one, but similarly they cannot say what makes *it* one. And this is a natural result; for the same reason is applicable, and substance is one in the sense which we have explained, and not, as some say, by being a sort of unit or point; each is a complete reality and a definite nature.
10 And (4) as number does not admit of the more and the less, neither does substance, in the sense of form, but if any substance does, it is only the substance which involves matter. Let this, then, suffice for an account of the generation and destruction of so-called substances —in what sense it is possible and in what sense impossible—and of the reduction of things to number.

15 **4**   Regarding material substance we must not forget that even if all things come from the same first cause [18] or have the same things for their first causes, and if the same matter serves as starting-point for their generation, yet there is a matter proper to each, e. g. for phlegm the sweet or the fat, and for bile the bitter, or something else; though
20 perhaps these come from the same original matter. And there come to be several matters for the same thing, when the one matter is matter for the other; e. g. phlegm comes from the fat and from the sweet, if the fat comes from the sweet; and it comes from bile by analysis of

[17] The Pythagoreans and Platonists (Cf. xiii. 6, 7).   [18] *sc.* material cause.

the bile into its ultimate matter. For one thing comes from another in two senses, either because it will be found at a later stage, or because it is produced if the other is analysed into its original constituents. When the matter is one, different things may be produced owing to 25 difference in the moving cause; e. g. from wood may be made both a chest and a bed. But *some* different things must have their matter different; e. g. a saw could not be made of wood, nor is this in the power of the moving cause; for it could not make a saw of wool or of wood. But if, as a matter of fact, the same thing can be made of different material, clearly the art, i. e. the moving principle, is the 30 same; for if both the matter and the moving cause were different, the product would be so too.

When one inquires into the cause of something, one should, since 'causes' are spoken of in several senses, state all the possible causes. E. g. what is the material cause of man? Shall we say 'the menstrual 35 fluid'? What is the moving cause? Shall we say 'the seed'? The formal cause? His essence. The final cause? His end. But perhaps the latter two are the same.—It is the proximate causes we must state. What is 1044ᵇ the material cause? We must name not fire or earth, but the matter peculiar to the thing.

Regarding the substances that are natural and generable, *if* the causes are really these and of this number and we have to learn the causes, we must inquire thus, if we are to inquire rightly. But in the 5 case of natural but *eternal* substances another account must be given. For perhaps some have no matter, or not matter of this sort but only such as can be moved in respect of place. Nor does matter belong to those things which exist by nature but are not substances; their substratum is the *substance*. E. g. what is the cause of eclipse? What is 10 its matter? There is none; the *moon* is that which suffers eclipse.[19] What is the moving cause which extinguished the light? The earth. The final cause perhaps does not exist. The formal principle is the definitory formula, but this is obscure if it does not include the cause.[20] E. g. what is eclipse? Deprivation of light. But if we add 'by the earth's coming in between', this is the formula which includes the cause. In the case 15 of sleep it is not clear what it is that proximately has this affection. Shall we say that it is the animal? Yes, but the animal in virtue of what, i. e. what is the proximate subject? The heart or some other part. Next, by what is it produced? Next, what is the affection—that of the proximate subject, not of the whole animal? Shall we say that

[19] i. e. the substratum of a substance is bare matter, but the substratum of an attribute is a determinate substance such as the moon.

[20] *sc.* the efficient cause.

it is immobility of such and such a kind? Yes, but to what process in
20 the proximate subject is this due?

5   Since some things are and are not, without coming to be and ceasing to be, e. g. points, if they can be said to *be*, and in general forms
(for it is not 'white' that comes to be, but the wood comes to be white,
if everything that comes to be comes from something and comes to be
25 something), not all contraries can come from one another, but it is
in different senses that a pale man comes from a dark man, and pale
comes from dark. Nor has everything matter, but only those things
which come to be and change into one another. Those things which,
without ever being in course of changing, are or are not, have no
matter.
    There is difficulty in the question how the matter of each thing is
30 related to its contrary states. E. g. if the body is potentially healthy,
and disease is contrary to health, is it potentially both healthy and
diseased? And is water potentially wine and vinegar? We answer that
it is the matter of one in virtue of its positive state and its form, and of
the other in virtue of the privation of its positive state and the corruption of it contrary to its nature. It is also hard to say why wine is not
35 said to be the matter of vinegar nor potentially vinegar (though
vinegar is produced from it), and why a living man is not said to be
potentially dead. In fact they are not, but the corruptions in question
1045ᵃ are accidental, and it is the *matter* of the animal that is itself in virtue
of its corruption the potency and matter of a corpse, and it is water
that is the matter of vinegar. For the corpse comes from the animal,
and vinegar from wine, as night from day. And *all* the things which
change thus into one another must go back to their matter; e. g. if
from a corpse is produced an animal, the corpse first goes back to its
5 matter, and only then becomes an animal; and vinegar first goes back
to water, and only then becomes wine.

6   To return to the difficulty which has been stated ²¹ with respect
both to definitions and to numbers, what is the cause of their unity?
In the case of all things which have several parts and in which the
totality is not, as it were, a mere heap, but the whole is something
10 besides the parts, there is a cause; for even in bodies contact is the
cause of unity in some cases, and in others viscosity or some other
such quality. And a definition is a set of words which is one not by
being connected together, like the *Iliad*, but by dealing with one
object.—What, then, is it that makes man one; why is he one and
15 not many, e. g. animal + biped, especially if there are, as some say,

²¹ Cf. vii. 12, viii. 1044ᵃ 2–6.

an animal-itself and a biped-itself? Why are not those Forms themselves the man, so that men would exist by participation not in man, nor in one Form, but in two, animal and biped, and in general man would be not one but more than one thing, animal and biped?

Clearly, then, if people proceed thus in their usual manner of defini- 20 tion and speech, they cannot explain and solve the difficulty. But if, as we say, one element is matter and another is form, and one is potentially and the other actually, the question will no longer be thought a diffi- 25 culty. For this difficulty is the same as would arise if 'round bronze' were the definition of 'cloak';[22] for this word would be a sign of the definitory formula, so that the question is, what is the cause of the unity of 'round' and 'bronze'? The difficulty disappears, because the one is matter, the other form. What, then, causes this—that which was poten- 30 tially to be actually—except, in the case of things which are generated, the agent? For there is no other cause of the potential sphere's becoming actually a sphere, but this was the essence of either.[23] Of matter some is intelligible, some perceptible, and in a formula there is always an element of matter as well as one of actuality; e. g. the circle is 'a 35 plane figure'.[24] But of the things which have no matter, either intelligible or perceptible, each is by its nature essentially a kind of unity, as 1045[b] it is essentially a kind of being—individual substance, quality, or quantity (and so neither 'existent' nor 'one' is present in their definitions), and the essence of each of them is by its very nature a kind of unity as it is a kind of being—and so none of these has any reason outside itself for being one, nor for being a kind of being; for each is 5 by its nature a kind of being and a kind of unity, not as being in the genus 'being' or 'one' nor in the sense that being and unity can exist apart from particulars.

Owing to the difficulty about unity some speak of 'participation', and raise the question, what is the cause of participation and what is it to participate; and others speak of 'communion', as Lycophron 10 says knowledge is a communion of knowing with the soul; and others say life is a 'composition' or 'connexion' of soul with body. Yet the same account applies to all cases; for being healthy, too, will on this showing be either a 'communion' or a 'connexion' or a 'composition' of soul and health, and the fact that the bronze is a triangle will be a 'composition' of bronze and triangle, and the fact that a thing is white 15 will be a 'composition' of surface and whiteness. The reason is that

[22] Cf. vii. 1029[b] 28, de Int. 18[a] 19.

[23] i. e. it was the essence of the potential ball to become an actual ball, and of the actual ball to be produced from a potential ball.

[24] Aristotle does not give the whole definition, but only the genus, or 'material' element.

people look for a unifying formula, and a difference, between potency and complete reality. But, as has been said,[25] the proximate matter and the form are one and the same thing, the one potentially, and the other actually. Therefore it is like asking what in general is the cause

20 of unity and of a thing's being one; for each thing is a unity, and the potential and the actual are somehow one. Therefore there is no other cause here unless there is something which caused the movement from potency into actuality. And all things which have *no* matter are *without qualification* essentially unities.

BOOK ⊙ (IX)

1   We have treated [1] of that which *is* primarily and to which all the other categories of being are referred—i. e. of substance. For it is in

30 virtue of the concept of substance that the others also are said to be— quantity and quality and the like; for all will be found to involve the concept of substance, as we said in the first part of our work.[2] And since 'being' is in one way divided into individual thing, quality, and quantity, and is in another way distinguished in respect of potency and

35 complete reality, and of function, let us now add a discussion of potency and complete reality. And first let us explain potency in the strictest

1046ª sense, which is, however, not the most *useful* for our present purpose. For potency and actuality extend beyond the cases that involve a reference to motion. But when we have spoken of this first kind, we shall in our discussions of actuality [3] explain the other kinds of potency as well.

We have pointed out elsewhere [4] that 'potency' and the word 'can'

5 have several senses. Of these we may neglect all the potencies that are so called by an equivocation. For some are called so by analogy, as in geometry we say one thing is or is not a 'power' of another by virtue of the presence or absence of some relation between them. But all potencies that conform to the same type are originative sources of

10 some kind, and are called potencies in reference to one primary kind of potency, which is an originative source of change in another thing or in the thing itself *qua* other. For one kind is a potency of being acted on, i. e. the originative source, in the very thing acted on, of its being passively changed by another thing or by itself *qua* other; and another kind is a state of insusceptibility to change for the worse and to destruction by another thing or by the thing itself *qua* other by virtue of an

[25] Cf.ª23–33.
[1] Cf. vii, viii.   [2] Cf. vii. 1.   [3] Cf. ix. 1048ª 27–ᵇ 6.   [4] Cf. v. 12.

originative source of change. In all these definitions is implied the 15
formula of potency in the primary sense.—And again these so-called
potencies are potencies either of merely acting or being acted on, or
of acting or being acted on *well*, so that even in the formulae of the
latter the formulae of the prior kinds of potency are somehow implied.

Obviously, then, in a sense the potency of acting and of being acted
on is one (for a thing may be 'capable' either because it can itself be 20
acted on or because something else can be acted on by it), but in a
sense the potencies are different. For the one is in the thing acted on;
it is because it contains a certain originative source, and because even
the matter is an originative source, that the thing acted on is acted
on, and one thing by one, another by another; for that which is oily
can be burnt, and that which yields in a particular way can be crushed; [5] 25
and similarly in all other cases. But the other potency is in the agent,
e. g. heat and the art of building are present, one in that which can
produce heat and the other in the man who can build. And so, in so
far as a thing is an organic unity, it cannot be acted on by itself; for
it is one and not two different things. And 'impotence' and 'impotent'
stand for the privation which is contrary to potency of this sort, so 30
that every potency belongs to the same subject and refers to the same
process as a corresponding impotence. Privation has several senses;
for it means (1) that which has not a certain quality and (2) that
which might naturally have it but has not it, either (a) in general or
(b) when it might naturally have it, and either (α) in some particular
way, e. g. when it has not it completely, or (β) when it has not it at
all. And in certain cases if things which naturally have a quality lose 35
it by violence, we say they have suffered privation.

2   Since some such originative sources are present in soulless things,
and others in things possessed of soul, and in soul, and in the rational
part of the soul, clearly some potencies will be non-rational and some 1046ᵇ
will be accompanied by a rational formula. This is why all arts, i. e.
all productive forms of knowledge, are potencies; they are originative
sources of change in another thing or in the artist himself considered
as other.

And each of those which are accompanied by a rational formula is
alike capable of contrary effects, but one non-rational power produces 5
one effect; e. g. the hot is capable only of heating, but the medical art
can produce both disease and health. The reason is that science is a
rational formula, and the same rational formula explains a thing and

---

[5] i. e. the event would not happen if the passive factor were different. What is
oily cannot necessarily be crushed, nor what is yielding burnt.

its privation, only not in the same way; and in a sense it applies to
10 both, but in a sense it applies rather to the positive fact. Therefore
such sciences must deal with contraries, but with one in virtue of their
own nature and with the other not in virtue of their nature; for the
rational formula applies to one object in virtue of that object's nature,
and to the other, in a sense, accidentally. For it is by denial and
removal that it exhibits the contrary; for the contrary is the primary
15 privation, and this is the removal of the positive term. Now since
contraries do not occur in the same thing, but science is a potency
which depends on the possession of a rational formula, and the soul
possesses an originative source of movement; therefore, while the
wholesome produces only health and the calorific only heat and the
20 frigorific only cold, the scientific man produces both the contrary
effects. For the rational formula is one which applies to both, though
not in the same way, and it is in a soul which possesses an originative
source of movement; so that the soul will start both processes from
the same originative source, having linked them up with the same
thing.[6] And so the things whose potency is according to a rational
formula act contrariwise to the things whose potency is non-rational;
for the products of the former are included under one originative
source, the rational formula.
25   It is obvious also that the potency of merely doing a thing or having
it done to one is implied in that of doing it or having it done *well*,
but the latter is not always implied in the former: for he who does a
thing well must also do it, but he who does it merely need not also do
it well.

3   There are some who say, as the Megaric school does, that a thing
'can' act only when it is acting, and when it is not acting it 'cannot'
30 act, e. g. that he who is not building cannot build, but only he who
is building, when he is building; and so in all other cases. It is not hard
to see the absurdities that attend this view.
For it is clear that on this view a man will not be a builder unless
he is building (for to be a builder is to be able to build), and so with
35 the other arts. If, then, it is impossible to have such arts if one has
not at some time learnt and acquired them, and it is then impossible
1047ᵃ not to have them if one has not sometime lost them (either by forgetfulness or by some accident or by time; for it cannot be by the destruction of the *object*,[7] for that lasts for ever), a man will not have the

6 i. e. with the rational formula.
7 The object of knowledge is always a form, which is eternal. The matter which
makes things perishable is no object for knowledge.

art when he has ceased to use it, and yet he may immediately build again; how then will he have got the art? And similarly with regard to lifeless things; nothing will be either cold or hot or sweet or per-⁵ ceptible at all if people are not perceiving it; so that the upholders of this view will have to maintain the doctrine of Protagoras.[8] But, indeed, nothing will even have perception if it is not perceiving, i. e. exercising its perception. If, then, that is blind which has not sight though it would naturally have it, when it would naturally have it and when it still exists, the same people will be blind many times in the day—and deaf too.

Again, if that which is deprived of potency is incapable, that which ¹⁰ is not happening will be incapable of happening; but he who says of that which is incapable of happening either that it is or that it will be will say what is untrue; for this is what incapacity meant. Therefore these views do away with both movement and becoming. For that ¹⁵ which stands will always stand, and that which sits will always sit, since if it is sitting it will not get up; for that which, as we are told, cannot get up will be incapable of getting up. But we cannot say this, so that evidently potency and actuality are different (but these views make potency and actuality the same, and so it is no small thing they are seeking to annihilate), so that it is possible that a thing may be ²⁰ capable of being and not *be*, and capable of not being and yet *be*, and similarly with the other kinds of predicate; it may be capable of walking and yet not walk, or capable of not walking and yet walk. And a thing is capable of doing something if there will be nothing impossible in its having the actuality of that of which it is said to have ²⁵ the capacity. I mean, for instance, if a thing is capable of sitting and it is open to it to sit, there will be nothing impossible in its actually sitting; and similarly if it is capable of being moved or moving, or of standing or making to stand, or of being or coming to be, or of not being or not coming to be.

The word 'actuality', which we connect with 'complete reality', ³⁰ has, in the main, been extended from movements to other things; for actuality in the strict sense is thought to be identical with movement. And so people do not assign movement to non-existent things, though they do assign some other predicates. E. g. they say that non-existent things are objects of thought and desire, but not that they are moved; and this because, while *ex hypothesi* they do not actually ³⁵ exist, they would have to exist actually if they were moved. For of non-existent things some exist potentially; but they do not *exist*, 1047ᵇ because they do not exist in complete reality.

[8] Cf. iv. 5, 6.

4 If what we have described [9] is identical with the capable or convertible with it, evidently it cannot be true to say 'this is capable of
5 being but will not be', which would imply that the things *in*capable of being would on this showing vanish. Suppose, for instance, that a man—one who did not take account of that which is incapable of being—were to say that the diagonal of the square is capable of being measured but will not be measured, because a thing may well be capable of being or coming to be, and yet not be or be about to be. But from the premises this necessarily follows, that if we actually
10 supposed that which is not, but is capable of being, to be or to have come to be, there will be nothing impossible in this; but the result *will* be impossible, for the measuring of the diagonal is impossible. For the false and the impossible are *not* the same; that you are standing now is false, but that you should be standing is not impossible.

At the same time it is clear that if, when A is real, B must be real,
15 then, when A is possible, B also must be possible. For if B need not be possible, there is nothing to prevent its not being possible. Now let A be supposed possible. Then, when A was possible, we agreed that nothing impossible followed if A were supposed to be real; and then B
20 must of course be real. But we supposed B to be impossible. Let it be impossible, then. If, then, B is impossible, A also must be so. But the first *was* supposed impossible; therefore the second also is impossible. If, then, A is possible, B also will be possible, if they were so related that if A is real, B must be real. If, then, A and B being thus related,[10]
25 B is not possible on this condition,[11] A and B will not be related as was supposed.[12] And if when A is possible, B must be possible, then if A is real, B also must be real. For to say that B must be possible, if A is possible, means this, that if A is real both at the time when and in the way in which it was supposed capable of being real, B also must
30 then and in that way be real.

5 As all potencies are either innate, like the senses, or come by practice, like the power of playing the flute, or by learning, like artistic power, those which come by practice or by rational formula we must acquire by previous exercise but this is not necessary with those which are not of this nature and which imply passivity.

---

[9] Cf. 1047ª 24–26.

[10] *sc.* so related that if the reality of A implies the reality of B the possibility of A implies the possibility of B.

[11] *sc.* if A is possible.

[12] *sc.* so related that the reality of A implies the reality of B.

Since that which is 'capable' is capable of something and at some 35
time and in some way (with all the other qualifications which must be 1048ᵃ
present in the definition), and since some things can produce change
according to a rational formula and their potencies involve such a
formula, while other things are non-rational and their potencies are
non-rational, and the former potencies must be in a living thing, while
the latter can be both in the living and in the lifeless; as regards 5
potencies of the latter kind, when the agent and the patient meet in
the way appropriate to the potency in question, the one must act and
the other be acted on, but with the former kind of potency this is not
necessary. For the non-rational potencies are all productive of one
effect each, but the rational produce contrary effects, so that if they
produced their effects necessarily they would produce contrary effects
at the same time; but this is impossible. There must, then, be some- 10
thing else that decides; I mean by this, desire or will. For whichever
of two things the animal desires decisively, it will do, when it is
present, and meets the passive object, in the way appropriate to the
potency in question. Therefore everything which has a rational
potency, when it desires that for which it has a potency and in the
circumstances in which it has the potency, must do this. And it has 15
the potency in question when the passive object is present and is in
a certain state; if not it will not be able to act. (To add the qualification 'if nothing external prevents it' is not further necessary; for
it has the potency on the terms on which this is a potency of acting,
and it is this not in all circumstances but on certain conditions, among
which will be the exclusion of external hindrances; for these are barred 20
by some of the positive qualifications.) And so even if one has a
rational wish, or an appetite, to do two things or contrary things at
the same time, one will not do them; for it is not on these terms
that one has the potency for them, nor is it a potency of doing both
at the same time, since one will do the things which it is a potency
of doing, on the terms on which one has the potency.

6 Since we have treated [13] of the kind of potency which is related 25
to movement, let us discuss actuality—what, and what kind of thing,
actuality is. For in the course of our analysis it will also become clear,
with regard to the potential, that we not only ascribe potency to that
whose nature it is to move something else, or to be moved by something
else, either without qualification or in some particular way, but also
use the word in another sense, which is the reason of the inquiry in
the course of which we have discussed these previous senses also. 30

[13] Cf. ix. 1–5.

Actuality, then, is the existence of a thing not in the way which we express by 'potentially'; we say that potentially, for instance, a statue of Hermes is in the block of wood and the half-line is in the whole, because it might be separated out, and we call even the man who is not studying a man of science, if he is capable of studying;

35 the thing that stands in contrast to each of these exists actually. Our meaning can be seen in the particular cases by induction, and we must not seek a definition of everything but be content to grasp the analogy, that it is as that which is building is to that which is capable of

1048ᵇ building, and the waking to the sleeping, and that which is seeing to that which has its eyes shut but has sight, and that which has been shaped out of the matter to the matter, and that which has been wrought up to the unwrought. Let actuality be defined by one mem-

5 ber of this antithesis, and the potential by the other. But all things are not said in the *same sense* to exist actually, but only by analogy—as *A* is in *B* or to *B*, *C* is in *D* or to *D*; for some are as movement to potency, and the others as substance to some sort of matter.

But also the infinite and the void and all similar things are said

10 to exist potentially and actually in a different sense from that which applies to many other things, e. g. to that which sees or walks or is seen. For of the latter class these predicates can at some time be also truly asserted without qualification; for the seen is so called sometimes because it is being seen, sometimes because it is capable of being seen. But the infinite does not exist potentially in the sense that it will ever actually have separate existence; it exists potentially only

15 for knowledge. For the fact that the process of dividing never comes to an end ensures that this activity exists potentially, but not that the infinite exists separately.

Since of the actions which have a limit none is an end but all are relative to the end, e. g. the removing of fat, or fat-removal, and the

20 bodily parts themselves when one is making them thin are in movement in this way (i. e. without being already that at which the movement aims), this is not an action or at least not a complete one (for it is not an end); but that movement in which the end is present is an action. E. g. at the same time we are seeing and have seen, are understanding and have understood, are thinking and have thought (while it is not true that at the same time we are learning and have

25 learnt, or are being cured and have been cured). At the same time we are living well and have lived well, and are happy and have been happy. If not, the process would have had sometime to cease, as the process of making thin ceases: but, as things are, it does not cease; we are living and have lived. Of these processes, then, we

must call the one set movements, and the other actualities. For every
movement is incomplete—making thin, learning, walking, building;
these are movements, and incomplete at that. For it is not true that 30
at the same time a thing is walking and has walked, or is building
and has built, or is coming to be and has come to be, or is being moved
and has been moved, but what is being moved is different from what
has been moved, and what is moving from what has moved. But it
is the same thing that at the same time has seen and is seeing, or is
thinking and has thought. The latter sort of process, then, I call an
actuality, and the former a movement.

7 What, and what kind of thing, the actual is, may be taken as 35
explained by these and similar considerations. But we must distinguish when a thing exists potentially and when it does not; for it
is not at any and every time. E. g. is earth potentially a man? No— 1049ᵃ
but rather when it has already become seed, and perhaps not even then.
It is just as it is with being healed; not everything can be healed
by the medical art or by luck, but there is a certain kind of thing
which is capable of it, and only this is potentially healthy. And (1)
the delimiting mark of that which as a result of *thought* comes to 5
exist in complete reality from having existed potentially is that if
the agent has willed it it comes to pass if nothing external hinders,
while the condition on the other side—viz. in that which is healed—
is that nothing in it hinders the result. It is on similar terms that we
have what is potentially a house; if nothing in the thing acted on—
i. e. in the matter—prevents it from becoming a house, and if there 10
is nothing which must be added or taken away or changed, this is
potentially a house; and the same is true of all other things the source
of whose becoming is external. And (2) in the cases in which the
source of the becoming is in the very thing which comes to be, a
thing is potentially all those things which it will be of itself if nothing
external hinders it. E. g. the seed is not yet potentially a man; for
it must be deposited in something other than itself and undergo a
change. But when through its own motive principle it has already 15
got such and such attributes, in this state it is already potentially
a man; while in the former state it needs another motive principle,
just as earth is not yet potentially a statue (for it must first change
in order to become brass).

It seems that when we call a thing not something else but 'thaten'
—e. g. a casket is not 'wood' but 'wooden', and wood is not 'earth' 20
but 'earthen', and again earth will illustrate our point if it is similarly
not something else but 'thaten'—that other thing is always poten-

tially (in the full sense of that word) the thing which comes after it in this series. E. g. a casket is not 'earthen' nor 'earth', but 'wooden'; for this is potentially a casket and this is the matter of a casket, wood in general of a casket in general, and this particular wood of this particular casket. And if there is a first thing, which is no longer, in reference to something else, called 'thaten', this is 25 prime matter; e. g. if earth is 'airy' and air is not 'fire' but 'fiery', fire is prime matter, which is not a 'this'. For the subject or substratum is differentiated by being a 'this' or not being one; i. e. the substratum of *modifications* is, e. g., a man, i. e. a body and a soul, 30 while the modification is 'musical' or 'pale'. (The subject is called, when music comes to be present in it, not 'music' but 'musical', and the man is not 'paleness' but 'pale', and not 'ambulation' or 'movement' but 'walking' or 'moving'—which is akin to the 'thaten'.) Wherever this is so, then, the ultimate subject is a substance; but 35 when this is not so but the predicate is a *form* and a 'this', the ultimate subject is matter and material substance. And it is only right that 'thaten' should be used with reference both to the matter 1049ᵇ and to the accidents; for both are indeterminates.

We have stated, then, when a thing is to be said to exist potentially and when it is not.

8   From our discussion of the various senses of 'prior',[14] it is clear 5 that actuality is prior to potency. And I mean by potency not only that definite kind which is said to be a principle of change in another thing or in the thing itself regarded as other, but in general every principle of movement or of rest. For nature also is in the same genus 10 as potency; for it is a principle of movement—not, however, in something else but in the thing itself *qua* itself. To all such potency, then, actuality is prior both in formula and in substantiality; and in time it is prior in one sense, and in another not.

(1) Clearly it is prior in formula; for that which is in the primary sense potential is potential because it is possible for it to become active; e. g. I mean by 'capable of building' that which can build, 15 and by 'capable of seeing' that which can see, and by 'visible' that which can be seen. And the same account applies to all other cases, so that the formula and the knowledge of the one must precede the knowledge of the other.

(2) In time it is prior in this sense: the actual which is identical in species though not in number with a potentially existing thing is prior to it. I mean that to this particular man who now exists actually

14 Cf. v. 11.

and to the corn and to the seeing subject the matter and the seed 20
and that which is capable of seeing, which are potentially a man and
corn and seeing, but not yet actually so, are prior in time; but prior
in time to these are other actually existing things, from which they
were produced. For from the potentially existing the actually existing
is always produced by an actually existing thing, e. g. man from
man, musician by musician; there is always a first mover, and the 25
mover already exists actually. We have said in our account of substance [15] that everything that is produced is something produced from
something and by something, and that the same in species as it.

This is why it is thought impossible to be a builder if one has
built nothing or a harper if one has never played the harp; for he 30
who learns to play the harp learns to play it by playing it, and all
other learners do similarly. And thence arose the sophistical quibble,
that one who does not possess a science will be doing that which is
the object of the science; for he who is learning it does not possess
it. But since, of that which is coming to be, some part must have 35
come to be, and, of that which, in general, is changing, some part
must have changed (this is shown in the treatise on movement [16]),
he who is learning must, it would seem, possess some part of the 1050ᵃ
science. But *here* too, then, it is clear that actuality is in this sense
also, viz. in order of generation and of time, prior to potency.

But (3) it is also prior in substantiality; firstly, (*a*) because the
things that are posterior in becoming are prior in form and in substantiality (e. g. man is prior to boy and human being to seed; for 5
the one already has its form, and the other has not), and because
everything that comes to be moves towards a principle, i. e. an end
(for that for the sake of which a thing is, is its principle, and the
becoming is for the sake of the end), and the actuality is the end,
and it is for the sake of this that the potency is acquired. For animals 10
do not see in order that they may have sight, but they have sight
that they may see. And similarly men have the art of building that
they may build, and theoretical science that they may theorize; but
they do not theorize that they may have theoretical science, except
those who are learning by practice; and these do not theorize except
in a limited sense, or because they have no need to theorize. Further, 15
matter exists in a potential state, just because it may come to its
form; and when it exists *actually,* then it is in its form. And the same
holds good in all cases, even those in which the end is a movement.
And so, as teachers think they have achieved their end when they

[15] Cf. vii. 7, 8.·   [16] Cf. *Phys.* vi. 6.

have exhibited the pupil at work, nature does likewise. For if this is
20 not the case, we shall have Pauson's Hermes over again, since
it will be hard to say about the knowledge, as about the figure in the
picture, whether it is within or without.[17] For the action is the end,
and the actuality is the action. And so even the *word* 'actuality' is
derived from 'action', and points to the complete reality.

And while in some cases the exercise is the ultimate thing (e. g.
in sight the ultimate thing is seeing, and no other product besides
25 this results from sight), but from some things a product follows
(e. g. from the art of building there results a house as well as the act
of building), yet none the less the act is in the former case the end
and in the latter more of an end than the potency is. For the act of
building is realized in the thing that is being built, and comes to be,
and is, at the same time as the house.

30   Where, then, the result is something apart from the exercise, the
actuality is in the thing that is being made, e. g. the act of building
is in the thing that is being built and that of weaving in the thing
that is being woven, and similarly in all other cases, and in general
the movement is in the thing that is being moved; but where there
35 is no product apart from the actuality, the actuality is present in
the agents, e. g. the act of seeing is in the seeing subject and that of
theorizing in the theorizing subject and the life is in the soul (and
1050ᵇ therefore well-being also; for it is a certain kind of life).

Obviously, therefore, the substance or form is actuality. According
to this argument, then, it is obvious that actuality is prior in substantial being to potency; and as we have said,[18] one actuality always
5 precedes another in time right back to the actuality of the eternal
prime mover.

But (*b*) actuality is prior in a stricter sense also; for eternal things
are prior in substance to perishable things, and no eternal thing
exists potentially. The reason is this. Every potency is at one and
the same time a potency of the opposite; for, while that which is not
10 capable of being present in a subject cannot be present, everything
that is capable of being may possibly not be actual. That, then,
which is capable of being may either be or not be; the same thing,
then, is capable both of being and of not being. And that which is
capable of not being may possibly not be; and that which may possibly not be is perishable, either in the full sense, or in the precise sense
15 in which it is said that it possibly may not be, i. e. in respect either

---

[17] The reference is apparently to a tricky painting in which the figure was
painted so as to stand out in high relief.
[18] 1049ᵇ 17–29.

of place or of quantity or quality; 'in the full sense' means 'in respect of substance'. Nothing, then, which is in the full sense imperishable is in the full sense potentially existent (though there is nothing to prevent its being so in some respect, e. g. potentially of a certain quality or in a certain place); all imperishable things, then, exist actually. Nor can anything which is of *necessity* exist potentially; yet these things are primary; for if these did not exist, nothing would exist. Nor does eternal movement, if there be such, exist potentially; 20 and, if there is an eternal *mobile*, it is not in motion in virtue of a potentiality, except in respect of 'whence' and 'whither' (there is nothing to prevent its having matter which makes it capable of movement in various directions). And so the sun and the stars and the whole heaven are ever active, and there is no fear that they may sometime stand still, as the natural philosophers fear they may.[19] Nor do they tire in this activity; for movement is not for them, as it is for perishable things, connected with the potentiality for opposites, 25 so that the continuity of the movement should be laborious; for it is that kind of substance which is matter and potency, not actuality, that causes this.

Imperishable things [20] are imitated by those that are involved in change, e. g. earth and fire. For these also are ever active; for they have their movement of themselves and in themselves.[21] But the 30 other potencies, according to our previous discussion,[22] are all potencies for opposites; for that which can move another in this way can also move it not in this way, i. e. if it acts according to a rational formula; and the same *non-rational* potencies will produce opposite results by their presence or absence.

If, then, there are any entities or substances such as the dialecti- 35 cians [23] say the Ideas are, there must be something much more scientific than science-itself and something more mobile than movement-itself; for these will be more of the nature of actualities, while 1051ᵃ science-itself and movement-itself are potencies for these.[24]

Obviously, then, actuality is prior both to potency and to every principle of change.

[19] e. g. Empedocles (Cf. *De Caelo,* 284ᵃ 24–6).
[20] *sc.* the heavenly bodies.
[21] i. e. they are both movers and moved.
[22] Cf. ᵇ 8–12.
[23] The Platonists are meant; Cf. i. 987ᵇ 31.
[24] The Idea, being the universal apart from its special manifestations, will be a potentiality, and will therefore be inferior to the corresponding particulars—e. g. the Idea of science will be inferior to particular acts of scientific thought.

9 That the actuality is also better and more valuable than the good
5 potency is evident from the following argument. Everything of which
we say that it can do something, is alike capable of contraries, e. g.
that of which we say that it can be well is the same as that which
can be ill, and has both potencies at once; for the same potency is a
potency of health and illness, of rest and motion, of building and
throwing down, of being built and being thrown down. The capacity
10 for contraries, then, is present at the same time; but contraries
cannot be present at the same time, and the actualities also cannot
be present at the same time, e. g. health and illness. Therefore, while
the good must be one of them, the capacity is both alike, or neither;
15 the actuality, then, is better. Also in the case of bad things the end
or actuality must be worse than the potency; for that which 'can'
is both contraries alike. Clearly, then, the bad does not exist apart
from bad things; for the bad is in its nature posterior to the
potency.[25] And therefore we may also say that in the things which
20 are from the beginning, i. e. in eternal things, there is nothing bad,
nothing defective, nothing perverted (for perversion is something
bad).[26]

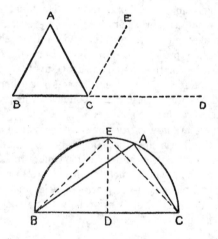

It is by an activity also that geometrical constructions are discovered; for we find them by dividing. If the figures had been already
divided, the constructions would have been obvious; but as it is they

[25] sc. while the eternal and substantial must be better than the potency.
[26] The paragraph seems to be directed against Plato: Cf. *Rep.* 402 c, 476 A,
Theaet. 176 E, *Laws* 896 E, 898 c.

are present only potentially. Why are the angles of the triangle equal to two right angles? Because the angles about one point are equal to two right angles. If, then, the line parallel to the side had been 25 already drawn upwards, the reason would have been evident to any one as soon as he saw the figure. Why is the angle in a semicircle in all cases a right angle? If three lines are equal—the two which form the base, and the perpendicular from the centre—the conclusion is evident at a glance to one who knows the former proposition. Obviously, therefore, the potentially existing constructions are discovered 30 by being brought to actuality; the reason is that the geometer's thinking is an actuality; so that the potency proceeds from an actuality; and therefore it is by making constructions that people come to know them (though the single actuality is later in generation than the corresponding potency).

10   The terms 'being' and 'non-being' are employed firstly with reference to the categories, and secondly with reference to the potency 35 or actuality of these or their non-potency or non-actuality, and 1051ᵇ thirdly in the sense of true and false. This depends, on the side of the objects, on their being combined or separated, so that he who thinks the separated to be separated and the combined to be combined has the truth, while he whose thought is in a state contrary to that of the objects is in error. This being so, when is what is 5 called truth or falsity present, and when is it not? We must consider what we mean by these terms. It is not because we think truly that you are pale, that you *are* pale, but because you are pale we who say this have the truth. If, then, some things are always combined and cannot be separated, and others are always separated and cannot 10 be combined, while others are capable either of combination or of separation, 'being' is being combined and one, and 'not being' is being not combined but more than one. Regarding contingent facts, then, the same opinion or the same statement comes to be false and true, and it is possible for it to be at one time correct and at another 15 erroneous; but regarding things that cannot be otherwise opinions are not at one time true and at another false, but the same opinions are always true or always false.

But with regard to *incomposites*, what is being or not being, and truth or falsity? A thing of this sort is not composite, so as to 'be' when it is compounded, and not to 'be' if it is separated, like 'that 20 the wood is white' or 'that the diagonal is incommensurable'; nor will truth and falsity be still present in the same way as in the previous cases. In fact, as truth is not the same in these cases, so also being is not the same; but (*a*) truth or falsity is as follows—contact and assertion are truth (assertion not being the same as affirmation), 25 and ignorance is non-contact. For it is not possible to be in *error* regarding the question what a thing is, save in an accidental sense; and the same holds good regarding non-composite substances (for it is not possible to be in error about them). And they all exist actually, not potentially; for otherwise they would have come to be and ceased to be; but, as it is, being itself does not come to be (nor 30 cease to be); for if it had done so it would have had to come out of something. About the things, then, which are essences and actualities, it is not possible to be in error, but only to know them or not to know them. But we do inquire what they are, viz. whether they are of such and such a nature or not.

(*b*) As regards the '*being*' that answers to truth and the 'non-being' that answers to falsity, in one case there is truth if the subject and the attribute are really combined, and falsity if they are not 35 combined; in the other case, if the object is existent it exists in a 1052ᵃ particular way, and if it does not exist in this way it does not exist at all.[27] And truth means knowing these objects, and falsity does not exist, nor error, but only ignorance—and not an ignorance which is like blindness; for blindness is akin to a total absence of the faculty of thinking.

5 It is evident also that about unchangeable things there can be no error in respect of time, if we assume them to be unchangeable. E. g. if we suppose that the triangle does not change, we shall not suppose that at one time its angles are equal to two right angles while at another time they are not (for that would imply change). It is possible, however, to suppose that one member of such a class has a certain attribute and another has not; e. g. while we *may* suppose that no even number is prime, we *may* suppose that some are and some are not. But regarding a numerically single number not even 10 this form of error is possible; for we cannot in this case suppose that one instance has an attribute and another has not, but whether our judgement be true or false, it is implied that the fact is eternal.

BOOK I (X)

15 1   We have said previously, in our distinction of the various meanings of words,[1] that 'one' has several meanings; the things that are

27 i. e. we have not here *A* and *B*, which may or may not be combined, but *A*, which if it exists at all exists as *A*.   1 v. 6.

directly and of their own nature and not accidentally called one may be summarized under four heads, though the word is used in more senses. (1) There is the continuous, either in general, or especially that which is continuous by nature and not by contact nor by being tied together; and of these, that has more unity and is prior, whose 20 movement [2] is more indivisible and simpler. (2) That which is a whole and has a certain shape and form is *one* in a still higher degree; and especially if a thing is of this sort by nature, and not by force like the things which are unified by glue or nails or by being tied together, i. e. if it has in itself the cause of its continuity. A thing is 25 of this sort because its movement is one and indivisible in place and time; so that evidently if a thing has by nature a principle of movement that is of the first kind (i. e. local movement) and the first in that kind (i. e. circular movement), this is in the primary sense one extended thing. Some things, then, are one in this way, *qua* continuous or whole, and the other things that are one are those whose definition is one. Of this sort are the things the thought of 30 which is one, i. e. those the thought of which is indivisible; and it is indivisible if the thing is indivisible in kind or in number. (3) In number, then, the individual is indivisible, and (4) in kind, that which in intelligibility and in knowledge is indivisible, so that that which causes substances to be one [3] must be one in the primary sense. 'One', then, has all these meanings—the naturally continuous and the whole, and the individual and the universal. And all these 35 are one because in some cases the movement, in others the thought or the definition is indivisible.

But it must be observed that the questions, what sort of things 1052ᵇ are said to be one, and what it is to be one and what is the definition of it, should not be assumed to be the same. 'One' has all these meanings, and each of the things to which one of these kinds of unity 5 belongs will be one; but 'to be one' will sometimes mean being one of these things, and sometimes being something else which is even nearer to the meaning of the *word* 'one' while these other things approximate to its *application*. This is also true of 'element' or 'cause', if one had both to specify the things of which it is predicable and to render the definition of the word. For in a sense fire is an 10 element (and doubtless also 'the indefinite' or something else of the sort is by its own nature the element), but in a sense it is not; for it is not the same thing to be fire and to be an element, but while as a particular thing with a nature of its own fire is an element, the name

---

[2] Nature is defined (v. 1015ᵃ 13) as 'the essence of things which have in themselves, as such, a source of movement'.   [3] *sc.* the form.

'element' means that it has this attribute, that there is something which is made of it as a primary constituent. And so with 'cause' and
15 'one' and all such terms. For this reason, too, 'to be one' means 'to be indivisible, being essentially a "this" and capable of being isolated either in place, or in form or thought'; or perhaps 'to be whole and indivisible'; but it means especially 'to be the first measure of a kind', and most strictly of quantity; for it is from this that it has been
20 extended to the other categories. For measure is that by which quantity is known; and quantity *qua* quantity is known either by a 'one' or by a number, and all number is known by a 'one'. Therefore all quantity *qua* quantity is known by the one, and that by which quantities are primarily known is the one itself; and so the one is the starting-point of number *qua* number. And hence in the other classes
25 too 'measure' means that by which each is first known, and the measure of each is a unit—in length, in breadth, in depth, in weight, in speed. (The words 'weight' and 'speed' are common to both contraries;[4] for each of them has two meanings—'weight' means both that which has any amount of gravity and that which has an excess of gravity, and 'speed' both that which has any amount of movement
30 and that which has an excess of movement; for even the slow has a certain speed and the comparatively light a certain weight.)

In all these, then, the measure and starting-point is something one and indivisible, since even in lines we treat as indivisible the line a foot long. For everywhere we seek as the measure something one
35 and indivisible; and this is that which is simple either in quality or in quantity. Now where it is thought impossible to take away or to add, there the measure is exact (hence that of number is most exact;
1053ᵃ for we posit the unit as indivisible in every respect); but in all other cases we imitate this sort of measure. For in the case of a furlong or a talent or of anything comparatively large any addition or subtraction might more easily escape our notice than in the case
5 of something smaller; so that the first thing from which, as far as our perception goes, nothing can be subtracted, all men make the measure, whether of liquids or of solids, whether of weight or of size; and they think they know the quantity when they know it by means of this measure. And indeed they know movement too by the
10 simple movement and the quickest; for this occupies least time. And so in astronomy a 'one' of this sort is the starting-point and measure (for they assume the movement of the heavens to be uniform and the quickest, and judge the others by reference to it), and in music the quarter-tone (because it is the least interval), and in speech

---

[4] *sc.* heavy and light, fast and slow.

the letter. And all these are ones in this sense—not that 'one' is something predicable in the same sense of all of these, but in the sense we have mentioned.

But the measure is not always one in number—sometimes there are several; e. g. the quarter-tones (not to the ear, but as determined 15 by the ratios) are two, and the articulate sounds by which we measure are more than one, and the diagonal of the square and its side are measured by two quantities, and all spatial magnitudes reveal similar varieties of unit. Thus, then, the one is the measure of all things, because we come to know the elements in the substance by dividing the things either in respect of quantity or in respect of kind. 20 And the one is indivisible just because the first of each class of things is indivisible. But it is not in the same way that every 'one' is indivisible, e. g. a foot and a unit; the latter is indivisible in every respect, while the former must be placed among things which are undivided to perception, as has been said already [5]—only to perception, for doubtless every continuous thing is divisible.

The measure is always homogeneous with the thing measured; the measure of spatial magnitudes is a spatial magnitude, and in particu- 25 lar that of length is a length, that of breadth a breadth, that of articulate sound an articulate sound, that of weight a weight, that of units a unit. (For we must state the matter so, and not say that the measure of numbers is a number; we ought indeed to say this if we were to use the corresponding form of words, but the claim does not really correspond—it is as if one claimed that the measure of units 30 is units, and not a unit; number is a plurality of *units*.)

Knowledge, also, and perception, we call the measure of things for the same reason, because we come to know something by them—while as a matter of fact they are measured rather than measure other things. But it is with us as if some one else measured us and we came to know how big we are by seeing that he applied the cubit-measure to such and such a fraction of us. But Protagoras says 'man is the 35 measure of all things', as if he had said 'the man who knows' or 'the man who perceives'; and these because they have respectively 1053^b knowledge and perception, which we say are the measures of objects. Such thinkers are saying nothing, then, while they appear to be saying something remarkable.

Evidently, then, unity in the strictest sense, if we define it according to the meaning of the word, is a measure, and most properly of 5 quantity, and secondly of quality. And some things will be one if they are indivisible in quantity, and others if they are indivisible in

[5] Cf. 1052^b 33, 1053^a 5.

quality; and so that which is one is indivisible, either absolutely or *qua* one.

2   With regard to the substance and nature of the one we must ask
10 in which of two ways it exists. This is the very question that we
reviewed [6] in our discussion of problems, viz. what the one is and how
we must conceive of it, whether we must take the one itself as being
a substance (as both the Pythagoreans say in earlier and Plato in
later times), or there is, rather, an underlying nature and the one
should be described more intelligibly and more in the manner of the
15 physical philosophers, of whom one says the one is love, another says
it is air, and another the indefinite.[7]

If, then, no universal can be a substance, as has been said [8] in our
discussion of substance and being, and if being itself cannot be a
substance in the sense of a one apart from the many (for it is com-
20 mon to the many), but is only a predicate, clearly unity also cannot be a
substance; for being and unity are the most universal of all predicates.
Therefore, on the one hand, genera are not certain entities and substances separable from other things; and on the other hand the one
cannot be a genus, for the same reasons for which being and substance
cannot be genera.

Further, the position must be similar in all the kinds of unity. Now
'unity' has just as many meanings as 'being'; so that since in the
25 sphere of qualities the one is something definite—some particular
kind of thing—and similarly in the sphere of quantities, clearly we
must in every category ask what the one is, as we must ask what the
existent is, since it is not enough to say that its nature is just to be
one or existent. But in colours the one is a colour, e. g. white, and
then the other colours are observed to be produced out of this and
30 black, and black is the privation of white, as darkness of light.
Therefore if all existent things were colours, existent things would
have been a number, indeed, but of what? Clearly of colours; and the
'one' would have been a particular 'one', i. e. white. And similarly if
all existing things were tunes, they would have been a number, but
35 a number of quarter-tones, and their essence would not have been
number; and the one would have been something whose substance
1054ᵃ was not to be one but to be the quarter-tone. And similarly if all
existent things had been articulate sounds, they would have been a
number of letters, and the one would have been a vowel. And if all

[6] iii. 1001ᵃ 4–ᵇ25.
[7] The three thinkers referred to are Empedocles, Anaximenes, Anaximander.
[8] vii. 13.

existent things were rectilinear figures, they would have been a number of figures, and the one would have been the triangle. And the same argument applies to all other classes. Since, therefore, while there are numbers and a one both in affections and in qualities and in 5 quantities and in movement, in all cases the number is a number of particular things and the one is one something, and its substance is not just to be one, the same must be true of substances also; for it is true of all cases alike.

That the one, then, in every class is a definite thing, and in no case 10 is its nature just this, unity, is evident; but as in colours the one-itself which we must seek is one colour, so too in substance the one-itself is one substance. That in a sense unity means the same as being is clear from the facts that its meanings correspond to the categories one to one, and it is not comprised within any category (e. g. it is 15 comprised neither in 'what a thing is' nor in quality, but is related to them just as being is); that in 'one man' nothing more is predicated than in 'man' (just as being is nothing apart from substance or quality or quantity); and that to be one is just to be a particular thing.

3   The one and the many are opposed in several ways, of which one 20 is the opposition of the one and plurality as indivisible and divisible; for that which is either divided or divisible is called a plurality, and that which is indivisible or not divided is called one. Now since opposition is of four kinds, and one of these two terms is privative in meaning, they must be contraries, and neither contradictory nor 25 correlative in meaning.[9] And the one derives its name and its explanation from its contrary, the indivisible from the divisible, because plurality and the divisible is more perceptible than the indivisible, so that in definition plurality is prior to the indivisible, because of the conditions of perception.

To the one belong, as we indicated graphically in our distinction 30 of the contraries,[10] the same and the like and the equal, and to plurality belong the other and the unlike and the unequal. 'The same' has several meanings; (1) we sometimes mean 'the same numerically'; again, (2) we call a thing the same if it is one both in definition and in number, e. g. you are one with yourself both in form and in matter; and again, (3) if the definition of its primary essence is 35 one; e. g. equal straight lines are the same, and so are equal and 1054ᵇ

[9] Two of the kinds, contrariety and privation, are not mutually exclusive, for contrariety is the relation between a form and its complete privation. Cf. iv. 1004ᵇ 27, x. 1055ᵇ 26.   [10] Cf. iv. 1004ᵃ 2.

equal-angled quadrilaterals; there are many such, but in these equality constitutes unity.

Things are like if, not being absolutely the same, nor without difference in respect of their concrete substance, they are the same in form; 5 e. g. the larger square is like the smaller, and unequal straight lines are like; they are like, but not absolutely the same. Other things are like, if, having the same form, and being things in which difference of degree is possible, they have no difference of degree. Other things, if they have a quality that is in form one and the same—e. g. white- 10 ness—in a greater or less degree, are called like because their form is one. Other things are called like if the qualities they have in common are more numerous than those in which they differ—either the qualities in general or the prominent qualities; e. g. tin is like silver, *qua* white, and gold is like fire, *qua* yellow and red.

Evidently, then, 'other' and 'unlike' also have several meanings. And the other in one sense is the opposite of the same (so that every- 15 thing is either the same as or other than everything else). In another sense things are other unless both their matter and their definition are one (so that you are other than your neighbour). The other in the third sense is exemplified in the objects of mathematics. 'Other or the same' can therefore be predicated of everything with regard to every- thing else—but only if the things are one and existent, for 'other' is 20 not the *contradictory* of 'the same'; which is why it is not predicated of non-existent things (while 'not the same' *is* so predicated). It *is* predicated of all *existing* things; for everything that is existent and one is by its very nature either one or not one with anything else.

The other, then, and the same are thus opposed. But difference is not the same as otherness. For the other and that which it is other than need not be other in some definite respect (for everything that 25 is existent is either other or the same), but that which is different is different from some particular thing in some particular respect, so that there must be something identical whereby they differ. And this identical thing is genus or species; for everything that differs differs either in genus or in species, in genus if the things have not their matter in common and are not generated out of each other (i. e. if they belong to different figures of predication), and in species if they 30 have the same genus ('genus' meaning that identical thing which is essentially predicated of both the different things).

Contraries are different, and contrariety is a kind of difference. That we are right in this supposition is shown by induction. For all 35 of these too are seen to be different; they are not merely other, but 1055ᵃ some are other in genus, and others are in the same line of predication, and therefore in the same genus, and the same in genus. We have distinguished [11] elsewhere what sort of things are the same or other in genus.

4   Since things which differ may differ from one another more or less, there is also a greatest difference, and this I call contrariety. That contrariety is the greatest difference is made clear by induction. For things which differ in *genus* have no way to one another, but are too far distant and are not comparable; and for things that differ in *species* the extremes from which generation takes place are the contraries, and the distance between extremes—and therefore that between the contraries—is the greatest.

But surely that which is greatest in each class is complete. For that is greatest which cannot be exceeded, and that is complete beyond which nothing can be found. For the complete difference marks the end of a series (just as the other things which are called complete are so called because they have attained an end), and beyond the end there is nothing; for in everything it is the extreme and includes all else, and therefore there is nothing beyond the end, and the complete needs nothing further. From this, then, it is clear that contrariety is complete difference; and as contraries are so called in several senses, their modes of completeness will answer to the various modes of contrariety which attach to the contraries.

This being so, it is clear that one thing cannot have more than one contrary (for neither can there be anything more extreme than the extreme, nor can there be more than two extremes for the one interval), and, to put the matter generally, this is clear if contrariety is a difference, and if difference, and therefore also the complete difference, must be between two things.

And the other commonly accepted definitions of contraries are also necessarily true. For not only is (1) the complete difference the greatest difference (for we can get no difference beyond it of things differing either in genus or in species; for it has been shown [12] that there is *no* 'difference' between anything and the things outside its *genus*, and among the things which differ in *species* the complete difference is the greatest); but also (2) the things in the same genus which differ most are contrary (for the complete difference is the greatest difference between species of the same genus); and (3) the things in the same receptive material which differ most are contrary (for the matter is the same for contraries); and (4) of the things which fall under the same faculty the most different are contrary

[11] v. 9.   [12] Cf. [a] 6.

(for one science deals with one class of things, and in these the complete difference is the greatest).

The primary contrariety is that between positive state and privation—not every privation, however (for 'privation' has several mean
35 ings), but that which is complete. And the other contraries must be called so with reference to these, some because they possess these, others because they produce or tend to produce them, others because they are acquisitions or losses of these or of other contraries. Now if the kinds of opposition are contradiction and privation and contrariety
1055ᵇ and relation, and of these the first is contradiction, and contradiction admits of no intermediate, while contraries admit of one, clearly contradiction and contrariety are not the same. But privation is a kind of contradiction; for what suffers privation, either in general or in some determinate way, is either that which is quite incapable of
5 having some attribute or that which, being of such a nature as to have it, has it not; here we have already a variety of meanings, which have been distinguished [13] elsewhere. Privation, therefore, is a contradiction or incapacity which is determinate or taken along with the receptive material. This is the reason why, while contradiction does not
10 admit of an intermediate, privation sometimes does; for everything is equal or not equal, but not everything is equal or unequal, or if it is, it is only within the sphere of that which is receptive of equality. If, then, the comings-to-be which happen to the matter start from the contraries, and proceed either from the form and the possession of the form or from a privation of the form or shape, clearly all con
15 trariety must be privation, but presumably not all privation is contrariety (the reason being that that which has suffered privation may have suffered it in several ways); for it is only the *extremes* from which changes proceed that are contraries.

And this is obvious also by induction. For every contrariety involves, as one of its terms, a privation, but not all cases are alike; inequality is the privation of equality and unlikeness of likeness, and
20 on the other hand vice is the privation of virtue. But the cases differ in a way already described; [14] in one case we mean simply that the thing has suffered privation, in another case that it has done so either at a certain time or in a certain part (e. g. at a certain age or in the dominant part), or throughout. This is why in some cases there is a mean (there are men who are neither good nor bad), and in others there is not (a number must be either odd or even). Further,
25 some contraries have their subject defined, others have not.—There-

[13] v. 22.   [14] 1055ᵇ 4–6.

fore it is evident that one of the contraries is always privative; but it is enough if this is true of the first—i. e. the generic—contraries, e. g. the one and the many; for the others can be reduced to these.

5   Since one thing has one contrary, we might raise the question how 30 the one is opposed to the many, and the equal to the great and the small. For if we use the word 'whether' only in an antithesis such as 'whether it is white or black', or 'whether it is white or not white' (we do not ask 'whether it is a man or white'), unless we are proceeding on a prior assumption and asking something such as 'whether it was 35 Cleon or Socrates that came'—but this is not a *necessary* disjunction in any class of things; yet even this is an extension from the case of opposites; for opposites alone cannot be present together; and we assume this incompatibility here too in asking which of the two came; for if they might both have come, the question would have been 1056ᵃ absurd; but if they might, even so this falls just as much into an antithesis, that of the 'one or many', i. e. 'whether both came or one of the two':—if, then, the question 'whether' is always concerned with opposites, and we can ask 'whether it is greater or less or equal', what is the opposition of the equal to the other two? It is not contrary 5 either to one alone or to both; for why should it be contrary to the greater rather than to the less? Further, the equal is contrary to the *unequal*. Therefore if it is contrary to the greater and the less, it will be contrary to more things than one. But if the unequal means the same as both the greater and the less together, the equal *will* be opposite to both (and the difficulty supports those who say the un- 10 equal is a 'two' [15]), but it follows that one thing is contrary to two others, which is impossible. Again, the equal is evidently intermediate between the great and the small, but no contrariety is either observed to be intermediate, or, from its definition, can be so; for it would not be complete [16] if it were intermediate between any two things, but rather it always has something intermediate between its own terms.

It remains, then, that it is opposed either as negation or as priva- 15 tion. It cannot be the negation or privation of one of the two; for why of the great rather than of the small? It is, then, the privative negation of both. This is why 'whether' is said with reference to both, not to one of the two (e. g. 'whether it is greater or equal' or 'whether it is equal or less'); there are always three cases. But it is not a 20 *necessary* privation; for not everything which is not greater or less is equal, but only the things which are of such a nature as to have these attributes.

[15] This is a Platonic doctrine; Cf. xiv. 1087ᵇ 7.   [16] Cf. 1055ᵃ 16.

The equal, then, is that which is neither great nor small but is naturally fitted to be either great or small; and it is opposed to both as a privative negation (and therefore is also intermediate). And that
25 which is neither good nor bad is opposed to both, but has no name; for each of these has several meanings and the recipient subject is not one; but that which is neither white nor black has more claim to unity. Yet even this has not one name, though the colours of which this negation is privately predicated are in a way limited; for they
30 must be either grey or yellow or something else of the kind. Therefore it is an incorrect criticism that is passed by those who think that all such phrases are used in the same way, so that that which is neither a shoe nor a hand would be intermediate between a shoe and a hand, since that which is neither good nor bad is intermediate between the good and the bad—as if there must be an intermediate in all cases.
35 But this does not necessarily follow. For the one phrase is a joint denial of opposites between which there is an intermediate and a
1056ᵇ certain natural interval; but between the other two there is no 'difference'; for the things, the denials of which are combined, belong to different classes, so that the substratum is not one.

6 We might raise similar questions about the one and the many. For if the many are absolutely opposed to the one, certain impossible
5 results follow. One will then be few, whether few be treated here as singular or plural; for the many are opposed also to the few. Further, two will be many, since the double is multiple and 'double' derives its meaning from 'two'; therefore one will be few; for what is that in comparison with which two are many, except one, which must therefore be few? For there is nothing fewer. Further, if the much and
10 the little are in plurality what the long and the short are in length, and whatever is much is also many, and the many are much (unless, indeed, there is a difference in the case of an easily-bounded continuum),[17] the little (or few) will be a plurality. Therefore one is a plurality *if* it is few; and this it must be, if two are many. But perhaps, while the 'many' are in a sense said to be also 'much', it is
15 with a difference; e. g. water is much but not many. But 'many' is applied to the things that are divisible; in one sense it means a plurality which is excessive either absolutely or relatively (while 'few' is similarly a plurality which is deficient), and in another sense it means number, in which sense alone it is opposed to the one. For we
20 say 'one or many', just as if one were to say 'one and ones' or 'white thing and white things', or to compare the things that have been

[17] i. e. a fluid. Cf. l. 16.

measured with the measure. It is in this sense also that multiples are so called. For each number is said to be many because it consists of ones and because each number is measurable by one; and it is 'many' as that which is opposed to one, not to the few. In *this* sense, then, even two is many—not, however, in the sense of a plurality which is 25 excessive either relatively or absolutely; it is the *first* plurality. But *without qualification* two is few; for it is the first plurality which is deficient (for this reason Anaxagoras was not right in leaving the subject with the statement that 'all things were together, boundless both in plurality and in smallness'—where for 'and in smallness' he 30 should have said 'and in fewness'; for they could not have been boundless in fewness), since it is not one, as some say, but two, that make a few.

The one is opposed then to the many in numbers as measure to thing measurable; and these are opposed as are the relatives which are not from their very nature relatives. We have distinguished [18] elsewhere the two senses in which relatives are so called:—(1) as 35 contraries; (2) as knowledge to thing known, a term being called relative because another is relative to it. There is nothing to prevent 1057ᵃ one from being fewer than something, e. g. than two; for if it is fewer, it is not therefore few. Plurality is as it were the class to which number belongs; for number is plurality measurable by one, and one and number are in a sense opposed, not as contrary, but as we have said some relative terms are opposed; for inasmuch as one is measure and 5 the other measurable, they are opposed. This is why not everything that is one is a number; i. e. if the thing is indivisible it is not a number. But though knowledge is similarly spoken of as relative to the knowable, the relation does not work out similarly; for while knowledge might be thought to be the measure, and the knowable the thing measured, the fact is that all knowledge is knowable, but 10 not all that is knowable is knowledge, because in a sense knowledge is measured by the knowable.—Plurality is contrary neither to the few (the *many* being contrary to this as excessive plurality to plurality exceeded), nor to the one in every sense; but in one sense these are contrary, as has been said, because the former is divisible and the latter indivisible, while in another sense they are relative as knowl- 15 edge is to knowable, if plurality is number and the one is a measure.

7   Since contraries admit of an intermediate and in some cases have it, intermediates must be composed of the contraries. For (1) all

[18] v. 1021ᵃ 26–30.

20 intermediates are in the same genus as the things between which they
stand. For we call those things intermediates, into which that which
changes must change first; e. g. if we were to pass from the highest
string to the lowest by the smallest intervals, we should come sooner
to the intermediate notes, and in colours if we were to pass from white
25 to black, we should come sooner to crimson and grey than to black;
and similarly in all other cases. But to change from one genus to
another genus is not possible except in an incidental way, as from
colour to figure. Intermediates, then, must be in the same genus both
as one another and as the things they stand between.

30   But (2) all intermediates stand between opposites of some kind;
for only between these can change take place in virtue of their own
nature (so that an intermediate is impossible between things which
are not opposite; for then there would be change which was not from
one opposite towards the other). Of opposites, contradictories admit
35 of no middle term; for this is what contradiction is—an opposition,
one or other side of which must attach to anything whatever, i. e.
which has no intermediate. Of other opposites, some are relative, others
privative, others contrary. Of relative terms, those which are not contrary have no intermediate; the reason is that they are not in the same
genus. For what intermediate could there be between knowledge, and
1057ᵇ knowable? But between great and small there *is* one.

(3) If intermediates are in the same genus, as has been shown, and
stand between contraries, they must be composed of these contraries.
For either there will be a genus including the contraries or there will
be none. And if (*a*) there is to be a genus in such a way that it is
5 something prior to the contraries, the differentiae which constituted
the contrary species-of-a-genus will be contraries prior to the species;
for species are composed of the genus and the differentiae. (E. g. if
white and black are contraries, and one is a piercing colour and the
other a compressing colour, these differentiae—'piercing' and 'com-
10 pressing'—are prior; so that these are prior contraries of one another.) But, again, the species which differ contrarywise are the more
truly contrary species. And the other species, i. e. the intermediates,
must be composed of their genus and their differentiae. (E. g. all
colours which are between white and black must be said to be com-
15 posed of the genus, i. e. colour, and certain differentiae. But these
differentiae will not be the primary contraries; otherwise every colour
would be either white or black. They are different, then, from the
primary contraries; and therefore they will be between the primary
contraries; the primary differentiae are 'piercing' and 'compressing'.)

Therefore it is (*b*) with regard to these contraries which do not fall within a genus that we must first ask of what their intermediates 20 are composed. (For things which *are* in the same genus must be composed of terms in which the genus is not an element, or else be themselves incomposite.) Now contraries do not involve one another in their composition, and are therefore first principles; but the intermediates are either all incomposite, or none of them. But there is something compounded out of the contraries, so that there can be a change from a contrary to it sooner than to the other contrary; for it will have less of the quality in question than the one contrary and 25 more than the other. This also,[19] then, will come between the contraries. All the other intermediates also, therefore, are *composite*; for that which has more of a quality than one thing and less than another is compounded somehow out of the things than which it is said to have more and less respectively of the quality. And since there are no other things prior to the contraries and homogeneous with the inter- 30 mediates, all intermediates must be compounded *out of the contraries*. Therefore also all the inferior classes, both the contraries and their intermediates, will be compounded out of the primary contraries. Clearly, then, intermediates are (1) all in the same genus and (2) intermediate between contraries, and (3) all compounded out of the contraries.

8   That which is other in species is other than something in some- 35 thing, and this must belong to both; e. g. if it is an animal other in species, both are animals. The things, then, which are other in species must be in the same genus. For by genus I mean that one identical thing which is predicated of both and is differentiated in no merely accidental way, whether conceived as matter or otherwise. For not 1058ᵃ only must the common nature attach to the different things, e. g. not only must both be animals, but this very animality must also be different for each (e. g. in the one case equinity, in the other humanity), and so this common nature is specifically different for each from what it is for the other. One, then, will be in virtue of its own nature 5 one sort of animal, and the other another, e. g. one a horse and the other a man. This difference, then, must be an otherness of the genus. For I give the name of 'difference in the genus' to an otherness which makes the genus itself other.

This, then, will be a contrariety (as can be shown also by induction). For all things are divided by opposites, and it has been proved 10

19 i. e. this intermediate differentia comes between the extreme differentiae, as the intermediate species comes between the extreme species.

that contraries are in the same genus.[20] For contrariety was seen [21]
to be complete difference; and all difference in species is a difference
from something *in something*; so that this is the same for both and is
their genus. (Hence also all contraries which are different in species
and not in genus are in the same line of predication, and other than
15 one another in the highest degree—for the difference is complete—
and cannot be present along with one another.) The difference, then,
is a contrariety.

This, then, is what it is to be 'other in species'—to have a contrariety, being in the same genus and being indivisible [22] (and those
things are the same in species which have no contrariety, being indivisible [23]); we say 'being indivisible', for in the process of division
20 contrarieties arise even in the intermediate stages before we come to
the indivisibles.[22] Evidently, therefore, with reference to that which
is called the genus, none of the species-of-a-genus is either the same
as it or other than it in species (and this is fitting; for the matter is
indicated by negation,[24] and the genus is the matter of that of which
it is called the genus, not in the sense in which we speak of the genus
or family of the Heraclidae, but in that in which the genus is an
element in a thing's nature), nor is it so with reference to things
25 which are not in the same genus, but it will differ in *genus* from them,
and in species from things in the same genus. For a thing's difference
from that from which it differs in species must be a contrariety; and
this belongs only to things in the same genus.

9   One might raise the question, why woman does not differ from
30 man in species, when female and male are contrary and their difference is a contrariety; and why a female and a male animal are not
different in species, though this difference belongs to animal in virtue
of its own nature, and not as paleness or darkness does; both 'female'
and 'male' belong to it *qua* animal. This question is almost the same
as the other, why one contrariety makes things different in species and
35 another does not, e. g. 'with feet' and 'with wings' do, but paleness
and darkness do not. Perhaps it is because the former are modifications peculiar to the genus, and the latter are less so. And since one
1058ᵇ element is definition and one is matter, contrarieties which are in the
definition make a difference in species, but those which are in the
thing taken as including its matter do not make one. And so paleness

---

[20] Ch. 4.   [21] 1055ᵃ 16.
[22] *sc.* individuals or *infimae species*.   [23] *sc.* individuals.
[24] i. e. by eliminating the form which characterizes the concrete thing.

in a man, or darkness, does not make one, nor is there a difference in species between the pale man and the dark man, not even if each of them be denoted by one word. For man is here being considered on 5 his material side, and matter does not create a difference; for it does not make individual men species of man, though the flesh and the bones of which this man and that man consist are other. The concrete thing is other, but not other in species, because in the definition there is no contrariety. This 25 is the ultimate indivisible kind. Callias is definition + *matter*; the pale man, then, is so also, because it is the 10 individual Callias that is pale; man, then, is pale only incidentally. Neither do a brazen and a wooden circle, then, differ in species; and if a brazen triangle and a wooden circle differ in species, it is not because of the matter, but because there is a contrariety in the definition. But does the matter not make things other in species, when it 15 is other in a certain way, or is there a sense in which it does? For why is this horse other than this man in species, although their matter is included with their definitions? Doubtless because there is a contrariety in the *definition*. For while there is a contrariety also between pale man and dark horse, and it is a contrariety in species, it does not depend on the paleness of the one and the darkness of the other, since 20 even if both had been pale, yet they would have been other in species. But male and female, while they are modifications peculiar to 'animal', are so not in virtue of its essence but in the matter, i. e. the body. This is why the same seed becomes female or male by being acted on in a certain way. We have stated, then, what it is to be other in species, and why some things differ in species and others do not. 25

10   Since contraries are other in form, and the perishable and the imperishable are contraries (for privation is a determinate incapacity), the perishable and the imperishable must be different in kind.

Now so far we have spoken of the general terms themselves, so that it might be thought not to be necessary that every imperishable thing 30 should be different from every perishable thing in form, just as not every pale thing is different in form from every dark thing. For the same thing can be both, and even at the same time if it is a universal (e.g. man can be both pale and dark), and if it is an individual it can still be both; for the same man can be, though not at the same time, 35 pale and dark. Yet pale is contrary to dark.

But while some contraries belong to certain things by accident (e. g. both those now mentioned and many others), others cannot, and among these are 'perishable' and 'imperishable'. For nothing is by

25 i. e. that in whose definition no contrarieties are included.

1059ª accident perishable. For what is accidental is capable of not being present, but perishableness is one of the attributes that belong of necessity to the things to which they belong; or else one and the same
5 thing may be perishable and imperishable, if perishableness is capable of not belonging to it. Perishableness then must either be the essence or be present in the essence of each perishable thing. The same account holds good for imperishableness also; for both are attributes which are present of necessity. The characteristics, then, in respect of which and in direct consequence of which one thing is perishable and another imperishable, are opposite, so that the things must be different in kind.
10   Evidently, then, there cannot be Forms such as some maintain, for then one man [26] would be perishable and another [27] imperishable. Yet the Forms are said to be the same in form with the individuals and not merely to have the same name; but things which differ in kind [28] are farther apart than those which differ in form.

BOOK K (XI)

1 That Wisdom is a science of first principles is evident from the introductory chapters,[1] in which we have raised objections to the
20 statements of others about the first principles; but one might ask the question whether Wisdom is to be conceived as one science or as several. If as one, it may be objected that one science always deals with contraries, but the first principles are not contrary. If it is *not* one, what sort of sciences are those with which it is to be identified? [2]
       Further, is it the business of one science, or of more than one, to examine the first principles of demonstration? If of one, why of this
25 rather than of any other? If of more, what sort of sciences must these be said to be? [3]
       Further, does Wisdom investigate all substances or not? If not all, it is hard to say which; but if, being one, it investigates them all, it is doubtful how the same science can embrace several subject-matters.[4]
       Further, does it deal with substances only or also with their at-
30 tributes? If in the case of *attributes* demonstration is possible, in that of *substances* it is not. But if the two sciences are different, what is each of them and which is Wisdom? If we think of it as demonstra-

---

[26] The sensible individual.   [27] The ideal man.
[28] As the perishable and the imperishable have been shown to do.

[1] Cf. Bk. i. 3–10.   [2] Cf. ii. 996ª 18–ᵇ 26.
[3] Cf. ii. 996ᵇ 26–997ª 15.   [4] Cf. ii. 997ª 15–25.

tive, the science of the attributes is Wisdom, but if as dealing with what is primary, the science of substances claim the title.[5]

But again the science we are looking for must not be supposed to deal with the causes which have been mentioned in the *Physics*.[6] 35 For (A) it does not deal with the final cause (for that is the nature of the good, and this is found in the field of action and movement; and it is the first mover—for that is the nature of the end—but in the case of things unmovable there is nothing that moved them first),[7] and (B) in general it is hard to say whether perchance the science we are now looking for deals with perceptible substances or not with them, but with certain others. If with others, it must deal either 1059ᵇ with the Forms or with the objects of mathematics. Now (*a*) evidently the Forms do not exist. (But it is hard to say, even if one suppose them to exist, why in the world the same is not true of the other things of which there are Forms, as of the objects of mathematics. I mean that these thinkers place the objects of mathematics 5 between the Forms and perceptible things, as a kind of third set of things apart both from the Forms and from the things in this world; but there is not a third man or horse besides the ideal and the individuals. If on the other hand it is not as they say, with what sort of things must the mathematician be supposed to deal? Certainly not with the things in this world; for none of these is the sort of thing 10 which the mathematical sciences demand.) Nor (*b*) does the science which we are now seeking treat of the objects of mathematics; for none of them can exist separately. But again it does not deal with perceptible substances; for they are perishable.[8]

In general one might raise the question, to what kind of science it 15 belongs to discuss the difficulties about the matter of the objects of mathematics. Neither to physics (because the whole inquiry of the physicist is about the things that have in themselves a principle of movement and rest), nor yet to the science which inquires into demonstration and science; for *this* is just the subject which *it* investigates. It remains then that it is the philosophy which we have set before 20 ourselves that treats of those subjects.

One might discuss the question whether the science we are seeking should be said to deal with the principles which are by some called elements; all men suppose these to be present in composite things. But it might be thought that the science we seek should treat rather of universals; for every definition and every science is of 25

[5] Cf. ii. 997ᵃ 25–34.

[6] The material, formal, efficient, and final causes (*Phys.* ii. 3).

[7] Cf. ii. 996ᵃ 21–ᵇ 1.   [8] Cf. ii. 997ᵃ 34–998ᵃ 19.

universals and not of *infimae species*,[9] so that as far as this goes
it would deal with the highest genera. These would turn out to be
being and unity; for these might most of all be supposed to contain
all things that are, and to be most like principles because they are
30 first by nature; for if they perish all other things are destroyed with
them; for everything *is* and is one. But inasmuch as, if one is to suppose them to be genera, they must be predicable of their differentiae,
and no genus is predicable of any of its differentiae, in this way it
would seem that we should not make them genera nor principles.
Further, if the simpler is more of a principle than the less simple,
35 and the ultimate members of the genus are simpler than the genera
(for they are indivisible, but the genera are divided into many and
differing species), the species might seem to be the principles, rather
than the genera. But inasmuch as the species are involved in the
destruction of the genera, the genera are more like principles; for that
which involves another in its destruction is a principle of it.[10] These
1060ª and others of the kind are the subjects that involve difficulties.

2 Further, must we suppose something apart from individual
things, or is it these that the science we are seeking treats of? But
5 these are infinite in number. Yet the things that are apart from the
individuals are genera or species; but the science we now seek treats
of neither of these. The reason why this is impossible has been
stated.[11] Indeed, it is in general hard to say whether one must assume
that there is a separable substance besides the sensible substances
(i. e. the substances in this world), or that these are the real things
10 and Wisdom is concerned with them. For we seem to seek another
kind of substance, and this is our problem, i. e. to see if there is
something which can exist apart by itself and belongs to no sensible
thing.—Further, if there is another substance apart from and corresponding to sensible substances, which kinds of sensible substance
must be supposed to have this corresponding to them? Why should
15 one suppose men or horses to have it, more than either the other
animals or even all lifeless things? On the other hand to set up other
and eternal substances equal in number to the sensible and perishable substances would seem to fall beyond the bounds of probability.
.—But if the principle we now seek is not separable from corporeal
things, what has a better claim to the name than matter? This,
20 however, does not exist in actuality, but exists in potency. And it

⁹ Cf. ii. 998ᵇ 15.   ¹⁰ Cf. ii. 998ª 20–999ª 23.   ¹¹ 1059ᵇ 24–38.

would seem rather that the form or shape is a more important principle than this; but the form is perishable,[12] so that there is no
eternal substance at all which can exist apart and independent. But
this is paradoxical; for such a principle and substance seems to
exist and is sought by nearly all the most refined thinkers as some- 25
thing that exists; for how is there to be order unless there is something eternal and independent and permanent? [13]

Further, if there is a substance or principle of such a nature as
that which we are now seeking, and if this is one for all things,
and the same for eternal and for perishable things, it is hard to say
why in the world, if there is the same principle, some of the things
that fall under the principle are eternal, and others are not eternal; 30
this is paradoxical. But if there is one principle of perishable and
another of eternal things, we shall be in a like difficulty if the
principle of perishable things, as well as that of eternal, is eternal;
for why, if the principle is eternal, are not the things that fall under
the principle also eternal? But if it is perishable another principle
is involved to account for it, and another to account for that, and
this will go on to infinity.[14]   35

If on the other hand we are to set up what are thought to be the
most unchangeable principles, being and unity, firstly, if each of
these does not indicate a 'this' or substance, how will they be separable and independent? Yet we expect the eternal and primary prin- 1060ᵗ
ciples to be so. But if each of them does signify a 'this' or substance,
all things that are are substances; for being is predicated of all
things (and unity also of some); but that all things that are are sub- 5
stance is false. Further, how can they [15] be right who say that the
first principle is unity and this is substance, and generate number
as the first product from unity and from matter, and assert that 10
number is substance? How are we to think of 'two', and each of the
other numbers composed of units, as one? On this point neither do
they say anything nor is it easy to say anything. But if we are to
suppose lines or what comes after these (I mean the primary surfaces) to be principles, these at least are not separable substances,
but sections and divisions—the former of surfaces, the latter of
bodies (while points are sections and divisions of lines); and fur- 15
ther they are limits of these same things; and all these are in other

---

[12] It must be remembered that A. is only stating common opinions and the
consequent difficulties.

[13] Cf. ii. 999ᵃ 24–ᵇ 24.   [14] Cf. ii. 1000ᵃ 5–1001ᵃ 3.

[15] The Pythagoreans and Plato.

things and none is separable. Further, how are we to suppose that there is a substance of unity and the point? Every substance comes into being by a gradual process, but a point does not; for the point is a division.[16]

20 A further difficulty is raised by the fact that all knowledge is of universals and of the 'such', but substance is not a universal, but is rather a 'this'—a separable thing, so that if there is knowledge about the first principles, the question arises, how are we to suppose the first principle to be substance? [17]

Further, is there anything apart from the concrete thing (by which I mean the matter and that which is joined with it), or not? If 25 not, we are met by the objection that all things that *are* in matter are perishable. But if there *is* something, it must be the form or shape. Now it is hard to determine in which cases this exists apart and in which it does not; for in some cases the form is evidently not separable, e. g. in the case of a house.[18]

Further, are the principles the same in kind or in number? If they 30 are one in number, all things will be the same.[19]

3 Since the science of the philosopher treats of being *qua* being universally and not in respect of a part of it, and 'being' has many senses and is not used in one only, it follows that if the word is used equivocally and in virtue of nothing common to its various uses, being does not fall under one science (for the meanings of an equivocal 35 term do not form one genus); but if the word is used in virtue of something common, being will fall under one science. The term seems to be used in the way we have mentioned, like 'medical' and 'healthy'. For each of these also we use in many senses. Terms are used in this 1061ᵃ way by virtue of some kind of reference, in the one case to medical science, in the other to health, in others to something else, but in each case to one identical concept. For a discussion and a knife are called medical because the former proceeds from medical science, and 5 the latter is useful to it. And a thing is called healthy in a similar way; one thing because it is indicative of health, another because it is productive of it. And the same is true in the other cases. Everything that is, then, is said to 'be' in this same way; each thing that is is said to 'be' because it is a modification of being *qua* being or a permanent or a transient state or a movement of it, or something 10 else of the sort. And since everything that is may be referred to something single and common, each of the contrarieties also may be re-

16 Cf. ii. 1001ᵃ 4–1002ᵇ 11.   17 Cf. ii. 1003ᵃ 5–17.
18 Cf. ii. 999ᵃ 24–ᵇ 24.   19 Cf. ii. 999ᵇ 24–1000ᵃ 4.

ferred to the first differences and contrarieties of being, whether the first differences of being are plurality and unity, or likeness and unlikeness, or some other differences; let these be taken as already discussed. It makes no difference whether that which is be referred to 15 being or to unity. For even if they are not the same but different, at least they are convertible; for that which is one is also somehow being, and that which is being is one.

But since every pair of contraries falls to be examined by one and the same science, and in each pair one term is the privative of the other—though one might regarding some contraries raise the ques- 20 tion, how they can be privately related, viz. those which have an intermediate, e. g. unjust and just—in all such cases one must maintain that the privation is not of the whole definition, but of the *infima species*. E. g. if the just man is 'by virtue of some permanent disposition obedient to the laws', the unjust man will not in every case 25 have the whole definition denied of him, but may be merely 'in some respect deficient in obedience to the laws', and in this respect the privation will attach to him; and similarly in all other cases.

As the mathematician investigates abstractions (for before beginning his investigation he strips off all the sensible qualities, e. g. 30 weight and lightness, hardness and its contrary, and also heat and cold and the other sensible contrarieties, and leaves only the quantitative and continuous, sometimes in one, sometimes in two, sometimes in three dimensions, and the attributes of these *qua* quantitative and 35 continuous, and does not consider them in any other respect, and examines the relative positions of some and the attributes of these, and the commensurabilities and incommensurabilities of others, 1061ᵇ and the ratios of others; but yet we posit one and the same science of all these things—geometry)—the same is true with regard to being. For the attributes of this in so far as it is being, and the con- 5 trarieties in it *qua* being, it is the business of no other science than philosophy to investigate; for to physics one would assign the study of things not *qua* being, but rather *qua* sharing in movement; while dialectic and sophistic deal with the attributes of things that are, but not of things *qua* being, and not with being itself in so far as 10 it is being; therefore it remains that it is the philosopher who studies the things we have named, in so far as they are being. Since all that is is said to 'be' in virtue of something single and common, though the term has many meanings, and contraries are in the same case (for they are referred to the first contrarieties and differences of being), and things of this sort can fall under one science, the diffi- 15 culty we stated at the beginning [20] appears to be solved—I mean the question how there can be a single science of things which are many and different in genus.

4   Since even the mathematician uses the common axioms only in a special application, it must be the business of first philosophy to examine the principles of mathematics also. That when equals are taken from equals the remainders are equal, is common to all quanti-
20 ties, but mathematics studies a part of its proper matter which it has detached, e. g. lines or angles or numbers or some other kind of quan-tity—not, however, *qua* being but in so far as each of them is con-
25 tinuous in one or two or three dimensions; but philosophy does not inquire about particular subjects in so far as each of them has some attribute or other, but speculates about being, in so far as each par-ticular thing *is*.—Physics is in the same position as mathematics; for physics studies the attributes and the principles of the things
30 that are, *qua* moving and not *qua* being (whereas the primary science, we have said, deals with these, only in so far as the underlying subjects are existent, and not in virtue of any other character); and so both physics and mathematics must be classed as *parts* of Wisdom.[21]

5   There is a principle in things, about which we cannot be de-
35 ceived, but must always, on the contrary, recognize the truth—viz. that the same thing cannot at one and the same time be and not
1062ᵃ be, or admit any other similar pair of opposites.[22] About such mat-ters there is no proof in the full sense, though there is proof *ad hominem*. For it is not possible to infer this truth itself from a more certain principle, yet this is *necessary* if there is to be completed proof
5 of it in the full sense.[23] But he who wants to prove to the asserter of opposites that he is wrong must get from him an admission which shall *be* identical with the principle that the same thing cannot be and not be at one and the same time, but shall not *seem* to be identical;
10 for thus alone can his thesis be demonstrated to the man who as-serts that opposite statements can be truly made about the same subject. Those, then, who are to join in argument with one another must to some extent understand one another; for if this does not

---

[20] 1059ᵃ 20–23. Cf. iv. 2. The question raised in 1059ᵃ 29–34 has also incidentally been answered.
[21] Cf. iv. 1005ᵃ 19–ᵇ 2, xi. 1059ᵃ 23–26.
[22] Cf. iv. 1005ᵇ 8–34.   [23] Cf. iv. 1006ᵃ 5–18.

happen how are they to join in argument with one another? Therefore every word must be intelligible and indicate something, and not many things but only one; and if it signifies more than one thing, it must be made plain to which of these the word is being applied. He, then, who says 'this is and is not' denies what he affirms, so that what the word signifies, he says it does not signify; and this is impossible. Therefore if 'this is' signifies something, one cannot truly assert its contradictory.[24]

Further, if the word signifies something and this is asserted truly,[25] this connexion must be necessary; and it is not possible that that which necessarily is should ever not be; it is not possible therefore to make the opposed affirmations and negations truly of the same subject.[26] Further, if the affirmation is no more true than the negation, he who says 'man' will be no more right than he who says 'not-man'. It would seem also that in saying the man is not a horse one would be either more or not less right than in saying he is not a man, so that one will also be right in saying that the same person *is* a horse; for it was assumed to be possible to make opposite statements equally truly. It follows then that the same person is a man and a horse, or any other animal.[27]

While, then, there is no proof of these things in the full sense, there is a proof which may suffice against one who will make these suppositions. And perhaps if one had questioned Heraclitus himself in this way one might have forced him to confess that opposite statements can never be true of the same subjects. But, as it is, he adopted this opinion without understanding what his statement involves.[28] But in any case if what is said by him is true, not even this itself will be true—viz. that the same thing can at one and the same time both be and not be. For as, when the statements are separated, the affirmation is no more true than the negation, in the same way—the combined and complex statement being like a single affirmation —the whole taken as an affirmation will be no more true than the negation.[29] Further, if it is not possible to affirm anything truly, this itself will be false—the assertion that there is no true affirmation.[30] But if a true affirmation exists, this appears to refute what is said by those who raise such objections and utterly destroy rational discourse.

[24] Cf. iv. 1006ᵃ 18–1007ᵃ 20.　　[25] *sc.* of that of which the word is asserted.
[26] Cf. iv. 1006ᵇ 28–34.　　[27] Cf. iv. 1007ᵇ 18–1008ᵃ 2.
[28] Cf. iv. 1005ᵇ 23–26.　　[29] Cf. iv. 1008ᵃ 6–7.　　[30] Cf. iv. 1012ᵇ 13–18.

6 The saying of Protagoras is like the views we have mentioned; he said that man is the measure of all things, meaning simply that that which seems to each man also assuredly is. If this is so, it fol-
15 lows that the same thing both is and is not, and is bad and good, and that the contents of all other opposite statements are true, because often a particular thing appears beautiful to some and the contrary of beautiful to others, and that which appears to each man
20 is the measure. This difficulty may be solved by considering the source of this opinion. It seems to have arisen in some cases from the doctrine of the natural philosophers, and in others from the fact that all men have not the same views about the same things, but a particular thing appears pleasant to some and the contrary of pleasant to others.[31]

That nothing comes to be out of that which is not, but every-
25 thing out of that which is, is a dogma common to nearly all the natural philosophers. Since, then, white cannot come to be if the perfectly white and in no respect not-white existed before, that which becomes white must come from that which is not white; so that it must come to be out of that which is not (so they argue), unless
30 the same thing was at the beginning white and not-white. But it is not hard to solve this difficulty; for we have said in our works on physics [32] in what sense things that come to be come to be from that which is not, and in what sense from that which is.[33]

But to attend equally to the opinions and the fancies of disputing parties is childish; for clearly one of them must be mistaken. And
35 this is evident from what happens in respect of sensation; for the
1063ᵃ same thing never appears sweet to some and the contrary of sweet to others, unless in the one case the sense-organ which discriminates the aforesaid flavours has been perverted and injured. And if this is so the one party must be taken to be the measure, and the other
5 must not. And I say the same of good and bad, and beautiful and ugly, and all other such qualities. For to maintain the view we are opposing is just like maintaining that the things that appear to people who put their finger under their eye and make the object appear two instead of one must be two (because they appear to be of that number) and again one (for to those who do not interfere with their eye the one object appears one).[34]
10 In general, it is absurd to make the fact that the things of this earth are observed to change and never to remain in the same state,

[31] Cf. iv. 1009ᵃ 6–16, 22–30.
[32] *Phys.* i. 7–9, *De Gen. et Corr.* i. 317ᵇ 14–319ᵇ 5.
[33] Cf. iv. 1009ᵃ 30–36. [34] Cf. iv. 1010ᵇ 1–26, 1011ᵃ 31–4.

the basis of our judgment about the truth. For in pursuing the truth one must start from the things that are always in the same state and suffer no change. Such are the heavenly bodies; for these do not appear to be now of one nature and again of another, but are manifestly always the same and share in no change.[35]

Further, if there is movement, there is also something moved, and everything is moved out of something and into something; it follows that that which is moved must first be in that out of which it is to be moved, and then not be in it, and move into the other and come to be in it, and that the contradictory statements are not true at the same time, as these thinkers assert they are.

And if the things of this earth continuously flow and move in respect of quantity—if one were to suppose this, although it is not true—why should they not endure in respect of *quality*? For the assertion of contradictory statements about the same thing seems to have arisen largely from the belief that the quantity of bodies does not endure, which, our opponents hold, justifies them in saying that the same thing both is and is not four cubits long. But essence depends on quality, and this is of determinate nature, though quantity is of indeterminate.[36]

Further, when the doctor orders people to take some particular food, why do they take it? In what respect is 'this is bread' truer than 'this is not bread'? And so it would make no difference whether one ate or not. But as a matter of fact they take the food which is ordered, assuming that they know the truth about it and that it is bread. Yet they should not, if there were no fixed constant nature in sensible things, but all natures moved and flowed for ever.[37]

Again, if we are always changing and never remain the same, what wonder is it if to us, as to the sick, things never appear the same? (For to them also, because they are not in the same condition as when they were well, sensible qualities do not appear alike; yet, for all that, the sensible things themselves need not share in any change, though they produce different, and not identical, sensations in the sick. And the same must surely happen to the healthy if the aforesaid [38] change takes place.) But if we do not change but remain the same, there will be something that endures.[39]

As for those to whom the difficulties mentioned are suggested by *reasoning*, it is not easy to solve the difficulties to their satisfaction, unless they will posit something and no longer demand a reason for

---

[35] Cf. iv. 1010ᵃ 25–32.
[37] Cf. iv. 1008ᵇ 12–27.
[39] Cf. iv. 1009ᵃ 38–ᵇ 33.

[36] Cf. iv. 1010ᵃ 22–25.
[38] Cf. iv. 1063ᵃ 35.

10 it; for it is only thus that all reasoning and all proof is accomplished; if they posit nothing, they destroy discussion and all reasoning. Therefore with such men there is no reasoning. But as for those who are perplexed by the traditional difficulties, it is easy to meet them and to dissipate the causes of their perplexity. This is evident from what has been said.[40]

15   It is manifest, therefore, from these arguments that contradictory statements cannot be truly made about the same subject at one time,[41] nor can contrary statements, because every contrariety depends on privation. This is evident if we reduce the definitions of contraries to their principle.[42]

Similarly, no intermediate between contraries can be predicated of one and the same subject, of which one of the contraries is predi-
20 cated. If the subject is white we shall be wrong in saying it is neither black nor white, for then it follows that it is and is not white; for the second of the two terms we have put together[43] is true of it, and this is the contradictory of white.[44]

We could not be right, then, in accepting the views either of
25 Heraclitus[45] or of Anaxagoras. If we were, it would follow that contraries would be predicated of the same subject; for when Anaxagoras says that in everything there is a part of everything, he says nothing is sweet any more than it is bitter, and so with any other pair of contraries, since in everything everything is present not poten-
30 tially only, but actually and separately. And similarly all statements cannot be false nor all true, both because of many other difficulties which might be adduced as arising from this position, and because if all are false it will not be true to say even this, and if all are true
35 it will not be false to say all are false.[46]

7   Every science seeks certain principles and causes for each of its
1064ᵃ objects—e. g. medicine and gymnastics and each of the other sciences, whether productive or mathematical. For each of these marks off a certain class of things for itself and busies itself about this as about something existing and real—not however *qua* real; the science that does *this* is another distinct from these. Of the sciences men-
5 tioned each gets somehow the 'what' in some class of things and tries to prove the other truths, with more or less precision. Some

[40] In 1062ᵇ 20–1063ᵇ 7.
[41] Cf. iv. 1009ᵃ 16–22, 1011ᵃ 3–16.
[42] Cf. iv. 1011ᵇ 15–22.
[43] *sc.* 'not white' and 'not black'.
[44] Cf. iv. 1011ᵇ 23–1012ᵃ 24.
[45] Cf. 1062ᵃ 31–ᵇ 2.
[46] Cf. iv. 1012ᵃ 24–ᵇ 18.

get the 'what' through perception, others by hypothesis; so that it is clear from an induction of this sort that there is no *demonstration* of the substance or 'what'.

There is a science of nature, and evidently it must be different both 10 from practical and from productive science. For in the case of productive science the principle of movement is in the producer and not in the product, and is either an art or some other faculty. And similarly in practical science the movement is not in the thing done, but rather in the doers. But the science of the natural philosopher deals 15 with the things that have *in themselves* a principle of movement. It is clear from these facts, then, that natural science must be neither practical nor productive, but theoretical (for it must fall into some one of these classes). And since each of the sciences must somehow know the 'what' and use this as a principle, we must not fail to observe how 20 the natural philosopher should define things and how he should state the definition of the essence—whether as akin to 'snub' or rather to 'concave'. For of these the definition of 'snub' includes the matter of the thing, but that of 'concave' is independent of the matter; for snub- 25 ness is found in a nose, so that we look for its definition without eliminating the nose, for what is snub is a concave nose. Evidently then the definition of flesh also and of the eye and of the other parts must always be stated without eliminating the matter.

Since there is a science of being *qua* being and capable of existing apart, we must consider whether this is to be regarded as the same as physics or rather as different. Physics deals with the things that have 30 a principle of movement in themselves; mathematics is theoretical, and *is* a science that deals with things that are at rest, but its subjects cannot exist apart. Therefore about that which can exist apart and is unmovable there is a science different from both of these, if there *is* a substance of this nature (I mean separable and unmovable), as we 35 shall try to prove there is.[47] And if there is such a kind of thing in the world, here must surely be the divine, and this must be the first and most dominant principle. Evidently, then, there are three kinds of 1064ᵇ theoretical sciences—physics, mathematics, theology. The class of theoretical sciences is the best, and of these themselves the last named is best; for it deals with the highest of existing things, and each science 5 is called better or worse in virtue of its proper object.

One might raise the question whether the science of being *qua* being is to be regarded as universal or not. Each of the mathematical sciences deals with some one determinate class of things, but universal mathematics applies alike to all. Now if natural substances are the first of

[47] Cf. v. 6, 7.

10 existing things, physics must be the first of sciences; but if there is
another entity and substance, separable and unmovable, the knowledge of it must be different and prior to physics and universal because
it is prior.[48]

15 8   Since 'being' in general has several senses, of which one is 'being
by accident', we must consider first that which 'is' in this sense. Evidently none of the traditional sciences busies itself about the accidental. For neither does architecture consider what will happen to
20 those who are to use the house (e. g. whether they will have a painful
life in it or not), nor does weaving, or shoemaking, or the confectioner's
art, do the like; but each of these sciences considers only what is
peculiar to it, i. e. its proper end. And as for the argument that 'when
he who is musical becomes lettered he will be both at once, not having
25 been both before; and that which is, not always having been, must
have come to be; therefore he must have at once become musical and
lettered'—this none of the recognized sciences considers, but only
sophistic; for this alone busies itself about the accidental, so that Plato
is not far wrong when he says [49] that the sophist spends his time on
non-being.
30   That a science of the accidental is not even possible will be evident
if we try to see what the accidental really is. We say that everything
either is always and of necessity (necessity not in the sense of violence,
35 but that which we appeal to in demonstrations), or is for the most part,
or is neither for the most part, nor always and of necessity, but merely
as it chances; e. g. there might be cold in the dog-days, but this occurs
1065ᵃ neither always and of necessity, nor for the most part, though it might
happen sometimes. The accidental, then, is what occurs, but not always
nor of necessity, nor for the most part. Now we have said what the
accidental is, and it is obvious why there is no science of such a thing;
5 for all science is of that which is always or for the most part, but the
accidental is in neither of these classes.
    Evidently there are not causes and principles of the accidental, of
the same kind as there are of the essential; for if there were, everything
would be of necessity. If A is when B is, and B is when C is, and if C
10 exists not by chance but of necessity, that also of which C was cause
will exist of necessity, down to the last *causatum* as it is called (but
this was supposed to be accidental). Therefore all things will be of
necessity, and chance and the possibility of a thing's either occurring
or not occurring are removed entirely from the range of events. And if
the cause be supposed not to exist but to be coming to be, the same

---

[48] Cf. vi. 1, xi. 1059ᵃ 26–29.   [49] Cf. *Sophistes* 254 A.

results will follow; everything will occur of necessity. For to-morrow's 15
eclipse will occur if A occurs, and A if B occurs, and B if C occurs; and
in this way if we subtract time from the limited time between now and
to-morrow we shall come sometime to the already existing condition.
Therefore since this exists, everything after this will occur of necessity, 20
so that all things occur of necessity.

As to that which 'is' in the sense of being true or of being by accident,
the *former* depends on a combination in thought and is an affection of
thought (which is the reason why it is the principles, not of that
which 'is' in this sense, but of that which is outside and can exist apart,
that are sought); and the *latter* is not necessary but indeterminate
(I mean the accidental); and of such a thing the causes are unordered 25
and indefinite.[50]

Adaptation to an end is found in events that happen by nature or
as the result of thought. It is 'luck' when one of these events [51] happens
by accident. For as a thing may exist, so it may be a cause, either by
its own nature or by accident.[52] Luck is an accidental cause at work in 30
such events adapted to an end as are usually effected in accordance
with purpose. And so luck and thought are concerned with the same
sphere; for purpose cannot exist without thought. The causes from
which lucky results might happen are indeterminate; and so luck is
obscure to human calculation and is a cause by accident, but in the
unqualified sense a cause of nothing.[53] It is good or bad luck when 35
the result is good or evil; and prosperity or misfortune when the 1065ᵇ
scale of the results is large.[54]

Since nothing accidental is prior to the essential, neither are accidental causes prior. If, then, luck or spontaneity is a cause of the
material universe, reason and nature are causes before it.[55]

9   Some things are only actually, some potentially, some potentially 5
and actually, what they are, viz. in one case a particular reality, in
another, characterized by a particular quantity, or the like.[56] There
is no movement apart from things; for change is always according to
the categories of being, and there is nothing common to these and in
no one category. But each of the categories belongs to all its subjects
in either of two ways (e. g. 'this-ness'—for one kind of it is 'positive 10
form', and the other is 'privation'; and as regards quality one kind is
'white' and the other 'black', and as regards quantity one kind is

[50] Cf. vi. 2–4.
[51] *sc.* which happen *usually* by nature or as the result of thought.
[52] Cf. *Phys.* ii. 196ᵇ 21–25.
[53] Cf. *Phys.* ii. 197ᵃ 5–14.   [54] Cf. *Phys.* ii. 197ᵃ 25–27.
[55] Cf. *Phys.* ii. 198ᵃ 5–13.   [56] Cf. *Phys.* iii. 200ᵇ 26–28.

'complete' and the other 'incomplete', and as regards spatial movement one is 'upwards' and the other 'downwards', or one thing is 'light' and another 'heavy') ; so that there are as many kinds of movement and
15 change as of being. There being a distinction in each class of things between the potential and the completely real, I call the actuality of the potential as such, movement. That what we say is true, is plain from the following facts. When the 'buildable', in so far as it is what we mean by 'buildable',[57] exists actually, it is being built, and this is the process of building. Similarly with learning, healing, walking,
20 leaping, ageing, ripening.[58] Movement takes place when the complete reality itself exists, and neither earlier nor later.[59] The complete reality, then, of that which exists potentially, when it is completely real and actual, not *qua* itself, but *qua* movable, is movement. By *qua* I mean this: bronze is potentially a statue; but yet it is not the complete
25 reality of bronze *qua* bronze that is movement. For it is not the same thing to be bronze and to be a certain potency. If it were absolutely the same in its definition, the complete reality of bronze would have been a movement. But it is not the same. (This is evident in the case of contraries; for to be capable of being well and to be capable of being ill are not the same—for if they were, being well and being ill
30 would have been the same—it is that which underlies and is healthy or diseased, whether it is moisture or blood, that is one and the same.) And since it is not the same, as colour and the visible are not the same, it is the complete reality of the potential, and *as potential*, that is move-
35 ment. That it is this, and that movement takes place when the com-
1066ᵃ plete reality itself exists, and neither earlier nor later, is evident. For each thing is capable of being sometimes actual, sometimes not, e. g. the buildable *qua* buildable; and the actuality of the buildable *qua* buildable is building. For the actuality is either this—the act of build-ing—or the house. But when the *house* exists, it is no longer buildable;
5 the buildable is what *is being* built. The actuality, then, must be the *act of building*, and this is a movement. And the same account applies to all other movements.

That what we have said is right is evident from what all others say about movement, and from the fact that it is not easy to define it otherwise. For firstly one cannot put it in any other class. This is
10 evident from what people say. Some call it otherness and inequality and the unreal;[60] none of these, however, is necessarily moved, and

---

[57] i. e. not as so much matter, but as matter capable of being made into a building.
[58] Cf. *Phys*. iii. 200ᵇ 32–201ᵃ 19.   [59] Cf. *Phys*. iii. 201ᵇ 6, 7.
[60] The Pythagoreans and Platonists are meant; Cf. Pl. *Soph*. 256 D, *Tim*. 57 E ff.

further, change is not either to these or from these any more than from their opposites. The reason why people put movement in these classes is that it is thought to be something indefinite, and the principles in one of the two 'columns of contraries' are indefinite because they are 15 privative, for none of them is either a 'this' or a 'such' or in any of the other categories. And the reason why movement is thought to be indefinite is that it cannot be classed either with the potency of things or with their actuality; for neither that which is capable of being of a certain quantity, nor that which is actually of a certain quantity, is of necessity moved, and movement is thought to be an actuality, but 20 incomplete; the reason is that the potential, whose actuality it is, is incomplete. And therefore it is hard to grasp what movement is; for it must be classed either under privation or under potency or under absolute actuality, but evidently none of these is possible. Therefore what remains is that it must be what we said—both actuality and the 25 actuality we have described—which is hard to detect but capable of existing.[61]

And evidently movement is in the movable; for it is the complete realization of this by that which is capable of causing movement. And the actuality of that which is capable of causing movement is no other than that of the movable. For it must be the complete reality of both. For while a thing is capable of causing movement because it *can* do this, it is a mover because it is *active*; but it is on the movable that it 30 is capable of acting, so that the actuality of both is one, just as there is the same interval from one to two as from two to one, and as the steep ascent and the steep descent are one, but the being of them is not one; the case of the mover and the moved is similar.[62]

10   The infinite is either that which is incapable of being traversed 35 because it is not its nature to be traversed (this corresponds to the sense in which the voice is 'invisible'), or that which admits only of incomplete traverse or scarcely admits of traverse, or that which, though it naturally admits of traverse, is not traversed or limited; further, a thing may be infinite in respect of addition or of subtraction, or both. The infinite cannot be a separate, independent thing. For if 1066ᵇ it is neither a spatial magnitude nor a plurality, but infinity itself is its substance and not an accident of it, it will be indivisible; for the divisible is either magnitude or plurality. But if indivisible, it is not infinite, except as the voice is invisible; but people do not mean this, 5

---

[61] With 1065ᵇ 22–1066ᵃ 27 cf. *Phys*. iii. 201ᵃ 27–202ᵃ 3.
[62] Cf. *Phys*. iii. 202ᵃ 13–21.

nor are we examining this sort of infinite, but the infinite as untraversable.[63] Further, how can an infinite exist by itself, unless number and magnitude also exist by themselves—since infinity is an attribute of these?[64] Further, if the infinite is an accident of something else, it
10 cannot be *qua* infinite an element in things, as the invisible is not an element in speech, though the voice is invisible.[65] And evidently the infinite cannot exist actually. For then any part of it that might be taken would be infinite (for 'to be infinite' and 'the infinite' are the same, if the infinite is substance and not predicated of a subject). Therefore it is either indivisible, or if it is partible, it is divisible into
15 infinites; but the same thing cannot be many infinites (as a part of air is air, so a part of the infinite would be infinite, if the infinite is a substance and a principle). Therefore it must be impartible and indivisible. But the actually infinite cannot be indivisible; for it must be of a certain quantity. Therefore infinity belongs to its subject inci-
20 dentally. But if so, then (as we have said [66]) it cannot be it that is a principle, but that of which it is an accident—the air or the even number.[67]

   This inquiry is universal; but that the infinite is not *among sensible things*, is evident from the following argument. If the definition of a body is 'that which is bounded by planes', there cannot be an infinite
25 body either sensible or intelligible; nor a separate and infinite number, for number or that which has a number is numerable.[68] Concretely, the truth is evident from the following argument. The infinite can neither be composite nor simple. For (*a*) it cannot be a composite body, since the elements are limited in multitude. For the contraries must be equal and no *one* of them must be infinite; for if one of the two
30 bodies falls at all short of the other in potency, the finite will be destroyed by the infinite. And that *each* should be infinite is impossible. For body is that which has extension in all directions, and the infinite is the boundlessly extended, so that if the infinite is a body it will be infinite in every direction. Nor (*b*) can the infinite body be
35 one and simple—neither, as some say,[69] something apart from the elements, from which they generate these [70] (for there is no such body apart from the elements; for everything can be resolved into that of which it consists, but no such product of analysis is observed except
1067ᵃ the simple bodies), nor fire nor any other of the elements. For apart from the question how any of them could be infinite, the All, even if

---

[63] Cf. *Phys.* iii. 204ᵃ 3–14.   [64] Cf. *Phys.* iii. 204ᵃ 17–19.
[65] Cf. *Phys.* iii. 204ᵃ 14–17.   [66] l. 9.
[67] Cf. *Phys.* iii. 204ᵃ 20–32.   [68] Cf. *Phys.* iii. 204ᵃ 34–ᵇ 8.
[69] Anaximander is meant.   [70] Cf. *Phys.* iii. 204ᵇ 10–24.

it is finite, cannot either be or become any one of them, as Heraclitus says all things sometimes become fire. The same argument applies to this as to the One which the natural philosophers posit *besides* the elements. For everything changes from contrary to contrary, e. g. from hot to cold.[71]

Further, a sensible body is somewhere, and whole and part have the same proper place, e. g. the whole earth and part of the earth. Therefore if (*a*) the infinite body is homogeneous, it will be unmovable or it will be always moving. But this is impossible; for why should it rather rest, or move, down, up, or anywhere, rather than anywhere else? E. g. if there were a clod which were part of an infinite body, where will this move or rest? The proper place of the body which is homogeneous with it is infinite. Will the clod occupy the whole place, then? And how? [This is impossible.] What then is its rest or its movement? It will either rest everywhere, and then it cannot move; or it will move everywhere, and then it cannot be still. But (*b*) if the All has unlike parts, the proper places of the parts are unlike also, and, firstly, the body of the All is not one except by contact, and, secondly, the parts will be either finite or infinite in variety of kind. *Finite* they cannot be; for then those of one kind will be infinite in quantity and those of another will not (if the All is infinite), e. g. fire or water would be infinite, but such an infinite element would be destruction to the contrary elements. But if the parts are *infinite* and simple, their places also are infinite and there will be an infinite number of elements; and if this is impossible, and the places are finite, the All also must be limited.[72]

In general, there cannot be an infinite body and also a proper place for bodies, if every sensible body has either weight or lightness. For it must move either towards the middle or upwards, and the infinite— either the whole or the half of it—cannot do either; for how will you divide it? Or how will part of the infinite be down and part up, or part extreme and part middle? Further, every sensible body is in a place, and there are six kinds of place,[73] but these cannot exist in an infinite body. In general, if there cannot be an infinite place, there cannot be an infinite body; [and there cannot be an infinite place,] for that which is in a place is somewhere, and this means either up or down or in one of the other directions, and each of these is a limit.[74]

The infinite is not the same in the sense that it is a single thing whether exhibited in distance or in movement or in time, but the

[71] Cf. *Phys.* iii. 204^b 32–205^a 7.   [72] Cf. *Phys.* iii. 205^a 29–32.

[73] *sc.* up and down, right and left, before and behind.

[74] Cf. *Phys.* iii. 205^b 24–206^a 7.

posterior among these is called infinite in virtue of its relation to the
35 prior; i. e. a movement is called infinite in virtue of the distance
covered by the spatial movement or alteration or growth, and a time
is called infinite because of the movement which occupies it.[75]

1067ᵇ 11 Of things which change, some change in an accidental sense,
like that in which 'the musical' may be said to walk, and others are
said, without qualification, to change, because something in them
changes, i. e. the things that change in parts; the body becomes
healthy, because the eye does. But there is something which is by its
5 own nature moved directly, and this is the essentially movable. The
same distinction is found in the case of the mover; for it causes movement either in an accidental sense or in respect of a part of itself or
essentially. There is something that directly causes movement; and
there is something that is moved, also the time in which it is moved,
and that from which and that into which it is moved.[76] But the forms
and the affections and the place, which are the terminals of the move-
10 ment of moving things, are unmovable, e. g. knowledge or heat; it is
not heat that is a movement, but heating.[77] Change which is not
accidental is found not in all things, but between contraries, and their
intermediates, and between contradictories. We may convince ourselves
of this by induction.[78]

15   That which changes changes either from positive into positive, or
from negative into negative, or from positive into negative, or from
negative into positive. (By positive I mean that which is expressed by
an affirmative term.) Therefore there must be three changes; for that
20 from negative into negative is not change, because (since the terms
are neither contraries nor contradictories) there is no opposition. The
change from the negative into the positive which is its contradictory
is generation—absolute change absolute generation, and partial change
partial generation; and the change from positive to negative is destruction—absolute change absolute destruction, and partial change partial
25 destruction. If, then, 'that which is not' has several senses,[79] and
movement can attach neither to that which implies putting together
or separating,[80] nor to that which implies potency and is opposed to
that which is in the full sense [81] (true, the not-white or not-good *can*

---

[75] Cf. *Phys.* iii. 207ᵇ 21–25.   [76] Cf. *Phys.* v. 224ᵃ 21–ᵇ 1.
[77] Cf. *Phys.* v. 224ᵇ 11–16.   [78] Cf. *Phys.* v. 224ᵇ 28–30.
[79] Cf. vi. 1026ᵃ 33–ᵇ 2, 1027ᵇ 18–19.
[80] i. e. to 'that which is not' in the sense of 'the judgment which is false'.
[81] i. e. a thing cannot be moved when it does not exist actually, but exists
potentially.

be moved *incidentally*, for the not-white might be a man; but that
which is not a particular thing at all can in no wise be moved), that
which is not cannot be moved (and if this is so, generation cannot be 30
movement; for that which is not *is* generated; for even if we admit to
the full that its generation is accidental, yet it is true to say that 'not-
being' is predicable of that which is generated absolutely).[82] Similarly
rest cannot belong to that which is not. These consequences, then, turn
out to be awkward, and also this, that everything that is moved is in 35
a place, but that which is not is not in a place; for then it would be
somewhere. Nor is destruction movement; for the contrary of movement is movement or rest, but the contrary of destruction is generation. Since every movement is a change, and the kinds of change are 1068ᵃ
the three named above,[83] and of these those in the way of generation
and destruction are not movements, and these are the changes from
a thing to its contradictory, it follows that only the change from positive into positive is movement. And the positives are either contrary or 5
intermediate (for even privation must be regarded as contrary), and
are expressed by an affirmative term, e. g. 'naked' or 'toothless' or
'black'.

12　If the categories are classified as substance, quality, place, acting
or being acted on, relation, quantity, there must be three kinds of
movement—of quality, of quantity, of place. There is no movement in 10
respect of substance (because there is nothing contrary to substance),
nor of relation (for it is possible that if one of two things in relation
changes, the relative term which was true of the other thing ceases to
be true, though this other does not change at all—so that their movement is accidental), nor of agent and patient, or mover and moved,
because there is no movement of movement nor generation of genera- 15
tion, nor, in general, change of change. For there *might* be movement
of movement in two senses; (1) movement might be the subject moved,
as a man is moved because he changes from pale to dark—so that on
this showing movement, too, may be either heated or cooled or change
its place or increase. But this is impossible; for change is not a subject.
Or (2) some other subject might change from change into some other 20
form of existence (e. g. a man from disease into health). But this also
is not possible except incidentally. For every movement is change from

---

[82] i. e. even if the not-being (privation) which is the starting-point of generation can exist only as an accident of prime matter, still not-being *is* the starting-
point of absolute generation (i. e. generation of a substance, not of a quality).

[83] In 1067ᵇ 19.

25 something into something. (And so are generation and destruction; only, these are changes into things opposed in certain ways while the other, movement, is into things opposed in another way.[84]) A thing changes, then, at the same time from health into illness, and from this changes itself into another. Clearly, then, if it has become ill, it will have changed into whatever may be the other change concerned (though it *may* be at rest [85]), and, further, into a determinate change each time; and that new change will be from something definite into 30 some other definite thing; therefore it will be the opposite change, that of growing well. We answer that this happens only incidentally; e. g. there is a change from the process of recollection to that of forgetting, only because *that to which the process attaches* is changing, now into a state of knowledge, now into one of ignorance.

Further, the process will go on to infinity, if there is to be change of change and coming to be of coming to be. What is true of the later, 35 then, must be true of the earlier; e. g. if the simple coming to be was 1068ᵇ once coming to be, that which comes to be something was also once coming to be; therefore that which simply comes to be something was not yet in existence, but something which was coming to be coming to be something was already in existence. And this was once coming to be, so that at that time it was not yet coming to be something else. Now since of an infinite number of terms there is not a first, the first in this series will not exist, and therefore no following term will exist. 5 Nothing, then, can either come to be or move or change. Further, that which is capable of a movement is also capable of the contrary movement and rest, and that which comes to be also ceases to be. Therefore that which is coming to be is ceasing to be when it has come to be coming to be; for it cannot cease to be as soon as it is coming to be coming to be, nor after it has come to be; for that which is ceasing to 10 be must *be*. Further, there must be a matter underlying that which comes to be and changes. What will this be, then—what is it that becomes movement or becoming, as body or soul is that which suffers alteration? And, again, what is it that they move into? For it must be the movement or becoming of something from something into something. How, then, can this condition be fulfilled? There can be no learning of learning, and therefore no becoming of becoming.[86]

15   Since there is not movement either of substance or of relation or of activity and passivity, it remains that movement is in respect of

---

[84] Change between contraries is movement, change between contradictories is generation or destruction.

[85] This is possible, though excluded by the theory in question.

[86] With 1067ᵇ 14–1068ᵇ 15 Cf. *Phys.* v. 225ᵃ 3–226ᵃ 16.

quality and quantity and place; for each of these admits of contrariety. By quality I mean not that which is in the substance (for even the differentia is a quality), but the passive quality, in virtue of which a thing is said to be acted on or to be incapable of being acted on.[87] The immobile is either that which is wholly incapable of being moved, or that which is moved with difficulty in a long time or begins slowly, or that which is of a nature to be moved and can be moved but is not moved when and where and as it would naturally be moved. This alone among immobiles I describe as being at rest; for rest is contrary to movement, so that it must be a privation, in that which is *receptive of movement*.[88]

Things which are in one proximate place are *together in place*, and things which are in different places are *apart*: things whose extremes are together *touch*: that at which a changing thing, if it changes continuously according to its nature, naturally arrives before it arrives at the extreme into which it is changing, is *between*.[89] That which is most distant in a straight line is *contrary in place*. That is *successive* which is after the beginning (the order being determined by position or form or in some other way) and has nothing of the same class between it and that which it succeeds, e. g. lines in the case of a line, units in that of a unit, or a house in that of a house. (There is nothing to prevent a thing of some *other* class from being between.) For the successive succeeds something and is something later; 'one' does not succeed 'two', nor the first day of the month the second. That which, being successive, touches, is *contiguous*. (Since all change is between opposites, and these are either contraries or contradictories, and there is no middle term for contradictories, clearly that which is *between* is between contraries.) The *continuous* is a species of the contiguous. I call two things continuous when the limits of each, with which they touch and by which they are kept together, become one and the same, so that plainly the continuous is found in the things out of which a unity naturally arises in virtue of their contact. And plainly the successive is the first of these concepts (for the successive does not necessarily touch, but that which touches is successive; and if a thing is continuous, it touches, but if it touches, it is not necessarily continuous; and in things in which there is no touching, there is no organic unity); therefore a point is not the same as a unit; for contact belongs to points, but not to units, which have only succession; and there is something between two of the former, but not between two of the latter.[90]

[87] Cf. *Phys.* v. 226ᵃ 23–29.
[88] Cf. *Phys.* v. 226ᵇ 10–16.
[89] Cf. *Phys.* v. 226ᵇ 21–25.
[90] Cf. *Phys.* v. 226ᵇ 32–227ᵃ 31.

BOOK Λ (XII)

1   The subject of our inquiry is substance; for the principles and the causes we are seeking are those of substances. For if the universe is of 20 the nature of a whole, substance is its first part; and if it coheres merely by virtue of serial succession, on this view also substance is first, and is succeeded by quality, and then by quantity. At the same time these latter are not even being in the full sense, but are qualities and movements of it—or else even the not-white and the not-straight would be being; at least we say even these *are*, e. g. 'there is a not-white'.[1] 25 Further, none of the categories other than substance can exist apart. And the early philosophers also in practice testify to the primacy of substance; for it was of substance that they sought the principles and elements and causes. The thinkers of the present [2] day tend to rank universals as substances (for genera are universals, and these they tend to describe as principles and substances, owing to the abstract nature of their inquiry); but the thinkers of old ranked particular things as substances, e. g. fire and earth, not what is common to both, body.

30   There are three kinds of substance—one that is sensible (of which one subdivision is eternal and another is perishable; the latter is recognized by all men, and includes e. g. plants and animals), of which we must grasp the elements, whether one or many; and another that is immovable, and this certain thinkers assert to be capable of existing 35 apart, some dividing it into two, others identifying the Forms and the objects of mathematics, and others positing, of these two, only the objects of mathematics.[3] The former two kinds of substance are the 1069ᵇ subject of physics (for they imply movement); but the third kind belongs to another science, if there is no principle common to it and to the other kinds.

2   Sensible substance is changeable. Now if change proceeds from opposites or from intermediates, and not from all opposites (for the 5 voice is not-white [but it does not therefore change to white]), but from the contrary, there must be something underlying which changes into the contrary state; for the *contraries* do not change. Further, something persists, but the contrary does not persist; there is, then, some third thing besides the contraries, viz. the matter. Now since changes are of four kinds—either in respect of the 'what' or of the quality or 10 of the quantity or of the place, and change in respect of 'thisness' is

---

[1] This is an implication of the ordinary type of judgement, '*x* is not white'.
[2] The Platonists.
[3] The three views appear to have been held respectively by Plato, Xenocrates, and Speusippus.

simple generation and destruction, and change in quantity is increase
and diminution, and change in respect of an affection is alteration,
and change of place is motion, changes will be from given states into
those contrary to them in these several respects. The matter, then,
which changes must be capable of both states. And since that which 15
'is' has two senses, we must say that everything changes from that
which is potentially to that which is actually, e. g. from potentially
white to actually white, and similarly in the case of increase and
diminution. Therefore not only can a thing come to be, incidentally,
out of that which is not, but also all things come to be out of that
which is, but is potentially, and is not actually. And this is the 'One' 20
of Anaxagoras; for instead of 'all things were together'—and the
'Mixture' of Empedocles and Anaximander and the account given by
Democritus—it is better to say 'all things were together potentially
but not actually'. Therefore these thinkers seem to have had some
notion of matter. Now all things that change have matter, but different 25
matter; and of eternal things those which are not generable but are
movable in space have matter—not matter for generation, however,
but for motion from one place to another.

One might raise the question from what sort of non-being generation
proceeds; for 'non-being' has three senses. If, then, one form of non-
being exists potentially, still it is not by virtue of a potentiality for any
and every thing, but different things come from different things; nor
is it satisfactory to say that 'all things were together'; for they differ 30
in their matter, since otherwise why did an infinity of things come to
be, and not one thing? For 'reason' is one, so that if matter also were
one, that must have come to be in actuality which the matter was in
potency.[4] The causes and the principles, then, are three, two being the
pair of contraries of which one is definition and form and the other
is privation, and the third being the matter.

3   Note, next, that neither the matter nor the form comes to be—and 35
I mean the last matter and form. For everything that changes is something and is changed by something and into something. That by which 1070ᶠ
it is changed is the immediate mover; that which is changed, the
matter; that into which it is changed, the form. The process, then, will
go on to infinity, if not only the bronze comes to be round but also the
round or the bronze comes to be; therefore there must be a stop.

Note, next, that each substance comes into being out of something
that shares its name. (Natural objects and other things both rank as 5
substances.) For things come into being either by art or by nature or

---

[4] *sc.* an undifferentiated unity.

by luck or by spontaneity. Now art is a principle of movement in something other than the thing moved, nature is a principle in the thing itself (for man begets man), and the other causes are privations of these two.

There are three kinds of substance—the matter, which is a 'this'
10 in appearance (for all things that are characterized by contact and not
19 by organic unity are matter and substratum, e. g. fire, flesh, head; for these are all matter, and the last matter is the matter of that
11 which is in the full sense substance); the nature, which is a 'this' or positive state towards which movement takes place; and again, thirdly, the particular substance which is composed of these two, e. g. Socrates or Callias. Now in some cases the 'this' does not exist apart from the composite substance, e. g. the form of house does not so
15 exist, unless the art of building exists apart (nor is there generation and destruction of these forms, but it is in another way that the house apart from its matter, and health, and all ideals of art, exist and do not exist); but if the 'this' exists apart from the concrete thing, it is only in the case of natural objects. And so Plato was not far wrong when he said that there are as many Forms as there are kinds of natural object (if there *are* Forms distinct from the things of this
21 earth). The moving causes exist as things preceding the effects, but causes in the sense of definitions are simultaneous with their effects. For when a man is healthy, then health also exists; and the shape of a bronze sphere exists at the same time as the bronze sphere. (But
25 we must examine whether any form also survives afterwards. For in some cases there is nothing to prevent this; e. g. the soul may be of this sort—not all soul but the reason; for presumably it is impossible that *all* soul should survive.) Evidently then there is no necessity, on this ground at least, for the existence of the Ideas. For man is begotten by man, a given man by an individual father; and similarly
30 in the arts; for the medical art is the formal cause of health.

4   The causes and the principles of different things are in a sense different, but in a sense, if one speaks universally and analogically, they are the same for all. For one might· raise the question whether the principles and elements are different or the same for substances
35 and for relative terms, and similarly in the case of each of the categories. But it would be paradoxical if they were the same for all. For then from the same elements will proceed relative terms and sub-
1070ᵇ stances. What then will this common element be? For (1) (a) there is nothing common to and distinct from substance and the other categories, viz. those which are predicated; but an element is prior

to the things of which it is an element. But again (*b*) substance is not an element in relative terms, nor is any of these an element in substance. Further, (2) how can all things have the same elements? For none of the elements can be the same as that which is composed 5 of elements, e. g. *b* or *a* cannot be the same as *ba*. (None, therefore, of the intelligibles, e. g. being or unity, is an element; for these are predicable of each of the compounds as well.) None of the elements, then, will be either a substance or a relative term; but it must be one or other. All things, then, have not the same elements.

Or, as we are wont to put it, in a sense they have and in a sense 10 they have not; e. g. perhaps the elements of perceptible bodies are, as *form*, the hot, and in another sense the cold, which is the *privation*; and, as *matter*, that which directly and of itself potentially has these attributes; and substances comprise both these and the things composed of these, of which these are the principles, or any unity which is produced out of the hot and the cold, e. g. flesh or bone; for the 15 product must be different from the elements. These things then have the same elements and principles (though specifically different things have specifically different elements); but *all* things have not the same elements in this sense, but only analogically; i. e. one might say that there are three principles—the form, the privation, and the matter. But each of these is different for each class; e. g. in colour they are 20 white, black, and surface, and in day and night they are light, darkness, and air.

Since not only the elements present in a thing are causes, but also something external, i. e. the moving cause, clearly while 'principle' and 'element' are different both are causes, and 'principle' is divided into these two kinds [5] and that which acts as producing movement or rest is a principle and a substance. Therefore analogically there are 25 three elements, and four causes and principles; but the elements are different in different things, and the proximate moving cause is different for different things. Health, disease, body; the moving cause is the medical art. Form, disorder of a particular kind, bricks; the moving cause is the building art. And since the moving cause in the 30 case of natural things is—for man, for instance, man, and in the products of thought the form or its contrary, there will be in a sense three causes, while in a sense there are four. For the medical art is in some sense health, and the building art is the form of the house, and man begets man; [6] further, besides these there is that which as first 35 of all things moves all things.

[5] i. e. the principles which are elements and those which are not.
[6] i. e. the efficient cause is identical with the formal.

5   Some things can exist apart and some cannot, and it is the former
1071ᵃ that are substances. And therefore all things have the same causes,[7]
because, without substances, modifications and movements do not
exist. Further, these causes will probably bé soul and body, or reason
and desire and body.

5   And in yet another way, analogically identical things are principles, i. e. actuality and potency; but these also are not only different
for different things but also apply in different ways to them. For in
some cases the same thing exists at one time actually and at another
potentially, e. g. wine or flesh or man does so. (And these two fall
under the above-named causes.[8] For the form exists actually, if it
can exist apart, and so does the complex of form and matter, and the
10 privation, e. g. darkness or disease; but the matter exists potentially;
for this is that which can become qualified either by the form or by
the privation.) But the distinction of actuality and potentiality
applies in another way to cases where the matter of cause and of effect
is not the same, in some of which cases the form is not the same but
different; e. g. the cause of man is (1) the elements in man (viz. fire
and earth as matter, and the peculiar form), and further (2) some-
15 thing else outside, i. e. the father, and (3) besides these the sun and
its oblique course, which are neither matter nor form nor privation
of man nor of the same species with him, but moving causes.

Further, one must observe that some causes can be expressed in
universal terms, and some cannot. The proximate principles of all
things are the 'this' which is proximate in actuality, and another
which is proximate in potentiality.[9] The universal causes, then, of
20 which we spoke [10] do not *exist*. For it is the individual that is the
originative principle of the individuals. For while man is the originative
principle of man universally, there *is* no universal man, but Peleus is
the originative principle of Achilles, and your father of you, and this
particular *b* of this particular *ba*, though *b* in general is the originative
principle of *ba* taken without qualification.

Further, if the causes of substances are the causes of all things,
yet different things have different causes and elements, as was said [11];
25 the causes of things that are not in the same class, e. g. of colours and
sounds, of substances and quantities, are different except in an analogi-

[7] i. e. the causes of substance are the causes of all things.

[8] i. e. the division into potency and actuality stands in a definite relation to the
previous division into matter, form, and privation.

[9] e. g. the proximate causes of a child are the individual father (who on Aristotle's view is the efficient and contains the formal cause) and the germ contained
in the individual mother (which is the material cause).

[10] In l. 17.   [11] In 1070ᵇ 17.

cal sense; and those of things in the same species are different, not in species, but in the sense that the causes of different individuals are different, your matter and form and moving cause being different from mine, while in their universal definition they are the same. And if we inquire what are the principles or elements of substances and 30 relations and qualities—whether they are the same or different —clearly when the names of the causes are used in several senses the causes of each are the same, but when the senses are distinguished the causes are not the same but different, except that in the following senses the causes of all are the same. They are (1) the same or analogous in this sense, that matter, form, privation, and the moving cause are common to all things; and (2) the causes of substances may be treated as causes of all things in this sense, that when substances are removed all things are removed; further, (3) that which 35 is first in respect of complete reality is the cause of all things. But in another sense there are different first causes, viz. all the contraries which are neither generic nor ambiguous terms; and, further, the matters of different things are different. We have stated, then, what 1071ᵛ are the principles of sensible things and how many they are, and in what sense they are the same and in what sense different.

6   Since there were [12] three kinds of substance, two of them physical and one unmovable, regarding the latter we must assert that it is necessary that there should be an eternal unmovable substance. For substances are the first of existing things, and if they are all destructi- 5 ble, all things are destructible. But it is impossible that movement should either have come into being or cease to be (for it must always have existed), or that time should. For there could not be a before and an after if time did not exist. Movement also is continuous, then, in the sense in which time is; for time is either the same thing as movement or an attribute of movement. And there is no continuous 10 movement except movement in place, and of this only that which is circular is continuous.

But if there is something which is capable of moving things or acting on them, but is not actually doing so, there will not necessarily be movement; for that which has a potency need not exercise it. Nothing, then, is gained even if we suppose eternal substances, as the believers in the Forms do, unless there is to be in them some prin- 15 ciple which can cause change; nay, even this is not enough, nor is another substance besides the Forms enough; for if it is not to *act*, there will be no movement. Further, even if it acts, this will not be

[12] Cf. 1069ᵃ 30.

enough, if its essence is potency; for there will not be *eternal* movement, since that which is potentially may possibly not be. There must,
20 then, be such a principle, whose very essence is actuality. Further,
then, these substances must be without matter; for they must be
eternal, if *anything* is eternal. Therefore they must be actuality.

Yet there is a difficulty; for it is thought that everything that acts
is able to act, but that not everything that is able to act acts, so that
25 the potency is prior. But if this is so, nothing that is need be; for
it is possible for all things to be capable of existing but not yet to
exist.

Yet if we follow the theologians who generate the world from night,
or the natural philosophers who say that 'all things were together',[13]
the same impossible result ensues. For how will there be movement,
if there is no actually existing cause? Wood will surely not move
30 itself—the carpenter's art must act on it; nor will the menstrual
blood nor the earth set themselves in motion, but the seeds must
act on the earth and the *semen* on the menstrual blood.

This is why some suppose eternal actuality—e. g. Leucippus [14] and
Plato [15]; for they say there is always movement. But why and what
this movement is they do not say, nor, if the world moves in this way
or that, do they tell us the cause of its doing so. Now nothing is
moved at random, but there must always be something present to
35 move it; e. g. as a matter of fact a thing moves in one way by nature,
and in another by force or through the influence of reason or something else. (Further, what sort of movement is primary? This makes
a vast difference.) But again for Plato, at least, it is not permissible
1072ᵃ to name here that which he sometimes supposes to be the source of
movement—that which moves itself; [16] for the soul is later, and coeval
with the heavens, according to his account.[17] To suppose potency
prior to actuality, then, is in a sense right, and in a sense not; and we
have specified these senses.[18] That actuality is prior is testified by
5 Anaxagoras (for his 'reason' is actuality) and by Empedocles in his
doctrine of love and strife, and by those who say that there is always
movement, e. g. Leucippus. Therefore chaos or night did not exist
for an infinite time, but the same things have always existed (either
passing through a cycle of changes or obeying some other law), since
actuality is prior to potency. If, then, there is a constant cycle, some-
10 thing must always remain,[19] acting in the same way. And if there is

13 Anaxagoras.
14 Cf. *De Caelo*, iii. 300ᵇ 8.
15 Cf. *Timaeus*, 30 A.
16 Cf. *Phaedrus*, 245 C; *Laws*, 894 E.
17 Cf. *Timaeus*, 34 B.
18 Cf. 1071ᵇ 22-26.
19 i. e. the sphere of the fixed stars.

to be generation and destruction, there must be something else [20]
which is always acting in different ways. This must, then, act in one
way in virtue of itself, and in another in virtue of something else—
either of a third agent, therefore, or of the first. Now it must be in
virtue of the first. For otherwise this again causes the motion both
of the second agent and of the third. Therefore it is better to say [15]
'the first'. For it was the cause of eternal uniformity; and something
else is the cause of variety, and evidently both together are the cause
of eternal variety. This, accordingly, is the character which the
motions actually exhibit. What need then is there to seek for other
principles?

7   Since (1) this is a possible account of the matter, and (2) if it
were not true, the world would have proceeded out of night and 'all
things together' and out of non-being, these difficulties may be taken [20]
as solved. There is, then, something which is always moved with an
unceasing motion, which is motion in a circle; and this is plain not
in theory only but in fact. Therefore the first heaven [21] must be
eternal. There is therefore also something which moves it. And since
that which is moved and moves is intermediate, there is something
which moves without being moved, being eternal, substance, and [25]
actuality. And the object of desire and the object of thought move
in this way; they move without being moved. The primary objects
of desire and of thought are the same. For the apparent good is the
object of appetite, and the real good is the primary object of rational
wish. But desire is consequent on opinion rather than opinion on
desire; for the thinking is the starting-point. And thought is moved [30]
by the object of thought, and one of the two columns of opposites is
in itself the object of thought; and in this, substance is first, and in
substance, that which is simple and exists actually. (The one and
the simple are not the same; for 'one' means a measure, but 'simple'
means that the thing itself has a certain nature.) But the beautiful,
also, and that which is in itself desirable are in the same column; and [35]
the first in any class is always best, or analogous to the best.

   That a final cause may exist among unchangeable entities is shown 1072[h]
by the distinction of its meanings. For the final cause is (a) some
being for whose good an action is done, and (b) something at which
the action aims; and of these the latter exists among unchangeable
entities though the former does not. The final cause, then, produces
motion as being loved, but all other things move by being moved.

[20] i. e. the sun. Cf. *De Gen. et Corr.* ii. 336[a] 23 ff.
[21] i. e. the outer sphere of the universe, that in which the fixed stars are set.

Now if something is moved it is capable of being otherwise than
5 as it is. Therefore if its actuality is the primary form of spatial motion,
then in so far as it is subject to change, in *this* respect it is capable
of being otherwise—in place, even if not in substance. But since there
is something which moves while itself unmoved, existing actually,
this can in no way be otherwise than as it is. For motion in space is
the first of the kinds of change, and motion in a circle the first kind
10 of spatial motion; and this the first mover *produces*.[22] The first
mover, then, exists of necessity; and in so far as it exists by necessity,
its mode of being is good, and it is in this sense a first principle. For
the necessary has all these senses—that which is necessary perforce
because it is contrary to the natural impulse, that without which the
good is impossible, and that which cannot be otherwise but can exist
only in a single way.

On such a principle, then, depend the heavens and the world of
nature. And it is a life such as the best which we enjoy, and enjoy
15 for but a short time (for it is ever in this state, which we cannot be),
since its actuality is also pleasure. (And for this reason [23] are waking,
perception, and thinking most pleasant, and hopes and memories are
so on account of these.) And thinking in itself deals with that which
is best in itself, and that which is thinking in the fullest sense with
that which is best in the fullest sense. And thought thinks on itself
20 because it shares the nature of the object of thought; for it becomes
an object of thought in coming into contact with and thinking its
objects, so that thought and object of thought are the same. For that
which is *capable* of receiving the object of thought, i. e. the essence,
is thought. But it is *active* when it *possesses* this object. Therefore the
possession rather than the receptivity is the divine element which
thought seems to contain, and the act of contemplation is what is
most pleasant and best. If, then, God is always in that good state in
which we sometimes are, this compels our wonder; and if in a better
25 this compels it yet more. And God *is* in a better state. And life also
belongs to God; for the actuality of thought is life, and God is that
actuality; and God's self-dependent actuality is life most good and
eternal. We say therefore that God is a living being, eternal, most
good, so that life and duration continuous and eternal belong to God;
for this *is* God.

---

[22] If it had any movement, it would have the first. But it produces this and
therefore cannot share in it; for if it did, we should have to look for something
that is prior to the first mover and imparts this motion to it.

[23] *sc.* because they are activities or actualities.

Those who suppose, as the Pythagoreans [24] and Speusippus [25] do, 30 that supreme beauty and goodness are not present in the beginning, because the beginnings both of plants and of animals are *causes*, but beauty and completeness are in the *effects* of these,[26] are wrong in their opinion. For the seed comes from other individuals which are 35 prior and complete, and the first thing is not seed but the complete being; e. g. we must say that before the seed there is a man—not the 1073ᵃ man produced from the seed, but another from whom the seed comes.

It is clear then from what has been said that there is a substance which is eternal and unmovable and separate from sensible things. It has been shown also that this substance cannot have any magni- 5 tude, but is without parts and indivisible (for it produces movement through infinite time, but nothing finite has infinite power; and, while every magnitude is either infinite or finite, it cannot, for the above reason, have finite magnitude, and it cannot have infinite mag- 10 nitude because there is no infinite magnitude at all). But it has also been shown that it is impassive and unalterable; for all the other changes are posterior to [27] change of place.

8   It is clear, then, why these things are as they are. But we must not ignore the question whether we have to suppose one such sub- stance or more than one, and if the latter, how many; we must also 15 mention, regarding the opinions expressed by others, that they have said nothing about the number of the substances that can even be clearly stated. For the theory of Ideas has no special discussion of the subject; for those who speak of Ideas say the Ideas are numbers, and they speak of numbers now as unlimited, now [28] as limited by the number 10; but as for the reason why there should be just so 20 many numbers, nothing is said with any demonstrative exactness. We however must discuss the subject, starting from the presuppositions and distinctions we have mentioned. The first principle or primary being is not movable either in itself or accidentally, but produces the 25 primary eternal and single movement. But since that which is moved must be moved by something, and the first mover must be in itself unmovable, and eternal movement must be produced by something eternal and a single movement by a single thing, and since we see that besides the simple spatial movement of the universe, which we say the

---

[24] Cf. 1075ᵃ 36.

[25] Cf. vii. 1028ᵇ 21, xiv. 1091ᵃ 34, 1092ᵃ 11.

[26] i. e. the animal or plant is more beautiful and perfect than the seed.

[27] i. e. impossible without.

[28] The reference is to Plato (Cf. *Phys.* 206ᵇ 32).

30 first and unmovable substance produces, there are other spatial movements—those of the planets—which are eternal (for a body which
moves in a circle is eternal and unresting; we have proved these points
in the physical treatises [29]), each of *these* movements also must be
caused by a substance both unmovable in itself and eternal. For the
nature of the stars [30] is eternal just because it is a certain kind of
35 substance, and the mover is eternal and prior to the moved, and that
which is prior to a substance must be a substance. Evidently, then,
there must be substances which are of the same number as the movements of the stars, and in their nature eternal, and in themselves
unmovable, and without magnitude, for the reason before mentioned.[31]

1073ᵇ   That the movers are substances, then, and that one of these is first
and another second according to the same order as the movements of
the stars, is evident. But in the number of the movements we reach a
problem which must be treated from the standpoint of that one of
the mathematical sciences which is most akin to philosophy—viz. of
5 astronomy; for this science speculates about substance which is perceptible but eternal, but the other mathematical sciences, i. e. arithmetic and geometry, treat of no substance. That the movements are
more numerous than the bodies that are moved is evident to those
who have given even moderate attention to the matter; for each of
10 the planets has more than one movement. But as to the actual number
of these movements, we now—to give some notion of the subject—
quote what some of the mathematicians say, that our thought may
have some definite number to grasp; but, for the rest, we must partly
15 investigate for ourselves, partly learn from other investigators, and
if those who study this subject form an opinion contrary to what we
have now stated, we must esteem both parties indeed, but follow the
more accurate.

Eudoxus supposed that the motion of the sun or of the moon involves, in either case, three spheres, of which the first is the sphere
of the fixed stars, and the second moves in the circle which runs along
20 the middle of the zodiac, and the third in the circle which is inclined
across the breadth of the zodiac; but the circle in which the moon
moves is inclined at a greater angle than that in which the sun moves.
And the motion of the planets involves, in each case, four spheres,
and of these also the first and second are the same as the first two
25 mentioned above (for the sphere of the fixed stars is that which moves

---

[29] Cf. *Phys.* viii. 8, 9; *De Caelo*, i. 2, ii. 3–8.

[30] This is to be understood as a general term including both fixed stars and
planets.   [31] Cf. ll. 5–11.

all the other spheres, and that which is placed beneath this and has
its movement in the circle which bisects the zodiac is common to all),
but the *poles* of the third sphere of each planet are in the circle which
bisects the zodiac, and the motion of the fourth sphere is in the circle
which is inclined at an angle to the equator of the third sphere; and
the poles of the third sphere are different for each of the other planets, 30
but those of Venus and Mercury are the same.

Callippus made the position of the spheres the same as Eudoxus
did, but while he assigned the same number as Eudoxus did to Jupiter
and to Saturn, he thought two more spheres should be added to the 35
sun and two to the moon, if one is to explain the observed facts; and
one more to each of the other planets.

But it is necessary, if all the spheres combined are to explain the
observed facts, that for each of the planets there should be other 1074ᵃ
spheres (one fewer than those hitherto assigned) which counteract
those already mentioned and bring back to the same position the
outermost sphere of the star which in each case is situated below [32]
the star in question; for only thus can all the forces at work produce 5
the observed motion of the planets. Since, then, the spheres involved
in the movement of the planets themselves are—eight for Saturn and
Jupiter and twenty-five for the others, and of these only those involved in the movement of the lowest-situated planet need not be
counteracted, the spheres which counteract those of the outermost
two planets will be six in number, and the spheres which counteract
those of the next four planets will be sixteen; therefore the number 10
of all the spheres—both those which move the planets and those
which counteract these—will be fifty-five. And if one were not to add
to the moon and to the sun the movements we mentioned,[33] the whole
set of spheres will be forty-seven in number.

Let this, then, be taken as the number of the spheres, so that the
unmovable substances and principles also may probably be taken as 15
just so many; the assertion of *necessity* must be left to more powerful
thinkers. But if there can be no spatial movement which does not
conduce to the moving of a star, and if further every being and every
substance which is immune from change and in virtue of itself has
attained to the best must be considered an end, there can be no other
being apart from these we have named, but this must be the number 20
of the substances. For if there are others, they will cause change as
being a final cause of movement; but there cannot *be* other movements besides those mentioned. And it is reasonable to infer this from

[32] i. e. inwards from, the universe being thought of as a system of concentric
spheres encircling the earth.   [33] In 1073ᵇ 35, 38–1074ᵃ 4.

25 a consideration of the bodies that are moved; for if everything that
moves is for the sake of that which is moved, and every movement
belongs to something that is moved, no movement can be for the sake
of itself or of another movement, but all the movements must be for
the sake of the stars. For if there is to be a movement for the sake of
a movement, this latter also will have to be for the sake of something
30 else; so that since there cannot be an infinite regress, the end of every
movement will be one of the divine bodies which move through the
heaven.

(Evidently there is but one heaven. For if there are many heavens
as there are many men, the moving principles, of which each heaven
will have one, will be one in form but in *number* many. But all things
that are many in number have matter; for one and the same defini-
35 tion, e. g. that of man, applies to many things, while Socrates is one.
But the primary essence has not matter; for it is complete reality. So
the unmovable first mover is one both in definition and in number;
so too, therefore, is that which is moved always and continuously;
therefore there is one heaven alone.)

1074ᵇ   Our forefathers in the most remote ages have handed down to their
posterity a tradition, in the form of a myth, that these bodies are
gods and that the divine encloses the whole of nature. The rest of the
tradition has been added later in mythical form with a view to the
5 persuasion of the multitude and to its legal and utilitarian expediency; they say these gods are in the form of men or like some of the
other animals, and they say other things consequent on and similar to
these which we have mentioned. But if one were to separate the first
point from these additions and take it alone—that they thought the
10 first substances to be gods, one must regard this as an inspired utterance, and reflect that, while probably each art and each science has
often been developed as far as possible and has again perished, these
opinions, with others, have been preserved until the present like relics
of the ancient treasure. Only thus far, then, is the opinion of our
ancestors and of our earliest predecessors clear to us.

15 9   The nature of the divine thought involves certain problems; for
while thought is held to be the most divine of things observed by us,
the question how it must be situated in order to have that character
involves difficulties. For if it thinks of nothing, what is there here
of dignity? It is just like one who sleeps. And if it thinks, but this
depends on something else, then (since that which is its substance is
not the act of thinking, but a potency) it cannot be the best sub-
20 stance; for it is through thinking that its value belongs to it. Further,

whether its substance is the faculty of thought or the act of thinking, what does it think of? Either of itself or of something else; and if of something else, either of the same thing always or of something different. Does it matter, then, or not, whether it thinks of the good or of any chance thing? Are there not some things about which it is incredi- 25 ble that it should think? Evidently, then, it thinks of that which is most divine and precious, and it does not change; for change would be change for the worse, and this would be already a movement. First, then, if 'thought' is not the act of thinking but a potency, it would be reasonable to suppose that the continuity of its thinking is wearisome to it. Secondly, there would evidently be something else more precious than thought, viz. that which is thought of. For both thinking and 30 the act of thought will belong even to one who thinks of the worst thing in the world, so that if this ought to be avoided (and it ought, for there are even some things which it is better not to see than to see), the act of thinking cannot be the best of things. Therefore it must be of itself that the divine thought thinks (since it is the most excellent of things), and its thinking is a thinking on thinking.

But evidently knowledge and perception and opinion and under- 35 standing have always something else as their object, and themselves only by the way. Further, if thinking and being thought of are different, in respect of which does goodness belong to thought? For to *be* an act of thinking and to *be* an object of thought are not the same thing. We answer that in some cases the knowledge is the object. In 1075ᵃ the productive sciences it is the substance or essence of the object, matter omitted, and in the theoretical sciences the definition or the act of thinking is the object. Since, then, thought and the object of thought are not different in the case of things that have not matter, the divine thought and its object will be the same, i. e. the thinking will be one with the object of its thought.

A further question is left—whether the object of the divine thought 5 is composite; for if it were, thought would change in passing from part to part of the whole. We answer that everything which has not matter is indivisible—as human thought, or rather the thought of composite beings, is in a certain period of time (for it does not possess the good at this moment or at that, but its best, being something *different* from it, is attained only in a whole period of time), so 10 throughout eternity is the thought which has *itself* for its object.

10   We must consider also in which of two ways the nature of the universe contains the good and the highest good, whether as something separate and by itself, or as the order of the parts. Probably in

both ways, as an army does; for its good is found both in its order
15 and in its leader, and more in the latter; for he does not depend on
the order but it depends on him. And all things are ordered together
somehow, but not all alike—both fishes and fowls and plants; and
the world is not such that one thing has nothing to do with another,
but they are connected. For all are ordered together to one end, but
20 it is as in a house, where the freemen are least at liberty to act at
random, but all things or most things are already ordained for them,
while the slaves and the animals do little for the common good, and
for the most part live at random; for this is the sort of principle that
constitutes the nature of each. I mean, for instance, that all must at
least come to be dissolved into their elements,[34] and there are other
functions similarly in which all share for the good of the whole.

25   We must not fail to observe how many impossible or paradoxical
results confront those who hold different views from our own, and
what are the views of the subtler thinkers, and which views are
attended by fewest difficulties. All make all things out of contraries.
But neither 'all things' nor 'out of contraries' is right; nor do these
thinkers tell us how all the things in which the contraries are present
30 can be made out of the contraries; for contraries are not affected by
one another. Now for us this difficulty is solved naturally by the fact
that there is a third element.[35] These thinkers however make one of
the two contraries matter; this is done for instance by those who
make the unequal matter for the equal, or the many matter for the
one.[36] But this also is refuted in the same way; for the one matter
which underlies any pair of contraries is contrary to nothing. Further,
all things, except the one, will, on the view we are criticizing, partake
35 of evil; for the bad itself is one of the two elements. But the other
school [37] does not treat the good and the bad even as principles; yet
in all things the good is in the highest degree a principle. The school
we first mentioned is right in saying that it is a principle, but *how*
the good is a principle they do not say—whether as end or as mover
or as form.

1075ᵇ   Empedocles [38] also has a paradoxical view; for he identifies the
good with love, but this is a principle both as mover (for it brings
things together) and as matter (for it is part of the mixture). Now
5 even if it happens that the same thing is a principle both as matter

[34] *sc.* in order that higher forms of being may be produced by new combinations of the elements.
[35] i. e. the substratum.   [36] The reference is to Platonists.
[37] The reference is to the Pythagoreans and Speusippus; Cf. xii. 1072ᵇ 31.
[38] Cf. i. 985ᵃ 4.

and as mover, still the being, at least, of the two is not the same. In which respect then is love a principle? It is paradoxical also that strife should be imperishable; the nature of his 'evil' is just strife.

Anaxagoras makes the good a motive principle; for his 'reason' moves things. But it moves them for an end, which must be something other than it, except according to *our* way of stating the case; for, on our view, the medical art is in a sense health. It is paradoxical also not to suppose a contrary to the good, i. e. to reason. But all who speak of the contraries make no use of the contraries, unless we bring their views into shape. And why some things are perishable and others imperishable, no one tells us; for they make all existing things out of the same principles. Further, some make existing things out of the non-existent; and others to avoid the necessity of this make all things one.

Further, why should there always be becoming, and what is the cause of becoming?—this no one tells us. And those who suppose two principles must suppose another, a superior principle, and so must those who believe in the Forms; for why did things come to participate, or why do they participate, in the Forms? And all other think- 20 ers[39] are confronted by the necessary consequence that there is something contrary to Wisdom, i. e. to the highest knowledge; but *we* are not. For there is nothing contrary to that which is primary; for all contraries have matter, and things that have matter exist only potentially; and the ignorance which is contrary to any knowledge leads to an object contrary to the object of the knowledge; but what is primary has no contrary.

Again, if besides sensible things no others exist, there will be no 25 first principle, no order, no becoming, no heavenly bodies, but each principle will have a principle before it, as in the accounts of the theologians and all the natural philosophers. But if the Forms or the numbers are to exist, they will be causes of nothing; or if not that, at least not of movement. Further, how is extension, i. e. a *continuum*, to be produced out of unextended parts? For number will not, either as mover or as form, produce a *continuum*. But again there cannot 30 be any *contrary* that is also essentially a productive or moving principle; or it would be possible not to be.[40] Or at least its action would be posterior to its potency. The world, then, would not be eternal. But it is; one of these premises, then, must be denied. And

[39] The special reference is to Plato; Cf. *Rep.* 477.

[40] Since contraries must contain matter, and matter implies potentiality and contingency.

we have said how this must be done.[41] Further, in virtue of what the
35 numbers, or the soul and the body, or in general the form and the
thing, are one—of this no one tells us anything; nor can any one
tell, unless he says, as we do, that the mover makes them one. And
those who say [42] mathematical number is first and go on to generate
one kind of substance after another and give different principles for
1076ª each, make the substance of the universe a mere series of episodes
(for one substance has no influence on another by its existence or
non-existence), and they give us many governing principles; but the
world refuses to be governed badly.

'The rule of many is not good; one ruler let there be.' [43]

BOOK M (XIII)

1 We have stated what is the substance of sensible things, dealing
in the treatise on physics [1] with matter, and later [2] with the substance
10 which has actual existence. Now since our inquiry is whether there
is or is not besides the sensible substances any which is immovable
and eternal, and, if there is, what it is, we must first consider what
is said by others, so that, if there is anything which they say wrongly,
we may not be liable to the same objections, while, if there is any
opinion common to them and us, we shall have no private grievance
15 against ourselves on that account; for one must be content to state
some points better than one's predecessors, and others no worse.

Two opinions are held on this subject; it is said that the objects
of mathematics—i.e. numbers and lines and the like—are substances, and again that the Ideas are substances. And since (1) some
20 recognize these as two different classes—the Ideas and the mathematical numbers, and (2) some recognize both as having one nature,
while (3) some others say that the mathematical substances are the
only substances,[3] we must consider first [4] the objects of mathematics,
not qualifying them by any other characteristic—not asking, for
instance, whether they are in fact Ideas or not, or whether they are
the principles and substances of existing things or not, but only
25 whether as objects of mathematics they exist or not, and if they exist,
how they exist. Then after this we must separately consider [5] the Ideas

---

[41] Cf. 1071ᵇ 19, 20.

[42] Speusippus is meant; Cf. vii. 1028ᵇ 21, xiv. 1090ᵇ 13–20.

[43] Cf. *Iliad*, ii. 204.

[1] *Phys.* i.   [2] *Met.* vii, viii, ix.

[3] Plato, Xenocrates, and the Pythagoreans and Speusippus, respectively, are meant.

[4] Cf. chs. 2, 3.   [5] Cf. chs. 4, 5.

themselves in a general way, and only as far as the accepted mode
of treatment demands; for most of the points have been repeatedly
made even by the discussions outside our school, and, further, the
greater part of our account must finish by throwing light on that 30
inquiry, viz. when we examine [6] whether the substances and the principles of existing things are numbers and Ideas; for after the discussion of the Ideas this remains as a third inquiry.

If the objects of mathematics exist, they must exist either in sensible objects, as some say, or separate from sensible objects (and this
also is said by some); or if they exist in neither of these ways, 35
either they do not exist, or they exist only in some special sense. So that
the subject of our discussion will be not whether they exist but how
they exist.

2   That it is impossible for mathematical objects to exist *in* sensible
things, and at the same time that the doctrine in question is an
artificial one, has been said already in our discussion of difficulties [7];
we have pointed out that it is impossible for two solids to be in the 1076ᵇ
same place, and also that according to the same argument the other
powers and characteristics also [8] should exist in sensible things and
none of them separately. This we have said already. But, further, it
is obvious that on this theory it is impossible for any body whatever 5
to be divided; for it would have to be divided at a plane, and the
plane at a line, and the line at a point, so that if the point cannot
be divided, neither can the line, and if the line cannot, neither can
the plane nor the solid. What difference, then, does it make whether
sensible things are such indivisible entities, or, without being so
themselves, have indivisible entities in them? The result will be the 10
same; if the sensible entities are divided the others will be divided
too, or else not even the sensible entities can be divided.

But, again, it is not possible that such entities should exist *separately.* For if besides the sensible solids there are to be other solids
which are separate from them and prior to the sensible solids, it is
plain that besides the planes also there must be other and separate 15
planes and points and lines; for consistency requires this. But if
these exist, again besides the planes and lines and points of the mathematical solid there must be others which are separate. (For incomposites are prior to compounds; and if there are, prior to the sensible
bodies, bodies which are not sensible, by the same argument the 20

---

[6] Cf. chs. 6–9.   [7] Cf. iii. 998ᵃ 7–19.
[8] Which nevertheless the theory in question represents as Ideas apart from
sensible things.

planes which exist by themselves must be prior to those which are
in the motionless solids. Therefore these will be planes and lines
other than those that exist along with the mathematical solids to which
these thinkers assign separate existence; for the latter exist along
with the mathematical solids, while the others are prior to the mathe-
25 matical solids.) Again, therefore, there will be, belonging to these
planes, lines, and prior to them there will have to be, by the same
argument, other lines and points; and prior to these points in the
prior lines there will have to be other points, though there will be no
others prior to these. Now (1) the accumulation becomes absurd;
30 for we find ourselves with one set of solids apart from the sensible
solids; three sets of planes apart from the sensible planes—those which
exist apart from the sensible planes, and those in the mathematical
solids, and those which exist apart from those in the mathematical solids; four sets of lines, and five sets of points. With which
of these, then, will the mathematical sciences deal? Certainly not
35 with the planes and lines and points in the motionless solid; for
science always deals with what is prior. And (2) the same account
will apply also to numbers; for there will be a different set of units
apart from each set of points, and also apart from each set of
realities, from the objects of sense and again from those of thought;
so that there will be various classes of mathematical numbers.

Again, how is it possible to solve the questions which we have
already enumerated in our discussion of difficulties [9]? For the objects
1077ᵃ of astronomy will exist apart from sensible things just as the objects
of geometry will; but how is it possible that a heaven and its parts
—or anything else which has movement—should exist apart? Similarly also the objects of optics and of harmonics will exist apart; for
5 there will be both voice and sight besides the sensible or individual
voices and sights. Therefore it is plain that the other senses as well,
and the other objects of sense, will exist apart; for why should one
set of them do so and another not? And if this is so, there will also
be animals existing apart, since there will be senses.

Again, there are certain mathematical theorems that are universal,
10 extending beyond these substances. Here then we shall have another
intermediate substance separate both from the Ideas and from the
intermediates—a substance which is neither number nor points nor
spatial magnitude nor time. And if this is impossible, plainly it is also
impossible that the *former* entities should exist separate from sensible things.

<hr>

9 iii. 997ᵇ 12–34.

And, in general, conclusions contrary alike to the truth and to the usual views follow, if one is to suppose the objects of mathematics 15 to exist thus as separate entities. For because they exist thus they must be prior to sensible spatial magnitudes, but in truth they must be posterior; for the incomplete spatial magnitude is in the order of generation prior, but in the order of substance posterior, as the lifeless is to the living.

Again, by virtue of what, and when, will mathematical magnitudes 20 be one? For things in our perceptible world are one in virtue of soul, or of a part of soul, or of something else that is reasonable enough; when these are not present, the thing is a plurality, and splits up into parts. But in the case of the subjects of mathematics, which are divisible and are quantities, what is the cause of their being one and holding together?.

Again, the modes of generation of the objects of mathematics show that we are right. For the dimension first generated is length, then comes breadth, lastly depth, and the process is complete. If, then, 25 that which is posterior in the order of generation is prior in the order of substantiality, the solid will be prior to the plane and the line. And in *this* way also it is both more complete and more whole, because it can become animate. How, on the other hand, could a line or a plane be animate? The supposition passes the power of our senses. 30

Again, the solid is a sort of substance; for it already has in a sense completeness. But how can lines be substances? Neither as a form or shape, as the soul perhaps is, nor as matter, like the solid; for we have no experience of anything that can be put together out of lines or planes or points, while if these had been a sort of material sub- 35 stance, we should have observed things which could be put together out of them.

Grant, then, that they are prior in definition. Still not all things 1077ᵇ that are prior in definition are also prior in substantiality. For those things are prior in substantiality which when separated from other things surpass them in the power of independent existence, but things are prior in definition to those whose definitions are compounded out of their definitions; and these two properties are not co-extensive. For if attributes do not exist apart from their substances (e. g. a 'mobile' 5 or a 'pale'), pale is prior to the pale man in definition, but not in substantiality. For it cannot exist separately, but is always along with the concrete thing; and by the concrete thing I mean the pale man. Therefore it is plain that neither is the result of abstraction prior nor that which is produced by adding determinants posterior; for it is by adding a determinant to pale that we speak of the pale man. 10

3 It has, then, been sufficiently pointed out that the objects of mathematics are not substances in a higher degree than bodies are, and that they are not prior to sensibles in being, but only in definition, and that they cannot exist somewhere apart. But since it was not 15 possible for them to exist *in* sensibles either,[10] it is plain that they either do not exist at all or exist in a special sense and therefore do not 'exist' without qualification. For 'exist' has many senses. For just as the universal propositions of mathematics deal not with objects which exist separately, apart from extended magnitudes and from numbers, but with magnitudes and numbers, not however *qua* 20 such as to have magnitude or to be divisible,[11] clearly it is possible that there should also be both propositions and demonstrations about sensible magnitudes, not however *qua* sensible but *qua* possessed of certain definite qualities. For as there are many propositions about things merely considered as in motion, apart from what each such thing 25 is and from their accidents, and as it is not therefore necessary that there should be either a mobile separate from sensibles, or a distinct mobile entity in the sensibles, so too in the case of mobiles there will be propositions and sciences, which treat them however not *qua* mobile but only *qua* bodies, or again only *qua* planes, or only *qua* 30 lines, or *qua* divisibles, or *qua* indivisibles having position, or only *qua* indivisibles. Thus since it is true to say without qualification that not only things which are separable but also things which are inseparable exist (for instance, that mobiles exist), it is true also to say without qualification that the objects of mathematics exist, and with the character ascribed to them by mathematicians. And as it is true to say of the other sciences too, without qualification, that they 35 deal with such and such a subject—not with what is accidental to it (e. g. not with the pale, if the healthy thing is pale, and the science has the healthy as its subject), but with that which is the subject of 1078ᵃ each science—with the healthy if it treats its object *qua* healthy, with man if *qua* man:—so too is it with geometry; if its subjects happen to be sensible, though it does not treat them *qua* sensible, the mathematical sciences will not for that reason be sciences of sensibles 5 —nor, on the other hand, of other things separate from sensibles. Many properties attach to things in virtue of their own nature as possessed of each such character; e. g. there are attributes peculiar to the animal *qua* female or *qua* male (yet there is no 'female' nor 'male' separate from animals); so that there are also attributes which belong to things merely as lengths or as planes. And in proportion as we are dealing with things which are prior in definition and simpler, our

---

¹⁰ Cf. 1076ᵃ 38–ᵇ 11.   ¹¹ Cf. vi. 1026ᵃ 25, xiii. 1077ᵃ 9.

knowledge has more accuracy, i. e. simplicity. Therefore a science 10
which abstracts from spatial magnitude is more precise than one
which takes it into account; and a science is most precise if it
abstracts from movement, but if it takes account of movement, it is
most precise if it deals with the primary movement, for this is the
simplest; and of this again uniform movement is the simplest form.

The same account may be given of harmonics and optics; for
neither considers its objects *qua* sight or *qua* voice, but *qua* lines and 15
numbers; but the latter are attributes proper to the former. And
mechanics too proceeds in the same way. Therefore if we suppose
attributes separated from their fellow-attributes and make any inquiry concerning them as such, we shall not for this reason be in
error, any more than when one draws a line on the ground and calls
it a foot long when it is not; for the error is not included in the 20
premisses.

Each question will be best investigated in this way—by setting up
by an act of separation what is not separate, as the arithmetician
and the geometer do. For a man *qua* man·is one indivisible thing;
and the arithmetician supposed one indivisible thing, and then considered whether any attribute belongs to a man *qua* indivisible. But 25
the geometer treats him neither *qua* man nor *qua* indivisible, but as
a solid. For evidently the properties which would have belonged to
him even if perchance he had not been indivisible, can belong to him
even apart from these attributes.[12] Thus, then, geometers speak correctly; they talk about existing things, and their subjects do exist; 30
for being has two forms—it exists not only in complete reality but
also materially.

Now since the good and the beautiful are different (for the former
always implies conduct as its subject, while the beautiful is found
also in motionless things), those who assert that the mathematical
sciences say nothing of the beautiful or the good [13] are in error. For
these sciences say and prove a great deal about them; if they do 35
not expressly mention them, but prove attributes which are their
results or their definitions, it is not true to say that they tell us
nothing about them. The chief forms of beauty are order and 1078ᵇ
symmetry and definiteness, which the mathematical sciences demonstrate in a special degree. And since these (e. g. order and definiteness) are obviously causes of many things, evidently these sciences
must treat this sort of causative principle also (i. e. the beautiful)

[12] *sc.* indivisibility and humanity.
[13] The reference is apparently to Aristippus; Cf. iii. 996ᵃ 32.

5 as in some sense a cause. But we shall speak more plainly elsewhere [14] about these matters.

4 So much then for the objects of mathematics; we have said that
they exist and in what sense they exist,[15] and in what sense they are
prior and in what sense not prior.[16] Now, regarding the Ideas, we
10 must first examine the ideal theory itself, not connecting it in any
way with the nature of numbers, but treating it in the form in which
it was originally understood by those who first maintained the existence of the Ideas. The supporters of the ideal theory were led to it
because on the question about the truth of things they accepted the
15 Heraclitean sayings which describe all sensible things as ever passing
away, so that if knowledge or thought is to have an object, there
must be some other and permanent entities, apart from those which
are sensible; for there could be no knowledge of things which were
in a state of flux. But when Socrates was occupying himself with the
excellences of character, and in connexion with them became the first
to raise the problem of universal definition (for of the physicists
20 Democritus only touched on the subject to a small extent, and
defined, after a fashion, the hot and the cold; while the Pythagoreans
had before this treated of a few things, whose definitions—e. g. those
of opportunity, justice, or marriage—they connected with numbers;
but it was natural that Socrates should be seeking the essence, for he
was seeking to syllogize, and 'what a thing is' is the starting-point
25 of syllogisms; for there was as yet none of the dialectical power
which enables people even without knowledge of the essence to speculate about contraries and inquire whether the same science deals with
contraries; for two things may be fairly ascribed to Socrates—inductive arguments and universal definition, both of which are concerned
30 with the starting-point of science):—but Socrates did not make the
universals or the definitions exist apart; *they*, however, gave them
separate existence, and this was the kind of thing they called Ideas.
Therefore it followed for them, almost by the same argument, that
there must be Ideas of all things that are spoken of universally, and
it was almost as if a man wished to count certain things, and while
35 they were few thought he would not be able to count them, but made
more of them and then counted them; for the Forms are, one may
say, more numerous than the particular sensible things, yet it was in
1079ᵃ seeking the causes of these that they proceeded from them to the
Forms. For to each thing there answers an entity which has the same

[14] Apparently an unfulfilled promise.   [15] Chs. 2, 3.
[16] 1077ᵃ 17–20, 24–ᵇ 11.

name and exists apart from the substances, and so also in the case of all other groups there is a one over many, whether these be of this world or eternal.

Again, of the ways in which it is proved that the Forms exist, none is convincing; for from some no inference necessarily follows, and from some arise Forms even of things of which they think there are no Forms. For according to the arguments from the sciences there will be Forms of all things of which there are sciences, and according to the argument of the 'one over many' there will be Forms even of negations, and according to the argument that thought has an object when the individual object has perished, there will be Forms of perishable things; for we have an image of these. Again, of the most accurate arguments, some lead to Ideas of relations, of which they say there is no independent class, and others introduce the 'third man'.[17]

And in general the arguments for the Forms destroy things for whose existence the believers in Forms are more zealous than for the existence of the Ideas; for it follows that not the dyad but number is first, and that prior to number is the relative, and that this is prior to the absolute [18]—besides all the other points on which certain people, by following out the opinions held about the Forms, came into conflict with the principles of the theory.

Again, according to the assumption on which the belief in the Ideas rests, there will be Forms not only of substances but also of many other things; for the concept is single not only in the case of substances, but also in that of non-substances, and there are sciences of other things than substance; and a thousand other such difficulties confront them. But according to the necessities of the case and the opinions about the Forms, if they can be shared in there must be Ideas of substances only. For they are not shared in incidentally, but each Form must be shared in as something not predicated of a subject. (By 'being shared in incidentally' I mean that if a thing snares in 'double itself', it shares also in 'eternal', but incidentally; for 'the double' happens to be eternal.) Therefore the Forms will be substance. But the same names indicate substance in this and in the ideal world (or what will be the meaning of saying that there is something apart from the particulars—the one over many?). And if the Ideas and the things that share in them have the same form, there will be

---

[17] Cf. vii. 1039[a] 2, *Soph. El.* 178[b] 36–179[a] 10, and Plato, *Parmenides*, 132 AB, D–133 A.

[18] i. e. the relative in general is more general than, and therefore (on Platonic principles) prior to, number. Number is similarly prior to the dyad. Therefore the relative is prior to the dyad, which yet is held to be absolute.

something common: for why should '2' be one and the same in the
35 perishable 2's, or in the 2's which are many but eternal, and not
the same in the '2 itself' as in the individual 2? But if they have not
1079^b the same form, they will have only the name in common, and it is
as if one were to call both Callias and a piece of wood a 'man', without observing any community between them.[19]

But if we are to suppose that in other respects the common definitions apply to the Forms, e. g. that 'plane figure' and the other parts
5 of the definition apply to the circle-itself, but 'what really is' has to
be added, we must inquire whether this is not absolutely meaningless.
For to what is this to be added? To 'centre' or to 'plane' or to all
the parts of the definition? For all the elements in the essence are
Ideas, e. g. 'animal' and 'two-footed'.[20] Further, there must be some
10 Idea answering to 'plane' above, some nature which will be present in
all the Forms as their genus.

5 Above all one might discuss the question what in the world the
Forms contribute to sensible things, either to those that are eternal
or to those that come into being and cease to be; for they cause
15 neither movement nor any change in them. But again they help in no
wise either towards the knowledge of other things (for they are not
even the substance of these, else they would have been in them), or
towards their being, if they are not *in* the individuals which share in
them; though if they were, they might be thought to be causes, as
white causes whiteness in a white object by entering into its com-
20 position. But this argument, which was used first by Anaxagoras, and
later by Eudoxus in his discussion of difficulties and by certain
others, is very easily upset; for it is easy to collect many and insuperable objections to such a view.

But, further, all other things cannot come from the Forms in any
25 of the usual senses of 'from'. And to say that they are patterns and
the other things share in them is to use empty words and poetical
metaphors. For what is it that works, looking to the Ideas? And any
thing can both be and come into being without being copied from
something else, so that, whether Socrates exists or not, a man like
30 Socrates might come to be. And evidently this might be so even
if Socrates were eternal. And there will be several patterns of the
same thing, and therefore several Forms; e. g. 'animal' and 'two-
footed', and also 'man-himself', will be Forms of man. Again, the
Forms are patterns not only of sensible things, but of Forms them-

---

[19] With 1078^b 34–1079^b 3 Cf. i. 990^b 2–991^a 8.
[20] *sc.* in the essence of man.

selves also; i. e. the genus is the pattern of the various forms-of-a-genus; therefore the same thing will be pattern and copy.

Again, it would seem impossible that substance and that whose 35 substance it is should exist apart; how, therefore, could the Ideas, 1080ᵃ being the substances of things, exist apart?

In the *Phaedo* ²¹ the case is stated in this way—that the Forms are causes both of being and of becoming. Yet though the Forms exist, still things do not come into being, unless there is something to originate movement; and many other things come into being (e. g. a house or a ring) of which they say there are no Forms. Clearly 5 therefore even the things of which they say there are Ideas can both be and come into being owing to such causes as produce the things just mentioned,²² and not owing to the Forms. But regarding the Ideas it is possible, both in this way and by more abstract and 10 accurate arguments, to collect many objections like those we have considered.

6   Since we have discussed these points, it is well to consider again the results regarding numbers which confront those who say that numbers are separable substances and first causes of things. If number is an entity and its substance is nothing other than just number, 15 as some say, it follows that either (1) there is a first in it and a second, each being different in species—and either (a) this is true of the units without exception, and any unit is inassociable with any unit, or (b) they are all without exception successive, and any of 20 them are associable with any, as they say is the case with mathematical number; for in mathematical number no one unit is in any way different from another. Or (c) some units must be associable and some not; e. g. suppose that 2 is first after 1, and then comes 3 and then the rest of the number series, and the units in each number are 25 associable, e. g. those in the first 2 are associable with one another, and those in the first 3 with one another, and so with the other numbers; but the units in the '2-itself' are inassociable with those in the '3-itself'; and similarly in the case of the other successive numbers. 30 And so while mathematical number is counted thus—after 1, 2 (which consists of another 1 besides the former 1), and 3 (which consists of another 1 besides these two), and the other numbers similarly, ideal number is counted thus—after 1, a distinct 2 which does not include the first 1, and a 3 which does not include the 2, and the rest of the number series similarly. Or (2) one kind of number must be like the 35

²¹ 100 d.   ²² With 1079ᵇ 12–1080ᵃ 8 Cf. i. 991ᵃ 8–ᵇ 9.

first that was named,[23] one like that which the mathematicians speak of, and that which we have named last [24] must be a third kind.

Again, these kinds of numbers must either be separable from things, 1080[b] or not separable but in objects of perception (not however in the way which we first considered,[25] but in the sense that objects of perception consist of numbers which are present in them)—either one kind and not another, or all of them.

5 These are of necessity the only ways in which the numbers can exist. And of those who say that the 1 is the beginning and substance and element of all things, and that number is formed from the 1 and something else, almost every one has described number in one of these ways; only no one has said *all* the units are inassociable. And 10 this has happened reasonably enough; for there can be no way besides those mentioned. Some [26] say both kinds of number exist, that which has a before and after [27] being identical with the Ideas, and mathematical number being different from the Ideas and from sensible things, and both being separable from sensible things; and 15 others [28] say mathematical number alone exists, as the first of realities, separate from sensible things. And the Pythagoreans, also, believe in one kind of number—the mathematical; only they say it is not separate but sensible substances are formed out of it. For they construct the whole universe out of numbers—only not numbers con- 20 sisting of abstract units; they suppose the units to have spatial magnitude. But how the first 1 was constructed so as to have magnitude, they seem unable to say.

Another thinker [29] says the first kind of number, that of the Forms, alone exists, and some [30] say mathematical number is identical with this.

The case of lines, planes, and solids is similar. For some think that those which are the objects of mathematics are different from those 25 which come after the Ideas;[31] and of those who express themselves otherwise some speak of the objects of mathematics and in a mathematical way—viz. those who do not make the Ideas numbers nor say that Ideas exist;[32] and others speak of the objects of mathematics, but not mathematically; for they say that neither is every spatial magnitude divisible into magnitudes, nor do any two units taken at 30 random make 2.[33] All who say the 1 is an element and principle of

[23] ll. 15–20.
[25] Cf. 1076[a] 38–[b] 11.
[27] i. e. in which the numbers differ in kind.
[29] Some unknown Platonist.
[31] This refers to Plato; Cf. i. 992[b] 13–18.
[33] Xenocrates is meant.

[24] ll. 23–35.
[26] Plato is meant.
[28] Speusippus is meant.
[30] Xenocrates is meant.
[32] Speusippus is meant.

things suppose numbers to consist of abstract units, except the Pythagoreans; but *they* suppose the numbers to have magnitude, as has
been said before.[34] It is clear from this statement, then, in how many
ways numbers may be described, and that all the ways have been
mentioned; and all these views are impossible, but some perhaps more 35
than others.

7   First, then, let us inquire if the units are associable or inassociable,
and if inassociable, in which of the two ways we distinguished.[35] For 1081ᵃ
it is possible that any unit is inassociable with any, and it is possible
that those in the '2-itself' are inassociable with those in the '3-itself',
and, generally, that those in each ideal number are inassociable with
those in other ideal numbers. Now (1) if all units are associable and 5
without difference, we get mathematical number—only one kind of
number, and the Ideas cannot be the numbers. For what sort of number will man-himself or animal-itself or any other Form be? There
is one Idea of each thing, e. g. one of man-himself and another one 10
of animal-itself; but the similar and undifferentiated numbers are
infinitely many, so that any particular 3 is no more man-himself than
any other 3. But if the Ideas are not numbers, neither can they exist
at all. For from what principles will the Ideas come? It is number
that comes from the 1 and the indefinite dyad, and the principles or 15
elements are said to be principles and elements of number, and the
Ideas cannot be ranked as either prior or posterior to the numbers.

   But (2) if the units are inassociable, and inassociable in the sense
that any is inassociable with any other, number of this sort cannot
be mathematical number; for mathematical number consists of undifferentiated units, and the truths proved of it suit this character. 20
Nor can it be ideal number. For 2 will not proceed immediately from
1 and the indefinite dyad, and be followed by the successive numbers,
as they say '2, 3, 4'—for the units in the ideal 2 are generated at the
same time, whether, as the first holder of the theory [36] said, from
unequals (coming into being when these were equalized) or in some
other way—since, if one unit is to be prior to the other, it will be 25
prior also to the 2 composed of these; for when there is one thing
prior and another posterior, the resultant of these will be prior to one
and posterior to the other.[37]

---

[34] l. 19.   [35] Cf. 1080ᵃ 18–20, 23–35.   [36] Plato.

[37] The theory of ideal number holds that 2 comes next after the original 1,
which with the 'indefinite 2' is the source of number. But if all units are different
in species, one of the units in 2 is prior to the other and ∴ to 2, and comes next
after the original 1. Similarly between 2 and 3 there will be the first unit in 3, and
so on.

30   Again, since the 1-itself is first, and then there is a particular 1 which is first among the others and next after the 1-itself, and again a third which is next after the second and next but one after the first 1—so the units must be prior to the numbers after which they are named when we count them; e. g. there will be a third unit in 2 before 3 exists, and a fourth and a fifth in 3 before the numbers 4 and 5

35 exist.—Now none of these thinkers has said the units are inassociable in this way, but according to their principles it is reasonable that they

1081ᵇ should be so even in this way, though in truth it is impossible. For it is reasonable both that the units should have priority and posteriority if there is a first unit or first 1, and also that the 2's should if there is a first 2; for after the first it is reasonable and necessary that there

5 should be a second, and if a second, a third, and so with the others successively. (And to say both things at the same time, that a *unit* is first and another unit is second after the ideal 1, and that a 2 is first after it, is impossible.) But they make a first unit or 1, but not also a second and a third, and a first 2, but not also a second and a third.

10   Clearly, also, it is not possible, if all the units are inassociable, that there should be a 2-itself and a 3-itself; and so with the other numbers. For whether the units are undifferentiated or different each from each, number must be counted by addition, e. g. 2 by adding

15 another 1 to the one, 3 by adding another 1 to the two, and 4 similarly. This being so, numbers cannot be generated as they generate them, from the 2 and the 1; for 2 becomes part of 3, and 3 of 4, and

20 the same happens in the case of the succeeding numbers, but *they* say 4 came from the first 2 and the indefinite 2—which makes it two 2's *other* than the 2-itself; if not, the 2-itself will be a part of 4 and one other 2 will be added. And similarly 2 will consist of the 1-itself

25 and another 1; but if this is so, the other element cannot be an indefinite 2; for it generates one unit, not, as the indefinite 2 does, a definite 2.

Again, besides the 3-itself and the 2-itself how can there be other 3's and 2's? And how do they consist of prior and posterior units?

30 All this is absurd and fictitious, and there cannot be a first 2 and then a 3-itself. Yet there must, if the 1 and the indefinite dyad are to be the elements. But if the results are impossible, it is also impossible that these are the generating principles.

If the units, then, are differentiated, each from each, these results

35 and others similar to these follow of necessity. But (3) if those in different numbers are differentiated, but those in the same number are alone undifferentiated from one another, even so the difficulties that

follow are no less. E. g. in the 10-itself there are ten units, and the 1082ª
10 is composed both of them and of two 5's. But since the 10-itself
is not any chance number nor composed of any chance 5's—or, for
that matter, units—the units in this 10 must differ. For if they do
not differ, neither will the 5's of which the 10 consists differ; but 5
since these differ, the units also will differ. But if they differ, will
there be no other 5's in the 10 but only these two, or will there be
others? If there are not, this is paradoxical; and if there are, what
sort of 10 will consist of them? For there is no other 10 in *the* 10 but 10
itself. But it is actually *necessary* on their view that the 4 should
not consist of any chance 2's; for the indefinite 2, as they say,
received the definite 2 and made two 2's; for its nature was to double
what it received.

Again, as to the 2 being an entity apart from its two units, and the 15
3 an entity apart from its three units, how is this possible? Either
by one's sharing in the other, as 'pale man' is different from 'pale'
and 'man' (for it shares in these), or when one is a differentia of
the other, as 'man' is different from 'animal' and 'two-footed'.

Again, some things are one by contact, some by intermixture, 20
some by position; none of which can belong to the units of which
the 2 or the 3 consists; but as two men are not a unity apart from
both, so must it be with the units. And their being indivisible will
make no difference to them; for points too are indivisible, but yet a 25
pair of them is nothing apart from the two.

But this consequence also we must not forget, that it follows that
there are prior and posterior 2's, and similarly with the other numbers. For let the 2's in the 4 be simultaneous; yet these are prior to 30
those in the 8, and as the 2 generated them, they generated the 4's
in the 8-itself. Therefore if the first 2 is an Idea, these 2's also will
be Ideas of some kind. And the same account applies to the units;
for the units in the first 2 generate the four in 4, so that all the units 35
come to be Ideas and an Idea will be composed of Ideas. Clearly
therefore those things also of which these happen to be the Ideas will
be composite, e. g. one might say that animals are composed of
animals, if there are Ideas of them.

In general, to differentiate the units in any way is an absurdity and 1082ᵇ
a fiction; and by a fiction I mean a forced statement made to suit a
hypotɥesis. For neither in quantity nor in quality do we see unit 5
differing from unit, and number must be either equal or unequal—all
number but especially that which consists of abstract units—so that
if one number is neither greater nor less than another, it is equal to it;

but things that are equal and in no wise differentiated we take to be
the same when we are speaking of numbers. If not, not even the 2's
10 in the 10-itself will be undifferentiated, though they are equal; for
what reason will the man who alleges that they are not differentiated
be able to give?

Again, if every unit + another unit makes two, a unit from the
2-itself and one from the 3-itself will make a 2. Nów (*a*) this will
consist of differentiated units; and (*b*) will it be prior to the 3 or
15 posterior? It rather seems that it must be prior; for one of the units
is simultaneous with the 3, and the other is simultaneous with the 2.
And we, for our part, suppose that in general 1 and 1, whether the
things are equal or unequal, is 2, e. g. the good and the bad, or a man
and a horse; but those who hold these views say that not even two
units are 2.

20   If the number of the 3-itself is not greater than that of the 2, this
is surprising; and if it *is* greater, clearly there is also a number in it
equal to the 2, so that *this* is not different from the 2-itself. But this
is not possible, if there is a first and a second number.[38]

Nor will the Ideas be numbers. For in this particular point they
are right who claim that the units must be different, if there are to be
25 Ideas; as has been said before.[39] For the Form is unique; but if the
units are not different, the 2's and the 3's also will not be different.
This is also the reason why they must say that when we count thus—
'1, 2'—we do not proceed by adding to the given number; for if we
30 do, neither will the numbers be generated from the indefinite dyad,
nor can a number be an Idea; for then one Idea will be in another,
and all the Forms will be parts of one Form. And so with a view to
their hypothesis their statements are right, but as a whole they are
wrong; for their view is very destructive, since they will admit that
35 *this* question itself affords some difficulty—whether, when we count
and say '1, 2, 3,' we count by addition or by separate portions. But
we do both; and so it is absurd to reason back from this problem to
so great a difference of essence.

1083ᵃ 8   First of all it is well to determine what is the differentia of a number—and of a unit, if it has a differentia. Units must differ either in
quantity or in quality; and neither of these seems to be possible.
But number *qua* number differs in quantity. And if the units also did
5 differ in quantity, number would differ from number, though equal

---

[38] i. e. if there is a difference of kind between the numbers.
[39] 1081ᵃ 5-17.

in number of units. Again, are the first units greater or smaller, and do the later ones increase or diminish? All these are irrational suppositions. But neither can they differ in *quality*. For no attribute can attach to them; for even to numbers quality is said to belong *after* 10 quantity. Again, quality could not come to them either from the 1 or from the dyad; for the former has no quality, and the latter gives *quantity*; for this entity is what makes things to be many. If the facts are really otherwise, they should state this quite at the beginning and 15 determine if possible, regarding the differentia of the unit, why it must exist, and, failing this, what differentia they mean.

Evidently then, if the Ideas are numbers, the units cannot all be associable, nor can they be inassociable in either of the two ways.[40] But neither is the way in which some others speak about numbers 20 correct. These are those who do not think there are Ideas, either without qualification or as identified with certain numbers, but think the objects of mathematics exist and the numbers are the first of existing things, and the 1-itself is the starting-point of them. It is paradoxical that there should be a 1 which is first of 1's, as *they* say, 25 but not a 2 which is first of 2's, nor a 3 of 3's; for the same reasoning applies to all. If, then, the facts with regard to number are so, and one supposes mathematical number alone to exist, the 1 is not the starting-point (for this sort of 1 must differ from the other units; 30 and if this is so, there must also be a 2 which is first of 2's, and similarly with the other successive numbers). But if the 1 is the starting-point, the truth about the numbers must rather be what Plato used to say, and there must be a first 2 and 3, and the numbers must not be associable with one another. But if on the other hand one supposes this, many impossible results, as we have said,[41] follow. 35 But either this or the other *must* be the case, so that if neither is, number cannot exist separately.

It is evident, also, from this that the third version [42] is the worst— 1083ᵇ the view ideal and mathematical number is the same. For two mistakes must then meet in the one opinion. (1) Mathematical number cannot be of this sort, but the holder of this view has to spin it 5 out by making suppositions peculiar to himself. And (2) he must also admit all the consequences that confront those who speak of number in the sense of 'Forms'.

The Pythagorean version in one way affords fewer difficulties than those before named, but in another way has others peculiar to itself.

---

[40] Cf. 1080ᵃ 18–20, 23–35.   [41] Cf. 1080ᵇ 37–1083ᵃ 17.
[42] That of Xenocrates; Cf. 1080ᵇ 22.

10 For not thinking of number as capable of existing separately removes many of the impossible consequences; but that bodies should be composed of numbers, and that this should be mathematical number, is impossible. For it is not true to speak of indivisible spatial magnitudes; and however much there might be magnitudes of this sort, 15 units at least have not magnitude; and how can a magnitude be composed of indivisibles? But arithmetical number, at least, consists of units, while these thinkers identify number with real things; at any rate they apply their propositions to bodies as if they consisted of those numbers.

If, then, it is necessary, if number is a self-subsistent real thing, 20 that it should exist in one of these ways which have been mentioned,[43] and if it cannot exist in any of these, evidently number has no such nature as those who make it separable set up for it.

Again, does each unit come from the great and the small, equalized, or one from the small, another from the great? (*a*) If the latter, 25 neither does each thing contain all the elements, nor are the units without difference; for in one there is the great and in another the small, which is contrary in its nature to the great. Again, how is it with the units in the 3-itself? One of them is an odd unit. But perhaps it is for this reason that they give 1-itself the middle place in odd 30 numbers. (*b*) But if each of the two units consists of both the great and the small, equalized, how will the 2, which is a single thing, consist of the great and the small? Or how will it differ from the unit? Again, the unit is prior to the 2; for when it is destroyed the 2 is destroyed. It must, then, be the Idea of an Idea since it is prior to 35 an Idea, and it must have come into being before it. From what, then? Not from the indefinite dyad, for *its* function was to double.

Again, number must be either infinite or finite; for these thinkers think of number as capable of existing separately, so that it is not 1084ª possible that neither of those alternatives should be true. Clearly it cannot be *infinite*; for infinite number is neither odd nor even, but the generation of numbers is always the generation either of an odd or of an even number; in one way, when 1 operates on an even num- 5 ber, an odd number is produced; in another way, when 2 operates, the numbers got from 1 by doubling are produced; in another way, when the odd numbers operate, the other even numbers are produced. Again, if every Idea is an Idea of something, and the numbers are Ideas, infinite number itself will be an Idea of something, either of some sensible thing or of something else. Yet this is not possible in

[43] 1080ª 15–ᵇ 36.

view of their thesis any more than it is reasonable in itself, at least if they arrange the Ideas as they do.

But if number is *finite*, how far does it go? With regard to this 10 not only the fact but the reason should be stated. But if number goes only up to 10, as some say,[44] firstly the Forms will soon run short; e. g. if 3 is man-himself, what number will be the horse-itself? The series of the numbers which are the several things-themselves goes 15 up to 10. It must, then, be one of the numbers within these limits; for it is these that are substances and Ideas. Yet they will run short; for the various forms of animal will outnumber them. At the same time it is clear that if in this way *the* 3 is man-himself, the other 3's are so also (for those in identical numbers are similar), so that there 20 will be an infinite number of men; if each 3 is an Idea, each of the numbers will be man-himself, and if not, they will at least be men. And if the smaller number is part of the greater (being number of such a sort that the units in the same number are associable), then if the 4-itself is an Idea of something, e. g. of 'horse' or of 'white', man will be a part of horse, if man is 2. It is paradoxical also that 25 there should be an Idea of 10, but not of 11, nor of the succeeding numbers. Again, there both are and come to be certain things of which there are no Forms; why, then, are there not Forms of them also? We infer that the Forms are not causes. Again, it is paradoxical if the number-series up to 10 is more of a real thing and a Form than 10 30 itself. There is no generation of the former as one thing, and there is of the latter. But they try to work on the assumption that the series of numbers up to 10 is a complete series. At least they generate the derivatives—e. g. the void, proportion, the odd, and the others of this kind—within the decade. For some things, e. g. movement and rest, good and bad, they assign to the originative principles, and the others 35 to the numbers. This is why they identify the odd with 1; for if the odd implied 3, how would 5 be odd?[45] Again, spatial magnitudes and all such things are explained without going beyond a definite number; e. g. the first, the indivisible, line,[46] then the 2, &c.; these entities 1084ᵇ also extend only up to 10.[47]

Again, if number can exist separately, one might ask which is

---

[44] This includes Plato (Cf. *Phys.* 206ᵇ 32) and probably Speusippus.

[45] i. e. to account for the oddness of odd numbers they identify the odd with the 1, which is a principle present in all numbers, not with the 3, which on their theory is not present in other numbers.　　　　　　　　　　[46] Cf. i. 992ᵃ 22.

[47] Cf. xiv. 1090ᵇ 21–24. 1 answers to the point (the 'indivisible line'), 2 to the line, 3 to the plane, 4 to the solid, and 1 + 2 + 3 + 4 = 10.

prior—1, or 3 or 2? Inasmuch as the number is composite, 1 is prior,
but inasmuch as the universal and the form is prior, the number is
5 prior; for each of the units is part of the number as its matter, and
the number acts as form. And in a sense the right angle is prior to
the acute, because it is determinate and in virtue of its definition;
but in a sense the acute is prior, because it is a part and the right angle
is divided into acute angles. As matter, then, the acute angle and the
10 element and the unit are prior, but in respect of the form and of the
substance as expressed in the definition, the right angle, and the whole
consisting of the matter and the form, are prior; for the concrete thing
is nearer to the form and to what is expressed in the definition, though
in generation it is later. How then is 1 the starting-point? Because
it is not divisible, they say; but both the universal, and the particular
15 or the element, are indivisible. But they are starting-points in different ways, one in definition and the other in time. In which way,
then, is 1 the starting-point? As has been said, the right angle is
thought to be prior to the acute, and the acute to the right, and each
is one. Accordingly they make 1 the starting-point in both ways.
But this is impossible. For the universal is one as form or substance,
20 while the element is one as a part or as matter. For each of the two is
in a sense one—in *truth* each of the two units exists potentially (at
least if the number is a unity and not like a heap, i. e. if different
numbers consist of differentiated units, as they say), but not in complete reality; and the cause of the *error* they fell into is that they were
conducting their inquiry at the same time from the standpoint of
25 mathematics and from that of universal definitions, so that (1) from
the former standpoint they treated unity, their first principle, as a
point; for the unit is a point without position. They put things together out of the smallest parts, as some others [48] also have done.
Therefore the unit becomes the matter of numbers and at the same
30 time prior to 2; and again posterior, 2 being treated as a whole, a
unity, and a form. But (2) because they were seeking the universal
they treated the unity which can be predicated of a number, as in
this sense also [49] a part of the number. But these characteristics
cannot belong at the same time to the same thing.

If the 1-itself must be unitary (for it differs in nothing from other
1's except that it is the starting-point), and the 2 is divisible but
the unit is not, the unit must be liker the 1-itself than the 2 is.

---

[48] *sc.* the Atomists.
[49] i. e. they treated the unity which is predicable of a number, as well as the
unit in a number, as a part of the number.

But if the unit is liker it, *it* must be liker to the unit than to the 2; 35 therefore each of the units in 2 must be prior to the 2. But they deny this; at least they generate the 2 first. Again, if the 2-itself is a 1085ᵃ unity and the 3-itself is one also, both form a 2. From what, then, is this 2 produced?

9　Since there is not contact in numbers, but succession, viz. between the units between which there is nothing, e. g. between those 5 in 2 or in 3, one might ask whether these succeed the 1-itself or not, and whether, of the terms that succeed it, 2 or either of the units in 2 is prior.

Similar difficulties occur with regard to the classes of things posterior to number—the line, the plane, and the solid. For some [50] construct these out of the species of the 'great and small'; e. g. lines 10 from the 'long and short', planes from the 'broad and narrow', masses from the 'deep and shallow'; which are species of the 'great and small'. And the originative principle of such things which answers to the 1 [51] different thinkers describe in different ways. And in these also the impossibilities, the fictions, and the contradictions of all 15 probability are seen to be innumerable. For (i) the geometrical classes are severed from one another, unless the principles of these are implied in one another in such a way that the 'broad and narrow' is also 'long and short' (but if this is so, the plane will be a line and the solid a plane; [52] again, how will angles and figures and such things be explained?). And (ii) the same happens as in regard to number; 20 for 'long and short', &c., are attributes of magnitude, but magnitude does not *consist* of these, any more than the line consists of 'straight and curved', or solids of 'smooth and rough'.[53]

(All these views share a difficulty which occurs with regard to species-of-a-genus, when one posits the universals, viz. whether it is animal-itself or something other than animal-itself that is in the 25 particular animal. True, if the universal is not separable from sensible things, this will present no difficulty; but if the 1 and the numbers *are* separable, as those who express these views say, it is not easy to solve the difficulty, if one may apply the words 'not easy' to the impossible. For when we apprehend the unity in 2, or in general in a number, do we apprehend a thing-itself or something else?) 30

---

[50] This probably includes Plato himself.

[51] i. e. that which is to the geometrical forms as the primary 1 is (according to the Platonic theory) to numbers.

[52] With 1085ᵃ 7–19 Cf. i. 992ᵃ 10–19:

[53] Cf. i. 992ᵇ 1–7, xiv. 1088ᵃ 15–21.

Some, then, generate spatial magnitudes from matter of this sort, others [54] from the point—and the point is thought by them to be not 1 but something like 1—and from other matter like plurality, but not 35 identical with it; about which principles none the less the same difficulties occur. For if the matter is one, line and plane and solid will be the same; for from the same elements will come one and the same 1085[b] thing. But if the matters are more than one, and there is one for the line and a second for the plane and another for the solid, they either are implied in one another or not, so that the same results will follow even so; for either the plane will not contain a line or it will *be* a line.

Again, how number can consist of the one and plurality, they make 5 no attempt to explain; but however they express themselves, the same objections arise as confront those who construct number out of the one and the indefinite dyad.[55] For the one view generates number from the universally predicated plurality, and not from a particular plurality; and the other generates it from a particular plurality, but the first; for 2 is said to be a 'first plurality'. Therefore there is 10 practically no difference, but the same difficulties will follow—is it intermixture or position or blending or generation? and so on. Above all one might press the question 'if each unit is one, what does it come from?' Certainly each is not the one-itself. It must, then, come from the one-itself and plurality, or a part of plurality. To say that the 15 unit is a plurality is impossible, for it is indivisible; and to generate it from a part of plurality involves many other objections; for (*a*) each of the parts must be indivisible (or it will be a plurality and the unit will be divisible) and the elements will not be the one and 20 *plurality*; for the single units do not come from plurality and the one. Again, (*b*) the holder of this view does nothing but presuppose another number; for his plurality of indivisibles is a number. Again, we must inquire, in view of this theory also,[56] whether the number is infinite or finite. For there was at first, as it seems, a plurality that 25 was itself finite, from which and from the one comes the finite number of units. And there is another plurality that is plurality-itself and infinite plurality; which sort of plurality, then, is the element which co-operates with the one? One might inquire similarly about the point, i. e. the element out of which they make spatial magnitudes. For surely this is not the one and only point; at any rate, then, let them say out of what each of the other points is formed. Certainly

[54] Speusippus is probably meant.   [55] i. e. probably Plato and Xenocrates.
[56] Cf. 1083[b] 36.

not of some *distance* + the point-itself. Nor again can there be in- 30
divisible parts of a distance, as the elements out of which the units are
said to be made are indivisible parts of plurality; for number consists
of indivisibles, but spatial magnitudes do not.⁵⁷

All these objections, then, and others of the sort make it evident
that number and spatial magnitudes cannot exist apart from things. 35
Again, the discord about numbers between the various versions is a
sign that it is the incorrectness of the alleged facts themselves that 1086ᵃ
brings confusion into the theories. For those who make the objects
of mathematics alone exist apart from sensible things,⁵⁸ seeing the
difficulty about the Forms and their fictitiousness, abandoned ideal
number and posited mathematical. But those who wished to make the 5
Forms at the same time also numbers, but did not see, if one assumed these principles, how mathematical number was to exist apart
from ideal,⁵⁹ made ideal and mathematical number the same—in
words, since in *fact* mathematical number has been destroyed; for 10
they state hypotheses peculiar to themselves and not those of mathematics. And he who first supposed that the Forms exist and that the
Forms are numbers and that the objects of mathematics exist,⁶⁰
naturally separated the two. Therefore it turns out that all of them
are right in some respect, but on the whole not right. And they themselves confirm this, for their statements do not agree but conflict. 15
The cause is that their hypotheses and their principles are false. And
it is hard to make a good case out of bad materials, according to
Epicharmus: 'as soon as 'tis said, 'tis seen to be wrong.'

But regarding numbers the questions we have raised and the conclusions we have reached are sufficient (for while he who is already
convinced might be further convinced by a longer discussion, one
not yet convinced would not come any nearer to conviction); re- 20
garding the first principles and the first causes and elements, the views
expressed by those who discuss only sensible substance have been
partly stated in our works on nature,⁶¹ and partly do not belong to
the present inquiry; but the views of those who assert that there are
other substances besides the sensible must be considered next after 25
those we have been mentioning. Since, then, some say that the Ideas
and the numbers are such substances, and that the elements of these

⁵⁷ The point cannot have for an element of it (*a*) a distance, for this would
destroy the simplicity of the point; or (*b*) part of a distance, for any part of a
distance must be a distance.   ⁵⁸ Speusippus is meant.
⁵⁹ Xenocrates is meant.   ⁶⁰ Plato.
⁶¹ *Phys.* i. 4–6; *De Caelo*, iii. 3–4; *De Gen. et Corr.* i. 1.

are elements and principles of real things, we must inquire regarding these what they say and in what sense they say it.

30 Those who posit numbers only, and these mathematical, must be considered later; [62] but as regards those who believe in the Ideas one might survey at the same time their way of thinking and the difficulty into which they fall. For they at the same time make the Ideas universal and again treat them as separable and as individuals. That 35 this is not possible has been argued before.[63] The reason why those who described their substances as universal combined these two characteristics in one thing, is that they did not make substances identical with sensible things. They thought that the particulars in 1086[b] the sensible world were in a state of flux and none of them remained, but that the universal was apart from these and something different. And Socrates gave the impulse to this theory, as we said in our earlier discussion,[64] by reason of his definitions, but he did not *separate* universals from individuals; and in this he thought rightly, in not 5 separating them. This is plain from the results; for without the universal it is not possible to get knowledge, but the separation is the cause of the objections that arise with regard to the Ideas. His successors, however, treating it as necessary, if there are to be any substances besides the sensible and transient substances, that they must be separable, had no others, but gave separate existence to these 10 universally predicated substances, so that it followed that universals and individuals were almost the same sort of thing. This in itself, then, would be one difficulty in the view we have mentioned.

10 Let us now mention a point which presents a certain difficulty both to those who believe in the Ideas and to those who do not, and 15 which was stated before, at the beginning, among the problems.[65] If we do not suppose substances to be separate, and in the way in which individual things are said to be separate, we shall destroy substance in the sense in which we understand 'substance'; but if we conceive substances to be separable, how are we to conceive their elements and their principles?

20 If they are individual and not universal, (a) real things will be just of the same number as the elements, and (b) the elements will not be knowable. For (a) let the syllables in speech be substances, and their elements elements of substances; then there must be only 25 one *ba* and one of each of the syllables, since they are not universal and the same in form but each is one in number and a 'this' and not

---

[62] Speusippus is meant; Cf. N. 1090 [a] 7–15, 20–[b] 20.   [63] iii. 1003[a] 7–17.
[64] 1078[b] 17–30.   [65] iii. 999[b] 24–1000[a] 4, 1003[a] 5–17.

a kind possessed of a common name (and again they suppose that the 'just what a thing is' [66] is in each case one). And if the syllables are unique, so too are the parts of which they consist; there will not, then, be more a's than one, nor more than one of any of the other elements, on the same principle on which an identical syllable can- 30 not exist in the plural number. But if this is so, there will not be other things existing besides the elements, but only the elements. (b) Again, the elements will not be even knowable; for they are not universal, and knowledge is of universals. This is clear from demonstrations and from definitions; for we do not conclude that this triangle has its angles equal to two right angles, unless every triangle has its angles 35 equal to two right angles, nor that this man is an animal, unless every man is an animal.

But if the principles *are* universal, either the substances composed of them are also universal, or non-substance will be prior to 1087ª substance; for the universal is not a substance, but the element or principle is universal, and the element or principle is prior to the things of which it is the principle or element.

All these difficulties follow naturally, when they make the Ideas 5 out of elements and at the same time claim that apart from the substances which have the same form there are Ideas, a single separate entity. But if, e. g., in the case of the elements of speech, the a's and the b's may quite well be many and there need be no a-itself and b-itself besides the many, there may be, so far as this goes, an infinite number of similar syllables. The statement that all knowledge is uni- 10 versal, so that the principles of things must also be universal and not separate substances, presents indeed, of all the points we have mentioned, the greatest difficulty, but yet the statement is in a sense true, although in a sense it is not. For knowledge, like the verb 'to 15 know', means two things, of which one is potential and one actual. The potency, being, as matter, universal and indefinite, deals with the universal and indefinite; but the actuality, being definite, deals with a definite object—being a 'this', it deals with a 'this'. But *per accidens* sight sees universal colour, because this individual colour which it sees is colour; and this individual a which the grammarian investigates is 20 an a. For if the principles must be universal, what is derived from them must also be universal, as in demonstrations [67]; and if this is so, there will be nothing capable of separate existence—i. e. no substance. But evidently in a sense knowledge is universal, and in a sense it is not. 25

[66] i. e. the Idea; Cf, 1079ᵇ 6.
[67] *sc.* universal premisses do not give singular conclusions.

BOOK N (XIV)

1   Regarding this kind of substance, what we have said must be taken as sufficient. All philosophers make the first principles con-
30 traries: as in natural things, so also in the case of unchangeable substances. But since there cannot be anything prior to the first principle of all things, the principle cannot be the principle and yet be an attribute of something else. To suggest this is like saying that the white is a first principle, not *qua* anything else but *qua* white, but yet that it is predicable of a subject, i. e. that its being white presup-
35 poses its being something else; this is absurd, for then that subject will be prior. But all things which are generated from their contraries involve an underlying subject; a subject, then, must be pres-
1087ᵇ ent in the case of contraries, if anywhere. All contraries, then, are always predicable of a subject, and none can exist apart, but just as appearances suggest that there is nothing contrary to substance, argument confirms this. No contrary, then, is the first principle of all things in the full sense; the first principle is something different.

But these thinkers make one of the contraries matter, some [1]
5 making the unequal—which they take to be the essence of plurality —matter for the One, and others [2] making plurality matter for the One. (The former generate numbers out of the dyad of the unequal, i. e. of the great and small, and the other thinker we have referred to generates them out of plurality, while according to both it is generated *by* the essence of the One.) For even the philosopher who says the unequal and the One are the elements, and the unequal is
10 a dyad composed of the great and small, treats the unequal, or the great and the small, as being one, and does not draw the distinction that they are one in definition, but not in number. But they do not describe rightly even the principles which they call elements, for some [3] name the great and the small with the One and treat these
15 three as elements of numbers, two being matter, one the form; while others [4] name the many and few, because the great and the small are more appropriate in their nature to magnitude than to number; and others [5] name rather the universal character common to these—'that which exceeds and that which is exceeded'. None of these varieties of opinion makes any difference to speak of, in view of some of the
20 consequences; they affect only the abstract objections, which these

---

[1] Plato is meant.   [2] Speusippus is probably referred to.
[3] This includes Plato.   [4] Unidentifiable Platonists.
[5] Perhaps Pythagoreans.

thinkers take care to avoid because the demonstrations they themselves offer are abstract—with this exception, that if the exceeding
and the exceeded are the principles, and not the great and the small,
consistency requires that number should come from the elements
before 2 does; for number is more universal than 2, as the exceeding
and the exceeded are more universal than the great and the small. But 25
as it is, they say one of these things but do not say the other. Others
oppose the different and the other to the One,[6] and others oppose
plurality to the One.[7] But if, as they claim, things consist of contraries, and to the One either there is nothing contrary, or if there
is to be anything it is plurality, and the unequal is contrary to the
equal, and the different to the same, and the other to the thing itself, 30
those who oppose the One to plurality have most claim to plausibility,
but even their view is inadequate, for the One would on their view
be a few; for plurality is opposed to fewness, and the many to the few.

'The one' evidently means a measure. And in every case there is
some underlying thing with a distinct nature of its own, e. g. in the 35
scale a quarter-tone, in spatial magnitude a finger or a foot or something of the sort, in rhythms a beat or a syllable; and similarly in
gravity it is a definite weight; and in the same way in all cases, in 1088[a]
qualities a quality, in quantities a quantity (and the measure is
indivisible, in the former case in kind, and in the latter to the sense);
which implies that the one is not in itself the substance of anything.
And this is reasonable; for 'the one' means the measure of some plurality, and 'number' means a measured plurality and a plurality of 5
measures. (Thus it is natural that one is not a number; for the
measure is not measures, but both the measure and the one are starting-points.) The measure must always be some identical thing predicable of all the things it measures, e. g. if the things are horses, the
measure is 'horse', and if they are men, 'man'. If they are a man, a
horse, and a god, the measure is perhaps 'living being', and the num- 10
ber of them will be a number of living beings. If the things are 'man'
and 'pale' and 'walking', these will scarcely have a number, because
all belong to a subject which is one and the same in number, yet the
number of these will be a number of 'kinds' or of some such term.

Those who treat the unequal as one thing, and the dyad as an in- 15
definite compound of great and small, say what is very far from being
probable or possible. For (a) these are modifications and accidents,
rather than substrata, of numbers and magnitudes—the many and

---

[6] Probably certain Pythagoreans are referred to.
[7] Probably Speusippus is meant.

few of number, and the great and small of magnitude—like even
20 and odd, smooth and rough, straight and curved. Again, (*b*) apart
from this mistake, the great and the small, and so on, must be relative to something; but what is relative is least of all things a kind of
entity or substance, and is posterior to quality and quantity; and the
25 relative is an accident of quantity, as was said, not its matter, since
something with a distinct nature of its own must serve as matter both
to the relative in general and to its parts and kinds. For there is nothing either great or small, many or few, or, in general, relative to something else, which without having a nature of its own is many or few,
great or small, or relative to something else. A sign that the relative is
30 least of all a substance and a real thing is the fact that it alone has
no proper generation or destruction or movement, as in respect of
quantity there is increase and diminution, in respect of quality
alteration, in respect of place locomotion, in respect of substance
simple generation and destruction. In respect of relation there is
no proper change; for, without changing, a thing will be now
greater and now less or equal, if that with which it is com-
35 pared has changed in quantity. And (*c*) the matter of each
1088ᵇ thing, and therefore of substance, must be that which is potentially
of the nature in question; but the relative is neither potentially nor
actually substance. It is strange, then, or rather impossible, to make
not-substance an element in, and prior to, substance; for all the categories are posterior to substance. Again, (*d*) elements are not predi-
5 cated of the things of which they are elements, but many and few are
predicated both apart and together of number, and long and short
of the line, and both broad and narrow apply to the plane. If there
is a plurality, then, of which the one term, viz. few, is always predicated, e. g. 2 (which cannot be many, for if it were many, 1 would
10 be few), there must be also one which is absolutely many, e. g. 10 is
many (if there is no number which is greater than 10), or 10,000.
How then, in view of this, can number consist of few and many?
Either both ought to be predicated of it, or neither; but in fact only
the one *or* the other is predicated.

2   We must inquire generally, whether eternal things can consist
15 of elements. If they do, they will have matter; for everything that
consists of elements is composite. Since, then, even if a thing exists
for ever, out of that of which it consists it would necessarily also, if
it *had* come into being, have come into being, and since everything
comes to be what it comes to be out of that which is it potentially
(for it could not have come to be out of that which had not this

capacity, nor could it consist of such elements), and since the potential can be either actual or not—this being so, however everlasting 20
number or anything else that has matter is, it must be capable of not
existing, just as that which is any number of years old is as capable
of not existing as that which is a day old; if this is capable of not
existing, so is that which has lasted for a time so long that it has no
limit. They cannot, then, be eternal, since that which is capable of
not existing is not eternal, as we had occasion to show in another context.[8] If that which we are now saying is true universally—that no 25
substance is eternal unless it is actuality—and if the elements are
matter that underlies substance, no eternal substance can have elements present in it, of which it consists.

There are some [9] who describe the element which acts with the
One as an indefinite dyad, and object to 'the unequal', reasonably
enough, because of the ensuing difficulties; but they have got rid 30
only of those objections which inevitably arise from the treatment of
the unequal, i. e. the relative, as an element; those which arise apart
from this opinion must confront even these thinkers, whether it is
ideal number, or mathematical, that they construct out of those
elements.

There are many causes which led them off into these explana- 35
tions, and especially the fact that they framed the difficulty in an 1089ᵃ
obsolete form. For they thought that all things that are would be one
(viz. Being itself), if one did not join issue with and refute the saying of Parmenides:

'For never will this be proved, that things that are not are.'

They thought it necessary to prove that that which is not is; for only
thus—of that which is *and something else*—could the things that are 5
be composed, if they are many.

But, first, if 'being' has many senses (for it means sometimes
substance, sometimes that it is of a certain quality, sometimes that
it is of a certain quantity, and at other times the other categories),
what sort of 'one', then, are all the things that are, if non-being is to
be supposed not to be? Is it the substances that are one, or the af- 10
fections and similarly the other categories as well, or all together—
so that the 'this' and the 'such' and the 'so much' and the other categories that indicate each some one class of being will all be one?
But it is strange, or rather impossible, that the coming into play of

---

[8] Cf. ix. 1050ᵇ 7 ff., *De Caelo*, i. 12.   [9] Probably Xenocrates is meant.

a single thing [10] should bring it about that part of that which is is a 'this', part a 'such', part a 'so much', part a 'here'.

15   Secondly, of what sort of non-being and being do the things that are consist? For 'non-being' also has many senses, since 'being' has; and 'not being a man' means not being a certain substance, 'not being straight' not being of a certain quality, 'not being three cubits long' not being of a certain quantity. What sort of being and non-being, then, by their union pluralize the things that are? This

20 thinker [11] means by the non-being, the union of which with being pluralizes the things that are, the false and the character of falsity. This is also why it used to be said that we must assume something that is false, as geometers assume the line which is not a foot long to be a foot long. But this cannot be so. For neither do geometers assume anything false (for the enunciation is extraneous to the in-

25 ference), nor is it non-being in this sense that the things that are are generated from or resolved into. But since 'non-being' taken in its various cases [12] has as many senses as there are categories, and be-sides this the false is said not to be, and so is the potential, it is from this that generation proceeds, man from that which is not man but

30 potentially man, and white from that which is not white but poten-tially white, and this whether it is some one thing that is generated or many.

The question evidently is, how being, in the sense of 'the *sub-stances*', is many; for the things that are generated are numbers and lines and bodies. Now it is strange to inquire how being in the sense

35 of the 'what' is many, and not how either qualities or quantities are many. For surely the indefinite dyad or 'the great and the small' is not a reason why there should be two kinds of white or many colours

1089^b or flavours or shapes; for then these also would be numbers and units. But if they *had* attacked these other categories, they would have seen the cause of the plurality in substances also; for the same thing or something analogous is the cause. This aberration is the

5 reason also why in seeking the opposite of being and the one, from which with being and the one the things that are proceed, they posited the relative term (i. e. the unequal), which is neither the contrary nor the contradictory of these, and is one kind of being as 'what' and quality also are.

They should have asked this question also, how relative terms are many and not one. But as it is, they inquire how there are many

_____

[10] i. e. non-being.   [11] Plato; Cf. *Soph.* 237 A. 240.
[12] Cf. ll. 16–19.

units besides the first 1, but do not go on to inquire how there are 10
many unequals besides *the* unequal. Yet they use them and speak
of great and small, many and few (from which proceed numbers),
long and short (from which proceeds the line), broad and narrow
(from which proceeds the plane), deep and shallow (from which
proceed solids); and they speak of yet more kinds of relative term.
What is the reason, then, why there is a plurality of these?

It is necessary, then, as we say, to presuppose for each thing that 15
which is it potentially; and the holder of these views further declared what that is which is potentially a 'this' and a substance but
is not in itself being—viz. that it is the relative (as if he had said
'the qualitative'), which is neither potentially the one or being, nor
the negation of the one nor of being, but one among beings. And it 20
was much *more* necessary, as we said,[13] if he was inquiring how
beings are many, not to inquire about those in the same category—
how there are many substances or many qualities—but how beings
as a whole are many; for some are substances, some modifications,
some relations. In the categories other than substance there is yet
another problem involved in the existence of plurality. Since they
are not separable from substances, qualities and quantities are many 25
just because their substratum becomes and is many; yet there *ought*
to be a matter for each category; only it cannot be separable from
substances. But in the case of 'thises', it is possible to explain how
the 'this' is many things, unless a thing is to be treated as both a
'this' and a general character.[14] The difficulty arising from the facts 30
about substances is rather this, how there are actually many substances and not one.

But further, if the 'this' and the quantitative are not the same,
we are not told how and why the things that are are many, but how
quantities are many. For all 'number' means a quantity, and so does 35
the 'unit', unless it means a measure or the quantitatively indivisible.
If, then, the quantitative and the 'what' are different, we are not
told whence or how the 'what' is many; but if any one says they are 1090ᵃ
the same, he has to face many inconsistencies.

One might fix one's attention also on the question, regarding the
numbers, what justifies the belief that they exist. To the believer in
Ideas they provide some sort of cause for existing things, since each 5
number is an Idea, and the Idea is to other things somehow or other
the cause of their being; for let this supposition be granted them.

---

13 ᵃ34.
14 Which, Aristotle thinks, the Platonists assert the Idea to be.

But as for him who does not hold this view because he sees the inherent objections to the Ideas (so that it is not for *this* reason that he posits numbers), but who posits *mathematical* number,[15] why 10 must we believe his statement that such number exists, and of what use is such number to other things? Neither does he who says it exists maintain that it is the cause of anything (he rather says it is a thing existing by itself), nor is it observed to be the cause of anything; for the theorems of arithmeticians will all be found true 15 even of sensible things, as was said before.[16]

3 As for those, then, who suppose the Ideas to exist and to be numbers, by their assumption—in virtue of the method of setting out each term apart from its instances—of the unity of each general term they try at least to explain somehow why number must exist. Since their reasons, however, are neither conclusive nor in themselves possible, one must not, for these reasons at least, assert the 20 existence of number. Again, the Pythagoreans, because they saw many attributes of numbers belonging to sensible bodies, supposed real things to be numbers—not separable numbers, however, but numbers of which real things consist. But why? Because the attributes of numbers are present in a musical scale and in the heavens 25 and in many other things.[17] Those, however, who say that mathematical number alone exists [18] cannot according to their hypotheses say anything of this sort, but it used to be urged that these sensible things could not be the subject of the sciences. But we maintain that they are, as we said before.[19] And it is evident that the objects of mathematics do not exist apart; for if they existed apart their 30 attributes would not have been present in bodies. Now the Pythagoreans in this point are open to no objection; but in that they construct natural bodies out of numbers, things that have lightness and weight out of things that have not weight or lightness, they seem to speak of another heaven and other bodies, not of the sensi- 35 ble. But those who make number separable [20] assume that it both exists and is separable because the axioms would not be true of sensible things, while the statements of mathematics *are* true and 'greet the soul'; and similarly with the spatial magnitudes of mathe- 1090ᵇ matics. It is evident, then, both that the rival theory [21] will say the contrary of this, and that the difficulty we raised just now,[22] why if

---

[15] Speusippus is meant.

[17] Cf. i. 989ᵇ 29–990ᵃ 29.

[19] Cf. xiii. 3.

[21] *sc.* of the Pythagoreans; Cf. ll. 20–25.

[16] Cf. xiii. 3, esp. 1077ᵇ 17–22.

[18] Speusippus is meant.

[20] The Platonists.

[22] ᵃ29.

numbers are in no way present in sensible things their attributes are present in sensible things, has to be solved by those who hold these views.

There are some who, because the point is the limit and extreme 5 of the line, the line of the plane, and the plane of the solid, think there must be real things of this sort. We must therefore examine this argument too, and see whether it is not remarkably weak. For (i) extremes are not substances, but rather all these things are 10 limits. For even walking, and movement in general, has a limit, so that on their theory this will be a 'this' and a substance. But that is absurd. Not but what (ii) even if they are substances, they will all be the substances of the sensible things in this world; for it is to these that the argument applied. Why then should they be capable of existing apart?

Again, if we are not too easily satisfied, we may, regarding all number and the objects of mathematics, press this difficulty, that they contribute nothing to one another, the prior to the posterior; 15 for if number did not exist, none the less spatial magnitudes would exist for those who maintain the existence of the objects of mathematics only,[23] and if spatial magnitudes did not exist, soul and sensible bodies would exist. But the observed facts show that nature is 20 not a series of episodes, like a bad tragedy. As for the believers in the Ideas, this difficulty misses them; for they construct spatial magnitudes out of matter and number, lines out of the number 2, planes doubtless out of 3, solids out of 4—or they use other numbers, which makes no difference. But will these magnitudes be Ideas, or what is their manner of existence, and what do they contribute 25 to things? These contribute nothing, as the objects of mathematics contribute nothing. But not even is any theorem true of them, unless we want to change the objects of mathematics and invent doctrines of our own. But it is not hard to assume any random hypotheses and 30 spin out a long string of conclusions. These thinkers,[24] then, are wrong in this way, in wanting to unite the objects of mathematics with the Ideas. And those who first posited two kinds of number, that of the Forms and that which is mathematical, neither have said nor can say how mathematical number is to exist and of what it is to consist. For they place it between ideal and sensible number. If 35 (i) it consists of the great and small, it will be the same as the other —ideal—number (he[25] makes spatial magnitudes out of some other

[23] Speusippus is meant.   [24] ll. 20-32 seem to refer to Xenocrates.
[25] sc. Plato.

1091ᵃ small and great [26]). And if (ii) he names some other element, he will
be making his elements rather many. And if the principle of each of
the two kinds of number is a 1, unity will be something common to
these, and we must inquire how the one is these *many* things, while at
the same time *number*, according to him, cannot be generated except
from one *and an indefinite dyad*.

5   All this is absurd, and conflicts both with itself and with the probabilities, and we seem to see in it Simonides' 'long rigmarole'; for the
long rigmarole comes into play, like those of slaves, when men have
nothing sound to say. And the very elements—the great and the small
10 —seem to cry out against the violence that is done to them; for they
cannot in any way generate numbers other than those got from 1 by
doubling.

It is strange also to attribute generation to things that are eternal,
or rather this is one of the things that are impossible. There need be
15 no doubt whether the Pythagoreans attribute generation to them or
not; for they say plainly that when the one had been constructed,
whether out of planes or of surface or of seed or of elements which
they cannot express, immediately the nearest part of the unlimited
began to be constrained and limited by the limit. But since they are
constructing a world and wish to speak the language of natural science,
it is fair to make some examination of their physical theories, but to
20 let them off from the present inquiry; for we are investigating the
principles at work in *unchangeable* things, so that it is numbers of
this kind whose genesis we must study.

4   These thinkers say there is no generation of the odd number, which
evidently implies that there *is* generation of the even; and some present
the even as produced first from unequals—the great and the small—
25 when these are equalized. The inequality, then, must belong to them
before they are equalized. If they had always been equalized, they
would not have been unequal before; for there is nothing before
that which is always. Therefore evidently they are not giving their
account of the generation of numbers merely to assist contemplation of
their nature.[27]

A difficulty, and a reproach to any one who finds it *no* difficulty,
30 are contained in the question how the elements and the principles are
related to the good and the beautiful; the difficulty is this, whether
any of the elements is such a thing as we mean by the good itself and
the best, or this is not so, but these are later in origin than the elements.

[26] Cf. 1090ᵇ 21, 22.   [27] Cf. *De Caelo*, i. 279ᵇ 32–280ᵃ 10.

The theologians seem to agree with some thinkers of the present day,[28] who answer the question in the negative, and say that both the good 35 and the beautiful appear in the nature of things only when that nature has made some progress. (This they do to avoid a real objection which confronts those who say, as some do, that the one is a first principle. 1091^{b} The objection arises not from their ascribing goodness to the first principle as an attribute, but from their making the one a principle— and a principle in the sense of an element—and generating number from the one.) The old poets agree with this inasmuch as they say that not those who are first in time, e. g. Night and Heaven or Chaos or 5 Ocean, reign and rule, but Zeus. These poets, however, are led to speak thus only because they think of the rulers of the world as *changing*; for those of them who combine the two characters in that they do not use mythical language throughout, e. g. Pherecydes and some others, make the original generating agent the Best, and so do the Magi, and 10 some of the later sages also, e. g. both Empedocles and Anaxagoras, of whom one made love an element, and the other made reason a principle. Of those who maintain the existence of the *unchangeable* substances some say the One itself is the good itself; but they thought its substance lay mainly in its unity.

This, then, is the problem—which of the two ways of speaking is 15 right. It would be strange if to that which is primary and eternal and most self-sufficient this very quality—self-sufficiency and self-main- tenance—belongs primarily in some other way than *as a good*. But indeed it can be for no other reason indestructible or self-sufficient than because its nature is good. Therefore to say that the first prin- ciple is good is probably correct; but that this principle should be the 20 One or, if not that, at least an element, and an element of numbers, is impossible. Powerful objections arise, to avoid which some have given up the theory [29] (viz. those who agree that the One is a first principle and element, but only of *mathematical* number). For on this view all the units become identical with species of good, and there is a great 25 profusion of goods. Again, if the Forms are numbers, all the Forms are identical with species of good. But let a man assume Ideas of anything he pleases. If these are Ideas only of goods, the Ideas will not be substances; but if the Ideas are also Ideas of substances, all animals and plants and all individuals that share in Ideas will be good.

These absurdities follow, and it also follows that the contrary ele- 30 ment, whether it is plurality or the unequal, i. e. the great and small,

[28] Speusippus is meant; Cf. xii. 1072^{b} 31.
[29] i. e. Speusippus gave up the identity of the One with the Good.

is the bad-itself. (Hence one thinker [30] avoided attaching the good to
the One, because it would necessarily follow, since generation is from
contraries, that badness is the fundamental nature of plurality; while
35 others [31] say inequality is the nature of the bad.) It follows, then,
that all things partake of the bad except one—the One itself, and that
1092ᵃ numbers partake of it in a more undiluted form than spatial magnitudes, and that the bad is the space in which the good is realized,[32]
and that it partakes in and desires that which tends to destroy it; for
contrary tends to destroy contrary. And if, as we were saying,[33] the
matter is that which is potentially each thing, e. g. that of actual fire
is that which is potentially fire, the bad will be just the potentially good.
5   All these objections, then, follow, partly because they make every
principle an element, partly because they make contraries principles,
partly because they make the One a principle, partly because they
treat the numbers as the first substances, and as capable of existing
apart, and as Forms.

5 If, then, it is equally impossible not to put the good among the
first principles and to put it among them in this way, evidently the
10 principles are not being correctly described, nor are the first substances.
Nor does any one conceive the matter correctly if he compares the
principles of the universe to that of animals and plants, on the ground
that the more complete always comes from the indefinite and incomplete—which is what leads this thinker [34] to say that this is also true
of the first principles of reality, so that the One itself is not even an
15 existing thing. This is incorrect, for even in this world of animals and
plants the principles from which these come are complete; for it is a
man that produces a man, and the seed is not first.

It is out of place, also, to generate place simultaneously with the
mathematical solids (for place is peculiar to the individual things, and
20 hence they are separate in place; but mathematical objects are nowhere), and to say that they must be somewhere, but not say what
kind of thing their place is.

Those who say that existing things come from elements and that the
first of existing things are the numbers, should have first distinguished
the senses in which one thing comes from another, and then said in
which sense number comes from its first principles.

By intermixture? But (1) not everything is capable of intermixture,
25 and (2) that which is produced by it is different from its elements, and

---

[30] Speusippus.   [31] Plato and Xenocrates.
[32] Cf. Pl. *Tim.* 52 ᴀ, ʙ.   [33] 1088ᵇ 1.
[34] Speusippus; Cf. xii. 1072ᵇ 30–34.

on this view the one will not remain separate or a distinct entity; but they want it to be so.

By juxtaposition, like a syllable? But then (1) the elements must have position; and (2) he who thinks of number will be able to think of the unity and the plurality apart; number then will be this—a unit *and* plurality, or the one *and* the unequal.

Again, coming from certain things means in one sense that these are still to be found in the product, and in another that they are not; in which sense does number come from these elements? Only things 30 that are generated can come from elements which are present in them. Does number come, then, from its elements as from seed? But nothing can be excreted from that which is indivisible. Does it come from its contrary, its contrary not persisting? But all things that come in this way come also from something else which does persist.[35] Since, then, 35 one thinker [36] places the 1 as contrary to plurality, and another [37] places it as contrary to the unequal, treating the 1 as equal, number 1092[b] must be being treated as coming from contraries. There is, then, something else that persists, from which and from one contrary the compound is or has come to be. Again, why in the world do the other things that come from contraries, or that have contraries, perish (even when all of the contrary is used to produce them), while number does not? Nothing is said about this. Yet whether present or not present in the 5 compound the contrary destroys it, e. g. 'strife' destroys the 'mixture' [38] (yet it *should* not; for it is not to that that it is contrary).[39]

Once more, it has not been determined at all in which way numbers are the causes of substances and of being—whether (1) as boundaries (as points are of spatial magnitudes). This is how Eurytus decided 10 what was the number of what (e. g. one of man and another of horse), viz. by imitating the figures of living things with pebbles, as some people bring numbers into the forms of triangle and square. Or (2) is it because harmony is a ratio of numbers, and so is man and everything else? But how are the attributes—white and sweet and hot— 15 numbers? Evidently it is not the numbers that are the essence or the causes of the form; for the ratio is the essence, while the number is the matter. E. g. the essence of flesh or bone is number only in this way, 'three parts of fire and two of earth'.[40] And a number, whatever number it is, is always a number of certain things, either of parts of fire or earth or of units; but the essence is that there is so much of one 20

[35] Cf. xii. 1069[b] 3–9, *Phys.* i. 7.   [36] Speusippus.   [37] Plato.
[38] Empedocles.   [39] [a] 17–[b] 8 seem to refer mainly to Speusippus.
[40] Empedocles.

thing to so much of another in the mixture; and this is no longer a number but a ratio of mixture of numbers, whether these are corporeal or of any other kind.

Number, then, whether it be number in general or the number which consists of abstract units, is neither the cause as agent, nor the matter, 25 nor the ratio and form of things. Nor, of course, is it the final cause.

6   One might also raise the question what the good is that things get from numbers because their composition is expressible by a number, either by one which is easily calculable or by an odd number. For in fact honey-water is no more wholesome if it is mixed in the proportion of three times three, but it would do more good if it were in no particu- lar ratio but well diluted than if it were numerically expressible but 30 strong. Again, the ratios of mixtures are expressed by the *adding* of numbers, not by mere numbers; e. g. it is 'three parts to two', not 'three times two'. For in any multiplication the genus of the things multiplied must be the same; therefore the product $1 \times 2 \times 3$ must be measurable by 1, and $4 \times 5 \times 6$ by 4, and therefore all products into which the 35 same factor enters must be measurable by that factor. The number of fire, then, cannot be $2 \times 5 \times 3 \times 6$, and at the same time that of water 2×3.

1093ª   If all things must share in number, it must follow that many things are the same, and the same number must belong to one thing and to another. Is number the cause, then, and does the thing exist because of its number, or is this not certain? E. g. the motions of the sun have 5 a number, and again those of the moon—yes, and the life and prime of each animal. Why, then, should not some of these numbers be squares, some cubes, and some equal, others double? There is no reason why they should not, and indeed they must move within these limits, since all things were assumed to share in number. And it was assumed that things that differed might fall under the same number. Therefore 10 if the same number had belonged to certain things, these would have been the same as one another, since they would have had the same form of number; e. g. sun and moon would have been the same. But why need these numbers be causes? There are seven vowels, the scale consists of seven strings, the Pleiades are seven, at seven animals lose 15 their teeth (at least some do, though some do not), and the champions who fought against Thebes were seven. Is it then because the number is the kind of number it is, that the champions were seven or the Pleiad consists of seven stars? Surely the champions were seven because there were seven gates or for some other reason, and the Pleiad *we* count as seven, as we count the Bear as twelve, while other peoples count more stars in both. Nay, they even say that Ξ, Ψ, and Z are concords, and that because there are three concords, the double consonants also are three. They quite neglect the fact that there might be a thousand such letters; for one symbol might be assigned to ΓΡ. But if they say that each of these three is equal to two of the other letters, and no other is so, and if the cause is that there are three parts of the mouth and one letter is in each applied to sigma, it is for this reason that there are only three, not because the concords are three; since as a matter of fact the concords are more than three, but of double consonants there cannot be more. These people are like the old-fashioned Homeric scholars, who see small resemblances but neglect great ones. Some say that there are many such cases, e. g. that the middle strings are repre- sented by nine and eight,[41] and that the epic verse has seventeen sylla- bles, which is equal in number to the two strings, and that the scansion is, in the right,[42] half of the line nine syllables, and in the left eight. And they say that the distance in the letters from alpha to omega is equal to that from the lowest note of the flute to the highest, and that the number of this note is equal to that of the whole choir of heaven. It may be suspected that no one could find difficulty either in stating such analogies or in finding them in eternal things, since they can be found even in perishable things.

But the lauded characteristics of numbers, and the contraries of these, and generally the mathematical relations, as some describe them, making them causes of nature, seem, when we inspect them in *this* way, to vanish; for none of them is a cause in any of the senses that have been distinguished in reference to the first principles.[43] In a sense, however, they make it plain that goodness belongs to numbers, and that the odd, the straight, the square, the potencies of certain numbers, are in the column of the beautiful. For the seasons and a particular kind of number go together; and the other agreements that they col- lect from the theorems of mathematics all have this meaning.[44] Hence they are like coincidences. For they are accidents, but the things that agree are all appropriate to one another, and one by analogy. For in each category of being an analogous term is found—as the straight is

---

[41] The ratios corresponding to the fourth and the fifth are respectively 8 to 6 and 9 to 6.

[42] i. e. first.   [43] Cf. v. 1, 2.

[44] *sc.* that numerical relations are found in things, but are not the *cause* of anything that happens.

20 in length, so is the level in surface, perhaps the odd in number, and the white in colour.

Again, it is not the *ideal* numbers that are the causes of musical phenomena and the like (for equal ideal numbers differ from one another in form; for even the units do); so that we need not assume Ideas for this reason at least.

These, then, are the results of the theory, and yet more might be 25 brought together. The fact that our opponents have much trouble with the generation of numbers and can in no way make a system of them, seems to indicate that the objects of mathematics are not separable from sensible things, as some say, and that they are not the first principles.

Ethica Nicomachea

Translated by W. D. Ross

CONTENTS

B. *Temperance.*

C. *Virtues concerned with money.*

D. *Virtues concerned with honour.*

E. *The virtue concerned with anger.*

F. *Virtues of social intercourse.*

G. *A quasi-virtue.*

H. *Justice.*

ETHICA NICOMACHEA

(*Nicomachean Ethics*)

BOOK I

1 Every art and every inquiry, and similarly every action and pur- 1094ᵃ
suit, is thought to aim at some good; and for this reason the good has
rightly been declared [1] to be that at which all things aim. But a certain
difference is found among ends; some are activities, others are
products apart from the activities that produce them. Where there are 5
ends apart from the actions, it is the nature of the products to be
better than the activities. Now, as there are many actions, arts, and
sciences, their ends also are many; the end of the medical art is health,
that of shipbuilding a vessel, that of strategy victory, that of economics wealth. But where such arts fall under a single capacity—as 10
bridle-making and the other arts concerned with the equipment of
horses fall under the art of riding, and this and every military action
under strategy, in the same way other arts fall under yet others—
in all of these the ends of the master arts are to be preferred to all
the subordinate ends; for it is for the sake of the former that the 15
latter are pursued. It makes no difference whether the activities themselves are the ends of the actions, or something else apart from the
activities, as in the case of the sciences just mentioned.

2 If, then, there is some end of the things we do, which we desire
for its own sake (everything else being desired for the sake of this),
and if we do not choose everything for the sake of something else
(for at that rate the process would go on to infinity, so that our desire 20
would be empty and vain), clearly this must be the good and the
chief good. Will not the knowledge of it, then, have a great influence
on life? Shall we not, like archers who have a mark to aim at, be more
likely to hit upon what is right? If so, we must try, in outline at least 25
to determine what it is, and of which of the sciences or capacities it
is the object. It would seem to belong to the most authoritative art

[1] Perhaps by Eudoxus; Cf. 1172ᵇ 9.

935

and that which is most truly the master art. And politics appears to
be of this nature; for it is this that ordains which of the sciences
1094ᵇ should be studied in a state, and which each class of citizens should
learn and up to what point they should learn them; and we see even
the most highly esteemed of capacities to fall under this, e. g. strategy,
5 economics, rhetoric; now, since politics uses the rest of the sciences,
and since, again, it legislates as to what we are to do and what we are
to abstain from, the end of this science must include those of the
others, so that this end must be the good for man. For even if the end
is the same for a single man and for a state, that of the state seems
at all events something greater and more complete whether to attain
or to preserve; though it is worth while to attain the end merely for
one man, it is finer and more godlike to attain it for a nation or for
10 city-states. These, then, are the ends at which our inquiry aims, since
it is political science, in one sense of that term.

3   Our discussion will be adequate if it has as much clearness as the
subject-matter admits of, for precision is not to be sought for alike
in all discussions, any more than in all the products of the crafts. Now
15 fine and just actions, which political science investigates, admit of
much variety and fluctuation of opinion, so that they may be thought
to exist only by convention, and not by nature. And goods also give
rise to a similar fluctuation because they bring harm to many people;
for before now men have been undone by reason of their wealth, and
others by reason of their courage. We must be content, then, in speak-
20 ing of such subjects and with such premisses to indicate the truth
roughly and in outline, and in speaking about things which are only for
the most part true and with premisses of the same kind to reach conclusions that are no better. In the same spirit, therefore, should each
type of statement be *received*; for it is the mark of an educated man
25 to look for precision in each class of things just so far as the nature
of the subject admits; it is evidently equally foolish to accept probable
reasoning from a mathematician and to demand from a rhetorician
scientific proofs.

Now each man judges well the things he knows, and of these he is
a good judge. And so the man who has been educated in a subject is
1095ᵃ a good judge of that subject, and the man who has received an all-
round education is a good judge in general. Hence a young man is not
a proper hearer of lectures on political science; for he is inexperienced
in the actions that occur in life, but its discussions start from these
and are about these; and, further, since he tends to follow his passions,

his study will be vain and unprofitable, because the end aimed at is not knowledge but action. And it makes no difference whether he is 5 young in years or youthful in character; the defect does not depend on time, but on his living, and pursuing each successive object, as passion directs. For to such persons, as to the incontinent, knowledge brings no profit; but to those who desire and act in accordance with 10 a rational principle knowledge about such matters will be of great benefit.

These remarks about the student, the sort of treatment to be expected, and the purpose of the inquiry, may be taken as our preface.

4 Let us resume our inquiry and state, in view of the fact that all knowledge and every pursuit aims at some good, what it is that we say political science aims at and what is the highest of all goods 15 achievable by action. Verbally there is very general agreement; for both the general run of men and people of superior refinement say that it is happiness, and identify living well and doing well with being happy; but with regard to what happiness is they differ, and 20 the many do not give the same account as the wise. For the former think it is some plain and obvious thing, like pleasure, wealth, or honour; they differ, however, from one another—and often even the same man identifies it with different things, with health when he is ill, with wealth when he is poor; but, conscious of their ignorance, 25 they admire those who proclaim some great ideal that is above their comprehension. Now some [2] thought that apart from these many goods there is another which is self-subsistent and causes the goodness of all these as well. To examine all the opinions that have been held were perhaps somewhat fruitless; enough to examine those that are most prevalent or that seem to be arguable.

Let us not fail to notice, however, that there is a difference between 30 arguments from and those to the first principles. For Plato, too, was right in raising this question and asking, as he used to do, 'are we on the way from or to the first principles?' [3] There is a difference, as there is in a race-course between the course from the judges to the turning-point and the way back. For, while we must begin with what 1095ᵇ is known, things are objects of knowledge in two senses—some to us, some without qualification. Presumably, then, we must begin with things known to us. Hence any one who is to listen intelligently to lectures about what is noble and just and, generally, about the subjects 5 of political science must have been brought up in good habits. For the

[2] The Platonic School; Cf. ch. 6.   [3] Cf. *Rep.* 511 B.

fact is the starting-point, and if this is sufficiently plain to him, he will not at the start need the reason as well; and the man who has been well brought up has or can easily get starting-points. And as for him who neither has nor can get them, let him hear the words of Hesiod:

10
>Far best is he who knows all things himself;
>Good, he that hearkens when men counsel right;
>But he who neither knows, nor lays to heart
>Another's wisdom, is a useless wight.

5 Let us, however, resume our discussion from the point at which we digressed. To judge from the lives that men lead, most men, and men
15 of the most vulgar type, seem (not without some ground) to identify the good, or happiness, with pleasure; which is the reason why they love the life of enjoyment. For there are, we may say, three prominent types of life—that just mentioned, the political, and thirdly the contemplative life. Now the mass of mankind are evidently quite slavish
20 in their tastes, preferring a life suitable to beasts, but they get some ground for their view from the fact that many of those in high places share the tastes of Sardanapallus. A consideration of the prominent types of life shows that people of superior refinement and of active disposition identify happiness with honour; for this is, roughly speaking, the end of the political life. But it seems too superficial to be what we are looking for, since it is thought to depend on those who bestow
25 honour rather than on him who receives it, but the good we divine to be something proper to a man and not easily taken from him. Further, men seem to pursue honour in order that they may be assured of their goodness; at least it is by men of practical wisdom that they seek to be honoured, and among those who know them, and on the ground of their virtue; clearly, then, according to them, at any rate, virtue
30 is better. And perhaps one might even suppose this to be, rather than honour, the end of the political life. But even this appears somewhat incomplete; for possession of virtue seems actually compatible with being asleep, or with lifelong inactivity, and, further, with the greatest
1096ª sufferings and misfortunes; but a man who was living so no one would call happy, unless he were maintaining a thesis at all costs. But enough of this; for the subject has been sufficiently treated even in the current discussions. Third comes the contemplative life, which we shall consider later.[4]

---

[4] 1177ª 12–1178ª 8, 1178ª 22–1179ª 32.

The life of money-making is one undertaken under compulsion, and 5
wealth is evidently not the good we are seeking; for it is merely useful
and for the sake of something else. And so one might rather take the
aforenamed objects to be ends; for they are loved for themselves. But
it is evident that not even these are ends; yet many arguments have
been thrown away in support of them. Let us leave this subject, then. 10

6 We had perhaps better consider the universal good and discuss
thoroughly what is meant by it, although such an inquiry is made an
uphill one by the fact that the Forms have been introduced by friends
of our own. Yet it would perhaps be thought to be better, indeed to
be our duty, for the sake of maintaining the truth even to destroy what
touches us closely, especially as we are philosophers or lovers of 15
wisdom; for, while both are dear, piety requires us to honour truth
above our friends.

The men who introduced this doctrine did not posit Ideas of classes
within which they recognized priority and posteriority (which is the
reason why they did not maintain the existence of an Idea embracing
all numbers); but the term 'good' is used both in the category of
substance and in that of quality and in that of relation, and that 20
which is *per se*, i. e. substance, is prior in nature to the relative (for
the latter is like an offshoot and accident of being); so that there could
not be a common Idea set over all these goods. Further, since 'good'
has as many senses as 'being' (for it is predicated both in the category
of substance, as of God and of reason, and in quality, i. e. of the 25
virtues, and in quantity, i. e. of that which is moderate, and in relation, i. e. of the useful, and in time, i. e. of the right opportunity,
and in place, i. e. of the right locality and the like), clearly it cannot
be something universally present in all cases and single; for then it
could not have been predicated in all the categories but in one only.
Further, since of the things answering to one Idea there is one science, 30
there would have been one science of all the goods; but as it is there
are many sciences even of the things that fall under one category, e. g.
of opportunity, for opportunity in war is studied by strategics and in
disease by medicine, and the moderate in food is studied by medicine
and in exercise by the science of gymnastics. And one might ask the
question, what in the world they *mean* by 'a thing itself', if (as is
the case) in 'man himself' and in a particular man the account of man 35
is one and the same. For in so far as they are man, they will in no 1096^b
respect differ; and if this is so, neither will 'good itself' and particular
goods, in so far as they are good. But again it will not be good any
the more for being eternal, since that which lasts long is no whiter

5 than that which perishes in a day. The Pythagoreans seem to give a
more plausible account of the good, when they place the one in the
column of goods; and it is they that Speusippus seems to have followed.

But let us discuss these matters elsewhere [5]; an objection to what
we have said, however, may be discerned in the fact that the Platonists
10 have not been speaking about *all* goods, and that the goods that are
pursued and loved for themselves are called good by reference to a
single Form, while those which tend to produce or to preserve these
somehow or to prevent their contraries are called so by reference to
these, and in a secondary sense. Clearly, then, goods must be spoken
of in two ways, and some must be good in themselves, the others by
reason of these. Let us separate, then, things good in themselves from
15 things useful, and consider whether the former are called good by
reference to a single Idea. What sort of goods would one call good in
themselves? Is it those that are pursued even when isolated from
others, such as intelligence, sight, and certain pleasures and honours?
Certainly, if we pursue these also for the sake of something else, yet
one would place them among things good in themselves. Or is nothing
20 other than the Idea of good good in itself? In that case the Form will be
empty. But if the things we have named are also things good in themselves, the account of the good will have to appear as something
identical in them all, as that of whiteness is identical in snow and in
white lead. But of honour, wisdom, and pleasure, just in respect of
25 their goodness, the accounts are distinct and diverse. The good, therefore, is not some common element answering to one Idea.

But what then do we mean by the good? It is surely not like the
things that only chance to have the same name. Are goods one, then,
by being derived from one good or by all contributing to one good,
or are they rather one by analogy? Certainly as sight is in the body,
30 so is reason in the soul, and so on in other cases. But perhaps these
subjects had better be dismissed for the present; for perfect precision
about them would be more appropriate to another branch of philosophy.[6] And similarly with regard to the Idea; even if there is some
one good which is universally predicable of goods or is capable of
separate and independent existence, clearly it could not be achieved
or attained by man; but we are now seeking something attainable.
35 Perhaps, however, some one might think it worth while to recognize
this with a view to the goods that *are* attainable and achievable; for

[5] Cf. *Met.* 986ª 22–6, 1028ᵇ 21–4, 1072ᵇ 30–1073ª 3, 1091ª 29–ᵇ 3, ᵇ 13–1092ª 17.
[6] Cf. *Met.* iv. 2.

having this as a sort of pattern we shall know better the goods that 1097ª
are good for us, and if we know them shall attain them. This argument
has some plausibility, but seems to clash with the procedure of the
sciences; for all of these, though they aim at some good and seek to 5
supply the deficiency of it, leave on one side the knowledge of *the*
good. Yet that all the exponents of the arts should be ignorant of, and
should not even seek, so great an aid is not probable. It is hard, too,
to see how a weaver or a carpenter will be benefited in regard to his
own craft by knowing this 'good itself', or how the man who has 10
viewed the Idea itself will be a better doctor or general thereby. For
a doctor seems not even to study health in this way, but the health
of man, or perhaps rather the health of a particular man; it is individuals that he is healing. But enough of these topics.

7   Let us again return to the good we are seeking, and ask what it 15
can be. It seems different in different actions and arts; it is different
in medicine, in strategy, and in the other arts likewise. What then is
the good of each? Surely that for whose sake everything else is done.
In medicine this is health, in strategy victory, in architecture a house, 20
in any other sphere something else, and in every action and pursuit
the end; for it is for the sake of this that all men do whatever else they
do. Therefore, if there is an end for all that we do, this will be the
good achievable by action, and if there are more than one, these will
be the goods achievable by action.

So the argument has by a different course reached the same point;
but we must try to state this even more clearly. Since there are evidently more than one end, and we choose some of these (e. g. wealth, 25
flutes, and in general instruments) for the sake of something else,
clearly not all ends are final ends; but the chief good is evidently
something final. Therefore, if there is only one final end, this will be
what we are seeking, and if there are more than one, the most final
of these will be what we are seeking. Now we call that which is in 30
itself worthy of pursuit more final than that which is worthy of pursuit
for the sake of something else, and that which is never desirable for
the sake of something else more final than the things that are desirable
both in themselves and for the sake of that other thing, and therefore we call final without qualification that which is always desirable
in itself and never for the sake of something else.

Now such a thing happiness, above all else, is held to be; for this
we choose always for itself and never for the sake of something else, 1097ᵇ
but honour, pleasure, reason, and every virtue we choose indeed for
themselves (for if nothing resulted from them we should still choose

each of them), but we choose them also for the sake of happiness,
5 judging that by means of them we shall be happy. Happiness, on the
other hand, no one chooses for the sake of these, nor, in general, for
anything other than itself.

From the point of view of self-sufficiency the same result seems to
follow; for the final good is thought to be self-sufficient. Now by
self-sufficient we do not mean that which is sufficient for a man by
10 himself, for one who lives a solitary life, but also for parents, children,
wife, and in general for his friends and fellow citizens, since man is
born for citizenship. But some limit must be set to this; for if we
extend our requirement to ancestors and descendants and friends'
friends we are in for an infinite series. Let us examine this question,
however, on another occasion;[7] the self-sufficient we now define as
15 that which when isolated makes life desirable and lacking in nothing;
and such we think happiness to be; and further we think it most
desirable of all things, without being counted as one good thing among
others—if it were so counted it would clearly be made more desirable
by the addition of even the least of goods; for that which is added
20 becomes an excess of goods, and of goods the greater is always more
desirable. Happiness, then, is something final and self-sufficient, and is
the end of action.

Presumably, however, to say that happiness is the chief good seems a
platitude, and a clearer account of what it is is still desired. This might
25 perhaps be given, if we could first ascertain the function of man. For
just as for a flute-player, a sculptor, or any artist, and, in general,
for all things that have a function or activity, the good and the 'well'
is thought to reside in the function, so would it seem to be for man,
if he has a function. Have the carpenter, then, and the tanner certain
30 functions or activities, and has man none? Is he born without a function? Or as eye, hand, foot, and in general each of the parts evidently
has a function, may one lay it down that man similarly has a function
apart from all these? What then can this be? Life seems to be common
even to plants, but we are seeking what is peculiar to man. Let us
1098ᵃ exclude, therefore, the life of nutrition and growth. Next there would
be a life of perception, but *it* also seems to be common even to the
horse, the ox, and every animal. There remains, then, an active life
of the element that has a rational principle; of this, one part has such
a principle in the sense of being obedient to one, the other in the sense
5 of possessing one and exercising thought. And, as 'life of the rational
element' also has two meanings, we must state that life in the sense of
activity is what we mean; for this seems to be the more proper sense

[7] i. 10, 11, ix. 10.

of the term. Now if the function of man is an activity of soul which follows or implies a rational principle, and if we say 'a so-and-so' and 'a good so-and-so' have a function which is the same in kind, e. g. a lyre-player and a good lyre-player, and so without qualification in all cases, eminence in respect of goodness being added to the name 10 of the function (for the function of a lyre-player is to play the lyre, and that of a good lyre-player is to do so well): if this is the case, [and we state the function of man to be a certain kind of life, and this to be an activity or actions of the soul implying a rational principle, and the function of a good man to be the good and noble performance of these, and if any action is well performed when it is 15 performed in accordance with the appropriate excellence: if this is the case,] human good turns out to be activity of soul in accordance with virtue, and if there are more than one virtue, in accordance with the best and most complete.

But we must add 'in a complete life'. For one swallow does not make a summer, nor does one day; and so too one day, or a short time, does not make a man blessed and happy.

Let this serve as an outline of the good; for we must presumably 20 first sketch it roughly, and then later fill in the details. But it would seem that any one is capable of carrying on and articulating what has once been well outlined, and that time is a good discoverer or partner in such a work; to which facts the advances of the arts are due; for any one can add what is lacking. And we must also remember what 25 has been said before,[8] and not look for precision in all things alike, but in each class of things such precision as accords with the subject-matter, and so much as is appropriate to the inquiry. For a carpenter and a geometer investigate the right angle in different ways; the former does so in so far as the right angle is useful for his work, 30 while the latter inquires what it is or what sort of thing it is; for he is a spectator of the truth. We must act in the same way, then, in all other matters as well, that our main task may not be subordinated to minor questions. Nor must we demand the cause in all matters alike; it is enough in some cases that the *fact* be well established, as 1098ᵇ in the case of the first principles; the fact is the primary thing or first principle. Now of first principles we see some by induction, some by perception, some by a certain habituation, and others too in other ways. But each set of principles we must try to investigate in the natural way, and we must take pains to state them definitely, since 5 they have a great influence on what follows. For the beginning is

<hr>

[8] 1094ᵇ 11-27.

thought to be more than half of the whole, and many of the questions we ask are cleared up by it.

8   We must consider it, however, in the light not only of our conclu-
10 sion and our premisses, but also of what is commonly said about it; for with a true view all the data harmonize, but with a false one the facts soon clash. Now goods have been divided into three classes,[9] and some are described as external, others as relating to soul or to body; we call those that relate to soul most properly and truly goods, and
15 physical actions and activities we class as relating to soul. Therefore our account must be sound, at least according to this view, which is an old one and agreed on by philosophers. It is correct also in that we identify the end with certain actions and activities; for thus it falls among goods of the soul and not among external goods. Another belief
20 which harmonizes with our account is that the happy man lives well and does well; for we have practically defined happiness as a sort of good life and good action. The characteristics that are looked for in happiness seem also, all of them, to belong to what we have defined happiness as being. For some identify happiness with virtue, some with practical wisdom, others with a kind of philosophic wisdom,
25 others with these, or one of these, accompanied by pleasure or not without pleasure; while others include also external prosperity. Now some of these views have been held by many men and men of old, others by a few eminent persons; and it is not. probable that either of these should be entirely mistaken, but rather that they should be right in at least some one respect or even in most respects.
30   With those who identify happiness with virtue or some one virtue our account is in harmony; for to virtue belongs virtuous activity. But it makes, perhaps, no small difference whether we place the chief good in possession or in use, in state of mind or in activity. For the
1099ª state of mind may exist without producing any good result, as in a man who is asleep or in some other way quite inactive, but the activity cannot; for one who has the activity will of necessity be acting, and acting well. And as in the Olympic Games it is not the most beautiful and the strongest that are crowned but those who compete (for it is
5 some of these that are victorious), so those who act win, and rightly win, the noble and good things in life.

Their life is also in itself pleasant. For pleasure is a state of *soul*, and to each man that which he is said to be a lover of is pleasant; e. g. not only is a horse pleasant to the lover of horses, and a spectacle
10 to the lover of sights, but also in the same way just acts are pleasant

[9] Pl. *Euthyd.* 279 AB, *Phil.* 48 E, *Laws,* 743 E.

to the lover of justice and in general virtuous acts to the lover of virtue. Now for most men their pleasures are in conflict with one another because these are not by nature pleasant, but the lovers of what is noble find pleasant the things that are by nature pleasant; and virtuous actions are such, so that these are pleasant for such men as well as in their own nature. Their life, therefore, has no further need of 15 pleasure as a sort of adventitious charm, but has its pleasure in itself. For, besides what we have said, the man who does not rejoice in noble actions is not even good; since no one would call a man just who did not enjoy acting justly, nor any man liberal who did not enjoy liberal actions; and similarly in all other cases. If this is so, virtuous actions 20 must be in themselves pleasant. But they are also *good* and *noble*, and have each of these attributes in the highest degree, since the good man judges well about these attributes; his judgement is such as we have described.[10] Happiness then is the best, noblest, and most pleasant thing in the world, and these attributes are not severed as in the 25 inscription at Delos—

> Most noble is that which is justest, and best is health;
> But pleasantest is it to win what we love.

For all these properties belong to the best activities; and these, or one— the best—of these, we identify with happiness.   30

Yet evidently, as we said,[11] it needs the external goods as well; for it is impossible, or not easy, to do noble acts without the proper equip- 1099ᵇ ment. In many actions we use friends and riches and political power as instruments; and there are some things the lack of which takes the lustre from happiness, as good birth, goodly children, beauty; for the man who is very ugly in appearance or ill-born or solitary and childless is not very likely to be happy, and perhaps a man would be still less 5 likely if he had thoroughly bad children or friends or had lost good children or friends by death. As we said,[11] then, happiness seems to need this sort of prosperity in addition; for which reason some identify happiness with good fortune, though others identify it with virtue.

9   For this reason also the question is asked, whether happiness is to be acquired by learning or by habituation or some other sort of train- ing, or comes in virtue of some divine providence or again by chance. 10 Now if there is *any* gift of the gods to men, it is reasonable that happi- ness should be god-given, and most surely god-given of all human things inasmuch as it is the best. But this question would perhaps be more

[10] i. e., he judges that virtuous actions are good and noble in the highest degree.
[11] 1098ᵇ 26–9.

appropriate to another inquiry; happiness seems, however, even if it
15 is not god-sent but comes as a result of virtue and some process of
learning or training, to be among the most god-like things; for that
which is the prize and end of virtue seems to be the best thing in the
world, and something godlike and blessed.

It will also on this view be very generally shared; for all who are
not maimed as regards their potentiality for virtue may win it by a
20 certain kind of study and care. But if it is better to be happy thus
than by chance, it is reasonable that the facts should be so, since everything that depends on the action of nature is by nature as good as it
can be, and similarly everything that depends on art or any rational
cause, and especially if it depends on the best of all causes. To entrust
to chance what is greatest and most noble would be a very defective
arrangement.

25   The answer to the question we are asking is plain also from the
definition of happiness; for it has been said [12] to be a virtuous activity
of soul, of a certain kind. Of the remaining goods, some must necessarily pre-exist as conditions of happiness, and others are naturally
co-operative and useful as instruments. And this will be found to agree
with what we said at the outset; [13] for we stated the end of political
30 science to be the best end, and political science spends most of its pains
on making the citizens to be of a certain character, viz. good and
capable of noble acts.

It is natural, then, that we call neither ox nor horse nor any other
of the animals happy; for none of them is capable of sharing in such
1100ᵃ activity. For this reason also a boy is not happy; for he is not yet
capable of such acts, owing to his age; and boys who are called happy
are being congratulated by reason of the hopes we have for them. For
there is required, as we said,[14] not only complete virtue but also a
5 complete life, since many changes occur in life, and all manner of
chances, and the most prosperous may fall into great misfortunes in
old age, as is told of Priam in the Trojan Cycle; and one who has
experienced such chances and has ended wretchedly no one calls happy.

10 **10**   Must no one at all, then, be called happy while he lives; must
we, as Solon says, see the end? Even if we are to lay down this doctrine,
is it also the case that a man *is* happy when he is *dead?* Or is not this
quite absurd, especially for us who say that happiness is an activity?
15 But if we do not call the dead man happy, and if Solon does not mean
this, but that one can then safely *call* a man blessed as being at last
beyond evils and misfortunes, this also affords matter for discussion;

_____

¹² 1098ᵃ 16.   ¹³ 1094ᵃ 27.   ¹⁴ 1098ᵃ 16–18.

for both evil and good are thought to exist for a dead man, as much as for one who is alive but not aware of them; e. g. honours and dishonours and the good or bad fortunes of children and in general of descendants. And this also presents a problem; for though a man has lived happily up to old age and has had a death worthy of his life, many reverses may befall his descendants—some of them may be good and attain the life they deserve, while with others the opposite may be the case; and clearly too the degrees of relationship between them and their ancestors may vary indefinitely. It would be odd, then, if the dead man were to share in these changes and become at one time happy, at another wretched; while it would also be odd if the fortunes of the descendants did not for *some* time have *some* effect on the happiness of their ancestors.

But we must return to our first difficulty; for perhaps by a consideration of it our present problem might be solved. Now if we must see the end and only then call a man happy, not as being happy but as having been so before, surely this is a paradox, that when he is happy the attribute that belongs to him is not to be truly predicated of him because we do not wish to call living men happy, on account of the changes that may befall them, and because we have assumed happiness to be something permanent and by no means easily changed, while a single man may suffer many turns of fortune's wheel. For clearly if we were to keep pace with his fortunes, we should often call the same man happy and again wretched, making the happy man out to be a 'chameleon and insecurely based'. Or is this keeping pace with his fortunes quite wrong? Success or failure in life does not depend on these, but human life, as we said,[15] needs these as mere additions, while virtuous activities or their opposites are what constitute happiness or the reverse.

The question we have now discussed confirms our definition. For no function of man has so much permanence as virtuous activities (these are thought to be more durable even than knowledge of the sciences), and of these themselves the most valuable are more durable because those who are happy spend their life most readily and most continuously in these; for this seems to be the reason why we do not forget them. The attribute in question,[16] then, will belong to the happy man, and he will be happy throughout his life; for always, or by preference to everything else, he will be engaged in virtuous action and contemplation, and he will bear the chances of life most nobly and altogether decorously, if he is 'truly good' and 'foursquare beyond reproach'.[17]

---

[15] 1099ᵃ 31–ᵇ 7.   [16] Durability.   [17] Simonides.

Now many events happen by chance, and events differing in importance; small pieces of good fortune or of its opposite clearly do not weigh down the scales of life one way or the other, but a multitude of
25 great events if they turn out well will make life happier (for not only are they themselves such as to add beauty to life, but the way a man deals with them may be noble and good), while if they turn out ill they crush and maim happiness; for they both bring pain with them and
30 hinder many activities. Yet even in these nobility shines through, when a man bears with resignation many great misfortunes, not through insensibility to pain but through nobility and greatness of soul.

If activities are, as we said,[18] what gives life its character, no happy man can become miserable; for he will never do the acts that are
35 hateful and mean. For the man who is truly good and wise, we think,
1101ᵃ bears all the chances of life becomingly and always makes the best of circumstances, as a good general makes the best military use of the army at his command and a good shoemaker makes the best shoes out
5 of the hides that are given him; and so with all other craftsmen. And if this is the case, the happy man can never become miserable—though he will not reach *blessedness*, if he meet with fortunes like those of Priam.

Nor, again, is he many-coloured and changeable; for neither will
10 he be moved from his happy state easily or by any ordinary misadventures, but only by many great ones, nor, if he has had many great misadventures, will he recover his happiness in a short time, but if at all, only in a long and complete one in which he has attained many splendid successes.

Why then should we not say that he is happy who is active in
15 accordance with complete virtue and is sufficiently equipped with external goods, not for some chance period but throughout a complete life? Or must we add 'and who is destined to live thus and die as befits his life'? Certainly the future is obscure to us, while happiness, we claim, is an end and something in every way final. If so, we shall call happy those among living men in whom these conditions are, and are
20 to be, fulfilled—but happy *men*. So much for these questions.

11   [19]That the fortunes of descendants and of all a man's friends should not affect his happiness at all seems a very unfriendly doctrine, and one opposed to the opinions men hold; but since the events that
25 happen are numerous and admit of all sorts of difference, and some

---

[18] l. 9.   [19] Aristotle now returns to the question stated in 1100ᵃ 18–30.

come more near to us and others less so, it seems a long—nay, an infinite—task to discuss each in detail; a general outline will perhaps suffice. If, then, as some of a man's own misadventures have a certain weight and influence on life while others are, as it were, lighter, so too there are differences among the misadventures of our friends taken 30 as a whole, and it makes a difference whether the various sufferings befall the living or the dead (much more even than whether lawless and terrible deeds are presupposed in a tragedy or done on the stage), this difference also must be taken into account; or rather, perhaps, the fact that doubt is felt whether the dead share in any good or evil. 35 For it seems, from these considerations, that even if anything whether 1101ᵇ good or evil penetrates to them, it must be something weak and negligible, either in itself or for them, or if not, at least it must be such in degree and kind as not to make happy those who are not happy nor to take away their blessedness from those who are. The good or bad fortunes of friends, then, seem to have some effects on the dead, 5 but effects of such a kind and degree as neither to make the happy unhappy nor to produce any other change of the kind.

12   These questions having been definitely answered, let us consider 10 whether happiness is among the things that are praised or rather among the things that are prized; for clearly it is not to be placed among *potentialities*.[20] Everything that is praised seems to be praised because it is of a certain kind and is related somehow to something else; for we praise the just or brave man and in general both the good man and virtue itself because of the actions and functions involved, and we 15 praise the strong man, the good runner, and so on, because he is of a certain kind and is related in a certain way to something good and important. This is clear also from the praises of the gods; for it seems absurd that the gods should be referred to our standard, but this *is* done because praise involves a reference, as we said, to something else. But 20 if praise is for things such as we have described, clearly what applies to the best things is not praise, but something greater and better, as is indeed obvious; for what we do to the gods and the most godlike of men is to call them blessed and happy. And so too with good *things*; no one 25 praises happiness as he does justice, but rather calls it blessed, as being something more divine and better.

Eudoxus also seems to have been right in his method of advocating the supremacy of pleasure; he thought that the fact that, though a good, it is not praised indicated it to be better than the things that are praised, and that this is what God and the good are; for by reference 30

---

[20] Cf. *Top.* 126ᵇ 4; *M. M.* 1183ᵇ 20.

to these all other things are judged. *Praise* is appropriate to virtue, for as a result of virtue men tend to do noble deeds; but *encomia* are bestowed on acts, whether of the body or of the soul. But perhaps 35 nicety in these matters is more proper to those who have made a study of encomia; to us it is clear from what has been said that happiness is 1102ᵃ among the things that are prized and perfect. It seems to be so also from the fact that it is a first principle; for it is for the sake of this that we all do all that we do, and the first principle and cause of goods is, we claim, something prized and divine.

5 13   Since happiness is an activity of soul in accordance with perfect virtue, we must consider the nature of virtue; for perhaps we shall thus see better the nature of happiness. The true student of politics, too, is thought to have studied virtue above all things; for he wishes to make 10 his fellow citizens good and obedient to the laws. As an example of this we have the lawgivers of the Cretans and the Spartans, and any others of the kind that there may have been. And if this inquiry belongs to political science, clearly the pursuit of it will be in accordance with our original plan. But clearly the virtue we must study is human virtue; for the good we were seeking was human good and the happiness 15 human happiness. By human virtue we mean not that of the body but that of the soul; and happiness also we call an activity of soul. But if this is so, clearly the student of politics must know somehow the facts about soul, as the man who is to heal the eyes or the body as a whole must know about the eyes or the body; and all the more since politics 20 is more prized and better than medicine; but even among doctors the best educated spend much labour on acquiring knowledge of the body. The student of politics, then, must study the soul, and must study it with these objects in view, and do so just to the extent which is suffi-cient for the questions we are discussing; for further precision is 25 perhaps something more laborious than our purposes require.

Some things are said about it, adequately enough, even in the discus-sions outside our school, and we must use these; e. g. that one element in the soul is irrational and one has a rational principle. Whether these 30 are separated as the parts of the body or of anything divisible are, or are distinct by definition but by nature inseparable, like convex and concave in the circumference of a circle, does not affect the present question.

Of the irrational element one division seems to be widely distributed, and vegetative in its nature, I mean that which causes nutrition and growth; for it is this kind of power of the soul that one must assign to 1102ᵇ all nurslings and to embryos, and this same power to full-grown creatures; this is more reasonable than to assign some different power to them. Now the excellence of this seems to be common to all species and not specifically human; for this part or faculty seems to function 5 most in sleep, while goodness and badness are least manifest in sleep (whence comes the saying that the happy are no better off than the wretched for half their lives; and this happens naturally enough, since sleep is an inactivity of the soul in that respect in which it is called good or bad), unless perhaps to a small extent some of the movements 10 actually penetrate to the soul, and in this respect the dreams of good men are better than those of ordinary people. Enough of this subject, however; let us leave the nutritive faculty alone, since it has by its nature no share in human excellence.

There seems to be also another irrational element in the soul—one which in a sense, however, shares in a rational principle. For we praise the rational principle of the continent man and of the incontinent, and 15 the part of their soul that has such a principle, since it urges them aright and towards the best objects; but there is found in them also another element naturally opposed to the rational principle, which fights against and resists that principle. For exactly as paralysed limbs when we intend to move them to the right turn on the contrary 20 to the left, so is it with the soul; the impulses of incontinent people move in contrary directions. But while in the body we see that which moves astray, in the soul we do not. No doubt, however, we must none the less suppose that in the soul too there is something contrary to the 25 rational principle, resisting and opposing it. In what sense it is distinct from the other elements does not concern us. Now even this seems to have a share in a rational principle, as we said;[21] at any rate in the continent man it obeys the rational principle—and presumably in the temperate and brave man it is still more obedient; for in him it speaks, on all matters, with the same voice as the rational principle.

Therefore the irrational element also appears to be twofold. For the vegetative element in no way shares in a rational principle, but the 30 appetitive, and in general the desiring element in a sense shares in it, in so far as it listens to and obeys it; this is the sense in which we speak of 'taking account' of one's father or one's friends, not that in which we speak of 'accounting' for a mathematical property. That the irrational element is in some sense persuaded by a rational principle is indicated also by the giving of advice and by all reproof and exhorta- 1103[a] tion. And if this element also must be said to have a rational principle, that which has a rational principle (as well as that which has not) will be twofold, one subdivision having it in the strict sense and in itself, and the other having a tendency to obey as one does one's father.

Virtue too is distinguished into kinds in accordance with this difference; for we say that some of the virtues are intellectual and others
5 moral, philosophic wisdom and understanding and practical wisdom
being intellectual, liberality and temperance moral. For in speaking
about a man's character we do not say that he is wise or has understanding but that he is good-tempered or temperate; yet we praise
the wise man also with respect to his state of mind; and of states of
10 mind we call those which merit praise virtues.

BOOK II

1 Virtue, then, being of two kinds, intellectual and moral, intellectual
15 virtue in the main owes both its birth and its growth to teaching (for
which reason it requires experience and time), while moral virtue
comes about as a result of habit, whence also its name *ethike* is one
that is formed by a slight variation from the word *ethos* (habit). From
this it is also plain that none of the moral virtues arises in us by nature;
20 for nothing that exists by nature can form a habit contrary to its nature.
For instance the stone which by nature moves downwards cannot be
habituated to move upwards, not even if one tries to train it by throwing
it up ten thousand times; nor can fire be habituated to move downwards, nor can anything else that by nature behaves in one way be
trained to behave in another. Neither by nature, then, nor contrary
to nature do the virtues arise in us; rather we are adapted by nature to
25 receive them, and are made perfect by habit.

Again, of all the things that come to us by nature we first acquire
the potentiality and later exhibit the activity (this is plain in the case
30 of the senses; for it was not by often seeing or often hearing that we
got these senses, but on the contrary we had them before we used
them, and did not come to have them by using them); but the virtues
we get by first exercising them, as also happens in the case of the arts
as well. For the things we have to learn before we can do them, we
learn by doing them, e. g. men become builders by building and lyre-
1103ᵇ players by playing the lyre; so too we become just by doing just acts,
temperate by doing temperate acts, brave by doing brave acts.

This is confirmed by what happens in states; for legislators make
the citizens good by forming habits in them, and this is the wish of
5 every legislator, and those who do not effect it miss their mark, and
it is in this that a good constitution differs from a bad one.

Again, it is from the same causes and by the same means that every
virtue is both produced and destroyed, and similarly every art; for it
is from playing the lyre that both good and bad lyre-players are pro-

duced. And the corresponding statement is true of builders and of all the rest; men will be good or bad builders as a result of building well or badly. For if this were not so, there would have been no need of a teacher, but all men would have been born good or bad at their craft. This, then, is the case with the virtues also; by doing the acts that we do in our transactions with other men we become just or unjust, and by doing the acts that we do in the presence of danger, and being habituated to feel fear or confidence, we become brave or cowardly. The same is true of appetities and feelings of anger; some men become temperate and good-tempered, others self-indulgent and irascible, by behaving in one way or the other in the appropriate circumstances. Thus, in one word, states of character arise out of like activities. This is why the activities we exhibit must be of a certain kind; it is because the states of character correspond to the differences between these. It makes no small difference, then, whether we form habits of one kind or of another from our very youth; it makes a very great difference, or rather *all* the difference.

2   Since, then, the present inquiry does not aim at theoretical knowledge like the others (for we are inquiring not in order to know what virtue is, but in order to become good, since otherwise our inquiry would have been of no use), we must examine the nature of actions, namely how we ought to do them; for these determine also the nature of the states of character that are produced, as we have said.[1] Now, that we must act according to the right rule is a common principle and must be assumed—it will be discussed later,[2] i. e. both what the right rule is, and how it is related to the other virtues. But this must be agreed 1104[a] upon beforehand, that the whole account of matters of conduct must be given in outline and not precisely, as we said at the very beginning [3] that the accounts we demand must be in accordance with the subject-matter; matters concerned with conduct and questions of what is good for us have no fixity, any more than matters of health. The general account being of this nature, the account of particular cases is yet more lacking in exactness; for they do not fall under any art or precept but the agents themselves must in each case consider what is appropriate to the occasion, as happens also in the art of medicine or of navigation.

But though our present account is of this nature we must give what help we can. First, then, let us consider this, that it is the nature of such things to be destroyed by defect and excess, as we see in the case of strength and of health (for to gain light on things imperceptible we must use the evidence of sensible things); both excessive and defective

---

[1] [a] 31–[b] 25.   [2] vi. 13.   [3] 1094[b] 11–27.

exercise destroys the strength, and similarly drink or food which is above or below a certain amount destroys the health, while that which is proportionate both produces and increases and preserves it. So too 20 is it, then, in the case of temperance and courage and the other virtues. For the man who flies from and fears everything and does not stand his ground against anything becomes a coward, and the man who fears nothing at all but goes to meet every danger becomes rash; and similarly the man who indulges in every pleasure and abstains from none becomes self-indulgent, while the man who shuns every pleasure, as 25 boors do, becomes in a way insensible; temperance and courage, then, are destroyed by excess and defect, and preserved by the mean.

But not only are the sources and causes of their origination and growth the same as those of their destruction, but also the sphere of their actualization will be the same; for this is also true of the things 30 which are more evident to sense, e. g. of strength; it is produced by taking much food and undergoing much exertion, and it is the strong man that will be most able to do these things. So too is it with the virtues; by abstaining from pleasures we become temperate, and it is 35 when we have become so that we are most able to abstain from them; 1104ᵇ and similarly too in the case of courage; for by being habituated to despise things that are terrible and to stand our ground against them we become brave, and it is when we have become so that we shall be most able to stand our ground against them.

3 We must take as a sign of states of character the pleasure or pain 5 that ensues on acts; for the man who abstains from bodily pleasures and delights in this very fact is temperate, while the man who is annoyed at it is self-indulgent, and he who stands his ground against things that are terrible and delights in this or at least is not pained is brave, while the man who is pained is a coward. For moral excellence is concerned with pleasures and pains; it is on account of the pleasure 10 that we do bad things, and on account of the pain that we abstain from noble ones. Hence we ought to have been brought up in a particular way from our very youth, as Plato says,[4] so as both to delight in and to be pained by the things that we ought; for this is the right education. Again, if the virtues are concerned with actions and passions, and every passion and every action is accompanied by pleasure and pain, 15 for this reason also virtue will be concerned with pleasures and pains. This is indicated also by the fact that punishment is inflicted by these means; for it is a kind of cure, and it is the nature of cures to be effected by contraries.

[4] *Laws*, 653 A ff., *Rep.* 401 E–402 A.

Again, as we said but lately,[5] every state of soul has a nature relative to and concerned with the kind of things by which it tends to be made 20 worse or better; but it is by reason of pleasures and pains that men become bad, by pursuing and avoiding these—either the pleasures and pains they ought not or when they ought not or as they ought not, or by going wrong in one of the other similar ways that may be distinguished. Hence men [6] even define the virtues as certain states of impassivity and 25 rest; not well, however, because they speak absolutely, and do not say 'as one ought' and 'as one ought not' and 'when one ought or ought not', and the other things that may be added. We assume, then, that this kind of excellence tends to do what is best with regard to pleasures and pains, and vice does the contrary.

The following facts also may show us that virtue and vice are concerned with these same things. There being three objects of choice and 30 three of avoidance, the noble, the advantageous, the pleasant, and their contraries, the base, the injurious, the painful, about all of these the good man tends to go right and the bad man to go wrong, and especially about pleasure; for this is common to the animals, and also it accompanies all objects of choice; for even the noble and the advantageous 35 appear pleasant.

Again, it has grown up with us all from our infancy; this is why it 1105ᵃ is difficult to rub off this passion, engrained as it is in our life. And we measure even our actions, some of us more and others less, by the rule 5 of pleasure and pain. For this reason, then, our whole inquiry must be about these; for to feel delight and pain rightly or wrongly has no small effect on our actions.

Again, it is harder to fight with pleasure than with anger, to use Heraclitus' phrase, but both art and virtue are always concerned with what is harder; for even the good is better when it is harder. Therefore 10 for this reason also the whole concern both of virtue and of political science is with pleasures and pains; for the man who uses these well will be good, he who uses them badly bad.

That virtue, then, is concerned with pleasures and pains, and that by the acts from which it arises it is both increased and, if they are done differently, destroyed, and that the acts from which it arose are those 15 in which it actualizes itself—let this be taken as said.

4   The question might be asked, what we mean by saying [7] that we must become just by doing just acts, and temperate by doing temperate acts; for if men do just and temperate acts, they are already just and

---

[5] ᵃ 27–ᵇ 3.

[6] Probably Speusippus is referred to.   [7] 1103ᵃ 31–ᵇ 25, 1104ᵃ 27–ᵇ 3.

20 temperate, exactly as, if they do what is in accordance with the laws of grammar and of music, they are grammarians and musicians.

Or is this not true even of the arts? It is possible to do something that is in accordance with the laws of grammar, either by chance or at the suggestion of another. A man will be a grammarian, then, only when 25 he has both done something grammatical and done it grammatically; and this means doing it in accordance with the grammatical knowledge in himself.

Again, the case of the arts and that of the virtues are not similar; for the products of the arts have their goodness in themselves, so that it is enough that they should have a certain character, but if the acts that are in accordance with the virtues have themselves a certain 30 character it does not follow that they are done justly or temperately. The agent also must be in a certain condition when he does them; in the first place he must have knowledge, secondly he must choose the acts, and choose them for their own sakes, and thirdly his action must proceed from a firm and unchangeable character. These are not reckoned in as conditions of the possession of the arts, except the 1105ᵇ bare knowledge; but as a condition of the possession of the virtues knowledge has little or no weight, while the other conditions count not for a little but for everything, i. e. the very conditions which result from often doing just and temperate acts.

5 Actions, then, are called just and temperate when they are such as the just or the temperate man would do; but it is not the man who does these that is just and temperate, but the man who also does them *as* just and temperate men do them. It is well said, then, that it is by 10 doing just acts that the just man is produced, and by doing temperate acts the temperate man; without doing these no one would have even a prospect of becoming good.

But most people do not do these, but take refuge in theory and think they are being philosophers and will become good in this way, 15 behaving somewhat like patients who listen attentively to their doctors, but do none of the things they are ordered to do. As the latter will not be made well in body by such a course of treatment, the former will not be made well in soul by such a course of philosophy.

5 Next we must consider what virtue is. Since things that are found 20 in the soul are of three kinds—passions, faculties, states of character, virtue must be one of these. By passions I mean appetite, anger, fear, confidence, envy, joy, friendly feeling, hatred, longing, emulation, pity, and in general the feelings that are accompanied by pleasure or pain; by faculties the things in virtue of which we are said to be capable

of feeling these, e. g. of becoming angry or being pained or feeling pity; by states of character the things in virtue of which we stand well or badly with reference to the passions, e. g. with reference to anger we stand badly if we feel it violently or too weakly, and well if we feel it moderately; and similarly with reference to the other passions.

Now neither the virtues nor the vices are *passions*, because we are not called good or bad on the ground of our passions, but are so called on the ground of our virtues and our vices, and because we are neither praised nor blamed for our passions (for the man who feels fear or anger is not praised, nor is the man who simply feels anger blamed, but the man who feels it in a certain way), but for our virtues and our vices we *are* praised or blamed.

Again, we feel anger and fear without choice, but the virtues are modes of choice or involve choice. Further, in respect of the passions we are said to be moved, but in respect of the virtues and the vices we are said not to be moved but to be disposed in a particular way.

For these reasons also they are not *faculties*; for we are neither called good nor bad, nor praised nor blamed, for the simple capacity of feeling the passions; again, we have the faculties by nature, but we are not made good or bad by nature; we have spoken of this before.[8]

If, then, the virtues are neither passions nor faculties, all that remains is that they should be *states of character*.

Thus we have stated what virtue is in respect of its genus.

6   We must, however, not only describe virtue as a state of character, but also say what sort of state it is. We may remark, then, that every virtue or excellence both brings into good condition the thing of which it is the excellence and makes the work of that thing be done well; e. g. the excellence of the eye makes both the eye and its work good; for it is by the excellence of the eye that we see well. Similarly the excellence of the horse makes a horse both good in itself and good at running and at carrying its rider and at awaiting the attack of the enemy. Therefore, if this is true in every case, the virtue of man also will be the state of character which makes a man good and which makes him do his own work well.

How this is to happen we have stated already,[9] but it will be made plain also by the following consideration of the specific nature of virtue. In everything that is continuous and divisible it is possible to take more, less, or an equal amount, and that either in terms of the

---

[8] 1103ᵃ 18–ᵇ 2.   [9] 1104ᵃ 11–27.

thing itself or relatively to us; and the equal is an intermediate between
excess and defect. By the intermediate in the object I mean that which
30 is equidistant from each of the extremes, which is one and the same
for all men; by the intermediate relatively to us that which is neither
too much nor too little—and this is not one, nor the same for all.
For instance, if ten is many and two is few, six is the intermediate,
taken in terms of the object; for it exceeds and is exceeded by an equal
35 amount; this is intermediate according to arithmetical proportion. But
the intermediate relatively to us is not to be taken so; if ten pounds
1106ᵇ are too much for a particular person to eat and two too little, it does
not follow that the trainer will order six pounds; for this also is perhaps
too much for the person who is to take it, or too little—too little for
5 Milo,¹⁰ too much for the beginner in athletic exercises. The same is true
of running and wrestling. Thus a master of any art avoids excess and
defect, but seeks the intermediate and chooses this—the intermediate
not in the object but relatively to us.

If it is thus, then, that every art does its work well—by looking to
the intermediate and judging its works by this standard (so that we
10 often say of good works of art that it is not possible either to take away
or to add anything, implying that excess and defect destroy the goodness of works of art, while the mean preserves it; and good artists,
as we say, look to this in their work), and if, further, virtue is more
exact and better than any art, as nature also is, then virtue must have
15 the quality of aiming at the intermediate. I mean moral virtue; for it
is this that is concerned with passions and actions, and in these there
is excess, defect, and the intermediate. For instance, both fear and confidence and appetite and anger and pity and in general pleasure and
pain may be felt both too much and too little, and in both cases not
20 well; but to feel them at the right times, with reference to the right
objects, towards the right people, with the right motive, and in the
right way, is what is both intermediate and best, and this is characteristic of virtue. Similarly with regard to actions also there is excess,
defect, and the intermediate. Now virtue is concerned with passions
25 and actions, in which excess is a form of failure, and so is defect, while
the intermediate is praised and is a form of success; and being praised
and being successful are both characteristics of virtue. Therefore virtue
is a kind of mean, since, as we have seen, it aims at what is intermediate.

Again, it is possible to fail in many ways (for evil belongs to the
class of the unlimited, as the Pythagoreans conjectured, and good to
30 that of the limited), while to succeed is possible only in one way (for
which reason also one is easy and the other difficult—to miss the mark

¹⁰ A famous wrestler.

easy, to hit it difficult); for these reasons also, then, excess and defect are characteristic of vice, and the mean of virtue;

For men are good in but one way, but bad in many.   35

Virtue, then, is a state of character concerned with choice, lying in a mean, i. e. the mean relative to us, this being determined by a rational 1107ᵃ principle, and by that principle by which the man of practical wisdom would determine it. Now it is a mean between two vices, that which depends on excess and that which depends on defect; and again it is a mean because the vices respectively fall short of or exceed what is right in both passions and actions, while virtue both finds and chooses that 5 which is intermediate. Hence in respect of its substance and the definition which states its essence virtue is a mean, with regard to what is best and right an extreme.

But not every action nor every passion admits of a mean; for some have names that already imply badness, e. g. spite, shamelessness, 10 envy, and in the case of actions adultery, theft, murder; for all of these and suchlike things imply by their names that they are themselves bad, and not the excesses or deficiencies of them. It is not possible, then, ever to be right with regard to them; one must always be wrong. Nor does goodness or badness with regard to such things depend on com- 15 mitting adultery with the right woman, at the right time, and in the right way, but simply to do any of them is to go wrong. It would be equally absurd, then, to expect that in unjust, cowardly, and voluptuous action there should be a mean, an excess, and a deficiency; for at that 20 rate there would be a mean of excess and of deficiency, an excess of excess, and a deficiency of deficiency. But as there is no excess and deficiency of temperance and courage because what is intermediate is in a sense an extreme, so too of the actions we have mentioned there is no mean nor any excess and deficiency, but however they are done they are wrong; for in general there is neither a mean of excess and 25 deficiency, nor excess and deficiency of a mean.

7   We must, however, not only make this general statement, but also apply it to the individual facts. For among statements about conduct those which are general apply more widely, but those which are particular are more genuine, since conduct has to do with individual 30 cases, and our statements must harmonize with the facts in these cases. We may take these cases from our table. With regard to feelings of fear and confidence courage is the mean; of the people who exceed, 1107ᵇ he who exceeds in fearlessness has no name (many of the states have no name), while the man who exceeds in confidence is rash, and he who

exceeds in fear and falls short in confidence is a coward. With regard
to pleasures and pains—not all of them, and not so much with regard
5 to the pains—the mean is temperance, the excess self-indulgence. Persons deficient with regard to the pleasures are not often found; hence
such persons also have received no name. But let us call them 'insensible'.

With regard to giving and taking of money the mean is liberality, the
10 excess and the defect prodigality and meanness. In these actions people
exceed and fall short in contrary ways; the prodigal exceeds in spending
and falls short in taking, while the mean man exceeds in taking and falls
short in spending. (At present we are giving a mere outline or summary,
15 and are satisfied with this; later these states will be more exactly
determined.[11]) With regard to money there are also other dispositions
—a mean, magnificence (for the magnificent man differs from the
liberal man; the former deals with large sums, the latter with small
ones), an excess, tastelessness and vulgarity, and a deficiency, nig-
20 gardliness; these differ from the states opposed to liberality, and the
mode of their difference will be stated later.[12]

With regard to honour and dishonour the mean is proper pride, the
excess is known as a sort of 'empty vanity', and the deficiency is undue
humility; and as we said [13] liberality was related to magnificence,
25 differing from it by dealing with small sums, so there is a state similarly related to proper pride, being concerned with small honours while
that is concerned with great. For it is possible to desire honour as one
ought, and more than one ought, and less, and the man who exceeds
in his desires is called ambitious, the man who falls short unambitious,
30 while the intermediate person has no name. The dispositions also are
nameless, except that that of the ambitious man is called ambition.
Hence the people who are at the extremes lay claim to the middle place;
and we ourselves sometimes call the intermediate person ambitious
and sometimes unambitious, and sometimes praise the ambitious man
1108ᵃ and sometimes the unambitious. The reason of our doing this will be
stated in what follows;[14] but now let us speak of the remaining states
according to the method which has been indicated.

With regard to anger also there is an excess, a deficiency, and a
5 mean. Although they can scarcely be said to have names, yet since we
call the intermediate person good-tempered let us call the mean good
temper; of the persons at the extremes let the one who exceeds be
called irascible, and his vice irascibility, and the man who falls short
an inirascible sort of person, and the deficiency inirascibility.

---

11 iv. 1.   12 1122ᵃ 20–9, ᵇ 10–18.
13 ll. 17–19.   14 ᵇ 11–26, 1125ᵇ 14–18.

There are also three other means, which have a certain likeness to one another, but differ from one another: for they are all concerned 10 with intercourse in words and actions, but differ in that one is concerned with truth in this sphere, the other two with pleasantness; and of this one kind is exhibited in giving amusement, the other in all the circumstances of life. We must therefore speak of these too, that we may the better see that in all things the mean is praiseworthy, and 15 the extremes neither praiseworthy nor right, but worthy of blame. Now most of these states also have no names, but we must try, as in the other cases, to invent names ourselves so that we may be clear and easy to follow. With regard to truth, then, the intermediate is a truthful 20 sort of person and the mean may be called truthfulness, while the pretence which exaggerates is boastfulness and the person characterized by it a boaster, and that which understates is mock modesty and the person characterized by it mock-modest. With regard to pleasantness in the giving of amusement the intermediate person is ready-witted and the disposition ready wit, the excess is buffoonery and the person characterized by it a buffoon, while the man who falls short 25 is a sort of boor and his state is boorishness. With regard to the remaining kind of pleasantness, that which is exhibited in life in general, the man who is pleasant in the right way is friendly and the mean is friendliness, while the man who exceeds is an obsequious person if he has no end in view, a flatterer if he is aiming at his own advantage, and the man who falls short and is unpleasant in all circumstances is a quarrelsome and surly sort of person.

There are also means in the passions and concerned with the pas- 30 sions; since shame is not a virtue, and yet praise is extended to the modest man. For even in these matters one man is said to be intermediate, and another to exceed, as for instance the bashful man who is ashamed of everything; while he who falls short or is not ashamed of anything at all is shameless, and the intermediate person is modest. Righteous indignation is a mean between envy and spite, and these 35 states are concerned with the pain and pleasures that are felt at the 1108^b fortunes of our neighbours; the man who is characterized by righteous indignation is pained at undeserved good fortune, the envious man, going beyond him, is pained at all good fortune, and the spiteful man 5 falls so far short of being pained that he even rejoices. But these states there will be an opportunity of describing elsewhere;[15] with regard

---

[15] The reference may be to the whole treatment of the moral virtues in iii. 6–iv. 9, or to the discussion of shame in iv. 9 and an intended corresponding discussion of righteous indignation, or to the discussion of these two states in *Rhet*. ii. 6, 9, 10.

to justice, since it has not one simple meaning, we shall, after describing the other states, distinguish its two kinds and say how each of them
10 is a mean; [16] and similarly we shall treat also of the rational virtues.[17]

8   There are three kinds of disposition, then, two of them vices, involving excess and deficiency respectively, and one a virtue, viz. the mean, and all are in a sense opposed to all; for the extreme states are contrary both to the intermediate state and to each other, and the
15 intermediate to the extremes; as the equal is greater relatively to the less, less relatively to the greater, so the middle states are excessive relatively to the deficiencies, deficient relatively to the excesses, both in passions and in actions. For the brave man appears rash relatively
20 to the coward, and cowardly relatively to the rash man; and similarly the temperate man appears self-indulgent relatively to the insensible man, insensible relatively to the self-indulgent, and the liberal man prodigal relatively to the mean man, mean relatively to the prodigal. Hence also the people at the extremes push the intermediate man each over to the other, and the brave man is called rash by the coward,
25 cowardly by the rash man, and correspondingly in the other cases.
    These states being thus opposed to one another, the greatest contrariety is that of the extremes to each other, rather than to the intermediate; for these are further from each other than from the intermediate, as the great is further from the small and the small
30 from the great than both are from the equal. Again, to the intermediate some extremes show a certain likeness, as that of rashness to courage and that of prodigality to liberality; but the extremes show the greatest unlikeness to each other; now contraries are defined as the things that are furthest from each other, so that things that are
35 further apart are more contrary.
1109ᵃ   To the mean in some cases the deficiency, in some the excess is more opposed; e. g. it is not rashness, which is an excess, but cowardice, which is a deficiency, that is more opposed to courage, and not insensibility, which is a deficiency, but self-indulgence, which
5 is an excess, that is more opposed to temperance. This happens from two reasons, one being drawn from the thing itself; for because one extreme is nearer and liker to the intermediate, we oppose not this but rather its contrary to the intermediate. E. g., since rashness is thought liker and nearer to courage, and cowardice more unlike, we
10 oppose rather the latter to courage; for things that are further from the intermediate are thought more contrary to it. This, then, is one

[16] 1129ᵃ 26–ᵇ 1, 1130ᵃ 14–ᵇ 5, 1131ᵇ 9–15, 1132ᵃ 24–30, 1133ᵇ 30–1134ᵃ 1.
[17] Bk. vi.

cause, drawn from the thing itself; another is drawn from ourselves; for the things to which we ourselves more naturally tend seem more contrary to the intermediate. For instance, we ourselves tend more 15 naturally to pleasures, and hence are more easily carried away towards self-indulgence than towards propriety. We describe as contrary to the mean, then, rather the directions in which we more often go to great lengths; and therefore self-indulgence, which is an excess, is the more contrary to temperance.

9   That moral virtue is a mean, then, and in what sense it is so, and 20 that it is a mean between two vices, the one involving excess, the other deficiency, and that it is such because its character is to aim at what is intermediate in passions and in actions, has been sufficiently stated. Hence also it is no easy task to be good. For in everything it is no easy task to find the middle, e. g. to find the middle of a circle is not 25 for every one but for him who knows; so, too, any one can get angry —that is easy—or give or spend money; but to do this to the right person, to the right extent, at the right time, with the right motive, and in the right way, *that* is not for every one, nor is it easy; wherefore goodness is both rare and laudable and noble.

Hence he who aims at the intermediate must first depart from what 30 is the more contrary to it, as Calypso advises—

Hold the ship out beyond that surf and spray.[18]

For of the extremes one is more erroneous, one less so; therefore, since to hit the mean is hard in the extreme, we must as a second best, as people say, take the least of the evils; and this will be done 35 best in the way we describe.

But we must consider the things towards which we ourselves also 1109^b are easily carried away; for some of us tend to one thing, some to another; and this will be recognizable from the pleasure and the pain we feel. We must drag ourselves away to the contrary extreme; for 5 we shall get into the intermediate state by drawing well away from error, as people do in straightening sticks that are bent.

Now in everything the pleasant or pleasure is most to be guarded against; for we do not judge it impartially. We ought, then, to feel towards pleasure as the elders of the people felt towards Helen, and in all circumstances repeat their saying;[19] for if we dismiss pleasure 10

[18] *Od*. xii. 219 f. (Mackail's trans.). But it was Circe who gave the advice (xii. 108), and the actual quotation is from Odysseus' orders to his steersman.
[19] *Il*. iii. 156–60.

thus we are less likely to go astray. It is by doing this, then, (to sum the matter up) that we shall best be able to hit the mean.

But this is no doubt difficult, and especially in individual cases;
15 for it is not easy to determine both how and with whom and on what provocation and how long one should be angry; for we too sometimes praise those who fall short and call them good-tempered, but sometimes we praise those who get angry and call them manly. The man, however, who deviates little from goodness is not blamed, whether he do so in the direction of the more or of the less, but only the man who deviates more widely; for *he* does not fail to be noticed. But up
20 to what point and to what extent a man must deviate before he becomes blameworthy it is not easy to determine by reasoning, any more than anything else that is perceived by the senses; such things depend on particular facts, and the decision rests with perception. So much, then, is plain, that the intermediate state is in all things
25 to be praised, but that we must incline sometimes towards the excess, sometimes towards the deficiency; for so shall we most easily hit the mean and what is right.

BOOK III

30 1   Since virtue is concerned with passions and actions, and on voluntary passions and actions praise and blame are bestowed, on those that are involuntary pardon, and sometimes also pity, to distinguish the voluntary and the involuntary is presumably necessary for those who are studying the nature of virtue, and useful also for legislators with a view to the assigning both of honours and of punishments.
35   Those things, then, are thought involuntary, which take place
1110ᵃ under compulsion or owing to ignorance; and that is compulsory of which the moving principle is outside, being a principle in which nothing is contributed by the person who is acting or is feeling the passion, e. g. if he were to be carried somewhere by a wind, or by men who had him in their power.

But with regard to the things that are done from fear of greater
5 evils or for some noble object (e. g. if a tyrant were to order one to do something base, having one's parents and children in his power, and if one did the action they were to be saved, but otherwise would be put to death), it may be debated whether such actions are involuntary or voluntary. Something of the sort happens also with regard to the throwing of goods overboard in a storm; for in the abstract no
10 one throws goods away voluntarily, but on condition of its securing

the safety of himself and his crew any sensible man does so. Such actions, then, are mixed, but are more like voluntary actions; for they are worthy of choice at the time when they are done, and the end of an action is relative to the occasion. Both the terms, then, 'voluntary' and 'involuntary', must be used with reference to the moment of action. Now the man acts voluntarily; for the principle that moves 15 the instrumental parts of the body in such actions is in him, and the things of which the moving principle is in a man himself are in his power to do or not to do. Such actions, therefore, are voluntary, but in the abstract perhaps involuntary; for no one would choose any such act in itself.

For such actions men are sometimes even praised, when they 20 endure something base or painful in return for great and noble objects gained; in the opposite case they are blamed, since to endure the greatest indignities for no noble end or for a trifling end is the mark of an inferior person. On some actions praise indeed is not bestowed, but pardon is, when one does what he ought not under pressure which 25 overstrains human nature and which no one could withstand. But some acts, perhaps, we cannot be forced to do, but ought rather to face death after the most fearful sufferings; for the things that 'forced' Euripides' Alcmaeon to slay his mother seem absurd. It is difficult sometimes to determine what should be chosen at what cost, and what should be endured in return for what gain, and yet more difficult to 30 abide by our decisions; for as a rule what is expected is painful, and what we are forced to do is base, whence praise and blame are bestowed on those who have been compelled or have not.

What sort of acts, then, should be called compulsory? We answer 1110ᵇ that without qualification actions are so when the cause is in the external circumstances and the agent contributes nothing. But the things that in themselves are involuntary, but now and in return for these gains are worthy of choice, and whose moving principle is in the agent, are in themselves involuntary, but now and in return 5 for these gains voluntary. They are more like voluntary acts; for actions are in the class of particulars, and the particular acts here are voluntary. What sort of things are to be chosen, and in return for what, it is not easy to state; for there are many differences in the particular cases.

But if some one were to say that pleasant and noble objects have a compelling power, forcing us from without, all acts would be for him compulsory; for it is for these objects that all men do every- 10 thing they do. And those who act under compulsion and unwillingly act with pain, but those who do acts for their pleasantness and nobility do them with pleasure; it is absurd to make external circumstances responsible, and not oneself, as being easily caught by such attractions, and to make oneself responsible for noble acts but the pleasant objects responsible for base acts. The compulsory, then, seems to be that whose moving principle is outside, the person compelled contributing nothing.

Everything that is done by reason of ignorance is *not* voluntary; it is only what produces pain and repentance that is *in*voluntary. for the man who has done something owing to ignorance, and feels not the least vexation at his action, has not acted voluntarily, since he did not know what he was doing, nor yet involuntarily, since he is not pained. Of people, then, who act by reason of ignorance he who repents is thought an involuntary agent, and the man who does not repent may, since he is different, be called a not voluntary agent; for, since he differs from the other, it is better that he should have a name of his own.

Acting by reason of ignorance seems also to be different from acting *in* ignorance; for the man who is drunk or in a rage is thought to act as a result not of ignorance but of one of the causes mentioned, yet not knowingly but in ignorance.

Now every wicked man is ignorant of what he ought to do and what he ought to abstain from, and it is by reason of error of this kind that men become unjust and in general bad; but the term 'involuntary' tends to be used not if a man is ignorant of what is to his advantage—for it is not mistaken purpose that causes involuntary action (it leads rather to wickedness), nor ignorance of the universal (for *that* men are *blamed*), but ignorance of particulars, i. e. of the circumstances of the action and the objects with which it is concerned.

1111ᵃ For it is on these that both pity and pardon depend, since the person who is ignorant of any of these acts involuntarily.

Perhaps it is just as well, therefore, to determine their nature and number. A man may be ignorant, then, of who he is, what he is doing, what or whom he is acting on, and sometimes also what (e. g. what instrument) he is doing it with, and to what end (e. g. he may think his act will conduce to some one's safety), and how he is doing it (e. g. whether gently or violently). Now of all of these no one could be ignorant unless he were mad, and evidently also he could not be ignorant of the agent; for how could he not know himself? But of what he is doing a man might be ignorant, as for instance people say 'it slipped out of their mouths as they were speaking', or 'they did not know it was a secret', as Aeschylus said of the mysteries, or a man might say he 'let it go off when he merely wanted to show its working', as the man did with the catapult. Again, one might think one's son was an enemy, as Merope did, or that a pointed spear had a button on it, or that a stone was pumice-stone; or one might give a man a draught to save him, and really kill him; or one might want to touch a man, as people do in sparring, and really wound him. The 15 ignorance may relate, then, to any of these things, i. e. of the circumstances of the action, and the man who was ignorant of any of these is thought to have acted involuntarily, and especially if he was ignorant on the most important points; and these are thought to be the circumstances of the action and its end. Further, the doing of an act that is called involuntary in virtue of ignorance of this sort must be painful 20 and involve repentance.

Since that which is done under compulsion or by reason of ignorance is involuntary, the voluntary would seem to be that of which the moving principle is in the agent himself, he being aware of the particular circumstances of the action. Presumably acts done by reason of anger or appetite are not rightly called involuntary.[1] For in the 25 first place, on that showing none of the other animals will act voluntarily, nor will children; and secondly, is it meant that we do not do voluntarily *any* of the acts that are due to appetite or anger, or that we do the noble acts voluntarily and the base acts involuntarily? Is not this absurd, when one and the same thing is the cause? But it would surely be odd to describe as involuntary the things one ought to desire; 30 and we ought both to be angry at certain things and to have an appetite for certain things, e. g. for health and for learning. Also what is involuntary is thought to be painful, but what is in accordance with appetite is thought to be pleasant. Again, what is the difference in respect of involuntariness between errors committed upon calculation and those committed in anger? Both are to be avoided, but the irra- 1111ᵇ tional passions are thought not less human than reason is, and therefore also the actions which proceed from anger or appetite are the man's actions. It would be odd, then, to treat them as involuntary.

2   Both the voluntary and the involuntary having been delimited, we must next discuss choice; for it is thought to be most closely bound 5 up with virtue and to discriminate characters better than actions do.

Choice, then, seems to be voluntary, but not the same thing as the voluntary; the latter extends more widely. For both children and the

---

[1] A reference to Pl. *Laws* 863 B, ff., where anger and appetite are coupled with ignorance as sources of wrong action.

lower animals share in voluntary action, but not in choice, and acts done on the spur of the moment we describe as voluntary, but not as chosen.

10   Those who say it is appetite or anger or wish or a kind of opinion do not seem to be right. For choice is not common to irrational creatures as well, but appetite and anger are. Again, the incontinent man acts with appetitie, but not with choice; while the continent man on the 15 contrary acts with choice, but not with appetite. Again, appetite is contrary to choice, but not appetite to appetite. Again, appetite relates to the pleasant and the painful, choice neither to the painful nor to the pleasant.

Still less is it anger; for acts due to anger are thought to be less than any others objects of choice.

20   But neither is it wish, though it seems near to it; for choice cannot relate to impossibles, and if any one said he chose them he would be thought silly; but there may be a wish even for impossibles, e. g. for immortality. And wish may relate to things that could in no way be brought about by one's own efforts, e. g. that a particular actor or 25 athlete should win in a competition; but no one chooses such things, but only the things that he thinks could be brought about by his own efforts. Again, wish relates rather to the end, choice to the means; for instance, we wish to be healthy, but we choose the acts which will make us healthy, and we wish to be happy and say we do, but we cannot well say we choose to be so; for, in general, choice seems to relate to the things that are in our own power.

30   For this reason, too, it cannot be opinion; for opinion is thought to relate to all kinds of things, no less to eternal things and impossible things than to things in our own power; and it is distinguished by its falsity or truth, not by its badness or goodness, while choice is distinguished rather by these.

Now with opinion in general perhaps no one even says it is identical. 1112ᵃ But it is not identical even with any kind of opinion; for by choosing what is good or bad we are men of a certain character, which we are not by holding certain opinions. And we choose to get or avoid something good or bad, but we have opinions about what a thing is or whom it is good for or how it is good for him; we can hardly be said 5 to opine to get or avoid anything. And choice is praised for being related to the right object rather than for being rightly related to it, opinion for being truly related to its object. And we choose what we best know to be good, but we opine what we do not quite know; and it is not the same people that are thought to make the best choices

and to have the best opinions, but some are thought to have fairly
good opinions, but by reason of vice to choose what they should not. 10
If opinion precedes choice or accompanies it, that makes no difference;
for it is not this that we are considering, but whether it is *identical* with
some kind of opinion.

What, then, or what kind of thing is it, since it is none of the things
we have mentioned? It seems to be voluntary, but not all that is voluntary to be an object of choice. Is it, then, what has been decided on 15
by previous deliberation? At any rate choice involves a rational principle and thought. Even the name seems to suggest that it is what is
chosen before other things.

3 Do we deliberate about everything, and is everything a possible
subject of deliberation, or is deliberation impossible about some 20
things? We ought presumably to call not what a fool or a madman
would deliberate about, but what a sensible man would deliberate
about, a subject of deliberation. Now about eternal things no one
deliberates, e. g. about the material universe or the incommensurability
of the diagonal and the side of a square. But no more do we deliberate
about the things that involve movement but always happen in the
same way, whether of necessity or by nature or from any other cause, 25
e. g. the solstices and the risings of the stars; nor about things that
happen now in one way, now in another, e. g. droughts and rains; nor
about chance events, like the finding of treasure. But we do not deliberate even about all human affairs; for instance, no Spartan deliberates
about the best constitution for the Scythians. For none of these things
can be brought about by our own efforts.

We deliberate about things that are in our power and can be done; 30
and these are in fact what is left. For nature, necessity, and chance are
thought to be causes, and also reason and everything that depends on
man. Now every class of men deliberates about the things that can be
done by their own efforts. And in the case of exact and self-contained
sciences there is no deliberation, e. g. about the letters of the alphabet 1112ᵇ
(for we have no doubt how they should be written); but the things
that are brought about by our own efforts, but not always in the same
way, are the things about which we deliberate, e. g. questions of medical
treatment or of money-making. And we do so more in the case of the 5
art of navigation than in that of gymnastics, inasmuch as it has been
less exactly worked out, and again about other things in the same
ratio, and more also in the case of the arts than in that of the sciences;
for we have more doubt about the former. Deliberation is concerned

with things that happen in a certain way for the most part, but in
10 which the event is obscure, and with things in which it is indeterminate.
We call in others to aid us in deliberation on important questions,
distrusting ourselves as not being equal to deciding.

We deliberate not about ends but about means. For a doctor does
not deliberate whether he shall heal, nor an orator whether he shall
persuade, nor a statesman whether he shall produce law and order,
15 nor does any one else deliberate about his end. They assume the end
and consider how and by what means it is to be attained; and if it
seems to be produced by several means they consider by which it is
most easily and best produced, while if it is achieved by one only they
consider how it will be achieved by this and by what means *this* will
be achieved, till they come to the first cause, which in the order of
20 discovery is last. For the person who deliberates seems to investigate
and analyse in the way described as though he were analysing a
geometrical construction [2] (not all investigation appears to be deliberation—for instance mathematical investigations—but all deliberation is investigation), and what is last in the order of analysis seems
to be first in the order of becoming. And if we come on an impossibility,
25 we give up the search, e. g. if we need money and this cannot be got;
but if a thing appears possible we try to do it. By 'possible' things I
mean things that might be brought about by our own efforts; and these
in a sense include things that can be brought about by the efforts of
our friends, since the moving principle is in ourselves. The subject of
investigation is sometimes the instruments, sometimes the use of them;
30 and similarly in the other cases—sometimes the means, sometimes the
mode of using it or the means of bringing it about. It seems, then, as
has been said, that man is a moving principle of actions; now deliberation is about the things to be done by the agent himself, and actions
are for the sake of things other than themselves. For the end cannot
be a subject of deliberation, but only the means; nor indeed can the
1113ᵃ particular facts be a subject of it, as whether this is bread or has been
baked as it should; for these are matters of perception. If we are to
be always deliberating, we shall have to go on to infinity.

The same thing is deliberated upon and is chosen, except that the
object of choice is already determinate, since it is that which has been
5 decided upon as a result of deliberation that is the object of choice.

---

[2] Aristotle has in mind the method of discovering the solution of a geometrical
problem. The problem being to construct a figure of a certain kind, we suppose
it constructed and then analyse it to see if there is some figure by constructing
which we can construct the required figure, and so on till we come to a figure
which our existing knowledge enables us to construct.

For every one ceases to inquire how he is to act when he has brought the moving principle back to himself and to the ruling part of himself; for this is what chooses. This is plain also from the ancient constitutions, which Homer represented; for the kings announced their choices to the people. The object of choice being one of the things in our own 10 power which is desired after deliberation, choice will be deliberate desire of things in our own power; for when we have decided as a result of deliberation, we desire in accordance with our deliberation.

We may take it, then, that we have described choice in outline, and stated the nature of its objects and the fact that it is concerned with means.

4   That *wish* is for the end has already been stated;[3] some think it 15 is for the good, others for the apparent good. Now those who say that the good is the object of wish must admit in consequence that that which the man who does not choose aright wishes for is not an object of wish (for if it is to be so, it must also be good; but it was, if it so happened, bad); while those who say the apparent good is the object 20 of wish must admit that there is no natural object of wish, but only what seems good to each man. Now different things appear good to different people, and, if it so happens, even contrary things.

If these consequences are unpleasing, are we to say that absolutely and in truth the good is the object of wish, but for each person the 25 apparent good; that that which is in truth an object of wish is an object of wish to the good man, while any chance thing may be so to the bad man, as in the case of bodies also the things that are in truth wholesome are wholesome for bodies which are in good condition, while for those that are diseased other things are wholesome—or bitter or sweet or hot or heavy, and so on; since the good man judges each class of things rightly, and in each the truth appears to him? For each state 30 of character has its own ideas of the noble and the pleasant, and perhaps the good man differs from others most by seeing the truth in each class of things, being as it were the norm and measure of them. In most things the error seems to be due to pleasure; for it appears a good when it is not. We therefore choose the pleasant as a good, and 1113ᵇ avoid pain as an evil.

5   The end, then, being what we wish for, the means what we deliberate about and choose, actions concerning means must be according to choice and voluntary. Now the exercise of the virtues is concerned 5

with means. Therefore virtue also is in our own power, and so too vice. For where it is in our power to act it is also in our power not to act, and *vice versa*; so that, if to act, where this is noble, is in our power, not to act, which will be base, will also be in our power, and if not to
10 act, where this is noble, is in our power, to act, which will be base, will also be in our power. Now if it is in our power to do noble or base acts, and likewise in our power not to do them, and this was what being good or bad meant,[4] then it is in our power to be virtuous or vicious.

The saying that 'no one is voluntarily wicked nor involuntarily
15 happy' seems to be partly false and partly true; for no one is involuntarily happy, but wickedness *is* voluntary. Or else we shall have to dispute what has just been said, at any rate, and deny that man is a moving principle or begetter of his actions as of children. But if these facts are evident and we cannot refer actions to moving principles
20 other than those in ourselves, the acts whose moving principles are in us must themselves also be in our power and voluntary.

Witness seems to be borne to this both by individuals in their private capacity and by legislators themselves; for these punish and take vengeance on those who do wicked acts (unless they have acted under compulsion or as a result of ignorance for which they are not them-
25 selves responsible), while they honour those who do noble acts, as though they meant to encourage the latter and deter the former. But no one is encouraged to do the things that are neither in our power nor voluntary; it is assumed that there is no gain in being persuaded not to be hot or in pain or hungry or the like, since we shall experience
30 these feelings none the less. Indeed, we punish a man for his very ignorance, if he is thought responsible for the ignorance, as when penalties are doubled in the case of drunkenness; for the moving principle is in the man himself, since he had the power of not getting drunk and his getting drunk was the cause of his ignorance. And we punish those who are ignorant of anything in the laws that they ought
1114ᵃ to know and that is not difficult, and so too in the case of anything else that they are thought to be ignorant of through carelessness; we assume that it is in their power not to be ignorant, since they have the power of taking care.

But perhaps a man is the kind of man not to take care. Still they are themselves by their slack lives responsible for becoming men of
5 that kind, and men make themselves responsible for being unjust or self-indulgent, in the one case by cheating and in the other by spending

4 1112ᵃ 1 f.

their time in drinking bouts and the like; for it is activities exercised
on particular objects that make the corresponding character. This is
plain from the case of people training for any contest or action; they
practise the activity the whole time. Now not to know that it is from
the exercise of activities on particular objects that states of char- 10
acter are produced is the mark of a thoroughly senseless person.
Again, it is irrational to suppose that a man who acts unjustly does
not wish to be unjust or a man who acts self-indulgently to be self-
indulgent. But if *without* being ignorant a man does the things which
will make him unjust, he will be unjust voluntarily. Yet it does not
follow that if he wishes he will cease to be unjust and will be just.
For neither does the man who is ill become well on those terms. We 15
may suppose a case in which he is ill voluntarily, through living incontinently and disobeying his doctors. In that case it was *then* open to
him not to be ill, but not now, when he has thrown away his chance,
just as when you have let a stone go it is too late to recover it; but yet
it was in your power to throw it, since the moving principle was in you.
So, too, to the unjust and to the self-indulgent man it was open at the 20
beginning not to become men of this kind, and so they are unjust and
self-indulgent voluntarily; but now that they have become so it is not
possible for them not to be so.

But not only are the vices of the soul voluntary, but those of the
body also for some men, whom we accordingly blame; while no one
blames those who are ugly by nature, we blame those who are so owing
to want of exercise and care. So it is, too, with respect to weakness 25
and infirmity; no one would reproach a man blind from birth or by
disease or from a blow, but rather pity him, while every one would
blame a man who was blind from drunkenness or some other form of
self-indulgence. Of vices of the body, then, those in our own power are
blamed, those not in our power are not. And if this be so, in the other 30
cases also the vices that are blamed must be in our own power.

Now some one may say that all men desire the apparent good, but
have no control over the appearance, but the end appears to each man
in a form answering to his character. We reply that if each man is 1114^b
somehow responsible for his state of mind, he will also be himself
somehow responsible for the appearance; but if not, no one is responsible for his own evildoing, but every one does evil acts through
ignorance of the end, thinking that by these he will get what is best, 5
and the aiming at the end is not self-chosen but one must be born with
an eye, as it were, by which to judge rightly and choose what is truly
good, and he is well endowed by nature who is well endowed with this.

For it is what is greatest and most noble, and what we cannot get or
10 learn from another, but must have just such as it was when given
us at birth, and to be well and nobly endowed with this will be perfect
and true excellence of natural endowment. If this is true, then, how
will virtue be more voluntary than vice? To both men alike, the good
15 and the bad, the end appears and is fixed by nature or however it may
be, and it is by referring everything else to this that men do whatever
they do.

Whether, then, it is not by nature that the end appears to each man
such as it does appear, but something also depends on him, or the end is
natural but because the good man adopts the means voluntarily virtue
20 is voluntary, vice also will be none the less voluntary; for in the case of
the bad man there is equally present that which depends on himself
in his actions even if not in his end. If, then, as is asserted, the virtues
are voluntary (for we are ourselves somehow partly responsible for our
states of character, and it is by being persons of a certain kind that
we assume the end to be so and so), the vices also will be voluntary;
25 for the same is true of them.

With regard to the virtues in *general* we have stated their genus
in outline, viz. that they are means and that they are states of character, and that they tend, and by their own nature, to the doing of
the acts by which they are produced, and that they are in our power
30 and voluntary, and act as the right rule prescribes. But actions and
states of character are not voluntary in the same way; for we are
masters of our actions from the beginning right to the end, if we know
the particular facts, but though we control the beginning of our states
1115ᵃ of character the gradual progress is not obvious, any more than it is in
illnesses; because it was in our power, however, to act in this way or not
in this way, therefore the states are voluntary.

Let us take up the several virtues, however, and say which they
are and what sort of things they are concerned with and how they are
5 concerned with them; at the same time it will become plain how many
they are. And first let us speak of courage.

6   That it is a mean with regard to feelings of fear and confidence has
already been made evident;[5] and plainly the things we fear are terrible
things, and these are, to speak without qualification, evils; for which
10 reason people even define fear as expectation of evil. Now we fear all
evils, e. g. disgrace, poverty, disease, friendlessness, death, but the
brave man is not thought to be concerned with all; for to fear some

[5] 1107ᵃ 33–ᵇ 4.

things is even right and noble, and it is base not to fear them—e. g. disgrace; he who fears this is good and modest, and he who does not is shameless. He is, however, by some people called brave, by a transference of the word to a new meaning; for he has in him something which 15 is like the brave man, since the brave man also is a fearless person. Poverty and disease we perhaps ought not to fear, nor in general the things that do not proceed from vice and are not due to a man himself. But not even the man who is fearless of these is brave. Yet we apply the word to him also in virtue of a similarity; for some who in 20 the dangers of war are cowards are liberal and are confident in face of the loss of money. Nor is a man a coward if he fears insult to his wife and children or envy or anything of the kind; nor brave if he is confident when he is about to be flogged. With what sort of terrible things, then, is the brave man concerned? Surely with the greatest; for no one 25 is more likely than he to stand his ground against what is awe-inspiring. Now death is the most terrible of all things; for it is the end, and nothing is thought to be any longer either good or bad for the dead. But the brave man would not seem to be concerned even with death in *all* circumstances, e. g. at sea or in disease. In what circumstances, then? Surely in the noblest. Now such deaths are those in battle; for these 30 take place in the greatest and noblest danger. And these are correspondingly honoured in city-states and at the courts of monarchs. Properly, then, he will be called brave who is fearless in face of a noble death, and of all emergencies that involve death; and the emergencies of war are in the highest degree of this kind. Yet at sea also, and in 35 disease; the brave man is fearless, but not in the same way as the sea- 1115^b men; for he has given up hope of safety, and is disliking the thought of death in this shape, while they are hopeful because of their experience. At the same time, we show courage in situations where there is the 5 opportunity of showing prowess or where death is noble; but in these forms of death neither of these conditions is fulfilled.

7 What is terrible is not the same for all men; but we say there are things terrible even beyond human strength. These, then, are terrible to every one—at least to every sensible man; but the terrible things that are *not* beyond human strength differ in magnitude and degree, and so too do the things that inspire confidence. Now the brave man 10 is as dauntless as man may be. Therefore, while he will fear even the things that are not beyond human strength, he will face them as he ought and as the rule directs, for honour's sake; for this is the end of virtue. But it is possible to fear these more, or less, and again to fear

15 things that are not terrible as if they were. Of the faults that are committed one consists in fearing what one should not, another in fearing as we should not, another in fearing when we should not, and so on; and so too with respect to the things that inspire confidence. The man, then, who faces and who fears the right things and from the right motive, in the right way and at the right time, and who feels confidence under the corresponding conditions, is brave; for the brave man feels and acts according to the merits of the case and in whatever way 20 the rule directs. Now the end of every activity is conformity to the corresponding state of character. This is true, therefore, of the brave man as well as of others. But courage is noble. Therefore the end also is noble; for each thing is defined by its end. Therefore it is for a noble end that the brave man endures and acts as courage directs.

Of those who go to excess he who exceeds in fearlessness has no name 25 (we have said previously that many states of character have no names [6]), but he would be a sort of madman or insensible person if he feared nothing, neither earthquakes nor the waves, as they say the Celts do not; while the man who exceeds in confidence about what really is terrible is rash. The rash man, however, is also thought to 30 be boastful and only a pretender to courage; at all events, as the brave man *is* with regard to what is terrible, so the rash man wishes to *appear*; and so he imitates him in situations where he can. Hence also most of them are a mixture of rashness and cowardice; for, while in these situations they display confidence, they do not hold their ground against what is really terrible. The man who exceeds in fear is a 35 coward; for he fears both what he ought not and as he ought not, and 1116ª all the similar characterizations attach to him. He is lacking also in confidence; but he is more conspicuous for his excess of fear in painful situations. The coward, then, is a despairing sort of person; for he fears everything. The brave man, on the other hand, has the opposite disposition; for confidence is the mark of a hopeful disposition. The coward, the rash man, and the brave man, then, are concerned with 5 the same objects but are differently disposed towards them; for the first two exceed and fall short, while the third holds the middle, which is the right, position; and rash men are precipitate, and wish for dangers beforehand but draw back when they are in them, while brave men are keen in the moment of action, but quiet beforehand.

10 As we have said, then, courage is a mean with respect to things that inspire confidence or fear, in the circumstances that have been stated; [7] and it chooses or endures things because it is noble to do so, or because

[6] 1107ᵇ 2, Cf. 1107ᵇ 29, 1108ª 5.   [7] Ch. 6.

it is base not to do so.[8] But to die to escape from poverty or love or anything painful is not the mark of a brave man, but rather of a coward; for it is softness to fly from what is troublesome, and such a man endures death not because it is noble but to fly from evil.

8   Courage, then, is something of this sort, but the name is also 15 applied to five other kinds. (1) First comes the courage of the citizen-soldier; for this is most like true courage. Citizen-soldiers seem to face dangers because of the penalties imposed by the laws and the reproaches they would otherwise incur, and because of the honours they win by such action; and therefore those peoples seem to be bravest among 20 whom cowards are held in dishonour and brave men in honour. This is the kind of courage that Homer depicts, e. g. in Diomede and in Hector:

First will Polydamas be to heap reproach on me then; [9]

and

For Hector one day 'mid the Trojans shall utter his vaulting 25
    harangue:
"Afraid was Tydeides, and fled from my face." [10]

This kind of courage is most like to that which we described earlier,[11] because it is due to virtue; for it is due to shame and to desire of a noble object (i. e. honour) and avoidance of disgrace, which is ignoble. One might rank in the same class even those who are compelled by 30 their rulers; but they are inferior, inasmuch as they do what they do not from shame but from fear, and to avoid not what is disgraceful but what is painful; for their masters compel them, as Hector [12] does:

But if I shall spy any dastard that cowers far from the fight,
Vainly will such an one hope to escape from the dogs.   35

And those who give them their posts, and beat them if they retreat, do the same, and so do those who draw them up with trenches or something 1116[b] of the sort behind them; all of these apply compulsion. But one ought to be brave not under compulsion but because it is noble to be so.

(2) Experience with regard to particular facts is also thought to be courage; this is indeed the reason why Socrates thought courage was knowledge. Other people exhibit this quality in other dangers, 5 and professional soldiers exhibit it in the dangers of war; for there

---

[8] 1115[b] 11-24.   [9] *Il.* xxii. 100.   [10] *Il.* viii. 148, 149.   [11] Chs. 6, 7.
[12] Aristotle's quotation is more like *Il.* ii. 391-3, where Agamemnon speaks, than xv. 348-51, where Hector speaks.

seem to be many empty alarms in war, of which these have had the most comprehensive experience; therefore they seem brave, because the others do·not know the nature of the facts. Again, their experience
10 makes them most capable in attack and in defence, since they can use their arms and have the kind that are likely to be best both for attack and for defence; therefore they fight like armed men against unarmed or like trained athletes against amateurs; for in such contests too it is not the bravest men that fight best, but those who are strongest
15 and have their bodies in the best condition. Professional soldiers turn cowards, however, when the danger puts too great a strain on them and they are inferior in numbers and equipment; for they are the first to fly, while citizen-forces die at their posts, as in fact happened at the temple of Hermes.¹³ For to the latter flight is disgraceful and death is
20 preferable to safety on those terms; while the former from the very beginning faced the danger on the assumption that they were stronger, and when they know the facts they fly, fearing death more than disgrace; but the brave man is not that sort of person.

(3) Passion also is sometimes reckoned as courage; those who act from passion, like wild beasts rushing at those who have wounded them,
25 are thought to be brave, because brave men also are passionate; for passion above all things is eager to rush on danger, and hence Homer's 'put strength into his passion'¹⁴ and 'aroused their spirit and passion'¹⁵ and 'hard he breathed panting'¹⁶ and 'his blood boiled'.¹⁷ For all such expressions seem to indicate the stirring and onset of
30 passion. Now brave men act for honour's sake, but passion aids them; while wild beasts act under the influence of pain; for they attack because they have been wounded or because they are afraid, since if they are in a forest they do not come near one. Thus they are not brave because, driven by pain and passion, they rush on danger with-
35 out foreseeing any of the perils, since at that rate even asses would be brave when they are hungry; for blows will not drive them from
1117ᵃ their food; and lust also makes adulterers do many daring things. [Those creatures are not brave, then, which are driven on to danger by pain or passion.] The 'courage' that is due to passion seems to be the most natural, and to be courage if choice and motive be added.
5   Men, then, as well as beasts, suffer pain when they are angry, and are pleased when they exact their revenge; those who fight for these

---

¹³ The reference is to a battle at Coronea in the Sacred War, c. 353 ʙ. c., in which the Phocians defeated the citizens of Coronea and some Boeotian regulars.
¹⁴ This is a conflation of *Il.* xi. 11 or xiv. 151 and xvi. 529.
¹⁵ Cf. *Il.* v. 470, xv. 232, 594.   ¹⁶ Cf. *Od.* xxiv. 318 f.
¹⁷ The phrase does not occur in Homer; it is found in Theocr. xx. 15.

reasons, however, are pugnacious but not brave; for they do not act for honour's sake nor as the rule directs, but from strength of feeling; they have, however, something akin to courage.

(4) Nor are sanguine people brave; for they are confident in danger 10 only because they have conquered often and against many foes. Yet they closely resemble brave men, because both are confident; but brave men are confident for the reasons stated earlier,[18] while these are so because they think they are the strongest and can suffer nothing. (Drunken men also behave in this way; they become sanguine.) When their adventures do not succeed, however, they run away; but 15 it was [18] the mark of a brave man to face things that are, and seem, terrible for a man, because it is noble to do so and disgraceful not to do so. Hence also it is thought the mark of a braver man to be fearless and undisturbed in sudden alarms than to be so in those that are foreseen; for it must have proceeded more from a state of character, because less from preparation; acts that are foreseen may be chosen 20 by calculation and rule, but sudden actions must be in accordance with one's state of character.

(5) People who are ignorant of the danger also appear brave, and they are not far removed from those of a sanguine temper, but are inferior inasmuch as they have no self-reliance while these have. Hence also the sanguine hold their ground for a time; but those who have 25 been deceived about the facts fly if they know or suspect that these are different from what they supposed, as happened to the Argives when they fell in with the Spartans and took them for Sicyonians.[19]

9   We have, then, described the character both of brave men and of those who are thought to be brave.

Though courage is concerned with feelings of confidence and of fear, it is not concerned with both alike, but more with the things that inspire fear; for he who is undisturbed in face of these and bears 30 himself as he should towards these is more truly brave than the man who does so towards the things that inspire confidence. It is for facing what is painful, then, as has been said,[20] that men are called brave. Hence also courage involves pain, and is justly praised; for it is harder to face what is painful than to abstain from what is pleasant. Yet the end which courage sets before it would seem to be pleasant, but to be 35 concealed by the attending circumstances, as happens also in athletic 1117ᵇ

---

[18] 1115ᵇ 11–24.
[19] At the Long Walls of Corinth, 392 ʙ. ᴄ. Cf. Xen. *Hell.* iv. 4. 10.
[20] 1115ᵇ 7–13.

contests; for the end at which boxers aim is pleasant—the crown and
the honours—but the blows they take are distressing to flesh and
5 blood, and painful, and so is their whole exertion; and because the blows
and the exertions are many the end, which is but small, appears to have
nothing pleasant in it. And so, if the case of courage is similar, death
and wounds will be painful to the brave man and against his will, but
he will face them because it is noble to do so or because it is base not to
do so. And the more he is possessed of virtue in its entirety and the
10 happier he is, the more he will be pained at the thought of death; for
life is best worth living for such a man, and he is knowingly losing the
greatest goods, and this is painful. But he is none the less brave, and
perhaps all the more so, because he chooses noble deeds of war at that
15 cost. It is not the case, then, with all the virtues that the exercise of
them is pleasant, except in so far as it reaches its end. But it is quite
possible that the best soldiers may be not men of this sort but those
who are less brave but have no other good; for these are ready to face
danger, and they sell their life for trifling gains.
20   So much, then, for courage; it is not difficult to grasp its nature in
outline, at any rate, from what has been said.

After courage let us speak of temperance; for these seem to be the
virtues of the irrational parts.

10   We have said [21] that temperance is a mean with regard to pleas-
25 ures (for it is less, and not in the same way, concerned with pains);
self-indulgence also is manifested in the same sphere. Now, therefore,
let us determine with what sort of pleasures they are concerned. We
may assume the distinction between bodily pleasures and those of the
soul, such as love of honour and love of learning; for the lover of each
30 of these delights in that of which he is a lover, the body being in no way
affected, but rather the mind; but men who are concerned with such
pleasures are called neither temperate nor self-indulgent. Nor, again,
are those who are concerned with the other pleasures that are not bodily; for those who are fond of hearing and telling stories and who spend
35 their days on anything that turns up are called gossips, but not self-
indulgent, nor are those who are pained at the loss of money or of friends.
1118ᵃ   Temperance must be concerned with bodily pleasures, but not all
even of these; for those who delight in objects of vision, such as colours
5 and shapes and painting, are called neither temperate nor self-
indulgent; yet it would seem possible to delight even in these either as
one should or to excess or to a deficient degree.

[21] 1107ᵇ 4–6.

And so too is it with objects of hearing; no one calls those who delight extravagantly in music or acting self-indulgent, nor those who do so as they ought temperate.

Nor do we apply these names to those who delight in odour, unless it be incidentally; we do not call those self-indulgent who delight in the odour of apples or roses or incense, but rather those who delight in 10 the odour of unguents or of dainty dishes; for self-indulgent people delight in these because these remind them of the objects of their appetite. And one may see even other people, when they are hungry, delighting in the smell of food; but to delight in this kind of thing is 15 the mark of the self-indulgent man; for these are objects of appetite to him.

Nor is there in animals other than man any pleasure connected with these senses, except incidentally. For dogs do not delight in the scent of hares, but in the eating of them, but the scent told them the hares 20 were there; nor does the lion delight in the lowing of the ox, but in eating it; but he perceived by the lowing that it was near, and therefore appears to delight in the lowing; and similarly he does not delight because he sees 'a stag or a wild goat',[22] but because he is going to make a meal of it. Temperance and self-indulgence, however, are concerned with the kind of pleasures that the other animals share in, which there- 25 fore appear slavish and brutish; these are touch and taste. But even of taste they appear to make little or no use; for the business of taste is the discriminating of flavours, which is done by wine-tasters and people who season dishes; but they hardly take pleasure in making these discriminations, or at least self-indulgent people do not, but in 30 the actual enjoyment, which in all cases comes through touch, both in the case of food and in that of drink and in that of sexual inter- course. This is why a certain gourmand prayed that his throat might become longer than a crane's, implying that it was the contact that he 1118ᵇ took pleasure in. Thus the sense with which self-indulgence is con- nected is the most widely shared of the senses; and self-indulgence would seem to be justly a matter of reproach, because it attaches to us not as men but as animals. To delight in such things, then, and to love them above all others, is brutish. For even of the pleasures of touch the most liberal have been eliminated, e. g. those produced in the gym- nasium by rubbing and by the consequent heat; for the contact char- 5 acteristic of the self-indulgent man does not affect the whole body but only certain parts.

---

[22] *Il.* iii. 24.

11   Of the appetites some seem to be common, others to be peculiar
to individuals and acquired; e. g. the appetite for food is natural, since
10 every one who is without it craves for food or drink, and sometimes for
both, and for love also (as Homer says) [23] if he is young and lusty; but
not every one craves for this or that kind of nourishment or love, nor
for the same things. Hence such craving appears to be our very own.
Yet it has of course something natural about it; for different things
are pleasant to different kinds of people, and some things are more
15 pleasant to every one than chance objects. Now in the natural appetites few go wrong, and only in one direction, that of excess; for to eat
or drink whatever offers itself till one is surfeited is to exceed the natural
amount, since natural appetite is the replenishment of one's deficiency.
Hence these people are called belly-gods, this implying that they
20 fill their belly beyond what is right. It is people of entirely slavish
character that become like this. But with regard to the pleasures
peculiar to individuals many people go wrong and in many ways.
For while the people who are 'fond of so and so' are so called because
they delight either in the wrong things, or more than most people do,
25 or in the wrong way, the self-indulgent exceed in all three ways; they
both delight in some things that they ought not to delight in (since
they are hateful), and if one ought to delight in some of the things
they delight in, they do so more than one ought and than most men do.
   Plainly, then, excess with regard to pleasures is self-indulgence and
is culpable; with regard to pains one is not, as in the case of courage,
30 called temperate for facing them or self-indulgent for not doing so, but
the self-indulgent man is so called because he is pained more than he
ought at not getting pleasant things (even his pain being caused by
pleasure), and the temperate man is so called because he is not pained
at the absence of what is pleasant and at his abstinence from it.
1119ᵃ   The self-indulgent man, then, craves for all pleasant things or those
that are most pleasant, and is led by his appetite to choose these at the
cost of everything else; hence he is pained both when he fails to get
them and when he is merely craving for them (for appetite involves
5 pain); but it seems absurd to be pained for the sake of pleasure. People
who fall short with regard to pleasures and delight in them less than
they should are hardly found; for such insensibility is not human.
Even the other animals distinguish different kinds of food and enjoy
some and not others; and if there is any one who finds nothing pleasant
and nothing more attractive than anything else, he must be something
10 quite different from a man; this sort of person has not received a name

---

[23] *Il.* xxiv. 130.

because he hardly occurs. The temperate man occupies a middle position with regard to these objects. For he neither enjoys the things that the self-indulgent man enjoys most—but rather dislikes them—nor in general the things that he should not, nor anything of this sort to excess, nor does he feel pain or craving when they are absent, or does so only to a moderate degree, and not more than he should, nor when he should 15 not, and so on; but the things that, being pleasant, make for health or for good condition, he will desire moderately and as he should, and also other pleasant things if they are not hindrances to these ends, or contrary to what is noble, or beyond his means. For he who neglects these conditions loves such pleasures more than they are worth, but the temperate man is not that sort of person, but the sort of person that 20 the right rule prescribes.

12   Self-indulgence is more like a voluntary state than cowardice. For the former is actuated by pleasure, the latter by pain, of which the one is to be chosen and the other to be avoided; and pain upsets and destroys the nature of the person who feels it, while pleasure does nothing of the sort. Therefore self-indulgence is more voluntary. Hence also it is more 25 a matter of reproach; for it is easier to become accustomed to its objects, since there are many things of this sort in life, and the process of habituation to them is free from danger, while with terrible objects the reverse is the case. But cowardice would seem to be voluntary in a different degree from its particular manifestations; for it is itself painless, but in these we are upset by pain, so that we even throw down our arms and disgrace ourselves in other ways; hence our acts are even 30 thought to be done under compulsion. For the self-indulgent man, on the other hand, the particular acts are voluntary (for he does them with craving and desire), but the whole state is less so; for no one craves to be self-indulgent.

The name self-indulgence is applied also to childish faults; for they bear a certain resemblance to what we have been considering. Which is called after which, makes no difference to our present purpose; plainly, 1119^b however, the later is called after the earlier. The transference of the name seems not a bad one; for that which desires what is base and which develops quickly ought to be kept in a chastened condition, and these characteristics belong above all to appetite and to the child, since children in fact live at the beck and call of appetite, and it is in them 5 that the desire for what is pleasant is strongest. If, then, it is not going to be obedient and subject to the ruling principle, it will go to great lengths; for in an irrational being the desire for pleasure is insatiable

even if it tries every source of gratification, and the exercise of appetite
10 increases its innate force, and if appetites are strong and violent they
even expel the power of calculation. Hence they should be moderate
and few, and should in no way oppose the rational principle—and this
is what we call an obedient and chastened state—and as the child should
live according to the direction of his tutor, so the appetitive element
15 should live according to rational principle. Hence the appetitive element in a temperate man should harmonize with the rational principle;
for the noble is the mark at which both aim, and the temperate man
craves for the things he ought, as he ought, and when he ought; and
this is what rational principle directs.

Here we conclude our account of temperance.

20   *BOOK IV*

1   Let us speak next of liberality. It seems to be the mean with regard
to wealth; for the liberal man is praised not in respect of military
matters, nor of those in respect of which the temperate man is praised,
25 nor of judicial decisions, but with regard to the giving and taking of
wealth, and especially in respect of giving. Now by 'wealth' we mean
all the things whose value is measured by money. Further, prodigality
and meanness are excesses and defects with regard to wealth; and
30 meanness we always impute to those who care more than they ought for
wealth, but we sometimes apply the word 'prodigality' in a complex
sense; for we call those men prodigals who are incontinent and spend
money on self-indulgence. Hence also they are thought the poorest
characters; for they combine more vices than one. Therefore the application of the word to them is not its proper use; for a 'prodigal' means
1120ª a man who has a single evil quality, that of wasting his substance;
since a prodigal is one who is being ruined by his own fault, and the
wasting of substance is thought to be a sort of ruining of oneself, life
being held to depend on possession of substance.

This, then, is the sense in which we take the word 'prodigality'. Now
5 the things that have a use may be used either well or badly; and riches
is a useful thing; and everything is used best by the man who has the
virtue concerned with it; riches, therefore, will be used best by the man
who has the virtue concerned with wealth; and this is the liberal man.
Now spending and giving seem to be the using of wealth; taking and
keeping rather the possession of it. Hence it is more the mark of the
10 liberal man to give to the right people than to take from the right
sources and not to take from the wrong. For it is more characteristic

of virtue to do good than to have good done to one, and more characteristic to do what is noble than not to do what is base; and it is
not hard to see that giving implies doing good and doing what is noble,
and taking implies having good done to one or not acting basely. And 15
gratitude is felt towards him who gives, not towards him who does not
take, and praise also is bestowed more on him. It is easier, also, not to
take than to give; for men are apter to give away their own too little
than to take what is another's. Givers, too, are called liberal; but those
who do not take are not praised for liberality but rather for justice; 20
while those who take are hardly praised at all. And the liberal are almost
the most loved of all virtuous characters, since they are useful; and this
depends on their giving.

Now virtuous actions are noble and done for the sake of the noble.
Therefore the liberal man, like other virtuous men, will give for the sake
of the noble, and rightly; for he will give to the right people, the right 25
amounts, and at the right time, with all the other qualifications that
accompany right giving; and that too with pleasure or without pain;
for that which is virtuous is pleasant or free from pain—least of all
will it be painful. But he who gives to the wrong people or not for the
sake of the noble but for some other cause, will be called not liberal but
by some other name. Nor is he liberal who gives with pain; for he would 30
prefer the wealth to the noble act, and this is not characteristic of a
liberal man. But no more will the liberal man take from wrong sources;
for such taking is not characteristic of the man who sets no store by
wealth. Nor will he be a ready asker; for it is not characteristic of a
man who confers benefits to accept them lightly. But he will take from
the right sources, e. g. from his own possessions, not as something 1120^b
noble but as a necessity, that he may have something to give. Nor
will he neglect his own property, since he wishes by means of this
to help others. And he will refrain from giving to anybody and everybody, that he may have something to give to the right people, at the
right time, and where it is noble to do so. It is highly characteristic of a
liberal man also to go to excess in giving, so that he leaves too little for 5
himself; for it is the nature of a liberal man not to look to himself.
The term 'liberality' is used relatively to a man's substance; for liberality resides not in the multitude of the gifts but in the state of character of the giver, and this is relative to the giver's substance. There is
therefore nothing to prevent the man who gives less from being the
more liberal man, if he has less to give. Those are thought to be more 10
liberal who have not made their wealth but inherited it; for in the first
place they have no experience of want, and secondly all men are fonder

of their own productions, as are parents and poets. It is not easy for the
15 liberal man to be rich, since he is not apt either at taking or at keeping,
but at giving away, and does not value wealth for its own sake but as a
means to giving. Hence comes the charge that is brought against fortune, that those who deserve riches most get it least. But it is not unreasonable that it should turn out so; for he cannot have wealth, any more
20 than anything else, if he does not take pains to have it. Yet he will not
give to the wrong people nor at the wrong time, and so on; for he would
no longer be acting in accordance with liberality, and if he spent on
these objects he would have nothing to spend on the right objects.
For, as has been said, he is liberal who spends according to his sub-
25 stance and on the right objects; and he who exceeds is prodigal. Hence
we do not call despots prodigal; for it is thought not easy for them to
give and spend beyond the amount of their possessions. Liberality,
then, being a mean with regard to giving and taking of wealth, the liberal man will both give and spend the right amounts and on the right
30 objects, alike in small things and in great, and that with pleasure; he
will also take the right amounts and from the right sources. For, the
virtue being a mean with regard to both, he will do both as he ought;
since this sort of taking accompanies proper giving, and that which is
not of this sort is contrary to it, and accordingly the giving and taking
that accompany each other are present together in the same man,
1121ᵃ while the contrary kinds evidently are not. But if he happens to spend
in a manner contrary to what is right and noble, he will be pained, but
moderately and as he ought; for it is the mark of virtue both to be
pleased and to be pained at the right objects and in the right way.
5 Further, the liberal man is easy to deal with in money matters; for he
can be got the better of, since he sets no store by money, and is more
annoyed if he has not spent something that he ought than pained if
he has spent something that he ought not, and does not agree with the
saying of Simonides.

The prodigal errs in these respects also; for he is neither pleased nor
pained at the right things or in the right way; this will be more evident
10 as we go on. We have said [1] that prodigality and meanness are excesses
and deficiencies, and in two things, in giving and in taking; for we
include spending under giving. Now prodigality exceeds in giving and
not taking, and falls short in taking, while meanness falls short in giv-
15 ing, and exceeds in taking, except in small things.

The characteristics of prodigality are not often combined; for it is
not easy to give to all if you take from none; private persons soon

[1] 1119ᵇ 27.

exhaust their substance with giving, and it is to these that the name of prodigals is applied—though a man of this sort would seem to be in no small degree better than a mean man. For he is easily cured both 20 by age and by poverty, and thus he may move towards the middle state. For he has the characteristics of the liberal man, since he both gives and refrains from taking, though he does neither of these in the right manner or well. Therefore if he were brought to do so by habituation or in some other way, he would be liberal; for he will then give to the right people, and will not take from the wrong sources. This is why 25 he is thought to have not a bad character; it is not the mark of a wicked or ignoble man to go to excess in giving and not taking, but only of a foolish one. The man who is prodigal in this way is thought much better than the mean man both for the aforesaid reasons and because he benefits many while the other benefits no one, not even himself.

But most prodigal people, as has been said,[2] also take from the 30 wrong sources, and are in this respect mean. They become apt to take because they wish to spend and cannot do this easily; for their possessions soon run short. Thus they are forced to provide means from some other source. At the same time, because they care nothing for honour, 1121ᵇ they take recklessly and from any source; for they have an appetite for giving, and they do not mind how or from what source. Hence also their giving is not liberal; for it is not noble, nor does it aim at nobility, nor is it done in the right way; sometimes they make rich those who 5 should be poor, and will give nothing to people of respectable character, and much to flatterers or those who provide them with some other pleasure. Hence also most of them are self-indulgent; for they spend lightly and waste money on their indulgences, and incline towards pleasures because they do not live with a view to what is noble. 10

The prodigal man, then, turns into what we have described if he is left untutored, but if he is treated with care he will arrive at the intermediate and right state. But meanness is both incurable (for old age and every disability is thought to make men mean) and more innate 15 in men than prodigality; for most men are fonder of getting money than of giving. It also extends widely, and is multiform, since there seem to be many kinds of meanness.

For it consists in two things, deficiency in giving and excess in taking, and is not found complete in all men but is sometimes divided; some men go to excess in taking, others fall short in giving. Those who are 20 called by such names as 'miserly', 'close', 'stingy', all fall short in giving, but do not covet the possessions of others nor wish to get them. In

[2] ll. 16–19.

some this is due to a sort of honesty and avoidance of what is disgrace-
25 ful (for some seem, or at least profess, to hoard their money for this
reason, that they may not some day be forced to do something disgraceful; to this class belong the cheeseparer and every one of the sort; he is
so called from his excess of unwillingness to give anything); while
others again keep their hands off the property of others from fear, on
the ground that it is not easy, if one takes the property of others oneself, to avoid having one's own taken by them; they are therefore
content neither to take nor to give.

30   Others again exceed in respect of taking by taking anything and
from any source, e. g. those who ply sordid trades, pimps and all such
people, and those who lend small sums and at high rates. For all of
1122ᵃ these take more than they ought and from wrong sources. What is
common to them is evidently sordid love of gain; they all put up with
a bad name for the sake of gain, and little gain at that. For those who
make great gains but from wrong sources, and not the right gains,
5 e. g. despots when they sack cities and spoil temples, we do not call
mean but rather wicked, impious, and unjust. But the gamester and
the footpad [and the highwayman] belong to the class of the mean,
since they have a sordid love of gain. For it is for gain that both of
them ply their craft and endure the disgrace of it, and the one faces
the greatest dangers for the sake of the booty, while the other makes
10 gain from his friends, to whom he ought to be giving. Both, then,
since they are willing to make gain from wrong sources, are sordid
lovers of gain; therefore all such forms of taking are mean.

And it is natural that meanness is described as the contrary of
liberality; for not only is it a greater evil than prodigality, but men err
15 more often in this direction than in the way of prodigality as we have
described it.

So much, then, for liberality and the opposed vices.

2   It would seem proper to discuss magnificence next. For this also
20 seems to be a virtue concerned with wealth; but it does not like liberality extend to all the actions that are concerned with wealth, but only
to those that involve expenditure; and in these it surpasses liberality
in scale. For, as the name itself suggests, it is a fitting expenditure
involving largeness of scale. But the scale is relative; for the expense
of equipping a trireme is not the same as that of heading a sacred
25 embassy. It is what is fitting, then, in relation to the agent, and to the
circumstances and the object. The man who in small or middling things
spends according to the merits of the case is not called magnificent

(e. g. the man who can say 'many a gift I gave the wanderer'),[3] but only the man who does so in great things. For the magnificent man is liberal, but the liberal man is not necessarily magnificent. The deficiency of this state of character is called niggardliness, the excess vulgarity, lack of taste, and the like, which do not go to excess in the amount spent on right objects, but by showy expenditure in the wrong circumstances and the wrong manner; we shall speak of these vices later.[4]

The magnificent man is like an artist; for he can see what is fitting and spend large sums tastefully. For, as we said at the beginning,[5] a state of character is determined by its activities and by its objects. 1122^b Now the expenses of the magnificent man are large and fitting. Such, therefore, are also his results; for thus there will be a great expenditure and one that is fitting to its result. Therefore the result should be worthy of the expense, and the expense should be worthy of the result, or should even exceed it. And the magnificent man will spend such sums for honour's sake; for this is common to the virtues. And further he will do so gladly and lavishly; for nice calculation is a niggardly thing. And he will consider how the result can be made most beautiful and most becoming rather than for how much it can be produced and how it can be produced most cheaply. It is necessary, then, that the magnificent man be also liberal. For the liberal man also will spend what he ought and as he ought; and it is in these matters that the greatness implied in the name of the magnificent man—his bigness, as it were—is manifested, since liberality is concerned with these matters; and at an equal expense he will produce a more magnificent work of art. For a possession and a work of art have not the same excellence. The most valuable possession is that which is worth most, e. g. gold, but the most valuable work of art is that which is great and beautiful (for the contemplation of such a work inspires admiration, and so does magnificence); and a work has an excellence—viz. magnificence—which involves magnitude. Magnificence is an attribute of expenditures of the kind which we call honourable, e. g. those connected with the gods—votive offerings, buildings, and sacrifices—and similarly with any form of religious worship, and all those that are proper objects of public-spirited ambition, as when people think they ought to equip a chorus or a trireme, or entertain the city, in a brilliant way. But in all cases, as has been said,[6] we have regard to the agent as well and ask who he is and what means he has; for the expenditure

---

[3] *Od.* xvii. 420.

[4] 1123^a 19–33.

[5] Not in so many words, but Cf. 1103^b 21–23, 1104^a 27–29.   [6] ^{a} 24–26.

should be worthy of his means, and suit not only the result but also
the producer. Hence a poor man cannot be magnificent, since he has
not the means with which to spend large sums fittingly; and he who
tries is a fool, since he spends beyond what can be expected of him and
what is proper, but it is *right* expenditure that is virtuous. But great
30 expenditure is becoming to those who have suitable means to start with,
acquired by their own efforts or from ancestors or connexions, and
to people of high birth or reputation, and so on; for all these things
bring with them greatness and prestige. Primarily, then, the magnificent
35 man is of this sort, and magnificence is shown in expenditures of
this sort, as has been said; [7] for these are the greatest and most
honourable. Of *private* occasions of expenditure the most suitable
are those that take place once for all, e. g. a wedding or anything of
1123ª the kind, or anything that interests the whole city or the people of
position in it, and also the receiving of foreign guests and the sending
of them on their way, and gifts and counter-gifts; for the magnificent
5 man spends not on himself but on public objects, and gifts bear some
resemblance to votive offerings. A magnificent man will also furnish
his house suitably to his wealth (for even a house is a sort of public
ornament), and will spend by preference on those works that are lasting (for these are the most beautiful), and on every class of things he
will spend what is becoming; for the same things are not suitable for
10 gods and for men, nor in a temple and in a tomb. And since each
expenditure may be great of its kind, and what is most magnificent
absolutely is great expenditure on a great object, but what is magnificent *here* is what is great in *these* circumstances, and greatness in the
work differs from greatness in the expense (for the most beautiful ball
15 or bottle is magnificent as a gift to a child, but the price of it is small
and mean)—therefore it is characteristic of the magnificent man,
whatever kind of result he is producing, to produce it magnificently
(for such a result is not easily surpassed) and to make it worthy of the
expenditure.

Such, then, is the magnificent man; the man who goes to excess and
is vulgar exceeds, as has been said, [8] by spending beyond what is
20 right. For on small objects of expenditure he spends much and displays
a tasteless showiness; e.g. he gives a club dinner on the scale of a wedding banquet, and when he provides the chorus for a comedy he brings
them on to the stage in purple, as they do at Megara. And all such
25 things he will do not for honour's sake but to show off his wealth, and
because he thinks he is admired for these things, and where he ought

[7] ll. 19–23.

[8] 1122ª 31–33.

to spend much he spends little and where little, much. The niggardly man on the other hand will fall short in everything, and after spending the greatest sums will spoil the beauty of the result for a trifle, and whatever he is doing he will hesitate and consider how he may spend 30 least, and lament even that, and think he is doing everything on a bigger scale than he ought.

These states of character, then, are vices; yet they do not bring *disgrace* because they are neither harmful to one's neighbour nor very unseemly.

3   Pride seems even from its name [9] to be concerned with great things; what sort of great things, is the first question we must try to answer. It makes no difference whether we consider the state of char- 35 acter or the man characterized by it. Now the man is thought to be proud who thinks himself worthy of great things, being worthy of 1123[b] them; for he who does so beyond his deserts is a fool, but no virtuous man is foolish or silly. The proud man, then, is the man we have described. For he who is worthy of little and thinks himself worthy of 5 little is temperate, but not proud; for pride implies greatness, as beauty implies a good-sized body, and little people may be neat and well-proportioned but cannot be beautiful. On the other hand, he who thinks himself worthy of great things, being unworthy of them, is vain; though not every one who thinks himself worthy of more than he really is worthy of is vain. The man who thinks himself worthy of less than he is really worthy of is unduly humble, whether his deserts be great or moderate, or his deserts be small but his claims yet smaller. 10 And the man whose deserts are great would seem *most* unduly humble; for what would he have done if they had been less? The proud man, then, is an extreme in respect of the greatness of his claims, but a mean in respect of the rightness of them; for he claims what is in accordance with his merits, while the others go to excess or fall short.

If, then, he deserves and claims great things, and above all the great- 15 est things, he will be concerned with one thing in particular. Desert is relative to external goods; and the greatest of these, we should say, is that which we render to the gods, and which people of position most aim at, and which is the prize appointed for the noblest deeds; and this 20 is honour; that is surely the greatest of external goods. Honours and dishonours, therefore, are the objects with respect to which the proud man is as he should be. And even apart from argument it is with honor

---

[9] 'Pride' of course has not the etymological associations of *megalopsychia*, but seems in other respects the best translation.

that proud men appear to be concerned; for it is honour that they chiefly claim, but in accordance with their deserts. The unduly humble man falls short both in comparison with his own merits and in com-
25 parison with the proud man's claims. The vain man goes to excess in comparison with his own merits, but does not exceed the proud man's claims.

Now the proud man, since he deserves most, must be good in the highest degree; for the better man always deserves more, and the best
30 man most. Therefore the truly proud man must be good. And greatness in every virtue would seem to be characteristic of a proud man. And it would be most unbecoming for a proud man to fly from danger, swinging his arms by his sides, or to wrong another; for to what end should he do disgraceful acts, he to whom nothing is great? If we consider him point by point, we shall see the utter absurdity of a proud man who is not good. Nor, again, would he be worthy of honour if
35 he were bad; for honour is the prize of virtue, and it is to the good
1124ᵃ that it is rendered. Pride, then, seems to be a sort of crown of the virtues; for it makes them greater, and it is not found without them. Therefore it is hard to be truly proud; for it is impossible without nobility and goodness of character. It is chiefly with honours and dis-
5 honours, then, that the proud man is concerned; and at honours that are great and conferred by good men he will be moderately pleased, thinking that he is coming by his own or even less than his own; for there can be no honour that is worthy of perfect virtue, yet he will at
10 any rate accept it since they have nothing greater to bestow on him; but honour from casual people and on trifling grounds he will utterly despise, since it is not this that he deserves, and dishonour too, since in his case it cannot be just. In the first place, then, as has been said,[10] the proud man is concerned with honours; yet he will also bear himself with moderation towards wealth and power and all good or evil
15 fortune, whatever may befall him, and will be neither over-joyed by good fortune nor over-pained by evil. For not even towards honour does he bear himself as if it were a very great thing. Power and wealth are desirable for the sake of honour (at least those who have them wish to get honour by means of them); and for him to whom even honour is a little thing the others must be so too. Hence proud men are thought to be disdainful.
20   The goods of fortune also are thought to contribute towards pride. For men who are well-born are thought worthy of honour, and so are those who enjoy power or wealth; for they are in a superior position,

[10] 1123ᵇ 15–22.

and everything that has a superiority in something good is held in
greater honour. Hence even such things make men prouder; for they
are honoured by some for having them; but in truth the good man 25
alone is to be honoured; he, however, who has both advantages is
thought the more worthy of honour. But those who without virtue
have such goods are neither justified in making great claims nor entitled to the name of 'proud'; for these things imply perfect virtue.
Disdainful and insolent, however, even those who have such goods become. For without virtue it is not easy to bear gracefully the goods of 30
fortune; and, being unable to bear them, and thinking themselves
superior to others, they despise others and themselves do what they 1124ᵇ
please. They imitate the proud man without being like him, and this
they do where they can; so they do not act virtuously, but they do
despise others. For the proud man despises justly (since he thinks 5
truly), but the many do so at random.

He does not run into trifling dangers, nor is he fond of danger, because he honours few things; but he will face great dangers, and when
he is in danger he is unsparing of his life, knowing that there are conditions on which life is not worth having. And he is the sort of man to
confer benefits, but he is ashamed of receiving them; for the one is the 10
mark of a superior, the other of an inferior. And he is apt to confer
greater benefits in return; for thus the original benefactor besides being
paid will incur a debt to him, and will be the gainer by the transaction.
They seem also to remember any service they have done, but not those
they have received (for he who receives a service is inferior to him who
has done it, but the proud man wishes to be superior), and to hear of
the former with pleasure, of the latter with displeasure; this, it seems, 15
is why Thetis did not mention to Zeus the services she had done him,[11]
and why the Spartans did not recount their services to the Athenians,
but those they had received. It is a mark of the proud man also to ask
for nothing or scarcely anything, but to give help readily, and to be
dignified towards people who enjoy high position and good fortune,
but unassuming towards those of the middle class; for it is a difficult 20
and lofty thing to be superior to the former, but easy to be so to the
latter, and a lofty bearing over the former is no mark of ill-breeding,
but among humble people it is as vulgar as a display of strength against
the weak. Again, it is characteristic of the proud man not to aim at
the things commonly held in honour, or the things in which others
excel; to be sluggish and to hold back except where great honour or 25
a great work is at stake, and to be a man of few deeds, but of great and

---

[11] In fact she did, *Il.* i. 503.

notable ones. He must also be open in his hate and in his love (for to conceal one's feelings, i. e. to care less for truth than for what people will think, is a coward's part), and must speak and act openly; for he is free of speech because he is contemptuous, and he is given to telling
30 the truth, except when he speaks in irony to the vulgar. He must be
1125ᵃ unable to make his life revolve round another, unless it be a friend; for this is slavish, and for this reason all flatterers are servile and people lacking in self-respect are flatterers. Nor is he given to admiration; for nothing to him is great. Nor is he mindful of wrongs; for it is not the part of a proud man to have a long memory, especially for wrongs, but
5 rather to overlook them. Nor is he a gossip; for he will speak neither about himself nor about another, since he cares not to be praised nor for others to be blamed; nor again is he given to praise; and for the same reason he is not an evil-speaker, even about his enemies, except from haughtiness. With regard to necessary or small matters he is least
10 of all men given to lamentation or the asking of favours; for it is the part of one who takes such matters seriously to behave so with respect to them. He is one who will possess beautiful and profitless things rather than profitable and useful ones; for this is more proper to a character that suffices to itself.

Further, a slow step is thought proper to the proud man, a deep voice, and a level utterance; for the man who takes few things seriously is not likely to be hurried, nor the man who thinks nothing great
15 to be excited, while a shrill voice and a rapid gait are the results of hurry and excitement.

Such, then, is the proud man; the man who falls short of him is unduly humble, and the man who goes beyond him is vain. Now even these are not thought to be bad (for they are not malicious), but only mistaken. For the unduly humble man, being worthy of good
20 things, robs himself of what he deserves, and seems to have something bad about him from the fact that he does not think himself worthy of good things, and seems also not to know himself; else he would have desired the things he was worthy of, since these were good. Yet such people are not thought to be fools, but rather unduly retiring. Such a
25 reputation, however, seems actually to make them worse; for each class of people aims at what corresponds to its worth, and these people stand back even from noble actions and undertakings, deeming themselves unworthy, and from external goods no less. Vain people, on the other hand, are fools and ignorant of themselves, and that manifestly; for, not being worthy of them, they attempt honourable undertakings, and
30 then are found out; and they adorn themselves with clothing and out-

ward show and such things, and wish their strokes of good fortune to be made public, and speak about them as if they would be honoured for them. But undue humility is more opposed to pride than vanity is; for it is both commoner and worse.

Pride, then, is concerned with honour on the grand scale, as has been said.[12]   35

4 There seems to be in the sphere of honour also, as was said in our 1125ᵇ first remarks on the subject,[13] a virtue which would appear to be related to pride as liberality is to magnificence. For neither of these has anything to do with the grand scale, but both dispose us as is right with 5 regard to middling and unimportant objects; as in getting and giving of wealth there is a mean and an excess and defect, so too honour may be desired more than is right, or less, or from the right sources and in the right way. We blame both the ambitious man as aiming at honour more than is right and from wrong sources, and the unambitious man 10 as not willing to be honoured even for noble reasons. But sometimes we praise the ambitious man as being manly and a lover of what is noble, and the unambitious man as being moderate and self-controlled, as we said in our first treatment of the subject.[14] Evidently, since 'fond of such and such an object' has more than one meaning, we do not assign the term 'ambition' or 'love of honour' always to the same thing, but when we praise the quality we think of the man who loves honour 15 more than most people, and when we blame it we think of him who loves it more than is right. The mean being without a name, the extremes seem to dispute for its place as though that were vacant by default. But where there is excess and defect, there is also an intermediate; now men desire honour both more than they should and less; therefore it is possible also to do so as one should; at all events this is 20 the state of character that is praised, being an unnamed mean in respect of honour. Relatively to ambition it seems to be unambitiousness, and relatively to unambitiousness it seems to be ambition, while relatively to both severally it seems in a sense to be both together. This appears to be true of the other virtues also. But in this case the extremes seem to be contradictories because the mean has not received a name.   25

5 Good temper is a mean with respect to anger; the middle state being unnamed, and the extremes almost without a name as well, we place good temper in the middle position, though it inclines towards

---

[12] 1107ᵇ 26, 1123ᵃ 34–ᵇ 22.   [13] Ib. 24–27.   [14] 1107ᵇ 33.

the deficiency, which is without a name. The excess might be called
30 a sort of 'irascibility'. For the passion is anger, while its causes are
many and diverse.

The man who is angry at the right things and with the right people,
and, further, as he ought, when he ought, and as long as he ought, is
praised. This will be the good-tempered man, then, since good temper
is praised. For the good-tempered man tends to be unperturbed and
35 not to be led by passion, but to be angry in the manner, at the things,
1126ᵃ and for the length of time, that the rule dictates; but he is thought to
err rather in the direction of deficiency; for the good-tempered man
is not revengeful, but rather tends to make allowances.

The deficiency, whether it is a sort of 'inirascibility' or whatever
it is, is blamed. For those who are not angry at the things they should
5 be angry at are thought to be fools, and so are those who are not angry
in the right way, at the right time, or with the right persons; for such
a man is thought not to feel things nor to be pained by them, and,
since he does not get angry, he is thought unlikely to defend himself;
and to endure being insulted and put up with insult to one's friends
is slavish.

The excess can be manifested in all the points that have been named
(for one can be angry with the wrong persons, at the wrong things,
10 more than is right, too quickly, or too long); yet *all* are not found
in the same person. Indeed they could not; for evil destroys even itself,
and if it is complete becomes unbearable. Now *hot-tempered* people
get angry quickly and with the wrong persons and at the wrong things
and more than is right, but their anger ceases quickly—which is the
15 best point about them. This happens to them because they do not
restrain their anger but retaliate openly owing to their quickness of
temper, and then their anger ceases. By reason of excess *choleric* people
are quick-tempered and ready to be angry with everything and on
every occasion; whence their name. *Sulky* people are hard to appease,
20 and retain their anger long; for they repress their passion. But it ceases
when they retaliate; for revenge relieves them of their anger, producing
in them pleasure instead of pain. If this does not happen they retain
their burden; for owing to its not being obvious no one even reasons
with them, and to digest one's anger in oneself takes time. Such people
25 are most troublesome to themselves and to their dearest friends. We
call *bad-tempered* those who are angry at the wrong things, more than
is right, and longer, and cannot be appeased until they inflict vengeance
or punishment.

To good temper we oppose the excess rather than the defect; for

not only is it commoner (since revenge is the more human), but bad-
tempered people are worse to live with.   30

What we have said in our earlier treatment of the subject [15] is plain
also from what we are now saying; viz. that it is not easy to define
how, with whom, at what, and how long one should be angry, and at
what point right action ceases and wrong begins. For the man who 35
strays a little from the path, either towards the more or towards the
less, is not blamed; since sometimes we praise those who exhibit the
deficiency, and call them good-tempered, and sometimes we call angry 1126ᵇ
people manly, as being capable of ruling. How far, therefore, and how
a man must stray before he becomes blameworthy, it is not easy to
state in words; for the decision depends on the particular facts and on
perception. But so much at least is plain, that the middle state is praise- 5
worthy—that in virtue of which we are angry with the right people,
at the right things, in the right way, and so on, while the excesses and
defects are blameworthy—slightly so if they are present in a low
degree, more if in a higher degree, and very much if in a high degree.
Evidently, then, we must cling to the middle state.—Enough of the
states relative to anger.   10

6   In gatherings of men, in social life and the interchange of words
and deeds, some men are thought to be obsequious, viz. those who to
give pleasure praise everything and never oppose, but think it their
duty 'to give no pain to the people they meet'; while those who, on 15
the contrary, oppose everything and care not a whit about giving pain
are called churlish and contentious. That the states we have named
are culpable is plain enough, and that the middle state is laudable—
that in virtue of which a man will put up with, and will resent, the
right things and in the right way; but no name has been assigned to
it, though it most resembles friendship. For the man who corresponds 20
to this middle state is very much what, with affection added, we call a
good friend. But the state in question differs from friendship in that
it implies no passion or affection for one's associates; since it is not by
reason of loving or hating that such a man takes everything in the
right way, but by being a man of a certain kind. For he will behave so 25
alike towards those he knows and those he does not know, towards
intimates and those who are not so, except that in each of these cases he
will behave as is befitting; for it is not proper to have the same care
for intimates and for strangers, nor again is it the same conditions that

---

[15] 1109ᵇ 14–26.

make it right to give pain to them. Now we have said generally that he will associate with people in the right way; but it is by reference to what is honourable and expedient that he will aim at not giving pain
30 or at contributing pleasure. For he seems to be concerned with the pleasures and pains of social life; and wherever it is not honourable, or is harmful, for him to contribute pleasure, he will refuse, and will choose rather to give pain; also if his acquiescence in another's action would bring disgrace, and that in a high degree, or injury, *on that other*,
35 while his opposition brings a little pain, he will not acquiesce but will decline. He will associate differently with people in high station and
1127ᵃ with ordinary people, with closer and more distant acquaintances, and so too with regard to all other differences, rendering to each class what is befitting, and while for its own sake he chooses to contribute pleasure, and avoids the giving of pain, he will be guided by the consequences,
5 if these are greater, i. e. honour and expediency. For the sake of a great future pleasure, too, he will inflict small pains.

The man who attains the mean, then, is such as we have described, but has not received a name; of those who contribute pleasure, the man who aims at being pleasant with no ulterior object is obsequious, but the man who does so in order that he may get some advantage in the
10 direction of money or the things that money buys is a flatterer; while the man who quarrels with everything is, as has been said,[16] churlish and contentious. And the extremes seem to be contradictory to each other because the mean is without a name.

7   The mean opposed to boastfulness is found in almost the same sphere; and this also is without a name. It will be no bad plan to
15 describe these states as well; for we shall both know the facts about character better if we go through them in detail, and we shall be convinced that the virtues are means if we see this to be so in all cases. In the field of social life those who make the giving of pleasure or pain their object in associating with others have been described;[17] let us now describe those who pursue truth or falsehood alike in words and
20 deeds and in the claims they put forward. The boastful man, then, is thought to be apt to claim the things that bring glory, when he has not got them, or to claim more of them than he has, and the mockmodest man on the other hand to disclaim what he has or belittle it, while the man who observes the mean is one who calls a thing by its own name, being truthful both in life and in word, owning to what he
25 has, and neither more nor less. Now each of these courses may be

---

[16] 1125ᵇ 14–16.   [17] Ch. 6.

adopted either with or without an object. But each man speaks and acts and lives in accordance with his character, if he is *not* acting for some ulterior object. And falsehood is *in itself* [18] mean and culpable, and truth noble and worthy of praise. Thus the truthful man is another 30 case of a man who, being in the mean, is worthy of praise, and both forms of untruthful man are culpable, and particularly the boastful man.

Let us discuss them both, but first of all the truthful man. We are not speaking of the man who keeps faith in his agreements, i. e. in the things that pertain to justice or injustice (for this would belong to another virtue), but the man who in the matters in which nothing of 1127^b this sort is at stake is true both in word and in life because his character is such. But such a man would seem to be as a matter of fact equitable. For the man who loves truth, and is truthful where nothing is at stake, will still more be truthful where something is at stake; he will avoid 5 falsehood as something base, seeing that he avoided it even for its own sake; and such a man is worthy of praise. He inclines rather to understate the truth; for this seems in better taste because exaggerations are wearisome.

He who claims more than he has with no ulterior object is a contemptible sort of fellow (otherwise he would not have delighted in 10 falsehood), but seems futile rather than bad; but if he does it for an object, he who does it for the sake of reputation or honour is (for a boaster) not very much to be blamed, but he who does it for money, or the things that lead to money, is an uglier character (it is not the capacity that makes the boaster, but the purpose; for it is in virtue of his state of character and by being a man of a certain kind that he is a boaster); as one man is a liar because he enjoys the lie itself, and 15 another because he desires reputation or gain. Now those who boast for the sake of reputation claim such qualities as win praise or congratulation, but those whose object is gain claim qualities which are of value to one's neighbours and one's lack of which is not easily detected, e. g. the powers of a seer, a sage, or a physician. For this reason it is such 20 things as these that most people claim and boast about; for in them the above-mentioned qualities are found.

Mock-modest people, who understate things, seem more attractive in character; for they are thought to speak not for gain but to avoid parade; and here too it is qualities which bring reputation that they 25 disclaim, as Socrates used to do. Those who disclaim trifling and obvious qualities are called humbugs and are more contemptible; and

---

[18] i. e. apart from any ulterior object it may serve.

sometimes this seems to be boastfulness, like the Spartan dress; for both excess and great deficiency are boastful. But those who use under-
30 statement with moderation and understate about matters that do not very much force themselves on our notice seem attractive. And it is the boaster that seems to be opposed to the truthful man; for he is the worse character.

8 Since life includes rest as well as activity, and in this is included leisure and amusement, there seems here also to be a kind of intercourse
1128ᵃ which is tasteful; there is such a thing as saying—and again listening to—what one should and as one should. The kind of people one is speaking or listening to will also make a difference. Evidently here also there is both an excess and a deficiency as compared with the
5 mean. Those who carry humour to excess are thought to be vulgar buffoons, striving after humour at all costs, and aiming rather at raising a laugh than at saying what is becoming and at avoiding pain to the object of their fun; while those who can neither make a joke themselves nor put up with those who do are thought to be boorish and unpolished. But those who joke in a tasteful way are called ready-witted, which
10 implies a sort of readiness to turn this way and that; for such sallies are thought to be movements of the character, and as bodies are dis-criminated by their movements, so too are characters. The ridiculous side of things is not far to seek, however, and most people delight more than they should in amusement and in jesting, and so even buffoons
15 are called ready-witted because they are found attractive; but that they differ from the ready-witted man, and to no small extent, is clear from what has been said.

To the middle state belongs also tact; it is the mark of a tactful man to say and listen to such things as befit a good and well-bred man;
20 for there are some things that it befits such a man to say and to hear by way of jest, and the well-bred man's jesting differs from that of a vulgar man, and the joking of an educated man from that of an un-educated. One may see this even from the old and the new comedies; to the authors of the former indecency of language was amusing, to those of the latter innuendo is more so; and these differ in no small
25 degree in respect of propriety. Now should we define the man who jokes well by his saying what is not unbecoming to a well-bred man, or by his not giving pain, or even giving delight, to the hearer? Or is the latter definition, at any rate, itself indefinite, since different things are hateful or pleasant to different people? The kind of jokes he will listen to will be the same; for the kind he can put up with are also the kind

he seems to make. There are, then, jokes he will not make; for the
jest is a sort of abuse, and there are things that lawgivers forbid us 30
to abuse; and they should, perhaps, have forbidden us even to make
a jest of such. The refined and well-bred man, therefore, will be as we
have described, being as it were a law to himself.

Such, then, is the man who observes the mean, whether he be called
tactful or ready-witted. The buffoon, on the other hand, is the slave of
his sense of humour, and spares neither himself nor others if he 35
can raise a laugh, and says things none of which a man of refinement
would say, and to some of which he would not even listen. The boor, 1128ᵇ
again, is useless for such social intercourse; for he contributes nothing
and finds fault with everything. But relaxation and amusement are
thought to be a necessary element in life.

The means in life that have been described, then, are three in number, and are all concerned with an interchange of words and deeds of 5
some kind. They differ, however, in that one is concerned with truth,
and the other two with pleasantness. Of those concerned with pleasure,
one is displayed in jests, the other in the general social intercourse
of life.

9   Shame should not be described as a virtue; for it is more like a 10
feeling than a state of character. It is defined, at any rate, as a kind
of fear of dishonour, and produces an effect similar to that produced by
fear of danger; for people who feel disgraced blush, and those who fear
death turn pale. Both, therefore, seem to be in a sense bodily conditions,
which is thought to be characteristic of feeling rather than of a state
of character.

The feeling is not becoming to every age, but only to youth. For we 15
think young people should be prone to the feeling of shame because
they live by feeling and therefore commit many errors, but are restrained by shame; and we praise young people who are prone to this
feeling, but an older person no one would praise for being prone to the
sense of disgrace, since we think he should not do anything that need 20
cause this sense. For the sense of disgrace is not even characteristic
of a good man,[19] since it is consequent on bad actions (for such actions
should not be done; and if some actions are disgraceful in very truth
and others only according to common opinion, this makes no difference;
for neither class of actions should be done, so that no disgrace should 25
be felt); and it is a mark of a bad man even to be such as to do any
disgraceful action. To be so constituted as to feel disgraced if one does

---

[19] *sc.* still less is it itself a virtue.

such an action, and for this reason to think oneself good, is absurd; for it is for voluntary actions that shame is felt, and the good man will
30 never voluntarily do bad actions. But shame may be said to be conditionally a good thing; *if* a good man does such actions, he will feel disgraced; but the virtues are not subject to such a qualification. And if shamelessness—not to be ashamed of doing base actions—is bad, that does not make it good to be ashamed of doing such actions. Continence
35 too is not virtue, but a mixed sort of state; this will be shown later.[20] Now, however, let us discuss justice.

BOOK V

1129ª 1 With regard to justice and injustice we must consider (1) what kind of actions they are concerned with, (2) what sort of mean justice
5 is, and (3) between what extremes the just act is intermediate. Our investigation shall follow the same course as the preceding discussions.

We see that all men mean by justice that kind of state of character which makes people disposed to do what is just and makes them act justly and wish for what is just; and similarly by injustice that state
10 which makes them act unjustly and wish for what is unjust. Let us too, then, lay this down as a general basis. For the same is not true of the sciences and the faculties as of states of character. A faculty or a science which is one and the same is held to relate to contrary objects, but a state of character which is one of two contraries does *not* produce
15 the contrary results; e. g. as a result of health we do not do what is the opposite of healthy, but only what is healthy; for we say a man walks healthily, when he walks as a healthy man would.

Now often one contrary state is recognized from its contrary, and often states are recognized from the subjects that exhibit them; for
20 (A) if good condition is known, bad condition also becomes known, and (B) good condition is known from the things that are in good condition, and they from it. If good condition is firmness of flesh, it is necessary both that bad condition should be flabbiness of flesh and that the wholesome should be that which causes firmness in flesh. And it follows for the most part that if one contrary is ambiguous the other
25 also will be ambiguous; e. g. if 'just' is so, that 'unjust' will be so too.

Now 'justice' and 'injustice' seem to be ambiguous, but because their different meanings approach near to one another the ambiguity escapes notice and is not obvious as it is, comparatively, when the

[20] vii. 1–10.

meanings are far apart, e. g. (for here the difference in outward form is great) as the ambiguity in the use of *kleis* for the collar-bone of an 30 animal and for that with which we lock a door. Let us take as a starting-point, then, the various meanings of 'an unjust man'. Both the lawless man and the grasping and unfair man are thought to be unjust, so that evidently both the law-abiding and the fair man will be just. The just, then, is the lawful and the fair, the unjust the unlawful and the unfair.

Since the unjust man is grasping, he must be concerned with goods 1129ᵇ —not all goods, but those with which prosperity and adversity have to do, which taken absolutely are always good, but for a particular person are not always good. Now men pray for and pursue these things; 5 but they should not, but should pray that the things that are good absolutely may also be good for them, and should choose the things that *are* good for them. The unjust man does not always choose the greater, but also the less—in the case of things bad absolutely; but because the lesser evil is itself thought to be in a sense good, and graspingness is directed at the good, therefore he is thought to be 10 grasping. And he is unfair; for this contains and is common to both.

Since the lawless man was seen to be unjust and the law-abiding man just, evidently all lawful acts are in a sense just acts; for the acts laid down by the legislative art are lawful, and each of these, we say, is just. Now the laws in their enactments on all subjects aim at the 15 common advantage either of all or of the best or of those who hold power, or something of the sort; so that in one sense we call those acts just that tend to produce and preserve happiness and its components for the political society. And the law bids us do both the acts of a brave 20 man (e. g. not to desert our post nor take to flight nor throw away our arms), and those of a temperate man (e. g. not to commit adultery nor to gratify one's lust), and those of a good-tempered man (e. g. not to strike another nor to speak evil), and similarly with regard to the other virtues and forms of wickedness, commanding some acts and forbidding others; and the rightly-framed law does this rightly, and the hastily conceived one less well.

This form of justice, then, is complete virtue, but not absolutely, 25 but in relation to our neighbour. And therefore justice is often thought to be the greatest of virtues, and 'neither evening nor morning star' is so wonderful; and proverbially 'in justice is every virtue compre-hended'. And it is complete virtue in its fullest sense, because it is the 30 actual exercise of complete virtue. It is complete because he who possesses it can exercise his virtue not only in himself but towards

his neighbour also; for many men can exercise virtue in their own
1130ᵃ affairs, but not in their relations to their neighbour. This is why the
saying of Bias is thought to be true, that 'rule will show the man';
for a ruler is necessarily in relation to other men and a member of a
society. For this same reason justice, alone of the virtues, is thought to
be 'another's good',[1] because it is related to our neighbour; for it does
5 what is advantageous to another, either a ruler or a copartner. Now
the worst man is he who exercises his wickedness both towards himself
and towards his friends, and the best man is not he who exercises his
virtue towards himself but he who exercises it towards another; for
this is a difficult task. Justice in this sense, then, is not part of virtue
10 but virtue entire, nor is the contrary injustice a part of vice but vice
entire. What the difference is between virtue and justice in this sense
is plain from what we have said; they are the same but their essence is
not the same; what, as a relation to one's neighbour, is justice is, as
a certain kind of state without qualification, virtue.

2 But at all events what we are investigating is the justice which is
a *part* of virtue; for there is a justice of this kind, as we maintain.
15 Similarly it is with injustice in the particular sense that we are concerned.

That there is such a thing is indicated by the fact that while the
man who exhibits in action the other forms of wickedness acts wrongly
indeed, but not graspingly (e. g. the man who throws away his shield
through cowardice or speaks harshly through bad temper or fails to
help a friend with money through meanness), when a man acts grasp-
20 ingly he often exhibits none of these vices—no, nor all together, but
certainly wickedness of some kind (for we blame him) and injustice.
There is, then, another kind of injustice which is a part of injustice
in the wide sense, and a use of the word 'unjust' which answers to a
part of what is unjust in the wide sense of 'contrary to the law'. Again,
if one man commits adultery for the sake of gain and makes money
25 by it, while another does so at the bidding of appetite though he loses
money and is penalized for it, the latter would be held to be self-
indulgent rather than grasping, but the former is unjust, but not
self-indulgent; evidently, therefore, he is unjust by reason of his making gain by his act. Again, all other unjust acts are ascribed invariably
30 to some particular kind of wickedness, e. g. adultery to self-indulgence,
the desertion of a comrade in battle to cowardice, physical violence to
anger; but if a man makes gain, his action is ascribed to no form of

[1] Pl. *Rep.* 343 c.

wickedness but injustice. Evidently, therefore, there is apart from injustice in the wide sense another, 'particular', injustice which shares the name and nature of the first, because its definition falls within the same genus; for the significance of both consists in a relation to one's 1130ᵇ neighbour, but the one is concerned with honour or money or safety —or that which includes all these, if we had a single name for it—and its motive is the pleasure that arises from gain; while the other is concerned with all the objects with which the good man is concerned. 5

It is clear, then, that there is more than one kind of justice, and that there is one which is distinct from virtue entire; we must try to grasp its genus and differentia.

The unjust has been divided into the unlawful and the unfair, and the just into the lawful and the fair. To the unlawful answers the afore-mentioned sense of injustice. But since the unfair and the unlaw- ful are not the same, but are different as a part is from its whole (for 10 all that is unfair is unlawful, but not all that is unlawful is unfair), the unjust and injustice in the sense of the unfair are not the same as but different from the former kind, as part from whole; for injustice in this sense is a part of injustice in the wide sense, and similarly justice in the one sense of justice in the other. Therefore we must speak also 15 about particular justice and particular injustice, and similarly about the just and the unjust. The justice, then, which answers to the whole of virtue, and the corresponding injustice, one being the exercise of virtue as a whole, and the other that of vice as a whole, towards one's neighbour, we may leave on one side. And how the meanings of 'just' 20 and 'unjust' which answer to these are to be distinguished is evident; for practically the majority of the acts commanded by the law are those which are prescribed from the point of view of virtue taken as a whole; for the law bids us practise every virtue and forbids us to practise any vice. And the things that tend to produce virtue taken 25 as a whole are those of the acts prescribed by the law which have been prescribed with a view to education for the common good. But with regard to the education of the individual as such, which makes him without qualification a good *man*, we must determine later [2] whether this is the function of the political art or of another; for perhaps it is not the same to be a good man and a good citizen of any state taken at random.

Of particular justice and that which is just in the corresponding 30 sense, (ᴀ) one kind is that which is manifested in distributions of

---

[2] 1179ᵇ 20–1181ᵇ 12. *Pol.* 1276ᵇ 16–1277ᵇ 32, 1278ᵃ 40–ᵇ5, 1288ᵃ 32–ᵇ2, 1333ᵃ 11–16, 1337ᵃ 11–14.

honour or money or the other things that fall to be divided among those who have a share in the constitution (for in these it is possible for one man to have a share either unequal or equal to that of another), and (B) one is that which plays a rectifying part in transactions between 1131ᵃ man and man. Of this there are two divisions; of transactions (1) some are voluntary and (2) others involuntary—voluntary such transactions as sale, purchase, loan for consumption, pledging, loan for use, depositing, letting (they are called voluntary because the origin of 5 these transactions is voluntary), while of the involuntary (a) some are clandestine, such as theft, adultery, poisoning, procuring, enticement of slaves, assassination, false witness, and (b) others are violent, such as assault, imprisonment, murder, robbery with violence, mutilation, abuse, insult.

10 3   (A) We have shown that both the unjust man and the unjust act are unfair or unequal; now it is clear that there is also an intermediate between the two unequals involved in either case. And this is the equal; for in any kind of action in which there is a more and a less there is also what is equal. If, then, the unjust is unequal, the just is equal, as all men suppose it to be, even apart from argument. And since the equal is intermediate, the just will be an intermediate. Now equality 15 implies at least two things. The just, then, must be both intermediate and equal and relative (i. e. for certain persons). And *qua* intermediate it must be between certain things (which are respectively greater and less); *qua* equal, it involves *two* things; *qua* just, it is for certain people. The just, therefore, involves at least four terms; for the persons for whom it is in fact just are two, and the things in which it is 20 manifested, the objects distributed, are two. And the same equality will exist between the persons and between the things concerned; for as the latter—the things concerned—are related, so are the former; if they are not equal, they will not have what is equal, but this is the origin of quarrels and complaints—when either equals have and are awarded unequal shares, or unequals equal shares. Further, this is 25 plain from the fact that awards should be 'according to merit'; for all men agree that what is just in distribution must be according to merit in some sense, though they do not all specify the same sort of merit, but democrats identify it with the status of freeman, supporters of oligarchy with wealth (or with noble birth), and supporters of aristocracy with excellence.

30   The just, then, is a species of the proportionate (proportion being not a property only of the kind of number which consists of abstract

units, but of number in general). For proportion is equality of ratios, and involves four terms at least (that discrete proportion involves four terms is plain, but so does continuous proportion, for it uses one term as two and mentions it twice; e. g. 'as the line A is to the line B, so is 1131ᵇ the line B to the line C'; the line B, then, has been mentioned twice, so that if the line B be assumed twice, the proportional terms will be four); and the just, too, involves at least four terms, and the ratio between one pair is the same as that between the other pair; for there is a similar distinction between the persons and between the things. 5 As the term A, then, is to B, so will C be to D, and therefore, *alternando*, as A is to C, B will be to D. Therefore also the whole is in the same ratio to the whole;³ and this coupling the distribution effects, and, if the terms are so combined, effects justly. The conjunction, then, of the term A with C and of B with D is what is just in distribution,⁴ and this species of the just is intermediate, and the unjust is 10 what violates the proportion; for the proportional is intermediate, and the just is proportional. (Mathematicians call this kind of proportion geometrical; for it is in geometrical proportion that it follows that the whole is to the whole as either part is to the corresponding part.) This 15 proportion is not continuous; for we cannot get a single term standing for a person and a thing.

This, then, is what the just is—the proportional; the unjust is what violates the proportion. Hence one term becomes too great, the other too small, as indeed happens in practice; for the man who acts unjustly has too much, and the man who is unjustly treated too little, of what is good. In the case of evil the reverse is true; for the lesser 20 evil is reckoned a good in comparison with the greater evil, since the lesser evil is rather to be chosen than the greater, and what is worthy of choice is good, and what is worthier of choice a greater good.

This, then, is one species of the just.

4   (B) The remaining one is the rectificatory, which arises in con- 25 nexion with transactions both voluntary and involuntary. This form of the just has a different specific character from the former. For the justice which distributes common possessions is always in accord-

---

³ Person A + thing C to person B + thing D.

⁴ The problem of distributive justice is to divide the distributable honour or reward into parts which are to one another as are the merits of the persons who are to participate. If

A (first person) : B (second person) :: C (first portion) : D (second portion),

then (*alternando*) A : C :: B : D,

and therefore (*componendo*) A + C : B + D :: A : B.

In other words the position established answers to the relative merits of the parties.

ance with the kind of proportion mentioned above [5] (for in the case also in which the distribution is made from the common funds of a
30 partnership it will be according to the same ratio which the funds put into the business by the partners bear to one another); and the injustice opposed to this kind of justice is that which violates the proportion. But the justice in transactions between man and man
1132ª is a sort of equality indeed, and the injustice a sort of inequality; not according to that kind of proportion, however, but according to arithmetical proportion.[6] For it makes no difference whether a good man has defrauded a bad man or a bad man a good one, nor whether it is a good or a bad man that has committed adultery; the law looks only to the distinctive character of the injury, and treats the
5 parties as equal, if one is in the wrong and the other is being wronged, and if one inflicted injury and the other has received it. Therefore, this kind of injustice being an inequality, the judge tries to equalize it; for in the case also in which one has received and the other has inflicted a wound, or one has slain and the other been slain, the suffering and the action have been unequally distributed; but the judge tries to equalize things by means of the penalty, taking
10 away from the gain of the assailant. For the term 'gain' is applied generally to such cases, even if it be not a term appropriate to certain cases, e. g. to the person who inflicts a wound—and 'loss' to the sufferer; at all events when the suffering has been estimated, the one is called loss and the other gain. Therefore the equal is intermediate
15 between the greater and the less, but the gain and the loss are respectively greater and less in contrary ways; more of the good and less of the evil are gain, and the contrary is loss; intermediate between them is, as we saw,[7] the equal, which we say is just; therefore corrective justice will be the intermediate between loss and gain. This is why,
20 when people dispute, they take refuge in the judge; and to go to the

[5] l. 12 f.

[6] The problem of 'rectificatory justice' has nothing to do with punishment proper but is only that of rectifying a wrong that has been done, by awarding damages; i. e. rectificatory justice is that of the civil, not that of the criminal courts. The parties are treated by the court as equal (since a law court is not a court of morals), and the wrongful act is reckoned as having brought equal gain to the wrong-doer and loss to his victim; it brings A to the position $A + C$, and B to the position $B - C$. The judge's task is to find the arithmetical mean between these, and this he does by transferring C from A to B. Thus (A being treated as $= B$) we get the arithmetical 'proportion'

$$(A + C) - (A + C - C) = (A + C - C) - (B - C)$$
or $$(A + C) - (B - C + C) = (B - C + C) - (B - C).$$

[7] l. 14.

judge is to go to justice; for the nature of the judge is to be a sort of animate justice; and they seek the judge as an intermediate, and in some states they call judges mediators, on the assumption that if they get what is intermediate they will get what is just. The just, then, is an intermediate, since the judge is so. Now the judge restores equality; it is as though there were a line divided into unequal parts, and he 25 took away that by which the greater segment exceeds the half, and added it to the smaller segment. And when the whole has been equally divided, then they say they have 'their own'—i. e. when they have got what is equal. The equal is intermediate between the greater and the lesser line according to arithmetical proportion. It is for this reason 30 also that it is called just (*dikaion*), because it is a division into two equal parts (*dicha*), just as if one were to call it (*dichaion*); and the judge (*dicastes*) is one who bisects (*dichastes*). For when something is subtracted from one of two equals and added to the other, the other is in excess by these two; since if what was taken from the one had not been added to the other, the latter would have been in excess by one only. It therefore exceeds the intermediate by one, and the inter- 1132^{b} mediate exceeds by one that from which something was taken. By this, then, we shall recognize both what we must subtract from that which has more, and what we must add to that which has less; we must add to the latter that by which the intermediate exceeds it, and subtract 5 from the greatest that by which it exceeds the intermediate. Let the lines AA', BB', CC' be equal to one another; from the line AA' let the segment AE have been subtracted, and to the line CC' let the segment CD [8] have been added, so that the whole line DCC' exceeds the line EA' by the segment CD and the segment CF; therefore it exceeds the line BB' by the segment CD.   9

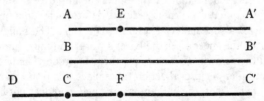

These names, both loss and gain, have come from voluntary exchange; 11 for to have more than one's own is called gaining, and to have less than one's original share is called losing, e. g. in buying and selling and 15 in all other matters in which the law has left people free to make their own terms; but when they get neither more nor less but just what

[8] *sc.* equal to AE.

belongs to themselves, they say that they have their own and that they neither lose nor gain.

Therefore the just is intermediate between a sort of gain and a sort of loss, viz. those which are involuntary;[9] it consists in having an
20 equal amount before and after the transaction.

5 Some think that *reciprocity* is without qualification just, as the Pythagoreans said; for they defined justice without qualification as reciprocity. Now 'reciprocity' fits neither distributive nor rectificatory
25 justice—yet people *want* even the justice of Rhadamanthus to mean this:

Should a man suffer what he did, right justice would be done

—for in many cases reciprocity and rectificatory justice are not in accord, e. g. (1) if an official has inflicted a wound, he should not be wounded in return, and if some one has wounded an official, he ought
30 not to be wounded only but punished in addition. Further (2) there is a great difference between a voluntary and an involuntary act. But in associations for exchange this sort of justice does hold men together —reciprocity in accordance with a proportion and not on the basis of precisely equal return. For it is by proportionate requital that the city holds together. Men seek to return either evil for evil—and if they
1133ᵃ cannot do so, think their position mere slavery—or good for good— and if they cannot do so there is no exchange, but it is by exchange that they hold together. This is why they give a prominent place to the temple of the Graces—to promote the requital of services; for this is characteristic of grace—we should serve in return one who has shown grace to us, and should another time take the initiative in showing it.
5 Now proportionate return is secured by cross-conjunction. Let A be a builder, B a shoemaker, C a house, D a shoe. The builder, then, must get from the shoemaker the latter's work, and must himself give
10 him in return his own. If, then, first there is proportionate equality of goods, and then reciprocal action takes place, the result we mention will be effected. If not, the bargain is not equal, and does not hold; for there is nothing to prevent the work of the one being better than that of the other; they must therefore be equated. (And this is true of the other
15 arts also; for they would have been destroyed if what the patient suf- fered had not been just what the agent did, and of the same amount and kind.) For it is not two doctors that associate for exchange, but a

[9] i. e. for the loser.

doctor and a farmer, or in general people who are different and unequal; but these must be equated. This is why all things that are exchanged must be somehow comparable. It is for this end that money has been introduced, and it becomes in a sense an intermediate; for it measures all things, and therefore the excess and the defect—how 20 many shoes are equal to a house or to a given amount of food. The number of shoes exchanged for a house [or for a given amount of food] must therefore correspond to the ratio of builder to shoemaker. For if this be not so, there will be no exchange and no intercourse. And this proportion will not be effected unless the goods are somehow 25 equal. All goods must therefore be measured by some one thing, as we said before. Now this unit is in truth demand, which holds all things together (for if men did not need one another's goods at all, or did not need them equally, there would be either no exchange or not the same exchange); but money has become by convention a sort of representa- 30 tive of demand; and this is why it has the name 'money' (*nomisma*) —because it exists not by nature but by law (*nomos*) and it is in our power to change it and make it useless. There will, then, be reciprocity when the terms have been equated so that as farmer is to shoemaker, the amount of the shoemaker's work is to that of the farmer's work for which it exchanges. But we must not bring them into a figure of 1133ᵇ proportion when they have already exchanged (otherwise one extreme will have both excesses), but when they still have their own goods. Thus they are equals and associates just because this equality can be effected in their case. Let A be a farmer, C food, B a shoemaker, D 5 his product equated to C. If it had not been possible for reciprocity to be thus effected, there would have been no association of the parties. That demand holds things together as a single unit is shown by the fact that when men do not need one another, i. e. when neither needs the other or one does not need the other, they do not exchange, as we do when some one wants what one has oneself, e. g. when people permit the exportation of corn in exchange for wine. This equation therefore 10 must be established. And for the future exchange—that if we do not need a thing now we shall have it if ever we do need it—money is as it were our surety; for it must be possible for us to get what we want by bringing the money. Now the same thing happens to money itself as to goods—it is not always worth the same; yet it tends to be steadier. This is why all goods must have a price set on them; for then there will 15 always be exchange, and if so, association of man with man. Money, then, acting as a measure, makes goods commensurate and equates

them; for neither would there have been association if there were not exchange, nor exchange if there were not equality, nor equality if there were not commensurability. Now in truth it is impossible that things differing so much should become commensurate, but with reference to demand they may become so sufficiently. There must, then, be a
20 unit, and that fixed by agreement (for which reason it is called money); for it is this that makes all things commensurate, since all things are measured by money. Let A be a house, B ten minae, C a bed. A is half of B, if the house is worth five minae or equal to them; the bed,
25 C, is a tenth of B; it is plain, then, how many beds are equal to a house, viz. five. That exchange took place thus before there was money is plain; for it makes no difference whether it is five beds that exchange for a house, or the money value of five beds.

30   We have now defined the unjust and the just. These having been marked off from each other, it is plain that just action is intermediate between acting unjustly and being unjustly treated; for the one is to have too much and the other to have too little. Justice is a kind of mean, but not in the same way as the other virtues, but because it relates to an intermediate amount, while injustice relates to the extremes. And
1134ᵃ justice is that in virtue of which the just man is said to be a doer, by choice, of that which is just, and one who will distribute either between himself and another or between two others not so as to give more of what is desirable to himself and less to his neighbour (and conversely
5 with what is harmful), but so as to give what is equal in accordance with proportion; and similarly in distributing between two other persons. Injustice on the other hand is similarly related to the unjust, which is excess and defect, contrary to proportion, of the useful or hurtful. For which reason injustice is excess and defect, viz. because it is productive of excess and defect—in one's own case excess of what is
10 in its own nature useful and defect of what is hurtful, while in the case of others it is as a whole like what it is in one's own case, but proportion may be violated in either direction. In the unjust act to have too little is to be unjustly treated; to have too much is to act unjustly.

    Let this be taken as our account of the nature of justice and
15 injustice, and similarly of the just and the unjust in general.

    6   Since acting unjustly does not necessarily imply being unjust, we must ask what sort of unjust acts imply that the doer is unjust with respect to each type of injustice, e. g. a thief, an adulterer, or a brigand. Surely the answer does not turn on the difference between these types.

For a man might even lie with a woman knowing who she was, but the origin of his act might be not deliberate choice but passion. He acts unjustly, then, but is not unjust; e. g. a man is not a thief, yet he stole, nor an adulterer, yet he committed adultery; and similarly in all other cases.

Now we have previously stated how the reciprocal is related to the just;[10] but we must not forget that what we are looking for is not only what is just without qualification but also political justice. This is found among men who share their life with a view to self-sufficiency, men who are free and either proportionately or arithmetically equal, so that between those who do not fulfil this condition there is no political justice but justice in a special sense and by analogy. For justice exists only between men whose mutual relations are governed by law; and law exists for men between whom there is injustice; for legal justice is the discrimination of the just and the unjust. And between men between whom there is injustice there is also unjust action (though there is not injustice between all between whom there is unjust action), and this is assigning too much to oneself of things good in themselves and too little of things evil in themselves. This is why we do not allow a *man* to rule, but *rational principle*, because a man behaves thus in his own interests and becomes a tyrant. The magistrate on the other hand is the guardian of justice, and, if of justice, then of equality also. And since he is assumed to have no more than his share, if he is just (for he does not assign to himself more of what is good in itself, unless such a share is proportional to his merits—so that it is for others that he labours, and it is for this reason that men, as we stated previously,[11] say that justice is 'another's good'), therefore a reward must be given him, and this is honour and privilege; but those for whom such things are not enough become tyrants.

The justice of a master and that of a father are not the same as the justice of citizens, though they are like it; for there can be no injustice in the unqualified sense towards things that are one's own, but a man's chattel,[12] and his child until it reaches a certain age and sets up for itself, are as it were part of himself, and no one chooses to hurt himself (for which reason there can be no injustice towards oneself). Therefore the justice or injustice of citizens is not manifested in these relations; for it was as we saw[13] according to law, and between people naturally subject to law, and these as we saw[14] are people who have an equal share in ruling and being ruled. Hence justice can

---

[10] 1132^b 21–1133^b 28.   [11] 1130^a 3.   [12] i. e. his slave.
[13] ^{a} 30.   [14] ^{a} 26–8.

15 more truly be manifested towards a wife than towards children and chattels, for the former is household justice; but even this is different from political justice.

7   Of political justice part is natural, part legal—natural, that which everywhere has the same force and does not exist by people's thinking 20 this or that; legal, that which is originally indifferent, but when it has been laid down is not indifferent, e. g. that a prisoner's ransom shall be a mina, or that a goat and not two sheep shall be sacrificed, and again all the laws that are passed for particular cases, e. g. that sacrifice shall be made in honour of Brasidas, and the provisions of 25 decrees. Now some think that all justice is of this sort, because that which is by nature is unchangeable and has everywhere the same force (as fire burns both here and in Persia), while they see change in the things recognized as just. This, however, is not true in this unqualified way, but is true in a sense; or rather, with the gods it is perhaps not true at all, while with us there is something that is just even by nature, yet all of it is changeable; but still some is by nature, some not by 30 nature. It is evident which sort of thing, among things capable of being otherwise, is by nature; and which is not but is legal and conventional, assuming that both are equally changeable. And in all other things the same distinction will apply; by nature the right hand is stronger, yet it is possible that all men should come to be ambidextrous. The things 1135ᵃ which are just by virtue of convention and expediency are like measures; for wine and corn measures are not everywhere equal, but larger in wholesale and smaller in retail markets. Similarly, the things which are just not by nature but by human enactment are not everywhere the same, since constitutions also are not the same, though there is but one which is everywhere by nature the best.

5   Of things just and lawful each is related as the universal to its particulars; for the things that are done are many, but of *them* each is one, since it is universal.

There is a difference between the act of injustice and what is unjust, and between the act of justice and what is just; for a thing is unjust by 10 nature or by enactment; and this very thing, when it has been done, is an act of injustice, but before it is done is not yet that but is unjust. So, too, with an act of justice (though the general term is rather 'just action', and 'act of justice' is applied to the correction of the act of injustice).

Each of these must later ¹⁵ be examined separately with regard to

¹⁵ Possibly a reference to an intended (or now lost) book of the *Politics* on laws.

the nature and number of its species and the nature of the things with which it is concerned.

8   Acts just and unjust being as we have described them, a man acts 15 unjustly or justly whenever he does such acts voluntarily; when involuntarily, he acts neither unjustly nor justly except in an incidental way; for he does things which happen to be just or unjust. Whether an act is or is not one of injustice (or of justice) is determined by its voluntariness or involuntariness; for when it is voluntary it is blamed, 20 and at the same time is then an act of injustice; so that there will be things that are unjust but not yet acts of injustice, if voluntariness be not present as well. By the voluntary I mean, as has been said before,[16] any of the things in a man's own power which he does with knowledge, i. e. not in ignorance either of the person acted on or of the instrument used or of the end that will be attained (e. g. whom he is striking, with 25 what, and to what end), each such act being done not incidentally nor under compulsion (e. g. if A takes B's hand and therewith strikes C, B does not act voluntarily; for the act was not in his own power). The person struck may be the striker's father, and the striker may know that it is a man or one of the persons present, but not know that it is his 30 father; a similar distinction may be made in the case of the end, and with regard to the whole action. Therefore that which is done in ignorance, or though not done in ignorance is not in the agent's power, or is done under compulsion, is involuntary (for many natural processes, even, we knowingly both perform and experience, none of which is 1135[b] either voluntary or involuntary; e. g. growing old or dying). But in the case of unjust and just acts alike the injustice or justice may be only incidental; for a man might return a deposit unwillingly and from fear, and then he must not be said either to do what is just or to act 5 justly, except in an incidental way. Similarly the man who under compulsion and unwillingly fails to return the deposit must be said to act unjustly, and to do what is unjust, only incidentally. Of voluntary acts we do some by choice, others not by choice; by choice those which we 10 do after deliberation, not by choice those which we do without previous deliberation. Thus there are three kinds of injury in transactions between man and man; those done in ignorance are *mistakes* when the person acted on, the act, the instrument, or the end that will be attained is other than the agent supposed; the agent thought either that he was not hitting any one or that he was not hitting with this missile

---

[16] 1109[b]35–1111[a]24.

or not hitting this person or to this end, but a result followed other
15 than that which he thought likely (e. g. he threw not with intent to
wound but only to prick), or the person hit or the missile was other
than he supposed. Now when (1) the injury takes place contrary to
reasonable expectation, it is a *misadventure*. When (2) it is not contrary to reasonable expectation, but does not imply vice, it is a *mistake*
(for a man makes a mistake when the fault originates in him, but
is the victim of accident when the origin lies outside him). When (3)
he acts with knowledge but not after deliberation, it is an *act of injus-*
20 *tice*—e. g. the acts due to anger or to other passions necessary or natural to man; for when men do such harmful and mistaken acts they act
unjustly, and the acts are acts of injustice, but this does not imply that
the doers are unjust or wicked; for the injury is not due to vice. But
25 when (4) a man acts from choice, he is an *unjust man* and a vicious man.

Hence acts proceeding from anger are rightly judged not to be done
of malice aforethought; for it is not the man who acts in anger but he
who enraged him that starts the mischief. Again, the matter in dispute
is not whether the thing happened or not, but its justice; for it is
apparent injustice that occasions rage. For they do not dispute about
30 the occurrence of the act—as in commercial transactions where one
of the two parties *must* be vicious [17]—unless they do so owing to forgetfulness; but, agreeing about the fact, they dispute on which side
justice lies (whereas a man who has deliberately injured another
cannot help knowing that he has done so), so that the one thinks he is
being treated unjustly and the other disagrees.

1136ª   But if a man harms another by choice, he acts unjustly; and *these*
are the acts of injustice which imply that the doer is an unjust man, provided that the act violates proportion or equality. Similarly, a man
is just when he acts justly by choice; but he *acts justly* if he merely
acts voluntarily.
5   Of involuntary acts some are excusable, others not. For the mistakes
which men make not only in ignorance but also from ignorance are
excusable, while those which men do not from ignorance but (though
they do them *in* ignorance) owing to a passion which is neither natural
nor such as man is liable to, are not excusable.

10 9   Assuming that we have sufficiently defined the suffering and doing
of injustice, it may be asked (1) whether the truth is expressed
in Euripides' paradoxical words:

---

[17] The plaintiff, if he brings a false accusation; the defendant, if he denies a
true one.

> 'I slew my mother, that's my tale in brief.'
> 'Were you both willing, or unwilling both?'

Is it truly possible to be willingly treated unjustly, or is all suffering of 15
injustice on the contrary involuntary, as all unjust action is voluntary?
And is all suffering of injustice of the latter kind or else all of the former,
or is it sometimes voluntary, sometimes involuntary? So, too, with the
case of being justly treated; all just action is voluntary, so that it is
reasonable that there should be a similar opposition in either case—
that both being unjustly and being justly treated should be either alike 20
voluntary or alike involuntary. But it would be thought paradoxical
even in the case of being justly treated, if it were always voluntary;
for some are unwillingly treated justly. (2) One might raise this question also, whether every one who has suffered what is unjust is being
unjustly treated, or on the other hand it is with suffering as with acting. 25
In action and in passivity alike it is possible to partake of justice
incidentally, and similarly (it is plain) of injustice; for to do what is
unjust is not the same as to act unjustly, nor to suffer what is unjust
as to be treated unjustly, and similarly in the case of acting justly and
being justly treated; for it is impossible to be unjustly treated if the
other does not act unjustly, or justly treated unless he acts justly. Now 30
if to act unjustly is simply to harm some one voluntarily, and 'voluntarily' means 'knowing the person acted on, the instrument, and the
manner of one's acting', and the incontinent man voluntarily harms
himself, not only will he voluntarily be unjustly treated but it will be
possible to treat oneself unjustly. (This also is one of the questions
in doubt, whether a man can treat himself unjustly.) Again, a man may 1136ᵇ
voluntarily, owing to incontinence, be harmed by another who acts
voluntarily, so that it would be possible to be voluntarily treated
unjustly. Or is our definition incorrect; must we to 'harming another,
with knowledge both of the person acted on, of the instrument, and of
the manner' add 'contrary to the wish of the person acted on'? Then a 5
man may be voluntarily harmed and voluntarily suffer what is unjust,
but no one is voluntarily treated unjustly; for no one wishes to be
unjustly treated, not even the incontinent man. He acts contrary to
his wish; for no one *wishes* for what he does not think to be good, but
the incontinent man does *do* things that he does not think he ought to
do. Again, one who gives what is his own, as Homer says Glaucus gave
Diomede

> *Armour of gold for brazen, the price of a hundred beeves for nine,*[18] 10

[18] *Il.* vi. 236.

is not unjustly treated; for though to give is in his power, to be unjustly treated is not, but there must be some one to treat him unjustly. It is plain, then, that being unjustly treated is not voluntary.

15   Of the questions we intended to discuss two still remain for discussion; (3) whether it is the man who has assigned to another more than his share that acts unjustly, or he who has the excessive share, and (4) whether it is possible to treat oneself unjustly. The questions are connected; for if the former alternative is possible and the distributor acts unjustly and not the man who has the excessive share, then if a man assigns more to another than to himself, knowingly and volun-
20   tarily, he treats himself unjustly; which is what modest people seem to do, since the virtuous man tends to take less than his share. Or does this statement too need qualification? For (a) he perhaps gets more than his share of some other good, e. g. of honour or of intrinsic nobility. (b) The question is solved by applying the distinction we applied to unjust action; [19] for he suffers nothing contrary to his own wish, so that he is not unjustly treated as far as this goes, but at most only suffers harm.

25   It is plain too that the distributor acts unjustly, but not always the man who has the excessive share; for it is not he to whom what is unjust appertains that acts unjustly, but he to whom it appertains to do the unjust act voluntarily, i. e. the person in whom lies the origin of the action, and this lies in the distributor, not in the receiver. Again,
30   since the word 'do' is ambiguous, and there is a sense in which lifeless things, or a hand, or a servant who obeys an order, may be said to slay, he who gets an excessive share does not act unjustly, though he 'does' what is unjust.

Again, if the distributor gave his judgment in ignorance, he does not act unjustly in respect of legal justice, and his judgment is not unjust in this sense, but in a sense it *is* unjust (for legal justice and primordial
1137ª   justice are different); but if with knowledge he judged unjustly, he is himself aiming at an excessive share either of gratitude or of revenge. As much, then, as if he were to share in the plunder, the man who has judged unjustly for these reasons has got too much; the fact that what he gets is different from what he distributes makes no difference, for even if he awards land with a view to sharing in the plunder he gets not land but money.

5   Men think that acting unjustly is in their power, and therefore that being just is easy. But it is not; to lie with one's neighbour's wife, to wound another, to deliver a bribe, is easy and in our power, but to do

these things as a result of a certain state of character is neither easy nor in our power. Similarly to know what is just and what is unjust requires, men think, no great wisdom, because it is not hard to understand the 10 matters dealt with by the laws (though these are not the things that are just, except incidentally); but how actions must be done and distributions effected in order to be just, to know *this* is a greater achievement than knowing what is good for the health; though even there, while it is easy to know that honey, wine, hellebore, cautery, and the use of the knife are so, to know how, to whom, and when these should 15 be applied with a view to producing health, is no less an achievement than that of being a physician. Again, for this very reason [20] men think that acting unjustly is characteristic of the just man no less than of the unjust, because he would be not less but even more capable of doing each of these unjust acts; [21] for he could lie with a woman or wound a neighbour; and the brave man could throw away his shield and turn 20 to flight in this direction or in that. But to play the coward or to act unjustly consists not in doing these things, except incidentally, but in doing them as the result of a certain state of character, just as to practise medicine and healing consists not in applying or not applying the knife, in using or not using medicines, but in doing so in a certain way. 25

Just acts occur between people who participate in things good in themselves and can have too much or too little of them; for some beings (e. g. presumably the gods) cannot have too much of them, and to others, those who are incurably bad, not even the smallest share in them is beneficial but all such goods are harmful, while to others they are beneficial up to a point; therefore justice is essentially something 30 human.

10 Our next subject is equity and the equitable (*to epieikes*), and their respective relations to justice and the just. For on examination they appear to be neither absolutely the same nor generically different; and while we sometimes praise what is equitable and the equitable man 35 (so that we apply the name by way of praise even to instances of the other virtues, instead of 'good,' meaning by *epieikesteron* that a 1137^{b} thing is better), at other times, when we reason it out, it seems strange if the equitable, being something different from the just, is yet praiseworthy; for either the just or the equitable is not good, if they are different; or, if both are good, they are the same.

[20] i. e. that stated in l. 4 f., that acting unjustly is in our own power.
[21] Cf. ll. 6–8.

5   These, then, are pretty much the considerations that give rise to the problem about the equitable; they are all in a sense correct and not opposed to one another; for the equitable, though it is better than one kind of justice, yet is just, and it is not as being a different class of thing that it is better than the just. The same thing, then, is just and
10 equitable, and while both are good the equitable is superior. What creates the problem is that the equitable is just, but not the legally just but a correction of legal justice. The reason is that all law is universal but about some things it is not possible to make a universal statement which shall be correct. In those cases, then, in which it is
15 necessary to speak universally, but not possible to do so correctly, the law takes the usual case, though it is not ignorant of the possibility of error. And it is none the less correct; for the error is not in the law nor in the legislator but in the nature of the thing, since the matter of practical affairs is of this kind from the start. When the law speaks uni-
20 versally, then, and a case arises on it which is not covered by the universal statement, then it is right, where the legislator fails us and has erred by over-simplicity, to correct the omission—to say what the legislator himself would have said had he been present, and would have put into his law if he had known. Hence the equitable is just, and
25 better than one kind of justice—not better than absolute justice but better than the error that arises from the absoluteness of the statement. And this is the nature of the equitable, a correction of law where it is defective owing to its universality. In fact this is the reason why all things are not determined by law, viz. that about some things it is impossible to lay down a law, so that a decree is needed. For when the thing is indefinite the rule also is indefinite, like the leaden rule used in
30 making the Lesbian moulding; the rule adapts itself to the shape of the stone and is not rigid, and so too the decree is adapted to the facts.

It is plain, then, what the equitable is, and that it is just and is better than one kind of justice. It is evident also from this who the
35 equitable man is; the man who chooses and does such acts, and is no
1138ᵃ stickler for his rights in a bad sense but tends to take less than his share though he has the law on his side, is equitable, and this state of character is equity, which is a sort of justice and not a different state of character.

11 Whether a man can treat himself unjustly or not, is evident from
5   what has been said.[22] For (a) one class of just acts are those acts in

---

[22] Cf. 1129ᵃ 32–ᵇ 1, 1136ᵃ 10–1137ᵃ 4.

accordance with any virtue which are prescribed by the law; e. g. the law does not expressly permit suicide, and what it does not expressly permit it forbids. Again, when a man in violation of the law harms another (otherwise than in retaliation) voluntarily, he acts unjustly, and a voluntary agent is one who knows both the person he is affecting by his action and the instrument he is using; and he who through anger voluntarily stabs himself does this contrary to the right rule of 10 life, and this the law does not allow; therefore he is acting unjustly. But towards whom? Surely towards the state, not towards himself. For he suffers voluntarily, but no one is voluntarily treated unjustly. This is also the reason why the state punishes; a certain loss of civil rights attaches to the man who destroys himself, on the ground that he is treating the state unjustly.

Further (b) in that sense of 'acting unjustly' in which the man who 'acts unjustly' is unjust only and not bad all round, it is not possible to treat oneself unjustly (this is different from the former sense; the 15 unjust man in one sense of the term is wicked in a particularized way just as the coward is, not in the sense of being wicked all round, so that his 'unjust act' does not manifest wickedness in general). For (i) that would imply the possibility of the same thing's having been subtracted from and added to the same thing at the same time; but this is impossible—the just and the unjust always involve more than one person. Further, (ii) unjust action is voluntary and done by choice, 20 and *takes the initiative* (for the man who because he has suffered does the same in return is not thought to act unjustly); but if a man harms himself he suffers and does the same things *at the same time*. Further, (iii) if a man could treat himself unjustly, he could be voluntarily treated unjustly. Besides, (iv) no one acts unjustly without committing particular acts of injustice; but no one can commit adultery with 25 his own wife or housebreaking on his own house or theft on his own property.

In general, the question 'can a man treat himself unjustly?' is solved also by the distinction we applied to the question 'can a man be voluntarily treated unjustly?' [23]

(It is evident too that both are bad, being unjustly treated and acting unjustly; for the one means having less and the other having more than the intermediate amount, which plays the part here that 30 the healthy does in the medical art, and that good condition does in the art of bodily training. But still acting unjustly is the worse, for it

[23] Cf. 1136ᵃ 31–ᵇ 5.

involves vice and is blameworthy—involves vice which is either of the complete and unqualified kind or almost so (we must admit the latter alternative, because not all voluntary unjust action implies injustice as a state of character), while being unjustly treated does not involve
35   vice and injustice in oneself. In itself, then, being unjustly treated is
1138ᵇ   less bad, but there is nothing to prevent its being incidentally a greater evil. But theory cares nothing for this; it calls pleurisy a more serious mischief than a stumble; yet the latter may become incidentally the more serious, if the fall due to it leads to your being taken prisoner or put to death by the enemy.)
5   Metaphorically and in virtue of a certain resemblance there is a justice, not indeed between a man and himself, but between certain parts of him; yet not every kind of justice but that of master and servant or that of husband and wife.²⁴ For these are the ratios in which the part of the soul that has a rational principle stands to the irrational part; and it is with a view to these parts that people also
10   think a man can be unjust to himself, viz. because these parts are liable to suffer something contrary to their respective desires; there is therefore thought to be a mutual justice between them as between ruler and ruled.

Let this be taken as our account of justice and the other, i. e. the other moral, virtues.

BOOK VI

1   Since we have previously said that one ought to choose that which is intermediate, not the excess nor the defect,¹ and that the intermediate is determined by the dictates of the right rule,² let us discuss the
20   nature of these dictates. In all the states of character we have mentioned,³ as in all other matters, there is a mark to which the man who has the rule looks, and heightens or relaxes his activity accordingly, and there is a standard which determines the mean states which we say are intermediate between excess and defect, being in accordance with
25   the right rule. But such a statement, though true, is by no means clear; for not only here but in all other pursuits which are objects of knowledge it is indeed true to say that we must not exert ourselves nor relax

²⁴Cf. 1134ᵇ 15-17.   ¹ 1104ᵃ 11-27, 1106ᵃ 26-1107ᵃ 27.
² 1107ᵃ 1, Cf. 1103ᵇ 31, 1114ᵇ 29.   ³ In iii. 6-v. 11.

our efforts too much nor too little, but to an intermediate extent and as the right rule dictates; but if a man had only this knowledge he would be none the wiser—e. g. we should not know what sort of medi- 30 cines to apply to our body if some one were to say 'all those which the medical art prescribes, and which agree with the practice of one who possesses the art.' Hence it is necessary with regard to the states of the soul also not only that this true statement should be made, but also that it should be determined what is the right rule and what is the standard that fixes it.

We divided the virtues of the soul and said that some are virtues 35 of character and others of intellect.[4] Now we have discussed in detail 1139ᵃ the moral virtues;[3] with regard to the others let us express our view as follows, beginning with some remarks about the soul. We said before [5] that there are two parts of the soul—that which grasps a rule or rational principle, and the irrational; let us now draw a similar 5 distinction within the part which grasps a rational principle. And let it be assumed that there are two parts which grasp a rational principle —one by which we contemplate the kind of things whose originative causes are invariable, and one by which we contemplate variable things; for where objects differ in kind the part of the soul answering to each of the two is different in kind, since it is in virtue of a certain 10 likeness and kinship with their objects that they have the knowledge they have. Let one of these parts be called the scientific and the other the calculative; for to deliberate and to calculate are the same thing, but no one deliberates about the invariable. Therefore the calculative is one part of the faculty which grasps a rational principle. We must, then, learn what is the best state of each of these two parts; for this 15 is the virtue of each.

2   The virtue of a thing is relative to its proper work. Now there are three things in the soul which control action and truth—sensation, reason, desire.

Of these sensation originates no action; this is plain from the fact that the lower animals have sensation but no share in action.   20

What affirmation and negation are in thinking, pursuit and avoidance are in desire; so that since moral virtue is a state of character concerned with choice, and choice is deliberate desire, therefore both the reasoning must be true and the desire right, if the choice is to be good, 25 and the latter must pursue just what the former asserts. Now this kind

[4] 1103ᵃ 3–7.   [5] 1102ᵃ 26–8.

of intellect and of truth is practical; of the intellect which is contemplative, not practical nor productive, the good and the bad state are truth
and falsity respectively (for this is the work of everything intellec-
30 tual); while of the part which is practical and intellectual the good
state is truth in agreement with right desire.

The origin of action—its efficient, not its final cause—is choice,
and that of choice is desire and reasoning with a view to an end. This
is why choice cannot exist either without reason and intellect or without a moral state; for good action and its opposite cannot exist with-
35 out a combination of intellect and character. Intellect itself, however,
moves nothing, but only the intellect which aims at an end and is
1139ᵇ practical; for this rules the productive intellect as well, since every one
who makes makes for an end, and that which is made is not an end in
the unqualified sense (but only an end in a particular relation, and the
end of a particular operation)—only that which is *done* is that; for
good action is an end, and desire aims at this. Hence choice is either
desiderative reason or ratiocinative desire, and such an origin of action
5 is a man. (It is to be noted that nothing that is past is an object of
choice, e. g. no one chooses to have sacked Troy; for no one *deliberates*
about the past, but about what is future and capable of being otherwise, while what is past is not capable of not having taken place; hence
Agathon is right in saying

10   For this alone is lacking even to God,
        To make undone things that have once been done.)

The work of both the intellectual parts, then, is truth. Therefore the
states that are most strictly those in respect of which each of these parts
will reach truth are the virtues of the two parts.

3 Let us begin, then, from the beginning, and discuss these states
15 once more. Let it be assumed that the states by virtue of which the soul
possesses truth by way of affirmation or denial are five in number, i. e.
art, scientific knowledge, practical wisdom, philosophic wisdom, intuitive reason; we do not include judgement and opinion because in these
we may be mistaken.

Now what *scientific knowledge* is, if we are to speak exactly and
not follow mere similarities, is plain from what follows. We all suppose
20 that what we know is not even capable of being otherwise; of things
capable of being otherwise we do not know, when they have passed
outside our observation, whether they exist or not. Therefore the
object of scientific knowledge is of necessity. Therefore it is eternal;

for things that are of necessity in the unqualified sense are all eternal; and things that are eternal are ungenerated and imperishable. Again, every science is thought to be capable of being taught, and its object of being learned. And all teaching starts from what is already known, as we maintain in the *Analytics* [6] also; for it proceeds sometimes through induction and sometimes by syllogism. Now induction is the starting-point which knowledge even of the universal presupposes, while syllogism proceeds *from* universals. There are therefore starting-points from which syllogism proceeds, which are not reached by syllogism; it is therefore by induction that they are acquired. Scientific knowledge is, then, a state of capacity to demonstrate, and has the other limiting characteristics which we specify in the *Analytics*; [7] for it is when a man believes in a certain way and the starting-points are known to him that he has scientific knowledge, since if they are not better known to him than the conclusion, he will have his knowledge only incidentally.

Let this, then, be taken as our account of scientific knowledge.

4   In the variable are included both things made and things done; making and acting are different (for their nature we treat even the discussions outside our school as reliable); so that the reasoned state of capacity to act is different from the reasoned state of capacity to make. Hence too they are not included one in the other; for neither is acting making nor is making acting. Now since architecture is an art and is essentially a reasoned state of capacity to make, and there is neither any art that is not such a state nor any such state that is not an art, *art* is identical with a state of capacity to make, involving a true course of reasoning. All art is concerned with coming into being, i. e. with contriving and considering how something may come into being which is capable of either being or not being, and whose origin is in the maker and not in the thing made; for art is concerned neither with things that are, or come into being, by necessity, nor with things that do so in accordance with nature (since these have their origin in themselves). Making and acting being different, art must be a matter of making, not of acting. And in a sense chance and art are concerned with the same objects; as Agathon says, 'art loves chance and chance loves art'. Art, then, as has been said,[8] is a state concerned with making, involving a true course of reasoning, and lack of art on the contrary is a

----

[6] *An. Post.* 71ª 1.   [7] Ib. ᵇ 9–23.   [8] l. 9.

state concerned with making, involving a false course of reasoning;
both are concerned with the variable.

5   Regarding *practical wisdom* we shall get at the truth by consider-
25 ing who are the persons we credit with it. Now it is thought to be the
mark of a man of practical wisdom to be able to deliberate well about
what is good and expedient for himself, not in some particular respect,
e. g. about what sorts of thing conduce to health or to strength, but
about what sorts of thing conduce to the good life in general. This is
shown by the fact that we credit men with practical wisdom in some
particular respect when they have calculated well with a view to some
30 good end which is one of those that are not the object of any art. It
follows that in the general sense also the man who is capable of deliberating has practical wisdom. Now no one deliberates about things that
are invariable, nor about things that it is impossible for him to do.
Therefore, since scientific knowledge involves demonstration, but
there is no demonstration of things whose first principles are variable
35 (for all such things might actually be otherwise), and since it is impossible to deliberate about things that are of necessity, practical wis-
1140ᵇ dom cannot be scientific knowledge nor art; not science because that
which can be done is capable of being otherwise, not art because action
and making are different kinds of thing. The remaining alternative,
5   then, is that it is a true and reasoned state of capacity to act with regard
to the things that are good or bad for man. For while making has an
end other than itself, action cannot; for good action itself is its end.
It is for this reason that we think Pericles and men like him have practical wisdom, viz. because they can see what is good for themselves
10 and what is good for men in general; we consider that those can do this
who are good at managing households or states. (This is why we call
temperance (*sophrosyne*) by this name; we imply that it preserves
one's practical wisdom (*sodsousa ten phronesin*). Now what it preserves is a judgement of the kind we have described. For it is not
any and every judgement that pleasant and painful objects destroy and
pervert, e. g. the judgement that the triangle has or has not its angles
15 equal to two right angles, but only judgements about what is to be done.
For the originating causes of the things that are done consist in the end
at which they are aimed; but the man who has been ruined by pleasure
or pain forthwith fails to see any such originating cause—to see that
for the sake of this or because of this he ought to choose and do whatever he chooses and does; for vice is destructive of the originating
cause of action.)

Practical wisdom, then, must be a reasoned and true state of 20 capacity to act with regard to human goods. But further, while there is such a thing as excellence in art, there is no such thing as excellence in practical wisdom; and in art he who errs willingly is preferable, but in practical wisdom, as in the virtues, he is the reverse. Plainly, then, practical wisdom is a virtue and not an art. There being two parts of the 25 soul that can follow a course of reasoning, it must be the virtue of one of the two, i. e. of that part which forms opinions; for opinion is about the variable and so is practical wisdom. But yet it is not only a reasoned state; this is shown by the fact that a state of that sort may be forgotten but practical wisdom cannot.   30

6   Scientific knowledge is judgement about things that are universal and necessary, and the conclusions of demonstration, and all scientific knowledge, follow from first principles (for scientific knowledge involves apprehension of a rational ground). This being so, the first principle from which what is scientifically known follows cannot be an object of scientific knowledge, of art, or of practical wisdom; for that 35 which can be scientifically known can be demonstrated, and art and practical wisdom deal with things that are variable. Nor are these first 1141ᵃ principles the objects of philosophic wisdom, for it is a mark of the philosopher to have *demonstration* about some things. If, then, the states of mind by which we have truth and are never deceived about things invariable or even variable are scientific knowledge, practical wisdom, philosophic wisdom, and intuitive reason, and it cannot be 5 any of the three (i. e. practical wisdom, scientific knowledge, or philosophic wisdom), the remaining alternative is that it is *intuitive reason* that grasps the first principles.

7   *Wisdom* (1) in the arts we ascribe to their most finished exponents, e. g. to Phidias as a sculptor and to Polyclitus as a maker of 10 portrait-statues, and here we mean nothing by wisdom except excellence in art; but (2) we think that some people are wise in general, not in some particular field or in any other limited respect, as Homer says in the *Margites*,

> Him did the gods make neither a digger nor yet a ploughman   15
> Nor wise in anything else.

Therefore wisdom must plainly be the most finished of the forms of knowledge. It follows that the wise man must not only know what follows from the first principles, but must also possess truth about the first principles. Therefore wisdom must be intuitive reason combined with scientific knowledge—scientific knowledge of the highest objects which has received as it were its proper completion.

20   Of the highest objects, we say; for it would be strange to think that the art of politics, or practical wisdom, is the best knowledge, since man is not the best thing in the world. Now if what is healthy or good is different for men and for fishes, but what is white or straight is always 25 the same, any one would say that what is wise is the same but what is practically wise is different; for it is to that which observes well the various matters concerning itself that one ascribes practical wisdom, and it is to this that one will entrust such matters. This is why we say that some even of the lower animals have practical wisdom, viz. those which are found to have a power of foresight with regard to their own life. It is evident also that philosophic wisdom and the art of politics cannot be the same; for if the state of mind concerned with a man's 30 own interests is to be called philosophic wisdom, there will be many philosophic wisdoms; there will not be one concerned with the good of all animals (any more than there is one art of medicine for all existing things), but a different philosophic wisdom about the good of each species.

But if the argument be that man is the best of the animals, this 1141ᵇ makes no difference; for there are other things much more divine in their nature even than man, e. g., most conspicuously, the bodies of which the heavens are framed. From what has been said it is plain, then, that philosophic wisdom is scientific knowledge, combined with intuitive reason, of the things that are highest by nature. This is why we say Anaxagoras, Thales, and men like them have philosophic but 5 not practical wisdom, when we see them ignorant of what is to their own advantage, and why we say that they know things that are remarkable, admirable, difficult, and divine, but useless; viz. because it is not human goods that they seek.

Practical wisdom on the other hand is concerned with things human and things about which it is possible to deliberate; for we say this is 10 above all the work of the man of practical wisdom, to deliberate well, but no one deliberates about things invariable, nor about things which have not an end, and that a good that can be brought about by action. The man who is without qualification good at deliberating is the man who is capable of aiming in accordance with calculation at the best for man of things attainable by action. Nor is practical wisdom concerned with universals only—it must also recognize the particulars; 15 for it is practical, and practice is concerned with particulars. This is why some who do not know, and especially those who have experience,

are more practical than others who know; for if a man knew that
light meats are digestible and wholesome, but did not know which sorts
of meat are light, he would not produce health, but the man who knows 20
that chicken is wholesome is more likely to produce health.

Now practical wisdom is concerned with action; therefore one
should have both forms of it, or the latter in preference to the former.
But of practical as of philosophic wisdom there must be a controlling kind.

8   Political wisdom and practical wisdom are the same state of mind,
but their essence is not the same. Of the wisdom concerned with the
city, the practical wisdom which plays a controlling part is legislative
wisdom, while that which is related to this as particulars to their uni- 25
versal is known by the general name 'political wisdom'; this has to
do with action and deliberation, for a decree is a thing to be carried out in the form of an individual act. This is why the exponents
of this art are alone said to 'take part in politics'; for these alone
'do things' as manual labourers 'do things'.

Practical wisdom also is identified especially with that form of
it which is concerned with a man himself—with the individual; and
this is known by the general name 'practical wisdom'; of the other 30
kinds one is called household management, another legislation, the
third politics, and of the latter one part is called deliberative and the
other judicial. Now knowing what is good for oneself will be one kind
of knowledge, but it is very different from the other kinds; and the 1142ª
man who knows and concerns himself with his own interests is
thought to have practical wisdom, while politicians are thought to be
busybodies; hence the words of Euripides,

> But how could I be wise, who might at ease,
> Numbered among the army's multitude,
> Have had an equal share? . . .
> For those who aim too high and do too much   5

Those who think thus seek their own good, and consider that one
ought to do so. From this opinion, then, has come the view that such
men have practical wisdom; yet perhaps one's own good cannot exist
without household management, nor without a form of government. 10
Further, how one should order one's own affairs is not clear and needs
inquiry.

What has been said is confirmed by the fact that while young men
become geometricians and mathematicians and wise in matters like

these, it is thought that a young man of practical wisdom cannot be found. The cause is that such wisdom is concerned not only with universals but with particulars, which become familiar from experience,
15 but a young man has no experience, for it is length of time that gives experience; indeed one might ask this question too, why a boy may become a mathematician, but not a philosopher or a physicist. Is it because the objects of mathematics exist by abstraction, while the first principles of these other subjects come from experience, and because young men have no conviction about the latter but merely use the proper language, while the essence of mathematical objects is plain enough to them?

20   Further, error in deliberation may be either about the universal or about the particular; we may fail to know either that all water that weighs heavy is bad, or that this particular water weighs heavy.

That practical wisdom is not scientific knowledge is evident; for it is, as has been said,[9] concerned with the ultimate particular fact, since the
25 thing to be done is of this nature. It is opposed, then, to intuitive reason; for intuitive reason is of the limiting premisses, for which no reason can be given, while practical wisdom is concerned with the ultimate particular, which is the object not of scientific knowledge but of perception—not the perception of qualities peculiar to one sense but a perception akin to that by which we perceive that the particular figure before us is a triangle; for in that direction as well as in that of the major premiss there will be a limit. But this is rather perception
30 than practical wisdom, though it is another kind of perception than that of the qualities peculiar to each sense.

9   There is a difference between inquiry and deliberation; for deliberation is inquiry into a particular kind of thing. We must grasp the nature of excellence in deliberation as well—whether it is a form of scientific knowledge, or opinion, or skill in conjecture, or some other kind of thing. *Scientific knowledge* it is not; for men do not inquire
1142ᵇ about the things they know about, but good deliberation is a kind of deliberation, and he who deliberates inquires and calculates. Nor is it *skill in conjecture*; for this both involves no reasoning and is something that is quick in its operation, while men deliberate a long time, and they say that one should carry out quickly the conclusions
5 of one's deliberation, but should deliberate slowly. Again, *readiness of mind* is different from excellence in deliberation; it is a sort of skill in conjecture. Nor again is excellence in deliberation *opinion* of any

9 1141ᵇ 14–22.

sort. But since the man who deliberates badly makes a mistake, while he who deliberates well does so correctly, excellence in deliberation is clearly a kind of correctness, but neither of knowledge nor of opinion; for there is no such thing as correctness of knowledge (since there is no such thing as error of knowledge), and correctness of opinion is truth; and at the same time everything that is an object of opinion is already determined. But again excellence in deliberation involves reasoning. The remaining alternative, then, is that it is *correctness of thinking*; for this is not yet assertion, since, while even opinion is not inquiry but has reached the stage of assertion, the man who is deliberating, whether he does so well or ill, is searching for something and calculating.

But excellence in deliberation is a certain correctness of deliberation; hence we must first inquire what deliberation is and what it is about. And, there being more than one kind of correctness, plainly excellence in deliberation is not any and every kind; for (1) the incontinent man and the bad man, if he is clever, will reach as a result of his calculation what he sets before himself, so that he will have deliberated correctly, but he will have got for himself a great evil. Now to have deliberated well is thought to be a good thing; for it is this kind of correctness of deliberation that is excellence in deliberation, viz. that which tends to attain what is good. But (2) it is possible to attain even good by a false syllogism, and to attain what one ought to do but not by the right means, the middle term being false; so that this too is not yet excellence in deliberation—this state in virtue of which one attains what one ought but not by the right means. Again (3) it is possible to attain it by long deliberation while another man attains it quickly. Therefore in the former case we have not yet got excellence in deliberation, which is rightness with regard to the expedient—rightness in respect both of the end, the manner, and the time. (4) Further it is possible to have deliberated well either in the unqualified sense or with reference to a particular end. Excellence in deliberation in the unqualified sense, then, is that which succeeds with reference to what is the end in the unqualified sense, and excellence in deliberation in a particular sense is that which succeeds relatively to a particular end. If, then, it is characteristic of men of practical wisdom to have deliberated well, excellence in deliberation will be correctness with regard to what conduces to the end of which practical wisdom is the true apprehension.

10   Understanding, also, and goodness of understanding, in virtue of which men are said to be men of understanding or of good under-

1143ᵃ standing, are neither entirely the same as opinion or scientific knowledge (for at that rate all men would have been men of understanding),
nor are they one of the particular sciences, such as medicine, the
science of things connected with health, or geometry, the science of
5 spatial magnitudes. For understanding is neither about things that
are always and are unchangeable, nor about any and every one of
the things that come into being, but about things which may become
subjects of questioning and deliberation. Hence it is about the same
objects as practical wisdom; but understanding and practical wisdom
are not the same. For practical wisdom issues commands, since its end
is what ought to be done or not to be done; but understanding only
10 judges. (Understanding is identical with goodness of understanding,
men of understanding with men of good understanding.) Now understanding is neither the having nor the acquiring of practical wisdom;
but as learning is called understanding when it means the exercise of
the faculty of knowledge, so 'understanding' is applicable to the exercise of the faculty of opinion for the purpose of judging of what some
one else says about matters with which practical wisdom is concerned
15 —and of judging soundly; for 'well' and 'soundly' are the same thing.
And from this has come the use of the name 'understanding' in virtue
of which men are said to be 'of good understanding', viz. from the
application of the word to the grasping of scientific truth; for we
often call such grasping understanding.

11   What is called judgement, in virtue of which men are said to 'be
20 sympathetic judges' and to 'have judgement', is the right discrimination of the equitable. This is shown by the fact that we say the equitable man is above all others a man of sympathetic judgement, and
identify equity with sympathetic judgement about certain facts. And
sympathetic judgement is judgement which discriminates what is
equitable and does so correctly; and correct judgement is that which
judges what is true.
25   Now all the states we have considered converge, as might be expected, to the same point; for when we speak of judgement and
understanding and practical wisdom and intuitive reason we credit
the same people with possessing judgement and having reached years
of reason and with having practical wisdom and understanding. For
all these faculties deal with ultimates, i. e. with particulars; and being
a man of understanding and of good or sympathetic judgement con-
30 sists in being able to judge about the things with which practical
wisdom is concerned; for the equities are common to all good men in

relation to other men. Now all things which have to be done are included among particulars or ultimates; for not only must the man
of practical wisdom know particular facts, but understanding and
judgement are also concerned with things to be done, and these are
ultimates. And intuitive reason is concerned with the ultimates in 35
both directions; for both the first terms and the last are objects of
intuitive reason and not of argument, and the intuitive reason which 1143ᵇ
is presupposed by demonstrations grasps the unchangeable and first
terms, while the intuitive reason involved in practical reasonings
grasps the last and variable fact, i.e. the minor premiss. For these
variable facts are the starting-points for the apprehension of the end,
since the universals are reached from the particulars; of these there- 5
fore we must have perception, and this perception is intuitive reason.

This is why these states are thought to be natural endowments—
why, while no one is thought to be a philosopher by nature, people
are thought to have by nature judgement, understanding, and intuitive reason. This is shown by the fact that we think our powers
correspond to our time of life, and that a particular age brings with it
intuitive reason and judgement; this implies that nature is the cause.
[Hence intuitive reason is both beginning and end; for demonstra- 10
tions are from these and about these.] Therefore we ought to attend
to the undemonstrated sayings and opinions of experienced and older
people or of people of practical wisdom not less than to demonstrations; for because experience has given them an eye they see aright.

We have stated, then, what practical and philosophic wisdom are,
and with what each of them is concerned, and we have said that each 15
is the virtue of a different part of the soul.

12   Difficulties might be raised as to the utility of these qualities of
mind. For (1) philosophic wisdom will contemplate none of the things
that will make a man happy (for it is not concerned with any coming into being), and though practical wisdom has *this* merit, for 20
what purpose do we need it? Practical wisdom is the quality of mind
concerned with things just and noble and good for man, but these are
the things which it is the mark of a *good* man to do, and we are none
the more able to act for *knowing* them if the virtues are states of
character, just as we are none the better able to act for knowing the 25
things that are healthy and sound, in the sense not of producing but
of issuing from the state of health; for we are none the more able to
act for having the art of medicine or of gymnastics. But (2) if we
are to say that a man should have practical wisdom not for the sake
of knowing moral truths but for the sake of becoming good, prac-

30 tical wisdom will be of no use to those who *are* good; but again it is of no use to those who have *not* virtue; for it will make no difference whether they have practical wisdom themselves or obey others who have it, and it would be enough for us to do what we do in the case of health; though we wish to become healthy, yet we do not learn the art of medicine. (3) Besides this, it would be thought strange if practical wisdom, being inferior to philosophic wisdom, is to be put in authority over it, as seems to be implied by the fact that the art which produces anything rules and issues commands about that thing.

35   These, then, are the questions we must discuss; so far we have only stated the difficulties.

1144ᵃ   (1) Now first let us say that in themselves these states must be worthy of choice because they are the virtues of the two parts of the soul respectively, even if neither of them produce anything.

(2) Secondly, they do produce something, not as the art of medicine produces health, however, but as health produces health; [10] so does philosophic wisdom produce happiness; for, being a part of

5 virtue entire, by being possessed and by actualizing itself it makes a man happy.

(3) Again, the work of man is achieved only in accordance with practical wisdom as well as with moral virtue; for virtue makes us aim at the right mark, and practical wisdom makes us take the right means. (Of the fourth part of the soul—the nutritive [11]—there is no

10 such virtue; for there is nothing which it is in its power to do or not to do.)

(4) With regard to our being none the more able to do because of our practical wisdom what is noble and just, let us begin a little further back, starting with the following principle. As we say that some people who do just acts are not necessarily just, i. e. those who do the

15 acts ordained by the laws either unwillingly or owing to ignorance or for some other reason and not for the sake of the acts themselves (though, to be sure, they do what they should and all the things that the good man ought), so is it, it seems, that in order to be good one must be in a certain state when one does the several acts, i. e. one

20 must do them as a result of choice and for the sake of the acts themselves. Now virtue makes the choice right, but the question of the things which should naturally be done to carry out our choice belongs not to virtue but to another faculty. We must devote our attention to these matters and give a clearer statement about them. There

----

10 i. e. as health, as an inner state, produces the activities which we know as constituting health.

11 The other three being the scientific, the calculative, and the desiderative.

is a faculty which is called cleverness; and this is such as to be able 25
to do the things that tend towards the mark we have set before ourselves, and to hit it. Now if the mark be noble, the cleverness is
laudable, but if the mark be bad, the cleverness is mere smartness;
hence we call even men of practical wisdom clever or smart. Practical wisdom is not the faculty, but it does not exist without this
faculty. And this eye of the soul acquires its formed state not with- 30
out the aid of virtue, as has been said [12] and is plain; for the syllogisms which deal with acts to be done are things which involve a
starting-point, viz. 'since the end, i. e. what is best, is of such and
such a nature', whatever it may be (let it for the sake of argument
be what we please); and this is not evident except to the good man;
for wickedness perverts us and causes us to be deceived about the 35
starting-points of action. Therefore it is evident that it is impossible
to be practically wise without being good.

13   We must therefore consider virtue also once more; for virtue 1144ᵇ
too is similarly related; as practical wisdom is to cleverness—not the
same, but like it—so is natural virtue to virtue in the strict sense. For
all men think that each type of character belongs to its possessors in
some sense by nature; for from the very moment of birth we are just or 5
fitted for self-control or brave or have the other moral qualities; but
yet we seek something else as that which is good in the strict sense—
we seek for the presence of such qualities in another way. For both
children and brutes have the natural dispositions to these qualities,
but without reason these are evidently hurtful. Only we seem to see 10
this much, that, while one may be led astray by them, as a strong
body which moves without sight may stumble badly because of its lack
of sight, still, if a man once acquires reason, that makes a difference in
action; and his state, while still like what it was, will then be virtue
in the strict sense. Therefore, as in the part of us which forms opinions
there are two types, cleverness and practical wisdom, so too in the 15
moral part there are two types, natural virtue and virtue in the strict
sense, and of these the latter involves practical wisdom. This is why
some say that all the virtues are forms of practical wisdom, and
why Socrates in one respect was on the right track while in another
he went astray; in thinking that all the virtues were forms of practical wisdom he was wrong, but in saying they implied practical wisdom 20
he was right. This is confirmed by the fact that even now all men, when
they define virtue, after naming the state of character and its objects
add 'that (state) which is in accordance with the right rule'; now the

[12] ll. 6–26.

right rule is that which is in accordance with practical wisdom. All men,
then, seem somehow to divine that this kind of state is virtue, viz. that
25 which is in accordance with practical wisdom. But we must go a little
further. For it is not merely the state in accordance with the right
rule, but the state that implies the *presence* of the right rule, that is
virtue; and practical wisdom is a right rule about such matters.
Socrates, then, thought the virtues were rules or rational principles
(for he thought they were, all of them, forms of scientific knowledge),
while we think they *involve* a rational principle.

30   It is clear, then, from what has been said, that it is not possible
to be good in the strict sense without practical wisdom, nor practically
wise without moral virtue. But in this way we may also refute the
dialectical argument whereby it might be contended that the virtues
exist in separation from each other; the same man, it might be said,
is not best equipped by nature for all the virtues, so that he will have
35 already acquired one when he has not yet acquired another. This is
possible in respect of the natural virtues, but not in respect of those
1145ᵃ in respect of which a man is called without qualification good; for with
the presence of the one quality, practical wisdom, will be given all
the virtues. And it is plain that, even if it were of no practical value,
we should have needed it because it is the virtue of the part of us
in question; plain too that the choice will not be right without prac-
5 tical wisdom any more than without virtue; for the one determines
the end and the other makes us do the things that lead to the end.

But again it is not *supreme* over philosophic wisdom, i. e. over the
superior part of us, any more than the art of medicine is over health;
for it does not use it but provides for its coming into being; it issues
10 orders, then, for its sake, but not to it. Further, to maintain its
supremacy would be like saying that the art of politics rules the gods
because it issues orders about all the affairs of the state.

BOOK VII

15 1   Let us now make a fresh beginning and point out that of moral
states to be avoided there are three kinds—vice, incontinence,
brutishness. The contraries of two of these are evident—one we call
virtue, the other continence; to brutishness it would be most fitting
20 to oppose superhuman virtue, a heroic and divine kind of nature, as
Homer has represented Priam saying of Hector that he was very good,

For he seemed not, he,
The child of a mortal man, but as one that of God's seed came.[1]

---

[1] *Il.* xxiv. 258 f.

Therefore if, as they say, men become gods by excess of virtue, of this kind must evidently be the state opposed to the brutish state; for as a brute has no vice or virtue, so neither has a god; his state is higher than virtue, and that of a brute is a different kind of state from vice.

Now, since it is rarely that a godlike man is found—to use the epithet of the Spartans, who when they admire any one highly call him a 'godlike man'—so too the brutish type is rarely found among men; it is found chiefly among barbarians, but some brutish quali- ties are also produced by disease or deformity; and we also call by this evil name those men who go beyond all ordinary standards by reason of vice. Of this kind of disposition, however, we must later make some mention,[2] while we have discussed vice before;[3] we must now discuss incontinence and softness (or effeminacy), and con- tinence and endurance; for we must treat each of the two neither as identical with virtue or wickedness, nor as a different genus. We must, as in all other cases, set the observed facts before us and, after first discussing the difficulties, go on to prove, if possible, the truth of all the common opinions about these affections of the mind, or, failing this, of the greater number and the most authoritative; for if we both refute the objections and leave the common opinions un- disturbed, we shall have proved the case sufficiently.

Now (1) both continence and endurance are thought to be included among things good and praiseworthy, and both incontinence and soft- ness among things bad and blameworthy; and the same man is thought to be continent and ready to abide by the result of his calcu- lations, or incontinent and ready to abandon them. And (2) the in- continent man, knowing that what he does is bad, does it as a result of passion, while the continent man, knowing that his appetites are bad, refuses on account of his rational principle to follow them. (3) The temperate man all men call continent and disposed to endurance, while the continent man some maintain to be always temperate but others do not; and some call the self-indulgent man incontinent and the incontinent man self-indulgent indiscriminately while others dis- tinguish them. (4) The man of practical wisdom, they sometimes say, cannot be incontinent, while sometimes they say that some who are practically wise and clever *are* incontinent. Again (5) men are said to be incontinent even with respect to anger, honour, and gain.— These, then, are the things that are said.

[2] Ch. 5.   [3] Bks. II–V.

2 Now we may ask (1) how a man who judges rightly can behave
incontinently. That he should behave so when he has knowledge,
some say is impossible; for it would be strange—so Socrates [4] thought
—if when knowledge was in a man something else could master it and
25 drag it about like a slave. For *Socrates* was entirely opposed to the view
in question, holding that there is no such thing as incontinence; no
one, he said, when he judges acts against what he judges best—people
act so only by reason of ignorance. Now this view plainly contradicts
the observed facts, and we must inquire about what happens to such
a man; if he acts by reason of ignorance, what is the manner of his
30 ignorance? For that the man who behaves incontinently does not,
before he gets into this state, *think* he ought to act so, is evident. But
there are *some* who concede certain of Socrates' contentions but not
others; that nothing is stronger than knowledge they admit, but not
that no one acts contrary to what has seemed to him the better course,
and therefore they say that the incontinent man has not knowledge
when he is mastered by his pleasures, but opinion. But *if* it is
35 opinion and not knowledge, if it is not a strong conviction that resists
1146ᵃ but a weak one, as in men who hesitate, we sympathize with their
failure to stand by such convictions against strong appetites; but we
do not sympathize with wickedness, nor with any of the other blameworthy states. Is it then *practical wisdom* whose resistance is mastered?
5 That is the strongest of all states. But this is absurd; the same man
will be at once practically wise and incontinent, but *no one* would say
that it is the part of a practically wise man to do willingly the basest
acts. Besides, it has been shown before that the man of practical
wisdom is one who will *act* [5] (for he is a man concerned with the
individual facts) [6] and who has the other virtues. [7]

(2) Further, if continence involves having strong and bad appe-
10 tites, the temperate man will not be continent nor the continent man
temperate; for a temperate man will have neither excessive nor bad
appetites. But the continent man *must*; for if the appetites are good,
the state of character that restrains us from following them is bad, so
15 that not all continence will be good; while if they are weak and not
bad, there is nothing admirable in resisting them, and if they are weak
and bad, there is nothing great in resisting these either.

(3) Further, if continence makes a man ready to stand by any and
every opinion, it is bad, i. e. if it makes him stand even by a false
opinion; and if incontinence makes a man apt to abandon any and

[4] Pl. *Prot.* 352 ʙ, ᴄ.   [5] 1140ᵇ 4–6.
[6] 1141ᵇ 16, 1142ᵃ 24.   [7] 1144ᵇ 30–1145ᵃ 2.

every opinion, there will be a good incontinence, of which Sophocles' Neoptolemus in the *Philoctetes* [8] will be an instance; for he is to be praised for not standing by what Odysseus persuaded him to do, because he is pained at telling a lie.

(4) Further, the sophistic argument presents a difficulty; the syllogism arising from men's wish to expose paradoxical results arising from an opponent's view, in order that they may be admired when they succeed, is one that puts us in a difficulty (for thought is bound fast when it will not rest because the conclusion does not satisfy it, and cannot advance because it cannot refute the argument). There is an argument from which it follows that folly coupled with incontinence is virtue; for a man does the opposite of what he judges, owing to incontinence, but judges what is good to be evil and something that he should not do, and in consequence he will do what is good and not what is evil.

(5) Further, he who on conviction does and pursues and chooses what is pleasant would be thought to be better than one who does so as a result not of calculation but of incontinence; for he is easier to cure since he may be persuaded to change his mind. But to the incontinent man may be applied the proverb 'when water chokes, what is one to wash it down with?' If he had been persuaded of the rightness of what he does, he would have desisted when he was persuaded to change his mind; but now he acts in spite of his being persuaded of something quite different.

(6) Further, if incontinence and continence are concerned with any and every kind of object, who is it that is incontinent in the unqualified sense? No one has all the forms of incontinence, but we say some people are incontinent without qualification.

3   Of some such kind are the difficulties that arise; some of these points must be refuted and the others left in possession of the field; for the solution of the difficulty is the discovery of the truth. (1) We must consider first, then, whether incontinent people act knowingly or not, and in what sense knowingly; then (2) with what sorts of object the incontinent and the continent man may be said to be concerned (i. e. whether with any and every pleasure and pain or with certain determinate kinds), and whether the continent man and the man of endurance are the same or different; and similarly with regard to the other matters germane to this inquiry. The starting-point of our investigation is (*a*) the question whether the continent man and the incontinent are differentiated by their objects or by their attitude, i. e.

[8] ll. 895–916.

whether the incontinent man is incontinent simply by being concerned with such and such objects, or, instead, by his attitude, or, instead of that, by both these things; (b) the second question is whether incontinence and continence are concerned with any and every object or not. The man who is incontinent in the unqualified sense is neither concerned with any and every object, but with precisely those with which 20 the self-indulgent man is concerned, nor is he characterized by being simply related to these (for then his state would be the same as self-indulgence), but by being related to them in a certain way. For the one is led on in accordance with his own choice, thinking that he ought always to pursue the present pleasure; while the other does not think so, but yet pursues it.

(1) As for the suggestion that it is true opinion and not knowledge against which we act incontinently, that makes no difference to the 25 argument; for some people when in a state of opinion do not hesitate, but think they know exactly. If, then, the notion is that owing to their weak conviction those who have opinion are more likely to act against their judgement than those who know, we answer that there need be no difference between knowledge and opinion in this respect; for some men are no less convinced of what they think than others of what they 30 know; as is shown by the case of Heraclitus. But (a), since we use the word 'know' in two senses (for both the man who has knowledge but is not using it and he who is using it are said to know), it *will* make a difference whether, when a man does what he should not, he has the knowledge but is not exercising it, or *is* exercising it; for the latter seems strange, but not the former.

35 (b) Further, since there are two kinds of premisses, there is 1147ᵃ nothing to prevent a man's having both premisses and acting against his knowledge, provided that he is using only the universal premiss and not the particular; for it is particular acts that have to be done. And there are also two kinds of universal term; one is predicable of 5 the agent, the other of the object; e. g. 'dry food is good for every man', and 'I am a man', or 'such and such food is dry'; but whether 'this food is such and such', of this the incontinent man either has not or is not exercising the knowledge.[9] There will, then, be, firstly, an enormous difference between these manners of knowing, so that to

---

[9] i. e., if I am to be able to deduce from (a) 'dry food is good for all men' that 'this food is good for me', I must have (b) the premiss 'I am a man' and (c) the premisses (i) 'x food is dry', (ii) 'this food is x'. I cannot fail to know (b), and I may know (c i); but if I do not know (c ii), or know it only 'at the back of my my mind', I shall not draw the conclusion.

know in one way when we act incontinently would not seem anything strange, while to know in the other way would be extraordinary.

And further (c) the possession of knowledge in another sense than those just named is something that happens to men; for within the case of having knowledge but not using it we see a difference of state, admitting of the possibility of having knowledge in a sense and yet not having it, as in the instance of a man asleep, mad, or drunk. But now this is just the condition of men under the influence of passion; for outbursts of anger and sexual appetites and some other such passions, it is evident, actually alter our bodily condition, and in some men even produce fits of madness. It is plain, then, that incontinent people must be said to be in a similar condition to men asleep, mad, or drunk. The fact that men use the language that flows from knowledge proves nothing; for even men under the influence of these passions utter scientific proofs and verses of Empedocles, and those who have just begun to learn a science can string together its phrases, but do not yet know it; for it has to become part of themselves, and that takes time; so that we must suppose that the use of language by men in an incontinent state means no more than its utterance by actors on the stage.

(d) Again, we may also view the cause as follows with reference to the facts of human nature. The one opinion is universal, the other is concerned with the particular facts, and here we come to something within the sphere of perception; when a single opinion results from the two, the soul must in one type of case [10] affirm the conclusion, while in the case of opinions concerned with production it must immediately act (e. g. if 'everything sweet ought to be tasted', and 'this is sweet', in the sense of being one of the particular sweet things, the man who can act and is not prevented must at the same time actually act accordingly). When, then, the universal opinion is present in us forbidding us to taste, and there is also the opinion that 'everything sweet is pleasant', and that 'this is sweet' (now this is the opinion that is active), [11] and when appetite happens to be present in us, the one opinion bids us avoid the object, but appetite leads us towards it (for it can move each of our bodily parts); so that it turns out that a man behaves incontinently under the influence (in a sense) of a rule and an opinion, and of one not contrary in itself, but only incidentally—for 1147ᵇ the appetite is contrary, not the opinion—to the right rule. It also follows that this is the reason why the lower animals are not incontinent, viz. because they have no universal judgment but only imagination and memory of particulars.

---

[10] i. e. in scientific reasoning.   [11] i. e. determines action (Cf. ᵇ10).

The explanation of how the ignorance is dissolved and the incontinent man regains his knowledge, is the same as in the case of the man drunk or asleep and is not particular to this condition; we must go to the students of natural science for it. Now, the last premiss both being an opinion about a perceptible object, and being what
10 determines our actions, this a man either has not when he is in the state of passion, or has it in the sense in which having knowledge did not mean knowing but only talking, as a drunken man may mutter the verses of Empedocles.[12] And because the last term is not universal nor equally an object of scientific knowledge with the universal term,
15 the position that Socrates sought to establish [13] actually seems to result; for it is not in the presence of what is thought to be knowledge proper that the affection of incontinence arises (nor is it this that is dragged about' as a result of the state of passion), but in that of perceptual knowledge.[14]

This must suffice as our answer to the question of action with and without knowledge, and how it is possible to behave incontinently with knowledge.

20 4   (2) We must next discuss whether there is any one who is incontinent without qualification, or all men who are incontinent are so in a particular sense, and if there is, with what sort of objects he is concerned. That both continent persons and persons of endurance, and incontinent and soft persons, are concerned with pleasures and pains, is evident.

Now of the things that produce pleasure some are necessary, while others are worthy of choice in themselves but admit of excess, the
25 bodily causes of pleasure being necessary (by such I mean both those concerned with food and those concerned with sexual intercourse, i. e. the bodily matters with which we defined [15] self-indulgence and temperance as being concerned), while the others are not necessary but worthy of choice in themselves (e. g. victory, honour, wealth, and
30 good and pleasant things of this sort). This being so, (a) those who go to excess with reference to the latter, contrary to the right rule which is in themselves, are not called incontinent simply, but incontinent with the qualification 'in respect of money, gain, honour, or anger',

---

[12] Cf. ᵃ10–24.   [13] 1145ᵇ 22–24.
[14] Even before the minor premiss of the practical syllogism has been obscured by passion, the incontinent man has not scientific knowledge in the strict sense, since his minor premiss is not universal but has for its subject a sensible particular, e. g. 'this glass of wine'.
[15] III. 10.

—not simply incontinent, on the ground that they are different from incontinent people and are called incontinent by reason of a resemblance. (Compare the case of Anthropos (Man), who won a contest at 35 the Olympic games; in his case the general definition of man differed 1148ᵃ little from the definition peculiar to *him,* but yet it *was* different.) [16] This is shown by the fact that incontinence either without qualification or in respect of some particular bodily pleasure is blamed not only as a fault but as a kind of vice, while none of the people who are incontinent in these other respects is so blamed.

But (*b*) of the people who are incontinent with respect to bodily enjoyments, with which we say the temperate and the self-indulgent 5 man are concerned, he who pursues the excesses of things pleasant— and shuns those of things painful, of hunger and thirst and heat and cold and all the objects of touch and taste—not by choice but contrary to his choice and his judgment, is called incontinent, not with the 10 qualification 'in respect of this or that', e. g. of anger, but just simply. This is confirmed by the fact that men are called 'soft' with regard to these pleasures, but not with regard to any of the others. And for this reason we group together the incontinent and the self-indulgent, the continent and the temperate man—but not any of these other types—because they are concerned somehow with the same pleasures 15 and pains; but though these are concerned with the same objects, they are not similarly related to them, but some of them make a deliberate choice while the others do not.[17]

This is why we should describe as self-indulgent rather the man who without appetite or with but a slight appetite pursues the excesses of pleasure and avoids moderate pains, than the man who does so because of his strong appetites; for what would the former do, if he had in 20 addition a vigorous appetite, and a violent pain at the lack of the 'necessary' objects?

Now of appetites and pleasures some belong to the class of things generically noble and good—for some pleasant things are by nature worthy of choice, while others are contrary to these, and others are intermediate, to adopt our previous distinction [18]—e. g. wealth, gain, 25 victory, honour. And with reference to all objects whether of this or of the intermediate kind men are not blamed for being affected by them, for desiring and loving them, but for doing so in a certain way,

---

[16] i. e. the definition appropriate to him was not 'rational animal' but 'rational animal who won the boxing contest at Olympia in 456 ʙ. ᴄ.'

[17] i. e. the temperate and the self-indulgent, not the continent and the incontinent.

[18] 1147ᵇ 23–31, where, however, the 'contraries' are not mentioned.

i. e. for going to excess. (This is why all those who contrary to the
rule either are mastered by or pursue one of the objects which are
30 naturally noble and good, e. g. those who busy themselves more than
they ought about honour or about children and parents, [are not
wicked]; for these too are goods, and those who busy themselves about
them are praised; but yet there is an excess even in them—if like
Niobe one were to f'ght even against the gods, or were to be as much
1148ᵇ devoted to one's father as Satyrus nicknamed 'the filial', who was
thought to be very silly on this point.[19]) There is no wickedness, then,
with regard to these objects, for the reason named, viz. because each of
them is by nature a thing worthy of choice for its own sake; yet
excesses in respect of them are bad and to be avoided. Similarly there
5 is no incontinence with regard to them; for incontinence is not only
to be avoided but is also a thing worthy of blame; but owing to a similarity in the state of feeling people apply the name incontinence,
adding in each case what it is in respect of, as we may describe as a
bad doctor or a bad actor one whom we should not call bad, simply.
As, then, in this case we do not apply the term without qualification
because each of these conditions is not badness but only analogous
10 to it, so it is clear that in the other case also that alone must be taken
to be incontinence and continence which is concerned with the same
objects as temperance and self-indulgence, but we apply the term to
anger by virtue of a resemblance; and this is why we say with a
qualification 'incontinent in respect of anger' as we say 'incontinent in
respect of honour, or of gain'.

15 5   (1) Some things are pleasant by nature, and of these (a) some are
so without qualification, and (b) others are so with reference to particular classes either of animals or of men; while (2) others are not
pleasant by nature, but (a) some of them become so by reason of
injuries to the system, and (b) others by reason of acquired habits,
and (c) others by reason of originally bad natures. This being so, it
is possible with regard to each of the latter kinds to discover similar
states of character to those recognized with regard to the former;
20 I mean (A) the brutish states,[20] as in the case of the female who,
they say, rips open pregnant women and devours the infants, or of the
things in which some of the tribes about the Black Sea that have gone
savage are said to delight—in raw meat or in human flesh, or in lending

[19] Nothing is really known about the Satyrus referred to, but Prof. Burnet's
suggestion that he was a king of Bosporus who deified his father seems probable.

[20] Answering to (2 c).

their children to one another to feast upon—or of the story told of Phalaris.[21]

These states are brutish, but (B) others arise as a result of disease [22] (or, in some cases, of madness, as with the man who sacrificed and ate [25] his mother, or with the slave who ate the liver of his fellow), and others are morbid states (C) resulting from custom,[23] e. g. the habit of plucking out the hair or of gnawing the nails, or even coals or earth, and in addition to these paederasty; for these arise in some by nature and in others, as in those who have been the victims of lust from [30] childhood, from habit.

Now those in whom nature is the cause of such a state no one would call incontinent, any more than one would apply the epithet to women because of the passive part they play in copulation; nor would one apply it to those who are in a morbid condition as a result of habit. To have these various types of habit is beyond the limits of vice, as brutishness is too; for a man who has them to master or be [1149ᵃ] mastered by them is not simple [continence or] incontinence but that which is so by analogy, as the man who is in this condition in respect of fits of anger is to be called incontinent in respect of that feeling, but not incontinent simply.

For every excessive state whether of folly, of cowardice, of self- [5] indulgence, or of bad temper, is either brutish or morbid; the man who is by nature apt to fear everything, even the squeak of a mouse, is cowardly with a brutish cowardice, while the man who feared a weasel did so in consequence of disease; and of foolish people those who by nature are thoughtless and live by their senses alone are brutish, like some races of the distant barbarians, while those who are [10] so as a result of disease (e. g. of epilepsy) or of madness are morbid. Of these characteristics it is possible to have some only at times, and not to be mastered by them, e. g. Phalaris may have restrained a desire to eat the flesh of a child or an appetite for unnatural sexual pleasure; but it is also possible to be mastered, not merely to have the [15] feelings. Thus, as the wickedness which is on the human level is called wickedness simply, while that which is not is called wickedness not simply but with the qualification 'brutish' or 'morbid', in the same way it is plain that some incontinence is brutish and some morbid, while [20] only that which corresponds to *human* self-indulgence is incontinence simply.

That incontinence and continence, then, are concerned only with the

[21] *sc.* and the bull. But Cf. 1149ᵃ 14.   [22] Answering to (2 *a*).
[23] Answering to (2 *b*).

same objects as self-indulgence and temperance and that what is concerned with other objects is a type distinct from incontinence, and called incontinence by a metaphor and not simply, is plain.

6   That incontinence in respect of anger is less disgraceful than that in respect of the appetites is what we will now proceed to see. (1) Anger
25 seems to listen to argument to some extent, but to mishear it, as do hasty servants who run out before they have heard the whole of what one says, and then muddle the order, or as dogs bark if there is but a knock at the door, before looking to see if it is a friend; so anger by
30 reason of the warmth and hastiness of its nature, though it hears, does not hear an order, and springs to take revenge. For argument or imagination informs us that we have been insulted or slighted, and anger, reasoning as it were that anything like this must be fought against, boils up straightway; while appetite, if argument or percep-
35 tion merely says that an object is pleasant, springs to the enjoyment
1149ᵇ of it. Therefore anger obeys the argument in a sense, but appetite does not. It is therefore more disgraceful; for the man who is incontinent in respect of anger is in a sense conquered by argument, while the other is conquered by appetite and not by argument.

(2) Further, we pardon people more easily for following natural
5 desires, since we pardon them more easily for following such appetites as are common to all men, and in so far as they are common; now anger and bad temper are more natural than the appetites for excess, i. e. for unnecessary objects. Take for instance the man who defended himself on the charge of striking his father by saying 'yes, but *he* struck *his*
10 father, and *he* struck *his,* and' (pointing to his child) 'this boy will strike *me* when he is a man; it runs in the family'; or the man who when he was being dragged along by his son bade him stop at the doorway, since he himself had dragged his father only as far as that.

(3) Further, those who are more given to plotting against others are more criminal. Now a passionate man is not given to plotting, nor is
15 anger itself—it is open; but the nature of appetite is illustrated by what the poets call Aphrodite, 'guile-weaving daughter of Cyprus', and by Homer's words about her 'embroidered girdle':

> And the whisper of wooing is there,
> Whose subtlety stealeth the wits of the wise, how prudent soe'er.[24]

Therefore if this form of incontinence is more criminal and disgraceful than that in respect of anger, it is both incontinence without qualification and in a sense vice.

[24] *Il.* xiv. 214, 217.

(4) Further, no one commits wanton outrage with a feeling of pain, [20] but every one who acts in anger acts with pain, while the man who commits outrage acts with pleasure. If, then, those acts at which it is most just to be angry are more criminal than others, the incontinence which is due to appetite is the more criminal; for there is no wanton outrage involved in anger.

Plainly, then, the incontinence concerned with appetite is more disgraceful than that concerned with anger, and continence and incon- [25] tinence are concerned with bodily appetites and pleasures; but we must grasp the differences among the latter themselves. For, as has been said at the beginning,[25] some are human and natural both in kind and in magnitude, others are brutish, and others are due to organic injuries and diseases. Only with the first of these are temper- [30] ance and self-indulgence concerned; this is why we call the lower animals neither temperate nor self-indulgent except by a metaphor, and only if some one race of animals exceeds another as a whole in wantonness, destructiveness, and omnivorous greed; these have no power of choice or calculation, but they *are* departures from the natural norm,[26] [35] as, among men, madmen are. Now brutishness is a less evil than vice, [1150ᵃ] though more alarming; for it is not that the better part has been perverted, as in man—they *have* no better part. Thus it is like comparing a lifeless thing with a living in respect of badness; for the badness of that which has no originative source of movement is always less hurtful, and reason is an originative source. Thus it is like comparing [5] injustice in the abstract with an unjust man. Each is in some sense worse; for a bad man will do ten thousand times as much evil as a brute.

7   With regard to the pleasures and pains and appetites and aversions arising through touch and taste, to which both self-indulgence [10] and temperance were formerly narrowed down,[27] it is possible to be in such a state as to be defeated even by those of them which most people master, or to master even those by which most people are defeated; among these possibilities, those relating to pleasures are incontinence and continence, those relating to pains softness and endurance. The state of most people is intermediate, even if they lean more [15] towards the worse states.

Now, since some pleasures are necessary while others are not, and

[25] 1148ᵇ 15-31.
[26] And therefore cannot be called self-indulgent properly, but *can* be so called by a metaphor.
[27] III. 10.

are necessary up to a point while the excesses of them are not, nor the deficiencies, and this is equally true of appetites and pains, the man who pursues the excesses of things pleasant, or pursues to excess neces-
20 sary objects, and does so by choice, for their own sake and not at all for the sake of any result distinct from them, is self-indulgent; for such a man is of necessity unlikely to repent, and therefore incurable, since a man who cannot repent cannot be cured. The man who is deficient in his pursuit of them is the opposite of self-indulgent; the man who is intermediate is temperate. Similarly, there is the man who avoids bodily pains not because he is defeated by them but by choice. (Of
25 those who do not *choose* such acts, one kind of man is led to them as a result of the pleasure involved, another because he avoids the pain arising from the appetite, so that these types differ from one another. Now any one would think worse of a man if with no appetite or with weak appetite he were to do something disgraceful, than if he did it under the influence of powerful appetite, and worse of him if he struck a blow not in anger than if he did it in anger; for what would he have
30 done if he *had* been strongly affected? This is why the self-indulgent man is worse than the incontinent.) Of the states named, then,[28] the latter is rather a kind of softness;[29] the former is self-indulgence. While to the incontinent man is opposed the continent, to the soft is opposed the man of endurance; for endurance consists in resisting,
35 while continence consists in conquering, and resisting and conquering are different, as not being beaten is different from winning; this is why
1150ᵇ continence is also more worthy of choice than endurance. Now the man who is defective in respect of resistance to the things which most men both resist and resist successfully is soft and effeminate; for effeminacy too is a kind of softness; such a man trails his cloak to avoid the pain of lifting it, and plays the invalid without thinking himself wretched, though the man he imitates is a wretched man.

5   The case is similar with regard to continence and incontinence. For if a man is defeated by violent and excessive pleasures or pains, there is nothing wonderful in that; indeed we are ready to pardon him if he has resisted, as Theodectes' Philoctetes does when bitten by the snake,
10 or Carcinus' Cercyon in the *Alope,* and as people who try to restrain their laughter burst out in a guffaw, as happened to Xenophantus. But it is surprising if a man is defeated by and cannot resist pleasures or pains which most men can hold out against, when this is not due to heredity or disease, like the softness that is hereditary with the

[28] In ll. 19–25.
[29] Not softness proper, which is non-deliberate avoidance of pain (ll. 13–15).

kings of the Scythians, or that which distinguishes the female sex from 15 the male.

The lover of amusement, too, is thought to be self-indulgent, but is really soft. For amusement is a relaxation, since it is a rest from work; and the lover of amusement is one of the people who go to excess in this.

Of incontinence one kind is impetuosity, another weakness. For some men after deliberating fail, owing to their emotion, to stand 20 by the conclusions of their deliberation, others because they have not deliberated are led by their emotion; since some men (just as people who first tickle others are not tickled themselves), if they have first perceived and seen what is coming and have first roused themselves and their calculative faculty, are not defeated by their emotion, whether it be pleasant or painful. It is keen and excitable people that 25 suffer especially from the impetuous form of incontinence; for the former by reason of their quickness and the latter by reason of the violence of their passions do not await the argument, because they are apt to follow their imagination.

8   The self-indulgent man, as was said,[30] is not apt to repent; for he stands by his choice; but any incontinent man is likely to repent. This 30 is why the position is not as it was expressed in the formulation of the problem,[31] but the self-indulgent man is incurable and the incontinent man curable; for wickedness is like a disease such as dropsy or consumption, while incontinence is like epilepsy; the former is a permanent, the latter an intermittent badness. And generally inconti- 35 nence and vice are different in kind; vice is unconscious of itself, incontinence is not (of incontinent men themselves, those who become 1151ᵃ temporarily beside themselves are better than those who have the rational principle but do not abide by it, since the latter are defeated by a weaker passion, and do not act without previous deliberation like the others); for the incontinent man is like the people who get drunk quickly and on little wine, i. e. on less than most people.

Evidently, then, incontinence is not·vice (though perhaps it is so 5 in a qualified sense); for incontinence is contrary to choice while vice is in accordance with choice; not but what they are similar in respect of the actions they lead to; as in the saying of Demodocus about the Milesians, 'the Milesians are not without sense, but they do the things that senseless people do', so too incontinent people are not criminal, but 10 they will do criminal acts.

Now, since the incontinent man is apt to pursue, not on conviction, bodily pleasures that are excessive and contrary to the right rule, while the self-indulgent man is convinced because he is the sort of man to pursue them, it is on the contrary the former that is easily per-
15 suaded to change his mind, while the latter is not. For virtue and vice respectively preserve and destroy the first principle, and in actions the final cause is the first principle, as the hypotheses [32] are in mathematics; neither in that case is it argument that teaches the first principles, nor is it so here—virtue either natural or produced by habituation is what teaches right opinion about the first principle. Such a man as this, then, is temperate; his contrary is the self-indulgent.
20   But there is a sort of man who is carried away as a result of passion and contrary to the right rule—a man whom passion masters so that he does not act according to the right rule, but does not master to the extent of making him ready to believe that he ought to pursue such pleasures without reserve; this is the incontinent man, who is better
25 than the self-indulgent man, and not bad without qualification; for the best thing in him, the first principle, is preserved. And contrary to him is another kind of man, he who abides by his convictions and is not carried away, at least as a result of passion. It is evident from these considerations that the latter is a good state and the former a bad one.

9   Is the man continent who abides by any and every rule and any and every choice, or the man who abides by the right choice, and is he
30 incontinent who abandons any and every choice and any and every rule, or he who abandons the rule that is not false and the choice that is right; this is how we put it before in our statement of the problem.[33] Or is it incidentally any and every choice but *per se* the true rule and
35 the right choice by which the one abides and the other does not? If any
1151^b one chooses or pursues this for the sake of that, *per se* he pursues and chooses the latter, but incidentally the former. But when we speak without qualification we mean what is *per se*. Therefore in a sense the one abides by, and the other abandons, any and every opinion; but without qualification, the true opinion.
There are some who are apt to abide by their opinion, who are
5 called strong-headed, viz. those who are hard to persuade in the first instance and are not easily persuaded to change; these have in them something like the continent man, as the prodigal is in a way like the liberal man and the rash man like the confident man; but they are

---

[32] i. e. the assumptions of the existence of the primary objects of mathematics, such as the straight line or the unit.
[33] 1146^a 16–31.

different in many respects. For it is to passion and appetite that the one will not yield, since on occasion the continent man *will* be easy to persuade; but it is to argument that the others refuse to yield, for 10 they do form appetites and many of them are led by their pleasures. Now the people who are strong-headed are the opinionated, the ignorant, and the boorish—the opinionated being influenced by pleasure and pain; for they delight in the victory they gain if they are not persuaded to change, and are pained if their decisions become null and 15 void as decrees sometimes do; so that they are liker the incontinent than the continent man.

But there are some who fail to abide by their resolutions, not as a result of incontinence, e. g. Neoptolemus in Sophocles' *Philoctetes*; yet it was for the sake of pleasure that he did not stand fast—but a noble pleasure; for telling the truth was noble to him, but he had been 20 persuaded by Odysseus to tell the lie. For not every one who does anything for the sake of pleasure is either self-indulgent or bad or incontinent, but he who does it for a disgraceful pleasure.

Since there is also a sort of man who takes less delight than he should in bodily things, and does not abide by the rule, he who is intermediate between him and the incontinent man is the continent man; 25 for the incontinent man fails to abide by the rule because he delights too much in them, and this man because he delights in them too little; while the continent man abides by the rule and does not change on either account. Now if continence is good, both the contrary states must be bad, as they actually appear to be; but because the other 30 extreme is seen in few people and seldom, as temperance is thought to be contrary only to self-indulgence, so is continence to incontinence.

Since many names are applied analogically, it is by analogy that we have come to speak of the 'continence' of the temperate man; for both the continent man and the temperate man are such as to do 35 nothing contrary to the rule for the sake of the bodily pleasures, but 1152ᵃ the former has and the latter has not bad appetites, and the latter is such as not to feel pleasure contrary to the rule, while the former is such as to feel pleasure but not to be led by it. And the incontinent and the self-indulgent man are also like another; they are different, 5 but both pursue bodily pleasures—the latter, however, also thinking that he ought to do so, while the former does not think this.

10   Nor can the same man have practical wisdom and be incontinent; for it has been shown [34] that a man is at the same time practically wise,

[34] 1144ᵃ 11–ᵇ 32.

and good in respect of character. Further, a man has practical wisdom not by knowing only but by being able to act; but the incontinent man is unable to act—there is, however, nothing to prevent a *clever*
10 man from being incontinent; this is why it is sometimes actually thought that some people have practical wisdom but are incontinent, viz. because cleverness and practical wisdom differ in the way we have described in our first discussions,[35] and are near together in respect of their reasoning, but differ in respect of their purpose—nor yet is the incontinent man like the man who knows and is contemplating a truth,
15 but like the man who is asleep or drunk. And he acts willingly (for he acts in a sense with knowledge both of what he does and of the end to which he does it), but is not wicked, since his purpose is good; so that he is half-wicked. And he is not a criminal; for he does not act of malice aforethought; of the two types of incontinent man the one does not abide by the conclusions of his deliberation, while the excit-
20 able man does not deliberate at all. And thus the incontinent man is like a city which passes all the right decrees and has good laws, but makes no use of them, as in Anaxandrides' jesting remark,

> 'The city willed it, that cares nought for laws';

but the wicked man is like a city that uses its laws, but has wicked laws to use.
25   Now incontinence and continence are concerned with that which is in excess of the state characteristic of most men; for the continent man abides by his resolutions more and the incontinent man less than most men can.

Of the forms of incontinence, that of excitable people is more cur-able than that of those who deliberate but do not abide by their decisions, and those who are incontinent through habituation are more curable than those in whom incontinence is innate; for it is
30 easier to change a habit than to change one's nature; even habit is hard to change just because it is like nature, as Evenus says:

> I say that habit's but long practice, friend,
> And this becomes men's nature in the end.

We have now stated what continence, incontinence, endurance, and
35 softness are, and how these states are related to each other.

1152ᵇ 11   The study of pleasure and pain belongs to the province of the political philosopher; for he is the architect of the end, with a view to which we call one thing bad and another good without qualification.

---

[35] 1144ᵃ 23–ᵇ4.

Further, it is one of our necessary tasks to consider them; for not only did we lay it down that moral virtue and vice are concerned with pains and pleasures,[36] but most people say that happiness involves pleasure; this is why the blessed man is called by a name derived from a word meaning enjoyment.[37]

Now (1) some people think that no pleasure is a good, either in itself or incidentally, since the good and pleasure are not the same; (2) others think that some pleasures are good but that most are bad. (3) Again there is a third view, that even if all pleasures are goods, yet the best thing in the world cannot be pleasure. (1) The reasons given for the view that pleasure is not a good at all are (a) that every pleasure is a perceptible process to a natural state, and that no process is of the same kind as its end, e. g. no process of building of the same kind as a house. (b) A temperate man avoids pleasures. (c) A man of practical wisdom pursues what is free from pain, not what is pleasant. (d) The pleasures are a hindrance to thought, and the more so the more one delights in them, e. g. in sexual pleasure; for no one could think of anything while absorbed in this. (e) There is no art of pleasure; but every good is the product of some art. (f) Children and the brutes pursue pleasures. (2) The reasons for the view that not all pleasures are good are that (a) there are pleasures that are actually base and objects of reproach, and (b) there are harmful pleasures; for some pleasant things are unhealthy. (3) The reason for the view that the best thing in the world is not pleasure is that pleasure is not an end but a process.

12 These are pretty much the things that are said. That it does not follow from these grounds that pleasure is not a good, or even the chief good, is plain from the following considerations. (A)[38] (a) First, since that which is good may be so in either of two senses (one thing good simply and another good for a particular person), natural constitutions and states of being, and therefore also the corresponding movements and processes, will be correspondingly divisible. Of those which are thought to be bad some will be bad if taken without qualification but not bad for a particular person, but worthy of his choice, and some will not be worthy of choice even for a particular person, but only at a particular time and for a short period, though not without qualification; while others are not even pleasures, but seem to be so, viz. all those which involve pain and whose end is curative, e. g. the processes that go on in sick persons.

---

[36] 1104^b 8–1105^a 13. [37] *makarios* from *mala chairein!*
[38] (A) is the answer to (1 a) and (3).

(*b*) Further, one kind of good being activity and another being state, the processes that restore us to our natural state are only inci-
35 dentally pleasant; for that matter the activity at work in the appetites for them is the activity of so much of our state and nature as has remained unimpaired; for there are actually pleasures that involve *no*
1153ᵃ pain or appetite (e. g. those of contemplation), the nature in such a case not being defective at all. That the others are incidental is indicated by the fact that men do not enjoy the same pleasant objects when their nature is in its settled state as they do when it is being replenished, but in the former case they enjoy the things that are pleasant without qualification, in the latter the contraries of these as well; for then they
5 enjoy even sharp and bitter things, none of which is pleasant either by nature or without qualification. The states they produce, therefore, are not pleasures naturally or without qualification; for as pleasant things differ, so do the pleasures arising from them.

(*c*) Again, it is not necessary that there should be something else better than pleasure, as some say the end is better than the process;
10 for pleasures are not processes nor do they all involve process—they are activities and ends; nor do they arise when we are becoming something, but when we are exercising some faculty; and not all pleasures have an end different from themselves, but only the pleasures of persons who are being led to the perfecting of their nature. This is why it is not right to say that pleasure is perceptible process, but it should
15 rather be called activity of the natural state, and instead of 'perceptible' 'unimpeded'. It is thought by *some* people to be process just because they think it is in the strict sense *good*; for they think that activity is process, which it is not.

(B) ³⁹ The view that pleasures are bad because some pleasant things are unhealthy is like saying that healthy things are bad because some healthy things are bad for money-making; both are bad
20 in the respect mentioned, but they are not *bad* for *that* reason—indeed, thinking itself is sometimes injurious to health.

Neither practical wisdom nor any state of being is impeded by the pleasure arising from it; it is foreign pleasures that impede, for the pleasures arising from thinking and learning will make us think and learn all the more.

(C) ⁴⁰ The fact that no pleasure is the product of any art arises
25 naturally enough; there is no art of any other activity either, but only of the corresponding faculty; though for that matter the arts of the perfumer and the cook *are* thought to be arts of pleasure.

---

³⁹ Answer to (2 *b*) and (1 *d*).   ⁴⁰ Answer to (1 *e*).

(D) [41] The arguments based on the grounds that the temperate man avoids pleasure and that the man of practical wisdom pursues the painless life, and that children and the brutes pursue pleasure, are all refuted by the same consideration. We have pointed out [42] in what sense pleasures are good without qualification and in what sense some are not good; now both the brutes and children pursue pleasures of the latter kind (and the man of practical wisdom pursues tranquil freedom from that kind), viz. those which imply appetite and pain, i. e. the bodily pleasures (for it is these that are of this nature) and the excesses of them, in respect of which the self-indulgent man is self-indulgent. This is why the temperate man avoids these pleasures; for even he *has* pleasures of his own.

13   But further (E) it is agreed that pain is bad and to be avoided; for some pain is without qualification bad, and other pain is bad because it is in some respect an impediment to us. Now the contrary of that which is to be avoided, *qua* something to be avoided and bad, is good. Pleasure, then, is necessarily a good. For the answer of Speusippus, that pleasure is contrary both to pain and to good, as the greater is contrary both to the less and to the equal, is not successful; since he would not say that pleasure is essentially just a species of evil.

And (F) [43] if certain pleasures are bad, that does not prevent the chief good from being some pleasure, just as the chief good may be some form of knowledge though certain kinds of knowledge are bad. Perhaps it is even necessary, if each disposition has unimpeded activities, that, whether the activity (if unimpeded) of all our dispositions or that of some one of them is happiness, this should be the thing most worthy of our choice; and this activity is pleasure. Thus the chief good would be some pleasure, though most pleasures might perhaps be bad without qualification. And for this reason all men think that the happy life is pleasant and weave pleasure into their ideal of happiness—and reasonably too; for no activity is perfect when it is impeded, and happiness is a perfect thing; this is why the happy man needs the goods of the body and external goods, i. e. those of fortune, viz. in order that he may not be impeded in these ways. Those who say that the victim on the rack or the man who falls into great misfortunes is happy if he is good, are, whether they mean to or not, talking nonsense. Now because we need fortune as well as other things, some people

1153ᵇ

30

35

5

10

15

20

[41] Answer to (ɪ *b*), (ɪ *c*), (ɪ *f*).   [42] 1152ᵇ 26–1153ᵃ 7.
[43] Answer to (2 *a*).

think good fortune the same thing as happiness; but it is not that, for even good fortune itself when in excess is an impediment, and perhaps should then be no longer called good fortune; for its limit is fixed by reference to happiness.

25   And indeed the fact that all things, both brutes and men, pursue pleasure is an indication of its being somehow the chief good:

> No voice is wholly lost that many peoples . . .

But since no one nature or state either is or is thought the best for all, neither do all pursue the same pleasure; yet all pursue pleasure. And perhaps they actually pursue not the pleasure they think they pursue nor that which they would say they pursue, but the same pleasure; for all things have by nature something divine in them. But the bodily pleasures have appropriated the name both because we oftenest steer our course for them and because all men share in them; thus because they alone are familiar, men think there are no others.

1154ᵃ   It is evident also that if pleasure, i. e. the activity of our faculties, is not a good, it will not be the case that the happy man lives a pleasant life; for to what end should he need pleasure, if it is not a good but the happy man may even live a painful life? For pain is neither an evil nor a good, if pleasure is not; why then should he avoid it? Therefore, too, the life of the good man will not be pleasanter than that of any one else, if his activities are not more pleasant.

14   (G) [44] With regard to the bodily pleasures, those who say that *some* pleasures are very much to be chosen, viz. the noble pleasures, but not the bodily pleasures, i. e. those with which the self-indulgent man is concerned, must consider why, then, the contrary things are bad. For the contrary of bad is good. Are the necessary pleasures good in the sense in which even that which is not bad is good? Or are they good up to a point? Is it that where you have states and processes of which there cannot be too much, there cannot be too much of the corresponding pleasure, and that where there can be too much of the one there can be too much of the other also? Now there can be too much of bodily goods, and the bad man is bad by virtue of pursuing the excess, not by virtue of pursuing the necessary pleasures (for *all* men enjoy in some way or other both dainty foods and wines and sexual intercourse, but not all men do so as they ought). The contrary is the case with pain; for he does not avoid the excess of it, he avoids it altogether; and this is peculiar to him, for the alternative to excess of pleasure is not pain, except to the man who pursues this excess.

[44] Answer to (2).

Since we should state not only the truth, but also the cause of error—for this contributes towards producing conviction, since when a reasonable explanation is given of why the false view appears true, this tends to produce belief in the true view—therefore we must state 25 why the bodily pleasures appear the more worthy of choice. (a) Firstly, then, it is because they expel pain; owing to the excesses of pain that men experience, they pursue excessive and in general bodily pleasure as being a cure for the pain. Now curative agencies produce 30 intense feeling—which is the reason why they are pursued—because they show up against the contrary pain. (Indeed pleasure is thought not to be good for these two reasons, as has been said,[45] viz. that (a) some of them are activities belonging to a bad nature—either congenital, as in the case of a brute, or due to habit, i. e. those of bad men; while (β) others are meant to cure a defective nature, and it is better to be in a healthy state than to be getting into it, but these arise 1154^b during the process of being made perfect and are therefore only incidentally good.) (b) Further, they are pursued because of their violence by those who cannot enjoy other pleasures. (At all events they go out of their way to manufacture thirsts somehow for themselves. When these are harmless, the practice is irreproachable; when they are hurtful, it is bad.) For they have nothing else to enjoy, and, besides, a 5 neutral state is painful to many people because of their nature. For the animal nature is always in travail, as the students of natural science also testify, saying that sight and hearing are painful; but we have become used to this, as they maintain. Similarly, while, in youth, people are, owing to the growth that is going on, in a situation like that of drunken men, and youth is pleasant,[46] on the other hand people 10 of excitable nature [47] always need relief; for even their body is ever in torment owing to its special composition, and they are always under the influence of violent desire; but pain is driven out both by the contrary pleasure, and by any chance pleasure if it be strong; and for these reasons they become self-indulgent and bad. But the pleasures 15 that do not involve pains do not admit of excess; and these are among the things pleasant by nature and not incidentally. By things pleasant incidentally I mean those that act as cures (for because as a result people are cured, through some action of the part that remains healthy, for this reason the process is thought pleasant); by things naturally pleasant I mean those that stimulate the action of the healthy nature.

---

[45] 1152^b 26–33.
[46] i. e. the growth or replenishment that is going on produces exhilaration and pleasure.
[47] Lit., melancholic people, those characterized by an excess of black bile.

20   There is no one thing that is always pleasant, because our nature
is not simple but there is another element in us as well, inasmuch as
we are perishable creatures, so that if the one element does something,
this is unnatural to the other nature, and when the two elements are
evenly balanced, what is done seems neither painful nor pleasant; for
25 if the nature of anything were simple, the same action would always
be most pleasant to it. This is why God always enjoys a single and
simple pleasure; for there is not only an activity of movement but an
activity of immobility, and pleasure is found more in rest than in
movement. But 'change in all things is sweet', as the poet says, because
of some vice; for as it is the vicious man that is changeable, so the
30 nature that needs change is vicious; for it is not simple nor good.

We have now discussed continence and incontinence, and pleasure
and pain, both what each is and in what sense some of them are good
and others bad; it remains to speak of friendship.

BOOK VIII

1155ª 1   After what we have said, a discussion of friendship would naturally follow, since it is a virtue or implies virtue, and is besides most
5 necessary with a view to living. For without friends no one would
choose to live, though he had all other goods; even rich men and those
in possession of office and of dominating power are thought to need
friends most of all; for what is the use of such prosperity without the
opportunity of beneficence, which is exercised chiefly and in its most
laudable form towards friends? Or how can prosperity be guarded and
10 preserved without friends? The greater it is, the more exposed is it to
risk. And in poverty and in other misfortunes men think friends are
the only refuge. It helps the young, too, to keep from error; it aids
older people by ministering to their needs and supplementing the
activities that are failing from weakness; those in the prime of life
15 it stimulates to noble actions—'two going together' [1]—for with friends
men are more able both to think and to act. Again, parent seems by
nature to feel it for offspring and offspring for parent, not only among
men but among birds and among most animals; it is felt mutually
20 by members of the same race, and especially by men, whence we praise
lovers of their fellowmen. We may see even in our travels how near
and dear every man is to every other. Friendship seems too to hold
states together, and lawgivers to care more for it than for justice; for
unanimity seems to be something like friendship, and this they aim

[1] *Il.* x. 224.

at most of all, and expel faction as their worst enemy; and when men 25 are friends they have no need of justice, while when they are just they need friendship as well, and the truest form of justice is thought to be a friendly quality.

But it is not only necessary but also noble; for we praise those who love their friends, and it is thought to be a fine thing to have many 30 friends; and again we think it is the same people that are good men and are friends.

Not a few things about friendship are matters of debate. Some define it as a kind of likeness and say like people are friends, whence come the sayings 'like to like', 'birds of a feather flock together', and 35 so on; others on the contrary say 'two of a trade never agree'. On this 1155ᵇ very question they inquire for deeper and more physical causes, Euripides saying that 'parched earth loves the rain, and stately heaven when filled with rain loves to fall to earth', and Heraclitus that 'it is what opposes that helps' and 'from different tones comes the fairest 5 tune' and 'all things are produced through strife'; while Empedocles, as well as others, expresses the opposite view that like aims at like. The physical problems we may leave alone (for they do not belong to the present inquiry); let us examine those which are human and involve character and feeling, e. g. whether friendship can arise 10 between any two people or people cannot be friends if they are wicked, and whether there is one species of friendship or more than one. Those who think there is only one because it admits of degrees have relied on an inadequate indication; for even things different in species admit of 15 degree. We have discussed this matter previously.

2   The kinds of friendship may perhaps be cleared up if we first come to know the object of love. For not everything seems to be loved but only the lovable, and this is good, pleasant, or useful; but it would seem to be that by which some good or pleasure is produced that is useful, so that it is the good and the useful that are lovable as ends. Do 20 men love, then, *the* good, or what is good for *them*? These sometimes clash. So too with regard to the pleasant. Now it is thought that each loves what is good for himself, and that the good is without qualification lovable, and what is good for each man is lovable for him; but each man loves not what is good for him but what seems 25 good. This however will make no difference; we shall just have to say that this is 'that which seems lovable'. Now there are three grounds on which people love; of the love of lifeless objects we do not use the word 'friendship'; for it is not mutual love, nor is there a wishing of

good to the other (for it would surely be ridiculous to wish wine well;
30 if one wishes anything for it, it is that it may keep, so that one may
have it oneself); but to a friend we say we ought to wish what is good
for his sake. But to those who thus wish good we ascribe only goodwill,
if the wish is not reciprocated; goodwill when it *is* reciprocal being
friendship. Or must we add 'when it is recognized'? For many people
35 have goodwill to those whom they have not seen but judge to be good
1156ᵃ or useful; and one of these might return this feeling. These people
seem to bear goodwill to each other; but how could one call them
friends when they do not know their mutual feelings? To be friends,
then, they must be mutually recognized as bearing goodwill and wish-
5 ing well to each other for one of the aforesaid reasons.

3 Now these reasons differ from each other in kind; so, therefore, do
the corresponding forms of love and friendship. There are therefore
three kinds of friendship, equal in number to the things that are love-
able; for with respect to each there is a mutual and recognized love,
and those who love each other wish well to each other in that respect
10 in which they love one another. Now those who love each other for
their utility do not love each other for themselves but in virtue of some
good which they get from each other. So too with those who love for the
sake of pleasure; it is not for their character that men love ready-
witted people, but because they find them pleasant. Therefore those
15 who love for the sake of utility love for the sake of what is good for
themselves, and those who love for the sake of pleasure do so for the
sake of what is pleasant to *themselves,* and not in so far as the other
is the person loved but in so far as he is useful or pleasant. And thus
these friendships are only incidental; for it is not as being the man he
is that the loved person is loved, but as providing some good or pleas-
20 ure. Such friendships, then, are easily dissolved, if the parties do
not remain like themselves; for if the one party is no longer pleasant
or useful the other ceases to love him.

Now the useful is not permanent but is always changing. Thus
when the motive of the friendship is done away, the friendship is
dissolved, inasmuch as it existed only for the ends in question. This
25 kind of friendship seems to exist chiefly between old people (for at
that age people pursue not the pleasant but the useful) and, of those
who are in their prime or young, between those who pursue utility.
And such people do not live much with each other either; for sometimes they do not even find each other pleasant; therefore they do
not need such companionship unless they are useful to each other; for

they are pleasant to each other only in so far as they rouse in each other hopes of something good to come. Among such friendships people also class the friendship of host and guest. On the other hand the friendship of young people seems to aim at pleasure; for they live under the guidance of emotion, and pursue above all what is pleasant to themselves and what is immediately before them; but with increasing age their pleasures become different. This is why they quickly become friends and quickly cease to be so; their friend- 35 ship changes with the object that is found pleasant, and such pleasure alters quickly. Young people are amorous too; for the greater part 1156ᵇ of the friendship of love depends on emotion and aims at pleasure; this is why they fall in love and quickly fall out of love, changing often within a single day. But these people do wish to spend their days and lives together; for it is thus that they attain the purpose of 5 their friendship.

Perfect friendship is the friendship of men who are good, and alike in virtue; for these wish well alike to each other *qua* good, and they are good in themselves. Now those who wish well to their friends for their sake are most truly friends; for they do this by reason of their 10 own nature and not incidentally; therefore their friendship lasts as long as they are good—and goodness is an enduring thing. And each is good without qualification and to his friend, for the good are both good without qualification and useful to each other. So too they are 15 pleasant; for the good are pleasant both without qualification and to each other, since to each his own activities and others like them are pleasurable, and the actions of the good *are* the same or like. And such a friendship is as might be expected permanent, since there meet in it all the qualities that friends should have. For all friendship is for the sake of good or of pleasure—good or pleasure either in the 20 abstract or such as will be enjoyed by him who has the friendly feeling—and is based on a certain resemblance; and to a friendship of good men all the qualities we have named belong in virtue of the nature of the friends themselves; for in the case of this kind of friendship the other qualities also [2] are alike in both friends, and that which is good without qualification is also without qualification pleasant, and these are the most lovable qualities. Love and friendship therefore are found most and in their best form between such men.

But it is natural that such friendships should be infrequent; for such men are rare. Further, such friendship requires time and famili- 25 arity; as the proverb says, men cannot know each other till they have

---

[2] i. e. absolute pleasantness, relative goodness, and relative pleasantness, as well as absolute goodness.

'eaten salt together'; nor can they admit each other to friendship or be friends till each has been found lovable and been trusted by each. Those who quickly show the marks of friendship to each other wish
30 to be friends, but are not friends unless they both are lovable and know the fact; for a wish for friendship may arise quickly, but friendship does not.

4   This kind of friendship, then, is perfect both in respect of duration and in all other respects, and in it each gets from each in all respects the same as, or something like what, he gives; which is what
35 ought to happen between friends. Friendship for the sake of pleas
1157ᵃ ure bears a resemblance to this kind; for good people too *are* pleasant to each other. So too does friendship for the sake of utility; for the good are also useful to each other. Among men of these inferior sorts too, friendships are most permanent when the friends get the same
5 thing from each other (e. g. pleasure), and not only that but also from the same source, as happens between ready-witted people, not as happens between lover and beloved. For these do not take pleasure in the same things, but the one in seeing the beloved and the other in receiving attentions from his lover; and when the bloom of youth is passing the friendship sometimes passes too (for the one finds no pleasure in the sight of the other, and the other gets no attentions
10 from the first); but many lovers on the other hand are constant, if familiarity has led them to love each other's characters, these being alike. But those who exchange not pleasure but utility in their amour are both less truly friends and less constant. Those who are friends
15 for the sake of utility part when the advantage is at an end; for they were lovers not of each other but of profit.

For the sake of pleasure or utility, then, even bad men may be friends of each other, or good men of bad, or one who is neither good nor bad may be a friend to any sort of person, but for their own sake clearly only good men can be friends; for bad men do not delight in each other unless some advantage come of the relation.
20   The friendship of the good too and this alone is proof against slander; for it is not easy to trust any one's talk about a man who has long been tested by oneself; and it is among good men that trust and the feeling that 'he would never wrong me' and all the other things that are demanded in true friendship are found. In the other kinds of friendship, however, there is nothing to prevent these evils arising.
25   For men apply the name of friends even to those whose motive is

utility, in which sense states are said to be friendly (for the alliances of states seem to aim at advantage), and to those who love each other for the sake of pleasure, in which sense children are called friends. Therefore we too ought perhaps to call such people friends, and say that there are several kinds of friendship—firstly and in the proper sense that of good men *qua* good, and by analogy the other kinds; for it is in virtue of something good and something akin to what is found in true friendship that they are friends, since even the pleasant is good for the lovers of pleasure. But these two kinds of friendship are not often united, nor do the same people become friends for the sake of utility and of pleasure; for things that are only incidentally connected are not often coupled together. 30 ... 35

Friendship being divided into these kinds, bad men will be friends for the sake of pleasure or of utility, being in this respect like each other, but good men will be friends for their own sake, i. e. in virtue of their goodness. These, then, are friends without qualification; the others are friends incidentally and through a resemblance to these. 1157ᵇ

5 As in regard to the virtues some men are called good in respect of a state of character, others in respect of an activity, so too in the case of friendship; for those who live together delight in each other and confer benefits on each other, but those who are asleep or locally separated are not performing, but are disposed to perform, the activities of friendship; distance does not break off the friendship absolutely, but only the activity of it. But if the absence is lasting, it seems actually to make men forget their friendship; hence the saying 'out of sight, out of mind'. Neither old people nor sour people seem to make friends easily; for there is little that is pleasant in them, and no one can spend his days with one whose company is painful, or not pleasant, since nature seems above all to avoid the painful and to aim at the pleasant. Those, however, who approve of each other but do not live together seem to be well-disposed rather than actual friends. For there is nothing so characteristic of friends as living together (since while it is people who are in need that desire benefits, even those who are supremely happy desire to spend their days together; for solitude suits such people least of all); but people cannot live together if they are not pleasant and do not enjoy the same things, as friends who are companions seem to do. 5 ... 10 ... 15 ... 20

The truest friendship, then, is that of the good, as we have frequently said;[3] for that which is without qualification good or 25

3 1156ᵇ 7, 23, 33, 1157ᵃ 30, ᵇ4.

pleasant seems to be lovable and desirable, and for each person that which is good or pleasant to him; and the good man is lovable and desirable to the good man for both these reasons. Now it looks as if love were a feeling, friendship a state of character; for love may be
30 felt just as much towards lifeless things, but mutual love involves choice and choice springs from a state of character; and men wish well to those whom they love, for their sake, not as a result of feeling but as a result of a state of character. And in loving a friend men love what is good for themselves; for the good man in becoming a friend becomes a good to his friend. Each, then, both loves what
35 is good for himself, and makes an equal return in goodwill and in pleasantness; for friendship is said to be equality, and both of these are found most in the friendship of the good.

1158ᵃ 6 Between sour and elderly people friendship arises less readily, inasmuch as they are less good-tempered and enjoy companionship less; for these are thought to be the greatest marks of friendship and most productive of it. This is why, while young men become
5 friends quickly, old men do not; it is because men do not become friends with those in whom they do not delight; and similarly sour people do not quickly make friends either. But such men may bear goodwill to each other; for they wish one another well and aid one another in need; but they are hardly *friends* because they do not spend their days together nor delight in each other, and these are thought the greatest marks of friendship.
10   One cannot be a friend to many people in the sense of having friendship of the perfect type with them, just as one cannot be in love with many people at once (for love is a sort of excess of feeling, and it is the nature of such only to be felt towards one person); and it is not easy for many people at the same time to please the same person very greatly, or perhaps even to be good in his eyes. One must, too, acquire some experience of the other person and become familiar
15 with him, and that is very hard. But with a view to utility or pleasure it is possible that many people should please one; for many people are useful or pleasant, and these services take little time.
    Of these two kinds that which is for the sake of pleasure is the more like friendship, when both parties get the same things from each other and delight in each other or in the same things, as in the
20 friendships of the young; for generosity is more found in such friend-ships. Friendship based on utility is for the commercially minded. People who are supremely happy, too, have no need of useful friends, but do need pleasant friends; for they wish to live with *some one* and,

though they can endure for a short time what is painful, no one could put up with it continuously, nor even with the Good itself if it were painful to him; this is why they look out for friends who are pleasant. 25 Perhaps they should look out for friends who, being pleasant, are also good, and good for them, too; for so they will have all the characteristics that friends should have.

People in positions of authority seem to have friends who fall into distinct classes; some people are useful to them and others are pleasant, but the same people are rarely both; for they seek neither those whose pleasantness is accompanied by virtue nor those whose 30 utility is with a view to noble objects, but in their desire for pleasure they seek for ready-witted people, and their other friends they choose as being clever at doing what they are told, and these characteristics are rarely combined. Now we have said that the *good* man *is* at the same time pleasant and useful; [4] but such a man does not become the friend of one who surpasses him in station, unless he is surpassed also in virtue; if this is not so, he does not establish equality 35 by being proportionally exceeded in both respects. But people who surpass him in both respects are not so easy to find.

However that may be, the aforesaid friendships involve equality; 1158[b] for the friends get the same things from one another and wish the same things for one another, or exchange one thing for another, e. g. pleasure for utility; we have said,[5] however, that they are both less truly friendships and less permanent. But it is from their likeness and 5 their unlikeness to the same thing that they are thought both to be and not to be friendships. It is by their likeness to the friendship of virtue that they seem to be friendships (for one of them involves pleasure and the other utility, and these characteristics belong to the friendship of virtue as well); while it is because the friendship of virtue is proof against slander and permanent, while these quickly change (besides differing from the former in many other respects), that they appear *not* to be friendships; i. e. it is because of their unlike- 10 ness to the friendship of virtue.

7 But there is another kind of friendship, viz. that which involves an inequality between the parties, e. g. that of father to son and in general of elder to younger, that of man to wife and in general that of ruler to subject. And these friendships differ also from each 15 other; for it is not the same that exists between parents and children and between rulers and subjects, nor is even that of father to son

---

[4] 1156[b] 13–15, 1157[a] 1–3.   [5] 1156[a] 16–24, 1157[a] 20–33.

the same as that of son to father, nor that of husband to wife the same as that of wife to husband. For the virtue and the function of each of these is different, and so are the reasons for which they love; 20 the love and the friendship are therefore different also. Each party, then, neither gets the same from the other, nor ought to seek it; but when children render to parents what they ought to render to those who brought them into the world, and parents render what they should to their children, the friendship of such persons will be abiding and excellent. In all friendships implying inequality the love also 25 should be proportional, i. e. the better should be more loved than he loves, and so should the more useful, and similarly in each of the other cases; for when the love is in proportion to the merit of the parties, then in a sense arises equality, which is certainly held to be characteristic of friendship.

But equality does not seem to take the same form in acts of justice 30 and in friendship; for in acts of justice what is equal in the primary sense is that which is in proportion to merit, while quantitative equality is secondary, but in friendship quantitative equality is primary and proportion to merit secondary. This becomes clear if there is a great interval in respect of virtue or vice or wealth or anything else between the parties; for then they are no longer friends, and do 35 not even expect to be so. And this is most manifest in the case of the gods; for they surpass us most decisively in all good things. But 1159ᵃ it is clear also in the case of kings; for with them, too, men who are much their inferiors do not expect to be friends; nor do men of no account expect to be friends with the best or wisest men. In such cases it is not possible to define exactly up to what point friends can remain friends; for much can be taken away and friendship remain, but when one party is removed to a great distance, as God is, the pos- 5 sibility of friendship ceases. This is in fact the origin of the question whether friends really wish for their friends the greatest goods, e. g. that of being gods; since in that case their friends will no longer be friends to them, and therefore will not be good things for them (for friends *are* good things). The answer is that if we were right in saying that friend wishes good to friend for his sake,[6] his friend must 10 remain the sort of being he is, whatever that may be; therefore it is for him only so long as he remains a man that he will wish the greatest goods. But perhaps not *all* the greatest goods; for it is for himself most of all that each man wishes what is good.

[6] 1155ᵇ 31.

8 Most people seem, owing to ambition, to wish to be loved rather than to love; which is why most men love flattery; for the flatterer is a friend in an inferior position, or pretends to be such and to love more than he is loved; and being loved seems to be akin to being 15 honoured, and this is what most people aim at. But it seems to be not for its own sake that people choose honour, but incidentally. For most people enjoy being honoured by those in positions of authority because of their hopes (for they think that if they want anything 20 they will get it from them; and therefore they delight in honour as a token of favour to come); while those who desire honour from good men, and men who know, are aiming at confirming their own opinion of themselves; they delight in honour, therefore, because they believe in their own goodness on the strength of the judgement of those who speak about them. In being loved, on the other hand, people delight for its own sake; whence it would seem to be better than being 25 honoured, and friendship to be desirable in itself. But it seems to lie in loving rather than in being loved, as is indicated by the delight mothers take in loving; for some mothers hand over their children to be brought up, and so long as they know their fate they love them 30 and do not seek to be loved in return (if they cannot have both), but seem to be satisfied if they see them prospering; and they themselves love their children even if these owing to their ignorance give them nothing of a mother's due. Now since friendship depends more on loving, and it is those who love their friends that are praised, loving seems to be the characteristic virtue of friends, so that it is only those 35 in whom this is found in due measure that are lasting friends, and only their friendship that endures.

It is in this way more than any other that even unequals can be 1159ᵇ friends; they can be equalized. Now equality and likeness are friendship, and especially the likeness of those who are like in virtue; for being steadfast in themselves they hold fast to each other, and neither 5 ask nor give base services, but (one may say) even prevent them; for it is characteristic of good men neither to go wrong themselves nor to let their friends do so. But wicked men have no steadfastness (for they do not remain even like to themselves), but become friends for a short time because they delight in each other's wickedness. 10 Friends who are useful or pleasant last longer; i. e. as long as they provide each other with enjoyments or advantages. Friendship for utility's sake seems to be that which most easily exists between contraries, e. g. between poor and rich, between ignorant and learned; for what a man actually lacks he aims at, and one gives something else

15 in return. But under this head, too, we might bring lover and beloved, beautiful and ugly. This is why lovers sometimes seem ridiculous, when they demand to be loved as they love; if they are equally lovable their claim can perhaps be justified, but when they have nothing lovable about them it is ridiculous. Perhaps, however, contrary does
20 not even aim at contrary by its own nature, but only incidentally, the desire being for what is intermediate; for that is what is good, e. g. it is good for the dry not to become wet [7] but to come to the intermediate state, and similarly with the hot and in all other cases. These subjects we may dismiss; for they are indeed somewhat foreign to our inquiry.

25 9   Friendship and justice seem, as we have said at the outset of our discussion,[8] to be concerned with the same objects and exhibited between the same persons. For in every community there is thought to be some form of justice, and friendship too; at least men address as friends their fellow-voyagers and fellow-soldiers, and so too those associated with them in any other kind of community. And the extent of their association is the extent of their friendship, as it is the
30 extent to which justice exists between them. And the proverb 'what friends have is common property' expresses the truth; for friendship depends on community. Now brothers and comrades have all things in common, but the others to whom we have referred have definite things in common—some more things, others fewer; for of friendships, too,
35 some are more and others less truly friendships. And the claims of jus-
1160ᵃ tice differ too; the duties of parents to children and those of brothers to each other are not the same nor those of comrades and those of fellow-citizens, and so, too, with the other kinds of friendship. There is a difference, therefore, also between the acts that are unjust towards each of these classes of associates, and the injustice increases by being exhibited towards those who are friends in a fuller sense; e. g. it is a more terrible thing to defraud a comrade than a fellow-citizen, more
5 terrible not to help a brother than a stranger, and more terrible to wound a father than any one else. And the demands of justice also seem to increase with the intensity of the friendship, which implies that friendship and justice exist between the same persons and have an equal extension.

Now all forms of community are like parts of the political community; for men journey together with a view to some particular
10 advantage, and to provide something that they need for the purposes

---

⁷ Cf. 1155ᵇ 3.   ⁸ 1155ᵃ 22–28.

of life; and it is for the sake of advantage that the political community too seems both to have come together originally and to endure, for this is what legislators aim at, and they call just that which is to the common advantage. Now the other communities aim at advantage bit by bit, e. g. sailors at what is advantageous on a voyage with a 15 view to making money or something of the kind, fellow-soldiers at what is advantageous in war, whether it is wealth or victory or the taking of a city that they seek, and members of tribes and demes act similarly [Some communities seem to arise for the sake of pleasure, viz. religious guilds and social clubs; for these exist respectively for 20 the sake of offering sacrifice and of companionship. But all these seem to fall under the political community; for it aims not at present advantage but at what is advantageous for life as a whole], offering sacrifices and arranging gatherings for the purpose, and assigning honours to the gods, and providing pleasant relaxations for themselves. For the ancient sacrifices and gatherings seem to take place 25 after the harvest as a sort of firstfruits, because it was at these seasons that people had most leisure. All the communities, then, seem to be parts of the political community; and the particular kinds of friendship will correspond to the particular kinds of community.   30

10   There are three kinds of constitution, and an equal number of deviation-forms—perversions, as it were, of them. The constitutions are monarchy, aristocracy, and thirdly that which is based on a property qualification, which it seems appropriate to call timocratic, though most people are wont to call it polity. The best of these is monarchy, 35 the worst timocracy. The deviation from monarchy is tyranny; for both are forms of one-man rule, but there is the greatest difference 1160ᵇ between them; the tyrant looks to his own advantage, the king to that of his subjects. For a man is not a king unless he is sufficient to himself and excels his subjects in all good things; and such a man needs nothing further; therefore he will not look to his own interests 5 but to those of his subjects; for a king who is not like that would be a mere titular king. Now tyranny is the very contrary of this; the tyrant pursues his own good. And it is clearer in the case of tyranny that it is the worst deviation-form; [9] but it is the contrary of the best that is worst.[10] Monarchy passes over into tyranny; for tyranny is the evil form of one-man rule and the bad king becomes 10 a tyrant. Aristocracy passes over into oligarchy by the badness of the rulers, who distribute contrary to equity what belongs to the city—all

[9] Than it is that monarchy is the best genuine form (ᵃ 35).
[10] Therefore monarchy must be the best.

or most of the good things to themselves, and office always to the
15 same people, paying most regard to wealth; thus the rulers are few
and are bad men instead of the most worthy. Timocracy passes over
into democracy; for these are coterminous, since it is the ideal even
of timocracy to be the rule of the majority, and all who have the
property qualification count as equal. Democracy is the least bad of
20 the deviations; for in its case the form of constitution is but a slight
deviation. These then are the changes to which constitutions are most
subject; for these are the smallest and easiest transitions.

One may find resemblances to the constitutions and, as it were,
patterns of them even in households. For the association of a father
25 with his sons bears the form of monarchy, since the father cares for
his children; and this is why Homer calls Zeus 'father'; it is the ideal
of monarchy to be paternal rule. But among the Persians the rule of
the father is tyrannical; they use their sons as slaves. Tyrannical too
is the rule of a master over slaves; for it is the advantage of the master
30 that is brought about in it. Now this seems to be a correct form of
government, but the Persian type is perverted; for the modes of rule
appropriate to different relations are diverse. The association of man
and wife seems to be aristocratic; for the man rules in accordance
with his worth, and in those matters in which a man should rule, but
35 the matters that befit a woman he hands over to her. If the man rules
in everything the relation passes over into oligarchy; for in doing so
he is not acting in accordance with their respective worth, and not
ruling in virtue of his superiority. Sometimes, however, women rule,
1161ª because they are heiresses; so their rule is not in virtue of excellence
but due to wealth and power, as in oligarchies. The association of
5 brothers is like timocracy; for they are equal, except in so far as they
differ in age; hence if they differ *much* in age, the friendship is no
longer of the fraternal type. Democracy is found chiefly in masterless
dwellings (for here every one is on an equality), and in those in
which the ruler is weak and every one has license to do as he pleases.

10 11   Each of the constitutions may be seen to involve friendship
just in so far as it involves justice. The friendship between a king and
his subjects depends on an excess of benefits conferred; for he confers
benefits on his subjects if being a good man he cares for them with
a view to their well-being, as a shepherd does for his sheep (whence
15 Homer called Agamemnon 'shepherd of the peoples'). Such too is the
friendship of a father, though this exceeds the other in the greatness
of the benefits conferred; for he is responsible for the existence of
his children, which is thought the greatest good, and for their nurture

and upbringing. These things are ascribed to ancestors as well. Further, by nature a father tends to rule over his sons, ancestors over descendants, a king over his subjects. These friendships imply superiority of one party over the other, which is why ancestors are honoured. 20 The justice therefore that exists between persons so related is not the same on both sides but is in every case proportioned to merit; for that is true of the friendship as well. The friendship of man and wife, again, is the same that is found in an aristocracy; for it is in accordance with virtue—the better gets more of what is good, and each gets what befits him; and so, too, with the justice in these relations. The friendship of brothers is like that of comrades; for they are equal 25 and of like age, and such persons are for the most part like in their feelings and their character. Like this, too, is the friendship appropriate to timocratic government; for in such a constitution the ideal is for the citizens to be equal and fair; therefore rule is taken in turn, and on equal terms; and the friendship appropriate here will correspond.

But in the deviation-forms, as justice hardly exists, so too does 30 friendship. It exists least in the worst form; in tyranny there is little or no friendship. For where there is nothing common to ruler and ruled, there is not friendship either, since there is not justice; e. g. between craftsman and tool, soul and body, master and slave; the 35 latter in each case is benefited by that which uses it, but there is 1161ᵇ no friendship nor justice towards lifeless things. But neither is there friendship towards a horse or an ox, nor to a slave *qua* slave. For there is nothing common to the two parties; the slave is a living tool and the tool a lifeless slave. *Qua* slave then, one cannot be friends 5 with him. But *qua* man one can; for there seems to be some justice between any man and any other who can share in a system of law or be a party to an agreement; therefore there can also be friendship with him in so far as he is a man. Therefore while in tyrannies friendship and justice hardly exist, in democracies they exist more fully; for where the citizens are equal they have much in common.   10

12 Every form of friendship, then, involves association, as has been said.[11] One might, however, mark off from the rest both the friendship of kindred and that of comrades. Those of fellow-citizens, fellow-tribesmen, fellow-voyagers, and the like are more like mere friendships of association; for they seem to rest on a sort of compact. With 15 them we might class the friendship of host and guest.

The friendship of kinsmen itself, while it seems to be of many

[11] 1159ᵇ 29–32.

kinds, appears to depend in every case on parental friendship; for parents love their children as being a part of themselves, and children their parents as being something originating from them. Now
20 (1) parents know their offspring better than their children know that they are their children, and (2) the originator feels his offspring to be his own more than the offspring do their begetter; for the product belongs to the producer (e. g. a tooth or hair or anything else to him whose it is), but the producer does not belong to the product, or belongs in a less degree. And (3) the length of time produces the same
25 result; parents love their children as soon as these are born, but children love their parents only after time has elapsed and they have acquired understanding or the power of discrimination by the senses. From these considerations it is also plain why mothers love more than fathers do. Parents, then, love their children as themselves (for their issue are by virtue of their separate existence a sort of other selves), while children love their parents as being born of them, and brothers
30 love each other as being born of the same parents; for their identity with them makes them identical with each other (which is the reason why people talk of 'the same blood', 'the same stock', and so on). They are, therefore, in a sense the same thing, though in separate individuals. Two things that contribute greatly to friendship are a common upbringing and similarity of age; for 'two of an age take
35 to each other', and people brought up together tend to be comrades;
1162ᵃ whence the friendship of brothers is akin to that of comrades. And cousins and other kinsmen are bound up together by derivation from brothers, viz. by being derived from the same parents. They come to be closer together or farther apart by virtue of the nearness or distance of the original ancestor.

The friendship of children to parents, and of men to gods, is a rela-
5 tion to them as to something good and superior; for they have conferred the greatest benefits, since they are the causes of their being and of their nourishment, and of their education from their birth; and this kind of friendship possesses pleasantness and utility also, more than that of strangers, inasmuch as their life is lived more in common. The friendship of brothers has the characteristics found in
10 that of comrades (and especially when these are good), and in general between people who are like each other, inasmuch as they belong more to each other and start with a love for each other from their very birth, and inasmuch as those born of the same parents and brought up together and similarly educated are more akin in character; and the test of time has been applied most fully and convincingly in their case.

Between other kinsmen friendly relations are found in due pro- 15
portion. Between man and wife friendship seems to exist by nature;
for man is naturally inclined to form couples—even more than to
form cities, inasmuch as the household is earlier and more necessary
than the city, and reproduction is more common to man with the
animals. With the other animals the union extends only to this point,
but human beings live together not only for the sake of reproduc- 20
tion but also for the various purposes of life; for from the start the
functions are divided, and those of man and woman are different;
so they help each other by throwing their peculiar gifts into the
common stock. It is for these reasons that both utility and pleasure 25
seem to be found in this kind of friendship. But this friendship may
be based also on virtue, if the parties are good; for each has its own
virtue and they will delight in the fact. And children seem to be a bond
of union (which is the reason why childless people part more easily);
for children are a good common to both and what is common holds
them together.

How man and wife and in general friend and friend ought mutually to behave seems to be the same question as how it is just for 30
them to behave; for a man does not seem to have the same duties to
a friend, a stranger, a comrade, and a schoolfellow.

13   There are three kinds of friendship, as we said at the outset of
our inquiry,[12] and in respect of each some are friends on an equality 35
and others by virtue of a superiority (for not only can equally good
men become friends but a better man can make friends with a worse, 1162^{b}
and similarly in friendships of pleasure or utility the friends may be
equal or unequal in the benefits they confer). This being so, equals
must effect the required equalization on a basis of equality in love
and in all other respects, while unequals must render what is in proportion to their superiority or inferiority.

Complaints and reproaches arise either only or chiefly in the friend- 5
ship of utility, and this is only to be expected. For those who are
friends on the ground of virtue are anxious to do well by each other
(since that is a mark of virtue and of friendship), and between men
who are emulating each other in this there cannot be complaints or
quarrels; no one is offended by a man who loves him and does well
by him—if he is a person of nice feeling he takes his revenge by doing 10
well by the other. And the man who excels the other in the services he
renders will not complain of his friend, since he gets what he aims at;

[12] 1156^{a} 7.

for each man desires what is good. Nor do complaints arise much even in friendships of pleasure; for both get at the same time what they desire, if they enjoy spending their time together; and even a
15 man who complained of another for *not* affording him pleasure would seem ridiculous, since it is in his power not to spend his days with him.

But the friendship of utility is full of complaints; for as they use each other for their own interests they always want to get the better of the bargain, and think they have got less than they should, and blame their partners because they do not get all they 'want and deserve'; and
20 those who do well by others cannot help them as much as those whom they benefit want.

Now it seems that, as justice is of two kinds, one unwritten and the other legal, one kind of friendship of utility is moral and the other legal. And so complaints arise most of all when men do not dissolve the relation in the spirit of the same type of friendship in which they
25 contracted it. The *legal* type is that which is on fixed terms; its purely commercial variety is on the basis of immediate payment, while the more liberal variety allows time but stipulates for a definite *quid pro quo*. In this variety the debt is clear and not ambiguous, but in the postponement it contains an element of friendliness; and so some
30 states do not allow suits arising out of such agreements, but think men who have bargained on a basis of credit ought to accept the consequences. The *moral* type is not on fixed terms; it makes a gift, or does whatever it does, as to a friend; but one expects to receive as much or more, as having not given but lent; and if a man is worse off when the relation is dissolved than he was when it was contracted he
35 will complain. This happens because all or most men, while they wish for what is noble, choose what is advantageous; now it is noble to do well by another without a view to repayment, but it is the receiving of benefits that is advantageous.

1163ᵃ   Therefore if we can we should return the equivalent of what we have received (for we must not make a man our friend against his will; we must recognize that we were mistaken at the first and took a benefit from a person we should not have taken it from—since it was not from a friend, nor from one who did it just for the sake of acting
5 so—and we must settle up just as if we had been benefited on fixed terms). Indeed, one would agree to repay if one could (if one could not, even the giver would not have expected one to do so); therefore if it is possible we must repay. But at the outset we must consider the man by whom we are being benefited and on what terms he is acting, in order that we may accept the benefit on these terms, or else decline it.

It is disputable whether we ought to measure a service by its utility 10
to the receiver and make the return with a view to that, or by the
benevolence of the giver. For those who have received say they have
received from their benefactors what meant little to the latter and what
they might have got from others—minimizing the service; while the
givers, on the contrary, say it was the biggest thing they had, and
what could not have been got from others, and that it was given in 15
times of danger or similar need. Now if the friendship is one that aims
at *utility*, surely the advantage to the receiver is the measure. For it is
he that asks for the service, and the other man helps him on the assumption that he will receive the equivalent; so the assistance has
been precisely as great as the advantage to the receiver, and therefore he must return as much as he has received, or even more (for that 20
would be nobler). In friendships based on *virtue* on the other hand,
complaints do not arise, but the purpose of the doer is a sort of
measure; for in purpose lies the essential element of virtue and
character.

14 Differences arise also in friendships based on superiority; for
each expects to get more out of them, but when this happens the 25
friendship is dissolved. Not only does the better man think he ought
to get more, since more should be assigned to a good man, but the
more useful similarly expects this; they say a useless man should not
get as much as they should, since it becomes an act of public service
and not a friendship if the proceeds of the friendship do not answer
to the worth of the benefits conferred. For they think that, as in a 30
commercial partnership those who put more in get more out, so it
should be in friendship. But the man who is in a state of need and
inferiority makes the opposite claim; they think it is the part of a
good friend to help those who are in need; what, they say, is the use
of being the friend of a good man or a powerful man, if one is to 35
get nothing out of it?

At all events it seems that each party is justified in his claim, and 1163ᵇ
that each should get more out of the friendship than the other—not
more of the same thing, however, but the superior more honour and
the inferior more gain; for honour is the prize of virtue and of beneficence, while gain is the assistance required by inferiority.

It seems to be so in constitutional arrangements also; the man who 5
contributes nothing good to the common stock is not honoured; for
what belongs to the public is given to the man who benefits the public, and honour does belong to the public. It is not possible to get
wealth from the common stock and at the same time honour. For no

10 one puts up with the smaller share in *all* things; therefore to the man who loses in wealth they assign honour and to the man who is willing to be paid, wealth, since the proportion to merit equalizes the parties and preserves the friendship, as we have said.[13]

This then is also the way in which we should associate with un- equals; the man who is benefited in respect of wealth or virtue must give honour in return, repaying what he can. For friendship asks a man to do what he can, not what is proportional to the merits of the 15 case; since that cannot always be done, e. g. in honours paid to the gods or to parents; for no one could ever return to them the equiva- lent of what he gets, but the man who serves them to the utmost of his power is thought to be a good man.

This is why it would not seem open to a man to disown his father 20 (though a father may disown his son; being in debt, he should repay, but there is nothing by doing which a son will have done the equiva- lent of what he has received, so that he is always in debt. But creditors can remit a debt; and a father can therefore do so too. At the same time it is thought that presumably no one would repudiate a son who was not far gone in wickedness; for apart from the natural friendship of father and son it is human nature not to reject a son's assistance. 25 But the son, if he *is* wicked, will naturally avoid aiding his father, or not be zealous about it; for most people wish to get benefits, but avoid doing them, as a thing unprofitable.—So much for these questions.

BOOK IX

1 In all friendships between dissimilars it is, as we have said,[1] pro- portion that equalizes the parties and preserves the friendship; e. g. in the political form of friendship the shoemaker gets a return for his 35 shoes in proportion to his worth, and the weaver and all other crafts- 1164ᵃ men do the same. Now here a common measure has been provided in the form of money, and therefore everything is referred to this and measured by this; but in the friendship of lovers sometimes the lover complains that his excess of love is not met by love in return (though 5 perhaps there is nothing lovable about him), while often the beloved complains that the lover who formerly promised everything now per- forms nothing. Such incidents happen when the lover loves the be- loved for the sake of pleasure while the beloved loves the lover for the sake of utility, and they do not both possess the qualities expected of

---

[13] 1162ᵃ 34–ᵇ 4, Cf. 1158ᵇ 27, 1159ᵃ 35–ᵇ 3.

[1] This has not been said precisely of friendship between dissimilars, but Cf. 1132ᵇ 31–33, 1158ᵇ 27, 1159ᵃ 35–ᵇ 3, 1162ᵃ 34–ᵇ 4, 1163ᵇ 11.

them. If these be the objects of the friendship it is dissolved when
they do not get the things that formed the motives of their love; for 10
each did not love the other person himself but the qualities he had,
and these were not enduring; that is why the friendships also are
transient. But the love of characters, as has been said, endures because it is self-dependent.[2] Differences arise when what they get is
something different and not what they desire; for it is like getting
nothing at all when we do not get what we aim at; compare the story 15
of the person who made promises to a lyre-player, promising him the
more, the better he sang, but in the morning, when the other demanded the fulfilment of his promises, said that he had given pleasure [3] for pleasure. Now if this had been what each wanted, all would
have been well; but if the one wanted enjoyment but the other gain,
and the one has what he wants while the other has not, the terms of
the association will not have been properly fulfilled; for what each in 20
fact wants is what he attends to, and it is for the sake of that that
he will give what he has.

But who is to fix the worth of the service; he who makes the sacrifice or he who has got the advantage? At any rate the other seems
to leave it to him. This is what they say Protagoras used to do; [4] 25
whenever he taught anything whatsoever, he bade the learner assess
the value of the knowledge, and accepted the amount so fixed. But in
such matters some men approve of the saying 'let a man have his fixed
reward'.

Those who get the money first and then do none of the things they
said they would, owing to the extravagance of their promises, naturally find themselves the objects of complaint; for they do not fulfil
what they agreed to. The sophists are perhaps compelled to do this 30
because no one would give money for the things they *do* know. These
people then, if they do not do what they have been paid for, are
naturally made the objects of complaint.

But where there is *no* contract of service, those who give up something for the sake of the other party cannot (as we have said [5]) be
complained of (for that is the nature of the friendship of virtue), 35
and the return to them must be made on the basis of their purpose 1164[b]
(for it is purpose that is the characteristic thing in a friend and in
virtue). And so too, it seems, should one make a return to those with
whom one has studied philosophy; for their worth cannot be measured against money, and they can get no honour which will balance

---

[2] 1156[b] 9–12.
[4] Cf. Pl. *Prot.* 328 B, C.
[3] i. e. the pleasure of expectation.
[5] 1162[b] 6–13.

5 their services, but still it is perhaps enough, as it is with the gods and with one's parents, to give them what one can.

If the gift was not of this sort, but was made with a view to a return, it is no doubt preferable that the return made should be one that seems fair to both parties, but if this cannot be achieved, it would seem not only necessary that the person who gets the first service 10 should fix the reward, but also just; for if the other gets in return the equivalent of the advantage the beneficiary has received, or the price he would have paid for the pleasure, he will have got what is fair as from the other.

We see this happening too with things put up for sale, and in some places there are laws providing that no actions shall arise out of voluntary contracts, on the assumption that one should settle with a person 15 to whom one has given credit, in the spirit in which one bargained with him. The law holds that it is more just that the person to whom credit was given should fix the terms than that the person who gave credit should do so. For most things are not assessed at the same value by those who have them and those who want them; each class values highly what is its own and what it is offering; yet the return is made 20 on the terms fixed by the receiver. But no doubt the receiver should assess a thing not at what it seems worth when he has it, but at what he assessed it at before he had it.

2 A further problem is set by such questions as, whether one should in all things give the preference to one's father and obey him, or whether when one is ill one should trust a doctor, and when one has 25 to elect a general should elect a man of military skill; and similarly whether one should render a service by preference to a friend or to a good man, and should show gratitude to a benefactor or oblige a friend, if one cannot do both.

All such questions are hard, are they not, to decide with precision? For they admit of many variations of all sorts in respect both of the 30 magnitude of the service and of its nobility and necessity. But that we should not give the preference in all things to the same person is plain enough; and we must for the most part return benefits rather than oblige friends, as we must pay back a loan to a creditor rather than make one to a friend. But perhaps even this is not always true; e. g. should a man who has been ransomed out of the hands of brigands 35 ransom his ransomer in return, whoever he may be (or pay him if he 1165ᵃ has not been captured but demands payment), or should he ransom his father? It would seem that he should ransom his father in preference even to himself. As we have said,[6] then, generally the debt should be paid, but if the gift is exceedingly noble or exceedingly necessary, one should defer to these considerations. For sometimes it is not even 5 fair to return the equivalent of what one has received, when the one man has done a service to one whom he knows to be good, while the other makes a return to one whom he believes to be bad. For that matter, one should sometimes not lend in return to one who has lent to oneself; for the one person lent to a good man, expecting to recover his loan, while the other has no hope of recovering from one who is believed to be bad. Therefore if the facts really are so, the demand 10 is not fair; and if they are not, but people think they are, they would be held to be doing nothing strange in refusing. As we have often pointed out,[7] then, discussions about feelings and actions have just as much definiteness as their subject-matter.

That we should not make the same return to everyone, nor give a father the preference in everything, as one does not sacrifice everything 15 to Zeus,[8] is plain enough; but since we ought to render different things to parents, brothers, comrades, and benefactors, we ought to render to each class what is appropriate and becoming. And this is what people seem in fact to do; to marriages they invite their kinsfolk; for these have a part in the family and therefore in the doings that affect the family; and at funerals also they think that kinsfolk, before all others, 20 should meet, for the same reason. And it would be thought that in the matter of food we should help our parents before all others, since we owe our own nourishment to them, and it is more honourable to help in this respect the authors of our being even before ourselves; and honour too one should give to one's parents as one does to the gods, but not any and every honour; for that matter one should not give 25 the same honour to one's father and one's mother, nor again should one give them the honour due to a philosopher or to a general, but the honour due to a father, or again to a mother. To all older persons, too, one should give honour appropriate to their age, by rising to receive them and finding seats for them and so on; while to comrades and brothers one should allow freedom of speech and common 30 use of all things. To kinsmen, too, and fellow-tribesmen and fellow-citizens and to every other class one should always try to assign what is appropriate, and to compare the claims of each class with respect to nearness of relation and to virtue or usefulness. The comparison is easier when the persons belong to the same class, and more laborious

---

[6] 1164^b 31–1165^a 2.   [7] 1094^b 11–27, 1098^a 26–29, 1103^b 34–1104^a 5.
[8] Cf. 1134^b 18–24.

35 when they are different. Yet we must not on *that* account shrink
from the task, but decide the question as best we can.

3 Another question that arises is whether friendships should or
should not be broken off when the other party does not remain the
1165ᵇ same. Perhaps we may say that there is nothing strange in breaking
off a friendship based on utility or pleasure, when our friends no
longer have these attributes. For it was of these attributes that we were
the friends; and when these have failed it is reasonable to love no
5 longer. But one might complain of another if, when he loved us for our
usefulness or pleasantness, he pretended to love us for our character.
For, as we said at the outset,⁹ most differences arise between friends
when they are not friends in the spirit in which they think they are.
So when a man has deceived himself and has thought he was being
loved for his character, when the other person was doing nothing of
10 the kind, he must blame himself; but when he has been deceived by
the pretences of the other person, it is just that he should complain
against his deceiver; he will complain with more justice than one does
against people who counterfeit the currency, inasmuch as the wrong-
doing is concerned with something more valuable.

But if one accepts another man as good, and he turns out badly
and is seen to do so, must one still love him? Surely it is impossible,
since not everything can be loved, but only what is good. What is evil
15 neither can nor should be loved; for it is not one's duty to be a lover
of evil, nor to become like what is bad; and we have said ¹⁰ that like
is dear to like. Must the friendship, then, be forthwith broken off? Or
is this not so in all cases, but only when one's friends are incurable in
their wickedness? If they are capable of being reformed one should
rather come to the assistance of their character or their property,
20 inasmuch as this is better and more characteristic of friendship. But
a man who breaks off such a friendship would seem to be doing nothing strange; for it was not to a man of this sort that he was a friend;
when his friend has changed, therefore, and he is unable to save him,
he gives him up.

But if one friend remained the same while the other became better
and far outstripped him in virtue, should the latter treat the former as a
25 friend? Surely he cannot. When the interval is great this becomes most
plain, e. g. in the case of childish friendships; if one friend remained a
child in intellect while the other became a fully developed man, how
could they be friends when they neither approved of the same things

⁹ 1162ᵇ 23–25.   ¹⁰ 1156ᵇ 19–21, 1159ᵇ 1.

nor delighted in and were pained by the same things? For not even
with regard to each other will their tastes agree, and without this (as
we saw [11]) they cannot be friends; for they cannot live together. But 30
we have discussed these matters.[12]

Should he, then, behave no otherwise towards him than he would if
he had never been his friend? Surely he should keep a remembrance
of their former intimacy, and as we think we ought to oblige friends
rather than strangers, so to those who have been our friends we ought 35
to make some allowance for our former friendship, when the breach
has not been due to excess of wickedness.

4   Friendly relations with one's neighbours, and the marks by which 1166ª
friendships are defined, seem to have proceeded from a man's relations
to himself. For (1) we define a friend as one who wishes and does
what is good, or seems so, for the sake of his friend, or (2) as one who
wishes his friend to exist and live, for his sake; which mothers do to 5
their children, and friends do who have come into conflict. And (3)
others define him as one who lives with and (4) has the same tastes as
another, or (5) one who grieves and rejoices with his friend; and this
too is found in mothers most of all. It is by some one of these characteristics that friendship too is defined.

Now each of these is true of the good man's relation to himself (and 10
of all other men in so far as they think themselves good; virtue and
the good man seem, as has been said,[13] to be the measure of every
class of things). For [14] his opinions are harmonious, and he desires the
same things with all his soul; and therefore [15] he wishes for himself
what is good and what seems so, and does it (for it is characteristic of 15
the good man to work out the good), and does so for his own sake
(for he does it for the sake of the intellectual element in him, which is
thought to be the man himself); and [16] he wishes himself to live and
be preserved, and especially the element by virtue of which he thinks.
For existence is good to the virtuous man, and each man wishes himself what is good, while no one chooses to possess the whole world if 20
he has first to become some one else (for that matter, even now God
possesses the good [17]); he wishes for this only on condition of being
whatever he is; and the element that thinks would seem to be the individual man, or to be so more than any other element in him. And [18]

---

[11] 1157ᵇ 22–24.   [12] ib. 17–24, 1158ᵇ 33–35.   [13] 1113ª 22–33, Cf. 1099ª 13.
[14] (4) above.   [15] (1) above.   [16] (2) above.
[17] sc. but as no one gains by God's now having the good, he would not gain if
a new person which was no longer himself were to possess it. Cf. 1159ª 5–11.
[18] (3) above.

such a man wishes to live with himself; for he does so with pleasure, since the memories of his past acts are delightful and his hopes for 25 the future are good, and therefore pleasant. His mind is well stored too with subjects of contemplation. And [19] he grieves and rejoices, more than any other, with himself; for the same thing is always painful, and the same thing always pleasant, and not one thing at one time and another at another; he has, so to speak, nothing to repent of.

Therefore, since each of these characteristics belongs to the good 30 man in relation to himself, and he is related to his friend as to himself (for his friend is another self), friendship too is thought to be one of these attributes, and those who have these attributes to be friends. Whether there is or is not friendship between a man and himself is a question we may dismiss for the present; [20] there would seem to be 35 friendship in so far as he is two or more, to judge from the afore- 1166ᵇ mentioned attributes of friendship, and from the fact that the extreme of friendship is likened to one's love for oneself.

But the attributes named seem to belong even to the majority of men, poor creatures though they may be. Are we to say then that in so far as they are satisfied with themselves and think they are good, 5 they share in these attributes? Certainly no one who is thoroughly bad and impious has these attributes, or even seems to do so. They hardly belong even to inferior people; for they [21] are at variance with themselves, and have appetites for some things and rational desires for others. This is true, for instance, of incontinent people; for they choose, instead of the things they themselves think good, things that 10 are pleasant but hurtful; while others again, through cowardice and laziness, shrink from doing what they think best for themselves. And [22] those who have done many terrible deeds and are hated for their wickedness even shrink from life and destroy themselves. And [23] wicked men seek for people with whom to spend their days, and shun 15 themselves; for they remember many a grievous deed, and anticipate others like them, when they are by themselves, but when they are with others they forget. And [24] having nothing lovable in them they have no feeling of love to themselves. Therefore [25] also such men do not rejoice or grieve with themselves; for their soul is rent by faction, and 20 one element in it by reason of its wickedness grieves when it abstains from certain acts, while the other part is pleased, and one draws them this way and the other that, as if they were pulling them in pieces. If a man cannot at the same time be pained and pleased, at all events after a short time he is pained *because* he was pleased, and he could

[19] (5) above.   [20] Cf. 1168ᵃ 28–1169ᵇ 2.   [21] (4) above.
[22] (2) above.   [23] (3) above.   [24] (1) above.   [25] (5) above.

have wished that these things had not been pleasant to him; for bad men are laden with repentance.

Therefore the bad man does not seem to be amicably disposed 25 even to himself, because there is nothing in him to love; so that if to be thus is the height of wretchedness, we should strain every nerve to avoid wickedness and should endeavour to be good; for so and only so can one be either friendly to oneself or a friend to another.

5   Goodwill is a friendly sort of relation, but is not *identical* with 30 friendship; for one may have goodwill both towards people whom one does not know, and without their knowing it, but not friendship. This has indeed been said already.[26] But goodwill is not even friendly feeling. For it does not involve intensity or desire, whereas these accompany friendly feeling; and friendly feeling implies intimacy while goodwill may arise of a sudden, as it does towards competitors 35 in a contest; we come to feel goodwill for them and to share in their 1167ᵃ wishes, but we would not *do* anything with them; for, as we said, we feel goodwill suddenly and love them only superficially.

Goodwill seems, then, to be a beginning of friendship, as the pleasure of the eye is the beginning of love. For no one loves if he has not first been delighted by the form of the beloved, but he who delights in 5 the form of another does not, for all that, love him, but only does so when he also longs for him when absent and craves for his presence; so too it is not possible for people to be friends if they have not come to feel goodwill for each other, but those who feel goodwill are not for all that friends; for they only *wish* well to those for whom they feel goodwill, and would not do anything with them nor take trouble for them. And so one might by an extension of the term friendship say 10 that goodwill is inactive friendship, though when it is prolonged and reaches the point of intimacy it becomes friendship—not the friendship based on utility nor that based on pleasure; for goodwill too does not arise on those terms. The man who has received a benefit bestows goodwill in return for what has been done to him, but in doing so is only doing what is just; while he who wishes some one to prosper 15 because he hopes for enrichment through him seems to have goodwill not to him but rather to himself, just as a man is not a friend to another if he cherishes him for the sake of some use to be made of him. In general, goodwill arises on account of some excellence and worth, when one man seems to another beautiful or brave or something of the sort, as we pointed out in the case of competitors in a 20 contest.

[26] 1155ᵇ 32–1156ᵃ 5.

6   Unanimity also seems to be a friendly relation. For this reason it is not identity of opinion; for that might occur even with people who do not know each other; nor do we say that people who have the same views on any and every subject are unanimous, e. g. those who
25 agree about the heavenly bodies (for unanimity about these is not a friendly relation), but we do say that a city is unanimous when men have the same opinion about what is to their interest, and choose the same actions, and do what they have resolved in common. It is about things to be done, therefore, that people are said to be unanimous, and, among these, about matters of consequence and in which it is possible for both or all parties to get what they want; e. g. a city is unani-
30 mous when all its citizens think that the offices in it should be elective, or that they should form an alliance with Sparta, or that Pittacus should be their ruler—at a time when he himself was also willing to rule. But when each of two people wishes himself to have the thing in question, like the captains in the *Phoenissae*,[27] they are in a state of
35 faction; for it is not unanimity when each of two parties thinks of the same thing, whatever that may be, but only when they think of the same thing in the same hands, e. g. when both the common people
1167ᵇ and those of the better class wish the best men to rule; for thus and thus alone do all get what they aim at. Unanimity seems, then, to be political friendship, as indeed it is commonly said to be; for it is concerned with things that are to our interest and have an influence on our life.

5   Now such unanimity is found among good men; for they are unanimous both in themselves and with one another, being, so to say, of one mind (for the wishes of such men are constant and not at the mercy of opposing currents like a strait of the sea), and they wish for what is just and what is advantageous, and these are the objects of their common endeavour as well. But bad men cannot be unanimous except to a small extent, any more than they can be friends, since they
10 aim at getting more than their share of advantages, while in labour and public service they fall short of their share; and each man wishing for advantage to himself criticizes his neighbour and stands in his way; for if people do not watch it carefully the common weal is soon destroyed. The result is that they are in a state of faction, putting com-
15 pulsion on each other but unwilling themselves to do what is just.

7   Benefactors are thought to love those they have benefited, more than those who have been well treated love those that have treated them well, and this is discussed as though it were paradoxical. Most

---

[27] Eteocles and Polynices (Eur. *Phoen.* 588 ff.).

people think it is because the latter are in the position of debtors and
the former of creditors; and therefore as, in the case of loans, debtors 20
wish their creditors did not exist, while creditors actually take care of
the safety of their debtors, so it is thought that benefactors wish the
objects of their action to exist since they will then get their gratitude,
while the beneficiaries take no interest in making this return. Epi- 25
charmus would perhaps declare that they say this because they 'look
at things on their bad side', but it is quite like human nature; for
most people are forgetful, and are more anxious to be well treated than
to treat others well. But the cause would seem to be more deeply
rooted in the nature of things; the case of those who have lent money
is not even analogous. For they have no friendly feeling to their debt- 30
ors, but only a wish that they may be kept safe with a view to what
is to be got from them; while those who have done a service to others
feel friendship and love for those they have served even if these are
not of any use to them and never will be. This is what happens with
craftsmen too; every man loves his own handiwork better than he 35
would be loved by it if it came alive; and this happens perhaps most 1168ᵃ
of all with poets; for they have an excessive love for their own
poems, doting on them as if they were their children. This is what the
position of benefactors is like; for that which they have treated well
is their handiwork, and therefore they love this more than the handiwork does its maker. The cause of this is that existence is to all men 5
a thing to be chosen and loved, and that we exist by virtue of activity (i. e. by living and acting), and that the handiwork *is* in a sense,
the producer in activity; he loves his handiwork, therefore, because
he loves existence. And this is rooted in the nature of things; for what
he is in potentiality, his handiwork manifests in activity.

At the same time to the benefactor that is noble which depends on
his action, so that he delights in the object of his action, whereas to 10
the patient there is nothing noble in the agent, but at most something
advantageous, and this is less pleasant and lovable. What *is* pleasant
is the activity of the present, the hope of the future, the memory of
the past; but most pleasant is that which depends on activity, and
similarly this is most lovable. Now for a man who has made some- 15
thing his work remains (for the noble is lasting), but for the person
acted on the utility passes away. And the memory of noble things is
pleasant, but that of useful things is not likely to be pleasant, or is
less so; though the reverse seems true of expectation.

Further, love is like activity, being loved like passivity; and loving
and its concomitants are attributes of those who are the more active.[28] 20

---

[28] i. e. benefactors.

Again, all men love more what they have won by labour; e. g. those who have made their money love it more than those who have inherited it; and to be well treated seems to involve no labour, while to treat others well is a laborious task. These are the reasons, too, why mothers
25 are fonder of their children than fathers; bringing them into the world costs them more pains, and they know better that the children are their own. This last point, too, would seem to apply to benefactors.

8   The question is also debated, whether a man should love himself most, or some one else. People criticize those who love themselves most, and call them self-lovers, using this as an epithet of disgrace, and a
30 bad man seems to do everything for his own sake, and the more so the more wicked he is—and so men reproach him, for instance, with doing nothing of his own accord—while the good man acts for honour's sake, and the more so the better he is, and acts for his friend's sake, and sacrifices his own interest.
35   But the facts clash with these arguments, and this is not surpris-
1168ᵇ ing. For men say that one ought to love best one's best friend, and a man's best friend is one who wishes well to the object of his wish for his sake, even if no one is to know of it; and these attributes are found most of all in a man's attitude towards himself, and so are all the other
5 attributes by which a friend is defined; for, as we have said,[29] it is from this relation that all the characteristics of friendship have extended to our neighbours. All the proverbs, too, agree with this, e. g. 'a single soul', and 'what friends have is common property', and 'friendship is equality', and 'charity begins at home'; for all these marks will be found most in a man's relation to himself; he is his own best friend and therefore ought to love himself best. It is there-
10 fore a reasonable question, which of the two views we should follow; for both are plausible.
    Perhaps we ought to mark off such arguments from each other and determine how far and in what respects each view is right. Now if we grasp the sense in which each school uses the phrase 'lover of self',
15 the truth may become evident. Those who use the term as one of reproach ascribe self-love to people who assign to themselves the greater share of wealth, honours, and bodily pleasures; for these are what most people desire, and busy themselves about as though they were the best of all things, which is the reason, too, why they become objects of competition. So those who are grasping with regard to these things
20 gratify their appetites and in general their feelings and the irrational element of the soul; and most men are of this nature (which is the

---

[29] Ch. 4.

reason why the epithet has come to be used as it is—it takes its meaning from the prevailing type of self-love, which is a bad one); it is
just, therefore, that men who are lovers of self in this way are reproached for being so. That it is those who give themselves the preference in regard to objects of this sort that most people usually call
lovers of self is plain; for if a man were always anxious that he him- 25
self, above all things, should act justly, temperately, or in accordance
with any other of the virtues, and in general were always to try to
secure for himself the honourable course, no one will call such a man a
lover of self or blame him.

But such a man would seem more than the other a lover of self; at
all events he assigns to himself the things that are noblest and best,
and gratifies the most authoritative element in himself and in all 30
things obeys this; and just as a city or any other systematic whole is
most properly identified with the most authoritative element in it,
so is a man; and therefore the man who loves this and gratifies it is
most of all a lover of self. Besides, a man is said to have or not to have
self-control according as his reason has or has not the control, on the
assumption that this is the man himself; and the things men have 35
done on a rational principle are thought most properly their own acts 1169ª
and voluntary acts. That this is the man himself, then, or is so more
than anything else, is plain, and also that the good man loves most
this part of him. Whence it follows that he is most truly a lover of
self, of another type than that which is a matter of reproach, and as
different from that as living according to a rational principle is from
living as passion dictates, and desiring what is noble from desiring 5
what seems advantageous. Those, then, who busy themselves in an
exceptional degree with noble actions all men approve and praise;
and if *all* were to strive towards what is noble and strain every nerve
to do the noblest deeds, everything would be as it should be for the
common weal, and every one would secure for himself the goods that 10
are greatest, since virtue is the greatest of goods.

Therefore the good man should be a lover of self (for he will both
himself profit by doing noble acts, and will benefit his fellows), but
the wicked man should not; for he will hurt both himself and his
neighbours, following as he does evil passions. For the wicked man, 15
what he does clashes with what he ought to do, but what the good
man ought to do he does; for reason in each of its possessors chooses
what is best for itself, and the good man obeys his reason. It is true of
the good man too that he does many acts for the sake of his friends
and his country, and if necessary dies for them; for he will throw away 20
both wealth and honours and in general the goods that are objects of

competition, gaining for himself nobility; since he would prefer a short period of intense pleasure to a long one of mild enjoyment, a twelve-month of noble life to many years of humdrum existence, and one
25 great and noble action to many trivial ones. Now those who die for others doubtless attain this result; it is therefore a great prize that they choose for themselves. They will throw away wealth too on condition that their friends will gain more; for while a man's friend gains wealth he himself achieves nobility; he is therefore assigning the greater good
30 to himself. The same too is true of honour and office; all these things he will sacrifice to his friend; for this is noble and laudable for himself. Rightly then is he thought to be good, since he chooses nobility before all else. But he may even give up actions to his friend; it may be nobler to become the cause of his friend's acting than to act himself.
35 In all the actions, therefore, that men are praised for, the good man is seen to assign to himself the greater share in what is noble. In this
1169ᵇ sense, then, as has been said, a man should be a lover of self; but in the sense in which most men are so, he ought not.

9   It is also disputed whether the happy man will need friends or not. It is said that those who are supremely happy and self-sufficient
5 have no need of friends; for they have the things that are good, and therefore being self-sufficient they need nothing further, while a friend, being another self, furnishes what a man cannot provide by his own effort; whence the saying 'when fortune is kind, what need of friends?' But it seems strange, when one assigns all good things to the happy
10 man, not to assign friends, who are thought the greatest of external goods. And if it is more characteristic of a friend to do well by another than to be well done by, and to confer benefits is characteristic of the good man and of virtue, and it is nobler to do well by friends than by strangers, the good man will need people to do well by. This is why the
15 question is asked whether we need friends more in prosperity or in adversity, on the assumption that not only does a man in adversity need people to confer benefits on him, but also those who are prospering need people to do well by. Surely it is strange, too, to make the supremely happy man a solitary; for no one would choose the whole world on condition of being alone, since man is a political creature and one whose nature is to live with others. Therefore even the happy man lives with others; for he has the things that are by nature good. And
20 plainly it is better to spend his days with friends and good men than with strangers or any chance persons. Therefore the happy man needs friends.

What then is it that the first school means, and in what respect is it right? Is it that most men identify friends with useful people? Of such friends indeed the supremely happy man will have no need, since he already has the things that are good; nor will he need those whom 25 one makes one's friends because of their pleasantness, or he will need them only to a small extent (for his life, being pleasant, has no need of adventitious pleasure); and because he does not need *such* friends he is thought not to need friends.

But that is surely not true. For we have said at the outset [30] that happiness is an activity; and activity plainly comes into being and is not present at the start like a piece of property. If (1) happiness lies 30 in living and being active, and the good man's activity is virtuous and pleasant in itself, as we have said at the outset,[31] and (2) a thing's being one's own is one of the attributes that make it pleasant, and (3) we can contemplate our neighbours better than ourselves and their actions better than our own, and if the actions of virtuous men who 35 are their friends are pleasant to good men (since these have both the 1170ª attributes that are naturally pleasant [32])—if this be so, the supremely happy man will need friends of this sort, since his purpose is to contemplate worthy actions and actions that are his own, and the actions of a good man who is his friend have both these qualities.

Further, men think that the happy man ought to live pleasantly. Now if he were a solitary, life would be hard for him; for by one- 5 self it is not easy to be continuously active; but with others and towards others it is easier. With others therefore his activity will be more continuous, and it is in itself pleasant, as it ought to be for the man who is supremely happy; for a good man *qua* good delights in virtuous actions and is vexed at vicious ones, as a musical man enjoys 10 beautiful tunes but is pained at bad ones. A certain training in virtue arises also from the company of the good, as Theognis has said before us.

If we look deeper into the nature of things, a virtuous friend seems to be naturally desirable for a virtuous man. For that which is good by nature, we have said,[33] is for the virtuous man good and pleasant 15 in itself. Now life is defined in the case of animals by the power of perception, in that of man by the power of perception or thought; and a power is defined by reference to the corresponding activity, which is the essential thing; therefore life seems to be essentially the act of perceiving or thinking. And life is among the things that are good

---

[30] 1098ª 16ᵇ, 31–1099ª 7.   [31] 1099ª 14, 21.
[32] i. e. the attribute of goodness and that of being their own.
[33] 1099ª 7–11, 1113ª 25–33.

20 and pleasant in themselves, since it is determinate and the determinate is of the nature of the good; and that which is good by nature is also good for the virtuous man (which is the reason why life seems pleasant to all men); but we must not apply this to a wicked and corrupt life nor to a life spent in pain; for such a life is indeterminate, as 25 are its attributes. The nature of pain will become plainer in what follows.[34] But if life itself is good and pleasant (which it seems to be, from the very fact that all men desire it, and particularly those who are good and supremely happy; for to such men life is most desirable, and their existence is the most supremely happy); and if he who sees perceives that he sees, and he who hears, that he hears, and he who walks, 30 that he walks, and in the case of all other activities similarly there is something which perceives that we are active, so that if we perceive, we perceive that we perceive, and if we think, that we think; and if to perceive that we perceive or think is to perceive that we exist (for 1170ᵇ existence was defined as perceiving or thinking); and if perceiving that one lives is in itself one of the things that are pleasant (for life is by nature good, and to perceive what is good present in oneself is pleasant); and if life is desirable, and particularly so for good men, because to them existence is good and pleasant (for they are pleased 5 at the consciousness of the presence in them of what is in itself good); and if as the virtuous man is to himself, he is to his friend also (for his friend is another self):—if all this be true, as his own being is desirable for each man, so, or almost so, is that of his friend. Now his being was seen to be desirable because he perceived his own goodness, and 10 such perception is pleasant in itself. He needs, therefore, to be conscious of the existence of his friend as well, and this will be realized in their living together and sharing in discussion and thought; for this is what living together would seem to mean in the case of man, and not, as in the case of cattle, feeding in the same place.

If, then, being is in itself desirable for the supremely happy man 15 (since it is by its nature good and pleasant), and that of his friend is very much the same, a friend will be one of the things that are desirable. Now that which is desirable for him he must have, or he will be deficient in this respect. The man who is to be happy will therefore need virtuous friends.

20 10   Should we, then, make as many friends as possible, or—as in the case of hospitality it is thought to be suitable advice, that one should be 'neither a man of many guests nor a man with none'—will that

[34] x. 1–5.

apply to friendship as well; should a man neither be friendless nor have an excessive number of friends?

To friends made with a view to *utility* this saying would seem thoroughly applicable; for to do services to many people in return is a laborious task and life is not long enough for its performance. 25 Therefore friends in excess of those who are sufficient for our own life are superfluous, and hindrances to the noble life; so that we have no need of them. Of friends made with a view to *pleasure,* also, few are enough, as a little seasoning in food is enough.

But as regards *good* friends, should we have as many as possible, or is there a limit to the number of one's friends, as there is to the 30 size of a city? You cannot make a city of ten men, and if there are a hundred thousand it is a city no longer. But the proper number is presumably not a single number, but anything that falls between certain fixed points. So for friends too there is a fixed number— 1171ᵃ perhaps the largest number with whom one can live together (for that, we found,[35] is thought to be very characteristic of friendship); and that one cannot live with many people and divide oneself up among them is plain. Further, they too must be friends of one another, if they are all to spend their days together; and it is a hard business for this condition to be fulfilled with a large number. It is 5 found difficult, too, to rejoice and to grieve in an intimate way with many people, for it may likely happen that one has at once to be happy with one friend and to mourn with another. Presumably, then, it is well not to seek to have as many friends as possible, but as many as are enough for the purpose of living together; for it would seem actually impossible to be a great friend to many people. This 10 is why one cannot love several people; love is ideally a sort of excess of friendship, and that can only be felt towards one person; therefore great friendship too can only be felt towards a few people. This seems to be confirmed in practice; for we do not find many people who are friends in the comradely way of friendship, and the famous friendships of this sort are always between two people. Those who 15 have many friends and mix intimately with them all are thought to be no one's friend, except in the way proper to fellow-citizens, and such people are also called obsequious. In the way proper to fellow-citizens, indeed, it is possible to be the friend of many and yet not be obsequious but a genuinely good man; but one cannot have with many people the friendship based on virtue and on the character of

---

[35] 1157ᵇ 19, 1158ᵃ 3, 10.

20 our friends themselves, and we must be content if we find even a few such.

11   Do we need friends more in good fortune or in bad? They are sought after in both; for while men in adversity need help, in prosperity they need people to live with and to make the objects of their beneficence; for they wish to do well by others. Friendship, then, is more necessary in bad fortune, and so it is useful friends 25 that one wants in this case; but it is more noble in good fortune, and so we also seek for good men as our friends, since it is more desirable to confer benefits on these and to live with these. For the very presence of friends is pleasant both in good fortune and also in bad, since 30 grief is lightened when friends sorrow with us. Hence one might ask whether they share as it were our burden, or—without that happening—their presence by its pleasantness, and the thought of their grieving with us, make our pain less. Whether it is for these reasons or for some other that our grief is lightened, is a question that may be dismissed; at all events what we have described appears to take place.

But their presence seems to contain a mixture of various factors. 35 The very seeing of one's friends is pleasant, especially if one is in 1171ᵇ adversity, and becomes a safeguard against grief (for a friend tends to comfort us both by the sight of him and by his words, if he is tactful, since he knows our character and the things that please or pain 5 us); but to see him pained at our misfortunes is painful; for every one shuns being a cause of pain to his friends. For this reason people of a manly nature guard against making their friends grieve with them, and, unless he be exceptionally insensible to pain, such a man cannot stand the pain that ensues for his friends, and in general does not admit fellow-mourners because he is not himself given to mourn- 10 ing; but women and womanly men enjoy sympathisers in their grief, and love them as friends and companions in sorrow. But in all things one obviously ought to imitate the better type of person.

On the other hand, the presence of friends in our *prosperity* implies both a pleasant passing of our time and the pleasant thought of their pleasure at our own good fortune. For this cause it would 15 seem that we ought to summon our friends readily to share our good fortunes (for the beneficent character is a noble one), but summon them to our bad fortunes with hesitation; for we ought to give them as little a share as possible in our evils—whence the saying 'enough is *my* misfortune'. We should summon friends to us most of all when they are likely by suffering a few inconveniences to do us a great service.

Conversely, it is fitting to go unasked and readily to the aid of 20 those in adversity (for it is characteristic of a friend to render services, and especially to those who are in need and have not demanded them; such action is nobler and pleasanter for both persons); but when our friends are prosperous we should join readily in their activities (for they need friends for these too), but be tardy in coming forward to be the objects of their kindness; for it is not noble to be keen to receive benefits. Still, we must no doubt avoid getting the 25 reputation of kill-joys by repulsing them; for that sometimes happens.

The presence of friends, then, seems desirable in all circumstances.

12   Does it not follow, then, that, as for lovers the sight of the beloved is the thing they love most, and they prefer this sense to the 30 others because on it love depends most for its being and for its origin, so for friends the most desirable thing is living together? For friendship is a partnership, and as a man is to himself, so is he to his friend; now in his own case the consciousness of his being is desirable, and so therefore is the consciousness of his friend's being, and the activity 35 of this consciousness is produced when they live together, so that it 1172ᵃ is natural that they aim at this. And whatever existence means for each class of men, whatever it is for whose sake they value life, in *that* they wish to occupy themselves with their friends; and so some drink together, others dice together, others join in athletic exercises and hunting, or in the study of philosophy, each class spending their 5 days together in whatever they love most in life; for since they wish to live with their friends, they do and share in those things which give them the sense of living together. Thus the friendship of bad men turns out an evil thing (for because of their instability they 10 unite in bad pursuits, and besides they become evil by becoming like each other), while the friendship of good men is good, being augmented by their companionship; and they are thought to become better too by their activities and by improving each other; for from each other they take the mould of the characteristics they approve —whence the saying 'noble deeds from noble men'.—So much, then, for friendship; our next task must be to discuss pleasure. 15

BOOK X

1   After these matters we ought perhaps next to discuss pleasure. For it is thought to be most intimately connected with our human nature, which is the reason why in educating the young we steer them 20 by the rudders of pleasure and pain; it is thought, too, that to enjoy

the things we ought and to hate the things we ought has the greatest
bearing on virtue of character. For these things extend right through
life, with a weight and power of their own in respect both to virtue
25 and to the happy life, since men choose what is pleasant and avoid
what is painful; and such things, it will be thought, we should least
of all omit to discuss, especially since they admit of much dispute.
For some [1] say pleasure is the good, while others,[2] on the contrary,
say it is thoroughly bad—some no doubt being persuaded that the
facts are so, and others thinking it has a better effect on our life
30 to exhibit pleasure as a bad thing even if it is not; for most people
(they think) incline towards it and are the slaves of their pleasures,
for which reason they ought to lead them in the opposite direction,
since thus they will reach the middle state. But surely this is not correct. For arguments about matters concerned with feelings and ac-
35 tions are less reliable than facts: and so when they clash with the
facts of perception they are despised, and discredit the truth as well;
1172ᵇ if a man who runs down pleasure is once seen to be aiming at it, his
inclining towards it is thought to imply that it is all worthy of being
aimed at; for most people are not good at drawing distinctions. True
arguments seem, then, most useful, not only with a view to knowledge,
5 but with a view to life also; for since they harmonize with the facts
they are believed, and so they stimulate those who understand them
to live according to them.—Enough of such questions; let us proceed to review the opinions that have been expressed about pleasure.

2   Eudoxus thought pleasure was the good because he saw all things,
10 both rational and irrational, aiming at it, and because in all things
that which is the object of choice is what is excellent, and that which
is most the object of choice the greatest good; thus the fact that all
things moved towards the same object indicated that this was for
all things the chief good (for each thing, he argued, finds its own good,
as it finds its own nourishment); and that which is good for all things
15 and at which all aim was *the* good. His arguments were credited more
because of the excellence of his character than for their own sake; he
was thought to be remarkably self-controlled, and therefore it was
thought that he was not saying what he did say as a friend of pleasure, but that the facts really were so. He believed that the same conclusion followed no less plainly from a study of the contrary of
pleasure; pain was in itself an object of aversion to all things, and

---

[1] The school of Eudoxus, Cf. ᵇ9. Aristippus is perhaps also referred to.
[2] The school of Speusippus, Cf. 1153ᵇ 5.

therefore its contrary must be similarly an object of choice. And 20 again that is most an object of choice which we choose not because or for the sake of something else, and pleasure is admittedly of this nature; for no one asks to what end he is pleased, thus implying that pleasure is in itself an object of choice. Further, he argued that pleasure when added to any good, e. g. to just or temperate action, makes it more worthy of choice, and that it is only by itself that the good 25 can be increased.

This argument seems to show it to be one of the goods, and no more a good than any other; for every good is more worthy of choice along with another good than taken alone. And so it is by an argument of this kind that Plato [3] proves the good *not* to be pleasure; he argues that the pleasant life is more desirable with wisdom than with- 30 out, and that if the mixture is better, pleasure is not the good; for the good cannot become more desirable by the addition of anything to it. Now it is clear that nothing else, any more than pleasure, can be the good if it is made more desirable by the addition of any of the things that are good in themselves. What, then, is there that satisfies this criterion, which at the same time we can participate in? It is something of this sort that we are looking for.

Those who object that that at which all things aim is not neces- 35 sarily good are, we may surmise, talking nonsense. For we say that that which every one thinks really is so; and the man who attacks 1173[a] this belief will hardly have anything more credible to maintain instead. If it is senseless creatures that desire the things in question, there might be something in what they say; but if intelligent creatures do so as well, what sense can there be in this view? But perhaps even in inferior creatures there is some natural good stronger than themselves which aims at their proper good.

Nor does the argument about the contrary of pleasure seem to 5 be correct. They say that if pain is an evil it does not follow that pleasure is a good; for evil is opposed to evil and at the same time both are opposed to the neutral state—which is correct enough but does not apply to the things in question. For if both pleasure and 10 pain belonged to the class of evils they ought both to be objects of aversion, while if they belonged to the class of neutrals neither should be an object of aversion or they should both be equally so; but in fact people evidently avoid the one as evil and choose the other as good; that then must be the nature of the opposition between them.

[3] *Phil.* 60 b–e.

3   Nor again, if pleasure is not a quality, does it follow that it is not a good; for the activities of virtue are not qualities either, nor is happiness.

15   They say,[4] however, that the good is determinate, while pleasure is indeterminate, because it admits of degrees. Now if it is from the feeling of pleasure that they judge thus, the same will be true of justice and the other virtues, in respect of which we plainly say that people of a certain character are so more or less, and act more or less 20 in accordance with these virtues; for people may be more just or brave, and it is possible also to act justly or temperately more or less. But if their judgement is based on the various pleasures, surely they are not stating the real cause,[5] if in fact some pleasures are unmixed and others mixed. Again, just as health admits of degrees without 25 being indeterminate, why should not pleasure? The same proportion is not found in all things, nor a single proportion always in the same thing, but it may be relaxed and yet persist up to a point, and it may differ in degree. The case of pleasure also may therefore be of this kind.

Again, they assume [6] that the good is perfect while movements 30 and comings into being are imperfect, and try to exhibit pleasure as being a movement and a coming into being. But they do not seem to be right even in saying that it is a movement. For speed and slowness are thought to be proper to every movement, and if a movement, e. g. that of the heavens, has not speed or slowness in itself, it has it in relation to something else; but of pleasure neither of these things is true. For while we may *become* pleased quickly as 1173[b] we may become angry quickly, we cannot *be* pleased quickly, not even in relation to some one else, while we *can* walk, or grow, or the like, quickly. While, then, we can change quickly or slowly into a state of pleasure, we cannot quickly exhibit the activity of pleasure, i. e. be pleased. Again, how can it be a coming into being? It is not thought that any chance thing can come out of any chance thing, 5 but that a thing is dissolved into that out of which it comes into being; and pain would be the destruction of that of which pleasure is the coming into being.

They say, too,[7] that pain is the lack of that which is according to nature, and pleasure is replenishment. But these experiences are bodily. If then pleasure is replenishment with that which is according to nature, that which feels pleasure will be that in which the

---

[4] Ib. 24 E–25 A, 31 A.   [5] *sc.*, of the badness of (some) pleasures.
[6] Pl. *Phil.* 53 C–54 D.   [7] Ib. 31 E–32 B, 42 C, D.

replenishment takes place, i.e. the body; but that is not thought 10
to be the case; therefore the replenishment is not pleasure, though
one would be pleased when replenishment was taking place, just as
one would be pained if one was being operated on.[8] This opinion
seems to be based on the pains and pleasures connected with nutrition; on the fact that when people have been short of food and have
felt pain beforehand they are pleased by the replenishment. But this
does not happen with all pleasures; for the pleasures of learning and, 15
among the sensuous pleasures, those of smell, and also many sounds
and sights, and memories and hopes, do not presuppose pain. Of what
then will these be the coming into being? There has not been lack
of anything of which they could be the supplying anew.

In reply to those who bring forward the disgraceful pleasures one 20
may say that these are not pleasant; if things are pleasant to people
of vicious constitution, we must not suppose that they are also pleasant to others than these, just as we do not reason so about the
things that are wholesome or sweet or bitter to sick people, or ascribe
whiteness to the things that seem white to those suffering from a
disease of the eye. Or one might answer thus—that the pleasures are 25
desirable, but not from *these* sources, as wealth is desirable, but
not as the reward of betrayal, and health, but not at the cost of
eating anything and everything. Or perhaps pleasures differ in kind;
for those derived from noble sources are different from those derived
from base sources, and one cannot get the pleasure of the just man
without being just, nor that of the musical man without being musical, 30
and so on.

The fact, too, that a friend is different from a flatterer seems to
make it plain that pleasure is not a good or that pleasures are different in kind; for the one is thought to consort with us with a
view to the good, the other with a view to our pleasure, and the one
is reproached for his conduct while the other is praised on the ground
that he consorts with us for different ends. And no one would choose 1174ᵃ
to live with the intellect of a child throughout his life, however much
he were to be pleased at the things that children are pleased at, nor
to get enjoyment by doing some most disgraceful deed, though he
were never to feel any pain in consequence. And there are many
things we should be keen about even if they brought no pleasure, 5
e.g. seeing, remembering, knowing, possessing the virtues. If pleasures necessarily do accompany these, that makes no odds; we should
choose these even if no pleasure resulted. It seems to be clear, then,

---

[8] The point being that the being replenished no more *is* pleasure than the being
operated on *is* pain. For the instance, Cf. Pl. *Tim.* 65 B.

that neither is pleasure the good nor is all pleasure desirable, and that
10 some pleasures *are* desirable in kind or in their sources from the
others. So much for the things that are said about pleasure and pain.

4 What pleasure is, or what kind of thing it is, will become plainer
if we take up the question again from the beginning. Seeing seems
15 to be at any moment complete, for it does not lack anything which
coming into being later will complete its form; and pleasure also
seems to be of this nature. For it is a whole, and at no time can one
find a pleasure whose form will be completed if the pleasure lasts
longer. For this reason, too, it is not a movement. For every movement (e. g. that of building) takes time and is for the sake of an end,
20 and is complete when it has made what it aims at. It is complete,
therefore, only in the whole time or at that final moment. In their
parts and during the time they occupy, all movements are incomplete,
and are different in kind from the whole movement and from each
other. For the fitting together of the stones is different from the flut-
ing of the column, and these are both different from the making of
25 the temple; and the making of the temple is complete (for it lacks
nothing with a view to the end proposed), but the making of the base
or of the triglyph is incomplete; for each is the making of only a part.
They differ in kind, then, and it is not possible to find at any and
every time a movement complete in form, but if at all, only in the
whole time. So, too, in the case of walking and all other movements.
30 For if locomotion is a movement from here to there, it, too, has differences in kind—flying, walking, leaping, and so on. And not only so,
but in walking itself there are such differences; for the whence and
whither are not the same in the whole racecourse and in a part of
it, nor in one part and in another, nor is it the same thing to traverse
1174ᵇ this line and that; for one traverses not only a line but one which is
in a place, and this one is in a different place from that. We have
discussed movement with precision in another work,[9] but it seems
that it is not complete at any and every time, but that the many movements are incomplete and different in kind, since the whence and
5 whither give them their form. But of pleasure the form is complete
at any and every time. Plainly, then, pleasure and movement must be
different from each other, and pleasure must be one of the things
that are whole and complete. This would seem to be the case, too, from
the fact that it is not possible to move otherwise than in time, but it
is possible to be pleased; for that which takes place in a moment
is a whole.

9 *Phys.* vi-viii.

From these considerations it is clear, too, that these thinkers are not right in saying there is a movement or a coming into being *of* pleasure. For these cannot be ascribed to all things, but only to those that are divisible and not wholes; there is no coming into being of seeing nor of a point nor of a unit, nor is any of these a movement or coming into being; therefore there is no movement or coming into being of pleasure either; for it is a whole.

Since every sense is active in relation to its object, and a sense which is in good condition acts perfectly in relation to the most beautiful of its objects (for perfect activity seems to be ideally of this nature; whether we say that *it* is active, or the organ in which it resides, may be assumed to be immaterial), it follows that in the case of each sense the best activity is that of the best-conditioned organ in relation to the finest of its objects. And this activity will be the most complete and pleasant. For, while there is pleasure in respect of any sense, and in respect of thought and contemplation no less, the most complete is pleasantest, and that of a well-conditioned organ in relation to the worthiest of its objects is the most complete; and the pleasure completes the activity. But the pleasure does not complete it in the same way as the combination of object and sense, both good, just as health and the doctor are not in the same way the cause of a man's being healthy. (That pleasure is produced in respect to each sense is plain; for we speak of sights and sounds as pleasant. It is also plain that it arises most of all when both the sense is at its best and it is active in reference to an object which corresponds; when both object and perceiver are of the best there will always be pleasure, since the requisite agent and patient are both present.) Pleasure completes the activity not as the corresponding permanent state does, by its immanence, but as an end which supervenes as the bloom of youth does on those in the flower of their age. So long, then, as both the intelligible or sensible object and the discriminating or contemplative faculty are as they should be, the pleasure will be involved in the activity; for when both the passive and the active factor are unchanged and are related to each other in the same way, the same result naturally follows.

How, then, is it that no one is continuously pleased? Is it that we grow weary? Certainly all human things are incapable of continuous activity. Therefore pleasure also is not continuous; for it accompanies activity. Some things delight us when they are new, but later do so less, for the same reason; for at first the mind is in a state of stimulation and intensely active about them, as people are with respect to their vision when they look hard at a thing, but afterwards our activity is not of this kind, but has grown relaxed; for which reason the pleasure also is dulled.

10   One might think that all men desire pleasure because they all aim at life; life is an activity, and each man is active about those things and with those faculties that he loves most; e. g. the musician is active with his hearing in reference to tunes, the student with his mind 15 in reference to theoretical questions, and so on in each case; now pleasure completes the activities, and therefore life, which they desire. It is with good reason, then, that they aim at pleasure too, since for every one it completes life, which is desirable. But whether we choose life for the sake of pleasure or pleasure for the sake of life is a question we may dismiss for the present. For they seem to be bound up to-20 gether and not to admit of separation, since without activity pleasure does not arise, and every activity is completed by the attendant pleasure.

5   For this reason pleasures seem, too, to differ in kind. For things different in kind are, we think, completed by different things (we see this to be true both of natural objects and of things produced by art, 25 e. g. animals, trees, a painting, a sculpture, a house, an implement); and, similarly, we think that activities differing in kind are completed by things differing in kind. Now the activities of thought differ from those of the senses, and both differ among themselves, in kind; so, therefore, do the pleasures that complete them.

This may be seen, too, from the fact that each of the pleasures is bound up with the activity it completes. For an activity is intensi-30 fied by its proper pleasure, since each class of things is better judged of and brought to precision by those who engage in the activity with pleasure; e. g. it is those who enjoy geometrical thinking that become geometers and grasp the various propositions better, and, similarly, those who are fond of music or of building, and so on, make progress 35 in their proper function by enjoying it; so the pleasures intensify the activities, and what intensifies a thing is proper to it, but things different in kind have properties different in kind.

1175ᵇ   This will be even more apparent from the fact that activities are hindered by pleasures arising from other sources. For people who are fond of playing the flute are incapable of attending to arguments if they overhear some one playing the flute, since they enjoy flute-5 playing more than the activity in hand; so the pleasure connected with flute-playing destroys the activity concerned with argument. This happens, similarly, in all other cases, when one is active

about two things at once; the more pleasant activity drives out
the other, and if it is much more pleasant does so all the more, so
that one even ceases from the other. This is why when we enjoy 10
anything very much we do not throw ourselves into anything else, and
do one thing only when we are not much pleased by another; e.g. in
the theatre the people who eat sweets do so most when the actors are
poor. Now since activities are made precise and more enduring and
better by their proper pleasure, and injured by alien pleasures, evi- 15
dently the two kinds of pleasure are far apart. For alien pleasures do
pretty much what proper pains do, since activities are destroyed by
their proper pains; e.g. if a man finds writing or doing sums unpleasant and painful, he does not write, or does not do sums, because
the activity is painful. So an activity suffers contrary effects from its 20
proper pleasures and pains, i.e. from those that supervene on it in
virtue of its own nature. And alien pleasures have been stated to do
much the same as pain; they destroy the activity, only not to the
same degree.

Now since activities differ in respect of goodness and badness, and
some are worthy to be chosen, others to be avoided, and others neutral, 25
so, too, are the pleasures; for to each activity there is a proper pleasure. The pleasure proper to a worthy activity is good and that proper
to an unworthy activity bad; just as the appetites for noble objects
are laudable, those for base objects culpable. But the pleasures in- 30
volved in activities are more proper to them than the desires; for the
latter are separated both in time and in nature, while the former are
close to the activities, and so hard to distinguish from them that it
admits of dispute whether the activity is not the same as the pleasure.
(Still, pleasure does not seem to *be* thought or perception—that
would be strange; but because they are not found apart they appear 35
to some people the same.) As activities are different, then, so are
the corresponding pleasures. Now sight is superior to touch in purity, 1176ᵃ
and hearing and smell to taste; the pleasures, therefore, are similarly
superior, and those of thought superior to these, and within each of
the two kinds some are superior to others.

Each animal is thought to have a proper pleasure, as it has a
proper function; viz. that which corresponds to its activity. If
we survey them species by species, too, this will be evident; horse, 5
dog, and man have different pleasures, as Heraclitus says 'asses
would prefer sweepings to gold'; for food is pleasanter than gold to
asses. So the pleasures of creatures different in kind differ in kind,
and it is plausible to suppose that those of a single species do not
differ. But they vary to no small extent, in the case of men at least; 10

the same things delight some people and pain others, and are painful
and odious to some, and pleasant to and liked by others. This happens, too, in the case of sweet things; the same things do not seem
sweet to a man in a fever and a healthy man—nor hot to a weak man
and one in good condition. The same happens in other cases. But in
15 all such matters that which appears to the good man is thought to
be really so. If this is correct, as it seems to be, and virtue and the
good man as such are the measure of each thing, those also will be
pleasures which appear so to him, and those things pleasant which he
enjoys. If the things he finds tiresome seem pleasant to some one, that
20 is nothing surprising; for men may be ruined and spoilt in many
ways; but the things are not pleasant, but only pleasant to these
people and to people in this condition. Those which are admittedly
disgraceful plainly should not be said to be pleasures, except to a perverted taste; but of those that are thought to be good what kind of
pleasure or what pleasure should be said to be that proper to man?
25 Is it not plain from the corresponding activities? The pleasures follow these. Whether, then, the perfect and supremely happy man has
one or more activities, the pleasures that perfect these will be said
in the strict sense to be pleasures proper to man, and the rest will be
so in a secondary and fractional way, as are the activities.

30 6   Now that we have spoken of the virtues, the forms of friendship,
and the varieties of pleasure, what remains is to discuss in outline
the nature of happiness, since this is what we state the end of human
nature to be. Our discussion will be the more concise if we first sum
up what we have said already. We said,[10] then, that it is not a disposition; for if it were it might belong to some one who was asleep
35 throughout his life, living the life of a plant, or, again, to some one
1176ᵇ who was suffering the greatest misfortunes. If these implications are
unacceptable, and we must rather class happiness as an activity, as
we have said before,[11] and if some activities are necessary, and desirable for the sake of something else, while others are so in themselves,
evidently happiness must be placed among those desirable in them-
5 selves, not among those desirable for the sake of something else;
for happiness does not lack anything, but is self-sufficient. Now those
activities are desirable in themselves from which nothing is sought
beyond the activity. And of this nature virtuous actions are thought
to be; for to do noble and good deeds is a thing desirable for its
own sake.

[10] 1095ᵇ 31–1096ᵃ 2, 1098ᵇ 31–1099ᵃ 7.   [11] 1098ᵃ 5–7.

Pleasant amusements also are thought to be of this nature; we choose them not for the sake of other things; for we are injured rather than benefited by them, since we are led to neglect our bodies 10 and our property. But most of the people who are deemed happy take refuge in such pastimes, which is the reason why those who are ready-witted at them are highly esteemed at the courts of tyrants; they make themselves pleasant companions in the tyrants' favourite pur- 15 suits, and that is the sort of man they want. Now these things are thought to be of the nature of happiness because people in despotic positions spend their leisure in them, but perhaps such people prove nothing; for virtue and reason, from which good activities flow, do not depend on despotic position; nor, if these people, who have never tasted pure and generous pleasure, take refuge in the bodily pleas- 20 ures, should these for that reason be thought more desirable; for boys, too, think the things that are valued among themselves are the best. It is to be expected, then, that, as different things seem valu-able to boys and to men, so they should to bad men and to good. Now, as we have often maintained,[12] those things are both valuable 25 and pleasant which are such to the good man; and to each man the activity in accordance with his own disposition is most desirable, and, therefore, to the good man that which is in accordance with virtue. Happiness, therefore, does not lie in amusement; it would, indeed, be strange if the end were amusement, and one were to take trouble and suffer hardship all one's life in order to amuse oneself. For, in a 30 word, everything that we choose we choose for the sake of some-thing else—except happiness, which is an end. Now to exert oneself and work for the sake of amusement seems silly and utterly childish. But to amuse oneself in order that one may exert oneself, as Ana-charsis puts it, seems right; for amusement is a sort of relaxation, and we need relaxation because we cannot work continuously. 35 Relaxation, then, is not an end; for it is taken for the sake of activity.

The happy life is thought to be virtuous; now a virtuous life 1177ª requires exertion, and does not consist in amusement. And we say that serious things are better than laughable things and those con-nected with amusement, and that the activity of the better of any two things—whether it be two elements of our being or two men—is the more serious; but the activity of the better is *ipso facto* superior 5 and more of the nature of happiness. And any chance person—even a slave—can enjoy the bodily pleasures no less than the best man; but

12 1099ª 13, 1113ª 22–33, 1166ª 12, 1170ª 14–16, 1176ª 15–22.

no one assigns to a slave a share in happiness—unless he assigns to
10 him also a share in human life. For happiness does not lie in such
occupations, but, as we have said before,[13] in virtuous activities.

7   If happiness is activity in accordance with virtue, it is reasonable that it should be in accordance with the highest virtue; and
this will be that of the best thing in us. Whether it be reason or
something else that is this element which is thought to be our natural
15 ruler and guide and to take thought of things noble and divine,
whether it be itself also divine or only the most divine element in us,
the activity of this in accordance with its proper virtue will be perfect happiness. That this activity is contemplative we have already
said.[14]

Now this would seem to be in agreement both with what we said
20 before [15] and with the truth. For, firstly, this activity is the best
(since not only is reason the best thing in us, but the objects of
reason are the best of knowable objects); and, secondly, it is the
most continuous, since we can contemplate truth more continuously
than we can *do* anything. And we think happiness has pleasure
mingled with it, but the activity of philosophic wisdom is admittedly
25 the pleasantest of virtuous activities; at all events the pursuit of it
is thought to offer pleasures marvellous for their purity and their
enduringness, and it is to be expected that those who know will pass
their time more pleasantly than those who inquire. And the self-sufficiency that is spoken of must belong most to the contemplative
activity. For while a philosopher, as well as a just man or one possess-
30 ing any other virtue, needs the necessaries of life, when they are
sufficiently equipped with things of that sort the just man needs
people towards whom and with whom he shall act justly, and the
temperate man, the brave man, and each of the others is in the same
case, but the philosopher, even when by himself, can contemplate
truth, and the better the wiser he is; he can perhaps do so better if
1177ᵇ he has fellow-workers, but still he is the most self-sufficient. And
this activity alone would seem to be loved for its own sake; for nothing arises from it apart from the contemplating, while from practical
activities we gain more or less apart from the action. And happiness
5 is thought to depend on leisure; for we are busy that we may have

---

[13] 1098ᵃ 16, 1176ᵃ 35–ᵇ9.

[14] This has not been said, but Cf. 1095ᵇ 14–1096ᵃ 5, 1141ᵃ 18–ᵇ 3, 1143ᵇ 33–
1144ᵃ 6, 1145ᵃ 6–11.

[15] 1097ᵃ 25–ᵇ 21, 1099ᵃ 7–21, 1173ᵇ 15–19, 1174ᵇ 20–23, 1175ᵇ 36–1176ᵃ 3.

leisure, and make war that we may live in peace. Now the activity of the practical virtues is exhibited in political or military affairs, but the actions concerned with these seem to be unleisurely. Warlike actions are completely so (for no one chooses to be at war, or provokes war, for the sake of being at war; any one would seem absolutely murderous if he were to make enemies of his friends in order to bring about battle and slaughter); but the action of the statesman is also unleisurely, and—apart from the political action itself—aims at despotic power and honours, or at all events happiness, for him and his fellow citizens—a happiness different from political action, and evidently sought as being different. So if among virtuous actions political and military actions are distinguished by nobility and greatness, and these are unleisurely and aim at an end and are not desirable for their own sake, but the activity of reason, which is contemplative, seems both to be superior in serious worth and to aim at no end beyond itself, and to have its pleasure proper to itself (and this augments the activity), and the self-sufficiency, leisureliness, unweariedness (so far as this is possible for man), and all the other attributes ascribed to the supremely happy man are evidently those connected with this activity, it follows that this will be the complete happiness of man, if it be allowed a complete term of life (for none of the attributes of happiness is *in*complete).

But such a life would be too high for man; for it is not in so far as he is man that he will live so, but in so far as something divine is present in him; and by so much as this is superior to our composite nature is its activity superior to that which is the exercise of the other kind of virtue. If reason is divine, then, in comparison with man, the life according to it is divine in comparison with human life. But we must not follow those who advise us, being men, to think of human things, and, being mortal, of mortal things, but must, so far as we can, make ourselves immortal, and strain every nerve to live in accordance with the best thing in us; for even if it be small in bulk, much more does it in power and worth surpass everything. This would seem, too, to be each man himself, since it is the authoritative and better part of him. It would be strange, then, if he were to choose not the life of his self but that of something else. And what we said before[16] will apply now; that which is proper to each thing is by nature best and most pleasant for each thing; for man, therefore, the life according to reason is best and pleasantest, since reason more than anything else *is* man. This life therefore is also the happiest.

[16] 1169^b 33, 1176^b 26.

8 But in a secondary degree the life in accordance with the other kind of virtue is happy; for the activities in accordance with this
10 befit our human estate. Just and brave acts, and other virtuous acts, we do in relation to each other, observing our respective duties with regard to contracts and services and all manner of actions and with regard to passions; and all of these seem to be typically human. Some
15 of them seem even to arise from the body, and virtue of character to be in many ways bound up with the passions. Practical wisdom, too, is linked to virtue of character, and this to practical wisdom, since the principles of practical wisdom are in accordance with the moral virtues and rightness in morals is in accordance with practical wisdom. Being connected with the passions also, the moral virtues must belong to our composite nature; and the virtues of
20 our composite nature are human; so, therefore, are the life and the happiness which correspond to these. The excellence of the reason is a thing apart; we must be content to say this much about it, for to describe it precisely is a task greater than our purpose requires. It would seem, however, also to need external equipment
25 but little, or less than moral virtue does. Grant that both need the necessaries, and do so equally, even if the statesman's work is the more concerned with the body and things of that sort; for there will be little difference there; but in what they need for the exercise of their activities there will be much difference. The liberal man will need money for the doing of his liberal deeds, and the just man too
30 will need it for the returning of services (for wishes are hard to discern, and even people who are not just pretend to wish to act justly); and the brave man will need power if he is to accomplish any of the acts that correspond to his virtue, and the temperate man will need opportunity; for how else is either he or any of the others to be recognized? It is debated, too, whether the will or the deed is more
35 essential to virtue, which is assumed to involve both; it is surely
1178b clear that its perfection involves both; but for deeds many things are needed, and more, the greater and nobler the deeds are. But the man who is contemplating the truth needs no such thing, at least with a view to the exercise of his activity; indeed they are, one may say,
5 even hindrances, at all events to his contemplation; but in so far as he is a man and lives with a number of people, he chooses to do virtuous acts; he will therefore need such aids to living a human life.

But that perfect happiness is a contemplative activity will appear from the following consideration as well. We assume the gods to be above all other beings blessed and happy; but what sort of

actions must we assign to them? Acts of justice? Will not the gods 10
seem absurd if they make contracts and return deposits, and so
on? Acts of a brave man, then, confronting dangers and running
risks because it is noble to do so? Or liberal acts? To whom will
they give? It will be strange if they are really to have money or
anything of the kind. And what would their temperate acts be? 15
Is not such praise tasteless, since they have no bad appetites?
If we were to run through them all, the circumstances of action
would be found trivial and unworthy of gods. Still, every one supposes that they *live* and therefore that they are active; we cannot
suppose them to sleep like Endymion. Now if you take away from 20
a living being action, and still more production, what is left but
contemplation? Therefore the activity of God, which surpasses all
others in blessedness, must be contemplative; and of human activities, therefore, that which is most akin to this must be most of the
nature of happiness.

This is indicated, too, by the fact that the other animals have no
share in happiness, being completely deprived of such activity. For
while the whole life of the gods is blessed, and that of men too in 25
so far as some likeness of such activity belongs to them, none of
the other animals is happy, since they in no way share in contemplation. Happiness extends, then, just so far as contemplation does,
and those to whom contemplation more fully belongs are more
truly happy, not as a mere concomitant but in virtue of the 30
contemplation; for this is in itself precious. Happiness, therefore,
must be some form of contemplation.

But, being a man, one will also need external prosperity; for our
nature is not self-sufficient for the purpose of contemplation, but
our body also must be healthy and must have food and other at- 35
tention. Still, we must not think that the man who is to be happy 1179a
will need many things or great things, merely because he cannot be
supremely happy without external goods; for self-sufficiency and
action do not involve excess, and we can do noble acts without
ruling earth and sea; for even with moderate advantages one can 5
act virtuously (this is manifest enough; for private persons are
thought to do worthy acts no less than despots—indeed even more);
and it is enough that we should have so much as that; for the life
of the man who is active in accordance with virtue will be happy.
Solon, too, was perhaps sketching well the happy man when he 10
described him as moderately furnished with externals but as having
done (as Solon thought) the noblest acts, and lived temperately;
for one can with but moderate possessions do what one ought. An-

axagoras also seems to have supposed the happy man not to be
· rich nor a despot, when he said that he would not be surprised if
the happy man were to seem to most people a strange person;
15 for they judge by externals, since these are all they perceive. The
opinions of the wise seem, then, to harmonize with our arguments.
But while even such things carry some conviction, the truth in
practical matters is discerned from the facts of life; for these are the
20 decisive factor. We must therefore survey what we have already
said, bringing it to the test of the facts of life, and if it harmonizes
with the facts we must accept it, but if it clashes with them we must
suppose it to be mere theory. Now he who exercises his reason and
cultivates it seems to be both in the best state of mind and most
dear to the gods. For if the gods have any care for human affairs,
25 as they are thought to have, it would be reasonable both that they
should delight in that which was best and most akin to them (i. e.
reason) and that they should reward those who love and honour
this most, as caring for the things that are dear to them and acting
both rightly and nobly. And that all these attributes belong most
30 of all to the philosopher is manifest. He, therefore, is the dearest
to the gods. And he who is that will presumably be also the
happiest; so that in this way too the philosopher will more than
any other be happy.

9 If these matters and the virtues, and also friendship and pleasure,
have been dealt with sufficiently in outline, are we to suppose that
35 our programme has reached its end? Surely, as the saying goes,
where there are things to be done the end is not to survey and
1179ᵇ recognize the various things, but rather to do them; with regard to
virtue, then, it is not enough to know, but we must try to have and
use it, or try any other way there may be of becoming good.
Now if arguments were in themselves enough to make men good,
5 they would justly, as Theognis says, have won very great rewards,
and such rewards should have been provided; but as things are,
while they seem to have power to encourage and stimulate the gen-
erous-minded among our youth, and to make a character which is
gently born, and a true lover of what is noble, ready to be possessed
10 by virtue, they are not able to encourage the many to nobility
and goodness. For these do not by nature obey the sense of shame,
but only fear, and do not abstain from bad acts because of their
baseness but through fear of punishment; living by passion they
pursue their own pleasures and the means to them, and avoid the op-
15 posite pains, and have not even a conception of what is noble and

truly pleasant, since they have never tasted it. What argument would
remould such people? It is hard, if not impossible, to remove by argument the traits that have long since been incorporated in the
character; and perhaps we must be content if, when all the influences
by which we are thought to become good are present, we get some
tincture of virtue.

Now some think that we are made good by nature, others by 20
habituation, others by teaching. Nature's part evidently does not depend on us, but as a result of some divine causes is present in those
who are truly fortunate; while argument and teaching, we may suspect, are not powerful with all men, but the soul of the student must
first have been cultivated by means of habits for noble joy and noble 25
hatred, like earth which is to nourish the seed. For he who lives as
passion directs will not hear argument that dissuades him, nor understand it if he does; and how can we persuade one in such a state
to change his ways? And in general passion seems to yield not to
argument but to force. The character, then, must somehow be there
already with a kinship to virtue, loving what is noble and hating 30
what is base.

But it is difficult to get from youth up a right training for virtue if one has not been brought up under right laws; for to live temperately and hardily is not pleasant to most people, especially when
they are young. For this reason their nurture and occupations should 35
be fixed by law; for they will not be painful when they have become customary. But it is surely not enough that when they are 1180ᵃ
young they should get the right nurture and attention; since they
must, even when they are grown up, practise and be habituated to
them, we shall need laws for this as well, and generally speaking to
cover the whole of life; for most people obey necessity rather than
argument, and punishments rather than the sense of what is noble.

This is why some think [17] that legislators ought to stimulate men 5
to virtue and urge them forward by the motive of the noble, on the
assumption that those who have been well advanced by the formation of habits will attend to such influences; and that punishments
and penalties should be imposed on those who disobey and are of
inferior nature, while the incurably bad should be completely banished.[18] A good man (they think), since he lives with his mind fixed
on what is noble, will submit to argument, while a bad man, whose 10
desire is for pleasure, is corrected by pain like a beast of burden. This
is, too, why they say the pains inflicted should be those that are
most opposed to the pleasures such men love.

[17] Pl. *Laws* 722 D ff.   [18] Pl. *Prot.* 325 A.

However that may be, if (as we have said)¹⁹ the man who is to be
15 good must be well trained and habituated, and go on to spend his
time in worthy occupations and neither willingly nor unwillingly do
bad actions, and if this can be brought about if men live in accordance with a sort of reason and right order, provided this has force—
if this be so, the paternal command indeed has not the required
20 force or compulsive power (nor in general has the command of one
man, unless he be a king or something similar), but the law *has* compulsive power, while it is at the same time a rule proceeding from
a sort of practical wisdom and reason. And while people hate *men*
who oppose their impulses, even if they oppose them rightly, the law
in its ordaining of what is good is not burdensome.

25   In the Spartan state alone, or almost alone, the legislator seems
to have paid attention to questions of nurture and occupations; in
most states such matters have been neglected, and each man lives
as he pleases, Cyclops-fashion, 'to his own wife and children dealing
law'.²⁰ Now it is best that there should be a public and proper care for
30 such matters; but if they are neglected by the community it would
seem right for each man to help his children and friends towards
virtue, and that they should have the power, or at least the will, to do
this.

It would seem from what has been said that he can do this better
if he makes himself capable of legislating. For public control is
plainly effected by laws, and good control by good laws; whether
35 written or unwritten would seem to make no difference, nor whether
1180ᵇ they are laws providing for the education of individuals or of groups
—any more than it does in the case of music or gymnastics and
other such pursuits. For as in cities laws and prevailing types of character have force, so in households do the injunctions and the habits
5 of the father, and these have even more because of the tie of blood
and the benefits he confers; for the children start with a natural
affection and disposition to obey. Further, private education has an
advantage over public, as private medical treatment has; for while in
general rest and abstinence from food are good for a man in a fever,
10 for a particular man they may not be; and a boxer presumably does
not prescribe the same style of fighting to all his pupils. It would
seem, then, that the detail is worked out with more precision if the
control is private; for each person is more likely to get what suits his
case.

But the details can be best looked after, one by one, by a doctor or gymnastic instructor or any one else who has the general

¹⁹ 1179ᵇ 31–1180ᵃ 5.   ²⁰ *Od.* ix. 114 f.

knowledge of what is good for every one or for people of a certain kind (for the sciences both are said to be, and are, concerned 15 with what is universal); not but what some particular detail may perhaps be well looked after by an unscientific person, if he has studied accurately in the light of experience what happens in each case, just as some people seem to be their own best doctors, though they could give no help to any one else. None the less, it will perhaps be agreed 20 that if a man does wish to become master of an art or science he must go to the universal, and come to know it as well as possible; for, as we have said, it is with this that the sciences are concerned.

And surely he who wants to make men, whether many or few, better by his care must try to become capable of legislating, if it is through laws that we can become good. For to get any one whatever 25 —any one who is put before us—into the right condition is not for the first chance comer; if any one can do it, it is the man who knows, just as in medicine and all other matters which give scope for care and prudence.

Must we not, then, next examine whence or how one can learn how to legislate? Is it, as in all other cases, from statesmen? Certainly it was thought to be a part of statesmanship.[21] Or is a difference ap- 30 parent between statesmanship and the other sciences and arts? In the others the same people are found offering to teach the arts and practising them, e. g. doctors or painters; but while the sophists profess 35 to teach politics, it is practised not by any of them but by the poli- 1181ª ticians, who would seem to do so by dint of a certain skill and experience rather than of thought; for they are not found either writing or speaking about such matters (though it were a nobler occupation perhaps than composing speeches for the law-courts and the assembly), nor again are they found to have made statesmen of their 5 own sons or any other of their friends. But it was to be expected that they should if they could; for there is nothing better than such a skill that they could have left to their cities, or could prefer to have for themselves, or, therefore, for those dearest to them. Still, experience seems to contribute not a little; else they could not have become 10 politicians by familiarity with politics; and so it seems that those who aim at knowing about the art of politics need experience as well.

But those of the sophists who profess the art seem to be very far from teaching it. For, to put the matter generally, they do not even know what kind of thing it is nor what kinds of things it is about; otherwise they would not have classed it as identical with rhetoric

21 1141ᵇ 24.

15 or even inferior to it,[22] nor have thought it easy to legislate by collecting the laws that are thought well of;[23] they say it is possible
to select the best laws, as though even the selection did not demand
intelligence and as though right judgement were not the greatest
thing, as in matters of music. For while people experienced in any
20 department judge rightly the works produced in it, and understand
by what means or how they are achieved, and what harmonizes with
what, the inexperienced must be content if they do not fail to see
whether the work has been well or ill made—as in the case of painting. Now laws are as it were the 'works' of the political art;
1181ᵇ how then can one learn from them to be a legislator, or judge which
are best? Even medical men do not seem to be made by a study of
text-books. Yet people try, at any rate, to state not only the treatments, but also how particular classes of people can be cured and
5 should be treated—distinguishing the various habits of body; but
while this seems useful to experienced people, to the inexperienced it is
valueless. Surely, then, while collections of laws, and of constitutions
also, may be serviceable to those who can study them and judge
what is good or bad and what enactments suit what circumstances,
10 those who go through such collections without a practised faculty
will not have right judgement (unless it be as a spontaneous gift
of nature), though they may perhaps become more intelligent in such
matters.

Now our predecessors have left the subject of legislation to us un-
examined; it is perhaps best, therefore, that we should ourselves
study it, and in general study the question of the constitution, in
15 order to complete to the best of our ability our philosophy of human
nature. First, then, if anything has been said well in detail by
earlier thinkers, let us try to review it; then in the light of the
constitutions we have collected let us study what sorts of influence
preserve and destroy states, and what sorts preserve or destroy the
particular kinds of constitution, and to what causes it is due that
20 some are well and others ill administered. When these have been
studied we shall perhaps be more likely to see with a comprehensive
view, which constitution is best, and how each must be ordered, and
what laws and customs it must use, if it is to be at its best.[24] Let us
make a beginning of our discussion.

---

[22] Isoc. *Antid.* § 80.   [23] Ib. §§ 82, 83.
[24] 1181ᵇ 12–23 is a programme for the *Politics,* agreeing to a large extent with
the existing contents of that work.

Politica

Translated by Benjamin Jowett

CONTENTS

BOOK I

CHAPTER

Chapters 1, 2. Definition and structure of the State.

Chapters 3–13. Household economy. The Slave. Property.
Children and Wives.

10. Also in their subject-matter; for natural finance is only concerned with the fruits of the earth and animals.

11. Natural finance is necessary to the householder; he must therefore know about live stock, agriculture, possibly about the exchange of the products of the earth, such as wood and minerals, for money. Special treatises on finance exist, and the subject should be specially studied by statesmen.

12. Lastly, we must discuss and distinguish the relations of husband to wife, of father to child.

13. In household management persons call for more attention than things; free persons for more than slaves. Slaves are only capable of an inferior kind of virtue. Socrates was wrong in denying that there are several kinds of virtue. Still the slave must be trained in virtue. The education of the free man will be subsequently discussed.

BOOK II

Chapters 1–8. Ideal Commonwealths—Plato, Phaleas, Hippodamus.

1. To ascertain the nature of the ideal state we should start by examining both the best states of history and the best that theorists have imagined. Otherwise we might waste our time over problems which others have already solved.

   Among theorists, Plato in the *Republic* raises the most fundamental questions. He desires to abolish private property and the family.

2. But the end which he has in view is wrong. He wishes to make all his citizens absolutely alike; but the differentiation of functions is a law of nature. There can be too much unity in a state.

3. And the means by which he would promote unity are wrong.
   The abolition of property will produce, not remove, dissension.
   Communism of wives and children will destroy natural affection.

4. Other objections can be raised; but this is the fatal one.

5. To descend to details. The advantages to be expected from communism of property would be better secured if private property were used in a liberal spirit to relieve the wants of others. Private property makes men happier, and enables them to cultivate such virtues as generosity. The *Republic* makes unity the result of uniformity among the citizens, which is not the case. The good sense of mankind has always been against Plato, and experiment would show that his idea is impracticable.

6. Plato sketched another ideal state in the *Laws;* it was meant to be

more practicable than the other. In the *Laws* he abandoned communism, but otherwise upheld the leading ideas of the earlier treatise, except that he made the new state larger and too large. He forgot to discuss foreign relations, and to fix a limit of private property, and to restrict the increase of population, and to distinguish between ruler and subject. The form of government which he proposed was bad.

7. Phaleas of Chalcedon made equal distribution of property the main feature of his scheme. This would be difficult to effect, and would not meet the evils which Phaleas had in mind. Dissensions arise from deeper causes than inequality of wealth. His state would be weak against foreign foes. His reforms would anger the rich and not satisfy the poor.

8. Hippodamus, who was not a practical politician, aimed at symmetry. In his state there were to be three classes, three kinds of landed property, three sorts of laws. He also proposed to (1) create a Court of Appeal, (2) let juries qualify their verdicts, (3) reward those who made discoveries of public utility. His classes and his property system were badly devised. Qualified verdicts are impossible since jurymen may not confer together. The law about discoveries would encourage men to tamper with the Constitution. Now laws when obsolete and absurd should be changed; but needless changes diminish the respect for law.

Chapters 9–12. The best existent states—Sparta, Crete, and Carthage— Greek lawgivers.

9. The Spartans cannot manage their serf population. Their women are too influential and too luxurious. Their property system has concentrated all wealth in a few hands. Hence the citizen body has decreased. There are points to criticize in the Ephorate, the Senate, the Kingship, the common meals, the Admiralty. The Spartan and his state are only fit for war. Yet even in war Sparta is hampered by the want of a financial system.

10. The Cretan cities resemble Sparta in their constitutions, but are more primitive. Their common meals are better managed. But the Cosmi are worse than the Ephors. The Cretan constitution is a narrow and factious oligarchy; the cities are saved from destruction only by their inaccessibility.

11. The Carthaginian polity is highly praised, and not without reason. It may be compared with the Spartan; it is an oligarchy with some democratic features. It lays stress upon wealth; in Carthage all offices are bought and sold. Also, one man may hold several offices

together. These are bad features. But the discontent of the people is soothed by schemes of emigration.

12. Of lawgivers, Solon was the best; conservative when possible, and a moderate democrat. About Philolaus, Charondas, Phaleas, Draco, Pittacus, and Androdamas there is little to be said.

BOOK III
Chapters 1–5. The Citizen, civic virtue, and the civic body.

1. How are we to define a citizen? He is more than a mere denizen; private rights do not make a citizen. He is ordinarily one who possesses political power; who sits on juries and in the assembly. But it is hard to find a definition which applies to all so-called citizens. To define him as the son of citizen parents is futile.

2. Some say that his civic rights must have been justly acquired. But he is a citizen who has political power, however acquired.

3. Similarly the state is defined by reference to the distribution of political power; when the mode of distribution is changed a new state comes into existence.

4. The good citizen may not be a good man; the good citizen is one who does good service to his state, and this state may be bad in principle. In a constitutional state the good citizen knows both how to rule and how to obey. The good man is one who is fitted to rule. But the citizen in a constitutional state learns to rule by obeying orders. Therefore citizenship in such a state is a moral training.

5. Mechanics will not be citizens in the best state. Extreme democracies, and some oligarchies, neglect this rule. But circumstances oblige them to do this. They have no choice.

Chapters 6–13. The Classification of Constitutions; Democracy and Oligarchy; Kingship.

6. The aims of the state are two: to satisfy man's social instinct, and to fit him for the good life. Political rule differs from that over slaves in aiming primarily at the good of those who are ruled.

7. Constitutions are bad or good according as the common welfare is, or is not, their aim. Of good Constitutions there are three: Monarchy, Aristocracy, and Polity. Of bad there are also three: Tyranny, Oligarchy, Extreme Democracy. The bad are perversions of the good.

8. Democracies and Oligarchies are not made by the numerical propor-

tion of the rulers to the ruled. Democracy is the rule of the poor; oligarchy is that of the rich.

9. Democrats take Equality for their motto; oligarchs believe that political rights should be unequal and proportionate to wealth. But both sides miss the true object of the state, which is virtue. Those who do most to promote virtue deserve the greatest share of power.

10. On the same principle, Justice is not the will of the majority or of the wealthier, but that course of action which the moral aim of the state requires.

11. But are the Many or the Few likely to be the better rulers? It would be unreasonable to give the highest offices to the Many. But they have a faculty of criticism which fits them for deliberative and judicial power. The good critic need not be an expert; experts are sometimes bad judges. Moreover, the Many have a greater stake in the city than the Few. But the governing body, whether Few or Many, must be held in check by the laws.

12. On what principle should political power be distributed? Granted that equals deserve equal shares; who are these equals? Obviously those who are equally able to be of service to the state.

13. Hence there is something in the claims advanced by the wealthy, the free born, the noble, the highly gifted. But no one of these classes should be allowed to rule the rest. A state should consist of men who are equal, or nearly so, in wealth, in birth, in moral and intellectual excellence. The principle which underlies Ostracism is plausible. But in the ideal state, if a pre-eminent individual be found, he should be made a king.

Chapters 14–18. *The Forms of Monarchy.*

14. Of Monarchy there are five kinds, (1) the Spartan, (2) the Barbarian, (3) the elective dictatorship, (4) the Heroic, (5) Absolute Kingship.

15. The last of these forms might appear the best polity to some; that is, if the king acts as the embodiment of law. For he will dispense from the law in the spirit of the law. But this power would be less abused if reserved for the Many. Monarchy arose to meet the needs of primitive society; it is now obsolete and on various grounds objectionable.

16. It tends to become hereditary; it subjects equals to the rule of an equal. The individual monarch may be misled by his passions, and no single man can attend to all the duties of government.

17. One case alone can be imagined in which Absolute Kingship would be just.

18. Let us consider the origin and nature of the best polity, now that we have agreed not to call Absolute Kingship the best.

BOOK IV (VI)

Chapters 1–10. Variations of the main types of Constitutions.

1. Political science should study (1) the ideal state, (2) those states which may be the best obtainable under special circumstances, and even (3) those which are essentially bad. For the statesman must sometimes make the best of a bad Constitution.

2. Of our six main types of state, Kingship and Aristocracy have been discussed (cf. Bk. III, c. 14 fol.). Let us begin by dealing with the other four and their divisions, inquiring also when and why they may be desirable.

3. First as to Democracy and Oligarchy. The common view that Democracy and Oligarchy should be taken as the main types of Constitution is at variance with our own view and wrong. So is the view that the numerical proportion of rulers to ruled makes the difference between these two types; in a Democracy the Many are also the poor, in an Oligarchy the Few are also the wealthy. In every state the distinction between rich and poor is the most fundamental of class-divisions. Still Oligarchy and Democracy are important types; and their variations arise from differences in the character of the rich and the poor by whom they are ruled.

4. Of Democracies there are four kinds. The worst, extreme Democracy, is that in which all offices are open to all, and the will of the people overrides all law.

5. Of Oligarchies too there are four kinds; the worst is that in which offices are hereditary and the magistrates uncontrolled by law.

6. These variations arise under circumstances which may be briefly described.

7. Of Aristocracy in the strict sense there is but one form, that in which the best men alone are citizens.

8. Polity is a compromise between Democracy and Oligarchy, but inclines to the Democratic side. Many so-called Aristocracies are really Polities.

9. There are different ways of effecting the compromise which makes a Polity. The Laconian Constitution is an example of a successful compromise.

10. Tyranny is of three kinds: (1) the barbarian despotism, and (2) the elective dictatorship have already been discussed; in both there is rule according to law over willing subjects. But in (3) the strict form of tyranny, there is the lawless rule of one man over unwilling subjects.

Chapters 11–13. *Of the Best State both in general and under special circumstances.*

11. For the average city-state the best constitution will be a mean between the rule of rich and poor; the middle-class will be supreme. No state will be well administered unless the middle-class holds sway. The middle-class is stronger in large than in small states. Hence in Greece it has rarely attained to power; especially as democracy and oligarchy were aided by the influence of the leading states.

12. No constitution can dispense with the support of the strongest class in the state. Hence Democracy and Oligarchy are the only constitutions possible in some states. But in these cases the legislator should conciliate the middle-class.

13. Whatever form of constitution be adopted there are expedients to be noted which may help in preserving it.

Chapters 14–16. *How to proceed in framing a Constitution.*

14. The legislator must pay attention to three subjects in particular: (*a*) The Deliberative Assembly which is different in each form of constitution.

15. (*b*) The Executive. Here he must know what offices are indispensable and which of them may be conveniently combined in the person of one magistrate; also whether the same offices should be supreme in every state; also which of the twelve or more methods of making appointments should be adopted in each case.

16. (*c*) The Courts of Law. Here he must consider the kinds of law-courts, their spheres of action, their methods of procedure.

BOOK V (VIII)

Chapters 1–4. *Of Revolutions, and their causes in general.*

1. Ordinary states are founded on erroneous ideas of justice, which lead to discontent and revolution. Of revolutions some are made to introduce a new Constitution, others to modify the old, others to put the working of the Constitution in new hands. Both Democracy and Oligarchy contain inherent flaws which lead to revolution, but Democracy is the more stable of the two types.

2. We may distinguish between the frame of mind which fosters revolution, the objects for which it is started, and the provocative causes.

3. The latter deserve a more detailed account.

4. Trifles may be the occasion but are never the true cause of a sedition. One common cause is the aggrandizement of a particular class; another is a feud between rich and poor when they are evenly balanced and there is no middle-class to mediate. As to the manner of effecting a revolution: it may be carried through by force or fraud.

Chapters 5–12. Revolutions in particular States, and how revolutions may be avoided.

5. (a) In Democracies revolutions may arise from a persecution of the rich; or when a demagogue becomes a general, or when politicians compete for the favour of the mob.

6. (b) In Oligarchies the people may rebel against oppression; ambitious oligarchs may conspire, or appeal to the people, or set up a tyrant. Oligarchies are seldom destroyed except by the feuds of their own members; unless they employ a mercenary captain, who may become a tyrant.

7. (c) In Aristocracies and Polities the injustice of the ruling class may lead to revolution, but less often in Polities. Aristocracies may also be ruined by an unprivileged class, or an ambitious man of talent. Aristocracies tend to become oligarchies. Also they are liable to gradual dissolution; which is true of Polities as well.

8. The best precautions against sedition are these: to avoid illegality and frauds upon the unprivileged; to maintain good feeling between rulers and ruled; to watch destructive agencies; to alter property qualifications from time to time; to let no individual or class become too powerful; not to let magistracies be a source of gain; to beware of class-oppression.

9. In all magistrates we should require loyalty, ability, and justice; we should not carry the principle of the constitution to extremes; we should educate the citizens in the spirit of a constitution.

10. (d) The causes which destroy and the means which preserve a Monarchy must be considered separately. Let us first distinguish between Tyranny and Kingship. Tyranny combines the vices of Democracy and Oligarchy. Kingship is exposed to the same defects as Aristocracy. But both these kinds of Monarchy are especially endangered by the insolence of their representatives and by the fear or contempt which they inspire in others. Tyranny is weak against both external and domestic foes; Kingship is strong against invasion, weak against sedition.

11. Moderation is the best preservative of Kingship. Tyranny may rely

on the traditional expedients of demoralizing and dividing its subjects, or it may imitate Kingship by showing moderation in expenditure, and courtesy and temperance in social relations, by the
wise use of ministers, by holding the balance evenly between the
rich and poor.

12. But the Tyrannies of the past have been short-lived.

Plato's discussion of revolutions in the *Republic* is inadequate; e. g. he
does not explain the results of a revolution against a tyranny, and
could not do so on his theory; nor is he correct about the cause of
revolution in an Oligarchy; nor does he distinguish between the
different varieties of Oligarchy and Democracy.

BOOK VI (VII)

Chapters 1–8. *Concerning the proper organization of Democracies and
Oligarchies.*

1. (A) Democracies differ *inter se* (1) according to the character of the
   citizen body, (2) according to the mode in which the characteristic
   features of democracy are combined.

2. Liberty is the first principle of democracy. The results of liberty are
   that the numerical majority is supreme, and that each man lives as
   he likes. From these characteristics we may easily infer the other
   features of democracy.

3. In oligarchies it is not the numerical majority, but the wealthier men,
   who are supreme. Both these principles are unjust if the supreme
   authority is to be absolute and above the law. Both numbers and
   wealth should have their share of influence. But it is hard to find the
   true principles of political justice, and harder still to make men act
   upon them.

4. Democracy has four species (cf. Bk. IV, c. 4). The best is (1) an
   Agricultural Democracy, in which the magistrates are elected by,
   and responsible to, the citizen body, while each office has a property
   qualification proportionate to its importance. These democracies
   should encourage agriculture by legislation. The next best is (2) the
   Pastoral Democracy. Next comes (3) the Commercial Democracy.
   Worst of all is (4) the Extreme Democracy with manhood suffrage.

5. It is harder to preserve than to found a Democracy. To preserve it we
   must prevent the poor from plundering the rich; we must not exhaust the public revenues by giving pay for the performance of
   public duties; we must prevent the growth of a pauper class.

6. (B) The modes of founding Oligarchies call for little explanation.

Careful organization is the best way of preserving these governments.

7. Much depends on the military arrangements; oligarchs must not make their subjects too powerful an element in the army. Admission to the governing body should be granted on easy conditions. Office should be made a burden, not a source of profit.

8. Both in oligarchies and democracies the right arrangement of offices is important. Some kinds of office are necessary in every state; others are peculiar to special types of state.

BOOK VII (IV)

Chapters 1–3. The Summum Bonum for individuals and states.

1. Before constructing the ideal state we must know what is the most desirable life for states and individuals. True happiness flows from the possession of wisdom and virtue, and not from the possession of external goods. But a virtuous life must be equipped with external goods as instruments. These laws hold good of both states and individuals.

2. But does the highest virtue consist in contemplation or in action? The states of the past have lived for action in the shape of war and conquest. But war cannot be regarded as a reasonable object for a state.

3. A virtuous life implies activity, but activity may be speculative as well as practical. Those are wrong who regard the life of a practical politician as degrading. But again they are wrong who treat political power as the highest good.

Chapters 4–12. A picture of the Ideal State.

4. We must begin by considering the population and the territory. The former should be as small as we can make it without sacrificing independence and the capacity for a moral life. The smaller the population the more manageable it will be.

5. The territory must be large enough to supply the citizens with the means of living liberally and temperately, with an abundance of leisure. The city should be in a central position.

6. Communication with the sea is desirable for economic and military reasons; but the moral effects of sea-trade are bad. If the state has a marine, the port town should be at some distance from the city.

7. The character of the citizens should be a mean between that of Asiatics and that of the northern races; intelligence and high spirit should be harmoniously blended as they are in some Greek races.

8. We must distinguish the members of the state from those who are necessary as its servants, but no part of it. There must be men who are able to provide food, to practise the arts, to bear arms, to carry on the work of exchange, to supervise the state religion, to exercise political and judicial functions.

9. But of these classes we should exclude from the citizen body (1) the mechanics, (2) the traders, (3) the husbandmen. Warriors, rulers, priests remain as eligible for citizenship. The same persons should exercise these three professions, but at different periods of life. Ownership of land should be confined to them.

10. Such a distinction between a ruling and a subject class, based on a difference of occupation, is nothing new. It still exists in Egypt, and the custom of common meals in Crete and Italy proves that it formerly existed there. Most of the valuable rules of politics have been discovered over and over again in the course of history.

    In dealing with the land of the state we must distinguish between public demesnes and private estates. Both kinds of land should be tilled by slaves or barbarians of a servile disposition.

11. The site of the city should be chosen with regard (1) to public health, (2) to political convenience, (3) to strategic requirements. The ground-plan of the city should be regular enough for beauty, not so regular as to make defensive warfare difficult. Walls are a practical necessity.

12. It is well that the arrangement of the buildings in the city should be carefully thought out.

Chapters 13–17. The Educational System of the Ideal State, its aim, and early stages.

13. The nature and character of the citizens must be determined with reference to the kind of happiness which we desire them to pursue. Happiness was defined in the *Ethics* as the perfect exercise of virtue, the latter term being understood not in the conditional, but in the absolute sense. Now a man acquires virtue of this kind by the help of nature, habit, and reason.

    Habit and reason are the fruits of education, which must therefore be discussed.

14. The citizens should be educated to obey when young and to rule when they are older. Rule is their ultimate and highest function. Since

the good ruler is the same as the good man, our education must be so framed as to produce the good man. It should develop all man's powers and fit him for all the activities of life; but the highest powers and the highest activities must be the supreme care of education. An education which is purely military, like the Laconian, neglects this principle.

15. The virtues of peace (intellectual culture, temperance, justice) are the most necessary for states and individuals; war is nothing but a means towards securing peace. But education must follow the natural order of human development, beginning with the body, dealing next with the appetites, and training the intellect last of all.

16. To produce a healthy physique the legislator must fix the age of marriage, regulate the physical condition of the parents, provide for the exposure of infants, and settle the duration of marriage.

17. He must also prescribe a physical training for infants and young children. For their moral education the very young should be committed to overseers; these should select the tales which they are told, their associates, the pictures, plays, and statues which they see. From five to seven years of age should be the period of preparation for intellectual training.

BOOK VIII (V).

Chapters 1–7. The Ideal Education continued. Its Music and Gymnastic.

1. Education should be under state-control and the same for all the citizens.

2. It should comprise those useful studies which every one must master, but none which degrade the mind or body.

3. Reading, writing, and drawing have always been taught on the score of their utility; gymnastic as producing valour. Music is taught as a recreation, but it serves a higher purpose. The noble employment of leisure is the highest aim which a man can pursue; and music is valuable for this purpose. The same may be said of drawing, and other subjects of education have the same kind of value.

4. Gymnastic is the first stage of education; but we must not develop the valour and physique of our children at the expense of the mind, as they do in Sparta. Until puberty, and for three years after, bodily exercise should be light.

5. Music, if it were a mere amusement, should not be taught to children; they would do better by listening to professionals. But music is a moral discipline and a rational enjoyment.

6. By learning music children become better critics and are given a suitable occupation. When of riper age they should abandon music; professional skill is not for them; nor should they be taught difficult instruments.

7. The various musical harmonies should be used for different purposes. Some inspire virtue, others valour, others enthusiasm. The ethical harmonies are those which children should learn. The others may be left to professionals. The Dorian harmony is the best for education. The Phrygian is bad; but the Lydian may be beneficial to children.

Cetera desunt.

POLITICA
(*Politics*)

BOOK I

1 Every state is a community of some kind, and every community 1252ᵃ
is established with a view to some good; for mankind always act in
order to obtain that which they think good. But, if all communities
aim at some good, the state or political community, which is the
highest of all, and which embraces all the rest, aims at good in a 5
greater degree than any other, and at the highest good.

Some people think [1] that the qualifications of a statesman, king,
householder, and master are the same, and that they differ, not in
kind, but only in the number of their subjects. For example, the ruler 10
over a few is called a master; over more, the manager of a household;
over a still larger number, a statesman or king, as if there were no
difference between a great household and a small state. The distinction which is made between the king and the statesman is as follows:
When the government is personal, the ruler is a king; when, accord- 15
'ing to the rules of the political science, the citizens rule and are
ruled in turn, then he is called a statesman.

But all this is a mistake; for governments differ in kind, as will
be evident to any one who considers the matter according to the
method [2] which has hitherto guided us. As in other departments of 20
science, so in politics, the compound should always be resolved into
the simple elements or least parts of the whole. We must therefore
look at the elements of which the state is composed, in order that we
may see in what the different kinds of rule differ from one another,
and whether any scientific result can be attained about each one of
them.

2 He who thus considers things in their first growth and origin,
whether a state or anything else, will obtain the clearest view of 25
them. In the first place there must be a union of those who cannot
exist without each other; namely, of male and female, that the race
may continue (and this is a union which is formed, not of deliberate

---

[1] Cp. Plato, *Politicus*, 258 E–259 D.   [2] Cp. 1256ᵃ2.

purpose, but because, in common with other animals and with plants,
30 mankind have a natural desire to leave behind them an image of
themselves), and of natural ruler and subject, that both may be preserved. For that which can foresee by the exercise of mind is by
nature intended to be lord and master, and that which can with its
body give effect to such foresight is a subject, and by nature a slave;
1252ᵇ hence master and slave have the same interest. Now nature has
distinguished between the female and the slave. For she is not
niggardly, like the smith who fashions the Delphian knife for many
uses; she makes each thing for a single use, and every instrument
is best made when intended for one and not for many uses. But
5 among barbarians no distinction is made between women and slaves,
because there is no natural ruler among them: they are a community
of slaves, male and female. Wherefore the poets say—

'It is meet that Hellenes should rule over barbarians';

as if they thought that the barbarian and the slave were by nature
one.

Out of these two relationships between man and woman, master
10 and slave, the first thing to arise is the family, and Hesiod is right
when he says—

'First house and wife and an ox for the plough',

for the ox is the poor man's slave. The family is the association estab-
blished by nature for the supply of men's everyday wants, and the
members of it are called by Charondas 'companions of the cupboard',
and by Epimenides the Cretan, 'companions of the manger.' But when
15 several families are united, and the association aims at something more
than the supply of daily needs, the first society to be formed is the
village. And the most natural form of the village appears to be that of
a colony from the family, composed of the children and grand-
children, who are said to be suckled with the same milk'. And this
20 is the reason why Hellenic states were originally governed by kings;
because the Hellenes were under royal rule before they came together,
as the barbarians still are. Every family is ruled by the eldest, and
therefore in the colonies of the family the kingly form of government prevailed because they were of the same blood. As Homer
says: [3]

'Each one gives law to his children and to his wives.'

[3] *Od.* ix. 114, quoted by Plato, *Laws,* iii. 680 B, and in *N. Eth.* x. 1180ª 28.

For they lived dispersedly, as was the manner in ancient times. Wherefore men say that the Gods have a king, because they themselves either are or were in ancient times under the rule of a king. 25 For they imagine, not only the forms of the Gods, but their ways of life to be like their own.

When several villages are united in a single complete community, large enough to be nearly or quite self-sufficing, the state comes into existence, originating in the bare needs of life, and continuing in existence for the sake of a good life. And therefore, if the earlier 30 forms of society are natural, so is the state, for it is the end of them, and the nature of a thing is its end. For what each thing is when fully developed, we call its nature, whether we are speaking of a man, a horse, or a family. Besides, the final cause and end of a thing is the best, and to be self-sufficing is the end and the best.   1253ᵃ

Hence it is evident that the state is a creation of nature, and that man is by nature a political animal. And he who by nature and not by mere accident is without a state, is either a bad man or above humanity; he is like the

'Tribeless, lawless, hearthless one,'

whom Homer [4] denounces—the natural outcast is forthwith a lover of war; he may be compared to an isolated piece at draughts.

Now, that man is more of a political animal than bees or any other gregarious animals is evident. Nature, as we often say, makes nothing in vain,[5] and man is the only animal whom she has endowed with the gift of speech.[6] And whereas mere voice is but an indication 10 of pleasure or pain, and is therefore found in other animals (for their nature attains to the perception of pleasure and pain and the intimation of them to one another, and no further), the power of speech is intended to set forth the expedient and inexpedient, and therefore likewise the just and the unjust. And it is a characteristic of man that he 15 alone has any sense of good and evil, of just and unjust, and the like, and the association of living beings who have this sense makes a family and a state.

Further, the state is by nature clearly prior to the family and to the individual, since the whole is of necessity prior to the part; 20 for example, if the whole body be destroyed, there will be no foot or hand, except in an equivocal sense, as we might speak of a stone hand; for when destroyed the hand will be no better than that. But things are defined by their working and power; and we ought not to

[4] *Il.* ix. 63.   [5] Cp. 1256ᵇ 20.
[6] Cp. vii. 1332ᵇ 5.

say that they are the same when they no longer have their proper
25 quality, but only that they have the same name. The proof that
the state is a creation of nature and prior to the individual is that the
individual, when isolated, is not self-sufficing; and therefore he is like
a part in relation to the whole. But he who is unable to live in society,
or who has no need because he is sufficient for himself, must be either
a beast or a god: he is no part of a state. A social instinct is im-
30 planted in all men by nature, and yet he who first founded the
state was the greatest of benefactors. For man, when perfected, is the
best of animals, but, when separated from law and justice, he is the
worst of all; since armed injustice is the more dangerous, and he is
equipped at birth with arms, meant to be used by intelligence and
35 virtue, which he may use for the worst ends. Wherefore, if he have not
virtue, he is the most unholy and the most savage of animals, and the
most full of lust and gluttony. But justice is the bond of men in states,
for the administration of justice, which is the determination of what
is just,[7] is the principle of order in political society.

3   Seeing then that the state is made up of households, before speaking of the state we must speak of the management of the household.
1253[b] The parts of household management correspond to the persons who
compose the household, and a complete household consists of slaves
and freemen. Now we should begin by examining everything in its
5 fewest possible elements; and the first and fewest possible parts of
a family are master and slave, husband and wife, father and children.
We have therefore to consider what each of these three relations
is and ought to be:—I mean the relation of master and servant,
10 the marriage relation (the conjunction of man and wife has no name
of its own), and thirdly, the procreative relation (this also has no
proper name). And there is another element of a household, the so-
called art of getting wealth, which, according to some, is identical
with household management, according to others, a principal part of
it; the nature of this art will also have to be considered by us.

15   Let us first speak of master and slave, looking to the needs of
practical life and also seeking to attain some better theory of their
relation than exists at present. For some are of opinion that the rule
of a master is a science, and that the management of a household,
and the mastership of slaves, and the political and royal rule, as I
20 was saying at the outset,[8] are all the same. Others affirm that the
rule of a master over slaves is contrary to nature, and that the dis-

[7] Cp. *N. Eth.* v. 1134[a] 31.
[8] Plato in *Pol.* 258 E–259 D, referred to already in 1252[a] 7–16.

tinction between slave and freeman exists by law only, and not by nature; and being an interference with nature is therefore unjust.

4   Property is a part of the household, and the art of acquiring property is a part of the art of managing the household; for no man can live well, or indeed live at all, unless he be provided with 25 necessaries. And as in the arts which have a definite sphere the workers must have their own proper instruments for the accomplishment of their work, so it is in the management of a household. Now instruments are of various sorts; some are living, others lifeless; in the rudder, the pilot of a ship has a lifeless, in the look-out man, a living instrument; for in the arts the servant is a kind of instrument. Thus, too, a possession is an instrument for maintaining life. And so, 30 in the arrangement of the family, a slave is a living possession, and property a number of such instruments; and the servant is himself an instrument which takes precedence of all other instruments. For if every instrument could accomplish its own work, obeying or anticipating the will of others, like the statues of Daedalus, or the tripods 35 of Hephaestus, which, says the poet,[9]

'of their own accord entered the assembly of the Gods';

if, in like manner, the shuttle would weave and the plectrum touch the lyre without a hand to guide them, chief workmen would not want servants, nor masters slaves. Here, however, another distinc- 1254 tion must be drawn; the instruments commonly so called are instruments of production, whilst a possession is an instrument of action. The shuttle, for example, is not only of use; but something else is made by it, whereas of a garment or of a bed there is only the use. Further, as production and action are different in kind, and both 5 require instruments, the instruments which they employ must likewise differ in kind. But life is action and not production, and therefore the slave is the minister of action. Again, a possession is spoken of as a part is spoken of; for the part is not only a part of something else, but wholly belongs to it; and this is also true of a possession. 10 The master is only the master of the slave; he does not belong to him, whereas the slave is not only the slave of his master, but wholly belongs to him. Hence we see what is the nature and office of a slave; he who is by nature not his own but another's man, is by nature a 15 slave; and he may be said to be another's man who, being a human

9 Hom. *Il.* xviii. 376.

being, is also a possession. And a possession may be defined as an instrument of action, separable from the possessor.

5   But is there any one thus intended by nature to be a slave, and for whom such a condition is expedient and right, or rather is not all slavery a violation of nature?

20   There is no difficulty in answering this question, on grounds both of reason and of fact. For that some should rule and others be ruled is a thing not only necessary, but expedient; from the hour of their birth, some are marked out for subjection, others for rule.

And there are many kinds both of rulers and subjects (and that
25   rule is the better which is exercised over better subjects—for example, to rule over men is better than to rule over wild beasts; for the work is better which is executed by better workmen, and where one man rules and another is ruled, they may be said to have a work); for in all things which form a composite whole and which are made up of
30   parts, whether continuous or discrete, a distinction between the ruling and the subject element comes to light. Such a duality exists in living creatures, but not in them only; it originates in the constitution of the universe; even in things which have no life there is a ruling principle, as in a musical mode. But we are wandering from the subject. We will therefore restrict ourselves to the living creature, which,
35   in the first place, consists of soul and body: and of these two, the one is by nature the ruler, and the other the subject. But then we must look for the intentions of nature in things which retain their nature, and not in things which are corrupted. And therefore we must study the man who is in the most perfect state both of body and soul, for in him we shall see the true relation of the two; although in bad or
1254ᵇ   corrupted natures the body will often appear to rule over the soul, because they are in an evil and unnatural condition. At all events we may firstly observe in living creatures both a despotical and a constitutional rule; for the soul rules the body with a despotical rule, whereas the intellect rules the appetites with a constitutional and
5   royal rule. And it is clear that the rule of the soul over the body, and of the mind and the rational element over the passionate, is natural and expedient; whereas the equality of the two or the rule of the inferior is always hurtful. The same holds good of animals in relation
10   to men; for tame animals have a better nature than wild, and all tame animals are better off when they are ruled by man; for then they are preserved. Again, the male is by nature superior, and the female inferior; and the one rules, and the other is ruled; this principle, of neces-
15   sity, extends to all mankind. Where then there is such a difference as

that between soul and body, or between men and animals (as in the case of those whose business is to use their body, and who can do nothing better), the lower sort are by nature slaves, and it is better for them as for all inferiors that they should be under the rule of a master. For he who can be, and therefore is, another's, and he who partici- 20 pates in rational principle enough to apprehend, but not to have, such a principle, is a slave by nature. Whereas the lower animals cannot even apprehend a principle; they obey their instincts. And indeed the use made of slaves and of tame animals is not very different; for both with their bodies minister to the needs of life. Nature would like 25 to distinguish between the bodies of freemen and slaves, making the one strong for servile labour, the other upright, and although useless for such services, useful for political life in the arts both of war and 30 peace. But the opposite often happens—that some have the souls and others have the bodies of freemen. And doubtless if men differed from one another in the mere forms of their bodies as much as the statues of the Gods do from men, all would acknowledge that the inferior class 35 should be slaves of the superior. And if this is true of the body, how much more just that a similar distinction should exist in the soul? but the beauty of the body is seen, whereas the beauty of the soul is not 1255ᵃ seen. It is clear, then, that some men are by nature free, and others slaves, and that for these latter slavery is both expedient and right.

6   But that those who take the opposite view have in a certain way right on their side, may be easily seen. For the words slavery and slave are used in two senses. There is a slave or slavery by law as well as by 5 nature. The law of which I speak is a sort of convention—the law by which whatever is taken in war is supposed to belong to the victors. But this right many jurists impeach, as they would an orator who brought forward an unconstitutional measure: they detest the notion that, because one man has the power of doing violence and is superior in brute strength, another shall be his slave and subject. Even among 10 philosophers there is a difference of opinion. The origin of the dispute, and what makes the views invade each other's territory, is as follows: in some sense virtue, when furnished with means, has actually the greatest power of exercising force: and as superior power is only found where there is superior excellence of some kind, power seems to imply virtue, and the dispute to be simply one about justice (for it is 15 due to one party identifying justice with goodwill,¹⁰ while the other identifies it with the mere rule of the stronger). If these views are thus

10 i. e. mutual goodwill, which is held to be incompatible with the relation of master and slave.

set out separately, the other views[11] have no force or plausibility
20 against the view that the superior in virtue ought to rule, or be master.
Others, clinging, as they think, simply to a principle of justice (for
law and custom are a sort of justice), assume that slavery in accordance with the custom of war is justified by law, but at the same
moment they deny this. For what if the cause of the war be unjust?
25 And again, no one would ever say that he is a slave who is unworthy
to be a slave. Were this the case, men of the highest rank would be
slaves and the children of slaves if they or their parents chance to
have been taken captive and sold. Wherefore Hellenes do not like to
call Hellenes slaves, but confine the term to barbarians. Yet, in using
30 this language, they really mean the natural slave of whom we spoke
at first;[12] for it must be admitted that some are slaves everywhere,
others nowhere. The same principle applies to nobility. Hellenes regard themselves as noble everywhere, and not only in their own
35 country, but they deem the barbarians noble only when at home,
thereby implying that there are two sorts of nobility and freedom, the
one absolute, the other relative. The Helen of Theodectes says:

'Who would presume to call me servant who am on both sides
sprung from the stem of the Gods?'

What does this mean but that they distinguish freedom and slavery,
40 noble and humble birth, by the two principles of good and evil? They
1255b think that as men and animals beget men and animals, so from
good men a good man springs. But this is what nature, though she
may intend it, cannot always accomplish.

We see then that there is some foundation for this difference of
5 opinion, and that all are not either slaves by nature or freemen by
nature, and also that there is in some cases a marked distinction between the two classes, rendering it expedient and right for the one to
be slaves and the others to be masters: the one practising obedience,
the others exercising the authority and lordship which nature intended them to have. The abuse of this authority is injurious to both;
10 for the interests of part and whole,[13] of body and soul, are the same,
and the slave is a part of the master, a living but separated part of his
bodily frame. Hence, where the relation of master and slave between

---

[11] i. e. those stated in ll. 5–12, that the stronger always has, and that he never
has, a right to enslave the weaker. Aristotle finds that these views cannot
maintain themselves against his intermediate view, that the superior in *virtue*
should rule.

[12] Chap. 5.

[13] Cp. 1254ª 8.

them is natural they are friends and have a common interest, but
where it rests merely on law and force the reverse is true.   15

7   The previous remarks are quite enough to show that the rule of a
master is not a constitutional rule, and that all the different kinds of
rule are not, as some affirm, the same with each other.[14] For there is
one rule exercised over subjects who are by nature free, another over
subjects who are by nature slaves. The rule of a household is a monarchy, for every house is under one head: whereas constitutional rule
is a government of freemen and equals. The master is not called a   20
master because he has science,[15] but because he is of a certain character, and the same remark applies to the slave and the freeman. Still
there may be a science for the master and a science for the slave. The
science of the slave would be such as the man of Syracuse taught, who
made money by instructing slaves in their ordinary duties. And such   25
a knowledge may be carried further, so as to include cookery and
similar menial arts. For some duties are of the more necessary, others
of the more honourable sort; as the proverb says, 'slave before slave,
master before master'. But all such branches of knowledge are servile.   30
There is likewise a science of the master, which teaches the use of
slaves; for the master as such is concerned, not with the acquisition,
but with the use of them. Yet this so-called science is not anything
great or wonderful; for the master need only know how to order that
which the slave must know how to execute. Hence those who are in a   35
position which places them above toil have stewards who attend to
their households while they occupy themselves with philosophy or
with politics. But the art of acquiring slaves, I mean of justly acquiring them, differs both from the art of the master and the art of the
slave, being a species of hunting or war.[16] Enough of the distinction
between master and slave.   40

8   Let us now inquire into property generally, and into the art of   1256ª
getting wealth, in accordance with our usual method,[17] for a slave has
been shown [18] to be a part of property. The first question is whether
the art of getting wealth is the same with the art of managing a household or a part of it, or instrumental to it; and if the last, whether in
the way that the art of making shuttles is instrumental to the art of
weaving, or in the way that the casting of bronze is instrumental to   5
the art of the statuary, for they are not instrumental in the same

---

[14] Plato, *Polit.* 258 E–259 D, referred to already in 1252ª 7–16, 1253ᵇ 18–20.
[15] *Polit.* 259 C, 293 C.   [16] Cp. vii. 1333ᵇ 38.
[17] Of understanding the whole by the part, Cp. 1252ª 17.   [18] Chap. 4.

way, but the one provides tools and the other material; and by material I mean the substratum out of which any work is made; thus wool

10 is the material of the weaver, bronze of the statuary. Now it is easy to see that the art of household management is not identical with the art of getting wealth, for the one uses the material which the other provides. For the art which uses household stores can be no other than the art of household management. There is, however, a doubt whether the art of getting wealth is a part of household management or a dis-

15 tinct art. If the getter of wealth has to consider whence wealth and property can be procured, but there are many sorts of property and riches, then are husbandry, and the care and provision of food in general, parts of the wealth-getting art or distinct arts? Again, there are many sorts of food, and therefore there are many kinds of lives both

20 of animals and men; they must all have food, and the differences in their food have made differences in their ways of life. For of beasts, some are gregarious, others are solitary; they live in the way which is best adapted to sustain them, accordingly as they are carnivorous

25 or herbivorous or omnivorous: and their habits are determined for them by nature in such a manner that they may obtain with greater facility the food of their choice. But, as different species have different tastes, the same things are not naturally pleasant to all of them; and therefore the lives of carnivorous or herbivorous animals further dif-

30 fer among themselves. In the lives of men too there is a great difference. The laziest are shepherds, who lead an idle life, and get their subsistence without trouble from tame animals; their flocks having to wander from place to place in search of pasture, they are compelled

35 to follow them, cultivating a sort of living farm. Others support themselves by hunting, which is of different kinds. Some, for example, are brigands, others, who dwell near lakes or marshes or rivers or a sea in which there are fish, are fishermen, and others live by the pursuit of birds or wild beasts. The greater number obtain a living from the cul-

40 tivated fruits of the soil. Such are the modes of subsistence which prevail among those whose industry springs up of itself, and whose

1256ᵇ food is not acquired by exchange and retail trade—there is the shepherd, the husbandman, the brigand, the fisherman, the hunter. Some gain a comfortable maintenance out of two employments, eking out the deficiencies of one of them by another: thus the life of a shepherd

5 may be combined with that of a brigand, the life of a farmer with that of a hunter. Other modes of life are similarly combined in any way which the needs of men may require. Property, in the sense of a bare livelihood, seems to be given by nature herself to all, both when they

are first born, and when they are grown up. For some animals bring 10
forth, together with their offspring, so much food as will last until they
are able to supply themselves; of this the vermiparous or oviparous
animals are an instance; and the viviparous animals have up to a certain time a supply of food for their young in themselves, which is
called milk. In like manner we may infer that, after the birth of ani- 15
mals, plants exist for their sake, and that the other animals exist for
the sake of man, the tame for use and food, the wild, if not all, at least
the greater part of them, for food, and for the provision of clothing
and various instruments. Now if nature makes nothing incomplete, 20
and nothing in vain, the inference must be that she has made all
animals for the sake of man. And so, in one point of view, the art of
war is a natural art of acquisition, for the art of acquisition includes
hunting, an art which we ought to practise against wild beasts, and
against men who, though intended by nature to be governed, will not 25
submit; for war of such a kind is naturally just.[19]

Of the art of acquisition then there is one kind which by nature is
a part of the management of a household, in so far as the art of household management must either find ready to hand, or itself provide,
such things necessary to life, and useful for the community of the 30
family or state, as can be stored. They are the elements of true riches;
for the amount of property which is needed for a good life is not unlimited, although Solon in one of his poems says that

'No bound to riches has been fixed for man'.

But there is a boundary fixed, just as there is in the other arts; for the
instruments of any art are never unlimited, either in number or size, 35
and riches may be defined as a number of instruments to be used in a
household or in a state. And so we see that there is a natural art of
acquisition which is practised by managers of households and by
statesmen, and what is the reason of this.

9   There is another variety of the art of acquisition which is com- 40
monly and rightly called an art of wealth-getting, and has in fact suggested the notion that riches and property have no limit. Being nearly 1257ʳ
connected with the preceding, it is often identified with it. But though
they are not very different, neither are they the same. The kind already
described is given by nature, the other is gained by experience and art.

Let us begin our discussion of the question with the following 5
considerations:

Of everything which we possess there are two uses: both belong

[19] Cp. 1255ᵇ38, 1333ᵇ38.

to the thing as such, but not in the same manner, for one is the proper, and the other the improper or secondary use of it. For example, a shoe is used for wear, and is used for exchange; both are uses of the shoe.

10 He who gives a shoe in exchange for money or food to him who wants one, does indeed use the shoe as a shoe, but this is not its proper or primary purpose, for a shoe is not made to be an object of barter. The same may be said of all possessions, for the art of exchange

15 extends to all of them, and it arises at first from what is natural, from the circumstance that some have too little, others too much. Hence we may infer that retail trade is not a natural part of the art of getting wealth; had it been so, men would have ceased to exchange when they had enough. In the first community, indeed, which is the

20 family, this art is obviously of no use, but it begins to be useful when the society increases. For the members of the family originally had all things in common; later, when the family divided into parts, the parts shared in many things, and different parts in different things, which they had to give in exchange for what they wanted, a kind of

25 barter which is still practised among barbarous nations who exchange with one another the necessaries of life and nothing more; giving and receiving wine, for example, in exchange for corn, and the like. This sort of barter is not part of the wealth-getting art and is not con-

30 trary to nature, but is needed for the satisfaction of men's natural wants. The other or more complex form of exchange grew, as might have been inferred, out of the simpler. When the inhabitants of one country became more dependent on those of another, and they im-ported what they needed, and exported what they had too much of,

35 money necessarily came into use. For the various necessaries of life are not easily carried about, and hence men agreed to employ in their dealings with each other something which was intrinsically useful and easily applicable to the purposes of life, for example, iron, silver, and the like. Of this the value was at first measured simply by size and

40 weight, but in process of time they put a stamp upon it, to save the trouble of weighing and to mark the value.

1257ᵇ   When the use of coin had once been discovered, out of the barter of necessary articles arose the other art of wealth-getting, namely, retail trade; which was at first probably a simple matter, but became more complicated as soon as men learned by experience whence and by what exchanges the greatest profit might be made. Originating in

5 the use of coin, the art of getting wealth is generally thought to be chiefly concerned with it, and to be the art which produces riches and wealth; having to consider how they may be accumulated. Indeed,

riches is assumed by many to be only a quantity of coin, because the
arts of getting wealth and retail trade are concerned with coin. Others 10
maintain that coined money is a mere sham, a thing not natural, but
conventional only, because, if the users substitute another commodity
for it, it is worthless, and because it is not useful as a means to any
of the necessities of life, and, indeed, he who is rich in coin may often
be in want of necessary food. But how can that be wealth of which a
man may have a great abundance and yet perish with hunger, like 15
Midas in the fable, whose insatiable prayer turned everything that was
set before him into gold?

Hence men seek after a better notion of riches and of the art of getting
wealth than the mere acquisition of coin, and they are right. For natural riches and the natural art of wealth-getting are a different thing;
in their true form they are part of the management of a household; 20
whereas retail trade is the art of producing wealth, not in every way,
but by exchange. And it is thought to be concerned with coin; for coin
is the unit of exchange and the measure or limit of it. And there is no
bound to the riches which spring from this art of wealth-getting.[20] As
in the art of medicine there is no limit to the pursuit of health, and 25
as in the other arts there is no limit to the pursuit of their several
ends, for they aim at accomplishing their ends to the uttermost (but
of the means there is a limit, for the end is always the limit), so, too,
in this art of wealth-getting there is no limit of the end, which is
riches of the spurious kind, and the acquisition of wealth. But the art 30
of wealth-getting which consists in household management, on the
other hand, has a limit; the unlimited acquisition of wealth is not its
business. And, therefore, in one point of view, all riches must have a
limit; nevertheless, as a matter of fact, we find the opposite to be the
case; for all getters of wealth increase their hoard of coin without limit.
The source of the confusion is the near connexion between the two
kinds of wealth-getting; in either, the instrument is the same, although 35
the use is different, and so they pass into one another; for each is a
use of the same property, but with a difference: accumulation is the
end in the one case, but there is a further end in the other. Hence
some persons are led to believe that getting wealth is the object of
household management, and the whole idea of their lives is that they
ought either to increase their money without limit, or at any rate not to 40
lose it. The origin of this disposition in men is that they are intent upon
living only, and not upon living well; and, as their desires are unlim- 1258ᵃ
ited, they also desire that the means of gratifying them should be
without limit. Those who do aim at a good life seek the means of ob-

[20] Cp. 1256ᵇ 32.

5 taining bodily pleasures; and, since the enjoyment of these appears to depend on property, they are absorbed in getting wealth: and so there arises the second species of wealth-getting. For, as their enjoyment is in excess, they seek an art which produces the excess of enjoyment; and, if they are not able to supply their pleasures by the art of getting wealth, they try other arts, using in turn every faculty in 10 a manner contrary to nature. The quality of courage, for example, is not intended to make wealth, but to inspire confidence; neither is this the aim of the general's or of the physician's art; but the one aims at victory and the other at health. Nevertheless, some men turn every quality or art into a means of getting wealth; this they conceive to be the end, and to the promotion of the end they think all things must contribute.

Thus, then, we have considered the art of wealth-getting which 15 is unnecessary, and why men want it; and also the necessary art of wealth-getting, which we have seen to be different from the other, and to be a natural part of the art of managing a household, concerned with the provision of food, not, however, like the former kind, unlimited, but having a limit.

10   And we have found the answer to our original question,[21] Whether the art of getting wealth is the business of the manager of a household 20 and of the statesman or not their business?—viz. that wealth is presupposed by them. For as political science does not make men, but takes them from nature and uses them, so too nature provides them with earth or sea or the like as a source of food. At this stage begins the duty of the manager of a household, who has to order the things which 25 nature supplies;—he may be compared to the weaver who has not to make but to use wool, and to know, too, what sort of wool is good and serviceable or bad and unserviceable. Were this otherwise, it would be difficult to see why the art of getting wealth is a part of the management of a household and the art of medicine not; for surely the members of a household must have health just as they must have life or 30 any other necessary. The answer is that as from one point of view the master of the house and the ruler of the state have to consider about health, from another point of view not they but the physician; so in one way the art of household management, in another way the subordinate art, has to consider about wealth. But, strictly speaking, as I have already said, the means of life must be provided beforehand by nature; 35 for the business of nature is to furnish food to that which is born, and the food of the offspring is always what remains over of that from

[21] 1256[a] 3.

which it is produced.[22] Wherefore the art of getting wealth out of fruits and animals is always natural.

There are two sorts of wealth-getting, as I have said [23]; one is a part of household management, the other is retail trade: the former necessary and honourable, while that which consists in exchange is 40 justly censured; for it is unnatural, and a mode by which men gain 1258[b] from one another. The most hated sort, and with the greatest reason, is usury, which makes a gain out of money itself, and not from the natural object of it. For money was intended to be used in exchange, but not to increase at interest. And this term interest,[24] which means the 5 birth of money from money, is applied to the breeding of money because the offspring resembles the parent. Wherefore of all modes of getting wealth this is the most unnatural.

11   Enough has been said about the theory of wealth-getting; we will now proceed to the practical part. The discussion of such matters is 10 not unworthy of philosophy, but to be engaged in them practically is illiberal and irksome. The useful parts of wealth-getting are, first, the knowledge of live-stock—which are most profitable, and where, and how—as, for example, what sort of horses or sheep or oxen or any other animals are most likely to give a return. A man ought to know which 15 of these pay better than others, and which pay best in particular places, for some do better in one place and some in another. Secondly, husbandry, which may be either tillage or planting, and the keeping of bees and of fish, or fowl, or of any animals which may be useful to man. These are the divisions of the true or proper art of wealth-getting 20 and come first. Of the other, which consists in exchange, the first and most important division is commerce (of which there are three kinds— the provision of a ship, the conveyance of goods, exposure for sale —these again differing as they are safer or more profitable), the second is usury, the third, service for hire—of this, one kind is em- 25 ployed in the mechanical arts, the other in unskilled and bodily labour. There is still a third sort of wealth-getting intermediate between this and the first or natural mode which is partly natural, but is also concerned with exchange, viz. the industries that make their profit from the earth, and from things growing from the earth which, although 30 they bear no fruit, are nevertheless profitable; for example, the cutting of timber and all mining. The art of mining, by which minerals are obtained, itself has many branches, for there are various kinds of things dug out of the earth. Of the several divisions of wealth-getting I now speak generally; a minute consideration of them might be use-

---

[22] Cp. 1256[b] 10.   [23] 1256[a] 15–1258[a] 18.   [24] *tokos*, lit. 'offspring'.

ful in practice, but it would be tiresome to dwell upon them at greater length now.

35   Those occupations are most truly arts in which there is the least element of chance; they are the meanest in which the body is most deteriorated, the most servile in which there is the greatest use of the body, and the most illiberal in which there is the least need of excellence.

Works have been written upon these subjects by various persons;
40 for example, by Chares the Parian, and Apollodorus the Lemnian, who
1259ᵃ have treated of Tillage and Planting, while others have treated of other branches; any one who cares for such matters may refer to their writings. It would be well also to collect the scattered stories of the ways in which individuals have succeeded in amassing a fortune; for all
5 this is useful to persons who value the art of getting wealth. There is the anecdote of Thales the Milesian and his financial device, which involves a principle of universal application, but is attributed to him on account of his reputation for wisdom. He was reproached for his
10 poverty, which was supposed to show that philosophy was of no use. According to the story, he knew by his skill in the stars while it was yet winter that there would be a great harvest of olives in the coming year; so, having a little money, he gave deposits for the use of all the olive-presses in Chios and Miletus, which he hired at a low price because no one bid against him. When the harvest-time came, and
15 many were wanted all at once and of a sudden, he let them out at any rate which he pleased, and made a quantity of money. Thus he showed the world that philosophers can easily be rich if they like, but that their ambition is of another sort. He is supposed to have given a striking proof of his wisdom, but, as I was saying, his device for get-
20 ting wealth is of universal application, and is nothing but the creation of a monopoly. It is an art often practised by cities when they are in want of money; they make a monopoly of provisions.

There was a man of Sicily, who, having money deposited with him, bought up all the iron from the iron mines; afterwards, when the
25 merchants from their various markets came to buy, he was the only seller, and without much increasing the price he gained 200 per cent. Which when Dionysius heard, he told him that he might take away his money, but that he must not remain at Syracuse, for he thought
30 that the man had discovered a way of making money which was injurious to his own interests. He made the same discovery as Thales; they both contrived to create a monopoly for themselves. And statesmen as well ought to know these things; for a state is often as much in want of money and of such devices for obtaining it as a household,

or even more so; hence some public men devote themselves entirely 35
to finance.

12   Of household management we have seen [25] that there are three
parts—one is the rule of a master over slaves, which has been discussed
already,[26] another of a father, and the third of a husband. A husband
and father, we saw, rules over wife and children, both free, but the 40
rule differs, the rule over his children being a royal, over his wife a
constitutional rule. For although there may be exceptions to the order 1259ᵇ
of nature, the male is by nature fitter for command than the female,
just as the elder and full-grown is superior to the younger and more
immature. But in most constitutional states the citizens rule and are 5
ruled by turns, for the idea of a constitutional state implies that the
natures of the citizens are equal, and do not differ at all.[27] Nevertheless, when one rules and the other is ruled we endeavour to create a
difference of outward forms and names and titles of respect, which
may be illustrated by the saying of Amasis about his foot-pan.[28] The
relation of the male to the female is of this kind, but there the inequality is permanent. The rule of a father over his children is royal, for 10
he rules by virtue both of love and of the respect due to age, exercising a kind of royal power. And therefore Homer has appropriately
called Zeus 'father of Gods and men', because he is the king of them
all. For a king is the natural superior of his subjects, but he should
be of the same kin or kind with them, and such is the relation of 15
elder and younger, of father and son.

13   Thus it is clear that household management attends more to men
than to the acquisition of inanimate things, and to human excellence
more than to the excellence of property which we call wealth, and to 20
the virtue of freemen more than to the virtue of slaves. A question
may indeed be raised, whether there is any excellence at all in a slave
beyond and higher than merely instrumental and ministerial qualities
—whether he can have the virtues of temperance, courage, justice,
and the like; or whether slaves possess only bodily and ministerial 25
qualities. And, whichever way we answer the question, a difficulty
arises; for, if they have virtue, in what will they differ from freemen?
On the other hand, since they are men and share in rational principle,
it seems absurd to say that they have no virtue. A similar question
may be raised about women and children, whether they too have vir- 30
tues: ought a woman to be temperate and brave and just, and is a child

[25] 1253ᵇ 3–11.   [26] 1253ᵇ 14–1255ᵇ 39.
[27] Cp. ii. 1261ᵃ 39, iii. 1288ᵃ 12.   [28] Herod. ii. 172.

to be called temperate, and intemperate, or not? So in general we may
ask about the natural ruler, and the natural subject, whether they
have the same or different virtues. For if a noble nature is equally
35 required in both, why should one of them always rule, and the other
always be ruled? Nor can we say that this is a question of degree,
for the difference between ruler and subject is a difference of kind,
which the difference of more and less never is. Yet how strange is the
supposition that the one ought, and that the other ought not, to have
40 virtue! For if the ruler is intemperate and unjust, how can he rule
1260ª well? if the subject, how can he obey well? If he be licentious and
cowardly, he will certainly not do his duty. It is evident, therefore,
that both of them must have a share of virtue, but varying as natural
subjects also vary among themselves. Here the very constitution of the
5 soul has shown us the way; in it one part naturally rules, and the
other is subject, and the virtue of the ruler we maintain to be different
from that of the subject;—the one being the virtue of the rational,
and the other of the irrational part. Now, it is obvious that the same
principle applies generally, and therefore almost all things rule and
are ruled according to nature. But the kind of rule differs;—the freeman rules over the slave after another manner from that in which
10 the male rules over the female, or the man over the child; although
the parts of the soul are present in all of them, they are present in
different degrees. For the slave has no deliberative faculty at all; the
woman has, but it is without authority, and the child has, but it is
15 immature. So it must necessarily be supposed to be with the moral
virtues also; all should partake of them, but only in such manner and
degree as is required by each for the fulfilment of his duty. Hence the
ruler ought to have moral virtue in perfection, for his function, taken
absolutely, demands a master artificer, and rational principle is such
an artificer; the subjects, on the other hand, require only that measure
20 of virtue which is proper to each of them. Clearly, then, moral virtue
belongs to all of them; but the temperance of a man and of a woman,
or the courage and justice of a man and of a woman, are not, as Socrates
maintained,[29] the same; the courage of a man is shown in commanding, of a woman in obeying. And this holds of all other virtues, as will
25 be more clearly seen if we look at them in detail, for those who say
generally that virtue consists in a good disposition of the soul, or in
doing rightly, or the like, only deceive themselves. Far better than
such definitions is their mode of speaking, who, like Gorgias,[30] enu-

29 Plato, *Meno*, 72 A–73 C.   30 *Meno*, 71 E, 72 A.

merate the virtues. All classes must be deemed to have their special attributes; as the poet says of women,

> 'Silence is a woman's glory', 30

but this is not equally the glory of man. The child is imperfect, and therefore obviously his virtue is not relative to himself alone, but to the perfect man and to his teacher, and in like manner the virtue of the slave is relative to a master. Now we determined [31] that a slave is useful for the wants of life, and therefore he will obviously require only so much virtue as will prevent him from failing in his duty 35 through cowardice or lack of self-control. Some one will ask whether, if what we are saying is true, virtue will not be required also in the artisans, for they often fail in their work through the lack of self-control? But is there not a great difference in the two cases? For the slave shares in his master's life; the artisan is less closely connected 40 with him, and only attains excellence in proportion as he becomes a slave. The meaner sort of mechanic has a special and separate slavery; 1260ᵇ and whereas the slave exists by nature, not so the shoemaker or other artisan. It is manifest, then, that the master ought to be the source of such excellence in the slave, and not a mere possessor of the art of mastership which trains the slave in his duties. [32] Wherefore they are 5 mistaken who forbid us to converse with slaves and say that we should employ command only, [33] for slaves stand even more in need of admonition than children.

So much for this subject; the relations of husband and wife, parent and child, their several virtues, what in their intercourse with one another is good, and what is evil, and how we may pursue the good 10 and escape the evil, will have to be discussed when we speak of the different forms of government. [34] For, inasmuch as every family is a part of a state, and these relationships are the parts of a family, and the virtue of the part must have regard to the virtue of the whole, women and children must be trained by education with an eye to the 15 constitution, [35] if the virtues of either of them are supposed to make any difference in the virtues of the state. And they must make a difference: for the children grow up to be citizens, and half the free persons in a state are women. [36]

Of these matters, enough has been said; of what remains, let us 20

---

[31] 1254ᵇ 16–39, Cf. 1259ᵇ 25 sq. [32] Cp. 1255ᵇ 23, 31–35.
[33] Plato, *Laws*, vi. 777 ᴇ.
[34] The question is not actually discussed in the *Politics*.
[35] Cp. v. 1310ª 12–36, viii. 1337ª 11–18. [36] Plato, *Laws*, vi. 781 ᴀ.

speak at another time. Regarding, then, our present inquiry as complete, we will make a new beginning. And, first, let us examine the various theories of a perfect state.

BOOK II

1   Our purpose is to consider what form of political community is best of all for those who are most able to realize their ideal of life.
30 We must therefore examine not only this but other constitutions, both such as actually exist in well-governed states, and any theoretical forms which are held in esteem; that what is good and useful may be brought to light. And let no one suppose that in seeking for something beyond them we are anxious to make a sophistical display at any
35 cost; we only undertake this inquiry because all the constitutions with which we are acquainted are faulty.

We will begin with the natural beginning of the subject. Three alternatives are conceivable: The members of a state must either have (1) all things or (2) nothing in common, or (3) some things in common and some not. That they should have nothing in common is clearly
40 impossible, for the constitution is a community, and must at any
1261ª rate have a common place—one city will be in one place, and the citizens are those who share in that one city. But should a well-ordered state have all things, as far as may be, in common, or some only and not others? For the citizens might conceivably have wives and chil-
5 dren and property in common, as Socrates proposes in the *Republic* of Plato.[1] Which is better, our present condition, or the proposed new order of society?

10 2   There are many difficulties in the community of women. And the principle on which Socrates rests the necessity of such an institution evidently is not established by his arguments. Further, as a means to the end which he ascribes to the state, the scheme, taken literally, is impracticable, and how we are to interpret it is nowhere precisely
15 stated. I am speaking of the premiss from which the argument of Socrates proceeds, 'that the greater the unity of the state the better'. Is it not obvious that a state may at length attain such a degree of unity as to be no longer a state?—since the nature of a state is to be a plurality, and in tending to greater unity, from being a state, it
20 becomes a family, and from being a family, an individual; for the

---

[1] *Rep.* iv. 423 E, v. 457 C, 462 B.

family may be said to be more than the state, and the individual than the family. So that we ought not to attain this greatest unity even if we could, for it would be the destruction of the state. Again, a state is not made up only of so many men, but of different kinds of men; for similars do not constitute a state. It is not like a military alliance. The usefulness of the latter depends upon its quantity even where there is no difference in quality (for mutual protection is the end aimed at), just as a greater weight of anything is more useful than a less (in like manner, a state differs from a nation, when the nation has not its population organized in villages, but lives an Arcadian sort of life); but the elements out of which a unity is to be formed differ in kind. Wherefore the principle of compensation, as I have already remarked in the *Ethics*,[2] is the salvation of states. Even among freemen and equals this is a principle which must be maintained, for they cannot all rule together, but must change at the end of a year or some other period of time or in some order of succession. The result is that upon this plan they all govern; just as if shoemakers and carpenters were to exchange their occupations, and the same persons did not always continue shoemakers and carpenters. And since it is better that this should be so in politics as well, it is clear that while there should be continuance of the same persons in power where this is possible, yet where this is not possible by reason of the natural equality of the citizens, and at the same time 1261ᵇ it is just that all should share in the government (whether to govern be a good thing or a bad [3]), an approximation to this is that equals should in turn retire from office and should, apart from official position, be treated alike.[4] Thus the one party rule and the others are ruled in turn, as if they were no longer the same persons. In like manner when they hold office there is a variety in the offices held. Hence it is evident that a city is not by nature one in that sense which some persons affirm; and that what is said to be the greatest good of cities is in reality their destruction; but surely the good of things must be that which preserves them.[5] Again, in another point of view, this extreme unification of the state is clearly not good; for a family is more self-sufficing than an individual, and a city than a family, and a city only comes into being when the community is large enough to be self-sufficing. If then self-sufficiency is to be desired, the lesser degree of unity is more desirable than the greater.

[2] *N. Eth.* v. 1132ᵇ 32.

[4] Cp. i. 1259ᵇ 4, iii. 1288ᵃ 12.

[3] Cp. Pl. *Rep.* i. 345–6.

[5] Cp. Pl. *Rep.* i. 353.

3   But, even supposing that it were best for the community to have
the greatest degree of unity, this unity is by no means proved to
follow from the fact 'of all men saying "mine" and "not mine" at the
same instant of time', which, according to Socrates,[6] is the sign of
20 perfect unity in a state. For the word 'all' is ambiguous. If the meaning be that every individual says 'mine' and 'not mine' at the same
time, then perhaps the result at which Socrates aims may be in some
degree accomplished; each man will call the same person his own son
and the same person his own wife, and so of his property and of all
that falls to his lot. This, however, is not the way in which people
would speak who had their wives and children in common; they
25 would say 'all' but not 'each.' In like manner their property would be
described as belonging to them, not severally but collectively. There is
an obvious fallacy in the term 'all': like some other words, 'both', 'odd',
'even', it is ambiguous, and even in abstract argument becomes a
30 source of logical puzzles. That all persons call the same thing mine in
the sense in which each does so may be a fine thing, but it is impracticable; or if the words are taken in the other sense, such a unity in no
way conduces to harmony. And there is another objection to the
proposal. For that which is common to the greatest number has the
least care bestowed upon it. Every one thinks chiefly of his own,
hardly at all of the common interest; and only when he is himself
35 concerned as an individual. For besides other considerations, everybody is more inclined to neglect the duty which he expects another to
fulfil; as in families many attendants are often less useful than a few.
Each citizen will have a thousand sons who will not be his sons in-
1262ª dividually, but anybody will be equally the son of anybody, and will
therefore be neglected by all alike. Further, upon this principle, every
one will use the word 'mine' of one who is prospering or the reverse,[7]
however small a fraction he may himself be of the whole number;
the same boy will be 'my son', 'so and so's son', the son of each of
the thousand, or whatever be the number of the citizens; and even
5 about this he will not be positive; for it is impossible to know who
chanced to have a child, or whether, if one came into existence, it has
survived. But which is better—for each to say 'mine' in this way,
making a man the same relation to two thousand or ten thousand
citizens, or to use the word 'mine' in the ordinary and more restricted
10 sense? For usually the same person is called by one man his own son
whom another calls his own brother or cousin or kinsman—blood
relation or connexion by marriage either of himself or of some relation
of his, and yet another his clansman or tribesman; and how much

⁶ Pl. *Rep.* v. 462 c.   ⁷ Cp. *Rep.* v. 463 e.

better is it to be the real cousin of somebody than to be a son after
Plato's fashion! Nor is there any way of preventing brothers and
children and fathers and mothers from sometimes recognizing one 15
another; for children are born like their parents, and they will
necessarily be finding indications of their relationship to one another.
Geographers declare such to be the fact; they say that in part of
Upper Libya, where the women are common, nevertheless the chil- 20
dren who are born are assigned to their respective fathers on the
ground of their likeness. And some women, like the females of other
animals—for example, mares and cows—have a strong tendency to
produce offspring resembling their parents, as was the case with the
Pharsalian mare called Honest.

4   Other evils, against which it is not easy for the authors of such a 25
community to guard, will be assaults and homicides, voluntary as well
as involuntary, quarrels and slanders, all which are most unholy acts
when committed against fathers and mothers and near relations, but
not equally unholy when there is no relationship. Moreover, they are 30
much more likely to occur if the relationship is unknown, and, when
they have occurred, the customary expiations of them cannot be made.
Again, how strange it is that Socrates,[8] after having made the children
common, should hinder lovers from carnal intercourse only, but should
permit love and familiarities between father and son or between 35
brother and brother, than which nothing can be more unseemly,
since even without them love of this sort is improper. How strange,
too, to forbid intercourse for no other reason than the violence of the
pleasure, as though the relationship of father and son or of brothers
with one another made no difference.

   This community of wives and children seems better suited to the 40
husbandmen than to the guardians, for if they have wives and children 1262^b
in common, they will be bound to one another by weaker ties, as a
subject class should be, and they will remain obedient and not rebel.[9]
In a word, the result of such a law would be just the opposite of that
which good laws ought to have, and the intention of Socrates in making 5
these regulations about women and children would defeat itself.
For friendship we believe to be the greatest good of states [10] and the
preservative of them against revolutions; neither is there anything
which Socrates so greatly lauds as the unity of the state which he and 10
all the world declare to be created by friendship. But the unity which

[8] *Rep.* iii. 403 A–C.   [9] Cp. vii. 1330^a 28.
[10] Cp. *N. Eth.* viii. 1155^a 22.

he commends [11] would be like that of the lovers in the *Symposium*,[12] who, as Aristophanes says, desire to grow together in the excess of their affection, and from being two to become one, in which case
15 one or both would certainly perish. Whereas in a state having women and children common, love will be watery; and the father will certainly not say 'my son', or the son 'my father'.[13] As a little sweet wine mingled with a great deal of water is imperceptible in the mixture, so, in this sort of community, the idea of relationship which
20 is based upon these names will be lost; there is no reason why the so-called father should care about the son, or the son about the father, or brothers about one another. Of the two qualities which chiefly inspire regard and affection—that a thing is your own and that it is your only one—neither can exist in such a state as this.

Again, the transfer of children as soon as they are born from the
25 rank of husbandmen or of artisans to that of guardians, and from the rank of guardians into a lower rank,[14] will be very difficult to arrange; the givers or transferrers cannot but know whom they are giving and transferring, and to whom. And the previously mentioned [15]
30 evils, such as assaults, unlawful loves, homicides, will happen more often amongst those who are transferred to the lower classes, or who have a place assigned to them among the guardians; for they will no longer call the members of the class they have left brothers, and children, and fathers, and mothers, and will not, therefore, be afraid of committing any crimes by reason of consanguinity. Touch-
35 ing the community of wives and children, let this be our conclusion.

5 Next let us consider what should be our arrangements about property: should the citizens of the perfect state have their posses-
40 sions in common or not? This question may be discussed separately
1263ᵃ from the enactments about women and children. Even supposing that the women and children belong to individuals, according to the custom which is at present universal, may there not be an advantage in having and using possessions in common? Three cases are possible: (1) the soil may be appropriated, but the produce may be thrown for consumption into the common stock; and this is the prac-
5 tice of some nations. Or (2), the soil may be common, and may be cultivated in common, but the produce divided among individuals for their private use; this is a form of common property which is said

[11] Cp. c. 2.   [12] *Symp*. 191 A, 192 C.   [13] Cp. c. 3.
[14] *Rep*. iii. 415 B.   [15] ᵃ 25–40.

to exist among certain barbarians. Or (3), the soil and the produce may be alike common.

When the husbandmen are not the owners, the case will be different and easier to deal with; but when they till the ground for themselves the question of ownership will give a world of trouble. If they do not share equally in enjoyments and toils, those who labour much and get little will necessarily complain of those who labour little and receive or consume much. But indeed there is always a difficulty in men living together and having all human relations in common, but especially in their having common property. The partnerships of fellow-travellers are an example to the point; for they generally fall out over everyday matters and quarrel about any trifle which turns up. So with servants: we are most liable to take offense at those with whom we most frequently come into contact in daily life.

These are only some of the disadvantages which attend the community of property; the present arrangement, if improved as it might be by good customs and laws, would be far better, and would have the advantages of both systems. Property should be in a certain sense common, but, as a general rule, private; for, when every one has a distinct interest,[16] men will not complain of one another, and they will make more progress, because every one will be attending to his own business. And yet by reason of goodness, and in respect of use, 'Friends', as the proverb says, 'will have all things common.'[17] Even now there are traces of such a principle, showing that it is not impracticable, but, in well-ordered states, exists already to a certain extent and may be carried further. For, although every man has his own property, some things he will place at the disposal of his friends, while of others he shares the use with them. The Lacedaemonians, for example, use one another's slaves, and horses, and dogs, as if they were their own; and when they lack provisions on a journey, they appropriate what they find in the fields throughout the country. It is clearly better that property should be private, but the use of it common; and the special business of the legislator is to create in men this benevolent disposition. Again, how immeasurably greater is the pleasure, when a man feels a thing to be his own; for surely the love of self[18] is a feeling implanted by nature and not given in vain, although selfishness is rightly censured; this, however, is not the mere love of self, but the love of self in excess, like the miser's love of money; for all, or almost all, men love money and other such objects in a measure. And further, there is the greatest pleasure in doing a

---

[16] Cp. *Rep.* ii. 374.　　　[17] Cp. *Rep.* iv. 424 A.　　　[18] Cp. *N. Eth.* ix. 8.

kindness or service to friends or guests or companions, which can only be rendered when a man has private property. These advantages are lost by excessive unification of the state. The exhibition of two virtues, besides, is visibly annihilated in such a state: first, temper-
10 ance towards women (for it is an honourable action to abstain from another's wife for temperance sake); secondly, liberality in the matter of property. No one, when men have all things in common, will any longer set an example of liberality or do any liberal action; for liberality consists in the use which is made of property.[19]

15   Such legislation may have a specious appearance of benevolence; men readily listen to it, and are easily induced to believe that in some wonderful manner everybody will become everybody's friend, especially when some one [20] is heard denouncing the evils now existing
20 in states, suits about contracts, convictions for perjury, flatteries of rich men and the like, which are said to arise out of the possession of private property. These evils, however, are due to a very different cause—the wickedness of human nature. Indeed, we see that there is much more quarrelling among those who have all things in com-
25 mon, though there are not many of them when compared with the vast numbers who have private property.

Again, we ought to reckon, not only the evils from which the citizens will be saved, but also the advantages which they will lose.
30 The life which they are to lead appears to be quite impracticable. The error of Socrates must be attributed to the false notion of unity from which he starts.[21] Unity there should be, both of the family and of the state, but in some respects only. For there is a point at which a state may attain such a degree of unity as to be no longer a state, or at which, without actually ceasing to exist, it
35 will become an inferior state, like harmony passing into unison, or rhythm which has been reduced to a single foot. The state, as I was saying, is a plurality,[22] which should be united and made into a community by education; and it is strange that the author of a system of education which he thinks will make the state virtuous, should expect to improve his citizens by regulations of this sort, and
40 not by philosophy or by customs and laws, like those which prevail at Sparta and Crete respecting common meals, whereby the
1264ᵃ legislator has made property common. Let us remember that we should not disregard the experience of ages; in the multitude of

---

[19] Cp. N. Eth. iv. 1119ᵇ 22.   [20] Rep. v. 464, 465.
[21] Cp. c. 2.   [22] Cp. 1261ᵃ 18.

years these things, if they were good, would certainly not have been unknown; for almost everything has been found out, although sometimes they are not put together; in other cases men do not use the knowledge which they have. Great light would be thrown on this sub- 5 ject if we could see such a form of government in the actual process of construction; for the legislator could not form a state at all without distributing and dividing its constituents into associations for common meals, and into phratries and tribes. But all this legislation ends only in forbidding agriculture to the guardians, a prohibition 10 which the Lacedaemonians try to enforce already.

But, indeed, Socrates has not said, nor is it easy to decide, what in such a community will be the general form of the state. The citizens who are not guardians are the majority, and about them nothing has been determined: are the husbandmen, too, to have their property in common? Or is each individual to have his own? and are the wives 15 and children to be individual or common? If, like the guardians, they are to have all things in common, in what do they differ from them, or what will they gain by submitting to their government? Or, upon what principle would they submit, unless indeed the governing class 20 adopt the ingenious policy of the Cretans, who give their slaves the same institutions as their own, but forbid them gymnastic exercises and the possession of arms. If, on the other hand, the inferior classes are to be like other cities in respect of marriage and property, what will be the form of the community? Must it not contain two states in 25 one,[23] each hostile to the other? He makes the guardians into a mere occupying garrison, while the husbandmen and artisans and the rest are the real citizens. But if so the suits and quarrels, and all the evils which Socrates affirms [24] to exist in other states, will exist equally among them. He says indeed that, having so good an education, the 30 citizens will not need many laws, for example laws about the city or about the markets; [25] but then he confines his education to the guardians. Again, he makes the husbandmen owners of the property upon condition of their paying a tribute.[26] But in that case they are likely to be much more unmanageable and conceited than the Helots, or Penestae, or slaves in general.[27] And whether community of wives 35 and property be necessary for the lower equally with the higher class or not, and the questions akin to this, what will be the education, form of government, laws of the lower class, Socrates has nowhere

23 Cp. *Rep.* iv. 422 E.　　　　　　24 *Rep.* v. 464, 465.
25 *Rep.* iv. 425 D.　　　　　　　26 *Rep.* v. 464 C.
27 Cp. 1269ᵃ 36.

determined: neither is it easy to discover this, nor is their char-
40 acter of small importance if the common life of the guardians is to be
maintained.

1264ᵇ　　Again, if Socrates makes the women common, and retains private
property, the men will see to the fields, but who will see to the
house? And who will do so if the agricultural class have both their
property and their wives in common? Once more: it is absurd to
5 argue, from the analogy of the animals, that men and women should
follow the same pursuits,[28] for animals have not to manage a household. The government, too, as constituted by Socrates, contains elements of danger; for he makes the same persons always rule. And
if this is often a cause of disturbance among the meaner sort, how
10 much more among high-spirited warriors? But that the persons whom
he makes rulers must be the same is evident; for the gold which the
God mingles in the souls of men is not at one time given to one,
at another time to another, but always to the same: as he says, 'God
mingles gold in some, and silver in others, from their very birth; but
15 brass and iron in those who are meant to be artisans and husbandmen.'[29] Again, he deprives the guardians even of happiness, and
says that the legislator ought to make the whole state happy.[30] But
the whole cannot be happy unless most, or all, or some of its parts
enjoy happiness.[31] In this respect happiness is not like the even prin-
20 ciple in numbers, which may exist only in the whole, but in neither
of the parts; not so happiness. And if the guardians are not happy,
who are? Surely not the artisans, or the common people. The Republic of which Socrates discourses has all these difficulties, and
25 others quite as great.

6　The same, or nearly the same, objections apply to Plato's later
work, the *Laws,* and therefore we had better examine briefly the constitution which is therein described. In the *Republic,* Socrates has
30 definitely settled in all a few questions only; such as the community
of women and children, the community of property, and the constitution of the state. The population is divided into two classes—
one of husbandmen, and the other of warriors;[32] from this latter
is taken a third class of counsellors and rulers of the state.[33] But
Socrates has not determined whether the husbandmen and artisans
35 are to have a share in the government, and whether they, too, are to

28 Cp. *Rep.* v. 451 ᴅ.　　　　　　　29 Cp. *Rep.* iii. 415 ᴀ.
30 *Rep.* iv. 419, 420.　　　　　　　31 Cp. vii. 1329ᵃ 23.
32 *Rep.* ii. 373 ᴇ.　　　　　　　　33 *Rep.* iii. 412 ʙ.

carry arms and share in military service, or not. He certainly thinks [34] that the women ought to share in the education of the guardians, and to fight by their side. The remainder of the work is filled up with digressions foreign to the main subject, and with discussions about [40] the education of the guardians. In the *Laws* there is hardly any- [1265ᵃ] thing but laws; not much is said about the constitution. This, which he had intended to make more of the ordinary type, he gradually brings round to the other or ideal form. For with the exception of the community of women and property, he supposes everything to [5] be the same in both states; there is to be the same education; the citizens of both are to live free from servile occupations, and there are to be common meals in both. The only difference is that in the *Laws*, the common meals are extended to women,[35] and the warriors number 5000,[36] but in the *Republic* only 1000.[37]

The discourses of Socrates are never commonplace; they always [10] exhibit grace and originality and thought; but perfection in every- thing can hardly be expected. We must not overlook the fact that the number of 5000 citizens, just now mentioned, will require a terri- tory as large as Babylon, or some other huge site, if so many persons [15] are to be supported in idleness, together with their women and at- tendants, who will be a multitude many times as great. In framing an ideal we may assume what we wish, but should avoid impos- sibilities.[38]

It is said that the legislator ought to have his eye directed to two points—the people and the country.[39] But neighbouring [20] countries also must not be forgotten by him,[40] firstly because the state for which he legislates is to have a political and not an isolated life.[41] For a state must have such a military force as will be service- able against her neighbours, and not merely useful at home. Even if [25] the life of action is not admitted to be the best, either for individuals or states;[42] still a city should be formidable to enemies, whether invading or retreating.

There is another point: Should not the amount of property be defined in some way which differs from this by being clearer? For Socrates says that a man should have so much property as will enable him to live temperately,[43] which is only a way of saying [30] 'to live well'; this is too general a conception. Further, a man may

---

[34] *Rep.* v. 451 E.
[35] *Laws*, vi. 780 E.
[36] *Laws*, v. 737 E.
[37] *Rep.* iv. 423 A.
[38] Cp. vii. 1325ᵇ 38.
[39] Perhaps *Laws*, iv. 704–709, and v. 747 D.
[40] Cp. 1267ᵃ 19.
[41] Cp. vii. 1327ᵃ 41.
[42] Cp. vii. c. 2. and 3.
[43] *Laws*, v. 737 D.

live temperately and yet miserably. A better definition would be that a man must have so much property as will enable him to live not only temperately but liberally;[44] if the two are parted, liberality will combine with luxury; temperance will be associated with toil. For liberality and temperance are the only eligible qualities which have
35 to do with the use of property. A man cannot use property with mildness or courage, but temperately and liberally he may; and therefore the practice of these virtues is inseparable from property. There is an inconsistency, too, in equalizing the property and not regulating the number of the citizens; [45] the population is to remain
40 unlimited, and he thinks that it will be sufficiently equalized by
1265b a certain number of marriages being unfruitful, however many are born to others, because he finds this to be the case in existing states. But greater care will be required than now; for among ourselves, whatever may be the number of citizens, the property is always distributed among them, and therefore no one is in want; but, if the property
5 were incapable of division as in the *Laws*, the supernumeraries, whether few or many, would get nothing. One would have thought that it was even more necessary to limit population than property; and that the limit should be fixed by calculating the chances of mortality in the children, and of sterility in married persons. The
10 neglect of this subject, which in existing states is so common, is a never-failing cause of poverty among the citizens; and poverty is the parent of revolution and crime. Pheidon the Corinthian, who was one of the most ancient legislators, thought that the families and the
15 number of citizens ought to remain the same, although originally all the lots may have been of different sizes: but in the *Laws* the opposite principle is maintained. What in our opinion is the right arrangement will have to be explained hereafter.[46]

There is another omission in the *Laws*: Socrates does not tell us how the rulers differ from their subjects; he only says that they
20 should be related as the warp and the woof, which are made out of different wools.[47] He allows that a man's whole property may be increased fivefold,[48] but why should not his land also increase to a certain extent? Again, will the good management of a household be
25 promoted by his arrangement of homesteads? for he assigns to each individual two homesteads in separate places,[49] and it is difficult to live in two houses.

---

[44] Cp. vii. 1326b 30.   [45] But see *Laws*, v. 740 B–741 A.
[46] Cp. vii. 1326b 26–32, 1330a 9–18, 1335b 19–26; but the promise is hardly fulfilled.   [47] *Laws*, v. 734 E, 735 A.
[48] *Laws*, v. 744 E.   [49] *Laws*, v. 745 C, but Cp. infra, vii. 1330a 9–18.

The whole system of government tends to be neither democracy nor oligarchy, but something in a mean between them, which is usually called a polity, and is composed of the heavy-armed soldiers. Now, if he intended to frame a constitution which would suit the greatest number of states, he was very likely right, but not if he meant to say that this constitutional form came nearest to his first or ideal state; for many would prefer the Lacedaemonian, or, possibly, some other more aristocratic government. Some, indeed, say that the best constitution is a combination of all existing forms, and they praise the Lacedaemonian [50] because it is made up of oligarchy, monarchy, and democracy, the king forming the monarchy, and the council of elders the oligarchy, while the democratic element is represented by the Ephors; for the Ephors are selected from the people. Others, however, declare the Ephoralty to be a tyranny, and find the element of democracy in the common meals and in the habits of daily life. In the *Laws* [51] it is maintained that the best constitution is made up of democracy and tyranny, which are either not constitutions at all, or are the worst of all. But they are nearer the truth who combine many forms; for the constitution is better which is made up of more numerous elements. The constitution proposed in the *Laws* has no element of monarchy at all; it is nothing but oligarchy and democracy, leaning rather to oligarchy. This is seen in the mode of appointing magistrates; [52] for although the appointment of them by lot from among those who have been already selected combines both elements, the way in which the rich are compelled by law to attend the assembly [53] and vote for magistrates or discharge other political duties, while the rest may do as they like, and the endeavour [54] to have the greater number of the magistrates appointed out of the richer classes and the highest officers selected from those who have the greatest incomes, both these are oligarchical features. The oligarchical principle prevails also in the choice of the council,[55] for all are compelled to choose, but the compulsion extends only to the choice out of the first class, and of an equal number out of the second class and out of the third class, but not in this latter case to all the voters but to those of the first three classes; and the selection of candidates out of the fourth class is only com-

---

[50] Cp. iv. 1293ᵇ 16, 1294ᵇ 18–34.

[51] iii. 693 ᴅ, 701 ᴇ, iv. 710, vi. 756 ᴇ.

[52] *Laws,* vi. 756, 763 ᴇ, 765.

[53] *Laws,* vi. 764 ᴀ; and *Pol.* iv. 1294ᵃ 37, 1298ᵇ 16.

[54] *Laws,* vi. 763 ᴅ ᴇ.

[55] *Laws,* vi. 756 ʙ–ᴇ.

pulsory on the first and second. Then, from the persons so chosen, he
20 says that there ought to be an equal number of each class selected.
Thus a preponderance will be given to the better sort of people,
who have the larger incomes, because many of the lower classes, not
being compelled, will not vote. These considerations, and others which
25 will be adduced [56] when the time comes for examining similar polities,
tend to show that states like Plato's should not be composed of
democracy and monarchy. There is also a danger in electing the
magistrates out of a body who are themselves elected; [57] for, if but a
small number choose to combine, the elections will always go as
30 they desire. Such is the constitution which is described in the *Laws*.

7   Other constitutions have been proposed; some by private persons, others by philosophers and statesmen, which all come nearer to
established or existing ones than either of Plato's. No one else has in-
35 troduced such novelties as the community of women and children,
or public tables for women: other legislators begin with what is
necessary. In the opinion of some, the regulation of property is the
chief point of all, that being the question upon which all revolutions
turn. This danger was recognized by Phaleas of Chalcedon, who
was the first to affirm that the citizens of a state ought to have equal
40 possessions. He thought that in a new colony the equalization might
1266ᵇ be accomplished without difficulty, not so easily when a state was
already established; and that then the shortest way of compassing
the desired end would be for the rich to give and not to receive
marriage portions, and for the poor not to give but to receive them.
5   Plato in the *Laws* [58] was of opinion that, to a certain extent, accumulation should be allowed, forbidding, as I have already observed,[59]
any citizen to possess more than five times the minimum qualification. But those who make such laws should remember what they are
apt to forget [60]—that the legislator who fixes the amount of prop-
10 erty should also fix the number of children; for, if the children are
too many for the property, the law must be broken. And, besides the
violation of the law, it is a bad thing that many from being rich
should become poor; for men of ruined fortunes are sure to stir up
revolutions. That the equalization of property exercises an influence
15 on political society was clearly understood even by some of the old
legislators. Laws were made by Solon and others prohibiting an

[56] iv. 7–9, 12. 1296ᵇ 34–38, 1297ᵃ 7–13.   [57] *Laws*, vi. 753 ᴅ.
[58] v. 744 ᴇ.   [59] 1265ᵇ 21
[60] Cp. 1265ᵃ 38–ᵇ 16.

individual from possessing as much land as he pleased; and there are other laws in states which forbid the sale of property: among the Locrians, for example, there is a law that a man is not to sell his property unless he can prove unmistakably that some misfortune has befallen him. Again, there have been laws which enjoin the preservation of the original lots. Such a law existed in the island of Leucas, and the abrogation of it made the constitution too democratic, for the rulers no longer had the prescribed qualification. Again, where there is equality of property, the amount may be either too large or too small, and the possessor may be living either in luxury or penury. Clearly, then, the legislator ought not only to aim at the equalization of properties, but at moderation in their amount. Further, if he prescribe this moderate amount equally to all, he will be no nearer the mark; for it is not the possessions but the desires of mankind which require to be equalized,[61] and this is impossible, unless a sufficient education is provided by the laws. But Phaleas will probably reply that this is precisely what he means; and that, in his opinion, there ought to be in states, not only equal property, but equal education. Still he should tell precisely what he means; and that, in his opinion, there ought to be in having one and the same for all, if it is of a sort that predisposes men to avarice, or ambition, or both. Moreover, civil troubles arise, not only out of the inequality of property, but out of the inequality of honour, though in opposite ways. For the common people quarrel about the inequality of property, the higher class about the equality of honour; as the poet says—

'The bad and good alike in honour share.'[62]

There are crimes of which the motive is want; and for these Phaleas expects to find a cure in the equalization of property, which will take away from a man the temptation to be a highwayman, because he is hungry or cold. But want is not the sole incentive to crime; men also wish to enjoy themselves and not to be in a state of desire—they wish to cure some desire, going beyond the necessities of life, which preys upon them; nay, this is not the only reason—they may desire superfluities in order to enjoy pleasures unaccompanied with pain, and therefore they commit crimes.

Now what is the cure of these three disorders? Of the first, moderate possessions and occupation; of the second, habits of temperance; as to the third, if any desire pleasures which depend on themselves,

---

[61] Cp. 1263[b] 22.   [62] Il. ix. 319.

they will find the satisfaction of their desires nowhere but in philosophy; for all other pleasures we are dependent on others. The fact is that the greatest crimes are caused by excess and not by necessity. Men do not become tyrants in order that they may not suffer cold;
15 and hence great is the honour bestowed, not on him who kills a thief, but on him who kills a tyrant. Thus we see that the institutions of Phaleas avail only against petty crimes.

There is another objection to them. They are chiefly designed to promote the internal welfare of the state. But the legislator should consider also its relation to neighbouring nations, and to all who are
20 outside of it.[63] The government must be organized with a view to military strength; and of this he has said not a word. And so with respect to property: there should not only be enough to supply the internal wants of the state, but also to meet dangers coming from without. The property of the state should not be so large that more
25 powerful neighbours may be tempted by it, while the owners are unable to repel the invaders; nor yet so small that the state is unable to maintain a war even against states of equal power, and of the same character. Phaleas has not laid down any rule; but we should bear in mind that abundance of wealth is an advantage. The best limit will probably be, that a more powerful neighbour must have no
30 inducement to go to war with you by reason of the excess of your wealth, but only such as he would have had if you had possessed less. There is a story that Eubulus, when Autophradates was going to besiege Atarneus, told him to consider how long the operation would take, and then reckon up the cost which would be incurred in the time. 'For', said he, 'I am willing for a smaller sum than that to leave Atar-
35 neus at once.' These words of Eubulus made an impression on Autophradates, and he desisted from the siege.

The equalization of property is one of the things that tend to prevent the citizens from quarrelling. Not that the gain in this direction is very great. For the nobles will be dissatisfied because they think
40 themselves worthy of more than an equal share of honours; and this is often found to be a cause of sedition and revolution.[64] And the avarice
1267b of mankind is insatiable; at one time two obols was pay enough; but now, when this sum has become customary, men always want more and more without end; for it is of the nature of desire not to be
5 satisfied, and most men live only for the gratification of it. The beginning of reform is not so much to equalize property as to train the nobler sort of natures not to desire more, and to prevent the lower

from getting more; that is to say, they must be kept down, but not ill-treated. Besides, the equalization proposed by Phaleas is imperfect; 10 for he only equalizes land, whereas a man may be rich also in slaves, and cattle, and money, and in the abundance of what are called his movables. Now either all these things must be equalized, or some limit must be imposed on them, or they must all be let alone. It would appear that Phaleas is legislating for a small city only, if, as he supposes, 15 all the artisans are to be public slaves and not to form a supplementary part of the body of citizens. But if there is a law that artisans are to be public slaves, it should only apply to those engaged on public works, as at Epidamnus, or at Athens on the plan which Diophantus once introduced.

From these observations any one may judge how far Phaleas was 20 wrong or right in his ideas.

8 Hippodamus, the son of Euryphon, a native of Miletus, the same who invented the art of planning cities, and who also laid out the Piraeus—a strange man, whose fondness for distinction led him into a general eccentricity of life, which made some think him affected (for he 25 would wear flowing hair and expensive ornaments; but these were worn on a cheap but warm garment both in winter and summer); he, besides aspiring to be an adept in the knowledge of nature, was the first person not a statesman who made inquiries about the best form of government.

The city of Hippodamus was composed of 10,000 citizens divided 30 into three parts—one of artisans, one of husbandmen, and a third of armed defenders of the state. He also divided the land into three parts, one sacred, one public, the third private:—the first was set apart to maintain the customary worship of the gods, the second was to support the warriors, the third was the property of the husbandmen. He also 35 divided laws into three classes, and no more, for he maintained that there are three subjects of lawsuits—insult, injury, and homicide. He likewise instituted a single final court of appeal, to which all causes seeming to have been improperly decided might be referred; this court 40 he formed of elders chosen for the purpose. He was further of opinion 1268ᵃ that the decisions of the courts ought not to be given by the use of a voting pebble, but that every one should have a tablet on which he might not only write a simple condemnation, or leave the tablet blank for a simple acquittal; but, if he partly acquitted and partly condemned, he was to distinguish accordingly. To the existing law he 5 objected that it obliged the judges to be guilty of perjury, whichever

way they voted. He also enacted that those who discovered anything for the good of the state should be honoured; and he provided that the children of citizens who died in battle should be maintained at the public expense, as if such an enactment had never been heard of
10 before, yet it actually exists at Athens and in other places. As to the magistrates, he would have them all elected by the people, that is, by the three classes already mentioned, and those who were elected were to watch over the interests of the public, of strangers, and of orphans. These are the most striking points in the constitution of Hippodamus.
15 There is not much else.

The first of these proposals to which objection may be taken is the threefold division of the citizens. The artisans, and the husbandmen, and the warriors, all have a share in the government. But the husbandmen have no arms, and the artisans neither arms nor land, and therefore they become all but slaves of the warrior class. That they
20 should share in all the offices is an impossibility; for generals and guardians of the citizens, and nearly all the principal magistrates, must be taken from the class of those who carry arms. Yet, if the two other classes have no share in the government, how can they be loyal
25 citizens? It may be said that those who have arms must necessarily be masters of both the other classes, but this is not so easily accomplished unless they are numerous; and if they are, why should the other classes share in the government at all, or have power to appoint
30 magistrates? Further, what use are farmers to the city? Artisans there must be, for these are wanted in every city, and they can live by their craft, as elsewhere; and the husbandmen, too, if they really provided the warriors with food, might fairly have a share in the government. But in the republic of Hippodamus they are supposed to have land of
35 their own, which they cultivate for their private benefit. Again, as to this common land out of which the soldiers are maintained, if they are themselves to be the cultivators of it, the warrior class will be identical with the husbandmen, although the legislator intended to make a distinction between them. If, again, there are to be other cultivators distinct both from the husbandmen, who have land of their own, and from the warriors, they will make a fourth class, which has
40 no place in the state and no share in anything. Or, if the same persons are to cultivate their own lands, and those of the public as well, they will have a difficulty in supplying the quantity of produce which will
1268ᵇ maintain two households: and why, in this case, should there be any division, for they might find food themselves and give to the warriors from the same land and the same lots? There is surely a great confusion in all this.

Neither is the law to be commended which says that the judges, 5
when a simple issue is laid before them, should distinguish in their
judgement; for the judge is thus converted into an arbitrator. Now, in
an arbitration, although the arbitrators are many, they confer with one
another about the decision, and therefore they can distinguish; but in
courts of law this is impossible, and, indeed, most legislators take pains 10
to prevent the judges from holding any communication with one another. Again, will there not be confusion if the judge thinks that
damages should be given, but not so much as the suitor demands?
He asks, say, for twenty minae, and the judge allows him ten minae
(or in general the suitor asks for more and the judge allows less),
while another judge allows five, another four minae. In this way they 15
will go on splitting up the damages, and some will grant the whole
and others nothing: how is the final reckoning to be taken? Again, no
one contends that he who votes for a simple acquittal or condemnation perjures himself, if the indictment has been laid in an unqualified
form; and this is just, for the judge who acquits does not decide that 20
the defendant owes nothing, but that he does not owe the twenty
minae. He only is guilty of perjury who thinks that the defendant
ought not to pay twenty minae, and yet condemns him.

To honour those who discover anything which is useful to the state
is a proposal which has a specious sound, but cannot safely be enacted
by law, for it may encourage informers, and perhaps even lead to
political commotions. This question involves another. It has been 25
doubted whether it is or is not expedient to make any changes in the
laws of a country, even if another law be better. Now, if all changes
are inexpedient, we can hardly assent to the proposal of Hippodamus;
for, under pretence of doing a public service, a man may introduce 30
measures which are really destructive to the laws or to the constitution. But, since we have touched upon this subject, perhaps we had
better go a little into detail, for, as I was saying, there is a difference
of opinion, and it may sometimes seem desirable to make changes.
Such changes in the other arts and sciences have certainly been bene- 35
ficial; medicine, for example, and gymnastic, and every other art and
craft have departed from traditional usage. And, if politics be an art,
change must be necessary in this as in any other art. That improvement has occurred is shown by the fact that old customs are exceedingly simple and barbarous. For the ancient Hellenes went about 40
armed and bought their brides of each other. The remains of ancient
laws which have come down to us are quite absurd; for example, 1269ᵃ
at Cumae there is a law about murder, to the effect that if the accuser

produce a certain number of witnesses from among his own kinsmen, the accused shall be held guilty. Again, men in general desire the good, and not merely what their fathers had. But the primaeval in-
5 habitants, whether they were born of the earth or were the survivors of some destruction, may be supposed to have been no better than ordinary or even foolish people among ourselves (such is certainly the tradition [65] concerning the earth-born men); and it would be ridiculous to rest contented with their notions. Even when laws have been written down, they ought not always to remain unaltered. As in other
10 sciences, so in politics, it is impossible that all things should be precisely set down in writing; for enactments must be universal, but actions are concerned with particulars.[66] Hence we infer that sometimes and in certain cases laws may be changed; but when we look at the matter from another point of view, great caution would seem to
15 be required. For the habit of lightly changing the laws is an evil, and, when the advantage is small, some errors both of lawgivers and rulers had better be left; the citizen will not gain so much by making the change as he will lose by the habit of disobedience. The analogy of the arts [67] is false; a change in a law is a very different thing from a
20 change in an art. For the law has no power to command obedience except that of habit, which can only be given by time, so that a readiness to change from old to new laws enfeebles the power of the law. Even if we admit that the laws are to be changed, are they all to be
25 changed, and in every state? And are they to be changed by anybody who likes, or only by certain persons? These are very important questions; and therefore we had better reserve the discussion of them to a more suitable occasion.[68]

9   In the governments of Lacedaemon and Crete, and indeed in all
30 governments, two points have to be considered: first, whether any particular law is good or bad, when compared with the perfect state; secondly, whether it is or is not consistent with the idea and character which the lawgiver has set before his citizens. That in a well-ordered state the citizens should have leisure and not have to provide for
35 their daily wants is generally acknowledged, but there is a difficulty in seeing how this leisure is to be attained. The Thessalian Penestae have often risen against their masters, and the Helots in like manner

---

[65] Cp. Plato, *Laws*, iii. 677 B; *Polit.* 274 C; *Tim.* 22 D.
[66] Cp. Plato, *Polit.* 295 A.   [67] 1268[b] 34 sqq.
[68] These questions are not actually discussed in the *Politics*.

against the Lacedaemonians, for whose misfortunes they are always
lying in wait. Nothing, however, of this kind has as yet happened to
the Cretans; the reason probably is that the neighbouring cities, even 40
when at war with one another, never form an alliance with rebellious 1269^b
serfs, rebellions not being for their interest, since they themselves have
a dependent population.[69] Whereas all the neighbours of the Lacedaemonians, whether Argives, Messenians, or Arcadians, were their enemies. In Thessaly, again, the original revolt of the slaves occurred 5
because the Thessalians were still at war with the neighbouring
Achaeans, Perrhaebians and Magnesians. Besides, if there were no
other difficulty, the treatment or management of slaves is a troublesome affair; for, if not kept in hand, they are insolent, and think
that they are as good as their masters, and, if harshly treated, they 10
hate and conspire against them. Now it is clear that when these are
the results the citizens of a state have not found out the secret of
managing their subject population.

Again, the licence of the Lacedaemonian women defeats the intention of the Spartan constitution, and is adverse to the happiness of the
state. For, a husband and a wife being each a part of every family, 15
the state may be considered as about equally divided into men and
women; and, therefore, in those states in which the condition of the
women is bad, half the city [70] may be regarded as having no laws. And
this is what has actually happened at Sparta; the legislator wanted to
make the whole state hardy and temperate, and he has carried out 20
his intention in the case of the men, but he has neglected the women,
who live in every sort of intemperance and luxury. The consequence is
that in such a state wealth is too highly valued, especially if the citizens fall under the dominion of their wives, after the manner of most 25
warlike races, except the Celts and a few others who openly approve of
male loves. The old mythologer would seem to have been right in uniting Ares and Aphrodite, for all warlike races are prone to the love
either of men or of women. This was exemplified among the Spartans 30
in the days of their greatness; many things were managed by their
women. But what difference does it make whether women rule, or the
rulers are ruled by women? The result is the same. Even in regard to
courage, which is of no use in daily life, and is needed only in war, the 35
influence of the Lacedaemonian women has been most mischievous.
The evil showed itself in the Theban invasion, when, unlike the women
in other cities, they were utterly useless and caused more confusion

[69] Cp. 1271^b 41.　　　　　　　　　　　　　　　[70] Cp. i. 1260^b 18.

than the enemy. This licence of the Lacedaemonian women existed
40 from the earliest times, and was only what might be expected. For,
1270ᵃ during the wars of the Lacedaemonians, first against the Argives, and
afterwards against the Arcadians and Messenians, the men were long
away from home, and, on the return of peace, they gave themselves
5 into the legislator's hand, already prepared by the discipline of a soldier's life (in which there are many elements of virtue), to receive
his enactments. But, when Lycurgus, as tradition says, wanted to bring
the women under his laws, they resisted, and he gave up the attempt.
These then are the causes of what then happened, and this defect in
the constitution is clearly to be attributed to them. We are not, how-
10 ever, considering what is or is not to be excused, but what is right or
wrong, and the disorder of the women, as I have already said,[71] not
only gives an air of indecorum to the constitution considered in itself,
but tends in a measure to foster avarice.
15   The mention of avarice naturally suggests a criticism on the inequality of property. While some of the Spartan citizens have quite
small properties, others have very large ones; hence the land has
passed into the hands of a few. And this is due also to faulty laws;
20 for, although the legislator rightly holds up to shame the sale or purchase of an inheritance, he allows anybody who likes to give or be-
queath it. Yet both practices lead to the same result. And nearly
two-fifths of the whole country are held by women; this is owing to
the number of heiresses and to the large dowries which are customary.
25 It would surely have been better to have given no dowries at all, or, if
any, but small or moderate ones. As the law now stands, a man may
bestow his heiress on any one whom he pleases, and, if he die intestate,
the privilege of giving her away descends to his heir.[72] Hence, although
30 the country is able to maintain 1500 cavalry and 30,000 hoplites, the
whole number of Spartan citizens [73] fell below 1000. The result
proves the faulty nature of their laws respecting property; for the
city sank under a single defeat; the want of men was their ruin. There
is a tradition that, in the days of their ancient kings, they were in
35 the habit of giving the rights of citizenship to strangers, and therefore, in spite of their long wars, no lack of population was experienced
by them; indeed, at one time Sparta is said to have numbered not
less than 10,000 citizens. Whether this statement is true or not, it
would certainly have been better to have maintained their numbers
by the equalization of property. Again, the law which relates to the

---

[71] 1269ᵇ 12, 23.   [72] i. e. to the person who 'inherits' the heiress.
[73] At the time of the Theban invasion.

procreation of children is adverse to the correction of this inequality. 40
For the legislator, wanting to have as many Spartans as he could, 1270ᵇ
encouraged the citizens to have large families; and there is a law at
Sparta that the father of three sons shall be exempt from military
service, and he who has four from all the burdens of the state. Yet it is
obvious that, if there were many children, the land being distributed 5
as it is, many of them must necessarily fall into poverty.

The Lacedaemonian constitution is defective in another point; I
mean the Ephoralty. This magistracy has authority in the highest
matters, but the Ephors are chosen from the whole people, and so the
office is apt to fall into the hands of very poor men, who, being badly 10
off, are open to bribes. There have been many examples at Sparta of
this evil in former times; and quite recently, in the matter of the
Andrians, certain of the Ephors who were bribed did their best to ruin
the state. And so great and tyrannical is their power, that even the
kings have been compelled to court them, so that, in this way as well, 15
together with the royal office the whole constitution has deteriorated,
and from being an aristocracy has turned into a democracy. The
Ephoralty certainly does keep the state together; for the people are
contented when they have a share in the highest office, and the result,
whether due to the legislator or to chance, has been advantageous.
For if a constitution is to be permanent, all the parts of the state must 20
wish that it should exist and the same arrangements be maintained.
This is the case at Sparta, where the kings desire its permanence because they have due honour in their own persons; the nobles because
they are represented in the council of elders (for the office of elder is a
reward of virtue); and the people, because all are eligible to the 25
Ephoralty. The election of Ephors out of the whole people is perfectly
right, but ought not to be carried on in the present fashion, which is
too childish. Again, they have the decision of great causes, although
they are quite ordinary men, and therefore they should not determine them merely on their own judgement, but according to written 30
rules, and to the laws. Their way of life, too, is not in accordance with
the spirit of the constitution—they have a deal too much licence;
whereas, in the case of the other citizens, the excess of strictness is so
intolerable that they run away from the law into the secret indulgence
of sensual pleasures.

Again, the council of elders is not free from defects. It may be said 35
that the elders are good men and well trained in manly virtue; and
that, therefore, there is an advantage to the state in having them. But
that judges of important causes should hold office for life is a disputable thing, for the mind grows old as well as the body. And when 40

1271ᵃ men have been educated in such a manner that even the legislator himself cannot trust them, there is real danger. Many of the elders are well known to have taken bribes and to have been guilty of par-
5 tiality in public affairs. And therefore they ought not to be irresponsible; yet at Sparta they are so. But (it may be replied), 'All magistracies are accountable to the Ephors.' Yes, but this prerogative is too great for them, and we maintain that the control should be exercised in some other manner. Further, the mode in which the Spartans elect
10 their elders is childish; and it is improper that the person to be elected should canvass for the office; the worthiest should be appointed, whether he chooses or not. And here the legislator clearly indicates the same intention which appears in other parts of his constitution; he would have his citizens ambitious, and he has reckoned
15 upon this quality in the election of the elders; for no one would ask to be elected if he were not. Yet ambition and avarice, almost more than any other passions, are the motives of crime.

Whether kings are or are not an advantage to states, I will consider
20 at another time [74]; they should at any rate be chosen, not as they are now, but with regard to their personal life and conduct. The legislator himself obviously did not suppose that he could make them really good men; at least he shows a great distrust of their virtue. For this
25 reason the Spartans used to join enemies with them in the same embassy, and the quarrels between the kings were held to be conservative of the state.

Neither did the first introducer of the common meals, called 'phiditia', regulate them well. The entertainment ought to have been provided at the public cost, as in Crete [75]; but among the Lacedae-
30 monians every one is expected to contribute, and some of them are too poor to afford the expense; thus the intention of the legislator is frustrated. The common meals were meant to be a popular institution, but the existing manner of regulating them is the reverse of popular. For
35 the very poor can scarcely take part in them; and, according to ancient custom, those who cannot contribute are not allowed to retain their rights of citizenship.

The law about the Spartan admirals has often been censured, and with justice; it is a source of dissension, for the kings are per-
40 petual generals and this office of admiral is but the setting up of another king.
1271ᵇ 　The charge which Plato brings, in the *Laws*,[76] against the inten-

---

[74] iii. 14–17.　　　　[75] Cp. 1272ᵃ 13–21.　　　　[76] *Laws*, i. 625 ᴇ, 630.

tion of the legislator, is likewise justified; the whole constitution has regard to one part of virtue only—the virtue of the soldier, which gives victory in war. So long as they were at war, therefore, their power was preserved, but when they had attained empire they fell,[77] for of 5 the arts of peace they knew nothing, and had never engaged in any employment higher than war. There is another error, equally great, into which they have fallen. Although they truly think that the goods for which men contend are to be acquired by virtue rather than by vice, they err in supposing that these goods are to be preferred to the virtue which gains them.

Once more: the revenues of the state are ill-managed; there is no 10 money in the treasury, although they are obliged to carry on great wars, and they are unwilling to pay taxes. The greater part of the land being in the hands of the Spartans, they do not look closely into one another's contributions. The result which the legislator has produced 15 is the reverse of beneficial; for he has made his city poor, and his citizens greedy.

Enough respecting the Spartan constitution, of which these are the principal defects.

10   The Cretan constitution nearly resembles the Spartan, and in 20 some few points is quite as good; but for the most part less perfect in form. The older constitutions are generally less elaborate than the later, and the Lacedaemonian is said to be, and probably is, in a very great measure, a copy of the Cretan. According to tradition, Lycurgus, when he ceased to be the guardian of King Charillus, went abroad 25 and spent most of his time in Crete. For the two countries are nearly connected; the Lyctians are a colony of the Lacedaemonians, and the colonists, when they came to Crete, adopted the constitution which they found existing among the inhabitants. Even to this day the Peri- 30 oeci, or subject population of Crete, are governed by the original laws which Minos is supposed to have enacted. The island seems to be intended by nature for dominion in Hellas, and to be well situated; it extends right across the sea, around which nearly all the Hellenes are settled; and while one end is not far from the Peloponnese, the other 35 almost reaches to the region of Asia about Triopium and Rhodes. Hence Minos acquired the empire of the sea, subduing some of the islands and colonizing others; at last he invaded Sicily, where he died near Camicus.

The Cretan institutions resemble the Lacedaemonian. The Helots are the husbandmen of the one, the Perioeci of the other, and both 40

_____
[77] Cp. vii. 1334ᵃ 6.

1272ᵃ Cretans and Lacedaemonians have common meals, which were
anciently called by the Lacedaemonians not 'phiditia' but 'andria';
and the Cretans have the same word, the use of which proves that the
common meals originally came from Crete. Further, the two constitu-
5 tions are similar; for the office of the Ephors is the same as that of the
Cretan Cosmi, the only difference being that whereas the Ephors are
five, the Cosmi are ten in number. The elders, too, answer to the elders
in Crete, who are termed by the Cretans the council. And the kingly
office once existed in Crete, but was abolished, and the Cosmi have
10 now the duty of leading them in war. All classes share in the ecclesia,
but it can only ratify the decrees of the elders and the Cosmi.

The common meals of Crete are certainly better managed than the
Lacedaemonian; for in Lacedaemon every one pays so much per
15 head, or, if he fails, the law, as I have already explained,[78] forbids
him to exercise the rights of citizenship. But in Crete they are of a
more popular character. There, of all the fruits of the earth and cattle
raised on the public lands, and of the tribute which is paid by the
Perioeci, one portion is assigned to the gods and to the service of the
20 state, and another to the common meals, so that men, women, and
children are all supported out of a common stock.[79] The legislator has
many ingenious ways of securing moderation in eating, which he conceives to be a gain; he likewise encourages the separation of men
from women, lest they should have too many children, and the com-
25 panionship of men with one another—whether this is a good or bad
thing I shall have an opportunity of considering at another time.[80] But
that the Cretan common meals are better ordered than the Lacedaemonian there can be no doubt.

On the other hand, the Cosmi are even a worse institution than the
Ephors, of which they have all the evils without the good. Like the
30 Ephors, they are any chance persons, but in Crete this is not counter-
balanced by a corresponding political advantage. At Sparta every one
is eligible, and the body of the people, having a share in the highest
office, want the constitution to be permanent.[81] But in Crete the Cosmi
are elected out of certain families, and not out of the whole people, and
the elders out of those who have been Cosmi.

35   The same criticism may be made about the Cretan, which has been
already made about the Lacedaemonian elders.[82] Their irresponsibil-
ity and life tenure is too great a privilege, and their arbitrary power of

78 1271ᵃ 35.   79 Cp. vii. 1330ᵃ 5.
80 The question is nowhere discussed by Aristotle.
81 Cp. *supra*, 1270ᵇ 25.   82 1270ᵇ 35–1271ᵃ 18.

acting upon their own judgement, and dispensing with written law, is dangerous. It is no proof of the goodness of the institution that the people are not discontented at being excluded from it. For there is no 40 profit to be made out of the office as out of the Ephoralty, since, 1272^b unlike the Ephors, the Cosmi, being in an island, are removed from temptation.

The remedy by which they correct the evil of this institution is an extraordinary one, suited rather to a close oligarchy than to a constitutional state. For the Cosmi are often expelled by a conspiracy of their own colleagues, or of private individuals; and they are allowed also to resign before their term of office has expired. Surely all matters of this kind are better regulated by law than by the will of man, which 5 is a very unsafe rule. Worst of all is the suspension of the office of Cosmi, a device to which the nobles often have recourse when they will not submit to justice. This shows that the Cretan government, although possessing some of the characteristics of a constitutional 10 state, is really a close oligarchy.

The nobles have a habit, too, of setting up a chief; they get together a party among the common people and their own friends and then quarrel and fight with one another. What is this but the temporary destruction of the state and dissolution of society? A city is in a 15 dangerous condition when those who are willing are also able to attack her. But, as I have already said,[83] the island of Crete is saved by her situation; distance has the same effect as the Lacedaemonian prohibition of strangers; and the Cretans have no foreign dominions. This is the reason why the Perioeci are contented in Crete, whereas the Helots are perpetually revolting. But when lately foreign invaders 20 found their way into the island, the weakness of the Cretan constitution was revealed. Enough of the government of Crete.

11 The Carthaginians are also considered to have an excellent form of government, which differs from that of any other state in several respects, though it is in some very like the Lacedaemonian. Indeed, 25 all three states—the Lacedaemonian, the Cretan, and the Carthaginian —nearly resemble one another, and are very different from any others. Many of the Carthaginian institutions are excellent. The superiority of their constitution is proved by the fact that the common people 30 remains loyal to the constitution; the Carthaginians have never had any rebellion worth speaking of, and have never been under the rule of a tyrant.

Among the points in which the Carthaginian constitution resembles

[83] ^a41 sq.

the Lacedaemonian are the following:—The common tables of the
35 clubs answer to the Spartan phiditia, and their magistracy of the 104
to the Ephors; but, whereas the Ephors are any chance persons, the
magistrates of the Carthaginians are elected according to merit—
this is an improvement. They have also their kings and their gerusia,
or council of elders, who correspond to the kings and elders of Sparta.
Their kings, unlike the Spartan, are not always of the same family, nor
40 that an ordinary one, but if there is some distinguished family they
are selected out of it and not appointed by seniority—this is far better.
1273ᵃ Such officers have great power, and therefore, if they are persons of
little worth, do a great deal of harm, and they have already done
harm at Lacedaemon.

Most of the defects or deviations from the perfect state, for which
the Carthaginian constitution would be censured, apply equally to all
the forms of government which we have mentioned. But of the de-
5 flections from aristocracy and constitutional government, some incline
more to democracy and some to oligarchy. The kings and elders, if
unanimous, may determine whether they will or will not bring a
matter before the people, but when they are not unanimous, the people
decide on such matters as well. And whatever the kings and elders
10 bring before the people is not only heard but also determined by them,
and any one who likes may oppose it; now this is not permitted in
Sparta and Crete. That the magistracies of five who have under them
many important matters should be co-opted, that they should choose
15 the supreme council of 100, and should hold office longer than other
magistrates (for they are virtually rulers both before and after they
hold office)—these are oligarchical features; their being without salary
and not elected by lot, and any similar points, such as the practice of
20 having all suits tried by the magistrates,[84] and not some by one class
of judges or jurors and some by another, as at Lacedaemon, are characteristic of aristocracy. The Carthaginian constitution deviates from
aristocracy and inclines to oligarchy, chiefly on a point where popular
opinion is on their side. For men in general think that magistrates
should be chosen not only for their merit, but for their wealth: a man,
they say, who is poor cannot rule well—he has not the leisure. If, then,
25 election of magistrates for their wealth be characteristic of oligarchy,
and election for merit of aristocracy, there will be a third form under
which the constitution of Carthage is comprehended; for the Carthaginians choose their magistrates, and particularly the highest of
30 them—their kings and generals—with an eye both to merit and to
wealth.

---

[84] Cp. iii. 1275ᵇ 8–12.

But we must acknowledge that, in thus deviating from aristocracy, the legislator has committed an error. Nothing is more absolutely necessary than to provide that the highest class, not only when in office, but when out of office, should have leisure and not disgrace themselves in any way; and to this his attention should be first directed. Even if you must have regard to wealth, in order to secure 35 leisure, yet it is surely a bad thing that the greatest offices, such as those of kings and generals, should be bought. The law which allows this abuse makes wealth of more account than virtue, and the whole state becomes avaricious. For, whenever the chiefs of the state deem anything honourable, the other citizens are sure to follow their 40 example; and, where virtue has not the first place, their aristocracy 1273ᵇ cannot be firmly established. Those who have been at the expense of purchasing their places will be in the habit of repaying themselves; and it is absurd to suppose that a poor and honest man will be wanting to make gains, and that a lower stamp of man who has incurred a great expense will not. Wherefore they should rule who are able to rule 5 best. And even if the legislator does not care to protect the good from poverty, he should at any rate secure leisure for them when in office.[85]

It would seem also to be a bad principle that the same person should hold many offices, which is a favourite practice among the Carthaginians, for one business is better done by one man.[86] The legis- 10 lator should see to this and should not appoint the same person to be a flute-player and a shoemaker. Hence, where the state is large, it is more in accordance both with constitutional and with democratic principles that the offices of state should be distributed among many persons. For, as I said,[87] this arrangement is fairer to all, and any action familiarized by repetition is better and sooner performed. We have a proof in military and naval matters; the duties of command 15 and of obedience in both these services extend to all.

The government of the Carthaginians is oligarchical, but they successfully escape the evils of oligarchy by enriching one portion of the people after another by sending them to their colonies. This is their panacea and the means by which they give stability to the state. 20 Accident favours them, but the legislator should be able to provide against revolution without trusting to accidents. As things are, if any misfortune occurred, and the bulk of the subjects revolted, there would be no way of restoring peace by legal methods.

[85] Cp. 1269ᵃ 34.   [86] Cp. Plato, *Rep.* ii. 374 A.   [87] 1261ᵇ 1.

25   Such is the character of the Lacedaemonian, Cretan, and Carthaginian constitutions, which are justly celebrated.

12   Of those who have treated of governments, some have never taken any part at all in public affairs, but have passed their lives in a private station; about most of them, what was worth telling has been already
30 told.[88] Others have been lawgivers, either in their own or in foreign cities, whose affairs they have administered; and of these some have only made laws, others have framed constitutions; for example, Lycurgus and Solon did both. Of the Lacedaemonian constitution I
35 have already spoken.[89] As to Solon, he is thought by some to have been a good legislator, who put an end to the exclusiveness of the oligarchy, emancipated the people, established the ancient Athenian democracy, and harmonized the different elements of the state. According to their view, the council of Areopagus was an oligarchical
40 element, the elected magistracy, aristocratical, and the courts of law,
1274ᵃ democratical. The truth seems to be that the council and the elected magistracy existed before the time of Solon, and were retained by him, but that he formed the courts of law out of all the citizens, thus creating the democracy, which is the very reason why he is sometimes blamed. For in giving the supreme power to the law courts, which
5 are elected by lot, he is thought to have destroyed the non-democratic element. When the law courts grew powerful, to please the people who were now playing the tyrant the old constitution was changed into the existing democracy. Ephialtes and Pericles curtailed the power of the Areopagus; Pericles also instituted the payment of the juries, and
10 thus every demagogue in turn increased the power of the democracy until it became what we now see. All this is true; it seems, however, to be the result of circumstances, and not to have been intended by Solon. For the people, having been instrumental in gaining the empire of the sea in the Persian War,[90] began to get a notion of itself, and followed worthless demagogues, whom the better class opposed. Solon,
15 himself, appears to have given the Athenians only that power of electing to offices and calling to account the magistrates which was absolutely necessary;[91] for without it they would have been in a state of slavery and enmity to the government. All the magistrates he appointed from the notables and the men of wealth, that is to say, from the
20 pentacosio-medimni, or from the class called zeugitae, or from a third

---

[88] cc. 1–8.   [89] c. 9.
[90] Cp. v. 1304ᵃ 20, viii. 1341ᵃ 29.   [91] Cp. iii. 1281ᵇ 32.

class of so-called knights or cavalry. The fourth class were labourers who had no share in any magistracy.

Mere legislators were Zaleucus, who gave laws to the Epizephyrian Locrians, and Charondas, who legislated for his own city of Catana, and for the other Chalcidian cities in Italy and Sicily. Some people 25 attempt to make out that Onomacritus was the first person who had any special skill in legislation, and that he, although a Locrian by birth, was trained in Crete, where he lived in the exercise of his prophetic art; that Thales was his companion, and that Lycurgus and Zaleucus were disciples of Thales, as Charondas was of Zaleucus. But 30 their account is quite inconsistent with chronology.

There was also Philolaus, the Corinthian, who gave laws to the Thebans. This Philolaus was one of the family of the Bacchiadae, and a lover of Diocles, the Olympic victor, who left Corinth in horror of the incestuous passion which his mother Halcyone had conceived for him, and retired to Thebes, where the two friends together ended 35 their days. The inhabitants still point out their tombs, which are in full view of one another, but one is visible from the Corinthian territory, the other not. Tradition says the two friends arranged them thus, Diocles out of horror at his misfortunes, so that the land of 40 Corinth might not be visible from his tomb; Philolaus that it might. 1274ᵇ This is the reason why they settled at Thebes, and so Philolaus legislated for the Thebans, and, besides some other enactments, gave them laws about the procreation of children, which they call the 'Laws of Adoption'. These laws were peculiar to him, and were intended to preserve the number of the lots.

In the legislation of Charondas there is nothing remarkable, except 5 the suits against false witnesses. He is the first who instituted denunciation for perjury. His laws are more exact and more precisely expressed than even those of our modern legislators.

(Characteristic of Phaleas is the equalization of property; of Plato, the community of women, children, and property, the common meals 10 of women, and the law about drinking, that the sober shall be masters of the feast;⁹² also the training of soldiers to acquire by practice equal skill with both hands, so that one should be as useful as the other.) ⁹³

Draco has left laws, but he adapted them to a constitution which 15 already existed, and there is no peculiarity in them which is worth mentioning, except the greatness and severity of the punishments.

Pittacus, too, was only a lawgiver, and not the author of a constitution; he has a law which is peculiar to him, that, if a drunken man do

---

⁹² Cp. *Laws,* i. 640 D, ii. 671 D–672 A.   ⁹³ Cp. *Laws,* vii. 794 D.

20 something wrong, he shall be more heavily punished than if he were
sober;[94] he looked not to the excuse which might be offered for the
drunkard, but only to expediency, for drunken more often than sober
people commit acts of violence.

Androdamas of Rhegium gave laws to the Chalcidians of Thrace.
25 Some of them relate to homicide, and to heiresses; but there is nothing
remarkable in them.

And here let us conclude our inquiry into the various constitutions
which either actually exist, or have been devised by theorists.

BOOK III

1 He who would inquire into the essence and attributes of various
kinds of governments must first of all determine 'What is a state?'
At present this is a disputed question. Some say that the state has done
35 a certain act; others, no, not the state,[1] but the oligarchy or the
tyrant. And the legislator or statesman is concerned entirely with the
state; a constitution or government being an arrangement of the
inhabitants of a state. But a state is composite, like any other whole
40 made up of many parts;—these are the citizens, who compose it. It is
1275ᵃ evident, therefore, that we must begin by asking, Who is the citizen,
and what is the meaning of the term? For here again there may be a
difference of opinion. He who is a citizen in a democracy will often not
5 be a citizen in an oligarchy. Leaving out of consideration those who
have been made citizens, or who have obtained the name of citizen in
any other accidental manner, we may say, first, that a citizen is not a
citizen because he lives in a certain place, for resident aliens and slaves
share in the place; nor is he a citizen who has no legal right except
10 that of suing and being sued; for this right may be enjoyed under the
provisions of a treaty. Nay, resident aliens in many places do not
possess even such rights completely, for they are obliged to have a
patron, so that they do but imperfectly participate in citizenship, and
we call them citizens only in a qualified sense, as we might apply the
15 term to children who are too young to be on the register, or to old men
who have been relieved from state duties. Of these we do not say
quite simply that they are citizens, but add in the one case that they
are not of age, and in the other, that they are past the age, or some-
20 thing of that sort; the precise expression is immaterial, for our meaning is clear. Similar difficulties to those which I have mentioned may
be raised and answered about deprived citizens and about exiles. But

---

[94] Cp. *N. Eth.* 1113ᵇ 31.   [1] Cp. 1276ᵃ 8.

the citizen whom we are seeking to define is a citizen in the strictest sense, against whom no such exception can be taken, and his special characteristic is that he shares in the administration of justice, and in offices. Now of offices some are discontinuous, and the same persons are not allowed to hold them twice, or can only hold them after a fixed 25 interval; others have no limit of time—for example, the office of dicast or ecclesiast.[2] It may, indeed, be argued that these are not magistrates at all, and that their functions give them no share in the government. But surely it is ridiculous to say that those who have the supreme power do not govern. Let us not dwell further upon this, which is a purely verbal question; what we want is a common term including 30 both dicast and ecclesiast. Let us, for the sake of distinction, call it 'indefinite office', and we will assume that those who share in such office are citizens. This is the most comprehensive definition of a citizen, and best suits all those who are generally so called.

But we must not forget that things of which the underlying prin- 35 ciples differ in kind, one of them being first, another second, another third, have, when regarded in this relation, nothing, or hardly anything, worth mentioning in common. Now we see that governments differ in kind, and that some of them are prior and that others are posterior; those which are faulty or perverted are necessarily posterior 1275[b] to those which are perfect. (What we mean by perversion will be hereafter explained.[3]) The citizen then of necessity differs under each form of government; and our definition is best adapted to the citizen 5 of a democracy; but not necessarily to other states. For in some states the people are not acknowledged, nor have they any regular assembly, but only extraordinary ones; and suits are distributed by sections among the magistrates. At Lacedaemon, for instance, the Ephors determine suits about contracts, which they distribute among themselves, 10 while the elders are judges of homicide, and other causes are decided by other magistrates. A similar principle prevails at Carthage;[4] there certain magistrates decide all causes. We may, indeed, modify our definition of the citizen so as to include these states. In them it is the holder of a definite, not of an indefinite office, who legislates and 15 judges, and to some or all such holders of definite offices is reserved the right of deliberating or judging about some things or about all things. The conception of the citizen now begins to clear up.

He who has the power to take part in the deliberative or judicial administration of any state is said by us to be a citizen of that state;

---

[2] 'Dicast' = juryman and judge in one: 'ecclesiast' = member of the ecclesia or assembly of the citizens.

[3] Cp. 1279[a] 19.   [4] Cp. ii. 1273[a] 19.

20 and, speaking generally, a state is a body of citizens sufficing for the purposes of life.

2 But in practice a citizen is defined to be one of whom both the parents are citizens; others insist on going further back; say to two
25 or three or more ancestors. This is a short and practical definition; but there are some who raise the further question: How this third or fourth ancestor came to be a citizen? Gorgias of Leontini, partly because he was in a difficulty, partly in irony, said—'Mortars are what is made by the mortar-makers, and the citizens of Larissa are those who are made by the magistrates;[5] for it is their trade to make Larissaeans.'
30 Yet the question is really simple, for, if according to the definition just given they shared in the government, they were citizens. This is a better definition than the other. For the words, 'born of a father or mother who is a citizen', cannot possibly apply to the first inhabitants or founders of a state.

There is a greater difficulty in the case of those who have been
35 made citizens after a revolution, as by Cleisthenes at Athens after the expulsion of the tyrants, for he enrolled in tribes many metics, both strangers and slaves. The doubt in these cases is, not who is, but
1276ª whether he who is ought to be a citizen; and there will still be a further ing the state, whether a certain act is or is not an act of the state; for what ought not to be is what is false. Now, there are some who hold office, and yet ought not to hold office, whom we describe as ruling, but ruling unjustly. And the citizen was defined [6] by the fact of his holding some kind of rule or office—he who holds a judicial or legislative office
5 fulfils our definition of a citizen. It is evident, therefore, that the citizens about whom the doubt has arisen must be called citizens.

3 Whether they ought to be so or not is a question which is bound up with the previous inquiry.[7] For a parallel question is raised respecting the state, whether a certain act is or is not an act of the state; for example, in the transition from an oligarchy or a tyranny to a democ-
10 racy. In such cases persons refuse to fulfil their contracts or any other obligations, on the ground that the tyrant, and not the state, contracted them; they argue that some constitutions are established by force, and not for the sake of the common good. But this would apply equally to democracies, for they too may be founded on violence, and
15 then the acts of the democracy will be neither more nor less acts of

---

[5] An untranslatable play upon the word *demiourgos,* which means either 'a magistrate' or 'an artisan'.

[6] 1275ª 22 sqq.

[7] Cp. 1274ᵇ 34.

the state in question than those of an oligarchy or of a tyranny. This question runs up into another:—on what principle shall we ever say that the state is the same, or different? It would be a very superficial view which considered only the place and the inhabitants (for the soil and the population may be separated, and some of the inhabitants may 20 live in one place and some in another). This, however, is not a very serious difficulty; we need only remark that the word 'state' is ambiguous.[8]

It is further asked: When are men, living in the same place, to be 25 regarded as a single city—what is the limit? Certainly not the wall of the city, for you might surround all Peloponnesus with a wall. Like this, we may say, is Babylon,[9] and every city that has the compass of a nation rather than a city; Babylon, they say, had been taken for three days before some part of the inhabitants became aware of the 30 fact. This difficulty may, however, with advantage be deferred [10] to another occasion; the statesman has to consider the size of the state, and whether it should consist of more than one nation or not.

Again. shall we say that while the race of inhabitants, as well as 35 their place of abode, remain the same, the city is also the same, although the citizens are always dying and being born, as we call rivers and fountains the same, although the water is always flowing away and coming again? Or shall we say that the generations of men, like the rivers, are the same, but that the state changes? For, since 40 the state is a partnership, and is a partnership of citizens in a consti- 1276[b] tution, when the form of the government changes, and becomes different, then it may be supposed that the state is no longer the same, just as a tragic differs from a comic chorus, although the members of 5 both may be identical. And in this manner we speak of every union or composition of elements as different when the form of their composition alters; for example, a scale containing the same sounds is said to be different, accordingly as the Dorian or the Phrygian mode is 10 employed. And if this is true it is evident that the sameness of the state consists chiefly in the sameness of the constitution, and it may be called or not called by the same name, whether the inhabitants are the same or entirely different. It is quite another question, whether a state ought or ought not to fulfil engagements when the form of 15 government changes.

---

[8] i. e. *Polis* means both 'state' and 'city'.   [9] Cp. ii. 1265[a] 14.

[10] The size of the state is discussed in vii. 1326[a] 8–1327[a] 3; the question whether it should consist of more than one nation is barely touched upon, in v. 1303[a] 25–[b] 3.

4 There is a point nearly allied to the preceding: Whether the virtue of a good man and a good citizen is the same or not.[11] But, before entering on this discussion, we must certainly first obtain some
20 general notion of the virtue of the citizen. Like the sailor, the citizen is a member of a community. Now, sailors have different functions, for one of them is a rower, another a pilot, and a third a look-out man, a fourth is described by some similar term; and while the precise
25 definition of each individual's virtue applies exclusively to him, there is, at the same time, a common definition applicable to them all. For they have all of them a common object, which is safety in navigation. Similarly, one citizen differs from another, but the salvation of the community is the common business of them all. This community is the
30 constitution; the virtue of the citizen must therefore be relative to the constitution of which he is a member. If, then, there are many forms of government, it is evident that there is not one single virtue of the good citizen which is perfect virtue. But we say that the good man is he who has one single virtue which is perfect virtue. Hence it is evident that the good citizen need not of necessity possess the virtue
35 which makes a good man.

The same question may also be approached by another road, from a consideration of the best constitution. If the state cannot be entirely composed of good men, and yet each citizen is expected to do his own
40 business well, and must therefore have virtue, still, inasmuch as all
1277ᵃ the citizens cannot be alike, the virtue of the citizen and of the good man cannot coincide. All must have the virtue of the good citizen— thus, and thus only, can the state be perfect; but they will not have the virtue of a good man, unless we assume that in the good state all the citizens must be good.

5   Again, the state, as composed of unlikes, may be compared to the living being: as the first elements into which a living being is resolved are soul and body, as soul is made up of rational principle and appetite, the family of husband and wife, property of master and slave, so of all these, as well as other dissimilar elements, the state is composed; and,
10 therefore, the virtue of all the citizens cannot possibly be the same, any more than the excellence of the leader of a chorus is the same as that of the performer who stands by his side. I have said enough to show why the two kinds of virtue cannot be absolutely and always the same.

But will there then be no case in which the virtue of the good citizen
15 and the virtue of the good man coincide? To this we answer that the good *ruler* is a good and wise man, and that he who would be a states-

---

[11] Cp. *N. Eth.* v. 1130ᵇ 28.

man must be a wise man. And some persons say that even the education of the ruler should be of a special kind; for are not the children of kings instructed in riding and military exercises? As Euripides says:

> 'No subtle arts for me, but what the state requires.'

As though there were a special education needed by a ruler. If then the virtue of a good ruler is the same as that of a good man, and we 20 assume further that the subject is a citizen as well as the ruler, the virtue of the good citizen and the virtue of the good man cannot be absolutely the same, although in some cases they may; for the virtue of a ruler differs from that of a citizen. It was the sense of this difference which made Jason say that 'he felt hungry when he was not a tyrant', meaning that he could not endure to live in a private station. But, on the other hand, it may be argued that men are praised for knowing 25 both how to rule and how to obey, and he is said to be a citizen of approved virtue who is able to do both. Now if we suppose the virtue of a good man to be that which rules, and the virtue of the citizen to include ruling and obeying, it cannot be said that they are equally worthy of praise. Since, then, it is sometimes thought that the ruler 30 and the ruled must learn different things and not the same, but that the citizen must know and share in them both, the inference is obvious. There is, indeed, the rule of a master, which is concerned with menial offices[12]—the master need not know how to perform these, but may employ others in the execution of them: the other would be degrading; 35 and by the other I mean the power actually to do menial duties, which vary much in character and are executed by various classes of slaves, such, for example, as handicraftsmen, who, as their name signifies, live by the labour of their hands:—under these the mechanic is included. 1277ᵇ Hence in ancient times, and among some nations, the working classes had no share in the government—a privilege which they only acquired under the extreme democracy. Certainly the good man and the statesman and the good citizen ought not to learn the crafts of inferiors except for their own occasional use;[13] if they habitually practise them, 5 there will cease to be a distinction between master and slave.

This is not the rule of which we are speaking; but there is a rule of another kind, which is exercised over freemen and equals by birth— a constitutional rule, which the ruler must learn by obeying, as he 10 would learn the duties of a general of cavalry by being under the orders of a general of cavalry, or the duties of a general of infantry by being under the orders of a general of infantry, and by having had the

---

[12] Cp. i. 1255ᵇ 20–37.   [13] Cp. viii. 1337ᵇ 15.

command of a regiment and of a company. It has been well said that 'he who has never learned to obey cannot be a good commander'. The two are not the same, but the good citizen ought to be capable of both; he should know how to govern like a freeman,
15 and how to obey like a freeman—these are the virtues of a citizen. And, although the temperance and justice of a ruler are distinct from those of a subject, the virtue of a good man will include both; for the virtue of the good man who is free and also a subject, e. g. his justice, will not be one but will comprise distinct kinds, the one qualifying him to rule, the other to obey, and differing as the tem-
20 perance and courage of men and women differ.[14] For a man would be thought a coward if he had no more courage than a courageous woman, and a woman would be thought loquacious if she imposed no more restraint on her conversation than the good man; and indeed their part in the management of the household is different, for the duty of the
25 one is to acquire, and of the other to preserve. Practical wisdom only is characteristic of the ruler:[15] it would seem that all other virtues must equally belong to ruler and subject. The virtue of the subject is certainly not wisdom, but only true opinion; he may be compared to the maker of the flute, while his master is like the flute-player or user of the flute.[16]
30   From these considerations may be gathered the answer to the question, whether the virtue of the good man is the same as that of the good citizen, or different, and how far the same, and how far different.[17]

5   There still remains one more question about the citizen: Is he only
35 a true citizen who has a share of office, or is the mechanic to be included? If they who hold no office are to be deemed citizens, not every citizen can have this virtue of ruling and obeying; for this man is a citizen. And if none of the lower class are citizens, in which part of the state are they to be placed? For they are not resident aliens, and
1278ᵃ they are not foreigners. May we not reply, that as far as this objection goes there is no more absurdity in excluding them than in excluding slaves and freedmen from any of the above-mentioned classes? It must be admitted that we cannot consider all those to be citizens who are necessary to the existence of the state; for example, children are not citizens equally with grown-up men, who are citizens absolutely, but
5 children, not being grown up, are only citizens on a certain assump-

[14] Cp. i. 1260ᵃ 20.   [15] Cp. *Rep.* iv. 428.
[16] Cp. *Rep.* x. 601 ᴅ, ᴇ.
[17] Cp. 1278ᵃ 40, 1288ᵃ 39, iv. 1293ᵇ 5, vii. 1333ᵃ 11.

tion.[18] Nay, in ancient times, and among some nations, the artisan class *were* slaves or foreigners, and therefore the majority of them are so now. The best form of state will not admit them to citizenship; but if they are admitted, then our definition of the virtue of a citizen will not apply to every citizen, nor to every free man as such, but only to those who are freed from necessary services. The necessary people are either slaves who minister to the wants of individuals, or mechanics and labourers who are the servants of the community. These reflections carried a little further will explain their position; and indeed what has been said already [19] is of itself, when understood, explanation enough.

Since there are many forms of government there must be many varieties of citizens, and especially of citizens who are subjects; so that under some governments the mechanic and the labourer will be citizens, but not in others, as, for example, in aristocracy or the so-called government of the best (if there be such an one), in which honours are given according to virtue and merit; for no man can practise virtue who is living the life of a mechanic or labourer. In oligarchies the qualification for office is high, and therefore no labourer can ever be a citizen; but a mechanic may, for an actual majority of them are rich. At Thebes [20] there was a law that no man could hold office who had not retired from business for ten years. But in many states the law goes to the length of admitting aliens; for in some democracies a man is a citizen though his mother only be a citizen; and a similar principle is applied to illegitimate children; the law is relaxed when there is a dearth of population. But when the number of citizens increases, first the children of a male or a female slave are excluded; then those whose mothers only are citizens; and at last the right of citizenship is confined to those whose fathers and mothers are both citizens.

Hence, as is evident, there are different kinds of citizens; and he is a citizen in the highest sense who shares in the honours of the state. Compare Homer's words 'like some dishonoured stranger'; [21] he who is excluded from the honours of the state is no better than an alien. But when this exclusion is concealed, then the object is that the privileged class may deceive their fellow inhabitants.

As to the question whether the virtue of the good man is the same as that of the good citizen, the considerations already adduced prove that in some states the good man and the good citizen are the

---

[18] *sc.* that they grow up to be men.   [19] 1275ᵃ 38 sqq.
[20] Cp. vi. 1321ᵃ 28.
[21] Achilles complains of Agamemnon's so treating him, *Il.* ix. 648, xvi. 59.

same, and in others different.When they are the same it is not every
citizen who is a good man, but only the statesman and those who
5 have or may have, alone or in conjunction with others, the conduct
of public affairs.

6 Having determined these questions, we have next to consider
whether there is only one form of government or many, and if many,
what they are, and how many, and what are the differences between them.

10 A constitution is the arrangement of magistracies in a state,[22]
especially of the highest of all. The government is everywhere sovereign
in the state, and the constitution is in fact the government. For
example, in democracies the people are supreme, but in oligarchies,
the few; and, therefore, we say that these two forms of government
also are different: and so in other cases.

15 First, let us consider what is the purpose of a state, and how many
forms of government there are by which human society is regulated.
We have already said, in the first part of this treatise,[23] when discussing household management and the rule of a master, that man
20 is by nature a political animal. And therefore, men, even when they
do not require one another's help, desire to live together; not but that
they are also brought together by their common interests in proportion as they severally attain to any measure of well-being. This is
certainly the chief end, both of individuals and of states. And also
25 for the sake of mere life (in which there is possibly some noble element so long as the evils of existence do not greatly overbalance the
good) mankind meet together and maintain the political community.
And we all see that men cling to life even at the cost of enduring great misfortune, seeming to find in life a natural sweetness and
happiness.

30 There is no difficulty in distinguishing the various kinds of
authority; they have been often defined already in discussions outside the school. The rule of a master, although the slave by nature
and the master by nature have in reality the same interests, is
35 nevertheless exercised primarily with a view to the interest of the
master, but accidentally considers the slave, since, if the slave perish,
the rule of the master perishes with him. On the other hand, the
government of a wife and children and of a household, which we have
called household management, is exercised in the first instance for
the good of the governed or for the common good of both parties,
40 but essentially for the good of the governed, as we see to be the case

[22] Cp. 1274[b] 38, iv. 1289[a] 15.   [23] Cp. i. 1253[a] 2.

in medicine, gymnastic, and the arts in general, which are only 1279ᵃ
accidentally concerned with the good of the artists themselves.²⁴ For
there is no reason why the trainer may not sometimes practise gymnastics, and the helmsman is always one of the crew. The trainer
or the helmsman considers the good of those committed to his care.
But, when he is one of the persons taken care of, he accidentally ⁵
participates in the advantage, for the helmsman is also a sailor, and
the trainer becomes one of those in training. And so in politics: when
the state is framed upon the principle of equality and likeness, the
citizens think that they ought to hold office by turns. Formerly, ¹⁰
as is natural, every one would take his turn of service; and then
again, somebody else would look after his interest, just as he, while
in office, had looked after theirs.²⁵ But nowadays, for the sake of the
advantage which is to be gained from the public revenues and from
office, men want to be always in office. One might imagine that the
rulers, being sickly, were only kept in health while they continued in ¹⁵
office; in that case we may be sure that they would be hunting after
places. The conclusion is evident: that governments which have a
regard to the common interest are constituted in accordance with
strict principles of justice, and are therefore true forms; but those
which regard only the interest of the rulers are all defective and per- ²⁰
verted forms, for they are despotic, whereas a state is a community
of freemen.

7　Having determined these points, we have next to consider how
many forms of government there are, and what they are; and in the
first place what are the true forms, for when they are determined the
perversions of them will at once be apparent. The words constitu- ²⁵
tion and government have the same meaning, and the government,
which is the supreme authority in states, must be in the hands of one,
or of a few, or of the many. The true forms of government, therefore,
are those in which the one, or the few, or the many, govern with a view
to the common interest; but governments which rule with a view to the ³⁰
private interest, whether of the one, or of the few, or of the many,
are perversions.²⁶ For the members of a state, if they are truly citizens,
ought to participate in its advantages. Of forms of government
in which one rules, we call that which regards the common interests,
kingship or royalty; that in which more than one, but not many, rule, ³⁵
aristocracy; and it is so called, either because the rulers are the best
men, or because they have at heart the best interests of the state and
of the citizens. But when the citizens at large administer the state

²⁴ Cp. Pl. *Rep.* i. 341 ᴅ.　　²⁵ Cp. ii. 1261ᵃ 37-ᵇ 6.　　²⁶ Cp. *N. Eth.* viii. 10.

for the common interest, the government is called by the generic
name—a constitution. And there is a reason for this use of language.
40 One man or a few may excel in virtue; but as the number increases
1279ᵇ it becomes more difficult for them to attain perfection in every kind
of virtue, though they may in military virtue, for this is found in the
masses. Hence in a constitutional government the fighting-men have
the supreme power, and those who possess arms are the citizens.

Of the above-mentioned forms, the perversions are as follows:—of
5 royalty, tyranny; of aristocracy, oligarchy; of constitutional government, democracy. For tyranny is a kind of monarchy which has in
view the interest of the monarch only; oligarchy has in view the
interest of the wealthy; democracy, of the needy: none of them the
10 common good of all.

8 But there are difficulties about these forms of government,
and it will therefore be necessary to state a little more at length the
nature of each of them. For he who would make a philosophical study
of the various sciences, and does not regard practice only, ought not to
15 overlook or omit anything, but to set forth the truth in every particular. Tyranny, as I was saying, is monarchy exercising the rule of
a master over the political society; oligarchy is when men of property
have the government in their hands; democracy, the opposite, when
the indigent, and not the men of property, are the rulers. And here
arises the first of our difficulties, and it relates to the distinction
20 just drawn. For democracy is said to be the government of the
many. But what if the many are men of property and have the power
in their hands? In like manner oligarchy is said to be the government
of the few; but what if the poor are fewer than the rich, and have
25 the power in their hands because they are stronger? In these cases
the distinction which we have drawn between these different forms of
government would no longer hold good.

Suppose, once more, that we add wealth to the few and poverty
to the many, and name the governments accordingly—an oligarchy is
said to be that in which the few and the wealthy, and a democracy
30 that in which the many and the poor are the rulers—there will still
be a difficulty. For, if the only forms of government are the ones
already mentioned, how shall we describe those other governments
also just mentioned by us, in which the rich are the more numerous
and the poor are the fewer, and both govern in their respective
states?

35 The argument seems to show that, whether in oligarchies or in
democracies, the number of the governing body, whether the greater

number, as in a democracy, or the smaller number, as in an oligarchy, is an accident due to the fact that the rich everywhere are few, and the poor numerous. But if so, there is a misapprehension of the causes of the difference between them. For the real difference between 40 democracy and oligarchy is poverty and wealth. Wherever men rule 1280ᵃ by reason of their wealth, whether they be few or many, that is an oligarchy, and where the poor rule, that is a democracy. But as a fact the rich are few and the poor many; for few are well-to-do, whereas freedom is enjoyed by all, and wealth and freedom are the grounds on 5 which the oligarchical and democratical parties respectively claim power in the state.

9 Let us begin by considering the common definitions of oligarchy and democracy, and what is justice oligarchical and democratical. For all men cling to justice of some kind, but their conceptions are imper- 10 fect and they do not express the whole idea. For example, justice is thought by them to be, and is, equality, not, however, for all, but only for equals. And inequality is thought to be, and is, justice; neither is this for all, but only for unequals. When the persons are omitted, then men judge erroneously. The reason is that they are passing judge- ment on themselves, and most people are bad judges in their own 15 case. And whereas justice implies a relation to persons as well as to things, and a just distribution, as I have already said in the *Ethics*,²⁷ implies the same ratio between the persons and between the things, they agree about the equality of the things, but dispute about the equality of the persons, chiefly for the reason which I have just 20 given—because they are bad judges in their own affairs; and secondly, because both the parties to the argument are speaking of a limited and partial justice, but imagine themselves to be speaking of absolute justice. For the one party, if they are unequal in one respect, for example wealth, consider themselves to be unequal in all; and the other party, if they are equal in one respect, for example free birth, consider themselves to be equal in all. But they leave out the 25 capital point. For if men met and associated out of regard to wealth only, their share in the state would be proportioned to their property, and the oligarchical doctrine would then seem to carry the day. It would not be just that he who paid one mina should have the same share of a hundred minae, whether of the principal or of the profits, 30 as he who paid the remaining ninety-nine. But a state exists for the sake of a good life, and not for the sake of life only: if life only were the object, slaves and brute animals might form a state, but they

<hr>

²⁷ v. 1131ᵃ 15.

cannot, for they have no share in happiness or in a life of free choice.
35 Nor does a state exist for the sake of alliance and security from injustice, nor yet for the sake of exchange and mutual intercourse;
for then the Tyrrhenians and the Carthaginians, and all who have
commercial treaties with one another,[28] would be the citizens of one
state. True, they have agreements about imports, and engagements
40 that they will do no wrong to one another, and written articles
1280ᵇ of alliance. But there are no magistracies common to the contracting
parties who will enforce their engagements; different states have
each their own magistracies. Nor does one state take care that the
citizens of the other are such as they ought to be, nor see that those
who come under the terms of the treaty do no wrong or wickedness at
all, but only that they do no injustice to one another. Whereas,
5 those who care for good government take into consideration virtue
and vice in states. Whence it may be further inferred that virtue must
be the care of a state which is truly so called, and not merely enjoys
the name: for without this end the community becomes a mere
alliance which differs only in place from alliances of which the members live apart; and law is only a convention, 'a surety to one
10 another of justice,' as the sophist Lycophron says, and has no real
power to make the citizens good and just.

This is obvious; for suppose distinct places, such as Corinth
and Megara, to be brought together so that their walls touched,
still they would not be one city, not even if the citizens had the
15 right to intermarry, which is one of the rights peculiarly characteristic of states. Again, if men dwelt at a distance from one another,
but not so far off as to have no intercourse, and there were laws
among them that they should not wrong each other in their exchanges,
20 neither would this be a state. Let us suppose that one man is a carpenter, another a husbandman, another a shoemaker, and so on, and
that their number is ten thousand: nevertheless, if they have nothing
in common but exchange, alliance, and the like, that would not con-
25 stitute a state. Why is this? Surely not because they are at a distance
from one another: for even supposing that such a community were
to meet in one place, but that each man had a house of his own, which
was in a manner his state, and that they made alliance with one
another, but only against evil-doers; still an accurate thinker would
not deem this to be a state, if their intercourse with one another was
30 of the same character after as before their union. It is clear then
that a state is not a mere society, having a common place, established
for the prevention of mutual crime and for the sake of exchange.[29]

---

[28] Cp. 1275ᵃ 10.   [29] Cp. *Protag.* 322 B.

These are conditions without which a state cannot exist; but all of them together do not constitute a state, which is a community of families and aggregations of families in well-being, for the sake of a perfect and self-sufficing life. Such a community can only be estab- 35 lished among those who live in the same place and intermarry. Hence arise in cities family connexions, brotherhoods, common sacri- fices, amusements which draw men together. But these are created by friendship, for the will to live together is friendship. The end of the state is the good life, and these are the means towards it. And the 40 state is the union of families and villages in a perfect and self-sufficing 1281ᵃ life, by which we mean a happy and honourable life.[30]

Our conclusion, then, is that political society exists for the sake of noble actions, and not of mere companionship. Hence they who con- tribute most to such a society have a greater share in it than those 5 who have the same or a greater freedom or nobility of birth but are inferior to them in political virtue; or than those who exceed them in wealth but are surpassed by them in virtue.

From what has been said it will be clearly seen that all the partisans of different forms of government speak of a part of justice only.   10

10   There is also a doubt as to what is to be the supreme power in the state:—Is it the multitude? Or the wealthy? Or the good? Or the one best man? Or a tyrant? Any of these alternatives seems to involve disagreeable consequences. If the poor, for example, because they are more in number, divide among themselves the property of the rich—is not this unjust? No, by heaven (will be the reply), for 15 the supreme authority justly willed it. But if this is not injustice, pray what is? Again, when in the first division all has been taken, and the majority divide anew the property of the minority, is it not evident, if this goes on, that they will ruin the state? Yet surely, virtue is not the ruin of those who possess her, nor is justice destructive of a state; and therefore this law of confiscation clearly cannot be just. If it were, 20 all the acts of a tyrant must of necessity be just; for he only coerces other men by superior power, just as the multitude coerce the rich. But is it just then that the few and the wealthy should be the rulers? 25 And what if they, in like manner, rob and plunder the people—is this just? If so, the other case will likewise be just. But there can be no doubt that all these things are wrong and unjust.

Then ought the good to rule and have supreme power? But in that

[30] Cp. i. 1252ᵇ 27; *N. Eth.* i. 1097ᵇ 6.

30 case everybody else, being excluded from power, will be dishonoured. For the offices of a state are posts of honour; and if one set of men always hold them, the rest must be deprived of them. Then will it be well that the one best man should rule? Nay, that is still more oligarchical, for the number of those who are dishonoured is thereby increased. Some one may say that it is bad in any case for a man, sub-

35 ject as he is to all the accidents of human passion, to have the supreme power, rather than the law. But what if the law itself be democratical or oligarchical, how will that help us out of our difficulties? [31] Not at all; the same consequences [32] will follow.

11   Most of these questions may be reserved for another occasion.[33]

40 The principle that the multitude ought to be supreme rather than the few best is one that is maintained, and, though not free from difficulty, yet seems to contain an element of truth. For the many, of

1281ᵇ whom each individual is but an ordinary person, when they meet together may very likely be better than the few good, if regarded not individually but collectively, just as a feast to which many contribute is better than a dinner provided out of a single purse. For each individual among the many has a share of virtue and prudence, and

5 when they meet together, they become in a manner one man, who has many feet, and hands, and senses; that is a figure of their mind and disposition. Hence the many are better judges than a single man of music and poetry; for some understand one part, and some an-

10 other, and among them they understand the whole. There is a similar combination of qualities in good men, who differ from any individual of the many, as the beautiful are said to differ from those who are not beautiful, and works of art from realities, because in them the scattered elements are combined, although, if taken separately, the eye of one person or some other feature in another person would be

15 fairer than in the picture. Whether this principle can apply to every democracy, and to all bodies of men, is not clear. Or rather, by heaven, in some cases it is impossible of application; for the argument would equally hold about brutes; and wherein, it will be asked, do some

20 men differ from brutes? But there may be bodies of men about whom our statement is nevertheless true. And if so, the difficulty which has been already raised,[34] and also another which is akin to it—viz. what power should be assigned to the mass of freemen and

25 citizens, who are not rich and have no personal merit—are both solved. There is still a danger in allowing them to share the great

³¹ Cp. 1282ᵇ 6.   ³² Cp. ll. 11–34.   ³³ cc. 12–17, iv., vi.
³⁴ c. 10.

offices of state, for their folly will lead them into error, and their dis-
honesty into crime. But there is a danger also in not letting them
share, for a state in which many poor men are excluded from office 30
will necessarily be full of enemies. The only way of escape is to assign
to them some deliberative and judicial functions. For this reason
Solon [35] and certain other legislators give them the power of electing to offices, and of calling the magistrates to account, but they
do not allow them to hold office singly. When they meet together
their perceptions are quite good enough, and combined with the bet- 35
ter class they are useful to the state (just as impure food when mixed
with what is pure sometimes makes the entire mass more wholesome
than a small quantity of the pure would be), but each individual,
left to himself, forms an imperfect judgement. On the other hand,
the popular form of government involves certain difficulties. In the
first place, it might be objected that he who can judge of the healing 40
of a sick man would be one who could himself heal his disease, and
make him whole—that is, in other words, the physician; and so in 1282ᵃ
all professions and arts. As, then, the physician ought to be called to
account by physicians, so ought men in general to be called to account
by their peers. But physicians are of three kinds:—there is the ordinary practitioner, and there is the physician of the higher class, and
thirdly the intelligent man who has studied the art: in all arts there
is such a class; and we attribute the power of judging to them quite 5
as much as to professors of the art. Secondly, does not the same
principle apply to elections? For a right election can only be made
by those who have knowledge; those who know geometry, for example, will choose a geometrician rightly, and those who know how to
steer, a pilot; and, even if there be some occupations and arts in which 10
private persons share in the ability to choose, they certainly cannot
choose better than those who know. So that, according to this argument, neither the election of magistrates, nor the calling of them to
account, should be entrusted to the many. Yet possibly these objections are to a great extent met by our old answer,[36] that if the people 15
are not utterly degraded, although individually they may be worse
judges than those who have special knowledge—as a body they are
as good or better. Moreover, there are some arts whose products
are not judged of solely, or best, by the artists themselves, namely
those arts whose products are recognized even by those who do not
possess the art; for example, the knowledge of the house is not 20
limited to the builder only; the user, or, in other words, the master,

---

[35] Cp. ii. 1274ᵃ 15.   [36] 1281ᵃ 40–ᵇ 21.

of the house will even be a better judge than the builder, just as the pilot will judge better of a rudder than the carpenter, and the guest will judge better of a feast than the cook.

This difficulty seems now to be sufficiently answered, but there is
25 another akin to it. That inferior persons should have authority in greater matters than the good would appear to be a strange thing, yet the election and calling to account of the magistrates is the greatest of all. And these, as I was saying,[37] are functions which in some states are assigned to the people, for the assembly is supreme in all
30 such matters. Yet persons of any age, and having but a small property qualification, sit in the assembly and deliberate and judge, although for the great officers of state, such as treasurers and generals, a high qualification is required. This difficulty may be solved in the same manner as the preceding, and the present practice of democracies may be really defensible. For the power does not reside
35 in the dicast, or senator, or ecclesiast, but in the court, and the senate, and the assembly, of which individual senators, or ecclesiasts, or dicasts, are only parts or members. And for this reason the many may claim to have a higher authority than the few; for the people, and the senate, and the courts consist of many persons, and their
40 property collectively is greater than the property of one or of a few individuals holding great offices. But enough of this.

1282ᵇ The discussion of the first question [38] shows nothing so clearly as that laws, when good, should be supreme; and that the magistrate or magistrates should regulate those matters only on which the laws are
5 unable to speak with precision owing to the difficulty of any general principle embracing all particulars.[39] But what are good laws has not yet been clearly explained; the old difficulty remains.[40] The goodness or badness, justice or injustice, of laws varies of necessity with the
10 constitutions of states. This, however, is clear, that the laws must be adapted to the constitutions. But if so, true forms of government will of necessity have just laws, and perverted forms of government will have unjust laws.

15 12 In all sciences and arts the end is a good, and the greatest good and in the highest degree a good in the most authoritative of all [41]— this is the political science of which the good is justice, in other words, the common interest. All men think justice to be a sort of equality; and to a certain extent [42] they agree in the philosophical

[37] 1281ᵇ 32.
[39] Cp. N. Eth. v. 1137ᵇ 19.
[41] Cp. i. 1252ª 2; N. Eth. i. 1094ª 1.

[38] c. 10.
[40] Cp. 1281ª 36.
[42] Cp. 1280ª 9.

distinctions which have been laid down by us about Ethics.[43] For 20
they admit that justice is a thing and has a relation to persons, and
that equals ought to have equality. But there still remains a question: equality or inequality of what? here is a difficulty which calls for
political speculation. For very likely some persons will say that offices
of state ought to be unequally distributed according to superior excellence, in whatever respect, of the citizen, although there is no other 25
difference between him and the rest of the community; for that those
who differ in any one respect have different rights and claims. But,
surely, if this is true, the complexion or height of a man, or any other
advantage, will be a reason for his obtaining a greater share of political 30
rights. The error here lies upon the surface, and may be illustrated
from the other arts and sciences. When a number of flute-players are
equal in their art, there is no reason why those of them who are better
born should have better flutes given to them; for they will not play
any better on the flute, and the superior instrument should be reserved
for him who is the superior artist. If what I am saying is still obscure,
it will be made clearer as we proceed. For if there were a superior flute- 35
player who was far inferior in birth and beauty, although either of
these may be a greater good than the art of flute-playing, and may
excel flute-playing in a greater ratio than he excels the others in his 40
art, still he ought to have the best flutes given to him, unless the ad- 1283ᵃ
vantages of wealth and birth contribute to excellence in flute-playing,
which they do not. Moreover, upon this principle any good may be
compared with any other. For if a given height may be measured
against wealth and against freedom, height in general may be so 5
measured. Thus if A excels in height more than B in virtue, even if
virtue in general excels height still more, all goods will be commensurable; for if a certain amount is better than some other, it is clear
that some other will be equal. But since no such comparison can be 10
made, it is evident that there is good reason why in politics men do
not ground their claim to office on every sort of inequality any more
than in the arts. For if some be slow, and others swift, that is no reason
why the one should have little and the others much; it is in gymnastic contests that such excellence is rewarded. Whereas the rival claims
of candidates for office can only be based on the possession of ele- 15
ments which enter into the composition of a state. And therefore the
noble, or free-born, or rich, may with good reason claim office; for
holders of offices must be freemen and tax-payers: a state can be no
more composed entirely of poor men than entirely of slaves. But if
wealth and freedom are necessary elements, justice and valour are

---

[43] Cp. *N. Eth.* v. 3.

equally so;[44] for without the former qualities a state cannot exist at
20 all, without the latter not well.

13 If the existence of the state is alone to be considered, then it
would seem that all, or some at least, of these claims are just; but, if
25 we take into account a good life, then, as I have already said,[45] education and virtue have superior claims. As, however, those who are
equal in one thing ought not to have an equal share in all, nor those
who are unequal in one thing to have an unequal share in all, it is
certain that all forms of government which rest on either of these principles are perversions. All men have a claim in a certain sense, as I
30 have already admitted,[46] but all have not an absolute claim. The rich
claim because they have a greater share in the land, and land is the
common element of the state; also they are generally more trustworthy in contracts. The free claim under the same title as the noble;
for they are nearly akin. For the noble are citizens in a truer sense
than the ignoble, and good birth is always valued in a man's own
35 home and country.[47] Another reason is, that those who are sprung
from better ancestors are likely to be better men, for nobility is excellence of race. Virtue, too, may be truly said to have a claim, for justice has been acknowledged by us to be a social[48] virtue, and it implies
40 all others.[49] Again, the many may urge their claim against the few;
for, when taken collectively, and compared with the few, they are
1283ᵇ stronger and richer and better. But, what if the good, the rich, the
noble, and the other classes who make up a state, are all living together in the same city, will there, or will there not, be any doubt who
shall rule?—No doubt at all in determining who ought to rule in each
5 of the above-mentioned forms of government. For states are characterized by differences in their governing bodies—one of them has a government of the rich, another of the virtuous, and so on. But a difficulty
arises when all these elements coexist. How are we to decide? Suppose
10 the virtuous to be very few in number: may we consider their numbers in relation to their duties, and ask whether they are enough to
administer the state, or so many as will make up a state? Objections
may be urged against all the aspirants to political power. For those
15 who found their claims on wealth or family might be thought to have
no basis of justice; on this principle, if any one person were richer
than all the rest, it is clear that he ought to be ruler of them. In like

44 Cp. iv. 1291ᵃ 19–33.   45 Cp. 1281ᵃ 4.
46 1280ᵃ 9 sqq.   47 Cp. i. 1255ᵃ 32.
48 Cp. i. 1253ᵃ 37.   49 Cp. N. Eth. v. 1129ᵇ 25.

manner he who is very distinguished by his birth ought to have the superiority over all those who claim on the ground that they are freeborn. In an aristocracy, or government of the best, a like difficulty 20 occurs about virtue; for if one citizen be better than the other members of the government, however good they may be, he too, upon the same principle of justice, should rule over them. And if the people are to be supreme because they are stronger than the few, then if one man, or more than one, but not a majority, is stronger than the many, 25 they ought to rule, and not the many.

All these considerations appear to show that none of the principles on which men claim to rule and to hold all other men in subjection to them are strictly right. To those who claim to be masters of the gov- 30 ernment on the ground of their virtue or their wealth, the many might fairly answer that they themselves are often better and richer than the few—I do not say individually, but collectively. And another ingenious objection which is sometimes put forward may be 35 met in a similar manner. Some persons doubt whether the legislator who desires to make the justest laws ought to legislate with a view to the good of the higher classes or of the many, when the case which we have mentioned occurs.[50] Now what is just or right is to be inter- 40 preted in the sense of 'what is equal'; and that which is right in the sense of being equal is to be considered with reference to the advantage of the state, and the common good of the citizens. And a citizen is one who shares in governing and being governed. He differs under different forms of government, but in the best state he 1284ᵃ is one who is able and willing to be governed and to govern with a view to the life of virtue.

If, however, there be some one person, or more than one, although not enough to make up the full complement of a state, whose virtue is so pre-eminent that the virtues or the political capacity of all the 5 rest admit of no comparison with his or theirs, he or they can be no longer regarded as part of a state; for justice will not be done to the superior, if he is reckoned only as the equal of those who are so far inferior to him in virtue and in political capacity. Such an one may 10 truly be deemed a God among men. Hence we see that legislation is necessarily concerned only with those who are equal in birth and in capacity; and that for men of pre-eminent virtue there is no law— they are themselves a law. Any one would be ridiculous who attempted to make laws for them: they would probably retort what, 15 in the fable of Antisthenes, the lions said to the hares,[51] when in the

---

[50] i. e. when the many collectively are better than the few.
[51] i. e. 'where are your claws and teeth?'

council of the beasts the latter began haranguing and claiming equality for all. And for this reason democratic states have instituted
20 ostracism; equality is above all things their aim, and therefore they
ostracized and banished from the city for a time those who seemed to
predominate too much through their wealth, or the number of their
friends, or through any other political influence. Mythology tells us
that the Argonauts left Heracles behind for a similar reason; the ship
25 Argo would not take him because she feared that he would have been
too much for the rest of the crew. Wherefore those who denounce
tyranny and blame the counsel which Periander gave to Thrasybulus
cannot be held altogether just in their censure. The story is that
Periander, when the herald was sent to ask counsel of him, said noth-
30 ing, but only cut off the tallest ears of corn till he had brought the
field to a level. The herald did not know the meaning of the action,
but came and reported what he had seen to Thrasybulus, who understood that he was to cut off the principal men in the state;[52] and this
35 is a policy not only expedient for tyrants or in practice confined to
them, but equally necessary in oligarchies and democracies. Ostracism[53] is a measure of the same kind, which acts by disabling and
banishing the most prominent citizens. Great powers do the same to
whole cities and nations, as the Athenians did to the Samians, Chians,
40 and Lesbians; no sooner had they obtained a firm grasp of the em-
1284^b pire, than they humbled their allies contrary to treaty; and the
Persian king has repeatedly crushed the Medes, Babylonians, and
other nations, when their spirit has been stirred by the recollection of
their former greatness.

The problem is a universal one, and equally concerns all forms of
government, true as well as false; for, although perverted forms with
5 a view to their own interests may adopt this policy, those which
seek the common interest do so likewise. The same thing may be observed in the arts and sciences;[54] for the painter will not allow the
figure to have a foot which, however beautiful, is not in proportion,
10 nor will the ship-builder allow the stern or any other part of the
vessel to be unduly large, any more than the chorus-master will allow
any one who sings louder or better than all the rest to sing in the choir.
Monarchs, too, may practise compulsion and still live in harmony with
15 their cities, if their own government is for the interest of the state.
Hence where there is an acknowledged superiority the argument in
favour of ostracism is based upon a kind of political justice. It would
certainly be better that the legislator should from the first so order

---

[52] Cp. v. 1311^a 20.   [53] Cp. v. 1302^b 18.
[54] Cp. v. 1302^b 34, 1309^b 21; vii. 1326^a 35; *Rep.* iv. 420.

his state as to have no need of such a remedy. But if the need arises, the next best thing is that he should endeavour to correct the evil by this or some similar measure. The principle, however, has not been 20 fairly applied in states; for, instead of looking to the good of their own constitution, they have used ostracism for factious purposes. It is true that under perverted forms of government, and from their special point of view, such a measure is just and expedient, but it is also clear that it is not absolutely just. In the perfect state there 25 would be great doubts about the use of it, not when applied to excess in strength, wealth, popularity, or the like, but when used against some one who is pre-eminent in virtue—what is to be done with him? Mankind will not say that such an one is to be expelled and exiled; on the other hand, he ought not to be a subject—that would be as 30 if mankind should claim to rule over Zeus, dividing his offices among them. The only alternative is that all should joyfully obey such a ruler, according to what seems·to be the order of nature, and that men like him should be kings in their state for life.

14   The preceding discussion, by a natural transition, leads to the 35 consideration of royalty, which we admit to be one of the true forms of government. Let us see whether in order to be well governed a state or country should be under the rule of a king or under some other form of government; and whether monarchy, although good for some, may not be bad for others. But first we must determine 40 whether there is one species of royalty or many. It is easy to see that 1285ᵃ there are many, and that the manner of government is not the same in all of them.

Of royalties according to law, (1) the Lacedaemonian is thought to answer best to the true pattern; but there the royal power is not absolute, except when the kings go on an expedition, and then they 5 take the command. Matters of religion are likewise committed to them. The kingly office is in truth a kind of generalship, irresponsible and perpetual. The king has not the power of life and death, except in a specified case, as for instance, in ancient times, he had it when upon a campaign, by right of force. This custom is described in 10 Homer. For Agamemnon is patient when he is attacked in the assembly, but when the army goes out to battle he has the power even of life and death. Does he not say?—'When I find a man skulking apart from the battle, nothing shall save him from the dogs and vultures, for in my hands is death.' [55]

[55] *Il.* ii. 391–393. The last clause is not found in our Homer.

15 This, then, is one form of royalty—a generalship for life: and of such royalties some are hereditary and others elective.

(2) There is another sort of monarchy not uncommon among the barbarians, which nearly resembles tyranny. But this is both legal 20 and hereditary. For barbarians, being more servile in character than Hellenes, and Asiatics than Europeans, do not rebel against a despotic government. Such royalties have the nature of tyrannies because the people are by nature slaves;[56] but there is no danger of their being overthrown, for they are hereditary and legal. Wherefore also their 25 guards are such as a king and not such as a tyrant would employ, that is to say, they are composed of citizens, whereas the guards of tyrants are mercenaries.[57] For kings rule according to law over voluntary subjects, but tyrants over involuntary; and the one are guarded by their fellow-citizens, the others are guarded against them.

30 These are two forms of monarchy, and there was a third (3) which existed in ancient Hellas, called an Aesymnetia or dictatorship. This may be defined generally as an elective tyranny, which, like the barbarian monarchy, is legal, but differs from it in not being hereditary. Sometimes the office was held for life, sometimes for a term of years, 35 or until certain duties had been performed. For example, the Mytilenaeans elected Pittacus leader against the exiles, who were headed by Antimenides and Alcaeus the poet. And Alcaeus himself shows in one of his banquet odes that they chose Pittacus tyrant, for he reproaches his fellow-citizens for 'having made the low-born Pittacus tyrant of 1285ᵇ the spiritless and ill-fated city, with one voice shouting his praises'.

These forms of government have always had the character of tyrannies, because they possess despotic power; but inasmuch as they are elective and acquiesced in by their subjects, they are kingly.

(4) There is a fourth species of kingly rule—that of the heroic times—which was hereditary and legal, and was exercised over will-5 ing subjects. For the first chiefs were benefactors of the people [58] in arts or arms; they either gathered them into a community, or procured land for them; and thus they became kings of voluntary subjects, and their power was inherited by their descendants. They took 10 the command in war and presided over the sacrifices, except those which required a priest. They also decided causes either with or without an oath; and when they swore, the form of the oath was the stretching out of their sceptre. In ancient times their power extended continuously to all things whatsoever, in city and country, as well as 15 in foreign parts; but at a later date they relinquished several of these

---

[56] Cp. i. 1252ᵇ 7. [57] Cp. v. 1311ᵃ 7. [58] Cp. v. 1310ᵇ 10.

privileges, and others the people took from them, until in some states nothing was left to them but the sacrifices; and where they retained more of the reality they had only the right of leadership in war beyond the border.

These, then, are the four kinds of royalty. First the monarchy of 20 the heroic ages; this was exercised over voluntary subjects, but limited to certain functions; the king was a general and a judge, and had the control of religion. The second is that of the barbarians, which is an hereditary despotic government in accordance with law. A third is the power of the so-called Aesymnete or Dictator; this is an elective 25 tyranny. The fourth is the Lacedaemonian, which is in fact a general-ship, hereditary and perpetual. These four forms differ from one another in the manner which I have described.

(5) There is a fifth form of kingly rule in which one has the disposal of all, just as each nation or each state has the disposal of public 30 matters; this form corresponds to the control of a household. For as household management is the kingly rule of a house, so kingly rule is the household management of a city, or of a nation, or of many nations.

15 Of these forms we need only consider two, the Lacedaemonian and the absolute royalty; for most of the others lie in a region be- 35 tween them, having less power than the last, and more than the first. Thus the inquiry is reduced to two points: first, is it advantageous to the state that there should be a perpetual general, and if so, should the office be confined to one family, or open to the citizens in turn? 1286ᵃ Secondly, is it well that a single man should have the supreme power in all things? The first question falls under the head of laws rather than of constitutions; for perpetual generalship might equally exist under any form of government, so that this matter may be dismissed for the present.[59] The other kind of royalty is a sort of constitution; 5 this we have now to consider, and briefly to run over the difficulties involved in it. We will begin by inquiring whether it is more advan-tageous to be ruled by the best man or by the best laws.[60]

The advocates of royalty maintain that the laws speak only in 10 general terms, and cannot provide for circumstances; and that for any science to abide by written rules is absurd. In Egypt the physician is allowed to alter his treatment after the fourth day, but if sooner, he takes the risk. Hence it is clear that a government acting according 15 to written laws is plainly not the best. Yet surely the ruler cannot

[59] It is not discussed later.   [60] Cp. Plato, *Polit.* 294 ᴀ–295 ᴄ.

dispense with the general principle which exists in law; and that is a better ruler which is free from passion than that in which it is innate. Whereas the law is passionless, passion must ever sway the heart of 20 man. Yes, it may be replied, but then on the other hand an individual will be better able to deliberate in particular cases.

The best man, then, must legislate, and laws must be passed, but these laws will have no authority when they miss the mark, though 25 in all other cases retaining their authority. But when the law cannot determine a point at all, or not well, should the one best man or should all decide? According to our present practice assemblies meet, sit in judgement, deliberate, and decide, and their judgements all relate to individual cases. Now any member of the assembly, taken separately, is certainly inferior to the wise man. But the state is made up of many individuals. And as a feast to which all the guests contribute is better than a banquet furnished by a single man,[61] so a 30 multitude is a better judge of many things than any individual.

Again, the many are more incorruptible than the few; they are like the greater quantity of water which is less easily corrupted than a little. The individual is liable to be overcome by anger or by some 35 other passion, and then his judgement is necessarily perverted; but it is hardly to be supposed that a great number of persons would all get into a passion and go wrong at the same moment. Let us assume that they are the freemen, and that they never act in violation of the law, but fill up the gaps which the law is obliged to leave. Or, if such virtue is scarcely attainable by the multitude, we need only suppose that the majority are good men and good citizens, and ask 40 which will be the more incorruptible, the one good ruler, or the many 1286ᵇ who are all good? Will not the many? But, you will say, there may be parties among them, whereas the one man is not divided against himself. To which we may answer that their character is as good as 5 his. If we call the rule of many men, who are all of them good, aristocracy, and the rule of one man royalty, then aristocracy will be better for states than royalty, whether the government is supported by force or not,[62] provided only that a number of men equal in virtue can be found.

The first governments were kingships, probably for this reason, because of old, when cities were small, men of eminent virtue were 10 few. Further, they were made kings because they were benefactors,[63] and benefits can only be bestowed by good men. But when many persons equal in merit arose, no longer enduring the pre-eminence of

[61] Cp. 1281ᵃ 42.   [62] Cp. l. 27.   [63] Cp. 1285ᵇ 6.

one, they desired to have a commonwealth, and set up a constitution. The ruling class soon deteriorated and enriched themselves out of the public treasury; riches became the path to honour, and so oli- 15 garchies naturally grew up. These passed into tyrannies and tyrannies into democracies; for love of gain in the ruling classes was always tending to diminish their number, and so to strengthen the masses, who in the end set upon their masters and established democracies. 20 Since cities have increased in size, no other form of government appears to be any longer even easy to establish.[64]

Even supposing the principle to be maintained that kingly power is the best thing for states, how about the family of the king? Are his children to succeed him? If they are no better than anybody else, that will be mischievous. But, says the lover of royalty, the king, 25 though he might, will not hand on his power to his children. That, however, is hardly to be expected, and is too much to ask of human nature. There is also a difficulty about the force which he is to employ; should a king have guards about him by whose aid he may be able to coerce the refractory? if not, how will he administer his 30 kingdom? Even if he be the lawful sovereign who does nothing arbitrarily or contrary to law, still he must have some force wherewith to maintain the law. In the case of a limited monarchy there is not much difficulty in answering this question; the king must have such 35 force as will be more than a match for one or more individuals, but not so great as that of the people. The ancients observe this principle when they have guards to any one whom they appointed dictator or tyrant. Thus, when Dionysius asked the Syracusans to allow him guards, somebody advised that they should give him only 40 such a number.

16   At this place in the discussion there impends the inquiry re- 1287[a] specting the king who acts solely according to his own will; he has now to be considered. The so-called limited monarchy, or kingship according to law, as I have already remarked,[65] is not a distinct form of government, for under all governments, as, for example, in a 5 democracy or aristocracy, there may be a general holding office for life, and one person is often made supreme over the administration of a state. A magistracy of this kind exists at Epidamnus,[66] and also at Opus, but in the latter city has a more limited power. Now, 10 absolute monarchy, or the arbitrary rule of a sovereign over all the citizens, in a city which consists of equals, is thought by some to be

[64] Cp. iv. 1293[a] 1, 1297[b] 22.   [65] 1286[a] 2.   [66] Cp. v. 1301[b] 21.

quite contrary to nature; it is argued that those who are by nature equals must have the same natural right and worth, and that for unequals to have an equal share, or for equals to have an unequal 15 share, in the offices of state, is as bad as for different bodily constitutions to have the same food and clothing. Wherefore it is thought to be just that among equals every one be ruled as well as rule, and therefore that all should have their turn. We thus arrive at law; for an order of succession implies law. And the rule of the law, it is 20 argued, is preferable to that of any individual. On the same principle, even if it be better for certain individuals to govern, they should be made only guardians and ministers of the law. For magistrates there must be—this is admitted; but then men say that to give authority to any one man when all are equal is unjust. Nay, there may indeed be cases which the law seems unable to determine, but 25 in such cases can a man? Nay, it will be replied, the law trains officers for this express purpose, and appoints them to determine matters which are left undecided by it, to the best of their judgement. Further, it permits them to make any amendment of the existing laws which experience suggests. Therefore he who bids the law rule may be deemed to bid God and Reason alone rule, but he who bids 30 man rule adds an element of the beast; for desire is a wild beast, and passion perverts the minds of rulers, even when they are the best of men. The law is reason unaffected by desire. We are told [67] that a patient should call in a physician; he will not get better if he is doctored out of a book. But the parallel of the arts is clearly not in 35 point; for the physician does nothing contrary to rule from motives of friendship; he only cures a patient and takes a fee; whereas magistrates do many things from spite and partiality. And, indeed, if a man suspected the physician of being in league with his enemies 40 to destroy him for a bribe, he would rather have recourse to the book. But certainly physicians, when they are sick, call in other 1287ᵇ physicians, and training-masters, when they are in training, other training-masters, as if they could not judge truly about their own case and might be influenced by their feelings. Hence it is evident that in seeking for justice men seek for the mean or neutral,[68] for 5 the law is the mean. Again, customary laws have more weight, and relate to more important matters, than written laws, and a man may be a safer ruler than the written law, but not safer than the customary law.

Again, it is by no means easy for one man to superintend many

[67] Cp. 1286ᵃ 12–14, *Polit.* 296 ʙ.   [68] Cp. *N. Eth.* v. 1132ᵃ 22.

things; he will have to appoint a number of subordinates, and what difference does it make whether these subordinates always existed or 10 were appointed by him because he needed them? If, as I said before,[69] the good man has a right to rule because he is better, still two good men are better than one: this is the old saying—

'two going together',[70]

and the prayer of Agamemnon—

'would that I had ten such counsellors!'[71]

And at this day there are magistrates, for example judges, who have 15 authority to decide some matters which the law is unable to determine, since no one doubts that the law would command and decide in the best manner whatever it could. But some things can, and other things cannot, be comprehended under the law, and this is the origin of the 20 vexed question whether the best law or the best man should rule. For matters of detail about which men deliberate cannot be included in legislation. Nor does any one deny that the decision of such matters must be left to man, but it is argued that there should be many judges, and not one only. For every ruler who has been trained by the law 25 judges well; and it would surely seem strange that a person should see better with two eyes, or hear better with two ears, or act better with two hands or feet, than many with many; indeed, it is already the practice of kings to make to themselves many eyes and ears and hands and feet. For they make colleagues of those who are the friends of 30 themselves and their governments. They must be friends of the monarch and of his government; if not his friends, they will not do what he wants; but friendship implies likeness and equality; and, therefore, if he thinks that his friends ought to rule, he must think that those who are equal to himself and like himself ought to rule equally with 35 himself. These are the principal controversies relating to monarchy.

17 But may not all this be true in some cases and not in others? for there is by nature both a justice and an advantage appropriate to the rule of a master, another to kingly rule, another to constitutional rule; but there is none naturally appropriate to tyranny, or to any other perverted form of government; for these come into being contrary to nature. Now, to judge at least from what has been said, it is manifest 40 that, where men are alike and equal, it is neither expedient nor just 1288ᵃ that one man should be lord of all, whether there are laws, or whether there are no laws, but he himself is in the place of law. Neither should

---

[69] 1283ᵇ 21, 1284ᵇ 32.   [70] Il. x. 224.   [71] Il. ii. 372.

a good man be lord over good men, nor a bad man over bad; nor, even
if he excels in virtue, should he have a right to rule, unless in a particular case, at which I have already hinted, and to which I will once
5 more recur.[72] But first of all, I must determine what natures are suited
for government by a king, and what for an aristocracy, and what for
a constitutional government.

A people who are by nature capable of producing a race superior in
the virtue needed for political rule are fitted for kingly government;
10 and a people submitting to be ruled as freemen by men whose virtue
renders them capable of political command are adapted for an aristocracy: while the people who are suited for constitutional freedom
are those among whom there naturally exists a warlike multitude [73]
able to rule and to obey in turn by a law which gives office to the well-
15 to-do according to their desert. But when a whole family, or some
individual, happens to be so pre-eminent in virtue as to surpass all
others, then it is just that they should be the royal family and supreme
over all, or that this one citizen should be king of the whole nation.
20 For, as I said before,[74] to give them authority is not only agreeable to
that ground of right which the founders of all states, whether aristocratical, or oligarchical, or again democratical, are accustomed to put
forward (for these all recognize the claim of excellence, although not
25 the same excellence), but accords with the principle already laid
down. For surely it would not be right to kill, or ostracize, or exile such
a person, or require that he should take his turn in being governed.
The whole is naturally superior to the part, and he who has this
pre-eminence is in the relation of a whole to a part. But if so, the
only alternative is that he should have the supreme power, and that
30 mankind should obey him, not in turn, but always. These are the conclusions at which we arrive respecting royalty and its various forms,
and this is the answer to the question, whether it is or is not advantageous to states, and to which, and how.

18   We maintain [75] that the true forms of government are three, and
35 that the best must be that which is administered by the best, and in
which there is one man, or a whole family, or many persons, excelling
all the others together in virtue, and both rulers and subjects are fitted,
the one to rule, the others to be ruled, in such a manner as to
attain the most eligible life. We showed at the commencement of
our inquiry [76] that the virtue of the good man is necessarily the same

---

[72] 1284ᵃ 3, and 1288ᵃ 15.   [73] Cp. 1279ᵇ 2.
[74] 1283ᵇ 20, 1284ᵃ 3–17, ᵇ25.   [75] Cp. 1279ᵃ 22–ᵇ4.   [76] cc. 4, 5.

as the virtue of the citizen of the perfect state. Clearly then in the
same manner, and by the same means through which a man becomes 40
truly good, he will frame a state that is to be ruled by an aristocracy 1288ᵇ
or by a king, and the same education and the same habits will be found
to make a good man and a man fit to be a statesman or king.

Having arrived at these conclusions, we must proceed to speak of
the perfect state, and describe how it comes into being and is estab- 5
lished.

BOOK IV

1   In all arts and sciences which embrace the whole of any subject, 10
and do not come into being in a fragmentary way, it is the province of
a single art or science to consider all that appertains to a single subject. For example, the art of gymnastic considers not only the suitable-
ness of different modes of training to different bodies (2), but what
sort is absolutely the best (1); (for the absolutely best must suit that
which is by nature best and best furnished with the means of life), and
also what common form of training is adapted to the great majority of 15
men (4). And if a man does not desire the best habit of body, or the
greatest skill in gymnastics, which might be attained by him, still the
trainer or the teacher of gymnastic should be able to impart any lower
degree of either (3). The same principle equally holds in medicine and
ship-building, and the making of clothes, and in the arts generally.¹   20

Hence it is obvious that government too is the subject of a single
science, which has to consider what government is best and of what sort
it must be, to be most in accordance with our aspirations, if there were
no external impediment, and also what kind of government is adapted
to particular states. For the best is often unattainable, and therefore 25
the true legislator and statesman ought to be acquainted, not only
with (1) that which is best in the abstract, but also with (2) that
which is best relatively to circumstances. We should be able further to
say how a state may be constituted under any given conditions (3);
both how it is originally formed and, when formed, how it may be
longest preserved; the supposed state being so far from having the 30
best constitution that it is unprovided even with the conditions necessary for the best; neither is it the best under the circumstances, but of
an inferior type.

He ought, moreover, to know (4) the form of government which is
best suited to states in general; for political writers, although they 35

¹ The numbers in this paragraph are made to correspond with the numbers
in the next.

have excellent ideas, are often unpractical. We should consider, not only what form of government is best, but also what is possible and what is easily attainable by all. There are some who would have none
40 but the most perfect; for this many natural advantages are required. Others, again, speak of a more attainable form, and, although they reject the constitution under which they are living, they extol some one in particular, for example the Lacedaemonian.[2] Any change of
1289ᵃ government which has to be introduced should be one which men, starting from their existing constitutions, will be both willing and able to adopt, since there is quite as much trouble in the reformation of an old constitution as in the establishment of a new one, just as to un-
5 learn is as hard as to learn. And therefore, in addition to the qualifications of the statesman already mentioned, he should be able to find remedies for the defects of existing constitutions, as has been said before.[3] This he cannot do unless he knows how many forms of government there are. It is often supposed that there is only one kind of
10 democracy and one of oligarchy. But this is a mistake; and, in order to avoid such mistakes, we must ascertain what differences there are in the constitutions of states, and in how many ways they are combined. The same political insight will enable a man to know which laws are the best, and which are suited to different constitutions; for the laws are, and ought to be, relative to the constitution, and not the
15 constitution to the laws. A constitution is the organization of offices in a state, and determines what is to be the governing body, and what is the end of each community. But laws are not to be confounded with the principles of the constitution; they are the rules according to which the magistrates should administer the state, and proceed against
20 offenders. So that we must know the varieties, and the number of varieties, of each form of government, if only with a view to making laws. For the same laws cannot be equally suited to all oligarchies or to all democracies, since there is certainly more than one form both of
25 democracy and of oligarchy.

2   In our original discussion [4] about governments we divided them into three true forms: kingly rule, aristocracy, and constitutional government, and three corresponding perversions—tyranny, oligarchy,
30 and democracy. Of kingly rule and of aristocracy we have already spoken,[5] for the inquiry into the perfect state is the same thing with the discussion of the two forms thus named, since both imply a prin-

---

[2] Cp. ii. 1265ᵇ 35.   [3] Cp. 1288ᵇ 29.   [4] iii. 7; Cp. *N. Eth.* viii. 10.
[5] iii. 14–18.

ciple of virtue provided with external means. We have already determined in what aristocracy and kingly rule differ from one another, and when the latter should be established.[6] In what follows we have 35 to describe the so-called constitutional government, which bears the common name of all constitutions, and the other forms, tyranny, oligarchy, and democracy.

It is obvious which of the three perversions is the worst, and which is the next in badness. That which is the perversion of the first and most 40 divine is necessarily the worst. And just as a royal rule, if not a mere 1289[b] name, must exist by virtue of some great personal superiority in the king,[7] so tyranny, which is the worst of governments, is necessarily the farthest removed from a well-constituted form; oligarchy is little better, for it is a long way from aristocracy, and democracy is the most tolerable of the three.

A writer [8] who preceded me has already made these distinctions, 5 but his point of view is not the same as mine. For he lays down the principle that when all the constitutions are good (the oligarchy and the rest being virtuous), democracy is the worst, but the best when all are bad. Whereas we maintain that they are in any case defective, and that one oligarchy is not to be accounted better than another, 10 but only less bad.

Not to pursue this question further at present, let us begin by determining (1)[9] how many varieties of constitution there are (since of democracy and oligarchy there are several); (2)[10] what constitution 15 is the most generally acceptable, and what is eligible in the next degree after the perfect state; and besides this what other there is which is aristocratical and well-constituted, and at the same time adapted to states in general; (3)[11] of the other forms of government to whom each is suited. For democracy may meet the needs of some better than oligarchy, and conversely. In the next place (4)[12] we have to con- 20 sider in what manner a man ought to proceed who desires to establish some one among these various forms, whether of democracy or of oligarchy; and lastly, (5)[13] having briefly discussed these subjects to the best of our power, we will endeavour to ascertain the modes of ruin and preservation both of constitutions generally and of each separately, and to what causes they are to be attributed.   25

[6] iii. 1279ª 32–37, 1286ᵇ 3–5, 1284ª 3–ᵇ34, ch. 17.
[7] Cp. iii. 1284ª 3–ᵇ34, chs. 17, 18, v. 1310ᵇ 10 sq., vii. 1325ᵇ 10–12.
[8] Plato, *Polit.* 302 E, 303 A.   [9] C. 3–10.
[10] C. 11.   [11] C. 12.
[12] Book vi. 1–7.   [13] Book v.

3   The reason why there are many forms of government is that every
state contains many elements. In the first place we see that all states
30 are made up of families, and in the multitude of citizens there must
be some rich and some poor, and some in a middle condition; the rich
are heavy-armed, and the poor not. Of the common people, some are
husbandmen, and some traders, and some artisans. There are also
among the notables differences of wealth and property—for example,
35 in the number of horses which they keep, for they cannot afford to
keep them unless they are rich. And therefore in old times the cities
whose strength lay in their cavalry were oligarchies, and they used
cavalry in wars against their neighbours; as was the practice of the
Eretrians and Chalcidians, and also of the Magnesians on the river
40 Maeander, and of other peoples in Asia. Besides differences of wealth
1290ᵃ there are differences of rank and merit, and there are some other elements which were mentioned by us when in treating of aristocracy we
enumerated the essentials of a state.[14] Of these elements, sometimes
all, sometimes the lesser and sometimes the greater number, have a
5 share in the government. It is evident then that there must be many
forms of government, differing in kind, since the parts of which they
are composed differ from each other in kind. For a constitution is an
organization of offices, which all the citizens distribute among themselves, according to the power which different classes possess, for ex-
10 ample the rich or the poor, or according to some principle of equality
which includes both. There must therefore be as many forms of
government as there are modes of arranging the offices, according to
the superiorities and the differences of the parts of the state.

There are generally thought to be two principal forms: as men say
of the winds that there are but two—north and south, and that the
15 rest of them are only variations of these, so of governments there are
said to be only two forms—democracy and oligarchy. For aristocracy
is considered to be a kind of oligarchy, as being the rule of a few, and
the so-called constitutional government to be really a democracy, just
as among the winds we make the west a variation of the north, and
20 the east of the south wind. Similarly of musical modes there are said
to be two kinds, the Dorian and the Phrygian; the other arrangements
of the scale are comprehended under one or other of these two. About
forms of government this is a very favourite notion. But in either case
the better and more exact way is to distinguish, as I have done,[15] the
25 one or two which are true forms, and to regard the others as perversions, whether of the most perfectly attempered mode or of the best

---

[14] iii. 1283ᵃ 14 sq., and Cp. vii. 8, 9.

[15] 1289ᵃ 31–33, 40 sqq., Cp. viii. 1340ᵃ 40–ᵇ 5, 1342ᵃ 28 sqq., ᵇ 29 sqq.

form of government: we may compare the severer and more over-powering modes to the oligarchical forms, and the more relaxed and gentler ones to the democratic.

4   It must not be assumed, as some are fond of saying, that democ- 30 racy is simply that form of government in which the greater number are sovereign,[16] for in oligarchies, and indeed in every government, the majority rules; nor again is oligarchy that form of government in which a few are sovereign. Suppose the whole population of a city to be 1300, and that of these 1000 are rich, and do not allow the re- 35 maining 300 who are poor, but free, and in all other respects their equals, a share of the government—no one will say that this is a democracy. In like manner, if the poor were few and the masters of the rich who outnumber them, no one would ever call such a government, in which the rich majority have no share of office, an oligarchy. Therefore we should rather say that democracy is the form of gov- 40 ernment in which the free are rulers, and oligarchy in which the rich; 1290ᵇ it is only an accident that the free are the many and the rich are the few. Otherwise a government in which the offices were given accord-ing to stature, as is said to be the case in Ethiopia, or according to 5 beauty, would be an oligarchy; for the number of tall or good-looking men is small. And yet oligarchy and democracy are not sufficiently distinguished merely by these two characteristics of wealth and free-dom. Both of them contain many other elements, and therefore we must carry our analysis further, and say that the government is not a democracy in which the freemen, being few in number, rule over the 10 many who are not free, as at Apollonia, on the Ionian Gulf, and at Thera; (for in each of these states the nobles, who were also the earliest settlers, were held in chief honour, although they were but a few out of many). Neither is it a democracy when the rich have the government because they exceed in number; as was the case formerly at Colophon, where the bulk of the inhabitants were possessed of large 15 property before the Lydian War. But the form of government is a democracy when the free, who are also poor and the majority, govern, and an oligarchy when the rich and the noble govern, they being at the same time few in number.   20

I have said that there are many forms of government, and have explained to what causes the variety is due. Why there are more than those already mentioned,[17] and what they are, and whence they arise, I will now proceed to consider, starting from the principle already

----

[16] Cp. iii. 1279ᵇ 21.   [17] i. e. democracy and oligarchy, Cp. 1290ᵃ 13.

admitted,[18] which is that every state consists, not of one, but of many
25 parts. If we were going to speak of the different species of animals, we·
should first of all determine the organs which are indispensable to
every animal, as for example some organs of sense and the instruments of receiving and digesting food, such as the mouth and the
stomach, besides organs of locomotion. Assuming now that there are
30 only so many kinds of organs, but that there may be differences in
them—I mean different kinds of mouths, and stomachs, and perceptive and locomotive organs—the possible combinations of these differences will necessarily furnish many varieties of animals. (For animals
cannot be the same which have different kinds of mouths or of ears.)
35 And when all the combinations are exhausted, there will be as many
sorts of animals as there are combinations of the necessary organs.
The same, then, is true of the forms of government which have been
described; states, as I have repeatedly said,[19] are composed, not of
40 one, but of many elements. One element is the food-producing class,
1291ª who are called husbandmen; a second, the class of mechanics who
practise the arts without which a city cannot exist;—of these arts
some are absolutely necessary, others contribute to luxury or to the
grace of life. The third class is that of traders, and by traders I mean
5 those who are engaged in buying and selling, whether in commerce
or in retail trade. A fourth class is that of the serfs or labourers. The
warriors make up the fifth class, and they are as necessary as any of
the others, if the country is not to be the slave of every invader. For
how can a state which has any title to the name be of a slavish
nature? The state is independent and self-sufficing, but a slave is the
10 reverse of independent. Hence we see that this subject, though ingeniously, has not been satisfactorily treated in the *Republic*.[20] Socrates
says that a state is made up of four sorts of people who are absolutely
necessary; these are a weaver, a husbandman, a shoemaker, and a
15 builder; afterwards, finding that they are not enough, he adds a
smith, and again a herdsman, to look after the necessary animals; then
a merchant, and then a retail trader. All these together form the
complement of the first state, as if a state were established merely to
supply the necessaries of life, rather than for the sake of the good, or
stood equally in need of shoemakers and of husbandmen. But he does
20 not admit into the state a military class until the country has increased in size, and is beginning to encroach on its neighbour's land,

[18] 1289ᵇ 27 sq.

[19] ii. 1261ª 22 sqq., iii. 1283ª 14 sqq., iv. 1289ᵇ 27–1290ª 5, 1290ᵇ 23 sq., Cp.
iii. 1277ª 5 sqq.   [20] *Rep.* ii. 369.

whereupon they go to war. Yet even amongst his four original citizens, or whatever be the number of those whom he associates in the state, there must be some one who will dispense justice and determine what is just. And as the soul may be said to be more truly part of an animal than the body, so the higher parts of states, that is to say, the 25 warrior class, the class engaged in the administration of justice, and that engaged in deliberation, which is the special business of political common sense—these are more essential to the state than the parts which minister to the necessaries of life. Whether their several functions are the functions of different citizens, or of the same—for it may 30 often happen that the same persons are both warriors and husbandmen—is immaterial to the argument. The higher as well as the lower elements are to be equally considered parts of the state, and if so, the military element at any rate must be included. There are also the wealthy who minister to the state with their property; these form the seventh class. The eighth class is that of magistrates and of officers; for the state cannot exist without rulers. And therefore some must be 35 able to take office and to serve the state, either always or in turn. There only remains the class of those who deliberate and who judge between disputants; we were just now distinguishing them. If presence of all these elements, and their fair and equitable organization, is 40 necessary to states, then there must also be persons who have the abil- 1291ᵇ ity of statesmen. Different functions appear to be often combined in the same individual; for example, the warrior may also be a husbandman, or an artisan; or, again, the counsellor a judge. And all claim to 5 possess political ability, and think that they are quite competent to fill most offices. But the same persons cannot be rich and poor at the same time. For this reason the rich and the poor are regarded in an especial sense as parts of a state. Again, because the rich are generally few in number, while the poor are many, they appear to be antagonis- 10 tic, and as the one or the other prevails they form the government. Hence arises the common opinion that there are two kinds of government—democracy and oligarchy.

I have already explained [21] that there are many forms of constitution, and to what causes the variety is due. Let me now show that there are different forms both of democracy and oligarchy, as will 15 indeed be evident from what has preceded. For both in the common people and in the notables various classes are included; of the common people, one class are husbandmen, another artisans; another traders, who are employed in buying and selling; another are the sea- 20

[21] Cp. iii. c. 6.

faring class, whether engaged in war or in trade, as ferrymen or as
fishermen. (In many places any one of these classes forms quite a large
population; for example, fishermen at Tarentum and Byzantium,
crews of triremes at Athens, merchant seamen at Aegina and Chios,
25 ferrymen at Tenedos.) To the classes already mentioned may be
added day-labourers, and those who, owing to their needy circumstances, have no leisure, or those who are not of free birth on both
sides; and there may be other classes as well. The notables again
may be divided according to their wealth, birth, virtue, education,
and similar differences.

30   Of forms of democracy first comes that which is said to be based
strictly on equality. In such a democracy the law says that it is just
for the poor to have no more advantage than the rich; and that
neither should be masters, but both equal. For if liberty and equality,
35 as is thought by some, are chiefly to be found in democracy, they
will be best attained when all persons alike share in the government to the utmost. And since the people are the majority, and the
opinion of the majority is decisive, such a government must necessarily be a democracy. Here then is one sort of democracy. There is
another, in which the magistrates are elected according to a certain
40 property qualification, but a low one; he who has the required amount
of property has a share in the government, but he who loses his prop-
1292ᵃ erty loses his rights. Another kind is that in which all the citizens who
are under no disqualification share in the government, but still the law
is supreme. In another, everybody, if he be only a citizen, is admitted
to the government, but the law is supreme as before. A fifth form of
5 democracy, in other respects, the same, is that in which, not the law,
but the multitude, have the supreme power, and supersede the law by
their decrees. This is a state of affairs brought about by the demagogues. For in democracies which are subject to the law the best citi-
10 zens hold the first place, and there are no demagogues; but where the
laws are not supreme, there demagogues spring up. For the people
becomes a monarch, and is many in one; and the many have the
power in their hands, not as individuals, but collectively. Homer says
that 'it is not good to have a rule of many',²² but whether he means
this corporate rule, or the rule of many individuals, is uncertain. At
15 all events this sort of democracy, which is now a monarch, and no
longer under the control of law, seeks to exercise monarchical sway,
and grows into a despot; the flatterer is held in honour; this sort of
democracy being relatively to other democracies what tyranny is to

²² *Il.* ii. 204.

other forms of monarchy. The spirit of both is the same, and they alike exercise a despotic rule over the better citizens. The decrees of the demos correspond to the edicts of the tyrant; and the demagogue is 20 to the one what the flatterer is to the other. Both have great power;— the flatterer with the tyrant, the demagogue with democracies of the kind which we are describing. The demagogues make the decrees of the people override the laws, by referring all things to the popular assembly. And therefore they grow great, because the people have all 25 things in their hands, and they hold in their hands the votes of the people, who are too ready to listen to them. Further, those who have any complaint to bring against the magistrates say, 'let the people be judges'; the people are too happy to accept the invitation; and so the authority of every office is undermined. Such a democracy is fairly 30 open to the objection that it is not a constitution at all; for where the laws have no authority, there is no constitution. The law ought to be supreme over all, and the magistracies should judge of particulars, and only this should be considered a constitution. So that if democracy be a real form of government, the sort of system in which all 35 things are regulated by decrees is clearly not even a democracy in the true sense of the word, for decrees relate only to particulars.[23]

These then are the different kinds of democracy.

5   Of oligarchies, too, there are different kinds:—one where the property qualification for office is such that the poor, although they 40 form the majority, have no share in the government, yet he who acquires a qualification may obtain a share. Another sort is when there 1292[b] is a qualification for office, but a high one, and the vacancies in the governing body are filled by co-optation. If the election is made out of all the qualified persons, a constitution of this kind inclines to an aristocracy, if out of a privileged class, to an oligarchy. Another sort of oligarchy is when the son succeeds the father. There is a fourth form, 5 likewise hereditary, in which the magistrates are supreme and not the law. Among oligarchies this is what tyranny is among monarchies, and the last-mentioned form of democracy among democracies; and in fact this sort of oligarchy receives the name of a dynasty (or 10 rule of powerful families).

These are the different sorts of oligarchies and democracies. It should however be remembered that in many states [24] the constitution which is established by law, although not democratic, owing to the education and habits of the people may be administered demo-

<hr/>

[23] Cp. *N. Eth.* v. 1137[b] 27.   [24] Cp. v. 1301[b] 10.

15 cratically, and conversely in other states the established constitution may incline to democracy, but may be administered in an
oligarchical spirit. This most often happens after a revolution: for
governments do not change at once; at first the dominant party are
20 content with encroaching a little upon their opponents. The laws
which existed previously continue in force, but the authors of the
revolution have the power in their hands.

6   From what has been already said we may safely infer that there
are so many different kinds of democracies and of oligarchies.
For it is evident that either all the classes whom we mentioned [25]
25 must share in the government, or some only and not others. When
the class of husbandmen and of those who possess moderate fortunes have the supreme power, the government is administered according to law. For the citizens being compelled to live by their
labour have no leisure; and so they set up the authority of the
law, and attend assemblies only when necessary. They all obtain a
share in the government when they have acquired the qualification
30 which is fixed by the law—the absolute exclusion of any class would
be a step towards oligarchy; hence all who have acquired the property qualification are admitted to a share in the constitution. But
leisure cannot be provided for them unless there are revenues to
support them. This is one sort of democracy, and these are the
causes which give birth to it. Another kind is based on the distinc-
35 tion which naturally comes next in order; in this, every one to
whose birth there is no objection is eligible, but actually shares in
the government only if he can find leisure. Hence in such a democracy the supreme power is vested in the laws, because the state has
no means of paying the citizens. A third kind is when all freemen
have a right to share in the government, but do not actually share,
40 for the reason which has been already given; so that in this form
again the law must rule. A fourth kind of democracy is that which
1293ᵃ comes latest in the history of states. In our own day, when cities
have far outgrown their original size, and their revenues have increased, all the citizens have a place in the government, through
the great preponderance of the multitude; and they all, including
5 the poor who receive pay, and therefore have leisure to exercise their
rights, share in the administration. Indeed, when they are paid, the
common people have the most leisure, for they are not hindered
by the care of their property, which often fetters the rich, who are
thereby prevented from taking part in the assembly or in the courts,

[25] 1291ᵇ 17–30.

and so the state is governed by the poor, who are a majority, and not by the laws. So many kinds of democracies there are, and they 10 grow out of these necessary causes.

Of oligarchies, one form is that in which the majority of the citizens have some property, but not very much; and this is the first form, which allows to any one who obtains the required amount the right of sharing in the government. The sharers in the govern- 15 ment being a numerous body, it follows that the law must govern, and not individuals. For in proportion as they are further removed from a monarchical form of government, and in respect of property have neither so much as to be able to live without attending to business, nor so little as to need state support, they must admit the rule 20 of law and not claim to rule themselves. But if the men of property in the state are fewer than in the former case, and own more property, there arises a second form of oligarchy. For the stronger they are, the more power they claim, and having this object in view, they themselves select those of the other classes who are to be ad- mitted to the government; but, not being as yet strong enough to 25 rule without the law, they make the law represent their wishes.[26] When this power is intensified by a further diminution of their num- bers and increase of their property, there arises a third and further stage of oligarchy, in which the governing class keep the offices in their own hands, and the law ordains that the son shall succeed the 30 father. When, again, the rulers have great wealth and numerous friends, this sort of family despotism approaches a monarchy; indi- viduals rule and not the law. This is the fourth sort of oligarchy, and is analogous to the last sort of democracy.

7   There are still two forms besides democracy and oligarchy; 35 one of them is universally recognized and included among the four principal forms of government, which are said to be (1) monarchy, (2) oligarchy, (3) democracy, and (4) the so-called aristocracy or government of the best. But there is also a fifth, which retains the generic name of polity or constitutional government; this is not common, and therefore has not been noticed by writers who attempt 40 to enumerate the different kinds of government; like Plato,[27] in their books about the state, they recognize four only. The term 1293ᵇ 'aristocracy' is rightly applied to the form of government which is described in the first part of our treatise; [28] for that only can be

---

[26] i. e. they make a law that the governing class shall have the power of co-optation from other classes.

[27] *Rep.* viii, ix.   [28] iii. 1279ᵃ 34, 1286ᵇ 3, Cp. vii. 1328ᵇ 37.

rightly called aristocracy which is a government formed of the best
men absolutely, and not merely of men who are good when tried
5 by any given standard. In the perfect state the good man is absolutely the same as the good citizen; whereas in other states the good
citizen is only good relatively to his own form of government. But
there are some states differing from oligarchies and also differing
from the so-called polity or constitutional government; these are
termed aristocracies, and in them magistrates are certainly chosen,
10 both according to their wealth and according to their merit. Such
a form of government differs from each of the two just now mentioned, and is termed an aristocracy. For indeed in states which do
not make virtue the aim of the community, men of merit and reputation for virtue may be found. And so where a government has
15 regard to wealth, virtue, and numbers, as at Carthage,[29] that is
aristocracy; and also where it has regard only to two out of the
three, as at Lacedaemon, to virtue and numbers, and the two principles of democracy and virtue temper each other. There are these
two forms of aristocracy in addition to the first and perfect state,
20 and there is a third form, viz. the constitutions which incline more
than the so-called polity towards oligarchy.

8 I have yet to speak of the so-called polity and of tyranny. I
put them in this order, not because a polity or constitutional government is to be regarded as a perversion any more than the above-
25 mentioned aristocracies. The truth is, that they all fall short of the
most perfect form of government, and so they are reckoned among
perversions, and the really perverted forms are perversions of these,
as I said in the original discussion.[30] Last of all I will speak of
tyranny, which I place last in the series because I am inquiring into
the constitutions of states, and this is the very reverse of a constitution.
30   Having explained why I have adopted this order, I will proceed
to consider constitutional government; of which the nature will be
clearer now that oligarchy and democracy have been defined. For
polity or constitutional government may be described generally as
a fusion of oligarchy and democracy; but the term is usually ap-
35 plied to those forms of government which incline towards democracy, and the term aristocracy to those which incline towards
oligarchy, because birth and education are commonly the accom-

---

[29] Cp. ii. 1273[a] 21–30.   [30] iii. 7.

paniments of wealth. Moreover, the rich already possess the external advantages the want of which is a temptation to crime, and hence they are called noblemen and gentlemen. And inasmuch as aristocracy seeks to give predominance to the best of the citizens, 40 people say also of oligarchies that they are composed of noblemen and gentlemen. Now it appears to be an impossible thing that the 1294ᵃ state which is governed not by the best citizens but by the worst should be well-governed, and equally impossible that the state which is ill-governed should be governed by the best. But we must remember that good laws, if they are not obeyed, do not constitute good government. Hence there are two parts of good government; one is the actual obedience of citizens to the laws, the other part is 5 the goodness of the laws which they obey; they may obey bad laws as well as good. And there may be a further subdivision; they may obey either the best laws which are attainable to them, or the best absolutely.

The distribution of offices according to merit is a special characteristic of aristocracy, for the principle of an aristocracy is virtue, 10 as wealth is of an oligarchy, and freedom of a democracy. In all of them there of course exists the right of the majority, and whatever seems good to the majority of those who share in the government has authority. Now in most states the form called polity exists, 15 for the fusion goes no further than the attempt to unite the freedom of the poor and the wealth of the rich, who commonly take the place of the noble. But as there are three grounds on which men claim an equal share in the government, freedom, wealth, and virtue (for the fourth or good birth is the result of the two last, being only 20 ancient wealth and virtue), it is clear that the admixture of the two elements, that is to say, of the rich and poor, is to be called a polity or constitutional government; and the union of the three is to be called aristocracy or the government of the best, and more than any other form of government, except the true and ideal, has a right to this name.

Thus far I have shown the existence of forms of states other than 25 monarchy, democracy, and oligarchy, and what they are, and in what aristocracies differ from one another, and polities from aristocracies—that the two latter are not very unlike is obvious.

9 Next we have to consider how by the side of oligarchy and de- 30 mocracy the so-called polity or constitutional government springs up, and how it should be organized. The nature of it will be at once understood from a comparison of oligarchy and democracy; we

must ascertain their different characteristics, and taking a portion
from each, put the two together, like the parts of an indenture.
35 Now there are three modes in which fusions of government may be
effected. In the first mode we must combine the laws made by both
governments, say concerning the administration of justice. In
oligarchies they impose a fine on the rich if they do not serve as
judges, and to the poor they give no pay; but in democracies they
40 give pay to the poor and do not fine the rich. Now (1) the union
of these two modes [31] is a common or middle term between them,
1294ᵇ and is therefore characteristic of a constitutional government, for
it is a combination of both. This is one mode of uniting the two
elements. Or (2) a mean may be taken between the enactments of
the two: thus democracies require no property qualification, or
only a small one, from members of the assembly, oligarchies a high
5 one; here neither of these is the common term, but a mean between them. (3) There is a third mode, in which something is
borrowed from the oligarchical and something from the democratical
principle. For example, the appointment of magistrates by lot is
thought to be democratical, and the election of them oligarchical;
democratical again when there is no property qualification, oli-
10 garchical when there is. In the aristocratical or constitutional state,
one element will be taken from each—from oligarchy the principle
of electing to offices, from democracy the disregard of qualification.
Such are the various modes of combination.

There is a true union of oligarchy and democracy when the
15 same state may be termed either a democracy or an oligarchy; those
who use both names evidently feel that the fusion is complete. Such
a fusion there is also in the mean; for both extremes appear in it.
The Lacedaemonian constitution, for example, is often described as
20 a democracy, because it has many democratical features. In the
first place the youth receive a democratical education. For the sons
of the poor are brought up with the sons of the rich, who are
educated in such a manner as to make it possible for the sons of
the poor to be educated like them. A similar equality prevails in
25 the following period of life, and when the citizens are grown up to
manhood the same rule is observed; there is no distinction between
the rich and poor. In like manner they all have the same food at
their public tables, and the rich wear only such clothing as any poor
man can afford. Again, the people elect to one of the two greatest
offices of state, and in the other they share; [32] for they elect the

---

[31] Cp. 1297ᵃ 38.   [32] Cp. ii. 1270ᵇ 17.

Senators and share in the Ephoralty. By others the Spartan consti- 30
tution is said to be an oligarchy, because it has many oligarchical
elements. That all offices are filled by election and none by lot, is one
of these oligarchical characteristics; that the power of inflicting
death or banishment rests with a few persons is another; and there
are others. In a well attempered polity there should appear to be 35
both elements and yet neither; also the government should rely on
itself, and not on foreign aid, and on itself not through the good
will of a majority—they might be equally well-disposed when there
is a vicious form of government—but through the general willing-
ness of all classes in the state to maintain the constitution.

Enough of the manner in which a constitutional government, and 40
in which the so-called aristocracies ought to be framed.

10 Of the nature of tyranny I have still to speak, in order that 1295ᵃ
it may have its place in our inquiry (since even tyranny is reckoned
by us to be a form of government), although there is not much to
be said about it. I have already in the former part of this treatise [33]
discussed royalty or kingship according to the most usual meaning 5
of the term, and considered whether it is or is not advantageous to
states, and what kind of royalty should be established, and from
what source, and how.

When speaking of royalty we also spoke [34] of two forms of
tyranny, which are both according to law, and therefore easily pass 10
into royalty. Among Barbarians there are elected monarchs who
exercise a despotic power; despotic rulers were also elected in ancient
Hellas, called Aesymnetes or dictators. These monarchies, when
compared with one another, exhibit certain differences. And they 15
are, as I said before,[35] royal, in so far as the monarch rules according to law over willing subjects; but they are tyrannical in so far
as he is despotic and rules according to his own fancy. There is also
a third kind of tyranny, which is the most typical form, and is the
counterpart of the perfect monarchy. This tyranny is just that arbitrary power of an individual which is responsible to no one, and 20
governs all alike, whether equals or better, with a view to its own advantage, not to that of its subjects, and therefore against their will.
No freeman, if he can escape from it, will endure such a government.

The kinds of tyranny are such and so many, and for the reasons
which I have given.

[33] iii. 14–17.   [34] iii. 1285ᵃ 16–ᵇ3.   [35] iii. 1285ᵇ 2.

²⁵ **11** We have now to inquire what is the best constitution for most states, and the best life for most men, neither assuming a standard of virtue which is above ordinary persons, nor an education which is exceptionally favoured by nature and circumstances, nor yet an ideal state which is an aspiration only, but having regard to the life ³⁰ in which the majority are able to share, and to the form of government which states in general can attain. As to those aristocracies, as they are called, of which we were just now speaking,[36] they either lie beyond the possibilities of the greater number of states, or they approximate to the so-called constitutional government, and therefore need no separate discussion. And in fact the conclusion at which ³⁵ we arrive respecting all these forms rests upon the same grounds. For if what was said in the *Ethics* [37] is true, that the happy life is the life according to virtue lived without impediment, and that virtue is a mean, then the life which is in a mean, and in a mean attainable by every one, must be the best. And the same principles of virtue ⁴⁰ and vice are characteristic of cities and of constitutions; for the con-^{1295ᵇ} stitution is in a figure the life of the city.

Now in all states there are three elements: one class is very rich, another very poor, and a third in a mean. It is admitted that moderation and the mean are best, and therefore it will clearly be best to ⁵ possess the gifts of fortune in moderation; for in that condition of life men are most ready to follow rational principle. But he who greatly excels in beauty, strength, birth, or wealth, or on the other hand who is very poor, or very weak, or very much disgraced, finds it difficult to follow rational principle.[38] Of these two the one sort grow ¹⁰ into violent and great criminals, the others into rogues and petty rascals. And two sorts of offences correspond to them, the one committed from violence, the other from roguery. Again, the middle class is least likely to shrink from rule, or to be over-ambitious for it; both of which are injuries to the state. Again, those who have too ¹⁵ much of the goods of fortune, strength, wealth, friends, and the like, are neither willing nor able to submit to authority. The evil begins at home; for when they are boys, by reason of the luxury in which they are brought up,[39] they never learn, even at school, the habit of obedience. On the other hand, the very poor, who are in the opposite extreme, are too degraded. So that the one class cannot obey, ²⁰ and can only rule despotically; the other knows not how to command

[36] 1293ᵇ 7–21, Cp. 1293ᵇ 36–1294ᵃ 25.
[37] *N. Eth.* i. 1098ᵃ 16. vii. 1153ᵇ 10, x. 1177ᵃ 12.
[38] Cp. Pl. *Rep.* iv. 421 ᴅ ff. [39] Cp. v. 1310ᵃ 22.

and must be ruled like slaves. Thus arises a city, not of freemen, but of masters and slaves, the one despising, the other envying; and nothing can be more fatal to friendship and good fellowship in states than this: for good fellowship springs from friendship; when men are at enmity with one another, they would rather not even share the same path. But a city ought to be composed, as far as possible, of 25 equals and similars; and these are generally the middle classes. Wherefore the city which is composed of middle-class citizens is necessarily best constituted in respect of the elements of which we say the fabric of the state naturally consists.[40] And this is the class of citizens which is most secure in a state, for they do not, like the poor, 30 covet their neighbours' goods; nor do others covet theirs, as the poor covet the goods of the rich; and as they neither plot against others, nor are themselves plotted against, they pass through life safely. Wisely then did Phocylides pray—'Many things are best in the mean; I desire to be of a middle condition in my city.'

Thus it is manifest that the best political community is formed by 35 citizens of the middle class, and that those states are likely to be well-administered, in which the middle class is large, and stronger if possible than both the other classes, or at any rate than either singly; for the addition of the middle class turns the scale, and prevents either of the extremes from being dominant. Great then is the good fortune 40 of a state in which the citizens have a moderate and sufficient prop- 1296ᵃ erty; for where some possess much, and the others nothing, there may arise an extreme democracy, or a pure oligarchy; or a tyranny may grow out of either extreme—either out of the most rampant democracy, or out of an oligarchy; but it is not so likely to arise out of the middle constitutions and those akin to them. I will explain the reason 5 of this hereafter, when I speak of the revolutions of states.[41] The mean condition of states is clearly best, for no other is free from faction; and where the middle class is large, there are least likely to be factions and dissensions. For a similar reason large states are less liable to faction than small ones, because in them the middle class is large; 10 whereas in small states it is easy to divide all the citizens into two classes who are either rich or poor, and to leave nothing in the middle. And democracies are safer[42] and more permanent than oligarchies, because they have a middle class which is more numerous and has a 15 greater share in the government; for when there is no middle class, and the poor greatly exceed in number, troubles arise, and the state

[40] Cp. ll. 1–3.　　　[41] v. 1308ᵃ 18–24.　　　[42] Cp. v. 1302ᵃ 8, 1307ᵃ 16.

soon comes to an end. A proof of the superiority of the middle class
is that the best legislators have been of a middle condition; for ex-
20 ample, Solon, as his own verses testify; and Lycurgus, for he was not
a king; and Charondas, and almost all legislators.

These considerations will help us to understand why most governments are either democratical or oligarchical. The reason is that the
middle class is seldom numerous in them, and whichever party,
25 whether the rich or the common people, transgresses the mean and pre-
dominates, draws the constitution its own way, and thus arises either
oligarchy or democracy. There is another reason—the poor and the
rich quarrel with one another, and whichever side gets the better,
30 instead of establishing a just or popular government, regards political
supremacy as the prize of victory, and the one party sets up a democracy and the other an oligarchy. Further, both the parties which
had the supremacy in Hellas looked only to the interest of their own
form of government, and established in states, the one, democracies,
35 and the other, oligarchies; they thought of their own advantage, of
the public not at all. For these reasons the middle form of government has rarely, if ever, existed, and among a very few only. One
man alone of all who ever ruled in Hellas was induced to give this
40 middle constitution to states. But it has now become a habit among
1296ᵇ the citizens of states, not even to care about equality; all men are
seeking for dominion, or, if conquered, are willing to submit.

What then is the best form of government, and what makes it
the best, is evident; and of other constitutions, since we say ⁴³ that
there are many kinds of democracy and many of oligarchy, it is not
5 difficult to see which has the first and which the second or any
other place in the order of excellence, now that we have determined
which is the best. For that which is nearest to the best must of
necessity be better, and that which is furthest from it worse, if we
are judging absolutely and not relatively to given conditions: I say
10 'relatively to given conditions', since a particular government may
be preferable, but another form may be better for some people.

12   We have now to consider what and what kind of government
is suitable to what and what kind of men. I may begin by assuming,
15 as a general principle common to all governments, that the portion of
the state which desires the permanence of the constitution ought to
be stronger than that which desires the reverse. Now every city is
composed of quality and quantity. By quality I mean freedom, wealth,

⁴³ 1289ᵃ 8, ᵇ13, 1291ᵇ 15–1292ᵇ 10, 1292ᵇ 22–1293ᵃ 10.

education, good birth, and by quantity, superiority of numbers. Qual- 20
ity may exist in one of the classes which make up the state, and
quantity in the other. For example, the meanly-born may be more
in number than the well-born, or the poor than the rich, yet they
may not so much exceed in quantity as they fall short in quality; and
therefore there must be a comparison of quantity and quality. Where 25
the number of the poor is more than proportioned to the wealth of
the rich, there will naturally be a democracy, varying in form with
the sort of people who compose it in each case. If, for example, the
husbandmen exceed in number, the first form of democracy will
then arise; if the artisans and labouring class, the last; and so with 30
the intermediate forms. But where the rich and the notables exceed
in quality more than they fall short in quantity, there oligarchy
arises, similarly assuming various forms according to the kind of
superiority possessed by the oligarchs.

The legislator should always include the middle class in his gov- 35
ernment; if he makes his laws oligarchical, to the middle class let him
look; if he makes them democratical, he should equally by his laws
try to attach this class to the state. There only can the government
ever be stable where the middle class exceeds one or both of the
others, and in that case there will be no fear that the rich will unite 40
with the poor against the rulers. For neither of them will ever be 1297ᵃ
willing to serve the other, and if they look for some form of government more suitable to both, they will find none better than this,
for the rich and the poor will never consent to rule in turn, because 5
they mistrust one another. The arbiter is always the one trusted,
and he who is in the middle is an arbiter. The more perfect the admixture of the political elements, the more lasting will be the constitution. Many even of those who desire to form aristocratical governments make a mistake, not only in giving too much power to the
rich, but in attempting to overreach the people. There comes a time 10
when out of a false good there arises a true evil, since the encroach-
ments of the rich are more destructive to the constitution than those
of the people.

13   The devices by which oligarchies deceive the people are five in
number; they relate to (1) the assembly; (2) the magistracies; (3) 15
the courts of law; (4) the use of arms; (5) gymnastic exercises. (1)
The assemblies are thrown open to all, but either the rich only are
fined for non-attendance, or a much larger fine is inflicted upon them.
(2) As to the magistracies, those who are qualified by property cannot decline office upon oath, but the poor may. (3) In the law-courts 20

the rich, and the rich only, are fined if they do not serve, the poor are let off with impunity, or, as in the laws of Charondas, a larger fine is inflicted on the rich, and a smaller one on the poor. In some states all citizens who have registered themselves are allowed to attend the assembly and to try causes; but if after registration they do not attend either in the assembly or at the courts, heavy fines are imposed upon them. The intention is that through fear of the fines they may avoid registering themselves, and then they cannot sit in the law-courts or in the assembly. Concerning (4) the possession of arms, and (5) gymnastic exercises, they legislate in a similar spirit. For the poor are not obliged to have arms, but the rich are fined for not having them; and in like manner no penalty is inflicted on the poor for non-attendance at the gymnasium, and consequently, having nothing to fear, they do not attend, whereas the rich are liable to a fine, and therefore they take care to attend.

These are the devices of oligarchical legislators, and in democracies they have counter devices. They pay the poor for attending the assemblies and the law-courts, and they inflict no penalty on the rich for non-attendance. It is obvious that he who would duly mix the two principles should combine the practice of both, and provide that the poor should be paid to attend, and the rich fined if they do not attend, for then all will take part; if there is no such combination, power will be in the hands of one party only. The government should be confined to those who carry arms. As to the property qualification, no absolute rule can be laid down, but we must see what is the highest qualification sufficiently comprehensive to secure that the number of those who have the rights of citizens exceeds the number of those excluded. Even if they have no share in office, the poor, provided only that they are not outraged or deprived of their property, will be quiet enough.

But to secure gentle treatment for the poor is not an easy thing, since a ruling class is not always humane. And in time of war the poor are apt to hesitate unless they are fed; when fed, they are willing enough to fight. In some states the government is vested, not only in those who are actually serving, but also in those who have served; among the Malians, for example, the governing body consisted of the latter, while the magistrates were chosen from those actually on service. And the earliest government which existed among the Hellenes, after the overthrow of the kingly power, grew up out of the warrior class, and was originally taken from the knights (for strength and superiority in war at that time depended on cavalry; [44]

[44] Cp. 1289ᵇ 36, vi. 1321ᵃ 8.

indeed, without discipline, infantry are useless, and in ancient times 20
there was no military knowledge or tactics, and therefore the strength
of armies lay in their cavalry). But when cities increased and the
heavy-armed grew in strength, more had a share in the government;
and this is the reason why the states which we call constitutional governments have been hitherto called democracies. Ancient constitu- 25
tions, as might be expected, were oligarchical and royal; their population being small they had no considerable middle class; the people
were weak in numbers and organization, and were therefore more
contented to be governed.

I have explained why there are various forms of government,
and why there are more than is generally supposed; for democracy,
as well as other constitutions, has more than one form: also what 30
their differences are, and whence they arise, and what is the best
form of government, speaking generally, and to whom the various
forms of government are best suited; all this has now been explained.

14   Having thus gained an appropriate basis of discussion we will 35
proceed to speak of the points which follow next in order. We will
consider the subject not only in general but with reference to particular constitutions. All constitutions have three elements, concerning which the good lawgiver has to regard what is expedient for each
constitution. When they are well-ordered, the constitution is well-
ordered, and as they differ from one another, constitutions differ. 40
There is (1) one element which deliberates about public affairs;
secondly (2) that concerned with the magistracies—the questions 1298ᵃ
being, what they should be, over what they should exercise authority,
and what should be the mode of electing to them; and thirdly (3)
that which has judicial power.

The deliberative element has authority in matters of war and
peace, in making and unmaking alliances; it passes laws, inflicts 5
death, exile, confiscation, elects magistrates and audits their accounts.
These powers must be assigned either all to all the citizens or all to
some of them (for example, to one or more magistracies, or different
causes to different magistracies), or some of them to all, and others of
them only to some. That all things should be decided by all is char- 10
acteristic of democracy; this is the sort of equality which the people
desire. But there are various ways in which all may share in the government; they may deliberate, not all in one body, but by turns, as
in the constitution of Telecles the Milesian. There are other constitutions in which the boards of magistrates meet and deliberate, but 15
come into office by turns, and are elected out of the tribes and the

very smallest divisions of the state, until every one has obtained office in his turn. The citizens, on the other hand, are assembled only for the purposes of legislation, and to consult about the constitution, and to hear the edicts of the magistrates. In another variety
20 of democracy the citizens form one assembly, but meet only to elect magistrates, to pass laws, to advise about war and peace, and to make scrutinies. Other matters are referred severally to special magistrates, who are elected by vote or by lot out of all the citizens. Or again,
25 the citizens meet about election to offices and about scrutinies, and deliberate concerning war or alliances while other matters are administered by the magistrates, who, as far as is possible,[45] are elected by vote. I am speaking of those magistracies in which special knowledge is required. A fourth form of democracy is when all the citizens
30 meet to deliberate about everything, and the magistrates decide nothing, but only make the preliminary inquiries; and that is the way in which the last and worst form of democracy, corresponding, as we maintain,[46] to the close family oligarchy and to tyranny, is at present administered. All these modes are democratical.

On the other hand, that some should deliberate about all is
35 oligarchical. This again is a mode which, like the democratical, has many forms. When the deliberative class being elected out of those who have a moderate qualification are numerous and they respect and obey the prohibitions of the law without altering it, and any one who has the required qualification shares in the government, then, just
40 because of this moderation, the oligarchy inclines towards polity. But when only selected individuals and not the whole people share
1298ᵇ in the deliberations of the state, then, although, as in the former case, they observe the law, the government is a pure oligarchy. Or, again, when those who have the power of deliberation are self-elected, and son succeeds father, and they and not the laws are
5 supreme—the government is of necessity oligarchical. Where, again, particular persons have authority in particular matters;—for example, when the whole people decide about peace and war and hold scrutinies, but the magistrates regulate everything else, and they are elected by vote—there the government is an aristocracy. And if some questions are decided by magistrates elected by vote, and others by magistrates elected by lot, either absolutely or out of select candidates,
10 or elected partly by vote, partly by lot—these practices are partly characteristic of an aristocratical government, and partly of a pure constitutional government.

---

[45] *sc.* in an advanced democracy. Cp. vi. 1317ᵇ 21.
[46] 1292ᵃ 17–21, ᵇ7–10, 1293ᵃ 32–34.

These are the various forms of the deliberative body; they correspond to the various forms of government. And the government of each state is administered according to one or other of the principles which have been laid down. Now it is for the interest of democracy, according to the most prevalent notion of it (I am speaking of that extreme form of democracy in which the people are supreme even over the laws), with a view to better deliberation to 15 adopt the custom of oligarchies respecting courts of law. For in oligarchies the rich who are wanted to be judges are compelled to attend under pain of a fine, whereas in democracies the poor are paid to attend. And this practice of oligarchies should be adopted by democracies in their public assemblies, for they will advise better if they all deliberate together—the people with the notables and the 20 notables with the people. It is also a good plan that those who deliberate should be elected by vote or by lot in equal numbers out of the different classes; and that if the people greatly exceed in number those who have political training, pay should not be given to all, but 25 only to as many as would balance the number of the notables, or that the number in excess should be eliminated by lot. But in oligarchies either certain persons should be co-opted from the mass, or a class of officers should be appointed such as exist in some states, who are termed probuli and guardians of the law; and the citizens should occupy themselves exclusively with matters on which these have previously deliberated; for so the people will have a share in the 30 deliberations of the state, but will not be able to disturb the principles of the constitution. Again, in oligarchies either the people ought to accept the measures of the government, or not to pass anything contrary to them; or, if all are allowed to share in counsel, the decision should rest with the magistrates. The opposite of what is done in constitutional governments should be the rule in oligarchies; the veto 35 of the majority should be final, their assent not final, but the proposal should be referred back to the magistrates. Whereas in constitutional governments they take the contrary course; the few have the negative, not the affirmative power; the affirmation of every- 40 thing rests with the multitude.
1299ª

These, then, are our conclusions respecting the deliberative, that is, the supreme element in states.

15 Next we will proceed to consider the distribution of offices; this too, being a part of politics concerning which many questions arise:— 5 What shall their number be? Over what shall they preside, and what

shall be their duration? Sometimes they last for six months, sometimes for less; sometimes they are annual, whilst in other cases offices
are held for still longer periods. Shall they be for life or for a long term
of years; or, if for a short term only, shall the same persons hold them
10 over and over again, or once only? Also about the appointment to them
—from whom are they to be chosen, by whom, and how? We should
first be in a position to say what are the possible varieties of them,
and then we may proceed to determine which are suited to different
forms of government. But what are to be included under the term
'offices'? That is a question not quite so easily answered. For a politi-
15 cal community requires many officers; and not every one who is
chosen by vote or by lot is to be regarded as a ruler. In the first place
there are the priests, who must be distinguished from political officers;
masters of choruses and heralds, even ambassadors, are elected by
20 vote. Some duties of superintendence again are political, extending either to all the citizens in a single sphere of action, like the
office of the general who superintends them when they are in the field,
or to a section of them only, like the inspectorships of women or of
youth. Other offices are concerned with household management, like
that of the corn measurers who exist in many states and are elected
officers. There are also menial offices which the rich have executed by
25 their slaves. Speaking generally, those are to be called offices to
which the duties are assigned of deliberating about certain measures
and of judging and commanding, especially the last; for to command is the especial duty of a magistrate. But the question is not of
any importance in practice; no one has ever brought into court the
30 meaning of the word, although such problems have a speculative
interest.

What kinds of offices, and how many, are necessary to the existence
of a state, and which, if not necessary, yet conduce to its well-being,
are much more important considerations, affecting all constitutions,
35 but more especially small states. For in great states it is possible,
and indeed necessary, that every office should have a special function;
where the citizens are numerous, many may hold office. And so it
happens that some offices a man holds a second time only after a long
interval, and others he holds once only; and certainly every work
1299ᵇ is better done which receives the sole, and not the divided attention
of the worker. But in small states it is necessary to combine many
offices in a few hands, since the small number of citizens does not
admit of many holding office:—for who will there be to succeed
5 them? And yet small states at times require the same offices and laws
as large ones; the difference is that the one want them often, the

others only after long intervals. Hence there is no reason why the care of many offices should not be imposed on the same person, for they will not interfere with each other. When the population is small, offices should be like the spits which also serve to hold a lamp.[47] 10 We must first ascertain how many magistrates are necessary in every state, and also how many are not exactly necessary, but are nevertheless useful, and then there will be no difficulty in seeing what offices can be combined in one. We should also know over which 15 matters several local tribunals are to have jurisdiction, and in which authority should be centralized: for example, should one person keep order in the market and another in some other place, or should the same person be responsible everywhere? Again, should offices be divided according to the subjects with which they deal, or according to the persons with whom they deal: I mean to say, should one person see to good order in general, or one look after the boys, another after the women, and so on? Further, under different con- 20 stitutions, should the magistrates be the same or different? For example, in democracy, oligarchy, aristocracy, monarchy, should there be the same magistrates, although they are elected, not out of equal or similar classes of citizens, but differently under different con- stitutions—in aristocracies, for example, they are chosen from the edu- cated, in oligarchies from the wealthy, and in democracies from the 25 free—or are there certain differences in the offices answering to them as well, and may the same be suitable to some, but different offices to others? For in some states it may be convenient that the same office should have a more extensive, in other states a narrower sphere. Special offices are peculiar to certain forms of government:—for 30 example that of probuli, which is not a democratic office, although a bule or council is. There must be some body of men whose duty is to prepare measures for the people in order that they may not be diverted from their business; when these are few in number, the state inclines to an oligarchy: or rather the probuli must always be few, and are 35 therefore an oligarchical element. But when both institutions exist in a state, the probuli are a check on the council; for the counsellor is a democratic element, but the probuli are oligarchical. Even the power of the council disappears when democracy has taken that ex- 1300[a] treme form in which the people themselves are always meeting and de- liberating about everything. This is the case when the members of the assembly receive abundant pay; for they have nothing to do and are always holding assemblies and deciding everything for themselves. A

[47] Cp. 1252[b] 2.

magistracy which controls the boys or the women, or any similar office,
5 is suited to an aristocracy rather than to a democracy; for how can
the magistrates prevent the wives of the poor from going out of doors?
Neither is it an oligarchical office; for the wives of the oligarchs are
too fine to be controlled.

.Enough of these matters. I will now inquire into appointments to
10 offices. The varieties depend on three terms, and the combinations
of these give all possible modes: first, who appoints? secondly,
from whom? and thirdly, how? Each of these three admits of three
15 varieties: (A) All the citizens, or (B) only some, appoint. Either (1)
the magistrates are chosen out of all or (2) out of some who are
distinguished either by a property qualification, or by birth, or merit,
or for some special reason, as at Megara only those were eligible who
had returned from exile and fought together against the democracy.
They may be appointed either (a) by vote or (b) by lot. Again, these
20 several varieties may be coupled, I mean that (C) some officers may
be elected by some, others by all, and (3) some again out of some,
and others out of all, and (c) some by vote and others by lot. Each
variety of these terms admits of four modes.

For either (A 1 a) all may appoint from all by vote, or (A 1 b)
all from all by lot, or (A 2 a) all from some by vote, or (A 2 b)
25 all from some by lot (and if from all, either by sections, as, for
example, by tribes, and wards, and phratries, until all the citizens
have been gone through; or the citizens may be in all cases eligible
indiscriminately); or again (A 1 c, A 2 c) to some offices in the one
way, to some in the other. Again, if it is only some that appoint,
they may do so either (B 1 a) from all by vote, or (B 1 b) from all
by lot, or (B 2 a) from some by vote, or (B 2 b) from some by lot,
or to some offices in the one way, to others in the other, i. e.
(B 1 c) from all, to some offices by vote, to some by lot, and
30 (B 2 c) from some, to some offices by vote, to some by lot. Thus
the modes that arise, apart from two (C, 3) out of the three couplings,
number twelve. Of these systems two are popular, that all should
appoint from all (A 1 a) by vote or (A 1 b) by lot—or (A 1 c)
35 by both. That all should not appoint at once, but should appoint from
all or from some either by lot or by vote or by both, or appoint to
some offices from all and to others from some ('by both' meaning to
some offices by lot, to others by vote), is characteristic of a polity.
And (B 1 c) that some should appoint from all, to some offices
by vote, to others by lot, is also characteristic of a polity, but more
40 oligarchical than the former method. And (A 3 a, b, c, B 3 a, b, c)
to appoint from both, to some offices from all, to others from some,

is characteristic of a polity with a leaning towards aristocracy. That (B 2) some should appoint from some is oligarchical—even (B 2 b) 1300^b that some should appoint from some by lot (and if this does not actually occur, it is none the less oligarchical in character), or (B 2 c) that some should appoint from some by both. (B 1 a) that some should appoint from all, and (A 2 a) that all should appoint from some, by vote, is aristocratic.

These are the different modes of constituting magistrates, and 5 these correspond to different forms of government:—which are proper to which, or how they ought to be established, will be evident when we determine the nature of their powers. [48] By powers I mean such powers as a magistrate exercises over the revenue or in defence of 10 the country; for there are various kinds of power: the power of the general, for example, is not the same with that which regulates contracts in the market.

16 Of the three parts of government, the judicial remains to be considered, and this we shall divide on the same principle. There are three points on which the varieties of law-courts depend: The 15 persons from whom they are appointed, the matters with which they are concerned, and the manner of their appointment. I mean, (1) are the judges taken from all, or from some only? (2) how many kinds of law-courts are there? (3) are the judges chosen by vote or by lot?

First, let me determine how many kinds of law-courts there are. There are eight in number: One is the court of audits or scrutinies; 20 a second takes cognizance of ordinary offences against the state; a third is concerned with treason against the constitution; the fourth determines disputes respecting penalties, whether raised by magistrates or by private persons; the fifth decides the more important civil cases; the sixth tries cases of homicide, which are of various 25 kinds, (a) premeditated, (b) involuntary, (c) cases in which the guilt is confessed but the justice is disputed; and there may be a fourth court (d) in which murderers who have fled from justice are tried after their return; such as the Court of Phreatto is said to be at Athens. But cases of this sort rarely happen at all even in large cities. 30 The different kinds of homicide may be tried either by the same or by different courts. (7) There are courts for strangers:—of these there are two subdivisions, (a) for the settlement of their disputes with one another, (b) for the settlement of disputes between them and the citizens. And besides all these there must be (8) courts for small suits about sums of a drachma up to five drachmas, or a little

[48] The promise is not fulfilled in the *Politics*.

more, which have to be determined, but they do not require many judges.

35 Nothing more need be said of these small suits, nor of the courts for homicide and for strangers:—I would rather speak of political cases, which, when mismanaged, create division and disturbances in constitutions.

Now if all the citizens judge, in all the different cases which I have
40 distinguished, they may be appointed by vote or by lot, or sometimes by lot and sometimes by vote. Or when a single class of causes are tried, the judges who decide them may be appointed, some by vote,
1301ª and some by lot. These then are the four modes of appointing judges from the whole people, and there will be likewise four modes, if they are elected from a part only; for they may be appointed from some by vote and judge in all causes; or they may be appointed from some by lot and judge in all causes; or they may be elected in some cases by vote, and in some cases taken by lot, or some courts, even when judging the same causes, may be composed of members some
5 appointed by vote and some by lot. These modes, then, as was said, answer to those previously mentioned.

Once more, the modes of appointment may be combined; I mean, that some may be chosen out of the whole people, others out of some, some out of both; for example, the same tribunal may be composed of some who were elected out of all, and of others who were elected out of some, either by vote or by lot or by both.

10 In how many forms law-courts can be established has now been considered. The first form, viz. that in which the judges are taken from all the citizens, and in which all causes are tried, is democratical; the second, which is composed of a few only who try all causes, oligarchical; the third, in which some courts are taken from
15 all classes, and some from certain classes only, aristocratical and constitutional.

BOOK V

1 The design which we proposed to ourselves is now nearly com-
20 pleted.[1] Next in order follow the causes of revolution in states, how many, and of what nature they are; what modes of destruction apply to particular states, and out of what, and into what they mostly change; also what are the modes of preservation in states generally, or in a particular state, and by what means each state may be best preserved: these questions remain to be considered.

[1] Cp. iv. c. 2.

In the first place we must assume as our starting-point that in 25
the many forms of government which have sprung up there has always been an acknowledgement of justice and proportionate equality,
although mankind fail in attaining them, as indeed I have already
explained.[2] Democracy, for example, arises out of the notion that those
who are equal in any respect are equal in all respects; because men are
equally free, they claim to be absolutely equal. Oligarchy is based on 30
the notion that those who are unequal in one respect are in all respects
unequal; being unequal, that is, in property, they suppose themselves
to be unequal absolutely. The democrats think that as they are equal
they ought to be equal in all things; while the oligarchs, under the idea
that they are unequal, claim too much, which is one form of inequality. All these forms of government have a kind of justice, but, 35
tried by an absolute standard, they are faulty; and, therefore, both
parties, whenever their share in the government does not accord with
their preconceived ideas, stir up revolution. Those who excel in
virtue have the best right of all to rebel (for they alone can with 40
reason be deemed absolutely unequal),[3] but then they are of all 1301ᵇ
men the least inclined to do so.[4] There is also a superiority which
is claimed by men of rank; for they are thought noble because they
spring from wealthy and virtuous ancestors.[5] Here then, so to speak,
are opened the very springs and fountains of revolution; and hence 5
arise two sorts of changes in governments; the one affecting the constitution, when men seek to change from an existing form into some
other, for example, from democracy into oligarchy, and from oligarchy
into democracy, or from either of them into constitutional government or aristocracy, and conversely; the other not affecting the con- 10
stitution, when, without disturbing the form of government, whether
oligarchy, or monarchy, or any other, they try to get the administration into their own hands.[6] Further, there is a question of degree; an
oligarchy, for example, may become more or less oligarchical, and a
democracy more or less democratical; and in like manner the charac- 15
teristics of the other forms of government may be more or less strictly
maintained. Or the revolution may be directed against a portion of
the constitution only, e. g. the establishment or overthrow of a particular office: as at Sparta it is said that Lysander attempted to overthrow the monarchy, and king Pausanias,[7] the ephoralty. At Epi- 20
damnus, too, the change was partial. For instead of phylarchs or

[2] iii. 1282ᵇ 18–30, Cp. 1280ᵃ 9 sqq.　　　[3] Cp. iii. 1284ᵇ 28–34.

[4] Cp. 1304ᵇ 4.　　　[5] Cp. iv. 1294ᵃ 21.

[6] Cp. iv. 1292ᵇ 11.　　　[7] Cp. vii. 1333ᵇ 34.

heads of tribes, a council was appointed; but to this day the magistrates are the only members of the ruling class who are compelled to
25 go to the Heliaea when an election takes places, and the office of the
single archon [8] was another oligarchical feature. Everywhere inequality is a cause of revolution, but an inequality in which there is
no proportion—for instance, a perpetual monarchy among equals;
and always it is the desire of equality which rises in rebellion.

Now equality is of two kinds, numerical and proportional; by the
30 first I mean sameness or equality in number or size; by the second,
equality of ratios. For example, the excess of three over two is numerically equal to the excess of two over one; whereas four exceeds
two in the same ratio in which two exceeds one, for two is the same
35 part of four that one is of two, namely, the half. As I was saying before,[9] men agree that justice in the abstract is proportion, but they
differ in that some think that if they are equal in any respect they are
equal absolutely, others that if they are unequal in any respect they
should be unequal in all. Hence there are two principal forms of
40 government, democracy and oligarchy; for good birth and virtue
1302ª are rare, but wealth and numbers are more common. In what city shall
we find a hundred persons of good birth and of virtue? whereas the
rich everywhere abound. That a state should be ordered, simply and
wholly, according to either kind of equality, is not a good thing;
5 the proof is the fact that such forms of government never last. They
are originally based on a mistake, and, as they begin badly, cannot
fail to end badly. The inference is that both kinds of equality should
be employed; numerical in some cases, and proportionate in others.

Still democracy appears to be safer and less liable to revolution
10 than oligarchy.[10] For in oligarchies [11] there is the double danger of the
oligarchs falling out among themselves and also with the people; but
in democracies [12] there is only the danger of a quarrel with the
oligarchs. No dissension worth mentioning arises among the people
themselves. And we may further remark that a government which is
composed of the middle class more nearly approximates to democracy
15 than to oligarchy, and is the safest of the imperfect forms of government.

2　In considering how dissensions and political revolutions arise, we
must first of all ascertain the beginnings and causes of them which
affect constitutions generally. They may be said to be three in num-

---

8 Cp. iii. 1287ª 7.　　　　　9 ª26.　　　　　10 Cp. iv. 1296ª 13.
11 Cp. c. 6.　　　　　　　　　　　　　　　　　12 Cp. c. 5.

ber; and we have now to give an outline of each. We want to know 20
(1) what is the feeling? (2) what are the motives of those who
make them? (3) whence arise political disturbances and quarrels?
The universal and chief cause of this revolutionary feeling has been
already mentioned; [13] viz. the desire of equality, when men think 25
that they are equal to others who have more than themselves; or,
again, the desire of inequality and superiority, when conceiving themselves to be superior they think that they have not more but the same
or less than their inferiors; pretensions which may and may not be
just. Inferiors revolt in order that they may be equal, and equals 30
that they may be superior. Such is the state of mind which creates
revolutions. The motives for making them are the desire of gain
and honour, or the fear of dishonour and loss; the authors of
them want to divert punishment or dishonour from themselves or
their friends. The causes and reasons of revolutions, whereby men 35
are themselves affected in the way described, and about the things
which I have mentioned, viewed in one way may be regarded as
seven, and in another as more than seven. Two of them have been
already noticed; [14] but they act in a different manner, for men are
excited against one another by the love of gain and honour—not,
as in the case which I have just supposed, in order to obtain them 40
for themselves, but at seeing others, justly or unjustly, engrossing 1302ᵇ
them. Other causes are insolence, fear, excessive predominance, contempt, disproportionate increase in some part of the state; causes of
another sort are election intrigues, carelessness, neglect about trifles,
dissimilarity of elements.

3 ·   What share insolence and avarice have in creating revolutions, 5
and how they work, is plain enough. When the magistrates are insolent and grasping they conspire against one another and also against
the constitution from which they derive their power, making their
gains either at the expense of individuals or of the public. It is evi- 10
dent, again, what an influence honour exerts and how it is a cause
of revolution. Men who are themselves dishonoured and who see
others obtaining honours rise in rebellion; the honour or dishonour
when undeserved is unjust; and just when awarded according to
merit. Again, superiority is a cause of revolution when one or more 15
persons have a power which is too much for the state and the power
of the government; this is a condition of affairs out of which there
arises a monarchy, or a family oligarchy. And therefore, in some

[13] 1301ᵃ 33 sqq., ᵇ35 sqq.   [14] l. 32.

places, as at Athens and Argos, they have recourse to ostracism.[15]
But how much better to provide from the first that there should be
20 no such pre-eminent individuals instead of letting them come into
existence and then finding a remedy.

Another cause of revolution is fear. Either men have committed
wrong, and are afraid of punishment, or they are expecting to
suffer wrong and are desirous of anticipating their enemy. Thus at
Rhodes the notables conspired against the people through fear of
25 the suits that were brought against them.[16] Contempt is also a
cause of insurrection and revolution; for example, in oligarchies—
when those who have no share in the state are the majority, they
revolt, because they think that they are the stronger. Or, again, in
democracies, the rich despise the disorder and anarchy of the state;
at Thebes, for example, where, after the battle of Oenophyta, the
30 bad administration of the democracy led to its ruin. At Megara the
fall of the democracy was due to a defeat occasioned by disorder and
anarchy. And at Syracuse the democracy aroused contempt before the
tyranny of Gelo arose; at Rhodes, before the insurrection.

Political revolutions also spring from a disproportionate increase
35 in any part of the state. For as a body is made up of many members,
and every member ought to grow in proportion,[17] that symmetry
may be preserved; but loses its nature if the foot be four cubits long
and the rest of the body two spans; and, should the abnormal
increase be one of quality as well as of quantity, may even take the
40 form of another animal: even so a state has many parts, of which
1303ᵃ some one may often grow imperceptibly; for example, the number of
poor in democracies and in constitutional states. And this disproportion may sometimes happen by an accident, as at Tarentum, from
a defeat in which many of the notables were slain in a battle with the
5 Iapygians just after the Persian War, the constitutional government
in consequence becoming a democracy; or as was the case at Argos,
where the Argives, after their army had been cut to pieces on the
seventh day of the month by Cleomenes the Lacedaemonian, were
compelled to admit to citizenship some of their perioeci; and at
Athens, when, after frequent defeats of their infantry at the time of
the Peloponnesian War, the notables were reduced in number, be-
10 cause the soldiers had to be taken from the roll of citizens. Revolutions arise from this cause as well, in democracies as in other forms of
government, but not to so great an extent. When the rich grow numerous or properties increase, the form of government changes into an

---

[15] Cp. iii. 1284ᵃ 17.   [16] Cp. 1304ᵇ 27.   [17] Cp. iii. 1284ᵇ 8.

oligarchy or a government of families. Forms of government also change—sometimes even without revolution, owing to election contests, as at Heraea (where, instead of electing their magistrates, 15 they took them by lot, because the electors were in the habit of choosing their own partisans); or owing to carelessness, when disloyal persons are allowed to find their way into the highest offices, as at Oreum, where, upon the accession of Heracleodorus to office, the oligarchy was overthrown, and changed by him into a constitutional and democratical government.

Again, the revolution may be facilitated by the slightness of 20 the change; I mean that a great change may sometimes slip into the constitution through neglect of a small matter; at Ambracia, for instance, the qualification for office, small at first, was eventually reduced to nothing. For the Ambraciots thought that a small qualification was much the same as none at all.

Another cause of revolution is difference of races which do not at 25 once acquire a common spirit; for a state is not the growth of a day, any more than it grows out of a multitude brought together by accident. Hence the reception of strangers in colonies, either at the time of their foundation or afterwards, has generally produced revolution; for example, the Achaeans who joined the Troezenians in the foundation of Sybaris, becoming later the more numerous, 30 expelled them; hence the curse fell upon Sybaris. At Thurii the Sybarites quarrelled with their fellow-colonists; thinking that the land belonged to them, they wanted too much of it and were driven out. At Byzantium the new colonists were detected in a conspiracy, and were expelled by force of arms; the people of Antissa, who had received the Chian exiles, fought with them, and drove them out; and the 35 Zancleans, after having received the Samians, were driven by them out of their own city. The citizens of Apollonia on the Euxine, after the introduction of a fresh body of colonists, had a revolution; the Syracusans, after the expulsion of their tyrants, having admitted 1303ᵇ strangers and mercenaries to the rights of citizenship, quarrelled and came to blows; the people of Amphipolis, having received Chalcidian colonists, were nearly all expelled by them.

Now, in oligarchies the masses make revolution under the idea that 5 they are unjustly treated, because, as I said before,[18] they are equals, and have not an equal share, and in democracies the notables revolt, because they are not equals, and yet have only an equal share.

Again, the situation of cities is a cause of revolution when the coun-

[18] 1301ᵃ 33.

try is not naturally adapted to preserve the unity of the state. For example, the Chytians at Clazomenae did not agree with the people 10 of the island; and the people of Colophon quarrelled with the Notians; at Athens too, the inhabitants of the Piraeus are more democratic than those who live in the city. For just as in war the impediment of a ditch, though ever so small, may break a regiment, so every cause 15 of difference, however slight, makes a breach in a city. The greatest opposition is confessedly that of virtue and vice; next comes that of wealth and poverty; and there are other antagonistic elements, greater or less, of which one is this difference of place.

4   In revolutions the occasions may be trifling, but great interests are at stake. Even trifles are most important when they concern the 20 rulers, as was the case of old at Syracuse; for the Syracusan constitution was once changed by a love-quarrel of two young men, who were in the government. The story is that while one of them was away from home his beloved was gained over by his companion, and he to revenge himself seduced the other's wife. They then drew the mem- 25 bers of the ruling class into their quarrel and so split all the people into portions. We learn from this story that we should be on our guard against the beginnings of such evils, and should put an end to the quarrels of chiefs and mighty men. The mistake lies in the beginning 30 —as the proverb says—'Well begun is half done'; so an error at the beginning, though quite small, bears the same ratio to the errors in the other parts. In general, when the notables quarrel, the whole city is involved, as happened in Hestiaea after the Persian War. The occasion was the division of an inheritance; one of two brothers 35 refused to give an account of their father's property and the treasure which he had found: so the poorer of the two quarrelled with him and enlisted in his cause the popular party, the other, who was very rich, the wealthy classes.

   At Delphi, again, a quarrel about a marriage was the beginning 1304ᵃ of all the troubles which followed. In this case the bridegroom, fancying some occurrence to be of evil omen, came to the bride, and went away without taking her. Whereupon her relations, thinking that they were insulted by him, put some of the sacred treasure among his offerings while he was sacrificing, and then slew him, pretending that he had been robbing the temple. At Mytilene, too, a dispute about 5 heiresses was the beginning of many misfortunes, and led to the war with the Athenians in which Paches took their city. A wealthy citizen, named Timophanes, left two daughters; Dexander, another citizen, wanted to obtain them for his sons; but he was rejected in his suit, whereupon he stirred up a revolution, and instigated the Athenians (of whom he was proxenus) to interfere. A similar quarrel about an heiress arose at Phocis between Mnaseas the father of Mnason, and Euthycrates the father of Onomarchus; this was the beginning of the Sacred War. A marriage-quarrel was also the cause of a change in the government of Epidamnus. A certain man betrothed his daughter to a person whose father, having been made a magistrate, fined the father of the girl, and the latter, stung by the insult, conspired with the unenfranchised classes to overthrow the state.

Governments also change into oligarchy or into democracy or into a constitutional government because the magistrates, or some other section of the state, increase in power or renown. Thus at Athens the reputation gained by the court of the Areopagus, in the Persian War, seemed to tighten the reins of government. On the other hand, the victory of Salamis,[19] which was gained by the common people who served in the fleet, and won for the Athenians the empire due to command of the sea, strengthened the democracy. At Argos, the notables, having distinguished themselves against the Lacedaemonians in the battle of Mantinea, attempted to put down the democracy. At Syracuse, the people, having been the chief authors of the victory in the war with the Athenians, changed the constitutional government into democracy. At Chalcis, the people, uniting with the notables, killed Phoxus the tyrant, and then seized the government. At Ambracia,[20] the people, in like manner, having joined with the conspirators in expelling the tyrant Periander, transferred the government to themselves. And generally, it should be remembered that those who have secured power to the state, whether private citizens, or magistrates, or tribes, or any other part or section of the state, are apt to cause revolutions. For either envy of their greatness draws others into rebellion, or they themselves, in their pride of superiority, are unwilling to remain on a level with others.

Revolutions also break out when opposite parties, e. g. the rich and the people, are equally balanced, and there is little or no middle class; for, if either party were manifestly superior, the other would not risk an attack upon them. And, for this reason, those who are eminent in virtue usually do not stir up insurrections, always a minority. Such are the beginnings and causes of the disturbances and revolutions to which every form of government is liable.

Revolutions are effected in two ways, by force and by fraud. Force may be applied either at the time of making the revolution or afterwards. Fraud, again, is of two kinds; for (1) sometimes the citizens

---

[19] Cp. ii. 1274ᵃ 12; viii. 1341ᵃ 29.   [20] Cp. 1311ᵃ 39.

are deceived into acquiescing in a change of government, and afterwards they are held in subjection against their will. This was what
happened in the case of the Four Hundred, who deceived the people
by telling them that the king would provide money for the war against
the Lacedaemonians, and, having cheated the people, still en-
15 deavoured to retain the government. (2) In other cases the people are
persuaded at first, and afterwards, by a repetition of the persuasion,
their goodwill and allegiance are retained. The revolutions which effect
constitutions generally spring from the above-mentioned causes.[21]

5 And now, taking each constitution separately, we must see what
follows from the principles already laid down.
20   Revolutions in democracies are generally caused by the intemperance of demagogues, who either in their private capacity lay information against rich men until they compel them to combine (for a common danger unites even the bitterest enemies), or coming forward in
public stir up the people against them. The truth of this remark is
25 proved by a variety of examples. At Cos the democracy was overthrown because wicked demagogues arose, and the notables combined. At Rhodes the demagogues not only provided pay for the multitude, but prevented them from making good to the trierarchs the sums
which had been expended by them; and they, in consequence of the
30 suits which were brought against them, were compelled to combine
and put down the democracy.[22] The democracy at Heraclea was overthrown shortly after the foundation of the colony by the injustice of
the demagogues, which drove out the notables, who came back in a
body and put an end to the democracy. Much in the same manner the
35 democracy at Megara [23] was overturned; there the demagogues drove
out many of the notables in order that they might be able to confiscate their property. At length the exiles, becoming numerous,
returned, and, engaging and defeating the people, established the
1305ᵃ oligarchy. The same thing happened with the democracy of Cyme,
which was overthrown by Thrasymachus. And we may observe that in
most states the changes have been of this character. For sometimes the
demagogues, in order to curry favour with the people, wrong the
notables and so force them to combine;—either they make a division of their property, or diminish their incomes by the imposition
5 of public services, and sometimes they bring accusations against the
rich that they may have their wealth to confiscate.[24]
    Of old, the demagogue was also a general, and then democracies

---

[21] Cp. 1302ᵃ 17.   [22] Cp. 1302ᵇ 23.
[23] Cp. 1302ᵇ 31, iv. 1300ᵃ 17.   [24] Cp. 1309ᵃ 14.

changed into tyrannies. Most of the ancient tyrants were originally 10
demagogues.[25] They are not so now, but they were then; and the reason
is that they were generals and not orators, for oratory had not yet
come into fashion. Whereas in our day, when the art of rhetoric has
made such progress, the orators lead the people, but their ignorance of military matters prevents them from usurping power; at any
rate instances to the contrary are few and slight. Tyrannies were 15
more common formerly than now, for this reason also, that great
power was placed in the hands of individuals; thus a tyranny arose
at Miletus out of the office of the Prytanis, who had supreme
authority in many important matters.[26] Moreover, in those days,
when cities were not large, the people dwelt in the fields, busy at their
work; and their chiefs, if they possessed any military talent, seized 20
the opportunity, and winning the confidence of the masses by professing their hatred of the wealthy, they succeeded in obtaining the
tyranny. Thus at Athens Peisistratus led a faction against the men of
the plain, and Theagenes at Megara slaughtered the cattle of the
wealthy, which he found by the river side, where they had put them to 25
graze in land not their own. Dionysius, again, was thought worthy of
the tyranny because he denounced Daphnaeus and the rich; his
enmity to the notables won for him the confidence of the people.
Changes also take place from the ancient to the latest form of democracy; for where there is a popular election of the magistrates and no 30
property qualification, the aspirants for office get hold of the people,
and contrive at last even to set them above the laws. A more or less
complete cure for this state of things is for the separate tribes, and
not the whole people, to elect the magistrates.

These are the principal causes of revolutions in democracies. 35

6　There are two patent causes of revolutions in oligarchies: (1)
First, when the oligarchs oppress the people, for then anybody is
good enough to be their champion, especially if he be himself a member of the oligarchy, as Lygdamis at Naxos, who afterwards came to be 40
tyrant. But revolutions which commence outside the governing class 1305ᵇ
may be further subdivided. Sometimes, when the government is very
exclusive, the revolution is brought about by persons of the wealthy
class who are excluded, as happened at Massalia and Istros and Her-　5
aclea, and other cities. Those who had no share in the government
created a disturbance, until first the elder brothers, and then the
younger, were admitted; for in some places father and son, in others

---

[25] Cp. 1310ᵇ 14; Plato, *Rep*. viii. 565 ᴅ.　　　　[26] Cp. 1310ᵇ 20.

10 elder and younger brothers, do not hold office together. At Massalia the oligarchy became more like a constitutional government, but at Istros ended in a democracy, and at Heraclea was enlarged to 600. At Cnidos, again, the oligarchy underwent a considerable change. For the notables fell out among themselves, because only a few shared in the government; there existed among them the rule already mentioned, that
15 father and son could not hold office together, and, if there were several brothers, only the eldest was admitted. The people took advantage of the quarrel, and choosing one of the notables to be their leader, attacked and conquered the oligarchs, who were divided, and division is always a source of weakness. The city of Erythrae, too, in old times
20 was ruled, and ruled well, by the Basilidae, but the people took offence at the narrowness of the oligarchy and changed the constitution.

(2) Of internal causes of revolutions in oligarchies one is the personal rivalry of the oligarchs, which leads them to play the demagogue. Now, the oligarchical demagogue is of two sorts: either (a) he practises upon the oligarchs themselves (for, although the oligarchy are
25 quite a small number, there may be a demagogue among them, as at Athens Charicles' party won power by courting the Thirty, that of Phrynichus by courting the Four Hundred); or (b) the oligarchs may play the demagogue with the people. This was the case at Larissa, where the guardians of the citizens endeavoured to gain over the
30 people because they were elected by them; and such is the fate of all oligarchies in which the magistrates are elected, as at Abydos, not by the class to which they belong, but by the heavy-armed or by the people, although they may be required to have a high qualification, or to be members of a political club; or, again, where the law-courts are composed of persons outside the government, the oligarchs flatter
35 the people in order to obtain a decision in their own favour, and so they change the constitution; this happened at Heraclea in Pontus. Again, oligarchies change whenever any attempt is made to narrow them; for then those who desire equal rights are compelled to call in the people. Changes in the oligarchy also occur when the
40 oligarchs waste their private property by extravagant living; for then
1306ᵃ they want to innovate, and either try to make themselves tyrants, or install some one else in the tyranny, as Hipparinus did Dionysius at Syracuse, and as at Amphipolis ²⁷ a man named Cleotimus introduced Chalcidian colonists, and when they arrived, stirred them up against the rich. For a like reason in Aegina the person who carried on the
5 negotiation with Chares endeavoured to revolutionize the state. Some-

---

²⁷ Cp. 1303ᵇ 2.

times a party among the oligarchs try directly to create a political change; sometimes they rob the treasury, and then either the thieves or, as happened at Apollonia in Pontus, those who resist them in their thieving quarrel with the rulers. But an oligarchy which is at unity with itself is not easily destroyed from within; of this we may 10 see an example at Pharsalus, for there, although the rulers are few in number, they govern a large city, because they have a good understanding among themselves.

Oligarchies, again, are overthrown when another oligarchy is created within the original one, that is to say, when the whole governing body is small and yet they do not all share in the highest 15 offices. Thus at Elis the governing body was a small senate; and very few ever found their way into it, because the senators were only ninety in number, and were elected for life and out of certain families in a manner similar to the Lacedaemonian elders. Oligarchy is liable 20 to revolutions alike in war and in peace; in war because, not being able to trust the people, the oligarchs are compelled to hire mercenaries, and the general who is in command of them often ends in becoming a tyrant, as Timophanes did at Corinth; or if there are more generals than one they make themselves into a company of tyrants. 25 Sometimes the oligarchs, fearing this danger, give the people a share in the government because their services are necessary to them. And in time of peace, from mutual distrust, the two parties hand over the defence of the state to the army and to an arbiter between the two factions, who often ends the master of both. This happened at Larissa when Simos the Aleuad had the government, and at Abydos in the 30 days of Iphiades and the political clubs. Revolutions also arise out of marriages or lawsuits which lead to the overthrow of one party among the oligarchs by another. Of quarrels about marriages I have already mentioned [28] some instances; another occurred at Eretria, where 35 Diagoras overturned the oligarchy of the knights because he had been wronged about a marriage. A revolution at Heraclea, and another at Thebes, both arose out of decisions of law-courts upon a charge of adultery; in both cases the punishment was just, but executed in the spirit of party, at Heraclea upon Eurytion, and at Thebes upon 1306b Archias; for their enemies were jealous of them and so had them pilloried in the agora. Many oligarchies have been destroyed by some members of the ruling class taking offence at their excessive despot- 5 ism; for example, the oligarchy at Cnidus and at Chios.

Changes of constitutional governments, and also of oligarchies which limit the office of counsellor, judge, or other magistrate to per-

[28] 1303b 37–1304a 17.

sons having a certain money qualification, often occur by accident.
The qualification may have been originally fixed according to the
10 circumstances of the time, in such a manner as to include in an oligarchy a few only, or in a constitutional government the middle class.
But after a time of prosperity, whether arising from peace or some
other good fortune, the same property becomes many times as
valuable, and then everybody participates in every office; this hap-
15 pens sometimes gradually and insensibly, and sometimes quickly.
These are the causes of changes and revolutions in oligarchies.

We must remark generally, both of democracies and oligarchies,
that they sometimes change, not into the opposite forms of government, but only into another variety of the same class; I mean to
20 say, from those forms of democracy and oligarchy which are regulated by law into those which are arbitrary, and conversely.

7 In aristocracies revolutions are stirred up when a few only share
in the honours of the state; a cause which has been already shown [29]
25 to affect oligarchies; for an aristocracy is a sort of oligarchy, and, like
an oligarchy, is the government of a few, although few not for the
same reason; hence the two are often confounded. And revolutions
will be most likely to happen, and must happen, when the mass of the
people are of the high-spirited kind, and have a notion that they
are as good as their rulers. Thus at Lacedaemon the so-called
30 Partheniae, who were the sons [30] of the Spartan peers, attempted a
revolution, and, being detected, were sent away to colonize Tarentum.
Again, revolutions occur when great men who are at least of equal
merit are dishonoured by those higher in office, as Lysander was by
the kings of Sparta; or, when a brave man is excluded from the
35 honours of the state, like Cinadon, who conspired against the Spartans in the reign of Agesilaus; or, again, when some are very poor and
others very rich, a state of society which is most often the result of
war, as at Lacedaemon in the days of the Messenian War; this is
1307ª proved from the poem of Tyrtaeus, entitled 'Good Order'; for he
speaks of certain citizens who were ruined by the war and wanted to
have a redistribution of the land. Again, revolutions arise when an
individual who is great, and might be greater, wants to rule alone,
as, at Lacedaemon, Pausanias, who was general in the Persian War, or
like Hanno at Carthage.
5 Constitutional governments and aristocracies are commonly overthrown owing to some deviation from justice in the constitution itself;
the cause of the downfall is, in the former, the ill-mingling of the two

---

[29] 1305ᵇ 2 sqq.   [30] i. e. the illegitimate sons.

elements democracy and oligarchy; in the latter, of the three elements, democracy, oligarchy, and virtue, but especially democracy 10
and oligarchy. For to combine these is the endeavour of constitutional
governments; and most of the so-called aristocracies have a like aim,[31]
but differ from polities in the mode of combination; hence some of
them are more and some less permanent. Those which incline more to 15
oligarchy are called aristocracies, and those which incline to democracy constitutional governments. And therefore the latter are the
safer of the two; for the greater the number, the greater the strength,
and when men are equal they are contented. But the rich, if the constitution gives them power, are apt to be insolent and avaricious; and, 20
in general, whichever way the constitution inclines, in that direction
it changes as either party gains strength, a constitutional government
becoming a democracy, an aristocracy an oligarchy. But the process
may be reversed, and aristocracy may change into democracy. This
happens when the poor, under the idea that they are being wronged,
force the constitution to take an opposite form. In like manner constitutional governments change into oligarchies. The only stable prin- 25
ciple of government is equality according to proportion, and for every
man to enjoy his own.

What I have just mentioned actually happened at Thurii,[32] where
the qualification for office, at first high, was therefore reduced, and the
magistrates increased in number. The notables had previously acquired the whole of the land contrary to law; for the government 30
tended to oligarchy, and they were able to encroach. . . . But the people, who had been trained by war, soon got the better of the guards
kept by the oligarchs, until those who had too much gave up their land.

Again, since all aristocratical governments incline to oligarchy, the
notables are apt to be grasping; thus at Lacedaemon, where property 35
tends to pass into few hands,[33] the notables can do too much as they
like, and are allowed to marry whom they please. The city of Locri
was ruined by a marriage connexion with Dionysius, but such a thing
could never have happened in a democracy, or in a well-balanced
aristocracy.

I have already remarked that in all states revolutions are occa- 40
sioned by trifles.[34] In aristocracies, above all, they are of a gradual 1307ᵇ
and imperceptible nature. The citizens begin by giving up some part
of the constitution, and so with greater ease the government change
something else which is a little more important, until they have under- 5
mined the whole fabric of the state. At Thurii there was a law that

[31] Cp. iv. c. 7.   [32] Cp. 1303ᵃ 31.
[33] Cp. ii. 1270ᵃ 18.   [34] 1302ᵇ 4, 1303ᵃ 20–25, ᵇ17.

generals should only be re-elected after an interval of five years, and
some young men who were popular with the soldiers of the guard for
their military prowess, despising the magistrates and thinking that
10 they would easily gain their purpose, wanted to abolish this law and
allow their generals to hold perpetual commands; for they well knew
that the people would be glad enough to elect them. Whereupon the
magistrates who had charge of these matters, and who are called
councillors, at first determined to resist, but they afterwards consented,
15 thinking that, if only this one law was changed, no further inroad
would be made on the constitution. But other changes soon followed
which they in vain attempted to oppose; and the state passed into the
hands of the revolutionists, who established a dynastic oligarchy.

All constitutions are overthrown either from within or from with-
20 out; the latter, when there is some government close at hand having
an opposite interest, or at a distance, but powerful. This was exemplified in the old times of the Athenians and the Lacedaemonians; the
Athenians everywhere put down the oligarchies, and the Lacedaemonians the democracies.[35]

I have now explained what are the chief causes of revolutions and
25 dissensions in states.

8   We have next to consider what means there are of preserving constitutions in general, and in particular cases. In the first place it is
evident that if we know the causes which destroy constitutions, we
also know the causes which preserve them; for opposites produce opposites, and destruction is the opposite of preservation.[36]
30   In all well-attempered governments there is nothing which should
be more jealously maintained than the spirit of obedience to law,
more especially in small matters; for transgression creeps in unper-
ceived and at last ruins the state, just as the constant recurrence of
small expenses in time eats up a fortune. The expense does not take
35 place all at once, and therefore is not observed; the mind is deceived,
as in the fallacy which says that 'if each part is little, then the whole
is little'. And this is true in one way, but not in another, for the whole
and the all are not little, although they are made up of littles.

In the first place, then, men should guard against the beginning of
40 change, and in the second place they should not rely upon the political
1308ª devices of which I have already spoken [37] invented only to deceive the
people, for they are proved by experience to be useless. Further, we
note that oligarchies as well as aristocracies may last, not from any
inherent stability in such forms of government, but because the rulers

[35] Cp. iv. 1296ª 32.   [36] Cp. *Nic. Eth.* v. 1129ª 13.   [37] Cp. iv. 1297ª 13–38.

are on good terms both with the unenfranchised and with the govern- 5
ing classes, not maltreating any who are excluded from the government, but introducing into it the leading spirits among them.[38] They
should never wrong the ambitious in a matter of honour, or the common people in a matter of money; and they should treat one another 10
and their fellow-citizens in a spirit of equality. The equality which
the friends of democracy seek to establish for the multitude is not
only just but likewise expedient among equals. Hence, if the governing class are numerous, many democratic institutions are useful; for 15
example, the restriction of the tenure of offices to six months, that all
those who are of equal rank may share in them. Indeed, equals or
peers when they are numerous become a kind of democracy, and
therefore demagogues are very likely to arise among them, as I have
already remarked.[39] The short tenure of office prevents oligarchies and
aristocracies from falling into the hands of families; it is not easy for
a person to do any great harm when his tenure of office is short, 20
whereas long possession begets tyranny in oligarchies and democracies.
For the aspirants to tyranny are either the principal men of the state,
who in democracies are demagogues and in oligarchies members of ruling houses, or those who hold great offices, and have a long tenure of
them.[40]

Constitutions are preserved when their destroyers are at a dis- 25
tance, and sometimes also because they are near, for the fear of them
makes the government keep in hand the constitution. Wherefore the
ruler who has a care of the constitution should invent terrors, and
bring distant dangers near, in order that the citizens may be on their
guard, and, like sentinels in a night-watch, never relax their attention. He should endeavour too by help of the laws to control the con- 30
tentions and quarrels of the notables, and to prevent those who have
not hitherto taken part in them from catching the spirit of contention. No ordinary man can discern the beginning of evil,[41] but only
the true statesman.

As to the change produced in oligarchies and constitutional gov- 35
ernments [42] by the alteration of the qualification, when this arises,
not out of any variation in the qualification but only out of the increase of money, it is well to compare the general valuation of property with that of past years, annually in those cities in which the 40
census is taken annually, and in larger cities every third or fifth year. 1308ᵇ
If the whole is many times greater or many times less than when the
ratings recognized by the constitution were fixed, there should be

[38] Cp. vi. 1321ᵃ 26.   [39] 1305ᵇ 23 sqq.   [40] Cp. 1305ᵃ 7.
[41] Cp. 1303ᵇ 17-31.   [42] Cp. 1306ᵇ 6-16.

5 power given by law to raise or lower the qualification as the amount
is greater or less. Where this is not done a constitutional government
passes into an oligarchy, and an oligarchy is narrowed to a rule of
families; or in the opposite case constitutional government becomes
democracy, and oligarchy either constitutional government or democracy.

10 It is a principle common to democracy, oligarchy, and every other
form of government not to allow the disproportionate increase of any
citizen, but to give moderate honour for a long time rather than great
honour for a short time. For men are easily spoilt; not every one can
15 bear prosperity. But if this rule is not observed, at any rate the honours which are given all at once should be taken away by degrees
and not all at once. Especially should the laws provide against any
one having too much power, whether derived from friends or money;
20 if he has, he should be sent clean out of the country.[43] And since inno-
vations creep in through the private life of individuals also, there ought
to be a magistracy which will have an eye to those whose life is not in
harmony with the government, whether oligarchy or democracy or
any other. And for a like reason an increase of prosperity in any part
25 of the state should be carefully watched. The proper remedy for this
evil is always to give the management of affairs and offices of state to
opposite elements; such opposites are the virtuous and the many, or
the rich and the poor. Another way is to combine the poor and the
rich in one body, or to increase the middle class: thus an end will be
30 put to the revolutions which arise from inequality.

But above all every state should be so administered and so regulated by law that its magistrates cannot possibly make money.[44] In
oligarchies special precautions should be used against this evil. For the
people do not take any great offence at being kept out of the govern-
35 ment—indeed they are rather pleased than otherwise at having leisure
for their private business—but what irritates them is to think that
their rulers are stealing the public money; then they are doubly annoyed; for they lose both honour and profit. If office brought no profit,
then and then only could democracy and aristocracy be combined;
40 for both notables and people might have their wishes gratified. All
1309ᵃ would be able to hold office, which is the aim of democracy, and the
notables would be magistrates, which is the aim of aristocracy. And
this result may be accomplished when there is no possibility of making money out of the offices; for the poor will not want to have them
5 when there is nothing to be gained from them—they would rather be
attending to their own concerns; and the rich, who do not want

---

[43] Cp. 1302ᵇ 18; iii. 1284ᵃ 17. [44] Cp. 1316ᵃ 39.

money from the public treasury, will be able to take them; and so the poor will keep to their work and grow rich, and the notables will not be governed by the lower class. In order to avoid peculation of the 10 public money, the transfer of the revenue should be made at a general assembly of the citizens, and duplicates of the accounts deposited with the different brotherhoods, companies, and tribes. And honours should be given by law to magistrates who have the reputation of being incorruptible. In democracies the rich should be spared; not only 15 should their property not be divided, but their incomes also, which in some states are taken from them imperceptibly, should be protected. It is a good thing to prevent the wealthy citizens, even if they are willing, from undertaking expensive and useless public services, such as the giving of choruses, torch-races, and the like. In an oligarchy, on the other hand, great care should be taken of the poor, and lucrative 20 offices should go to them; if any of the wealthy classes insult them, the offender should be punished more severely than if he had wronged one of his own class. Provision should be made that estates pass by inheritance and not by gift, and no person should have more than one 25 inheritance; for in this way properties will be equalized, and more of the poor rise to competency. It is also expedient both in a democracy and in an oligarchy to assign to those who have less share in the government (i. e. to the rich in a democracy and to the poor in an oligarchy) an equality or preference in all but the principal offices of 30 state. The latter should be entrusted chiefly or only to members of the governing class.

9　There are three qualifications required in those who have to fill the highest offices—(1) first of all, loyalty to the established constitution; (2) the greatest administrative capacity; (3) virtue and 35 justice of the kind proper to each form of government; for, if what is just is not the same in all governments, the quality of justice must also differ. There may be a doubt, however, when all these qualities do not meet in the same person, how the selection is to be made; suppose, 40 for example, a good general is a bad man and not a friend to the constitution, and another man is loyal and just, which should we choose? In making the election ought we not to consider two points? what qualities are common, and what are rare. Thus in the choice of a general, we should regard his skill rather than his virtue; for few 5 have military skill, but many have virtue. In any office of trust or stewardship, on the other hand, the opposite rule should be observed; for more virtue than ordinary is required in the holder of such an office, but the necessary knowledge is of a sort which all men possess.

It may, however, be asked what a man wants with virtue if he have
10 political ability and is loyal, since these two qualities alone will make
him do what is for the public interest. But may not men have both of
them and yet be deficient in self-control? If, knowing and loving their
own interests, they do not always attend to them, may they not be
equally negligent of the interests of the public?

Speaking generally, we may say that whatever legal enactments
15 are held to be for the interest of various constitutions, all these preserve them. And the great preserving principle is the one which has
been repeatedly mentioned [45]—to have a care that the loyal citizens
should be stronger than the disloyal. Neither should we forget the
mean, which at the present day is lost sight of in perverted forms of
20 government; for many practices which appear to be democratical are
the ruin of democracies, and many which appear to be oligarchical
are the ruin of oligarchies. Those who think that all virtue is to be
found in their own party principles push matters to extremes; they do
not consider that disproportion destroys a state. A nose which varies
from the ideal of straightness to a hook or snub may still be of good
25 shape and agreeable to the eye; but if the excess be very great, all
symmetry is lost, and the nose at last ceases to be a nose at all on
account of some excess in one direction or defect in the other; and this
30 is true of every other part of the human body. The same law of proportion equally holds in states. Oligarchy or democracy, although a
departure from the most perfect form, may yet be a good enough
government, but if any one attempts to push the principles of either to
an extreme, he will begin by spoiling the government and end by hav-
35 ing none at all. Wherefore the legislator and the statesman ought to
know what democratical measures save and what destroy a democracy, and what oligarchical measures save or destroy an oligarchy.
For neither the one nor the other can exist or continue to exist unless
both rich and poor are included in it. If equality of property is intro-
40 duced, the state must of necessity take another form; for when by
1310ᵃ laws carried to excess one or other element in the state is ruined, the
constitution is ruined.

There is an error common both to oligarchies and to democracies:—
in the latter the demagogues, when the multitude are above the law,
5 are always cutting the city in two by quarrels with the rich, whereas
they should always profess to be maintaining their cause; just as in oligarchies the oligarchs should profess to maintain the cause of the
people, and should take oaths the opposite of those which they now
take. For there are cities in which they swear—'I will be an enemy to

⁴⁵ iv. 1296ᵇ 15, vi. 1320ᵃ 14. Cᴅ. ii. 1270ᵇ 21 sq., iv. 1294ᵇ 37.

the people, and will devise all the harm against them which I can';
But they ought to exhibit and to entertain the very opposite feeling; 10
in the form of their oath there should be an express declaration—'I
will do no wrong to the people.'

But of all the things which I have mentioned that which most
contributes to the permanence of constitutions is the adaptation of
education to the form of government,[46] and yet in our own day this
principle is universally neglected. The best laws, though sanctioned by 15
every citizen of the state, will be of no avail unless the young are
trained by habit and education in the spirit of the constitution, if the
laws are democratical, democratically, or oligarchically, if the laws are
oligarchical. For there may be a want of self-discipline in states as well
as in individuals. Now, to have been educated in the spirit of the constitution is not to perform the actions in which oligarchs or demo- 20
crats delight, but those by which the existence of an oligarchy or of a
democracy is made possible. Whereas among ourselves the sons of the
ruling class in an oligarchy live in luxury,[47] but the sons of the poor
are hardened by exercise and toil, and hence they are both more inclined and better able to make a revolution.[48] And in democracies of 25
the more extreme type there has arisen a false idea of freedom which
is contradictory to the true interests of the state. For two principles
are characteristic of democracy, the government of the majority and
freedom. Men think that what is just is equal; and that equality is the 30
supremacy of the popular will; and that freedom means the doing
what a man likes. In such democracies every one lives as he pleases,
or in the words of Euripides, 'according to his fancy'. But this is all
wrong; men should not think it slavery to live according to the rule 35
of the constitution; for it is their salvation.

I have now discussed generally the causes of the revolution and
destruction of states, and the means of their preservation and continuance.

10　I have still to speak of monarchy, and the causes of its destruction and preservation. What I have said already respecting forms of 40
constitutional government applies almost equally to royal and to 1310[b]
tyrannical rule. For royal rule is of the nature of an aristocracy, and a
tyranny is a compound of oligarchy and democracy in their most extreme forms; it is therefore most injurious to its subjects, being made 5
up of two evil forms of government, and having the perversions and
errors of both. These two forms of monarchy are contrary in their very
origin. The appointment of a king is the resource of the better classes

---

[46] Cp. viii. 1337ᵃ 14.　　[47] Cp. iv. 1295ᵇ 17.　　[48] Cp. Pl. *Rep.* viii. 556 D.

10 against the people, and he is elected by them out of their own number, because either he himself or his family excel in virtue and virtuous actions; whereas a tyrant is chosen from the people to be their protector against the notables, and in order to prevent them from being injured. History shows that almost all tyrants have been demagogues
15 who gained the favour of the people by their accusation of the notables.[49] At any rate this was the manner in which the tyrannies arose in the days when cities had increased in power. Others which were older originated in the ambition of kings wanting to overstep the limits of their hereditary power and become despots. Others again grew out
20 of the class which were chosen to be chief magistrates; for in ancient times the people who elected them gave the magistrates, whether civil or religious, a long tenure. Others arose out of the custom which oligarchies had of making some individual supreme over the highest offices. In any of these ways an ambitious man had no difficulty, if he
25 desired, in creating a tyranny, since he had the power in his hands already, either as king or as one of the officers of state.[50] Thus Pheidon at Argos and several others were originally kings, and ended by becoming tyrants; Phalaris, on the other hand, and the Ionian tyrants, acquired the tyranny by holding great offices. Whereas Panaetius at
30 Leontini, Cypselus at Corinth, Peisistratus at Athens, Dionysius at Syracuse, and several others who afterwards became tyrants, were at first demagogues.

And so, as I was saying,[51] royalty ranks with aristocracy, for it is based upon merit, whether of the individual or of his family, or on benefits conferred,[52] or on these claims with power added to them. For
35 all who have obtained this honour have benefited, or had in their power to benefit, states and nations; some, like Codrus, have prevented the state from being enslaved in war; others, like Cyrus, have given their country freedom, or have settled or gained a territory, like
40 the Lacedaemonian, Macedonian, and Molossian kings. The idea of a
1311ᵃ king is to be a protector of the rich against unjust treatment, of the people against insult and oppression. Whereas a tyrant, as has often been repeated,[53] has no regard to any public interest, except as conducive to his private ends; his aim is pleasure, the aim of a king,
5 honour. Wherefore also in their desires they differ; the tyrant is desirous of riches, the king, of what brings honour. And the guards of a king are citizens, but of a tyrant mercenaries.[54]

That tyranny has all the vices both of democracy and oligarchy is

---

[49] Cp. 1305ᵃ 8; Plato, *Rep.* viii. 565 D.
[50] Cp. 1305ᵃ 15.
[51] l. 2 sq.
[52] Cp. iii. 1285ᵇ 6.
[53] iii. 1279ᵇ 6 sq., iv. 1295ᵃ 19.
[54] Cp. iii. 1285ᵃ 24.

evident. As of oligarchy so of tyranny, the end is wealth; (for by 10
wealth only can the tyrant maintain either his guard or his luxury).
Both mistrust the people, and therefore deprive them of their arms.
Both agree too in injuring the people and driving them out of the city
and dispersing them. From democracy tyrants have borrowed the art 15
of making war upon the notables and destroying them secretly or
openly, or of exiling them because they are rivals and stand in the
way of their power; and also because plots against them are contrived
by men of this class, who either want to rule or to escape subjection. 20
Hence Periander advised Thrasybulus [55] by cutting off the tops of the
tallest ears of corn, meaning that he must always put out of the way
the citizens who overtop the rest. And so, as I have already inti-
mated,[56] the beginnings of change are the same in monarchies as in
forms of constitutional government; subjects attack their sovereigns 25
out of fear or contempt, or because they have been unjustly treated
by them. And of injustice, the most common form is insult, another
is confiscation of property.

The ends sought by conspiracies against monarchies, whether tyrannies or royalties, are the same as the ends sought by conspiracies
against other forms of government. Monarchs have great wealth and 30
honour, which are objects of desire to all mankind. The attacks are
made sometimes against their lives, sometimes against the office; where
the sense of insult is the motive, against their lives. Any sort of insult
(and there are many) may stir up anger, and when men are angry,
they commonly act out of revenge, and not from ambition. For exam- 35
ple, the attempt made upon the Peisistratidae arose out of the public
dishonour offered to the sister of Harmodius and the insult to himself.
He attacked the tyrant for his sister's sake, and Aristogeiton joined in
the attack for the sake of Harmodius. A conspiracy was also formed
against Periander, the tyrant of Ambracia, because, when drinking 40
with a favourite youth, he asked him whether by this time he was not 1311[b]
with child by him. Philip, too, was attacked by Pausanias because he
permitted him to be insulted by Attalus and his friends, and Amyntas
the little, by Derdas, because he boasted of having enjoyed his youth.
Evagoras of Cyprus, again, was slain by the eunuch to revenge an 5
insult; for his wife had been carried off by Evagoras's son. Many
conspiracies have originated in shameful attempts made by sovereigns
on the persons of their subjects. Such was the attack of Crataeas upon
Archelaus; he had always hated the connexion with him, and so, when
Archelaus, having promised him one of his two daughters in marriage, 10
did not give him either of them, but broke his word and married the

---

[55] Cp. 1284[a] 26.   [56] 1310[a] 40 sqq.

elder to the king of Elymeia, when he was hard pressed in a war
against Sirrhas and Arrhabaeus, and the younger to his own son Amyntas, under the idea that Amyntas would then be less likely to quarrel
15 with his son by Cleopatra—Crataeas made this slight a pretext for
attacking Archelaus, though even a less reason would have sufficed,
for the real cause of the estrangement was the disgust which he felt at
his connexion with the king. And from a like motive Hellanocrates of
Larissa conspired with him; for when Archelaus, who was his lover,
did not fulfil his promise of restoring him to his country, he thought
that the connexion between them had originated, not in affection, but
20 in the wantonness of power. Pytho, too, and Heracleides of Aenos,
slew Cotys in order to avenge their father, and Adamas revolted
from Cotys in revenge for the wanton outrage which he had committed in mutilating him when a child.

Many, too, irritated at blows inflicted on the person which they
25 deemed an insult, have either killed or attempted to kill officers of
state and royal princes by whom they have been injured. Thus, at
Mytilene, Megacles and his friends attacked and slew the Penthilidae,
as they were going about and striking people with clubs. At a later
date Smerdis, who had been beaten and torn away from his wife by
30 Penthilus, slew him. In the conspiracy against Archelaus, Decamnichus stimulated the fury of the assassins and led the attack; he
was enraged because Archelaus had delivered him to Euripides to be
scourged; for the poet had been irritated at some remark made by
Decamnichus on the foulness of his breath. Many other examples
35 might be cited of murders and conspiracies which have arisen from
similar causes.

Fear is another motive which, as we have said,[57] has caused conspiracies as well in monarchies as in more popular forms of government. Thus Artapanes conspired against Xerxes and slew him, fearing that he would be accused of hanging Darius against his orders—
he having been under the impression that Xerxes would forget what
he had said in the middle of a meal, and that the offence would be
forgiven.

40   Another motive is contempt, as in the case of Sardanapalus, whom
1312ᵃ some one saw carding wool with his women, if the story-tellers say
truly; and the tale may be true, if not of him, of some one else.[58]
5 Dion attacked the younger Dionysius because he despised him, and
saw that he was equally despised by his own subjects, and that he
was always drunk. Even the friends of a tyrant will sometimes attack
him out of contempt; for the confidence which he reposes in them

---

⁵⁷ Cp. 1302ᵇ 2, 21, 1311ᵃ 25.   ⁵⁸ Cp. i. 1259ᵃ 7.

breeds contempt, and they think that they will not be found out. The
expectation of success is likewise a sort of contempt; the assailants
are ready to strike, and think nothing of the danger, because they 10
seem to have the power in their hands. Thus generals of armies
attack monarchs; as, for example, Cyrus attacked Astyages, despising
the effeminacy of his life, and believing that his power was worn out.
Thus again, Seuthes the Thracian conspired against Amadocus,
whose general he was.

And sometimes men are actuated by more than one motive, like 15
Mithridates, who conspired against Ariobarzanes, partly out of contempt and partly from the love of gain.

Bold natures, placed by their sovereigns in a high military position,
are most likely to make the attempt in the expectation of success;
for courage is emboldened by power, and the union of the two in- 20
spires them with the hope of an easy victory.

Attempts of which the motive is ambition arise in a different way as
well as in those already mentioned. There are men who will not risk 25
their lives in the hope of gains and honours however great, but who
nevertheless regard the killing of a tyrant simply as an extraordinary action which will make them famous and honourable in the
world; they wish to acquire, not a kingdom, but a name. It is rare, 30
however, to find such men; he who would kill a tyrant must be prepared to lose his life if he fail. He must have the resolution of Dion,
who, when he made war upon Dionysius, took with him very few 35
troops, saying 'that whatever measure of success he might attain
would be enough for him, even if he were to die the moment he landed;
such a death would be welcome to him'. But this is a temper to which
few can attain.

Once more, tyrannies, like all other governments, are destroyed 40
from without by some opposite and more powerful form of govern- 1312ᵇ
ment. That such a government will have the will to attack them is
clear; for the two are opposed in principle; and all men, if they can,
do what they will. Democracy is antagonistic to tyranny, on the principle of Hesiod, 'Potter hates Potter', because they are nearly akin, for
the extreme form of democracy is tyranny; and royalty and aristoc- 5
racy are both alike opposed to tyranny, because they are constitutions
of a different type. And therefore the Lacedaemonians put down most
of the tyrannies, and so did the Syracusans during the time when they
were well governed.

Again, tyrannies are destroyed from within, when the reigning
family are divided among themselves, as that of Gelo was, and more 10
recently that of Dionysius; in the case of Gelo because Thrasybulus,

the brother of Hiero, flattered the son of Gelo and led him into excesses in order that he might rule in his name. Whereupon the family got together a party to get rid of Thrasybulus and save the tyranny;
15 but those of the people who conspired with them seized the opportunity and drove them all out. In the case of Dionysius, Dion, his own relative, attacked and expelled him with the assistance of the people; he afterwards perished himself.

There are two chief motives which induce men to attack tyrannies—
20 hatred and contempt. Hatred of tyrants is inevitable, and contempt is also a frequent cause of their destruction. Thus we see that most of those who have acquired, have retained their power, but those who have inherited,[59] have lost it, almost at once; for, living in luxurious ease, they have become contemptible, and offer many opportunities to
25 their assailants. Anger, too, must be included under hatred, and produces the same effects. It is oftentimes even more ready to strike—the angry are more impetuous in making an attack, for they do not follow rational principle. And men are very apt to give way to their passions
30 when they are insulted. To this cause is to be attributed the fall of the Peisistratidae and of many others. Hatred is more reasonable, for anger is accompanied by pain, which is an impediment to reason, whereas hatred is painless.[60]

In a word, all the causes which I have mentioned [61] as destroying
35 the last and most unmixed form of oligarchy, and the extreme form of democracy, may be assumed to affect tyranny; indeed the extreme forms of both are only tyrannies distributed among several persons. Kingly rule is little affected by external causes, and is therefore last-
40 ing; it is generally destroyed from within. And there are two ways in
1313ᵃ which the destruction may come about; (1) when the members of the royal family quarrel among themselves, and (2) when the kings attempt to administer the state too much after the fashion of a tyranny, and to extend their authority contrary to the law. Royalties do not now come into existence; where such forms of government arise, they
5 are rather monarchies or tyrannies. For the rule of a king is over voluntary subjects, and he is supreme in all important matters; but in our own day men are more upon an equality, and no one is so immeasurably superior to others as to represent adequately the greatness and dignity of the office. Hence mankind will not, if they can help,
10 endure it, and any one who obtains power by force or fraud is at once thought to be a tyrant. In hereditary monarchies a further cause of destruction is the fact that kings often fall into contempt, and, al-

---

[59] Cp. Plato, *Laws*, iii. 695.   [60] Cp. *Rhetoric*, ii. 1382ᵃ 12.
[61] 1302ᵇ 25–33, 1304ᵇ 20–1306ᵇ 21.

though possessing not tyrannical power, but only royal dignity, are
apt to outrage others. Their overthrow is then readily effected; for
there is an end to the king when his subjects do not want to have him, 15
but the tyrant lasts, whether they like him or not.

The destruction of monarchies is to be attributed to these and the
like causes.

11 And they are preserved, to speak generally, by the opposite
causes; or, if we consider them separately, (1) royalty is preserved
by the limitation of its powers. The more restricted the functions of 20
kings, the longer their power will last unimpaired; for then they are
more moderate and not so despotic in their ways; and they are less
envied by their subjects. This is the reason why the kingly office has
lasted so long among the Molossians. And for a similar reason it has 25
continued among the Lacedaemonians, because there it was always
divided between two, and afterwards further limited by Theopompus
in various respects, more particularly by the establishment of the
Ephoralty. He diminished the power of the kings, but established on a
more lasting basis the kingly office, which was thus made in a certain
sense not less, but greater. There is a story that when his wife once 30
asked him whether he was not ashamed to leave to his sons a royal
power which was less than he had inherited from his father, 'No indeed,' he replied, 'for the power which I leave to them will be more
lasting.'

As to (2) tyrannies, they are preserved in two most opposite ways.
One of them is the old traditional method in which most tyrants 35
administer their government. Of such arts Periander of Corinth is
said to have been the great master, and many similar devices may be
gathered from the Persians in the administration of their government. There are firstly the prescriptions mentioned some distance
back,[62] for the preservation of a tyranny, in so far as this is possible;
viz. that the tyrant should lop off those who are too high; he must put 40
to death men of spirit; he must not allow common meals, clubs, educa- 1313ᵇ
tion, and the like; he must be upon his guard against anything which is
likely to inspire either courage or confidence among his subjects; he
must prohibit literary assemblies or other meetings for discussion, and
he must take every means to prevent people from knowing one another (for acquaintance begets mutual confidence). Further, he must 5
compel all persons staying in the city to appear in public and live at
his gates; then he will know what they are doing: if they are always
kept under, they will learn to be humble. In short, he should practise

[62] 1311ᵃ 15–22.

these and the like Persian and barbaric arts, which all have the same
10 object. A tyrant should also endeavour to know what each of his
subjects says or does, and should employ spies, like the 'female
detectives' at Syracuse, and the eavesdroppers whom Hiero was in the
15 habit of sending to any place of resort or meeting; for the fear of
informers prevents people from speaking their minds, and if they do,
they are more easily found out. Another art of the tyrant is to sow
quarrels among the citizens; friends should be embroiled with friends,
the people with the notables, and the rich with one another. Also he
should impoverish his subjects; he thus provides against the mainte-
20 nance of a guard by the citizens, and the people, having to keep hard
at work, are prevented from conspiring. The Pyramids of Egypt afford
an example of this policy; also the offerings of the family of Cypselus,
and the building of the temple of Olympian Zeus by the Peisistratidae,
and the great Polycratean monuments at Samos; all these works were
25 alike intended to occupy the people and keep them poor. Another
practice of tyrants is to multiply taxes, after the manner of Dionysius
at Syracuse, who contrived that within five years his subjects should
bring into the treasury their whole property. The tyrant is also fond
of making war in order that his subjects may have something to do
30 and be always in want of a leader. And whereas the power of a king is
preserved by his friends, the characteristic of a tyrant is to distrust his
friends, because he knows that all men want to overthrow him, and
they above all have the power.

Again, the evil practices of the last and worst form of democracy [63]
are all found in tyrannies. Such are the power given to women in their
families in the hope that they will inform against their husbands, and
the licence which is allowed to slaves in order that they may betray
35 their masters; for slaves and women do not conspire against tyrants;
and they are of course friendly to tyrannies and also to democracies,
since under them they have a good time. For the people too would
fain be a monarch, and therefore by them, as well as by the tyrant,
40 the flatterer is held in honour; in democracies he is the demagogue;
and the tyrant also has those who associate with him in a humble
1314[a] spirit, which is a work of flattery.

Hence tyrants are always fond of bad men, because they love to be
flattered, but no man who has the spirit of a freeman in him will lower
himself by flattery; good men love others, or at any rate do not flatter
them. Moreover, the bad are useful for bad purposes; 'nail knocks
5 out nail', as the proverb says. It is characteristic of a tyrant to dislike
every one who has dignity or independence; he wants to be alone in

[63] Cp. vi. 1319[b] 27.

his glory, but any one who claims a like dignity or asserts his independence encroaches upon his prerogative, and is hated by him as an
enemy to his power. Another mark of a tyrant is that he likes for- 10
eigners better than citizens, and lives with them and invites them to
his table; for the one are enemies, but the others enter into no rivalry
with him.

Such are the notes of the tyrant and the arts by which he preserves
his power; there is no wickedness too great for him. All that we have
said may be summed up under three heads, which answer to the three 15
aims of the tyrant. These are, (1) the humiliation of his subjects; he
knows that a mean-spirited man will not conspire against anybody:
(2) the creation of mistrust among them; for a tyrant is not overthrown until men begin to have confidence in one another; and this
is the reason why tyrants are at war with the good; they are under
the idea that their power is endangered by them, not only because they 20
will not be ruled despotically, but also because they are loyal to one
another, and to other men, and do not inform against one another or
against other men: (3) the tyrant desires that his subjects shall be
incapable of action, for no one attempts what is impossible, and they
will not attempt to overthrow a tyranny, if they are powerless. Under
these three heads the whole policy of a tyrant may be summed up, and 25
to one or other of them all his ideas may be referred: (1) he sows
distrust among his subjects; (2) he takes away their power; (3) he
humbles them.

This then is one of the two methods by which tyrannies are pre- 30
served; and there is another which proceeds upon an almost opposite
principle of action. The nature of this latter method may be gathered
from a comparison of the causes which destroy kingdoms, for as one
mode of destroying kingly power is to make the office of king more
tyrannical, so the salvation of a tyranny is to make it more like the
rule of a king. But of one thing the tyrant must be careful; he must 35
keep power enough to rule over his subjects, whether they like him or
not, for if he once gives this up he gives up his tyranny. But though
power must be retained as the foundation, in all else the tyrant should
act or appear to act in the character of a king. In the first place he 40
should pretend a care of the public revenues, and not waste money in 1314ᵇ
making presents of a sort at which the common people get excited when
they see their hard-won earnings snatched from them and lavished on
courtesans and strangers and artists. He should give an account of 5
what he receives and of what he spends (a practice which has been
adopted by some tyrants); for then he will seem to be a steward of the

public rather than a tyrant; nor need he fear that, while he is the lord of the city, he will ever be in want of money. Such a policy is at all events much more advantageous for the tyrant when he goes from home, than to leave behind him a hoard, for then the garrison who remain in the city will be less likely to attack his power; and a tyrant, when he is absent from home, has more reason to fear the guardians of his treasure than the citizens, for the one accompany him, but the others remain behind. In the second place, he should be seen to collect taxes and to require public services only for state purposes, and that he may form a fund in case of war, and generally he ought to make himself the guardian and treasurer of them, as if they belonged, not to him, but to the public. He should appear, not harsh, but dignified, and when men meet him they should look upon him with reverence, and not with fear. Yet it is hard for him to be respected if he inspires no respect, and therefore whatever virtues he may neglect, at least he should maintain the character of a great soldier, and produce the impression that he is one. Neither he nor any of his associates should ever be guilty of the least offence against modesty towards the young of either sex who are his subjects, and the women of his family should observe a like self-control towards other women; the insolence of women has ruined many tyrannies. In the indulgence of pleasures he should be the opposite of our modern tyrants, who not only begin at dawn and pass whole days in sensuality, but want other men to see them, that they may admire their happy and blessed lot. In these things a tyrant should if possible be moderate, or at any rate should not parade his vices to the world; for a drunken and drowsy tyrant is soon despised and attacked; not so he who is temperate and wide awake. His conduct should be the very reverse of nearly everything which has been said before [64] about tyrants. He ought to adorn and improve his city, as though he were not a tyrant, but the guardian of the state. Also he should appear to be particularly earnest in the service of the Gods; for if men think that a ruler is religious and has a reverence for the Gods, they are less afraid of suffering injustice at his hands, and they are less disposed to conspire against him, because they believe him to have the very Gods fighting on his side. At the same time his religion must not be thought foolish. And he should honour men of merit, and make them think that they would not be held in more honour by the citizens if they had a free government. The honour he should distribute himself, but the punishment should be inflicted by officers and courts of law. It is a precaution which is

[64] 1313[a] 35–1314[a] 29.

taken by all monarchs not to make one person great; but if one, then two or more should be raised, that they may look sharply after one another. If after all some one has to be made great, he should not 10 be a man of bold spirit; for such dispositions are ever most inclined to strike. And if any one is to be deprived of his power, let it be diminished gradually, not taken from him all at once.[65] The tyrant should abstain from all outrage; in particular from personal violence and 15 from wanton conduct towards the young. He should be especially careful of his behaviour to men who are lovers of honour; for as the lovers of money are offended when their property is touched, so are the lovers of honour and the virtuous when their honour is affected. 20 Therefore a tyrant ought either not to commit such acts at all; or he should be thought only to employ fatherly correction, and not to trample upon others—and his acquaintance with youth should be supposed to arise from affection, and not from the insolence of power, and in general he should compensate the appearance of dishonour by the increase of honour.

Of those who attempt assassination they are the most dangerous, 25 and require to be most carefully watched, who do not care to survive, if they effect their purpose. Therefore special precaution should be taken about any who think that either they or those for whom they care have been insulted; for when men are led away by passion to assault others they are regardless of themselves. As Heracleitus says, 'It is difficult to fight against anger; for a man will buy revenge with 30 his soul.'

And whereas states consist of two classes, of poor men and of rich, the tyrant should lead both to imagine that they are preserved and prevented from harming one another by his rule, and whichever of the 35 two is stronger he should attach to his government; for, having this advantage, he has no need either to emancipate slaves or to disarm the citizens; either party added to the force which he already has, will make him stronger than his assailants.

But enough of these details;—what should be the general policy of 40 the tyrant is obvious. He ought to show himself to his subjects in the light, not of a tyrant, but of a steward and a king. He should not 1315[b] appropriate what is theirs, but should be their guardian; he should be moderate, not extravagant in his way of life; he should win the notables by companionship, and the multitude by flattery. For then his rule will of necessity be nobler and happier, because he will rule 5 over better men [66] whose spirits are not crushed, over men to whom he himself is not an object of hatred, and of whom he is not afraid.

[65] Cp. 1308[b] 15.   [66] Cp. i. 1254[a] 25.

His power too will be more lasting. His disposition will be virtuous,
10 or at least half virtuous; and he will not be wicked, but half wicked
only.

12 Yet no forms of government are so short-lived as oligarchy and
tyranny. The tyranny which lasted longest was that of Orthagoras and
his sons at Sicyon; this continued for a hundred years. The reason was
15 that they treated their subjects with moderation, and to a great extent observed the laws; and in various ways gained the favour of the
people by the care which they took of them. Cleisthenes, in particular,
was respected for his military ability. If report may be believed, he
crowned the judge who decided against him in the games; and, as
20 some say, the sitting statue in the Agora of Sicyon is the likeness of
this person. (A similar story is told of Peisistratus, who is said on one
occasion to have allowed himself to be summoned and tried before the
Areopagus.)

Next in duration to the tyranny of Orthagoras was that of the
Cypselidae at Corinth, which lasted seventy-three years and six
25 months: Cypselus reigned thirty years, Periander forty and a half, and
Psammetichus the son of Gorgus three. Their continuance was due to
similar causes: Cypselus was a popular man, who during the whole
time of his rule never had a body-guard; and Periander, although he
was a tyrant, was a great soldier. Third in duration was the rule of the
30 Peisistratidae at Athens, but it was interrupted; for Peisistratus was
twice driven out, so that during three and thirty years he reigned
only seventeen; and his sons reigned eighteen—altogether thirty-five
years. Of other tyrannies, that of Hiero and Gelo at Syracuse was the
35 most lasting. Even this, however, was short, not more than eighteen
years in all; for Gelo continued tyrant for seven years, and died in
the eighth; Hiero reigned for ten years, and Thrasybulus was driven
out in the eleventh month. In fact, tyrannies generally have been of
quite short duration.

40 I have now gone through almost all the causes by which constitu-
1316ᵃ tional governments and monarchies are either destroyed or preserved.

In the *Republic* of Plato,[67] Socrates treats of revolutions, but not
well, for he mentions no cause of change which peculiarly affects the
first, or perfect state. He only says that the cause is that nothing is
5 abiding, but all things change in a certain cycle; and that the origin
of the change consists in those numbers 'of which 4 and 3, married
with 5, furnish two harmonies'—(he means when the number of this
figure becomes solid); he conceives that nature at certain times pro-

[67] This is an extract from the much fuller account in *Rep.* viii. 546 ʙ.ᴄ.

duces bad men who will not submit to education; in which latter particular he may very likely be not far wrong, for there may well be
some men who cannot be educated and made virtuous. But why is such 10
a cause of change peculiar to his ideal state, and not rather common
to all states, nay, to everything which comes into being at all? And
is it by the agency of time, which, as he declares, makes all things
change, that things which did not begin together, change together? 15
For example, if something has come into being the day before the
completion of the cycle, will it change with things that came into being
before? Further, why should the perfect state change into the Spartan? [68] For governments more often take an opposite form than one
akin to them. The same remark is applicable to the other changes; he 20
says that the Spartan constitution changes into an oligarchy, and this
into a democracy, and this again into a tyranny. And yet the contrary
happens quite as often; for a democracy is even more likely to change
into an oligarchy than into a monarchy. Further, he never says 25
whether tyranny is, or is not, liable to revolutions, and if it is, what is
the cause of them, or into what form it changes. And the reason is,
that he could not very well have told: for there is no rule; according
to him it should revert to the first and best, and then there would be
a complete cycle. But in point of fact a tyranny often changes into a 30
tyranny, as that at Sicyon changed from the tyranny of Myron into
that of Cleisthenes; into oligarchy, as the tyranny of Antileon did at
Chalcis; into democracy, as that of Gelo's family did at Syracuse;
into aristocracy, as at Carthage, and the tyranny of Charilaus at Lace- 35
daemon. Often an oligarchy changes into a tyranny, like most of the
ancient oligarchies in Sicily; for example, the oligarchy at Leontini
changed into the tyranny of Panaetius; that at Gela into the tyranny
of Cleander; that at Rhegium into the tyranny of Anaxilaus; the same
thing has happened in many other states. And it is absurd to suppose
that the state changes into oligarchy merely because the ruling class 40
are lovers and makers of money,[69] and not because the very rich 1316ᵇ
think it unfair that the very poor should have an equal share in the
government with themselves. Moreover, in many oligarchies there are
laws against making money in trade. But at Carthage, which is a 5
democracy, there is no such prohibition; and yet to this day the
Carthaginians have never had a revolution. It is absurd too for him to
say that an oligarchy is two cities, one of the rich, and the other of the
poor.[70] Is not this just as much the case in the Spartan constitution,
or in any other in which either all do not possess equal property, or
all are not equally good men? Nobody need be any poorer than he was 10

[68] *Rep*. viii. 544 C.   [69] *Rep*. viii. 550 E.   [70] *Rep*. viii. 551 D.

before, and yet the oligarchy may change all the same into a democracy, if the poor form the majority; and a democracy may change into an oligarchy, if the wealthy class are stronger than the people, and the
15 one are energetic, the other indifferent. Once more, although the causes of the change.[71] are very numerous, he mentions only one,[72] which is, that the citizens become poor through dissipation and debt, as though he thought that all, or the majority of them, were originally rich. This is not true: though it is true that when any of the leaders lose their property they are ripe for revolution; but, when anybody
20 else, it is no great matter, and an oligarchy does not even then more often pass into a democracy than into any other form of government. Again, if men are deprived of the honours of state, and are wronged, and insulted, they make revolutions, and change forms of government, even although they have not wasted their substance because they might do what they liked—of which extravagance he declares excessive freedom to be the cause.[73]
25   Finally, although there are many forms of oligarchies and democracies, Socrates speaks of their revolutions as though there were only one form of either of them.

BOOK VI

1 We have now considered the varieties of the deliberative or supreme power in states, and the various arrangements of law-courts and state offices, and which of them are adapted to different forms of government.[1] We have also spoken of the destruction and preservation
35 of constitutions, how and from what causes they arise.[2]

Of democracy and all other forms of government there are many kinds; and it will be well to assign to them severally the modes of organization which are proper and advantageous to each, adding what
40 remains to be said about them.[3] Moreover, we ought to consider the
1317ª various combinations of these modes themselves; for such combinations make constitutions overlap one another, so that aristocracies have an oligarchical character, and constitutional governments incline to democracies.[4]

When I speak of the combinations which remain to be considered, and thus far have not been considered by us, I mean such as these:—
5 when the deliberative part of the government and the election of officers is constituted oligarchically, and the law-courts aristocratically,

[71] sc. from oligarchy to democracy.   [72] Rep. viii. 555 D.
[73] Rep. viii. 557 C, 564.
[1] Bk. iv. 14–16.   [2] Bk. v.
[3] 1318ᵇ 6–1319ª 6.   [4] Cp. iv. 1293ᵇ 34.

or when the courts and the deliberative part of the state are oligarchical, and the election to offices aristocratical, or when in any other way
there is a want of harmony in the composition of a state.[5]

I have shown already [6] what forms of democracy are suited to par- 10
ticular cities, and what of oligarchy to particular peoples, and to whom
each of the other forms of government is suited. Further, we must not
only show which of these governments is the best for each state, but
also briefly proceed to consider [7] how these and other forms of gov- 15
ernment are to be established.

First of all let us speak of democracy, which will also bring to light
the opposite form of government commonly called oligarchy. For
the purposes of this inquiry we need to ascertain all the elements and
characteristics of democracy, since from the combinations of these 20
the varieties of democratic government arise. There are several of
these differing from each other, and the difference is due to two
causes. One (1) has been already mentioned [8]—differences of population; for the popular element may consist of husbandmen, or of 25
mechanics, or of labourers, and if the first of these be added to the
second, or the third to the two others, not only does the democracy
become better or worse, but its very nature is changed. A second cause
(2) remains to be mentioned: the various properties and character- 30
istics of democracy, when variously combined, make a difference. For
one democracy will have less and another will have more, and another will have all of these characteristics. There is an advantage in
knowing them all, whether a man wishes to establish some new form
of democracy, or only to remodel an existing one.[9] Founders of 35
states try to bring together all the elements which accord with the
ideas of the several constitutions; but this is a mistake of theirs, as
I have already remarked [10] when speaking of the destruction and
preservation of states. We will now set forth the principles, characteristics, and aims of such states.

2　The basis of a democratic state is liberty; which, according to the 40
common opinion of men, can only be enjoyed in such a state;—this 1317ᵇ
they affirm to be the great end of every democracy.[11] One principle
of liberty is for all to rule and be ruled in turn, and indeed democratic justice is the application of numerical not proportionate equality;
whence it follows that the majority must be supreme, and that what- 5

[5] These questions are not actually discussed by A.　　　　[6] iv. 12.
[7] Cp. iv. 1289ᵇ 20.　　　　[8] iv. 1291ᵇ 17–28, 1292ᵇ 25 sqq., 1296ᵇ 26–31.
[9] Cp. iv. 1289ᵃ 1.　　　　　　　　　[10] v. 1309ᵇ 18–1310ᵃ 36.
[11] Cp. Plato, *Rep.* viii. 557 sqq.

ever the majority approve must be the end and the just. Every citizen, it is said, must have equality, and therefore in a democracy the poor have more power than the rich, because there are more of them, and the will of the majority is supreme. This, then, is one note
10 of liberty which all democrats affirm to be the principle of their state. Another is that a man should live as he likes.[12] This, they say, is the privilege of a freeman, since, on the other hand, not to live as .a man likes is the mark of a slave. This is the second characteristic of democracy, whence has arisen the claim of men to be ruled by
15 none, if possible, or, if this is impossible, to rule and be ruled in turns; and so it contributes to the freedom based upon equality.

Such being our foundation and such the principle from which we start, the characteristics of democracy are as follows:—the election
20 of officers by all out of all; and that all should rule over each, and each in his turn over all; that the appointment to all offices, or to all but those which require experience and skill,[13] should be made by lot; that no property qualification should be required for offices, or only a very low one; that a man should not hold the same office twice, or not often, or in the case of few except military offices: that the
25 tenure of all offices, or of as many as possible, should be brief; that all men should sit in judgement, or that judges selected out of all should judge, in all matters, or in most and in the greatest and most important—such as the scrutiny of accounts, the constitution, and private contracts; that the assembly should be supreme over all causes, or at any rate over the most important, and the magistrates
30 over none or only over a very few. Of all magistracies, a council is the most democratic[14] when there is not the means of paying all the citizens, but when they are paid even this is robbed of its power; for the people then draw all cases to themselves, as I said in the pre-
35 vious discussion.[15] The next characteristic of democracy is payment for services; assembly, law-courts, magistrates, everybody receives pay, when it is to be had; or when it is not to be had for all, then it is given to the law-courts and to the stated assemblies, to the council and to the magistrates, or at least to any of them who are compelled to have their meals together. And whereas oligarchy is characterized
40 by birth, wealth, and education, the notes of democracy appear to be the opposite of these—low birth, poverty, mean employment. Another
1318ᵃ note is that no magistracy is perpetual, but if any such have survived some ancient change in the constitution it should be stripped of its power, and the holders should be elected by lot and no longer by vote.

[12] Cp. v. 1310ᵃ 31.   [13] Cp. iv. 1298ᵃ 27.
[14] Cp. iv. 1299ᵇ 32   [15] Cp. iv. 1299ᵇ 38.

These are the points common to all democracies; but democracy and
demos in their truest form are based upon the recognized principle 5
of democratic justice, that all should count equally; for equality implies that the poor should have no more share in the government
than the rich, and should not be the only rulers, but that all should
rule equally according to their numbers.[16] And in this way men think
that they will secure equality and freedom in their state.   10

3 Next comes the question, how is this equality to be obtained?
Are we to assign to a thousand poor men the property qualifications
of five hundred rich men? and shall we give the thousand a power
equal to that of the five hundred? or, if this is not to be the mode,
ought we, still retaining the same ratio, to take equal numbers from 15
each and give them the control of the elections and of the courts?—
Which, according to the democratical notion, is the juster form of the
constitution—this or one based on numbers only? Democrats say
that justice is that to which the majority agree, oligarchs that to which 20
the wealthier class; in their opinion the decision should be given according to the amount of property. In both principles there is some
inequality and injustice. For if justice is the will of the few, any one
person who has more wealth than all the rest of the rich put together, ought, upon the oligarchical principle, to have the sole power
—but this would be tyranny; or if justice is the will of the majority, 25
as I was before saying,[17] they will unjustly confiscate the property
of the wealthy minority. To find a principle of equality in which they
both agree we must inquire into their respective ideas of justice.

  Now they agree in saying that whatever is decided by the majority
of the citizens is to be deemed law. Granted:—but not without some
reserve; since there are two classes out of which a state is composed 30
—the poor and the rich—that is to be deemed law, on which both
or the greater part of both agree; and if they disagree, that which is
approved by the greater number, and by those who have the higher
qualification. For example, suppose that there are ten rich and twenty
poor, and some measure is approved by six of the rich and is dis-
approved by fifteen of the poor, and the remaining four of the rich 35
join with the party of the poor, and the remaining five of the poor
with that of the rich; in such a case the will of those whose qualifications, when both sides are added up, are the greatest, should prevail. If they turn out to be equal, there is no greater difficulty than at
present, when, if the assembly or the courts are divided, recourse 40
is had to the lot, or to some similar expedient. But, although it may 1318ᵇ

---

[16] Cp. iv. 1291ᵇ 30.   [17] Cp. iii. 1281ᵃ 14.

be difficult in theory to know what is just and equal, the practical
difficulty of inducing those to forbear who can, if they like, encroach,
is far greater, for the weaker are always asking for equality and
5 justice, but the stronger care for none of these things.

4   Of the four kinds of democracy, as was said in the previous discussion,[18] the best is that which comes first in order; it is also the
oldest of them all. I am speaking of them according to the natural
classification of their inhabitants. For the best material of democracy
10 is an agricultural population; [19] there is no difficulty in forming a
democracy where the mass of the people live by agriculture or tending of cattle. Being poor, they have no leisure, and therefore do not
often attend the assembly, and not having the necessaries of life
they are always at work, and do not covet the property of others. Indeed, they find their employment pleasanter than the cares of govern-
15 ment or office where no great gains can be made out of them, for
the many are more desirous of gain than of honour.[20] A proof is that
even the ancient tyrannies were patiently endured by them, as they
still endure oligarchies, if they are allowed to work and are not de-
20 prived of their property; for some of them grow quickly rich and the
others are well enough off. Moreover, they have the power of electing
the magistrates and calling them to account; [21] their ambition, if
they have any, is thus satisfied; and in some democracies, although
they do not all share in the appointment of offices, except through
representatives elected in turn out of the whole people, as at Mantinea;
25 —yet, if they have the power of deliberating, the many are contented.
Even this form of government may be regarded as a democracy, and
was such at Mantinea. Hence it is both expedient and customary in
the afore-mentioned [22] type of democracy that all should elect to
30 offices, and conduct scrutinies, and sit in the law-courts, but that the
great offices should be filled up by election and from persons having
a qualification; the greater requiring a greater qualification, or, if
there be no offices for which a qualification is required, then those
who are marked out by special ability should be appointed. Under
such a form of government the citizens are sure to be governed well
(for the offices will always be held by the best persons; the people
35 are willing enough to elect them and are not jealous of the good).
The good and the notables will then be satisfied, for they will not be
governed by men who are their inferiors, and the persons elected will
rule justly, because others will call them to account. Every man

---

[18] iv. 1292^b 22–1293^a 10.   [19] Cp. iv. 1292^b 25–33.
[20] Cp. iv. 1297^b 6.   [21] Cp. ii. 1274^a 15.   [22] l. 6.

should be responsible to others, nor should any one be allowed to do just as he pleases; for where absolute freedom is allowed there is 40 nothing to restrain the evil which is inherent in every man. But the 1319ᵃ principle of responsibility secures that which is the greatest good in states; the right persons rule and are prevented from doing wrong, and the people have their due. It is evident that this is the best kind of democracy, and why? Because the people are drawn from a cer- 5 tain class. Some of the ancient laws of most states were, all of them, useful with a view to making the people husbandmen. They provided either that no one should possess more than a certain quantity of land, or that, if he did, the land should not be within a certain distance from the town or the acropolis. Formerly in many states there was a 10 law forbidding any one to sell his original allotment of land.[23] There is a similar law attributed to Oxylus, which is to the effect that there should be a certain portion of every man's land on which he could not borrow money. A useful corrective to the evil of which I am speaking would be the law of the Aphytaeans, who, although 15 they are numerous, and do not possess much land, are all of them husbandmen. For their properties are reckoned in the census, not entire, but only in such small portions that even the poor may have more than the amount required.

Next best to an agricultural, and in many respects similar, are a 20 pastoral people, who live by their flocks; they are the best trained of any for war, robust in body and able to camp out. The people of whom other democracies consist are far inferior to them, for their 25 life is inferior; there is no room for moral excellence in any of their employments, whether they be mechanics or traders or labourers. Besides, people of this class can readily come to the assembly, because they are continually moving about in the city and in the agora; 30 whereas husbandmen are scattered over the country and do not meet, or equally feel the want of assembling together. Where the territory also happens to extend to a distance from the city, there is no difficulty in making an excellent democracy or constitutional govern- 35 ment; for the people are compelled to settle in the country, and even if there is a town population the assembly ought not to meet, in democracies, when the country people cannot come. We have thus explained how the first and best form of democracy should be constituted; it is clear that the other or inferior sorts will deviate in a 40 regular order, and the population which is excluded will at each stage 1319ᵇ be of a lower kind.

[23] Cp. ii. 1266ᵇ 21.

The last form of democracy, that in which all share alike, is one which cannot be borne by all states, and will not last long unless well regulated by laws and customs. The more general causes which tend
5 to destroy this or other kinds of government have been pretty fully considered.[24] In order to constitute such a democracy and strengthen the people, the leaders have been in the habit of including as many as they can, and making citizens not only of those who are legitimate, but even of the illegitimate, and of those who have only one parent a
10 citizen, whether father or mother; [25] for nothing of this sort comes amiss to such a democracy. This is the way in which demagogues proceed. Whereas the right thing would be to make no more additions when the number of the commonalty exceeds that of the notables and of the middle class—beyond this not to go. When in excess of this
15 point, the constitution becomes disorderly, and the notables grow excited and impatient of the democracy, as in the insurrection at Cyrene; for no notice is taken of a little evil, but when it increases it strikes the eye. Measures like those which Cleisthenes [26] passed when
20 he wanted to increase the power of the democracy at Athens, or such as were taken by the founders of popular government at Cyrene, are useful in the extreme form of democracy. Fresh tribes and brotherhoods should be established; the private rites of families should be restricted and converted into public ones; in short, every contrivance
25 should be adopted which will mingle the citizens with one another and get rid of old connexions. Again, the measures which are taken by tyrants appear all of them to be democratic; such, for instance, as the licence permitted to slaves (which may be to a certain extent advantageous) and also that of women and children, and the allow-
30 ing everybody to live as he likes.[27] Such a government will have many supporters, for most persons would rather live in a disorderly than in a sober manner.

5 The mere establishment of a democracy is not the only or principal business of the legislator, or of those who wish to create
35 such a state, for any state, however badly constituted, may last one, two, or three days; a far greater difficulty is the preservation of it. The legislator should therefore endeavour to have a firm foundation according to the principles already laid down concerning the preservation and destruction of states; [28] he should guard against

---

[24] v. 2–7, 1311ᵃ 22–1313ᵃ 16.
[26] Cp. iii. 1275ᵇ 35.
[28] Cp. Bk. v.

[25] Cp. iii. 1278ᵃ 27.
[27] Cp. v. 1313ᵇ 32.

the destructive elements, and should make laws, whether written 40
or unwritten, which will contain all the preservatives of states. He 1320ᵃ
must not think the truly democratical or oligarchical measure to be
that which will give the greatest amount of democracy or oligarchy,
but that which will make them last longest.[29] The demagogues of
our own day often get property confiscated [30] in the law-courts in 5
order to please the people. But those who have the welfare of the
state at heart should counteract them, and make a law that the property of the condemned should not be public and go into the treasury
but be sacred. Thus offenders will be as much afraid, for they will be
punished all the same, and the people, having nothing to gain, will 10
not be so ready to condemn the accused. Care should also be taken
that state trials are as few as possible, and heavy penalties should
be inflicted on those who bring groundless accusations; for it is the
practice to indict, not members of the popular party, but the notables,
although the citizens ought to be all attached to the constitution 15
as well, or at any rate should not regard their rulers as enemies.

Now, since in the last and worst form of democracy the citizens are
very numerous, and can hardly be made to assemble unless they
are paid, and to pay them when there are no revenues presses hardly 20
upon the notables (for the money must be obtained by a property-
tax and confiscations and corrupt practices of the courts, things
which have before now overthrown many democracies); where, I say,
there are no revenues, the government should hold few assemblies,
and the law-courts should consist of many persons, but sit for a
few days only. This system has two advantages: first, the rich do
not fear the expense, even although they are unpaid themselves when 25
the poor are paid; and secondly, causes are better tried, for wealthy
persons, although they do not like to be long absent from their
own affairs, do not mind going for a few days to the law-courts. Where
there are revenues the demagogues should not be allowed after their
manner to distribute the surplus; the poor are always receiving and 30
always wanting more and more, for such help is like water poured
into a leaky cask. Yet the true friend of the people should see that
they be not too poor, for extreme poverty lowers the character of the 35
democracy; measures therefore should be taken which will give them
lasting prosperity; and as this is equally the interest of all classes,
the proceeds of the public revenues should be accumulated and distributed among its poor, if possible, in such quantities as may enable
them to purchase a little farm, or, at any rate, make a beginning in

[29] Cp. v. 1313ᵃ 20–33.   [30] Cp. v. 1305ᵃ 3.

1320^b trade or husbandry. And if this benevolence cannot be ·extended to all, money should be distributed in turn according to tribes or other divisions, and in the meantime the rich should pay the fee for the attendance of the poor at the necessary assemblies; and should in return be excused from useless public services. By administering the state in this spirit the Carthaginians retain the affections of the people;

5 their policy is from time to time to send some of them into their dependent towns, where they grow rich.[31] It is also worthy of a generous and sensible nobility to divide the poor amongst them, and give them the means of going to work. The example of the people of

10 Tarentum is also well deserving of imitation, for, by sharing the use of their own property with the poor, they gain their good will.[32] Moreover, they divide all their offices into two classes, some of them being elected by vote, the others by lot; the latter, that the people may participate in them, and the former, that the state may be better administered. A like result may be gained by dividing the same offices,

15 so as to have two classes of magistrates, one chosen by vote, the other by lot.

Enough has been said of the manner in which democracies ought to be constituted.

6 From these considerations there will be no difficulty in seeing what should be the constitution of oligarchies. We have only to reason from opposites and compare each form of oligarchy with the

20 corresponding form of democracy.

The first and best attempered of oligarchies is akin to a constitutional government. In this there ought to be two standards of qualification; the one high, the other low—the lower qualifying for the humbler yet indispensable offices and the higher for the superior

25 ones. He who acquires the prescribed qualification should have the rights of citizenship. The number of those admitted should be such as will make the entire governing body stronger than those who are excluded, and the new citizen should be always taken out of the better class of the people. The principle, narrowed a little, gives another

30 form of oligarchy; until at length we reach the most cliquish and tyrannical of them all, answering to the extreme democracy, which, being the worst, requires vigilance in proportion to its badness. For as

35 healthy bodies and ships well provided with sailors may undergo many mishaps and survive them, whereas sickly constitutions and rotten ill-manned ships are ruined by the very least mistake, so do

[31] Cp. ii. 1273^b 18.   [32] Cp. ii. 1263^a 37.

the worst forms of government require the greatest care. The popu-
lousness of democracies generally preserves them (for number is to   1321ᵃ
democracy in the place of justice based on proportion); whereas the
preservation of an oligarchy clearly depends on an opposite principle,
viz. good order.

7   As there are four chief divisions of the common people—husband-   5
men, mechanics, retail traders, labourers; so also there are four kinds
of military forces—the cavalry, the heavy infantry, the light-armed
troops, the navy.³³ When the country is adapted for cavalry, then a
strong oligarchy is likely to be established. For the security of the   10
inhabitants depends upon a force of this sort, and only rich men can
afford to keep horses. The second form of oligarchy prevails when
the country is adapted to heavy infantry; for this service is better
suited to the rich than to the poor. But the light-armed and the naval
element are wholly democratic; and nowadays, where they are   15
numerous, if the two parties quarrel, the oligarchy are often worsted
by them in the struggle. A remedy for this state of things may be
found in the practice of generals who combine a proper contingent
of light-armed troops with cavalry and heavy-armed. And this is
the way in which the poor get the better of the rich in civil contests;   20
being lightly armed, they fight with advantage against cavalry and
heavy infantry. An oligarchy which raises such a force out of the
lower classes raises a power against itself. And therefore, since the
ages of the citizens vary and some are older and some younger, the
fathers should have their own sons, while they are still young, taught
the agile movements of light-armed troops; and these, when they   25
have been taken out of the ranks of the youth, should become light-
armed warriors in reality. The oligarchy should also yield a share in
the government to the people, either, as I said before, to those
who have a property qualification,³⁴ or, as in the case of Thebes,³⁵ to
those who have abstained for a certain number of years from mean   30
employments, or, as at Massalia, to men of merit who are selected
for their worthiness, whether previously citizens or not. The magistracies of the highest rank, which ought to be in the hands of the
governing body, should have expensive duties attached to them,
and then the people will not desire them and will take no offence at the
privileges of their rulers when they see that they pay a heavy fine
for their dignity. It is fitting also that the magistrates on entering   35
office should offer magnificent sacrifices or erect some public edifice,
and then the people who participate in the entertainments, and see the

³³ Cp. iv. 1289ᵇ 32–40.   ³⁴ 1320ᵇ 25.   ³⁵ Cp. iii. 1278ᵃ 25.

city decorated with votive offerings and buildings, will not desire an
alteration in the government, and the notables will have memorials
40 of their munificence. This, however, is anything but the fashion of
our modern oligarchs, who are as covetous of gain as they are of
1321ᵇ honour; oligarchies like theirs may be well described as petty democracies. Enough of the manner in which democracies and oligarchies
should be organized.

8 Next in order follows the right distribution of offices, their num-
5 ber, their nature, their duties, of which indeed we have already
spoken.[36] No state can exist not having the necessary offices, and no
state can be well administered not having the offices which tend to
preserve harmony and good order. In small states, as we have already
remarked,[37] there must not be many of them, but in larger there
10 must be a larger number, and we should carefully consider which
offices may properly be united and which separated.

First among necessary offices is that which has the care of the
market; a magistrate should be appointed to inspect contracts and
15 to maintain order. For in every state there must inevitably be buyers
and sellers who will supply one another's wants; this is the readiest
way to make a state self-sufficing and so fulfil the purpose for which
men come together into one state.[38] A second office of a similar kind
20 undertakes the supervision and embellishment of public and private
buildings, the maintaining and repairing of houses and roads, the
prevention of disputes about boundaries, and other concerns of a
like nature. This is commonly called the office of City-warden, and
25 has various departments, which, in more populous towns, are shared
among different persons, one, for example, taking charge of the walls,
another of the fountains, a third of harbours. There is another equally
necessary office, and of a similar kind, having to do with the same
matters without the walls and in the country—the magistrates who
hold this office are called Wardens of the country, or Inspectors of
30 the woods. Besides these three there is a fourth office of receivers of
taxes, who have under their charge the revenue which is distributed
among the various departments; these are called Receivers or Treasurers. Another officer registers all private contracts, and decisions
35 of the courts, all public indictments, and also all preliminary pro-
ceedings. This office again is sometimes subdivided, in which case one
officer is appointed over all the rest. These officers are called Recorders or Sacred Recorders, Presidents, and the like.

[36] iv. 15.   [37] iv. 1299ᵃ 34–ᵇ10.
[38] Cp. i. 1252ᵇ 27; *Nic. Eth* ᵛ. 1134ᵃ 26; Pl. *Rep* ii. 369.

Next to these comes an office of which the duties are the most 40 necessary and also the most difficult, viz. that to which is committed the execution of punishments, or the exaction of fines from those who are posted up according to the registers; and also the custody 1322ᵃ of prisoners. The difficulty of this office arises out of the odium which is attached to it; no one will undertake it unless great profits are to be made, and any one who does is loath to execute the law. Still the office is necessary; for judicial decisions are useless if they take 5 no effect; and if society cannot exist without them, neither can it exist without the execution of them. It is an office which, being so unpopular, should not be entrusted to one person, but divided among several taken from different courts. In like manner an effort should be made to distribute among different persons the writing up of those who are on the register of public debtors. Some sentences should 10 be executed by the magistrates also, and in particular penalties due to the outgoing magistrates should be exacted by the incoming ones; and as regards those due to magistrates already in office, when one court has given judgement, another should exact the penalty; for example, the wardens of the city should exact the fines imposed by the wardens of the agora, and others again should exact the fines imposed by *them*. For penalties are more likely to be exacted when 15 less odium attaches to the exaction of them; but a double odium is incurred when the judges who have passed also execute the sentence, and if they are always the executioners, they will be the enemies of all.

In many places, while one magistracy executes the sentence, another has the custody of the prisoners, as, for example, 'the Eleven' at Athens. It is well to separate off the jailorship also, and try by 20 some device to render the office less unpopular. For it is quite as necessary as that of the executioners; but good men do all they can to avoid it, and worthless persons cannot safely be trusted with it; for they themselves require a guard, and are not fit to guard others. 25 There ought not therefore to be a single or permanent officer set apart for this duty; but it should be entrusted to the young, wherever they are organized into a band or guard, and different magistrates acting in turn should take charge of it.

These are the indispensable officers, and should be ranked first;— next in order follow others, equally necessary, but of higher rank, 30 and requiring great experience and fidelity. Such are the officers to which are committed the guard of the city, and other military functions. Not only in time of war but of peace their duty will be to de- 35 fend the walls and gates, and to muster and marshal the citizens. In some states there are many such offices; in others there are a few

only, while small states are content with one; these officers are called
1322ᵇ generals or commanders. Again, if a state has cavalry or light-armed
troops or archers or a naval force, it will sometimes happen that
each of these departments has separate officers, who are called admirals, or generals of cavalry or of light-armed troops. And there are
subordinate officers called naval captains, and captains of light-armed
5 troops and of horse; having others under them:—all these are included in the department of war. Thus much of military command.

But since many, not to say all, of these offices handle the public
money, there must of necessity be another office which examines and
10 audits them, and has no other functions. Such officers are called by
various names—Scrutineers, Auditors, Accountants, Controllers. Besides all these offices there is another which is supreme over them,
and to this is often entrusted both the introduction and the ratifica-
tion of measures, or at all events it presides, in a democracy, over
15 the assembly. For there must be a body which convenes the supreme
authority in the state. In some places they are called 'probuli', because they hold previous deliberations, but in a democracy more
commonly 'councillors'.³⁹ These are the chief political offices.

Another set of officers is concerned with the maintenance of re-
20 ligion; priests and guardians see to the preservation and repair of
the temples of the gods and to other matters of religion. One office
of this sort may be enough in small places, but in larger ones there
are a great many besides the priesthood; for example superintendents
25 of public worship, guardians of shrines, treasurers of the sacred
revenues. Nearly connected with these there are also the officers appointed for the performance of the public sacrifices, except any
which the law assigns to the priests; such sacrifices derive their dignity
from the public hearth of the city. They are sometimes called archons,
sometimes kings,⁴⁰ and sometimes prytanes.

30 These, then, are the necessary offices, which may be summed up
as follows: offices concerned with matters of religion, with war, with
the revenue and expenditure, with the market, with the city, with
the harbours, with the country; also with the courts of law, with the
35 records of contracts, with execution of sentences, with custody of
prisoners, with audits and scrutinies and accounts of magistrates;
lastly, there are those which preside over the public deliberations
of the state. There are likewise magistracies characteristic of states
which are peaceful and prosperous, and at the same time have a
regard to good order: such as the offices of guardians of women,

---

³⁹ Cp. iv. 1299ᵇ 31.　　　　　　　　　⁴⁰ Cp. iii. 1285ᵇ 23.

guardians of the laws, guardians of children, and directors of gymnastics; also superintendents of gymnastic and Dionysiac contests, 1323[a] and of other similar spectacles. Some of these are clearly not democratic offices; for example, the guardianships of women and children [41]—the poor, not having any slaves, must employ both their women and children as servants. 5

Once more: there are three offices according to whose directions the highest magistrates are chosen in certain states—guardians of the law, probuli, councillors—of these, the guardians of the law are an aristocratical, the probuli an oligarchical, the council a democratical institution. Enough of the different kinds of offices. 10

BOOK VII

1 He who would duly inquire about the best form of a state ought first to determine which is the most eligible life; while this remains uncertain the best form of the state must also be uncertain; 15 for, in the natural order of things, those may be expected to lead the best life who are governed in the best manner of which their circumstances admit. We ought therefore to ascertain, first of all, which is the most generally eligible life, and then whether the same life is or 20 is not best for the state and for individuals.

Assuming that enough has been already said in discussions outside the school concerning the best life, we will now only repeat what is contained in them. Certainly no one will dispute the propriety of that partition of goods which separates them into three classes,[1] 25 viz. external goods, goods of the body, and goods of the soul, or deny that the happy man must have all three. For no one would maintain that he is happy who has not in him a particle of courage or temperance or justice or prudence, who is afraid of every insect which flutters past him, and will commit any crime, however great, in order 30 to gratify his lust of meat or drink, who will sacrifice his dearest friend for the sake of half-a-farthing, and is as feeble and false in mind as a child or a madman. These propositions are almost universally acknowledged as soon as they are uttered, but men differ 35 about the degree or relative superiority of this or that good. Some think that a very moderate amount of virtue is enough, but set no limit to their desires of wealth, property, power, reputation, and the like. To whom we reply by an appeal to facts, which easily prove that 40

---

[41] Cp. iv. 1300[a] 4.
[1] Cp. *Laws*, iii. 697 B, v. 743 E; *N. Eth.* i. 1098[b] 12.

mankind do not acquire or preserve virtue by the help of external
1323ᵇ goods, but external goods by the help of virtue, and that happiness,
whether consisting in pleasure or virtue, or both, is more often found
with those who are most highly cultivated in their mind and in their
character, and have only a moderate share of external goods, than
5 among those who possess external goods to a useless extent but are
deficient in higher qualities; and this is not only matter of experience, but, if reflected upon, will easily appear to be in accordance
with reason. For, whereas external goods have a limit, like any other
instrument,[2] and all things useful are of such a nature that where
there is too much of them they must either do harm, or at any rate
10 be of no use, to their possessors, every good of the soul, the greater
it is, is also of greater use, if the epithet useful as well as noble is
appropriate to such subjects. No proof is required to show that the
best state of one thing in relation to another corresponds in degree
15 of excellence to the interval between the natures of which we say
that these very states are states: so that, if the soul is more noble
than our possessions or our bodies, both absolutely and in relation
to us, it must be admitted that the best state of either has a similar
ratio to the other. Again, it is for the sake of the soul that goods
external and goods of the body are eligible at all, and all wise men
20 ought to choose them for the sake of the soul, and not the soul for
the sake of them.

Let us acknowledge then that each one has just so much of
happiness as he has of virtue and wisdom, and of virtuous and wise
action. God is a witness to us of this truth, for he is happy and blessed,
not by reason of any external good, but in himself and by reason of
25 his own nature. And herein of necessity lies the difference between
good fortune and happiness; for external goods come of themselves,
and chance is the author of them, but no one is just or temperate by
30 or through chance.[3] In like manner, and by a similar train of argument, the happy state may be shown to be that which is best and
which acts rightly; and rightly it cannot act without doing right
actions, and neither individual nor state can do right actions without virtue and wisdom. Thus the courage, justice, and wisdom of a
35 state have the same form and nature as the qualities which give the
individual who possesses them the name of just, wise, or temperate.

Thus much may suffice by way of preface: for I could not avoid
touching upon these questions, neither could I go through all the
arguments affecting them; these are the business of another science.

² Cp. i. 1256ᵇ 35.   ³ *N. Eth.* i. 1099ᵇ 20.

Let us assume then that the best life, both for individuals and 40
states, is the life of virtue, when virtue has external goods enough for 1324ᵃ
the performance of good actions. If there are any who controvert our
assertion, we will in this treatise pass them over, and consider their
objections hereafter.

2 There remains to be discussed the question, Whether the happi- 5
ness of the individual is the same as that of the state, or different?
Here again there can be no doubt—no one denies that they are the
same. For those who hold that the well-being of the individual consists in his wealth, also think that riches make the happiness of the
whole state, and those who value most highly the life of a tyrant deem 10
that city the happiest which rules over the greatest number; while
they who approve an individual for his virtue say that the more
virtuous a city is, the happier it is. Two points here present themselves for consideration: first (1), which is the more eligible life, 15
that of a citizen who is a member of a state, or that of an alien who
has no political ties; and again (2), which is the best form of constitution or the best condition of a state, either on the supposition
that political privileges are desirable for all, or for a majority only?
Since the good of the state and not of the individual is the proper 20
subject of political thought and speculation, and we are engaged in a
political discussion, while the first of these two points has a secondary
interest for us, the latter will be the main subject of our inquiry.

Now it is evident that the form of government is best in which
every man, whoever he is, can act best and live happily. But even 25
those who agree in thinking that the life of virtue is the most eligible
raise a question, whether the life of business and politics is or is not
more eligible than one which is wholly independent of external goods,
I mean than a contemplative life, which by some is maintained to
be the only one worthy of a philosopher. For these two lives—
the life of the philosopher and the life of the statesman—appear to
have been preferred by those who have been most keen in the pursuit 30
of virtue, both in our own and in other ages. Which is the better is
a question of no small moment; for the wise man, like the wise state,
will necessarily regulate his life according to the best end. There are
some who think that while a despotic rule over others is the greatest 35
injustice, to exercise a constitutional rule over them, even though not
unjust, is a great impediment to a man's individual well-being. Others
take an opposite view; they maintain that the true life of man is
the practical and political, and that every virtue admits of being 40

1324ᵇ practised, quite as much by statesmen and rulers as by private individuals. Others, again, are of opinion that arbitrary and tyrannical rule alone consists with happiness; indeed, in some states the entire aim both of the laws and of the constitution is to give men despotic
5 power over their neighbours. And, therefore, although in most cities the laws may be said generally to be in a chaotic state, still, if they aim at anything, they aim at the maintenance of power: thus in Lacedaemon and Crete the system of education and the greater part of the laws are framed with a view to war.[4] And in all nations which
10 are able to gratify their ambition military power is held in esteem, for example among the Scythians and Persians and Thracians and Celts. In some nations there are even laws tending to stimulate the warlike virtues, as at Carthage, where we are told that men obtain
15 the honour of wearing as many armlets as they have served campaigns. There was once a law in Macedonia that he who had not killed an enemy should wear a halter, and among the Scythians no one who had not slain his man was allowed to drink out of the cup which was handed round at a certain feast. Among the Iberians, a warlike nation, the number of enemies whom a man has slain is indicated by the
20 number of obelisks which are fixed in the earth round his tomb; and there are numerous practices among other nations of a like kind, some of them established by law and others by custom. Yet to a reflecting mind it must appear very strange that the statesman should
25 be always considering how he can dominate and tyrannize over others, whether they will or not. How can that which is not even lawful be the business of the statesman or the legislator? Unlawful it certainly is to rule without regard to justice, for there may be might where there is no right. The other arts and sciences offer no parallel; a
30 physician is not expected to persuade or coerce his patients, nor a pilot the passengers in his ship. Yet most men appear to think that the art of despotic government is statesmanship, and what men affirm to be unjust and inexpedient in their own case they are not ashamed
35 of practising towards others; they demand just rule for themselves, but where other men are concerned they care nothing about it. Such behaviour is irrational; unless the one party is, and the other is not, born to serve, in which case men have a right to command, not indeed all their fellows, but only those who are intended to be subjects; just as we ought not to hunt mankind, whether for food or sacrifice,
40 but only the animals which may be hunted for food or sacrifice, this is to say, such wild animals as are eatable. And surely there may
1325ᵃ be a city happy in isolation, which we will assume to be well-governed

---

[4] Cp. Plato, *Laws*, i. 633 ff.

(for it is quite possible that a city thus isolated might be well-administered and have good laws); but such a city would not be constituted with any view to war or the conquest of enemies—all that sort of thing must be excluded. Hence we see very plainly that war- 5 like pursuits, although generally to be deemed honourable, are not the supreme end of all things, but only means. And the good lawgiver should inquire how states and races of men and communities may participate in a good life, and in the happiness which is attainable by them. His enactments will not be always the same; and where there 10 are neighbours [5] he will have to see what sort of studies should be practised in relation to their several characters, or how the measures appropriate in relation to each are to be adopted. The end at which the best form of government should aim may be properly made a matter of future consideration.[6]   15

3 Let us now address those who, while they agree that the life of virtue is the most eligible, differ about the manner of practising it. For some renounce political power, and think that the life of 20 the freeman is different from the life of the statesman and the best of all; but others think the life of the statesman best. The argument of the latter is that he who does nothing cannot do well, and that virtuous activity is identical with happiness. To both we say: 'you are partly right and partly wrong.' The first class are right in affirming that the life of the freeman is better than the life of the despot; 25 for there is nothing grand or noble in having the use of a slave, in so far as he is a slave; or in issuing commands about necessary things. But it is an error to suppose that every sort of rule is despotic like that of a master over slaves, for there is as great a difference between the rule over freemen and the rule over slaves as there is between slavery by nature and freedom by nature, about which I have said enough at 30 the commencement of this treatise.[7] And it is equally a mistake to place inactivity above action, for happiness is activity, and the actions of the just and wise are the realization of much that is noble.

But perhaps some one, accepting these premises, may still maintain that supreme power is the best of all things, because the possessors of it are able to perform the greatest number of noble 35 actions. If so, the man who is able to rule, instead of giving up anything to his neighbour, ought rather to take away his power; and the father should make no account of his son, nor the son of his father, nor friend of friend; they should not bestow a thought on one another in comparison with this higher object, for the best

[5] Cp. ii. 1265ᵃ 20, 1267ᵃ 19.   [6] 1333ᵃ 11 sqq.   [7] i. 4–7.

40 is the most eligible and 'doing well' is the best. There might be some
1325ᵇ truth in such a view if we assume that robbers and plunderers
attain the chief good. But this can never be; their hypothesis is
false. For the actions of a ruler cannot really be honourable, unless
he is as much superior to other men as a husband is to a wife, or a
5 father to his children, or a master to his slaves. And therefore he
who violates the law can never recover by any success, however great,
what he has already lost in departing from virtue. For equals the
honourable and the just consist in sharing alike, as is just and equal.
But that the unequal should be given to equals, and the unlike to
those who are like, is contrary to nature, and nothing which is
10 contrary to nature is good. If therefore, there is any one [8] superior in
virtue and in the power of performing the best actions, him we ought
to follow and obey, but he must have the capacity for action as
well as virtue.

If we are right in our view, and happiness is assumed to be
15 virtuous activity, the active life will be the best, both for every city
collectively, and for individuals. Not that a life of action must
necessarily have relation to others, as some persons think, nor are
those ideas only to be regarded as practical which are pursued for the
sake of practical results, but much more the thoughts and contempla-
20 tions which are independent and complete in themselves; since virtuous activity, and therefore a certain kind of action, is an end, and
even in the case of external actions the directing mind is most truly
said to act. Neither, again, is it necessary that states which are cut
off from others and choose to live alone should be inactive; for
25 activity, as well as other things, may take place by sections; there are
many ways in which the sections of a state act upon one another.
The same thing is equally true of every individual. If this were otherwise, God and the universe, who have no external actions over and
above their own energies, would be far enough from perfection. Hence
30 it is evident that the same life is best for each individual, and for
states and for mankind collectively.

4 Thus far by way of introduction. In what has preceded [9] I have
35 discussed other forms of government; in what remains the first point
to be considered is what should be the conditions of the ideal or perfect state; for the perfect state cannot exist without a due supply of
the means of life. And therefore we must pre-suppose many purely
imaginary conditions,[10] but nothing impossible. There will be a cer-

---

[8] Cp. iii. 1284ᵇ 32 and 1288ᵃ 28.   [9] Bk. ii.
[10] Cp. ii. 1265ᵃ 17.

tain numbers of citizens, a country in which to place them, and the 40
like. As the weaver or shipbuilder or any other artisan must have
the material proper for his work (and in proportion as this is better 1326ᵃ
prepared, so will the result of his art be nobler), so the statesman or
legislator must also have the materials suited to him.

First among the materials required by the statesman is popula- 5
tion: he will consider what should be the number and character of the
citizens, and then what should be the size and character of the
country. Most persons think that a state in order to be happy ought
to be large; but even if they are right, they have no idea what is a
large and what a small state. For they judge of the size of the city by 10
the number of the inhabitants; whereas they ought to regard, not their
number, but their power. A city too, like an individual, has a work
to do; and that city which is best adapted to the fulfilment of its
work is to be deemed greatest, in the same sense of the word great in 15
which Hippocrates might be called greater, not as a man, but as a
physician, than some one else who was taller. And even if we reckon
greatness by numbers, we ought not to include everybody, for there
must always be in cities a multitude of slaves and sojourners and 20
foreigners; but we should include those only who are members of
the state, and who form an essential part of it. The number of the
latter is a proof of the greatness of a city; but a city which produces
numerous artisans and comparatively few soldiers cannot be great,
for a great city is not to be confounded with a populous one. Moreover, experience shows that a very populous city can rarely, if ever, be 25
well governed; since all cities which have a reputation for good
government have a limit of population. We may argue on grounds of
reason, and the same result will follow. For law is order, and good
law is good order; but a very great multitude cannot be orderly: to in- 30
troduce order into the unlimited is the work of a divine power—of such
a power as holds together the universe. Beauty is realized in number
and magnitude,[11] and the state which combines magnitude with good
order must necessarily be the most beautiful. To the size of states 35
there is a limit, as there is to other things, plants, animals, implements; for none of these retain their natural power when they are
too large or too small, but they either wholly lose their nature, or
are spoiled. For example,[12] a ship which is only a span long will not 40
be a ship at all, nor a ship a quarter of a mile long; yet there may be
a ship of a certain size, either too large or too small, which will still 1326ᵇ
be a ship, but bad for sailing. In like manner a state when composed
of too few is not, as a state ought to be, self-sufficing; when of too

---

[11] Cp. *Poet.* 1450ᵇ 36.   [12] Cp. v. 1309ᵇ 23.

many, though self-sufficing in all mere necessaries, as a nation may be,
5 it is not a state, being almost incapable of constitutional government.
For who can be the general of such a vast multitude, or who the
herald, unless he have the voice of a Stentor?

A state, then, only begins to exist when it has attained a population
sufficient for a good life in the political community: it may indeed,
10 if it somewhat exceed this number, be a greater state. But, as I was
saying, there must be a limit. What should be the limit will be
easily ascertained by experience. For both governors and governed
have duties to perform; the special functions of a governor are to com-
15 mand and to judge. But if the citizens of a state are to judge and to
distribute offices according to merit, then they must know each other's
characters; where they do not possess this knowledge, both the election to offices and the decision of lawsuits will go wrong. When the
population is very large they are manifestly settled at haphazard,
20 which clearly ought not to be. Besides, in an over-populous state
foreigners and metics will readily acquire the rights of citizens,
for who will find them out? Clearly then the best limit of the population of a state is the largest number which suffices for the purposes of
25 life, and can be taken in at a single view. Enough concerning the size
of a state.

5   Much the same principle will apply to the territory of the state:
every one would agree in praising the territory which is most entirely
self-sufficing; and that must be the territory which is all-producing,
30 for to have all things and to want nothing is sufficiency. In size and
extent it should be such as may enable the inhabitants to live at
once temperately and liberally in the enjoyment of leisure.[13]
Whether we are right or wrong in laying down this limit we will inquire
more precisely hereafter,[14] when we have occasion to consider what
35 is the right use of property and wealth: a matter which is much
disputed, because men are inclined to rush into one of two extremes,
some into meanness, others into luxury.

It is not difficult to determine the general character of the territory which is required (there are, however, some points on which
40 military authorities should be heard); it should be difficult of access
1327ᵃ to the enemy, and easy of egress to the inhabitants. Further, we
require that the land as well as the inhabitants of whom we were just
now speaking [15] should be taken in at a single view, for a country
which is easily seen can be easily protected. As to the position of the

---

[13] Cp. ii. 1265ᵃ 32.   [14] This promise is not fulfilled.
[15] 1326ᵇ 22–24.

city, if we could have what we wish, it should be well situated in regard 5
both to sea and land. This then is one principle, that it should be a
convenient centre for the protection of the whole country: the other
is, that it should be suitable for receiving the fruits of the soil, and
also for the bringing in of timber and any other products that are 10
easily transported.

6   Whether a communication with the sea is beneficial to a well-
ordered state or not is a question which has often been asked. It is
argued that the introduction of strangers brought up under other laws,
and the increase of population, will be adverse to good order; the 15
increase arises from their using the sea and having a crowd of merchants coming and going, and is inimical to good government.[16]
Apart from these considerations, it would be undoubtedly better, both
with a view to safety and to the provision of necessaries, that the 20
city and territory should be connected with the sea; the defenders of
a country, if they are to maintain themselves against an enemy,
should be easily relieved both by land and by sea; and even if they are
not able to attack by sea and land at once, they will have less difficulty in doing mischief to their assailants on one element, if they
themselves can use both. Moreover, it is necessary that they should 25
import from abroad what is not found in their own country, and that
they should export what they have in excess; for a city ought to be a
market, not indeed for others, but for herself.

Those who make themselves a market for the world only do so for
the sake of revenue, and if a state ought not to desire profit of this 30
kind it ought not to have such an emporium. Nowadays we often see in
countries and cities dockyards and harbours very conveniently placed
outside the city, but not too far off; and they are kept in dependence
by walls and similar fortifications. Cities thus situated manifestly 35
reap the benefit of intercourse with their ports; and any harm which
is likely to accrue may be easily guarded against by the laws, which
will pronounce and determine who may hold communication with one
another, and who may not.

There can be no doubt that the possession of a moderate naval 40
force is advantageous to a city; the city should be formidable not 1327[b]
only to its own citizens but to some of its neighbours,[17] or, if
necessary, able to assist them by sea as well as by land. The proper
number or magnitude of this naval force is relative to the character
of the state; for if her function is to take a leading part in politics,
her naval power should be commensurate with the scale of her enter- 5

16 Cp. Plato, *Laws*, iv. 704 D–705 B.   17 Cp. ii. 1265ᵃ 20.

prises. The population of the state need not be much increased, since there is no necessity that the sailors should be citizens: the marines who have the control and command will be freemen, and belong also 10 to the infantry; and wherever there is a dense population of Perioeci and husbandmen, there will always be sailors more than enough. Of this we see instances at the present day. The city of Heraclea, 15 for example, although small in comparison with many others, can man a considerable fleet. Such are our conclusions respecting the territory of the state, its harbours, its towns, its relations to the sea, and its maritime power.

7   Having spoken of the number of the citizens,[18] we will proceed to 20 speak of what should be their character. This is a subject which can be easily understood by any one who casts his eye on the more celebrated states of Hellas, and generally on the distribution of races in the habitable world. Those who live in a cold climate and in Europe 25 are full of spirit, but wanting in intelligence and skill; and therefore they retain comparative freedom, but have no political organization, and are incapable of ruling over others. Whereas the natives of Asia are intelligent and inventive, but they are wanting in spirit, and therefore they are always in a state of subjection and slavery. But the Hellenic race, which is situated between them, is likewise inter- 30 mediate in character, being high-spirited and also intelligent.[19] Hence it continues free, and is the best-governed of any nation, and, if it could be formed into one state, would be able to rule the world. There are also similar differences in the different tribes of Hellas; for some of them are of a one-sided nature, and are intelligent or courage- 35 ous only, while in others there is a happy combination of both qualities. And clearly those whom the legislator will most easily lead to virtue may be expected to be both intelligent and courageous. Some [20] say that the guardians should be friendly towards those whom 40 they know, fierce towards those whom they do not know. Now, pas- 1328ª sion is the quality of the soul which begets friendship and enables us to love; notably the spirit within us is more stirred against our friends and acquaintances than against those who are unknown to us, when we think that we are despised by them; for which reason Archilochus, complaining of his friends, very naturally addresses his soul in these words,

5   'For surely thou art plagued on account of friends'.

The power of command and the love of freedom are in all men

---

[18] 1326ª 9–ᵇ24.   [19] Cp. Plato, *Rep.* iv. 435 E, 436 A.
[20] *Rep.* ii. 375 C.

based upon this quality, for passion is commanding and invincible.
Nor is it right to say that the guardians should be fierce towards those
whom they do not know, for we ought not to be out of temper with
any one; and a lofty spirit is not fierce by nature, but only when
excited against evil-doers. And this, as I was saying before, is a 10
feeling which men show most strongly towards their friends if they
think they have received a wrong at their hands: as indeed is reasonable; for, besides the actual injury, they seem to be deprived of a
benefit by those who owe them one. Hence the saying,   15

'Cruel is the strife of brethren',

and again,

'They who love in excess also hate in excess'.

Thus we have nearly determined the number and character of the
citizens of our state, and also the size and nature of their territory.
I say 'nearly', for we ought not to require the same minuteness in 20
theory as in the facts given by perception.[21]

8 As in other natural compounds the conditions of a composite
whole are not necessarily organic parts of it, so in a state or in any
other combination forming a unity not everything is a part, which is
a necessary condition.[22] The members of an association have necessarily some one thing the same and common to all, in which they 25
share equally or unequally; for example, food or land or any other
thing. But where there are two things of which one is a means and
the other an end, they have nothing in common except that the one
receives what the other produces. Such, for example, is the relation 30
in which workmen and tools stand to their work; the house and the
builder have nothing in common, but the art of the builder is for the
sake of the house. And so states require property, but property, even 35
though living beings are included in it,[23] is no part of a state; for a
state is not a community of living beings only, but a community of
equals, aiming at the best life possible. Now, whereas happiness is
the highest good, being a realization and perfect practice of virtue,
which some can attain, while others have little or none of it, the
various qualities of men are clearly the reason why there are various 40
kinds of states and many forms of government; for different men
seek after happiness in different ways and by different means, and 1328ᵇ
so make for themselves different modes of life and forms of gov-

[21] Cp. 1331ᵇ 18.   [22] Cp. iii. 1278ᵃ 2.   [23] Cp. i. 1253ᵇ 32.

ernment. We must see also how many things are indispensable to the
existence of a state, for what we call the parts of a state will be found
among the indispensables. Let us then enumerate the functions of a
5 state, and we shall easily elicit what we want:

First, there must be food; secondly, arts, for life requires many
instruments; thirdly, there must be arms, for the members of a
community have need of them, and in their own hands, too, in order
10 to maintain authority both against disobedient subjects and against
external assailants; fourthly, there must be a certain amount of
revenue, both for internal needs, and for the purposes of war;
fifthly, or rather first, there must be a care of religion, which is commonly called worship; sixthly, and most necessary of all, there must
be a power of deciding what is for the public interest, and what is
just in men's dealings with one another.

15   These are the services which every state may be said to need. For
a state is not a mere aggregate of persons, but a union of them
sufficing for the purposes of life; and if any of these things be wanting, it is as we maintain [24] impossible that the community can be
absolutely self-sufficing. A state then should be framed with a view to
the fulfilment of these functions. There must be husbandmen to pro-
20 cure food, and artisans, and a warlike and a wealthy class, and
priests, and judges to decide what is necessary and expedient.

9   Having determined these points, we have in the next place to
consider whether all ought to share in every sort of occupation. Shall
25 every man be at once husbandman, artisan, councillor, judge, or shall
we suppose the several occupations just mentioned assigned to di-
ferent persons? or, thirdly, shall some employments be assigned to
individuals and others common to all? The same arrangement, how-
30 ever, does not occur in every constitution; as we were saying, all
may be shared by all, or not all by all, but only by some; and
hence arise the differences of constitutions, for in democracies all
share in all, in oligarchies the opposite practice prevails. Now, since
we are here speaking of the best form of government, i. e. that under
35 which the state will be most happy (and happiness, as has been already said, cannot exist without virtue [25]), it clearly follows that in
the state which is best governed and possesses men who are just absolutely, and not merely relatively to the principle of the constitution,
the citizens must not lead the life of mechanics or tradesmen, for
40 such a life is ignoble, and inimical to virtue.[26] Neither must they be

[24] Cp. ii. 1261ᵇ 12, iii. 1275ᵇ 20, v. 1303ᵃ 26.
[25] Cp. 1323ᵃ 21–1324ᵃ 4, 1328ᵃ 37 sq.   [26] Cp. Plato, *Laws*, xi. 919 c–ᴇ.

husbandmen, since leisure is necessary both for the development 1329ᵃ
of virtue and the performance of political duties.

Again, there is in a state a class of warriors, and another of councillors, who advise about the expedient and determine matters of law, and these seem in an especial manner parts of a state. Now, should 5 these two classes be distinguished, or are both functions to be assigned to the same persons? Here again there is no difficulty in seeing that both functions will in one way belong to the same, in another, to different persons. To different persons in so far as these employments are suited to different primes of life,²⁷ for the one requires wisdom and the other strength. But on the other hand, since it is an impossible thing that those who are able to use or to resist force should 10 be willing to remain always in subjection, from this point of view the persons are the same; for those who carry arms can always determine the fate of the constitution. It remains therefore that both functions should be entrusted by the ideal constitution to the same persons, not, however, at the same time, but in the order prescribed by nature, who has given to young men strength and to older men 15 wisdom. Such a distribution of duties will be expedient and also just, and is founded upon a principle of conformity to merit. Besides, the ruling class should be the owners of property, for they are citizens, and the citizens of a state should be in good circumstances; whereas 20 mechanics or any other class which is not a producer of virtue have no share in the state. This follows from our first principle,²⁸ for happiness cannot exist without virtue, and a city is not to be termed happy in regard to a portion of the citizens, but in regard to them all.²⁹ And clearly property should be in their hands, since the husband- 25 men will of necessity be slaves or barbarian Perioeci.³⁰

Of the classes enumerated there remain only the priests, and the manner in which their office is to be regulated is obvious. No husbandman or mechanic should be appointed to it; for the Gods should receive honour from the citizens only. Now since the body of the citi- 30 zens is divided into two classes, the warriors and the councillors, and it is beseeming that the worship of the Gods should be duly performed, and also a rest provided in their service for those who from age have given up active life, to the old men of these two classes should be assigned the duties of the priesthood.

We have shown what are the necessary conditions, and what the parts of a state: husbandmen, craftsmen, and labourers of all kinds 35 are necessary to the existence of states, but the parts of the state are

---

²⁷ i. e. the physical and the mental. ²⁸ Cp. 1328ᵇ 35.
²⁹ Cp. ii. 1264ᵇ 17–24. ³⁰ Cp. *infra*, 1330ᵃ 25–31.

the warriors and councillors. And these are distinguished severally from one another, the distinction being in some cases permanent, in others not.

40 10   It is now new or recent discovery of political philosophers that
1329ᵇ the state ought to be divided into classes, and that the warriors should be separated from the husbandmen. The system has continued in Egypt and in Crete to this day, and was established, as tradition says, by a law of Sesostris in Egypt and of Minos in Crete. The
5 institution of common tables also appears to be of ancient date, being in Crete as old as the reign of Minos, and in Italy far older. The Italian historians say that there was a certain Italus king of Oenotria,
10 from whom the Oenotrians were called Italians, and who gave the name of Italy to the promontory of Europe lying within the Scylletic and Lametic Gulfs,[31] which are distant from one another only half a day's journey. They say that this Italus converted the Oenotrians
15 from shepherds into husbandmen, and besides other laws which he gave them, was the founder of their common meals; even in our day some who are derived from him retain this institution and certain other laws of his. On the side of Italy towards Tyrrhenia dwelt the
20 Opici, who are now, as of old, called Ausones; and on the side towards Iapygia and the Ionian Gulf, in the district called Siritis, the Chones, who are likewise of Oenotrian race. From this part of the world originally came the institution of common tables; the separation into castes from Egypt, for the reign of Sesostris is of far greater antiquity than that of Minos. It is true indeed that these and many other
25 things have been invented several times over [32] in the course of ages, or rather times without number; for necessity may be supposed to have taught men the inventions which were absolutely required, and when these were provided, it was natural that other things which
30 would adorn and enrich life should grow up by degrees. And we may infer that in political institutions the same rule holds. Egypt [33] witnesses to the antiquity of all these things, for the Egyptians appear to be of all people the most ancient; and they have laws and a regular constitution existing from time immemorial. We should there-
35 fore make the best use of what has been already discovered, and try to supply defects.

[31] i. e. between these gulfs and the Strait of Messina.
[32] Cp. Plato, *Laws*, iii. 676; Aristotle, *Metaph.* xii. 1074ᵇ 10; and *Pol.* ii. 1264ᵃ 3.
[33] Cp. *Metaph.* i. 981ᵇ 23; *Meteor.* i. 14. 352ᵇ 19; Plato, *Timaeus*, 22 ʙ; *Laws*, ii. 656, 657.

I have already remarked that the land ought to belong to those who possess arms and have a share in the government,[34] and that the husbandmen ought to be a class distinct from them; and I have determined what should be the extent and nature of the territory. Let me proceed to discuss the distribution of the land, and the character of the agricultural class; for I do not think that property ought to be common, as some maintain,[35] but only that by friendly consent there should be a common use of it; and that no citizen should be in want of subsistence. 40 1330ᵃ

As to common meals, there is a general agreement that a well-ordered city should have them; and we will hereafter explain what are our own reasons for taking this view.[36] They ought, however, to be open to all the citizens.[37] And yet it is not easy for the poor to contribute the requisite sum out of their private means, and to provide also for their household. The expense of religious worship should likewise be a public charge. The land must therefore be divided into two parts, one public and the other private, and each part should be subdivided, part of the public land being appropriated to the service of the Gods, and the other part used to defray the cost of the common meals; while of the private land, part should be near the border, and the other near the city, so that, each citizen having two lots, they may all of them have land in both places; there is justice and fairness in such a division, and it tends to inspire unanimity among the people in their border wars. Where there is not this arrangement, some of them are too ready to come to blows with their neighbours, while others are so cautious that they quite lose the sense of honour. Wherefore there is a law in some places which forbids those who dwell near the border to take part in public deliberations about wars with neighbours, on the ground that their interests will pervert their judgment. For the reasons already mentioned, then, the land should be divided in the manner described. The very best thing of all would be that the husbandmen should be slaves taken from among men who are not all of the same race [38] and not spirited, for if they have no spirit they will be better suited for their work, and there will be no danger of their making a revolution. The next best thing would be that they should be Perioeci of foreign race,[39] and of a like inferior nature; some of them should be the slaves of individuals, and employed in the private estates of men of property, the remainder should be the

5

10

15

20

25

30

---

³⁴ 1328ᵇ 33–1329ᵃ 2, 1329ᵃ 17–26, 1326ᵇ 26–32.

³⁵ Cp. ii. 5, *Rep.* iii. 416 D.

³⁶ Aristotle does not give any explanation in the *Politics*.

³⁷ Cp. ii. 1271ᵃ 28.   ³⁸ Cp. Plato, *Laws*, vi. 777 C, D.   ³⁹ Cp. 1329ᵃ 26.

property of the state and employed on the common land.[40] I will hereafter explain [41] what is the proper treatment of slaves, and why it is
expedient that liberty should be always held out to them as the reward
of their services.

11   We have already said that the city should be open to the land and
35 to the sea,[42] and to the whole country as far as possible. In respect
of the place itself our wish would be that its situation should be
fortunate in four things. The first, health—this is a necessity: cities
which lie towards the east, and are blown upon by winds coming from
40 the east, are the healthiest; next in healthfulness are those which are
sheltered from the north wind, for they have a milder winter. The site
1330ᵇ of the city should likewise be convenient both for political administration and for war. With a view to the latter it should afford easy
egress to the citizens, and at the same time be inaccessible and difficult
of capture to enemies.[43] There should be a natural abundance of
5 springs and fountains in the town, or, if there is a deficiency of them,
great reservoirs may be established for the collection of rain-water,
such as will not fail when the inhabitants are cut off from the country
by war. Special care should be taken of the health of the inhabitants,
which will depend chiefly on the healthiness of the locality and of the
10 quarter to which they are exposed, and secondly, on the use of pure
water; this latter point is by no means a secondary consideration. For
the elements which we use most and oftenest for the support of the
body contribute most to health, and among these are water and air.
15 Wherefore, in all wise states, if there is a want of pure water, and
the supply is not all equally good, the drinking water ought to be
separated from that which is used for other purposes.

As to strongholds, what is suitable to different forms of government
20 varies: thus an acropolis is suited to an oligarchy or a monarchy, but
a plain to a democracy; neither to an aristocracy, but rather a number
of strong places. The arrangement of private houses is considered to
be more agreeable and generally more convenient, if the streets are
regularly laid out after the modern fashion which Hippodamus [44]
25 introduced, but for security in war the antiquated mode of building,
which made it difficult for strangers to get out of a town and for
assailants to find their way in, is preferable. A city should therefore
adopt both plans of building: it is possible to arrange the houses ir-
regularly, as husbandmen plant their vines in what are called 'clumps'

[40] Cp. ii. 1267ᵇ 16.
[41] A. does not do so in the *Politics*, but Cp. *Oec.* 1344ᵇ 15.
[42] 1327ᵃ 4-40.   [43] Repetition of 1326ᵇ 40.   [44] Cp. ii. 1267ᵇ 22.

The whole town should not be laid out in straight lines, but only cer- 30
tain quarters and regions; thus security and beauty will be combined.

As to walls, those who say [45] that cities making any pretension to
military virtue should not have them, are quite out of date in their
notions; and they may see the cities which prided themselves on this
fancy confuted by facts. True, there is little courage shown in seeking 35
for safety behind a rampart when an enemy is similar in character and
not much superior in number; but the superiority of the besiegers may
be and often is too much both for ordinary human valor and for that
which is found only in a few; and if they are to be saved and to 40
escape defeat and outrage, the strongest wall will be the truest 1331ᵃ
soldierly precaution, more especially now that missiles and siege engines
have been brought to such perfection. To have no walls would be as
foolish as to choose a site for a town in an exposed country, and to
level the heights; or as if an individual were to leave his house unwalled, 5
lest the inmates should become cowards. Nor must we forget that
those who have their cities surrounded by walls may either take advantage of them or not, but cities which are unwalled have no
choice.

If our conclusions are just, not only should cities have walls, but 10
care should be taken to make them ornamental, as well as useful for
warlike purposes, and adapted to resist modern inventions. For as the
assailants of a city do all they can to gain an advantage, so the de- 15
fenders should make use of any means of defence which have been
already discovered, and should devise and invent others, for when men
are well prepared no enemy even thinks of attacking them.

12   As the walls are to be divided by guard-houses and towers built
at suitable intervals, and the body of citizens must be distributed at 20
common tables,[46] the idea will naturally occur that we should establish
some of the common tables in the guard-houses. These might be arranged as has been suggested; while the principal common tables of
the magistrates will occupy a suitable place, and there also will be the 25
buildings appropriated to religious worship except in the case of those
rites which the law or the Pythian oracle has restricted to a special
locality.[47] The site should be a spot seen far and wide, which gives due
elevation to virtue and towers over the neighbourhood. Below this 30
spot should be established an agora, such as that which the Thessalians
call the 'freemen's agora'; from this all trade should be excluded, and
no mechanic, husbandman, or any such person allowed to enter, unless

⁴⁵ Cp. Plato, *Laws*, vi. 778 ᴅ.   ⁴⁶ Cp. 1330ᵃ 3.
⁴⁷ Cp. Plato, *Laws*, v. 738 ʙ–ᴅ, vi. 759 ᴄ, 778 ᴄ, viii. 848 ᴅ–ᴇ.

35 he be summoned by the magistrates. It would be a charming use of the place, if the gymnastic exercises of the elder men were performed there. For in this noble practice different ages should be separated, and some of the magistrates should stay with the boys, while the 40 grown-up men remain with the magistrates; for the presence of the magistrates is the best mode of inspiring true modesty and ingenuous 1331ᵇ fear. There should also be a traders' agora, distinct and apart from the other, in a situation which is convenient for the reception of goods both by sea and land.

But in speaking of the magistrates we must not forget another sec-5 tion of the citizens, viz. the priests, for whom public tables should likewise be provided in their proper place near the temples. The magistrates who deal with contracts, indictments, summonses, and the like, and those who have the care of the agora and of the city respectively, 10 ought to be established near an agora and some public place of meeting; the neighbourhood of the traders' agora will be a suitable spot; the upper agora we devote to the life of leisure, the other is intended for the necessities of trade.

The same order should prevail in the country, for there too the 15 magistrates, called by some 'Inspectors of Forests' and by others 'Wardens of the Country', must have guard-houses and common tables while they are on duty; temples should also be scattered throughout the country, dedicated, some to Gods, and some to heroes.

But it would be a waste of time for us to linger over details like these. The difficulty is not in imagining but in carrying them out. 20 We may talk about them as much as we like, but the execution of them will depend upon fortune. Wherefore let us say no more about these matters for the present.

13 Returning to the constitution itself, let us seek to determine out 25 of what and what sort of elements the state which is to be happy and well-governed should be composed. There are two things in which all well-being consists: one of them is the choice of a right end and aim of action, and the other the discovery of the actions which are means 30 towards it; for the means and the end may agree or disagree. Sometimes the right end is set before men, but in practice they fail to attain it; in other cases they are successful in all the means, but they propose to themselves a bad end; and sometimes they fail in both. Take, for example, the art of medicine; physicians do not always understand 35 the nature of health, and also the means which they use may not effect the desired end. In all arts and sciences both the end and the means should be equally within our control:

The happiness and well-being which all men manifestly desire, some have the power of attaining, but to others, from some accident 40 or defect of nature, the attainment of them is not granted; for a good life requires a supply of external goods, in a less degree when men 1332ᵃ are in a good state, in a greater degree when they are in a lower state. Others again, who possess the conditions of happiness, go utterly wrong from the first in the pursuit of it. But since our object is to discover the best form of government, that, namely, under which a city 5 will be best governed, and since the city is best governed which has the greatest opportunity of obtaining happiness, it is evident that we must clearly ascertain the nature of happiness.

We maintain, and have said in the *Ethics*,[48] if the arguments there adduced are of any value, that happiness is the realization and perfect exercise of virtue, and this not conditional, but absolute. And I used 10 the term 'conditional' to express that which is indispensable, and 'absolute' to express that which is good in itself. Take the case of just actions; just punishments and chastisements do indeed spring from a good principle, but they are good only because we cannot do without them—it would be better that neither individuals nor states should need anything of the sort—but actions which aim at honour and 15 advantage are absolutely the best. The conditional action is only the choice of a lesser evil; whereas these are the foundation and creation of good. A good man may make the best even of poverty and disease, and the other ills of life; but he can only attain happiness under the 20 opposite conditions [49] (for this also has been determined in accordance with ethical arguments,[50] that the good man is he for whom, because he is virtuous, the things that are absolutely good are good; it is also plain that his use of these goods must be virtuous and in the 25 absolute sense good). This makes men fancy that external goods are the cause of happiness, yet we might as well say that a brilliant performance on the lyre was to be attributed to the instrument and not to the skill of the performer.

It follows then from what has been said that some things the legislator must find ready to his hand in a state, others he must provide. And therefore we can only say: May our state be constituted in such a manner as to be blessed with the goods of which fortune disposes (for we acknowledge her power): whereas virtue and goodness 30 in the state are not a matter of chance but the result of knowledge and purpose. A city can be virtuous only when the citizens who have a

---

[48] *Nic. Eth.* i. 1098ᵃ 16, x. 1176ᵇ 4; and Cp. 1328ᵃ 37.
[49] *Nic. Eth.* i. 1100ᵇ 22, 1101ᵃ 13.
[50] *Nic. Eth.* iii. 1113ᵃ 22–ᵇ1; *E. E.* vii. 1248ᵇ 26; *M. M.* ii. 1207ᵇ 31.

share in the government are virtuous, and in our state all the citizens
35 share in the government; let us then inquire how a man becomes
virtuous. For even if we could suppose the citizen body to be virtuous, without each of them being so, yet the latter would be better,
for in the virtue of each the virtue of all is involved.

There are three things which make men good and virtuous; these
40 are nature, habit, rational principle.[51] In the first place, every one
must be born a man and not some other animal; so, too, he must have
a certain character, both of body and soul. But some qualities there
1332ᵇ is no use in having at birth, for they are altered by habit, and there
are some gifts which by nature are made to be turned by habit to good
or bad. Animals lead for the most part a life of nature, although in
lesser particulars some are influenced by habit as well. Man has
5 rational principle, in addition, and man only. Wherefore nature, habit,
rational principle must be in harmony with one another; for they do
not always agree; men do many things against habit and nature, if
rational principle persuades them that they ought. We have already
determined what natures are likely to be most easily moulded
by the hands of the legislator.[52] All else is the work of education; we
10 learn some things by habit and some by instruction.

14   Since every political society is composed of rulers and subjects
let us consider whether the relations of one to the other should inter-
15 change or be permanent.[53] For the education of the citizens will
necessarily vary with the answer given to this question. Now, if some
men excelled others in the same degree in which gods and heroes are
supposed to excel mankind in general (having in the first place a great
20 advantage even in their bodies, and secondly in their minds), so
that the superiority of the governors was undisputed and patent to
their subjects, it would clearly be better that once for all the one
class should rule and the others serve.[54] But since this is unattainable,
and kings have no marked superiority over their subjects, such as
25 Scylax affirms to be found among the Indians, it is obviously necessary on many grounds that all the citizens alike should take their
turn of governing and being governed. Equality consists in the same
treatment of similar persons, and no government can stand which is
not founded upon justice. For if the government be unjust every one
in the country unites with the governed in the desire to have a revolu-
30 tion, and it is an impossibility that the members of the government

[51] Cp. *N. Eth.* x. 1179ᵇ 20.   [52] 1327ᵇ 36.
[53] Cp. iii. 1279ᵃ 8.   [54] Cp. i. 1254ᵇ 16, 1284ᵃ 3.

can be so numerous as to be stronger than all their enemies put together. Yet that governors should excel their subjects is undeniable. How all this is to be effected, and in what way they will respectively share in the government, the legislator has to consider. The subject 35 has been already mentioned.[55] Nature herself has provided the distinction when she made a difference between old and young within the same species, of whom she fitted the one to govern and the other to be governed. No one takes offence at being governed when he is young, nor does he think himself better than his governors, especially 40 if he will enjoy the same privilege when he reaches the required age.

We conclude that from one point of view governors and governed are identical, and from another different. And therefore their education must be the same and also different. For he who would learn 1333ᵃ to command well must, as men say, first of all learn to obey.[56] As I observed in the first part of this treatise, there is one rule which is for the sake of the rulers and another rule which is for the sake of the ruled; [57] the former is a despotic, the latter a free government. Some 5 commands differ not in the thing commanded, but in the intention with which they are imposed. Wherefore, many apparently menial offices are an honour to the free youth by whom they are performed; for actions do not differ as honourable or dishonourable in themselves 10 so much as in the end and intention of them. But since we say [58] that the virtue of the citizen and ruler is the same as that of the good man, and that the same person must first be a subject and then a ruler, the legislator has to see that they become good men, and by 15 what means this may be accomplished, and what is the end of the perfect life.

Now the soul of man is divided into two parts, one of which has a rational principle in itself, and the other, not having a rational principle in itself, is able to obey such a principle.[59] And we call a man in any way good because he has the virtues of these two parts. In which of them the end is more likely to be found is no matter 20 of doubt to those who adopt our division; for in the world both of nature and of art the inferior always exists for the sake of the better or superior, and the better or superior is that which has a rational principle. This principle, too, in our ordinary way of speaking, is divided into two kinds, for there is a practical and a speculative principle.[60] 25

[55] 1329ᵃ 2–17.
[57] iii. 1278ᵇ 32–1279ᵃ 8, Cp. 1277ᵃ 33–ᵇ 30.
[59] Cp. *Nic. Eth.* i. 1102ᵇ 28.

[56] Cp. iii. 1277ᵇ 9.
[58] Cp. iii. 4, 5.
[60] Cp. *Nic. Eth.* vi. 1139ᵃ 6.

This part, then, must evidently be similarly divided. And there must
be a corresponding division of actions; the actions of the naturally
better part are to be preferred by those who have it in their power
to attain to two out of the three or to all, for that is always to every
one the most eligible which is the highest attainable by him. The
30 whole of life is further divided into two parts, business and leisure,[61]
war and peace, and of actions some aim at what is necessary and useful, and some at what is honourable. And the preference given to one
or the other class of actions must necessarily be like the preference
35 given to one or other part of the soul and its actions over the other;
there must be war for the sake of peace, business for the sake of leisure,
things useful and necessary for the sake of things honourable. All
these points the statesman should keep in view when he frames his
laws; he should consider the parts of the soul and their functions,
40 and above all the better and the end; he should also remember the
diversities of human lives and actions. For men must be able to
1333b engage in business and go to war, but leisure and peace are better;
they must do what is necessary and indeed what is useful, but what
is honourable is better. On such principles children and persons of
5 every age which requires education should be trained. Whereas even
the Hellenes of the present day who are reputed to be best governed,
and the legislators who gave them their constitutions, do not appear
to have framed their governments with a regard to the best end, or
to have given them laws and education with a view to all the virtues, but in a vulgar spirit have fallen back on those which promised
10 to be more useful and profitable. Many modern writers have taken a
similar view: they commend the Lacedaemonian constitution, and
praise the legislator for making conquest and war his sole aim,[62] a
15 doctrine which may be refuted by argument and has long ago been
refuted by facts. For most men desire empire in the hope of accumu-
lating the goods of fortune; and on this ground Thibron and all those
who have written about the Lacedaemonian constitution have praised
20 their legislator, because the Lacedaemonians, by being trained to
meet dangers, gained great power. But surely they are not a happy
people now that their empire has passed away, nor was their legislator right. How ridiculous is the result, if, while they are continuing
in the observance of his laws and no one interferes with them, they
25 have lost the better part of life! These writers further err about the
sort of government which the legislator should approve, for the
government of freemen is nobler and implies more virtue than despotic

61 Nic. Eth. x. 1177b 4.   62 Cp. Plato, Laws, i. 628, 638.

government.[63] Neither is a city to be deemed happy or a legislator to be praised because he trains his citizens to conquer and obtain domin- 30 ion over their neighbours, for there is great evil in this. On a similar principle any citizen who could, should obviously try to obtain the power in his own state—the crime which the Lacedaemonians accuse king Pausanias of attempting,[64] although he had so great honour already. No such principle and no law having this object is either 35 statesmanlike or useful or right. For the same things are best both for individuals and for states, and these are the things which the legislator ought to implant in the minds of his citizens. Neither should men study war with a view to the enslavement of those who do not deserve to be enslaved; but first of all they should provide against 40 their own enslavement, and in the second place obtain empire for the good of the governed, and not for the sake of exercising a general 1334ᵇ despotism, and in the third place they should seek to be masters only over those who deserve to be slaves. Facts, as well as arguments, prove that the legislator should direct all his military and other measures to 5 the provision of leisure and the establishment of peace. For most of these military states are safe only while they are at war,[65] but fall when they have acquired their empire; like unused iron they lose their temper in time of peace. And for this the legislator is to blame, he 10 never having taught them how to lead the life of peace.

15　Since the end of individuals and of states is the same, the end of the best man and of the best constitution must also be the same; it is therefore evident that there ought to exist in both of them the vir- tues of leisure; for peace, as has been often repeated,[66] is the end of 15 war, and leisure of toil. But leisure and cultivation may be promoted, not only by those virtues which are practised in leisure, but also by some of those which are useful to business.[67] For many necessaries of life have to be supplied before we can have leisure. Therefore a city must be temperate and brave, and able to endure: for truly, as the 20 proverb says, 'There is no leisure for slaves,' and those who cannot face danger like men are the slaves of any invader. Courage and endurance are required for business and philosophy for leisure, tem- perance and justice for both, and more especially in times of peace 25 and leisure, for war compels men to be just and temperate, whereas the enjoyment of good fortune and the leisure which comes with peace

---

[63] Cp. i. 1254ᵃ 25.　　　　　　　　　　[64] Cp. v. 1301ᵇ 20, 1307ᵃ 3.
[65] Cp. ii. 1271ᵇ 3.　　　　　　　　　　[66] 1333ᵃ 35, 1334ᵃ 2.
[67] i. e. 'not only by some of the speculative but also by some of the practical virtues'.

tend to make them insolent. Those then who seem to be the best-off and to be in the possession of every good, have special need of justice
30 and temperance—for example, those (if such there be, as the poets say) who dwell in the Islands of the Blest; they above all will need philosophy and temperance and justice, and all the more the more leisure they have, living in the midst of abundance. There is no dif-
35 ficulty in seeing why the state that would be happy and good ought to have these virtues. If it be disgraceful in men not to be able to use the goods of life, it is peculiarly disgraceful not to be able to use them in time of leisure—to show excellent qualities in action and war, and when they have peace and leisure to be no better than slaves. Where-
40 fore we should not practise virtue after the manner of the Lacedae-monians.[68] For they, while agreeing with other men in their concep-
1334b tion of the highest goods, differ from the rest of mankind in thinking that they are to be obtained by the practice of a single virtue. And since [they think] these goods and the enjoyment of them greater
5 than the enjoyment derived from the virtues . . . and that [it should be practised] for its own sake, is evident from what has been said; we must now consider how and by what means it is to be attained.

We have already determined that nature and habit and rational principle are required,[69] and, of these, the proper *nature* of the citizens has also been defined by us.[70] But we have still to consider whether the training of early life is to be that of rational principle or habit, for these two must accord, and when in accord they will then form
10 the best of harmonies. The rational principle may be mistaken and fail in attaining the highest ideal of life, and there may be a like evil influence of habit. Thus much is clear in the first place, that, as in all other things, birth implies an antecedent beginning,[71] and that there are beginnings whose end is relative to a further end. Now, in men rational principle and mind are the end towards which nature strives,[72]
15 so that the birth and moral discipline of the citizens ought to be ordered with a view to them. In the second place, as the soul and body are two, we see also that there are two parts of the soul, the rational and the irrational, and two corresponding states—reason and
20 appetite. And as the body is prior in order of generation to the soul, so the irrational is prior to the rational. The proof is that anger and wishing and desire are implanted in children from their very birth, but reason and understanding are developed as they grow older. Where-

---

[68] Cp. ii. 1271ᵃ 41.

[69] 1332ᵃ 39 sqq.

[70] c. 7.

[71] i. e. the union of the parents.

[72] i. e. the birth of the offspring, which is the end of the union of the parents, points to a further end, the development of mind.

25 fore, the care of the body ought to precede that of the soul, and the training of the appetitive part should follow: none the less our care of it must be for the sake of the reason, and our care of the body for the sake of the soul.

16   Since the legislator should begin by considering how the frames of the children whom he is rearing may be as good as possible, his 30 first care will be about marriage—at what age should his citizens marry, and who are fit to marry? In legislating on this subject he ought to consider the persons and the length of their life, that their procreative life may terminate at the same period, and that they may 35 not differ in their bodily powers, as will be the case if the man is still able to beget children while the woman is unable to bear them, or the woman able to bear while the man is unable to beget, for from these causes arise quarrels and differences between married persons. Secondly, he must consider the time at which the children will succeed to their parents; there ought not to be too great an interval of 40 age, for then the parents will be too old to derive any pleasure from their affection, or to be of any use to them. Nor ought they to be too 1335ª nearly of an age; to youthful marriages there are many objections— the children will be wanting in respect to the parents, who will seem to be their contemporaries, and disputes will arise in the management of the household. Thirdly, and this is the point from which we digressed,[73] the legislator must mould to his will the frames of newly- 5 born children. Almost all these objects may be secured by attention to one point. Since the time of generation is commonly limited within the age of seventy years in the case of a man, and of fifty in the case of a woman, the commencement of the union should conform to these 10 periods. The union of male and female when too young is bad for the procreation of children; in all other animals the offspring of the young are small and ill-developed, and with a tendency to produce female children, and therefore also in man, as is proved by the fact 15 that in those cities in which men and women are accustomed to marry young, the people are small and weak; in childbirth also younger women suffer more, and more of them die; some persons say that this was the meaning of the response once given to the Troezenians [74]— the oracle really meant that many died because they married too 20 young; it had nothing to do with the ingathering of the harvest. It also conduces to temperance not to marry too soon; for women who marry early are apt to be wanton; and in men too the bodily frame is stunted if they marry while the seed is growing (for there is a time 25

[73] 1334ᵇ 29 sqq.   [74] 'Plough not the young field'.

when the growth of the seed, also, ceases, or continues to but a slight extent). Women should marry when they are about eighteen years of age, and men at seven and thirty; then they are in the prime of life,
30 and the decline in the powers of both will coincide. Further, the children, if their birth takes place soon, as may reasonably be expected, will succeed in the beginning of their prime, when the fathers are already in the decline of life, and have nearly reached their term of
35 three-score years and ten.

Thus much of the age proper for marriage: the season of the year should also be considered; according to our present custom, people generally limit marriage to the season of winter, and they are right.
40 The precepts of physicians and natural philosophers about generation should also be studied by the parents themselves; the physicians give good advice about the favourable conditions of the body, and
1335ᵇ the natural philosophers about the winds; of which they prefer the north to the south.

What constitution in the parent is most advantageous to the offspring is a subject which we will consider more carefully [75] when we speak of the education of children, and we will only make a few gen-
5 eral remarks at present. The constitution of an athlete is not suited to the life of a citizen, or to health, or to the procreation of children, any more than the valetudinarian or exhausted constitution, but one which is in a mean between them. A man's constitution should be inured to labour, but not to labour which is excessive or of one sort only,
10 such as is practised by athletes; he should be capable of all the actions of a freeman. These remarks apply equally to both parents.

Women who are with child should be careful of themselves; they should take exercise and have a nourishing diet. The first of these
15 prescriptions the legislator will easily carry into effect by requiring that they shall take a walk daily to some temple, where they can worship the gods who preside over birth.[76] Their minds, however, unlike their bodies, they ought to keep quiet, for the offspring derive their natures from their mothers as plants do from the earth.
20 As to the exposure and rearing of children, let there be a law that no *deformed* child shall live, but that on the ground of an *excess* in the number of children, if the established customs of the state forbid this (for in our state population has a limit), no child is to be exposed, but when couples have children in excess, let abortion be procured
25 before sense and life have begun; what may or may not be lawfully done in these cases depends on the question of life and sensation.

And now, having determined at what ages men and women are to

[75] A. does not actually do so.   [76] Cp. Plato, *Laws*, vii. 789 E.

begin their union, let us also determine how long they shall continue
to beget and bear offspring for the state; men who are too old, like men
who are too young, produce children who are defective in body and 30
mind; the children of very old men are weakly. The limit, then, should
be the age which is the prime of their intelligence, and this in most
persons, according to the notion of some poets who measure life by periods of seven years, is about fifty; at four or five years later, they should 35
cease from having families; and from that time forward only cohabit
with one another for the sake of health; or for some similar reason.

As to adultery, let it be held disgraceful, in general, for any man
or woman to be found in any way unfaithful when they are married, 40
and called husband and wife. If during the time of bearing children 1336ª
anything of the sort occur, let the guilty person be punished with a
loss of privileges in proportion to the offence.[77]

17 After the children have been born, the manner of rearing them
may be supposed to have a great effect on their bodily strength. It 5
would appear from the example of animals, and of those nations who
desire to create the military habit, that the food which has most milk
in it is best suited to human beings; but the less wine the better, if
they would escape diseases. Also all the motions to which children can
be subjected at their early age are very useful. But in order to preserve 10
their tender limbs from distortion, some nations have had recourse to
mechanical appliances which straighten their bodies. To accustom
children to the cold from their earliest years is also an excellent practice, which greatly conduces to health, and hardens them for military
service. Hence many barbarians have a custom of plunging their chil- 15
dren at birth into a cold stream; others, like the Celts, clothe them in a
light wrapper only. For human nature should be early habituated to
endure all which by habit it can be made to endure; but the process
must be gradual. And children, from their natural warmth, may be 20
easily trained to bear cold. Such care should attend them in the first
stage of life.

The next period lasts to the age of five; during this no demand
should be made upon the child for study or labour, lest its growth be
impeded; and there should be sufficient motion to prevent the limbs 25
from being inactive. This can be secured, among other ways, by amusement, but the amusement should not be vulgar or tiring or effeminate. The Directors of Education, as they are termed, should be careful what tales or stories the children hear,[78] for all such things are 30
designed to prepare the way for the business of later life, and should

---

[77] Cp. *Laws*, viii. 841 D, E.   [78] Plato, *Rep.* ii. 377 ff.

be for the most part imitations of the occupations which they will
hereafter pursue in earnest.[79] Those are wrong who in their laws at-
35 tempt to check the loud crying and screaming of children, for these
contribute towards their growth, and, in a manner, exercise their
bodies.[80] Straining the voice has a strengthening effect similar to that
40 produced by the retention of the breath in violent exertions. The Directors of Education should have an eye to their bringing up, and in
particular should take care that they are left as little as possible with
1336ᵇ slaves. For until they are seven years old they must live at home; and
therefore, even at this early age, it is to be expected that they should
acquire a taint of meanness from what they hear and see. Indeed,
there is nothing which the legislator should be more careful to drive
5 away than indecency of speech; for the light utterance of shameful
words leads soon to shameful actions. The young especially should
never be allowed to repeat or hear anything of the sort. A freeman who
is found saying or doing what is forbidden, if he be too young as yet to
10 have the privilege of reclining at the public tables, should be disgraced
and beaten, and an elder person degraded as his slavish conduct
deserves. And since we do not allow improper language, clearly we
should also banish pictures or speeches from the stage which are inde-
15 cent. Let the rulers take care that there be no image or picture representing unseemly actions, except in the temples of those Gods at whose
festivals the law permits even ribaldry, and whom the law also permits to be worshipped by persons of mature age on behalf of themselves, their children, and their wives. But the legislator should not
20 allow youth to be spectators of iambi or of comedy until they are of
an age to sit at the public tables and to drink strong wine; by that
time education will have armed them against the evil influences of
such representations.

We have made these remarks in a cursory manner—they are enough
25 for the present occasion; but hereafter [81] we will return to the subject and after a fuller discussion determine whether such liberty
should or should not be granted, and in what way granted, if at all.
Theodorus, the tragic actor, was quite right in saying that he would
30 not allow any other actor, not even if he were quite second-rate, to
enter before himself, because the spectators grew fond of the voices
which they first heard. And the same principle applies universally to
association with things as well as with persons, for we always like
best whatever comes first. And therefore youth should be kept
35 strangers to all that is bad, and especially to things which suggest vice

---

[79] Plato, *Laws*, i. 643.   [80] Plato, *Laws*, vii. 792 A.
[81] An unfulfilled promise.

or hate. When the five years have passed away, during the two following years they must look on at the pursuits which they are hereafter to learn. There are two periods of life with reference to which education has to be divided, from seven to the age of puberty, and onwards to the age of one and twenty. The poets who divide ages by sevens [82] are in the main right: but we should observe the divisions actually made by nature; for the deficiencies of nature are what art and education seek to fill up.

Let us then first inquire if any regulations are to be laid down about children, and secondly, whether the care of them should be the concern of the state or of private individuals, which latter is in our own day the common custom, and in the third place, what these regulations should be.

BOOK VIII

1 No one will doubt that the legislator should direct his attention above all to the education of youth; for the neglect of education does harm to the constitution. The citizen should be moulded to suit the form of government under which he lives.[1] For each government has a peculiar character which originally formed and which continues to preserve it. The character of democracy creates democracy, and the character of oligarchy creates oligarchy; and always the better the character, the better the government.

Again, for the exercise of any faculty or art a previous training and habituation are required; clearly therefore for the practice of virtue. And since the whole city has one end, it is manifest that education should be one and the same for all, and that it should be public, and not private—not as at present, when every one looks after his own children separately, and gives them separate instruction of the sort which he thinks best; the training in things which are of common interest should be the same for all. Neither must we suppose that any one of the citizens belongs to himself, for they all belong to the state, and are each of them a part of the state, and the care of each part is inseparable from the care of the whole. In this particular as in some others the Lacedaemonians are to be praised, for they take the greatest pains about their children, and make education the business of the state.[2]

2 That education should be regulated by law and should be an affair of state is not to be denied, but what should be the character of

[82] Cp. 1335[b] 33.   [1] Cp. v. 1310[a] 12–36.   [2] Cp. *Nic. Eth.* x. 1180[a] 24.

this public education, and how young persons should be educated, are questions which remain to be considered. As things are, there is dis-
35 agreement about the subjects. For mankind are by no means agreed about the things to be taught, whether we look to virtue or the best life. Neither is it clear whether education is more concerned with intellectual or with moral virtue. The existing practice is perplexing;
40 no one knows on what principle we should proceed—should the useful in life, or should virtue, or should the higher knowledge, be the
1337ᵇ aim of our training; all three opinions have been entertained. Again, about the means there is no agreement; for different persons, starting with different ideas about the nature of virtue, naturally disagree about the practice of it. There can be no doubt that children should be taught those useful things which are really necessary, but not all
5 useful things; for occupations are divided into liberal and illiberal; and to young children should be imparted only such kinds of knowledge as will be useful to them without vulgarizing them. And any occu-
10 pation, art, or science, which makes the body or soul or mind of the freeman less fit for the practice or exercise of virtue, is vulgar; wherefore we call those arts vulgar which tend to deform the body, and likewise all paid employments, for they absorb and degrade the mind.
15 There are also some liberal arts quite proper for a freeman to acquire, but only in a certain degree, and if he attend to them too closely, in order to attain perfection in them, the same evil effects will follow. The object also which a man sets before him makes a great difference; if he does or learns anything for his own sake [3] or for the sake of his friends, or with a view to excellence, the action will not appear illib-
20 eral; but if done for the sake of others, the very same action will be thought menial and servile. The received subjects of instruction, as I have already remarked,[4] are partly of a liberal and partly of an illiberal character.

3 The customary branches of education are in number four; they are—(1) reading and writing, (2) gymnastic exercises, (3) music, to
25 which is sometimes added (4) drawing. Of these, reading and writing and drawing are regarded as useful for the purposes of life in a variety of ways, and gymnastic exercises are thought to infuse courage. Concerning music a doubt may be raised—in our own day most men cultivate it for the sake of pleasure, but originally it was included in
30 education, because nature herself, as has been often said,[5] requires that we should be able, not only to work well, but to use leisure well;

---

[3] Cp. iii. 1277ᵇ 3.　　　　　　　　　　　　　　　[4] ᵃ 39–ᵇ 3.
[5] ii. 1271ᵃ 41 sqq., vii. 1333ᵃ 16–1334ᵇ 3; *N. Eth.* x. 6.

for, as I must repeat once again, the first principle of all action is leisure. Both are required, but leisure is better than occupation and is
its end; and therefore the question must be asked, what ought we to
do when at leisure? Clearly we ought not to be amusing ourselves, 35
for then amusement would be the end of life. But if this is inconceivable, and amusement is needed more amid serious occupations than
at other times (for he who is hard at work has need of relaxation,
and amusement gives relaxation, whereas occupation is always accompanied with exertion and effort, we should introduce amusements 40
only at suitable times, and they should be our medicines, for the
emotion which they create in the soul is a relaxation, and from the
pleasure we obtain rest. But leisure of itself gives pleasure and happi- 1338ᴬ
ness and enjoyment of life, which are experienced, not by the busy
man, but by those who have leisure. For he who is occupied has in view
some end which he has not attained; but happiness is an end, since all 5
men deem it to be accompanied with pleasure and not with pain. This
pleasure, however, is regarded differently by different persons, and
varies according to the habit of individuals; the pleasure of the best
man is the best, and springs from the noblest sources. It is clear then
that there are branches of learning and education which we must study 10
merely with a view to leisure spent in intellectual activity, and these
are to be valued for their own sake; whereas those kinds of knowledge which are useful in business are to be deemed necessary, and
exist for the sake of other things. And therefore our fathers admitted
music into education, not on the ground either of its necessity or utility,
for it is not necessary, nor indeed useful in the same manner as reading 15
and writing, which are useful in money-making, in the management
of a household, in the acquisition of knowledge and in political life,
nor like drawing, useful for a more correct judgement of the works of
artists, nor again like gymnastic, which gives health and strength; 20
for neither of these is to be gained from music. There remains, then,
the use of music for intellectual enjoyment in leisure; which is in
fact evidently the reason of its introduction, this being one of the ways
in which it is thought that a freeman should pass his leisure; as
Homer says—

'But he who alone should be called [6] to the pleasant feast',　　25

and afterwards he speaks of others whom he describes as inviting

'The bard who would delight them all'.[7]

[6] The line does not occur in our text of Homer, but in Aristotle's text it
probably came instead of, or after, *Od*. xvii. 383.

[7] *Od*. xvii. 385.

And in another place Odysseus says there is no better way of passing life than when men's hearts are merry and

'The banqueters in the hall, sitting in order, hear the voice of the minstrel'.[8]

30　It is evident, then, that there is a sort of education in which parents should train their sons, not as being useful or necessary, but because it is liberal or noble. Whether this is of one kind only, or of more than one, and if so, what they are, and how they are to be imparted, must hereafter be determined.[9] Thus much we are now in a position to 35 say, that the ancients witness to us; for their opinion may be gathered from the fact that music is one of the received and traditional branches of education. Further, it is clear that children should be instructed in some useful things—for example, in reading and writing—not only for their usefulness, but also because many other sorts 40 of knowledge are acquired through them. With a like view they may be taught drawing, not to prevent their making mistakes in their own purchases, or in order that they may not be imposed upon in the 1338ᵇ buying or selling of articles, but perhaps rather because it makes them judges of the beauty of the human form. To be always seeking after the useful does not become free and exalted souls.[10] Now it is clear 5 that in education practice must be used before theory, and the body be trained before the mind; and therefore boys should be handed over to the trainer, who creates in them the proper habit of body, and to the wrestling-master, who teaches them their exercises.

4　Of those states which in our own day seem to take the greatest care of children, some aim at producing in them an athletic habit, 10 but they only injure their forms and stunt their growth. Although the Lacedaemonians have not fallen into this mistake, yet they brutalize their children by laborious exercises which they think will make them courageous. But in truth, as we have often repeated,[11] education 15 should not be exclusively, or principally, directed to this end. And even if we suppose the Lacedaemonians to be right in their end, they do not attain it. For among barbarians and among animals courage is found associated, not with the greatest ferocity, but with a gentle 20 and lion-like temper. There are many races who are ready enough to kill and eat men, such as the Achaeans and Heniochi, who both live about the Black Sea;[12] and there are other mainland tribes, as bad

---

[8] *Od.* ix. 7.　　　[9] An unfulfilled promise.　　　[10] Cp. Plato, *Rep.* vii. 525 ff.
[11] ii. 1271ᵃ 41–ᵇ10, vii. 1333ᵇ 5 sqq., 1334ᵃ 40 sqq.
[12] Cp. *N. Eth.* vii. 1148ᵇ 21.

or worse, who all live by plunder, but have no courage. It is notorious that the Lacedaemonians themselves, while they alone were assiduous 25 in their laborious drill, were superior to others, but now they are beaten both in war and gymnastic exercises. For their ancient superiority did not depend on their mode of training their youth, but only on the circumstance that they trained them when their only rivals did not. Hence we may infer that what is noble, not what is brutal, should have the first place; no wolf or other wild animal will face a really 30 noble danger; such dangers are for the brave man.[13] And parents who devote their children to gymnastics while they neglect their necessary education, in reality vulgarize them; for they make them useful to the art of statesmanship in one quality only, and even in this the argument 35 proves them to be inferior to others. We should judge the Lacedae-monians not from what they have been, but from what they are; for now they have rivals who compete with their education; formerly they had none.

It is an admitted principle, that gymnastic exercises should be employed in education, and that for children they should be of a lighter 40 kind, avoiding severe diet or painful toil, lest the growth of the body be impaired. The evil of excessive training in early years is strikingly proved by the example of the Olympic victors; for not more than 1339ᵃ two or three of them have gained a prize both as boys and as men;. their early training and severe gymnastic exercises exhausted their constitutions. When boyhood is over, three years should be spent in other studies; the period of life which follows may then be devoted 5 to hard exercise and strict diet. Men ought not to labour at the same time with their minds and with their bodies;[14] for the two kinds of labour are opposed to one another; the labour of the body impedes the mind, and the labour of the mind the body. 10

5 Concerning music there are some questions which we have al-ready raised;[15] these we may now resume and carry further; and our remarks will serve as a prelude to this or any other discussion of the subject. It is not easy to determine the nature of music, or why any 15 one should have a knowledge of it. Shall we say, for the sake of amusement and relaxation, like sleep or drinking, which are not good in themselves, but are pleasant, and at the same time 'make care to cease', as Euripides says? And for this end men also appoint music, and make use of all three alike—sleep, drinking, music—to which some 20 add dancing. Or shall we argue that music conduces to virtue, on

---

[13] Cp. *N. Eth.* iii. 1115ᵃ 29.　　　　　　　[14] Cp. Plato, *Rep.* vii. 537 ʙ.
[15] 1337ᵇ 27–1338ᵃ 30.

the ground that it can form our minds and habituate us to true pleasures as our bodies are made by gymnastic to be of a certain 25 character? Or shall we say that it contributes to the enjoyment of leisure and mental cultivation, which is a third alternative? Now obviously youths are not to be instructed with a view to their amusement, for learning is no amusement, but is accompanied with pain. 30 Neither is intellectual enjoyment suitable to boys of that age, for it is the end, and that which is imperfect cannot attain the perfect or end. But perhaps it may be said that boys learn music for the sake of the amusement which they will have when they are grown up. If so, why should they learn themselves, and not, like the Persian and 35 Median kings, enjoy the pleasure and instruction which is derived from hearing others? (for surely persons who have made music the business and profession of their lives will be better performers than those who practise only long enough to learn). If they must learn 40 music, on the same principle they should learn cookery, which is absurd. And even granting that music may form the character, the objection still holds: why should we learn ourselves? Why cannot 1339ᵇ we attain true pleasure and form a correct judgement from hearing others, like the Lacedaemonians?—for they, without learning music, nevertheless can correctly judge, as they say, of good and bad melodies. Or again, if music should be used to promote cheerfulness and 5 refined intellectual enjoyment, the objection still remains—why should we learn ourselves instead of enjoying the performances of others? We may illustrate what we are saying by our conception of the Gods; for in the poets Zeus does not himself sing or play on the lyre. Nay, we call professional performers vulgar; no freeman would play or sing unless he were intoxicated or in jest. But these matters 10 may be left for the present.[16]

The first question is whether music is or is not to be a part of education. Of the three things mentioned in our discussion, which does it produce?—education or amusement or intellectual enjoyment, for it may be reckoned under all three, and seems to share in the 15 nature of all of them. Amusement is for the sake of relaxation, and relaxation is of necessity sweet, for it is the remedy of pain caused by toil: and intellectual enjoyment is universally acknowledged to contain an element not only of the noble but of the pleasant, for 20 happiness is made up of both. All men agree that music is one of the pleasantest things, whether with or without song; as Musaeus says, 'Song is to mortals of all things the sweetest.'

[16] Cp. c. 6.

Hence and with good reason it is introduced into social gatherings and entertainments, because it makes the hearts of men glad: so that on this ground alone we may assume that the young ought to be trained 25 in it. For innocent pleasures are not only in harmony with the perfect end of life, but they also provide relaxation. And whereas men rarely attain the end, but often rest by the way and amuse themselves, not only with a view to a further end, but also for the pleasure's 30 sake, it may be well at times to let them find a refreshment in music. It sometimes happens that men make amusement the end, for the end probably contains some element of pleasure, though not any ordinary or lower pleasure; but they mistake the lower for the higher, and in seeking for the one find the other, since every pleasure has a likeness to the end of action.[17] For the end is not eligible for the sake 35 of any future good, nor do the pleasures which we have described exist for the sake of any future good but of the past, that is to say, they are the alleviation of past toils and pains. And we may infer this to be the reason why men seek happiness from these pleasures. 40

But music is pursued, not only as an alleviation of past toil, but also as providing recreation. And who can say whether, having this use, it may not also have a nobler one? In addition to this com- 1340ª mon pleasure, felt and shared in by all (for the pleasure given by music is natural, and therefore adapted to all ages and characters), 5 may it not have also some influence over the character and the soul? It must have such an influence if characters are affected by it. And that they are so affected is proved in many ways, and not least by the power which the songs of Olympus exercise; for beyond ques- 10 tion they inspire enthusiasm, and enthusiasm is an emotion of the ethical part of the soul. Besides, when men hear imitations, even apart from the rhythms and tunes themselves, their feelings move in 15 sympathy. Since then music is a pleasure, and virtue consists in rejoicing and loving and hating aright, there is clearly nothing which we are so much concerned to acquire and to cultivate as the power of forming right judgements, and of taking delight in good dispositions and noble actions.[18] Rhythm and melody supply imitations of anger and gentleness, and also of courage and temperance, and of all the 20 qualities contrary to these, and of the other qualities of character, which hardly fall short of the actual affections, as we know from our own experience, for in listening to such strains our souls undergo a change. The habit of feeling pleasure or pain at mere representa-

17 Cp. *N. Eth.* vii. 1153ᵇ 33.
18 Cp. Plato, *Rep.* iii. 401, 402; *Laws*, ii. 659 C-E.

tions is not far removed from the same feeling about realities; [19] for
25 example, if any one delights in the sight of a statue for its beauty only,
it necessarily follows that the sight of the original will be pleasant
to him. The objects of no other sense, such as taste or touch, have
30 any resemblance to moral qualities; in visible objects there is only
a little, for there are figures which are of a moral character, but
only to a slight extent, and all do not participate in the feeling about
them. Again, figures and colours are not imitations, but signs, of moral
habits, indications which the body gives of states of feeling. The
35 connexion of them with morals is slight, but in so far as there is any,
young men should be taught to look, not at the works of Pauson, but
at those of Polygnotus,[20] or any other painter or sculptor who expresses moral ideas. On the other hand, even in mere melodies there is
40 an imitation of character, for the musical modes differ essentially
from one another, and those who hear them are differently affected by
1340ᵇ each. Some of them make men sad and grave, like the so-called
Mixolydian, others enfeeble the mind, like the relaxed modes, another, again, produces a moderate and settled temper, which appears
to be the peculiar effect of the Dorian; the Phrygian inspires en-
5 thusiasm. The whole subject has been well treated by philosophical
writers [21] on this branch of education, and they confirm their arguments by facts. The same principles apply to rhythms; [22] some have
a character of rest, others of motion, and of these latter again, some
10 have a more vulgar, others a nobler movement. Enough has been said
to show that music has a power of forming the character, and should
therefore be introduced into the education of the young. The study
15 is suited to the stage of youth, for young persons will not, if they
can help, endure anything which is not sweetened by pleasure, and
music has a natural sweetness. There seems to be in us a sort of
affinity to musical modes and rhythms, which makes some philosophers say that the soul is a tuning, others, that it possesses tuning.

20 **6**   And now we have to determine the question which has been
already raised,[23] whether children should be themselves taught to
sing and play or not. Clearly there is a considerable difference made
in the character by the actual practice of the art. It is difficult, if not
impossible, for those who do not perform to be good judges of the
25 performance of others.[24] Besides, children should have something
to do, and the rattle of Archytas, which people give to their children

---

[19] Cp. Plato, *Rep.* iii. 395.
[21] Cp. *Rep.* 398 ᴇ sqq.
[23] 1339ᵃ 33–ᵇ 10.

[20] Cp. *Poet.* 1448ᵃ 5, 1450ᵃ 26.
[22] *Rep.* iii. 399 ᴇ, 400.
[24] Cp. 1339ᵃ 42.

in order to amuse them and prevent them from breaking anything in the house, was a capital invention, for a young thing cannot be quiet. The rattle is a toy suited to the infant mind, and education is a rattle 30 or toy for children of a larger growth. We conclude then that they should be taught music in such a way as to become not only critics but performers.

The question what is or is not suitable for different ages may be easily answered; nor is there any difficulty in meeting the objection of those who say that the study of music is vulgar.[25] We reply (1) 35 in the first place, that they who are to be judges must also be performers, and that they should begin to practise early, although when they are older they may be spared the execution; they must have learned to appreciate what is good and to delight in it, thanks to the knowledge which they acquired in their youth. As to (2) the 40 vulgarizing effect which music is supposed to exercise, this is a question which we shall have no difficulty in determining, when we have considered to what extent freemen who are being trained to political virtue should pursue the art, what melodies and what rhythms they 1341ᵃ should be allowed to use, and what instruments should be employed in teaching them to play; for even the instrument makes a difference. The answer to the objection turns upon these distinctions; for it is quite possible that certain methods of teaching and learning music do really have a degrading effect. It is evident then that the learning of 5 music ought not to impede the business of riper years, or to degrade the body or render it unfit for civil or military training, whether for bodily exercises at the time or for later studies.

The right measure will be attained if students of music stop short 10 of the arts which are practised in professional contests, and do not seek to acquire those fantastic marvels of execution which are now the fashion in such contests, and from these have passed into education. Let the young practise even such music as we have prescribed, only until they are able to feel delight in noble melodies and rhythms, and not merely in that common part of music in which every slave 15 or child and even some animals find pleasure.

From these principles we may also infer what instruments should be used. The flute, or any other instrument which requires great skill, as for example the harp, ought not to be admitted into education, but only such as will make intelligent students of music or of the 20 other parts of education. Besides, the flute is not an instrument which is expressive of moral character; it is too exciting. The proper time for using it is when the performance aims not at instruction, but at

²⁵ Cp. 1339ᵇ 8, 1341ᵇ 14.

the relief of the passions.[26] And there is a further objection; the impediment which the flute presents to the use of the voice detracts
25 from its educational value. The ancients therefore were right in forbidding the flute to youths and freemen, although they had once allowed it. For when their wealth gave them a greater inclination to leisure, and they had loftier notions of excellence, being also elated
30 with their success, both before and after the Persian War, with more zeal than discernment they pursued every kind of knowledge, and so they introduced the flute into education. At Lacedaemon there was a choragus who led the chorus with a flute, and at Athens the instrument became so popular that most freemen could play upon it. The popularity is shown by the tablet which Thrasippus dedicated when
35 he furnished the chorus to Ecphantides. Later experience enabled men to judge what was or was not really conducive to virtue, and they rejected both the flute and several other old-fashioned instru-
40 ments, such as the Lydian harp, the many-stringed lyre, the 'heptagon', 'triangle', 'sambuca', and the like—which are intended only
1341ᵇ to give pleasure to the hearer, and require extraordinary skill of hand.[27] There is a meaning also in the myth of the ancients, which tells how Athene invented the flute and then threw it away. It was not a bad
5 idea of theirs, that the Goddess disliked the instrument because it made the face ugly; but with still more reason may we say that she rejected it because the acquirement of flute-playing contributes nothing to the mind, since to Athene we ascribe both knowledge and art.

Thus then we reject the professional instruments and also the professional mode of education in music (and by professional we mean
10 that which is adopted in contests), for in this the performer practises the art, not for the sake of his own improvement, but in order to give pleasure, and that of a vulgar sort, to his hearers. For this reason the execution of such music is not the part of a freeman but of a paid performer, and the result is that the performers are vulgar-
15 ized, for the end at which they aim is bad.[28] The vulgarity of the spectator tends to lower the character of the music and therefore of the performers; they look to him—he makes them what they are, and fashions even their bodies by the movements which he expects them to exhibit.

7 We have also to consider rhythms and modes, and their use
20 in education. Shall we use them all or make a distinction? and shall the same distinction be made for those who practise music with a

---

[26] Cp. 1341ᵇ 38.   [27] Cp. Plato, *Rep.* iii. 399 c, d.
[28] Cp. Plato, *Laws*, iii. 700.

view to education, or shall it be some other? Now we see that music
is produced by melody and rhythm, and we ought to know what
influence these have respectively on education, and whether we 25
should prefer excellence in melody or excellence in rhythm. But as
the subject has been very well treated by many musicians of the
present day, and also by philosophers [29] who have had considerable
experience of musical education, to these we would refer the more 30
exact student of the subject; we shall only speak of it now after the
manner of the legislator, stating the general principles.

We accept the division of melodies proposed by certain philosophers into ethical melodies, melodies of action, and passionate or
inspiring melodies, each having, as they say, a mode corresponding
to it. But we maintain further that music should be studied, not for 35
the sake of one, but of many benefits, that is to say, with a view to
(1) education, (2) purgation (the word 'purgation' we use at present without explanation, but when hereafter we speak of poetry,[30]
we will treat the subject with more precision); music may also serve
(3) for intellectual enjoyment, for relaxation and for recreation after 40
exertion. It is clear, therefore, that all the modes must be employed 1342ᵃ
by us, but not all of them in the same manner. In education the most
ethical modes are to be preferred, but in listening to the performances of others we may admit the modes of action and passion also. 5
For feelings such as pity and fear, or, again, enthusiasm, exist very
strongly in some souls, and have more or less influence over all. Some
persons fall into a religious frenzy, whom we see as a result of the
sacred melodies—when they have used the melodies that excite the 10
soul to mystic frenzy—restored as though they had found healing
and purgation. Those who are influenced by pity or fear, and every
emotional nature, must have a like experience, and others in so far
as each is susceptible to such emotions, and all are in a manner 15
purged and their souls lightened and delighted. The purgative melodies likewise give an innocent pleasure to mankind. Such are the
modes and the melodies in which those who perform music at the
theatre should be invited to compete. But since the spectators are
of two kinds—the one free and educated, and the other a vulgar crowd
composed of mechanics, labourers, and the like—there ought to 20
be contests and exhibitions instituted for the relaxation of the
second class also. And the music will correspond to their minds; for
as their minds are perverted from the natural state, so there are

29 Cp. *Rep.* iii. 398 ᴅ sqq.

30 Cp. *Poet.* 1449ᵇ 27, though the promise is really unfulfilled. The reference is probably to a lost part of the *Poetics*.

perverted modes and highly strung and unnaturally coloured melo-
25 dies. A man receives pleasure from what is natural to him, and
therefore professional musicians may be allowed to practise this lower
sort of music before an audience of a lower type. But, for the purposes of education, as I have already said,[31] those modes and
melodies should be employed which are ethical, such as the Dorian,
30 as we said before;[32] though we may include any others which are
approved by philosophers who have had a musical education. The
Socrates of the *Republic*[33] is wrong in retaining only the Phrygian
1342ᵇ mode along with the Dorian, and the more so because he rejects
the flute; for the Phrygian is to the modes what the flute is to musical
instruments—both of them are exciting and emotional. Poetry proves
5 this, for Bacchic frenzy and all similar emotions are most suitably
expressed by the flute, and are better set to the Phrygian than to any
other mode. The dithyramb, for example, is acknowledged to be
Phrygian, a fact of which the connoisseurs of music offer many
proofs, saying, among other things, that Philoxenus, having at-
10 tempted to compose his *Mysians* as a dithyramb in the Dorian mode,
found it impossible, and fell back by the very nature of things into
the more appropriate Phrygian. All men agree that the Dorian music
15 is the gravest and manliest. And whereas we say that the extremes
should be avoided and the mean followed, and whereas the Dorian is
a mean between the other modes,[34] it is evident that our youth
should be taught the Dorian music.

Two principles have to be kept in view, what is possible, what is
becoming: at these every man ought to aim. But even these are
20 relative to age; the old, who have lost their powers, cannot very well
sing the high-strung modes, and nature herself seems to suggest that
their songs should be of the more relaxed kind. Wherefore the musicians likewise blame Socrates,[35] and with justice, for rejecting the
25 relaxed modes in education under the idea that they are intoxicat-
ing, not in the ordinary sense of intoxication (for wine rather tends
to excite men), but because they have no strength in them. And so,
with a view also to the time of life when men begin to grow old, they
ought to practise the gentler modes and melodies as well as the
others, and, further, any mode, such as the Lydian above all others
30 appears to be, which is suited to children of tender age, and possesses the elements both of order and of education. Thus it is clear
that education should be based upon three principles—the mean,
the possible, the becoming, these three.

[31] 1342ᵃ 2.   [32] 1340ᵇ 3 sq.   [33] Plato, *Rep*. iii. 399 ᴀ.
[34] Cp. 1340ᵃ 42.   [35] *Rep*. iii. 398 ᴇ sqq.

Rhetorica

Translated by W. Rhys Roberts

CONTENTS

BOOK I

3. There are three kinds of rhetoric: A. political (deliberative), B. forensic (legal), and C. epideictic (the ceremonial oratory of display). Their (*a*) divisions, (*b*) times, and (*c*) ends are as follows: A. Political (*a*) exhortation and dehortation, (*b*) future, (*c*) expediency and inexpediency; B. Forensic (*a*) accusation and defence, (*b*) past, (*c*) justice and injustice; C. Epideictic (*a*) praise and censure, (*b*) present, (*c*) honour and dishonour.

4. (A) The subjects of Political Oratory fall under five main heads: (1) ways and means, (2) war and peace, (3) national defence, (4) imports and exports, (5) legislation. The scope of each of these divisions.

5. In urging his hearers to take or to avoid a course of action, the political orator must show that he has an eye to their happiness. Four definitions (of a popular kind: as usual in the *Rhetoric*), and some fourteen constituents, of happiness.

6. The political speaker will also appeal to the interest of his hearers, and this involves a knowledge of what is good. Definition and analysis of things 'good'.

7. Comparison of 'good' things. Of two 'good' things, which is the better? This entails a consideration of degree—the lore of 'less or more'.

8. The political speaker will find his powers of persuasion most of all enhanced by a knowledge of the four sorts of government—democracy, oligarchy, aristocracy, monarchy, and their characteristic customs, institutions, and interests. Definition of the four sorts severally. Ends of each.

9. (C) The Epideictic speaker is concerned with virtue and vice, praising the one and censuring the other. The forms of virtue. Which are the greatest virtues?—Some rhetorical devices used by the epideictic speaker: 'amplification', especially. Amplification is particularly appropriate to epideictic oratory; examples, to political; Enthymemes, to forensic.

10. (B) The Forensic speaker should have studied wrongdoing—its motives, its perpetrators, and its victims. Definition of wrongdoing as injury voluntarily inflicted contrary to law. Law is either (*a*) special, viz. that written law which regulates the life of a particular community, or (*b*) general, viz. all those unwritten principles which are supposed to be acknowledged everywhere. Enumeration and elucidation of the seven causes of human action, viz. three involuntary, (1) chance, (2) nature, (3) compulsion; and four voluntary, viz. (4) habit, (5) reasoning, (6) anger, (7) appetite. All voluntary actions are good or apparently good, pleasant or apparently pleasant. The good (or expedient) has been discussed under political oratory. The pleasant has yet to be considered.

BOOK II

20. The two general modes of persuasion are: (1) the example, (2) the Enthymeme; the maxim being part of the Enthymeme. Examples are either (a) historical parallels, or (b) invented parallels, viz. either (i) illustrations, or (ii) fables, such as those of Aesop. Fables are suitable for popular addresses; and they have this advantage, that they are comparatively easy to invent, whereas it is hard to find parallels among actual past events.

21. Use of maxims. A maxim is a general statement about questions of practical conduct. It is an incomplete Enthymeme. Four kinds of maxims. Maxims should be used (a) by elderly men, and (b) to controvert popular sayings. Advantages of maxims: (a) they enable a speaker to gratify his commonplace hearers by expressing as a universal truth the opinions which they themselves hold about particular cases; (b) they invest a speech with moral character.

22. Enthymemes. In Enthymemes we must not carry our reasoning too far back, nor must we put in all the steps that lead to our conclusion. There are two kinds of Enthymemes: (a) the demonstrative, formed by the conjunction of compatible propositions; (b) the refutative, formed by the conjunction of incompatible propositions.

23. Enumeration of twenty-eight topics (lines of argument) on which Enthymemes, demonstrative and refutative, can be based. Two general remarks are added: (a) the refutative Enthymeme has a greater reputation than the demonstrative, because within a small space it works out two opposing arguments, and arguments put side by side are clearer to the audience; (b) of all syllogisms, whether refutative or demonstrative, those are most applauded of which we foresee the conclusions from the beginning, so long as they are not obvious at first sight—for part of the pleasure we feel is at our own intelligent anticipation; or those which we follow well enough to see the point of them as soon as the last work has been uttered.

24. Nine topics of apparent, or sham, Enthymemes.

25. Refutation. An argument may be refuted either by a counter-syllogism or by bringing an objection. Objections may be raised in four ways: (a) by directly attacking your opponent's own statement; (b) by putting forward another statement like it; (c) by putting forward a statement contrary to it; (d) by quoting previous decisions.

26. Correction of two errors, possible or actual; (1) Amplification and Depreciation do not constitute an element of Enthymeme, in the sense of 'a line of Enthymematic argument'; (2) refutative Enthymemes are not a different species from constructive. This brings to an end the treatment of the thought-element of rhetoric—the way to invent and refute persuasive arguments. There remain the subjects of (A) style and (B) arrangement.

BOOK III

1. (A) Style. It is not enough to know what to say; we must also say it in the right way. Upon the subject of delivery (which presents itself here) no systematic treatise has been composed, though this art has much to do with oratory (as with poetry). The matter has, however, been touched upon by Thrasymachus in his 'Appeals to Pity'. As to the place of style: the right thing in speaking really is that we should fight our case with no help beyond the bare facts; and yet the arts of language cannot help having a small but real importance, whatever it is we have to expound to others. Through the influence of the poets, the language of oratorical prose at first took a poetical colour, as in the case of Gorgias. But the language of prose is distinct from that of poetry; and, further, the writers of tragic poetry itself have now given up those words, not used in ordinary talk, which adorned the early drama.

[Chapters 2–12 omitted.]

13. (B) Arrangement. A speech has two essential parts: statement and proof. To these may be added introduction and epilogue.

14. Introduction. The introduction corresponds to the prologue in poetry and the prelude in flute-music. The most essential function and distinctive property of the introduction is to indicate the aim of the speech. An introduction may (1) excite or allay prejudice; (2) exalt or depreciate. In a political speech an introduction is seldom found, for the subject is usually familiar to the audience.

15. Prejudice. The various lines of argument suitable for exciting or allaying prejudice.

16. Narration. (1) In ceremonial oratory, narration should, as a rule, not be continuous but intermittent: variety is pleasant, and the facts in a celebrity's praise are usually well known. (2) In forensic oratory, the current rule that the narration should be rapid is wrong: rightness consists neither in rapidity nor in conciseness, but in the happy mean. The defendant will make less use of narration than the plaintiff. (3) In political oratory there is least opening for narration; nobody can narrate what has not yet happened. If there is narration at all, it will be of past events, the recollection of which will help the hearers to make better plans for the future. Or it may be employed to attack some one's character, or to eulogize him.

17. Arguments. The duty of the Arguments is to attempt conclusive proofs. (1) In forensic oratory, the question in dispute will fall under one of four heads: (a) the fact, (b) the existence of injury, (c) the amount of injury, (d) the justification. (2) In ceremonial oratory, the facts themselves will usually be taken on trust, and the speaker will maintain, say, the nobility or the utility of the deeds in question. (3) In political oratory, it will be urged that a proposal is imprac-

ticable; or that, though practicable, it is unjust, or will do no good, or is not so important as its proposer thinks. Argument by 'example' is highly suitable for political oratory, argument by 'Enthymeme' better suits forensic. Enthymemes should not be used in unbroken succession; they should be interspersed with other matter. 'If you have proofs to bring forward, bring them forward, and your moral discourse as well; if you have no Enthymemes, then fall back upon moral discourse: after all, it is more fitting for a good man to display himself as an honest fellow than as a subtle reasoner.' Hints as to the order in which arguments should be presented. As to character: you cannot well say complimentary things about yourself or abusive things about another, but you can put such remarks into the mouth of some third person.

18. Interrogation and Jests. The best moment to employ interrogation is when your opponent has so answered one question that the putting of just one more lands him in absurdity. In replying to questions, you must meet them, if they are ambiguous, by drawing reasonable distinctions, not by a curt answer.—Jests are supposed to be of some service in controversy. Gorgias said that you should kill your opponents' earnestness with jesting and their jesting with earnestness; in which he was right. Jests have been classified in the *Poetics*. 'Some are becoming to a gentleman, others are not; see that you choose such as become *you*. Irony better befits a gentleman than buffoonery; the ironical man jokes to amuse himself, the buffoon to amuse other people'.

19. Epilogue (Peroration, Conclusion). This has four parts. You must (1) make the audience well disposed towards yourself and ill disposed towards your opponent, (2) magnify or minimize the leading facts, (3) excite the required kind of emotion in your hearers, and (4) refresh their memories by means of a recapitulation.—In your closing words you may dispense with conjunctions, and thereby mark the difference between the oration and the peroration: 'I have done. You have heard me. The facts are before you. I ask for your judgement.'

RHETORICA

(*Rhetoric*)

BOOK I

1 Rhetoric is the counterpart of Dialectic.[1] Both alike are concerned 1354ᵃ
with such things as come, more or less, within the general ken of all
men and belong to no definite science. Accordingly all men make use,
more or less, of both; for to a certain extent all men attempt to
discuss statements and to maintain them, to defend themselves and 5
to attack others. Ordinary people do this either at random or through
practice and from acquired habit. Both ways being possible, the subject can plainly be handled systematically, for it is possible to inquire
the reason why some speakers succeed through practice and others 10
spontaneously; and every one will at once agree that such an inquiry
is the function of an art.

Now, the framers of the current treatises on rhetoric have constructed but a small portion of that art. The modes of persuasion are
the only true constituents of the art: everything else is merely accessory. These writers, however, say nothing about Enthymemes, which
are the substance of rhetorical persuasion, but deal mainly with non- 15
essentials. The arousing of prejudice, pity, anger, and similar emotions has nothing to do with the essential facts, but is merely a
personal appeal to the man who is judging the case. Consequently
if the rules for trials which are now laid down in some states—espe- 20
cially in well-governed states—were applied everywhere, such people
would have nothing to say. All men, no doubt, think that the laws
should prescribe such rules, but some, as in the court of Areopagus,
give practical effect to their thoughts and forbid talk about non-
essentials. This is sound law and custom. It is not right to pervert
the judge [2] by moving him to anger or envy or pity—one might as 25

---

[1] 'Rhetoric' and 'Dialectic' may be roughly Englished as 'the art of public speaking' and 'the art of logical discussion'. Aristotle's philosophical definition of
'Rhetoric' is given at the beginning of c. 2.

[2] Here, and in what follows, the English reader should understand 'judge' in a
broad sense, including 'jurymen' and others who 'judge'.

well warp a carpenter's rule before using it. Again, a litigant has clearly nothing to do but to show that the alleged fact is so or is not so, that it has or has not happened. As to whether a thing is important or unimportant, just or unjust, the judge must surely refuse to take his instructions from the litigants: he must decide for himself all such points as the law-giver has not already defined for him.

Now, it is of great moment that well-drawn laws should themselves define all the points they possibly can and leave as few as may be to the decision of the judges; and this for several reasons. First, to find one man, or a few men, who are sensible persons and capable of legislating and administering justice is easier than to find a large number. Next, laws are made after long consideration, whereas decisions in the courts are given at short notice, which makes it hard for those who try the case to satisfy the claims of justice and expediency. The weightiest reason of all is that the decision of the lawgiver is not particular but prospective and general, whereas members of the assembly and the jury find it *their* duty to decide on definite cases brought before them. They will often have allowed themselves to be so much influenced by feelings of friendship or hatred or self-interest that they lose any clear vision of the truth and have their judgement obscured by considerations of personal pleasure or pain. In general, then, the judge should, we say, be allowed to decide as few things as possible. But questions as to whether something has happened or has not happened, will be or will not be, is or is not, must of necessity be left to the judge, since the lawgiver cannot foresee them. If this is so, it is evident that any one who lays down rules about other matters, such as what must be the contents of the 'introduction' or the 'narration' or any of the other divisions of a speech, is theorizing about non-essentials as if they belonged to the art. The only question with which these writers here deal is how to put the judge into a given frame of mind. About the orator's proper modes of persuasion they have nothing to tell us; nothing, that is, about how to gain skill in Enthymemes.

Hence it comes that, although the same systematic principles apply to political as to forensic oratory,[3] and although the former is a nobler business, and fitter for a citizen, than that which concerns the relations of private individuals, these authors say nothing about political oratory, but try, one and all, to write treatises on the way to plead in court. The reason for this is that in political oratory there

---

[3] The words 'orator' and 'oratory' have the advantage of brevity, but the reader will bear in mind that 'public speaker' and 'public speaking' are in some ways nearer the Greek conception of 'rhetor' and 'rhetoric'.

is less inducement to talk about non-essentials. Political oratory is less given to unscrupulous practices than forensic, because it treats of wider issues. In a political debate the man who is forming a 30 judgement is making a decision about his own vital interests. There is no need, therefore, to prove anything except that the facts are what the supporter of a measure maintains they are. In forensic oratory this is not enough; to conciliate the listener is what pays here. It is 35 other people's affairs that are to be decided, so that the judges, intent on their own satisfaction and listening with partiality, surrender themselves to the disputants instead of judging between them. Hence 1355ᵃ in many places, as we have said already,⁴ irrelevant speaking is forbidden in the law-courts: in the public assembly those who have to form a judgement are themselves well able to guard against that.

It is clear, then, that rhetorical study, in its strict sense, is concerned with the modes of persuasion. Persuasion is clearly a sort of 5 demonstration, since we are most fully persuaded when we consider a thing to have been demonstrated. The orator's demonstration is an Enthymeme, and this is, in general, the most effective of the modes of persuasion. The Enthymeme is a sort of syllogism, and the consideration of syllogisms of all kinds, without distinction, is the business of dialectic, either of dialectic as a whole or of one of its branches. It 10 follows plainly, therefore, that he who is best able to see how and from what elements a syllogism is produced will also be best skilled in the Enthymeme, when he has further learnt what its subject-matter is and in what respects it differs from the syllogism of strict logic. The true and the approximately true are apprehended by the same faculty; it may also be noted that men have a sufficient natural 15 instinct for what is true, and usually do arrive at the truth. Hence the man who makes a good guess at truth is likely to make a good guess at probabilities.

It has now been shown that the ordinary writers on rhetoric treat of non-essentials; it has also been shown why they have inclined more towards the forensic branch of oratory.　　　　　　　　　20

Rhetoric is useful (1) because things that are true and things that are just have a natural tendency to prevail over their opposites, so that if the decisions of judges are not what they ought to be, the defeat must be due to the speakers themselves, and they must be blamed accordingly. Moreover, (2) before some audiences not even the possession of the exactest knowledge will make it easy for what 25 we say to produce conviction. For argument based on knowledge

⁴ 1354ᵃ 22.

implies instruction, and there are people whom one cannot instruct. Here, then, we must use, as our modes of persuasion and argument, notions possessed by everybody, as we observed in the *Topics*⁵ when dealing with the way to handle a popular audience. Further, (3) we must be able to employ persuasion, just as strict reasoning can
30 be employed, on opposite sides of a question, not in order that we may in practice employ it in both ways (for we must not make people believe what is wrong), but in order that we may see clearly what the facts are, and that, if another man argues unfairly, we on our part may be able to confute him. No other of the arts draws
35 opposite conclusions: dialectic and rhetoric alone do this. Both these arts draw opposite conclusions impartially. Nevertheless, the underlying facts do not lend themselves equally well to the contrary views. No; things that are true and things that are better are, by their nature, practically always easier to prove and easier to believe in.
1355ᵇ Again, (4) it is absurd to hold that a man ought to be ashamed of being unable to defend himself with his limbs, but not of being unable to defend himself with speech and reason, when the use of rational speech is more distinctive of a human being than the use of his limbs. And if it be objected that one who uses such power of speech unjustly might do great harm, *that* is a charge which may be made in common against all good things except virtue, and above
5 all against the things that are most useful, as strength, health, wealth, generalship. A man can confer the greatest of benefits by a right use of these, and inflict the greatest of injuries by using them wrongly.

It is clear, then, that rhetoric is not bound up with a single definite class of subjects, but is as universal as dialectic; it is clear, also, that it is useful. It is clear, further, that its function is not simply to
10 succeed in persuading, but rather to discover the means of coming as near such success as the circumstances of each particular case allow. In this it resembles all other arts. For example, it is not the function of medicine simply to make a man quite healthy, but to put him as far as may be on the road to health; it is possible to give excellent treatment even to those who can never enjoy sound health. Furthermore, it is plain that it is the function of one and
15 the same art to discern the real and the apparent means of persuasion, just as it is the function of dialectic to discern the real and the apparent syllogism. What makes a man a 'sophist' is not his faculty, but his moral purpose. In rhetoric, however, the term 'rhetorician' may describe either the speaker's knowledge of the art, or his moral

⁵ *Topics*, i. 2, 101ᵃ 30–4.

purpose. In dialectic it is different: a man is a 'sophist' because he [20] has a certain kind of moral purpose, a 'dialectician' in respect, not of his moral purpose, but of his faculty.

Let us now try to give some account of the systematic principles of Rhetoric itself—of the right method and means of succeeding in the object we set before us. We must make as it were a fresh start, and before going further define what rhetoric is.   [25]

2   Rhetoric may be defined as the faculty of observing in any given case the available means of persuasion. This is not a function of any other art. Every other art can instruct or persuade about its own particular subject-matter; for instance, medicine about what is healthy and unhealthy, geometry about the properties of magnitudes, [30] arithmetic about numbers, and the same is true of the other arts and sciences. But rhetoric we look upon as the power of observing the means of persuasion on almost any subject presented to us; and that is why we say that, in its technical character, it is not concerned [35] with any special or definite class of subjects.

Of the modes of persuasion some belong strictly to the art of rhetoric and some do not. By the latter I mean such things as are not supplied by the speaker but are there at the outset—witnesses, evidence given under torture, written contracts, and so on. By the former I mean such as we can ourselves construct by means of the principles of rhetoric. The one kind has merely to be used, the other has to be invented.

Of the modes of persuasion furnished by the spoken word there [1356ᵃ] are three kinds. The first kind depends on the personal character of the speaker; the second on putting the audience into a certain [6] frame of mind; the third on the proof, or apparent proof, provided by the words of the speech itself. Persuasion is achieved by the speaker's personal character when the speech is so spoken as to make [5] us think him credible. We believe good men more fully and more readily than others: this is true generally whatever the question is, and absolutely true where exact certainty is impossible and opinions are divided. This kind of persuasion, like the others, should be achieved by what the speaker says, not by what people think of his character before he begins to speak. It is not true, as some writers [10] assume in their treatises on rhetoric, that the personal goodness revealed by the speaker contributes nothing to his power of persuasion; on the contrary, his character may almost be called the most effective means of persuasion he possesses. Secondly, persuasion may

[6] i. e. the right, fit, required frame of mind.

come through the hearers, when the speech stirs their emotions. Our
15 judgements when we are pleased and friendly are not the same as
when we are pained and hostile. It is towards producing these effects,
as we maintain, that present-day writers on rhetoric direct the whole
of their efforts. This subject shall be treated in detail when we come
to speak of the emotions.[7] Thirdly, persuasion is effected through the
20 speech itself when we have proved a truth or an apparent truth by
means of the persuasive arguments suitable to the case in question.

There are, then, these three means of effecting persuasion. The
man who is to be in command of them must, it is clear, be able
(1) to reason logically, (2) to understand human character and goodness in their various forms, and (3) to understand the emotions—
that is, to name them and describe them, to know their causes and
25 the way in which they are excited. It thus appears that rhetoric is
an offshoot of dialectic and also of ethical studies. Ethical studies may
fairly be called political; and for this reason rhetoric masquerades as
political science, and the professors of it as political experts—sometimes from want of education, sometimes from ostentation, sometimes
30 owing to other human failings. As a matter of fact, it is a branch of
dialectic and similar to it, as we said at the outset.[8] Neither rhetoric
nor dialectic is the scientific study of any one separate subject: both
are faculties for providing arguments. This is perhaps a sufficient
35 account of their scope and of how they are related to each other.

With regard to the persuasion achieved by proof or apparent proof:
1356[b] just as in dialectic there is induction on the one hand and syllogism
or apparent syllogism on the other, so it is in rhetoric. The example
is an induction, the Enthymeme is a syllogism, and the apparent
Enthymeme is an apparent syllogism. I call the Enthymeme a
5 rhetorical syllogism, and the example a rhetorical induction. Every
one who effects persuasion through proof does in fact use either
Enthymemes or examples there is no other way. And since every one
who proves anything at all is bound to use either syllogisms or
inductions (and this is clear to us from the *Analytics* [9]), it must follow
10 that Enthymemes are syllogisms and examples are inductions. The
difference between example and Enthymeme is made plain by the
passages in the *Topics* [10] where induction and syllogism have already
been discussed. When we base the proof of a proposition on a number
of similar cases, this is induction in dialectic, example in rhetoric;
15 when it is shown that, certain propositions being true, a further and
quite distinct proposition must also be true in consequence, whether

[7] ii, cc. 2–11.   [8] i. 1. 1354[a] 1.
[9] *Anal. Pr.* ii. 23, 2a · *Anal. Post.* i. 1. Cp. 68[b] 13.   [10] *Top.* i. 1 and 12.

invariably or usually, this is called syllogism in dialectic, Enthymeme in rhetoric. It is plain also that each of these types of oratory has its advantages. Types of oratory, I say: for what has been said in the *Methodics* [11] applies equally well here; in some oratorical styles examples prevail, in others Enthymemes; and in like manner, some 20 orators are better at the former and some at the latter. Speeches that rely on examples are as persuasive as the other kind, but those which rely on Enthymemes excite the louder applause. The sources of examples and Enthymemes, and their proper uses, we will discuss later.[12] Our next step is to define the processes themselves more clearly. 25

A statement is persuasive and credible either because it is directly self-evident or because it appears to be proved from other statements that are so. In either case it is persuasive because there is somebody whom it persuades. But none of the arts theorize about individual cases. Medicine, for instance, does not theorize about what will help to cure Socrates or Callias, but only about what will help to cure any 30 or all of a given class of patients: this alone is its business: individual cases are so infinitely various that no systematic knowledge of them is possible. In the same way the theory of rhetoric is concerned not with what seems probable to a given individual like Socrates or Hippias, but with what seems probable to men of a given type; and this is true of dialectic also. Dialectic does not construct its syllogisms 35 out of any haphazard materials, such as the fancies of crazy people, but out of materials that call for discussion; and rhetoric, too, draws upon the regular subjects of debate. The duty of rhetoric is to deal 1357ᵃ with such matters as we deliberate upon without arts or systems to guide us, in the hearing of persons who cannot take in at a glance a complicated argument, or follow a long chain of reasoning. The subjects of our deliberation are such as seem to present us with alterna- 5 tive possibilities: about things that could not have been, and cannot now or in the future be, other than they are, nobody who takes them to be of this nature wastes his time in deliberation.

It is possible to form syllogisms and draw conclusions from the results of previous syllogisms; or, on the other hand, from premisses which have not been thus proved, and at the same time are so little 10 accepted that they call for proof. Reasonings of the former kind will necessarily be hard to follow owing to their length, for we assume an audience of untrained thinkers; those of the latter kind will fail to win assent, because they are based on premisses that are not generally admitted or believed.

---

[11] A lost logical treatise of Aristotle.　　　　　　　[12] ii, cc. 20–4.

The Enthymeme and the example must, then, deal with what is in the main contingent, the example being an induction, and the Enthymeme a syllogism, about such matters. The Enthymeme must consist of few propositions, fewer often than those which make up the normal syllogism. For if any of these propositions is a familiar fact, there is no need even to mention it; the hearer adds it himself. Thus, to show that Dorieus has been victor in a contest for which the prize is a crown, it is enough to say 'For he has been victor in the Olympic games', without adding 'And in the Olympic games the prize is a crown', a fact which everybody knows.

There are few facts of the 'necessary' type that can form the basis of rhetorical syllogisms. Most of the things about which we make decisions, and into which therefore we inquire, present us with alternative possibilities. For it is about our actions that we deliberate and inquire, and all our actions have a contingent character; hardly any of them are determined by necessity. Again, conclusions that state what is merely usual or possible must be drawn from premises that do the same, just as 'necessary' conclusions must be drawn from 'necessary' premises; this too is clear to us from the *Analytics*.[13] It is evident, therefore, that the propositions forming the basis of Enthymemes, though some of them may be 'necessary', will most of them be only usually true. Now the materials of Enthymemes are Probabilities and Signs, which we can see must correspond respectively with the propositions that are generally and those that are necessarily true. A Probability is a thing that usually happens; not, however, as some definitions would suggest, anything whatever that usually happens, but only if it belongs to the class of the 'contingent' or 'variable'. It bears the same relation to that in respect of which it is probable as the universal bears to the particular. Of Signs, one kind bears the same relation to the statement it supports as the particular bears to the universal, the other the same as the universal bears to the particular. The infallible kind is a 'complete proof'; the fallible kind has no specific name. By infallible signs I mean those on which syllogisms proper may be based: and this shows us why this kind of Sign is called 'complete proof': when people think that what they have said cannot be refuted, they then think that they are bringing forward a 'complete proof', meaning that the matter has now been demonstrated and completed; for the word *peras* has the same meaning (of 'end' or 'boundary') as the word *tekmar* in the ancient tongue. Now the one kind of Sign (that which bears to the proposition it supports the relation of particular to universal) may be illustrated thus. Suppose it

---

[13] *An. Pr.* i. 8, 12–14, 27.

were said, 'The fact that Socrates was wise and just is a sign that the wise are just'. Here we certainly have a Sign; but even though the proposition be true, the argument is refutable, since it does not form a syllogism. Suppose, on the other hand, it were said, 'The fact that he has a fever is a sign that he is ill', or, 'The fact that she is giving milk is 15 a sign that she has lately borne a child'. Here we have the infallible kind of Sign, the only kind that constitutes a complete proof, since it is the only kind that, if the particular statement is true, is irrefutable. The other kind of Sign, that which bears to the proposition it supports the relation of universal to particular, might be illustrated by saying, 'The fact that he breathes fast is a sign that he has a fever'. This argument also is refutable, even if the statement about the fast breathing be true, since a man may breathe hard without 20 having a fever.

It has, then, been stated above what is the nature of a Probability, of a Sign, and of a complete proof, and what are the differences between them. In the *Analytics* [14] a more explicit description has been given of these points; it is there shown why some of these reasonings can be put into syllogisms and some cannot.

The 'example' has already been described as one kind of induction; 25 and the special nature of the subject-matter that distinguishes it from the other kinds has also been stated above. Its relation to the proposition it supports is not that of part to whole, nor whole to part, nor whole to whole, but of part to part, or like to like. When two statements are of the same order, but one is more familiar than the other, the former is an 'example'. The argument may, for instance, 30 be that Dionysius, in asking as he does for a bodyguard, is scheming to make himself a despot. For in the past Peisistratus kept asking for a bodyguard in order to carry out such a scheme, and did make himself a despot as soon as he got it; and so did Theagenes at Megara; and in the same way all other instances known to the speaker are made into examples, in order to show what is not yet known, that Dionysius has the same purpose in making the same 35 request: all these being instances of the one general principle, that a man who asks for a bodyguard is scheming to make himself a despot. We have now described the sources of those means of persua- 1358[a] sion which are popularly supposed to be demonstrative.

There is an important distinction between two sorts of enthymemes that has been wholly overlooked by almost everybody—one that also subsists between the syllogisms treated of in dialectic. One sort of Enthymeme really belongs to rhetoric, as one sort of syllogism 5

[14] *An. Pr.* ii. 27.

really belongs to dialectic; but the other sort really belongs to other arts and faculties, whether to those we already exercise or to those we have not yet acquired. Missing this distinction, people fail to notice that the more correctly they handle their particular subject the further they are getting away from pure rhetoric or dialectic. This
10 statement will be clearer if expressed more fully. I mean that the proper subjects of dialectical and rhetorical syllogisms are the things with which we say the regular or universal Lines of Argument [15] are concerned, that is to say those lines of argument that apply equally to questions of right conduct, natural science, politics, and many other things that have nothing to do with one another. Take, for instance, the line of argument concerned with 'the more or less'.[16]
15 On this line of argument it is equally easy to base a syllogism or Enthymeme about any of what nevertheless are essentially disconnected subjects—right conduct, natural science, or anything else whatever. But there are also those special Lines of Argument which are based on such propositions as apply only to particular groups or classes of things. Thus there are propositions about natural science on which it is impossible to base any Enthymeme or syllogism about ethics, and other propositions about ethics on which nothing can be
20 based about natural science. The same principle applies throughout. The general Lines of Argument have no special subject-matter, and therefore will not increase our understanding of any particular class of things. On the other hand, the better the selection one makes of propositions suitable for special Lines of Argument, the nearer one comes, unconsciously, to setting up a science that is distinct from dialectic and rhetoric. One may succeed in stating the required
25 principles, but one's science will be no longer dialectic or rhetoric, but the science to which the principles thus discovered belong. Most Enthymemes are in fact based upon these particular or special Lines of Argument; comparatively few on the common or general kind. As in the *Topics*,[17] therefore, so in this work, we must distinguish,
30 in dealing with Enthymemes, the special and the general Lines of Argument on which they are to be founded. By special Lines of Argument I mean the propositions peculiar to each several class of things, by general those common to all classes alike. We may begin with the special Lines of Argument. But, first of all, let us classify rhetoric into its varieties. Having distinguished these we may deal with them one by one, and try to discover the elements of which
35 each is composed, and the propositions each must employ.

[15] Or Topics, Commonplaces.   [16] i. e. the topic of *degree*.
[17] Cp. *Top.* ɪ. 10, 14; iii. 5; *Soph. El.* 9.

3 Rhetoric falls into three divisions, determined by the three classes of listeners to speeches. For of the three elements in speech-making —speaker, subject, and person addressed—it is the last one, the hearer, that determines the speech's end and object. The hearer must be 1358ᵇ either a judge, with a decision to make about things past or future, or an observer. A member of the assembly decides about future events, a juryman about past events: while those who merely decide 5 on the orator's skill are observers. From this it follows that there are three divisions of oratory—(1) political, (2) forensic, and (3) the ceremonial oratory of display.[18]

Political speaking urges us either to do or not to do something: one of these two courses is always taken by private counsellors, as well as by men who address public assemblies. Forensic speaking 10 either attacks or defends somebody: one or other of these two things must always be done by the parties in a case. The ceremonial oratory of display either praises or censures somebody. These three kinds of rhetoric refer to three different kinds of time. The political orator is concerned with the future: it is about things to be done hereafter that he advises, for or against. The party in a case at law is concerned 15 with the past; one man accuses the other, and the other defends himself, with reference to things already done. The ceremonial orator is, properly speaking, concerned with the present, since all men praise or blame in view of the state of things existing at the time, though they often find it useful also to recall the past and to make guesses 20 at the future.

Rhetoric has three distinct ends in view, one for each of its three kinds. The political orator aims at establishing the expediency or the harmfulness of a proposed course of action; if he urges its acceptance, he does so on the ground that it will do good; if he urges its rejection, he does so on the ground that it will do harm; and all other points, such as whether the proposal is just or unjust, honourable or dishonourable, he brings in as subsidiary and relative to this main 25 consideration. Parties in a law-case aim at establishing the justice or injustice of some action, and they too bring in all other points as subsidiary and relative to this one. Those who praise or attack a man aim at proving him worthy of honour or the reverse, and they too treat all other considerations with reference to this one.

That the three kinds of rhetoric do aim respectively at the three

---

[18] Or: deliberative (advisory), legal, and epideictic—the oratory respectively of parliamentary assemblies, of law-courts, and of ceremonial occasions when there is an element of 'display', 'show', 'declamation', and the result is a 'set speech' or 'harangue'.

30 ends we have mentioned is shown by the fact that speakers will sometimes not try to establish anything else. Thus, the litigant will sometimes not deny that a thing has happened or that he has done harm. But that he is guilty of injustice he will never admit; otherwise there would be no need of a trial. So too, political orators often make any concession short of admitting that they are recommending
35 their hearers to take an inexpedient course or not to take an expedient one. The question whether it is not *unjust* for a city to enslave its innocent neighbours often does not trouble them at all. In like man-
1359ᵃ ner those who praise or censure a man do not consider whether his acts have been expedient or not, but often make it a ground of actual praise that he has neglected his own interest to do what was honourable. Thus, they praise Achilles because he championed his fallen friend Patroclus, though he knew that this meant death, and that otherwise he need not die: yet while to die thus was the nobler
5 thing for him to do, the expedient thing was to live on.

It is evident from what has been said that it is these three subjects, more than any others, about which the orator must be able to have propositions at his command. Now the propositions of Rhetoric are Complete Proofs, Probabilities, and Signs. Every kind
10 of syllogism is composed of propositions, and the enthymeme is a particular kind of syllogism composed of the aforesaid propositions.[19]

Since only possible actions, and not impossible ones, can ever have been done in the past or the present, and since things which have not occurred, or will not occur, also cannot have been done or be
15 going to be done, it is necessary for the political, the forensic, and the ceremonial speaker alike to be able to have at their command propositions about the possible and the impossible, and about whether a thing has or has not occurred, will or will not occur. Further, all men, in giving praise or blame, in urging us to accept or reject proposals for action, in accusing others or defending themselves, attempt
20 not only to prove the points mentioned but also to show that the good or the harm, the honour or disgrace, the justice or injustice, is great or small, either absolutely or relatively; and therefore it is plain that we must also have at our command propositions about greatness or smallness and the greater or the lesser—propositions both universal and particular. Thus, we must be able to say which
25 is the greater or lesser good, the greater or lesser act of justice or injustice; and so on.

Such, then, are the subjects regarding which we are inevitably

---

[19] i. e. of Complete Proofs, Probabilities, and Signs relating to the three subjects of the expedient, the just, and the noble.

bound to master the propositions relevant to them. We must now discuss each particular class of these subjects in turn, namely those dealt with in political, in ceremonial, and lastly in legal, oratory.

4   First, then, we must ascertain what are the kinds of things, good or bad, about which the political orator offers counsel. For he does not deal with all things, but only with such as may or may not take place. Concerning things which exist or will exist inevitably, or which cannot possibly exist or take place, no counsel can be given. Nor, again, can counsel be given about the whole class of things which may or may not take place; for this class includes some good things that occur naturally, and some that occur by accident; and about these it is useless to offer counsel. Clearly counsel can only be given on matters about which people deliberate; matters, namely, that ultimately depend on ourselves, and which we have it in our power to set going. For we turn a thing over in our mind until we have reached the point of seeing whether we can do it or not.

Now to enumerate and classify accurately the usual subjects of public business, and further to frame, as far as possible, true definitions of them, is a task which we must not attempt on the present occasion. For it does not belong to the art of rhetoric, but to a more instructive art and a more real branch of knowledge; and as it is, rhetoric has been given a far wider subject-matter than strictly belongs to it. The truth is, as indeed we have said already,[20] that rhetoric is a combination of the science of logic and of the ethical branch of politics; and it is partly like dialectic, partly like sophistical reasoning. But the more we try to make either dialectic or rhetoric not, what they really are, practical faculties, but sciences, the more we shall inadvertently be destroying their true nature; for we shall be re-fashioning them and shall be passing into the region of sciences dealing with definite subjects rather than simply with words and forms of reasoning. Even here, however, we will mention those points which it is of practical importance to distinguish, their fuller treatment falling naturally to political science.

The main matters on which all men deliberate and on which political speakers make speeches are some five in number: ways and means, war and peace, national defence, imports and exports, and legislation.

As to Ways and Means, then, the intending speaker will need to know the number and extent of the country's sources of revenue, so that, if any is being overlooked, it may be added, and, if any is

[20] i. 2. 1356ᵃ 25 ff.

defective, it may be increased. Further, he should know all the expenditure of the country, in order that, if any part of it is super-fluous, it may be abolished, or, if any is too large, it may be reduced. For men become richer not only by increasing their existing wealth but also by reducing their expenditure. A comprehensive view of 30 these questions cannot be gained solely from experience in home affairs; in order to advise on such matters a man must be keenly interested in the methods worked out in other lands.

As to Peace and War, he must know the extent of the military strength of his country, both actual and potential, and also the nature 35 of that actual and potential strength; and further, what wars his country has waged, and how it has waged them. He must know these facts not only about his own country, but also about neighbouring countries; and also about countries with which war is likely, in order that peace may be maintained with those stronger than his own, and that his own may have power to make war or not against those that 1360ᵃ are weaker. He should know, too, whether the military power of another country is like or unlike that of his own; for this is a matter that may affect their relative strength. With the same end in view he must, besides, have studied the wars of other countries as well as those of his own, and the way they ended; similar causes are likely 5 to have similar results.

With regard to National Defence: he ought to know all about the methods of defence in actual use, such as the strength and char-acter of the defensive force and the positions of the forts—this last means that he must be well acquainted with the lie of the country— 10 in order that a garrison may be increased if it is too small or removed if it is not wanted, and that the strategic points may be guarded with special care.

With regard to the Food Supply: he must know what outlay will meet the needs of his country; what kinds of food are produced at home and what imported; and what articles must be exported or imported. This last he must know in order that agreements and 15 commercial treaties may be made with the countries concerned. There are, indeed, two sorts of state to which he must see that his countrymen give no cause for offence, states stronger than his own, and states with which it is advantageous to trade.

But while he must, for security's sake, be able to take all this into account, he must before all things understand the subject of 20 legislation; for it is on a country's laws that its whole welfare depends. He must, therefore, know how many different forms of constitution there are; under what conditions each of these will prosper and by

what internal developments or external attacks each of them tends
to be destroyed. When I speak of destruction through internal developments I refer to the fact that all constitutions, except the best
one of all, are destroyed both by not being pushed far enough and by
being pushed too far. Thus, democracy loses its vigour, and finally 25
passes into oligarchy, not only when it is not pushed far enough,
but also when it is pushed a great deal too far; just as the aquiline
and the snub nose not only turn into normal noses by not being
aquiline or snub enough, but also by being too violently aquiline
or snub arrive at a condition in which they no longer look like noses
at all.

It is useful, in framing laws, not only to study the past history 30
of one's own country, in order to understand which constitution is
desirable for it now, but also to have a knowledge of the constitutions
of other nations, and so to learn for what kinds of nation the various
kinds of constitution are suited. From this we can see that books of
travel are useful aids to legislation, since from these we may learn
the laws and customs of different races. The political speaker will 35
also find the researches of historians useful. But all this is the business
of political science and not of rhetoric.

These, then, are the most important kinds of information which
the political speaker must possess. Let us now go back and state the 1360^b
premises from which he will have to argue in favour of adopting or
rejecting measures regarding these and other matters.

5   It may be said that every individual man and all men in common
aim at a certain end which determines what they choose and what 5
they avoid. This end, to sum it up briefly, is happiness and its constituents. Let us, then, by way of illustration only, ascertain what
is in general the nature of happiness, and what are the elements of
its constituent parts. For all advice to do things or not to do them
is concerned with happiness and with the things that make for or 10
against it; whatever creates or increases happiness or some part of
happiness, we ought to do; whatever destroys or hampers happiness,
or gives rise to its opposite, we ought not to do.

We may define happiness as prosperity combined with virtue;
or as independence of life; or as the secure enjoyment of the maximum 15
of pleasure; or as a good condition of property and body, together
with the power of guarding one's property and body and making
use of them. That happiness is one or more of these things, pretty
well everybody agrees.

From this definition of happiness it follows that its constituent parts are:—good birth, plenty of friends, good friends, wealth, good children, plenty of children, a happy old age, also such bodily excellences as health, beauty, strength, large stature, athletic powers, together with fame, honour, good luck, and virtue. A man cannot fail to be completely independent if he possesses these internal and these external goods; for besides these there are no others to have. (Goods of the soul and of the body are internal. Good birth, friends, money, and honour are external.) Further, we think that he should possess resources and luck, in order to make his life really secure. As we have already ascertained what happiness in general is, so now let us try to ascertain what each of these parts of it is.

Now good birth in a race or a state means that its members are indigenous or ancient; that its earliest leaders were distinguished men, and that from them have sprung many who were distinguished for qualities that we admire.

The good birth of an individual, which may come either from the male or the female side, implies that both parents are free citizens, and that, as in the case of the state, the founders of the line have been notable for virtue or wealth or something else which is highly prized, and that many distinguished persons belong to the family, men and women, young and old.

The phrases 'possession of good children' and 'of many children' bear a quite clear meaning. Applied to a community, they mean that its young men are numerous and of good quality: good in regard to bodily excellences, such as stature, beauty, strength, athletic powers; and also in regard to the excellences of the soul, which in a young man are temperance and courage. Applied to an individual, they mean that his own children are numerous and have the good qualities we have described. Both male and female are here included; the excellences of the latter are, in body, beauty and stature; in soul, self-command and an industry that is not sordid. Communities as well as individuals should lack none of these perfections, in their women as well as in their men. Where, as among the Lacedaemonians, the state of women is bad, almost half of human life is spoilt.

The constituents of wealth are: plenty of coined money and territory; the ownership of numerous, large, and beautiful estates; also the ownership of numerous and beautiful implements, live stock, and slaves. All these kinds of property are our own, are secure, gentlemanly, and useful. The useful kinds are those that are productive, the gentlemanly kinds are those that provide enjoyment. By 'productive' I mean those from which we get our income; by 'enjoyable', those from which we get nothing worth mentioning except the use of them. The criterion of 'security' is the ownership of property in such places and under such conditions that the use of it is in our 20 power; and it is 'our own' if it is in our own power to dispose of it or keep it. By 'disposing of it' I mean giving it away or selling it. Wealth as a whole consists in using things rather than in owning them; it is really the activity—that is, the use—of property that constitutes wealth.

Fame means being respected by everybody, or having some quality 25 that is desired by all men, or by most, or by the good, or by the wise.

Honour is the token of a man's being famous for doing good. It is chiefly and most properly paid to those who have already done good; but also to the man who can do good in future. Doing good 30 refers either to the preservation of life and the means of life, or to wealth, or to some other of the good things which it is hard to get either always or at that particular place or time—for many gain honour for things which seem small, but the place and the occasion account for it. The constituents of honour are: sacrifices; commem- 35 oration, in verse or prose; privileges; grants of land; front seats at civic celebrations; state burial; statues; public maintenance; among foreigners, obeisances and giving place; and such presents as are among various bodies of men regarded as marks of honour. For a present is not only the bestowal of a piece of property, but also a token of honour; which explains why honour-loving as well as money-loving persons desire it. The present brings to both what they want; 1361 it is a piece of property, which is what the lovers of money desire; and it brings honour, which is what the lovers of honour desire.

The excellence of the body is health; that is, a condition which allows us, while keeping free from disease, to have the use of our bodies; for many people are 'healthy' as we are told Herodicus was; and these no one can congratulate on their 'health', for they have to 5 abstain from everything or nearly everything that men do.—Beauty varies with the time of life. In a young man beauty is the possession of a body fit to endure the exertion of running and of contests of strength; which means that he is pleasant to look at; and therefore 10 all-round athletes are the most beautiful, being naturally adapted both for contests of strength and for speed also. For a man in his prime, beauty is fitness for the exertion of warfare, together with a pleasant but at the same time formidable appearance. For an old man, it is to be strong enough for such exertion as is necessary, and

to be free from all those deformities of old age which cause pain
15 to others. Strength is the power of moving some one else at will;
to do this, you must either pull, push, lift, pin, or grip him; thus
you must be strong in all of those ways or at least in some. Excellence
in size is to surpass ordinary people in height, thickness, and breadth
20 by just as much as will not make one's movements slower in consequence. Athletic excellence of the body consists in size, strength,
and swiftness; swiftness implying strength. He who can fling forward
his legs in a certain way, and move them fast and far, is good at
running; he who can grip and hold down is good at wrestling; he
25 who can drive an adversary from his ground with the right blow is a
good boxer: he who can do both the last is a good pancratiast, while
he who can do all is an 'all-round' athlete.

Happiness in old age is the coming of old age slowly and pain-
lessly; for a man has not this happiness if he grows old either quickly,
or tardily but painfully. It arises both from the excellences of the
body and from good luck. If a man is not free from disease, or if he
30 is not strong, he will not be free from suffering; nor can he continue
to live a long and painless life unless he has good luck. There is,
indeed, a capacity for long life that is quite independent of health
or strength; for many people live long who lack the excellences of
the body; but for our present purpose there is no use in going into
the details of this.

35 The terms 'possession of many friends' and 'possession of good
friends' need no explanation; for we define a 'friend' as one who will
always try, for your sake, to do what he takes to be good for you.
The man towards whom many feel thus has many friends; if these
are worthy men, he has good friends.

'Good luck' means the acquisition or possession of all or most, or
the most important, of those good things which are due to luck.
1362ᵃ Some of the things that are due to luck may also be due to artificial
contrivance; but many are independent of art, as for example those
which are due to nature—though, to be sure, things due to luck may
actually be contrary to nature. Thus health may be due to artificial
contrivance, but beauty and stature are due to nature. All such good
5 things as excite envy are, as a class, the outcome of good luck.
Luck is also the cause of good things that happen contrary to reasonable expectation: as when, for instance, all your brothers are ugly,
but you are handsome yourself; or when you find a treasure that
everybody else has overlooked; or when a missile hits the next man
and misses you; or when you are the only man not to go to a place

you have gone to regularly, while the others go there for the first 10
time and are killed. All such things are reckoned pieces of good luck.

As to virtue, it is most closely connected with the subject of Eulogy,
and therefore we will wait to define it until we come to discuss that
subject.[21]

6   It is now plain what our aims, future or actual, should be in urging 15
and what in deprecating, a proposal; the latter being the opposite of
the former. Now the political or deliberative orator's aim is utility:
deliberation seeks to determine not ends but the means to ends, i.e.
what it is most useful to do. Further, utility is a good thing. We ought 20
therefore to assure ourselves of the main facts about Goodness and
Utility in general.

We may define a good thing as that which ought to be chosen for
its own sake; or as that for the sake of which we choose something else;
or as that which is sought after by all things, or by all things that
have sensation or reason, or which will be sought after by any things
that acquire reason; or as that which must be prescribed for a given 25
individual by reason generally, or is prescribed for him by his individual reason, this being his individual good; or as that whose presence
brings anything into a satisfactory and self-sufficing condition; or as
self-sufficiency; or as what produces, maintains, or entails characteristics of this kind, while preventing and destroying their opposites.
One thing may entail another in either of two ways—(1) simulta- 30
neously, (2) subsequently. Thus learning entails knowledge subsequently, health entails life simultaneously. Things are productive of
other things in three senses: first as being healthy produces health;
secondly, as food produces health; and thirdly, as exercise does—
i. e. it does so usually. All this being settled, we now see that both
the acquisition of good things and the removal of bad things must be 35
good; the latter entails freedom from the evil things simultaneously,
while the former entails possession of the good things subsequently.
The acquisition of a greater in place of a lesser good, or of a lesser in
place of a greater evil, is also good, for in proportion as the greater
exceeds the lesser there is acquisition of good or removal of evil. The 1362[b]
virtues, too, must be something good; for it is by possessing these that
we are in a good condition, and they tend to produce good works and
good actions. They must be severally named and described elsewhere.[22] Pleasure, again, must be a good thing, since it is the nature 5
of all animals to aim at it. Consequently both pleasant and beautiful

[21] i. c. 9.   [22] in c. 9.

things must be good things, since the former are productive of pleasure, while of the beautiful things some are pleasant and some desirable in and for themselves.

10　　The following is a more detailed list of things that must be good. Happiness, as being desirable in itself and sufficient by itself, and as being that for whose sake we choose many other things. Also justice, courage, temperance, magnanimity, magnificence, and all such qualities, as being excellences of the soul. Further, health, beauty, and the 15 like, as being bodily excellences and productive of many other good things: for instance, health is productive both of pleasure and of life, and therefore is thought the greatest of goods, since these two things which it causes, pleasure and life, are two of the things most highly prized by ordinary people. Wealth, again: for it is the excellence of possession, and also productive of many other good things. Friends and friendship: for a friend is desirable in himself and also productive 20 of many other good things. So, too, honour and reputation, as being pleasant, and productive of many other good things, and usually accompanied by the presence of the good things that cause them to be bestowed. The faculty of speech and action; since all such qualities are productive of what is good. Further—good parts, strong memory, 25 receptiveness, quickness of intuition, and the like, for all such faculties are productive of what is good. Similarly, all the sciences and arts. And life: since, even if no other good were the result of life, it is desirable in itself. And justice, as the cause of good to the community.

　　The above are pretty well all the things admittedly good. In dealing with things whose goodness is disputed, we may argue in the following 30 ways:—That is good of which the contrary is bad. That is good the contrary of which is to the advantage of our enemies; for example, if it is to the particular advantage of our enemies that we should be cowards, clearly courage is of particular value to our countrymen. And generally, the contrary of that which our enemies desire, or of 35 that at which they rejoice, is evidently valuable. Hence the passage beginning:

Surely would Priam exult.[23]

This principle usually holds good, but not always, since it may well be that our interest is sometimes the same as that of our enemies. Hence it is said that 'evils draw men together'; that is, when the 1363ᵃ same thing is hurtful to them both.

　　Further: that which is not in excess is good, and that which is

[23] *Iliad*, i. 255.

greater than it should be is bad. That also is good on which much labour or money has been spent; the mere fact of this makes it seem good, and such a good is assumed to be an end—an end reached through a long chain of means; and any end is a good. Hence the 5 lines beginning:

And for Priam <and Troy-town's folk> should they leave behind them a boast; [24]

and

Oh, it were shame
To have tarried so long and return empty-handed as erst we came; [25]

and there is also the proverb about 'breaking the pitcher at the door'.

That which most people seek after, and which is obviously an object of contention, is also a good; for, as has been shown,[26] that is good which is sought after by everybody, and 'most people' is taken to be equivalent to 'everybody'. That which is praised is good, since no one praises what is not good. So, again, that which is praised by our 10 enemies [or by the worthless]; for when even those who have a grievance think a thing good, it is at once felt that every one must agree with them; our enemies can admit the fact only because it is evident, just as those must be worthless whom their friends censure and their enemies do not. (For this reason the Corinthians conceived themselves to be 15 insulted by Simonides when he wrote:

Against the Corinthians hath Ilium no complaint.)

Again, that is good which has been distinguished by the favour of a discerning or virtuous man or woman, as Odysseus was distinguished by Athena, Helen by Theseus, Paris by the goddesses, and Achilles by Homer. And, generally speaking, all things are good which men deliberately choose to do; this will include the things already mentioned, and also whatever may be bad for their enemies or good for their 20 friends, and at the same time practicable. Things are 'practicable' in two senses: (1) it is possible to do them, (2) it is easy to do them. Things are done 'easily' when they are done either without pain or quickly: the 'difficulty' of an act lies either in its painfulness or in the long time it takes. Again, a thing is good if it is as men wish; and they wish to have either no evil at all or at least a balance of good over 25 evil. This last will happen where the penalty is either imperceptible or slight. Good, too, are things that are a man's very own, possessed by no

----

[24] *Iliad*, ii. 160.　　　　[25] *Iliad*, ii. 298.　　　　[26] 1362ª 23.

one else, exceptional; for this increases the credit of having them. So
are things which befit the possessors, such as whatever is appropriate
to their birth or capacity, and whatever they feel they ought to have
30 but lack—such things may indeed be trifling, but none the less men
deliberately make them the goal of their action. And things easily
effected; for these are practicable (in the sense of being easy); such
things are those in which every one, or most people, or one's equals, or
one's inferiors have succeeded. Good also are the things by which we
shall gratify our friends or annoy our enemies: and the things chosen
35 by those whom we admire: and the things for which we are fitted by
nature or experience, since we think we shall succeed more easily in
these: and those in which no worthless man can succeed, for such
things bring greater praise: and those which we do in fact desire, for
what we desire is taken to be not only pleasant but also better. Further,
1363ᵇ a man of a given disposition makes chiefly for the corresponding
things: lovers of victory make for victory, lovers of honour for honour,
money-loving men for money, and so with the rest. These, then, are
the sources from which we must derive our means of persuasion about
Good and Utility.

5 7   Since, however, it often happens that people agree that two things
are both useful but do not agree about which is the more so, the next
step will be to treat of relative goodness and relative utility.

A thing which surpasses another may be regarded as being that other
thing plus something more, and that other thing which is surpassed as
being what is contained in the first thing. Now to call a thing 'greater'
or 'more' always implies a comparison of it with one that is 'smaller'
10 or 'less', while 'great' and 'small', 'much' and 'little', are terms used
in comparison with normal magnitude. The 'great' is that which surpasses the normal, the 'small' is that which is surpassed by the normal;
and so with 'many' and 'few'.

Now we are applying the term 'good' to what is desirable for its
own sake and not for the sake of something else; to that at which
all things aim; to what they would choose if they could acquire under-
15 standing and practical wisdom; and to that which tends to produce
or preserve such goods, or is always accompanied by them. Moreover,
that for the sake of which things are done is the end (an end being that
for the sake of which all else is done), and for each individual that thing
is a good which fulfils these conditions in regard to himself. It follows,
then, that a greater number of goods is a greater good than one or than
a smaller number, if that one or that smaller number is included in the

count; for then the larger number surpasses the smaller, and the smaller quantity is surpassed as being contained in the larger.   20

Again, if the largest number of one class surpasses the largest member of another, then the one class surpasses the other; and if one class surpasses another, then the largest member of the one surpasses the largest member of the other. Thus, if the tallest man is taller than the tallest woman, then men in general are taller than women. Conversely, if men in general are taller than women, then the tallest man   25 is taller than the tallest woman. For the superiority of class over class is proportionate to the superiority possessed by their largest specimens. Again, where one good is always accompanied by another, but does not always accompany it, it is greater than the other, for the use of the second thing is implied in the use of the first. A thing may be   30 accompanied by another in three ways, either simultaneously, subsequently, or potentially. Life accompanies health simultaneously (but not health life), knowledge accompanies the act of learning subsequently, cheating accompanies sacrilege potentially, since a man who has committed sacrilege is always capable of cheating. Again, when two things each surpass a third, that which does so by the greater amount is the greater of the two; for it must surpass the greater as well as the less of the other two. A thing productive of a greater good than another is productive of is itself a greater good than that other. For this conception of 'productive of a greater' has been implied in our argument.[27]   35 Likewise, that which is produced by a greater good is itself a greater good; thus, if what is wholesome is more desirable and a greater good than what gives pleasure, health too must be a greater good than pleasure. Again, a thing which is desirable in itself is a greater good   1364ª than a thing which is not desirable in itself, as for example bodily strength than what is wholesome, since the latter is not pursued for its own sake, whereas the former is; and this was our definition of the good.[28] Again, if one of two things is an end, and the other is not, the former is the greater good, as being chosen for its own sake and not for the sake of something else; as, for example, exercise is chosen   5 for the sake of physical well-being. And of two things that which stands less in need of the other, or of other things, is the greater good, since it is more self-sufficing. (That which stands 'less' in need of others is that which needs either *fewer* or *easier* things.) So when one thing does not exist or cannot come into existence without a second, while

---

[27] i.e. we have already (1363ᵇ 15) said that what is productive of good is good; it follows, then, from our way of looking at 'productivity' and 'degree', that what is productive of a greater good is a greater good.   [28] 1362ª 22.

the second can exist without the first, the second is the better. That which does not need something else is more self-sufficing than that which does, and presents itself as a greater good for that reason. Again,
10 that which is a beginning of other things is a greater good than that which is not, and that which is a cause is a greater good than that which is not; the reason being the same in each case, namely that without a cause and a beginning nothing can exist or come into existence. Again, where there are two sets of consequences arising from two different beginnings or causes, the consequences of the more important beginning or cause are themselves the more important; and conversely, that beginning or cause is itself the more important which has the more
15 important consequences. Now it is plain, from all that has been said, that one thing may be shown to be more important than another from two opposite points of view: it may appear the more important (1) because it is a beginning and the other thing is not, and also (2) because it is not a beginning and the other thing is—on the ground that the end is more important and is not a beginning. So Leodamas, when accusing Callistratus, said that the man who prompted the deed was
20 more guilty than the doer, since it would not have been done if he had not planned it. On the other hand, when accusing Chabrias he said that the doer was worse than the prompter, since there would have been no deed without some one to do it; men, said he, plot a thing only in order to carry it out.

Further, what is rare is a greater good than what is plentiful. Thus, gold is a better thing than iron, though less useful: it is harder to
25 get, and therefore better worth getting. Reversely, it may be argued that the plentiful is a better thing than the rare, because we can make more use of it. For what is often useful surpasses what is seldom useful, whence the saying

The best of things is water.[29]

More generally: the hard thing is better than the easy, because it is rarer: and reversely, the easy thing is better than the hard, for it is
30 as we wish it to be. That is the greater good whose contrary is the greater evil, and whose loss affects us more. Positive goodness and badness are more important than the mere *absence* of goodness and badness: for positive goodness and badness are ends, which the mere absence of them cannot be. Further, in proportion as the functions of things are noble or base, the things themselves are good or bad: conversely, in proportion as the things themselves are good or bad, their

29 Pindar, *Olympians,* i. 1.

ıunctions also are good or bad; for the nature of results corresponds with that of their causes and beginnings, and conversely the nature of 35 causes and beginnings corresponds with that of their results. Moreover, those things are greater goods, superiority in which is more desirable or more honourable. Thus, keenness of sight is more desirable than keenness of smell, sight generally being more desirable than smell generally; and similarly, unusually great love of friends being more 1364ᵇ honourable than unusually great love of money, ordinary love of friends is more honourable than ordinary love of money. Conversely, if one of two normal things is better or nobler than the other, an unusual degree of that thing is better or nobler than an unusual degree of the other. Again, one thing is more honourable or better than another if it is more honourable or better to desire it; the importance of the object of a given instinct corresponds to the importance of the 5 instinct itself; and for the same reason, if one thing is more honourable or better than another, it is more honourable and better to desire it. Again, if one science is more honourable and valuable than another, the activity with which it deals is also more honourable and valuable; as is the science, so is the reality that is its object, each science being authoritative in its own sphere. So, also, the more valuable and honour- 10 able the object of a science, the more valuable and honourable the science itself is in consequence. Again, that which would be judged, or which has been judged, a good thing, or a better thing than something else, by all or most people of understanding, or by the majority of men, or by the ablest, must be so; either without qualification, or in so far as they use their understanding to form their judgment. This is indeed a general principle, applicable to all other judgements also; not only the goodness of things, but their essence, magnitude, and general nature are in fact just what knowledge and understanding will 15 declare them to be. Here the principle is applied to judgements of goodness, since one definition of 'good' was 'what beings that acquire understanding will choose in any given case': [30] from which it clearly follows that that thing is *better* which understanding declares to be so. That, again, is a better thing which attaches to better men, either absolutely, or in virtue of their being better; as courage is better than 20 strength. And that is a greater good which would be chosen by a better man, either absolutely, or in virtue of his being better: for instance, to suffer wrong rather than to do wrong, for that would be the choice of the juster man. Again, the pleasanter of two things is the better, since *all* things pursue pleasure, and things instinctively desire pleas-

[30] Cp. 1363ᵇ 14.

urable sensation *for its own sake*; and these are two of the character-
25 istics by which the 'good' and the 'end' have been defined. One
pleasure is greater than another if it is more unmixed with pain, or
more lasting. Again, the nobler thing is better than the less
noble, since the noble is either what is pleasant or what is desirable
in itself. And those things also are greater goods which men desire
more earnestly to bring about for themselves or for their friends,
whereas those things which they least desire to bring about are greater
30 evils. And those things which are more lasting are better than those
which are more fleeting, and the more secure than the less; the enjoyment of the lasting has the advantage of being longer, and that of the
secure has the advantage of suiting our wishes, being there for us
whenever we like. Further, in accordance with the rule of co-ordinate
terms and inflexions of the same stem, what is true of one such related
35 word is true of all. Thus if the action qualified by the term 'brave' is
more noble and desirable than the action qualified by the term 'temperate', then 'bravery' is more desirable than 'temperance' and 'being
brave' than 'being temperate'. That, again, which is chosen by all is a
greater good than that which is not, and that chosen by the majority
1365ᵃ than that chosen by the minority. For that which *all* desire is good,
as we have said; ³¹ and so, the more a thing is desired, the better it is.
Further, that is the better thing which is considered so by competitors
or enemies, or, again, by authorized judges or those whom they select
to represent them. In the first two cases the decision is virtually that
of every one, in the last two that of authorities and experts. And sometimes it may be argued that what all share is the better thing, since
5 it is a dishonour not to share in it; at other times, that what none or
few share is better, since it is rarer. The more praiseworthy things are,
the nobler and therefore the better they are. So with the things that
earn greater honours than others—honour is, as it were, a measure
of value; and the things whose absence involves comparatively heavy
penalties; and the things that are better than others admitted or
10 believed to be good. Moreover, things look better merely by being
divided into their parts, since they then seem to surpass a greater
number of things than before. Hence Homer says that Meleager was
roused to battle by the thought of

All horrors that light on a folk whose city is ta'en of their foes,
When they slaughter the men, when the burg is wasted with ravening
flame,

³¹ 1363ᵇ 14.

When strangers are haling young children to thraldom, [fair women 15
    to shame].[32]

The same effect is produced by piling up facts in a climax after the
manner of Epicharmus. The reason is partly the same as in the case
of division (for combination too makes the impression of great superiority), and partly that the original thing appears to be the cause and
origin of important results. And since a thing is better when it is harder
or rarer than other things, its superiority may be due to seasons, ages,
places, times, or one's natural powers. When a man accomplishes some- 20
thing beyond his natural power, or beyond his years, or beyond the
measure of people like him, or in a special way, or at a special place or
time, his deed will have a high degree of nobleness, goodness, and
justice, or of their opposites. Hence the epigram on the victor at the 25
Olympic games:

In time past, bearing a yoke on my shoulders, of wood unshaven,
I carried my loads of fish from Argos to Tegea town.[33]

So Iphicrates used to extol himself by describing the low estate from
which he had risen. Again, what is natural is better than what is
acquired, since it is harder to come by. Hence the words of Homer:

I have learnt from none but myself.[34]   30

And the best part of a good thing is particularly good; as when Pericles
in his funeral oration said that the country's loss of its young men in
battle was 'as if the spring were taken out of the year'. So with those
things which are of service when the need is pressing; for example,
in old age and times of sickness. And of two things that which leads
more directly to the end in view is the better. So too is that which
is better for people generally as well as for a particular individual. 35
Again, what *can* be got is better than what cannot, for it is good in a
given case and the other thing is not. And what is at the end of life is
better than what is not, since those things are ends in a greater degree
which are nearer the end. What aims at reality is better than what aims
at appearance. We may define what aims at appearance as what a man 1365 ᵃ
will not choose if nobody is to know of his having it. This would seem
to show that to receive benefits is more desirable than to confer them,
since a man will choose the former even if nobody is to know of it, but
it is not the general view that he will choose the latter if nobody knows

[32] *Iliad*, ix. 592–4.   [33] Simonides.   [34] *Odyssey*, xxii. 347.

of it. What a man wants to *be* is better than what a man wants to *seem*,
for in aiming at that he is aiming more at reality. Hence men say that
justice is of small value, since it is more desirable to seem just than to
be just, whereas with health it is not so. That is better than other
things which is more useful than they are for a number of different
purposes; for example, that which promotes life, good life, pleasure,
and noble conduct. For this reason wealth and health are commonly
thought to be of the highest value, as possessing all these advantages.
Again, that is better than other things which is accompanied both with
less pain and with actual pleasure; for here there is more than one
advantage; and so here we have the good of feeling pleasure and also
the good of not feeling pain. And of two good things that is the better
whose addition to a third thing makes a better whole than the addition of the other to the same thing will make. Again, those things
which we are seen to possess are better than those which we are not
seen to possess, since the former have the air of reality. Hence wealth
may be regarded as a greater good if its existence is known to others.
That which is dearly prized is better than what is not—the sort of
thing that some people have only one of, though others have more
like it. Accordingly, blinding a one-eyed man inflicts worse injury than
half-blinding a man with two eyes; for the one-eyed man has been
robbed of what he dearly prized.

The grounds on which we must base our arguments, when we are
speaking for or against a proposal, have now been set forth more or
less completely.

8 The most important and effective qualification for success in persuading audiences and speaking well on public affairs is to understand
all the forms of government and to discriminate their respective customs, institutions, and interests. For all men are persuaded by considerations of their interest, and their interest lies in the maintenance
of the established order. Further, it rests with the supreme authority
to give authoritative decisions, and this varies with each form of government; there are as many different supreme authorities as there are
different forms of government. The forms of government are four—
democracy, oligarchy, aristocracy, monarchy. The supreme right to
judge and decide always rests, therefore, with either a part or the
whole of one or other of these governing powers.

A Democracy is a form of government under which the citizens
distribute the offices of state among themselves by lot, whereas under
oligarchy there is a property qualification, under aristocracy one of

education. By education I mean that education which is laid down by
the law; for it is those who have been loyal to the national institutions 35
that hold office under an aristocracy. These are bound to be looked
upon as 'the best men', and it is from this fact that this form of government has derived its name ('the rule of the best'). Monarchy, as the
word implies, is the constitution in which one man has authority over 1366ᵉ
all. There are two forms of monarchy: kingship, which is limited by
prescribed conditions, and 'tyranny', which is not limited by anything.

We must also notice the ends which the various forms of government pursue, since people choose in practice such actions as will lead
to the realization of their ends. The end of democracy is freedom; of
oligarchy, wealth; of aristocracy, the maintenance of education and 5
national institutions; of tyranny, the protection of the tyrant. It is
clear, then, that we must distinguish those particular customs, institutions, and interests which tend to realize the ideal of each constitution, since men choose their means with reference to their ends. But
rhetorical persuasion is effected not only by demonstrative but by
ethical argument; it helps a speaker to convince us, if we believe that
he has certain qualities himself, namely, goodness, or goodwill towards 10
us, or both together. Similarly, we should know the moral qualities
characteristic of each form of government, for the special moral character of each is bound to provide us with our most effective means
of persuasion in dealing with it. We shall learn the qualities of governments in the same way as we learn the qualities of individuals, since
they are revealed in their deliberate acts of choice; and these are 15
determined by the end that inspires them.

We have now considered the objects, immediate or distant, at which
we are to aim when urging any proposal, and the grounds on which
we are to base our arguments in favour of its utility. We have also
briefly considered the means and methods by which we shall gain a
good knowledge of the moral qualities and institutions peculiar to the 20
various forms of government—only, however, to the extent demanded
by the present occasion; a detailed account of the subject has been
given in the *Politics*.³⁵

9 We have now to consider Virtue and Vice, the Noble and the
Base, since these are the objects of praise and blame. In doing so, we
shall at the same time be finding out how to make our hearers take 25
the required view of our own characters—our second method of per-
suasion.³⁶ The ways in which to make them trust the goodness of other

³⁵ *Politics*, iii and iv.   ³⁶ 1356ᵃ 2 and 5.

people are also the ways in which to make them trust our own. Praise,
again, may be serious or frivolous; nor is it always of a human or divine
30 being but often of inanimate things, or of the humblest of the lower
animals. Here too we must know on what grounds to argue, and must,
therefore, now discuss the subject, though by way of illustration
only.[37]

The Noble is that which is both desirable for its own sake and also
worthy of praise; or that which is both good and also pleasant because
35 good. If this is a true definition of the Noble, it follows that virtue must
be noble, since it is both a good thing and also praiseworthy. Virtue is,
according to the usual view, a faculty of providing and preserving
good things; or a faculty of conferring many great benefits, and benefits
1366[b] of all kinds on all occasions. The forms of Virtue are justice, courage,
temperance, magnificence, magnanimity, liberality, gentleness, prudence, wisdom. If virtue is a faculty of beneficence, the highest kinds
of it must be those which are most useful to others, and for this reason
5 men honour most the just and the courageous, since courage is useful
to others in war, justice both in war and in peace. Next comes liberality; liberal people let their money go instead of fighting for it, whereas
other people care more for money than for anything else. Justice is the
virtue through which everybody enjoys his own possessions in accord-
10 ance with the law; its opposite is injustice, through which men enjoy
the possessions of others in defiance of the law. Courage is the virtue
that disposes men to do noble deeds in situations of danger, in accordance with the law and in obedience to its commands; cowardice is the
opposite. Temperance is the virtue that disposes us to obey the law
15 where physical pleasures are concerned; incontinence is the opposite.
Liberality disposes us to spend money for others' good; illiberality is
the opposite. Magnanimity is the virtue that disposes us to do good to
others on a large scale; [its opposite is meanness of spirit]. Magnificence is a virtue productive of greatness in matters involving the
spending of money. The opposites of these two are smallness of spirit
and meanness respectively. Prudence is that virtue of the understand-
20 ing which enables men to come to wise decisions about the relation to
happiness of the goods and evils that have been previously mentioned.[38]

The above is a sufficient account, for our present purpose, of virtue
and vice in general, and of their various forms. As to further aspects
of the subject, it is not difficult to discern the facts; it is evident

[37] i. e. enough to make our meaning clear.　　　[38] Cp. 1362[b] 10–28.

that things productive of virtue are noble, as tending towards virtue; 25
and also the effects of virtue, that is, the signs of its presence and the
acts to which it leads. And since the signs of virtue, and such acts as
it is the mark of a virtuous man to do or have done to him, are noble,
it follows that all deeds or signs of courage, and everything done cou-
rageously, must be noble things; and so with what is just and actions 30
done justly. (Not, however, actions justly done to us; here justice is
unlike the other virtues; 'justly' does not always mean 'nobly'; when a
man is punished, it is more shameful that this should be justly than
unjustly done to him.) The same is true of the other virtues. Again,
those actions are noble for which the reward is simply honour, or 35
honour more than money. So are those in which a man aims at something desirable for some one else's sake; actions good absolutely, such
as those a man does for his country without thinking of himself; actions
good in their own nature; actions that are not good simply for the individual, since individual interests are selfish. Noble also are those 1367ᵃ
actions whose advantage may be enjoyed after death, as opposed to
those whose advantage is enjoyed during one's lifetime: for the latter
are more likely to be for one's own sake only. Also, all actions done for
the sake of others, since these less than other actions are done for one's
own sake; and all successes which benefit others and not oneself; and 5
services done to one's benefactors, for this is just; and good deeds
generally, since they are not directed to one's own profit. And the
opposites of those things of which men feel ashamed, for men are
ashamed of saying, doing, or intending to do shameful things. So when
Alcaeus said

> Something I fain would say to thee,
> Only shame restraineth me,   10

Sappho wrote

> If for things good and noble thou wert yearning,
> If to speak baseness were thy tongue not burning,
> No load of shame would on thine eyelids weigh;
> What thou with honour wishest thou wouldst say.

Those things, also, are noble for which men strive anxiously, without 15
feeling fear; for they feel thus about the good things which lead to fair
fame. Again, one quality or action is nobler than another if it is that
of a naturally finer being: thus a man's will be nobler than a woman's.
And those qualities are noble which give more pleasure to other
people than to their possessors; hence the nobleness of justice and
just actions. It is noble to avenge oneself on one's enemies and not to 20

come to terms with them; for requital is just, and the just is noble; and not to surrender is a sign of courage. Victory, too, and honour belong to the class of noble things, since they are desirable even when they yield no fruits, and they prove our superiority in good qualities. Things that deserve to be remembered are noble, and the more they deserve this, the nobler they are. So are the things that continue even after

25 death; those which are always attended by honour; those which are exceptional; and those which are possessed by one person alone— these last are more readily remembered than others. So again are possessions that bring no profit, since they are more fitting than others for a gentleman. So are the distinctive qualities of a particular people, and the symbols of what it specially admires, like long hair in Sparta, where this is a mark of a free man, as it is not easy to perform any

30 menial task when one's hair is long. Again, it is noble not to practise any sordid craft, since it is the mark of a free man not to live at another's beck and call. We are also to assume, when we wish either to praise a man or blame him, that qualities closely allied to those which he actually has are identical with them; for instance, that the cautious man is cold-blooded and treacherous, and that the stupid man is an

35 honest fellow or the thick-skinned man a good-tempered one. We can always idealize any given man by drawing on the virtues akin to his actual qualities; thus we may say that the passionate and excitable man is 'outspoken'; or that the arrogant man is 'superb' or 'impres-

1367ᵇ sive'. Those who run to extremes will be said to possess the corresponding good qualities; rashness will be called courage, and extravagance generosity. That will be what most people think; and at the same time this method enables an advocate to draw a misleading inference from the motive, arguing that if a man runs into danger needlessly, much

5 more will he do so in a noble cause; and if a man is open-handed to any one and every one, he will be so to his friends also, since it is the extreme form of goodness to be good to everybody.

We must also take into account the nature of our particular audience when making a speech of praise; for, as Socrates used to say, it is not difficult to praise the Athenians to an Athenian audience.[39] If the audience esteems a given quality, we must say that our hero has

10 that quality, no matter whether we are addressing Scythians or Spartans or philosophers. Everything, in fact, that is esteemed we are to represent as noble. After all, people regard the two things as much the same.

All actions are noble that are appropriate to the man who does

39 Cp. Plato, *Menexenus*, 235 D.

them: if, for instance, they are worthy of his ancestors or of his own
past career. For it makes for happiness, and is a noble thing, that he
should add to the honour he already has. Even inappropriate actions 15
are noble if they are better and nobler than the appropriate ones would
be; for instance, if one who was just an average person when all went
well becomes a hero in adversity, or if he becomes better and easier to
get on with the higher he rises. Compare the saying of Iphicrates,
'Think what I was and what I am'; and the epigram on the victor at
the Olympic games,

In time past, bearing a yoke on my shoulders, of wood unshaven; [40]

and the encomium of Simonides,

A woman whose father, whose husband, whose brethren were
    princes all.   20

Since we praise a man for what he has actually done, and fine
actions are distinguished from others by being intentionally good, we
must try to prove that our hero's noble acts are intentional. This is all
the easier if we can make out that he has often acted so before, and
therefore we must assert coincidences and accidents to have been
intended. Produce a number of good actions, all of the same kind, and 25
people will think that they must have been intended, and that they
prove the good qualities of the man who did them.

Praise is the expression in words of the eminence of a man's good
qualities, and therefore we must display his actions as the product of
such qualities. Encomium refers to what he has actually done; the
mention of accessories, such as good birth and education, merely helps
to make our story credible—good fathers are likely to have good
sons, and good training is likely to produce good character. Hence 30
it is only when a man has already done something that we bestow
encomiums upon him. Yet the actual deeds are evidence of the doer's
character: even if a man has not actually done a given good thing, we
shall bestow *praise* on him, if we are sure that he is the sort of man
who *would* do it. To call any one blest is, it may be added, the same
thing as to call him happy; but these are not the same thing as to
bestow praise and encomium upon him; the two latter are a part of
'calling happy', just as goodness is a part of happiness.   35

To praise a man is in one respect akin to urging a course of action.
The suggestions which would be made in the latter case become
encomiums when differently expressed. When we know what action 1368ᵃ
or character is required, then, in order to express these facts as sug-

---

[40] Cp. i. 7, 1365ᵃ 24–8, for this and the previous quotation.

gestions for action, we have to change and reverse our form of words. Thus the statement 'A man should be proud not of what he owes to fortune but of what he owes to himself', if put like this, amounts to a 5 suggestion; to make it into praise we must put it thus, 'Since he is proud not of what he owes to fortune but of what he owes to himself.' [41] Consequently, whenever you want to praise any one, think what you would urge people to do; and when you want to urge the doing of anything, think what you would praise a man for having done. Since suggestion may or may not forbid an action, the praise into which we convert it must have one or other of two opposite forms of expression accordingly.

10   There are, also, many useful ways of heightening the effect of praise. We must, for instance, point out that a man is the only one, or the first, or almost the only one who has done something, or that he has done it better than any one else; all these distinctions are honourable. And we must, further, make much of the particular season and occasion of an action, arguing that we could hardly have looked for it just then. If a man has often achieved the same success, we must mention 15 this; that is a strong point; he himself, and not luck, will then be given the credit. So, too, if it is on his account that observances have been devised and instituted to encourage or honour such achievements as his own: thus we may praise Hippolochus because the first encomium ever made was for him, or Harmodius and Aristogeiton because their statues were the first to be put up in the market-place. And we may censure bad men for the opposite reason.

Again, if you cannot find enough to say of a man himself, you may 20 pit him against others, which is what Isocrates used to do owing to his want of familiarity with forensic pleading. The comparison should be with famous men; that will strengthen your case; it is a noble thing to surpass men who are themselves great. It is only natural that methods of 'heightening the effect' should be attached particularly to speeches of praise; they aim at proving superiority over others, and any such superiority is a form of nobleness. Hence if you cannot compare your 25 hero with famous men, you should at least compare him with other people generally, since any superiority is held to reveal excellence. And, in general, of the lines of argument which are common to all speeches, this 'heightening of effect' is most suitable for declamations, where we take our hero's actions as admitted facts, and our business is simply to invest these with dignity and nobility. 'Examples' are 30 most suitable to deliberative speeches; for we judge of future events by divination from past events. Enthymemes are most suitable to forensic

[41] Cp. Isocrates, *Evagoras* § 45 and *Panath.* § 32.

speeches; it is our doubts about past events that most admit of arguments showing why a thing must have happened or proving that it
did happen.

The above are the general lines on which all, or nearly all, speeches
of praise or blame are constructed. We have seen the sort of thing
we must bear in mind in making such speeches, and the materials 35
out of which encomiums and censures are made. No special treatment
of censure and vituperation is needed. Knowing the above facts, we
know their contraries; and it is out of these that speeches of censure
are made.

10　We have next to treat of Accusation and Defence, and to enu- 1368ᵇ
merate and describe the ingredients of the syllogisms used therein.
There are three things we must ascertain—first, the nature and number
of the incentives to wrong-doing; second, the state of mind of wrongdoers; third, the kind of persons who are wronged, and their condition. 5
We will deal with these questions in order. But before that let us define
the act of 'wrong-doing'.

We may describe 'wrong-doing' as injury voluntarily inflicted
contrary to law. 'Law' is either special or general. By special law I
mean that written law which regulates the life of a particular community; by general law, all those unwritten principles which are
supposed to be acknowledged everywhere. We do things 'voluntarily' 10
when we do them consciously and without constraint. (Not all voluntary ⁴² acts are deliberate, but all deliberate acts are conscious ⁴³—
no one is ignorant of what he deliberately intends.) The causes of
our deliberately intending harmful and wicked acts contrary to law
are (1) vice, (2) lack of self-control. For the wrongs a man does to
others will correspond to the bad quality or qualities that he himself 15
possesses. Thus it is the mean man who will wrong others about
money, the profligate in matters of physical pleasure, the effeminate
in matters of comfort, and the coward where danger is concerned—
his terror makes him abandon those who are involved in the same
danger. The ambitious man does wrong for the sake of honour, the
quick-tempered from anger, the lover of victory for the sake of victory, 20
the embittered man for the sake of revenge, the stupid man because
he has misguided notions of right and wrong, the shameless man
because he does not mind what people think of him; and so with the
rest—any wrong that any one does to others corresponds to his
particular faults of character.

---

⁴² i. e. and therefore conscious.　　　　　⁴³ i. e. and therefore voluntary.

25 However, this subject has already been cleared up in part in our discussions of the virtues [44] and will be further explained later when we treat of the emotions.[45] We have now to consider the motives and states of mind of wrongdoers, and to whom they do wrong.

Let us first decide what sort of things people are trying to get or avoid when they set about doing wrong to others. For it is plain that 30 the prosecutor must consider, out of all the aims that can ever induce us to do wrong to our neighbours, how many, and which, affect his adversary; while the defendant must consider how many, and which, do *not* affect him. Now every action of every person either is or is not due to that person himself. Of those not due to himself some are due to chance, the others to necessity; of these latter, again, some 35 are due to compulsion, the others to nature. Consequently all actions that are not due to a man himself are due either to chance or to nature 1369ª or to compulsion. All actions that *are* due to a man himself and caused by himself are due either to habit or to rational or irrational craving. Rational craving is a craving for good, i. e. a *wish*—nobody wishes for anything unless he thinks it good. Irrational craving is twofold, viz. anger and appetite.

5 Thus every action must be due to one or other of seven causes: chance, nature, compulsion, habit, reasoning, anger, or appetite. It is superfluous further to distinguish actions according to the doers' ages, moral states, or the like; it is of course true that, for instance, young men do have hot tempers and strong appetites; still, it is not 10 through youth that they act accordingly, but through anger or appetite. Nor, again, is action due to wealth or poverty; it is of course true that poor men, being short of money, do have an appetite for it, and that rich men, being able to command needless pleasures, do have an appetite for such pleasures: but here, again, their actions will be *due* not to wealth or poverty but to appetite. Similarly, with just 15 men, and unjust men, and all others who are said to act in accordance with their moral qualities, their actions will really be due to one of the causes mentioned—either reasoning or emotion: due, indeed, sometimes to good dispositions and good emotions, and sometimes to bad; but that good qualities should be followed by good emotions, 20 and bad by bad, is merely an accessory fact—it is no doubt true that the temperate man, for instance, because he is temperate, *is* always and at once attended by healthy opinions and appetites in regard to pleasant things, and the intemperate man by unhealthy ones. So we must ignore such distinctions. Still we must consider what kinds of actions and of people usually go together; for while there are no

[44] i, c. 9.   [45] ii, cc. 1–11.

definite kinds of action associated with the fact that a man is fair 25
or dark, tall or short, it does make a difference if he is young or old,
just or unjust. And, generally speaking, all those accessory qualities
that cause distinctions of human character are important: e. g. the
sense of wealth or poverty, of being lucky or unlucky. This shall be
dealt with later [46]—let us now deal first with the rest of the subject
before us.   30

The things that happen by chance are all those whose cause cannot
be determined, that have no purpose, and that happen neither always
nor usually nor in any fixed way. The definition of chance shows just
what they are. Those things happen by nature which have a fixed and 35
internal cause; they take place uniformly, either always or usually. 1369[b]
There is no need to discuss in exact detail the things that happen contrary to nature, nor to ask whether they happen in some sense naturally
or from some other cause; it would seem that chance is at least partly
the cause of such events. Those things happen through compulsion 5
which take place contrary to the desire or reason of the doer, yet
through his own agency. Acts are done from habit which men do
because they have often done them before. Actions are due to reasoning when, in view of any of the goods already mentioned,[47] they
appear useful either as ends or as means to an end, and are performed
for that reason: 'for that reason', since even licentious persons 10
perform a certain number of useful actions, but because they are
pleasant and not because they are useful. To passion and anger are
due all acts of revenge. Revenge and punishment are different things.
Punishment is inflicted for the sake of the person punished; revenge
for that of the punisher, to satisfy his feelings. (What anger is will
be made clear when we come to discuss the emotions.[48]) Appetite is 15
the cause of all actions that appear pleasant. Habit, whether acquired
by mere familiarity or by effort, belongs to the class of pleasant
things, for there are many actions not naturally pleasant which men
perform with pleasure, once they have become used to them. To sum
up then, all actions due to ourselves either are or seem to be either 20
good or pleasant. Moreover, as all actions due to ourselves are done
voluntarily and actions not due to ourselves are done involuntarily,
it follows that all voluntary actions must either be or seem to be either
good or pleasant; for I reckon among goods escape from evils or
apparent evils and the exchange of a greater evil for a less (since
these things are in a sense positively desirable), and likewise I count 25
among pleasures escape from painful or apparently painful things
and the exchange of a greater pain for a less. We must ascertain,

[46] ii, cc. 12–17.   [47] i, c. 6.   [48] ii, c. 2.

then, the number and nature of the things that are useful and pleasant. The useful has been previously examined in connexion with political
30 oratory;[49] let us now proceed to examine the pleasant. Our various definitions must be regarded as adequate, even if they are not exact, provided they are clear.

11   We may lay it down that Pleasure is a movement, a movement by which the soul as a whole is consciously brought into its normal
1370ª state of being; and that Pain is the opposite. If this is what pleasure is, it is clear that the pleasant is what tends to produce this condition, while that which tends to destroy it, or to cause the soul to be brought into the opposite state, is painful. It must therefore be pleasant as a rule to move towards a natural state of being, particularly when a
5 natural process has achieved the complete recovery of that natural state. Habits also are pleasant; for as soon as a thing has become habitual, it is virtually natural; habit is a thing not unlike nature; what happens often is akin to what happens always, natural events happening always, habitual events often. Again, that is pleasant which is not forced on us; for force is unnatural, and that is why what is
10 compulsory is painful, and it has been rightly said

All that is done on compulsion is bitterness unto the soul.[50]

So all acts of concentration, strong effort, and strain are necessarily painful; they all involve compulsion and force, unless we are accustomed to them, in which case it is custom that makes them pleasant.
15 The opposites to these are pleasant; and hence ease, freedom from toil, relaxation, amusement, rest, and sleep belong to the class of pleasant things; for these are all free from any element of compulsion. Everything, too, is pleasant for which we have the desire within us, since desire is the craving for pleasure. Of the desires some are irrational, some associated with reason. By irrational I mean those which do not arise from any opinion held by the mind. Of this kind
20 are those known as 'natural'; for instance, those originating in the body, such as the desire for nourishment, namely hunger and thirst, and a separate kind of desire answering to each kind of nourishment; and the desires connected with taste and sex and sensations of touch
25 in general; and those of smell, hearing, and vision. Rational desires are those which we are induced to have; there are many things we desire to see or get because we have been told of them and induced to believe them good. Further, pleasure is the consciousness through the senses of a certain kind of emotion; but imagination is a feeble

[49] i, c. 6.   [50] Evenus.

sort of sensation, and there will always be in the mind of a man who
remembers or expects something an image or picture of what he 30
remembers or expects. If this is so, it is clear that memory and
expectation also, being accompanied by sensation, may be accompanied by pleasure. It follows that anything pleasant is either present
and perceived, past and remembered, or future and expected, since
we perceive present pleasures, remember past ones, and expect future
ones. Now the things that are pleasant to remember are not only those 1370ᵇ
that, when actually perceived as present, *were* pleasant, but also some
things that were not, provided that their results have subsequently
proved noble and good. Hence the words

> Sweet 'tis when rescued to remember pain,[51]

and

> Even his griefs are a joy long after to one that remembers   5
> All that he wrought and endured.[52]

The reason of this is that it is pleasant even to be merely free from
evil. The things it is pleasant to expect are those that when present
are felt to afford us either great delight or great but not painful
benefit. And in general, all the things that delight us when they are
present also do so, as a rule, when we merely remember or expect 10
them. Hence even being angry is pleasant—Homer said of wrath that

> Sweeter it is by far than the honeycomb dripping with sweetness [53]—

for no one grows angry with a person on whom there is no prospect
of taking vengeance, and we feel comparatively little anger, or none
at all, with those who are much our superiors in power. Some pleasant 15
feeling is associated with most of our appetites; we are enjoying
either the memory of a past pleasure or the expectation of a future
one, just as persons down with fever, during their attacks of thirst,
enjoy remembering the drinks they have had and looking forward
to having more. So also a lover enjoys talking or writing about his 20
loved one, or doing any little thing connected with him; all these
things recall him to memory and make him actually present to the
eye of imagination. Indeed, it is always the first sign of love, that
besides enjoying some one's presence, we remember him when he is
gone, and feel pain as well as pleasure, because he is there no longer.
Similarly there is an element of pleasure even in mourning and lamen- 25
tation for the departed. There is grief, indeed, at his loss, but pleasure

---

51 Euripides.   52 Cp. *Odyssey*, xv. 400, 401.   53 *Iliad*, xviii. 109.

in remembering him and as it were seeing him before us in his deeds and in his life. We can well believe the poet when he says

He spake, and in each man's heart he awakened the love of lament.[54]

Revenge, too, is pleasant; it is pleasant to get anything that it is
30 painful to fail to get, and angry people suffer extreme pain when they fail to get their revenge; but they enjoy the prospect of getting it. Victory also is pleasant, and not merely to 'bad losers', but to every one; the winner sees himself in the light of a champion, and everybody has a more or less keen appetite for being that. The pleasantness of victory implies of course that combative sports and intel-
1371ᵃ lectual contests are pleasant (since in these it often happens that some one wins) and also games like knuckle-bones, ball, dice, and draughts. And similarly with the serious sports; some of these become pleasant when one is accustomed to them; while others are pleasant from the first, like hunting with hounds, or indeed any kind of hunt-
5 ing. For where there is competition, there is victory. That is why forensic pleading and debating contests are pleasant to those who are accustomed to them and have the capacity for them. Honour and good repute are among the most pleasant things of all; they make a man see himself in the character of a fine fellow, especially when he
10 is credited with it by people whom he thinks good judges. His neighbours are better judges than people at a distance; his associates and fellow-countrymen better than strangers; his contemporaries better than posterity; sensible persons better than foolish ones; a large number of people better than a small number: those of the former class, in each case, are the more likely to be good judges of him. Honour and credit bestowed by those whom you think much inferior
15 to yourself—e. g. children or animals—you do not value: not for its own sake, anyhow: if you do value it, it is for some other reason. Friends belong to the class of pleasant things; it is pleasant to love—if you love wine, you certainly find it delightful: and it is pleasant to be loved, for this too makes a man see
20 himself as the possessor of goodness, a thing that every being that has a feeling for it desires to possess: to be loved means to be valued for one's own personal qualities. To be admired is also pleasant, simply because of the honour implied. Flattery and flatterers are pleasant: the flatterer is a man who, you believe, admires and likes you. To do
25 the same thing often is pleasant, since, as we saw, anything habitual is pleasant.[55] And to change is also pleasant: change means an approach to nature, whereas invariable repetition of anything causes

---

[54] *Iliad*, xxiii. 108; *Odyssey*, iv. 183.   [55] i, c. 10, 1369ᵇ 16.

the excessive prolongation of a settled condition: therefore, says
the poet,

Change is in all things sweet.[56]

That is why what comes to us only at long intervals is pleasant,
whether it be a person or a thing; for it is a change from what we had
before, and, besides, what comes only at long intervals has the value 30
of rarity. Learning things and wondering at things are also pleasant
as a rule; wondering implies the desire of learning, so that the object
of wonder is an object of desire; while in learning one is brought into
one's natural condition. Conferring and receiving benefits belong to
the class of pleasant things; to receive a benefit is to get what one
desires; to confer a benefit implies both possession and superiority, 1371[b]
both of which are things we try to attain. It is because beneficent
acts are pleasant that people find it pleasant to put their neighbours
straight again and to supply what they lack. Again, since learning
and wondering are pleasant, it follows that such things as acts of 5
imitation must be pleasant—for instance, painting, sculpture, poetry
—and every product of skilful imitation; this latter, even if the object
imitated is not itself pleasant; for it is not the object itself which
here gives delight; the spectator draws inferences ('That is a
so-and-so') and thus learns something fresh.[57] Dramatic turns of 10
fortune and hairbreadth escapes from perils are pleasant, because we
feel all such things are wonderful.

And since what is natural is pleasant, and things akin to each other
seem natural to each other, therefore all kindred and similar things
are usually pleasant to each other; for instance, one man, horse, or
young person is pleasant to another man, horse, or young person. 15
Hence the proverbs 'mate delights mate', 'like to like',[58] 'beast knows
beast', 'jackdaw to jackdaw', and the rest of them. But since everything like and akin to oneself is pleasant, and since every man is
himself more like and akin to himself than any one else is, it follows
that all of us must be more or less fond of ourselves. For all this 20
resemblance and kinship is present particularly in the relation of an
individual to himself. And because we are all fond of ourselves, it
follows that what is our own is pleasant to all of us, as for instance
our own deeds and words. That is why we are usually fond of our
flatterers, [our lovers,] and honour; also of our children, for our
children are our own work. It is also pleasant to complete what is 25

[56] Euripides, *Orestes*, 234.   [57] Cp. *Poetics*, c. 4, 1448[b] 5–19.
[58] *Odyssey*, xvii. 218.

defective, for the whole thing thereupon becomes our own work. And since power over others is very pleasant, it is pleasant to be thought wise, for practical wisdom secures us power over others. (Scientific wisdom is also pleasant, because it is the knowledge of many wonderful things.) Again, since most of us are ambitious, it must be pleasant to disparage our neighbours as well as to have power over them. It 30 is pleasant for a man to spend his time over what he feels he can do best; just as the poet says,

> To that he bends himself,
> To that each day allots most time, wherein
> He is indeed the best part of himself.[59]

Similarly, since amusement and every kind of relaxation and laughter too belong to the class of pleasant things, it follows that ludicrous 1372ᵃ things are pleasant, whether men, words, or deeds. We have discussed the ludicrous separately in the treatise on the *Art of Poetry*.[60]

So much for the subject of pleasant things: by considering their opposites we can easily see what things are unpleasant.

12　The above are the motives that make men do wrong to others; 5 we are next to consider the states of mind in which they do it, and the persons to whom they do it.

They must themselves suppose that the thing can be done, and done by them: either that they can do it without being found out, or that if they are found out they can escape being punished, or that if they are punished the disadvantage will be less than the gain for themselves or those they care for. The general subject of apparent possibility and impossibility will be handled later on,[61] since it is 10 relevant not only to forensic but to all kinds of speaking. But it may here be said that people think that they can themselves most easily do wrong to others without being punished for it if they possess eloquence, or practical ability, or much legal experience, or a large body of friends, or a great deal of money. Their confidence is greatest if they personally possess the advantages mentioned: but even without them they are satisfied if they have friends or supporters or 15 partners who do possess them: they can thus both commit their crimes and escape being found out and punished for committing them. They are also safe, they think, if they are on good terms with their victims

---

[59] Euripides.

[60] Not found in the *Poetics,* as it exists to-day. Aristotle probably analysed the causes and conditions of laughter, when treating of Comedy in his lost Second Book.　　　　　　　　　　　　　　　　　　　　　　[61] ii, c. 19.

or with the judges who try them. Their victims will in that case not be on their guard against being wronged, and will make some arrangement with them instead of prosecuting; while their judges will favour them because they like them, either letting them off altogether or imposing light sentences. They are not likely to be found out if their appearance contradicts the charges that might be brought against them: for instance, a weakling is unlikely to be charged with violent assault, or a poor and ugly man with adultery. Public and open injuries are the easiest to do, because nobody could at all suppose them possible, and therefore no precautions are taken. The same is true of crimes so great and terrible that no man living could be suspected of them: here too no precautions are taken. For all men guard against ordinary offences, just as they guard against ordinary diseases; but no one takes precautions against a disease that nobody has ever had. You feel safe, too, if you have either no enemies or a great many; if you have none, you expect not to be watched and therefore not to be detected; if you have a great many, you will be watched, and therefore people will think you can never risk an attempt on them, and you can defend your innocence by pointing out that you could never have taken such a risk. You may also trust to hide your crime by the way you do it or the place you do it in, or by some convenient means of disposal.

You may feel that even if you are found out you can stave off a trial, or have it postponed, or corrupt your judges: or that even if you are sentenced you can avoid paying damages, or can at least postpone doing so for a long time: or that you are so badly off that you will have nothing to lose. You may feel that the gain to be got by wrongdoing is great or certain or immediate, and that the penalty is small or uncertain or distant. It may be that the advantage to be gained 1372ᵇ is greater than any possible retribution: as in the case of despotic power, according to the popular view. You may consider your crimes as bringing you solid profit, while their punishment is nothing more than being called bad names. Or the opposite argument may appeal to you: your crimes may bring you some credit (thus you may, incidentally, be avenging your father or mother, like Zeno), whereas the punishment may amount to a fine, or banishment, or something of that sort. People may be led on to wrong others by either of these motives or feelings; but no man by both—they will affect people of quite opposite characters. You may be encouraged by having often escaped detection or punishment already; or by having often tried and failed; for in crime, as in war, there are men who will always refuse to give up the struggle. You may get your pleasure on the spot

and the pain later, or the gain on the spot and the loss later. That is what appeals to weak-willed persons—and weakness of will may be shown with regard to all the objects of desire. It may on the contrary appeal to you—as it does appeal to self-controlled and sensible people
15 —that the pain and loss are immediate, while the pleasure and profit come later and last longer. You may feel able to make it appear that your crime was due to chance, or to necessity, or to natural causes, or to habit: in fact, to put it generally, as if you had failed to do right rather than actually done wrong. You may be able to trust other people to judge you equitably. You may be stimulated by being in
20 want: which may mean that you want necessaries, as poor people do, or that you want luxuries, as rich people do. You may be encouraged by having a particularly good reputation, because that will save you from being suspected: or by having a particularly bad one, because nothing you are likely to do will make it worse.

The above, then, are the various states of mind in which a man sets about doing wrong to others. The kind of people to whom he does wrong, and the ways in which he does it, must be considered next. The people to whom he does it are those who have what he
25 wants himself, whether this means necessities or luxuries and materials for enjoyment. His victims may be far off or near at hand. If they are near, he gets his profit quickly; if they are far off, vengeance is slow, as those think who plunder the Carthaginians. They may be those who are trustful instead of being cautious and watchful, since all such people are easy to elude. Or those who are too easy-going
30 to have enough energy to prosecute an offender. Or sensitive people, who are not apt to show fight over questions of money. Or those who have been wronged already by many people, and yet have not prosecuted; such men must surely be the proverbial 'Mysian prey'.[62] Or those who have either never or often been wronged before; in neither case will they take precautions; if they have never been wronged they think they never will, and if they have often been wronged they
35 feel that surely it cannot happen again. Or those whose character has been attacked in the past, or is exposed to attack in the future: they will be too much frightened of the judges to make up their minds
1373ª to prosecute, nor can they win their case if they do: this is true of those who are hated or unpopular. Another likely class of victim is those who their injurer can pretend have, themselves or through their ancestors or friends, treated badly, or intended to treat badly, the man himself, or his ancestors, or those he cares for; as the proverb says, 'wickedness needs but a pretext'. A man may wrong his enemies,

---

[62] i. e. an easy prey.

because that is pleasant: he may equally wrong his friends, because that is easy. Then there are those who have no friends, and those who lack eloquence and practical capacity; these will either not attempt to prosecute, or they will come to terms, or failing that they will lose their case. There are those whom it does not pay to waste time in waiting for trial or damages. such as foreigners and small farmers; they will settle for a trifle, and always be ready to leave off. Also those who have themselves wronged others, either often, or in the same way as they are now being wronged themselves—for it is felt that next to no wrong is done to people when it is the same wrong as they have often themselves done to others: if, for instance, you assault a man who has been accustomed to behave with violence to others. So too with those who have done wrong to others, or have meant to, or mean to, or are likely to do so; there is something fine and pleasant in wronging such persons, it seems as though almost no wrong were done. Also those by doing wrong to whom we shall be gratifying our friends, or those we admire or love, or our masters, or in general the people by reference to whom we mould our lives. Also those whom we may wrong and yet be sure of equitable treatment. Also those against whom we have had any grievance, or any previous differences with them, as Callippus had when he behaved as he did to Dion: here too it seems as if almost no wrong were being done. Also those who are on the point of being wronged by others if we fail to wrong them ourselves, since here we feel we have no time left for thinking the matter over. So Aenesidemus is said to have sent the 'cottabus' prize to Gelon, who had just reduced a town to slavery, because Gelon had got there first and forestalled his own attempt. Also those by wronging whom we shall be able to do many righteous acts; for we feel that we can then easily cure the harm done. Thus Jason the Thessalian said that it is a duty to do some unjust acts in order to be able to do many just ones.

Among the kinds of wrong done to others are those that are done universally, or at least commonly: one expects to be forgiven for doing these. Also those that can easily be kept dark, as where things that can rapidly be consumed like eatables are concerned, or things that can easily be changed in shape, colour, or combination, or things that can easily be stowed away almost anywhere—portable objects that you can stow away in small corners, or things so like others of which you have plenty already that nobody can tell the difference. There are also wrongs of a kind that shame prevents the victim speaking about, such as outrages done to the women in his household or to himself or to his sons. Also those for which you would be thought very litigious to prosecute any one—trifling wrongs, or wrongs for which people are usually excused.

The above is a fairly complete account of the circumstances under which men do wrong to others, of the sort of wrongs they do, of the sort of persons to whom they do them, and of their reasons for doing them.

1373ᵇ 13 It will now be well to make a complete classification of just and unjust actions. We may begin by observing that they have been defined relatively to two kinds of law, and also relatively to two classes of persons. By the two kinds of law I mean particular law and universal law. Particular law is that which each community lays down
5 and applies to its own members: this is partly written and partly unwritten. Universal law is the law of nature. For there really is, as every one to some extent divines, a natural justice and injustice that is binding on all men, even on those who have no association or covenant with each other. It is this that Sophocles' Antigone clearly
10 means when she says that the burial of Polyneices was a just act in spite of the prohibition: she means that it was just by nature.

> Not of to-day or yesterday it is,
> But lives eternal: none can date its birth.[63]

And so Empedocles, when he bids us kill no living creature, says that
15 doing this is not just for some people while unjust for others,

> Nay, but, an all-embracing law, through the realms of the sky
> Unbroken it stretcheth, and over the earth's immensity.

And as Alcidamas [64] says in his Messeniac Oration. . . .

The actions that we ought to do or not to do have also been divided into two classes as affecting either the whole community or some one
20 of its members. From this point of view we can perform just or unjust acts in either of two ways—towards one definite person, or towards the community. The man who is guilty of adultery or assault is doing wrong to some definite person; the man who avoids service in the army is doing wrong to the community.

25 Thus the whole class of unjust actions may be divided into two classes, those affecting the community, and those affecting one or more other persons. We will next, before going further, remind ourselves of what 'being wronged' means. Since it has already [65] been

[63] Sophocles, *Antigone*, 456, 7.
[64] According to the scholiast, the words of Alcidamas were, 'God has left all men free; Nature has made no man a slave'. [65] i, c. 10.

settled that 'doing a wrong' must be intentional, 'being wronged' must
consist in having an injury done to you by some one who *intends* to
do it. In order to be wronged, a man must (1) suffer actual harm, 30
(2) suffer it against his will. The various possible forms of harm are
clearly explained by our previous [66] separate discussion of goods and
evils. We have also seen that a voluntary action is one where the
doer knows what he is doing.[67] We now see that every accusation
must be of an action affecting either the community or some individual. The doer of the action must either understand and intend the
action, or not understand and intend it. In the former case, he must 35
be acting either from deliberate choice or from passion. (Anger will
be discussed when we speak of the passions [68]; the motives for crime
and the state of mind of the criminal have already [69] been discussed.)
Now it often happens that a man will admit an act, but will not admit 1374ᵃ
the prosecutor's label for the act nor the facts which that label
implies. He will admit that he took a thing but not that he 'stole' it;
that he struck some one first, but not that he committed 'outrage';
that he had intercourse with a woman, but not that he committed
'adultery'; that he is guilty of theft, but not that he is guilty of
'sacrilege', the object stolen not being consecrated; that he has encroached, but not that he has 'encroached on State lands'; that he 5
has been in communication with the enemy, but not that he has been
guilty of 'treason'. Here therefore we must be able to distinguish
what is theft, outrage, or adultery, from what is not, if we are to be
able to make the justice of our case clear, no matter whether our
aim is to establish a man's guilt or to establish his innocence. Wherever such charges are brought against a man, the question is whether 10
he is or is not guilty of a criminal offence. It is deliberate purpose
that constitutes wickedness and criminal guilt, and such names as
'outrage' or 'theft' imply deliberate purpose as well as the mere action.
A blow does not always amount to 'outrage', but only if it is struck
with some such purpose as to insult the man struck or gratify the
striker himself. Nor does taking a thing without the owner's knowl- 15
edge always amount to 'theft', but only if it is taken with the intention of keeping it and injuring the owner. And as with these charges,
so with all the others.

We saw that there are two kinds of right and wrong conduct
towards others, one provided for by written ordinances, the other by
unwritten. We have now discussed the kind about which the laws 20
have something to say. The other kind has itself two varieties. First,
there is the conduct that springs from exceptional goodness or bad-

[66] i, c. 6.   [67] i, c. 10.   [68] ii, c. 2.   [69] i, cc. 11 and 12.

ness, and is visited accordingly with censure and loss of honour, or with praise and increase of honour and decorations: for instance, gratitude to, or requital of, our benefactors, readiness to help our friends, and the like. The second kind makes up for the defects of
25 a community's written code of law. This is what we call equity; people regard it as just; it is, in fact, the sort of justice which goes beyond the written law. Its existence partly is and partly is not intended by legislators; not intended, where they have noticed no defect in the
30 law; intended, where they find themselves unable to define things exactly, and are obliged to legislate as if that held good always which in fact only holds good usually; or where it is not easy to be complete owing to the endless possible cases presented, such as the kinds and sizes of weapons that may be used to inflict wounds—a lifetime would be too short to make out a complete list of these. If, then, a precise statement is impossible and yet legislation is necessary, the law must
35 be expressed in wide terms; and so, if a man has no more than a finger-ring on his hand when he lifts it to strike or actually strikes another man, he is guilty of a criminal act according to the written
1374b words of the law; but he is innocent really, and it is equity that declares him to be so. From this definition of equity it is plain what sort of actions, and what sort of persons, are equitable or the reverse. Equity must be applied to forgivable actions; and it must make us
5 distinguish between criminal acts on the one hand, and errors of judgement, or misfortunes, on the other. (A 'misfortune' is an act, not due to moral badness, that has unexpected results: an 'error of judgement' is an act, also not due to moral badness, that has results that might have been expected: a 'criminal act' has results that might have been expected, but *is* due to moral badness, for that is the source
10 of all actions inspired by our appetites.) Equity bids us be merciful to the weakness of human nature; to think less about the laws than about the man who framed them, and less about what he said than about what he meant; not to consider the actions of the accused so much as his intentions, nor this or that detail so much as the whole
15 story; to ask not what a man is now but what he has always or usually been. It bids us remember benefits rather than injuries, and benefits received rather than benefits conferred; to be patient when we are wronged; to settle a dispute by negotiation and not by force; to
20 prefer arbitration to litigation—for an arbitrator goes by the equity of a case, a judge by the strict law, and arbitration was invented with the express purpose of securing full power for equity.

The above may be taken as a sufficient account of the nature of equity.

14 The worse of two acts of wrong done to others is that which is prompted by the worse disposition. Hence the most trifling acts may [25] be the worst ones; as when Callistratus charged Melanopus with having cheated the temple-builders of three consecrated half-obols. The converse is true of just acts. This is because the greater is here potentially contained in the less: there is no crime that a man who has stolen three consecrated half-obols would shrink from committing. Sometimes, however, the worse act is reckoned not in this way but [30] by the greater harm that it does. Or it may be because no punishment for it is severe enough to be adequate; or the harm done may be incurable—a difficult and even hopeless crime to defend; or the sufferer may not be able to get his injurer legally punished, a fact that makes the harm incurable, since legal punishment and chastisement are the proper cure. Or again, the man who has suffered wrong may have inflicted some fearful punishment on himself; then the doer of the wrong ought in justice to receive a still more fearful punish- [35] ment. Thus Sophocles, when pleading for retribution to Euctemon, who had cut his own throat because of the outrage done to him, said he would not fix a penalty less than the victim had fixed for himself. [1375a] Again, a man's crime is worse if he has been the first man, or the only man, or almost the only man, to commit it: or if it is by no means the first time he has gone seriously wrong in the same way: or if his crime has led to the thinking-out and invention of measures to prevent and punish similar crimes—thus in Argos a penalty is inflicted on a man on whose account a law is passed, and also on [5] those on whose account the prison was built: or if a crime is specially brutal, or specially deliberate: or if the report of it awakes more terror than pity. There are also such rhetorically effective ways of putting it as the following: That the accused has disregarded and broken not one but many solemn obligations like oaths, promises, pledges, or rights of intermarriage between states—here the crime [10] is worse because it consists of many crimes; and that the crime was committed in the very place where criminals are punished, as for example perjurers do—it is argued that a man who will commit a crime in a law-court would commit it anywhere. Further, the worse deed is that which involves the doer in special shame; that whereby a man wrongs his benefactors—for he does more than one wrong, by not merely doing them harm but failing to do them good; that which [15] breaks the unwritten laws of justice—the better sort of man will be just without being forced to be so, and the written laws depend on force while the unwritten ones do not. It may however be argued

otherwise, that the crime is worse which breaks the written laws: for
the man who commits crimes for which terrible penalties are provided
20 will not hesitate over crimes for which no penalty is provided at all.
—So much, then, for the comparative badness of criminal actions.

15 There are also the so-called 'non-technical' [70] means of persuasion; and we must now take a cursory view of these, since they are
specially characteristic of forensic oratory. They are five in number:
laws, witnesses, contracts, tortures, oaths.

25 First, then, let us take laws and see how they are to be used in
persuasion and dissuasion, in accusation and defence. If the written
law tells against our case, clearly we must appeal to the universal
law, and insist on its greater equity and justice. We must argue that
the juror's oath 'I will give my verdict according to my honest
30 opinion' means that one will not simply follow the letter of the written
law. We must urge that the principles of equity are permanent and
changeless, and that the universal law does not change either, for it
is the law of nature, whereas written laws often do change. This is
the bearing of the lines in Sophocles' *Antigone*, where Antigone pleads
that in burying her brother she had broken Creon's law, but not the
unwritten law:

1375ᵇ
Not of to-day or yesterday they are,
But live eternal: <none can date their birth.>
Not I would fear the wrath of any man,
<And brave Gods' vengeance> for defying these.[71]

We shall argue that justice indeed is true and profitable, but that
sham justice is not, and that consequently the written law is not,
because it does not fulfil the true purpose of law. Or that justice is
5 like silver, and must be assayed by the judges, if the genuine is to
be distinguished from the counterfeit. Or that the better a man is,
the more he will follow and abide by the unwritten law in preference
to the written. Or perhaps that the law in question contradicts some
other highly-esteemed law, or even contradicts itself. Thus it may
be that one law will enact that all contracts must be held binding,
10 while another forbids us ever to make illegal contracts. Or if a law
is ambiguous, we shall turn it about and consider which construction
best fits the interests of justice or utility, and then follow that way
of looking at it. Or if, though the law still exists, the situation to
meet which it was passed exists no longer, we must do our best to

---

[70] Cp. c. 2, *supra*.   [71] Sophocles, *Antigone*, 456.

prove this and to combat the law thereby. If however the written law 15
supports our case, we must urge that the oath 'to give my verdict
according to my honest opinion' is not meant to make the judges
give a verdict that is contrary to the law, but to save them from the
guilt of perjury if they misunderstand what the law really means.
Or that no one chooses what is absolutely good, but every one what
is good for himself.[72] Or that not to use the laws is as bad as to
have no laws at all. Or that, as in the other arts, it does not pay to 20
try to be cleverer than the doctor: for less harm comes from the
doctor's mistakes than from the growing habit of disobeying authority. Or that trying to be cleverer than the laws is just what is forbidden by those codes of law that are accounted best.—So far as
the laws are concerned, the above discussion is probably sufficient. 25

As to witnesses, they are of two kinds, the ancient and the recent;
and these latter, again, either do or do not share in the risks of the
trial. By 'ancient' witnesses I mean the poets and all other notable
persons whose judgements are known to all. Thus the Athenians
appealed to Homer [73] as a witness about Salamis; and the men of 30
Tenedos not long ago appealed to Periander of Corinth in their dispute with the people of Sigeum; and Cleophon supported his accusation of Critias by quoting the elegiac verse of Solon, maintaining
that discipline had long been slack in the family of Critias, or Solon
would never have written,

Pray thee, bid the red-haired Critias do what his father commands
   him.

These witnesses are concerned with past events. As to future
events we shall also appeal to soothsayers: thus Themistocles quoted 1376ᵃ
the oracle about 'the wooden wall' as a reason for engaging the
enemy's fleet. Further, proverbs are, as has been said,[74] one form of
evidence. Thus if you are urging somebody not to make a friend of
an old man, you will appeal to the proverb,

Never show an old man kindness.   5

Or if you are urging that he who has made away with fathers should
also make away with their sons, quote,

Fool, who slayeth the father and leaveth his sons to avenge him.[75]

---

[72] sc., and our written laws, which were made for us, may not reach the
abstract ideal of perfection, but they probably suit us better than if they did.

[73] *Iliad*, ii. 557.   [74] A general statement, apparently.

[75] Stasinus, *Cypria*.

'Recent' witnesses are well-known people who have expressed their
opinions about some disputed matter: such opinions will be useful
support for subsequent disputants on the same points: thus Eubulus
10 used in the law-courts against Chares the reply Plato [76] had made
to Archibius, 'It has become the regular custom in this country to
admit that one is a scoundrel'. There are also those witnesses who
share the risk of punishment if their evidence is pronounced false.
These are valid witnesses to the fact that an action was or was not
done, that something is or is not the case; they are not valid wit-
15 nesses to the quality of an action, to its being just or unjust, useful
or harmful. On such questions of *quality* the opinion of detached
persons is highly trustworthy. Most trustworthy of all are the
'ancient' witnesses, since they cannot be corrupted.

   In dealing with the evidence of witnesses, the following are useful
arguments. If you have no witnesses on your side, you will argue that
the judges must decide from what is probable; that this is meant
by 'giving a verdict in accordance with one's honest opinion'; that
20 probabilities cannot be bribed to mislead the court; and that probabilities are never convicted of perjury. If you *have* witnesses, and
the other man has not, you will argue that probabilities cannot be
put on their trial, and that we could do without the evidence of witnesses altogether if we need do no more than balance the pleas
advanced on either side.

   The evidence of witnesses may refer either to ourselves or to our
25 opponent; and either to questions of fact or to questions of personal
character: so, clearly, we need never be at a loss for useful evidence.
For if we have no evidence of fact supporting our own case or telling
against that of our opponent, at least we can always find evidence
to prove our own worth or our opponent's worthlessness. Other arguments about a witness—that he is a friend or an enemy or neutral, or
30 has a good, bad, or indifferent reputation, and any other such distinctions—we must construct upon the same general lines as we use for
the regular rhetorical proofs.[77]

   Concerning contracts argument can be so far employed as to
1376ᵇ increase or diminish their importance and their credibility; we shall
try to increase both if they tell in our favour, and to diminish both
if they tell in favour of our opponent. Now for confirming or upsetting
the credibility of contracts the procedure is just the same as for
dealing with witnesses, for the credit to be attached to contracts
5 depends upon the character of those who have signed them or have

[76] Disputed whether the Comic Poet or the Philosopher.
[77] 'enthymemes': Cp. ii, c. 23

the custody of them. The contract being once admitted genuine, we must insist on its importance, if it supports our case. We may argue that a contract is a law, though of a special and limited kind; and that, while contracts do not of course make the law binding, the law does make any lawful contract binding, and that the law itself as a whole is a sort of contract, so that any one who disregards or repu- 10 diates any contract is repudiating the law itself. Further, most business relations—those, namely, that are voluntary—are regulated by contracts, and if these lose their binding force, human intercourse ceases to exist. We need not go very deep to discover the other appropriate arguments of this kind. If, however, the contract tells against us and for our opponents, in the first place those arguments are suitable which 15 we can use to fight a law that tells against us. We do not regard ourselves as bound to observe a bad law which it was a mistake ever to pass: and it is ridiculous to suppose that we are bound to observe a bad and mistaken contract. Again, we may argue that the duty of the judge as umpire is to decide what is just, and therefore he must ask 20 where justice lies, and not what this or that document means. And that it is impossible to pervert justice by fraud or by force, since it is founded on nature, but a party to a contract may be the victim of either fraud or force. Moreover, we must see if the contract contravenes either universal law or any written law of our own or another country; 25 and also if it contradicts any other previous or subsequent contract; arguing that the subsequent is the binding contract, or else that the previous one was right and the subsequent one fraudulent—whichever way suits us. Further, we must consider the question of utility, noting whether the contract is against the interest of the judges or not; and so 30 on—these arguments are as obvious as the others.

Examination by torture is one form of evidence, to which great weight is often attached because it is in a sense compulsory. Here again it is not hard to point out the available grounds for magnifying its value, if it happens to tell in our favour, and arguing that it is the only form of evidence that is infallible; or, on the other hand, for refuting it it tells against us and for our opponent, when we may 1377ᵃ say what is true of torture of every kind alike, that people under its compulsion tell lies quite as often as they tell the truth, sometimes persistently refusing to tell the truth, sometimes recklessly making a 5 false charge in order to be let off sooner. We ought to be able to quote cases, familiar to the judges, in which this sort of thing has actually happened. [We must say that evidence under torture is not trustworthy, the fact being that many men whether thick-witted, tough-skinned, or stout of heart endure their ordeal nobly, while cowards and timid men are full of boldness till they see the ordeal of these others: so that no trust can be placed in evidence under torture.]

In regard to oaths, a fourfold division can be made. A man may either both offer and accept an oath,[78] or neither, or one without the other—that is, he may offer an oath but not accept one, or accept
10 an oath but not offer one. There is also the situation that arises when an oath has already been sworn either by himself or by his opponent.

If you refuse to offer an oath, you may argue that men do not hesitate to perjure themselves; and that if your opponent does swear, you lose your money, whereas, if he does not, you think the judges will decide against him; and that the risk of an unfavourable verdict
15 is preferable, since you trust the judges and do not trust him.

If you refuse to accept an oath, you may argue that an oath is always paid for; that you would of course have taken it if you had been a rascal, since if you *are* a rascal you had better make something by it, and you would in that case have to swear in order to succeed. Thus your refusal, you argue, must be due to high principle, not to fear of perjury: and you may aptly quote the saying of Xenophanes,

20 'Tis not fair that he who fears not God should challenge him who doth.

It is as if a strong man were to challenge a weakling to strike, or be struck by, him.

If you agree to accept an oath, you may argue that you trust yourself but not your opponent; and that (to invert the remark of Xenophanes) the fair thing is for the impious man to offer the oath and for the pious man to accept it; and that it would be monstrous if you yourself were unwilling to accept an oath in a case where you demand
25 that the judges should do so before giving their verdict. If you wish to offer an oath, you may argue that piety disposes you to commit the issue to the gods; and that your opponent ought not to want other judges than himself, since you leave the decision with him; and that it is outrageous for your opponents to refuse to swear about this question, when they insist that others should do so.

Now that we see how we are to argue in each case separately, we see also how we are to argue when they occur in pairs, namely, when
30 you are willing to accept the oath but not to offer it; to offer it but not to accept it; both to accept and to offer it; or to do neither. These
1377ᵇ are of course combinations of the cases already mentioned, and so

[78] i. e. both demand an oath from his adversary (call upon him to swear to the truth of his statements) and take an oath himself.

your arguments also must be combinations of the arguments already mentioned.

If you have already sworn an oath that contradicts your present one, you must argue that it is not perjury, since perjury is a crime, and a crime must be a voluntary action, whereas actions due to the 5 force or fraud of others are involuntary. You must further reason from this that perjury depends on the intention and not on the spoken words. But if it is your opponent who has already sworn an oath that contradicts his present one, you must say that if he does not abide by his oaths he is the enemy of society, and that this is the reason why men take an oath before administering the laws. 'My opponents insist that you, the judges, must abide by the oath you have sworn, and 10 yet they are not abiding by their own oaths.' And there are other arguments which may be used to magnify the importance of the oath.—[So much, then, for the 'non-technical' modes of persuasion.]

BOOK II

1   We have now considered the materials to be used in supporting or opposing a political measure, in pronouncing eulogies or censures, and for prosecution and defence in the law courts. We have considered the received opinions on which we may best base our arguments so as to convince our hearers—those opinions with which our enthymemes deal, and out of which they are built, in each of the three kinds of oratory, according to what may be called the special needs of each. 20

But since rhetoric exists to affect the giving of decisions—the hearers decide between one political speaker and another, and a legal verdict *is* a decision—the orator must not only try to make the argument of his speech demonstrative and worthy of belief; he must also make his own character look right and put his hearers, who are to decide, into the right frame of mind. Particularly in political oratory, but also in lawsuits, it adds much to an orator's influence that his own character 25 should look right and that he should be thought to entertain the right feelings toward his hearers; and also that his hearers themselves should be in just the right frame of mind. That the orator's own character should look right is particularly important in political speaking: that the audience should be in the right frame of mind, in lawsuits. 30 When people are feeling friendly and placable, they think one sort of thing; when they are feeling angry or hostile, they think either something totally different or the same thing with a different intensity: 1378ª when they feel friendly to the man who comes before them for judgement, they regard him as having done little wrong, if any; when they feel hostile, they take the opposite view. Again, if they are eager for, and have good hopes of, a thing that will be pleasant if it happens, they think that it certainly will happen and be good for them: whereas if 5 they are indifferent or annoyed, they do not think so.

There are three things which inspire confidence in the orator's own character—the three, namely, that induce us to believe a thing apart from any proof of it: good sense, good moral character, and goodwill. 10 False statements and bad advice are due to one or more of the following three causes. Men either form a false opinion through want of good sense; or they form a true opinion, but because of their moral badness do not say what they really think; or finally, they are both sensible and upright, but not well disposed to their hearers, and may fail in consequence to recommend what they know to be the best course. These are the only possible cases. It follows that any one who is 15 thought to have all three of these good qualities will inspire trust in his audience. The way to make ourselves thought to be sensible and morally good must be gathered from the analysis of goodness already given:[1] the way to establish your own goodness is the same as the way to establish that of others. Good will and friendliness of disposition will form part of our discussion of the emotions,[2] to which we must now turn.

20   The Emotions are all those feelings that so change men as to affect their judgements, and that are also attended by pain or pleasure. Such are anger, pity, fear and the like, with their opposites. We must arrange what we have to say about each of them under three heads. Take, for instance, the emotion of anger: here we must discover (1) what the state of mind of angry people is, (2) who the people are 25 with whom they usually get angry, and (3) on what grounds they get angry with them. It is not enough to know one or even two of these points; unless we know all three, we shall be unable to arouse anger in any one. The same is true of the other emotions. So just as earlier in this work we drew up a list of useful propositions for the orator, 30 let us now proceed in the same way to analyse the subject before us.

2   Anger may be defined as an impulse, accompanied by pain, to a conspicuous revenge for a conspicuous slight directed without justification towards what concerns oneself or towards what concerns one's friends. If this is a proper definition of anger, it must always be felt towards some particular individual, e. g. Cleon, and not 'man' in general. It must be felt because the other has done or intended to do 1378^b something to him or one of his friends. It must always be attended

---

[1] i, c. 9.   [2] ii, c. 4.

by a certain pleasure—that which arises from the expectation of revenge. For since nobody aims at what he thinks he cannot attain,
the angry man is aiming at what he can attain, and the belief that
you will attain your aim is pleasant. Hence it has been well said about 5
wrath,

Sweeter it is by far than the honeycomb dripping with sweetness,
And spreads through the hearts of men.[3]

It is also attended by a certain pleasure because the thoughts dwell
upon the act of vengeance, and the images then called up cause pleasure, like the images called up in dreams.

　　Now slighting is the actively entertained opinion of something as 10
obviously of no importance. We think bad things, as well as good
ones, have serious importance; and we think the same of anything
that tends to produce such things, while those which have little or no
such tendency we consider unimportant. There are three kinds of
slighting—contempt, spite, and insolence. (1) Contempt is one kind
of slighting: you feel contempt for what you consider unimportant, 15
and it is just such things that you slight. (2) Spite is another kind; it
is a thwarting another man's wishes, not to get something yourself
but to prevent his getting it. The slight arises just from the fact that
you do not aim at something for yourself: clearly you do not think
that he can do you harm, for then you would be afraid of him instead 20
of slighting him, nor yet that he can do you any good worth mentioning, for then you would be anxious to make friends with him. (3)
Insolence is also a form of slighting, since it consists in doing and
saying things that cause shame to the victim, not in order that anything may happen to yourself, or because anything has happened 25
to yourself, but simply for the pleasure involved. (Retaliation is not
'insolence', but vengeance.) The cause of the pleasure thus enjoyed
by the insolent man is that he thinks himself greatly superior to others
when ill-treating them. That is why youths and rich men are insolent;
they think themselves superior when they show insolence. One sort of
insolence is to rob people of the honour due to them; you certainly
slight them thus; for it is the unimportant, for good or evil, that 30
has no honour paid to it. So Achilles says in anger:

He hath taken my prize for himself and hath done me dishonour,[4]

and

　　　　　　　　　Like an alien honoured by none,[5]

meaning that this is why he is angry. A man expects to be especially

　³ *Iliad*, xviii. 109.　　　　⁴ *Iliad*, i. 356.　　　　⁵ *Ib.* ix. 648.

respected by his inferiors in birth, in capacity, in goodness, and gen-
1739ᵃ erally in anything in which he is much their superior: as where money
is concerned a wealthy man looks for respect from a poor man; where
speaking is concerned, the man with a turn for oratory looks for
respect from one who cannot speak; the ruler demands the respect of
the ruled, and the man who thinks he ought to be a ruler demands the
respect of the man whom he thinks he ought to be ruling. Hence it has
been said

> Great is the wrath of kings, whose father is Zeus almighty,[6]

and

5   Yea, but his rancour abideth long afterward also,[7]

their great resentment being due to their great superiority. Then
again a man looks for respect from those who he thinks owe him good
treatment, and these are the people whom he has treated or is treating
well, or means or has meant to treat well, either himself, or through
his friends, or through others at his request.

It will be plain by now, from what has been said, (1) in what frame
of mind, (2) with what persons, and (3) on what grounds people
10 grow angry. (1) The frame of mind is that in which any pain is being
felt. In that condition, a man is always aiming at something. Whether,
then, another man opposes him either directly in any way, as by
preventing him from drinking when he is thirsty, or indirectly, the
act appears to him just the same; whether some one works against him,
or fails to work with him, or otherwise vexes him while he is in this
15 mood, he is equally angry in all these cases. Hence people who are
afflicted by sickness or poverty or love or thirst or any other unsatis-
fied desires are prone to anger and easily roused: especially against
those who slight their present distress. Thus a sick man is angered
by disregard of his illness, a poor man by disregard of his poverty, a
man waging war by disregard of the war he is waging, a lover by dis-
20 regard of his love, and so throughout, any other sort of slight being
enough if special slights are wanting. Each man is predisposed, by the
emotion now controlling him, to his own particular anger. Further, we
are angered if we happen to be expecting a contrary result: for a quite
unexpected evil is especially painful, just as the quite unexpected ful-
25 filment of our wishes is specially pleasant. Hence it is plain what
seasons, times, conditions, and periods of life tend to stir men easily
to anger, and where and when this will happen; and it is plain that the
more we are under these conditions the more easily we are stirred.

[6] *Iliad,* ii. 196.   [7] *Ib.* i. 82.

These, then, are the frames of mind in which men are easily stirred to anger. The persons with whom we get angry are those who laugh, mock, or jeer at us, for such conduct is insolent. Also those who inflict injuries upon us that are marks of insolence. These injuries must be 30 such as are neither retaliatory nor profitable to the doers: for only then will they be felt to be due to insolence. Also those who speak ill of us, and show contempt for us, in connexion with the things we ourselves most care about: thus those who are eager to win fame as philosophers get angry with those who show contempt for their philosophy; those 35 who pride themselves upon their appearance get angry with those who show contempt for their appearance; and so on in other cases. We feel particularly angry on this account if we suspect that we are in fact, or that people think we are, lacking completely or to any effective extent in the qualities in question. For when we are convinced that 1379^b we excel in the qualities for which we are jeered at, we can ignore the jeering. Again, we are angrier with our friends than with other people, since we feel that our friends ought to treat us well and not badly. We are angry with those who have usually treated us with honour or regard, if a change comes and they behave to us otherwise: 5 for we think that they feel contempt for us, or they would still be behaving as they did before. And with those who do not return our kindnesses or fail to return them adequately, and with those who oppose us though they are our inferiors: for all such persons seem to feel contempt for us; those who oppose us seem to think us inferior to themselves, and those who do not return our kindnesses seem to think that those kindnesses were conferred by inferiors. And we feel particularly angry with men of no account at all, if they slight us. For, by our 10 hypothesis, the anger caused by the slight is felt towards people who are not justified in slighting us, and our inferiors are not thus justified. Again, we feel angry with friends if they do not speak well of us or treat us well; and still more, if they do the contrary; or if they do not perceive our needs, which is why Plexippus is angry with Meleager 15 in Antiphon's play; for this want of perception shows that they are slighting us—we do not fail to perceive the needs of those for whom we care. Again, we are angry with those who rejoice at our misfortunes or simply keep cheerful in the midst of our misfortunes, since this shows that they either hate us or are slighting us. Also with those who are indifferent to the pain they give us: this is why we get angry with 20 bringers of bad news. And with those who listen to stories about us or keep on looking at our weaknesses; this seems like either slighting us or hating us; for those who love us share in all our distresses and it must distress any one to keep on looking at his own weaknesses. Further, with those who slight us before five classes of people: namely, 25 (1) our rivals, (2) those whom we admire, (3) those whom we wish to admire us, (4) those for whom we feel reverence, (5) those who feel reverence for us: if any one slights us before such persons, we feel particularly angry. Again, we feel angry with those who slight us in connexion with what we are as honourable men bound to champion —our parents, children, wives, or subjects. And with those who do 30 not return a favour, since such a slight is unjustifiable. Also with those who reply with humorous levity when we are speaking seriously, for such behaviour indicates contempt. And with those who treat us less well than they treat everybody else; it is another mark of contempt that they should think we do not deserve what every one else deserves. 35 Forgetfulness, too, causes anger, as when our own names are forgotten, trifling as this may be; since forgetfulness is felt to be another sign that we are being slighted; it is due to negligence, and to neglect us is to slight us.

The persons with whom we feel anger, the frame of mind in which 1380ᵃ we feel it, and the reasons why we feel it, have now all been set forth. Clearly the orator will have to speak so as to bring his hearers into a frame of mind that will dispose them to anger, and to represent his adversaries as open to such charges and possessed of such qualities as do make people angry.

5 **3** Since growing calm is the opposite of growing angry, and calmness the opposite of anger, we must ascertain in what frames of mind men are calm, towards whom they feel calm, and by what means they are made so. Growing calm may be defined as a settling down or quieting of anger. Now we get angry with those who slight us; and since slighting is a voluntary act, it is plain that we feel calm towards those who 10 do nothing of the kind, or who do or seem to do it involuntarily. Also towards those who intended to do the opposite of what they did do. Also towards those who treat themselves as they have treated us: since no one can be supposed to slight himself. Also towards those who admit their fault and are sorry: since we accept their grief at what they 15 have done as satisfaction, and cease to be angry. The punishment of servants shows this: those who contradict us and deny their offence we punish all the more, but we cease to be incensed against those who agree that they deserved their punishment. The reason is that it is shameless to deny what is obvious, and those who are shameless to- 20 wards us slight us and show contempt for us: anyhow, we do not feel shame before those of whom we are thoroughly contemptuous. Also

we feel calm towards those who humble themselves before us and do not gainsay us; we feel that they thus admit themselves our inferiors, and inferiors feel fear, and nobody can slight any one so long as he feels afraid of him. That our anger ceases towards those who humble themselves before us is shown even by dogs, who do not bite people when they sit down. We also feel calm towards those who are serious when we are serious, because then we feel that we are treated seriously and not contemptuously. Also towards those who have done us more kindnesses than we have done them. Also towards those who pray to us and beg for mercy, since they humble themselves by doing so. Also towards those who do not insult or mock at or slight any one at all, or not any worthy person or any one like ourselves. In general, the things that make us calm may be inferred by seeing what the opposites are of those that make us angry. We are not angry with people we fear or respect, as long as we fear or respect them; you cannot be afraid of a person and also at the same time angry with him. Again, we feel no anger, or comparatively little, with those who have done what they did through anger; we do not feel that they have done it from a wish to slight us, for no one slights people when angry with them, since slighting is painless, and anger is painful. Nor do we grow angry with those who reverence us.

As to the frame of mind that makes people calm, it is plainly the opposite to that which makes them angry, as when they are amusing themselves or laughing or feasting; when they are feeling prosperous or successful or satisfied; when, in fine, they are enjoying freedom from pain, or inoffensive pleasure, or justifiable hope. Also when time has passed and their anger is no longer fresh, for time puts an end to anger. And vengeance previously taken on one person puts an end to even greater anger felt against another person. Hence Philocrates, being asked by some one, at a time when the public was angry with him, 'Why don't you defend yourself?' did right to reply, 'The time is not yet.' 'Why, when *is* the time?' 'When I see some one else calumniated.' For men become calm when they have spent their anger on somebody else. This happened in the case of Ergophilus: though the people were more irritated against him than against Callisthenes, they acquitted him because they had condemned Callisthenes to death the day before. Again, men become calm if they have convicted the offender; or if he has already suffered worse things than they in their anger would have themselves inflicted upon him; for they feel as if they were already avenged. Or if they feel that they themselves are in the wrong and are suffering justly (for anger is not excited by what is just), since men no longer think then that they are suffering without

justification; and anger, as we have seen, means this. Hence we ought
20 always to inflict a preliminary punishment·in words: if that is done,
even slaves are less aggrieved by the actual punishment. We also
feel calm if we think that the offender will not see that he is punished
on our account and because of the way he has treated us. For anger has
to do with individuals. This is plain from the definition.[8] Hence the
poet has well written:

> Say that it was Odysseus, sacker of cities,[9]

implying that Odysseus would not have considered himself avenged
unless the Cyclops perceived both by whom and for what he had been
25 blinded. Consequently we do not get angry with any one who cannot
be aware of our anger, and in particular we cease to be angry with
people once they are dead, for we feel that the worst has been done
to them, and that they will neither feel pain nor anything else that we
in our anger aim at making them feel. And therefore the poet has well
made Apollo say, in order to put a stop to the anger of Achilles against
the dead Hector,

> For behold in his fury he doeth despite to the senseless clay.[10]

30 It is now plain that when you wish to calm others you must draw
upon these lines of argument; you must put your hearers into the corresponding frame of mind, and represent those with whom they are
angry as formidable, or as worthy of reverence, or as benefactors, or
as involuntary agents, or as much distressed at what they have done.

4   Let us now turn to Friendship and Enmity, and ask towards whom
these feelings are entertained, and why. We will begin by defining
35 friendship and friendly feeling. We may describe friendly feeling towards any one as wishing for him what you believe to be good things,
1381ᵃ not for your own sake but for his, and being inclined, so far as you
can, to bring these things about. A friend is one who feels thus and
excites these feelings in return: those who think they feel thus towards
each other think themselves friends. This being assumed, it follows
that your friend is the sort of man who shares your pleasure in what
5 is good and your pain in what is unpleasant, for your sake and for no
other reason. This pleasure and pain of his will be the token of his good
wishes for you, since we all feel glad at getting what we wish for, and
pained at getting what we do not. Those, then, are friends to whom the
same things are good and evil; and those who are, moreover, friendly or

---

[8] ii, c. 2, init.   [9] *Odyssey*, ix. 504.   [10] *Iliad*, xxiv. 54.

unfriendly to the same people; for in that case they must have the same 10
wishes, and thus by wishing for each other what they wish for themselves, they show themselves each other's friends. Again, we feel
friendly to those who have treated us well, either ourselves or
those we care for, whether on a large scale, or readily, or at some particular crisis; provided it was for our own sake. And also to those who
we think *wish* to treat us well. And also to our friends' friends, and
to those who like, or are liked by, those whom we like ourselves. And 15
also to those who are enemies to those whose enemies we are, and dislike, or are disliked by, those whom we dislike. For all such persons
think the things good which we think good, so that they wish what is
good for us; and this, as we saw,[11] is what friends must do. And also
to those who are willing to treat us well where money or our personal 20
safety is concerned: and therefore we value those who are liberal,
brave, or just. The just we consider to be those who do not live on
others; which means those who work for their living, especially farmers
and others who work with their own hands. We also like temperate
men, because they are not unjust to others; and, for the same reason, 25
those who mind their own business. And also those whose friends we
wish to be, if it is plain that they wish to be our friends: such are the
morally good, and those well thought of by every one, by the best
men, or by those whom 'we admire or who admire us. And also those
with whom it is pleasant to live and spend our days: such are the 30
good-tempered, and those who are not too ready to show us our mistakes, and those who are not cantankerous or quarrelsome—such people are always wanting to fight us, and those who fight us we feel wish
for the opposite of what we wish for ourselves—and those who have
the tact to make and take a joke; here both parties have the same
object in view,[12] when they can stand being made fun of as well as do 35
it prettily themselves. And we also feel friendly towards those who
praise such good qualities as we possess, and especially if they praise
the good qualities that we are not too sure we *do* possess. And towards 1381ᵇ
those who are cleanly in their person, their dress, and all their way
of life. And towards those who do not reproach us with what we have
done amiss to them or they have done to help us, for both actions show
a tendency to criticize us. And towards those who do not nurse
grudges or store up grievances, but are always ready to make friends 5
again; for we take it that they will behave to us just as we find them
behaving to every one else. And towards those who are not evil
speakers and who are aware of neither their neighbours' bad points

---

[11] ii, c. 4, init.   [12] i. e. both wish to pass the time pleasantly.

nor our own, but of our good ones only, as a good man always will be. And towards those who do not try to thwart us when we are angry or
10 in earnest, which would mean being ready to fight us. And towards those who have some serious feeling towards us, such as admiration for us, or belief in our goodness, or pleasure in our company; especially if they feel like this about qualities in us for which we especially wish to be admired, esteemed, or liked. And towards those who are
15 like ourselves in character and occupation, provided they do not get in our way or gain their living from the same source as we do—for then it will be a case of 'potter against potter':

Potter to potter and builder to builder begrudge their reward.[13]

And those who desire the same things as we desire, if it is possible for us both to share them together; otherwise the same trouble arises here too. And towards those with whom we are on such terms that,
20 while we respect their opinions, we need not blush before them for doing what is conventionally wrong: as well as towards those before whom we should be ashamed to do anything really wrong. Again, our rivals, and those whom we should like to envy us—though without ill-feeling—either we like these people or at least we wish them to like us. And we feel friendly towards those whom we help to secure good for themselves, provided we are not likely to suffer heavily by it
25 ourselves. And those who feel as friendly to us when we are not with them as when we are—which is why all men feel friendly towards those who are faithful to their dead friends. And, speaking generally, towards those who are really fond of their friends and do not desert them in trouble; of all good men, we feel most friendly to those who show their goodness as friends. Also towards those who are honest with us, including those who will tell us of their own weak points: it
30 has just been said that with our friends we are not ashamed of what is conventionally wrong,[14] and if we do have this feeling, we do not love them; if therefore we do not have it, it looks as if we *did* love them. We also like those with whom we do not feel frightened or uncomfortable—nobody can like a man of whom he feels frightened. Friendship has various forms—comradeship, intimacy, kinship, and so on.
35   Things that cause friendship are: doing kindnesses; doing them unasked; and not proclaiming the fact when they are done, which shows that they were done for their own sake and not for some other reason.
1382ᵃ   Enmity and Hatred should clearly be studied by reference to their

---

¹³ Hesiod, *Works and Days*, 25.   ¹⁴ 1381ᵇ 20.

opposites. Enmity may be produced by anger or spite or calumny. Now whereas anger arises from offences against oneself, enmity may arise even without that; we may hate people merely because of what we take to be their character. Anger is always concerned with individuals—a Callias or a Socrates—whereas hatred is directed also 5 against classes: we all hate any thief and any informer. Moreover, anger can be cured by time; but hatred cannot. The one aims at giving pain to its object, the other at doing him harm; the angry man wants his victims to feel; the hater does not mind whether they feel or not. All painful things are felt; but the greatest evils, injustice and folly, 10 are the least felt, since their presence causes no pain. And anger is accompanied by pain, hatred is not; the angry man feels pain, but the hater does not. Much may happen to make the angry man pity those who offend him, but the hater under no circumstances wishes to pity a man whom he has once hated: for the one would have the offenders 15 suffer for what they have done; the other would have them cease to exist.

It is plain from all this that we can prove people to be friends or enemies; if they are not, we can make them out to be so; if they claim to be so, we can refute their claim; and if it is disputed whether an action was due to anger or to hatred, we can attribute it to whichever of these we prefer.

5 To turn next to Fear, what follows will show the things and persons of which, and the states of mind in which, we feel afraid. Fear 20 may be defined as a pain or disturbance due to a mental picture of some destructive or painful evil in the future. Of destructive or painful evils only; for there are some evils, e. g. wickedness or stupidity, the prospect of which does not frighten us: I mean only such as amount to great pains or losses. And even these only if they appear not remote but so near as to be imminent: we do not fear things that are 25 a very long way off: for instance, we all know we shall die, but we are not troubled thereby, because death is not close at hand. From this definition it will follow that fear is caused by whatever we feel has great power of destroying us, or of harming us in ways that tend to cause us great pain. Hence the very indications of such things are 30 terrible, making us feel that the terrible thing itself is close at hand; the approach of what is terrible is just what we mean by 'danger'. Such indications are the enmity and anger of people who have power to do something to us; for it is plain that they have the will to do it, and so they are on the point of doing it. Also injustice in possession of power; for it is the unjust man's will to do evil that makes him 35

1382ᵇ unjust. Also outraged virtue in possession of power; for it is plain that, when outraged, it always has the will to retaliate, and now it has the power to do so. Also fear felt by those who have the power to do something to us, since such persons are sure to be ready to do it. And since most men tend to be bad—slaves to greed, and cowards in
5 danger—it is, as a rule, a terrible thing to be at another man's mercy; and therefore, if we have done anything horrible, those in the secret terrify us with the thought that they may betray or desert us. And those who can do us wrong are terrible to us when we are liable to be wronged; for as a rule men do wrong to others whenever they have
10 the power to do it. And those who have been wronged, or believe themselves to be wronged, are terrible; for they are always looking out for their opportunity. Also those who have done people wrong, if they possess power, since they stand in fear of retaliation: we have already ¹⁵ said that wickedness possessing power is terrible. Again, our rivals for a thing cause us fear when we cannot both have it at once; for we are always at war with such men. We also fear those who are to
15 be feared by stronger people than ourselves: if they can hurt those stronger people, still more can they hurt us; and, for the same reason, we fear those whom those stronger people are actually afraid of. Also those who have destroyed people stronger than we are. Also those who are attacking people weaker than we are: either they are already formidable, or they will be so when they have thus grown stronger.
20 Of those we have wronged, and of our enemies or rivals, it is not the passionate and outspoken whom we have to fear, but the quiet, dissembling, unscrupulous; since we never know when they are upon us, we can never be sure they are at a safe distance. All terrible things are more terrible if they give us no chance of retrieving a blunder—either no chance at all, or only one that depends on our enemies and not
25 ourselves. Those things are also worse which we cannot, or cannot easily, help. Speaking generally, anything causes us to feel fear that when it happens to, or threatens, others causes us to feel pity.

The above are, roughly, the chief things that are terrible and are feared. Let us now describe the conditions under which we ourselves feel fear. If fear is associated with the expectation that something
30 destructive will happen to us, plainly nobody will be afraid who believes nothing can happen to him; we shall not fear things that we believe cannot happen to us, nor people who we believe cannot inflict them upon us; nor shall we be afraid at times when we think ourselves safe from them. It follows therefore that fear is felt by those who believe something to be likely to happen to them, at the

¹⁵ 1382ᵃ 34.

hands of particular persons, in a particular form, and at a particular 35
time. People do not believe this when they are, or think they are, in 1383[a]
the midst of great prosperity, and are in consequence insolent, contemptuous, and reckless—the kind of character produced by wealth,
physical strength, abundance of friends, power: nor yet when they
feel they have experienced every kind of horror already and have
grown callous about the future, like men who are being flogged and 5
are already nearly dead—if they are to feel the anguish of uncertainty,
there must be some faint expectation of escape. This appears from the
fact that fear sets us thinking what can be done, which of course
nobody does when things are hopeless. Consequently, when it is ad-
visable that the audience should be frightened, the orator must make
them feel that they really are in danger of something, pointing out that
it has happened to others who were stronger than they are, and is hap- 10
pening, or has happened, to people like themselves, at the hands of
unexpected people, in an unexpected form, and at an unexpected time.

Having now seen the nature of fear, and of the things that cause it,
and the various states of mind in which it is felt, we can also see
what Confidence is, about what things we feel it, and under what 15
conditions. It is the opposite of fear, and what causes it is the opposite
of what causes fear; it is, therefore, the expectation associated with a
mental picture of the nearness of what keeps us safe and the absence
or remoteness of what is terrible: it may be due either to the near
presence of what inspires confidence or to the absence of what causes
alarm. We feel it if we can take steps—many, or important, or both— 20
to cure or prevent trouble; if we have neither wronged others nor
been wronged by them; if we have either no rivals at all or no
strong ones; if our rivals who are strong are our friends or have treated
us well or been treated well by us; or if those whose interest is the
same as ours are the more numerous party, or the stronger, or both.

As for our own state of mind, we feel confidence if we believe we 25
have often succeeded and never suffered reverses, or have often met
danger and escaped it safely. For there are two reasons why human
beings face danger calmly: they may have no experience of it, or they
may have means to deal with it: thus when in danger at sea people 30
may feel confident about what will happen either because they have
no experience of bad weather, or because their experience gives them
the means of dealing with it. We also feel confident whenever there is
nothing to terrify other people like ourselves, or people weaker than
ourselves, or people than whom we believe ourselves to be stronger—
and we believe this if we have conquered them, or conquered others
who are as strong as they are, or stronger. Also if we believe ourselves 35

superior to our rivals in the number and importance of the advan-
1383^b tages that make men formidable—wealth, physical strength, strong
bodies of supporters, extensive territory, and the possession of all, or
the most important, appliances of war. Also if we have wronged no one,
or not many, or not those of whom we are afraid; and generally, if our
5 relations with the gods are satisfactory, as will be shown especially by
signs and oracles. The fact is that anger makes us confident—that
anger is excited by our knowledge that we are not the wrongers but
the wronged, and that the divine power is always supposed to be on
the side of the wronged. Also when, at the outset of an enterprise, we
10 believe that we cannot and shall not fail, or that we shall succeed
completely.—So much for the causes of fear and confidence.

6 We now turn to Shame and Shamelessness; what follows will
explain the things that cause these feelings, and the persons before
whom, and the states of mind under which, they are felt. Shame may
15 be defined as pain or disturbance in regard to bad things, whether
present, past, or future, which seem likely to involve us in discredit;
and shamelessness as contempt or indifference in regard to these same
bad things. If this definition be granted, it follows that we feel shame
at such bad things as we think are disgraceful to ourselves or to those
20 we care for. These evils are, in the first place, those due to moral badness. Such are throwing away one's shield or taking to flight; for these
bad things are due to cowardice. Also, withholding a deposit or otherwise wronging people about money; for these acts are due to injustice. Also, having carnal intercourse with forbidden persons, at wrong
times, or in wrong places; for these things are due to licentiousness.
Also, making profit in petty or disgraceful ways, or out of helpless
25 persons, e. g. the poor, or the dead—whence the proverb 'He would
pick a corpse's pocket'; for all this is due to low greed and meanness.
Also, in money matters, giving less help than you might, or none at all,
or accepting help from those worse off than yourself; so also borrowing when it will seem like begging; begging when it will seem like asking the return of a favour; asking such a return when it will seem like
30 begging; praising a man *in order that* it may seem like begging; and
going on begging in spite of failure: all such actions are tokens of
meanness. Also, praising people to their face, and praising extravagantly a man's good points and glozing over his weaknesses, and
showing extravagant sympathy with his grief when you are in his
35 presence, and all that sort of thing; all this shows the disposition of a
flatterer. Also, refusing to endure hardships that are endured by peo-
1384^a ple who are older, more delicately brought up, of higher rank, or gen-

erally less capable of endurance than ourselves; for all this shows effeminacy. Also, accepting benefits, especially accepting them often, from another man, and then abusing him for conferring them: all this shows a mean, ignoble disposition. Also, talking incessantly about yourself, making loud professions, and appropriating the merits of 5 others; for this is due to boastfulness. The same is true of the actions due to any of the other forms of badness of moral character, of the tokens of such badness, &c.: they are all disgraceful and shameless. Another sort of bad thing at which we feel shame is, lacking a share in the honourable things shared by every one else, or by all or nearly all who are like ourselves. By 'those like ourselves' I mean those 10 of our own race or country or age or family, and generally those who are on our own level. Once we are on a level with others, it is a disgrace to be, say, less well educated than they are; and so with other advantages: all the more so, in each case, if it is seen to be our own fault: wherever we are ourselves to blame for our present, past, or 15 future circumstances, it follows at once that this is to a greater extent due to our moral badness. We are moreover ashamed of having done to us, having had done, or being about to have done to us acts that involve us in dishonour and reproach; as when we surrender our persons, or lend ourselves to vile deeds, e. g. when we submit to outrage. And acts of yielding to the lust of others are shameful whether willing or unwilling (yielding to force being an instance of unwillingness), since 20 unresisting submission to them is due to unmanliness or cowardice.

These things, and others like them, are what cause the feeling of shame. Now since shame is a mental picture of disgrace, in which we shrink from the disgrace itself and not from its consequences, and we 25 only care what opinion is held of us because of the people who form that opinion, it follows that the people before whom we feel shame are those whose opinion of us matters to us. Such persons are: those who admire us, those whom we admire, those by whom we wish to be admired, those with whom we are competing, and those whose opinion of us we respect. We admire those, and wish those to admire us, who possess any good thing that is highly esteemed; or from whom we are 30 very anxious to get something that they are able to give us—as a lover feels. We compete with our equals. We respect, as true, the views of sensible people, such as our elders and those who have been well educated. And we feel more shame about a thing if it is done openly, before all men's eyes. Hence the proverb, 'shame dwells in the eyes'. For this reason we feel most shame before those who will always be with us and those who notice what we do, since in both cases eyes are upon us. We also feel it before those not open to the same imputation as our- 1384ᵇ

selves: for it is plain that their opinions about it are the opposite of ours. Also before those who are hard on any one whose conduct they think wrong; for what a man does himself, he is said not to resent when his neighbours do it: so that of course he does resent their doing
5 what he does not do himself. And before those who are likely to tell everybody about you; not telling others is as good as not believing you wrong. People are likely to tell others about you if you have wronged them, since they are on the look out to harm you; or if they speak evil of everybody, for those who attack the innocent will be still more ready to attack the guilty. And before those whose main occupa-
10 tion is with their neighbours' failings—people like satirists and writers of comedy; these are really a kind of evil-speakers and tell-tales. And before those who have never yet known us come to grief, since their attitude to us has amounted to admiration so far: that is why we feel ashamed to refuse those a favour who ask one for the first time—we have not as yet lost credit with them. Such are those who are just
15 beginning to wish to be our friends; for they have seen our best side only (hence the appropriateness of Euripides' [16] reply to the Syracusans): and such also are those among our old acquaintances who know nothing to our discredit. And we are ashamed not merely of the actual shameful conduct mentioned, but also of the evidences of it: not merely, for example, of actual sexual intercourse, but also of its
20 evidences; and not merely of disgraceful acts but also of disgraceful talk. Similarly we feel shame not merely in presence of the persons mentioned but also of those who will tell them what we have done, such as their servants or friends. And, generally, we feel no shame before those upon whose opinions we quite look down as untrustworthy (no one feels shame before small children or animals); nor are we
25 ashamed of the same things before intimates as before strangers, but before the former of what seem genuine faults, before the latter of what seem conventional ones.

The conditions under which we shall feel shame are these: first, having people related to us like those before whom, as has been said,[17] we feel shame. These are, as was stated, persons whom we admire, or
30 who admire us, or by whom we wish to be admired, or from whom we desire some service that we shall not obtain if we forfeit their good

---

[16] The scholiast tells us that Euripides was sent to negotiate peace with the Syracusans, and finding them unwilling said: 'You ought, men of Syracuse, to respect our expressions of esteem if only because we are new petitioners.' The Euripides in question may well have been the tragic poet: the popularity of whose poems at Syracuse, and whose turn for rhetorical argument, are beyond dispute.　　　　　　　　　　　　　　　　　[17] 1384ᵃ 27.

opinion. These persons may be actually looking on (as Cydias represented them in his speech on land assignments in Samos, when he told the Athenians to imagine the Greeks to be standing all around them, actually seeing the way they voted and not merely going to hear about it afterwards): or again they may be near at hand, or may 35 be likely to find out about what we do. This is why in misfortune we do not wish to be seen by those who once wished themselves like us; for such a feeling implies admiration. And men feel shame when they have acts or exploits to their credit on which they are bringing 1385ª dishonour, whether these are their own, or those of their ancestors, or those of other persons with whom they have some close connexion. Generally, we feel shame before those for whose own misconduct we should also feel it—those already mentioned; those who take us as their models; those whose teachers or advisers we have been; or other 5 people, it may be, like ourselves, whose rivals we are. For there are many things that shame before such people makes us do or leave undone. And we feel more shame when we are likely to be continually seen by, and go about under the eyes of, those who know of our disgrace. Hence, when Antiphon the poet was to be cudgelled to death by order of Dionysius, and saw those who were to perish with him covering 10 their faces as they went through the gates, he said, 'Why do you cover your faces? Is it lest some of these spectators should see you *tomorrow*?'

So much for Shame; to understand Shamelessness, we need only to consider the converse cases, and plainly we shall have all we need. 15

7   To take Kindness next: the definition of it will show us towards whom it is felt, why, and in what frames of mind. Kindness—under the influence of which a man is said to 'be kind'—may be defined as helpfulness towards some one in need, not in return for anything, nor for the advantage of the helper himself, but for that of the person 20 helped. Kindness is great if shown to one who is in great need, or who needs what is important and hard to get, or who needs it at an important and difficult crisis; or if the helper is the only, the first, or the chief person to give the help. Natural cravings constitute such needs; and in particular cravings, accompanied by pain, for what is not being attained. The appetites are cravings of this kind: sexual desire, for instance, and those which arise during bodily injuries and in dangers; for appetite is active both in danger and in pain. Hence 25 those who stand by us in poverty or in banishment, even if they do not help us much, are yet really kind to us, because our need is great and the occasion pressing; for instance, the man who gave the mat in

the Lyceum.[18] The helpfulness must therefore meet, preferably, just
this kind of need; and failing just this kind, some other kind as great
30 or greater. We now see to whom, why, and under what conditions
kindness is shown; and these facts must form the basis of our arguments. We must show that the persons helped are, or have been, in
such pain and need as has been described, and that their helpers gave,
35 or are giving, the kind of help described, in the kind of need described. We can also see how to eliminate the idea of kindness and
make our opponents appear unkind: we may maintain that they are
1385ᵇ being or have been helpful simply to promote their own interest—
this, as has been stated,[19] is not kindness: or that their action was
accidental, or was forced upon them; or that they were not doing a
favour, but merely returning one, whether they know this or not—
in either case the action *is* a mere return, and is therefore not a kindness even if the doer does *not* know how the case stands. In consider-
5 ing this subject we must look at all the 'categories':[20] an act may
be an act of kindness because (1) it is a particular thing, (2) it has a
particular magnitude or (3) quality, or (4) is done at a particular
time or (5) place. As evidence of the want of kindness, we may point
out that a smaller service had been refused to the man in need; or
that the same service, or an equal or greater one, has been given to his
enemies; these facts show that the service in question was not done
for the sake of the person helped. Or we may point out that the
10 thing desired was worthless and that the helper knew it: no one will
admit that he is in need of what is worthless.

8 So much for Kindness and Unkindness. Let us now consider
Pity, asking ourselves what things excite pity, and for what persons,
and in what states of our mind pity is felt. Pity may be defined as a
feeling of pain caused by the sight of some evil, destructive or painful, which befalls one who does not deserve it, and which we might
15 expect to befall ourselves or some friend of ours, and moreover to
befall us soon. In order to feel pity, we must obviously be capable
of supposing that some evil may happen to us or some friend of
ours, and moreover some such evil as is stated in our definition or is
more or less of that kind. It is therefore not felt by those completely
20 ruined, who suppose that no further evil can befall them, since the
worst has befallen them already; nor by those who imagine themselves immensely fortunate—their feeling is rather presumptuous
insolence, for when they think they possess all the good things of
life, it is clear that the impossibility of evil befalling them will be

[18] Particulars unknown.   [19] 1385ᵃ 18.   [20] Cp. *Categ.* 1ᵇ 25 ff.

included, this being one of the good things in question. Those who
think evil *may* befall them are such as have already had it befall them 25
and have safely escaped from it; elderly men, owing to their good
sense and their experience; weak men, especially men inclined to
cowardice; and also educated people, since these can take long
views. Also those who have parents living, or children, or wives; for
these are our own, and the evils mentioned above may easily befall
them. And those who are neither moved by any courageous emotion 30
such as anger or confidence (these emotions take no account of the
future), nor by a disposition to presumptuous insolence (insolent
men, too, take no account of the possibility that something evil will
happen to them), nor yet by great fear (panic-stricken people do not
feel pity, because they are taken up with what is happening to themselves); only those feel pity who are between these two extremes.
In order to feel pity we must also believe in the goodness of at least 35
some people; if you think nobody good, you will believe that every-   1386ᵃ
body deserves evil fortune. And, generally, we feel pity whenever we
are in the condition of remembering that similar misfortunes have
happened to us or ours, or expecting them to happen in future.

So much for the mental conditions under which we feel pity. What
we pity is stated clearly in the definition. All unpleasant and painful
things excite pity if they tend to destroy and annihilate; and all such 5
evils as are due to chance, if they are serious. The painful and
destructive evils are: death in its various forms, bodily injuries and
afflictions, old age, diseases, lack of food. The evils due to chance
are: friendlessness, scarcity of friends (it is a pitiful thing to be torn 10
away from friends and companions), deformity, weakness, mutilation; evil coming from a source from which good ought to have come;
and the frequent repetition of such misfortunes. Also the coming of
good when the worst has happened: e. g. the arrival of the Great
King's gifts for Diopeithes after his death. Also that either no good 15
should have befallen a man at all, or that he should not be able to
enjoy it when it has.

The grounds, then, on which we feel pity are these or like these.
The people we pity are: those whom we know, if only they are not
very closely related to us—in that case we feel about them as if we
were in danger ourselves. For this reason Amasis did not weep, they
say, at the sight of his son being led to death, but did weep when 20
he saw his friend begging: the latter sight was pitiful, the former
terrible, and the terrible is different from the pitiful; it tends to cast
out pity, and often helps to produce the opposite of pity. Again, we

feel pity when the danger is near ourselves. Also we pity those who
25 are like us in age, character, disposition, social standing, or birth; for
in all these cases it appears more likely that the same misfortune may
befall us also. Here too we have to remember the general principle
that what we fear for ourselves excites our pity when it happens to
others.[21] Further, since it is when the sufferings of others are close
to us that they excite our pity (we cannot remember what disasters
happened a hundred centuries ago, nor look forward to what will
30 happen a hundred centuries hereafter, and therefore feel little pity,
if any, for such things): it follows that those who heighten the effect
of their words with suitable gestures, tones, dress, and dramatic action
generally, are especially successful in exciting pity: they thus put the
disasters before our eyes, and make them seem close to us, just com-
1386ᵇ ing or just past. Anything that has just happened, or is going to
happen soon, is particularly piteous: so too therefore are the tokens
and the actions of sufferers—the garments and the like of those who
have already suffered; the words and the like of those actually suffering—of those, for instance, who are on the point of death. Most pite-
5 ous of all is it when, in such times of trial, the victims are persons of
noble character: whenever they are so, our pity is especially excited,
because their innocence, as well as the setting of their misfortunes
before our eyes, makes their misfortunes seem close to ourselves.

9   Most directly opposed to pity is the feeling called Indignation.
10 Pain at unmerited good fortune is, in one sense, opposite to pain at
unmerited bad fortune, and is due to the same moral qualities. Both
feelings are associated with good moral character; it is our duty both
to feel sympathy and pity for unmerited distress, and to feel indigna-
15 tion at unmerited prosperity; for whatever is undeserved is unjust,
and that is why we ascribe indignation even to the gods. It might
indeed be thought that envy is similarly opposed to pity, on the
ground that envy is closely akin to indignation, or even the same
thing. But it is not the same. It is true that it also is a disturbing
pain excited by the prosperity of others. But it is excited not by the
20 prosperity of the undeserving but by that of people who are like us or
equal with us. The two feelings have this in common, that they must
be due not to some untoward thing being likely to befall ourselves,
but only to what is happening to our neighbour. The feeling ceases to
be envy in the one case and indignation in the other, and becomes
fear, if the pain and disturbance are due to the prospect of some-

---

[21] Cp. 1382ᵇ 26, 27.

thing bad for ourselves as the result of the other man's good fortune. The feelings of pity and indignation will obviously be attended by 25 the converse feelings of satisfaction. If you are pained by the un- merited distress of others, you will be pleased, or at least not pained, by their merited distress. Thus no good man can be pained by the punishment of parricides or murderers. These are things we are bound to rejoice at, as we must at the prosperity of the deserving; 30 both these things are just, and both give pleasure to any honest man, since he cannot help expecting that what has happened to a man like him will happen to him too. All these feelings are associated with the same type of moral character. And their contraries are associated with the contrary type; the man who is delighted by others' mis- fortunes is identical with the man who envies others' prosperity. For 1387ᵃ any one who is pained by the occurrence or existence of a given thing must be pleased by that thing's non-existence or destruction. We can now see that all these feelings tend to prevent pity (though they differ among themselves, for the reasons given), so that all are equally useful for neutralizing an appeal to pity.   5

We will first consider Indignation—reserving the other emotions for subsequent discussion—and ask with whom, on what grounds, and in what states of mind we may be indignant. These questions are really answered by what has been said already. Indignation is pain caused by the sight of undeserved good fortune. It is, then, plain to begin with that there are some forms of good the sight of which 10 cannot cause it. Thus a man may be just or brave, or acquire moral goodness: but we shall not be indignant with him for that reason, any more than we shall pity him for the contrary reason. Indignation is roused by the sight of wealth, power, and the like—by all those things, roughly speaking, which are deserved by good men and by those who possess the goods of nature—noble birth, beauty, and so 15 on. Again, what is long established seems akin to what exists by na- ture; and therefore we feel more indignation at those possessing a given good if they have as a matter of fact only just got it and the prosperity it brings with it. The newly rich give more offence than those whose wealth is of long standing and inherited. The same is true of those who have office or power, plenty of friends, a fine family, 20 &c. We feel the same when these advantages of theirs secure them others. For here again, the newly rich give us more offence by ob- taining office through their riches than do those whose wealth is of long standing; and so in all other cases. The reason is that what the latter have is felt to be really their own, but what the others have is 25

not: what appears to have been always what it is is regarded as real, and so the possessions of the newly rich do not seem to be really their own. Further, it is not any and every man that deserves any given kind of good; there is a certain correspondence and appropriateness in such things; thus it is appropriate for brave men, not for
30 just men, to have fine weapons, and for men of family, not for parvenus, to make distinguished marriages. Indignation may therefore properly be felt when any one gets what is not appropriate for him, though he may be a good man enough. It may also be felt when any one sets himself up against his superior, especially against his superior in some particular respect—whence the lines

Only from battle he shrank with Aias Telamon's son;
Zeus had been angered with him, had he fought with a mightier one;[22]

1387ᵇ but also, even apart from that, when the inferior in any sense contends with his superior; a musician, for instance, with a just man, for justice is a finer thing than music.

Enough has been said to make clear the grounds on which, and the persons against whom, Indignation is felt—they are those mentioned, and others like them. As for the people who feel it; we feel it if we do
5 ourselves deserve the greatest possible goods and moreover have them, for it is an injustice that those who are not our equals should have been held to deserve as much as we have. Or, secondly, we feel it if we are really good and honest people; our judgement is then sound, and we loathe any kind of injustice. Also if we are ambitious
10 and eager to gain particular ends, especially if we are ambitious for· what others are getting without deserving to get it. And, generally, if we think that we ourselves deserve a thing and that others do not, we are disposed to be indignant with those others so far as that thing is concerned. Hence servile, worthless, unambitious persons are not inclined to Indignation, since there is nothing they can believe themselves to deserve.

From all this it is plain what sort of men those are at whose
15 misfortunes, distresses, or failures we ought to feel pleased, or at least not pained: by considering the facts described we see at once what their contraries are. If therefore our speech puts the judges in such a frame of mind as that indicated and shows that those who claim pity on certain definite grounds do not deserve to secure pity
20 but do deserve not to secure it, it will be impossible for the judges· to feel pity.

---

[22] *Iliad*, xi. 542. The second line is not found in the existing manuscripts of the *Iliad*.

10　To take Envy next: we can see on what grounds, against what persons, and in what states of mind we feel it. Envy is pain at the sight of such good fortune as consists of the good things already mentioned; we feel it towards our equals; not with the idea of getting something for ourselves, but because the other people have it. We shall feel it if we have, or think we have, equals; and by 'equals' I 25 mean equals in birth, relationship, age, disposition, distinction, or wealth. We feel envy also if we fall but a little short of having everything; which is why people in high place and prosperity feel it—they think every one else is taking what belongs to themselves. Also if we are exceptionally distinguished for some particular thing, and especially if that thing is wisdom or good fortune. Ambitious men are 30 more envious than those who are not. So also those who profess wisdom; they are ambitious—to be thought wise. Indeed, generally, those who aim at a reputation for anything are envious on this particular point. And small-minded men are envious, for everything seems great to them. The good things which excite envy have already been mentioned. The deeds or possessions which arouse the love of reputation 1388ᵃ and honour and the desire for fame, and the various gifts of fortune, are almost all subject to envy; and particularly if we desire the thing ourselves, or think we are entitled to it, or if having it puts us a little above others, or not having it a little below them. It is clear also what kind of people we envy; that was included in what has been 5 said already: we envy those who are near us in time, place, age, or reputation. Hence the line:

> Ay, kin can even be jealous of their kin.[23]

Also our fellow-competitors, who are indeed the people just mentioned—we do not compete with men who lived a hundred centuries ago, or those not yet born, or the dead, or those who dwell near the Pillars of Hercules,[24] or those whom, in our opinion or that of others, 10 we take to be far below us or far above us. So too we compete with those who follow the same ends as ourselves: we compete with our rivals in sport or in love, and generally with those who are after the same things; and it is therefore these whom we are bound to envy 15 beyond all others. Hence the saying:

> Potter against potter.

We also envy those whose possession of or success in a thing is a reproach to us: these are our neighbours and equals; for it is clear

23 Aeschylus.
24 i. e. those who dwell at the farthest limits of the western world.

that it is our own fault we have missed the good thing in question;
20 this annoys us, and excites envy in us. We also envy those who have
what we ought to have, or have got what we did have once. Hence old
men envy younger men, and those who have spent much envy those
who have spent little on the same thing. And men who have not got
a thing, or not got it yet, envy those who have got it quickly. We
can also see what things and what persons give pleasure to envious
people, and in what states of mind they feel it: the states of mind
25 in which they feel pain are those under which they will feel pleasure
in the contrary things. If therefore we ourselves with whom the decision rests are put into an envious state of mind, and those for whom
our pity, or the award of something desirable, is claimed are such
as have been described, it is obvious that they will win no pity
from us.

11   We will next consider Emulation, showing in what follows its
30 causes and objects, and the state of mind in which it is felt. Emulation is pain caused by seeing the presence, in persons whose nature
is like our own, of good things that are highly valued and are possible for ourselves to acquire; but it is felt not because others
have these goods, but because we have not got them ourselves. It is
therefore a good feeling felt by good persons, whereas envy is a bad
35 feeling felt by bad persons. Emulation makes us take steps to secure
the good things in question, envy makes us take steps to stop our
neighbour having them. Emulation must therefore tend to be felt
by persons who believe themselves to deserve certain good things that
1388ᵇ they have not got, it being understood that no one aspires to things
which appear impossible. It is accordingly felt by the young and by
persons of lofty disposition. Also by those who possess such good
things as are deserved by men held in honour—these are wealth,
5 abundance of friends, public office, and the like; on the assumption
that they ought to be good men, they are emulous to gain such goods
because they ought, in their belief, to belong to men whose state of
mind is good. Also by those whom all others think deserving. We
also feel it about anything for which our ancestors, relatives, personal
friends, race, or country are specially honoured, looking upon that
thing as really our own, and therefore feeling that we deserve to have
10 it. Further, since all good things that are highly honoured are objects
of emulation, moral goodness in its various forms must be such an
object, and also all those good things that are useful and serviceable
to others: for men honour those who are morally good, and also those
who do them service. So with those good things our possession of

which can give enjoyment to our neighbours—wealth and beauty rather than health. We can see, too, what persons are the objects of the feeling. They are those who have these and similar things—those already mentioned, as courage, wisdom, public office.[25] Holders of public office—generals, orators, and all who possess such powers— can do many people a good turn. Also those whom many people wish to be like; those who have many acquaintances or friends; those whom many admire, or whom we ourselves admire; and those who have been praised and eulogized by poets or prose-writers. Persons of the contrary sort are objects of contempt: for the feeling and notion of contempt are opposite to those of emulation. Those who are such as to emulate or be emulated by others are inevitably disposed to be contemptuous of all such persons as are subject to those bad things which are contrary to the good things that are the objects of emulation: despising them for just that reason. Hence we often despise the fortunate, when luck comes to them without their having those good things which are held in honour.

This completes our discussion of the means by which the several emotions may be produced or dissipated, and upon which depend the persuasive arguments connected with the emotions.

12   Let us now consider the various types of human character, in relation to the emotions and moral qualities, showing how they correspond to our various ages and fortunes. By emotions I mean anger, desire, and the like; these we have discussed already.[26] By moral qualities I mean virtues and vices; these also have been discussed already,[27] as well as the various things that various types of men tend to will and to do.[28] By ages I mean youth, the prime of life, and old age. By fortune I mean birth, wealth, power, and their opposites—in fact, good fortune and ill fortune.

To begin with the Youthful type of character. Young men have strong passions, and tend to gratify them indiscriminately. Of the bodily desires, it is the sexual by which they are most swayed and in which they show absence of self-control. They are changeable and fickle in their desires, which are violent while they last, but quickly over: their impulses are keen but not deep-rooted, and are like sick people's attacks of hunger and thirst. They are hot-tempered and quick-tempered, and apt to give way to their anger; bad temper often gets the better of them, for owing to their love of honour they cannot bear being slighted, and are indignant if they imagine themselves

---

25 Cp. 1388b 5 and i, c. 6.   26 ii, cc. 1 ff.
27 i, c. 9.   28 i, c. 6, 1363a 19.

unfairly treated. While they love honour, they love victory still more; for youth is eager for superiority over others, and victory is one form of this. They love both more than they love money, which indeed they love very little, not having yet learnt what it means to 15 be without it—this is the point of Pittacus' remark about Amphiaraus.[29] They look at the good side rather than the bad, not having yet witnessed many instances of wickedness. They trust others readily, because they have not yet often been cheated. They are sanguine; nature warms their blood as though with excess of wine; and besides 20 that, they have as yet met with few disappointments. Their lives are mainly spent not in memory but in expectation; for expectation refers to the future, memory to the past, and youth has a long future before it and a short past behind it: on the first day of one's life one has nothing at all to remember, and can only look forward. They are easily cheated, owing to the sanguine disposition just mentioned. 25 Their hot tempers and hopeful dispositions make them more courageous than older men are; the hot temper prevents fear, and the hopeful disposition creates confidence; we cannot feel fear so long as we are feeling angry, and any expectation of good makes us confident. They are shy, accepting the rules of society in which they 30 have been trained, and not yet believing in any other standard of honour. They have exalted notions, because they have not yet been humbled by life or learnt its necessary limitations; moreover, their hopeful disposition makes them think themselves equal to great things —and that means having exalted notions. They would always rather do noble deeds than useful ones: their lives are regulated more by moral feeling than by reasoning; and whereas reasoning leads us 35 to choose what is useful, moral goodness leads us to choose what is noble. They are fonder of their friends, intimates, and companions 1389b than older men are, because they like spending their days in the company of others, and have not yet come to value either their friends or anything else by their usefulness to themselves. All their mistakes are in the direction of doing things excessively and vehemently. They disobey Chilon's precept by overdoing everything; they love too 5 much and hate too much, and the same with everything else. They think they know everything, and are always quite sure about it; this, in fact, is why they overdo everything. If they do wrong to others, it is because they mean to insult them, not to do them actual harm. They are ready to pity others, because they think every one an honest man, or anyhow better than he is: they judge their neigh-

<hr>

[29] The remark is unknown.

bour by their own harmless natures, and so cannot think he deserves
to be treated in that way. They are fond of fun and therefore witty, 10
wit being well-bred insolence.

13   Such, then, is the character of the Young. The character of
Elderly Men—men who are past their prime—may be said to be
formed for the most part of elements that are the contrary of all
these. They have lived many years; they have often been taken in, 15
and often made mistakes; and life on the whole is a bad business.
The result is that they are sure about nothing and *under-do* everything. They 'think', but they never 'know'; and because of their hesitation they always add a 'possibly' or a 'perhaps', putting everything
this way and nothing positively. They are cynical; that is, they tend 20
to put the worse construction on everything. Further, their experience makes them distrustful and therefore suspicious of evil. Consequently they neither love warmly nor hate bitterly, but following
the hint of Bias they love as though they will some day hate and hate
as though they will some day love. They are small-minded, because they have been humbled by life: their desires are set upon 25
nothing more exalted or unusual than what will help them to keep
alive. They are not generous, because money is one of the things
they must have, and at the same time their experience has taught
them how hard it is to get and how easy to lose. They are cowardly,
and are always anticipating danger; unlike that of the young, who 30
are warm-blooded, their temperament is chilly; old age has paved
the way for cowardice; fear is, in fact, a form of chill. They love life;
and all the more when their last day has come, because the object
of all desire is something we have not got, and also because we desire
most strongly that which we need most urgently. They are too fond 35
of themselves; this is one form that small-mindedness takes. Because
of this, they guide their lives too much by considerations of what
is useful and too little by what is noble—for the useful is what is
good for oneself, and the noble what is good absolutely. They 1390ᵃ
are not shy, but shameless rather; caring less for what is noble than
for what is useful, they feel contempt for what people may think of
them. They lack confidence in the future; partly through experience—for most things go wrong, or anyhow turn out worse than one
expects; and partly because of their cowardice. They live by memory 5
rather than by hope; for what is left to them of life is but little as
compared with the long past; and hope is of the future, memory of
the past. This, again, is the cause of their loquacity; they are continually talking of the past, because they enjoy remembering it. 10

Their fits of anger are sudden but feeble. Their sensual passions have either altogether gone or have lost their vigour: consequently they do not feel their passions much, and their actions are inspired less by what they do feel than by the love of gain. Hence men at this time of life are often supposed to have a self-controlled char-
15 acter; the fact is that their passions have slackened, and they are slaves to the love of gain. They guide their lives by reasoning more than by moral feeling; reasoning being directed to utility and moral feeling to moral goodness. If they wrong others, they mean to injure them, not to insult them. Old men may feel pity, as well as young men, but not for the same reason. Young men feel it out of kindness;
20 old men out of weakness, imagining that anything that befalls any one else might easily happen to them, which, as we saw,[30] is a thought that excites pity. Hence they are querulous, and not disposed to jesting or laughter—the love of laughter being the very opposite of querulousness.

Such are the characters of Young Men and Elderly Men. People
25 always think well of speeches adapted to, and reflecting, their own character: and we can now see how to compose our speeches so as to adapt both them and ourselves to our audiences.

14   As for Men in their Prime, clearly we shall find that they have a character between that of the young and that of the old, free from
30 the extremes of either. They have neither that excess of confidence which amounts to rashness, nor too much timidity, but the right amount of each. They neither trust everybody nor distrust everybody, but judge people correctly. Their lives will be guided not by
1390ᵇ the sole consideration either of what is noble or of what is useful, but by both; neither by parsimony nor by prodigality, but by what is fit and proper. So, too, in regard to anger and desire; they will be
5 brave as well as temperate, and temperate as well as brave; these virtues are divided between the young and the old; the young are brave but intemperate, the old temperate but cowardly. To put it generally, all the valuable qualities that youth and age divide between them are united in the prime of life, while all their excesses or defects are replaced by moderation and fitness. The body is in
10 its prime from thirty to five-and-thirty; the mind about forty-nine.

15   So much for the types of character that distinguish youth, old age, and the prime of life. We will now turn to those Gifts of For-

<hr>

[30] ii, c. 8, 1386ᵃ 24 and 29.

tune by which human character is affected. First let us consider ¹⁵
Good Birth. Its effect on character is to make those who have it more
ambitious; it is the way of all men who have something to start with
to add to the pile, and good birth implies ancestral distinction. The
well-born man will look down even on those who are as good as his ²⁰
own ancestors, because any far-off distinction is greater than the
same thing close to us, and better to boast about. Being well-born,
which means coming of a fine stock, must be distinguished from
nobility, which means being true to the family nature—a quality not
usually found in the well-born, most of whom are poor creatures. In
the generations of men as in the fruits of the earth, there is a varying ²⁵
yield; now and then, where the stock is good, exceptional men are
produced for a while, and then decadence sets in. A clever stock will
degenerate towards the insane type of character, like the descendants
of Alcibiades or of the elder Dionysius; a steady stock towards the
fatuous and torpid type, like the descendants of Cimon, Pericles, ³⁰
and Socrates.

16   The type of character produced by Wealth lies on the surface
for all to see. Wealthy men are insolent and arrogant; their possession
of wealth affects their understanding; they feel as if they had every
good thing that exists; wealth becomes a sort of standard of value
for everything else, and therefore they imagine there is nothing 1391ᵃ
it cannot buy. They are luxurious and ostentatious; luxurious, because of the luxury in which they live and the prosperity which they
display; ostentatious and vulgar, because, like other people's, their
minds are regularly occupied with the object of their love and ad- ⁵
miration, and also because they think that other people's idea of
happiness is the same as their own. It is indeed quite natural that they
should be affected thus; for if you have money, there are always
plenty of people who come begging from you. Hence the saying of
Simonides about wise men and rich men, in answer to Hiero's wife,
who asked him whether it was better to grow rich or wise. 'Why, rich,' ¹⁰
he said; 'for I see the wise men spending their days at the rich men's
doors.' Rich men also consider themselves worthy to hold public
office; for they consider they already have the things that give a
claim to office. In a word, the type of character produced by wealth
is that of a prosperous fool. There is indeed one difference between
the type of the newly-enriched and those who have long been rich: ¹⁵
the newly-enriched have all the bad qualities mentioned in an exaggerated and worse form—to be newly-enriched means, so to speak,
no education in riches. The wrongs they do others are not meant to

injure their victims, but spring from insolence or self-indulgence, e. g. those that end in assault or in adultery.

20 **17** As to Power: here too it may fairly be said that the type of character it produces is mostly obvious enough. Some elements in this type it shares with the wealthy type, others are better. Those in power are more ambitious and more manly in character than the wealthy, because they aspire to do the great deeds that their power 25 permits them to do. Responsibility makes them more serious: they have to keep paying attention to the duties their position involves. They are dignified rather than arrogant, for the respect in which they are held inspires them with dignity and therefore with moderation—dignity being a mild and becoming form of arrogance. If they wrong others, they wrong them not on a small but on a great scale. 30 Good fortune in certain of its branches produces the types of character belonging to the conditions just described,[31] since these conditions are in fact more or less the kinds of good fortune that are regarded as most important. It may be added that good fortune leads us to gain all we can in the way of family happiness and bodily 1391ᵇ advantages.[32] It does indeed make men more supercilious and more reckless; but there is one excellent quality that goes with it—piety, and respect for the divine power, in which they believe because of events which are really the result of chance.

This account of the types of character that correspond to differ- 5 ences of age [33] or fortune [34] may end here; for to arrive at the opposite types to those described, namely, those of the poor, the unfortunate, and the powerless, we have only to ask what the opposite qualities are.

18 The use of persuasive speech is to lead to decisions. (When we know a thing, and have decided about it, there is no further use in speaking about it.) This is so even if one is addressing a single per- 10 son and urging him to do or not to do something, as when we scold a man for his conduct or try to change his views: the single person is as much your 'judge' as if he were one of many; we may say, without qualification, that any one is your judge whom you have to persuade. Nor does it matter whether we are arguing against an actual opponent or against a mere proposition; in the latter case we still 15 have to use speech and overthrow the opposing arguments, and we attack these as we should attack an actual opponent. Our principle

---

[31] viz. good birth, wealth, and power.　　[32] Cp. 1360ᵇ 19–23.
[33] ii, cc. 12–14.　　[34] ii, cc. 15–17.

holds good of ceremonial speeches also; the 'onlookers' for whom such a speech is put together are treated as the judges of it. Broadly speaking, however, the only sort of person who can strictly be called a judge is the man who decides the issue in some matter of public controversy; that is, in law suits and in political debates, in both of which there are issues to be decided. In the section on political oratory an account has already been given of the types of character that mark the different constitutions.[35]

The manner and means of investing speeches with moral character may now be regarded as fully set forth.

Each of the main divisions of oratory has, we have seen,[36] its own distinct purpose. With regard to each division, we have noted the accepted views and propositions upon which we may base our arguments—for political,[37] for ceremonial,[38] and for forensic speaking.[39] We have further determined completely by what means speeches may be invested with the required moral character. We are now to proceed to discuss the arguments common to *all* oratory. All orators, besides their special lines of argument, are bound to use, for instance, the topic of the Possible and Impossible; and to try to show that a thing has happened, or will happen in future. Again, the topic of Size is common to all oratory; all of us have to argue that things are bigger or smaller than they seem, whether we are making political speeches, speeches of eulogy or attack, or prosecuting or defending in the law-courts. Having analysed these subjects, we will try to say what we can about the general principles of arguing by 'enthymeme' and 'example', by the addition of which we may hope to complete the project with which we set out. Of the above-mentioned general lines of argument, that concerned with Amplification is—as has been already said[40]—most appropriate to ceremonial speeches; that concerned with the Past, to forensic speeches, where the required decision is always about the past; that concerned with Possibility and the Future, to political speeches.

19 Let us first speak of the Possible and Impossible. It may plausibly be argued: That if it is possible for one of a pair of contraries to be or happen, then it is possible for the other: e. g. if a man can be cured, he can also fall ill; for any two contraries are equally possible, in so far as they are contraries. That if of two similar things one is possible, so is the other. That if the harder of two things is possible, so is the easier. That if a thing can come into existence in a good and

35 i, c. 8.   36 i, c. 3.   37 i, cc. 4–8.
38 i, c. 9.   39 i, cc. 10–14.   40 i, c. 9.

beautiful form, then it can come into existence generally; thus a
15 house can exist more easily than a beautiful house. That if the beginning of a thing can occur, so can the end; for nothing impossible
occurs or begins to occur; thus the commensurability of the diagonal
of a square with its side neither occurs nor can begin to occur. That
20 if the end is possible, so is the beginning; for all things that occur
have a beginning. That if that which is posterior in essence or in
order of generation can come into being, so can that which is prior:
thus if a man can come into being, so can a boy, since the boy comes
first in order of generation; and if a boy can, so can a man, for the
man also is first. That those things are possible of which the love or
25 desire is natural; for no one, as a rule, loves or desires impossibilities.
That things which are the object of any kind of science or art are
possible and exist or come into existence. That anything is possible
the first step in whose production depends on men or things which
we can compel or persuade to produce it, by our greater strength,
our control of them, or our friendship with them. That where the
parts are possible, the whole is possible; and where the whole is
30 possible, the parts are usually possible. For if the slit in front,
the toe-piece, and the upper leather can be made, then shoes can
1392ᵇ be made; and if shoes, then also the front slit and toe-piece. That if
a whole genus is a thing that can occur, so can the species; and if the
species can occur, so can the genus: thus, if a sailing vessel can be
made, so also can a trireme; and if a trireme, then a sailing vessel
also. That if one of two things whose existence depends on each other
is possible, so is the other; for instance, if 'double', then 'half', and
5 if 'half', then 'double'. That if a thing can be produced without
art or preparation, it can be produced still more certainly by the careful application of art to it. Hence Agathon has said:

> To some things we by art must needs attain,
> Others by destiny or luck we gain.

10 That if anything is possible to inferior, weaker, and stupider people,
it is more so for their opposites; thus Isocrates said that it would be a
strange thing if he could not discover a thing that Euthynus had found
out.[41] As for Impossibility, we can clearly get what we want by taking
the contraries of the arguments stated above.

Questions of Past Fact may be looked at in the following ways:
15 First, that if the less likely of two things has occurred, the more likely
must have occurred also. That if one thing that usually follows another has happened, then that other thing has happened; that, for

[41] Cp. Isocr. xviii. 15.

instance, if a man has forgotten a thing, he has also once learnt it. That if a man had the power and the wish to do a thing, he has done it; for every one does do whatever he intends to do whenever he can do it, there being nothing to stop him. That, further, he has done the thing in question either if he intended it and nothing external prevented him; or if he had the power to do it and was angry at the time; or if he had the power to do it and his heart was set upon it—for people as a rule do what they long to do, if they can; bad people through lack of self-control; good people, because their hearts are set upon good things. Again, that if a thing was 'going to happen', it has happened; if a man was 'going to do something', he has done it, for it is likely that the intention was carried out. That if one thing has happened which naturally happens before another or with a view to it, the other has happened; for instance, if it has lightened, it has also thundered; and if an action has been attempted, it has been done. That if one thing has happened which naturally happens after another, or with a view to which that other happens, then that other (that which happens first, or happens with a view to this thing) has also happened; thus, if it has thundered it has also lightened, and if an action has been done it has been attempted. Of all these sequences some are inevitable and some merely usual. The arguments for the *non*-occurrence of anything can obviously be found by considering the opposites of those that have been mentioned.

How questions of Future Fact should be argued is clear from the same considerations: That a thing will be done if there is both the power and the wish to do it; or if along with the power to do it there is a craving for the result, or anger, or calculation, prompting it. That the thing will be done, in these cases, if the man is actually setting about it, or even if he means to do it later—for usually what we mean to do happens rather than what we do not mean to do. That a thing will happen if another thing which naturally happens before it has already happened; thus, if it is clouding over, it is likely to rain. That if the means to an end have occurred, then the end is likely to occur; thus, if there is a foundation, there will be a house.

For arguments about the Greatness and Smallness of things, the greater and the lesser, and generally great things and small, what we have already said will show the line to take. In discussing deliberative oratory we have spoken about the relative greatness of various goods, and about the greater and lesser in general.[42] Since therefore in each type of oratory the object under discussion is some kind of good—whether it is utility, nobleness, or justice—it is clear that

[Right margin line markers: 20, 25, 30, 1393ᵃ, 5, 10]

---

[42] i, c. 7.

every orator must obtain the materials of amplification through these
15 channels.⁴³ To go further than this, and try to establish abstract laws
of greatness and superiority, is to argue without an object; in practical life, particular facts count more than generalizations.

Enough has now been said about these questions of possibility and
20 the reverse, of past or future fact, and of the relative greatness or
smallness of things.

20   The special forms of oratorical argument having now been discussed, we have next to treat of those which are common to all kinds
of oratory. These are of two main kinds, 'Example' and 'Enthymeme';
for the 'Maxim' is part of an Enthymeme.
25   We will first treat of argument by Example, for it has the nature
of induction, which is the foundation of reasoning. This form of argument has two varieties; one consisting in the mention of actual past
facts, the other in the invention of facts by the speaker. Of the latter, again, there are two varieties, the illustrative parallel and the
30 fable (e. g. the fables of Aesop, or those from Libya). As an instance
of the mention of actual facts, take the following. The speaker
may argue thus: 'We must prepare for war against the king of Persia
and not let him subdue Egypt. For Darius of old did not cross
1393ᵇ the Aegean until he had seized Egypt; but once he had seized it, he did
cross. And Xerxes, again, did not attack us until he had seized Egypt;
but once he had seized it, he did cross. If therefore the present king
seizes Egypt, he also will cross, and therefore we must not let him.'

The illustrative parallel is the sort of argument Socrates used: e. g.
'Public officials ought not to be selected by lot. That is like using the
5 lot to select athletes, instead of choosing those who are fit for the contest; or using the lot to select a steersman from among a ship's crew,
as if we ought to take the man on whom the lot falls, and not the
man who knows most about it.'

Instances of the fable are that of Stesichorus about Phalaris, and
10 that of Aesop in defence of the popular leader. When the people of
Himera had made Phalaris military dictator, and were going to give
him a bodyguard, Stesichorus wound up a long talk by telling them the
fable of the horse who had a field all to himself. Presently there came a
stag and began to spoil his pasturage. The horse, wishing to revenge
15 himself on the stag, asked a man if he could help him to do so. The
man said, 'Yes, if you will let me bridle you and get on to your back
with javelins in my hand'. The horse agreed, and the man mounted;
but instead of getting his revenge on the stag, the horse found himself

⁴³ i. e. some kind of good.

the slave of the man. 'You too', said Stesichorus, 'take care lest, in
your desire for revenge on your enemies, you meet the same fate as 20
the horse. By making Phalaris military dictator, you have already let
yourselves be bridled. If you let him get on to your backs by giving
him a bodyguard, from that moment you will be his slaves.'

Aesop, defending before the assembly at Samos a popular leader
who was being tried for his life, told this story: A fox, in crossing a
river, was swept into a hole in the rocks; and, not being able to get 25
out, suffered miseries for a long time through the swarms of fleas that
fastened on her. A hedgehog, while roaming around, noticed the fox;
and feeling sorry for her asked if he might remove the fleas. But the
fox declined the offer; and when the hedgehog asked why, she replied, 'These fleas are by this time full of me and not sucking much
blood; if you take them away, others will come with fresh appetites 30
and drink up all the blood I have left.' 'So, men of Samos', said Aesop,
'my client will do you no further harm; he is wealthy already. But
if you put him to death, others will come along who are not rich, and
their peculations will empty your treasury completely.'   1394[a]

Fables are suitable for addresses to popular assemblies; and they
have one advantage—they are comparatively easy to invent, whereas
it is hard to find parallels among actual past events. You will in fact
frame them just as you frame illustrative parallels: all you require is 5
the power of thinking out your analogy, a power developed by intellectual training. But while it is easier to supply parallels by inventing
fables, it is more valuable for the political speaker to supply them by
quoting what has actually happened, since in most respects the future
will be like what the past has been.

Where we are unable to argue by Enthymeme, we must try to
demonstrate our point by this method of Example, and to convince 10
our hearers thereby. If we *can* argue by Enthymeme, we should use
our Examples as subsequent supplementary evidence. They should
not precede the Enthymemes: that will give the argument an inductive air, which only rarely suits the conditions of speech-making. If
they follow the Enthymemes, they have the effect of witnesses giving
evidence, and this always tells. For the same reason, if you put your 15
examples first you must give a large number of them; if you put them
last, a single one is sufficient; even a single witness will serve if he is a
good one. It has now been stated how many varieties of argument
by Example there are, and how and when they are to be employed.

21 We now turn to the use of maxims, in order to see upon what subjects and occasions, and for what kind of speaker, they will appro- 20

priately form part of a speech. This will appear most clearly when we have defined a maxim. It is a statement; not about a particular fact, such as the character of Iphicrates, but of a general kind; nor is it about any and every subject—e.g. 'straight is the contrary of curved' is not a maxim—but only about questions of practical con-
25 duct, courses of conduct to be chosen or avoided. Now an Enthymeme is a syllogism dealing with such practical subjects. It is therefore roughly true that the premises or conclusions of Enthymemes, considered apart from the rest of the argument, are maxims: e.g.

> Never should any man whose wits are sound
> 30   Have his sons taught more wisdom than their fellows.[44]

Here we have a maxim; add the reason or explanation, and the whole thing is an Enthymeme; thus—

> It makes them idle; and therewith they earn
> Ill-will and jealousy throughout the city.[45]

1394ᵇ Again,

> There is no man in all things prosperous,[46]

and

> There is no man among us all is free,

5 are maxims; but the latter, taken with what follows it, is an Enthymeme—

> For all are slaves of money or of chance.[47]

From this definition of a maxim it follows that there are four kinds of maxims. In the first place, the maxim may or may not have a supplement. Proof is needed where the statement is paradoxical or dis-
10 putable; no supplement is wanted where the statement contains nothing paradoxical, either because the view expressed is already a known truth, e. g.

> Chiefest of blessings is health for a man, as it seemeth to me,[48]

this being the general opinion: or because, as soon as the view is
15 stated, it is clear at a glance, e. g.

> No love is true save that which loves for ever.[49]

---

[44] Euripides, *Medea*, 295.   [45] ib. 297.
[46] Euripides, fragm.   [47] Euripides, *Hecuba*, 864 f.
[48] Possibly a fragment of Epicharmus.   [49] Euripides, *Troades*, 1051.

Of the maxims that do have a supplement attached, some are part
of an Enthymeme, e. g.

> Never should any man whose wits are sound, &c.[50]

Others have the essential character of Enthymemes, but are not
stated as parts of Enthymemes; these latter are reckoned the best;
they are those in which the reason for the view expressed is simply 20
implied, e. g.

> O mortal man, nurse not immortal wrath.

To say 'it is not right to nurse immortal wrath' is a maxim; the
added words 'O mortal man' give the reason. Similarly, with the
words

> Mortal creatures ought to cherish mortal, not immortal thoughts.[51]

What has been said has shown us how many kinds of maxim there 25
are, and to what subjects the various kinds are appropriate. They
must not be given without supplement if they express disputed or
paradoxical views: we must, in that case, either put the supplement
first and make a maxim of the conclusion, e. g. you might say, 'For my
part, since both unpopularity and idleness are undesirable, I hold that 30
it is better not to be educated'; or you may say this first, and then
add the previous clause. Where a statement, without being paradoxical, is not obviously true, the reason should be added as concisely
as possible. In such cases both laconic and enigmatic sayings are suitable: thus one might say what Stesichorus said to the Locrians, 1395ᵃ
'Insolence is better avoided, lest the cicalas chirp on the ground.' [52]

The use of maxims is appropriate only to elderly men, and in
handling subjects in which the speaker is experienced. For a young
man to use them is—like telling stories—unbecoming; to use them
in handling things in which one has no experience is silly and ill- 5
bred: a fact sufficiently proved by the special fondness of country
fellows for striking out maxims, and their readiness to air them.

To declare a thing to be universally true when it is not is most
appropriate when working up feelings of horror and indignation in our
hearers; especially by way of preface, or after the facts have been
proved. Even hackneyed and commonplace maxims are to be used, if 10
they suit one's purpose: just because they are commonplace, every
one seems to agree with them, and therefore they are taken for truth.

---

[50] Euripides, *Medea*, 295.   [51] Epicharmus?
[52] The cicalas would have to chirp on the ground if an enemy cut down the
trees.

Thus, any one who is calling on his men to risk an engagement without obtaining favourable omens may quote

> One omen of all is best, that we fight for our fatherland.[53]

Or, if he is calling on them to attack a stronger force—

15　　　　　　　　The War-God showeth no favour.[54]

Or, if he is urging people to destroy the innocent children of their enemies—

> Fool, who slayeth the father and leaveth his sons to avenge him.[55]

Some proverbs are also maxims, e. g. the proverb 'An Attic neighbour'. You are not to avoid uttering maxims that contradict such sayings 20 as have become public property (I mean such sayings as 'know thyself' and 'nothing in excess'), if doing so will raise your hearers' opinion of your character, or convey an effect of strong emotion— e. g. an angry speaker might well say, 'It is not true that we ought to know ourselves: anyhow, if this man had known himself, he would never have thought himself fit for an army command.' It will raise peo- 25 ple's opinion of our character to say, for instance, 'We ought not to follow the saying that bids us treat our friends as future enemies: much better to treat our enemies as future friends.' [56] The moral purpose should be implied partly by the very wording of our maxim. Failing this, we should add our reason: e. g. having said 'We should treat our friends, not as the saying advises, but as if they were going to be our friends always', we should add 'for the other behaviour 30 is that of a traitor': or we might put it, 'I disapprove of that saying. A true friend will treat his friend as if he were going to be his friend for ever'; and again, 'Nor do I approve of the saying "nothing in excess": we are bound to hate bad men excessively.'

1395ᵇ　　One great advantage of maxims to a speaker is due to the want of intelligence in his hearers, who love to hear him succeed in expressing as a universal truth the opinions which they hold themselves about particular cases. I will explain what I mean by this, indicating at the same time how we are to hunt down the maxims required. The 5 maxim, as has been already said,[57] is a general statement, and people love to hear stated in general terms what they already believe in some particular connexion: e. g. if a man happens to have bad neighbours or bad children, he will agree with any one who tells him, 'Nothing is more annoying than having neighbours', or, 'Nothing is more fool-

---

[53] *Iliad*, xii. 243.　　　[54] Ibid. xviii. 309.　　　[55] Cp. i, c. 15, 1376ᵃ 7.
[56] Cp. ii, c. 13, 1389ᵇ 23–5.　　　[57] 1394ᵃ 23.

ish than to be the parent of children.' The orator has therefore to guess the subjects on which his hearers really hold views already, and 10 what those views are, and then must express, as general truths, these same views on these same subjects. This is one advantage of using maxims. There is another which is more important—it invests a speech with moral character. There is moral character in every speech in which the moral purpose is conspicuous: and maxims always pro- 15 duce this effect, because the utterance of them amounts to a general declaration of moral principles: so that, if the maxims are sound, they display the speaker as a man of sound moral character. So much for the maxim—its nature, varieties, proper use, and advantages.

22 We now come to the Enthymemes, and will begin the subject with 20 some general consideration of the proper way of looking for them, and then proceed to what is a distinct question, the lines of argument to be embodied in them. It has already [58] been pointed out that the Enthymeme is a syllogism, and in what sense it is so. We have also noted the differences between it and the syllogism of dialectic. Thus we must not carry its reasoning too far back, or the length of our argu- 25 ment will cause obscurity: nor must we put in all the steps that lead to our conclusion, or we shall waste words in saying what is manifest. It is this simplicity that makes the uneducated more effective than the educated when addressing popular audiences—makes them, as the poets [59] tell us, 'charm the crowd's ears more finely'. Educated men lay down broad general principles; uneducated men argue from 30 common knowledge and draw obvious conclusions. We must not, therefore, start from any and every accepted opinion, but only from those we have defined—those accepted by our judges or by those whose authority they recognize: and there must, moreover, be no 1396[a] doubt in the minds of most, if not all, of our judges that the opinions put forward really are of this sort. We should also base our arguments upon probabilities as well as upon certainties.

The first thing we have to remember is this. Whether our argument concerns public affairs or some other subject, we must know some, if 5 not all, of the facts about the subject on which we are to speak and argue. Otherwise we can have no materials out of which to construct arguments. I mean, for instance, how could we advise the Athenians whether they should go to war or not, if we did not know their strength, whether it was naval or military or both, and how great it is; what their revenues amount to; who their friends and enemies 10 are; what wars, too, they have waged, and with what success;

---

[58] i, c. 2, 1356[b] 3, 1357[a] 16.   [59] Cp. Euripides, *Hippolytus*, 989.

and so on? Or how could we eulogize them if we knew nothing about
the sea-fight at Salamis, or the battle of Marathon, or what they did
for the Heracleidae, or any other facts like that? All eulogy is based
15 upon the noble deeds—real or imaginary—that stand to the credit of
those eulogized. On the same principle, invectives are based on facts
of the opposite kind: the orator looks to see what base deeds—real
or imaginary—stand to the discredit of those he is attacking, such
as treachery to the cause of Hellenic freedom, or the enslavement
of their gallant allies against the barbarians (Aegina,[60] Potidaea,[61]
20 &c.), or any other misdeeds of this kind that are recorded against
them. So, too, in a court of law: whether we are prosecuting or
defending, we must pay attention to the existing facts of the case.
It makes no difference whether the subject is the Lacedaemonians or
the Athenians, a man or a god; we must do the same thing. Suppose it
25 to be Achilles whom we are to advise, to praise or blame, to accuse
or defend; here too we must take the facts, real or imaginary;
these must be our material, whether we are to praise or blame him
for the noble or base deeds he has done, to accuse or defend him for
his just or unjust treatment of others, or to advise him about
30 what is or is not to his interest. The same thing applies to any subject whatever. Thus, in handling the question whether justice is or
is not a good, we must start with the real facts about justice and goodness. We see, then, that this is the only way in which any one ever
1396^b proves anything, whether his arguments are strictly cogent or not:
not all facts can form his basis, but only those that bear on the matter in hand: nor, plainly, can proof be effected otherwise by means
of the speech. Consequently, as appears in the *Topics,*[62] we must first
5 of all have by us a selection of arguments about questions that may
arise and are suitable for us to handle; and then we must try to think
out arguments of the same type for special needs as they emerge;
not vaguely and indefinitely, but by keeping our eyes on the actual
facts of the subject we have to speak on, and gathering in as many of
them as we can that bear closely upon it: for the more actual facts
10 we have at our command, the more easily we prove our case;
and the more closely they bear on the subject, the more they will
seem to belong to that speech only instead of being commonplaces.
By 'commonplaces' I mean, for example, eulogy of Achilles because
he is a human being, or a demi-god, or because he joined the expedition against Troy: these things are true of many others, so that this
15 kind of eulogy applies no better to Achilles than to Diomede. The

---

[60] Cp. Thucyd. ii. 27; iv. 57.   [61] Cp. Thucyd. ii. 70.
[62] Cp. *Top.* i, c. 14.

special facts here needed are those that are true of Achilles alone; such facts as that he slew Hector, the bravest of the Trojans, and Cycnus the invulnerable, who prevented all the Greeks from landing, and again that he was the youngest man who joined the expedition, and was not bound by oath to join it, and so on.

Here, then, we have our first principle of selection of Enthy- 20 memes—that which refers to the lines of argument selected. We will now consider the various elementary classes of Enthymemes. (By an 'elementary class' of Enthymeme I mean the same thing as a 'line of argument'.) We will begin, as we must begin, by observing that there are two kinds of Enthymemes. One kind proves some affirma- 25 tive or negative proposition; the other kind disproves one. The difference between the two kinds is the same as that between syllogistic proof and disproof in dialectic. The demonstrative Enthymeme is formed by the conjunction of compatible propositions; the refutative, by the conjunction of incompatible propositions.

We may now be said to have in our hands the lines of argument for the various *special* subjects that it is useful or necessary to handle, having selected the propositions suitable in various cases. We 30 have, in fact, already ascertained the lines of argument applicable to Enthymemes about good and evil, the noble and the base, justice and injustice, and also to those about types of character, emotions, and moral qualities.[63] Let us now lay hold of certain facts about the whole subject, considered from a different and more general point of 1397[a] view. In the course of our discussion we will take note of the distinction between lines of proof and lines of disproof: [64] and also of those lines of argument used in what seem to be Enthymemes, but are not, since they do not represent valid syllogisms.[65] Having made all this clear, we will proceed to classify Objections and Refuta- 5 tions, showing how they can be brought to bear upon Enthymemes.[66]

23　1. One line of positive proof [67] is based upon consideration of the opposite of the thing in question. Observe whether that opposite has the opposite quality.[68] If it has not, you refute the original proposition; if it has, you establish it. E. g. 'Temperance is beneficial; 10 for licentiousness is hurtful'. Or, as in the Messenian speech,[69] 'If war is the cause of our present troubles, peace is what we need to put things right again.' Or—

---

[63] i, cc. 4–14; ii, cc. 1–18.　　　[64] ii, c. 23.　　[65] ii, c. 24.　　[66] ii, c. 25.
[67] Positive proof, as opposed to Refutation.
[68] i. e. the quality opposite to that which, in the proposition under examination, is said to attach to the original thing.　　　[69] Cp. 1373[b] 18.

> For if not even evil-doers should
> Anger us if they meant not what they did,
> Then can we owe no gratitude to such
> 15 As were constrained to do the good they did us.

Or—

> Since in this world liars may win belief,
> Be sure of the opposite likewise—that this world
> Hears many a true word and believes it not.[70]

2. Another line of proof is got by considering some modification 20 of the key-word, and arguing that what can or cannot be said of the one, can or cannot be said of the other: e. g. 'just' does not always mean 'beneficial', or 'justly' would always mean 'beneficially', whereas it is *not* desirable to be justly put to death.[71]

3. Another line of proof is based upon correlative ideas. If it is true that one man *gave* noble or just treatment to another, you argue that the other must have *received* noble or just treatment; or that where it is right to command obedience, it must have been right 25 to obey the command. Thus Diomedon, the tax-farmer, said of the taxes: 'If it is no disgrace for you to sell them,[72] it is no disgrace for us to buy them'. Further, if 'well' or 'justly' is true of the person to whom a thing is done, you argue that it is true of the doer. But it is possible to draw a false conclusion here. It may be just that A should be treated in a certain way, and yet *not* just that he 30 should be so treated by B. Hence you must ask yourself two distinct 1397^b questions: (1) Is it right that A should be thus treated? (2) Is it right that B should thus treat him? and apply your results properly, according as your answers are Yes or No. Sometimes in such a case the two answers differ: you may quite easily have a position like that in the *Alcmaeon* of Theodectes:

> And was there none to loathe thy mother's crime?

to which question Alcmaeon in reply says,

> Why, there are two things to examine here.

5 And when Alphesiboea asks what he means, he rejoins:

> They judged *her* fit to die, not *me* to slay her.

Again there is the lawsuit about Demosthenes and the men who killed

[70] Euripides, *Thyestes*, fragm.   [71] Cp. i, c. 9, 1366^b 33.
[72] i. e. the right of collecting them.

Nicanor; as they were judged to have killed him justly, it was thought that he was killed justly. And in the case of the man who was killed at Thebes, the judges were requested to decide whether 10 it was unjust that he should be killed, since if it was not, it was argued that it could not have been unjust to kill him.

4. Another line of proof is the *a fortiori*. Thus it may be argued that if even the gods are not omniscient, certainly human beings are not. The principle here is that, if a quality does not in fact exist where it is *more* likely to exist, it clearly does not exist where it is *less* likely. Again, the argument that a man who strikes his father 15 also strikes his neighbours follows from the principle that, if the less likely thing is true, the more likely thing is true also; for a man is less likely to strike his father than to strike his neighbours. The argument, then, may run thus. Or it may be urged that, if a thing is not true where it is more likely, it is not true where it is less likely; or that, if it is true where it is less likely, it is true where it is more likely: according as we have to show that a thing *is* or is *not* true. This argument might also be used in a case of parity, as in the lines:

> Thou hast pity for *thy* sire, who has lost his sons:
> Hast none for Oeneus, whose brave son is dead?   20

And, again, 'if Theseus did no wrong, neither did Paris'; or 'if the sons of Tyndareus did no wrong, neither did Paris'; or 'if Hector did well to slay Patroclus, Paris did well to slay Achilles'. And 'if other followers of an art are not bad men, neither are philosophers'. And 'if generals are not bad men because it often happens that they are condemned to death, neither are sophists'. And the remark that 'if each 25 individual among you ought to think of his own city's reputation, you ought all to think of the reputation of Greece as a whole'.

5. Another line of argument is based on considerations of time. Thus Iphicrates, in the case against Harmodius, said, 'if before doing the deed I had bargained that, if I did it, I should have a statue, you would have given me one. Will you not give me one now that I *have* done the deed? You must not make promises when you are expecting 30 a thing to be done for you, and refuse to fulfil them when the thing has been done.' And, again, to induce the Thebans to let Philip pass through their territory into Attica, it was argued that 'if he had in- 1398ᵃ sisted on this before he helped them against the Phocians, they would have promised to do it. It is monstrous, therefore, that just because he threw away his advantage then, and trusted their honour, they should not let him pass through now'.

6. Another line is to apply to the other speaker what he has said

against yourself. It is an excellent turn to give to a debate, as may be
5 seen in the *Teucer*.[73] It was employed by Iphicrates in his reply to Aristophon. 'Would *you*', he asked, 'take a bribe to betray the fleet?' 'No',
said Aristophon; and Iphicrates replied, 'Very good: if you, who are
Aristophon, would not betray the fleet, would I, who am Iphicrates?'
Only, it must be recognized beforehand that the other man is more
likely than you are to commit the crime in question. Otherwise you
10 will make yourself ridiculous; if it is Aristeides who is prosecuting,
you cannot say that sort of thing to him. The purpose is to discredit
the prosecutor, who as a rule would have it appear that his character
is better than that of the defendant, a pretension which it is desirable
to upset. But the use of such an argument is in all cases ridiculous
if you are attacking others for what you do or would do yourself, or
are urging others to do what you neither do nor would do yourself.
15 7. Another line of proof is secured by defining your terms. Thus,
'What is the supernatural? Surely it is either a god or the work of a
god. Well, anyone who believes that the work of a god exists, cannot
help also believing that gods exist'. Or take the argument of Iphicrates,
'Goodness is true nobility; neither Harmodius nor Aristogeiton had
20 any nobility before they did a noble deed'. He also argued that he
himself was more akin to Harmodius and Aristogeiton than his
opponent was. 'At any rate, my deeds are more akin to those of Harmodius and Aristogeiton than yours are.' Another example may be
found in the *Alexander*. 'Every one will agree that by incontinent
people we mean those who are not satisfied with the enjoyment of
one love'. A further example is to be found in the reason given by
25 Socrates for not going to the court of Archelaus. He said that 'one is
insulted by being unable to requite benefits, as well as by being unable
to requite injuries'. All the persons mentioned define their term and
get at its essential meaning, and then use the result when reasoning
on the point at issue.

8. Another line of argument is founded upon the various senses of
a word. Such a word is 'rightly', as has been explained in the *Topics*.

9. Another line is based upon logical division. Thus, 'All men do
30 wrong from one of three motives, A, B, or C: in my case A and B
are out of the question, and even the accusers do not allege C'.

10. Another line is based upon induction. Thus from the case of
the woman of Peparethus it might be argued that women everywhere can settle correctly the facts about their children. Another
1398ᵇ example of this occurred at Athens in the case between the orator
Mantias [74] and his son, when the boy's mother revealed the true facts:

---

[73] Of Sophocles.   [74] Cp. Demosth., Or. xviii, *Boeot. de nom.*, §§ 7, 10.

and yet another at Thebes, in the case between Ismenias and Stilbon, when Dodonis proved that it was Ismenias who was the father of her son Thettaliscus, and he was in consequence always regarded as being so. A further instance of induction may be taken from the *Law* of Theodectes: 'If we do not hand over our horses to the care of men who 5 have mishandled other people's horses, nor ships to those who have wrecked other people's ships, and if this is true of everything else alike, then men who have failed to secure other people's safety are not to be employed to secure our own.' Another instance is the argument of Alcidamas: 'Every one honours the wise. Thus the Parians have 10 honoured Archilochus, in spite of his bitter tongue; the Chians Homer, though he was not their countryman; the Mytilenaeans Sappho, though she was a woman; the Lacedaemonians actually made Chilon a member of their senate, though they are the least literary of men; the Italian Greeks honoured Pythagoras; the inhabitants of Lamp- sacus gave public burial to Anaxagoras, though he was an alien, and 15 honour him even to this day. [It may be argued that peoples for whom philosophers legislate are always prosperous] on the ground that the Athenians became prosperous under Solon's laws and the Lacedaemonians under those of Lycurgus, while at Thebes no sooner did the leading men become philosophers than the country began to prosper.

11. Another line of argument is founded upon some decision al- ready pronounced, whether on the same subject or on one like it or contrary to it. Such a proof is most effective if every one has always 20 decided thus; but if not every one, then at any rate most people; or if all, or most, wise or good men have thus decided, or the actual judges of the present question, or those whose authority they accept, or any one whose decision they cannot gainsay because he has com- plete control over them, or those whom it is not seemly to gainsay, as the gods, or one's father, or one's teachers. Thus Autocles said, when attacking Mixidemides, that it was a strange thing that the 25 Dread Goddesses could without loss of dignity submit to the judge- ment of the Areopagus, and yet Mixidemides could not. Or as Sappho said, 'Death is an evil thing; the gods have so judged it, or they would die'. Or again as Aristippus said in reply to Plato when he spoke somewhat too dogmatically, as Aristippus thought: 'Well, 30 anyhow, our *friend*', meaning Socrates, 'never spoke like that'. And Hegesippus, having previously consulted Zeus at Olympia, asked Apollo at Delphi 'whether his opinion was the same as his father's', implying that it would be shameful for him to contradict his father. 1399ᵃ Thus too Isocrates argued that Helen must have been a good woman,

because Theseus decided that she was;[75] and Paris a good man, because the goddesses chose him before all others;[76] and Evagoras also, says Isocrates, was good, since when Conon met with his misfortune he betook himself to Evagoras without trying any one else on the way.[77]

12. Another line of argument consists in taking separately the parts of a subject. Such is that given in the *Topics*:[78] 'What *sort* of motion is the soul? for it must be this or that.' The *Socrates* of Theodectes provides an example: 'What temple has he profaned? What gods recognized by the state has he not honoured?'

13. Since it happens that any given thing usually has both good and bad consequences, another line of argument consists in using those consequences as a reason for urging that a thing should or should not be done, for prosecuting or defending any one, for eulogy or censure. E. g. education leads both to unpopularity, which is bad, and to wisdom, which is good. Hence you either argue, 'It is therefore not well to be educated, since it is not well to be unpopular': or you answer, 'No, it is well to be educated, since it is well to be wise'. The *Art of Rhetoric* of Callippus is made up of this line of argument, with the addition of those of Possibility and the others of that kind already described.[79]

14. Another line of argument is used when we have to urge or discourage a course of action that may be done in either of two opposite ways, and have to apply the method just mentioned to both. The difference between this one and the last is that, whereas in the last any two things are contrasted, here the things contrasted are opposites. For instance, the priestess enjoined upon her son not to take to public speaking: 'For', she said, 'if you say what is right, men will hate you; if you say what is wrong, the gods will hate you.' The reply might be, 'On the contrary, you *ought* to take to public speaking: for if you say what is right, the gods will love you; if you say what is wrong, men will love you.' This amounts to the proverbial 'buying the marsh with the salt'. It is just this situation, viz. when each of two opposites has both a good and a bad consequence opposite respectively to each other, that has been termed *divarication*.

15. Another line of argument is this: The things people approve of openly are not those which they approve of secretly: openly, their chief praise is given to justice and nobleness; but in their hearts they prefer their own advantage. Try, in face of this, to establish the point of view which your opponent has not adopted. This is the most

---

[75] Isocrates, *Helen*, 18–38.　　　[76] Ibid., 41–8.
[77] Isocrates, *Evagoras*, 51 ff.　　　[78] Cp. *Top.* ii. 4; iv. 1.
[79] ii, c. 19 *supra*.

effective of the forms of argument that contradict common opinion.

16. Another line is that of rational correspondence. E. g. Iphicrates, when they were trying to compel his son, a youth under the prescribed age, to perform one of the state duties because he was tall, said 'If you count tall boys men, you will next be voting short men boys'. And Theodectes in his *Law* [80] said, 'You make citizens of such mercenaries 1399ᵇ as Strabax and Charidemus, as a reward of their merits; will you not make exiles of such citizens as those who have done irreparable harm among the mercenaries?'

17. Another line is the argument that if two results are the same their antecedents are also the same. For instance, it was a saying of Xenophanes that to assert that the gods had birth is as impious as to say that they die; the consequence of both statements is that there is a time when the gods do not exist. This line of proof assumes generally that the result of any given thing is always the same: e. g. 'you are going to decide not about Isocrates, but about the value of the whole profession of philosophy.' Or, 'to give earth and water' means slavery; or, 'to share in the Common Peace' means obeying orders. We are to make either such assumptions or their opposite, as suits us best.

18. Another line of argument is based on the fact that men do not always make the same choice on a later as on an earlier occasion, but reverse their previous choice. E. g. the following Enthymeme: 'When we were exiles, we fought in order to return; now we have returned, it would be strange to choose exile in order not to have to fight.' [81] On one occasion, that is, they chose to be true to their homes at the cost of fighting, and on the other to avoid fighting at the cost of deserting their homes.

19. Another line of argument is the assertion that some *possible* motive for an event or state of things is the *real* one: e. g. that a gift was given in order to cause pain by its withdrawal. This notion underlies the lines:

> God gives to many great prosperity,
> Not of good will towards them, but to make
> The ruin of them more conspicuous.

Or take the passage from the *Meleager* of Antiphon:

> To slay no boar, but to be witnesses
> Of Meleager's prowess unto Greece.

Or the argument in the *Ajax* of Theodectes, that Diomede chose out Odysseus [82] not to do him honour, but in order that his companion

[80] Cp. 1398ᵇ 6.   [81] Cp. Lysias, Or. xxxiv, § 11.   [82] Cp. *Iliad*, x. 218–54.

30 might be a lesser man than himself—such a motive for doing so is quite possible.

20. Another line of argument is common to forensic and deliberative oratory, namely, to consider inducements and deterrents, and the motives people have for doing or avoiding the actions in question. These are the conditions which make us bound to act if they are for us, and to refrain from action if they are against us: that is, we are bound to act if the action is possible, easy, and useful to ourselves or 35 our friends or hurtful to our enemies; this is true even if the action entails loss, provided the loss is outweighed by the solid advantage. A speaker will urge action by pointing to such conditions, and discour-

1400ᵃ age it by pointing to the opposite. These same arguments also form the materials for accusation or defence—the deterrents being pointed out by the defence, and the inducements by the prosecution. As for the defence, . . . This topic forms the whole *Art of Rhetoric* both of Pamphilus and of Callippus.

5 21. Another line of argument refers to things which are supposed to happen and yet seem incredible. We may argue that people could not have believed them, if they had not been true or nearly true: even that they are the more likely to be true because they are incredible. For the things which men believe are either facts or probabilities: if, therefore, a thing that *is* believed is improbable and even incredible, it must be true, since it is certainly not believed because it is at all probable or credible. An example is what Androcles of the deme Pitthus said in his well-known arraignment of the law. The audience 10 tried to shout him down when he observed that the laws required a law to set them right. 'Why', he went on, 'fish need salt, improbable and incredible as this might seem for creatures reared in salt water; and olive-cakes ⁸³ need oil, incredible as it is that what produces oil should need it.'

22. Another line of argument is to refute our opponent's case by 15 noting any contrasts or contradictions of dates, acts, or words that it anywhere displays; and this in any of the three following connexions. (1) Referring to our opponent's conduct, e. g. 'He says he is devoted to you, yet he conspired with the Thirty.' (2) Referring to our own conduct, e. g. 'He says I am litigious, and yet he cannot prove that 20 I have been engaged in a single lawsuit.' (3) Referring to both of us together, e. g. '*He* has never even *lent* any one a penny, but *I* have *ransomed* quite a number of you.'

23. Another line that is useful for men and causes that have been really or seemingly slandered, is to show why the facts are not as

⁸³ i. e. cakes made of dried olives.

supposed; pointing out that there is a reason for the false impression given. Thus a woman, who had palmed off her son on another woman, was thought to be the lad's mistress because she embraced him; but when her action was explained the charge was shown to be groundless. Another example is from the *Ajax* of Theodectes, where Odysseus tells Ajax the reason why, though he is really braver than Ajax, he is not thought so.

24. Another line of argument is to show that if the *cause* is present, the *effect* is present, and if absent, absent. For by proving the cause you at once prove the effect, and conversely nothing can exist without its cause. Thus Thrasybulus accused Leodamas of having had his name recorded as a criminal on the slab in the Acropolis, and of erasing the record in the time of the Thirty Tyrants: to which Leodamas replied, 'Impossible: for the Thirty would have trusted me all the more if my quarrel with the commons had been inscribed on the slab.'

25. Another line is to consider whether the accused person can take or could have taken a better [84] course than that which he is recommending or taking, or has taken. If he has *not* taken this better course, it is clear that he is not guilty, since no one deliberately and consciously chooses what is bad.[85] This argument is, however, fallacious, for it often becomes clear after the event how the action could have been done better, though before the event this was far from clear.

26. Another line is, when a contemplated action is inconsistent with any past action, to examine them both together. Thus, when the people of Elea asked Xenophanes if they should or should not sacrifice to Leucothea and mourn for her, he advised them not to mourn for her if they thought her a goddess, and not to sacrifice to her if they thought her a mortal woman.

27. Another line is to make previous mistakes the grounds of accusation or defence. Thus, in the *Medea* of Carcinus the accusers allege that Medea has slain her children; 'at all events', they say, 'they are not to be seen'—Medea having made the mistake of sending her children away. In defence she argues that it is not her children, but Jason, whom she would have slain; for it would have been a mistake on her part not to do this if she *had* done the other. This special line of argument for enthymeme forms the whole of the *Art of Rhetoric* in use before Theodorus.

28. Another line is to draw meanings from names. Sophocles, for instance, says,

> O steel in heart as thou art steel in name.

[84] i. e. better suited to effect the evil purpose with which he is charged.
[85] i. e. bad *means* to effect his purpose.

This line of argument is common in praises of the gods. Thus, too, Conon called Thrasybulus *rash in counsel*. And Herodicus said of Thrasymachus, 'You are always *bold in battle*'; of Polus, 'you are always *a colt*'; and of the legislator Draco that his laws were those not of a human being but of *a dragon,* so savage were they. And, in Euripides, Hecuba says of Aphrodite,

> Her name and Folly's rightly begin alike,[86]

and Chaeremon writes

> Pentheus—a name foreshadowing grief to come.

The Refutative Enthymeme has a greater reputation than the Demonstrative, because within a small space it works out two opposing arguments, and arguments put side by side are clearer to the audience. But of all syllogisms, whether refutative or demonstrative, those are most applauded of which we foresee the conclusions from the beginning, so long as they are not obvious at first sight—for part of the pleasure we feel is at our own intelligent anticipation; or those which we follow well enough to see the point of them as soon as the last word has been uttered.

24 Besides genuine syllogisms, there may be syllogisms that look genuine but are not; and since an Enthymeme is merely a syllogism of a particular kind, it follows that, besides genuine Enthymemes, there may be those that look genuine but are not.

1. Among the lines of argument that form the Spurious Enthymeme the first is that which arises from the particular words employed.

(*a*) One variety of this is when—as in dialectic, without having gone through any reasoning process, we make a final statement as if it were the conclusion of such a process, 'Therefore so-and-so is not true', 'Therefore also so-and-so must be true'—so too in rhetoric a compact and antithetical utterance passes for an enthymeme, such language being the proper province of enthymeme, so that it is seemingly the form of wording here that causes the illusion mentioned. In order to produce the effect of genuine reasoning by our form of wording it is useful to summarize the results of a number of previous reasonings: as 'some he saved—others he avenged—the Greeks he freed'.[87] Each of these statements has been previously proved from other facts; but the mere collocation of them gives the impression of establishing some fresh conclusion.

(*b*) Another variety is based on the use of similar words for dif-

---

[86] Euripides, *Troades,* 990.　　　　[87] Isocrates, *Evagoras,* 65–9.

ferent things; e. g. the argument that the mouse must be a noble
creature, since it gives its name to the most august of all religious rites 15
—for such the Mysteries are. Or one may introduce, into a eulogy of
the dog, the dog-star; or Pan, because Pindar said:

> O thou blessed one!
> Thou whom they of Olympus call
> The hound of manifold shape
> That follows the Mother of Heaven:

or we may argue that, because there is much disgrace in there *not*
being a dog about, there is honour in *being* a dog.[88] Or that Hermes
is readier than any other god to go shares, since we never say 'shares 20
all round' except of him. Or that speech [89] is a very excellent thing,
since good men are not said to be worth money but to be worthy of
esteem—the phrase 'worthy of esteem' also having the meaning of
'worth speech'.

2. Another line is to assert of the whole what is true of the parts,
or of the parts what is true of the whole. A whole and its parts are
supposed to be identical, though often they are not. You have there- 25
fore to adopt whichever of these two lines better suits your purpose.
That is how Euthydemus argues: e. g. that any one knows that there
is a trireme in the Peiraeus, since he knows the separate details that
make up this statement. There is also the argument that one who
knows the letters knows the whole word, since the word is the same
thing as the letters which compose it; or that, if a double portion of a 30
certain thing is harmful to health, then a single portion must not be
called wholesome, since it is absurd that two good things should make
one bad thing. Put thus, the Enthymeme is refutative; put as follows,
demonstrative: 'For one good thing cannot be made up of two bad
things.' The whole line of argument is fallacious. Again, there is
Polycrates' saying that Thrasybulus put down thirty tyrants, where
the speaker adds them up one by one. Or the argument in the *Orestes*
of Theodectes, where the argument is from part to whole: 35

> 'Tis right that she who slays her lord should die.

'It is right, too, that the son should avenge his father. Very good:
these two things are what Orestes has done.' Still, perhaps the two 1401ᵇ
things, once they are put together, do not form a right act. The
fallacy might also be said to be due to omission, since the speaker
fails to say by whose hand a husband-slayer should die.

[88] viz. a dog-philosopher, a Cynic.
[89] The same Greek word *logos* is here used for 'speech' and 'esteem': hence
what follows.

3. Another line is the use of indignant language, whether to support your own case or to overthrow your opponent's. We do this when we paint a highly-coloured picture of the situation without having proved the facts of it: if the defendant does so, he produces an impression of his innocence; and if the prosecutor goes into a passion, he produces an impression of the defendant's guilt. Here there is no genuine Enthymeme: the hearer infers guilt or innocence, but no proof is given, and the inference is fallacious accordingly.

4. Another line is to use a 'Sign', or single instance, as certain evidence; which, again, yields no valid proof. Thus, it might be said that lovers are useful to their countries, since the love of Harmodius and Aristogeiton caused the downfall of the tyrant Hipparchus.[90] Or, again, that Dionysius is a thief, since he is a vicious man—there is, of course, no valid proof here; not every vicious man is a thief, though every thief is a vicious man.

5. Another line represents the accidental as essential. An instance is what Polycrates says of the mice, that they 'came to the rescue' because they gnawed through the bowstrings. Or it might be maintained that an invitation to dinner is a great honour, for it was because he was *not* invited that Achilles was 'angered' with the Greeks at Tenedos. As a fact, what angered him was the *insult* involved; it was a mere accident that this was the particular form that the insult took.

6. Another is the argument from consequence. In the *Alexander*, for instance, it is argued that Paris must have had a lofty disposition, since he despised society and lived by himself on Mount Ida: because lofty people do this kind of thing, therefore Paris too, we are to suppose, had a lofty soul. Or, if a man dresses fashionably and roams around at night, he is a rake, since that is the way rakes behave. Another similar argument points out that beggars sing and dance in temples, and that exiles can live wherever they please, and that such privileges are at the disposal of those we account happy; and therefore every one might be regarded as happy if only he has those privileges. What matters, however, is the *circumstances* under which the privileges are enjoyed. Hence this line too falls under the head of fallacies by omission.

7. Another line consists in representing as causes things which are not causes, on the ground that they happened along with or before the event in question. They assume that, because B happens *after* A, it happens *because* of A. Politicians are especially fond of taking this

[90] Cp. Plato, *Symposium*, 182 b, c.

line. Thus Demades said that the policy of Demosthenes was the cause of all the mischief, 'for after it the war occurred'.

8. Another line consists in leaving out any mention of time and circumstances. E. g. the argument that Paris was justified in taking 35 Helen, since her father left her free to choose: here the freedom was presumably not perpetual; it could only refer to her first choice, beyond which her father's authority could not go. Or again, one might 1402ʳ say that to strike a free man is an act of wanton outrage; but it is not so in every case—only when it is unprovoked.

9. Again, a spurious syllogism may, as in 'eristical' discussions, be based on the confusion of the absolute with that which is not absolute but particular. As, in dialectic, for instance, it may be argued that 5 what-is-not *is,* on the ground that what-is-not *is* what-is-not; or that the unknown can be known, on the ground that it can be known to *be* unknown: so also in rhetoric a spurious Enthymeme may be based on the confusion of some particular probability with absolute probability. Now no particular probability is universally probable: as Agathon says,

> One might perchance say this was probable—   10
> That things improbable oft will hap to men.

For what is improbable does happen, and therefore it is probable that improbable things *will* happen. Granted this, one might argue that 'what is improbable is probable'. But this is not true absolutely. As, in eristic, the imposture comes from not adding any clause specifying 15 relationship or reference or manner; so here it arises because the probability in question is not general but specific. It is of this line of argument that Corax's *Art of Rhetoric* is composed. If the accused is not open to the charge—for instance if a weakling be tried for violent assault—the defence is that he was not likely to do such a thing. But if he *is* open to the charge—i. e. if he is a *strong* man—the defence is still that he was not likely to do such a thing, since he could 20 be sure that people would think he *was* likely to do it. And so with any other charge: the accused must be either open or not open to it: there is in either case an appearance of probable innocence, but whereas in the latter case the probability is genuine, in the former it can only be asserted in the special sense mentioned. This sort of argument illustrates what is meant by making the worse argument seem the better. Hence people were right in objecting to the training Protagoras undertook to give them.[91] It was a fraud; the probability 25 it handled was not genuine but spurious, and has a place in no art except Rhetoric and Eristic.

[91] Cp. Plato, *Protag.,* 319 ᴀ.

25   Enthymemes, genuine and apparent, have now been described;
30 the next subject is their Refutation.

An argument may be refuted either by a counter-syllogism or by
bringing an objection. It is clear that counter-syllogisms can be built
up from the same lines of arguments as the original syllogisms: for
the materials of syllogisms are the ordinary opinions of men, and
such opinions often contradict each other. Objections, as appears in
35 the *Topics*,[92] may be raised in four ways—either by directly attacking
your opponent's own statement, or by putting forward another statement like it, or by putting forward a statement contrary to it, or by
quoting previous decisions.

1. By 'attacking your opponent's own statement' I mean, for instance, this: if his Enthymeme should assert that love is always good,
1402ᵇ the objection can be brought in two ways, either by making the general statement that 'all want is an evil', or by making the particular
one that there would be no talk of 'Caunian love'[93] if there were not
evil loves as well as good ones.

2. An objection 'from a contrary statement' is raised when, for
instance, the opponent's Enthymeme having concluded that a good
5 man does good to all his friends, you object, 'That proves nothing,
for a bad man does not do evil to all his friends'.

3. An example of an objection 'from a like statement' is, the
Enthymeme having shown that ill-used men always hate their ill-users,
to reply, 'That proves nothing, for well-used men do not always love
those who used them well'.

4. The 'decisions' mentioned are those proceeding from well-
known men; for instance, if the Enthymeme employed has concluded
10 that 'Some allowance ought to be made for drunken offenders, since
they did not know what they were doing', the objection will be, 'Pittacus, then, deserves no approval, or he would not have prescribed
specially severe penalties for offences due to drunkenness'.

Enthymemes are based upon one or other of four kinds of alleged
fact: (1) Probabilities, (2) Examples, (3) Infallible Signs, (4) Ordi-
15 nary Signs.[94] (1) Enthymemes based upon Probabilities are those
which argue from what is, or is supposed to be, usually true. (2)
Enthymemes based upon Example are those which proceed by induction from one or more similar cases, arrive at a general proposition,
and then argue deductively to a particular inference. (3) Enthymemes

---

[92] Cp. *Topics*, viii. 10, and *Anal. Pr.*, ii. 26.
[93] The incestuous love of Byblis for her brother Caunus.
[94] Fallible signs.

based upon Infallible Signs are those which argue from the inevitable
and invariable. (4) Enthymemes based upon ordinary Signs are those 20
which argue from some universal or particular proposition, true or
false.

Now (1) as a Probability is that which happens usually but not
always, Enthymemes founded upon Probabilities can, it is clear, always be refuted by raising some objection. The refutation is not
always genuine: it may be spurious: for it consists in showing not
that your opponent's premiss is not probable, but only in showing that 25
it is not inevitably true. Hence it is always in defence rather than in
accusation that it is possible to gain an advantage by using this fallacy.
For the accuser uses probabilities to prove his case: and to refute a
conclusion as improbable is not the same thing as to refute it as not
inevitable. Any argument based upon what usually happens is always
open to objection: otherwise it would not be a probability but an invariable and necessary truth. But the judges think, if the refutation 30
takes this form, either that the accuser's case is not probable or that
they must not decide it; which, as we said, is a false piece of reasoning.
For they ought to decide by considering not merely what *must* be true
but also what is *likely* to be true: this is, indeed, the meaning of
'giving a verdict in accordance with one's honest opinion'. Therefore
it is not enough for the defendant to refute the accusation by proving
that the charge is not *bound* to be true: he must do so by showing 35
that it is not *likely* to be true. For this purpose his objection must state
what is more usually true than the statement attacked. It may do so
in either of two ways: either in respect of frequency or in respect of
exactness. It will be most convincing if it does so in both respects;
for if the thing in question *both* happens *oftener* as we represent it *and* 1403ᵃ
happens more *as* we represent it, the probability is particularly great.

(2) Fallible Signs, and Enthymemes based upon them, can be
refuted even if the facts are correct, as was said at the outset.⁹⁵ For
we have shown in the *Analytics* ⁹⁶ that no Fallible Sign can form part
of a valid logical proof.

(3) Enthymemes depending on examples may be refuted in the 5
same way as probabilities. If we have a negative instance, the argument is refuted, in so far as it is proved not inevitable, even though
the positive examples are more similar and more frequent. And if the
positive examples *are* more numerous and more frequent, we must
contend that the present case is dissimilar, or that its conditions are
dissimilar, or that it is different in some way or other.

(4) It will be impossible to refute Infallible Signs, and Enthy- 10

⁹⁵ i, c. 2, 1357ᵇ 13, 14.   ⁹⁶ *Anal. Pr.*, ii. 27.

memes resting on them, by showing in any way that they do not form a valid logical proof: this, too, we see from the *Analytics*.[97] All we can do is to show that the fact alleged does not exist. If there is no doubt 15 that it does, and that it is an Infallible Sign, refutation now becomes impossible: for this is equivalent to a demonstration which is clear in every respect.

26 Amplification and Depreciation are not an element of Enthymeme. By 'an element [98] of Enthymeme' I mean the same thing as 'a line of Enthymematic argument'—a general class embracing a large number of particular kinds of Enthymeme. Amplification and Depreciation are 20 one kind of Enthymeme, viz. the kind used to show that a thing is great or small; just as there are other kinds used to show that a thing is good or bad, just or unjust, and anything else of the sort. All these things are the *subject-matter* of syllogisms and Enthymemes; none of these is the line of argument of an Enthymeme; no more, therefore, are Amplification and Depreciation.

25 Nor are Refutative Enthymemes a different species from Constructive. For it is clear that refutation consists either in offering positive proof or in raising an objection. In the first case we prove the opposite of our adversary's statements. Thus, if he shows that a thing has happened, we show that it has not; if he shows that it has not happened, we show that it has. This, then, could not be the distinc- 30 tion if there were one, since the same means are employed by both parties, Enthymemes being adduced to show that the fact is or is not so-and-so. An objection, on the other hand, is not an Enthymeme at all, but, as was said in the *Topics*,[99] it consists in stating some accepted opinion from which it will be clear that our opponent has not reasoned correctly or has made a false assumption.

Three points must be studied in making a speech; and we have 35 now completed the acccount of (1) Examples, Maxims, Enthymemes, and in general the *thought*-element—the way to invent and refute 1403ᵇ arguments. We have next to discuss (2) Style, and (3) Arrangement.

BOOK III

1 In making a speech one must study three points: first, the means of producing persuasion; second, the style, or language, to be used; third, the proper arrangement of the various parts of the speech'. We

---

[97] *Anal. Pr.*, ii. 27.
[98] i. e. an elementary class a primary type: cp. 1396ᵇ 21.
[99] Cp. *Top.*, viii. 10.

have already specified the sources of persuasion. We have shown that these are three in number;[1] what they are; and why there are only these three: for we have shown that persuasion must in every case be effected either (1) by working on the emotions of the judges themselves, (2) by giving them the right impression of the speakers' character, or (3) by proving the truth of the statements made.

Enthymemes also have been described, and the sources from which they should be derived; there being both special and general lines of argument for enthymemes.[2]

Our next subject will be the style of expression. For it is not enough to know *what* we ought to say; we must also say it *as* we ought; much help is thus afforded towards producing the right impression of a speech. The first question to receive attention was naturally the one that comes first naturally—how persuasion can be produced from the facts themselves. The second is how to set these facts out in language. A third would be the proper method of delivery; this is a thing that affects the success of a speech greatly; but hitherto the subject has been neglected. Indeed, it was long before it found a way into the arts of tragic drama and epic recitation: at first poets acted their tragedies themselves. It is plain that delivery has just as much to do with oratory as with poetry. (In connexion with poetry, it has been studied by Glaucon of Teos among others.) It is, essentially, a matter of the right management of the voice to express the various emotions —of speaking loudly, softly, or between the two; of high, low, or intermediate pitch; of the various rhythms that suit various subjects. These are the three things—volume of sound, modulation of pitch, and rhythm—that a speaker bears in mind. It is those who *do* bear them in mind who usually win prizes in the dramatic contests; and just as in drama the actors now count for more than the poets, so it is in the contests of public life, owing to the defects of our political institutions. No systematic treatise upon the rules of delivery has yet been composed; indeed, even the study of language made no progress till late in the day. Besides, delivery is—very properly—not regarded as an elevated subject of inquiry. Still, the whole business of rhetoric being concerned with appearances, we must pay attention to the subject of delivery, unworthy though it is, because we cannot do without it. The right thing in speaking really is that we should be satisfied not to annoy our hearers, without trying to delight them: we ought in fairness to fight our case with no help beyond the bare facts: nothing, therefore, should matter except the proof of those facts. Still, as has been already said, other things affect the result considerably, owing to the defects of our hearers. The arts of language cannot help having a small but real importance, whatever it is we have to expound to others: 10 the way in which a thing is said does affect its intelligibility. Not, however, so much importance as people think. All such arts are fanciful and meant to charm the hearer. Nobody uses fine language when teaching geometry.

When the principles of delivery have been worked out, they will produce the same effect as on the stage. But only very slight attempts to deal with them have been made and by a few people, as by Thrasy- 15 machus in his 'Appeals to Pity'. Dramatic ability is a natural gift, and can hardly be systematically taught. The principles of good diction can be so taught, and therefore we have men of ability in this direction too, who win prizes in their turn, as well as those speakers who excel in delivery—speeches of the written or literary kind owe more of their effect to their diction than to their thought.

20 It was naturally the poets who first set the movement going; for words represent things, and they had also the human voice at their disposal, which of all our organs can best represent other things. Thus the arts of recitation and acting were formed, and others as well. Now it was because poets seemed to win fame through their fine language when their thoughts were simple enough, that the language of 25 oratorical prose at first took a poetical colour, e g. that of Gorgias. Even now most uneducated people think that poetical language makes the finest discourses. That is not true: the language of prose is distinct from that of poetry. This is shown by the state of things to-day, when 30 even the language of tragedy has altered its character. Just as iambics were adopted, instead of tetrameters, because they are the most prose-like of all metres, so tragedy has given up all those words, not used in ordinary talk, which decorated the early drama and are still used by the writers of hexameter poems. It is therefore ridiculous to imitate a 35 poetical manner which the poets themselves have dropped; and it is now plain that we have not to treat in detail the whole question of style, but may confine ourselves to that part of it which concerns our present subject, rhetoric. The other—the poetical—part of it has been discussed in the treatise on the *Art of Poetry*.[3]

[Chapter 2-12 omitted.]

1414ᵃ **13** A speech has two parts. You must state your case, and you must prove it. You cannot either state your case and omit to prove it, or prove it without having first stated it; since any proof must be a proof of something, and the only use of a preliminary statement is

---

[3] *Poetics*, cc. 20-2.

the proof that follows it. Of these two parts the first part is [4] called the Statement of the case, the second part the Argument, just as we distinguish [5] between Enunciation and Demonstration. The current 35 division is absurd. For 'narration' surely is part of a forensic speech only: how in a political speech or a speech of display can there be 'narration' in the technical sense? or a reply to a forensic opponent? 1414[b] or an epilogue in closely-reasoned speeches? Again, introduction, comparison of conflicting arguments, and recapitulation are only found in political speeches when there is a struggle between two policies. They *may* occur then; so may even accusation and defence, often enough; but they form no essential part of a political speech. Even forensic speeches do not always need epilogues; not, for instance, a short 5 speech, nor one in which the facts are easy to remember, the effect of an epilogue being always a reduction in the apparent length.[6] It follows, then, that the only necessary parts of a speech are the Statement and the Argument. These are the essential features of a speech; and it cannot in any case have more than Introduction, Statement, Argument, and Epilogue. 'Refutation of the Opponent' is part of the arguments: so is 'Comparison' of the opponent's case with your own, for that process is a magnifying of your own case and therefore a part of 10 the arguments, since one who does this *proves* something. The Introduction does nothing like this; nor does the Epilogue—it merely reminds us of what has been said already. If we make such distinctions we shall end, like Theodorus and his followers, by distinguishing 'narration' proper from 'post-narration' and 'pre-narration', and 'refutation' from 'final refutation'. But we ought only to bring in a new 15 name if it indicates a real species with distinct specific qualities; otherwise the practice is pointless and silly, like the way Licymnius invented names in his *Art of Rhetoric*—'Secundation', 'Divagation', 'Ramification'.

14   The Introduction is the beginning of a speech, corresponding to the prologue in poetry and the prelude in flute-music; they are all 20 beginnings, paving the way, as it were, for what is to follow. The musical prelude resembles the introduction to speeches of display; as flute-players play first some brilliant passage they know well and then fit it on to the opening notes of the piece itself, so in speeches of display the writer should proceed in the same way; he should begin with what best takes his fancy, and then strike up his theme and lead into it;[25]

---

[4] *sc.* in rhetoric.   [5] *sc.* in dialectic.
[6] A good effect where a speech may seem too long; bad, where it may seem too short already.

which is indeed what *is* always done. (Take as an example the introduction to the *Helen* [7] of Isocrates—there is nothing in common between the 'eristics' [8] and Helen.) And here, even if you travel far from your subject, it is fitting, rather than that there should be sameness in the entire speech.

30   The usual subject for the introductions to speeches of display is some piece of praise or censure. Thus Gorgias writes in his *Olympic Speech*, 'You deserve widespread admiration, men of Greece', praising thus those who started the festival gatherings. Isocrates, on the other hand, censures them for awarding distinctions to fine athletes but giving no prize for intellectual ability.[9] Or one may begin with a

35 piece of advice, thus: 'We ought to honour good men and so I myself am praising Aristeides' or 'We ought to honour those who are unpopular but not bad men, men whose good qualities have never been

1415ᵃ noticed, like Alexander son of Priam.' Here the orator gives *advice*. Or we may begin as speakers do in the law-courts; that is to say, with appeals to the audience to excuse us if our speech is about something paradoxical, difficult, or hackneyed; like Choerilus in the lines—

> But now when allotment of all has been made . . .

5   Introductions to speeches of display, then, may be composed of some piece of praise or censure, of advice to do or not to do something, or of appeals to the audience; and you must choose between making these preliminary passages connected or disconnected with the speech itself.

    Introductions to forensic speeches, it must be observed, have the same value as the prologues of dramas and the introductions to epic

10 poems; the dithyrambic prelude resembling the introduction to a speech of display, as

> For thee, and thy gifts, and thy battle-spoils . . .

    In prologues, and in epic poetry, a foretaste of the theme is given, intended to inform the hearers of it in advance instead of keeping their minds in suspense. Anything vague puzzles them: so give them a grasp

15 of the beginning, and they can hold fast to it and follow the argument. So we find—

> Sing, O goddess of song, of the Wrath . . . [10]

> Tell me, O Muse, of the hero . . . [11]

---

[7] Isocrates, *Helena*, 1–13.

[8] i. e. the disputatious dialecticians to whom Isocrates refers in the introduction to his *Helena*, 3, 4: Protagoras, Gorgias, &c.

[9] Isocrates, *Paneg.* 1, 2.   [10] *Iliad*, i. 1.   [11] *Odyssey*, i. 1.

Lead me to tell a new tale, how there came great warfare to Europe
Out of the Asian land . . . [12]

The tragic poets, too, let us know the pivot of their play; if not at
the outset like Euripides, at least somewhere in the preface to a speech 20
like Sophocles—

Polybus was my father . . . ; [13]

and so in Comedy. This, then, is the most essential function and
distinctive property of the introduction, to show what the aim of the
speech is; and therefore no introduction ought to be employed where
the subject is not long or intricate.

The other kinds of introduction employed are remedial in purpose, 25
and may be used in any type of speech. They are concerned with the
speaker, the hearer, the subject, or the speaker's opponent. Those concerned with the speaker himself or with his opponent are directed to
removing or exciting prejudice. But whereas the defendant will begin
by dealing with this sort of thing, the prosecutor will take quite another line and deal with such matters in the closing part of his speech.
The reason for this is not far to seek. The defendant, when he is going 30
to bring himself on the stage, must clear away any obstacles, and
therefore must begin by removing any prejudice felt against him. But
if you are to *excite* prejudice, you must do so at the close, so that the
judges may more easily remember what you have said.

The appeal to the hearer aims at securing his goodwill, or at arousing his resentment, or sometimes at gaining his serious attention to the 35
case, or even at distracting it—for gaining it is not always an advantage, and speakers will often for that reason try to make him laugh.
You may use any means you choose to make your hearer receptive;
among others, giving him a good impression of your character, which
always helps to secure his attention. He will be ready to attend to any- 1415ᵇ
thing that touches himself, and to anything that is important, surprising, or agreeable; and you should accordingly convey to him the
impression that what you have to say is of this nature. If you wish to
distract his attention, you should imply that the subject does not affect
him, or is trivial or disagreeable. But observe, all this has nothing to 5
do with the speech itself. It merely has to do with the weak-minded
tendency of the hearer to listen to what is beside the point. Where this
tendency is absent, no introduction is wanted beyond a summary
statement of your subject, to put a sort of head on the main body of
your speech. Moreover, calls for attention, when required, may come

---

[12] Choerilus?   [13] Sophocles, *Oedipus Tyrannus*, 774.

10 equally well in any part of a speech; in fact, the beginning of it is just where there is least slackness of interest; it is therefore ridiculous to put this kind of thing at the beginning, when every one is listening with most attention. Choose therefore any point in the speech where such an appeal is needed, and then say 'Now I beg you to note this point—it concerns you quite as much as myself'; or

> I will tell you that whose like you have never yet

heard for terror, or for wonder. This is what Prodicus called 'slipping
15 in a bit of the fifty-drachma show-lecture for the audience whenever they began to nod'. It is plain that such introductions are addressed not to ideal hearers, but to hearers as we find them. The use of introductions to excite prejudice or to dispel misgivings is universal—

> My lord, I will not say that eagerly . . . [14]

20 or

> ### Why all this preface? [15]

Introductions are popular with those whose case is weak, or looks weak; it pays them to dwell on anything rather than the actual facts of it. That is why slaves, instead of answering the questions put to them, make indirect replies with long preambles. The means of excit-
25 ing in your hearers goodwill and various other feelings of the same kind have already been described.[16] The poet finely says

> May I find in Phaeacian hearts, at my coming, goodwill and compassion; [17]

and these are the two things we should aim at. In speeches of display we must make the hearer feel that the eulogy includes either himself or his family or his way of life or something or other of the kind. For it
30 is true, as Socrates says in the *Funeral Speech*,[18] that 'the difficulty is not to praise the Athenians at Athens but at Sparta'.

The introductions of political oratory will be made out of the same materials as those of the forensic kind, though the nature of political oratory makes them very rare. The subject is known already, and therefore the *facts* of the case need no introduction; but you may have to say something on account of yourself or your opponents; or those
35 present may be inclined to treat the matter either more or less seriously than you wish them to. You may accordingly have to excite or dispel some prejudice, or to make the matter under discussion seem

---

[14] Sophocles, *Antigone*, 223. [15] Cp. Euripides, *Iph. Taur.*, 1162.
[16] ii, cc. i ff. [17] *Odyssey*, vi. 327. [18] Cp. Plato, *Menexenus*, 235 D.

more or less important than before: for either of which purposes you will want an introduction. You may also want one to add elegance to your remarks, feeling that otherwise they will have a casual air, like Gorgias' eulogy of the Eleans, in which, without any preliminary spar- 1416ᵃ ring or fencing, he begins straight off with 'Happy city of Elis!'

15 In dealing with prejudice, one class of argument is that whereby you can dispel objectionable suppositions about yourself. It makes no practical difference whether such a supposition has been put into words 5 or not, so that this distinction may be ignored. Another way is to meet any of the issues directly: to deny the alleged fact; or to say that you have done no harm, or none to *him,* or not as much as he says; or that you have done him no injustice, or not much; or that you have done nothing disgraceful, or nothing disgraceful enough to matter: these are the sort of questions on which the dispute hinges. Thus Iphicrates, replying to Nausicrates, admitted that he had done the 10 deed alleged, and that he had done Nausicrates harm, but not that he had done him wrong. Or you may admit the wrong, but balance it with other facts, and say that, if the deed harmed him, at any rate it was honourable; or that, if it gave him pain, at least it did him good; or something else like that. Another way is to allege that your action was due to mistake, or bad luck, or necessity—as Sophocles said he was not trembling, as his traducer maintained, in order to make peo- 15 ple think him an old man, but because he could not help it; he would rather *not* be eighty years old.[19] You may balance your motive against your actual deed; saying, for instance, that you did not mean to injure him but to do so-and-so; that you did not do what you are falsely charged with doing—the damage was accidental—'I should indeed be a detestable person if I had deliberately intended this result.' Another way is open when your calumniator, or any of his connexions, 20 is or has been subject to the same grounds for suspicion. Yet another, when others are subject to the same grounds for suspicion but are admitted to be in fact innocent of the charge: e. g. 'Must I be a profligate because I am well-groomed? Then so-and-so must be one too.' Another, if other people have been calumniated by the same man or some one else, or, without being calumniated, have been suspected, 25 like yourself now, and yet have been proved innocent. Another way is to return calumny for calumny and say, 'It is monstrous to trust the man's statements when you cannot trust the man himself.' Another is when the question has been already decided. So with Euripides'

[19] *sc.* but he *was.*

reply to Hygiaenon, who, in the action for an exchange of properties,
30 accused him of impiety in having written a line encouraging perjury—

My tongue hath sworn: no oath is on my soul.[20]

Euripides said that his opponent himself was guilty in bringing into
the law-courts cases whose decision belonged to the Dionysiac contests. 'If I have not already answered for my words there, I am ready
to do so if you choose to prosecute me there.' Another method is to
denounce calumny, showing what an enormity it is, and in particular
35 that it raises false issues, and that it means a lack of confidence in
the merits of his case. The argument from evidential circumstances
1416ᵇ is available for both parties: thus in the *Teucer* Odysseus says that
Teucer is closely bound to Priam, since his mother Hesione was
Priam's sister. Teucer [21] replies that Telamon his father was Priam's
enemy, and that he himself did not betray the spies to Priam. Another
method, suitable for the caluminator, is to praise some trifling merit at
5 great length, and then attack some important' failing concisely; or
after mentioning a number of good qualities to attack one bad one
that really bears on the question. This is the method of thoroughly
skilful and unscrupulous prosecutors. By mixing up the man's merits
with what is bad, they do their best to make use of them to damage
him.

There is another method open to both calumniator and apologist.
Since a given action can be done from many motives, the former must
10 try to disparage it by selecting the worse motive of the two, the latter
to put the better construction on it. Thus one might argue that
Diomedes chose Odysseus as his companion [22] because he supposed
Odysseus to be the best man for the purpose; and you might reply
to this that it was, on the contrary, because he was the only hero so
worthless that Diomedes need not fear his rivalry.

16 We may now pass from the subject of calumny to that of Narra-
15 tion.

Narration in ceremonial oratory is not continuous but intermittent.
There must, of course, be some survey of the actions that form the
subject-matter of the speech. The speech is a composition containing
two parts. One of these is not provided by the orator's art, viz. the
actions themselves, of which the orator is in no sense author. The
20 other part is provided by his art, namely, the proof (where proof
is needed) that the actions were done, the description of their quality
or their extent, or even all these three things together. Now the reason

[20] Euripides, *Hippolytus*, 612.   [21] Sophocles.   [22] Cp. *Iliad*, x. 242–7.

why sometimes it is not desirable to make the whole narrative continuous is that the case thus expounded is hard to keep in mind. Show, therefore, from one set of facts that your hero is, e. g. brave, and from other sets of fact that he is able, just, &c. A speech thus arranged is comparatively simple, instead of being complicated and elaborate. You will have to recall well-known deeds among others; and because 25 they are well-known, the hearer usually needs no narration of them; none, for instance, if your object is the praise of Achilles; we all know the facts of his life—what you have to do is to apply those facts. But if your object is the praise of Critias, you *must* narrate his deeds, which not many people know of . . .

Nowadays it is said, absurdly enough, that the narration should be rapid. Remember what the man said to the baker who asked 30 whether he was to make the cake hard or soft: 'What, can't you make it *right*?' Just so here. We are not to make long narrations, just as we are not to make long introductions or long arguments. Here, again, rightness does not consist either in rapidity or in conciseness, but in 35 the happy mean; that is, in saying just so much as will make the facts plain, or will lead the hearer to believe that the thing has happened, 1417ᵃ or that the man has caused injury or wrong to some one, or that the facts are really as important as you wish them to be thought: or the opposite facts to establish the opposite arguments.

You may also narrate as you go anything that does credit to yourself, e. g. 'I kept telling him to do his duty and not abandon his children'; or discredit to your adversary, e. g. 'But he answered me that, wherever he might find himself, there he would find other children', 5 the answer Herodotus [23] records of the Egyptian mutineers. Slip in anything else that the judges will enjoy.

The defendant will make less of the narration. He has to maintain that the thing has not happened, or did no harm, or was not unjust, or not so bad as is alleged. He must therefore not waste time about 10 what is admitted fact, unless this bears on his own contention; e. g. that the thing was done, but was not wrong. Further, we must speak of events as past and gone, except where they excite pity or indignation by being represented as present. The Story told to Alcinous [24] is an example of a brief chronicle, when it is repeated to Penelope in sixty lines.[25] Another instance is the Epic Cycle as treated by Phayl- 15 lus, and the prologue to the *Oeneus*.[26]

The narration should depict character; to which end you must know what makes it do so. One such thing is the indication of moral

[23] Cp. Herodotus, ii. 30.   [24] *Odyssey*, ix–xii.
[25] *Odyssey*, xxiii. 264–84 and 310–43.   [26] Euripides.

purpose; the quality of purpose indicated determines the quality of
character depicted and is itself determined by the end pursued. Thus
it is that mathematical discourses depict no character; they have
nothing to do with moral purpose, for they represent nobody as pur-
20 suing any end. On the other hand, the Socratic dialogues do depict
character, being concerned with moral questions. This end will also
be gained by describing the manifestations of various types of character, e. g. 'he kept walking along as he talked', which shows the man's
recklessness and rough manners. Do not let your words seem inspired so much by intelligence, in the manner now current, as by
moral purpose: e. g. 'I willed this; aye, it was my moral purpose;
25 true, I gained nothing by it, still it is better thus.' For the other way
shows good sense, but this shows good character; good sense making
us go after what is useful, and good character after what is noble.
Where any detail may appear incredible, then add the cause of it;
of this Sophocles provides an example in the *Antigone*, where Antigone says she had cared more for her brother than for husband or
30 children, since if the latter perished they might be replaced,

> But since my father and mother in their graves
> Lie dead, no brother can be born to me.[27]

If you have no such cause to suggest, just say that you are aware
that no one will believe your words, but the fact remains that such is
35 your nature, however hard the world may find it to believe that a
man deliberately does anything except what pays him.

Again, you must make use of the emotions. Relate the familiar
manifestations of them, and those that distinguish yourself and your
opponent; for instance, 'he went away scowling at me'. So Aeschines
1417ᵇ described Cratylus as 'hissing with fury and shaking his fists'. These
details carry conviction: the audience take the truth of what they
know as so much evidence for the truth of what they do not. Plenty
of such details may be found in Homer:

5 Thus did she say: but the old woman buried her face in her hands: [28]

a true touch—people beginning to cry do put their hands over their
eyes.

Bring yourself on the stage from the first in the right character,
that people may regard you in that light; and the same with your
adversary; but do not let them see what you are about. How easily
such impressions may be conveyed we can see from the way in which
10 we get some inkling of things we know nothing of by the mere look

27 Sophocles, *Antigone*, 911, 912.   28 *Odyssey*, xix. 361.

of the messenger bringing news of them. Have some narrative in many different parts of your speech; and sometimes let there be none at the beginning of it.

In political oratory there is very little opening for narration; nobody can 'narrate' what has not yet happened. If there is narration at all, it will be of past events, the recollection of which is to help the hearers to make better plans for the future. Or it may be employed 15 to attack some one's character, or to eulogize him—only then you will not be doing what the political speaker, as such, has to do.

If any statement you make is hard to believe, you must guarantee its truth, and at once offer an explanation, and then furnish it with such particulars as will be expected. Thus Carcinus' Jocasta, in his *Oedipus,* keeps guaranteeing the truth of her answers to the inquiries of the man who is seeking her son; and so with Haemon in Sophocles.[29] 20

17 The duty of the Arguments is to attempt demonstrative proofs. These proofs must bear directly upon the question in dispute, which must fall under one of four heads. (1) If you maintain that the act *was not committed,* your main task in court is to prove this. (2) If you 25 maintain that the act *did no harm,* prove this. If you maintain that (3) the act was *less* than is alleged, or (4) *justified,* prove these facts, just as you would prove the act not to have been committed if you were maintaining that.

It should be noted that only where the question in dispute falls under the first of these heads can it be true that one of the two parties is necessarily a rogue. Here ignorance cannot be pleaded, as it might if the dispute were whether the act was justified or not. This argument must therefore be used in this case only, not in the others.   30

In ceremonial speeches you will develop your case mainly by arguing that what has been done is, e. g., noble and useful. The facts themselves are to be taken on trust; proof of them is only submitted on those rare occasions when they are not easily credible or when they have been set down to some one else.

In political speeches you may maintain that a proposal is impracti- 35 cable; or that, though practicable, it is unjust, or will do no good, or is not so important as its proposer thinks. Note any falsehoods about irrelevant matters—they will look like proof that his other statements also are false. Argument by 'example' is highly suitable for political ora- 1418ᵃ tory, argument by 'Enthymeme' better suits forensic. Political oratory deals with future events, of which it can do no more than quote past

[29] Cp. Sophocles, *Antigone,* 635–8, 701–4.

events as examples. Forensic oratory deals with what is or is not *now*
true, which can better be demonstrated, because not contingent—there
is no contingency in what has now already happened. Do not use a con-
5 tinuous succession of Enthymemes: intersperse them with other matter, or they will spoil one another's effect. There are limits to their
number—

> Friend, you have spoken *as much* as a sensible man would have
> spoken.[30]—

'as *much*' says Homer, not 'as *well*'. Nor should you try to make
10 Enthymemes on every point; if you do, you will be acting just like
some students of philosophy, whose conclusions are more familiar and
believable than the premises from which they draw them. And avoid
the Enthymeme form when you are trying to rouse feeling; for it will
either kill the feeling or will itself fall flat: all simultaneous motions
tend to cancel each other either completely or partially. Nor should
15 you go after the Enthymeme form in a passage where you are depict-
ing character—the process of demonstration can express neither moral
character nor moral purpose. Maxims should be employed in the Arguments—and in the Narration too—since these do express character:
'I have given him this, though I am quite aware that one should "Trust
no man".' Or if you are appealing to the emotions: 'I do not regret it,
20 though I have been wronged; if he has the profit on his side, I have
justice on mine.'

Political oratory is a more difficult task than forensic; and naturally
so, since it deals with the future, whereas the pleader deals with the
past, which, as Epimenides of Crete said, even the diviners already
know. (Epimenides did not practise divination about the future; only
25 about the obscurities of the past.) Besides, in forensic oratory you have
a basis in the law; and once you have a starting-point, you can prove
anything with comparative ease. Then again, political oratory affords
few chances for those leisurely digressions in which you may attack
your adversary, talk about yourself, or work on your hearers' emotions; fewer chances, indeed, than any other affords, unless your set
purpose is to divert your hearers' attention. Accordingly, if you find
30 yourself in difficulties, follow the lead of the Athenian speakers, and
that of Isocrates, who makes regular attacks upon people in the course
of a political speech, e. g. upon the Lacedaemonians in the *Pane-
gyricus*,[31] and upon Chares in the speech about the allies.[32] In cere-

---

[30] *Odyssey*, iv. 204.   [31] Isocrates, *Paneg.*, 110–14.
[32] Cp. Isocrates, *De Pace*, 27.

monial oratory, intersperse your speech with bits of episodic eulogy, like Isocrates, who is always bringing some one forward for this purpose.[33] And this is what Gorgias meant by saying that he always found something to talk about. For if he speaks of Achilles, he praises 35 Peleus, then Aeacus, then Zeus; and in like manner the virtue of valour, describing its good results, and saying what it is like.

Now if you have proofs to bring forward, bring them forward, and your moral discourse as well; if you have no Enthymemes, then fall back upon moral discourse: after all, it is more fitting for a good 1418[b] man to display himself as an honest fellow than as a subtle reasoner. Refutative Enthymemes are more popular than demonstrative ones: their logical cogency is more striking: the facts about two opposites always stand out clearly when the two are put side by side.

The 'Reply to the Opponent' is not a separate division of the 5 speech; it is part of the Arguments to break down the opponent's case, whether by objection or by counter-syllogism. Both in political speaking and when pleading in court, if you are the first speaker you should put your own arguments forward first, and then meet the arguments on the other side by refuting them and pulling them to pieces beforehand. If, however, the case for the other side contains a great variety of arguments, begin with these, like Callistratus in the Messenian assembly, when he demolished the arguments likely to be used 10 against him before giving his own. If you speak later, you must first, by means of refutation and counter-syllogism, attempt some answer to your opponent's speech, especially if his arguments have been well received. For just as our minds refuse a favourable reception to a *person* against whom they are prejudiced, so they refuse it to a speech when they have been favourably impressed by the speech on 15 the other side. You should, therefore, make room in the minds of the audience for your coming speech; and this will be done by getting your opponent's speech out of the way. So attack that first—either the whole of it, or the most important, successful, or vulnerable points in it, and thus inspire confidence in what you have to say your- 20 self—

> First, champion will I be of Goddesses . . .
> Never, I ween, would Hera . . . : [34]

where the speaker has attacked the silliest argument first. So much for the Arguments.

[33] Isocrates has episodic passages on Theseus (*Helena* 23–38), on Paris (*Helena* 41–8), on Pythagoras and the Egyptian priests (*Busiris* 21–9), on the poets (*Busiris* 38–40), and on Agamemnon (*Panathenaicus*, 72–84).
[34] Euripides, *Troades*, 969 and 971.

With regard to the element of moral character: there are assertions
25 which, if made about yourself, may excite dislike, appear tedious, or
expose you to the risk of contradiction; and other things which you
cannot say about your opponent without seeming abusive or ill-
bred. Put such remarks, therefore, into the mouth of some third person. This is what Isocrates does in the *Philippus* [35] and in the *Antidosis*,[36] and Archilochus in his satires. The latter represents the
father himself as attacking his daughter in the lampoon

> Think nought impossible at all,
> Nor swear that it shall not befall . . .

30 and puts into the mouth of Charon the carpenter the lampoon which
begins

> Not for the wealth of Gyges. . . .

So too Sophocles makes Haemon appeal to his father on behalf of
Antigone as if it were others who were speaking.[37]

Again, sometimes you should restate your Enthymemes in the form
35 of maxims; e. g. 'Wise men will come to terms in the hour of success;
for they will gain most if they do'.[38] Expressed as an Enthymeme, this
would run, '*If* we ought to come to terms when doing so will enable
us to gain the greatest advantage, *then* we ought to come to terms
in the hour of success.'

18   Next as to Interrogation. The best moment to employ this is
1419[a] when your opponent has so answered one question that the putting of
just one more lands him in absurdity. Thus Pericles questioned
Lampon about the way of celebrating the rites of the Saviour Goddess.[39] Lampon declared that no uninitiated person could be told of
them. Pericles then asked, 'Do you know them yourself?' 'Yes',
answered Lampon. 'Why,' said Pericles, 'how can that be, when you
5 are uninitiated?'

Another good moment is when one premiss of an argument is
obviously true, and you can see that your opponent must say 'yes'
if you ask him whether the other is true. Having first got this answer
about the other, do not go on to ask him about the obviously true
one, but just state the conclusion yourself. Thus, when Meletus
denied that Socrates believed in the existence of gods but admitted
10 that he talked about a supernatural power, Socrates proceeded to

---

[35] Isocrates, *Philippus*, 4–7.
[37] Sophocles, *Antigone*, 688–700.
[39] *sc.* Demeter.

[36] Ib., *Antidosis*, 132–9, 141–9.
[38] Cp. Isocrates, *Archidamus*, 50.

ask whether 'supernatural beings were not either children of the gods or in some way divine?' 'Yes', said Meletus. 'Then', replied Socrates, 'is there any one who believes in the existence of children of the gods and yet not in the existence of the gods themselves?' [40] Another good occasion is when you expect to show that your opponent is contradicting either his own words or what every one believes. A fourth is when it is impossible for him to meet your question except by an evasive answer. If he answers 'True, and yet not true', or 'Partly true and partly not true', or 'True in one sense but not in another', the audience thinks he is in difficulties, and applauds his discomfiture. In other cases do not attempt interrogation; for if your opponent gets in an objection, you are felt to have been worsted. You cannot ask a series of questions owing to the incapacity of the audience to follow them; and for this reason you should also make your enthymemes as compact as possible.

In replying, you must meet ambiguous questions by drawing reasonable distinctions, not by a curt answer. In meeting questions that seem to involve you in a contradiction, offer the explanation at the outset of your answer, before your opponent asks the next question or draws his conclusion. For it is not difficult to see the drift of his argument in advance. This point, however, as well as the various means of refutation, may be regarded as known to us from the *Topics*.[41]

When your opponent in drawing his conclusions puts it in the form of a question, you must justify your answer. Thus when Sophocles was asked by Peisander whether he had, like the other members of the Board of Safety, voted for setting up the Four Hundred, he said 'Yes.' 'Why, did you not think it wicked?'—'Yes.'—'So *you* committed this wickedness?'—'Yes', said Sophocles, 'for there was nothing better to do.' Again, the Lacedaemonian, when he was being examined on his conduct as ephor, was asked whether he thought that the other ephors had been justly put to death. 'Yes', he said. 'Well then', asked his opponent, 'did not *you* propose the same measures as they?'— 'Yes.'—'Well then, would not *you* too be justly put to death?'—'Not at all', said he; '*they* were bribed to do it, and I did it from conviction'. Hence you should not ask any further questions after drawing the conclusion, nor put the conclusion itself in the form of a further question, unless there is a large balance of truth on your side.

As to jests. These are supposed to be of some service in controversy. Gorgias said that you should kill your opponents' earnestness with jesting and their jesting with earnestness; in which he was right.

[40] Cp. Plato, *Apology*, 27 c.   [41] *Topics*, viii.

5 Jests have been classified in the *Poetics*.[42] Some are becoming to a gentleman, others are not; see that you choose such as become *you*. Irony better befits a gentleman than buffoonery; the ironical man jokes to amuse himself, the buffoon to amuse other people.

10 **19** The Epilogue has four parts. You must (1) make the audience well-disposed towards yourself and ill-disposed towards your opponent, (2) magnify or minimize the leading facts, (3) excite the required state of emotion in your hearers, and (4) refresh their memories.

(1) Having shown your own truthfulness and the untruthfulness of your opponent, the natural thing is to commend yourself, censure 15 him, and hammer in your points. You must aim at one of two objects —you must make yourself out a good man and him a bad one either in yourselves or in relation to your hearers. How this is to be managed —by what lines of argument you are to represent people as good or bad—this has been already explained.[43]

20 (2) The facts having been proved, the natural thing to do next is to magnify or minimize their importance. The facts must be admitted before you can discuss how important they are; just as the body cannot grow except from something already present. The proper lines of argument to be used for this purpose of amplification and depreciation have already been set forth.[44]

(3) Next, when the facts and their importance are clearly under- 25 stood, you must excite your hearers' emotions. These emotions are pity, indignation, anger, hatred, envy, emulation, pugnacity. The lines of argument to be used for these purposes also have been previously mentioned.[45]

(4) Finally you have to review what you have already said. Here you may properly do what some wrongly recommended doing in the introduction—repeat your points frequently so as to make them easily 30 understood. What you *should* do in your introduction is to state your subject, in order that the point to be judged may be quite plain; in the epilogue you should summarize the arguments by which your case has been proved. The first step in this reviewing process is to observe that you have done what you undertook to do. You must, then, state what you have said and why you have said it. Your method may be a comparison of your own case with that of your

---

[42] Not in the existing *Poetics*. Cp. 1372ᵃ 1.
[43] i, c. 9.   [44] ii, c. 19.   [45] ii, cc. 1–11.

opponent; and you may compare either the ways you have both 35
handled the same point or make your comparison less direct: 'My
opponent said so-and-so on this point; I said so-and-so, and this is
why I said it'. Or with modest irony, e. g. 'He certainly said so-and-so, 1420ᵃ
but I said so-and-so'. Or 'How vain he would have been if he had
proved all this instead of *that!*' Or put it in the form of a question,
'What has *not* been proved by me?' or 'What *has* my opponent
proved?' You may proceed, then, either in this way by setting point
against point, or by following the natural order of the arguments as
spoken, first giving your own, and then separately, if you wish, those 1420ᵇ
of your opponent.

For the conclusion, the disconnected style of language is appropriate, and will mark the difference between the oration and the peroration. 'I have done. You have heard me. The facts are before you. I
ask for your judgement.' ⁴⁶

⁴⁶ Cp. Lysias, *Eratosthenes,* fin.

De Poetica

Translated by Ingram Bywater

CONTENTS

(A) Preliminary discourse on tragedy, epic poetry, and comedy, as the chief forms of imitative poetry.

DE POETICA

(*Poetics*)

1 Our subject being Poetry, I propose to speak not only of the 1447ᵃ art in general but also of its species and their respective capacities; of the structure of plot required for a good poem; of the number and nature of the constituent parts of a poem; and likewise of 10 any other matters in the same line of inquiry. Let us follow the natural order and begin with the primary facts.

Epic poetry and Tragedy, as also Comedy, Dithyrambic poetry, and most flute-playing and lyre-playing, are all, viewed as a whole, 15 modes of imitation. But at the same time they differ from one another in three ways, either by a difference of kind in their means, or by differences in the objects, or in the manner of their imitations.

I. Just as colour and form are used as means ʼby some, who (whether by art or constant practice) imitate and portray many things by their aid, and the voice is used by others; so also in the 20 above-mentioned group of arts, the means with them as a whole are rhythm, language, and harmony—used, however, either singly or in certain combinations. A combination of harmony and rhythm alone is the means in flute-playing and lyre-playing, and any other arts there may be of the same description, e. g. imitative piping. Rhythm 25 alone, without harmony, is the means in the dancer's imitations; for even he, by the rhythms of his attitudes, may represent men's characters, as well as what they do and suffer. There is further an art which imitates by language alone, without harmony, in prose or in verse, and if in verse, either in some one or in a plurality of metres. 1447ᵇ This form of imitation is to this day without a name. We have no common name for a mime of Sophron or Xenarchus and a Socratic 10 Conversation; and we should still be without one even if the imitation in the two instances were in trimeters or elegiacs or some other kind of verse—though it is the way with people to tack on 'poet' to the name of a metre, and talk of elegiac-poets and epic-poets, thinking that they call them poets not by reason of the imitative nature of their 15 work, but indiscriminately by reason of the metre they write in. Even if a theory of medicine or physical philosophy be put forth in a metrical form, it is usual to describe the writer in this way; Homer

and Empedocles, however, have really nothing in common apart
from their metre; so that, if the one is to be called a poet, the other
20 should be termed a physicist rather than a poet. We should be in the
same position also, if the imitation in these instances were in all the
metres, like the *Centaur* (a rhapsody in a medley of all metres) of
Chaeremon; and Chaeremon one has to recognize as a poet. So much,
then, as to these arts. There are, lastly, certain other arts, which com-
25 bine all the means enumerated, rhythm, melody, and verse, e. g.
Dithyrambic and Nomic poetry, Tragedy and Comedy; with this
difference, however, that the three kinds of means are in some of them
all employed together, and in others brought in separately, one after
the other. These elements of difference in the above arts I term the
means of their imitation.

1448ª 2   II. The objects the imitator represents are actions, with agents
who are necessarily either good men or bad—the diversities of
human character being nearly always derivative from this primary
distinction, since the line between virtue and vice is one dividing the
whole of mankind. It follows, therefore, that the agents represented
must be either above our own level of goodness, or beneath it, or just
5 such as we are; in the same way as, with the painters, the personages
of Polygnotus are better than we are, those of Pauson worse, and
those of Dionysius just like ourselves. It is clear that each of the
above-mentioned arts will admit of these differences, and that it will
become a separate art by representing objects with this point of
difference. Even in dancing, flute-playing, and lyre-playing such
10 diversities are possible; and they are also possible in the nameless
art that uses language, prose or verse without harmony, as its means;
Homer's personages, for instance, are better than we are; Cleophon's
are on our own level; and those of Hegemon of Thasos, the first
writer of parodies, and Nicochares, the author of the *Diliad,* are be-
15 neath it. The same is true of the Dithyramb and the Nome: the personages may be presented in them with the difference exemplified in
the . . . of . . . and Argas, and in the Cyclopses of Timotheus and
Philoxenus. This difference it is that distinguishes Tragedy and
Comedy also; the one would make its personages worse, and the other
better, than the men of the present day.

3   III. A third difference in these arts is in the manner in which
20 each kind of object is represented. Given both the same means and
the same kind of object for imitation, one may either (1) speak
at one moment in narrative and at another in an assumed character,

as Homer does; or (2) one may remain the same throughout, without any such change; or (3) the imitators may represent the whole
story dramatically, as though they were actually doing the things described.

As we said at the beginning, therefore, the differences in the
imitation of these arts come under three heads, their means, their
objects, and their manner.

So that as an imitator Sophocles will be on one side akin to 25
Homer, both portraying good men; and on another to Aristophanes,
since both present their personages as acting and doing. This in
fact, according to some, is the reason for plays being termed dramas,
because in a play the personages act the story. Hence too both
Tragedy and Comedy are claimed by the Dorians as their discover- 30
ies; Comedy by the Megarians—by those in Greece as having arisen
when Megara became a democracy, and by the Sicilian Megarians
on the ground that the poet Epicharmus was of their country, and
a good deal earlier than Chionides and Magnes; even Tragedy also
is claimed by certain of the Peloponnesian Dorians. In support of
this claim they point to the words 'comedy' and 'drama'. Their word 35
for the outlying hamlets, they say, is *comae,* whereas Athenians call
them *demes*—thus assuming that comedians got the name not from
their *comoe* or revels, but from their strolling from hamlet to hamlet,
lack of appreciation keeping them out of the city. Their word also 1448^b
for 'to act', they say, is *dran,* whereas Athenians use *prattein.*

So much, then, as to the number and nature of the points of difference in the imitation of these arts.

4   It is clear that the general origin of poetry was due to two causes,
each of them part of human nature. Imitation is natural to man from 5
childhood, one of his advantages over the lower animals being this,
that he is the most imitative creature in the world, and learns at
first by imitation. And it is also natural for all to delight in works
of imitation. The truth of this second point is shown by experience: 10
though the objects themselves may be painful to see, we delight
to view the most realistic representations of them in art, the forms
for example of the lowest animals and of dead bodies. The explanation is to be found in a further fact: to be learning something is
the greatest of pleasures not only to the philosopher but also to
the rest of mankind, however small their capacity for it; the reason 15
of the delight in seeing the picture is that one is at the same time
learning—gathering the meaning of things, e. g. that the man there is
so-and-so; for if one has not seen the thing before, one's pleasure will

not be in the picture as an imitation of it, but will be due to the execu-
20 tion or colouring or some similar cause. Imitation, then, being
natural to us—as also the sense of harmony and rhythm, the metres
being obviously species of rhythms—it was through their original
aptitude, and by a series of improvements for the most part gradual
on their first efforts, that they created poetry out of their improvisations.

Poetry, however, soon broke up into two kinds according to the
25 differences of character in the individual poets; for the graver among
them would represent noble actions, and those of noble personages;
and the meaner sort the actions of the ignoble. The latter class produced invectives at first, just as others did hymns and panegyrics.
We know of no such poem by any of the pre-Homeric poets, though
there were probably many such writers among them; instances, however, may be found from Homer downwards, e. g. his *Margites,* and
30 the similar poems of others. In this poetry of invective its natural
fitness brought an iambic metre into use; hence our present term
'iambic', because it was the metre of their 'iambs' or invectives
against one another. The result was that the old poets became some
of them writers of heroic and others of iambic verse. Homer's position, however, is peculiar: just as he was in the serious style the
35 poet of poets, standing alone not only through the literary excellence,
but also through the dramatic character of his imitations, so too he
was the first to outline for us the general forms of Comedy by producing not a dramatic invective, but a dramatic picture of the Ridiculous; his *Margites* in fact stands in the same relation to our come-
1449ᵃ dies as the *Iliad* and *Odyssey* to our tragedies. As soon, however, as
Tragedy and Comedy appeared in the field, those naturally drawn
to the one line of poetry became writers of comedies instead of iambs,
5 and those naturally drawn to the other, writers of tragedies instead of
epics, because these new modes of art were grander and of more
esteem than the old.

If it be asked whether Tragedy is now all that it need be in its
formative elements, to consider that, and decide it theoretically and
in relation to the theatres, is a matter for another inquiry.
10 It certainly began in improvisations—as did also Comedy; the
one originating with the authors of the Dithyramb, the other with
those of the phallic songs, which still survive as institutions in many
of our cities. And its advance after that was little by little, through
their improving on whatever they had before them at each stage.
It was in fact only after a long series of changes that the movement
15 of Tragedy stopped on its attaining to its natural form. (1) The

number of actors was first increased to two by Aeschylus, who curtailed the business of the Chorus, and made the dialogue, or spoken
portion, take the leading part in the play. (2) A third actor and
scenery were due to Sophocles. (3) Tragedy acquired also its magnitude. Discarding short stories and a ludicrous diction, through its 20
passing out of its satyric stage, it assumed, though only at a late
point in its progress, a tone of dignity; and its metre changed then
from trochaic to iambic. The reason for their original use of the
trochaic tetrameter was that their poetry was satyric and more connected with dancing than it now is. As soon, however, as a spoken
part came in, nature herself found the appropriate metre. The iambic,
we know, is the most speakable of metres, as is shown by the fact 25
that we very often fall into it in conversation, whereas we rarely talk
hexameters, and only when we depart from the speaking tone of
voice. (4) Another change was a plurality of episodes or acts. As for
the remaining matters, the superadded embellishments and the account of their introduction, these must be taken as said, as it
would probably be a long piece of work to go through the details.   30

5   As for Comedy, it is (as has been observed [1]) an imitation of
men worse than the average; worse, however, not as regards any and
every sort of fault, but only as regards one particular kind, the
Ridiculous, which is a species of the Ugly. The Ridiculous may be
defined as a mistake or deformity not productive of pain or harm to 35
others; the mask, for instance, that excites laughter, is something
ugly and distorted without causing pain.
   Though the successive changes in Tragedy and their authors are
not unknown, we cannot say the same of Comedy; its early stages
passed unnoticed, because it was not as yet taken up in a serious 1449[b]
way. It was only at a late point in its progress that a chorus of
comedians was officially granted by the archon; they used to be mere
volunteers. It had also already certain definite forms at the time when
the record of those termed comic poets begins. Who it was who supplied it with masks, or prologues, or a plurality of actors and the like,
has remained unknown. The invented Fable, or Plot, however, origi- 5
nated in Sicily with Epicharmus and Phormis; of Athenian poets
Crates was the first to drop the Comedy of invective and frame
stories of a general and non-personal nature, in other words, Fables
or Plots.
   Epic poetry, then, has been seen to agree with Tragedy to this
extent, that of being an imitation of serious subjects in a grand kind of 10

[1] 1448[a] 17; 1448[b] 37.

verse. It differs from it, however, (1) in that it is in one kind of verse and in narrative form; and (2) in its length—which is due to its action having no fixed limit of time, whereas Tragedy endeavours to keep as far as possible within a single circuit of the sun, or something near that. This, I say, is another point of difference between
15 them, though at first the practice in this respect was just the same in tragedies as in epic poems. They differ also (3) in their constituents, some being common to both and others peculiar to Tragedy— hence a judge of good and bad in Tragedy is a judge of that in epic poetry also. All the parts of an epic are included in Tragedy; but those of Tragedy are not all of them to be found in the Epic.

20 **6** Reserving hexameter poetry and Comedy for consideration hereafter,[2] let us proceed now to the discussion of Tragedy; before doing so, however, we must gather up the definition resulting from what has been said. A tragedy, then, is the imitation of an action that is
25 serious and also, as having magnitude, complete in itself; in language with pleasurable accessories, each kind brought in separately in the parts of the work; in a dramatic, not in a narrative form; with incidents arousing pity and fear, wherewith to accomplish its catharsis of such emotions. Here by 'language with pleasurable accessories' I mean that with rhythm and harmony or song superadded; and by
30 'the kinds separately' I mean that some portions are worked out with verse only, and others in turn with song.

I. As they act the stories, it follows that in the first place the Spectacle (or stage-appearance of the actors) must be some part of the whole; and in the second Melody and Diction, these two being the means of their imitation. Here by 'Diction' I mean merely this,
35 the composition of the verses; and by 'Melody', what is too completely understood to require explanation. But further: the subject represented also is an action; and the action involves agents, who must necessarily have their distinctive qualities both of character and
1450ᵃ thought, since it is from these that we ascribe certain qualities to their actions. There are in the natural order of things, therefore, two causes, Thought and Character, of their actions, and consequently of their success or failure in their lives. Now the action (that which was done) is represented in the play by the Fable or Plot. The Fable, in our present sense of the term, is simply this, the combination of the incidents, or things done in the story; whereas Character
5 is what makes us ascribe certain moral qualities to the agents; and

[2] For hexameter poetry cf. chap. 23 f.; comedy was treated of in the lost Second Book.

Thought is shown in all they say when proving a particular point or, it may be, enunciating a general truth. There are six parts consequently of every tragedy, as a whole (that is) of such or such quality, viz. a Fable or Plot, Characters, Diction, Thought, Spectacle, and Melody; two of them arising from the means, one from the manner, 10 and three from the objects of the dramatic imitation; and there is nothing else besides these six. Of these, its formative elements, then, not a few of the dramatists have made due use, as every play, one may say, admits of Spectacle, Character, Fable, Diction, Melody, and Thought.

II. The most important of the six is the combination of the 15 incidents of the story. Tragedy is essentially an imitation not of persons but of action and life, of happiness and misery. All human happiness or misery takes the form of action; the end for which we live is a certain kind of activity, not a quality. Character gives us qualities, but it is in our actions—what we do—that we are happy or the reverse. In a play accordingly they do not act in order to portray the 20 Characters; they include the Characters for the sake of the action. So that it is the action in it, i. e. its Fable or Plot, that is the end and purpose of the tragedy; and the end is everywhere the chief thing. Besides this, a tragedy is impossible without action, but there may be one without Character. The tragedies of most of the moderns are 25 characterless—a defect common among poets of all kinds, and with its counterpart in painting in Zeuxis as compared with Polygnotus; for whereas the latter is strong in character, the work of Zeuxis is devoid of it. And again: one may string together a series of characteristic speeches of the utmost finish as regards Diction and Thought, and yet fail to produce the true tragic effect; but one will 30 have much better success with a tragedy which, however inferior in these respects, has a Plot, a combination of incidents, in it. And again: the most powerful elements of attraction in Tragedy, the Peripeties and Discoveries, are parts of the Plot. A further proof is in 35 the fact that beginners succeed earlier with the Diction and Characters than with the construction of a story; and the same may be said of nearly all the early dramatists. We maintain, therefore, that the first essential, the life and soul, so to speak, of Tragedy is the Plot; and that the Characters come second—compare the parallel in paint- 1450^b ing, where the most beautiful colours laid on without order will not give one the same pleasure as a simple black-and-white sketch of a portrait. We maintain that Tragedy is primarily an imitation of action, and that it is mainly for the sake of the action that it imitates the personal agents. Third comes the element of Thought, i. e. the power 5

of saying whatever can be said, or what is appropriate to the occasion. This is what, in the speeches in Tragedy, falls under the arts of Politics and Rhetoric; for the older poets make their personages discourse like statesmen, and the modern like rhetoricians. One must not confuse it with Character. Character in a play is that which reveals the moral purpose of the agents, i. e. the sort of thing they seek or avoid, where that is not obvious—hence there is no room for Character in a speech on a purely indifferent subject. Thought, on the
10 other hand, is shown in all they say when proving or disproving some particular point, or enunciating some universal proposition. Fourth among the literary elements is the Diction of the personages, i. e., as before explained,[3] the expression of their thoughts in words, which
15 is practically the same thing with verse as with prose. As for the two remaining parts, the Melody is the greatest of the pleasurable accessories of Tragedy. The Spectacle, though an attraction, is the least artistic of all the parts, and has least to do with the art of poetry. The tragic effect is quite possible without a public performance and actors; and besides, the getting-up of the Spectacle is more a matter
20 for the costumier than the poet.

7　Having thus distinguished the parts, let us now consider the proper construction of the Fable or Plot, as that is at once the first and the most important thing in Tragedy. We have laid it down that a tragedy is an imitation of an action that is complete in itself, as a whole of
25 some magnitude; for a whole may be of no magnitude to speak of. Now a whole is that which has beginning, middle, and end. A beginning is that which is not itself necessarily after anything else, and which has naturally something else after it; an end is that which
30 is naturally after something itself, either as its necessary or usual consequent, and with nothing else after it; and a middle, that which is by nature after one thing and has also another after it. A well-constructed Plot, therefore, cannot either begin or end at any point one likes; beginning and end in it must be of the forms just described. Again: to be beautiful, a living creature, and every whole made up of
35 parts, must not only present a certain order in its arrangement of parts, but also be of a certain definite magnitude. Beauty is a matter of size and order, and therefore impossible either (1) in a very minute creature, since our perception becomes indistinct as it approaches instantaneity; or (2) in a creature of vast size—one, say,
1,000　miles long—as in that case, instead of the object being seen
1451ª all at once, the unity and wholeness of it is lost to the beholder.

[3] 1449ᵇ 34.

Just in the same way, then, as a beautiful whole made up of parts, or a beautiful living creature, must be of some size, but a size to be taken in by the eye, so a story or Plot must be of some length, but of a 5 length to be taken in by the memory. As for the limit of its length, so far as that is relative to public performances and spectators, it does not fall within the theory of poetry. If they had to perform a hundred tragedies, they would be timed by water-clocks, as they are said to have been at one period. The limit, however, set by the 10 actual nature of the thing is this: the longer the story, consistently with its being comprehensible as a whole, the finer it is by reason of its magnitude. As a rough general formula, 'a length which allows of the hero passing by a series of probable or necessary stages from misfortune to happiness, or from happiness to misfortune', may suf- fice as a limit for the magnitude of the story. 15

8   The Unity of a Plot does not consist, as some suppose, in its hav- ing one man as its subject. An infinity of things befall that one man, some of which it is impossible to reduce to unity; and in like manner there are many actions of one man which cannot be made to form one action. One sees, therefore, the mistake of all the poets who have 20 written a *Heracleid,* a *Theseid,* or similar poems; they suppose that, because Heracles was one man, the story also of Heracles must be one story. Homer, however, evidently understood this point quite well, whether by art or instinct, just in the same way as he excels the rest in every other respect. In writing an *Odyssey,* he did not make the poem cover all that ever befell his hero—it befell him, for instance, 25 to get wounded on Parnassus and also to feign madness at the time of the call to arms, but the two incidents had no necessary or probable connexion with one another—instead of doing that, he took as the subject of the *Odyssey,* as also of the *Iliad,* an action with a Unity of the kind we are describing. The truth is that, just as in the other 30 imitative arts one imitation is always of one thing, so in poetry the story, as an imitation of action, must represent one action, a complete whole, with its several incidents so closely connected that the trans- posal or withdrawal of any one of them will disjoin and dislocate the whole. For that which makes no perceptible difference by its pres- ence or absence is no real part of the whole. 35

9   From what we have said it will be seen that the poet's function is to describe, not the thing that has happened, but a kind of thing that might happen, i. e. what is possible as being probable or neces- sary. The distinction between historian and poet is not in the one 1451ᵇ

writing prose and the other verse—you might put the work of Herodotus into verse, and it would still be a species of history; · it consists really in this, that the one describes the thing that has been,
5 and the other a kind of thing that might be. Hence poetry is something more philosophic and of graver import than history, since its statements are of the nature rather of universals, whereas those of history are singulars. By a universal statement I mean one as to what such or such a kind of man will probably or necessarily say or do—which is the aim of poetry, though it affixes proper names to the
10 characters; by a singular statement, one as to what, say, Alcibiades did or had done to him. In Comedy this has become clear by this time; it is only when their plot is already made up of probable incidents that they give it a basis of proper names, choosing for the purpose any names that may occur to them, instead of writing like the old
15 iambic poets about particular persons. In Tragedy, however, they still adhere to the historic names; and for this reason: what convinces is the possible; now whereas we are not yet sure as to the possibility of that which has not happened, that which has happened is manifestly possible, else it would not have come to pass. Nevertheless even in Tragedy there are some plays with but one or two known names in
20 them, the rest being inventions; and there are some without a single known name, e. g. Agathon's *Antheus,* in which both incidents and names are of the poet's invention; and it is no less delightful on that account. So that one must not aim at a rigid adherence to the tradi-
25 tional stories on which tragedies are based. It would be absurd, in fact, to do so, as even the known stories are only known to a few, though they are a delight none the less to all.

It is evident from the above that the poet must be more the poet of his stories or Plots than of his verses, inasmuch as he is a poet by virtue of the imitative element in his work, and it is actions that he imitates. And if he should come to take a subject from actual history,
30 he is none the less a poet for that; since some historic occurrences may very well be in the probable and possible order of things; and it is in that aspect of them that he is their poet.

Of simple Plots and actions the episodic are the worst. I call a Plot episodic when there is neither probability nor necessity in the
35 sequence of its episodes. Actions of this sort bad poets construct through their own fault, and good ones on account of the players. His work being for public performance, a good poet often stretches out a Plot beyond its capabilities, and is thus obliged to twist the sequence of incident.

1452ᵃ Tragedy, however, is an imitation not only of a complete action, but also of incidents arousing pity and fear. Such incidents have the very greatest effect on the mind when they occur unexpectedly and at the same time in consequence of one another; there is more of the marvellous in them then than if they happened of themselves or 5 by mere chance. Even matters of chance seem most marvellous if there is an appearance of design as it were in them; as for instance the statue of Mitys at Argos killed the author of Mitys' death by falling down on him when a looker-on at a public spectacle; for incidents like that we think to be not without a meaning. A Plot, there- 10 fore, of this sort is necessarily finer than others.

10   Plots are either simple or complex, since the actions they repre- sent are naturally of this twofold description. The action, proceeding in the way defined, as one continuous whole, I call simple, when the 15 change in the hero's fortunes takes place without Peripety or Dis- covery; and complex, when it involves one or the other, or both. These should each of them arise out of the structure of the Plot itself, so as to be the consequence, necessary or probable, of the antecedents. There is a great difference between a thing happening *propter hoc* and 20 *post hoc*.

11   A Peripety is the change of the kind described from one state of things within the play to its opposite, and that too in the way we are saying, in the probable or necessary sequence of events; as it is for instance in *Oedipus*: here the opposite state of things is produced 25 by the Messenger, who, coming to gladden Oedipus and to remove his fears as to his mother, reveals the secret of his birth.[4] And in *Lynceus*:[5] just as he is being led off for execution, with Danaus at his side to put him to death, the incidents preceding this bring it about that he is saved and Danaus put to death. A Discovery is, as the 30 very word implies, a change from ignorance to knowledge, and thus to either love or hate, in the personages marked for good or evil fortune. The finest form of Discovery is one attended by Peripeties, like that which goes with the Discovery in *Oedipus*. There are no doubt other forms of it; what we have said may happen in a way in reference to inanimate things, even things of a very casual kind; and it is also pos- 35 sible to discover whether some one has done or not done something. But the form most directly connected with the Plot and the action of the piece is the first-mentioned. This, with a Peripety, will arouse 1452ᵇ either pity or fear—actions of that nature being what Tragedy is as-

⁴ *O. T.* 911–1085.   ⁵ By Theodectes.

sumed to represent; and it will also serve to bring about the happy or
unhappy ending. The Discovery, then, being of persons, it may be that
of one party only to the other, the latter being already known; or
5 both the parties may have to discover themselves. Iphigenia, for
instance, was discovered to Orestes by sending the letter; [6] and another Discovery was required to reveal him to Iphigenia.

Two parts of the Plot, then, Peripety and Discovery, are on mat-
10 ters of this sort. A third part is Suffering; which we may define as an
action of a destructive or painful nature, such as murders on the stage,
tortures, woundings, and the like. The other two have been already
explained.

12 The parts of Tragedy to be treated as formative elements in the
15 whole were mentioned in a previous Chapter.[7] From the point of view,
however, of its quantity, i. e. the separate sections into which it is
divided, a tragedy has the following parts: Prologue, Episode,
Exode, and a choral portion, distinguished into Parode and Stasimon;
these two are common to all tragedies, whereas songs from the stage
20 and *Commoe* are only found in some. The Prologue is all that precedes
the Parode of the chorus; an Episode all that comes in between two
whole choral songs; the Exode all that follows after the last choral
song. In the choral portion the Parode is the whole first statement of
the chorus; a Stasimon, a song of the chorus without anapaests or
trochees; a *Commos,* a lamentation sung by chorus and actor in con-
25 cert. The parts of Tragedy to be used as formative elements in the
whole we have already mentioned; the above are its parts from the
point of view of its quantity, or the separate sections into which
it is divided.

13 The next points after what we have said above will be these:
(1) What is the poet to aim at, and what is he to avoid, in constructing his Plots? and (2) What are the conditions on which the
tragic effect depends?
30 We assume that, for the finest form of Tragedy, the Plot must
be not simple but complex; and further, that it must imitate actions
arousing fear and pity, since that is the distinctive function of this
kind of imitation. It follows, therefore, that there are three forms of
Plot to be avoided. (1) A good man must not be seen passing from
happiness to misery, or (2) a bad man from misery to happiness.
35 The first situation is not fear-inspiring or piteous, but simply odious
to us. The second is the most untragic that can be; it has no one of the

[6] *Iph. Taur.* 727 ff.   [7] Ch. 6.

requisites of Tragedy; it does not appeal either to the human feeling in us, or to our pity, or to our fears. Nor, on the other hand, should 1453ᵃ (3) an extremely bad man be seen falling from happiness into misery. Such a story may arouse the human feeling in us, but it will not move us to either pity or fear; pity is occasioned by undeserved 5 misfortune, and fear by that of one like ourselves; so that there will be nothing either piteous or fear-inspiring in the situation. There remains, then, the intermediate kind of personage, a man not pre-eminently virtuous and just, whose misfortune, however, is brought upon him not by vice and depravity but by some error of judgement, of the number of those in the enjoyment of great reputation and pros- 10 perity; e. g. Oedipus, Thyestes, and the men of note of similar families. The perfect Plot, accordingly, must have a single, and not (as some tell us) a double issue; the change in the hero's fortunes must be not from misery to happiness, but on the contrary from happiness to misery; and the cause of it must lie not in any depravity, but in some 15 great error on his part; the man himself being either such as we have described, or better, not worse, than that. Fact also confirms our theory. Though the poets began by accepting any tragic story that came to hand, in these days the finest tragedies are always on the story of some few houses, on that of Alcmeon, Oedipus, Orestes, 20 Meleager, Thyestes, Telephus, or any others that may have been in-volved, as either agents or sufferers, in some deed of horror. The theoretically best tragedy, then, has a Plot of this description. The critics, therefore, are wrong who blame Euripides for taking this line in his tragedies, and giving many of them an unhappy ending. It is, 25 as we have said, the right line to take. The best proof is this: on the stage, and in the public performances, such plays, properly worked out, are seen to be the most truly tragic; and Euripides, even if his execution be faulty in every other point, is seen to be nevertheless the most tragic certainly of the dramatists. After this comes the construc- 30 tion of Plot which some rank first, one with a double story (like the *Odyssey*) and an opposite issue for the good and the bad per-sonages. It is ranked as first only through the weakness of the audi-ences; the poets merely follow their public, writing as its wishes 35 dictate. But the pleasure here is not that of Tragedy. It belongs rather to Comedy, where the bitterest enemies in the piece (e. g. Orestes and Aegisthus) walk off good friends at the end, with no slaying of any one by any one.

14 The tragic fear and pity may be aroused by the Spectacle; but 1453ᵇ they may also be aroused by the very structure and incidents of the

play—which is the better way and shows the better poet. The Plot
in fact should be so framed that, even without seeing the things take
5 place, he who simply hears the account of them shall be filled with
horror and pity at the incidents; which is just the effect that the mere
recital of the story in *Oedipus* would have on one. To produce this
same effect by means of the Spectacle is less artistic, and requires
extraneous aid. Those, however, who make use of the Spectacle to
put before us that which is merely monstrous and not productive
10 of fear, are wholly out of touch with Tragedy; not every kind of
pleasure should be required of a tragedy, but only its own proper
pleasure.

The tragic pleasure is that of pity and fear, and the poet has to produce it by a work of imitation; it is clear, therefore, that the causes
should be included in the incidents of his story. Let us see, then, what
15 kinds of incident strike one as horrible, or rather as piteous. In a deed
of this description the parties must necessarily be either friends, or
enemies, or indifferent to one another. Now when enemy does it on
enemy, there is nothing to move us to pity either in his doing or in his
meditating the deed, except so far as the actual pain of the sufferer
is concerned; and the same is true when the parties are indifferent to
one another. Whenever the tragic deed, however, is done within the
20 family—when murder or the like is done or meditated by brother on
brother, by son on father, by mother on son, or son on mother—these
are the situations the poet should seek after. The traditional stories,
accordingly, must be kept as they are, e.g. the murder of
Clytaemnestra by Orestes and of Eriphyle by Alcmeon. At the same
25 time even with these there is something left to the poet himself;
it is for him to devise the right way of treating them. Let us explain
more clearly what we mean by 'the right way'. The deed of horror
may be done by the doer knowingly and consciously, as in the old
poets, and in Medea's murder of her children in Euripides.[8] Or he
30 may do it, but in ignorance of his relationship, and discover that afterwards, as does the Oedipus in Sophocles. Here the deed is outside the
play; but it may be within it, like the act of the Alcmeon in Astydamas,
or that of the Telegonus in *Ulysses Wounded*.[9] A third possibility is
35 for one meditating some deadly injury to another, in ignorance of his
relationship, to make the discovery in time to draw back. These exhaust the possibilities, since the deed must necessarily be either done
or not done, and either knowingly or unknowingly.

The worst situation is when the personage is with full knowledge on
the point of doing the deed, and leaves it undone. It is odious and

8 *Med.* 1236.   9 Perhaps by Sophocles.

also (through the absence of suffering) untragic; hence it is that no
one is made to act thus except in some few instances, e. g. Haemon 1454[a]
and Creon in *Antigone*.[10] Next after this comes the actual perpetra-
tion of the deed meditated. A better situation than that, however,
is for the deed to be done in ignorance, and the relationship discovered afterwards, since there is nothing odious in it, and the Discovery will serve to astound us. But the best of all is the last; what 5
we have in *Cresphontes*,[11] for example, where Merope, on the point
of slaying her son, recognizes him in time; in *Iphigenia,* where sister
and brother are in a like position; and in *Helle*,[12] where the son recognizes his mother, when on the point of giving her up to her enemy.

This will explain why our tragedies are restricted (as we said just
now)[13] to such a small number of families. It was accident rather than 10
art that led the poets in quest of subjects to embody this kind of incident in their Plots. They are still obliged, accordingly, to have recourse to the families in which such horrors have occurred.

On the construction of the Plot, and the kind of Plot required for
Tragedy, enough has now been said.   15

15 In the Characters there are four points to aim at. First and fore-
most, that they shall be good. There will be an element of character
in the play, if (as has been observed)[14] what a personage says or does
reveals a certain moral purpose; and a good element of character, if
the purpose so revealed is good. Such goodness is possible in every
type of personage, even in a woman or a slave, though the one is 20
perhaps an inferior, and the other a wholly worthless being. The second point is to make them appropriate. The Character before us may
be, say, manly; but it is not appropriate in a female Character to be
manly, or clever. The third is to make them like the reality, which
is not the same as their being good and appropriate, in our sense of 25
the term. The fourth is to make them consistent and the same
throughout; even if inconsistency be part of the man before one for
imitation as presenting that form of character, he should still be
consistently inconsistent. We have an instance of baseness of character, not required for the story, in the Menelaus in *Orestes*; of the
incongruous and unbefitting in the lamentation of Ulysses in *Scylla*,[15] 30
and in the (clever) speech of Melanippe;[16] and of inconsistency in
Iphigenia at Aulis,[17] where Iphigenia the suppliant is utterly unlike
the later Iphigenia. The right thing, however, is in the Characters

---

[10] l. 1231.   [11] By Euripides.   [12] Authorship unknown.
[13] 1453[a] 19.   [14] 1450[b] 8.   [15] A dithyramb by Timotheus.
[16] (Euripides).   [17] ll. 1211 ff., 1368 ff.

just as in the incidents of the play to endeavour always after the
35 necessary or the probable; so that whenever such-and-such a personage says or does such-and-such a thing, it shall be the necessary
or probable outcome of his character; and whenever this incident follows on that, it shall be either the necessary or the probable consequence of it. From this one sees (to digress for a moment) that the
1454ᵇ Dénouement also should arise out of the plot itself, and not depend
on a stage-artifice, as in *Medea*,[18] or in the story of the (arrested)
departure of the Greeks in the *Iliad*.[19] The artifice must be reserved
for matters outside the play—for past events beyond human knowl-
5 edge, or events yet to come, which require to be foretold or announced; since it is the privilege of the Gods to know everything.
There should be nothing improbable among the actual incidents. If
it be unavoidable, however, it should be outside the tragedy, like the
improbability in the *Oedipus* of Sophocles. But to return to the Characters. As Tragedy is an imitation of personages better than the
ordinary man, we in our way should follow the example of good
10 portrait-painters, who reproduce the distinctive features of a man,
and at the same time, without losing the likeness, make him hand-
somer than he is. The poet in like manner, in portraying men quick or
slow to anger, or with similar infirmities of character, must know
how to represent them as such, and at the same time as good men,
as Agathon and Homer have represented Achilles.
15   All these rules one must keep in mind throughout, and, further,
those also for such points of stage-effect as directly depend on the art
of the poet, since in these too one may often make mistakes. Enough,
however, has been said on the subject in one of our published writings.[20]

16   Discovery in general has been explained already.[21] As for the
20 species of Discovery, the first to be noted is (1) the least artistic form
of it, of which the poets make most use through mere lack of invention, Discovery by signs or marks. Of these signs some are congenital,
like the 'lance-head which the Earth-born have on them',[22] or 'stars',
such as Carcinus brings in his *Thyestes*; others acquired after birth—
these latter being either marks on the body, e. g. scars, or external
tokens, like necklaces, or (to take another sort of instance) the ark
25 in the Discovery in *Tyro*.[23] Even these, however, admit of two uses,
a better and a worse; the scar of Ulysses is an instance; the Discovery of him through it is made in one way by the nurse[24] and in

18 l. 1317.   19 ii. 155.   20 In the lost dialogue *On Poets*.   21 1452ᵃ 29.
22 Authorship unknown.   23 By Euripides.   24 *Od*. xix. 386–475.

another by the swineherds.[25] A Discovery using signs as a means of assurance is less artistic, as indeed are all such as imply reflection; whereas one bringing them in all of a sudden, as in the *Bath-story*,[26] is of a better order. Next after these are (2) Discoveries made directly by the poet; which are inartistic for that very reason; e. g. Orestes' Discovery of himself in *Iphigenia*: whereas his sister reveals who she is by the letter,[27] Orestes is made to say himself what the poet rather than the story demands.[28] This, therefore, is not far removed from the first-mentioned fault, since he might have presented certain tokens as well. Another instance is the 'shuttle's voice' in the *Tereus* of Sophocles. (3) A third species is Discovery through memory, from a man's consciousness being awakened by something seen. Thus in *The Cyprioe* of Dicaeogenes, the sight of the picture makes the man burst into tears; and in the *Tale of Alcinous*,[29] hearing the harper Ulysses is reminded of the past and weeps; the Discovery of them being the result. (4) A fourth kind is Discovery through reasoning; e. g. in *The Choephoroe*;[30] 'One like me is here; there is no one like me but Orestes; he, therefore, must be here.' Or that which Polyidus the Sophist suggested for *Iphigenia*; since it was natural for Orestes to reflect: 'My sister was sacrificed, and I am to be sacrificed like her.' Or that in the *Tydeus* of Theodectes: 'I came to find a son, and am to die myself.' Or that in *The Phinidae*:[31] on seeing the place the women inferred their fate, that they were to die there, since they had also been exposed there. (5) There is, too, a composite Discovery arising from bad reasoning on the side of the other party. An instance of it is in *Ulysses the False Messenger*:[31] he said he should know the bow—which he had not seen; but to suppose from that that he would know it again (as though he had once seen it) was bad reasoning. (6) The best of all Discoveries, however, is that arising from the incidents themselves, when the great surprise comes about through a probable incident, like that in the *Oedipus* of Sophocles; and also in *Iphigenia*;[32] for it was not improbable that she should wish to have a letter taken home. These last are the only Discoveries independent of the artifice of signs and necklaces. Next after them come Discoveries through reasoning.

17   At the time when he is constructing his Plots, and engaged on the Diction in which they are worked out, the poet should remember (1) to put the actual scenes as far as possible before his eyes. In this

---

[25] *Od.* xxi. 205–25.   [26] *Od.* xix. 392.   [27] *Iph. Taur.* 727 ff.

[28] Ib., 800 ff.   [29] *Od.* viii. 521 ff. (Cf. viii, 83 ff.).

[30] ll. 168–234.   [31] Authorship unknown.   [32] *Iph. Taur.* 582.

25 way, seeing everything with the vividness of an eye-witness as it were, he will devise what is appropriate, and be least likely to overlook incongruities. This is shown by what was censured in Carcinus, the return of Amphiaraus from the sanctuary; it would have passed unnoticed, if it had not been actually seen by the audience; but on the stage his play failed, the incongruity of the incident offending the spectators. (2) As far as may be, too, the poet should even act his story with 30 the very gestures of his personages. Given the same natural qualifications, he who feels the emotions to be described will be the most convincing; distress and anger, for instance, are portrayed most truthfully by one who is feeling them at the moment. Hence it is that poetry demands a man with a special gift for it, or else one with a touch of madness in him; the former can easily assume the required mood, and the latter may be actually beside himself with emotion. (3) His story, again, whether already made or of his own making,
1455b he should first simplify and reduce to a universal form, before proceeding to lengthen it out by the insertion of episodes. The following will show how the universal element in *Iphigenia*, for instance, may be viewed: A certain maiden having been offered in sacrifice, and spirited away from her sacrificers into another land, where the cus-
5 tom was to sacrifice all strangers to the Goddess, she was made there the priestess of this rite. Long after that the brother of the priestess happened to come; the fact, however, of the oracle having for a certain reason bidden him go thither, and his object in going, are outside the Plot of the play. On his coming he was arrested, and about to be sacrificed, when he revealed who he was—either as
10 Euripides puts it, or (as suggested by Polyidus) by the not improbable exclamation, 'So I too am doomed to be sacrificed, as my sister was'; and the disclosure led to his salvation. This done, the next thing, after the proper names have been fixed as a basis for the story, is to work in episodes or accessory incidents. One must mind, however, that the episodes are appropriate, like the fit of madness [33] in
15 Orestes, which led to his arrest, and the purifying,[34] which brought about his salvation. In plays, then, the episodes are short; in epic poetry they serve to lengthen out the poem. The argument of the *Odyssey* is not a long one. A certain man has been abroad many years; Poseidon is ever on the watch for him, and he is all alone. Matters at
20 home too have come to this, that his substance is being wasted and his son's death plotted by suitors to his wife. Then he arrives there himself after his grievous sufferings; reveals himself, and falls on his enemies; and the end is his salvation and their death. This being

[33] *Iph. Taur.* 281 ff.   [34] Ib., 1163 ff.

all that is proper to the *Odyssey,* everything else in it is episode.

18 (4) There is a further point to be borne in mind. Every tragedy is in part Complication and in part Dénouement; the incidents before the opening scene, and often certain also of those within the play, forming the Complication; and the rest the Dénouement. By 25 Complication I mean all from the beginning of the story to the point just before the change in the hero's fortunes; by Dénouement, all from the beginning of the change to the end. In the *Lynceus* of Theodectes, for instance, the Complication includes, together with the 30 presupposed incidents, the seizure of the child and that in turn of the parents; and the Dénouement all from the indictment for the 1456ᵃ7 murder to the end. Now it is right, when one speaks of a tragedy as the same or not the same as another, to do so on the ground before all else of their Plot, i. e. as having the same or not the same Complication and Dénouement. Yet there are many dramatists who, after a good Complication, fail in the Dénouement. But it is necessary for both points of construction to be always duly mastered. (5) There are four 1455ᵇ32 distinct species of Tragedy—that being the number of the constituents also that have been mentioned:³⁵ first, the complex Tragedy, which is all Peripety and Discovery; second, the Tragedy of suffering, e. g. the *Ajaxes* and *Ixions*; third, the Tragedy of character, e. g. 1456ᵃ *The Phthiotides*³⁶ and *Peleus.*³⁷ The fourth constituent is that of 'Spectacle', exemplified in *The Phorcides,*³⁸ in *Prometheus,*³⁹ and in all plays with the scene laid in the nether world. The poet's aim, then, should be to combine every element of interest, if possible, or else the more important and the major part of them. This is now especially necessary owing to the unfair criticism to which the poet is subjected in these days. Just because there have been poets before 5 him strong in the several species of tragedy, the critics now expect the one man to surpass that which was the strong point of each one of his predecessors. (6) One should also remember what has been said more 10 than once,⁴⁰ and not write a tragedy on an epic body of incident (i. e. one with a plurality of stories in it), by attempting to dramatize, for instance, the entire story of the *Iliad.* In the epic owing to its scale every part is treated at proper length; with a drama, however, on the same story the result is very disappointing. This is shown by the fact 15 that all who have dramatized the fall of Ilium in its entirety, and

³⁵ This does not agree with anything actually said before.   ³⁶ By Sophocles.
³⁷ Probably Sophocles' *Peleus* is incorrect.   ³⁸ By Aeschylus.
³⁹ Probably a satyric drama by Aeschylus.
⁴⁰ A loose reference to 1449ᵇ 12, 1455ᵇ 15.

not part by part, like Euripides, of the whole of the Niobe story, instead of a portion, like Aeschylus, either fail utterly or have but ill success on the stage; for that and that alone was enough to ruin even a play by Agathon. Yet in their Peripeties, as also in their simple
20 plots, the poets I mean show wonderful skill in aiming at the kind of effect they desire—a tragic situation that arouses the human feeling in one, like the clever villain (e. g. Sisyphus) deceived, or the brave wrongdoer worsted. This is probable, however, only in Agathon's sense, when he speaks of the probability of even improbabilities com-
25 ing to pass. (7) The Chorus too should be regarded as one of the actors; it should be an integral part of the whole, and take a share in the action—that which it has in Sophocles, rather than in Euripides. With the later poets, however, the songs in a play of theirs have no more to do with the Plot of that than of any other tragedy. Hence it is that they are now singing intercalary pieces, a practice first intro-
30 duced by Agathon. And yet what real difference is there between singing such intercalary pieces, and attempting to fit in a speech, or even a whole act, from one play into another?

19 The Plot and Characters having been discussed, it remains to consider the Diction and Thought. As for the Thought, we may
35 assume what is said of it in our Art of Rhetoric,[41] as it belongs more properly to that department of inquiry. The Thought of the person-ages is shown in everything to be effected by their language—in every effort to prove or disprove, to arouse emotion (pity, fear, anger, and
1456ᵇ the like), or to maximize or minimize things. It is clear, also, that their mental procedure must be on the same lines in their actions likewise, whenever they wish them to arouse pity or horror, or to
5 have a look of importance or probability. The only difference is that with the act the impression has to be made without explanation; whereas with the spoken word it has to be produced by the speaker, and result from his language. What, indeed, would be the good of the speaker, if things appeared in the required light even apart from any-thing he says?

As regards the Diction, one subject for inquiry under this head is the turns given to the language when spoken; e. g. the difference
10 between command and prayer, simple statement and threat, ques-tion and answer, and so forth. The theory of such matters, however, belongs to Elocution and the professors of that art. Whether the poet knows these things or not, his art as a poet is never seriously criti-
15 cized on that account. What fault can one see in Homer's 'Sing of the

---

[41] Cf. especially Rhet. 1356ᵃ 1.

wrath, Goddess'?—which Protagoras has criticizeα as being a command where a prayer was meant, since to bid one do or not do, he tells us, is a command. Let us pass over this, then, as appertaining to another art, and not to that of poetry.

20   The Diction viewed as a whole is made up of the following parts: 20 the Letter (or ultimate element), the Syllable, the Conjunction, the Article, the Noun, the Verb, the Case, and the Speech. (1) The Letter is an indivisible sound of a particular kind, one that may become a factor in an intelligible sound. Indivisible sounds are uttered by the brutes also, but no one of these is a Letter in our sense of the term. These elementary sounds are either vowels, semi-vowels, or mutes. A 25 vowel is a Letter having an audible sound without the addition of another Letter. A semi-vowel, one having an audible sound by the addition of another Letter; e. g. S and R. A mute, one having no sound at all by itself, but becoming audible by an addition, that of one of the Letters which have a sound of some sort of their own; e.g. 30 G and D. The Letters differ in various ways: as produced by different conformations or in different regions of the mouth; as aspirated, not aspirated, or sometimes one and sometimes the other; as long, short, or of variable quantity; and further as having an acute, grave, or intermediate accent. The details of these matters we must leave to the metricians. (2) A Syllable is a non-significant composite sound, 35 made up of a mute and a Letter having a sound (a vowel or semi-vowel); for GR, without an A, is just as much a Syllable as GRA, with an A. The various forms of the Syllable also belong to the theory of metre. (3) A Conjunction is (a) a non-significant sound which, when one significant sound is formable out of several, neither 1457ᵃ hinders nor aids the union, and which, if the Speech thus formed stands by itself (apart from other Speeches), must not be inserted at the beginning of it; e. g. μέν, δή, τοι, δέ. Or (b) a non-significant sound capable of combining two or more significant sounds into one; 5 e. g. ἀμφί, περί, &c. (4) An Article is a non-significant sound marking the beginning, end, or dividing-point of a Speech, its natural place being either at the extremities or in the middle. (5) A Noun 10 or name is a composite significant sound not involving the idea of time, with parts which have no significance by themselves in it. It is to be remembered that in a compound we do not think of the parts as having a significance also by themselves; in the name 'Theodorus', for instance, the δῶρον means nothing to us. (6) A Verb is a composite significant sound involving the idea of time, with parts which (just as in the Noun) have no significance by themselves in it. 15

Whereas the word 'man' or 'white' does not imply *when,* 'walks' and 'has walked,' involve in addition to the idea of walking that of time present or time past. (7) A Case of a Noun or Verb is when the word
20 means 'of' or 'to' a thing, and so forth, or for one or many (e. g. 'man' and 'men'); or it may consist merely in the mode of utterance, e. g. in question, command, &c. 'Walked?' and 'Walk!' are Cases of the verb 'to walk' of this last kind. (8) A Speech is a composite significant sound, some of the parts of which have a certain significance by themselves. It may be observed that a Speech
25 is not always made up of Noun and Verb; it may be without a Verb, like the definition of man; but it will always have some part with a certain significance by itself. In the Speech 'Cleon walks', 'Cleon' is an instance of such a part. A Speech is said to be one in two ways, either as signifying one thing, or as a union of several Speeches made into one by conjunction. Thus the *Illiad* is one Speech
30 by conjunction of several; and the definition of man is one through its signifying one thing.

21 Nouns are of two kinds, either (1) simple, i. e. made up of non-significant parts, like the word γῆ, or (2) double; in the latter case the word may be made up either of a significant and a non-significant part (a distinction which disappears in the compound),
35 or of two significant parts. It is possible also to have triple, quadruple, or higher compounds, like most of our amplified names; e. g. 'Hermocaïcoxanthus' and the like.

1457ᵇ   Whatever its structure, a Noun must always be either (1) the ordinary word for the thing, or (2) a strange word, or (3) a metaphor, or (4) an ornamental word, or (5) a coined word, or (6) a word lengthened out, or (7) curtailed, or (8) altered in form. By the ordinary word I mean that in general use in a country; and by a strange word, one in use elsewhere. So that the same word may obviously be at
5 once strange and ordinary, though not in reference to the same people; σίγυνον, for instance, is an ordinary word in Cyprus, and a strange word with us. Metaphor consists in giving the thing a name that belongs to something else; the transference being either from genus to species, or from species to genus, or from species to species, or on grounds of analogy. That from genus to species is
10 exemplified in 'Here stands my ship';[42] for lying at anchor is the 'standing' of a particular kind of thing. That from species to genus in 'Truly ten thousand good deeds has Ulysses wrought',[43] where 'ten thousand', which is a particular large number, is put in place

[42] *Od.* i. 185, xxiv. 308.   [43] *Il.* ii. 272.

of the generic 'a large number'. That from species to species in 'Drawing the life with the bronze',[44] and in 'Severing with the enduring
bronze';[44] where the poet uses 'draw' in the sense of 'sever' and 15
'sever' in that of 'draw', both words meaning to 'take away' something. That from analogy is possible whenever there are four terms
so related that the second (B) is to the first (A), as the fourth (D)
to the third (C); for one may then metaphorically put D in lieu of
B, and B in lieu of D. Now and then, too, they qualify the metaphor
by adding on to it that to which the word it supplants is relative. 20
Thus a cup (B) is in relation to Dionysus (A) what a shield (D) is to
Ares (C). The cup accordingly will be metaphorically described as
the 'shield *of Dionysus*' (D + A), and the shield as the 'cup *of
Ares*'[45] (B + C). Or to take another instance: As old age (D)
is to life (C), so is evening (B) to day (A). One will accordingly
describe evening (B) as the 'old age *of the day*' (D + A)—or by the
Empedoclean equivalent; and old age (D) as the 'evening'[46] or
'sunset *of life*'[47] (B + C). It may be that some of the terms thus 25
related have no special name of their own, but for all that they will
be metaphorically described in just the same way. Thus to cast forth
seed-corn is called 'sowing'; but to cast forth its flame, as said of the
sun, has no special name. This nameless act (B), however, stands in
just the same relation to its object, sunlight (A), as sowing (D) to
the seed-corn (C). Hence the expression in the poet, 'sowing around a
god-created *flame*'[48] (D + A). There is also another form of qualified 30
metaphor. Having given the thing the alien name, one may by a negative addition deny of it one of the attributes naturally associated
with its new name. An instance of this would be to call the shield not
the 'cup *of Ares*', as in the former case, but a 'cup *that holds no
wine*'. . . . A coined word is a name which, being quite unknown
among a people, is given by the poet himself; e. g. (for there are
some words that seem to be of this origin) ἔρνυγες for horns, and
ἀρητήρ for priest.[49] A word is said to be lengthened out, when 35
it has a short vowel made long, or an extra syllable inserted; 1458ᵃ
e. g. πόληος for πόλεως, Πηληιάδεω for Πηλείδου. It is said to be
curtailed, when it has lost a part; e. g. κρῖ, δῶ, and ὄψ in μία 5
γίνεται ἀμφοτέρων ὄψ.[50] It is an altered word, when part is left
as it was and part is of the poet's making; e. g. δεξιτερόν for δεξιόν,
in δεξιτερὸν κατὰ μαζόν.[51]

The Nouns themselves (to whatever class they may belong) are

[44] Empedocles.　　[45] Timotheus.　　[46] Alexis.　　[47] Pl., *Laws* 770 A.
[48] Authorship unknown.　[49] *Il.* i. 11.　　[50] Empedocles.　[51] *Il.* v. 393.

either masculines, feminines, or intermediates (neuter). All ending
in N, P, Σ, or in the two compounds of this last, Ψ and Ξ, are
10 masculines. All ending in the invariably long vowels, H and Ω, and
in A among the vowels that may be long, are feminines. So that there
is an equal number of masculine and feminine terminations, as Ψ
and Ξ are the same as Σ, and need not be counted. There is no Noun,
15 however, ending in a mute or in either of the two short vowels, E
and O. Only three (μέλι, κόμμι, πέπερι) end in I and five in Y.
The intermediates, or neuters, end in the variable vowels or in
N, P, Σ.

22   The perfection of Diction is for it to be at once clear and not
mean. The clearest indeed is that made up of the ordinary words
20 for things, but it is mean, as is shown by the poetry of Cleophon and
Sthenelus. On the other hand the Diction becomes distinguished and
non-prosaic by the use of unfamiliar terms, i. e. strange words, metaphors, lengthened forms, and everything that deviates from the ordinary modes of speech.—But a whole statement in such terms will be
25 either a riddle or a barbarism, a riddle, if made up of metaphors, a
barbarism, if made up of strange words. The very nature indeed of a
riddle is this, to describe a fact in an impossible combination of words
(which cannot be done with the real names for things, but can be with
their metaphorical substitutes); e. g. 'I saw a man glue brass on an-
30 other with fire',[52] and the like. The corresponding use of strange words
results in a barbarism.—A certain admixture, accordingly, of unfamiliar terms is necessary. These, the strange word, the metaphor,
the ornamental equivalent, &c., will save the language from seeming
mean and prosaic, while the ordinary words in it will secure the
1458ᵇ requisite clearness. What helps most, however, to render the Diction at once clear and non-prosaic is the use of the lengthened, curtailed, and altered forms of words. Their deviation from the ordinary
words will, by making the language unlike that in general use, give it
a non-prosaic appearance; and their having much in common with the
5 words in general use will give it the quality of clearness. It is not right,
then, to condemn these modes of speech, and ridicule the poet for
using them, as some have done; e. g. the elder Euclid, who said it was
easy to make poetry if one were to be allowed to lengthen the words
in the statement itself as much as one likes—a procedure he cari-
10 catured by reading Ἐπιχάρην εἶδον Μαραθῶνάδε βαδίζοντα, and οὐκ
ἄν γ' ἐράμενος τὸν ἐκείνου ἐλλέβορον as verses. A too apparent use of
these licences has certainly a ludicrous effect, but they are not alone

52 Cleobulina.

in that; the rule of moderation applies to all the constituents of the poetic vocabulary; even with metaphors, strange words, and the rest, the effect will be the same, if one uses them improperly and with a view to provoking laughter. The proper use of them is a very dif- 15 ferent thing. To realize the difference one should take an epic verse and see how it reads when the normal words are introduced. The same should be done too with the strange word, the metaphor, and the rest; for one has only to put the ordinary words in their place to see the truth of what we are saying. The same iambic, for instance, is found in Aeschylus and Euripides, and as it stands in the former it is a poor line; whereas Euripides, by the change of a single word, 20 the substitution of a strange for what is by usage the ordinary word, has made it seem a fine one. Aeschylus having said in his *Philoctetes*:

φαγέδαινα ἥ μου σάρκας ἐσθίει ποδός

Euripides has merely altered the ἐσθίει here into θοινᾶται. Or suppose

νῦν δέ μ' ἐὼν ὀλίγος τε καὶ οὐτιδανὸς καὶ ἀεικής [53]   25

to be altered, by the substitution of the ordinary words, into

νῦν δέ μ' ἐὼν μικρός τε καὶ ἀσθενικὸς καὶ ἀειδής.

Or the line

δίφρον ἀεικέλιον καταθεὶς ὀλίγην τε τράπεζαν [54]

into

δίφρον μοχθηρὸν καταθεὶς μικράν τε τράπεζαν.   30

Or ἠιόνες βοόωσιν [55] into ἠιόνες κράζουσιν.   Add to this that Ariphrades used to ridicule the tragedians for introducing expressions unknown in the language of common life, δωμάτων ἄπο (for ἀπὸ δωμάτων), σέθεν, ἐγὼ δέ νιν,[56] 'Αχιλλέως πέρι (for περὶ 'Αχιλλέως), and the like. The mere fact of their not being 1459ᵃ in ordinary speech gives the Diction a non-prosaic character; but Ariphrades was unaware of that. It is a great thing, indeed, to make a proper use of these poetical forms, as also of compounds and strange words. But the greatest thing by far is to be a master of 5 metaphor. It is the one thing that cannot be learnt from others; and it is also a sign of genius, since a good metaphor implies an intuitive perception of the similarity in dissimilars.

---

[53] *Od.* ix. 515.   [54] *Od.* xx. 259.   [55] *Il.* xvii. 265.   [56] Soph., *O. C.*, 986.

Of the kinds of words we have enumerated it may be observed
that compounds are most in place in the dithyramb, strange words
10 in heroic, and metaphors in iambic poetry. Heroic poetry, indeed,
may avail itself of them all. But in iambic verse, which models itself
as far as possible on the spoken language, only those kinds of
words are in place which are allowable also in an oration, i. e. the
ordinary word, the metaphor, and the ornamental equivalent.
15   Let this, then, suffice as an account of Tragedy, the art imitating by means of action on the stage.

23   As for the poetry which merely narrates, or imitates by means
of versified language (without action), it is evident that it has
several points in common with Tragedy.
    I. The construction of its stories should clearly be like that in a
drama; they should be based on a single action, one that is a
complete whole in itself, with a beginning, middle, and end, so as
20 to enable the work to produce its own proper pleasure with all the
organic unity of a living creature. Nor should one suppose that there
is anything like them in our usual histories. A history has to deal not
with one action, but with one period and all that happened in that
to one or more persons, however disconnected the several events
25 may have been. Just as two events may take place at the same time,
e. g. the sea-fight off Salamis and the battle with the Carthaginians
in Sicily, without converging to the same end, so too of two consecutive events one may sometimes come after the other with no one
end as their common issue. Nevertheless most of our epic poets,
one may say, ignore the distinction.
30   Herein, then, to repeat what we have said before,[57] we have a
further proof of Homer's marvellous superiority to the rest. He did
not attempt to deal even with the Trojan war in its entirety,
though it was a whole with a definite beginning and end—through a
feeling apparently that it was too long a story to be taken in in one
35 view, or if not that, too complicated from the variety of incident
in it. As it is, he has singled out one section of the whole; many of
the other incidents, however, he brings in as episodes, using the
Catalogue of the Ships, for instance, and other episodes to relieve
the uniformity of his narrative. As for the other epic poets, they
treat of one man, or one period; or else of an action which, although
1459ᵇ one, has a multiplicity of parts in it. This last is what the authors
of the *Cypria* [58] and *Little Iliad* [58] have done. And the result is

[57] 1451ᵃ 23 ff.   [58] Authorship unknown.

is that, whereas the *Iliad* or *Odyssey* supplies materials for only one, or at most two tragedies, the *Cypria* does that for several and the *Little Iliad* for more than eight: for an *Adjudgment of Arms,* a Philoctetes, a *Neoptolemus,* a *Eurypylus,* a *Ulysses as Beggar,* a *Laconian Women,* a *Fall of Ilium,* and a *Departure of the Fleet*; as also a *Sinon,* and a *Women of Troy.*

24   II. Besides this, Epic poetry must divide into the same species as Tragedy; it must be either simple or complex, a story of character or one of suffering. Its parts, too, with the exception of Song and Spectacle, must be the same, as it requires Peripeties, Discoveries, and scenes of suffering just like Tragedy. Lastly, the Thought and Diction in it must be good in their way. All these elements appear in Homer first; and he has made due use of them. His two poems are each examples of construction, the *Iliad* simple and a story of suffering, the *Odyssey* complex (there is Discovery throughout it) and a story of character. And they are more than this, since in Diction and Thought too they surpass all other poems.

There is, however, a difference in the Epic as compared with Tragedy, (1) in its length, and (2) in its metre. (1) As to its length, the limit already suggested [59] will suffice: it must be possible for the beginning and end of the work to be taken in in one view—a condition which will be fulfilled if the poem be shorter than the old epics, and about as long as the series of tragedies offered for one hearing. For the extension of its length epic poetry has a special advantage, of which it makes large use. In a play one cannot represent an action with a number of parts going on simultaneously; one is limited to the part on the stage and connected with the actors. Whereas in epic poetry the narrative form makes it possible for one to describe a number of simultaneous incidents; and these, if germane to the subject, increase the body of the poem. This then is a gain to the Epic, tending to give it grandeur, and also variety of interest and room for episodes of diverse kinds. Uniformity of incident by the satiety it soon creates is apt to ruin tragedies on the stage. (2) As for its metre, the heroic has been assigned it from experience; were any one to attempt a narrative poem in some one, or in several, of the other metres, the incongruity of the thing would be apparent. The heroic in fact is the gravest and weightiest of metres —which is what makes it more tolerant than the rest of strange words and metaphors, that also being a point in which the narrative form of poetry goes beyond all others. The iambic and trochaic, on

[59] 1451ᵃ 3.

the other hand, are metres of movement, the one representing that
1460ᵃ of life and action, the other that of the dance. Still more unnatural
would it appear, if one were to write an epic in a medley of metres,
as Chaeremon did.[60] Hence it is that no one has ever written a long
story in any but heroic verse; nature herself, as we have said,[61]
teaches us to select the metre appropriate to such a story.

5   Homer, admirable as he is in every other respect, is especially
so in this, that he alone among epic poets is not unaware of the part
to be played by the poet himself in the poem. The poet should say
very little *in propria persona,* as he is no imitator when doing
that. Whereas the other poets are perpetually coming forward in person, and say but little, and that only here and there, as imitators,
10 Homer after a brief preface brings in forthwith a man, a woman, or
some other Character—no one of them characterless, but each with
distinctive characteristics.

The marvellous is certainly required in Tragedy. The Epic, however, affords more opening for the improbable, the chief factor in the
marvellous, because in it the agents are not visibly before one. The
15 scene of the pursuit of Hector would be ridiculous on the stage—the
Greeks halting instead of pursuing him, and Achilles shaking his head
to stop them; [62] but in the poem the absurdity is overlooked. The
marvellous, however, is a cause of pleasure, as is shown by the fact
that we all tell a story with additions, in the belief that we are
doing our hearers a pleasure.

Homer more than any other has taught the rest of us the art of
20 framing lies in the right way. I mean the use of paralogism. Whenever, if A is or happens, a consequent, B, is or happens, men's notion
is that, if the B is, the A also is—but that is a false conclusion.
Accordingly, if A is untrue, but there is something else, B, that on the
assumption of its truth follows as its consequent, the right thing then
is to add on the B. Just because we know the truth of the consequent,
we are in our own minds led on to the erroneous inference of the
25 truth of the antecedent. Here is an instance, from the *Bath-story* in
the *Odyssey.*[63]

A likely impossibility is always preferable to an unconvincing
possibility. The story should never be made up of improbable incidents; there should be nothing of the sort in it. If, however, such
incidents are unavoidable, they should be outside the piece, like the
30 hero's ignorance in *Oedipus* of the circumstances of Laius' death;

[60] *Centaur,* cf. 1447ᵇ 21.
[12] *Il.* xxii. 205.

[61] 1449ᵃ 24.
[63] xix. 164–260.

not within it, like the report of the Pythian games in *Electra*,[64] or the man's having come to Mysia from Tegea without uttering a word on the way, in *The Mysians*.[65] So that it is ridiculous to say that one's Plot would have been spoilt without them, since it is fundamentally wrong to make up such Plots. If the poet has taken such a Plot, however, and one sees that he might have put it in a more probable form, he is guilty of absurdity as well as a fault of art. Even in [35] the *Odyssey* the improbabilities in the setting-ashore of Ulysses [66] would be clearly intolerable in the hands of an inferior poet. As [1460^b] it is, the poet conceals them, his other excellences veiling their absurdity. Elaborate Diction, however, is required only in places where there is no action, and no Character or Thought to be revealed. Where there is Character or Thought, on the other hand, an over-ornate Diction tends to obscure them.   [5]

25 As regards Problems and their Solutions, one may see the number and nature of the assumptions on which they proceed by viewing the matter in the following way. (1) The poet being an imitator just like the painter or other maker of likenesses, he must necessarily in all instances represent things in one or other of three aspects, either [10] as they were or are, or as they are said or thought to be or to have been, or as they ought to be. (2) All this he does in language, with an admixture, it may be, of strange words and metaphors, as also of the various modified forms of words, since the use of these is conceded in poetry. (3) It is to be remembered, too, that there is not the same kind of correctness in poetry as in politics, or indeed any other art. There is, however, within the limits of poetry itself [15] a possibility of two kinds of error, the one directly, the other only accidentally connected with the art. If the poet meant to describe the thing correctly, and failed through lack of power of expression, his art itself is at fault. But if it was through his having meant to describe it in some incorrect way (e. g. to make the horse in movement have both right legs thrown forward) that the technical error (one in a matter of, say, medicine or some other special science), [20] or impossibilities of whatever kind they may be, have got into his description, his error in that case is not in the essentials of the poetic art. These, therefore, must be the premisses of the Solutions in answer to the criticisms involved in the Problems.

I. As to the criticisms relating to the poet's art itself. Any impossibilities there may be in his descriptions of things are faults. But from another point of view they are justifiable, if they serve

---

[64] Soph. *El.* 660 ff.   [65] Probably by Aeschylus.   [66] xiii. 116 ff.

25 the end of poetry itself—if (to assume what we have said of that end) [67] they make the effect of either that very portion of the work or some other portion more astounding. The Pursuit of Hector is an instance in point. If, however, the poetic end might have been as well or better attained without sacrifice of technical correctness in such matters, the impossibility is not to be justified, since the description should be, if it can, entirely free from error. One may
30 ask, too, whether the error is in a matter directly or only accidentally connected with the poetic art; since it is a lesser error in an artist not to know, for instance, that the hind has no horns, than to produce an unrecognizable picture of one.

II. If the poet's description be criticized as not true to fact, one may urge perhaps that the object ought to be as described—an answer like that of Sophocles, who said that he drew men as they
35 ought to be, and Euripides as they were. If the description, however, be neither true nor of the thing as it ought to be, the answer must be then, that it is in accordance with opinion. The tales about Gods, for instance, may be as wrong as Xenophanes thinks, neither true nor the better thing to say; but they are certainly in accordance with
1461ᵃ opinion. Of other statements in poetry one may perhaps say, not that they are better than the truth, but that the fact was so at the time; e. g. the description of the arms: 'their spears stood upright, butt-end upon the ground'; [68] for that was the usual way of fixing them then, as it is still with the Illyrians. As for the question whether something said or done in a poem is morally right or not, in
5 dealing with that one should consider not only the intrinsic quality of the actual word or deed, but also the person who says or does it, the person to whom he says or does it, the time, the means, and the motive of the agent—whether he does it to attain a greater good, or to avoid a greater evil.

III. Other criticisms one must meet by considering the language
10 of the poet: (1) by the assumption of a strange word in a passage like οὐρῆας μὲν πρῶτον, [69] where by οὐρῆας Homer may perhaps mean not mules but sentinels. And in saying of Dolon, ὅς ῥ᾽ ἦ τοι εἶδος μὲν ἔην κακός, [70] his meaning may perhaps be, not that Dolon's body was deformed, but that his face was ugly, as εὐειδής is the Cretan word for handsome-faced. So, too, ζωρότε-
15 ρον δὲ κέραιε [71] may mean not 'mix the wine stronger', as though for topers, but 'mix it quicker', (2) Other expressions in Homer may be explained as metaphorical; e. g. in ἄλλοι μέν ῥα θεοί τε καὶ

---

[67] 1452ᵃ 4, 1454ᵃ 4, 1455ᵃ 17, 1460ᵃ 11.   [68] Il. x. 152.
[69] Il. i. 50.   [70] Il. x. 316.   [71] Il. ix. 202.

ἀνέρες εὗδον ⟨ἅπαντες⟩ παννύχιοι,[72] as compared with what he tells us at the same time, ἤ τοι ὅτ' ἐς πεδίον τὸ Τρωικὸν ἀθρήσειεν, αὐλῶν συρίγγων †τε ὁμαδόν†,[73] the word ἅπαντες, 'all', is metaphorically put for 'many', since 'all' is a species of 'many'. So also his οἴη δ' ἄμμορος[74] is metaphorical, the best known stand- 20 ing 'alone'. (3) A change, as Hippias of Thasos suggested, in the mode of reading a word will solve the difficulty in δίδομεν δέ οἱ,[75] and in τὸ μὲν οὗ καταπύθεται ὄμβρῳ.[76] (4) Other difficulties may be solved by another punctuation; e. g. in Empedocles, αἶψα δὲ θνήτ' ἐφύοντο, τὰ πρὶν μάθον ἀθάνατα ζωρά τε πρὶν κέκρητο. 25 Or (5) by the assumption of an equivocal term, as in παρῴχηκεν δὲ πλέω νύξ,[77] where πλέω is equivocal. Or (6) by an appeal to the custom of language. Wine-and-water we call 'wine'; and it is on the same principle that Homer speaks of a κνημὶς νεοτεύκτου κασσιτέροιο,[78] a 'greave of new-wrought *tin*'. A worker in iron we call a 'brazier'; and it is on the same principle that Ganymede is described as the '*wine*-server' of Zeus,[79] though the Gods do not drink wine. This latter, however, may be an instance of 30 metaphor. But whenever also a word seems to imply some contradiction, it is necessary to reflect how many ways there may be of understanding it in the passage in question; e. g. in Homer's τῇ ῥ' ἔσχετο χάλκεον ἔγχος[80] one should consider the possible senses of 'was stopped there'—whether by taking it in this sense or in that one will best avoid the fault of which Glaucon 35 speaks: 'They start with some improbable presumption; and hav- 1461ᵇ ing so decreed it themselves, proceed to draw inferences, and censure the poet as though he had actually said whatever they happen to believe, if his statement conflicts with their own notion of things.' This is how Homer's silence about Icarius has been treated. Starting with the notion of his having been a Lacedaemonian, the critics think it strange for Telemachus not to have met him when he went to 5 Lacedaemon. Whereas the fact may have been as the Cephallenians say, that the wife of Ulysses was of a Cephallenian family, and that her father's name was Icadius, not Icarius. So that it is probably a mistake of the critics that has given rise to the Problem.

Speaking generally, one has to justify (1) the Impossible by reference to the requirements of poetry, or to the better, or to opinion. 10 For the purposes of poetry a convincing impossibility is preferable to

---

[72] Cf. *Il.* x. 1, ii. 1.   [73] *Il.* x. 11–13.   [74] *Il.* xviii. 489 = *Od.* v. 275.
[75] Cf. *Soph. El.* 166ᵇ 1; *Il.* ii. 15.   [76] *Il.* xxiii. 327.   [77] *Il.* x. 251.
[78] *Il.* xxi. 592.   [79] *Il.* xx. 234.   [80] *Il.* xx. 267.

an unconvincing possibility; and if men such as Zeuxis depicted be impossible, the answer is that it is better they should be like that, as the artist ought to improve on his model. (2) The Improbable one has to justify either by showing it to be in accordance with opinion, or by urging that at times it is not improbable; for there is a probability of
15 things happening also against probability. (3) The contradictions found in the poet's language one should first test as one does an opponent's confutation in a dialectical argument, so as to see whether he means the same thing, in the same relation, and in the same sense, before admitting that he has contradicted either something he has said himself or what a man of sound sense assumes as true. But there is no possible apology for improbability of Plot or depravity of character,
20 when they are not necessary and no use is made of them, like the improbability in the appearance of Aegeus in *Medea* [81] and the baseness of Menelaus in *Orestes*.

The objections, then, of critics start with faults of five kinds: the allegation is always that something is either (1) impossible, (2) improbable, (3) corrupting, (4) contradictory, or (5) against technical correctness. The answers to these objections must be sought under one
25 or other of the above-mentioned heads, which are twelve in number.

26   The question may be raised whether the epic or the tragic is the higher form of imitation. It may be argued that, if the less vulgar is the higher, and the less vulgar is always that which addresses the better public, an art addressing any and every one is of a very vulgar order. It is a belief that their public cannot see the meaning, unless
30 they add something themselves, that causes the perpetual movements of the performers—bad flute-players, for instance, rolling about, if quoit-throwing is to be represented, and pulling at the conductor, if Scylla is the subject of the piece. Tragedy, then, is said to be an art of this order—to be in fact just what the later actors were in the eyes of their predecessors; for Mynniscus used to call Callippides 'the
35 ape', because he thought he so overacted his parts; and a similar
1462ᵃ view was taken of Pindarus also. All Tragedy, however, is said to stand to the Epic as the newer to the older school of actors. The one, accordingly, is said to address a cultivated audience, which does not need the accompaniment of gesture; the other, an uncultivated one. If,
5 therefore, Tragedy is a vulgar art, it must clearly be lower than the Epic.

The answer to this is twofold. In the first place, one may urge (1) that the censure does not touch the art of the dramatic poet, but only

81 l. 663.

that of his interpreter; for it is quite possible to overdo the gesturing even in an epic recital, as did Sosistratus, and in a singing contest, as did Mnasitheus of Opus. (2) That one should not condemn all movement, unless one means to condemn even the dance, but only that of ignoble people—which is the point of the criticism passed on Callippides and in the present day on others, that their women are not like gentlewomen. (3) That Tragedy may produce its effect even without movement or action in just the same way as Epic poetry; for from the mere reading of a play its quality may be seen. So that, if it be superior in all other respects, this element of inferiority is no necessary part of it.

In the second place, one must remember (1) that Tragedy has everything that the Epic has (even the epic metre being admissible), together with a not inconsiderable addition in the shape of the Music (a very real factor in the pleasure of the drama) and the Spectacle. (2) That its reality of presentation is felt in the play as read, as well as in the play as acted. (3) That the tragic imitation requires less space for the attainment of its end; which is a great advantage, since the more concentrated effect is more pleasurable than one with a large admixture of time to dilute it—consider the *Oedipus* of Sophocles, for instance, and the effect of expanding it into the number of lines of the *Iliad*. (4) That there is less unity in the imitation of the epic poets, as is proved by the fact that any one work of theirs supplies matter for several tragedies; the result being that, if they take what is really a single story, it seems curt when briefly told, and thin and waterish when on the scale of length usual with their verse. In saying that there is less unity in an epic, I mean an epic made up of a plurality of actions, in the same way as the *Iliad* and *Odyssey* have many such parts, each one of them in itself of some magnitude; yet the structure of the two Homeric poems is as perfect as can be, and the action in them is as nearly as possible one action. If, then, Tragedy is superior in these respects, and also, besides these, in its poetic effect (since the two forms of poetry should give us, not any or every pleasure, but the very special kind we have mentioned), it is clear that, as attaining the poetic effect better than the Epic, it will be the higher form of art.

So much for Tragedy and Epic poetry—for these two arts in general and their species; the number and nature of their constituent parts; the causes of success and failure in them; the Objections of the critics, and the Solutions in answer to them.

Modern Library is online at
www.modernlibrary.com

MODERN LIBRARY ONLINE IS YOUR GUIDE TO CLASSIC LITERATURE ON THE WEB

THE MODERN LIBRARY E-NEWSLETTER

Our free e-mail newsletter is sent to subscribers, and features sample chapters, interviews with and essays by our authors, upcoming books, special promotions, announcements, and news.

To subscribe to the Modern Library e-newsletter, send a blank e-mail to: **sub_modernlibrary@info.randomhouse.com** or visit **www.modernlibrary.com**

THE MODERN LIBRARY WEBSITE

Check out the Modern Library website at **www.modernlibrary.com** for:

- The Modern Library e-newsletter
- A list of our current and upcoming titles and series
- Reading Group Guides and exclusive author spotlights
- Special features with information on the classics and other paperback series
- Excerpts from new releases and other titles
- A list of our e-books and information on where to buy them
- The Modern Library Editorial Board's 100 Best Novels and 100 Best Nonfiction Books of the Twentieth Century written in the English language
- News and announcements

Questions? E-mail us at **modernlibrary@randomhouse.com**. For questions about examination or desk copies, please visit the Random House Academic Resources site at **www.randomhouse.com/academic**